VELÁZQUEZ
LARGE PRINT
Spanish and English
Dictionary

Spanish - English/ Inglés - Español

Created in Cooperation with the Editors of
Velázquez Press

Velázquez Press
www.VelazquezPress.com

PREFACE

For over 150 years, *Velázquez Spanish and English Dictionary* has been known as the preeminent authority in Spanish and English dictionaries. Velázquez Press is pleased to offer *Velázquez Large Print Spanish and English Dictionary* to readers who need bilingual large print references. Its vocabulary is based on *Velázquez World Wide Spanish and English Dictionary*. Due to its large font size, *Velázquez Large Print Spanish and English Dictionary* is designed as a quick reference, containing over 38, 000 common entries. By offering the only large print Spanish and English dictionary on the market, Velázquez Press hopes to support the underserved visual impaired bilingual readers around the world.

Claudia P. Huesca, *Editor*

PREFACIO

Por más de 150 años, el diccionario Velázquez ha sido conocido como la autoridad preeminente cuando a diccionarios de inglés-español se refiere. Velázquez Press se enorgullece en ofrecer el *Velázquez Large Print Spanish and English Dictionary* a lectores que tienen la necesidad de consultar un material de referencia bilingüe con letra grande. Su vocabulario está basado en el *Velázquez World Wide Spanish and English Dictionary*. Por su letra grande, *Velázquez Large Print Spanish and English Dictionary* está diseñado como una referencia rápida, contando con más de 38,000 palabras. Al ofrecer el único diccionario inglés-español con letra grande en el mercado, Velázquez Press apoya a los lectores bilingües alrededor del mundo que tienen algún impedimento visual.

Claudia P. Huesca, *Editora*

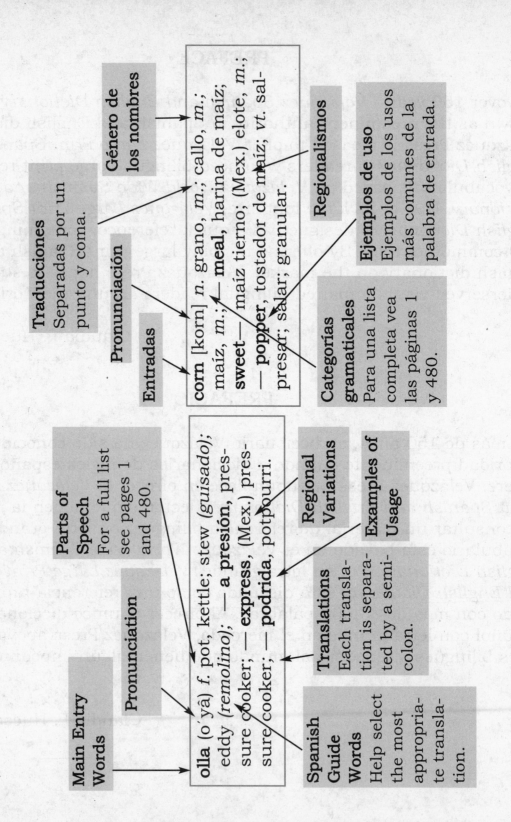

Guía del usuario

Género de los nombres

Traducciones
Separadas por un punto y coma.

Pronunciación

Entradas

Regionalismos

Ejemplos de uso
Ejemplos de los usos más comunes de la palabra de entrada.

Categorías gramaticales
Para una lista completa vea las páginas 1 y 480.

corn [korn] *n.* grano, *m.*; callo, *m.*; maíz, *m.*; **meal**, harina de maíz; **sweet** — maíz tierno; (Mex.) elote, *m.*; — **popper**, tostador de maíz; *vt.* salpresar; salar; granular.

User's Guide

Parts of Speech
For a full list see pages 1 and 480.

Pronunciation

Main Entry Words

Regional Variations

Examples of Usage

Translations
Each translation is separated by a semicolon.

Spanish Guide Words
Help select the most appropriate translation.

olla (o'yä) *f.* pot, kettle; stew (guisado); eddy (remolino); — **a presión,** pressure cooker; — **express,** (Mex.) pressure cooker; — **podrida,** potpourri.

Guide to Spanish Pronunciation
The Spanish Alphabet and Its Sounds

Spanish Letter	English Sound	Phonetic Symbol	Spanish Word	Phonetic Respelling
a	father	â	para	(pâ´râ)
b	bad	b	basta	(bâs´tâ)
	save	v	sabe	(sâ´ve)
c	kid	k	casa	(kâ´sâ)
	say	s	cinco	(sēng´ko)
	get	g	anécdota	(â•neg´tho•tâ)
ch	chip	ch	chico	(chē´ko)
d	day	d	dama	(dâ´mâ)
	though	th	mudo	(mū´tho)
e	they	e	leve	(le´ve)
	ten	e	el	(el)
f	few	f	finca	(fēng´kâ)
g	go	g	gana	(gâ´nâ)
	hot	h	gente	(hen´te)
h	(silent)		hacer	(â•ser´)
í	police	ē	Isla	(ēz´lâ)
	yes	y	bien	(byen)
j	hot	h	eje	(e´he)
k	kick	k	kilo	(kē´lo)
l	lamp	l	lana	(lâ´nâ)
ll	yes	y	llama	(yâ´mâ)
m	mama	m	mano	(mâ´no)
n	none	n	nota	(no´ta)
o	go	o	ocho	(o´cho)
	gone	o	ostra	(os´tra)
p	pop	p	papel	(pâ•pel´)
q	quit	k	aquí	(â•ke´)
r	very	r	clero	(kle´ro)
	(none)	rr	río	(rrē´o)
rr	(none)	rr	sierra	(sye´rrâ)

s		*s*ee	s	**saco**	(sâ′ko)
		ro*s*e	z	**desde**	(dez′the)
t		*t*ip	t	**todo**	(to′tho)
		though	th	**atleta**	(âth•le′tâ)
u		f*oo*d	ū	**luna**	(lū′nâ)
		q*u*it	w	**huevo**	(we′vo)
		silent		**guerra**	(ge′rrâ)
v		*b*ad	b	**vaca**	(bâ′kâ)
		sa*v*e	v	**grave**	(grâ′ve)
x		a*x*	ks	**taxi**	(tâk′sē)
		*s*ee	s	**sexto**	(ses′to)
Y		*y*es	y	**ya**	(yâ)
		pol*i*ce	ē	**ley**	(leē)
z		*s*ee	s	**zapa**	(sâ′pâ)
		*z*ero	z	**biznieto**	(bēz•nye′to)

Diphthongs

When two vowels occur together in words, they are usually pronounced as one syllable. Such one-syllable combinations are known as *diphthongs.* Some well-known English examples are *oi* in *boil* and *ou* in *house.* Diphthongs are frequent occurrences in Spanish, and it is therefore important to know how to pronounce them.

The five vowels occur in just about every possible combination. But the more common diphthongs combine *a strong* vowel with *a weak* one. Strong vowels (**a, e**, and **o**) are so called because they usually *sound* stronger (louder) than weak vowels (**i** and **u**) when combined. *Examples:* **aire** (â′ē•re), **causa** (kâ′ū•sâ), **diez** (dyes), **nueve** (nwe′ve), **boina** (bo′ē•nâ).

When two weak vowels combine to form a diphthong, the stress always falls on the second. *Examples:* **viuda** (byū′thâ), **huir** (wēr).

The combination of two strong vowels (**a, e, o**) results, not in a diphthong, but in two syllables. *Examples:* **nao** (nâ′o), **real** (rre · âl′), **boa** (bo′â), **poeta** (po•e′tâ), **caer** (kâ•er′).

When a weak vowel in combination with a strong vowel bears a written accent, the weak vowel is the one that is stressed and two syllables result. *Examples:* **día** (dē′â), **caído** (kâ•ē′tho), **dúo** (dū′o).

When a word ending in **i, u,** or **y** is followed in the same sentence by a second word beginning with a vowel, the two vowels are sometimes pronounced as a diphthong. *Examples:* **mi amor** (myâ•mor′), **su obra** (swo′-vrâ), **y usted** (yūs•teth′).

Triphthongs

When three vowels occur together they are usually pronounced as one syllable, with the middle vowel (always a or e) bearing the stress. *Examples:* **buey** (bwe′ē), **Paraguay** (pâ•râ•gwâ′ē).

Accentuation

Words ending in a vowel or in **n** or **s** are accented on the next-to-the-last syllable. *Examples:* **negro** (ne′gro), **hablan** (â′vlân), **comidas** (ko•mē′thâs).

Words ending in a consonant other than **n** or **s** are accented on the last syllable. *Examples:* **papel** (pâ•pel′), **escribir** (es•krē•vēr′), **feroz** (fe•ros′).

Words whose pronunciations do not conform to these rules are spelled with a written accent to indicate the stressed syllable. *Examples:* **francés** (frân•ses´), **lección** (lek•syon´), **ánimo** (â´nē•mo).

Syllabication

Spanish words have no silent vowels (except **u** preceded by **g** or **q** and followed by **e** or **i**), as many English words do *(were, fair, buy)*. This means that there are as many syllables as there are sounded vowels (counting diphthongs and triphthrongs as one-vowel sounds).

Single consonants between vowels (and that includes **ch, ll,** and **rr**) belong with the following vowel. *Examples:* **casa** (kâ´sâ), **viuda** (vyū´thâ), **echar** (e•châr).

The following two-consonant combinations are never divided between syllables: **bl, br, cl, cr, dr, fl, fr, gl, gr, pl, pr, tr.** They always start the syllable to which they belong. *Examples:* **hablar** (â•vlâr´), **copla** (ko´plâ), **madre** (mâ´thre), **otro** (o´tro).

All other two-consonant combinations (including **dl** and **tl**) are divided. *Examples:* **manta** (mân´tâ), **orbe** (or´ve), **atleta** (âth•le´tâ).

When vowels are separated by three consonants (except as noted below), the syllable division occurs after the first two. *Examples:* **instinto** (ēns•tēn´to), **obstaculizar** (ovs•tâ•kū•lē•sâr´).

When vowels are separated by three or more consonants the last two of which are **bl, br, cl, cr, dr, fl, fr, gl, gr, pl, pr,** or **tr,** the syllable division occurs before the aforesaid inseparable two-consonant combinations. *Examples:* **estrecho** (es•tre´cho), **instrumento** (ēns•trū•men´to), **implicar** (ēm•plē•kâr´).

CONJUGATION OF SPANISH VERBS

1 Regular Verbs

All regular verbs entered in the dictionary conform to one of the following basic patterns.

In the regular conjugations below, the verb forms are given in the following order: first, second, and third person singular; followed by first, second, and third person plural.

—AR VERBS *Example*: **hablar** (â•vlâr´) to speak

PRESENT PARTICIPLE **hablando** (â•vlân´do)
PAST PARTICIPLE **hablado** (â•vlâ´tho)
PRESENT **hablo** (â´vlo), **hablas** (â´vlâs), **habla** (â´vla), **hablamos** (â•vlâ´mos), **habláis** (â•vlâ´ēs), **hablan** (a´vlân)
FUTURE **hablaré** (â•vlâ•re´), **hablarás** (â•vlâ•râs´), **hablará** (â•vlâ•râ´), **hablaremos** (â•vlâ•re´mos), **hablaréis** (â•vlâ•re´ēs), **hablarán** (â•vlâ•rân´)
CONDITIONAL **hablaría** (â•vlâ•rē´â), **hablarías** (â•vlâ•rē´âs), **hablaría** (â•vlâ•rē´â), **hablaríamos** (â•vlâ•rē´â•mos), **hablaríais** (â•vlâ•rē´âēs), **hablarían** (â•vlâ•rē´ân)
PRESENT SUBJUNCTIVE **hable** (â´vle), **hables** (âvles), **hable** (â´vle), **hablemos** (â•vle´mos), **habléis** (â•vle´ēs), **hablen** (â´vlen)
IMPERFECT **hablaba** (â•vlâ´vâ), **hablabas** (â•vlâ´vâs), **hablaba** (â•vlâ´vâ), **hablábamos** (â•vlâ´vâ•mos), **hablabais** (â•vlâ´vâēs)) **hablaban** (â•vlâ´van)
PRETERITE **hablé** (â•vle´), **hablaste** (a.vlâs´te), **habló** (â•vlo´), **hablamos** (â•vlâ´mos), **hablasteis** (â•vlâs´teēs), **hablaron** (â•vlâ´ron)
PAST SUBJUNCTIVE (I) **hablase** (â•vlâ´se) **hablases** (â•vlâ´ses), **hablase** (â•vlâ´se), **hablásemos** (â•vlâ´se•mos), **hablaseis** (â•vla´seēs), **hablasen** (â•vlâ´sen)
PAST SUBJUNCTIVE (II) **hablara** (â•vlâ´râ), **hablaras** (â•vlâ´râs), **hablara** (â•vlâ´râ), **habláramos** (â•vlâ´râ•mos), **hablarais** (â•vlâ´râēs), **hablaran** (â•vlâ´rân)
IMPERATIVE **habla** (â´vlâ), **hablad** (â•vlâth´)

—ER VERBS Example: **comer** (ko•mer´) to eat

PRESENT PARTICIPLE **comiendo** (ko•myen´do)

PAST PARTICIPLE **comido** (ko•mē´tho)

PRESENT **como** (ko´mo), **comes** (ko´mes), **come** (ko´me), **comemos** (ko•me´mos), **coméis** (ko•me´ēs), **comen** (ko´men)

FUTURE **comeré** (ko•me•re´), **comerás** (ko•me•râs´), **comerá** (ko•me•râ´), **comeremos** (ko•me•re´mos), **comeréis** (ko•me•re´ēs), **comerán** (ko•me•ran´)

CONDITIONAL **comería** (ko•me•rē´â), **comerías** (ko•me•rē´âs), **comería** (ko•me•ē´â), **comeríamos** (ko•me•rē´â•mos), **comeríais** (ko•me•rē´âēs), **comerían** (ko•me•rē´ân)

PRESENT SUBJUNCTIVE **coma** (ko´mâ), **comas** (ko´mâs), **coma** (ko´mâ), **comamos** (ko•mâ´mos), **comáis** (ko•mâ´ēs), **coman** (ko´mân)

IMPERFECT **comía** (komē´â), **comías** (ko•mē´âs), **comía** (ko•mē´â), **comíamos** (ko•miâ•mos), **comíais** (ko•mē´âēs), **comían** (ko • mē´ân)

PRETERITE **comí** (ko•mē´), **comiste** (ko•mēs´te), **comió** (ko•myo´), **comimos** (ko •mē´mos), **comisteis** (ko•mēs´teēs), **comieron** (ko•mye´ron)

PAST SUBJUNCTIVE (I) **comiese** (ko•mye´se), **comieses** (ko•mye´ses), **comiese** (ko•mye´se), **comiésemos** (ko•mye´se•mos), **comieseis** (ko•mye´seēs), **comiesen** (ko•mye´sen)

PAST SUBJUNCTIVE (II) **comiera** (ko•mye´râ), **comieras** (ko•mye´râs), **comiera** (ko mye´râ), **comiéramos** (ko•mye´râ•mos), **comierais** (ko•mye´râes), **comieran** (ko•mye´•rân)

IMPERATIVE **come** (kome), **comed** (ko•meth´)

—IR VERBS *Example:* **vivir** (bē•vēr´) to live

PRESENT PARTICIPLE **viviendo** (bē•vyen´do)

PAST PARTICIPLE **vivido** (bē•vē´tho)

PRESENT **VIVO** (bē´vo), **vives** (bē´ves), **vive** (bē´ve), **vivimos** (bē•vē´mos), **vivís** (bē•vēs´), **viven** (bē´ven)

FUTURE **viviré** (bē•vē•re´), **vivirás** (bē•vē•râs´), **vivirá** (bē•vē•râ´), **viviremos** (bē•vē•re´mos), **viviréis** (bē•vē•re´ēs), **vivirán** (bē•vē•rân´)

CONDITIONAL **viviría** (bē•vē•rē´â), **vivirías** (bē•vē•re´âs), **viviría** (bē•vē•rē´â), **viviríamos** (bē•ve•rē´â•mos), **viviríais** (bē•vē•rē´âēs), **vivirían** (bē•ve•rē´ân)
PRESENT SUBJUNCTIVE **viva** (bē´vâ), **vivas** (bē´vâs), **viva** (bē´vâ), **vivamos** (bē•vâ´mos), **viváis** (bē•vâ´ēs), **vivan** (bē´vân)
IMPERFECT **vivía** (bē•vē´â), **vivías** (bē•vē´âs), **vivía** (bē•vē´â), **vivíamos** (bē•vē´â•mos), **vivíais** (bē•vē´aēs), **vivían** (bē•ve´ân)
PRETERITE **viví** (bē•vē´), **viviste** (bē•ves´te), **vivió** (bē•vyo´), **vivimos** (bē•vē´mos), **vivisteis** (bē•vēs´teēs) **vivieron** (bē•vye´ron)
PAST SUBJUNCTIVE (I) **viviese** (bē•vye´se), **vivieses** (bē•vye´ses), **viviese** (bē•vye´se), **viviésemos** (bē•vye´se•mos), **vivieseis** (bē•vye´seēs), **viviesen** (bē•vye´sen)
PAST SUBJUNCTIVE (n) **viviera** (bē•vye´râ), **vivieras** (bē•vye´râs), **viviera** (bē•vye´râ), **viviéramos** (bē•vye´râ•mos), **vivierais** (bē•vye´râes), **vivieran** (bē•vye´rân)
IMPERATIVE **vive** (bē´ve), **vivid** (bē•vēth´)

2 Irregular Verbs

The following list contains all the irregular Spanish verbs entered in this dictionary. The reader is referred to this list by an asterisk following the irregular verb at the point of entry. In the case of verb families all of whose conjugations follow one basic pattern, only one model verb is given and the others of the family are referred to the model (for example, **pertenecer** see **abastecer.**

In the conjugations offered below, only those tenses containing one or more irregular forms are given. Other tenses can be formed on the model of the regular verbs given previously.

The verb forms are given in the following order: first, second, and third person singular; followed by first, second, and third person plural.

abastecer to purvey
PRESENT **abastezco, abasteces, abastece, abastecemos, abastecéis,**

abastecen

abnegar to renounce, see **cegar**

abolir to abolish, see **blandir**

aborrecer to hate, see **abastecer**

abrir, to open
PAST PARTICIPLE **abierto**

absolver to absolve, see **volver**

abstenerse to abstain, see **tener**

abstraer to abstract, see **traer**

acertar to hit the mark
PRESENT **acierto, aciertas,
acierta,
acertamos, acertáis, aciertan**
PRESENT SUBJUNCTIVE **acierte, aciertes, acierte, acertemos,
acertéis, acierten**

aclocarse to brood
PRESENT **aclueco, acluecas,
aclueca, aclocamos, aclocáis,
acluecan**
PRESENT SUBJUNCTIVE
**aclueque, aclueques, aclueque,
acloquemos, acloquéis, aclue-
quen**

acontecer to happen
PRESENT SUBJUNCTIVE **acon-
tezca, acontezcan**
DEFECTIVE VERB: Used only in
the third person singular and
plural.

acostar to put to bed, see
mostrar

acrecentar to increase, see **acertar**

acrecer to augment, see **abastecer**

adherir to stick, see **invertir**

adolecer to be ill, see **abastecer**

adormecer to put to sleep see
abastecer

adquirir to acquire, see **inquirir**

advertir to notice, see **invertir**

afluir to flow, see **diluir**

agorar to divine
PRESENT **agüero, agüeras,
agüera, agoramos, agoráis,
agüeran**
PRESENT SUBJUNCTIVE **agüere, agüeres, agüere, agoremos,
agoréis agüeren**

agradecer to appreciate, see
abastecer

alentar to breathe, see **acertar**

almorzar to eat lunch, see **forzar**

amanecer to dawn, see **abastecer**

amolar to whet, see **mostrar**

andar to walk
PRETERITE **anduve, anduviste,
anduvo, anduvimos, anduvisteis,
anduvieron**

anochecer to grow dark, see
abastecer

anteponer to prefer, see **poner**

apacentar to pasture, see **acertar**

aparecer to appear, see **abastecer**

apetecer to long for, see **abaste
cer**

apostar to bet, see **mostrar**

apretar to squeeze, see **acertar**
aprobar to approve, see **mostrar**
argüir to argue, see **diluir**
arrendar to rent, see **acertar**
arrepentirse to repent, see
invertir
ascender to ascend, see **hender**
asentar to seat, see **acertar**
asentir to acquiesce, see **invertir**
aserrar to saw, see **acertar**
asir to grasp
  PRESENT **asgo, ases, ase, asi-**
  mos, asís, asen
atender to heed, see **hender**
atenerse to depend, see **tener**
atentar to attempt, see **acertar**
atestar to stuff, see **acertar**
atraer to attract, see **traer**
atravesar to cross, see **acertar**
atribuir to attribute, see **diluir**
avenir to reconcile, see **venir**
aventar to fan, see **acertar**
avergonzar to shame
  PRESENT **avergüenzo, avergüen-**
  zas, avergüenza, avergonzamos,
  avergonzáis, avergüenzan
  PRESENT SUBJUNCTIVE **aver-**
  güence, avergüences, aver-
  güence, avergoncemos, avergon-
  céis, avergüencen
  PRETERITE **avergoncé, avergon-**
  zaste, avergonzó, avergonzamos,
  avergonzasteis, avergonzaron

bendecir to bless
  PRESENT PARTICIPLE **bendi-**
  ciendo PRESENT **bendigo, ben-**
  dices, bendice, bendecimos,
  bendecís, bendicen
  PRETERITE **bendije bendijiste**
  bendijo, bendijimos, bendijisteis,
  bendijeron
blandir to brandish
  DEFECTIVE VERB: Used only in
  forms whose endings begin with
  i.
blanquecer to blanch, see **abaste-**
cer
bruñir to burnish, see **plañir**
caber to fit
  PRESENT **quepo, cabes, cabe,**
  cabemos, cabéis, caben
  FUTURE **cabré, cabrás, cabrá,**
  cabremos, cabréis, cabrán
  CONDITIONAL **cabría, cabrías,**
  cabría, cabríamos, cabríais,
  cabrían
  PRETERITE **cupe, cupiste,**
  cupo, cupimos, cupisteis,
  cupieron
caer to fall
  PRESENT PARTICIPLE **cayendo**
  PAST PARTICIPLE **caído**
  PRESENT **caigo, caes, cae, cae-**
  mos, caísteis, caen
  PRETERITE **caí, caíste, cayó,**
  caímos, caísteis, cayeron
calentar to warm, see **acertar**
carecer to lack, see **abastecer**

cegar to go blind
  PRESENT **ciego, ciegas, ciega, cegamos, cegáis, ciegan**
  PRESENT SUBJUNCTIVE **ciegue, ciegues, ciegue, ceguemos, ceguéis, cieguen**
ceñir to surround, see **teñir**
cerner to sift, see **hender**
cerrar to close, see **acertar**
cimentar to found, see **acertar**
circunscribir to circumscribe, see **escribir**
cocer to boil
  PRESENT **cuezo, cueces, cuece, cocemos, cocéis, cuecen**
  PRESENT SUBJUNCTIVE **cueza, cuezas, cueza, cozamos, cozáis, cuezan**
colar to strain, see **mostrar**
colgar to hang, see **rogar**
comenzar to commence, see **empezar**
compadecer to pity, see **abastecer**
comparecer to appear, see **abastecer**
competir to contend, see **pedir**
complacer to please, see **placer**
componer to compose, see **poner**
comprobar to verify, see **mostrar**
concebir to conceive, see **pedir**
concernir to regard
  PRESENT **concierne, conciernen** DEFECTIVE VERB: Used only in the third person singu

lar and plural.
concertar to concert, see **acertar**
concluir to conclude, see **diluir**
concordar to accord, see **mostrar**
condescender to consent, see **hender**
condolerse to condole, see **mover**
conducir to convey
  PRESENT **conduzco, conduces, conduce, conducimos, conducís, conducen**
  PRETERITE **conduje, condujiste, condujo, condujimos, condujisteis, condujeron**
conferir to confer, see **invertir**
confesar to confess, see **acertar**
confluir to join, see **diluir**
conmover to touch, see **mover**
conocer to know, see **abastecer**
conseguir to obtain, see **seguir**
consentir to consent to, see **invertir**
consolar to console, see **mostrar**
constituir to constitute, see **diluir**
constreñir to constrain, see **teñir**
construir to build, see **diluir**
contar to count, see **mostrar**
contender to contend, see **hender**
contener to contain, see **tener**
contorcerse to writhe, see **cocer**

contradecir to contradict, see
decir

contraer to catch, see **traer**

contravenir to contravene, see
  venir

contribuir to contribute, see
  diluir

convalecer to convalesce, see
  abastecer

convenir to agree, see **venir**

convertir to transform, see **inver**
tir

corregir to correct, see **elegir**

costar to cost, see **mostrar**

crecer to grow, see **abastecer**

creer to believe, see **leer**

cubrir to cover
  PAST PARTICIPLE **cubierto**

dar to **give**
  PRESENT **doy, das, da, damos,
  dais, dan**
  PRESENT SUBJUNCTIVE **dé,
  des, dé,
  demos, deis, den**
  PRETERITE **dí, diste, dio, dimos,
  disteis, dieron**

decaer to decay, see **caer**

decentar to cut the first piece of,
  see **acertar**

decir to say
  PRESENT PARTICIPLE **diciendo**
  PAST PARTICIPLE **dicho**
  PRESENT **digo, dices, dice, deci**

mos, decís, dicen
  FUTURE **diré, dirás, dirá, dire-
  mos, diréis, dirán**
  CONDITIONAL **diría, dirías,
  diría, diríamos, diríais, dirían**
  PRETERITE **dije, dijiste, dijo,
  dijimos, dijisteis, dijeron**
  IMPERATIVE **di, decid**

deducir to deduce, see **conducir**

defender to defend, see **hender**

degollar to behead, see **agorar**

demoler to demolish, see **mover**

demostrar to prove, see **mostrar**

denegar to deny, see **cegar**

derretir to melt, see **pedir**

derruir to demolish, see **diluir**

desaforar to violate the rights of,
  see **mostrar**

desalentar to wind, see **acertar**

desandar to retrace, see **andar**

desaparecer to disappear, see
  abastecer

desaprobar to disapprove of, see
  mostrar

desasir to let go of, see **asir**

desatender to disregard, see **hender**

desavenir to put at odds, see
  venir

descabullirse to escape, see
  engullir

descender to descend, see **hender**

descolgar to take down, see **rogar**

descollar to excel, see **mostrar**

descomedirse to be rude, see
pedir

descomponer to decompose, see
poner

desconcertar to disconcert, see
acertar

desconocer to disown, see **abaste-cer**

desconsolar to grieve, see **mostrar**

descontar to deduct, see **mostrar**

descreer to disbelieve, see **leer**

describir to describe, see **escribir**

descubrir to uncover, see **cubrir**

desdecir to go counter, see **decir**

desencordar to unstring, see
mostrar

desentenderse to pretend igno-rance, see **hender**

desenterrar to disinter, see **acer-tar**

desenvolver to unwrap, see **volver**

desfallecer to weaken, see **abaste-cer**

desfavorecer to disfavor, see
abastecer

desguarnecer to strip of orna-ments, see **abastecer**

deshacer to undo, see **hacer**

deshelar to thaw, see **acertar**

desherrar to unchain, see **acertar**

deshumedecer to dehumidify, see
abastecer

desleir to dissolve, see **reir**

deslucir to offset, see **lucir**

desmembrar to dismember, see
acertar

desmentir to contradict, see
invertir

desmerecer to be unworthy of,
see **abastecer**

desobedecer to disobey, see **abas-tecer**

desolar to desolate, see **mostrar**

desollar to skin, see **mostrar**

despedir to dismiss, see **pedir**

despertar to wake, see **acertar**

desplegar to unfold, see **cegar**

despoblar to depopulate, see
mostrar

desposeer to dispossess, see **leer**

desteñir to discolor, see **teñir**

desterrar to banish, see **acertar**

destituir to deprive, see **diluir**

destruir to destroy, see **diluir**

desvanecer to dispel, see **abaste-cer**

detener to stop, see **tener**

devolver to return, see **volver**

diferir to defer, see **invertir**

digerir to digest, see **invertir**

diluir to dilute

PRESENT PARTICIPLE diluyen-do

PRESENT diluyo diluyes, diluye, diluimos, diluís, diluyen

PRETERITE diluí, diluiste, dilu-yó, diluimos, diluisteis, diluye-ron

discernir to discern
PRESENT **discierno, disciernes, discierne, discernimos, discernís, disciernen**
PRESENT SUBJUNCTIVE **discierna, disciernas, discierna, discernamos, discernáis, disciernan**
discordar to disagree, see **mostrar**
disentir to dissent, see **invertir**
disolver to dissolve, see **volver**
disonar to be in disharmony, see **mostrar**
disponer to dispose, see **poner**
distender to distend, see **hender**
distraer to distract, see **traer**
distribuir to distribute, see **diluir**
divertir to amuse, see **invertir**
doler to hurt, see **mover**
dormir to sleep
PRESENT PARTICIPLE **durmiendo**
PRESENT **duermo, duermes, duerme, dormimos, dormís, duermen**
PRESENT SUBJUNCTIVE **duerma, duermas, duerma, durmamos, durmáis, duerman**
PRETERITE **dormí, dormiste, durmió, dormimos, dormisteis, durmieron**

elegir to choose
PRESENT PARTICIPLE **eligiendo**
PRESENT **elijo, eliges, elige, elegimos, elegís, eligen**
PRETERITE **elegí, elegiste, eligió, elegimos, elegisteis, eligieron**
embellecer to embellish, see **abastecer**
embestir to attack, see **pedir**
emblandecer to soften, see **abastecer**
embobecer to stupefy, see **abastecer**
emparentar to become related by marriage, see **acertar**
empedernir to harden, see **blandir**
empedrar to pave with stones, see **acertar**
empequeñecer to belittle, see **abastecer**
empezar to begin
PRESENT **empiezo, empiezas, empieza, empezamos, empezáis, empiezan**
PRESENT SUBJUNCTIVE **empiece, empieces, empiece, empecemos, empecéis, empiecen**
PRETERITE **empecé, empezaste, empezó, empezamos, empezasteis, empezaron**
emplumecer to grow feathers, see **abastecer**
empobrecer to impoverish, see **abastecer**

enaltecer to praise, see abastecer

enardecer to inflame, see abastecer

encalvecer to get bald, see abastecer

encandecer to bring to a white heat, see abastecer

encanecer to turn gray, see abastecer

encarecer to raise the price of, see abastecer

encender to light, see hender

encerrar to confine, see acertar

encomendar to recommend, see acertar

encontrar to meet, see mostrar

encrudecer to exasperate, see abastecer

endurecer to harden, see abastecer

enflaquecer to weaken, see abastecer

enfurecer to infuriate, see abastecer

engrandecer to augment, see abastecer

engreir to make proud, see reir

engrosar to thicken, see mostrar

engullir to gobble up
PRESENT PARTICIPLE engullendo
PRETERITE engullí, engulliste, engulló, engullimos, engullisteis, engulleron

enloquecer to madden, see abastecer

enmendar to correct, see acertar

enmohecer to mold, see abastecer

enmudecer to silence, see abastecer

ennegrecer to blacken, see abastecer

ennoblecer to ennoble, see abastecer

enorgullecer to fill with pride, see abastecer

enriquecer to enrich, see abastecer

enrojecer to redden, see abastecer

enronquecer to make hoarse, see abastecer

ensangrentar to bloody, see acertar

ensordecer to deafen, see abastecer

entender to understand, see hender

enternecer to soften, see abastecer

enterrar to inter, see acertar

entontecer to stupefy, see abastecer

entorpecer to dull, see abastecer

entreabrir to leave ajar, see abrir

entreoír to barely hear, see oir

entretener to amuse, see tener

entrever to catch a glimpse of,

see **ver**

entristecer to sadden, see **abastecer**

entumecer to numb, see **abastecer**

envanecer to make vain, see **abastecer**

envejecer to age, see **abastecer**

envestir to invest, see **pedir**

envilecer to degrade, see **abastecer**

envolver to involve, see **volver**

equivaler to be of equal value, see **salir**

erguir to raise
 PRESENT PARTICIPLE **irguiendo**
 PRESENT **yergo** or **irgo, yergues** or **irgues, yergue** or **irgue, erguimos, erguís, yerguen** or **irguen**
 PRESENT SUBJUNCTIVE **yerga** or **irga, yergas** or **irgas, yerga** or **irga, irgamos, igáis, yergan** or **irgan**
 PRETERITE **erguí, erguiste, erguimos, erguisteis, irguieron**

errar to miss
 PRESENT **yerro, yerras, yerra, erramos, erráis, yerran**
 PRESENT SUBJUNCTIVE **yerre, yerres, yerre, erremos, erréis, yerren**

escabullirse to escape, see **engullir**

escarmentar to take warning, see **acertar**

escarnecer to mock, see **abastecer**

esclarecer to illuminate, see **abastecer**

escribir to write
 PAST PARTICIPLE **escrito**

esforzar to strengthen, see **forzar**

establecer to establish, see **abastecer**

estar to be
 PRESENT **estoy, estás, está, estamos, estáis, están**
 PRESENT SUBJUNCTIVE **esté, estés, esté, estemos, estéis, estén**
 PRETERITE **estuve, estuviste, estuvo, estuvimos, estuvisteis, estuvieron**

estregar to rub, see **cegar**

estremecer to shake, see **abastecer**

estreñir to constipate, see **teñir**

excluir to exclude, see **diluir**

expedir to expedite, see **pedir**

exponer to expose, see **poner**

extender to extend, see **hender**

extraer to extract, see **traer**

fallecer to die, see **abastecer**

favorecer to favor, see **abastecer**

florecer to blossom, see **abastecer**
fluir to flow, see **diluir**
fortalecer to fortify, see **abastecer**
forzar to force
   PRESENT **fuerzo, fuerzas,
fuerza, forzamos, forzáis,
fuerzan**
   PRESENT SUBJUNCTIVE
**fuerce, fuerces, fuerce,
forcemos, forcéis, fuercen**
   PRETERITE **forcé, forzaste,
forzó, forzamos, forzasteis, for-
zaron**
fregar to scrub, see **cegar**
freír to fry
   PRESENT PARTICIPLE **friendo**
   PAST PARTICIPLE **frito**
   PRESENT **frío, fríes, fríe, freí-
mos, freís, fríen**
   PRETERITE **freí, freíste, frió, fre-
ímos, freísteis, frieron**

gemir to groan, see **pedir**
gobernar to govern, see **acertar**
gruñir to grunt, see **plañir**
guarnecer to set, see **abastecer**

haber to have
   PRESENT **he, has, ha, hemos,
habéis, han**
   FUTURE **habré, habrás, habrá,
habremos, habréis, habran**
   CONDITIONAL **habría, habrías,
habría, habríamos, habríais,**
habrían
   PRESENT SUBJUNCTIVE **haya,
hayas, haya, hayamos, hayáis ,
hayan**
   PRETERITE **hube, hubiste,
hubo, hubimos, hubisteis
hubieron**
   IMPERATIVE **hé, habed,**
hacer to make, to do
   PAST PARTICIPLE **hecho**
   PRESENT **hago, haces, hace,
hacemos, hacéis, hacen**
   FUTURE **haré, harás, hará,
haremos, haréis, harán**
   CONDITIONAL **haría, harías,
haría, haríamos, haríais, harían**
   PRETERITE **hice, hiciste, hizo,
hicimos, hicisteis, hicieron**
   IMPERATIVE **haz, haced**
heder to smell bad, see **hender**
helar to freeze, see **acertar**
henchir to fill, see **pedir**
hender to split
   PRESENT **hiendo, hiendes,
hiende, hendemos, hendéis,
hienden**
   PRESENT SUBJUNCTIVE **hienda, hiendas, hienda, hendamos,
hendáis, hiendan**
herir to wound, see **invertir**
herrar to shoe, see **acertar**
hervir to boil, see **invertir**
holgar to rest, see **rogar**
hollar to trample, see **mostrar**

huir to flee, see **diluir**

humedecer to moisten, see
  abastecer

imbuir to imbue, see **diluir**

impedir to impede, see **pedir**

imponer to impose, see **poner**

incluir to include, see **diluir**

indisponer to indispose, see **poner**

inducir to induce, see **conducir**

inferir to infer, see **invertir**

influir to influence, see **diluir**

ingerir to ingest, see **invertir**

inquirir to investigate
  PRESENT inquiero, inquieres,
  inquiere, inquirimos, inquirís,
  inquieren
  PRESENT SUBJUNCTIVE
  inquiera, inquieras, inquiera,
  inquiramos, inquiráis, inquieran

inscribir to inscribe, see **escribir**

instituir to institute, see **diluir**

instruir to instruct, see **diluir**

interponer to interpose, see **poner**

intervenir to happen, see **venir**

introducir to introduce, see conducir

invertir to invert
  PRESENT PARTICIPLE invirtien-
  do
  PRESENT invierto, inviertes,
  invierte, invertimos, invertís,
  invierten
  PRESENT SUBJUNCTIVE invier

ta, inviertas, invierta,
invirtamos, invirtáis, inviertan
PRETERITE invertí, invertiste,
invirtió, invertimos, invertisteis,
invirtieron,

investir to invest, see **pedir**

ir to go
  PRESENT PARTICIPLE yendo
  PRESENT voy, vas, va, vamos,
  vais, van
  PRESENT SUBJUNCTIVE vaya,
  vayas, vaya, vayamos, vayáis,
  vayan
  IMPERFECT iba, ibas, iba, íba-
  mos, ibais, iban
  PRETERITE fui, fuiste, fue, fui-
  mos, fuisteis, fueron
  IMPERATIVE vé, id

jugar to play
  PRESENT juego, juegas, juega,
  jugamos, jugáis, juegan
  PRESENT SUBJUNCTIVE juegue, juegues, juegue, juguemos,
  juguéis, jueguen

languidecer to languish, see
  abastecer

leer to read
  PRESENT PARTICIPLE leyendo
  PAST PARTICIPLE leído
  PRETERITE leí, leíste, leyó, leí-
  mos, leísteis, leyeron

lucir to shine

PRESENT luzco, luces, luce, lucimos, lucís, lucen

llover to rain, see mover

maldecir to curse, see bendecir

malquerer to have a grudge against, see querer

manifestar to manifest, see acertar

mantener to maintain, see tener

medir to measure, see pedir

mentar to mention, see acertar

mentir to lie, see invertir

merecer to deserve, see abastecer

merendar to have a snack, see acertar

moler to grind, see mover

morder to bite, see mover

morir to die

PRESENT PARTICIPLE muriendo

PAST PARTICIPLE muerto

PRESENT muero, mueres, muere, morimos, morís, mueren

PRESENT SUBJUNCTIVE muera, mueras, muera, muramos, muráis, mueran PRETERITE morí, moriste, murió, morimos, moristeis, murieron

mostrar to show

PRESENT muestro, muestras, muestra, mostramos, mostráis, muestran

PRESENT SUBJUNCTIVE mues

tre, muestres, muestre, mostremos, mostréis, muestren

mover to move

PRESENT muevo, mueves, mueve, movemos, movéis, mueven

PRESENT SUBJUNCTIVE mueva, muevas, mueva, movamos, mováis, muevan

mullir to fluff up, see engullir

nacer to be born, see abastecer

negar to deny, see cegar

nevar to snow, see acertar

obedecer to obey, see abastecer

obstruir to obstruct, see diluir

obtener to obtain, see tener

ofrecer to offer, see abastecer

oir to hear

PRESENT PARTICIPLE oyendo

PAST PARTICIPLE oído

PRESENT oigo, oyes, oye, oímos, oís, oyen

PRETERITE oí, oíste, oyó, oímos, oísteis, oyeron

IMPERATIVE oye, oíd

oler to smell

PRESENT huelo, hueles, huele, olemos, oléis, huelen

PRESENT SUBJUNCTIVE huela, huelas, huela, olamos, oláis, huelan

oponer to oppose, see poner

oscurecer to darken, see **abastecer**

padecer to suffer, see **abastecer**

palidecer to turn pale, see **abastecer**

parecer to appear, see **abastecer**

pedir to ask

PRESENT PARTICIPLE **pidiendo**
PRESENT **pido, pides, pide, pedimos, pedís, piden**
PRETERITE **pedí, pediste, pidió, pedimos, pedisteis, pidieron**

pensar to think, see **acertar**

perder to lose, see **hender**

perecer to perish, see **abastecer**

permanecer to remain, see **abastecer**

perseguir to persecute, see **seguir**

pertenecer to belong, see **abastecer**

pervertir to pervert, see **invertir**

placer to please

PRESENT **plazco, places, place, placemos, placéis, placen**
PRETERITE **placé, placiste, plació** or **plugo, placimos, placisteis, placieron** or **pluguieron**
PAST SUBJUNCTIVE **placiera, placieras, placiera** or **pluguiera, placiéramos, placierais, placieran**

plañir to lament

PRESENT PARTICIPLE **plañendo**

PRETERITE **plañí, plañiste, plañó, plañimos, plañisteis, plañeron**

plegar to fold, see **cegar**

poblar to populate, see **mostrar**

poder to be able

PRESENT PARTICIPLE **pudiendo**
PRESENT **puedo, puedes, puede, podemos, podéis, pueden**
FUTURE **podré, podrás, podrá, podremos, podréis, podrán**
CONDITIONAL **podría, podrías, podría, podríamos, podríais, podrían**
PRESENT SUBJUNCTIVE **pueda, puedas, pueda, podamos, podáis, puedan** PRETERITE **pude, pudiste, pudo, pudimos, pudisteis, pudieron**

podrir to rot, see **pudrir**

poner to put

PAST PARTICIPLE **puesto**
PRESENT **pongo, pones, pone, ponemos, ponéis, ponen**
FUTURE **pondré, pondrás, pondrá, pondremos, pondréis, pondrán**
CONDITIONAL **pondría, pondrías, pondría, pondríamos, pondríais, pondrían**
PRETERITE **puse, pusiste, puso, pusimos, pusisteis, pusieron**
IMPERATIVE **pon, poned**

poseer to possess, see **leer**

posponer to postpone, see **poner**

predecir to foretell, see **decir**

predisponer to predispose, see **poner**

preferir to prefer, see **invertir**

prescribir to prescribe, see **escribir**

presentir to have a premonition of, see **invertir**

presuponer to presuppose, see **poner**

prevalecer to prevail, see **abastecer**

prevenir to prepare, see **venir**

prever to foresee, see **ver**

probar to try, see **mostrar**

producir to produce, see **conducir**

proferir to utter, see **invertir**

promover to promote, see **mover**

proponer to propose, see **poner**

proscribir to exile, see escribir

proseguir to pursue, see **seguir**

proveer to provide, see **leer**

provenir to arise, see **venir**

pudrir to putrefy

  PAST PARTICIPLE **podrido**

quebrar to break, see **acertar**

querer to wish

  PRESENT **quiero, quieres, quiere, queremos, queréis, quieren**

  FUTURE **querré, querrás, querrá, querremos, querréis, querrán**

  CONDITIONAL **querría, querrías, querría, querríamos, querríais, querrían**

  PRESENT SUBJUNCTIVE **quiera, quieras, quiera, queramos, queráis, quieran**

  PRETERITE **quise, quisiste, quiso, quisimos, quisisteis, quisieron**

reaparecer to reappear, see **abastecer**

recaer to fall back, see **caer**

recalentar to reheat, see **acertar**

recluir to shut in, see **diluir**

recomendar to recommend, see **acertar**

reconocer to recognize, see **abastecer**

reconstruir to reconstruct, see **diluir**

reconvenir to retort with, see **venir**

recordar to remember, see **acertar**

recostar to lean, see **mostrar**

recubrir to cover, see **cubrir**

reducir to reduce, see **conducir**

reelegir to reelect, see **elegir**

referir to refer, see **invertir**

reforzar to strengthen, see **forzar**

regar to water, see **cegar**

regir to rule, see **elegir**

rehacer to repair, see **hacer**

reir to laugh
PRESENT PARTICIPLE riendo
PAST PARTICIPLE reído
PRESENT río, ríes, ríe, reímos,
reís, ríen PRETERITE reí, reíste,
rió, reímos, reísteis, rieron
rejuvenecer to rejuvenate, see
abastecer
relucir to shine, see lucir
remendar to repair, see acertar
remover to remove, see mover
renacer to be born again, see
abastecer
rendir to yield, see pedir
renegar to deny, see cegar
renovar to renovate, see mostrar
reñir to wrangle, see teñir
repetir to repeat, see pedir
reponer to replace, see poner
reprobar to fail, see mostrar
reproducir to reproduce, see conducir
requerir to notify, see invertir
resentirse to weaken, see invertir
resolver to resolve, see volver
resonar to resound, see mostrar
resplandecer to shine, see
abastecer
resquebrar to start to break, see
acertar
restablecer to restore, see abastecer
restituir to restore, see diluir
restregar to scrub hard, see cegar

restriñir to constrict, see plañir
retener to retain, see tener
retorcer to twist, see cocer
retraer to bring back, see traer
retribuir to repay, see diluir
reventar to break, see acertar
reverdecer to grow green again,
see abastecer
revestir to don, see pedir
revolcarse to wallow, see aclocarse
revolver to shake, see volver
robustecer to strengthen, see
abastecer
rodar to roll, see mostrar
roer to gnaw
PRESENT PARTICIPLE royendo
PAST PARTICIPLE roído
PRESENT roo or roigo or royo,
roes, roe, roemos, roéis, roen
PRESENT SUBJUNCTIVE roa,
roiga or roya, roas, roa, roamos,
roáis, roan
PRETERITE roí, roíste, royó, roí-
mos, roísteis, royeron
rogar to entreat
PRESENT ruego, ruegas, ruega,
rogamos, rogáis, ruegan
PRESENT SUBJUNCTIVE
ruegue, ruegues, ruegue, rogue-
mos, roguéis, rueguen
romper to break
PAST PARTICIPLE roto

saber to know
PRESENT sé, sabes, sabe, sabemos, sabéis, saben
FUTURE sabré, sabrás, sabrá, sabremos, sabréis, sabrán
CONDITIONAL sabría, sabrías, sabría, sabríamos, sabríais, sabrían
PRESENT SUBJUNCTIVE sepa, sepas, sepa, sepamos, sepáis, sepan
PRETERITE supe, supiste, supo, supimos, supisteis, supieron

salir to go out
PRESENT salgo, sales, sale, salimos, salís, salen
FUTURE saldré, saldrás, saldrá, saldremos, saldréis, saldrán
CONDITIONAL saldría, saldrías, saldría, saldríamos, saldríais, saldría
IMPERATIVE sal, salid

satisfacer to satisfy, see **hacer**
seducir to seduce, see **conducir**
segar to reap, see **cegar**
seguir to follow
PRESENT sigo, sigues, sigue, seguimos, seguís, siguen
PRETERITE seguí, seguiste, siguió, seguimos, seguisteis, siguieron

sembrar to sow, see **acertar**
sementar to seed, see **acertar**
sentar to seat, see **acertar**

sentir to feel, see **invertir**
ser to be
PRESENT soy, eres, es, somos, sois, son
PRESENT SUBJUNCTIVE sea, seas, sea, seamos, seáis, sean
IMPERFECT era, eras, era, éramos, erais, eran
PRETERITE fui, fuiste, fue, fuimos, fuisteis, fueron
IMPERATIVE sé, sed

servir to serve, see **invertir**
sobrentender to understand, see **hender**
sobreponer to superimpose, see **poner**
sobresalir to excel, see **salir**
sobrevenir to happen unexpectedly, see **venir**
soldar to solder, see **mostrar**
soler to be accustomed to, see **mover**
soltar to untie, see **mostrar**
sonar to sound, see **mostrar**
sonreir to smile, see **reir**
soñar to dream, see **mostrar**
sorber to sip, see **mover**
sosegar to calm, see **cegar**
sostener to sustain, see **tener**
subarrendar to sublet, see **acertar**
sugerir to suggest, see **invertir**
suponer to suppose, see **poner**

sustituir to replace, see diluir
sustraer to subtract, see traer

temblar to tremble, see acertar
tender to stretch out, see hender
tener to have
  PRESENT tengo, tienes, tiene, tenemos, tenéis, tienen
  FUTURE tendré, tendrás, tendrá, tendremos, tendréis, tendrán
  CONDITIONAL tendría, tendrías, tendría, tendríamos, tendríais, tendrían
  PRETERITE tuve, tuviste, tuvo, tuvimos, tuvisteis, tuvieron
  IMPERATIVE ten, tened
tentar to touch, see acertar
teñir to dye
  PRESENT PARTICIPLE tiñiendo
  PRESENT tiño, tiñes, tiñe, teñimos, teñís, tiñen
  PRETERITE teñí, teñiste, tiñó, teñimos, teñisteis, tiñeron
torcer to twist, see cocer
tostar to toast, see mostrar
traducir to translate, see conducir
traer to bring
  PRESENT PARTICIPLE trayendo
  PAST PARTICIPLE traído
  PRESENT traigo, traes, trae, traemos, traéis, traen
  IMPERFECT traía, traías, traía,
traíamos, traíais, traían
  PRETERITE traje, trajiste, trajo, trajimos, trajisteis, trajeron
trascender to spread, see hender
trascribir to transcribe, see escribir
trasferir to transfer, see invertir
traslucirse to be transparent, see lucir
trasponer to transfer, see poner
trocar to exchange, see aclocarse
tronar to thunder, see mostrar
tropezar to stumble, see empezar

valer to be worth, see salir
venir to arrive
  PRESENT PARTICIPLE viniendo
  PRESENT vengo, vienes, viene, venimos, venís, vienen
  FUTURE vendré, vendrás, vendrá, vendremos, vendréis, vendrán
  CONDITIONAL vendría, vendrías, vendría, vendríamos, vendríais, vendrían
  PRETERITE vine, viniste, vino, vinimos, vinisteis, vinieron
  IMPERATIVE ven, venid
ver to see
  PAST PARTICIPLE visto
  PRESENT veo, ves, ve, vemos, veis, ven IMPERFECT veía, veías, veía, veíamos, veíais, veían

PRETERITE **ví, viste, vio, vimos, visteis, vieron**

verter to spill, see **hender**

vestir to clothe, see **pedir**

volar to fly, see **mostrar**

volcar to upset, see **aclocarse**

volver to return

PAST PARTICIPLE **vuelto**

PRESENT **vuelvo, vuelves, vuelve, volvemos, volvéis, vuelven**

PRESENT SUBJUNCTIVE **vuelva, vuelvas, vuelva, volvamos, volváis, vuelvan**

yacer to lie

PRESENT **yazco** or **yazgo** or **yago, yaces, yace, yacemos, yacéis, yacen**

PRESENT SUBJUNCTIVE **yazca** or **yazga** or **yaga, yazcas, yazca, yazcamos, yazcáis, yazcan**

IMPERATIVE **yaz** or **yace, yaced**

zambullirse to dive, see **engullir**

Part I

SPANISH - ENGLISH

ESPAÑOL - INGLÉS

ABBREVIATIONS

adj.	adjective, *adjetivo*
adv.	adverb, *adverbio*
avi.	aviation, *aviación*
agr.	agriculture, *agricultura*
anat.	anatomy, *anatomía*
arch,	architecture, *arquitectura*
Arg.	Argentina, *Argentina*
art.	article, *artículo*
ast.	astronomy, *astronomía*
auto.	automobile, *automóvil*
biol.	biology, *biología*
Bol.	Bolivia, *Bolivia*
Bot.	botany, *botánica*
chem.	chemistry, *química*
Col.	Columbia, *Colombia*
coll.	colloquial, *familiar*
com.	commerce, *comercio*
conj.	conjunction, *conjunción*
dent.	dentistry, *dentistería*
eccl.	ecclesiastic, *eclesiástico*
Ecu.	Ecuador, *Ecuador*
elec.	electricity, *electricidad*
ent.	entomology, *entomología*
f.	feminine, *femenino*
fig.	figurative(ly), *figurado*
geog.	geography, *geografía*
geol.	geology, *geología*
gram.	grammar, *gramática*
Guat.	Guatemala, *Guatemala*
ichth.	ichthyology, *ictiología*
inter/.	interjection, *interjección*
interr.	interrogative, *interrogativo*
m.	masculine, *masculino*

math.	mathematics, *matemáticas*
mech.	mechanics, *mecánica*
med.	medicine, *medicina*
Mex.	Mexico, *Méjico*
mil.	military art, *milicia*
min.	mining, *minería*
mus,	music, *música*
n.	noun, *sustantivo*
naut.	nautical, *náutico* or *marino*
orn.	ornithology, *ornitología*
phot.	photography, *fotografía*
phy.	physics, *física*
pl.	plural, *plural*
poet.	poetry, *poética*
pol.	politics, *política*
p.p.	past participle, *participio pasado*
P.R.	Puerto Rico, *Puerto Rico*
prep.	preposition, *preposición*
print.	printing, *imprenta*
pron.	pronoun, *pronombre*
rad.	radio, *radiocomunica-ción*
rail.	railway, *ferrocarril*
rhet.	rhetoric, *retórica*
sing.	singular, *singular*
Sp.Am	Spanish America, *Hispanoamérica*
theat.	theater, *teatro*
TV.	television, *televisión*
Urug.	Uruguay, *Uruguay*
v.	verb, *verbo*
va.	transitive verb, *verbo activo*
Ven.	Venezuela, *Venezuela*
vet.	veterinary, *veterinaria*
vi., vn.	intransitive verb, *verbo neutro*
vr.	reflexive verb, *verbo reflexivo*
vt.	transitive verb, *verbo activo*
zool.	zoology, *zoología*

Spanish - English

A

a (â) *prep.* to; in, at *(lugar);* according to *(según);* by, through *(por);* for *(para);* toward *(hacia);* with *(con);* — **pie,** on foot; — **mi izquierda,** on my left.

ábaco (â´vâ•ko) *m.* abacus.

abad (â•vâth´) *m.* abbot.

abadejo (â•vâ•the´ho) *m.* codfish *(bacalao);* yellow wren *(reyezuelo);* Spanish fly *(cantárida).*

abadía (â•vâ•thē´â) *f.* abbey; abbacy *(dignidad).*

abajo (â•vâ´ho) *adv.* under, underneath, below; downstairs; **calle —,** down the street; **hacia —,** downward.

abalorio (â•vâ•lo´ryo) *m.* glass bead.

abanderar (â•vân•de•râr´) *va.* to register.

abandonamiento (â•vân•do•nâ•myen´to) *m.* abandonment; carelessness *(descuido);* debauchery *(vicio).*

abandonar (â•van•do•nâr´) *va.* to abandon, to desert, to leave; **—se,** to despond, to despair.

abandono (â•van•do´no) *m.* abandonment, carelessness *(descuido);* loneliness *(soledad);* debauchery *(vicio).*

abanico (â•vâ•nē´ko) *m.* fan: small crane, derrick *(cabria);* — **neumático,** suction fan.

abarcar (â•vâr•kâr´) *va.* to clasp, to embrace *(ceñir);* to contain, to comprise *(entrañar).*

abarrancar (â•va•rrâng•kâr´) *va.* to dig holes; **—se,** to get into a tight fix, to get into a predicament.

abarrote (â•vâ•rro´te) *m.* (naut.) small wedge; **—s,** *pl.* groceries; **tienda de —s,** grocery store.

abastecedor, ra (â•vâs•te•se•thor´, râ) *n.* purveyor, caterer.

abastecer* (â•vâs•te•ser´) *va.* to purvey, to supply.

abastecimiento, (â•vas•te•sē•myen´to) *m.* provisioning, supplying with provisions.

abatimiento (â•vâ•tē•myen´to) *m.* low spirits, depression.

abatir (â•vä•tēr´) va. to tear
down, to knock down (derribar); to take down, to take apart
(desarmar).

abdicación (âv•thē•kâ•syon´) f.
abdication.

abdicar (âv•thē•kâr´) va. to abdicate.

abdomen (âv•tho´men) m.
abdomen.

abecé (â•ve•se´) m. ABC´s,
alphabet.

abecedario (â•ve•se•thâ´ryo) m.
alphabet; spelling book, primer
(librito).

abedul (â•ve•thūl´) m. birch
tree.

abeja (â•ve´hâ) f. bee; — **maestra** or **madre,** queen bee.

abejarrón (â•ve•hâ•rron´) or

abejorro (â•ve•ho´rro) m. cock-
chafer (coleóptero); bumblebee
(himenóptero).

abejero (â•ve•he´ro) m. beekee-
per.

abejón (â•ve•hon´) m. hornet;
drone (zángano).

aberración (â•ve•rrâ•syon´) f.
aberration.

abertura (â•ver•tū´râ) f . cleft,
opening.

abierto, ta (â•vyer´to, tâ) adj.
open; sincere, frank (sincero).

abigarrar (â•vē•gâ•rrâr´) va. to
variegate, to dapple.

abismar (â•vēz•mâr´) va. to

throw into an abyss; to depress
(deprimir); to humble (humillar); to confound (confundir); —
se, (Sp. Am.) to be astonished.

abismo (â•vēz´mo) m. chasm,
abyss, gulf; hell (infierno).

ablandamiento
(â•vlân•dâ•myen´to) m. mollifi-
cation, softening.

ablandar (â•vlân•dâr´) va. and
vn. to mollify, to soften.

abnegación (ây•ne•gâ•syon´) f.
abnegation, self-denial.

abnegar* (ây•ne•gâr´) va. to
renounce.

abobar (â•vo•vâr´) va. to stupefy.

abochornar (â•vo•chor•nâr.´) va.
to swelter, to overheat (sobre-
calentar); to mortify (avergonzar); —**se**, to be embarrassed,
to blush (sonrojarse); to be
sweltering (padecer del calor).

abofetear (â•vo•fe•te•âr´) va. to
slap one´s face.

abogacía (â•vo•gâ•sē´â) f. legal
profession.

abogado (â•vo•gâ´tho) m. lawyer;
advocate, mediator (defensor).

abogar (â•vo•gâr´) vn. to mediate, to intercede.

abolir* (â•vo•lēr´) va. to abolish.

abolladura (â•vo•yâ•thū´râ) f .
dent; embossing (realce).

abollar (â•vo•yâr´) va. to dent; to
emboss (realzar).

abombado, da (â•vom•bâ´tho,

thâ) *adj.* stunned, confused.

abominable (â•vo•mē•nâ´vle) *adj.* abominable.

abominar (â•vo•mē•nâr´) *va.* to abominate, to detest.

abonar (â•vo•nâr´) *va.* to improve *(mejorar);* to make good an assertion *(acertar);* to fertilize *(fertilizar);* (com.) to credit *(acreditar);* to pay (on an account); —**se,** to subscribe to; — **en cuenta,** to credit to one´s account.

abono (â•vo´no) *m.* fertilizer *(fertilizante);* (com.) payment, installment *(pago);* season ticket (to a theater) *(suscripción);* — **de pasaje,** commutation ticket.

abordar (â•vor•thâr´) *va.* (naut.) to come alongside; to broach, to take up *(entablar);* —, *vn.* to put into port, to dock, to land.

aborigen (â•vo•rē´hen) *adj.* aboriginal, indigenous; —, *m.* aborigine.

aborrecer* (â•vo•rre•ser´) *va.* to hate, to abhor; to abandon, to desert *(las aves).*

aborrecimiento (â•vo•rre•sē•myen´to) *m.* abhorrence, hatred.

abortar (â•vor•târ´) *vn.* to miscarry, to have an abortion.

aborto (â•vor´to) *m.* miscarriage, abortion.

abotonar (â•vo•to•nâr´) *va.* and vr. to button; —, *vn.* to bud.

abovedar (â•vo•ve•thâr´) *va.* to arch, to vault.

abrasar (â•vrâ•sâr´) *va.* to burn, to scorch *(quemar);* to parch *(secar);* **tierra abrasada,** scorched earth.

abrazadera (â•vrâ•sâ•the´râ) *f.* bracket *(corchete);* loop *(sortija);* binding *(atadura).*

abrazar (â•vrâ•sâr´) *va.* to embrace, to hug; to surround *(rodear);* to comprise, to contain *(entrañar).*

abrazo (â•vrâ´so) *m.* embrace, hug.

abrebrechas (â•vre•vre´châs) *m.* bulldozer.

abrelatas (â•vre•lâ´tâs) *m.* can opener.

abrevadero (â•vre•vâ•the´ro) *m.* watering place for cattle.

abreviación (â•vre•vyâ•syon´) *f.* abbreviation, abridgment, shortening.

abreviar (â•vre•vyâr´) va. to abridge, to cut short *(acortar);* to accelerate *(acelerar).*

abreviatura (â•vre•vyâ•tū´râ) *f.* abbreviation.

abridor (â•vrē•thor´) *m.* opener; — **de latas,** can opener.

abrigar (â•vrē•gâr´) *va.* to shelter, to protect *(amparar);* to hold, to cherish *(tener);* — **la**

esperanza, to hope; **—se,** to take shelter *(refugiarse);* to protect oneself against the cold *(arroparse).*

abrigo (â•vrē´go) *m.* shelter, protection, aid *(amparo);* wrap, overcoat *(sobretodo);* **— de pieles,** fur coat.

abril (â•vrēl´) *m.* April.

abrir* (â•vrēr´) *va.* and *vr.* to open; to unlock, to open up *(soltar);* to disclose, to reveal *(descubrir).*

abrochador (â•vro•châ•thor´) *m.* buttonhook.

abrochar (a•vro•châr´) *va.* to button on, to clasp on.

abrumador, ra (â•vrū•mâ•thor´, râ) *adj.* troublesome, annoying *(fastidioso);* overwhelming *(agobiador).*

abrumar (â•vrū•mâr´) *va.* to overwhelm *(agobiar);* to importune *(molestar).*

absceso (âvs•se´so) *m.* abscess.

absentismo (âv•sen •tēz´mo) *m.* absenteeism.

absolución (âv•so•lū•syon´) *f.* forgiveness, absolution.

absolutamente (âv•lū•tâ•men´te) *adv.* absolutely.

absoluto, ta (âv•so•lū´to, tâ) *adj.* absolute, unconditional, sole; **en —,** at all, absolutely not.

absolver* (âv•sol•ver´) *va.* to absolve, to pardon.

absorbente (âv•sor•ven´te) *m.* and *adj.* (med.) absorbent, absorbing.

absorber (âv•sor•ver´) *va.* to absorb.

absorción (âv•sor•syon´) *f.* absorption.

absorto, ta (âv•sor´to, tâ) *adj.* absorbed, engrossed *(cautivo);* amazed *(pasmado).*

abstención (âvs•ten•syon´) *f.* abstention.

abstenerse* (âvs•te•ner´se) *vr.* to abstain, to refrain from.

abstinencia (âvs•te•nen´syâ) *f.* abstinence.

abstinente (âvs•tē•nen´te) *adj.* abstinent, abstemious.

abstracción (âvs•trâk•syon´) *f.* abstraction.

abstracto, ta (âvs•trâk´to, ta) *adj.* abstract.

abstraer* (âvs•trâ•er´) *va.* to abstract, to leave out, to leave aside; **—se,** to be lost in thought.

abstraído, da (âvs•trâ•ē´tho, thâ) *adj.* abstracted; absorbed *(absorto).*

absuelto, ta (âv•swel´to, ta) *adj.* absolved, acquitted.

absurdo, da (âv•sūr´tho, thâ) *adj.* absurd; **—,** *m.* absurdity.

abuela (â•vwe´lâ) *f.* grandmother.

abuelo (â•vwe´lo) *m.* grandfather; —**s,** *pl.* ancestors, forefathers.

abultar (â•vūl•târ´) *va.* to make bulky, to enlarge; —, *vn.* to be bulky.

abundancia (â•vūn•dân´syâ) *f.* abundance.

abundante (â•vūn•dân´te) *adj.* abundant, copious.

abundar (â•vūn•dâr´) *vn.* to abound.

aburrido, da (â•vū•rrē´tho, thâ) *adj.* bored, weary *(fastidiado);* boresome, tedious *(pesado).*

aburrir (â•vū•rrēr´) *va.* to vex, to weary, to bore; —**se,** to be bored.

abusar (â•vū•sâr´) *vn.* to take advantage of, to abuse; — **de,** to impose upon.

abusivo, va (â•vū•sē´vo, vâ) *adj.* abusive.

abuso (â•vū´so) *m.* abuse, misuse, harsh treatment; — **de confianza,** breach of trust.

abyecto, ta (âv•yek´to, tâ) *adj.* abject, low, dejected.

A.C. or **A. de C.: Año de Cristo,** A.D. in the year of Our Lord.

acá (â•kâ´) *adv.* here, this way.

acabado, da (â•kâ•vâ´tho, thâ) *adj.* finished, perfect, accomplished *(consumado);* concluded, terminated *(concluido).*

acabar (â•kâ•vâr´) *va.* to finish, to complete *(completar);* to

achieve *(alcanzar);* —, *vn.* to die *(morir);* to expire, to run out *(expirar);* **acaba de hacerlo,** he has just done it; —**se,** to grow feeble, to become run down.

academia (â•kâ•the´myâ) *f.* academy; literary society.

académico (â•kâ•the´mē•ko) *m.* academician; —, **ca,** *adj.* academic.

acaecimiento (â•kâ•e•sē•myen´-to) *m.* event, incident.

acalambrado, da (â•kâ•lâm•brâ´tho, thâ) *adj.* cramped.

acalenturarse (â•kâ•len•tū•râr´se) *vr.* to be feverish.

acalorar (â•kâ•lo•râr´) *va.* to heat; —**se,** to get excited *(irritarse);* to become warm.

acampamento (â•kâm•pâ•men´-to) *m.* (mil.) encampment.

acampar (â•kâm•pâr´) *va.* to camp; (mil.) to encamp.

acaparar (â•kâ•pa•râr´) *va.* to monopolize, to corner.

acaramelar (â•kâ•râ•me•lâr´) *va.* to ice, to candy; —**se,** to be cloying, to be overly attentive (toward).

acariciar (â•kâ•rē•syâr´) *va.* to fondle, to caress; to cherish *(abrigar).*

acarrear (â•kâ•rre•âr´) *va.* to

convey in a cart, to transport *(trasportar);* to bring about, to occasion, to cause *(causar).*

acaso (â•kâ´so) *m.* chance, happenstance, accident; —, *adv.* perhaps, by chance; **por si —.** just in case.

acatar (â•kâ•târ´) *va.* to revere, to respect, to show willingness to obey.

acaudalado, da (â•kâū•thâ•lâ´tho, thâ) *adj.* rich, wealthy.

acaudalar (â•kâū•thâ•lâr´) *va.* to hoard up, to store up.

acceder (âk•se•ther´) *vn.* to accede, to agree.

accesibilidad (âk•se•sē•vē•lē•thâth´) *f.* accessibility.

accessible (âk•se•sē´vle) *adj.* attainable, accessible.

acceso (âk•se´so) *m.* access, approach; **— de tos,** coughing fit.

accesorio, ria (âk•se•so´ryo, ryâ) *adj.* accessory, additional; —, *m.* accessory, addition, attachment.

accidental (âk•sē•then•tâl´) *adj.* accidental, casual.

accidentarse (âk•sē•then•târ´se) *vr.* to faint, to lose consciousness, to pass out.

accidente (âk•sē•then´te) *m.* accident *(desgracia);* attack, fit

(síncope).

acción (âk•syon´) *f.* act, action; operation *(operación);* battle *(combate);* (com.) share, stock.

accionar (âk•syo•nâr´) *vn.* to gesticulate.

accionista (âk•syo•nēs´tâ) *m.* and *f.* share-holder, stockholder.

acebo (â•se´vo) *m.* holly tree.

acechar (â´se•châr´) *va.* to watch closely, to spy on.

acecho (â•se´cho) *m.* lying in ambush, waylaying.

aceitar (â•see•târ´) *va.* to oil.

aceite (â•se´ē•te) *m.* oil; **— de comer** or **de oliva,** olive oil; **— de higado de bacalao,** cod-liver oil; **— de ricino,** castor oil.

aceitoso, sa (â•seē•to´so, sâ) *adj.* oily, greasy.

aceituna (â•seē•tu´nâ) *f.* olive.

aceleración (â•se•le•râ•syon´) *f.* acceleration.

acelerador (â•se•le•râ•thor´) *m.* accelerator; (auto.) gas pedal.

acelerar (â•se•le•râr´) *va.* to accelerate, to hurry.

acemita (â•se•mē´tâ) *f.* graham bread.

acendrado, da (â•sen•drâ´tho, thâ) *adj.* pure, spotless.

acendrar (â•sen•drâr´) *va.* to refine (metals); (fig.) to purify, to make flawless.

acento (â•sen´to) *m.* accent.

acentuación (â•sen•twâ•syon´) f. accentuation.

acentuar (â•sen•twâr´) va. to accentuate, to emphasize.

aceptable (â•sep•tâ´vle) adj. acceptable.

aceptación (â•sep•tâ•syon´) f. acceptance, approbation; (com.) acceptance (of a bill); **presentar a la —,** to present for acceptance; **falta de —,** nonacceptance.

aceptar (â•sep•târ´) va. to accept, to admit; (com.) to honor.

acequia (â•se´kyâ) f. canal, channel, drain, trench.

acera (â•se´râ) f. sidewalk.

acerado, da (â•se•râ´tho, thâ) adj. made of steel; (fig) mordant, caustic, biting.

acerar (â•se•rar´) va. to steel.

acerbo, ba (â•ser´vo, vâ) adj. bitter, sharptasting; (fig.) harsh, cruel.

acerca de (â•ser´kâ the) prep. about, relating to.

acercar (â•ser•kâr´) va. to bring near together; to approach; —se, to accost, to approach.

acero (â•se´ro) m. steel; (arma) blade; — **dulce,** soft steel; — **de aleación,** alloy steel; — **colado,** cast steel; — **fundido,** hard steel; — **inoxidable,** stainless steel; — **recocido,** tempered steel; — **al carbono,** carbon steel; — **al cromo,** chrome steel; — **al vanadio,** vanadium steel; — **en barras,** bar steel; — **en bruto,** raw steel; **pulmón de —,** iron lung.

acerrojar (â•se•rro•hâr´) va. to bolt, to lock.

acertado, da (â•ser•tâ´tho, thâ) adj. accurate (preciso); skillful (hábil).

acertar* (â•ser•târ´) va. to hit (the mark) (dar en); to conjecture correctly (adivinar); —, vn. to chance, to happen, to turn out right; — **con,** to discover.

acertijo (â•ser•tē´ho) m. riddle, conundrum.

acervo (â•ser´vo) m. heap, pile.

acetona (â•se•to´nâ) f. (chem.) acetone.

acial (â•syâl´) m. barnacle.

acicalar (â•sē•kâ•lâr´) va. to polish, to furbish; —se, to dress elegantly, to spruce up.

acidez (â•sē•thes´) f. acidity.

ácido (â´sē•tho) m. (chem.) acid; **exento de —,** acid-free; — **deoxiribonucleico,** deoxyribonucleic acid; —, **da,** adj. acid, sour.

acierto (â•syer´to) m. accuracy, exactness (exactitud); dexterity, ability, knack (habilidad).

aclamación (â•klâ•mâ•syon´) f. acclamation; **por —** unanimously.

aclamar (â•klâ•mâr´) *va.* to applaud, to acclaim.

aclaración (â•klâ•ra•syon´) *f.* explanation.

aclarar (â•klâ•râr´) *va.* to clear, to brighten; to explain, to clarify *(clarificar);* —, *vn.* to clear up (weather); **—se,** to become clear.

aclimatar (â•klē•mâ•târ) *va.* to acclimatize.

aclocarse* (â•klo•kâr´se) *vr.* to brood, to hatch.

acné (âg•ne´) *f.* (med.) acne.

acobardar (â•ko•vâr•thâr´) *va.* to intimidate; **— se,** to lose courage, to be afraid.

acogedor, ra (â•ko•he•thor´, râ) *adj.* cozy, inviting.

acoger (â•ko•her´) *va.* to receive *(recibir);* to protect, to harbor *(amparar);* **—se,** to resort to.

acogida (â•ko•hē´thâ) *f.* reception; asylum, protection *(amparo);* confluence, meeting place *(concurrencia);* **dar — a una letra,** to honor a draft; **tener excelente —,** to meet with favor, to be well received.

acogimiento (â•ko•hē•myēn´to) *m.* reception, good acceptance.

acometedor, ra (a•ko•me•te•thor´, râ) *n.* aggressor; enterpriser *(emprendedor);* —, *adj.* aggressive, enterprising.

acometer (â•ko•me•ter´) *va.* to attack *(atacar);* to undertake *(emprender);* to overtake, to overcome, to steal over *(alcanzar).*

acomodadizo, za (â•ko•mo•thâ•thē´so, sâ) *adj.* accommodating.

acomodado, da (â•ko•mo•thâ´-tho, thâ) *adj.* wealthy *(rico);* suitable, convenient, fit *(conveniente).*

acomodamiento (â•ko•mo•thâ•myen´to) *m.* transaction; convenience *(conveniencia);* adaptation *(ajuste).*

acomodar (â•ko•mo•thâr´) *va.* to accommodate, to arrange; —, *vn.* to fit, to suit; **—se,** to make oneself comfortable.

acompañador, ra (â•kom•pâ•nyâ•thor´, râ) *n.* companion *(compañero);* chaperon *(dueña);* (mus.) accompanist.

acompañamiento (â•kom•pâ•nyâ•myen´•to) *m.* accompaniment, escort; (mus.) accompaniment.

acompañante, ta (â•kom•pâ•nyân´te, tâ) *n.* attendant *(asistente);* companion; (mus.) accompanist.

acompañar (â•kom•pâ•nyâr´) *va.* to accompany, to join; (mus.)

to accompany; (com.) to attach, insert.

acompasado, da (â•kom•pâ•sâ´tho, thâ) *adj.* measured, well-proportioned, cadenced.

acondicionado, da (â•kon•dē•syo•nâ´tho, thâ) *adj.* conditioned; **bien** or **mal —,** well- or ill-prepared, well- or ill-qualified.

acondicionar (â•kon•dē•syo•nâr´) *va.* to prepare, to arrange, to fit, to put in condition.

acongojar (â•kong•go•hâr´) *va.* to oppress, to afflict; **—se,** to become sad, to grieve.

aconsejable (â•kon•se•hâ´vle) *adj.* advisable.

aconsejar (â•kon•se•hâr´) *va.* to advise; **—se,** to take advice.

acontecer* (â•kon•te•ser´) *vn.* to happen.

acontecimiento (â•kon•te•sē•myen´to) *m.* event, incident.

acopiamiento (â•ko•pyâ•myen´- to) or **acopio,** (â. ko´pyo) *m.* gathering, storing.

acopiar (â•ko•pyâr´) *va.* to gather, to store up.

acoplado, da (â•ko•plâ´tho, thâ) *adj.* coupled; fitted; **—,** *m.* trailer (vehicle).

acoplamiento (â•ko•plâ•myen´to) *m.* coupling, connection; (auto.) clutch.

acoplar (â•ko•plâr´) *va.* to couple, to adjust, to fit.

acorazado, da (â•ko•râ•sâ´tho, thâ) *adj.* iron-clad; **—,** *m.* battleship.

acorazonado, da (â•ko•râ•so•nâ´tho, thâ) *adj.* heart-shaped.

acorde (â•kor´the) *adj.* conformable, in agreement; **—,** *m.* accord; (mus.) chord.

acordeón (â•kor •the•on´) *m.* accordion.

acordonar (â•kor•tho•nâr´) *va.* (mil.) to form a cordon around; to lace, put laces on.

acorralar (â•ko•rrâ•lâr´) *va.* to corral *(encerrar);* to intimidate *(acobardar).*

acortar (â•kor•târ´) *va.* to abridge, to shorten; **— el paso,** to slow down.

acosar (â•ko•sâr´) *va.* to pursue closely *(perseguir);* to annoy, to harass *(molestar).*

acostar* (â•kos•târ´) *va.* to put to bed; **—se,** to go to bed, lie down *(tenderse);* to incline to one side *(inclinarse).*

acostumbrado, da (â•kos•tūm•brâ´tho, thâ) *adj.* customary, accustomed.

acostumbrar (â•kos•tūm•brâr´) *va.* to make accustomed; **—,**

vn. and *vr.* to be accustomed.

acre (â′kre) *adj.* acid, sharp, bitter; —, *m.* acre.

acrecentar* (â•kre•sen•târ′) or **acrecer*** (â•kre•ser′) *va.* to increase, to augment.

acreditado, da (â•kre•thē•tâ′tho, thâ) *adj.* accredited, authorized, creditable.

acreditar (â•kre•thē•târ′) *va.* to assure *(asegurar):* to authorize *(autorizar);* to credit *(abonar);* to accredit, to give credit *(elogiar);* **—se,** to gain credit, to get a good reputation.

acreedor, ra (â•kre•e•thor′, râ) *n.* creditor; —, *adj.* worthy, creditable; **saldo —,** credit balance.

acribillar (â•krē•vē•yâr′) *va.* to perforate *(perforar);* to annoy *(molestar);* to torment *(atormentar).*

acrílico, ca (â•krē′lē•ko, kâ) *adj.* acrylic.

acrobacia (â•kro•vâ′syâ) *f.* acrobatics; **— aérea,** stunt flying.

acróbata (â•kro′vâ•tâ) *m.* and *f.* acrobat.

acta (âk′tâ) *f.* act; minutes of proceedings; **— de venta,** bill of sale; **— de nacimiento,** birth certificate.

actitud (âk•tē•tūth′) *f.* attitude, outlook; position, posture *(postura).*

activador (âk•tē•va•thor′) *m.* (chem.) activator.

activar (âk•tē•vâr′) *va.* to make active *(animar);* to expedite, to hasten *(acelerar);* to activate.

actividad (âk•tē•vē•thâth′) *f.* activity *(acción);* liveliness *(animación).*

activo, va (âk•tē′vo, vâ) *adj.* active, diligent; —, *m.* (com.) assets.

acto (âk′to) *m.* act, action; function; **— continuo,** immediately; **en el —,** at once, immediately.

actor (âk•tor′) *m.* actor, player, comedian; plaintiff *(demandante).*

actriz (âk•trēs′) *f.* actress.

actuación (âk•twâ•syon′) *f.* action, performance.

actual (âk•twâl′) *adj.* present, of the present moment.

actualidad (âk•twâ•lē•thâth′) *f.* present time; current event *(suceso);* **en la —,** at present.

actuar (âk•twâr′) *vn.* to act, to take action, to proceed.

acuarela (â•kwâ•re′lâ) *f.* water coloring, water color.

acuarelista (â•kwâ•re•lēs′tâ) *m.* and *f.* watercolorist.

acuario (â•kwâ′ryo) *m.* aquarium, tank; Aquarius *(del Zodiaco).*

acuartelar (â•kwâr•te•lâr′) *va.* (mil.) to quarter troops; (naut.)

to furl sails.

acuático, ca (â•kwâ´tē•ko, kâ) *adj.* aquatic.

acuchillar (â•kū•chē•yâr´) *va.* to stab, to knife; **—se,** to fight with knives.

acudimiento (â•kū•thē•myen´to) *m.* aid, assistance.

acudir (â•kū•thēr´) *vn.* to assist, to succor *(socorrer);* to be present *(asistir);* — **a,** to resort to, to hasten to *(recurrir).*

acueducto (â•kwe•thūk´to) *m.* aqueduct.

acuerdo (â•kwer´tho) *m.* agreement, consent; resolution, court decision *(juicio);* **de —,** unanimously, by agreement; **de — con,** in accordance with; **ponerse de —,** to reach an agreement.

acumulación (â•kū•mū•lâ•syon´) *f.* accumulation.

acumulador (â•kū•mū•lâ•thor´) *m.* battery, electric storage battery; accumulator.

acumular (â•kū•mū•lâr´) *va.* to accumulate, to heap together *(juntar);* to impute *(atribuir).*

acuoso, sa (â•kwo´so, sâ) *adj.* watery.

acurrucado, da (â•kū•rrū•kâ´tho, thâ) *adj.* huddled, squatted.

acurrucarse (â•kū•rrū•kâr´se) *vr.* to huddle up.

acusación (â•kū•sâ•syon´) *f.* accusation.

acusado, da (â•kū•sâ´tho, thâ) *n.* defendant, accused.

acusador, ra (â•kū•sâ•thor´, râ) *n.* accuser.

acusar (â•kū•sâr´) *va.* to accuse, to reproach *(denunciar);* to meld *(anunciar);* —**se,** to make one´s confession, to confess.

acusatorio, ria (â•kū•sâ•to´ryo, ryâ) *adj.* accusing.

acústica (â•kūs´tē•kâ) *f.* acoustics.

acústico, ca (â•kūs´tē•ko, kâ) *adj.* acoustic.

achacar (â•châ•kâr´) *va.* to impute, to blame.

achacoso, sa (â•châ•ko´so, sâ) *adj.* sickly, habitually ailing.

achaque (â•châ´ke) *m.* unhealthiness, sickliness, ill health;(fig.) excuse, pretext.

Adán (â•thân´) *m.* Adam.

adaptabilidad (â•thâp•tâ•vē•lē•thâth´) *f.* adaptability.

adaptable (â•thâp•tâ´vle) *adj.* adaptable.

adaptar (â•thâp•târ´) *va.* to adapt, to fit, to adjust.

adecuado, da (â•the•kwâ´tho, thâ) *adj.* adequate, fit, able.

adecuar (â•the•kwâr´) *va.* to fit, to accommodate, to proportion.

A. de J.C.: antes de Jesucristo

B.C. before Christ.

adelantado, da
(â•the•lân•tâ´tho, thâ) *adj.*
anticipated *(anticipado);* forward, bold *(atrevido);* advanced
(avanzado); **por —do,** in
advance.

adelantar (â•the lân•târ´) *va.*
and *vn.* to advance, to further,
to accelerate *(promover);* to
ameliorate, to improve *(mejorar);* — **la paga,** to pay in
advance; —**se,** to take the lead,
to outdo, to outstrip.

adelante (â•the •lân´te) *adv.*
onward, further off; **en —,** from
now on, henceforth; **más —,**
farther on; later *(después);* **salir
—,** to go ahead, to come
through; **¡—!** come in! go on!
proceed!

adelanto (â•the•lân´to) *m.*
progress, advance.

adelgazar (â•thel•gâ•sâr´) *va.* to
make thin or slender; —**se,** to
lose weight.

ademán (â•the•mân´) *m.* gesture
(gesto); attitude *(actitud).*

además (â•the•mas´) *adv.* moreover, also, in addition; — **de,**
besides, aside from.

adentro (â•then´tro) *adv.* within,
inwardly; **tierra —,** inland.

aderezar (â•the•re•sâr´) *va.* to
dress, to adorn *(hermosear);* to
prepare *(disponer);* to season

(condimentar).

aderezo (â•the•re´so) *m.* adornment, finery; set of jewels; seasoning; dressing *(para ensaladas).*

adeudado, da (â•theū•thâ´tho,
thâ) *adj.* indebted.

adeudar (â•theū•thâr´) *va.* to
owe; — **en cuenta,** to charge to
one's account; —**se,** to be
indebted.

adeudo (â•the´ū•tho) *m.* indebtedness; (com.) debit.

adherencia (â•the•ren´syâ) *f.*
adherence, cohesion, adhesion;
(fig.) connection, relationship.

adherente (â•the•ren´te) *adj.*
adherent, cohesive.

adherir* (â •the•rēr´) *vn.* and *vr.*
to stick *(pegarse);* to believe, to
be faithful, to belong *(afiliarse);*
to hold, to cling to *(guardar).*

adhesión (â•the•syon´) *f.* adhesion, cohesion, adherence.

adición (â•thē•syon´) *f.* addition.

adicional (â•thē•syo•nâl´) *adj.*
additional, supplementary.

adicto, ta (â•thēk´to, tâ) *adj.*
addicted *(apegado);* devoted to
(dedicado); —, *n.* follower, supporter; addict.

adiestrar (â•thyes•trâr´) *va.* to
guide, to teach, to instruct, to
train; —**se,** to practice.

adinerado, da (â•thē•ne•râ´tho,
thâ) *adj.* moneyed, rich,

wealthy.

adiós (â•thyos´) *interj.* good-bye, adieu.

adivinador, ra (â•thē•vē•nâ•thor´, râ) *n.* diviner, soothsayer.

adivinanza (â•thē•vē•nân´sâ) *f.* riddle, conundrum.

adivinar (â•thē•vē•nâr´) *va.* to foretell *(predecir);* to conjecture, to guess *(conjeturar).*

adivino, na (â•thē•vē´no, nâ) *n.* diviner, soothsayer, fortune-teller.

adjetivo (âth•he•tē´vo) *m.* adjective.

adjuntar (âth•hūn•târ´) *va.* to enclose, to attach.

adjunto, ta (âth•hūn´to, ta) *adj.* united, joined, attached, annexed; —, *m.* attaché.

administración (âth•mē•nēs•trâ•syon´) *f.* administration, management, direction *(manejo);* headquarters *(jefatura);* **en —,** in trust.

administrador, ra (âth•mē•nēs•trâ•thor´, râ) *n.* administrator, trustee, manager; **—de aduanas,** collector of customs; **— de correos,** postmaster.

administrar (âth•mē•nēs•trâr´) *va.* to administer, to manage.

administrativo, va (âth•mē•nēs•trâ•tē´vo, vâ) *adj.*

administrative.

admirable (âth•mē•râ´vle) *adj.* admirable, marvelous.

admiración (âth•mē•râ•syon´) *f.* admiration, wonder.

admirador, ra (âth•mē•râ•thor´, râ) admirer.

admirar (âth•mē•râr´) *va.* to admire; **—se,** to be amazed, to be surprised.

admisible (âth•mē•sē´vle) *adj.* admissible, acceptable.

admisión (âth•mē•syon´) *f.* admission, acceptance.

admitir (âth•mē•tēr´) *va.* to admit, to accept *(aceptar);* to acknowledge *(reconocer);* to let in *(recibir);* to concede *(conceder).*

admonición (âth•mo•nē•syon´) *f.* Admonition, warning.

A.D.N.: ácido desoxirribonucleico D.N.A., deoxyribonucleic acid.

adobar (â•tho•vâr´) *va.* to dress *(aderezar);* to pickle *(encurtir);* to stew *(guisar);* to tan *(curtir).*

adobe (â•tho´ve) *m.* adobe, sundried brick.

adobo (â•tho´vo) *m.* stew *(guisado);* pickle sauce *(salsa);* rouge *(afeite);* ingredients for dressing leather or cloth *(curtiente).*

adolecer* (â•tho•le•ser´) *vn.* to be ill; **— de,** to suffer or ail from, to be subject to.

adolescencia (â•tho•les•sen´syâ) *f.* adolescence, youth.

adolescente (â•tho•les•sen´te) *adj.* adolescent, young; —, *m.* and *f.* adolescent, teen-ager.

adondequiera (â•thon•de•kye´râ) *adv.* wherever.

adopción (â•thop•syon´) *f.* adoption.

adoptar (â•thop•târ´) *va.* to adopt.

adoptivo, va (â•thop•tē´vo, vâ) *adj.* adoptive, adopted.

adoración (â•tho•râ•syon´) *f.* adoration, worship.

adorar (â•thó•râr´) *va.* to adore, to worship.

adormecer* (â•thor•me•ser´) *va.* to lull to sleep; —se, to fall asleep.

adormecido, da (â•thor•me•sē´tho, thâ) *adj.* drowsy, stilled, sleepy.

adormecimiento (â•thor•me•sē•myen´to) *m.* drowsiness, sleepiness.

adornar (â•thor•nâr´) *va.* to embellish, to ornament, to trim.

adorno (â•thor´no) *m.* adornment, ornament, decoration.

adquirir* (âth•kē•rēr´) *va.* to acquire, to gain.

adquisición (âth•kē•sē•syon´) *f.* acquisition, attainment; **poder de** —, purchasing power.

adrenalina (â•thre•nâ•lē´nâ) *f.* adrenalin.

aduana (â•thwâ´nâ) *f.* customhouse; **derechos de** —, customhouse duties.

aduanero (â•thwâ•ne´ro) *m.* Customhouse officer; —, **ra,** *adj.* pertaining to customs or customhouse.

adueñarse (â•thwe•nyâr´se) *vr.* to take possession (of).

adulador, ra (â•thu•lâ•thor´, râ) *n.* flatterer.

adular (â•thū•lâr´) *va.* to flatter, to admire excessively.

adulto, ta (â•thūl´to, tâ) *n.* and *adj.* adult, grown-up, mature.

adusto, ta (â•thūs´to, tâ) *adj.* excessively hot, scorching; (fig.) intractable, austere, gloomy.

advenimiento (âth•ve•nē•myen´-to) *m.* arrival, long-awaited advent; Advent.

adverbial (âth•ver•vyâl´) *adj.* adverbial.

adverbio (âth•ver´vyo) *m.* adverb.

adversario (âth•ver•sâ´ryo) *m.* adversary, antagonist.

adversidad (âth•ver•sē•thâth´) *f.* adversity, calamity.

adverso, sa (âth•ver´so, sâ) *adj.* adverse, calamitous.

advertencia (âth•ver•ten´syâ) *f.* admonition, warning *(admonición);* notice *(reparo).*

advertido, da (âth•ver•tē´tho, thâ) *adj.* forewarned *(avisado);* skillful *(capaz);* intelligent, clever, alert, aware *(listo).*

advertir* (âth•ver•tēr´) *va.* to advert, to notice *(reparar);* to call attention to, to warn *(avisar).*

adyacente (âth•yâ•sen´te) *adj.* adjacent.

aéreo, rea (â•e´re•o, re•â) *adj.* air, aerial; **correo —,** air mail.

aerodinámica (â•e•ro•thē•nâ´me•kâ) *f.* aerodynamics.

aerodinámico, ca (â•e•ro•thē•nâ´me•ko, kâ) *adj.* streamlined.

aeronauta (â•e•ro•nâ´ū•tâ) *m.* aeronaut, airman, aviator.

aeronáutica (â•e•ro•nâ´ū•tē•kâ) *f.* aeronautics.

aeronave (â•e•ro•nâ´ve) *f.* airship, dirigible, aircraft.

aeroplano (â•e•ro•plâ´no) *m.* airplane; **— de combate,** fighter plane.

aeropostal (â•e•ro pos•tâl´) *adj.* airmail.

aeropuerto (â•e•ro•pwer´to) *m.* airport; **— para helicópteros,** heliport.

aerosol (â•e•ro•sol´) *m.* aerosol.

aerospacio (â•e•ros•pâ´syo) *m.* aerospace.

afable (â•fâ´vle) *adj.* affable, ple-asant, courteous.

afán (â•fân´) *m.* anxiety, solicitude, worry *(ansia);* physical toil *(labor).*

afanar (â•fâ•nâr´) *va.* to press, to hurry; **—se,** to toil, to overwork *(fatigarse);* to work eagerly, to take pains *(esmerarse).*

afección (â•fek•syon´) *f.* affection fondness, attachment; (med.) affection, disease.

afectar (â•fek•târ´) *va.* to affect *(conmover);* to feign *(fingir).*

afectísimo, ma (â•fek•tē´sē•mo, mâ) *adj.* very affectionate, devoted; yours truly, very truly yours.

afecto (â•fek´to) *m.* affection, fondness, love; **—, ta,** *adj.* fond of, inclined to.

afectuoso, sa (â•fek•two´so, sâ) *adj.* affectionate, tender.

afeitada (â•feē•tâ´thâ) *f.* shave, shaving.

afeitar (â•feē•târ´) *va.* and *vr.* to shave; to apply make-up, to put on cosmetics *(poner afeites).*

afelpado, da (â•fel•pâ´tho, thâ) *adj.* plushlike, velvetlike.

afeminado, da (â•fe•mē•nâ´tho, thâ) *adj.* effeminate.

afeminar (â•fe•mē•nâr´) *va.* to make effeminate.

aferrado, da (â•fe•rrâ´tho, thâ) *adj.* stubborn, headstrong.

aferrar (â•fe•rrâr´) *va.* to grapple, to grasp, to seize.

afianzar (â•fyân•sâr´) *va.* to bail, to guarantee, to become security for *(garantizar);* to prop, to fix, to secure *(asegurar).*

afición (â•fē•syon´) *f.* affection *(cariño);* preference, fondness, fancy, liking *(inclinación);* hobby *(pasatiempo).*

aficionado, da (â•fē•syo•nâ´tho, thâ) *n.* devotee, fan, amateur.

afijo, ja (â•fē´ho, hâ) *adj.* suffixed; —, *m.* suffix.

afiladera (â•fē•lâ•the´râ) *f.* whetstone.

afilado, da (â•fē•lâ´tho, thâ) *adj.* sharp, clear-cut *(marcado);* thin *(adelgazado).*

afilador (â•fē•lâ•thor´) *m.* sharpener, grinder.

afilar (â•fē•lâr´) *va.* to whet, to sharpen, to grind.

afiliado, da (â•fē•lyâ´tho, thâ) *adj.* affiliated; —, *n.* subsidiary.

afin (â•fēn´) *m.* and *f.* relation, relative; —, *adj.* contiguous *(próximo);* related *(relacionado).*

afinación (â•fē•nâ•syon´) *f.* refining *(refinación);* tuning *(acuerdo).*

afinado, da (â•fē•nâ´tho, thâ) *adj.* refined *(purificado);* well-finished *(perfeccionado);* tuned *(acordado).*

afinador (â•fē•nâ•thor´) *m.* tuner.

afinar (â•fē•nâr´) *va.* to finish, to perfect *(perfeccionar);* to tune *(acordar);* to refine *(purificar).*

afinidad (â•fē•nē•thâth´) *f.* affinity, attraction *(atracción);* relationship, kinship *(parentesco);* analogy *(analogía).*

afirmación (â•fēr•mâ•syon´) *f.* affirmation *(aseguramiento);* statement *(declaración).*

afirmar (â•fēr•mâr´) *va.* to secure, to fasten *(fijar);* to affirm, to assure *(asegurar).*

afirmativo, va (â•fēr•mâ•tē´vo, vâ) *adj.* affirmative.

aflicción (â•flēk•syon´) *f.* affliction, grief, heartache, pain *(pena);* misfortune *(desgracia).*

afligido, da (â•flē•hē´tho, thâ) *adj.* afflicted, sad, despondent.

afligir (â•flē•hēr´) *va.* to afflict, to grieve, to torment; —se, to grieve *(entristecerse);* to lose heart *(desanimarse).*

aflojar (â•flo•hâr´) *va.* to loosen, to slacken, to relax *(soltar);* to relent *(ceder);* —, *vn.* to grow weak *(debilitarse);* to abate, to lose intensity *(moderarse).*

afluencia (â•flwen´syâ) *f.* inflow; plenty, abundance, affluence, *f.* *(copia).*

afluente (â•flwen´te) *adj.* affluent, abundant; tributary *(secundario);* loquacious *(hablador);* —, *m.* tributary stream.

afluir* (â•flwēr´) *vn.* to flow; to congregate, to assemble *(acudir).*

afortunadamente (â•for•tū•nâ•thâ•men´•te) *adv.* fortunately, luckily.

afortunado, da (â•for´tū•nâ´tho, thâ) *adj.* fortunate, lucky; successful *(exitoso).*

afrenta (â•fren´tâ) *f.* outrage, insult, injury *(ultraje);* infamy, disgrace *(deshonor).*

afrentar (â•fren•târ´) *va.* to affront, to offend.

africano, na (â•frē•kâ´no, nâ) *n.* and *adj.* African.

afrontar (â•fron•târ´) *va.* to confront.

aftoso, sa (âf•to´so, sâ) *adj.* (med.) aphthous; **fiebre —sa** (vet.) hoof-and-mouth disease.

afuera (â•fwe´râ) *adv.* out, outside, outward; ¡—! *interj.* out of the way!

afueras (â•fwe´râs) *f. pl.* environs, suburbs, outskirts.

agachar (â•gâ•châr´) *va.* to lower; —, *vn.* to crouch; —**se,** to stoop, to squat, to duck down.

agalla (â•gâ´yâ) *f.* gallnut; —**s,** *pl.* tonsils *(amígdalas);* fish gills.

agarradera (â•gâ•rrâ•the´râ) *f.* holder, handle.

agarrar (â•gâ•rrar´) *va.* to grasp, to seize; —**se,** to hold on.

agazapar (â•gâ•sâ•pâr´) *va.* (coll.) to catch, to grab; —**se,** to hide *(esconderse);* to crouch down *(agacharse).*

agencia (â•hen´syâ) *f.* agency; — **de turismo,** travel agency.

agenda (â•hen´dâ) *f.* agenda.

agente (â•hen´te) *m.* agent, representative *(intermediario);* attorney *(abogado);* — **viajero,** traveling salesman; — **de seguros,** insurance agent.

ágil (â´hēl) *adj.* nimble, fast, active, agile.

agilidad (â•hē•lē•thâth´) *f.* agility, nimbleness.

agitación (â•hē•tâ•syon´) *f.* agitation, excitement.

agitado, da (â•hē•tâ´tho, thâ) *adj.* excited, agitated.

agitar (â•hē•târ´) *va.* to agitate, to move; —**se,** to become excited.

agobiar (â•go•vyâr´) *va.* to weigh down, to oppress, to burden.

agonía (â•go•nē´â) *f.* agony, anguish.

agonizante (â•go•nē•sân´te) *m.* and *f.* dying person; —, *adj.* dying, agonizing.

agonizar (â•go•nē•sâr´) *va.* to assist dying persons; (coll.) to harass; —, *vn.* to be in the agony of death, to agonize.

agorar* (â•go•râr´) *va.* to divine, to augur.

agosto (â•gos´to) *m.* August; harvest time.

agotado, da (â•go•tâ´tho, thâ) *adj.* sold out *(terminado);* exhausted, spent, tired *(rendido).*

agotamiento (â•go•tâ•myen´to) *m.* exhaustion.

agotar (â•go•târ´) *va.* to misspend *(malgastar);* to exhaust, to use up *(gastar);* —**se,** to become run-down, to become exhausted *(rendirse);* to be sold out *(terminarse).*

agraciar (â•grâ•syâr´) *va.* to embellish *(embellecer);* to grace, to favor *(favorecer).*

agradable (â•grâ•thâ´vle) *adj.* agreeable, pleasant.

agradar (â•grâ•thâr´) *va.* to please, to gratify.

agradecer* (â•grâ•the•ser´) *va.* to be grateful for, to appreciate.

agradecido, da (â•grâ•the•sē´tho, thâ) *adj.* thankful, grateful.

agradecimiento (â•grâ•the•sē•myen´to) *m.* gratitude, gratefulness.

agrandamiento (â•gran•dâ•myen´to) *m.* enlargement.

agrandar (â•grân•dâr´) *va.* to enlarge; to extend.

agrario, da (â•grâ´ryo, ryâ) *adj.* agrarian.

agravante (â•grâ•vân´te) *adj.* aggravating, trying.

agravar (â•grâ•vâr´) *va.* to oppress *(oprimir);* to aggravate *(irritar);* to make worse, to exaggerate *(empeorar).*

agravio (â•grâ´vyo) *m.* offense, injury.

agregación (â•gre•gâ•syon´) *f.* aggregation; collection.

agregado (â•gre•gâ´tho) *m.* aggregate *(conjunto);* attaché *(funcionario).*

agregar (â•gre•gâr´) *va.* to aggregate, to heap together, to collect, to add.

agremiar (â•gre•myâr´) *va.* to organize into a union; —**se,** to unionize.

agresión (â•gre•syon´) *f.* aggression, attack.

agresivo, va (â•gre•sē´vo, vâ) *adj.* aggressive.

agresor (â•gre•sor´) *m.* aggressor, assaulter.

agrícola (â•grē´ko•lâ) *adj.* agricultural.

agricultor (â•grē•kūl•tor´) *m.* agriculturist, farmer.

agricultura (â•grē•kūl•tū´râ) *f.* agriculture.

agridulce (â•grē•thūl´se) *adj.* bittersweet.

agrio, ria (â´gryo, gryâ) *adj.* sour, acrid; rough, rocky, craggy *(peñascoso);* sharp, rude, unpleasant *(áspero).*

agrupación (â•grū•pâ•syon´) *f.* group, association, crowd.

agrupar (á• grū•pâr´) *va.* to group, to place together; **—se,** to cluster, to crowd together.

agrura (â•grū´râ) *f.* acidity.

agua (â´gwâ) *f.* water; slope *(vertiente);* **— potable,** drinking water.

aguacate (â•gwâ•kâ´te) *m.* avocado.

aguacero (â•gwâ•se´ro) *m.* short, heavy shower of rain.

aguadero (â•gwâ•the´ro) *m.* watering place for cattle, horsepond.

aguado, da (â•gwâ´tho, thâ) *adj.* watered down, watery, mixed with water; not firm, flaccid.

aguafiestas (â•gwâ•fyes´tâs), *m.* and *f.* killjoy, spoilsport.

aguafuerte (â•gwâ•fwer´te) *m.* or *f.* etching.

aguamarina (â•gwâ•mâ•rē´nâ) *f.* aquamarine.

aguantar (â•gwân•târ´) *va.* to sustain, to suffer, to endure, to bear.

aguante (â•gwân´te) *m.* patience, endurance.

aguar (â•gwâr´) *va.* to dilute with water *(diluir);* to spoil *(turbar).*

aguardar (â•gwâr•thâr´) *va.* to expect, to await, to wait for.

agudeza (â•gū•the´sâ) *f.* keenness, sharpness; acuteness, smartness.

agudo, da (â•gū´tho, thâ) *adj.* sharppointed, keen-edged, fine *(afilado);* acute, witty, bright *(perspicaz);* (fig.) shrill, glaring, loud.

aguijada (â•gē•hâ´thâ) *f.* spur, goad.

aguijón (â•gē•hon´) *m.* stinger of a bee or wasp *(dardo);* stimulation *(estímulo).*

aguijonear (â•gē•ho•ne•âr´) *va.* to prick; to spur on, to stimulate, to goad *(estimular).*

águila (â´gē•lâ) *f.* eagle; (fig.) sharp, clever person.

aguileño, ña (â•ge•le´nyo, nyâ) *adj.* aquiline; hawk-nosed.

aguilucho (â•gē•lū´cho) *m.* eaglet.

aguinaldo (â•gē•nâl´do) *m.* Christmas gift.

aguja (â•gū´hâ) *f.* needle; (rail.) switch.

agujerear (â•gū•he•re•âr´) *va.* to pierce, to bore.

agujero (â•gū•he´ro) *m.* hole *(abertura);* needlemaker *(fabricante);* needle seller *(vendedor).*

agujeta (â•gū•he´tâ) *f.* shoelace *(cordón);* muscular twinge *(punzada).*

ahí (â•ē´) *adv.* there; **de — que,** for this reason; **por —,** that direction; more or less.

ahijada (â•ē•hä´thâ) *f.* god-daughter.

ahijado (â•ē•hä´tho) *m.* godson.

ahínco (â•hēng´ko) *m.* zeal, earnestness, eagerness.

ahogar (â•o•gâr´) *va.* and *vr.* to smother, to suffocate *(sofocar);* to drown *(en agua);* —, *va.* to oppress *(oprimir);* to quench *(apagar).*

ahogo (â•o´go) *m.* suffocation; anguish *(angustia).*

ahondar (â•on•dâr´) *va.* to sink, to deepen; —, *vn.* to penetrate deeply *(penetrar);* to go into thoroughly *(profundizar).*

ahora (â•o´râ) *adv.* now, at present; —, *conj.* whether, or; — **mismo,** right now; **hasta —,** thus far; **por —,** for the present; — **bien,** now, then; **de — en adelante,** from now on.

ahorcajarse (â•or•kâ•hâr´se) *vr.* to sit astride.

ahorcar (â•or•kâr´) *va.* to kill by hanging; —**se,** to hang oneself, to commit suicide by hanging.

ahorita (â•o•rē´tâ) *adv.* (Sp. Am.) right now, in just a minute.

ahorrar (â•o•rrâr´) *va.* to econo-mize, to save.

ahorro (â•o´rro) *m.* saving, thrift; **caja** or **banco de —s,** savings bank.

ahuecar (â•we•kâr´) *va.* to hol-low, to scoop out.

ahumar (âū•mâr´) *va.* to smoke, to cure in smoke; —**se** (coll.) to get high, to become tipsy.

ahuyentar (âū•yen•târ´) *va.* to put to flight, to banish; —**se,** to flee; to escape.

airarse (âē•râr´se) *vr.* to become irritated, to become angry.

aire (â´ē•re) *m.* air; wind *(viento);* atmosphere; gracefulness, charm *(gracia);* aspect, counte-nance *(apariencia);* musical composition, melody *(melodía);* (auto.) choke; — **viciado,** foul air; **con — acondicionado,** air-conditioned; **al — libre,** out-doors.

airear (âē•re•âr´) *va.* to air, to ventilate.

airoso, sa (âē•ro´so, sâ) *adj.* airy, windy; graceful, charming *(gar-boso);* successful *(lucido).*

aislado, da (âēz•lä´tho, thâ) *adj.* isolated, cut off, insulated.

aislador, (âēz•lä•thor´) *m.* (elec.) insulator.

aislamiento (âēz•lä•myen´to) *m.* isolation, insulation; (fig.) soli-tude, loneliness; privacy.

aislar (âēz•lâr´) *va.* to surround with water; to isolate, to insu-late.

¡ajá! (â•hä´) *interj.* aha!

ajedrecista (â•he•thre•sēs´tâ) *m.* or *f.* chess player.

ajedrez (â•he•thres´) *m.* chess;
(naut.) netting, grating.

ajenjo (â•hen´ho) *m.* wormwood;
absinthe *(licor).*

ajeno, na (â•he´no, nâ) *adj.*
another´s, not one´s own;
strange, improper, contrary,
foreign *(impropio);* unknown to.

ajetrearse (â•he•tre•âr´se) *vr.* to
exert oneself, to bustle, to toil.

aji (â•hē´) *m.* chili pepper, chili.

ajo (â´ho) *m.* garlic; garlic sauce
(salsa); (coll.) shady deal, dishonest business transaction;
¡—! *interj.* darn! heck!

ajuar (â•hwâr´) *m.* bridal apparel and furniture, trousseau *(de
boda);* household furnishings
(muebles).

ajustable (â•hūs•tâ´vle) *adj.*
adjustable.

ajuste (â•hūs´te) *m.* agreement,
adjustment, settlement, accommodation.

al (âl) to the; **— fin,** at last; **—
instante,** at once.

ala (â´lâ) *f.* wing; brim *(parte lateral);* **—s,** *pl.* (naut.) upper
studding sails.

alabanza (â•lâ•vân´sâ) *f.* praise,
applause.

alabar (â•lâ•vâr´) *va.* to praise,
to applaud, to extol.

alabastrino, na (â•lâ•vâs•trē´no,
nâ) *adj.* of alabaster.

alacena (â•lâ•se´nâ) *f.* cupboard.

alacrán (â•lâ•krân´) *m.* scorpion;
ring of the mouthpiece of a bridle *(de freno).*

alacridad (â•lâ•krē•thâth´) *f.*
alacrity.

alado, da (â•lâ´tho, thâ) *adj.*
winged.

alambique (â•lâm•bē´ke) *m.* still,
distillery.

alambrado (â•lâm•brâ´tho) *m.*
wire fence, wire screen.

alambrar (â•lâm•brâr´) *va.* to
fence with wire.

alambre (â•lâm´bre) *m.* wire,
copper wire; **— de púas,**
barbed wire.

alameda (â•lâ•me´thâ) *f.* poplar
grove; tree-lined promenade
(paseo).

álamo (â´lâ•mo) *m.* poplar,
poplar tree; cottonwood tree
(chopo); **— temblón,** aspen
tree.

alarde (â•lâr´the) *m.* military
review *(desfile);* display, show,
exhibition *(ostentación);* **hacer
—,** to boast, to brag.

alardear (â•lâr•the•âr´) *vn.* to
brag, to boast.

alargado, da (â•lâr•gâ´tho, thâ)
adj. elongated.

alargar (â•lâr•gâr´) *va.* to length-
en, to extend, to prolong.

alarido (â•lâ•rē´tho) *m.* outcry,
shout, howl; **dar —s,** to howl.

alarma (â•lâr´mâ) *f.* alarm; **— de**

incendios, fire alarm; — **contra ladrones,** burglar alarm.

alarmante (â•lâr•mân´te) *adj.* alarming.

alarmar (â•lâr•mâr´) *va.* to alarm; —**se** to be alarmed.

alarmista (â•lâr•mēs´tâ) *m.* and *f.* alarmist.

alba (âl´vâ) *f.* dawn of day, day-break; alb, surplice *(vestidura).*

albañil (âl•vâ•nyēl´) *m.* mason, brick-layer.

albaricoque (âl•vâ•rē•ko´ke) *m.* apricot.

albatros (âl•vâ´tros) *m.* alba-tross.

albedrío (âl•ve•thrē´o) *m.* free will.

alberca (âl•ver´kâ) *f.* swimming pool *(piscina);* reservoir, cistern *(cisterna);* pond *(estanque).*

albergar (âl•ver•gâr´) *va.* to lodge, to house, to harbor; — **se,** to take shelter.

albergue (âl•ver´ge) *m.* shelter, refuge.

albino, na (âl•vē´no, nâ) *n.* albino.

albóndiga (âl•von´dē•gâ) *f.* meat-ball.

albor (âl•vor´) *m.* (poet.) dawn; —**es,** *pl.* beginnings.

alborada (âl•vo•râ´thâ) *f.* first dawn of day; (mus.) aubade.

alborotar (âl•vo•ro•târ´) *va.* to upset, to stir up, to disturb.

alboroto (âl•vo•ro´to) *m.* noise, disturbance, tumult, riot.

alborozar (âl•vo•ro•sâr´) *va.* to exhilarate.

alborozo (âl•vo•ro´so) *m.* joy, gaiety, rejoicing.

álbum (âl´vūn) *m.* album; — **de recortes,** scrap book.

albur (âl•vūr´) *m.* chance, haz-ard; **jugar** or **correr un —,** to leave to chance, to take a risk.

alcachofa (âl•kâ•cho´fâ) *f.* arti-choke.

alcaide (âl•kâ´ē•the) *m.* jailer, warden.

alcalde (âl•kâl´de) *m.* mayor.

alcaldía (âl•kâl•dē´â) *f.* mayor´s office.

alcalino, na (âl•kâ•lē´no, nâ) *adj.* alkaline.

alcance (âl•kân´se) *m.* reach, scope, range; ability, grasp *(tal-ento);* (fig.) import, significance; — **del oído,** earshot.

alcancía (âl•kân•sē´â) *f.* piggy bank; (eccl.) alms box.

alcanfor (âl•kâm•for´) *m.* cam-phor.

alcantarilla (âl•kân•tâ•rē´yâ) *f.* small bridge, culvert *(puente-cillo);* drain, sewer, conduit *(albañal).*

alcantarillado (âl•kân•tâ•rē•yâ´-tho) *m.* sewage.

alcanzar (âl•kan•sâr´) *va.* to overtake, to catch up with, to reach *(emparejar);* to get, to obtain *(obtener);* to perceive *(percibir);* — **a oir,** to overhear; **—,** *vn.* to suffice, to reach, to be enough.

alcatraz (âl•kâ•trâs´), *m.* pelican; (Mex.) calla ily.

alcázar (âl•kâ´sâr), *m.* castle; fortress; (naut.) quarterdeck.

alcoba (âl•ko´vâ), *f.* bedroom.

alcohol (âl•ko•ol´), *m.* alcohol.

alcohólico, ca (âl•ko´olē•ko, kâ), *adj.* alcoholic.

alcornoque (âl•kor•no´ke), *m.* cork tree; (coll.) dunce, blockhead.

aldea (âl•de´â), *f.* hamlet, small village.

aldeano, na (âl•de•â´no, nâ), *adj.* rustic, countried, uncultured; **—,** *n.* Peasant, countryman.

aledaño, ña (â•le•thâ´nyo, nyâ), *adj.* bordering, pertaining to a boundary line; **—,** *m.* border, boundary.

alegación (â•le•gâ•syon´), *f.* allegation.

alegar (â•le•gâr), *va.* to allege, to maintain, to affirm.

alegato (â•le•gâ´to), *m.* allegation, statement of plaintiff's case.

alegoría (â•le•go•rē´â), *f.* allegory.

alegórico, ca (â•le•go´rē•ko, kâ), *adj.* allegorical.

alegrar (â•le•grâr´), *va.* to gladden (regocijar); to lighten (aliviar); to exhilarate, to enliven (avivar); to beautify (hermosear); **—se,** to rejoice (regocijarse); to grow merry with drinking (achisparse).

alegre (â•le´gre), *adj.* glad, merry, joyful, content.

alegría (â•le•grē´â), *f.* mirth, gaiety, delight, cheer.

alejamiento (â•le•hâ•myen´to), *m.* distance, remoteness; removal, separation.

alejar (â•le•hâr´), *va.* to remove to a greater distance, to separate, to take away; **—se,** to withdraw, to move away.

aleluya (â•le•lū´yâ) *m.* or *f.* hallelujah; **—,** *m.* Easter time.

alemán, ana (â•le•mân´, â´nâ) *adj.* and *n.* German; **—,** *m.* German language.

Alemania (â•le•mâ´nyâ) *f.* Germany.

alentador, ra (â•len•tâ•thor´, râ) *adj.* encouraging.

alentar* (â•len•târ´) *vn.* to breathe; **—,** *va.* to animate, to cheer, to encourage, **—se,** to recover.

alergia (â•ler´hyâ) *f.* (med.) allergy.

alérgico, ca (â•ler´hē•ko, kâ) *adj.* allergic.

alero (â•le´ro) *m.* eaves.

alertar (â•ler•târ´) *va.* to alert.

alerto, ta (â•ler´to, tâ) *adj.* alert, vigilant, open-eyed.

aleta (â•le´tâ) *f.* fin *(de pez);* (mech.) blade *(de hélice).*

aletargarse (â•le•târ•gâr´se) *vr.* to fall into a lethargic state, to become torpid.

aletazo (â•le•tâ´so) *m.* blow, hit, from a wing.

aletear (â•le•te•âr´) *vn.* to flutter, to flap, to flick.

aleteo (â•le•te´o) *m.* flapping of wings, fluttering.

alfabéticamente (âl•fâ•ve•tē•kâ•men´te) *adv.* alphabetically.

alfabético, ca (âl•fâ•ve´tē•ko, kâ) *adj.* alphabetical.

alfabeto (âl•fa•ve´to) *m.* alphabet.

alfarería (âl•fâ•re•rē´â) *f.* art of pottery, ceramics.

alfarero (âl•fâ•re´ro) *m.* potter.

alfil (âl•fēl´) *m.* bishop (in chess).

alfiler (âl•fē•ler´) *m.* pin; —es, *pl.* pin money; — **de corbata,** stickpin; — **imperdible,** safety pin.

alfiletero (âl•fē•le•te´ro) *m.* pincushion.

alfombra (âl•fom´brâ) *f.* carpet, rug.

alfombrilla (âl•fom•brē´yâ) *f.* (med.) measles.

alforja (âl•for´hâ) *f.* saddlebag, knapsack.

alforza (âl•for´sâ) *f.* tuck, pleat.

alga (âl´gâ) *f.* (bot.) alga, seaweed.

algarada (âl•gâ•râ´thâ) *f.* uproar *(vocería);* sudden attack *(ataque).*

algazara (âl•gâ•sâ´râ) *f.* din, hubbub, uproar.

álgebra (âl´he•vrâ) *f.* algebra.

algo (âl´go) *pron.* some, something; anything; — **de,** a little; — **que comer,** something to eat; **en** —, somewhat, in some way, a bit; **por** —, for some reason; —, *adv.* a little, rather.

algodón (âl•go•thon´) *m.* cotton, cotton plant; cotton material *(tela);* — **en bruto** or **en rama,** raw cotton.

algoso, sa (âl•go´so, sâ) *adj.* full of algae or seaweed.

alguien (âl´gyen) *pron.* someone, somebody, anyone, anybody.

algún (âl•gūn´), **alguno, na** (âl•gū´no, nâ) *pron.* somebody, someone, some person, anybody, anyone; —, *adj.* some, any; **en modo** —, in any way; — **cosa,** anything; **en** —**na parte,** anywhere; —**s,** *pl.* a few.

alhaja (â•lâ´hâ) *f.* jewel, gem.

aliado, da (â•lyâ´tho, thâ) *adj.* allied; —, *n.* ally.

alianza (â•lyân´sâ) *f.* alliance, league.

aliarse (â•lyâr´se) *vr.* to ally oneself, to become allied.

alias (â´lyâs) *adv.* alias, otherwise known as.

alicates (â•lē•kâ´tes) *m. pl.* pincers, nippers, pliers.

aliciente (â•lē•syen´te) *m.* attraction, incitement, inducement.

alienista (â•lye•nēs´tâ) *m.* and *f.*
alienist.

aliento (â•lyen´to) *m.* breath;.
(fig.) support, encouragement;
dar —, to encourage; **sin** —,
without vigor, spiritless, dull.

aligar (â•lē•gâr´) *va.* to tie, to
unite.

aligerar (â•lē•he•râr´) *va.* to
lighten, to alleviate *(aliviar);* to
hasten, quicken *(acelerar).*

alimentación (â•lē•men•tâ•syon´)
f. maintenance, feeding, nour-
ishment, meals.

alimentar (â•lē•men•târ´) *va.* to
feed, to nourish.

alimenticio, cia (â•lē•men•tē´syo,
syâ) *adj.* nutritious, nutritive.

alimento (â•lē•men´to) *m.* nour-
ishment, food; —**s**, pl. alimony,
allowance.

alindar (â•lēn•dâr´) *va.* to fix
limits.

alineación (â•lē•ne•â•syon´) *f.*
alignment.

alinear (â•lē•ne•âr´) *va.* to align,
to arrange in a line, to line up;
—**se,** to fall in line, to fall in.

aliñar (â•lē•nyâr´) *va.* to adorn
(adornar); to season *(condimentar).*

aliño (â•lē´nyo) *m.* dress, ornament, decoration *(adorno);*
dressing, seasoning *(condimento).*

alisar (â•lē•sâr´) *va.* to plane, to
smooth; to polish *(pulir).*

aliso (â•lē´so) *m.* alder tree.

alistado, da (â•lēs•tâ´tho, thâ)
adj. striped.

alistar (â•lēs•târ´) *va.* to enlist,
to enroll; —**se,** to get ready, to
make ready.

aliviar (â•lē•vyâr´) *va.* to lighten,
to ease, to mollify, to alleviate.

alivio (â•lē´vyo) *m.* alleviation,
mitigation, comfort.

aljibe (âl•hē´ve) *m.* cistern.

alma (âl´mâ) *f.* soul; human
being *(individuo);* principal
part, heart *(ánimo);* (fig.) conscience, motivating force.

almacén (âl•mâ•sen´) *m.* department store *(tienda);* warehouse,
magazine *(depósito);* **tener en**
—, to have in stock.

almacenar (âl•mâ•se•nâr´) *va.* to
store, to lay up, to warehouse.

almanaque (âl•ma•nâ´ke) *m.*
almanac.

almeja (âl•me•hâ) *f.* clam.

almendra (âl•men´drâ) *f.*
almond; — **garapiñada,** sugared, honeyed almond.

almendrera (âl•men•dre´râ) *f.*
almendrero (âl•men•dre´ro) or
almendro, (âl•men´dro) *m.*
almond tree.

almez (âl•mes´) or **almezo**
(âl•me´so) *m.* lotus tree.

almiar (âl•myâr´) *m.* haystack.

almíbar (âl•mē´vâr) *m.* sirup.

almibarar (âl•mē•vâ•râr´) *va.* to
preserve fruit in sugar; (fig.) to
ply with soft and endearing
words.

almidón (âl•mē•thon´) *m.* starch,
farina.

almidonado, da
(âl•mē•tho•nâ´tho, thâ) *adj.*
starched; (fig.) affected, stiff in
mannerisms, overly prim.

almidonar (âl•mē•tho•nâr´) *va.*
to starch.

almirante (âl•mē•rân´te) *m.*
admiral.

almirez (âl•mē•res´) *m.* brass
mortar; — **y mano,** mortar and
pestle.

almizcle (âl•mēs´kle) *m.* musk.

almizclera (âl•mēs•kle´râ) *f.*
muskrat.

almodrote (âl•mo•thro´te) *m.*
(coll.) hodgepodge.

almohada (âl•mo•â´thâ) *f.* pillow,
cushion.

almohadón (âl•mo•â•thon´) *m.*
large cushion.

almorranas (âl•mo•rrâ´nâs) *f. pl.*
hemorrhoids, piles.

almorzar* (âl•mor•sâr´) *vn.* to
eat lunch, to have lunch.

almuerzo (âl•mwer´so) *m.* lunch,
luncheon.

alocado, da (â•lo•kâ´tho, thâ)
adj. crack-brained, foolish,
reckless.

alocución (â•lō•kū•syon´) *f.*
address, speech.

áloe (â´lo•e) or **aloe** (â•lo´e) *m.*
(bot.) aloe.

alojamiento, (â•lo•hâ•myen´to)
m. lodging, accommodation;
(naut.) steerage.

alojar (â•lo•hâr´) *va.* to lodge; —
se, to reside in lodgings, to
board.

alondra (â•lon´drâ) *f.* lark.

Alpes (âl´pes) *m. pl.* Alps.

alpinismo (âl•pē•nēz´mo) *m.*
mountain climbing.

alpinista (âl•pē•nēs´tâ) *m. and f.*
mountain climber.

alpino, na (âl•pē´no, nâ) *adj.*
Alpine.

alquilar (âl•kē•lâr´) *va.* to let, to
hire, to rent.

alquiler (âl•kē•ler´) *m.* hire; rent
(de casa); **de —,** for hire, for
rent.

alrededor (âl•rre•the•thor´) *adv.*
around; — **de,** about, around.

alrededores (âl•rre•the•tho´res)
m. pl. environs, neighborhood,
surroundings.

alta (âl´tâ) *f.* new member; **dar**

de —, to dismiss, to discharge.

altanería (âl•tâ•ne•rē´â) *f.*
haughtiness.

altanero, ra (âl•tâ•ne´ro, râ) *adj.*
haughty, arrogant, vain, proud.

altar (âl•târ´) *m.* altar; — **mayor,**
high altar.

altavoz (âl•tâ•vos´) *m.* loudspeaker.

alterable (âl•te•râ´vle) *adj.* alterable, mutable.

alteración (âl•te•râ•syon´) *f.* alteration, change, mutation; emotional upset, disturbance *(trastorno).*

alterar (âl•te•râr´) *va.* to alter, to
change *(cambiar);* to disturb, to
upset *(trastornar);* —**se,** to
become angry.

altercación (âl•ter•kâ•syon´) *f.*
altercation, controversy, quarrel, contention, strife.

altercado (âl•ter•kâ´tho) *m.* disagreement, quarrel.

altercar (âl•ter•kâr´) *va.* to dispute, to altercate, to quarrel.

alternar (âl•ter•nâr´) *va.* and *vn.*
to alternate.

alternativa (âl•ter•nâ•tē´vâ) *f.*
alternative.

Alteza (âl•te´sâ) *f.* Highness
(title).

alteza (âl•te´sâ) *f.* height, elevation.

altibajos (âl•tē•vâ´hos) *m. pl.*
unevenness of the ground; (fig.)
ups and downs of life.

altiplanicie (âl•tē•plâ•nē´sye) *f.*
highland.

altiplano (âl•tē•plâ´no) *m.* high
plateau.

altísimo, ma (âl•tē´sē•mo, ma)
adj. extremely high; **el A—,** the
Most High, God.

altisonante (âl•tē•so•nân´te) or
altísono, na (âl•tē•so•no, nâ)
adj. high-sounding, pompous.

altitud (âl•tē•tūth´) *f.* altitude.

altivez (âl•tē•ves´) *f.* pride,
haughtiness, huff.

altivo, va (âl•te´vo, vâ) *adj.*
haughty, proud.

alto, ta (âl´to, tâ) *adj.* tall, high,
elevated; loud *(fuerte);* —, *m.*
height; story, floor *(piso);* highland *(meseta);* (mil.) halt;
(mus.) tenor, tenor notes; ¡—!
or ¡—ahí! *interj.* stop there!

altoparlante (âl•to•pâr•lân´te) *m.*
loudspeaker.

altruismo (âl•trwēz´mo) *m.*
altruism, unselfishness.

altruista (âl•trwēs´tâ) *adj.* altru-
istic, unselfish; —, *m.* and *f.*
altruist, unselfish person.

altura (âl•tū´râ) *f.* height, highness, altitude; peak, summit
(cumbre); —**s,** *pl.* the heavens.

alubia (â•lū´vyâ) *f.* string bean.

alucinación (â•lū•sē•nâ•syon´)
f., **alucinamiento,**
(â•lū•sē•nâ•myen´to) *m.* hallu-

cination.

alucinar (â•lū•sē•nâr´) *va.* to delude, to deceive; to hallucinate; —**se,** to deceive oneself, to be deceived.

alud (â•lūth´) *m.* avalanche.

aludido, da (â•lū•thē´tho, thâ) *adj.* referred to, above-mentioned.

aludir (â•lū•thēr´) *vn.* to allude, to refer to.

alumbrado, da (â•lūm•brâ´tho, thâ) *adj.* illuminated; —, *m.* lighting; (avi.) flare.

alumbramiento (â•lūm•brâ•myen´to) *m.* illumination; childbirth *(parto).*

alumbrar (â•lūm•brâr´) *va.* to light, to illuminate; (fig.) to enlighten.

aluminio (â•lū•mē´nyo) *m.* aluminum.

alumno, na (â•lūm´no, nâ) *n.* student, pupil; (fig.) disciple, follower.

alusión (â•lū•syon´) *f.* allusion, hint.

alveolo (âl•ve•o´lo) or **alvéolo,** (âl•ve´o•lo) *m.* socket of a tooth; honeycomb cell *(de panal).*

alverjas (âl•ver´hâs) *f. pl.* peas.

alza (âl´sâ) *f.* advance in price; lift.

alzado, da (âl•sâ´tho, thâ) *adj.* raised, lifted; (coll.) proud,

insolent *(engreído);* fraudulent *(negociante).*

alzamiento (âl•sâ•myen´to) *m.* raising, elevation; uprising.

alzar (âl•sar´) *va.* to raise, to lift up, to heave *(levantar);* to construct, to build *(construir);* to hide, to lock up *(guardarse);* to cut cards *(cortar);* — **cabeza,** to recover from a calamity; —**se,** to rise in rebellion.

allá (á•yá´) *adv.* there; thither; **más** —, further on, beyond; **más** — **de,** beyond.

allanar (â•yâ•nar´) *va.* to level, to flatten *(aplanar);* to overcome, to rise above *(superar);* to pacify, to subdue *(sujetar);* — **se,** to submit, to abide by.

allegado, da (â•ye•gâ´tho, thâ) *adj.* related, similar, close; —, *n.* follower, ally.

allegar (â•ye•gâr´) *va.* to collect, to gather.

allí (â•yē´) *adv.* there, in that place; **por** —, yonder, over there.

A.M.: antemeridiano A.M. or a.m., before noon.

ama (â´mâ) *f.* mistress; — **de casa,** housewife; — **de llaves,** housekeeper.

amabilidad (â•mâ•vē•lē•thâth´) *f.* amiability, kindness.

amable (â•mâ´vle) *adj.* amiable, kind.

amado, da (â•mâ´tho, thâ) *n.* and *adj.* beloved, darling, loved.

amaestrar (â•mâ•es•trâr´) *va.* to teach, to train.

amagar (â•mâ•gâr´) *va.* and *vn.* to threaten, to hint at, to smack of.

amago (â•mâ´go) *m.* threat, indication, symptom.

amalgama (â•mâl•gâ´mâ) *f.* amalgam, alloy; (fig.) mixture, blend.

amalgamar (â•mâl•gâ•mâr´) *va.* (chem.) to amalgamate, to mix.

amamantar (â•mâ•man•tar´) *va.* to suckle, to nurse.

amancillar (â•man•sē•yâr´) *va.* to stain, to defile, to taint, to injure.

amanecer (â•mâ•ne•ser´) *m.* dawn, daybreak; **al —,** at daybreak; **—*,** *vn.* to dawn; to appear at daybreak *(aparecer);* to reach at daybreak *(llegar).*

amanerado, da (â•mâ•ne•râ´tho, thâ) *adj.* affected, artificial.

amaneramiento (â•mâ•ne•râ•myen´to) *m.* mannerism.

amansar (â•mân•sâr´) *va.* to tame, to domesticate *(domesticar);* to soften, to pacify *(apaciguar).*

amante (â•mân´te) *m.* and *f.* lover.

amapola (â•mâ•po´lâ) *f.* (bot.) poppy.

amar (â•mâr´) *va. to* love.

amargo, ga (â•mâr´go, gâ) *adj.* bitter, acrid; (fig.) painful, unpleasant; **—,** *m.* bitterness; **—s,** *m. pl.* bitters.

amargor (â•mar•gor´) *m.* bitterness; (fig.) sorrow, distress.

amargura (â•mar•gū´râ) *f.* bitterness; (fig.) sorrow, affliction.

amarillento, ta (â•ma´•rē•yen´to, tâ) *adj.* yellowish.

amarillo, lla (â•mâ•rē´yo, yâ) *adj.* yellow.

amarrar (â•mâ•rrâr´) *va.* to tie, to fasten.

amarre (â•mâ´rre) *m.* mooring; mooring line or cable.

amartillar (â•mâr•tē•yâr´) *va.* to hammer; to cock *(disparador).*

amasar (â•mâ•sâr´) *va.* to knead; (fig.) to arrange, to prepare, to plot.

amasijo (â•mâ•sē´ho) *m.* mixed mortar *(argamasa);* bread dough *(harina).*

amatista (â•mâ•tēs´tâ) *f.* amethyst.

amazona (â•mâ•so´nâ) *f.* amazon, masculine woman.

ámbar (âm´bâr) *m.* amber; **— gris,** amber-gris.

ambarino, na (âm•bâ•rē´no, nâ) *adj.* amber, amberlike.

Amberes (âm•be´res) *f.* Antwerp.

ambición (âm•bē•syon´) f. ambition; drive, desire (pasión).

ambicionar (âm•bē•syo•nâr´) va. to covet, to aspire to.

ambicioso, sa (âm•bē•syo´so, sâ) adj. ambitious.

ambiental (âm•byen•tâl´) adj. environmental.

ambientalismo (âm•byen•tâ•lēz´-mo) m. environmentalism.

ambiente (âm•byen´te) m. environment.

ambigüedad (âm•bē•gwe•thâth´) f. ambiguity.

ambigüo, güa (âm•bē´gwo, ucal.

ámbito (âm´bē•to) m. border, limit, enclosed area, realm.

ambos, bas (âm´bos, bâs) pron. and adj. pl. both.

ambulancia (âm•bū•lân´syâ) f. ambulance.

ambulante (âm•bū•lân´te) adj. ambulatory, roving; **músico —,** street musician; **vendedor —,** peddler.

ameliorar (â•me•lyo•râr´) va. to better, to improve.

amén (â•men´) interj. amen, so be it; **—,** n. acquiescence, consent; **en un decir —,** in an instant; **— de,** besides, in addition to.

amenaza (â•me•nâ´sâ) f. threat, menace.

amenazador, ra (â•me•nâ•sâ•thor´, râ) adj.

menancing, threatening.

amenazar (â•me•nâ•sâr´) va. to threaten, to menace.

amenidad (â•me•nē•thâth´) f. amenity, agreeableness.

amenizar (â•me•nē•sâr´) va. to make pleasant.

ameno, na (â•me´no, nâ) adj. pleasant, amusing, entertaining.

América del Norte (â•me´rē•kâ thel nor´te) f. North America.

América del Sur (â•me´rē•kâ thel sūr) f. South America.

americanismo (â•me•rē•kâ•nēz´-mo) m. Americanism; an expression or word used in Latin-American Spanish.

americanizado, da (â•me•rē•kâ•nē•sâ´•tho, thâ) adj. Americanized.

americano, na (â•me•rē•kâ´no, nâ) n. and adj. American.

ametralladora (â•me•trâ•y´â•tho´râ) f. machine gun.

amiba (â•mē´vâ) f. ameba or amoeba.

amigable (â•mē•gâ´vle) adj. amiable, friendly.

amígdala (â•mēg´thâ•lâ) f. tonsil.

amigo, ga (â•mē´go, gâ) n. friend, comrade; devotee, fan, lover (aficionado); **—, ga,** adj. friendly; fond, devoted.

amilanar (â•mē•lâ•nâr´) va. to

frighten, to terrify; **—se,** to become terrified.

aminoácido (â•mē•no•â′sē•tho) *m.* amino acid.

aminorar (â•mē•no•râr′) *va.* to reduce, to lessen.

amistad (â•mēs•tâth′) *f.* friendship; **hacer —,** to become acquainted.

amistoso, sa (â•mēs•to′so, sâ) *adj.* friendly, cordial.

amnesia (âm•ne′syâ) *f.* amnesia.

amnistía (âm•nēs•tē′â) *f.* amnesty.

amo (â′mo) *m.* master, proprietor, owner.

amolador (â•mo•lâ•thor′) *m.* grinder.

amolar* (â•mo•lâr′) *va.* to whet, to grind, to sharpen.

amoldar (â•mol•dâr′) *va.* to mold; to adapt, to adjust *(ajustar);* **—se,** to adapt oneself to, to live up to, to pattern oneself after.

amonestación (â•mo•nes•tâ•syon′) *f.* advice, admonition, warning.

amonio (â•mo′nyo) *m.* (chem.) ammonium.

amontonar (â•mon•to•nâr′) *va.* to heap together, to accumulate.

amor (â•mor′) *m.* love; **por — de,** for the sake of; **por — de Dios,** for God's sake; **— propio,** dig-

nity, pride; **—es,** pl. love affair.

amordazar (â•mor•thâ•sâr′) *va.* to gag, to muzzle.

amorfo, fa (â•mor′fo, fâ) *adj.* amorphous.

amorío (â•mo•rē′o) *m.* love-making, love.

amoroso, sa (â•mo•ro′so, sâ) *adj.* affectionate, loving.

amortiguador (â•mor•tē•gwâ•thor′) *m.* shock absorber.

amortiguar (â•mor•tē•gwâr′) *va.* to lessen, to mitigate, to soften *(apaciguar);* to deaden *(amortecer);* to temper *(moderar).*

amotinamiento (â•mo•tē•nâ•myen′to) *m.* mutiny.

amotinar (â•mo•tē•nâr′) *va.* to excite rebellion; **—se,** to mutiny.

amparar (âm•pâ•râr′) *va.* to shelter, to favor, to protect; **—se,** to claim protection.

amparo (âm•pâ′ro) *m.* protection, help, support; refuge, asylum *(abrigo);* (Mex.) habeas corpus.

ampliación (âm•plyâ•syon′) *f.* amplification, enlargement.

ampliar (âm•plyâr′) *va.* to amplify, to enlarge, to extend, to expand, to increase.

amplificador (âm•plē•fē•kâ•thor′) *m.* amplifier.

amplio, plia (âm´plyo, plyâ) *adj.* ample, vast, spacious.

amplitud (âm•plē•tūth´) *f.* amplitude, extension, largeness.

ampolla (âm•po´yâ) *f.* blister; vial, flask (frasco); (med.) ampoule.

ampollar (âm•po•yâr´) *va.* to raise blisters; **—se,** to rise in bubbles; **—,** *adj.* bubble-shaped; blister-like.

ampolleta (âm•po•ye´tâ) *f.* hour-glass.

amputación (âm•pū•tâ•syon´) *f.* amputation.

amputar (âm•pū•tar´) *va.* to amputate.

amueblar (â•mwe•vlâr´) *va.* to furnish.

amuleto (â•mū•le´to) *m.* amulet.

amurallar (â•mū•râ•yâr´) *va.* to surround with walls.

anacardo (â•nâ•kâr´tho) *m.* cashew tree or fruit.

anaconda (â•nâ•kon´dâ) *f.* anaconda, South American boa.

anacronismo (â•nâ•kro•nēz´mo) *m.* anachronism.

anafe (â•nâ´fe) *m.* portable stove.

anagrama (â•na•grâ´mâ) *m.* anagram.

anales (â•nâ´les) *m. pl.* annals.

analfabetismo (â•nâl•fa•ve•tēz´-mo) *m.* illiteracy.

analfabeto, ta (â•nâl•fâ•ve´to, tâ) *n.* illiterate person.

análisis (â•nâ´lē•sēs) *m. or f.* analysis.

analítico, ca (â•nâ•lē´tē•ko, kâ) *adj.* analytical.

analizar (â•nâ•lē•sâr´) *va.* to analyze.

analogía (â•nâ•lo•hē´â) *f.* analogy.

análogo, ga (â•nâ´lo•go, gâ) *adj.* analogous, similar.

anaquel (â•nâ•kel´) *m.* shelf in a bookcase.

anaranjado, da (â•nâ•ran•hâ´-tho, thâ) *adj.* orange-colored.

anarquía (â•nâr•kē´â) *f.* anarchy.

anarquismo (â•nâr•kēz´mo) *m.* anarchism.

anarquista (â•nâr•kēs´tâ) *m. and f.* anarchist.

anatema (â•nâ•te´mâ) *m. or f.* anathema.

anatomía (â•nâ•to•mē´â) *f.* anatomy. .

anatómico, ca (â•nâ•to´mē•ko, kâ) *adj.* anatomical.

anca (âng´kâ) *f.* buttock *(nalga);* hindquarter, haunch.

ancianidad (ân•syâ•nē•thâth´) *f.* old age, great age.

anciano, na (ân•syâ´no, nâ) *adj.* aged, ancient; **—,** *n.* ancient.

ancla (âng´klâ) *f.* anchor; **echar —s,** to anchor.

anclar (âng•klâr´) *vn.* to anchor.

áncora (âng´ko•râ) *f.* anchor.

ancho, cha (ân´cho, cha) *adj.* broad, wide, large; —, *m.* breadth, width.

anchoa (ân•cho´â) *f.* anchovy; —s, (Mex.) pin curls.

anchura (ân•chū´râ) *f.* width, breadth.

andaderas (ân•dâ•the´râs) *f. pl.* gocart.

Andalucía (ân•dâ•lū•sē´â) *f.* Andalusia.

andamio (ân•dâ´myo) *m.* scaffold, scaffolding; (naut.) gangplank, gangway.

andana (ân•dâ´nâ) *f.* row, rank, line; **llamarse** —, (coll.) to unsay, to retract a promise.

andante (ân•dân´te) *adj.* walking, errant; (mus.) andante.

andar* (ân•dâr´) *vn.* to go, to walk; to do, to fare *(estar);* to proceed, to behave *(proceder);* to work, to function, to move *(funcionar);* — **a tientas,** to grope; **¡ándale!** hurry up! move on! **¡anda!** you don´t say!

andén (ân•den´) *m.* pavement, sidewalk *(acera);* (rail.) platform; foot path *(senda);* dock, landing.

andrajo (ân•drâ´ho) *m.* rag, tatter of clothing.

Andrés (ân•dres´) Andrew.

andurriales (ân•dū•rrya´les) *m.*

pl. by-ways.

anécdota (â•neg´tho•ta) *f.* anecdote.

anegar (â•ne•gâr´) *va.* to inundate, to submerge —**se,** to drown or to be flooded.

anemia (â•ne´myâ) *f.* (med.) anemia.

anémico, ca (â•ne´mē•ko, kâ) *adj.* anemic.

anestesia (â•nes•te´syâ) *f.* (med.) anesthesia.

anestésico, ca (â•nes•te´sē•ko, kâ) *m.* and *adj.* anesthetic.

anexar (â•nek•sâr´) *va.* to annex, to join *(añadir);* to enclose *(adjuntar).*

anexo, xa (â•nek´so, sa) *adj.* annexed, joined; —, *m.* attachment on a letter or document; —**s,** *m. pl.* belongings.

anfibio, bia (âm•fē´vyo, vyá) *adj.* amphibious; —, *m.* amphibian.

anfiteatro (âm•fē•te•â´tro) *m.* amphitheater, auditorium *(auditorio);* (theat.) balcony.

anfitrión (âm•fē•tryon´) *m.* host.

anfitriona (âm•fē•tryo´nâ) *f.* hostess.

ánfora (âm´fo•râ) *f.* amphora; (Mex.) voting box.

ángel (ân•hēl) *m.* angel; **tener** —, to have a pleasing personality.

angelical (ân•he•lē•kâl´) *adj.* angelic.

angina (ân•hē´nâ) *f.* (med.) angina; — **de pecho,** angina pectoris.

anglicismo (âng•glē•sēz´mo) *m.* Anglicism.

anglosajón, ona (âng•glo•sâ•hon´, o´nâ) *n.* and *adj.* Anglo-Saxon.

angosto, ta (âng•gos´to, ta) *adj.* narrow, close.

angostura (âng•gos•tū´râ) *f.* narrowness; narrow passage *(paso).*

anguila (âng•gē´lâ) *f.* (zool.) eel.

angular (âng•gū•lâr´) *adj.* angular; **piedra —,** cornerstone.

ángulo (âng´gū•lo) *m.* angle, corner.

anguloso, sa (âng•gūl•lo´so, sa) *adj.* angular, cornered.

angustia (âng•gūs´tyâ) *f.* anguish, heartache.

angustiado, da (án•gūs•tyâ´tho, thâ) *adj.* worried, miserable.

angustiar, (âng•gūs•tyâr´) *va.* to cause anguish; **—se,** to feel anguish, to grieve.

angustioso, sa (án•gūs•tyo´so, sa) *adj.* distressing, alarming.

anhelante (â•ne•lân´te) *adj.* eager.

anhelar (â•ne•lâr´) *vn.* to long for, to desire *(ansiar);* to breathe with difficulty *(jadear).*

anhelo (â•ne´lo) *m.* vehement desire, longing.

anheloso, sa (â•ne•lo´so, sa) *adj.*

very desirous.

anidar (â•nē•thâr´) *va.* to inhabit; —, *vn.* to nestle, to make a nest.

anillo (â•nē´yo) *m.* ring, small circle.

ánima (â´nē•mâ) *f.* soul; bore of a gun *(de fusil);* **—s,** *pl.* church bells ringing at sunset.

animación (â•nē•mâ•syon´) *f.* animation, liveliness.

animado, da (â•nē•mâ´tho, thâ) *adj.* lively; animated.

animal (â•nē•mâl´) *m.* and *adj.* animal; brute.

animar (â•nē•mâr´) *va.* to animate, to enliven *(avivar);* to comfort, to encourage *(alentar);* **—se,** to cheer up, to be encouraged.

ánimo (â´nē•mo) *m.* soul, spirit; (fig.) energy, determination. ¡—! *interj.* cheer up!

animosidad (â•nē•mo•sē•thâth´) *f.* animosity.

animoso, sa (â•nē•mo´so, sâ) *adj.* courageous, spirited.

aniquilar (â•nē•kē•lâr´) *va.* to annihilate, to destroy; **—se,** to decay, to be consumed; (fig.) to be crushed, to be nonplussed.

anís (â•nēs´) *m.* (bot.) anise.

aniversario (â•nē•ver•sâ´ryo) *m.* anniversary; **—, ria,** *adj.* annual.

anoche (â•no´che) *adv.* last

night.

anochecer* (â•no•che•ser´) *vn.* to grow dark; to arrive by nightfall *(llegar).*

anodizar (â•no•thē•sar) *va.* to anodize.

ánodo (â´no•tho) *m.* (elec.) anode.

anomalía (â•no•ma•lē´â) *f.* anomaly.

anómalo, la (â•no´mâ•lo, lâ) *adj.* anomalous.

anónimo, ma (â•no´nē•mo, ma) *adj.* anonymous; —, *m.* anonymous message.

anormal (â•nor•mâl´) *adj.* abnormal.

anotación (â•no•tâ•syon´) *f.* annotation, note.

anotar (â•no•târ´) *va.* to jot down, to note.

ansia (ân´syâ) *f.* anxiety, worry *(inquietud);* eagerness, yearning *(anhelo).*

ansiar (ân•syâr´) *va.* to desire exceedingly, to long for.

ansiedad (ân•sye•thâth´) *f.* anxiety, worry.

ansioso, sa (ân•syo´so, sâ) *adj.* anxious, eager.

antagónico, ca (ân•tâ•go´nē•ko, kâ) *adj.* antagonistic.

antagonista (ân•tâ•go•nēs´tâ) *m.* and *f.* antagonist.

antaño (ân•tâ´nyo) *adv.* long ago; of old.

antártico, ca (ân•târ´tē•ko, kâ) *adj.* Antarctic.

ante (ân´te) *m.* (zool.) elk; elk skin; —, *prep.* before, in the presence of; — **todo,** above all else.

anteayer (ân•te•â•yer´) *adv.* day before yesterday.

antebrazo (ân•te•vrâ´so) *m.* forearm.

antecámara (ân•te•kâ´mâ•râ) *f.* antechamber, lobby, hall.

antecedente (ân•te•se•then´te) *m.* and *adj.* antecedent.

anteceder (ân•te•se•ther´) *va.* to precede, to antecede.

antecesor, ra (ân•te•se•sor´, râ) *n.* predecessor; forefather *(antepasado).*

antelación (ân•te•lâ•syon´) *f.* precedence.

antemano (ân•te•mâ´no) **de —,** *adv.* beforehand, in advance.

antemeridiano, na (ân•te•me•rē•thyâ´ no, nâ) *adj.* in the forenoon.

antena (ân•te´nâ) *f.* feeler; antenna, aerial.

antenoche (ân•te•no´che) *adv.* the night before last.

anteojo (ân•te•o´ho) *m.* spyglass, eyeglass; — **de larga vista,** telescope; —**s,** pl. spectacles, glasses.

antepagar (ân•te•pâ•gâr´) *va.* to pay in advance.

antepasado, da
(ân•te•pâ•sâ′tho, thâ) *adj.*
passed, elapsed; **semana —,**
week before last; **—dos,** *m. pl.*
ancestors.

anteponer* (ân•te•po•ner′) *va.* to
place before; to prefer *(preferir).*

anterior (ân•te•ryor′) *adj.* anterior, fore *(delantero);* former,
previous *(antecedente);* **año —,**
preceding year.

anterioridad
(ân•te•ryo•rē•thâth′) *f.* precedence; **pagar con —,** to pay in
advance.

antes (ân′tes) *adv.* first
(primero); formerly *(anterior-
mente);* before, before-hand *(de
antemano);* rather *(más bien);*
— bien, on the contrary; **— de,**
before (time); **— que,** before
(position) ; **cuanto —,** as soon
as possible; **— de J.C. B.C.**
before Christ.

antesala (ân•te•sâ′lâ) *f.*
antechamber, waiting room;
hacer —, to wait one's turn in
an office.

antibiótico (ân•tē•vyo′tē•ko) *m.*
antibiotic.

anticipación (ân•tē•sē•pâ•syon′)
f. anticipation; advance *(adelanto);* **pagar con —,** to pay in
advance.

anticipar (ân•tē•sē•pâr′) *va.* to
anticipate.

anticipo (ân•tē•sē′po) *m.*
advance; **— de pago,** payment
in advance, retainer.

anticonceptivo
(ân•tē•kon•sep•tē′vo) *m.* contraceptive.

anticuado, da (ân•tē•kwâ′tho,
thâ) *adj.* antiquated; obsolete
(desusado).

anticuario (ân•tē•kwâ′ryo) *m.*
antiquary, antiquarian.

antídoto (ân•tē′tho•to) *m.* antidote.

antier (ân•tyer′) *adv.* day before
yesterday.

antigüedad (ân•tē•gwe•thâth′) *f.*
antiquity, oldness; ancient
times *(tiempo);* **—es,** *f. pl.*
antiques.

antiguo, gua (ân•te′gwo, gwâ)
adj. antique, old, ancient.

antihigiénico, ca (ân•tē•e•hye-
′nē•ko, kâ) *adj.* unsanitary.

antihistamina
(ân•tē•ēs•tâ•mē′nâ) *f.* antihistamine.

antílope (ân•tē′lo•pe) *m.* antelope.

Antillas (ân•tē′yas) *f. pl.* Antilles
or West Indies.

antipático, ca (ân•tē•pâ′tē•ko,
kâ) *adj.* disagreeable, displeasing.

antisemítico, ca
(ân•tē•se•mē′tē•ko, kâ) *adj.*
anti-Semitic.

antiséptico, ca (ân•tē•sep´tē•ko, kâ) *adj.* antiseptic.

antisocial (ân•tē•so•syâl´) *adj.* antisocial.

antítesis (ân•tē´te•sēs) *f.* (gram.) antithesis.

antojadizo, za (ân•to•hâ•thē´so, sâ) *adj.* capricious, fanciful.

antojarse (ân•to•hâr´se) *vr.* to long, to desire earnestly, to take a fancy.

antojo (ân•to´ho) *m.* whim, fancy, longing, craving.

antología (ân•to•lo•hē´â) *f.* anthology.

antónimo (ân•to´nē•mo) *m.* antonym.

antorcha (ân•tor´châ) *f.* torch, taper.

antropoide (ân•tro•po´ē•the) *m.* and *adj.* anthropoid.

antropología (ân•tro•po•lo•hē´â) *f.* anthropology.

anual (â•nwâl´) *adj.* annual.

anualidad (â•nwâ•lē•thâth´) *f.* yearly recurrence; annuity *(renta).*

anuario (â•nwâ´ryo) *m.* annual, yearbook.

anublar (â•nū•vlâr´) *va.* to cloud, to obscure; **—se** to become clouded *(obscurecerse);* (fig.) to fall through, to fail *(fracasar).*

anudar (â•nū•thâr´) *va.* to knot, to tie, to join.

anular (â•nū•lâr´) *va.* to annul, to render void, to void; **—,** *adj.* annular; **dedo —,** ring finger, fourth finger.

anunciador (â•nūn•syâ•thor´) *m.* announcer.

anunciante (â•nūn•syân´te) *m.* advertiser.

anunciar (â•nūn•syâr´) *va.* to announce, to advertise.

anuncio (â•nūn´syo) *m.* advertisement, announcement.

anzuelo (ân•swe´lo) *m.* fishhook; (fig.) allurement, attraction.

añadidura (â•nyâ•thē•thū´râ) *f.* addition; **por —,** in addition, besides.

añadir (â•nyâ•thēr´) *va.* to add, to join, to attach.

añejar (â•nye•hâr´) *va.* to make old; **—se,** to get old, to become stale; to age *(mejorar).*

añejo, ja (â•nye´ho, hâ) *adj.* old, stale, musty, aged.

añicos (â•nyē´kos) *m. pl.* bits, small pieces; **hacer —,** to break into small pieces; **hacerse —,** to overexert oneself.

año (â´nyo) *m.* year; **— bisiesto,** leap year; **al** or **por —,** per annum; **cumplir —s,** to reach one's birthday; **día de A— Nuevo,** New Year's; **el — pasado,** last year; **el — que viene,** next year; **entrado en —s,** middle-aged; **hace un —,** a year ago; **tener dos —s,** to be two years old.

añoranza (â•nyo•rân´sâ) *f.* melancholy, nostalgia.

apacentar* (â•pâ•sen•tar´) *va* to pasture, to graze.

apacible (â•pâ•sē´vle) *adj.* affable, gentle, placid.

apaciguador (â•pâ•sē•gwâ•thor´) *m.* pacifier, appeaser.

apaciguamiento (â•pâ•sē•gwâ•myen´to) *m.* appeasement.

apaciguar (â•pâ•sē•gwâr´) *va.* to appease, to pacify, to calm; **— se,** to calm down.

apachurrar (â•pâ•chū•rrâr´) *va.* to crush, to flatten.

apadrinar (â•pâ•thrē•nâr´) *va.* to act as godfather to, to sponsor; to support, to favor, to patronize *(patrocinar).*

apagado, da (â•pâ•gâ´tho, thâ) *adj.* nut out, turned off *(extinguido);* low, dull, muffled *(amortiguado);* submissive *(sumiso).*

apagador (â•pâ•gâ•thor´) *m.* extinguisher; **— de incendios,** fire extinguisher.

apagar (â•pâ•gâr´) *va.* to quench, to extinguish, to put out, to turn off; to soften *(aplacar).*

apagón (â•pâ•gon´) *m.* blackout.

apalear (â•pâ•le•âr´) *va.* to whip, to beat with a stick.

aparador (â•pâ•râ•thor´) *m.* buffet; sideboard; workshop *(taller);* store window *(escaparate).*

aparato (â•pâ•râ´to) *m.* apparatus, appliance *(máquina);* preparation, ostentation, show.

aparatoso, sa (â•pâ•râ•to´so, sâ) *adj.* pompous showy.

aparear (â•pâ•re•âr´) *va.* to match, to pair; **—se,** to be paired off by twos.

aparecer* (â•pâ•re•ser´) *vn.* to appear, to be found.

aparecido (â•pâ•re•sē´tho) *m.* apparition, ghost.

aparejar (â•pâ•re•hâr´) *va.* to prepare; to harness *(arrear);* (naut.) to rig.

aparentar (â•pâ•ren•târ´) *va.* to assume, to simulate, to affect, to feign, to pretend, to sham.

aparente (â•pâ•ren´te) *adj.* apparent; fit, suitable *(conveniente);* evident; seeming, ilusory, deceptive *(engañoso).*

aparición (â•pâ•rē•syon´) *f.* apparition *(fantasma);* appearance *(manifestación).*

apariencia (â•pâ•ryen´syâ) *f.* appearance, looks.

apartadero (â•pâr•tâ•the´ro) *m.* (rail.) siding, side track; wide roadbed for passing.

apartado (â•pâr•tâ´tho) *m.* post-office box; —, **da,** *adj.* secluded, separated; (fig.) reserved, aloof.

apartamiento (â•par•tâ•myen´to) *m.* secluded place *(retiro);* apartment, flat; — **amueblado,** furnished apartment; — **sin muebles,** unfurnished apartment.

apartar (â•pâr•târ´) *va.* to separate, to divide *(separar);* to dissuade *(disuadir)* to remove *(sacar);* to sort *(clasificar);* —**se,** to withdraw; to desist.

aparte (â•pâr´te) *m.* (theat.) aside; new paragraph *(acápite);* —, *adv.* apart, separately.

apasionado, da (â•pâ•syo•nâ´tho, thâ) *adj.* passionate, impulsive; devoted to, fond of *(aficionado).*

apasionar (â•pá•syo•nâr´) *va.* to excite apassion; —**se,** to become very fond (of), to be prejudiced (about).

apatía (â•pâ•tē´â) *f.* apathy.

apático, ca (â•pâ´tē•ko, kâ) *adj.* apathetic, indifferent.

apeadero (â•pe•â•the´ro) *m.* horse block *(poyo);* rest stop, resting place; (rail.) flag stop, whistle-stop.

apegarse (â•pe•gâr´se) *vr.* to become attached, to become fond.

apego (â•pe´go) *m.* attachment, fondness.

apelación (â•pe•lâ•syon´) *f.* supplication, entreaty; appeal *(jurídica).*

apelar (â•pe•lar´) *vn.* to appeal, to have recourse, to supplicate.

apellidar (â•pe•yē•thâr´) *va.* to call by one´s last name; (mil.) to call to arms; —**se,** to be surnamed, to be one´s last name.

apellido (â•pe•yē´tho) *m.* surname, family name.

apenar (â•pe•nâr´) *va.* to cause pain; —**se,** to grieve.

apenas (â•pe´nâs) *adv.* scarcely, hardly.

apéndice (â•pen´dē•se) *m.* (med.) appendix; supplement *(suplemento).*

apendicitis (â•pen•dē•sē´tēs) *f.* appendicitis.

apercibir (â•per•sē•vēr) *va.* to prepare to provide *(disponer);* to warn, to advise *(avisar);* to sense.

aperitivo (â•pe•rē•tē´vo) *m.* appetizer, apéritif.

apertura (â•per•tū´râ) *f.* opening, inauguration.

apestar (â•pes•târ´) *vn.* to produce an offensive smell, to smell bad, to stink.

apetecer* (â•pe•te•ser´) *va.* to long for, to crave.

apetecible (â•pe•te•sē´vle) *adj.* desirable.

apetito (â•pe•tē′to) *m.* appetite;
entrar en —, to get hungry, to
work up an appetite.

apetitoso, sa (â•pe•tē•to•so, sâ)
adj. appetizing.

apiadarse (â•pyâ•thâr′se) *vr.* to
commiserate (with), to take pity
(on).

ápice (â′pē•se) *m.* summit,
point; (fig.) smallest part.

apiñar (a•pē•nyâr′) *va.* to press,
to crowd close together; **—se,**
to clog, to crowd.

apio (â′pyo) *m.* (bot.) celery.

aplacar (â•plâ•kâr′) *va.* to
appease, to pacify; **—se,** to
calm down.

aplanadora (â•plâ•nâ•tho′râ) *f.*
steamroller.

aplanar (â•plâ•nâr′) *va.* to level,
to flatten; to astonish *(pasmar);*
—se, to fall to the ground.

aplastado, da (â•plâs•tâ′tho,
thâ) *adj.* crushed, flattened;
(fig.) dispirited.

aplastar (â•plâs•târ′) *va.* to flatten, to crush; (fig.) to squelch
or crush (an opponent); **—se,**
to collapse; to feel squelched.

aplaudir (â•lâū•thēr′) *va.* to
applaud; to extol *(celebrar).*

aplauso (â•plâ′ū•so) *m.*
applause, approbation, praise.

aplazamiento (â•plâ•sâ•myen′to)
m. postponement; summons.

aplazar (â•plâ•sâr′) *va.* to call

together, to call into session; to
defer, to put off, to postpone
(diferir).

aplicable (â•plē•kâ′vle) *adj.*
applicable.

aplicación (â•plē•kâ•syon′) *f.*
application; attention, care,
industriousness *(esmero).*

aplicado, da (â•plē•kâ′tho, thâ)
adj. studious, industrious.

aplicar (â•plē•kâr′) *va.* to apply,
to stick; (fig.) to adapt, to make
use of; **—se,** to devote oneself,
to apply oneself.

aplomado, da (â•plo•mâ′tho,
thâ) *adj.* lead-colored, leaden;
(fig.) heavy, dull.

aplomo (â•plo′mo) *m.* composure, self-possession, poise.

apocar (â•po•kâr′) *va.* to lessen,
to diminish, to limit; **—se,** to
humble oneself.

apócope (â•po′ko•pe) *m.* apocope.

apodar (â•po•thâr′) *va.* to give
nicknames.

apoderado, da (â•po•the•râ′tho,
thâ) *adj.* authorized, empow-
ered; **—,** *m.* legal representative, proxy, attorney in fact.

apoderar (â•po•the•râr′) *va.* to
empower *(autorizar);* to grant
power of attorney; **—se,** to take
possession.

apodo (â•po′tho) *m.* nickname.

apogeo (â•po•he′o) *m.* (ast.)

apogee; (fig.) apex, culmination; **estar en su —,** to be at the height of one's fame or popularity.

apología (â•po•lo•hē´â) *f.* eulogy, apology.

apoplejía (â•po•ple•hē´â) *f.* apoplexy.

aporreado, da (â po•rre•â´tho, thâ) *adj.* cudgeled, beaten; **—,** *m.* (Cuba) kind of beef stew.

aporrear (â•po•rre•âr´) *va.* to thrash, to slug.

aportar (â•por•târ´) *va.* to bring, to contribute; **—,** *vn.* to land at a port.

aposento (â•po•sen´to) *m.* room, chamber; inn *(posada).*

apostar* (â•pos•târ´) *va.* to bet, to lay a wager; (mil.) to station; **—se,** to station oneself.

apostema (â•pos•te´mâ) *f.* abscess, tumor.

apóstol (â•pos´tol) *m.* apostle.

apostólico, ca (â•pos•to´lē•ko, kâ) *adj.* apostolic.

apóstrofe (â•pos´tro•fe) *m.* (rhet.) apostrophe.

apoyar (â•po•yâr´) *va.* to favor, to support; **—,** vn. to rest, to lie; **—se,** to lean upon.

apoyo (â•po´yo) *m.* prop, rest, stay, support *(sostén);* (fig.) protection, aegis.

apreciable (â•pre•syâ´vle) *adj.* appreciable, valuable,

respectable; **su —,** (corn.) your favor (letter).

apreciación (â•pre•syâ•syon´) *f.* estimation, evaluation, appreciation.

apreciar (â•pre•syâr´) *va.* to appreciate, to value.

aprecio (â•pre´syo) *m.* appreciation, esteem, regard.

aprehender (â•pre•en•der´) *va.* to apprehend, to seize.

aprehensión (â•pre•en•syon´) *f.* apprehension, seizure.

aprehensivo, va (â•pre•en•sē´vo, vâ) *adj.* apprehensive, fearful; quick to understand, bright *(listo).*

apremiante (â•pre•myân´te) *adj.* urgent, pressing.

apremiar (â•pre•myâr´) *va.* to hurry, to urge, to press; to oppress *(oprimir).*

apremio (â•pre´myo) *m.* pressure, urging; enjoinder *(jurídico).*

aprender (â•pren•der´) *va.* to learn; **— de memoria,** to learn by heart.

aprendiz, za (â•pren•dēs´, sâ) *n.* apprentice.

aprensión (â•pren•syon´) *f.* apprehension, fear, misgiving.

apresar (â•pre•sâr´) *va.* to seize, to grasp *(agarrar);* to capture *(aprisionar).* .

apresurado, da (â•pre•sū•râ´tho,

thâ) *adj.* hasty.

apresuramiento (â•pre•sū•râ•myen´to) *m.* haste.

apresurar (â•pre•sū•râr´) *va.* to accelerate, to hasten, to expedite; —se, to hurry, to hasten.

apretado, da (â•pre•tâ´tho, thâ) *adj.* tight, squeezed; mean, miserable, closehanded *(mezquino);* hard, difficult *(dificil).*

apretar* (â•pre•târ´) *va.* to close tight, to tighten, to squeeze *(estrechar);* to bother, to harass *(afligir);* to pinch, to be too tight *(calzado);* to urge, to entreat *(instar).*

apretón (â•pre•ton´) *m.* pressure; — **de manos,** strong handshake.

aprieto (â•prye´to) *m.* crowd *(gentío);* predicament, difficulty *(apuro);* **estar en un —,** to be in a pickle, to be in a jam.

aprisa (â•pre´sâ) *adv.* in a hurry, swiftly

aprisionar (â•prē•syo•nâr´) *va.* to imprison.

aprobación (â•pro•vâ•syon´) *f.* approval.

aprobado, da (â•pro•vâ´tho, thâ) *adj.* well-thought-of; *(en un examen)* passed; —, *m.* pass, passing grade.

aprobar* (â•pro•vâr´) *va.* to approve, to approve of, to OK.

apropiación (â•pro•pyâ•syon´) *f.* appropriation, assumption.

apropiado, da (â•pro•pyâ´tho, thâ) *adj.* appropriate, adequate.

apropiar (â•pro•pyâr´) *va.* to appropriate; —se, take possession of.

aprovechable (â•pro•ve•châ´vle) *adj.* available, usable.

aprovechamiento (â•pro•ve•châ•myen´to) *m.* taking advantage, profiting.

aprovechar (â•pro•ve•châr´) *va.* to avail oneself of, to make use of; —, *vn.* to make progress; —se de, to take advantage of, to avail oneself of.

aproximación (â•prok•sē•ma•syon´) *f.* approximation, approach.

aproximar (â•prok•sē•mar´) *va.* and *vr.* to approach, to move near, to approximate.

aptitud (âp•tē•tūth´) *f.* aptitude, fitness, ability, talent.

apto, ta (âp´to, tâ) *adj.* apt, fit, able, clever.

apuesta (â•pwes´tâ) *f.* bet, wager.

apuesto, ta (â•pwes´to, ta) *adj.* smart, elegant.

apuntado, da (â•pūn•tâ´tho, thâ) *adj.* pointed *(puntiagudo);* jotted, written down *(anotado).*

apuntar (â•pūn•târ´) *va.* to aim,

to level *(asestar);* to point out,
to note *(señalar);* to write down
(anotar); (theat.) to prompt; —,
vn. to begin to appear; —**se,** to
register, to enroll *(alistarse);* to
begin to turn (of wine) *(agriarse).*

apunte (â•pūn´te) *m.* annotation, note; sketch *(boceto);*
(theat.) stage prompting.

aquel, lla (â•kel´, yâ) *adj.* **aquél,
lla,** *pron.* that; the former; —
llos, llas, *pl.* those.

aquello (â•ke´yo) *pron.* that, the
former, the first mentioned,
that matter.

aquí (â•kē´) *adv.* here, in this
place; **de** —, hence; **por** —, this
way.

aquietar (â•kye•târ´) *va.* to quiet,
to appease, to lull; —**se,** to
become calm.

ara (â´râ) *f.* altar; **en —s de,** for
the sake of.

árabe (â´râ•ve) *m.* and *f.* Arab;
—, *adj.* Arabic; —, *m.* Arabic
language.

arabesco (â•râ•ves´ko) *m.* ara-
besque; —, **ca,** *adj.* Arabic.

arábico, ca (â•râ´vē•ko, kâ) or
arábigo, ga, (â•râ´vē•go, gâ)
adj. Arabian, Arabic.

arado (â•râ´tho) *m.* plow; — **de
azada,** hoe plow; — **giratorio,**
rotary plow.

arador (â•râ•thor´) *m.* plowman.

aragonés, esa (â•râ•go•nes´, esâ)
n. and *adj.* Aragonese.

araña (â•râ´nyâ) *f.* (ent.) spider;
chandelier *(candelabro).*

arañar (â•râ•nyâr´) *va.* to
scratch, to scrape.

arar (â•râr´) *va.* to plow, to till.

arbitraje (âr•vē•trâ´he) *m.* arbitration.

arbitrar (âr•vē•trâr´) *va.* to arbitrate.

arbitrario, ria (âr•vē•trâ´ryo, ryâ)
adj. arbitrary.

árbitro (âr´vē•tro) *m.* arbiter,
arbitrator; umpire *(del juego).*

árbol (âr´vol) *m.* tree; (mech.)
shaft; (naut.) mast; — **de eje,**
or de manivela, crankshaft; —
de levas, camshaft.

arbolado, da (âr•vo•lâ´tho, thâ)
adj. forested, wooded; —, *m.*
woodland.

arboleda (âr•vo•le´thâ) *f.* grove.

arbusto (âr•vūs´to) *m.* shrub.

arca (âr´kâ) *f.* chest, wooden
box; — **de hierro,** strongbox,
safe.

arcada (âr•kâ´thâ) *f.* (ârch.)
arcade, row of arches; retching
(vómito).

arcaico, ca (âr•kâ´ē•ko, kâ) *adj.*
archaic, ancient.

arcángel (âr•kân´hel) *m.* archan-
gel.

arcano, na (âr•kâ´no, nâ) *adj.*
secret, mysterious; —, *m.* very

important secret, mystery.

arce (âr´se) *m.* maple tree.

arcilla (âr•sē´yâ) *f.* argil, clay.

arco (âr´ko) *m.* arc; (ârch.) arch; (mus.) fiddle bow; hoop *(aro);* — **iris,** rainbow; **soldadura con** —, arc welding; —**adintelado,** straight, fiat arch.

arcón (âr•kon´) *m.* large chest, bin.

archiduque (âr•chē•thū´ke) *m.* archduke.

archipiélago (âr•chē•pye´lâ•go) *m.* archipelago.

archivar (âr•chē•vâr´) *va.* to file, to place in the archives.

archivero, ra (âr•chē•ve´ro, râ) *n.* or **archivista,** (âr•chē•vēs´tâ) *m.* and *f.* keeper of the archives; file clerk.

archivo (âr•chē´vo) *m.* archives, files.

arder (âr•ther´) *vn.* to burn, to blaze.

ardiente (âr•thyen´te) *adj.* ardent, fiery, intense.

ardilla (âr•thē´yâ) *f.* squirrel.

ardor (âr•thor´) *m.* great heat; energy, vivacity *(eficacia);* anxiety, longing *(anhelo);* fervor, zeal *(esfuerzo).*

ardoroso, sa (âr•tho•ro´so, sâ) *adj.* fiery, restless.

arduo, dua (âr´thwo, dwâ) *adj.* arduous, difficult.

área (â´re•â) *f.* area.

arena (â•re´nâ) *f.* sand, grains; arena *(palenque).*

arenal (â•re•nâl´) *m.* sandy ground, sand pit.

arenoso, sa (â•re•no´so, sa) *adj.* sandy.

arenque (â•reng´ke) *m.* herring; — **ahumado,** smoked herring; — **en escabeche,** pickled herring.

aretes (â•re´tes) *m. pl.* earrings.

argentado, da (âr•hen•tâ´tho, thâ) *adj.* silverlike.

argentino, na (âr•hen•tē´no, na) *adj.* silvery *(argénteo);* Argentine.

argüir* (âr•gwēr´) *vn.* to argue, to dispute, to oppose; —, *va.* to infer.

argumentar (âr•gū•men•târ´) *vn.* to argue, to dispute.

argumento (âr•gū•mento) *m.* argument; (theat.) plot, intrigue.

aria (â´ryâ) *f.* (mus.) aria.

aridez (â•rē•thes´) *f.* aridity, dryness; (fig.) barrenness.

árido, da (â´rē•tho, thâ) *adj.* arid, dry; barren *(estéril).*

arisco, ca (â•rēs´ko, kâ) *adj.* fierce, rude, surly.

aristocracia (â•res•to•krâ´syâ) *f.* aristocracy.

aristócrata (â•rēs•to´krâ•tâ) *m.* and *f.* aristocrat.

aristocrático, ca

(â•rēs•to•krâ′tē•ko, kâ) *adj.* aristocratic.

aritmética (â•rēth•me′tē•kâ) *f.* arithmetic.

arlequín (âr•le•kēn′) *m.* harlequin, buffoon.

arma (âr′mâ) *f.* weapon, arm; — s blancas, side arms; **alzarse en —s,** to revolt.

armada (âr•mâ′thâ) *f.* fleet, armada.

armadillo (âr•mâ•thē′yo) *m.* armadillo.

armado, da (âr•mâ′tho, thâ) *adj.* armed; assembled, put together *(montado).*

armadura (âr•mâ•thū′râ) *f.* armor; (arch.) framework.

armamento (âr•mâ•men′to) *m.* armament.

armar (âr•mâr′) *va.* to furnish with arms or troops; to put together, to set up, to assemble *(montar);* to cause, to bring about *(provocar).*

armario (âr•mâ′ryo) *m.* wall cabinet, cupboard.

armonía (âr•mo•nē′â) *f.* harmony.

armónico, ca (âr•mo′nē•ko, kâ) *adj.* harmonious, harmonic; —, *f.* harmonica, mouth organ.

armonioso, sa (âr•mo•nyo′so, sâ) *adj.* harmonious, sonorous.

armonizar (âr•mo•nē•sâr′) *va.* to harmonize.

aro (â′ro) *m.* hoop; (auto.) rim.

aroma (â•ro′mâ) *f.* flower of the aromatic myrrh tree; —, *m.* aroma, fragrance.

aromático, ca (â•ro•mâ′tē•ko, kâ) *adj.* aromatic.

aromatizar (â•ro•mâ•tē•sâr′) *va.* to perfume.

arpa (âr′pâ) *f.* (mus.) harp.

arpía (âr•pē′â) *f.* (poet.) harpy; (fig.) hag, witch.

arpista (âr•pēs′tâ) *m.* harpist.

arpón (âr•pon′) *m.* harpoon.

arponar (âr•po•nâr′) *va.* to harpoon.

arqueado, da (âr•ke•â′tho, thâ) *adj.* arched, vaulted; bent.

arquear (âr•ke•âr′) *va.* to arch.

arqueología (âr•ke•o•lo•hē′â) *f.* archaeology.

arquero (âr•ke′ró) *m.* archer *(soldado);* bow maker; goalkeeper *(portero);* cashier *(cajero).*

arquitecto (âr•kē•tek′to) *m.* architect.

arquitectura (âr•kē•tek•tū′râ) *f.* architecture.

arrabal (â•rrâ•vâl′) *m.* suburb; **—es,** *pl.* outskirts, outlying districts.

arraigar (â•rrâē•gâr′) *vn.* to take root; (fig.) to become established, to become deep-seated, to become fixed; **costumbre arraigada,** settled habit, second nature.

arraigo (â•rrä´ē•go) *m.* landed property, real estate *(bienes raíces);* settlement, establishment *(establecimiento).*

arrancar (â•rräng•kär´) *va.* to pull up by the roots, to pull out; (fig.) to wrest from, to drag from; —, *vn.* to start; (naut.) to set sail.

arranque (â•rräng´ke) *m.* extirpation, pulling out; burst of rage, scene, tantrum *(ímpetu);* (auto.) ignition, starter; (fig.) bright idea *(ocurrencia);* — **automático,** self-starter; **motor de —,** self-starting motor.

arrasar (â•rrä•sär´) *va.* to demolish, to destroy, to raze; —, *vn.* to clear up (of the sky).

arrastrado, da (â•rräs•trä´tho, thâ) *adj.* dragged along; (fig.) miserable, destitute.

arrastrar (â•rräs•trär´) *vn.* to creep, to crawl; to lead a trump in card playing; — *va.* to drag along the ground.

arrear (â•rre•är´) *va.* to drive (horses, mules); to urge on, hurry *(dar prisa).*

arrebatado, da (â•rre•vä•tä´tho, thâ) *adj.* rapid, violent, impetuous, rash, inconsiderate.

arrebatar (â•rre•vä•tär´) *va.* to carry off, to snatch hurriedly; (fig.) to enrapture, to thrill.

arrebato (â•rre•vä´to) *m.* surprise; sudden attack; (fig.) thrill, rapture, ecstasy.

arreciar (â•rre•syär´) *vn.* to increase in intensity.

arrecife (â•rre•sē´fe) *m.* reef; causeway *(calzada).*

arreglado, da (â•rre•glä´tho, thâ) *adj.* regular, moderate; (fig.) neat, organized *(ordenado).*

arreglar (â•rre•glâr´) *va.* to regulate, to adjust; to arrange *(disponer);* — **una cuenta,** to settle an account; **arreglárselas,** to manage, to make out, to get by.

arreglo (â•rre´glo)*m.* adjustment, arrangement, settlement; **con — a,** according to.

arremangar (â•rre•mâng•gär´) *va.* to roll up, to tuck up; **—se,** to resolve firmly.

arremeter (â•rre•me•ter´) *va.* to assail, to attack.

arremetida (â•rre•me•tē´thâ) *f.* attack, assault.

arrendado, da (â•rren•dâ´tho, thâ) *adj.* manageable, tractable, easily reined.

arrendador (â•rren•dâ•thor´) *m.* tenant, lessee *(inquilino);* hirer.

arrendajo (â•rren•dâ´ho) *m.* (orn.) mockingbird; (fig.) mimic, buffoon.

arrendamiento (â•rren•dâ•myen´to) *m.* lease, leasing, rental; **contrato de —,** lease.

arrendar* (â•rren•dâr´) *va.* to rent, to let out, to lease; to tie, to bridle *(atar);* to mimic, to imitate *(remedar).*

arrendatario, ria (â•rren•dâ•tâ´ryo, ryâ) *n.* tenant.

arrepentido, da (â•rre•pen•tē´-tho, thâ) *adj.* repentant.

arrepentimiento (â•rre•pen•tē•myen´to) *m.* remorse, penitence.

arrepentirse* (â•rre•pen•tēr•se)*vr.* to repent.

arrestado, da (â•rres•tâ´tho, thâ) *adj.* intrepid, bold.

arrestar (â•rres•târ´) *va.* to arrest, to imprison; **—se,** to be bold and enterprising.

arresto (â•rres´to)*m.* boldness, vigor, enterprise; imprisonment, arrest *(detención).*

arriata (â•rryâ´tâ) *f.,* **arriate,** *m.* flowerbed; roadway, causeway *(calzada).*

arriba (â•rrē´vâ) *adv.* up above, on high, overhead, upstairs; (naut.) aloft; **de — abajo,** from head to foot; **para —,** up, upwards.

arribar (â•rrē•vâr´) *vn.* to arrive; (naut.) to put into port; to fall off to leeward *(sotaventarse).*

arribo (â•rrē´vo) *m.* arrival.

arriendo (â•rryen´do) *m.* lease, farm rent.

arriero (â•rrye´ro) *m.* muleteer.

arriesgado (â•rryez•gâ´tho) *adj.* risky, dangerous.

arriesgar (â•rryez•gâr´) *va.* and *vr.* to risk, to hazard, to expose to danger.

arrinconar (â•rrēng•ko•nâr´) *va.* to put in a corner *(poner);* (fig.) to corner, to tree *(acosar);* to lay aside, to neglect, to forget; **—se,** to retire, to withdraw.

arrodillar (â•rro•thē•yâr´) *va.* to cause to kneel down; **—se,** to kneel.

arrogancia (â•rro•gân´syâ) *f.* arrogance, haughtiness.

arrogante (â•rro•gân•te) *adj.* haughty, proud, assuming, arrogant *(altanero);* bold, valiant, stout *(valiente).*

arrojadamente (â•rro•hâ•thâ•men´te) *adv.* daringly.

arrojado, da (â•rro•hâ´tho, thâ) *adj.* rash, inconsiderate *(arrebatado);* bold, fearless, unflinching *(resuelto).*

arrojar (â•rro•hâr´) *va.* to dart, to fling, to hurl, to dash *(lanzar);* to shed, to emit, to give off *(emitir).*

arrojo (â•rro´ho) *m.* boldness, intrepidity, fearlessness.

arropar (â•rro•pâr´) *va.* to dress warmly, to bundle up.

arroyo (â•rro´yo) *m.* creek; (Sp. Am.) gully, dry creek bed.

arroz (â•rros´) *m.* rice.

arruga (â•rrū´gâ) *f.* wrinkle, rumple.

arrugar (â•rrū•gâr´) *va.* to wrinkle, to rumple, to fold; — **el ceño,** to frown; — **la frente,** to knit one´s brow; —**se,** to shrivel.

arruinado, da (â•rrwē•nâ´tho, thâ) *adj.* fallen.

arruinar (â•rrwē•nâr´) *va.* to demolish, to ruin; —**se,** to lose one´s fortune.

arrullador, ra (â•rrū•yâ•thor´, râ) *adj.* flattering, cajoling.

arrullar (â•rrū•yâr´) *va.* to lull to rest; to court, to woo *(cortejar).*

arsenal (âr•se•nâl´) *m.* arsenal; (naut.) dockyard.

arsénico (âr•se´nē•ko) *m.* arsenic.

arte (âr´te) *m.* and *f.* art; skill, artfulness *(habilidad);* **bellas —s,** fine arts.

artefacto (âr•te•fâk´to) *m.* artifact, mechanism, device.

arteria (âr•te´ryâ) *f.* artery.

arterial (âr•te•ryâl´) *adj.* arterial; **presión —,** blood pressure.

artesano (âr•te•sâ´no) *m.* artisan, workman.

ártico, ca (âr´tē•ko, kâ) *adj.* Arctic.

articulación (âr•tē•kū•lâ•syon´) *f.* articulation, enunciation, way of speaking; (anat.) joining, joint; — **universal,** (mech.) universal joint.

articular (âr•tē•kū•lâr´) *va.* to articulate, to pronounce distinctly.

artículo (âr•tē´kū•lo) *m.* article; clause, point *(subdivisión);* (gram.) article; — **de fondo,** editorial; —**s de fantasia,** novelties; —**s de tocador,** toilet articles; —**s para escritorio,** office supplies.

artificial (âr•tē•fē•syâl´) *adj.* artificial.

artificio (âr•tē•fē´syo) *m.* workmanship, craft *(arte);* device, artifice *(mecanismo);* trickery, cunning, subterfuge *(disimulo).*

artificioso, sa (âr•tē•fē•syo´so, sâ) *adj.* skillful, ingenious; artful, cunning *(astuto).*

artillería (âr•tē•ye•rē´â) *f.* gunnery, artillery; ordnance *(material).*

artillero (âr•tē•ye´ro) *m.* artilleryman.

artimaña (âr•tē•mâ´nyâ) *f.* stratagem, deception *(astucia);* trap *(trampa).*

artista (âr•tēs´tâ) *m.* and *f.* artist.

artístico, ca (âr•tēs´tē•ko, kâ) *adj.* artistic.

artritis (âr•trē´tēs) *f.* (med.)

arthritis.

arzobispado (âr•so•vēs•pâ′tho) *m.* archdiocese.

arzobispo (âr•so•vēs′po) *m.* archbishop.

as (âs) *m.* ace; as *(moneda).*

asa (â′sâ) *f.* handle, haft.

asado, da (â•sâ′tho, thâ) *adj.* roasted; —, *m.* roast.

asador (â•sâ•thor′) *m.* barbecue *(aparato).*

asalariado, da (â•sâ•lâ•ryâ′tho, thâ) *adj.* and *n.* salaried, salaried person.

asaltador (â•sal•tâ•thor′) *m.* assailant, highwayman.

asaltar (â•sal•târ′) *va.* to attack, to storm, to assail, to fall upon.

asalto (â•sâl′to) *m.* assault, holdup.

asamblea (â•sâm•ble′â) *f.* assembly, meeting.

asar (â•sâr′) *va.* to roast.

asbesto (âz•ves′to) *m.* asbestos.

ascendencia (âs•sen•den′syâ) *f.* ascending line, line of ancestors.

ascendente (âs•sen•den′te) *adj.* ascending.

ascender* (âs sen•der′) *va.* and *vn.* to ascend, to climb; (corn.) to amount to.

ascendiente (âs•sen•dyen′te) *m.* ascendant, forefather; (fig.) influence.

ascensión (âs•sen•syon′) *f.*

(eccl.) feast of the Ascension; ascent.

ascenso (âs•sen′so) *m.* promotion, advance.

ascensor (âs•sen•sor′) *m.* elevator, lift.

ascetismo (âs•se•tēz′mo) *m.* asceticism.

asco (âs′ko) *m.* nausea; (fig.) loathing, disgust.

ascua (âs′kwâ) *f.* red-hot coal; **estar en** —**s,** (coll.) to be restless or excited; ¡—! *interj.* ouch!

aseado, da (â•se•â′tho, thâ) *adj.* clean; well-groomed, neat.

asear (â•se•âr′) *va.* to clean, to groom, to make neat.

asechanza (â•se•chân′sâ) *f.* snare.

asediar (â•se•thyâr′) *va.* to besiege; (fig.) to annoy, to nag.

asegurado, da (â•se•gū•râ′tho, thâ) *adj.* assured, secured; (corn.) insured; —, *n.* policyholder.

asegurador (â•se•gū•râ•thor″) *m.* fastener; (corn.) insurer, underwriter.

asegurar (â•se•gū•râr′) *va.* to secure, to fasten; (fig.) to assure, to affirm; (corn.) to insure.

asemejar (â•se•me•hâr′) *va.* to make similar; —**se,** to resemble.

asenso (â•sen′so) *m.* assent,

consent.

asentaderas (â•sen•ta•the´râs) *f. pl.* buttocks.

asentar* (â•sen•târ´) *va.* to seat, to place; (fig.) to assure, to establish, to base; — **al crédito de,** to place to the credit of; —, *vn.* to be becoming; —**se,** to settle, to distill (liquid).

asentimiento (â•sen•tē•myen´to) *m.* assent.

asentir* (â•sen•tēr´) *vn.* to acquiesce, to concede.

aseo (â•se´o) *m.* cleanliness, neatness.

asequible (â•se•kē´vle) *adj.* attainable, obtainable.

aserción (â•ser•syon´) *m.* assertion, affirmation.

aserrar* (â•se•rrâr´) *va.* to saw.

aserrín (â•se•rrēn´) *m.* sawdust.

asesinar (â•se•sē•nâr´) *va.* to assassinate.

asesinato (â•se•sē•nâ´to)*m.* assassination.

asesino, na (â•se•sē´no, nâ) *m.* assassin.

asesor (â•se•sor´) *m.* counselor, assessor.

asesorar (â•se•so•râr´) *va.* to give legal advice to; —**se,** to employ counsel; to take advice.

aseverar (â•se•ve•râr´) *va.* to asseverate, to affirm solemnly.

asfalto (âs•fâl´to) *m.* asphalt.

asfixia (âs•fēk´syâ) *f.* (med.) asphyxia,

asfixiante (âs•fēk•syân´te) *adj.* asphyxiating, suffocating.

asfixiar (âs•fēk•syâr´) *va.* and *vr.* to asphyxiate, to suffocate.

así (â•sē´) *adv.* so, thus, in this manner; therefore, as a result *(por esto);* even though *(aunque);* — **que,** as soon as, just after; **por decirlo —,** so to speak.

asiático, ca (â•syâ´tē•ko,•kâ) *n.* and *adj.* Asiatic.

asiduidad (â•se•thwē•thâth´) *f.* assiduity, diligence.

asiduo, dua (â•sē´thwo, thwâ) *adj.* assiduous, devoted, careful.

asiento (â•syen´to) *m.* chair, seat; (corn.) entry; (fig.) stability, permanence; — **trasero,** back seat.

asignación (â•sēg•nâ•syon´) *f.* allocation, distribution; destination.

asignar (â•sēg•nâr´) *va.* to allocate, to apportion, to assign, to distribute.

asignatura (â•sēg•nâ•tū´râ) *f.* subject of a school course.

asilo (â•sē´lo) *m.* asylum, refuge.

asimetría (â•sē•me•trē´â) *f.* asymmetry.

asimilar (â•sē•mē•lâr´) *vn.* to resemble; —. *va.* to assimilate.

asimismo (â•sē•mēz´mo) *adv.*

similarly, likewise.

asir* (â•sēr´) *va.* and *vn.* to grasp, to seize, to hold, to grip; (fig.) to take root, to take hold.

asistencia (â•sēs•ten´syâ) *f.* presence, attendance; assistance, help *(ayuda);* **falta de —,** absence (from class, etc.); — **social,** social work.

asistente (â•sēs•ten´te) *m.* assistant, helper; (mil.) orderly.

asistir (â•sēs•tēr´) *vn.* to be present, to attend; —, *va.* to help, to further; to attend, to take care of *(atender).*

asma (âz´mâ) *f.* asthma.

asmático, ca (âz•mâ´tē•ko, kâ) *adj.* asthmatic.

asno (âz´no) *m.* ass.

asociación (â•so•syâ•syon´) *f.* association; partnership *(conjunto).*

asociado, da (âs•so•syâ´tho, thâ) *n.* associate; —, *adj.* associated.

asociar (â•so•syâr´) *va.* to associate; —**se,** to form a partnership.

asoleado, da (â•so•le•â´tho, thâ) *adj.* sunny; suntanned *(bronceado).*

asolear (â•so•le•âr´) *va.* to expose to the sun; —**se,** to bask in the sun.

asomar (â•so•mâr´) *vn.* to begin to appear, to become visible, to show; —**se,** to look out, to lean out, to peer over, to peek.

asombrar (â•som•brâr´) *va.* to amaze, to astonish.

asombro (â•som´bro) *m.* amazement, astonishment.

asombroso, sa (â•som•bro´so, sâ) *adj.* astonishing *(sorprendente);* marvelous *(admirable).*

aspecto (âs•pek´to) *m.* appearance; aspect *(punto).*

aspereza (âs•pe•re´sâ) *f.* asperity, harshness, acerbity.

áspero, ra (âs´pe•ro, râ) *adj.* rough, rugged, craggy; (fig.) harsh, gruff.

aspiración (âs•pē•râ•syon´) *f.* aspiration, ambition.

aspiradora (âs•pē•râ•tho´râ) *f.* vacuum cleaner.

aspirar (âs•pē•râr´) *va.* (gram.) to aspirate; to suck in, to draw in.

aspirina (âs•pē•rē´nâ) *f.* aspirin.

asqueroso, sa (âs•ke•ro´so, sâ) *adj.* loathsome, repugnant.

asta (âs´tâ) *f.* lance; horn *(cuerno);* handle *(mango);* staff, pole *(palo).*

asterisco (âs•te•rēs´ko) *m.* asterisk.

astigmatismo (âs•tēg•mâ•tēz´mo) *m.* astigmatism.

astilla (âs•tē´yâ) *f.* chip, splinter, fragment.

astillar (âs•tē•yâr´) *va.* to chip.

astringente (âs•trēn•hen´te) *adj.*
and *m.* astringent.

astro (âs´tro) *m.* star.

astrofísica (âs•tro•fē´sē•kâ) *f.*
astrophysics.

astrología (âs•tro•lo•hē´â) *f.*
astrology.

astrólogo (âs•tro´lo•go) *m.* astro-
loger.

astronauta (âs•tro•nâ´ū•tâ) *m.*
astronaut.

astronomía (âs•tro•no•mē´â) *f.*
astronomy.

astronómico, ca
(âs•tro•no´mē•ko, kâ) *adj.*
astronomical.

astrónomo (âs•tro´no•mo) *m.*
astronomer.

astucia (âs•tū´syâ) *f.* cunning,
slyness *(maña)*.

asturiano, na (âs•tū•ryâ´no, nâ)
n. and *adj.* Asturian.

astuto, ta (âs•tū´to, tâ) *adj.* cunning, sly, astute.

asueto (â•swe´to) *m.* holiday,
vacation.

asumir (â•sū•mēr´) *va.* to assume.

asunto (â•sūn´to) *m.* subject,
matter *(materia);* affair, business deal *(negocio).*

asustadizo, za (â•sūs•tâ•thē´so,
sâ) *adj.* easily frightened, shy.

asustar (â•sūs•târ´) *va.* to fright-
en; —**se,** to be frightened.

atacado, da (â•tâ•kâ´tho, thâ)

adj. irresolute, timid; (fig.)
petty, mean.

atacar (â•tâ•kâr´) *va.* to attack,
to assail; to ram in, to jam in
(apretar); to button *(abrochar);*
to fit *(ceñir).*

atadura (â•tâ•thū´râ) *f.* knot,
fastening.

atajo (â•tâ´ho) *m.* bypass, short
cut.

atalaya (â•tâ•lâ´yâ) *f.* watchtower; —, *m.* guard in a watchtower.

ataque (â•tâ´ke) *m.* attack,
assault; (mil.) trenches; (med.)
siege of illness.

atar (â•târ´) *va.* to tie, to bind, to
fasten; (fig.) to hamstring, to
impede; —**se,** to be frustrated,
to be baffled.

atarear (â•tâ•re•âr´) *va.* to
impose a task; —**se,** to work
diligently.

atascar (â•tâs•kâr´) *va.* to stop
(a leak); (naut.) to caulk; (fig.)
to obstruct, to impede; —**se,** to
become clogged, to become
blocked, to become stuffed.

ataúd (â•tâ•u´th´) *m.* coffin.

ataviar (â•tâ•vyar´) *va.* to trim,
to adorn, to ornament.

atavío (â•tâ•vē´o) *m.* dress, ornament, finery.

ateísmo (â•te•ēz´mo) *m.* atheism.

atemorizar (â•te•mo•rē•sâr´) *va.*
to strike with terror, to daunt,

to frighten; **—se,** to become frightened.

Atenas (â•te´nâs) *f.* Athens.

atención (â•ten•syon´) *f.* attention, heedfulness, concentration; civility, politeness *(urbanidad).*

atender* (â•ten•der´) *vn.* to be attentive, to heed, to hearken; —, *va.* to wait for *(esperar);* to look after *(cuidar).*

atenerse* (â•te•ner´se) *vr.* to depend, to rely.

atenido, da (â•te•nē´tho, thâ) *adj.* dependent.

atentado, da (â•ten•tâ´tho, thâ) *adj.* sensible, moderate; careful, skillful *(con tiento);* —, *m.* aggression, offense, crime.

atentar* (â•ten•târ´) *va.* to attempt an illegal act, to try to commit a crime.

atento, ta (â•ten´to, tâ) *adj.* attentive, heedful, observant, mindful; courteous, considerate *(comedido).*

atenuar (â•te•nwâr´) *va.* to attenuate, to diminish, to lessen.

ateo, a (â•te´o, â) *n.* and *adj.* atheist, atheistic.

aterciopelado, da (â•ter•syo•pe•lâ´tho, tha) *adj.* velvetlike.

aterrado, da (â•te•rrâ´tho, thâ) *adj.* terrified, appalled.

aterrador, ra (â•te•rrâ•thor´, râ) *adj.* terrifying, frightful.

aterrar (â•te•rrâr´) *va.* to terrify; (fig.) to prostrate, to humble; **—se,** to be terrified.

aterrizaje (â•te•rrē•sâ´he) *m.* (avi.) landing (of airplane); **— accidentado,** crash landing; **— ciego,** blind landing; **— de emergencia,** crash landing; **— forzoso,** forced landing; **campo de —,** landing field; **pista de —,** landing strip; **tren de —,** landing gear.

aterrizar (â•te•rrē•sâr´) *vn.* (avi.) to land.

aterrorizar (â•te•rro•rē•sâr´) *va.* to frighten, to terrify.

atesorar (â•te•so•râr´) *va.* to save up, to put away.

atestar (â•tes•târ´) *va.* to attest, to testify, to witness.

atestar* (â•tes•târ´) *va.* to cram, to stuff, to crowd; **—se,** to overeat.

atestiguar (â•tes•tē•gwâr´) *va.* to witness, to attest.

ático (â´tē•ko) *m.* (arch.) attic; Attic.

atiesar (â•tye•sâr´) *va.* to make stiff, to make rigid.

atildado, da (â•tēl•dâ´tho, thâ) *adj.* correct, neat.

atildar (â•tēl•dâr´) *va.* to punctuate, to underline, to accent; to censure *(censurar);* to deck

out, to dress up, to adorn
(asear).

atisbadero (â•tēz•vâ•the´ro) *m.*
peephole, eyehole.

Atlántico, ca (âth•lân´tē•ko, kâ)
m. and *adj.* Atlantic.

atlas (âth´lâs) *m.* atlas.

atleta (âth•le´tâ) *m.* and *f.* athlete.

atlético, ca (âth•le´tē•ko, kâ) *adj.*
athletic.

atmósfera (âth•mos´fe•râ) *f.*
atmosphere.

atmosférico, ca
(âth•mos•fe´rē•ko, kâ) *adj.*
atmospheric.

atole (â•to´le) *m.* corn-flour
gruel; **dar — con el dedo,** (Mex.
coll.) to deceive, to cheat.

atolondrar (â•to•lon•drâr´) *va.*
to confuse, to stupefy; **—se,** to
be befuddled, to be confused.

atómico, ca (â•to´mē•ko, kâ) *adj.*
atomic.

átomo (â´to•mo) *m.* atom.

atónito, ta (â•to´nē•to, tâ) *adj.*
astonished, amazed.

atorarse (â•to•râr´se) *vr.* to
choke *(atragantarse);* to stick
in the mud *(atascarse).*

atormentar (â•tor•men•târ´) *va.*
to torment, to give pain.

atornillar (â•tor•nē•yâr´) *va.* to
screw.

atracción (â•trâk•syon´) *f.*
attraction.

atractivo, va (â•trâk•tē´vo, vâ)
adj. attractive, magnetic; **—,** *m.*
charm, grace.

atraer* (â•trâ•er´) *va.* to attract,
to allure.

atragantarse (â•trâ•gân•târ´se)
vr. to choke; (fig.) to get mixed
up in conversation *(turbarse).*

atrancar (â•trâng•kâr´) *va.* to
barricade.

atrapar (â•trâ•pâr´) *va.* (fig.) to
get, to obtain; to catch, to nab;
to deceive, to take in *(engañar).*

atrás (â•trâs´) *adv.* backwards,
back; be-hind *(detrás);* past
(pasado); **hacerse —,** to fall
back; **hacia —,** backwards,
back; **echarse —,** to change
one´s mind, to go back on
one´s word.

atrasado, da (â•trâ•sâ´tho, thâ)
adj. (fig.) backward, behind the
times; late, tardy *(tardío);* in
arrears *(adeudado);* slow *(de
reloj).*

atrasar (â•trâ•sâr´) *va.* to outstrip, to leave behind; to postpone, to delay *(demorar);* **— el
reloj,** to set a watch back; **—se,**
to be late, to fall behind; (corn.)
to be in arrears.

atraso (â•trâ´so) *m.* delay, falling
behind.

atravesado, da (â•trâ•ve•sâ´tho,
thâ) *adj.* squint-eyed *(bizco);* of
mixed breed. mongrel *(híbrido);*

(fig.) degenerate, perverse.

atravesar* (â•trâ•ve•sâr´) *va.* to lay across, to put across; to run through, to pierce *(penetrar);* to go across, to cross *(cruzar);* to trump *(meter triunfo);* —**se,** to get in the way, to thwart one's purpose.

atreverse (â•tre•ver´se) *vr.* to dare, to venture.

atrevido, da (â•tre•vē´tho, thâ) *adj.* bold, audacious, daring.

atrevimiento (â•tre•vē•myen´to) *m.* boldness, audacity.

atribución (â•trē•vū•syon´) *f.* attribution, imputation.

atribuir* (â•trē•vwēr´) *va.* to attribute, to ascribe, to impute; —**se** to assume.

atributo (â•trē•vū´to) *m.* attribute.

atrición (â•trē•syon´) *f.* contrition.

atrio (â´tryo) *m.* porch; portico.

atrocidad (â•tro•sē•thâth´) *f.* atrocity.

atropellado, da (â•tro•pe•yâ´tho, thâ) *adj.* hasty, precipitate; —, *n.* person who has been run over.

atropellar (â•tro•pe•yâr´) *va.* to trample, to run down, to knock down; —**se,** (fig.) to fall all over oneself, to overdo it.

atropello (â•tro•pe´yo) *m.* trampling, knocking down; (fig.)

abusiveness; — **de automóvil,** automobile collision.

atroz (â•tros´) *adj.* atrocious; (coll.) enormous.

atuendo (â•twen´do) *m.* attire, garb *(vestido);* pomp, ostentation.

atún (â•tūn´) *m.* tuna, tunny fish.

aturdido, da (â•tūr•thē´tho, thâ) *adj.* harebrained, rattled.

aturdimiento (â•tūr•thē•myen´to) *m.* stupefaction, dazed condition; (fig.) astonishment, bewilderment.

aturdir (â•tūr•thēr´) *va* (fig.) to bewilder, to confuse; to stupefy, to daze.

audacia (âū•thâ´syâ) *f.* audacity, boldness.

audaz (âū•thâs´) *adj.* audacious, bold.

audible (âū•thē´vle) *adj.* audible.

audición (âū•thē•syon´) *f.* audition, hearing

audiencia (âū•thyen´syâ) *f.* audience, hearing; hearing in court; circuit court; appellate court *(tribunal),*

audífono (âū•thē´fo•no) *m.* radio earphone.

audiología (âū•thyo•lo•hē´â) *f.* audiology.

audiovisual (âū•thyo•vē•swâl) *adj.* audiovisual.

auditivo, va (âū•thē•tē´vo, va)

adj. auditory.

auditorio (âū•thē•to´ryo) *m.* assembly, audience.

auge (â´ū•he) *m.* the pinnacle of power, height of success.

aula (â´ū•la) *f.* lecture room, classroom.

aullar (âu•yâr´) *vn.* to howl.

aullido (âū•yē´tho) or **aúllo** (â•ū´yo) *m.* howling, wailing, cry.

aumentar (âū•men•târ´) *va.* to augment, to increase; —, *vn.* to grow larger.

aumento (âū•men´to) *m.* increase, growth; promotion, advancement, progress *(adelantamiento).*

aun (â´ūn) *adv.* even, the very; — **cuando,** even though.

aún (â•ūn´) *adv.* still, yet.

aunque (â´ūn•ke) *conj.* though, notwithstanding.

áureo, rea (â´ū•re•o, re•â) *adj.* golden, gilt.

aureola (âū•re•o´lâ) or **auréola,** (âū•re´o lâ) *f.* halo; (fig.) glory, heavenly bliss; (ast.) corona.

auricular (âū•re•kū•lâr´) *adj.* within hearing, auricular; —, *m.* earphone; — **de casco,** headset.

aurora (âū•ro´râ) *f.* dawn, daybreak; (poet.) dawn, first beginnings.

ausencia (âū•sen´syâ) *f.*

absence.

ausentarse (âū•sen•târ´se) *vr.* to absent oneself.

ausente (âū•sen´te) *adj.* absent.

austeridad, (âūs•te•rē•thâth´) *f.* rigor, austerity.

austero, ra (âūs•te´ro, râ) *adj.* austere, severe.

austral (âūs•trâl´) *adj.* austral, southern.

austriaco, ca (âūs•tryâ´ko, kâ) or **austríaco, ca,** (âūs•trē´â•ko, kâ) *n.* and *adj.* Austrian.

autenticar (âū•ten•tē•kâr´) *va.* to authenticate.

autenticidad (âū•ten•tē•sē•thâth´) *f.* authenticity.

auténtico, ca (âū•ten´tē•ko, kâ) *adj.* authentic, true, genuine.

auto (â´ū•to) *m.* judicial decree, edict, ordinance; auto, car; — **de auxilio,** wrecker, tow car.

autobiografía (âū•to•vyo•grâ•fē´â) *f.* autobiography.

autobús (âū•to•vūs´) *m.* bus.

autocracia (âū•to•krâ´syâ) *f.* autocracy.

autócrata (âū•to´krâ•tâ) *m.* and *f.* autocrat.

autógrafo (âū•to´grâ•fo) *m.* autograph.

autohotel (âū•to•o•tel´) *m.* motel.

automático, ca (âū•to•mâ´tē•ko, ka) *adj.* automatic.

automatización
(āū•to•ma•tē•sā•syon´) *f.* automation.

automotor, ra (āū•to•mo•tor´,
râ) *adj.* automotive.

automotriz (āū•to•mo•trēs´) *f.*
adj. automotive.

automóvil (āū•to•mo´vēl) *m.*
automobile; — **acorazado,**
armored car.

automovilista (āū•to•mo•vē•lē´s-
tâ) *m.* motorist.

automovilístico, ca
(āū•to•mo•vē•lēs´tē ko, kâ) *adj.*
automobile.

autonomía (āū•to•no•mē´â) *f.*
autonomy.

autónomo, ma (āū•to´no•mo,
mâ) *adj.* autonomous.

autopista (āū•to•pēs´tâ) *f.* super-
highway, expressway; — **de**
acceso libre, freeway.

autopsia (āū•top´syâ) *f.* autopsy,
post mortem.

autor (āū•tor´) *m.* author.

autoridad (āū•to•rē•thâth´) *f.*
authority.

autoritativo, va
(āū•to•rē•tâ•tē´vo, vá) *adj.*
authoritative.

autorización (āū•to•rē•sâ•syon´)
f. authorization.

autorizado, da (āū•to•rē•sâ´tho,
thâ) *adj.* competent, reliable.

autorizar (āū•to•rē•sâr´) *va.* to
authorize.

autorretrato (āū•to•rre•trâ´to) *m.*
self-portrait.

auxiliar (âūk•sē•lyâr´) *va.* to
aid, to help, to assist; to keep a
deathwatch with; —, *adj.* auxiliary.

auxilio (âūk•sē´lyo) *m.* aid, help,
assistance; **acudir en — de,** to
go to the assistance of; **prime-**
ros —s, first aid.

aval *m.* backing, countersigna-
ture, collateral.

avalorar (â•vâ•lo•râr´) *va.* to
enhance the value of; (fig.) to
inspire, to enthuse.

avaluar (â•vâ•lwâr´) *va.* to estimate, to value, to evaluate, to
appraise, to set a price on.

avance (â•vân´se) *m.* (mil.)
advance, attack.

avanzada (â•vân•sâ´thâ) *f.* (mil.)
vanguard.

avanzar (â•vân•sâr´) *va.* and *vn.*
to advance, to push forward.

avaricia (â•vâ•rē´syâ) *f.* avarice.

avariento, ta (â•vâ•ryen´to, tâ)
adj. avaricious, covetous.

avaro, ra (â•vâ´ro, râ) *adj.* avaricious, miserly; —, *m.* miser.

ave (â´ve) *f.* bird; — **de corral,**
fowl.

avellana (â•ve•yâ´nâ) *f.* filbert,
hazelnut.

avellanarse (â•ve•yâ•nâr´se) *vr.*
to shrivel, to dry up.

¡Ave María! (â•ve mâ•rē´â) *interj.*

my goodness! golly!

avena (â•ve´nâ) *f.* oats.

avenida (â•ve•ne´thâ) flood, inundation; (fig.) coming toge- ther, concurrence, conjunction; avenue, boulevard.

avenir* (â•ve•ner´) *va.* to recon- cile, to bring into agreement; — **se** to be reconciled, to come to an agreement.

aventador (â•ven•tâ•thor´) *m.* (agr.) winnower; fan.

aventajado, da (â•ven•tâ•hâ´tho, thâ) *adj.* advantageous, exce- lling, superior.

aventajar (â•ven•tâ•hâr´) *va.* to surpass, to excel, to have the advantage.

aventar* (â•ven•târ´) *va.* to fan; (agr.) to winnow; to blow along; (fig.) to cast out, to expulse; — **se,** to puff up, to fill with air.

aventura (â•ven•tū´râ) *f.* adven- ture, event, incident, chance.

aventurar (â•ven•tū•râr´) *va.* to venture, to risk, to take chan- ces with.

aventurero, ra (â•ven•tū•re´ro, râ) *adj.* adventurous; —, *n.* adventurer, free lance.

avergonzado, da (â•ver•gon•sâ´- tho, thâ) *adj.* embarrassed, sheepish.

avergonzar* (â•ver•gon•sâr´) *va.* to shame, to abash; —**se,** to be ashamed.

avería (â ve•re´â) *f.* damage to goods; (orn.) aviary; (naut.) average.

averiguación (â•ve•re•gwâ•syon´) *f.* investigation.

averiguar (â•ve•re•gwâr´) *va.* to inquire into, to investigate, to ascertain, to find out.

aversión (â•ver•syon´) *f.* aver- sion, dislike, antipathy.

avestruz (â•ves•trūs´) *m.* ostrich.

aviación (â•vyâ•syon´) *f.* avia- tion.

aviador, ra (â•vyâ•thor´, râ) *n.*

avidez (â•vē•thes´) *f.* covetous- ness.

ávido, da (â´vē•tho, thâ) *adj.* greedy, covetous.

avillanar (â•vē•yâ•nâr´) *va.* to debase.

avión (â•vyon´) *m.* (orn.) martin, swallow; airplane; — **radioguia- do,** drone; — **de bombardeo,** bomber; — **de combate,** pur- suit plane; — **de turbohélice,** turboprop; — **de turborreac- ción,** turbo-jet; **por —,** by plane, by air mail.

avisar (â•vē•sâr´) *va.* to inform, to notify; to admonish, to advise *(aconsejar).*

aviso (â•vē´so) *m.* information, notice; advertisement *(anun- cio);* warning, hint *(adverten- cia);* prudence, discretion; counsel, advice *(consejo);* **sin**

otro —, without further advice; **según —,** as per advice.

avispa (â•vēs´pâ) *f.* wasp.

avispado, da (â•vés•pâ´tho, thâ) *adj.* lively, brisk, vivacious.

avispar (â•vēs•pâr´) *va.* to spur, to incite to alertness; **—se,** to grow restless.

avispero (â•vēs•pe´ro) *m.* wasps' nest.

avivar (â•vē•vâr´) *va.* to quicken, to encourage.

axila (âk•sē´lâ) *f.* armpit.

axioma (âk•syo´mâ) *m.* axiom, maxim.

¡ay! *inter.* alas!; ¡**— de mi!** alas! poor me!

ayer (â•yer´) *adv.* yesterday; (fig.) lately; **— mismo,** only yesterday; **— por la mañana,** yesterday morning; **— por la tarde,** yesterday afternoon.

ayuda (â•yū´thâ) *f.* help, aid, assistance, support; **—,** *m.* assistant; **— de cámara,** valet.

ayudante (â•yū•thân´te) *m.* assistant.

ayudar (â•yū•thâr´) *va.* to aid, to help, to assist; to further, to contribute to *(alentar).*

ayunar (â•yū•nâr´) *vn.* to fast, to abstain from food.

ayunas (â•yū´nâs) **en —,** *adv.* before breakfast, not having had breakfast; (fig.) unprepared, lacking information, ignorant (of a situation).

ayuno (â•yū´no) *m.* fast, abstinence from food.

ayuntamiento (â•yūn•tâ•myen´-to) *m.* town council *(junta);* city hall, town hall; city government *(corporación).*

azafata (â•sâ•fâ´tâ) *f.* plane stewardess.

azafrán (â•sâ•frân´) *m.* saffron.

azahar (â•sâ•âr´) *m.* orange or lemon blossom.

azar (â•sâr´) *m.* unforeseen disaster, unexpected accident *(desgracia);* chance, happenstance *(casualidad);* **al —,** at random.

azaroso, sa (â•sâ•ro´so, sâ) *adj.* ominous, hazardous, foreboding.

azorar (â•so•râr´) *va.* to frighten, to terrify; **—se,** to be terrified.

azotar (â•so•târ´) *va.* to whip, to lash.

azote (â•so´te) *m.* whip, scourge; lash given with a whip *(azotazo);* (fig.) calamity, great misfortune.

azotea (â•so•te´â) *f.* flat roof; roof garden.

azteca (âs•te´kâ) *m.* and *f.* and *adj.* Aztec; **—,** *m.* Mexican gold coin.

azúcar (â•sū´kâr) *m.* or *f.* sugar; **— blanco, ca,** refinedsugar; **— cubicado, da,** cube sugar; **— de**

remolacha, beet sugar; — morena, brown sugar.

azucarado, da (â•sū•kâ•râ´tho, thâ) *adj.* sugared; sugary.

azucarar (â•sū•kâ•râr´) *va.* to sugar, to sweeten.

azucarera (â•sū•kâ•re´râ) *f.* sugar bowl.

azucena (â•sū•se´nâ) *f.* white lily.

azufre (â•sū´fre) *m.* sulphur, brimstone.

azul (â•sūl´) *adj.* blue; — celeste, sky blue; — subido, bright blue; — turquí, turquoise blue.

azulado, da (â•sū•lâ´tho, thâ) *adj.* azure, bluish.

azulejo (â•sū•le´ho) *m.* glazed tile; (orn.) bluebird.

azuzar (â•sū•sâr´) *va.* to sic, to set on; (fig.) to irritate, to stir up.

B

baba (bâ´vâ) *f.* driveling, drooling, slobbering; (zool.) mucus, slime.

babear (bâ•ve•âr´) *vn.* to drivel, to drool, to slobber.

babel (bâ•vel´) *m.* babel, confusion.

babero (bâ•ve´ro) *m.* bib.

babosear (bâ•vo•se•âr´) *va.* and *vn.* to drool, to slobber.

baboso, sa (bâ•vo´so, sâ) *adj.* driveling, slobbery; (fig.) foolish, silly; —, *n.* (Sp. Am.) fool, idiot.

bacalao (bâ•kâ•lâ´o) *m.* codfish.

bacanales (bâ•kâ•nâ´les) *f. pl.* bacchanals.

bacilo (bâ•se´lo) *m.* bacillus.

bacteria (bak•te´ryâ) *f.* bacteria.

bactericida (bâk•te•rē•se´thâ) *adj.* germicidal; —, *m.* germici-

de.

bacteriología (bâk•te•ryo•lo•hē´â) *f.* bacteriology.

bacteriólogo, ga (bâk•te•ryo´lo•go, gâ) *n.* bacteriologist.

bache (bâ´che) *m.* rut, hole, pothole; (avi.) air pocket.

bachiller (bâ•chē•yer´) *m.* and *f.* holder of a bachelor's degree.

bachillerato (bâ•chē•ye•râ´to) *m.* bachelor's degree.

bahía (bâ•ē´a) *f.* bay.

bailador, ra (bâē•lâ•thor´, râ) *n.* dancer.

bailar (bâē•lâr´) *vn.* to dance.

bailarín (bâē•lâ•rēn´) *m.* male dancer.

bailarina (bâē•lâ•rē´nâ) *f.* ballerina, female, dancer.

baile (bâ´ē•le) *m.* dance, ball; bailiff *(magistrado);* — **de etiqueta,** dress ball; — **de máscaras,** masked ball.

baja (bâ´hâ) *f.* drop in prices, loss of value; (mil.) loss, casualty; withdrawal, resignation *(de una sociedad);* **dar de** — to discharge, to release; **darse de** — to withdraw, to resign, to drop out.

bajada (bâ•hâ´thâ) *f.* incline, slope; descent, going down *(acción).*

bajamar (bâ•hâ•mâr´) *f.* low water, low tide, ebb.

bajar (bâ•hâr´) *va.* to lower, to decrease *(precio);* to take down, to let down, to lead down.

bajeza (bâ•he´sâ) *f.* meanness, littleness, pettiness.

bajío (bâ•hē´o) *m.* shoal, sandbank; (Sp. Am.) lowland.

bajo, ja (bâ´ho, hâ) *adj.* low *(altura);* short *(persona);* abject, humble *(abatido);* coarse, common *(tosco);* dull, faint *(color);* downcast, cast down, bent over *(inclinado);* **tierra** —, lowland; **piso** or **planta** —, ground floor; —**jo,** *adv.* under; —**jo,** *prep.* underneath, below; — **techo,** indoors; — **cuerda,** underhandedly; —, *m. (mus.)* bass.

bajón (bâ•hon´) *m.* bassoon.

bajorrelieve (bâ•ho•rre•lye´ve) *m.* basrelief.

bala (bâ´lâ) *f.* bullet, shot *(proyectil);* bale *(de mercancías);* (print.) inking roller.

balacera (bâ•lâ•se´râ) *f.* (Mex.) shooting at random.

balada (bâ•lâ´thâ) *f.* ballad.

balance (bâ´lân´se) *m.* swaying, swinging; (fig.) indecisiveness, hesitation.

balancear (bâ•lân•se•âr´) *va.* to balance, to put in balance; — **se,** to rock, to sway, to swing; (fig.) to hesitate, to be doubtful.

balanceo (bâ•lân•se´o) *m.* rocking, swing; (avi. and naut.) rolling, pitching. (mech.) rocker arm.

balanza (bâ•lân´sâ) *f.* scale,

balar (bâ•lâr´) *vn.* to bleat.

balaustre (bâ•lâ´ūs•tre) or **balaústre** (bâ•lâ•us´tre)) *m.* banister.

balazo (bâ•lâ´so) *m.* shot; bullet wound *(herida).*

balboa (bâl•vo´â) *m.* monetary unit of Panama.

balbucear (bâl•vū•se•âr´) *va.* and *vn.* to speak indistinctly, to stammer.

balcón (bâl•kon´) *m.* balcony.

balde (bâl´de) *m.* bucket, pail; **de** —, gratis, for nothing; **en** —, in vain.

baldío, día (bâl•dē´o, dē´â) *adj.* (agr.) untilled, uncultivated;

idle, shiftless *(vagabundo)*; fruitless, useless *(vano)*.

baldosa (bâl•do´sâ) *f.* fine paving bricks or tile.

balido (bâ•lē´tho) *m.* bleating, bleat.

balín (bâ•lēn´) *m.* buckshot.

balística (bâ•lēs´tē•kâ) *f.* ballistics.

baliza (bâ•lē´sâ) *f.* buoy.

balneario (bâl•ne•â´ryo) *m.* bathing resort.

balón (bâ•lon´) *m.* balloon; bale *(fardo);* — **de fútbol,** football.

baloncesto (bâ•lon•ses´to) *m.* basketball.

balsa (bâl´sâ) *f.* raft, float; pool, large puddle *(charca).*

bálsamo (bâl´sâ•mo) *m.* balsam, balm.

balsear (bâl•se•âr´) *va.* to cross by ferry.

balsero (bâl•se´ro) *m.* ferryman.

baluarte (bâ•lwâr´te) *m.* bastion, bulwark, rampart.

ballena (bâ•ye´nâ) *f.* whale; whalebone *(producto).*

ballenato (bâ•ye•nâ´to) *m.* whale calf.

ballesta (bâ•yes´tâ) *f.* crossbow.

bambolear (bâm•bo•le•âr´) *vn.* to reel, to sway, to stagger.

bamboleo (bâm•bo•le´o) *m.* reeling, staggering.

bambú (bâm•bū´) *m.* bamboo.

banana (bâ•nâ´nâ) *f.* banana tree or fruit.

banano (bâ•nâ´no) *m.* banana tree or fruit.

banca (bâng´kâ) *f.* bench; (corn.) banking.

bancario, ria (bang•kâ´ryo, ryâ) *adj.* banking.

bancarrota (bang•kâ•rro´tâ) *f.* bankruptcy.

banco (bâng´ko) *m.* bench; bank, shoal *(bajo);* (ichth.) school; (corn.) bank; — **agrícola,** agricultural (or farmers') bank; — **de ahorros,** savings bank; — **de depósito,** trust bank; — **de emisión,** bank of issue; — **del estado,** state bank; — **de liquidación,** clearinghouse; — **de préstamos,** loan bank; — **de sangre,** blood bank; — **de taller,** workbench; — **hipotecario,** mortgage bank; **billete de** —, banknote; **empleado de** —, bank clerk; **libro de** —, passbook; **poner en el** —, to deposit in the bank.

banda (bân´dâ) *f.* band; sash, ribbon *(faja);* faction, party *(partido);* side, edge *(lado).*

bandeja (bân•de´hâ) *f.* tray;— **de entrada,** in-box *(internet);*— **de salida,** out-box *(internet).*

bandera (bân•de´râ) *f.* banner, standard *(estandarte);* flag; **a** — **s desplegadas,** freely, openly.

banderilla (bân•de•rē´yâ) *f.*

small decorated dart used at a bullfight.

bandido (ban•dē´tho) *m.* bandit, outlaw; highwayman *(bandolero).*

bandido, da (ban•dē´tho, thâ) *adj.* bandit-like, lawless.

bando (bân´do) *m.* faction, party; proclamation, decree *(edicto).*

bandola (ban•do´lâ) *f.* mandolin.

bandolero (bân•do•le´ro) *m.* highway-man, robber.

banquero, ra (bang•ke´ro, ra) *n.* banker.

banqueta (bang•ke´tâ) *f.* stool; (Mex. and Guat.) sidewalk.

banquete (bang•ke´te) *m.* banquet; feast.

bañar (bâ•nyâr´) *va.* to bathe; to dip *(sumergir);* to coat, to apply a coat (of a liquid) to *(cubrir);* —**se,** to take a bath.

bañera (bâ•nye´râ) *f.* bathtub.

baño (bâ´nyo) *m.* bath; bathtub *(pila);* bathroom *(cuarto);* coat, coating *(capa);* — **de ducha,** — **de regadera,** shower bath.

baqueta (bâ•ke´tâ) *f.* ramrod; (taus.) drumstick; (mil.) gauntlet *(castigo).*

baraja (bâ•râ´hâ) *f.* deck of playing cards; **jugar con dos —s** to deal from the bottom of the deck, to be a double-crosser.

barajar (bâ•râ•hâr´) *va.* to shuf- fle (cards); (fig.) to entangle, to mix up, to envolve.

baranda (bâ•rân´dâ) *f.* banister, railing.

barandal (bâ•ran•dâl´) *m.* railing.

barato, ta (bâ•râ´to, tâ) *adj.* cheap, low-priced; —**to,** *adv.* cheaply.

baratura (bâ•ra•tū´râ) *f.* cheapness.

baraúnda (bâ•râ•ūn´dâ) *f.* noise, confusion.

barba (bâr´vâ) *f.* chin; beard, whiskers *(pelo);* — **a** —, face to face; **hacer la** —, to fawn on, to play up to; to bother, to annoy *(fastidiar);* **por** —, per person.

barbacoa (bar•vâ•ko´â) *f.* barbecue.

barbada (bâr•vâ´thâ) *f.* lower jaw of a horse: (ichth.) dab.

barbaridad (bâr•vâ•rē•thâth´) *f.* barbarity, cruelty *(fiereza);* rudeness, grossness *(grosería);* piece of foolishness, hare-brained action *(disparate);* (coll.) tremendous amount, awful lot; ¡**qué** —! how terrible!

barbarie (bâr•vâ´rye) *f.* barbarism, cruelty; lack of culture, grossness.

barbarismo (bâr•vâ•rēz´mo) *m.* barbarism.

bárbaro, ra (bâr´vâ•ro, râ) *adj.* cruel, savage, barbaric *(fiero);*

rash, headstrong, impetuous *(arrojado);* rude, unpolished, gross *(inculto).*

barbería (bâr•ve•rē´â) *f.* barbershop.

barbero (bâr•ve´ro) *m.* barber.

barbilla (bâr•vē´yâ) *f.* point of the chin.

barbudo, da (bâr•vū´tho, thâ) *adj.* long-bearded.

barbulla (bar•vū´yâ) *f.* confused noise.

barca (bâr´kâ) *f.* boat, barge.

barco (bâr´ko) *m.* boat, (poet.) bark, ship; — **de guerra,** warship.

bardo (bâr´tho) *m.* bard, poet.

bario (bâ´ryo) *m.* barium.

barítono (bâ•rē´to•no) *m.* (mus.) baritone.

barniz (bâr•nēs´) *m.* varnish; — **para uñas,** nail polish.

barnizar (bar•nē•sâr´) *va.* to varnish.

barómetro (bâ•ro´me•tro) *m.* barometer; **indicación del —,** barometric reading.

barón (bâ•ron´) *m.* baron.

baronesa (bâ•ro•ne´sâ) *f.* baroness.

barquillo (bâr•·kē´yō) *m.* cone-shaped wafer; ice-cream cone *(de helado).*

barra (bâ´rrâ) *f.* bar; crowbar, lever *(palanca).*

barraca (bâ•rrâ´kâ) *f.* hut, cabin; (Sp. Am.) depository, warehouse, storage shed.

barranca (bâ•rrâng´kâ) *f.* precipice, cliff; ravine, gully *(quiebra).*

barranco (bâ•rrâng´ko) *m.* ravine, gorge; cliff; (fig.) difficult situation, predicament.

barrancoso, sa (bâ•rrâng•ko´so, sâ) *adj.* uneven, rugged, gullied, full of holes.

barredor, ra (bâ•rre•thor´, râ) *n.* sweeper.

barrendero, ra (bâ•rren•de´ro, râ) *n.* sweeper, dustman or woman.

barrer (bâ•rrer´) *va.* to sweep; (fig.) to sweep away, to clear away, to rid of.

barrera (bâ•rre´râ) *f.* clay pit *(de barro);* bar, barrier, barricade *(valla);* (fig.) obstruction; — **sónica,** sound barrier.

barricada (bâ•rre•kâ´thâ) *f.* barricade.

barrido (bâ•rre´thō) *m.* sweep; —, **da,** *adj.* swept.

barriga (bâ•rre´gâ) *f.* abdomen, belly; belly (de *vasija);* (fig.) bulge in a wall.

barrigón (bâ•rre•gon´) *m.* (Cuba) small child; —, **ona,** *adj.* big-bellied.

barrigudo, da (bâ•rre•gū´tho, thâ) *adj.* big-bellied.

barril (bâ•rrēl´) *m.* barrel, cask.

barrilero (bâ•rrē•le´ro) *in.* barrel-maker, cooper.

barrio (bâ´rryo) *m.* district or section of a town, neighborhood; —s bajos, slums.

barro (bâ´rro) *m.* clay *(arcilla);* mud *(lodo);* pimple *(granillo);* — cocido, terra cotta, baked clay.

barroco (bâ•rro´ko) *m.* baroque.

barroso, sa (bâ•rro´so, sâ) *adj.* muddy; like clay; pimpled, pimply.

barrote (bâ•rro´te) *m.* heavy bar,metal brace.

basar (bâ•sâr´) *va.* to base, to found, to support; — se en, to rely on, to have confidence in.

báscula (bâs´kū•lâ) *f.* platform scale.

base (bâ´se) *f.* base, basis;— de datos, database.

básico, ca (bâ´sē•ko, kâ) *adj.* basic, fundamental.

basilica (bâ•sē´lē•kâ) *f.* basilica.

básquetbol (bâs´ket•vol) *m.* basketball.

basquetbolista (bâs•ket•vo•lēs´-tâ) *m.* and *f.* basketball player.

basta (bâs´tâ) *f.* basting, loose stitching; ¡—! *interj.* enough!

bastante (bâs•tân´te) *adj.* sufficient, enough; considerable; —, *adv.* enough, sufficiently; quite a bit, quite, rather *(no poco).*

bastar (bâs•târ´) *vn.* to suffice, to be enough.

bastardilla (bâs•târ•thē´yâ) *f.* italic.

bastardo, da (bâs•târ´tho, thâ) *adj.* bastard, spurious; —, *m.* bastard.

bastón (bâs•ton´) *m.* staff, cane.

bastonero (bâs•to•ne´ro) *m.* cane maker or seller; dance director, dance manager *(de baile);* assistant jailer *(de la cárcel).*

basura (bâs•sū´râ) *f.* dirt, dust, sweepings; trash; horse manure *(estiércol).*

basurero (bâ•sū•re´ro) *m.* garbage man, trash collector; garbage dump, trash pile *(muladar).*

bata (bâ´tâ) *f.* dressing gown, robe; — de mujer, housecoat.

batalla (bâ•tâ´yâ) *f.* battle, combat, fight.

batallador, ra (bâ•tâ•yâ•thor´, râ) *adj.* battling, combative; —, *m.* combatant, warrior.

batallar (bâ•tâ•yâr´) *vn.* to battle, to fight, to struggle; to fence with foils *(esgrimir);* to dispute, to wrangle *(disputar)* ; to fluctuate, to waver *(vacilar).*

batallón (bâ•tâ•yon´) *m.* (mil.) battalion.

batata (bâ•tâ´tâ) *f.* sweet potato.

batear (bâ•te•âr´) *va* and *vn.* (baseball) to bat.

batería (bâ•te•rē´â) *f.* battery; (mus.) percussion instruments; — de acumuladores, storage battery; — **de cocina,** kitchen utensils; — **de teatro,** stage lights; — **líquida,** wet battery; — **seca,** dry battery.

batey (bâ•te´ē) *m.* (Cuba) premises of a sugar refinery; (P.R.) front yard.

batido, da (ba•tē´tho, thâ) *adj.* beaten; with a changeable luster, chatoyant *(tejido);* well-beaten, well-traveled *(camino);* —, *m.* batter.

batidor (bâ•tē•thor´) *m.* beater.

batidora (bâ•tē•tho´râ) *f.* beater.

batir (bâ•tēr´) *va.* to beat; to beat down, knock down, to demolish *(derribar);* to flap violently, to beat *(las alas).*

baturrillo (bâ•tū•rrē´yo) *m.* hodgepodge, potpourri, medley.

batuta (bâ•tū´tâ) *f.* baton; **llevar la —,** to lead, to preside.

baúl (bâ•ūl´) *m.* trunk, chest; — **ropero,** wardrobe trunk.

bautismal (bâu•tēz•mâl´) *adj.* baptismal.

bautismo (bâu•tēz´mo) *m.* baptism.

bautizar (bâu•tē•sâr´) *va.* to baptize, to christen.

bautizo (bâu•tē´so) *m.* baptism, christening.

baya (bâ´yâ) *f.* berry.

bayo, ya (bâ´yo, yâ) *adj.* bay.

bayoneta (bâ•yo•ne´tâ) *f.* bayonet.

bazar (bâ•sâr´) *m.* bazaar; department store *(tienda).*

beatitud (be•â•tē•tūth´) *f.* beatitude, blessedness.

beato, ta (be•â´to, tâ) *adj.* fortunate, blessed *(bienaventurado);* devout *(piadoso);* hypocritical, sanctimonious *(santurrón);* —, *n.* pious person, devout individual.

bebedero (be•ve•the´ro) *m.* drinking dish; watering trough *(abrevadero);* bird bath *(para aves);* —, **ra,** *adj.* drinkable, potable.

bebedor, ra (be•ve•thor´, râ) *n.* drinker; (fig.) tippler, drunkard.

beber (be•ver´) *va.* and *vn.* to drink; —, *m.* drinking.

bebida (be•vē´thâ) *f.* drink, beverage; — **alcohólica,** intoxicant.

bebido, da (be•vē´tho, thâ) *adj.* intoxicated.

beca (be´kâ) *f.* scholarship, fellowship.

becerra (be•se´rrâ) *f.* female calf; (bot.) snapdragon.

becerro (be•se´rro) *m.* yearling calf; calf-skin *(piel);* — **marino,** (zool.) seal.

beduino, na (be•thwē´no, nâ) *adj.* and *n.* Bedouin.

béisbol (be´ēz•vol) *m.* baseball.

bejuco (be•hū´ko) *m.* liana.

Belén (be•len´) *m.* Bethlehem; **estar en —,** not to pay atten-

tion, to have one´s mind elsewhere; **b—,** *m.* creche *(nacimiento);* bedlam *(confusión);*
meterse en —enes, to do things
at the wrong time.

belga (bel´gâ) *adj.* and *n.*
Belgian.

Bélgica (bel´hē•kâ) *f.* Belgium.

bélico, ca (be´lē•ko, kâ) *adj.* warlike, martial.

beligerante (be•lē•he•rân´te) *adj.*
belligerent.

Belice (be•lē´se) *f.* British
Honduras; Belize *(ciudad).*

bellaco, ca (be•yâ´ko, kâ) *adj.*
sly, cunning, roguish; —, *m.*
knave.

belladona (be•yâ•tho´nâ) *f.* (bot.)
deadly nightshade; (med.)
belladonna.

belleza (be•ye´sâ) *f.* beauty.

bello, lla (be´yo, yâ) *adj.* beautiful, handsome, fair, fine; **—llas
artes,** fine arts.

bencina (ben•sē´nâ) *f.* (chem.)
benzine.

bendecir* (ben•de•sēr´) *va.* to
consecrate, to bless *(consagrar);* to praise, to exalt *(alabar).*

bendición (ben•dē•syon´) *f.*
benediction, blessing.

bendito, ta (ben•dē´to, tâ) *adj.*
sainted, blessed; simple, naive,
simpleminded *(sencillo);* fortunate, happy *(dichoso);* **dormir**

como un —, to sleep soundly;
¡—s sean! bless their hearts!

benefactor (be•ne•fâk•tor´) *m.*
benefactor.

beneficencia (be•ne•fē•sen´syâ)
f. beneficence, charity.

beneficiar (be•ne•fē•syâr´) *va.* to
profit, to benefit; to work, to
cultivate *(tierras);* to exploit, to
work *(minas);* **—se con** or **por,**
to profit by, to benefit from.

beneficiario, ria (be•ne•fē•syâ´r-
yo, ryâ) *n.* beneficiary.

beneficio (be•ne•fē´syo) *m.* benefit, favor, kindness *(bien
hecho);* (agr.) working, cultivation; (min.) exploitation, working; profit, gain, advantage
(utilidad).

benéfico, ca (be•ne´fē•ko, kâ)
adj. beneficent, kind.

benemérito, ta (be•ne•me´rē•to,
tâ) *adj.* meritorious, worthy.

benevolencia (be•ne•vo•len´syâ)
f. benevolence, kindness, good
will, goodness of heart.

benévolo, la (be•ne´vo•lo, lâ) *adj.*
benevolent, charitable, kindhearted.

benignidad (be•nēg•nē•thâth´) *f.*
kindliness, mildness.

benigno, na (be•nēg´no, nâ) *adj.*
benign, kind, mild.

berenjena (be•ren•he´nâ) *f.* eggplant.

bergantín (ber•gân•tēn´) *m.*

(naut.) brigantine, brig.

bermejo, ja (ber•me′ho, hâ) *adj.* vermilion, reddish orange.

bermellón (ber•me•yon′) *m.* vermilion.

berrear (be•rre•âr′) *vn.* to low, to bellow.

berrido (be•rrē′tho) *m.* bleating of a calf.

berrinche (be•rrēn′che) *m.* fit of anger, temper tantrum.

berro (be′rro) *m.* watercress.

berza (ber′sâ) *f.* cabbage.

besar (be•sâr′) *va.* to kiss; (coll.) to touch, to be in contact; —**se**, (coll.) to bump heads, to knock heads together.

beso (be′so) *m.* kiss; touching, contact *(objetos);* knocking heads together *(personas).*

bestia (bes′tyâ) *f.* beast, animal; —, *m.* and *f.* dunce, idiot, nitwit.

bestial (bes•tyâl′) *adj.* bestial, brutal.

besuquear (be•sū•ke•âr′) *va.* (coll.) to smooch with, to smooch.

besuqueo (bū•sū•ke′o) *m.* (coll.) smooching.

betabel (be•tâ•vel′) *m.* (Mex.) beet.

betarraga (be•tâ•rrâ′gâ) or **betarrata** (be•tâ•rrâ′tâ) *f.* (bet.) beet.

betún (be•tūn′) *m.* shoe polish;

(Mex.) frosting.

biberón (bē•ve•ron′) *m.* nursing bottle.

Biblia (bē′vlyâ) *f.* Bible.

bíblico, ca (bē′vlē•ko, kâ) *adj.* Biblical.

bibliografía (bē•vlyo•grâ•fē′â) *f.* bibliography.

biblioteca (bē•vlyo•te′kâ) *f.* library.

bibliotecario, ria (bē•vlyo•te•kâ′ryo, ryâ) *n.* librarian.

bicarbonato (bē•kâr•vo•nâ′to) *m.* bicarbonate; — **de sosa,** baking soda.

biceps (bē′seps) *m.* (anat.) biceps.

bicicleta (bē•sē•kle′tâ) *f.* bicycle; **montar en** —to ride a bicycle.

biciclista (bē•sē•klēs′tâ) *m.* and *f.* bicyclist.

bicho (bē′cho) *m.* insect, bug; **todo** — **viviente,** every living soul, every man jack.

bien (byen′) *m.* good; use, benefit *(provecho);* welfare, good *(bienestar);* —**es**, *pl.* property, possessions, goods; —, *adv.* well, right, all right; very *(muy).*

bienal (bye•nâl′) *adj.* biennial.

bienestar (bye•nes•târ′) *m.* wellbeing, welfare, comfort.

bienhablado, da (bye•nâ•vlâ′tho, thâ) *adj.* courteous, well-spoken.

bienhechor, ra (bye•ne•chor´, râ) *adj.* humane; —, *n.* benefactor.

bienio (bye´nyo) *m.* period of two years, biennium.

bienvenida (byem•be•ne´thâ) *f.* welcome.

bienvenido, da (byem•be•ne´tho, thâ) *adj.* welcome.

bienvivir (byem•be•vēr´) *vn.* to live in comfort, to live well *(con holgura);* to live an honest life, to live right.

bifocal (bē•fo•kâl´) *adj.* bifocal; **lentes —es**, bifocal glasses.

bigamia (bē•gâ´myâ) *f.* bigamy.

bígamo, ma (bē´gâ•mo, mâ) *adj.* bigamous; —, *n.* bigamist.

bigote (bē•go´te) *m.* mustache; (print.) dash rule; **tener —a**, to be firm and undaunted.

bilateral (bē´lâ•te•râl´) *adj.* bilateral.

bilingüe (bē•lēng´gwe) *adj.* bilingual.

bilis (bē´lēs) *f.* bile.

billar (bē•yâr´) *m.* billiards.

billete (bē•ye´te) *m.* ticket *(cédula);* bill *(moneda);* note, short letter *(carta);* **— de banco**, banknote; **— de entrada**, admission ticket; **— de ida y vuelta**, round-trip ticket; **— del tesoro**, treasury note; **— direc-to**, through ticket; **— sencillo**, one-way ticket.

billón (bē•yon´) *m.* billion.

billonario, ria (bē•yo•nâ´ryo, ryâ) *n.* billionaire.

bimestral (bē•mes•trâl´) *adj.* bimonthly.

bimestre (bē•mes´tre) *adj.* bimonthly; —, *m.* period of two months; bimonthly payment *(pago);* bimonthly charge *(cobranza).*

bimotor, ra (bē•mo•tor´, râ) *adj.* two-motored.

binomio, mia (bē•no´myo, myâ) *m.* and *adj.* binomial.

biografía (byo•grâ•fē´â) *f.* biography.

biógrafo (byo´grâ•fo) *m.* biographer.

biología (byo•lo•hē´â) *f.* biology; **— molecular**, molecular biology.

biónica (byo´nē•kâ) bionics.

bioquímica (byo•kē´mē•kâ) *f.* biochemistry.

bípedo (bē´pe•tho) *m.* and *adj.* biped.

biplano (bē•plâ´no) *m.* biplane.

birrete (bē•rre´te) *m.* (eccl.) beretta; academic cap, graduation cap.

bisabuela (bē•sâ•vwe´lâ) *f.* great-grandmother.

bisabuelo (bē•sâ•vwe´lo) *m.* great-grandfather.

bisagra (bē•sâ´grâ) *f.* hinge; shoemaker´s polisher *(de zapatero).*

bisecar (bē•se•kâr´) *va.* to bisect.

bisección (bē•sek•syon´) *f.* bisection.

bisonte (bē•son´te) *m.* bison.

bistec (bēs•tek´) *m.* beefsteak; — **de filete,** tenderloin steak.

bisutería (bē•sū•te•rē´â) *f.* cheap or imitation jewelry.

bizco, ca (bēs´ko, kâ) *adj.* squint-eyed, cross-eyed.

bizcocho (bēs•ko´cho) *m.* biscuit; cake, ladyfinger, sponge cake *(pastel).*

biznieta (bēz•nye´tâ) *f.* great-granddaughter.

biznieto (bēz•nye´to) *m.* great-grandson.

blanco, â *adj.* white, blank; **ropa** — linens; —, *m.* blank; (print.) blank form; target; — **directo,** direct hit; **carta en —co,** blank credit; **dar en el —,** to hit the target; **en —co,** blank.

blancura (blâng•kū´râ) *f.* whiteness.

blancuzco, ca (blâng•kūs´ko, kâ) *adj.* whitish.

blandir* (blân•dēr´) *va.* to brandish, to swing.

blando, da (blân´do, dâ) *adj.* soft, smooth, bland; (fig.) mild, gentle, mellow; cowardly, soft, unmanly *(cobarde).*

blandura (blân•dū´râ) *f.* softness; daintiness, delicacy, mildness; cowardice, weakness.

blanquear (blâng•ke•âr´) *va.* to bleach, to whiten; to whitewash *(dar de yeso);* (ent.) to wax, to put wax on *(panales);* —, *vn.* to show whiteness, to turn white; to verge on white *(tirar a blanco).*

blanquecer* (blâng•ke•ser´) *va.* to blanch *(metales);* to whiten, to bleach.

blanqueo (blâng•ke´o) *m.* whitening, bleaching; whitewash.

blasfemar (blâs•fe•mâr´) *vn.* to blaspheme.

blasfemia (blâs•fe´myâ) *f.* blasphemy; oath; (fig.) gross insult, vituperation.

blasón (bla•son´) *m.* heraldry, blazonry; (fig.) honor, glory; escutcheon, coat of arms *(escudo).*

bledo (ble´tho) *m.* (bot.) wild amaranth; **no me importa un —,** I don´t give a rap, I just don´t care.

blindado, da (blēn•dâ´tho, thâ) *adj.* ironclad, ironplated, armored.

blog (blag) *n.* an easy-to-use web site, where one can quickly post thoughts and interact with others.

bloque (blo´ke) *m.* block; (poi.) bloc.

bloquear (blo•ke•âr´) *va.* to blockade.

bloqueo (blo•ke′o) *m.* blockade.

blusa (blū′sä) *f.* blouse.

boa (bo′ä) *f.* (zool.) boa; boa *(prenda)*.

bobada (bo•vä′thä) *f.* folly, foolish action.

bobería (bo•ve•rē′ä) *f.* folly, foolishness.

bobo, ba (bo′vo, va) *n.* dunce, fool; stage clown *(gracioso);* —, *adj.* stupid, silly, foolish; naive *(cándido)*.

boca (bo′kä) *f.* (anat.) mouth; entrance, opening, mouth *(entrada);* (fig.) taste.

bocacalle (bo•kä•kä′ye) *f.* street intersection.

bocadillo (bo•kä•thē′yo) *m.* snack; sandwich, stuffed roll *(panecillo);* narrow ribbon *(cinta);* very thin linen *(lienzo)*.

bocado (bo′kä′tho) *m.* morsel, mouthful.

bocanada (bo•kä•nä′thä) *f.* mouthful of liquid *(sorbo);* puff of smoke *(de humo);* — **de gente,** crowd of people; — **de viento,** gust of wind.

boceto (bo•se′to) *m.* sketch.

bocina (bo•sē′nä) *f.* horn, trumpet; mega-phone *(tornavoz);* (zool.) triton; (auto.) horn; (Chile and Col.) blowgun; (Sp. Am.) hearing trumpet; speaker *(del radio);* receiver *(del teléfono)*.

bocio (bo′syo) *m.* goiter.

bocón, ona (bo•kon′, o′nä) *n.* (coll.) wide-mouthed individual *(bocudo);* braggart *(fanfarrón)*.

bocudo, da (bo•kū′tho, thä) *adj.* large-mouthed.

bochorno (bo•chor′no) *m.* sultry weather, dog days, scorching heat *(vulturno);* flush, blush *(del rostro);* (fig.) humiliation, embarrassment.

boda (bo′thä) *f.* nuptials, wedding; —**s de plata** or **de oro,** silver or golden wedding.

bodega (bo•the′gä) *f.* wine cellar; harvest of wine *(cosecha);* dock warehouse *(almacén);* wine shop, tavern *(taberna);* (naut.) hold of a ship; pantry *(despensa)*

bofetón (bo•fe•ton′) *m.* hard slap in the face; (theat.) revolving flat.

boga (bo′gä) *f.* (fig.) vogue, popularity; (ichth.) boce; rowing; —, *m.* and *f.* rower; **estar en —,** to be fashionable, to be in vogue.

bohemio, mia (bo•e′myo, myä) *n.* and *adj.* Bohemian.

boicot (boē•kot′) *m.* boycott.

boicotear (boē•ko•te•är′) *va.* to boycott.

boina (bo′ē•nä) *f.* beret.

bola (bo′lä) *f.* ball, globe; shoe polish *(betun);* bowling *(juego);* (coll.) tall tale, fib; (Mex.) dis-

turbance, row; **hacerse
—s,** to get confused.

bolear (bo•le•âr´) *vn.* to play
billiards without keeping score;
—, *va.* to cast, to throw *(arrojar);* to blackball, to reject
(reprobar); (Mex.) to polish, to
put a shine on; (Arg.) to rope
with bolas; (fig.) to play a mean
trick on, to do a bad turn.

bolero (bo•le´ro) *m.* bolero;
(Mex.) boot-black, shoeshine
boy.

boletín (bo•le•tēn´) *m.* bulletin;
pay warrant *(libranza);* ticket,
permit, *(cédula);* (Cuba) railroad ticket; **— de cotización,** list
of quotations; **— meteorológico,**
weather report.

boleto (bo•le´to) *m. (Sp.* Am.) ticket; **— de entrada,** admission
ticket; **— de ferrocarril,** railroad
ticket; **— de avión,** airplane ticket; **— de ida y vuelta,** round-
trip ticket; **— sencillo,** one-way
ticket.

boliche (bo•lē´che) *m.* bowling;
jack; small dragnet *(jábega).*

bolígrafo (bo•lē´grâ•fo) *m.* ball-
point pen.

bolívar (bo•le´vâr) *m.* monetary
unit of Venezuela.

boliviano, na (bo•lē•vyâ´no, nâ)
adj. and *n.* Bolivian; —, *m.*
monetary unit of Bolivia.

bolsa (bol´sâ) *f.* purse, handbag

(de mujer); pouch; (com.) stock
exchange; (min.) main lode; **—
de comercio** or **financiera,**
stock exchange; **corredor de —,**
stockbroker, exchange broker,
jugar a la —, to speculate in
stocks, to play the stock market.

bolsillo (bol•sē´yo) *m.* pocket;
money, funds *(caudal).*

bolsista (bol•sēs´tâ) *m.* specula-
tor, stockbroker; jobber.

bomba (bom´bâ) *f.* pump; bomb,
bombshell *(proyectil);* **a prueba
de —,** bombproof; **— atómica,**
atomic bomb.

bombachos (bom•bâ´chos) *m. pl.*
slacks.

bombardear (bom•bâr•the•âr)
va. to bombard.

bombardeo (bom•bâr•the´o) *m.*
bombardment.

bombardero (bom•bâr•the´ro) *m.*
bomber; bombardier *(artillero);*
— de pique, dive bomber.

bombero (bom•be´ro) *m.* fireman
(mata-fuego); pumper; (mil.)
howitzer.

bombilla (bom•bē´yâ) *f.* light
bulb; (Sp. Am.) a tube to sip
maté; **— de destello,**
photoflash bulb.

bombón (bom•bon´) *m.* bonbon,
candy.

bonaerense (bo•nâ•e•ren´se) *m.*
and *f.* and *adj.* native of or per-

taining to Buenos Aires.

bonanza (bo•nân´sâ) *f.* (naut.) fair weather, calm seas; (min.) bonanza; (fig.) good fortune, success.

bondad (bon•dâth´) *f.* goodness, bounty kindness; **tenga la —de,** please be good enough to, please have the kindness to, please.

bondadoso, sa (bon•dâ•tho´so, sâ) *adj.* bountiful, kind, good; **poco —,** unkind.

bonete (bo•ne´te) *m.* (eccl.) secular biretta; (fig.) member of the secular clergy; graduation cap, academic cap *(de graduado).*

bonificación (bo•nē•fē•kâ•syon´) *f.* allowance, bonus.

bonito, ta (bo•nē´to, tâ) *adj.* quite good, pretty good *(bueno);* pretty, nice looking *(lindo);* —, *m.* tuna, bonito.

bono (bo´no) *m.* (com.) bond, certificate; **—s de gobierno,** government bonds.

boquear (bo•ke•âr´) *vn.* to gape, to gasp; to be breathing one´s last, to be dying *(expirar);* (fig.) to be winding up, to be just about finished; —, *va.* to pronounce, to utter.

boquilla (bo•kē´yâ) *f.* mouthpiece *(de instrumento);* stem *(de pipa);* cigarette holder, cigar holder *(de cigarro);* burner, jet

(de llama).

borbotón (bor•bo•ton´) *m.* bubbling, gushing of water; **hablar a —ones,** to speak in torrents, to ramble on.

bordado (bor•thâ´tho) *m.* embroidery.

bordar (bor•thâr´) *va.* to embroider; (fig.) to embellish, to elaborate; **seda de —,** embroidery silk.

borde (bor´the) *m.* border, edge; rim *(de vasija);* (naut.)board;— **de la acera,** curb.

bordear (bor•the•âr´) *vn.* to go along the edge, to stay on the outskirts; (naut.) to ply to windward; —, *va.* to skirt along the edge of.

bordo (bor´tho) *m.* (naut.) board; tack *(bordada);* **a —,** on board; **franco a —,** free on board (f.o.b.).

Boreal (bo•re•âl´) *adj.* boreal, northern.

borgoña (bor•go´nyâ) *m.* Burgundy wine; **B—,** Burgundy.

bórico (bo´rē•ko) *adj.* boric; **ácido —,** boric acid.

boricua (bo•rē•kuâ) *n.* and *adj.* Puerto Rican.

borla (bor´lâ) *f.* tassel; **— de empolvarse,** powder puff; **tomar la —,** to receive one´s doctorate.

borra (boˊrrâ) *f.* yearling ewe *(cordera);* goatˊs hair *(de cabra);* nap, fuzz, lint *(pelusa);* thick wool *(lana);* (fig.) dross, junk.

borrachera (bo•rrâ•cheˊrâ) *f.* drunkenness; bacchanal, carousing, revelry *(función);* (fig.) excess, exaltation.

borracho, cha (bo•rrâˊcho, châ) *adj.* drunk, intoxicated; (fig.) frenzied, infuriated.

borrador (bo•rrâ•thorˊ) *m.* rough draft, first draft; rubber eraser *(goma).*

borrar (bo•rrârˊ) *va.* to erase *(con goma);* to scratch out, to strike out *(tachar)* to blot, to blur *(manchar);* (fig.) to strike, to delete, to erase.

borrego, ga (bo•rreˊgo, gâ) *n.* lamb; (fig.) simpleton, easy mark.

borrón (bo•rronˊ) *m.* ink blot, splotch of ink, ink smudge; (fig.) blemish, imperfection; rough draft, first copy *(borrador);* preliminary sketch, outline of a painting *(de cuadro).*

borroso, sa (bo•rroˊso, sâ) *adj.* indistinct, blurred.

bosque (bosˊke) *m.* forest, grove, woods.

bosquejo (bos•keˊho) *m.* outline, sketch.

bostezar (bos•te•sârˊ) *vn.* to yawn, to gape.

bostezo (bos•teˊso) *m.* yawn, yawning.

bota (boˊtâ) *f.* wine bag *(odre);* water cask *(cuba);* boot *(calzado).*

botana (bo•tâˊnâ) *f.* plug, stopper *(remiendo);* (coll.) healing plaster *(parole);* (coll.) scar *(cicatriz);* (Mex.) appetizer.

botánica (bo•tâˊne•kâ) *f.* botany.

botar (bo•târˊ) *va.* to cast, to throw; to launch *(buque).*

bote (boˊte) *m.* rowboat, small boat; *(barco);* thrust blow *(de arma);* prance, caper *(de caballo);* rebound, bounce *(de pelota);* (Mex.) jail; — **de salvavidas,** lifeboat; **de — en —,** jammed, overcrowded.

botella (bo•teˊyâ) *f.* bottle, flask.

botica (bo•teˊkâ) *f.* drugstore, pharmacy.

boticario (bo•te•kâˊryo) *m.* druggist, pharmacist.

botín (bo•tenˊ) *m.* half boot *(botina);* short gaiter *(polaina);* booty, loot, spoils *(despojo);* (Chile) sock.

botón (bo•tonˊ) *m.* button; bud *(yema);* — **de contacto,** push button; — **de llamada,** call button; — **eléctrico,** push button.

bóveda (boˊve•thâ) *f.* dome, vault; crypt, vault *(cripta).*

bovino, na (bo•veˊno, nâ) *adj.*

bovine.

boxeador (bok•se•â•thor´) *m.* boxer.

boxear (bok•se•âr´) *vn.* to box.

boxeo (bok•se´o) *m.* boxing.

boya (bo´yâ) *f.* (naut.) buoy; float *(de red)*.

boyar (bo•yâr´) *vn.* to float, to be afloat; (naut.) to be returned to service, to be floated again.

bozal (bo•sâl´) *m.* muzzle; —, *adj.* green, inexperienced; foolish, stupid *(necio)*.

bracero (brâ•se´ro) *m.* day laborer *(peón);* man with a good throwing arm.

bragueta (brâ•ge´tâ) *f.* trousers' fly.

brama (brâ´mâ) *f.* rut, mating time.

bramadero (brâ•mâ•the´ro) *m.* rutting place, mating spot.

bramar (brâ•mâr´) *vn.* to roar, to bellow; (fig.) to storm, to bluster; to be in a fury.

bramido (brâ•me´tho) *m.* roar, bellow; furious outcry, shriek of rage *(del hombre)*.

brasa (brâ´sâ) *f.* live coal.

Brasil (brâ•se•l´) *m.* Brazil.

brasileño, ña (brâ•se•le´nyo, nyâ) *n. and adj.* Brazilian.

bravío, via (brâ•ve´o, ve´â) *adj.* ferocious, savage, wild; (fig.) coarse, uncultured *(rústico);* —, *m.* fierceness, savageness.

bravo, va (brâ´vo, vâ) *adj.* brave, valiant; blustering, bullying *(valentón);* savage, fierce *(fiero);* angry, enraged *(enojado);* very good, excellent, fine *(excelente);* ¡—vo! *interj,* bravo! well done!

braza (brâ´sâ) *f.* fathom; breast stroke *(natación)*.

brazado (brâ•sâ´tho) *m.* armful.

brazalete (brâ•sâ•le´te) *m.* bracelet.

brazo (brâ´so) *m.* arm; branch *(del árbol);* foreleg *(de cuadrúpedo);* (fig.) stamina, strength, power *(brío);* — a — man to man; a — **partido,** with bare hands; —s, *pl.* hands, man power; **huelga de —s caídos,** sit-down strike.

brea (bre´â) *f.* pitch, tar.

brebaje (bre•vâ´he) *m.* unpalatable brew; (naut.) grog.

brecha (bre´châ) *f.* breach, gap; (fig.) vivid impression, marked effect; **batir en —,** (mil.) to make a breach; (fig.) to impress on someone´s mind, to get through to someone; (Mex.) dirt road.

brega (bre´gâ) *f.* strife, struggle; joke, trick *(chasco)*.

bregar (bre•gâr´) *vn.* to contend, to struggle; —, *va.* to knead.

breña (bre´nyâ) *f.* craggy, brambly ground.

breñal (bre•nyâl´) or **breñar**

(bre•nyâr´) *m.* craggy, brambly area.

bresca (bres•kâ) *f.* honeycomb.

Bretaña (bre•tâ´nyâ) *f.* Brittany; **Gran —,** Great Britain.

bretones (bre•to´nes) *m. pl.* Brussels sprouts.

breve (bre´ve) *m.* apostolic brief; **—,** *f.* (mus.) breve; **—,** *adj.* brief, short; **en —,** shortly.

brevedad (bre•ve•thâth´) *f.* brevity, shortness, conciseness; **a la mayor — posible,** as soon as possible.

brezal (bre•sâl´) *m.* heath.

bribón, ona (bre•von´, o´nâ) *adj.* mischievous, impish; rascally roguish, scoundrel *(bellaco);* **—,** *n.* imp; rascal, rogue, scoundrel.

brida (bre´thâ) *f.* bridle; (fig.) restraint, check, curb; flange *(de tubo).*

brigada (bre•gâ´thâ) *f.* brigade.

brillante (bre•yân´te) *adj.* brilliant, bright, shining; **—,** *m.* brilliant, diamond.

brillantez (bre•yân•tes´) *f.* brilliancy, brightness.

brillar (bre•yâr´) *vn.* to shine, to sparkle, to glisten; (fig.) to stand out, to be preeminent, to be outstanding.

brillo (bre´yo) *m.* brilliancy, brightness, splendor.

brincar (breng•kâr´) *vn.* to leap, to jump; (fig.) to get upset, to flare up *(resentirse);* (fig.) to gloss over the details, to skip over the details *(pasar por alto).*

brinco (breng´ko) *m.* leap, jump; **dar —s,** to leap, to jump around.

brindar (bren•dâr´) *va.* to offer, to provide with; **— a,** to drink to the health of, to toast *(beber);* to invite to, to offer to *(ofrecer);* **—se** to offer one's help.

brindis (bren´des) *m.* health, toast.

brío (bre´o) *m,* strength, vigor; (fig.) spirit, verve, vivacity.

brioso, sa (bryo´so, sâ) *adj.* strong, vigorous; spirited, lively, vivacious.

brisa (bre´sâ) *f.* breeze.

británico, ca (bre•tâ´ne•ko, kâ) *adj.* British.

brizna (brez´na) *f.* wisp, thin strip, shred.

bróculi (bro´kū•lē) *m.* broccoli.

brocha (bro´châ) *f.* paintbrush; shaving brush *(para enjabonar).*

broche (bro´che) *m.* clasp, brooch.

broma (bro´mâ) *f.* hilarity, noisy fun; joke, jest prank *(chanza);* **dar —,** to tease, to have fun with; **tomar a —,** to take as a joke, to take in fun.

bromear (bro•me•âr´) *vn.* to jest, to joke, to play pranks.

bromista (bro•mēs´tâ) *m.* and *f.* joker, prankster; —, *adj.* fond of playing jokes.

bromuro (bro•mū´ro) *m.* bromide.

bronce (bron´se) *m.* bronze.

bronceado, da (bron•se•â´tho, thâ) *adj.* bronzed; suntanned *(piel);* —, *m.* bronze-color finish.

broncear (bron•se•âr´) *va.* to bronze; —**se,** to get a suntan, to get sun-tanned.

bronco, ca (brong´ko, ka) *adj.* rough, coarse, unfinished; brittle, easily broken *(metal);* harsh, gruff *(voz);* (fig.) crabby, vile-tempered *(genio);* (Mex.) untamed.

bronquio (brong´kyo) *m.* bronchial tube.

bronquitis (brong•kē´tēs) *f.* bronchitis.

broquel (bro•kel´) *m.* (mil.) buckler; (fig.) shield; protection; **rajar** —**es,** to play the bully, to lord it.

brotar (bro•târ´) *vn.* (bot.) to bud, to germinate, to sprout; to gush, to rush out *(agua);* (fig.) to erupt, to break out, to crop out; —, *va.* (bot.) to shoot out, to shoot forth; (fig.) to give rise

to.

brote (bro´te) *m.* bud, shoot; (fig.) outbreak, rash, outcrop.

broza (bro´sâ) *f.* plant trash *(vegetal);* rubbish, trash *(escoria);* underbrush *(maleza);* (print.) brush.

bruces (bru•´ses) **a** — or **de** —, head-long, face downward.

bruja (brū´hâ) *f.* witch, hag; —, *adj.* (Mex.) temporarily broke.

brujería (bru•he•rē´â)*f.* witchcraft.

brujo (brū´ho) *m.* sorcerer.

brújula (brū´hū•lâ) *f.* compass; magnetic needle *(aguja);* — **giroscópica,** gyrocompass.

bruma (brū´mâ) *f.* mist, haze.

brumoso, sa (brū•mo´so, sâ) *adj.* misty,

bruñido (brū•nyē´tho) *m.* polish, burnish; —, **da,** *adj.* polished, burnished.

bruñir* (brū•nyēr´) *va.* to burnish, to polish; (fig.) to put makeup on, to paint *(el rostro).*

brusco, ca (brūs´ko, kâ) *adj.* rude, gruff, brusque; abrupt, sudden *(súbito).*

Bruselas (brū•se´lâs) *f.* Brussels.

brusquedad (brūs•ke•thâth´) *f.* rudeness; abruptness, suddenness.

brutal (brū•tâl´) *adj.* brutal, brutish; (coll.) colossal, terrific; —, *m.* brute, beast.

brutalidad (brū•tâ•lē•thâth´) *f.* brutality; (fig.) brutal action.

bruto (brū´to) *m.* brute, beast, blockhead; —, **ta,** *adj.* brutal; stupid *(torpe);* (min.) crude; (com.) gross; coarse, unpolished, unrefined *(tosco);* **en —to,** in a raw, unmanufactured state, as **lino en —to,** raw flax; **peso —,** gross weight.

bubónico, ca (bū•vo´nē•ko, kâ) *adj.* bubonic.

bucanero (bū•kâ•ne´ro) *m.* buccaneer.

bucear (bū•se•âr´) *vn.* to skin-dive; to deepsea-dive *(con escafandra).*

buceo (bū•se´o) *m.* skin-diving; deepsea diving.

bucle (bū´kle) *m.* curl.

buche (bū´che) *m.* craw, crop, gullet *(de ave);* stomach *(de cuadrúpedo);* mouthful *(bocanada);* suckling ass *(borrico);* pucker, crease *(de ropa);* (fig.) bosom, heart.

bueno, na (bwe´no, nâ) *ad´.* good; fair, pleasant *(de tiempo);* kind, sociable *(bondadoso);* strong; well, fit, healthy *(de salud);* large, good-sized *(de tamaño);* **dar — acogida,** to honor (a draft); **de — gana,** freely, willingly; **—no,** *adv.* enough, sufficiently; **—no está,** enough, no more; ¡ **—no!** *interj.* all right! that´s enough!

buey (bwe´ē) *m.* ox, bullock.

búfalo (bū´fâ•lo) *m.* buffalo.

bufanda (bū•fân´dâ) *f.* scarf.

bufete (bū•fe´te) *m.* desk; (fig.) lawyer´s office *(despacho);* practice, clients *(clientela).*

bufo (bū´fo) *m.* (theat.) buffoon, clown; —, **fa,** *adj.* comic; **ópera —,** comic opera.

bufón (bū•fon´) *m.* buffoon, jester; —, **ona,** *adj.* funny, comical.

buhardilla (bwâr•thē´yâ) *f.* dormer; small garret, attic *(desván).*

búho (bū´o) *m.* owl; (fig.) unsociable individual.

buhonero (bwo•ne´ro) *m.* peddler, hawker.

buitre (bwē´tre) *m.* vulture.

bujía (bū•hē´a) *f.* candle; candlestick *(candelero);* (auto.) spark plug; candle, international candle *(medida);* **— de cera,** wax candle.

bula (bū´lâ) *f.* papal bull.

bulbo (būl´vo) *m.* (bot.) bulb.

bulevar (bū•le•vâr´) *m.* boulevard, parkway.

bulto (būl´to) *m.* bulk, mass; parcel, bundle *(fardo);* lump, swelling *(hinchazón);* bust *(busto);* piece of luggage *(maleta);* **en —,** in bulk.

bulla (bū´yâ) *f.* confused noise,

clatter; crowd *(gentío).*

bullicio (bū•yē´syo) *m.* bustle, tumult, uproar.

bullicioso, sa (bū•yē•syo´so, sâ) *adj.* lively, restless *(desasosegado);* noisy, clamorous, turbulent; boisterous, riotous *(alborotador).*

bumerang (bū•me•rân´) *m.* boomerang.

buñuelo (bū•nywe´lō) *m.* doughnut.

buque (bū´ke) *m.* ship, vessel; capacity *(cabida);* hull *(casco);* — **explorador,** scouting ship; — **fanal,** lightship; — **petrolero,** tanker; — **taller,** repair ship; — **de vela,** sailboat.

bureta (bū•re´tâ) *f.* (chem.) burette.

burgués, esa (būr•ges´, e´sâ) *adj.* and *n.* bourgeois.

burguesía (būr•ge•sē´â) *f.* bourgeoisie.

burla (būr´lâ) *f.* scoffing, mockery, sneering *(mofa);* trickery *(engaño);* joke, jest *(chanza);* **de —,** in jest; **hacer una —,** to play a joke.

burlar (būr•lâr´) *va.* to play a trick on, to deceive *(engañar);* to frustrate, to disappoint *(frustrar);* to mock; **—se de,** to make fun of.

burlesco, ca (būr•les´ko, kâ) *adj.* burlesque, comical, funny.

buró (bū•ro´) *m.* writing desk; (Mex.) night table.

burocracia (bū•ro•krâ´syâ) *f.* bureaucracy.

burocrático, ca (bū•ro•krâ´tē•ko, kâ) *adj.* bureaucratic.

burrada (bū•rrâ´thâ) *f.* drove of asses; (fig.) stupidity, asininity.

burro (bū´rro) *m.* ass, donkey; (fig.) workhorse; sawhorse *(armazón);* — **de plan-char,** ironing board.

bursátil (būr•sâ´tēl) *adj.* relating to the stock exchange.

busca (būs´kâ) *f.* search, examination.

buscar (būs•kâr´) *va.* to seek, to search for, to look for; **ir a —,** to get, to go after.

búsqueda (būs´ke•thâ) *f.* search.

busto (būs´to) *m.* bust.

butaca (bū•tâ´kâ) *f.* armchair; (theat.) orchestra seat.

buzo (bū´so) *m.* skin diver *(de superficie);* deepsea diver *(con escafandra).*

buzón (bū•son´) *m.* mailbox, letter drop; conduit, canal *(de desagüe).*

C

cabal (kâ•vâl´) *adj.* precise, exact; perfect, complete, accomplished *(acabado).*

cabalgada (kâ•vâl•gâ´thâ) *f.* mounted foray into the countryside.

cabalgar (kâ•vâl•gâr´) *vn.* to ride horseback.

cabalgata (kâ•vâl•gâ´tâ) *f.* cavalcade.

caballeresco, ca (kâ•va•ye•res´-ko, kâ) *adj.* knightly, chivalrous; (fig.) lofty, sublime.

caballería (kâ•vâ•ye•rē´â) *f.* (mil.) cavalry; mount *(animal);* chivalry, knighthood; — **andante,** knight-errantry.

caballero (kâ•vâ•ye´ro) *m.* gentleman; nobleman, knight *(hidalgo);* cavalier, rider, horseman *(jinete).*

caballerosidad (kâ•va•ye•ro•sē•thâth´) *f.* chivalry, nobleness, knightliness.

caballeroso, sa (kâ•vâ•ye•ro´so, sâ) *adj.* noble, gentlemanly, chivalrous.

caballitos (kâ•vâ•yē´tos) *m. pl.* merry-go-round *(tiovivo);* miniature mechanical horse race *(juego).*

caballo (kâ•vâ´yo) *m.* horse; knight *(de ajedrez);* **a —,** on horseback; — **de fuerza,** horsepower.

cabaña (kâ•vâ´nyâ) *f.* hut, cabin, cottage *(choza);* cabana *(de playa);* large number of livestock *(de ganado);* balkline *(de billar).*

cabaret (kâ•vâ•ret´) *m.* cabaret, night club.

cabecear (kâ•ve•se•âr´) *vn.* to nod with sleep; to shake one´s head *(de negación);* (naut., avi.) to pitch; to hit with one's head *(deportes).*

cabeceo (kâ•ve•se´o) *m.* nod; shaking of the head.

cabecera (kâ•ve•se´râ) *f.* head; head, headboard *(de la cama);* pillow *(almohada);* headwaters *(del río);* heading *(del libro);* **médico de —,** attending physician.

cabello (kâ•ve´yo) *m.* hair of the head.

cabelludo, da (kâ•ve•yū´tho, thâ) *adj.* hairy, overgrown with hair; **cuero —,** scalp.

caber* (kâ•ver´) *vn.* to fit; to be possible, to be likely *(ser posible);* to be admitted, to be allowed in *(tener entrada);* **el libro**

no cabe, there isn't room for the book.

cabeza (kâ•ve′sâ) *f.* head.

cabezada (kâ•ve•sâ′thâ) *f.* blow on the head *(recibida);* butt with the head *(dada);* nod; headstall *(correaje);* instep *(de bota).*

cabida (kâ•vē′thâ) *f.* content, capacity.

cabina (kâ•vé′nâ) *f.* cockpit.

cabizbajo, ja (kâ•vēz•vâ′ho, ha′) *adj.* crestfallen.

cable (kâ′vle) *m.* cable, rope; — **conductor,** electric cable; — **de remolque,** towline.

cabo (kâ′vo) *m.* (geog.) cape, headland; end *(fin);* tip, extremity *(extremo);* (mil.) corporal; **al —,** at last; **al — de,** at the end of; **llevar a** or **al —,** to finish, to carry out, to accomplish.

cabra (kâ′vrâ) *f.* goat.

cabrio (kâ•vrē′o) *m.* flock of goats; **macho —,** buck.

cabrito (kâ•vrē′to) *m.* kid.

cabrón (kâ•vron′) *m.* buck, he-goat; (fig.) cuckold.

cacahual (ka•kâ•wâl′) or **cacaotal** (kâ•o•tâl′) *m.* cocoa plantation.

cacahuate (kâ•kâ•wâ′te) or **cacahuete** (kâ•kâ•we′te) *m.* peanut.

cacao (kâ•kâ′o) *m.* (bot.) cacao; cocoa seed *(semilla).*

cacarear (kâ•kâ•re•âr′) *vn.* to crow *(gallo);* to cackle, to cluck *(gallina);* (fig.) to brag, to boast.

cacareo (kâ•kâ•re′o) *n.* crowing; cackling; (fig.) boasting, bragging.

cacería (kâ•se•rē′â) hunting party.

cacerola (kâ•se•ro′lâ) *f.* casserole.

cacique (kâ•sē′ke) *m.* cacique; (fig.) political boss.

caciquismo (kâ•sē•kēz′mo) *m.* (poi.) bossism.

cacofonía (kâ•ko•fo•nē′â) *f.* cacophony, dissonance.

cacto (kâk′to) *m.* cactus.

cacha (kâ′châ) *f.* knife handle; grip.

cachete (kâ•che′te) *m.* chubby cheek *(carrillo);* sock in the face *(golpe).*

cachetudo, da (kâ•che•tū′tho, thâ) *adj.* chubby-cheeked.

cachivache (kâ•chē•vâ′che) *m.* junky kitchen utensil, old piece of kitchen-ware; (fig.) phony, fake.

cacho (kâ′cho) *m.* slice, piece; (Sp. Am.) horn *(cuerno).*

cachorro, rra (kâ•cho′rro, rrâ) *n.* puppy *(perro);* cub.

cachupín, ina (kâ•chū•pēn′, ē′nâ) *n.* Spanish settler in America.

cada (kâ′thâ) *adj.* each, every;

every *(con numeral absoluto);* — **cual,** everyone, everybody; — **uno,** everyone, each one; — **vez,** every time; — **vez más,** more and more.

cadáver (kâ•thâ´ver) *m.* corpse, cadaver.

cadavérico, ca (kâ•thâ•ve´rē•ko, kâ) *adj.* cadaveric; *(fig.)* cadaverous.

cadena (kâ•the´nâ) *f.* chain; chain gang *(de galeotes);* network, series *(conjunto)* — **de montañas,** range of mountains; — **perpetua,** life sentence, life imprisonment.

cadencia (kâ•then´syâ) *f.* cadence.

cadente (kâ•then´te) *adj.* cadent, rythmical *(cadencioso);* declining, failing.

cadera (kâ•the´râ) *f.* hip.

cadete (kâ•the´te) *m.* (mil.) cadet.

caducar (ka•thū•kar´) *vn.* to be senile, to dote *(chochear);* to lose effect, to lapse *(perder fuerza);* (fig.) to fall into disuse, to be outmoded *(acabarse).*

caduco, ca (kâ•thū´ko, kâ) *adj.* senile, in one´s dotage; perishable, fleeting *(perecedero).*

caer* (kâ•er´) *vn.* to fall, to tumble down; to diminish, to lag *(debilitarse);* to befall, to happen *(una desgracia);* to come by chance, to happen to come *(llegar);* (com.) to fall due; to catch on, to understand *(comprender);* — **bien,** to suit, to be pleasing; — **de bruces,** to fall headlong; — **en gracia,** to be liked, to win favor; —**se de suyo,** to be self-evident; **dejar** —, to drop.

café (kâ•fe´) *m.* coffee tree *(cafeto);* coffee; coffeehouse, café *(sitio);* — **cargado,** strong coffee; — **claro,** weak coffee; — **molido,** ground coffee; —, *adj.* coffee-colored.

cafeína (kâ•fe•ē´nâ) *f.* caffeine.

cafetal (kâ•fe•tâl´) *m.* coffee plantation.

cafetalero, ra (kâ•fe•tâ•le´ro, râ) *n.* coffee grower, coffee planter.

cafetera (kâ•fe•te´râ) *f.* coffee pot *(vasija);* (coll.) jalopy *(automóvil).*

cafeteria (kâ•fe•te•rē´â) *f.* coffeehouse, coffee shop; cafeteria *(de autoservicio).*

cafeto (kâ•fe´to) *m.* coffee tree.

caída (kâ•ē´thâ) *f.* fall, falling; slope, de-scent *(declive);* — **de agua,** waterfall; — **de la tarde,** nightfall; — **incontrolada,** free fall.

caído, da (kâ•ē´tho, thâ) *adj.* fallen.

caimán (kaē•mân´) *m.* caiman, cayman; (fig.) crafty, tricky individual.

caja (kâ´hâ) *f.* box; case *(de instrumento);* casket, coffin *(ataúd);* strong box, cashbox *(para valores);* — **registradora,** (cash register); **libro de —,** cashbook.

cajero, ra (kâ•he´ro, râ) *n.* cashier;— **automático,** automatic teller machine (ATM).

cajeta (kâ•he´tâ) *f.* (Sp. Am.) small box; jelly jar *(para jaleas).*

cajetilla (kâ•he•tē´yâ) *f.* pack *(de cigarillos);* (Arg.) city swell, city slicker *(elegante).*

cajón (kâ•hon´) *m.* space between shelves *(de estante);* drawer *(gaveta);* (Sp. Am.)grocery store; **ser de —,** (coll.) to be the usual thing, to be customary.

cajuela (kâ•hwe´lâ) *f.* auto trunk.

cal (kâl) *f.* lime; — **viva,** quicklime.

cala (kâ´lâ) *f.* cove, inlet, small bay.

calabaza (kâ•lâ•vâ´sâ) *f.* pumpkin, gourd.

calabozo (kâ•lâ•vo´so) *m.* dungeon *(subterráneo);* isolated cell *(de cárcel).*

calambre (kâ•lâm´bre) *m.* cramp.

calamidad (kâ•lâ•mē•thâth´) *f.* calamity, general disaster.

calamitoso, sa (kâ•lâ•mē•to´so, sâ) *adj.* calamitous, disastrous.

calavera (kâ•lâ•ve´râ) *f.* skull; *m.* reckless individual, daredevil, madcap.

calcañal (kâl•kâ•nyâl´) or **calcañar** (kâl•kâ•nyâr´) *m.* heel bone *(calcáneo);* heel *(talón).*

calceta (kâl•se´tâ) *f.* stocking.

calcetín (kâl•se•tēn´) *m.* sock.

calcificar (kâl•sē•fē•kâr´) *va.* to calcify.

calcinar (kâl•sē•nâr´) *va.* to calcine; (fig.) to char, to reduce to ashes.

calcio (kâl´syo) *m.* calcium.

calcomanía (kâl•ko•mâ•nē´â) *f.* sticker.

calculable (kâl•kū•lâ´vle) *adj.* calculable.

calculador (kâl•kū•lâ•thor´) *m.* calculator, computer; estimator; —, **ra,** *adj.* calculating, scheming.

calculadora (kâl•kū•lâ•tho´râ) *f.* calculating machine, calculator.

calcular (kâl•kū•lâr´) *va.* to calculate, to compute; to estimate, to judge *(apreciar).*

cálculo (kâl´kū•lo) *m.* calculation, computation; estimate, judgment; — **biliario,** (med.) gallstone.

caldera (kâl•de´râ) *f.* kettle; — **de vapor,** steam boiler; —

tubular, hot-water boiler.

calderón (kâl•de•ron´) *m.* large kettle, caldron.

caldo (kâl´do) *m.* broth, bouillon; salad dressing *(de la ensalada);* — **de carne,** beef consommé.

calefacción (kâ•le•fâk•syon´) *f.* heating.

calendario (kâ•len•dâ´ryo) *m.* calendar.

calentador (kâ•len•tâ•thor´) *m.* heater, heating apparatus; — **de agua,** water heater.

calentar* (kâ•len•târ´) *va.* to warm, to heat; —**se,** (fig.) to get hot under the collar.

calentura (kâ•len•tū´râ) *f.* fever.

calenturiento, ta (kâ•len•tū•rye-n´to, tâ) *adj.* feverish.

calibración (kâ•lē•vrâ•syon´) *f.* calibration.

calibrador (kâ•lē´•vrâ•thor´) *m.* gauge.

calibrar (kâ•lē•vrâr´) *va.* to calibrate.

calibre (kâ•lē´vre) *m.* bore, caliber, gauge *(de un cañón);* caliber *(de un proyectil);* —**diameter** *(de un alambre);* (fig.) caliber.

calidad (kâ•lē•thâth´) *f.* quality; type, kind *(índole);* qualities, qualifications *(para un cargo);* term, condition *(para un contrato);* **en — de,** in one's position as.

cálido, da (kâ´lē•tho, thâ) *adj.* hot, warm.

calidoscopio (kâ•lē•thos•ko´pyo) *m.* kaleidoscope.

caliente (kâ•lyen´te) *adj.* hot, warm; (fig.) fiery, vehement *(acalorado);* **en —,** at once, immediately.

calificación (kâ•lē•fē•kâ•syon´) *f.* rating, classification, evaluation; grade, mark *(nota de examen).*

calificar (kâ•lē•fē•kâr´) *va.* to rate, to classify, to evaluate; to grade, to mark *(al alumno);* (fig.) to ennoble; —**se,** to prove one's noble birth.

caligrafía (kâ•lē•grâ•fē´â) *f.* calligraphy, penmanship.

cáliz (kâ´lēs) *m.* chalice, goblet; (bot.) calyx.

caliza (kâ•lē´sâ) *f.* limestone.

calma (kâl´mâ) *f.* calm, stillness; lull, let-up *(cesación);* (fig.) peace, quiet *(tranquilidad).*

calmante (kâl•mân´te) *m.* (med.) sedative; tranquilizer.

calmar (kâl•mâr´) *va.* to calm, to quiet; —**se,** to quiet down, to calm down.

calmoso, sa (kâl•mo´so, sâ) *adj.* calm; tranquil, peaceful.

caló (kâ•lo´) *m.* gypsy argot.

calor (kâ•lor´) *m.* heat, warmth; (fig.) ardor, enthusiasm *(ardimiento);* heat, flush *(de una* *acción);* **hacer —,** to be hot or warm, to be hot weather; **tener —,** to be hot or warm.

caloría (kâ•lo•rē´â) *f.* calorie.

calumnia (kâ•lūm´nyâ) *f.* calumny, slander.

calumniar (kâ•lūm•nyâr´) *vn.* to slander, to smear.

calumnioso, sa (kâ•lūm•nyo´so, sâ) *adj.* calumnious, slanderous.

caluroso, sa (kâ•lū•ro´so, sâ) *adj.* warm, hot; **— bienvenida,** cordial welcome.

calva (kâl´va) *f.* bald spot, bald place *(de la cabeza);* clearing *(del bosque).*

Calvario (kâl•vâ´ryo) *m.* Calvary; via dolorosa *(vía crucis);* **c—,** (fig.) cross to bear, via dolorosa.

calvicie (kâl•vē´sye) *f.* baldness.

calvo, va (kâl´vo, vâ) *adj.* bald; barren, bare *(terreno).*

calzada (kâl•sâ´thâ) *f.* causeway, highway.

calzado (kâl•sâ´tho) *m.* footwear.

calzador (kâl•sâ•thor´) *m.* shoe horn.

calzar (kâl•sâr´) *va.* to put on *(calzado);* to put a wedge under *(cuña);* to take *(calibre de bala);* to wear, to take *(número de zapato).*

calzón (kâl•son´) *m.* ombre *(tresillo);* (Mex.) sugar-cane blight;

—ones, *pl.* breeches, knee-length shorts *(hasta la rodilla);* trousers, pants *(pantalones).*

calzoncillos (kâl•son•sē´yos) *m. pl.* drawers, shorts.

callado, da (kâ•yâ´tho, thâ) *adj.* silent, noiseless, quiet *(silencioso),* quiet *(taciturno).*

callar (kâ•yâr´) *vn.* to keep quiet, to be silent *(guardar silencio);* to become quiet, to stop talking *(dejar de hablar);* **—,** *va.* not to mention, to keep quiet about; **hacer —,** to silence, to hush up.

calle (kâ´ye) *f.* street; lane *(en una competición);* **— trasversal,** crossroad; **cruce de —,** street crossing; **doblar la —,** to turn the corner; **—s céntricas,** downtown.

callejuela (kâ•ye•hwe´lâ) *f.* lane, narrow street; (fig.) subterfuge, shift.

callo (kâ´yo) *m.* corn, callus; **—s,** *pl.* tripe.

calloso, sa (kâ•yo´so, sâ) *adj.* callous.

cama (kâ´mâ) *f.* bed; litter *(para el ganado);* den, lair *(de animales);* **— plegadiza,** folding bed; **guardar —,** to stay in bed; **hacer la —,** to make the bed.

camaleón (kâ•mâ•le•on´) *m.* chameleon.

cámara (kâ´mâ•râ) *f.* hall, chamber; (pol.) house; (phot.) came-ra; (avi.) cockpit; (mech.) chamber; — **de aire,** inner tube; — **de combustión,** combustion chamber; — **de comercio,** chamber of commerce; — **de compensación,** clearing house; — **de escape,** exhaust; — **frigorífica,** cold-storage locker.

camarada (kâ•mâ•râ´thâ) *m.* comrade, companion.

camaradería (kâ•mâ•râ•the•rē´â) *f.* fellowship.

camarera (kâ•mâ•re´râ) *f.* waitress *(de restaurante);* maid.

camarero (kâ•mâ•re´ro) *m.* waiter *(de restaurante);* valet; (naut. and avi.) steward.

camarógrafo (kâ•mâ•ro´grâ•fo) *m.* cameraman.

camarón (kâ•mâ•ron´) *m.* (ichth.) shrimp; **coctel de — ones,** shrimp cocktail.

cambiable (kâm•byâ´vle) *adj.* changeable.

cambiante (kâm•byân´te) *adj.* changeable; iridescent *(tela);* — , *m.* iridescence.

cambiar (kâm•byâr´) *va.* to change; to exchange *(una cosa por otra);* to alter *(modificar);* to turn *(convertir);* to convert *(divisas);* to make change for *(billetes).*

cambio (kâm´byo) *m.* exchange; change; alteration; — **exterior**

or **extranjero,** foreign exchange; — **de marchas** or **de velocidad,** gearshift; — **de moneda,** money exchange; **a — de,** in exchange for; **al — de,** at the rate of exchange of; **en —,** on the other hand; **agente de —,** stockbroker; **casa de —,** exchange office; **corredor de —,** exchange broker; **letra de —,** bill of exchange; **tipo de —,** rate of exchange.

camelia (kâ•me´lyâ) *f.* (bot.) camellia.

camello (kâ•me´yo) *m.* camel.

camilla (kâ•mē´yâ) *f.* stretcher.

caminante (kâ•mē•nân´te) *m.* traveler, wayfarer; walker.

caminar (kâ•mē•nâr´) *vn.* to travel; to walk *(andar).*

camino (kâ•mē´no) *m.* road; — **trillado,** beaten path; — **de acceso,** access road; **en —,** on the way; **ponerse en —,** to start out.

camión (kâ•myon´) *m.* truck; (Mex.) bus.

camioneta (kâ•myo•ne´tâ) *f.* station wagon; small truck *(para mercancías).*

camisa (kâ•mē´sâ) *f.* shirt; chemise *(de señora);* — **de fuerza,** straitjacket.

camiseta (kâ•mē•se´tâ) *f.* undershirt.

camisola (kâ•mē•so´lâ) *f.* ruffled

shirt.

camisón (kâ•mē•son´) *m.* nightgown *(de dormir);* chemise.

camote (kâ•mo´te) *m.* sweet potato.

campamento (kâm•pâ•men´to) *m.* (mil.) encampment, camp.

campana (kâm•pâ´nâ) *f.* bell; — **de buzo,** diving bell; — **de chimenea,** funnel of a chimney; **juego de** —**s,** chimes.

campanada (kâm•pâ•nâ´thâ) *f.* peal, stroke of a bell; (fig.) scandal.

campanero (kâm•pâ•ne´ro) *m.* bell founder *(artífice);* bell ringer.

campanilla (kâm•pâ•nē´yâ) *f.* hand bell.

campanillazo (kâm•pâ•nē•yâ´so) *m.* loud ring of a bell.

campaña (kâm•pâ´nyâ) *f.* level countryside, fiat country; campaign *(serie de actos).*

campechano, na (kâm•pe •châ´-no, nâ) *adj.* (coll.) good-natured, cheerful.

campeón, ona (kâm•pe•on´, o´nâ) *n.* champion.

campeonato (kâm•pe•o•nâ´to) *m.* championship.

campesino, na (kâm•pe•sē´no, nâ) *adj.* rural; —, *n.* peasant.

campestre (kâm•pes´tre) *adj.* rural, rustic; **merienda** —, picnic lunch.

campo (kâm´po) *m.* country, countryside; field *(terreno);* (mil.) camp; — **de deportes,** playing field; — **de juegos,** playground; — **minado,** mine field.

camuflaje (kâ•mū•flâ´he) *m.* camouflage.

cana (kâ´nâ) *f.* gray hair; **peinar** —**s,** to grow old.

Canadá (kâ•nâ•thâ´) *m.* Canada.

canadiense (kâ•nâ•thyen´se) *m.* and *f.* and *adj.* Canadian.

canal (kâ•nâl´) *m.* channel; canal *(artificial);* gutter *(del tejado).*

Canal de la Mancha (kâ•nâl´ the lâ mân´-châ) *m.* English Channel.

canalizar (kâ•nâ•lē•sâr´) *va.* to channel; (elec.) to wire.

canalla (kâ•nâ´yâ) *f.* mob, rabble; —, *m.* scoundrel, heel, despicable person.

canallada (kâ•nâ•yâ´thâ) *f.* despicable act.

Canarias (kâ•nâ´ryâs) *f. pl.* Canary Islands.

canario (kâ•nâ´ryo) *m.* canary; (Sp. Am.) liberal tipper; —, **ria,** *adj.* from the Canary Islands.

canasta (kâ•nâs´tâ) *f.* basket, hamper; canasta *(juego).*

cancelación (kân •se•lâ•syon´) *f.* cancellation; erasure; settlement.

cancelar (kân•se•lâr´) *va.* to annul, to void *(un documento);* to pay, to liquidate *(una deuda);* to break, to cancel *(un compromiso).*

cáncer (kân´ser) *m.* (med.) cancer.

canceroso, sa (kân•se•ro´so, sâ) *adj.* cancerous.

canciller (kan•sē•yer´) *m.* chancellor; attaché *(de consulado).*

canción (kân•syon´) *f.* song.

cancionero (kân•syo•ne´ro) *m.* collection of songs and poetry.

cancha (kân´châ) *f.* playing field; — **de tenis,** tennis court.

candado (kân•dâ´tho) *m.* padlock.

candela (kân•de´lâ) *f.* (coll.) a light *(lumbre);* candle.

candelabro (kân•de•lâ´vro) *m.* candelabrum.

candelero (kân•de•le´ro) *m.* candlestick.

candente (kân•den´te) *adj.* red-hot.

candidato, ta (kân•dē•thâ´to, tâ) *n.* candidate, applicant.

candidatura (kân•dē•thâ•tū´râ) *f.* candidacy.

candidez (kân•dē•thes´) *f.* candor, frankness; whiteness *(blancura).*

cándido, da (kân´dē•tho, thâ) *adj.* frank, open, candid; white.

candor (kân•dor´) *m.* candor, frankness.

canela (ca•ne´lâ) *f.* cinnamon; — **en raja,** cinnamon stick; — **en polvo,** powdered cinnamon.

cangrejo (kâng•gre´ho) *m.* crawfish, crab.

canguro (kâng•gū´ro) *m.* kangaroo.

caníbal (kâ•nē´vâl) *m.* cannibal.

canino, na (kâ•nē´no, nâ) *adj.* canine.

canje (kân´he) exchange, interchange.

canjear (kân•he•âr´) *va.* to exchange, to interchange.

cano, na (kâ´no, nâ) *adj.* hoary, gray-haired.

canoa (kâ•no´â) *f.* canoe; (Sp. Am.) wooden trough *(artesa);* (Sp. Am.) wooden aqueduct *(canal).*

canon (kâ´non) *m.* catalogue, list; (eccl.) canon; **cánones,** *pl.* canon law.

canónico, ca (kâ•no´nē•ko, kâ) *adj.* canonical.

canónigo (kâ•no´nē•go) *m.* (eccl.) canon.

canonizar (kâ•no•nē•sâr´) *va.* to canonize.

canoso, sa (kâ•no´so, sâ) *adj.* whitehaired.

cansado, da (kân•sâ´tho, thâ) *adj.* weary, wearied, tired; tedious, tiresome *(fastidioso).*

cansancio (kan•sân´syo) *m.* lassitude, fatigue, weariness.

cansar (kân•sâr´) *va.* to weary, to fatigue; to annoy, to bore *(fastidiar);* —**se,** to grow weary, to get tired.

cantante (kân•tân´te) *m.* and *f.* singer.

cantar (kân•târ´) *m.* song; —, *va.* and *vn.* to sing.

cántara (kân´tâ•râ) *f.* pitcher; a liquid measure of 32 pints *(medida).*

cántaro (kân´tâ•ro) *m.* pitcher; ballot box *(electoral);* **llover a —s,** to rain heavily, to pour.

cantera (kân•te´râ) *f.* quarry.

cantero (kan•te´ro) *m.* stonecutter.

cántico (kân´tē•ko) *m.* song, canticle.

cantidad (kân•tē•thâth´) *f.* quantity, amount, number.

cantimplora (kân•tēm•plo´râ) *f.* siphon *(sifón);* decanter *(garrafa);* water bottle, canteen *(frasco).*

cantina (kân•tē´nâ) *f.* barroom, cantina; wine cellar *(sótano);* canteen *(caja).*

cantinero (kân•tē•ne´ro) *m.* bartender.

canto (kân´to) *m.* song; (eccl.) chant; edge *(de mesa);* chunk, piece *(de piedra);* canto *(del poema épico).*

cantor, ra (kân•tor´, râ) *n.* singer; —, *adj.* singing.

canturrear (kân•tū•rre•âr´) *vn.* to hum, to sing in a low voice.

caña (kâ´nyâ) *f.* cane, reed *(planta);* stalk *(tallo);* (Sp. Am.) rum; — **del timón,** helm; — **de azúcar,** sugar cane.

cañal (kâ•nyâl´) *m.* cane plantation *(plantío);* reed bank, canebrake.

cáñamo (kâ´nyâ•mo) *m.* hemp; hempen cloth *(lienzo).*

cañavera (kâ•nyâ•ve´râ) *f.* reed.

cañaveral (kâ•nyâ•ve•râl´) *m.* sugar-cane plantation.

cañería (kâ•nye•rē´â) *f.* pipe line; gas main *(del gas);* water main *(de las aguas).*

caño (kâ´nyo) *m.* tube, pipe; drain *(albañal)*

cañón (kâ•nyon´) *m.* pipe *(de órgano);* gorge, canyon *(paso estrecho);* cannon, gun *(de artillería);* barrel *(de fusil).*

cañonazo (ká•nyo•nâ´so) *m.* cannon shot.

cañonería (kâ•nyo•ne•rē´â) *f.* organ pipes; (mil.) battery of cannons.

cañonero, ra (kâ•nyo•ne´ro, râ) *adj.* carrying guns; —, *m.* gunboat.

cañutillo (kâ•nyū•tē´yo) *m.* slender glass tubing.

caoba (kâ•o´vâ) *f.* mahogany.

caos (kâ′os) *m.* chaos, confusion.

caótico, ca (kâ•o′tē•ko, kâ) *adj.* chaotic.

capa (kâ′pâ) *f.* cloak, cape *(prenda de vestir);* layer, coating *(de azucar);* stratum *(del terreno);* cover *(cubierta); (fig.)* pretext; **defender a — y espada,** to defend at all costs.

capacidad (ká•pâ•sē•thâth′) *f.* capacity.

capacitar (kâ•pâ•sē•târ′) *va.* to enable *(habilitar);* to empower, to authorize *(facultar).*

capataz (kâ•pâ•tâs′) *m.* overseer *(de hacienda);* foreman *(de operarios).*

capaz (kâ•pâs′) *adj.* spacious, roomy *(grande);* capable *(apto);* able, competent *(diestro).*

capellán (kâ•pe•yân′) *m.* chaplain; clergyman *(eclesiástico).*

caperuza (kâ•pe•rū′sâ) *f.* hood; **Caperucita Roja,** Little Red Riding Hood.

capilar (kâ•pē•lâr′) *adj.* capillary.

capilla (kâ•pē′yâ) *f.* hood *(capucha);* chapel.

capital (ká•pē•tâl′) *m.* capital *(valor permanente);* principal; estate, assets *(caudal);* **colocar un —,** to invest capital; **—,** *f.* capital; *adj.* capital; principal, main.

capitalismo (kâ•pē•tâ•lēz′mo) *m.* capitalism.

capitalista (kâ•pē•tâ•lēs′tâ) *m. and f. and adj.* capitalist; **socio —,** investor, investing member.

capitalización (kâ•pē•tâ•lē•sâ•syon′) *f.* capitalization.

capitalizar (kâ•pē•tâ•lē•sâr′) *va.* to capitalize.

capitán (kâ•pē•tân′) *m.* captain; chief, leader *(de forajidos);* **— de corbeta,** lieutenant commander; **— del puerto,** harbor master.

capitel (kâ•pē•tel′) *m.* steeple *(de una torre);* capital *(de una columna).*

capitolio (kâ•pē•to′lyo) *m.* capitol.

capítulo (kâ•pē′tū•lo) *m.* chapter; charge, count, allegation *(cargo).*

caporal (kâ•po•râl′) *m.* chief, ringleader.

capote (kâ•po′te) *m.* long cloak, capote; bullfighter′s cape *(de torero);* (coll.) stern look, frown *(ceño);* **decir para su —,** to say to oneself.

capricho (kâ•prē′cho) *m.* caprice, whim, fancy.

caprichoso, sa (kâ•prē•cho′so, sâ) *adj.* capricious, whimsical, fickle.

cápsula (kâp′sū•lâ) *f.* capsule

(envoltura); top, cap *(de botella);* cartridge *(del arma de fuego);* — **de escape** or **de emergencia,** escape capsule; — **fulminante,** detonator, percussion cap.

captar (kâp•târ´) *va.* to captivate; (rad.) to tune in; to understand, to perceive *(comprender).*

captura (kâp•tū´râ) *f.* capture, seizure.

capturar (kâp•tū•râr´) *va.* to capture.

capullo (kâ•pū´yo) *m.* cocoon *(de oruga);* bud *(de flor).*

caqui (kâ´kē) *adj.* khaki.

cara (kâ´râ) *f.* face, visage *(del hombre);* front *(fachada);* surface *(superficie);* — **a** —, face to face; — **o cruz** or — **o sello,** heads or tails; **de** —, opposite, facing; **buena** —, cheerful mien; **mala** —, frown; **tener mala** —, to look bad.

carabina (kâ•râ•vē´nâ) *f.* carbine; **ser como la** — **de Ambrosio,** to be good for nothing, to be worthless.

carabinero (kâ•râ•vē•ne´ro) *m.* carabineer.

caracol (kâ•râ•kol´) *m.* snail; **escalera de** —, winding staircase, spiral staircase.

carácter (kâ•râk´ter) *m.* character; nature, disposition *(genio);* characteristic *(rasgo);* position, rank *(condición).*

característica (kâ•râk•te•rēs´tē•kâ) *f.* characteristic; trait *(de una persona).*

característico, ca (kâ•râk•te•rēs´tē•ko, kâ) *adj.* characteristic.

caracterizar (kâ•râk•te•rē•sâr´) *va.* to characterize.

¡caramba! (kâ•râm´bâ) *interj.* heck! dam it!

caramelo (kâ•râ•me´lo) *m.* caramel.

carátula (kâ•râ´tū•lâ) *f.* mask; (fig.) theater, stage; (Sp. Am.) title page *(de un libro).*

caravana (kâ•râ•vâ´nâ) *f.* caravan; — **de automóviles,** autocade, motorcade.

carbohidrato (kâr•voē•thrâ´to) *m.* carbohydrate.

carbón (kâr•von´) *m.* coal; (elec.) carbon; **copia al** —, carbon copy; — **de leña,** charcoal; — **de piedra,** mineral coal; **papel** —, carbon paper; — **vegetal,** charcoal.

carbonera (kâr•vo•ne´râ) *f.* coal mine *(mina de hulla);* coal bin *(depósito).*

carbonero (kâr•vo•ne´ro) *m.* collier; — , **ra,** *adj.* pertaining to coal.

carbónico, ca (kâr•vo´nē•ko, kâ) *adj.* carbonic.

carbonífero, ra (kâr•vo•nē´fe•ro,

rã) *adj.* carboniferous, coal producing.

carbonizar (kâr•vo•nē•sâr´) *va.* to carbonize, to char.

carbono (kâr•vo´no) *m.* (chem.) carbon.

carburador (kâr•vū•râ•thor´)*m.*carburetor.

carcacha (kâr•kâ´chã) *f.* (coll. *Mex.)* jalopy, old dilapidated car.

carcajada (kâr•kâ•hâ´thâ)*f.* hearty laughter; **soltar una —,** to burst out laughing.

carcañal (kâr•kâ•nyâl´) or **carcaño** (kâr•kâ´nyo) *m.* heel bone.

cárcel (kâr´sel) *f.* jail; prison *(presidio).*

carcelero (kâr•se•le´ro) *m.* jailer.

carcinógeno (kâr•sē•no´he•no)*m.*carcinogen.

carcomer (kâr•ko•mer´) *va.* to gnaw; (fig.) to corrode, to waste, to eat away.

carcomido, da (kâr•ko•mē´tho, thâ) *adj.* worm-eaten.

carda (kâr´thã) *f.* teasel *(para los paños);* card *(para la lana);* (fig.) reprimand, rebuke.

cardador, ra (kâr•thâ•thor´, rã) *n.* carder.

cardar (kâr•thâr´) *va.* to card; to teasel.

cardenal (kâr•the•nâl´) *m.* cardinal; (orn.) cardinal; bruise *(equimosis).*

cardiaco, ca (kâr•thyâ´ko, kâ) or **cardiaco, ca** (kâr•thēâ•ko, kâ) *adj.* cardiac; **síncope —co,** heart attack.

cardinal (kâr•thē•nâl´) *adj.* cardinal.

cardiógrafo (kâr•thyo´grâ•fo) *m.* (med.) cardiograph.

cardiograma (kâr•thyo•grâ´mâ) *m.* (med.) cardiogram.

cardo (kâr´tho) *m.* thistle.

carecer* (kâ•re•ser´) *vn.* to want, to lack.

carencia (kâ•ren´syâ) *f.* lack, scarcity.

carey (kâ•re´ē) *m.* sea turtle, hawksbill turtle; tortoise shell *(concha).*

carga (kâr´gâ) *f.* load; burden, pack *(en hombros);* freight, cargo *(en vehículo);* load, charge *(de pólvera);* impost, tax *(gravamen);* (fig:) responsibility, obligation *(obligación);* worry, problem *(cuidado);* **— inútil** useless burden; **— de profundidad,** (mil.) depth charge.

cargado, da (kâr•gâ´tho, thâ) *adj.* loaded, full.

cargador (kâr•gâ•thor´) *m.* stoker *(fogonero);* stevedore, longshoreman *(estibador);* rammer, ramrod *(para armas de fuego);* carrier, porter *(portador).*

cargamento (kâr•gâ•men´to) *m.*

(naut.) load, cargo.

cargar (kâr•gâr´) *va.* to load, to freight *(un vehículo);* to charge *(una batería);* to impose, to charge *(imponer);* to assault; — **con,** to assume the responsibility for.

cargo (kâr´go) *m.* (com.) debits; charge, accusation *(falta);* position, office *(oficio);* care, responsibility *(obligación);* weight, load *(peso).*

cariancho, cha (kâ•ryân´cho, châ) *adj.* broad-faced, chubby-cheeked.

caribe (kâ•rē´ve) *adj.* Caribbean.

caricatura (kâ•rē•kâ•tū´râ) *f.* caricature, cartoon; — **animada,** animated cartoon.

caricia (kâ•rē´syâ) *f.* caress.

caridad (kâ•rē•thâth´) *f.* charity, benevolence; alms *(limosna).*

caries (kâ´ryes) *f.* (med.) caries, decay.

carigordo, da (kâ•rē•gor´tho, thâ) *adj.* full-faced.

carilargo, ga (kâ•rē•lâr´go, gâ) *adj.* long-faced.

carilleno, na (kâ•rē•ye´no, nâ) *adj.* full-faced.

cariño (kâ•rē´nyo) *m.* fondness, affection; term of endearment *(manifestación).*

cariñoso, sa (kâ•rē•nyo´so, sâ) *adj.* affectionate, fond, endearing.

caritativo, va (kâ•rē•tâ•tē´vo, vâ) *adj.* charitable.

carmelita (kâr•me•lē´tâ) *f.* and *adj.* Carmelite.

carmesí (kâr•me•sē´) *adj.* crimson; —, *m.* cochineal powder.

carmín (kâr•mēn´) *m.* and *adj.* carmine.

carnada ((kâr•nâ´thâ) *m.* and *f.* bait, lure.

carnal (kâr•nâl´) *adj.* carnal, fleshy; sensual *(lascivo);* blood, related by blood; **primo** —, first cousin; —, *m.* time of year other than Lent.

carnaval (kâr•nâ•vâl´) *m.* carnival.

carne (kâr´ne) *f.* flesh, meat; pulp *(de la fruta);* — **asada en horno,** baked meat; — **asada en parrilla,** broiled meat; — **de gallina,** (fig.) gooseflesh; — **de vaca,** beef.

carnero (kâr•ne´ro) *m.* sheep; mutton *(carne);* family vault *(sepulcro).*

carnicería (kâr•nē•se•rē´â) *f.* meat market, butcher shop; (fig.) massacre.

carnicero (kâr•nē•se´ro) *m.* butcher; —, **ra,** *adj.* fond of eating meat.

carnívoro, ra (kâr•nē´vo•ro, râ) *adj.* carnivorous.

carnoso, sa (kar•no´so, sâ) or **carnudo, da** (kâr•nū´tho, thâ) *adj.* fleshy; full of marrow *(meduloso).*

caro, ra (kâ´ro, râ) *adj.* expensive, dear; —**ra mitad,** better half.

carpa (kâr´pâ) *f.* (ichth.) carp; (Sp. Am.) camping tent.

carpeta (kâr•pe´tâ) *f.* table cover; folder *(de un legajo).*

carpintear (kâr•pēn•te•âr´) *vn.* to carpenter.

carpintería (kâr•pēn•te•rē´â) *f.* carpentry; carpenter's shop *(taller).*

carpintero (kâr•pēn•te´ro) *m.* carpenter; **pájaro —,** woodpecker.

carrasca (kâ•rrâs´kâ) *f.,* **carrasco** (kâ•rrâs´ko) *m.* live oak.

carrera (kâ•rre´râ) *f.* running *(acción);* run *(espacio);* track *(sitio);* race *(certamen);* row, line *(hilera);* course of one's life *(de la vida humana);* career, profession *(profesión);* **a — abierta,** at full speed; **— de armamentos,** arms race.

carretera (kâ•rre•te´râ) *f.* highway, main road.

carril (kâ•rrēl´) *m.* wheel rut *(huella);* furrow *(surco);* rail *(del ferrocarril);* lane, narrow road *(camino).*

carro (kâ´rro) *m.* (rail.) freight car; chariot *(de guerra);* cart, wagon *(de transporte);* (Sp. Am.) auto, car; carriage *(de la máquina de escribir);* — **entero,** carload; — **lateral,** side car of a motor-cycle; C— **Mayor,** Big Dipper; C— **Menor,** Little Dipper.

carrocería (kâ•rro•se•rē´â) *f.* body *(del coche automóvil);* body shop, auto-repair pair shop *(taller).*

carroña (kâ•rro´nyâ) *f.* carrion.

carruaje (kâ•rrwâ´he) *m.* wheeled vehicle.

carrusel (kâ•rrū•sel´) *m.* merry-go-round.

carta (kâr´tâ) *f.* letter; charter *(constitución);* (avi. and naut.) chart; card *(naipe);* — **aérea,** airmail letter; — **certificada,** registered letter; — **credencial** or **de crédito,** letter of credit; — **de amparo,** safe conduct; — **de ciudadanía** citizenship papers; — **de presentación,** letter of introduction; — **en lista,** general delivery letter; — **general,** form letter.

cartel (kâr•tel´) *m.* poster; show bill *(de teatro);* (poi.) cartel, organized crime; **no fijar —es,** post no bills.

cartelera (kâr•te•le´râ) *f.* billboard.

cartera (kâr•te´râ) *f.* brief case; flap *(del bolsillo);* — **de bolsillo,** billfold, wallet.

cartero (kâr•te′ro) *m.* letter carrier, postman, mailman.

cartílago (kâr•tē′lâ•go) *m.* cartilage.

cartilla (kâr•tē′yâ) *f.* primer.

cartografía (kâr•to•grâ•fē′â) *f.* cartography.

cartón (kâr•ton′) *m.* pasteboard, card-board.

cartucho (kâr•tū′cho) *m.* cartridge; — **en blanco,** blank cartridge.

cartulina (kâr•tū•lē′nâ) *f.* bristol.

casa (kâ′sâ) *f.* house; home *(hogar);* (corn.) firm, concern; — **al por mayor,** wholesale house; — **de banca,** banking house; — **de cambio,** exchange office; — **de campo,** country house; — **de comercio,** business house; — **de comisiones,** commission house; — **de compensación,** clearing house; — **de huéspedes,** boardinghouse; — **de locos,** madhouse; — **de máquinas,** engine house; — **de maternidad,** maternity hospital; — **de moneda,** mint; — **de préstamos or empeños,** pawnshop; — **editorial,** publishing house; — **matriz,** main office; — **mortuoria,** funeral parlor; **en** —, at home; **poner** —, to set up housekeeping.

casamiento (kâ•sâ•myen′to) *m.* marriage, wedding.

casar (kâ•sâr) *va.* to marry, to wed; (fig.) to join, to combine; to abrogate, to annul *(anular);* —**se,** to get married.

cascabel (kâs•kâ•vel′) *m.* sleigh bell; (zool.) rattlesnake.

cascada (kâ•kâ′thâ) *f.* cascade, waterfall.

cascajo (kâs•kâ′ho) *m.* gravel; (coll.) piece of junk *(trasto).*

cascanueces (kâs•kâ•nwe′ses) *m.* nutcracker.

cáscara (kâs′kâ•râ) *f.* rind, peel *(de la fruta);* husk; bark *(del árbol);* skin *(piel de fruta).*

cascarón (kâs•kâ•ron′) *m.* eggshell.

cascarrón, ona (kâs•kâ•rron′, o′nâ) *adj.* rough, harsh, tough.

casco (kâs′ko) *m.* skull, cranium *(cráneo);* fragment, piece *(fragmento);* helmet *(armadura);* (naut.) hulk; crown *(del sombrero);* hoof *(de caballería).*

casera (kâ•se′râ) *f.* housekeeper.

caserío (kâ•se•rē′o) *m.* village.

casero, ra (kâ•se′ro, râ) *adj.* domestic, homey; homemade *(hecho en casa);* —, *m.* landlord; —, *f.* landlady.

casi (kâ′sē) *adv.* almost, nearly; — **que,** or —, very nearly.

casilla (kâ•sē′yâ) *f.* booth, shelter; box office *(taquilla);* square *(del tablero);* postal box *(apar-*

tado); — **de correos,** mailbox; **sacar de sus —s,** to get out of one's rut, to make change one's ways; to infuriate, to exasperate *(irritar).*

casimir (kâ•sē•mēr´) *m.* cashmere.

casino (kâ•sē´no) *m.* casino; clubhouse *(centro de recreo).*

caso (kâ´so) *m.* case *(punto de consulta);* event *(circunstancia);* occurrence, happening *(acontecimiento);* (gram.) case.

caspa (kâs´pâ) *f.* dandruff; scab *(de una llaga).*

casquete (kâs•ke´te) *m.* helmet, cap; — **polar,** polar cap.

casquijo (kâs•kē´ho) *m.* gravel.

casta (kâs´tâ) *f.* caste *(clase);* race, lineage *(linaje);* (fig.) kind, quality *(especie).*

castaña (kâs•tâ´nyâ) *f.* chestnut; demijohn *(damajuana);* bun *(de pelo).*

castaño (kâs•tâ´nyo) *m.* chestnut tree; —, **ña,** *adj.* chestnut.

castañuela (kâs•tâ•nywe´lâ) *f.* castanet.

castellano, na (kâs•te•yâ´no, nâ) *n.* and *adj.* Castilian; —, *m.* Spanish language.

castidad (kâs•tē•thâth´) *f.* chastity.

castigador, ra (kâs•tē•gâ•thor´, râ) *n.* punisher; —, *adj.* punishing.

castigar (kâs•tē•gâr´) *va.* to chastise, to punish.

castigo (kâs•tē´go) *m.* chastisement, punishment.

Castilla (kâs•tē´yâ) *f.* Castile.

castillo (kâs•tē´yo) *m.* castle, fortress; cell of the queen bee *(maestril).*

castizo, za (kâs•tē´so, sâ) *adj.* of noble descent; pure, uncorrupt *(de lenguaje).*

casto, ta (kâs´to, tâ) *adj.* pure, chaste.

castor (kâs•tor´) *m.* beaver.

castración (kâs•trâ•syon´) *f.* castration, emasculation.

casual (kâ•swâl´) *adj.* accidental, happenstance.

casualidad (kâ•swâ•lē•thâth´) *f.* accident, chance, coincidence; **por —,** by chance, by coincidence.

casucha (kâ•sū´châ) *f.* hut, shack.

cata (kâ´tâ) *f.* tasting; (Sp. Am.) parrakeet *(cotorra).*

cataclismo (kâ•tâ•klēz´mo) *m.* cataclysm.

catacumbas (kâ•tâ•kūm´bâs) *f. pl.* catacombs.

catalán, ana (kâ•tâ•lân´, â´nâ) *n.* and *adj.* Catalan, Catalonian.

catalizador (kâ•tâ•lē•sâ•thor´) *m.* catalyst.

catalogar (kâ•tâ•lo•gâr´) *va.* to

catalogue, to list.

catálogo (kâ•tâ´lo•go) *m.* catalogue, list.

Cataluña (kâ•tâ•lū´nyâ) *f.* Catalonia.

catar (kâ•târ´) *va.* to taste *(saborear);* to inspect, to examine *(observar).*

catarata (kâ•tâ•râ´tâ) *f.* cataract, waterfall, cascade; (med.) cataract.

catarro (kâ•tâ´rro) *m.* catarrh, cold.

catártico, ca (ca•târ´tē•ko, kâ) *adj.* (med.) cathartic, purging.

catástrofe (kâ•tâs´tro•fe) *f.* catastrophe, disaster.

catecismo (kâ•te•sēz´mo) *m.* catechism.

cátedra (kâ´te•thrâ) *f.* professorate; class, course *(clase).*

catedral (kâ•te•thrâl´) *adj.* and *f.* cathedral.

catedrático (kâ•te•thrâ´tē•ko) *m.* professor.

categoría (kâ•te•go•rē´â) *f.* category, class.

categórico, ca (kâ•te•go´rē•ko, kâ) *adj.* categorical, decisive.

catequismo (kâ•te•kēz´mo) *m.* catechism.

cátodo (kâ´to•tho) *m.* cathode.

catolicismo (kâ•to•lē•sēz´mo) *m.* Catholicism.

católico, ca (kâ•to´lē•ko, kâ) *adj.* and *n.* Catholic.

catorce (kâ•tor´se) *m.* and *adj.* fourteen.

catre (kâ´tre) *m.* fieldbed, cot.

caucásico, ca (kâū•kâ´sē•ko, kâ) *adj.,* Caucasian.

cauce (kâ´ū•se) *m.* irrigation ditch *(acequia);* riverbed *(del río).*

caución (kâū•syon´) *f.* precaution; security, guaranty *(fianza).*

caucionar (kâū•syo•nâr´) *va.* to guarantee.

cauchera (kâū•che´râ) *f.* rubber plant.

caucho (ka´ū•cho) *m.* rubber; — **artificial,** synthetic rubber; — **endurecido,** hard rubber.

caudal (kâū•thâl´) *m.* property, fortune, wealth *(hacienda);* (com.) funds; abundance, plenty *(abundancia);* flow, discharge *(de agua).*

caudillo (kâū•thē´yo) *m.* chief, leader.

causa (kâ´ū•sâ) *f.* cause, origin *(fundamento);* motive, reason *(motivo);* case, lawsuit *(pleito);* **a — de,** owing to, because of, on account of, by reason of.

causar (kâū•sâr´) *va.* to cause, to pro-duce, to occasion.

cáustico (kâ´ūs•tē•ko) *m.* caustic; **—, ca,** *adj.* caustic.

cautela (kâū•te´lâ) *f.* caution, prudence, heedfulness.

cautelar (kâū•te•lâr´) *va.* to guard against; —, *vn.* to take precautions.

cauteloso, sa (kâū•te•lo´so, sâ) *adj.* cautious, prudent.

cauterizar (kâū•te•rē•sâr´) *va.* to cauterize; (fig.) to reproach severely.

cautivador, ra (kâū•tē•vâ•thor´, râ) *adj.* captivating, fascinating.

cautivar (kâū•tē•vâr´) *va.* to take prisoner, to capture; (fig.) to captivate, to charm, to attract.

cautiverio (kâū•tē•ve´ryo) *m.* captivity, confinement.

cautivo, va (kâū•tē´vo, vâ) *n.* captive, prisoner.

cauto, ta (kâ´ū•to, tâ) *adj.* cautious, wary, prudent.

cavar (kâ•vâr´) *va.* to dig, to excavate; —, *vn.* to penetrate deeply, to study thoroughly *(profundizar).*

caverna (kâ•ver´nâ) *f.* cavern, cave.

caviar (kâ•vyâr´) *m.* caviar.

cavidad (kâ•vē•thâth´) *f.* cavity, hollow.

cayo (kâ´yo) *m.* cay, key.

caza (kâ´sâ) *f.* game *(animales);* hunting, hunt *(acción);* (avi.) pursuit plane, fighter plane.

cazador (kâ•sâ•thor´) *m.* hunter, huntsman; — **furtivo,** poacher.

cazar (kâ•sâr´) *va.* to hunt.

cazo (kâ´so) *m.* saucepan.

cazuela (kâ•swe´lâ) *f.* stewpan.

cazuz (kâ•sūs´) *m.* (bot.) ivy.

CD: disco compacto, CD, compact disk; **reproductor de—,** CD player.

cebada (se•vâ´thâ) *f.* barley; — **fermentada,** malt.

cebo (se´vo) *m.* feed *(para engordar);* bait, lure *(para atraer);* priming *(del arma de fuego).*

cebolla (se•vo´ya) *f.* onion; bulb *(bulbo).*

cebollino (se•vo•yē´no) *f.* seedling onion.

cebra or **zebra** (se´vrâ) *f.* zebra.

cecear (se•se•âr´) *vn.* to lisp.

cecina (se•sē´nâ) *f.* jerked meat, jerky.

ceder (se•ther´) *va.* to cede, to yield; to transfer, to assign *(transferir);* —, *vn.* to submit, to comply, to give in *(rendirse);* to abate, to diminish *(disminuir).*

cedro (se´thro) *m.* cedar.

cédula (se•thū•lâ) *f.* slip, ticket; card *(documento);* — **de cambio,** bill of ex-change; — **personal** or **de vecindad,** identification papers; —**s hipotecarias,** bank stock in the form of mortgages.

céfiro (se´fē•ro) *m.* zephyr, breeze.

cegar* (se•gâr´) *vn.* to go blind; —, *va.* to blind; to shut *(cer-*

rar).

ceguedad (se•ge•thâth´) *f.* blindness.

ceguera (se•ge´râ) *f.* blindness.

ceja (se´hâ) *f.* eyebrow *(del ojo)*; edge, rim.

cejudo, da (se•hu´tho, thâ) *adj.* having bushy eyebrows.

celada (se•lâ´thâ) *f.* sallet; ambush *(emboscada)*; trick, trap *(engaño)*.

celar (se•lâr´) *va.* to fulfill carefully, to carry out to the letter *(esmerarse)*; to watch over, to guard *(vigilar)*; to hide, to conceal *(ocultar)*; to engrave *(esculpir)*.

celda (sel´dâ) *f.* cell.

celebración (se•le•vrâ•syon´) *f.* celebration; praise, acclamation *(aplauso)*.

celebrar (se•le•vrâr´) *va.* to celebrate *(una ceremonia)*; to praise, to acclaim, to be glad of *(aplaudir)*; —, *vi.* to take place; — **misa,** to say mass.

célebre (se´le•vre) *adj.* famous, renowned; humorous witty *(gracioso)*.

celebridad (se•le•vrē•thâth´) *f.* fame, renown; celebrity, famous person *(personaje)*.

celerímetro (se•le•rē´me•tro) *m.* speedometer.

celeste (se•les´te) *adj.* heavenly, celestial; sky-blue *(color)*.

celestial (se•les•tyâl´) *adj.* celestial, heavenly.

celo (se´lo) *m.* zeal *(entusiasmo)*; care *(esmero)*; rut, heat *(de los animales)*; — **s,** *pl.* jealousy; **tener — s de,** to be jealous of.

celofán (se•lo•fân´) *m.* cellophane.

celoso, sa (se•lo´so, sâ) *adj.* zealous, eager; jealous.

celta (sel´tâ) *adj.* Celtic; — , *m.* or *f.* Celt.

céltico, ca (sel´tē•ko, kâ) *adj.* Celtic.

célula (se´lū•lâ) *f.* cell.

celular (se•lū•lâr´) *adj.* cellular.

celuloide (se•lū•lo´e•the) *m.* celluloid.

celulosa (se•lū•lo´sâ) *f.* (chem.) cellulose.

cementar (se•men•târ´) *va.* to case harden.

cementerio (se•men•te´ryo) *m.* cemetery.

cemento (se•men´to) *m.* cement; — **armado,** reinforced concrete.

cena (se´nâ) *f.* supper.

cenagal (se•nâ•gâl´) *m.* slough, quagmire, marsh.

cenar (se•nâr´) *vn.* to have supper, to dine.

cencerrear (sen•se•rre•âr´) *vn. to* jangle *(los cencerros)*; to squeak *(los herrajes)*.

cencerro (sen•se´rro) *m.* cowbell;

a — s tapados, (fig.) quietly, unobtrusively.

cenicero (se•nē•se´ro) *m.* ash dump; ash pit *(del hogar);* ash tray *(platillo).*

ceniciento, ta (se•nē•syen´to, tâ) *adj.* ash, ash-colored; **La C— ,** Cinderella.

cenit (se´nēt) *m.* zenith, pinnacle.

ceniza (se•nē´sâ) *f.* ashes; **Miércoles de C— ,** Ash Wednesday.

cenote (se•no´te) *m.* cenote, limestone sinkhole.

censo (sen´so) *m.* census *(lista);* ground rent paid under contract and redeemable *(contrato).*

censor (sen•sor´) *m.* censor; critic, fault-finder *(crítico);* proctor, monitor *(en los colegios).*

censura (sen•sū´râ) *f.* censorship; censure *(reprobación).*

censurar (sen•sū•râr´) *va.* to censor *(notar por malo);* to judge, to estimate *(formar juicio);* to censure, to find fault with *(criticar).*

centavo (sen•tâ´vo) *m.* hundredth; cent *(moneda).*

centella (sen•te´yâ) *f.* thunderbolt *(rayo);* spark *(chispa).*

centellar (sen•te•yâr´) or **centellear** (sen•te•ye•âr´) *vn.* to sparkle, to glitter.

centelleo (sen•te•ye´o) *m.* glitter, sparkle.

centena (sen•te´nâ) *f.* hundred.

centenar (sen•te•nâr´) *m.* hundred.

centenario, ria (sen•te•nâ´ryo, ryâ) *adj.* and *n.* centenarian; — . *m.* centennial.

centeno (sen•te´no) *m.* (bot.) rye; — , **na,** *adj.* hundredth.

centésimo, ma (sen•te´sē•mo, ma) *adj.* centesimal, hundredth.

centígrado, da (sen•tē´grâ•tho, thâ) *adj.* and *m.* centigrade.

centigramo (sen•tē•grâ´mo) *m.* centigram.

centímetro (sen•tē´me•tro) *m.* centimeter.

céntimo (sen´tē•mo) *m.* cent; centime *(moneda francesa).*

centinela (sen•tē•ne´lâ) *m.* and *f.* sentinel; **estar de** or **hacer —,** (mil.) to be on guard.

central (sen•trâl´) *adj.* central, centric; *f.* headquarters; (Sp. Am.) sugar refinery *(de azúcar);* — **de electricidad,** powerhouse; — **telefónica,** telephone central.

centralización (sen•trâ•lē•sâ•syon´) *f.* centralization.

centralizar (sen•trâ•lē•sâr´) *va.* to centralize.

centrar (sen•trâr´) *va.* to center.

céntrico, ca (sen´trē•ko, kâ) *adj.* central, centric.

centro (sen´tro) *m.* center; downtown *(de una población);*— **comercial,** mall, shopping center.

Centroamérica (sen•tro•â•me´rē•kâ) *f.* Central America.

ceñir* (se•nyēr´) *vn.* to gird, to surround, to encircle *(rodear);* to curtail *(abreviar);* to fit around one´s waist; **—se,** to limit oneself, to take in one´s sails.

ceño (se´nyo) *m.* frown.

ceñudo, da (se•nyū´tho, thâ) *adj.* frowning, stern, gruff.

cepa (se´pâ) *f.* tree stump; (fig.) lineage, family; **de buena —,** of good stock.

cepillo (se•pē´yo) *m.* brush; plane *(de carpintero);* collection box *(para donativos);* — **de dientes,** toothbrush; — **para el cabello** or **para la cabeza,** hairbrush.

cera (se´râ) *f.* wax; — **s,** *pl.* honeycomb.

cerámica (se•râ´mē•kâ) *f.* ceramics.

cerca (ser´kâ) *f.* enclosure, fence; —, *adv.* near, at hand, close by; — **de,** close to, near; about *(aproximadamente).*

cercado (ser•kâ´tho) *m.* fenced-in garden *(huerto);* enclosure, fence *(cerca).*

cercanía (ser•kâ•nē´â) *f.* neighborhood, vicinity.

cercano, na (ser•kâ´no, nâ) *adj.* nearby, neighboring.

cercar (ser•kâr´) *va.* to enclose, to surround, to fence in; (mil.) to lay siege to.

cercenar (ser•se•nâr´) *va.* to pare off, to trim off, to cut off; to cut down, to re-duce *(disminuir).*

cerciorar (ser•syo•râr´) *va.* to assure, to reassure, to convince; — **se,** to make certain.

cerco (ser´ko) *m.* siege *(asedio);* hoop, ring *(aro);* circular motion *(movimiento);* enclosure.

cerdo (ser´tho) *m.* hog, pig.

cereal (se•re•âl´) *m.* cereal, grain.

cerebral (se•re•vrâl´) *adj.* cerebral; **parálisis —,** cerebral palsy.

cerebro (se•re´vro) *m.* brain.

ceremonia (se•re•mo´nyâ) ceremony.

ceremonial (se•re•mo•nyâl´) *adj.* and *m.* ceremonial.

ceremonioso, sa (se•re•mo•nyo´- so, sâ) *adj.* ceremonious.

cereza (se•re´sâ) *f.* cherry.

cerezo (se•re´so) *m.* cherry tree.

cerilla (se•rē´yâ) *f.* taper; wax *(de los oídos);* wax match *(fósforo).*

cerillo (se•rē´yo) *m.* (Mex.) wax match.

cernedera (ser•ne•the´râ) *f.* sifter.

cerner* (ser•ner´) *va.* to sift, to strain; (fig.) to examine closely; —, *vn.* to blossom; to rizzle *(llover);* **—se,** to sway, to waddle; to hover *(las aves).*

cernidura (ser•nē•thū´râ) *f.* sifting.

cero (se´ro) *m.* zero; **ser un — a la izquierda,** to be insignificant, to be of no account.

cerrado, da (se•rrâ´tho, thâ) *adj.* closed; closemouthed, reserved *(callado);* abstruse *(obscuro);* stupid, dense *(torpe).*

cerradura (se•rrâ•thū´râ) *f.* act of locking; lock *(mecanismo);* — **de golpe** or **de muelle,** spring lock.

cerrajero (se•rrâ•he´ro) *m.* locksmith.

cerrar* (se•rrâr´) *va.* and *vn.* to close, to shut; to obstruct, to block off *(impedir la entrada);* to lock *(con cerradura);* to shut up, to wall in *(tapar);* to seal *(una carta);* to bring to an end, to close *(terminar);* — **una operación,** to close a transaction, to arrange a deal; **—se,** to close ranks *(un batallón);* to persist.

cerro (se´rro) *m.* hill; neck *(del animal);* backbone *(espinazo);* **en —,** bareback.

cerrojo (se•rro´ho) *m.* bolt, latch.

certamen (ser•tâ´men) *m.* literary contest.

certero, ra (ser•te´ro, râ) *adj.* certain, sure; well-aimed, accurate *(en el tiro).*

certeza (ser•te´sâ) *f.* certainty, assurance.

certidumbre (ser•tē•thūm´bre) *f.* certainty, certitude.

certificación (ser•tē•fē•kâ•syon´) *f.* certification.

certificado (ser•tē•fē•kâ´tho) *m.* certificate; —, **da,** *adj.* certified; registered *(una carta).*

certificar (ser•tē•fē•kâr´) *va.* to certify, to affirm; to register *(una carta).*

cervecería (ser•ve•se•rē´â) *f.* brewery.

cerveza (ser•ve´sâ) *f.* beer.

cerviz (ser•vēs´) *f.* (anat.) cervix, nape of the neck; **doblar** or **bajar la —,** to humble oneself.

cesación (se•sâ•syon´) *f.* cessation, ceasing, pause, discontinuation.

cesante (se•sân´te) *m.* dismissed public official; —, *adj.* jobless, out of a job.

cesar (se•sâr´) *vn.* to cease, to quit, to stop.

cesáreo, rea (se•sâ´re•o, re•â) *adj.* Caesarean; **operación —**

rea, Caesarean section.

cesión (se•syon´) f. cession, transfer.

césped (ses´peth) m. grass, lawn.

cesta (ses´tâ) f. basket; scoop *(del pelotari).*

cesto (ses´to) m. large basket; cestus *(de pugilista).*

cetrino, na (se•trē´no, nâ) *adj.* citrine; jaundiced *(de rostro);* *(fig.)* melancholy, somber.

cetro (se´tro) m. scepter.

cibernética (sē•ver•ne´tē•kâ) f. cybernetics.

cicatriz (sē•kâ•trēs´) f. scar.

ciclismo (sē•klēz´mo) m. bicycling.

ciclista (sē•klēs´tâ) m. and f. cyclist, bicyclist.

ciclo (sē´klo) m. cycle.

ciclón (sē•klon´) m. cyclone.

cicuta (sē•sū´tâ) f. (bot.) hemlock.

cidro (sē´thro) m. citron tree.

ciego, ga (sye´go, gâ) *adj.* blind; —, *n.* blind person; **a —gas,** blindly; **vuelo a —gas,** blind flying.

cielo (sye´lo) m. sky, heaven; climate, weather; **— de la cama,** bed canopy; **— de la boca,** roof of the mouth, palate; **— máximo,** (avi.) ceiling.

ciempiés (syem•pyes´) m. centipede.

cien (syen´) *adj.* one hundred (used before a noun).

ciencia (syen´syâ) f. science; **—s físicas,** physical science; **a — cierta,** with certainty; **hombre de —,** scientist.

cieno (sye´no) m. mud, mire.

científicamente (syen•tē•fē•kâ•men´te) *adv.* scientifically.

científico, ca (syen•tē´fē•ko, kâ) *adj.* scientific; m. scientist.

ciento (syen´to) *adj.* one hundred; —, *m.* a hundred; **por —,** per cent; **tanto por —,** percentage.

cierre (sye´rre) m. closing; **— relámpago,** zipper; **— de los libros,** (com.) closing of the books.

cierto, ta (syer´to, tâ) *adj.* certain; confident, sure *(seguro);* **noticias —s,** definite news; **por — to,** certainly.

ciervo (syer´vo) m. deer, stag; **— volante,** stag beetle.

cifra (sē´frâ) f. cipher, number *(número);* abbreviation *(abreviatura);* monogram *(monograma);* code *(escritura secreta).*

cifrar (sē•frâr´) *va.* to write in code, to code; to abridge *(resumir);* **— la esperanza en,** to place one's hope in.

cigarra (sē•gâ´rrâ) f. cicada, locust.

cigarrero, ra (sē•gâ•rre´ro, râ) *m.* cigar maker.

cigarrillo (sē•gâ•rrē´yo) *m.* cigarette.

cigarro (sē•gâ´rro) *m.* cigar; cigarette *(de papel).*

cigüeña (sē•gwe´nyâ) *f.* (orn.) stork; (mech.) crank.

cilantro (sē•lân´tro) or **culantro** (kū•lân´tro) *m.* (bot.) coriander.

cilíndrico, ca (sē•lēn´drē•ko, kâ) *adj.* cylindncal.

cilindro (sē•lēn´dro) *m.* cylinder.

cima (sē´mâ) *f.* summit, peak, top.

cimbra (sēm´brâ) *f.* (arch.) intrados.

cimbrar (sēm•brâr´) or **cimbrear** (sēm•bre•âr´) *va.* to swing, to shake, to sway; to bend *(doblar);* — **a alguno,** to give someone a beating.

cimentar* (sē•men•târ´) *va.* to lay the foundation of; to found, to establish *(fundar);* (fig.) to affirm; (min.) to refine.

cimiento (se•myen´to) *m.* (fig.) foundation, base; —**s,** *pl.* (arch.) foundation.

cinc (sēngk) *m.* zinc.

cincel (sēn•sel´) *m.* chisel.

cincelar (sēn•se•lâr´) *va.* to chisel.

cinco (sēng´ko) *adj.* and *m.* five.

cincuenta (sēng•kwen´tâ) *m.* and *adj.* fifty.

cincha (sēn´châ) *f.* girth, cinch.

cine (sē´ne) or **cinematógrafo** (se•ne•mâ•to´grâ•fo) *m.* motion-picture projector *(aparato);* movie theater *(sala).*

cinematografía (sē•ne•mâ •to•grâ•fē´â) *f.* cinematography.

cinética (sē•ne´tē•kâ) *f.* kinetics.

cínico, ca (sē´nē• ko, kâ) *adj.* cynical.

cinta (sēn´tâ) *f.* ribbon, band; — **de medir,** tape measure; — **de teletipo,** (com.) ticker tape; — **trasportadora,** conveyor belt.

cinto (sēn´to) *m.* belt, girdle.

cintura (sēn•tū´râ) *f.* waist; belt *(ceñidor).*

cinturón (sēn•tū•ron´) *m.* belt; — **salvavidas,** life belt; — **de seguridad,** safety belt.

ciprés (sē•pres´) *m.* cypress tree.

circo (sēr´ko) *m.* circus.

circuito (sēr•kwē´to) *m.* circuit; hookup, network *(de comunicaciones).*

circulación (sēr•kū•lâ•syon´) *f.* circulation; traffic *(del tráfico).*

circular (sēr•kū•lâr´) *adj.* circular, round; **carta —,** circular letter; —, *va.* and *vn.* to circulate.

círculo (sēr´kū•lo) *m.* circle; circumference *(circumferencia);* sphere, province *(extensión);* club *(sociedad).*

circuncidar (sēr•kūn•sē•thâr´)

va. to circumcise.

circuncisión (sēr•kūn•sē•syon´)
f. circumcision.

circundar (sēr•kūn•dâr´) *va.* to
surround, to encircle.

circunferencia
(sēr•kūm•fe•ren´syâ) *f.* circumference.

circunscribir*
(sēr•kūns•krē•vēr´) *va.* to circumscribe.

circunstancia (sēr•kūns•tân´syâ)
f. circumstance.

circunstancial (sēr
•kūns•tân•syâl´) *adj.* circumstantial.

circunstante (sēr•kūns•tân´te)
adj. surrounding, attending; —
s, *m. pl.* bystanders, audience.

cirio (sē´ryo) *m.* wax candle.

ciruela (sē•rwe´lâ) *f.* plum; —
seca or — **pasa**, prune.

ciruelo (sē•rwe´lo) *m.* plum tree.

cirugía (sē•rū•hē´â) *f.* surgery.

cirujano (sē•rū•hâ´no) *m.* surgeon.

cisne (sēz´ne) *m.* swan; (fig.)
outstanding poet or musician.

cisterna (sēs•ter´nâ) *f.* cistern,
tank, reservoir.

cita (sē´tâ) *f.* date, appointment;
citation, quotation *(nota).*

citación (sē•tâ•syon´) *f.* summons, citation.

citado, da (sē•tâ´tho, thâ) *adj.*
mentioned, quoted.

citar (sē•tar´) *va.* to make an
appointment with; to call together, to convoke *(convocar);* to
cite, to quote *(alegar);* (law) to
summon, to cite.

cítrico, ca (sē´trē•ko, kâ) *adj.*
citric.

ciudad (syū•thâth´) *f.* city; —
natal, city of birth, home town.

ciudadanía (syū•thâ•thâ•nē´â) *f.*
citizenship.

ciudadano, na (syū•thâ•thâ´no,
nâ) *n.* citizen; —, *adj.* civic,
city.

ciudadela (syū•thâ•the´lâ) *f.*
citadel.

cívico, ca (sē´vē•ko, kâ) *adj.*
civic.

civil (sē•vēl´) *adj.* civil; polite,
courteous *(sociable).*

civilización (sē•vē•lē•sâ•syon´) *f.*
civilization.

civilizador, ra (sē•vē•lē•sâ•thor´,
râ) *adj.* civilizing.

civilizar (sē•vē•lē•sâr´) *va.* to
civilize.

civismo (sē•vēz´mo) *m.* patriotism.

cizaña (sē•sâ´nyâ) *f.* (bot.) dar-
nel; bad influence, rotten apple
(lo que daña); unrest, disagreement *(disensión);* **meter —,** to
sow discord.

clamar (klâ•mâr´) *vn.* to cry out,
to call out.

clamor (klâ•mor´) *m.* clamor,

outcry; death knells *(de campa-nas)*.

clamoroso, sa (klâ•mo•ro′so, sâ) *adj.* clamorous.

clan (klân) *m.* clan.

clandestino, na (klân•des•tē′no, nâ) *adj.* clandestine, secret, concealed.

clara (klâ′râ) *f.* egg white; brief letup in the rain *(de la lluvia)*.

clarete (klâ•re′te) or **vino —,** *m.* claret wine.

claridad (klâ•rē•thâth′) *f.* clearness, clarity.

clarificar (klâ•rē•fē•kâr′) *va.* to illuminate, to brighten; to clarify, to clear up *(aclarar)*.

clarín (klâ•rēn′) *m.* bugle, trumpet; trumpeter *(el que toca)*.

clarinete (klâ•rē•ne′te) *m.* clarinet; clarinet player *(músico)*.

clarividencia (klâ•rē•vē•then′syâ) *f.* clairvoyance.

claro, ra (klâ′ro, râ) *adj.* clear; bright *(luminoso)*; light *(de color)*; thin *(ralo)*; evident, obvious *(evidente)*; **poner en —ro,** to set right; **—,** *m.* opening *(abertura)*; space *(espacio)*; **¡—ro!** *interj.* of course!

clase (klâ′se) *f.* class; classroom *(aula)*; kind *(especie)*; **— media,** middle class.

clásico, ca (klâ′sē•ko, kâ) *adj.* classical, classic.

clasificación (klâ•sē•fē•kâ•syon′) *f.* classification.

clasificar (klâ•sē•fē•kâr′) *va.* to classify, to class, to put in order.

claustro (klâ′ūs•tro) *m.* cloister.

cláusula (klâ′ū•sū•lâ) *f.* clause.

clausura (klâū•sū′râ) *f.* cloister *(recinto)*; cloistered life *(vida religiosa)*; vows of seclusion *(obligación)*; closing *(cierre)*.

clausurar (klâū•sū•râr′) *va.* to close, to suspend operation of.

clavar (klâ•vâr′) *va.* to drive in, to stick *(introducir)*; to nail *(asegurar)*; (fig.) to cheat, to deceive *(engañar)*; **— la mirada en, — la vista en,** to stare at, to fix one′s gaze on.

clave (klâ′ve) *f.* key; (mus.) clef; **palabra —,** key word; **—,** *m.* harpsichord, clavichord.

clavícula (klâ•vē′kū•lâ) *f.* (anat.) clavicle, collarbone.

clavija (klâ•vē′hâ) *f.* pin; (elec.) plug; (mus.) peg.

clavo (klâ′vo) *m.* nail; corn *(callo)*; **— de olor, — de especia,** clove.

claxon (klâk′son) *m.* (Mex.) auto horn.

clemencia (kle•men′syâ) *f.* clemency, mercy.

clerical (kle•rē•kâl′) *adj.* clerical, pertaining to the clergy.

clérigo (kle′rē•go) *m.* clergyman.

clero (kleˊro) *m.* clergy.

cliente (klyenˊte) *m.* and *f.* client, customer.

clientela (klyen•teˊlâ) *f.* clientele, patronage.

clima (klēˊmâ) *m.* climate; — **artificial**, air conditioning.

climatérico, ca (klē•mâ•teˊrē•ko, kâ) *adj.* climacteric.

climatológico, ca (klē•mâ•to•loˊhē•ko, kâ) *adj.* climatological.

clínica (klēˊnē•kâ) *f.* clinic.

clínico, ca (klēˊnē•ko, kâ) *adj.* clinical.

cloaca (klo•âˊkâ) *f.* sewer.

cloro (kloˊro) *m.* (chem) chlorine.

clorofila (klo•ro•fēˊlâ) *f.* chlorophyll.

cloroformo (klo•ro•forˊmo) *m.* chloroform.

cloruro (klo•rūˊro) *m.* (chem.) chloride.

club (klūv) *m.* club, association.

clueca (klweˊkâ) *adj.* brooding; —, *f.* brooder.

clueco, ca (klweˊko, kâ) *adj.* (coll.) decrepit.

cm. or c/m: centímetro cm. centimeter.

coacción (ko•âk•syonˊ) *f.* coaction, compulsion.

coadyuvar (ko•âth•yū•vârˊ) *va.* to help, to assist.

coagular (ko•â•gū•lârˊ) *va.* and *vr.* to coagulate, to curd.

coágulo (ko•âˊgū•lo) *m.* blood clot *(de sangre);* coagulum, clot.

coalición (ko•â•lē•syonˊ) *f.* coalition, confederacy.

coartación (ko•âr•tâ•syonˊ). *f.* limitation, restriction.

coartada (ko•âr•tâˊthâ) *f.* (law) alibi.

coartar (ko•âr•târˊ) *va.* to limit, to restrict, to restrain.

cobarde (ko•vârˊthe) *adj.* cowardly, timid; —, *m.* and *f.* coward.

cobardía (ko•vâr•thēˊâ) *f.* cowardice.

cobertizo (ko•ver•tēˊso) *m.* shed; — **para automóvil**, carport.

cobija (ko•vēˊhâ) *f.* gutter tile *(teja);* covering *(cubierta);* (Mex.) blanket *(manta);* (Sp. Am.) thatch *(de paja).*

cobijar (ko•vē•hârˊ) *va.* to cover; (fig.) to shelter, to protect; (Sp. Am.) to thatch, to cover with thatch *(con paja).*

cobra (koˊvrâ) *f.* (zool.) cobra.

cobrador (ko•vrâ•thôrˊ) *m.* collector; conductor *(de tranvía).*

cobrar (ko•vrârˊ) *va.* to collect *(una cantidad);* to recover *(recuperar);* to charge *(un precio);* to cash *(un cheque);* to acquire *(adquirir);* to pull in *(una soga);* —**ánimo,** to take courage; — **fuerzas,** to gain strength; — **impuestos,** to tax; **letras** or **efectos a —,** bills receivable.

cobre (ko´vre) *m.* copper; set of copper kitchenware *(batería de cocina);* **moneda de —,** copper coin.

cobrizo, za (ko•vrē´so, sâ) *adj.* coppery.

cobro (ko´vro) *m.* collection; **presentar al —,** to present for payment or collection.

cocción (kok•syon´) *f.* cooking.

cocer* (ko•ser´) *va.* to boil *(el té);* to cook; to bake *(el pan);* —, *vn.* to boil; to ferment; —**se,** to suffer for a long time.

cocido, da (ko•sē´tho, thâ) *adj.* cooked; boiled; (fig.) skilled, experienced *(experimentado);* —, *m.* Spanish stew.

cociente (ko•syen´te) *m.* quotient.

cocina (ko•sē´nâ) *f.* kitchen; cuisine *(arte);* — **económica,** cooking range.

cocinar (ko•sē•nâr´) *va.* to cook; —, *vn.* to meddle.

cocinero, ra (ko•sē•ne´ro, râ) *n.* cook.

coco (ko´ko) *m.* coconut *(fruto);* coconut palm *(árbol);* bogeyman *(fantasma);* **agua de —,** coconut water; **hacer —s,** to flirt.

cocodrilo (ko•ko•thrē´lo) *m.* cro-

codile.

coctel (kok•tel´) *m.* cocktail.

coche (ko´che) *m.* coach, carriage; auto-mobile, car *(automóvil).*

cochera (ko•che´râ) *f.* coach house *(para carruajes);* garage.

cochina (ko•chē´nâ) *f. sow.*

cochinilla (ko•chē•nē´yâ) *f.* wood louse; cochineal *(colorante).*

cochino, na (ko•chē´no, nâ) *adj.* dirty, nasty, filthy, messy; —, *m. pig.*

codazo (ko•thâ´so) *m.* blow with the elbow.

codear (ko•the•âr´) *vn.* to elbow; —**se con,** to hobnob with.

códice (ko´thē•se) *m.* codex.

codicia (ko•thē´syâ) *f.* covetousness, greed, cupidity.

codiciar (ko•thē•syâr´) *va.* to covet, to desire eagerly.

codicioso, sa (ko•thē•syo´so, sâ) *adj.* greedy, covetous; diligent, laborious *(hacendoso).*

código (ko´thē•go) *m.* code.

codo (ko´tho) *m.* elbow; **dar de —,** to elbow; **charlar hasta por los —s,** to talk a blue streak.

codo, da (ko´tho, thâ) *adj.* (Mex. coll.) stingy, cheap.

codorniz (ko•thor•nēs´) *f.* (orn.) quail.

coeficiente (ko•e•fē•syen´te) *m.* coefficient; — **de seguridad,** safety factor.

coerción (ko•er•syon´) *f.* coercion, restraint.

coercitivo, va (ko•er•sē•tē´vo, vâ) *adj.* coercive.

coexistencia (ko•ek•sēs•ten´syâ) *f.* coexistence.

coexistir (ko•ek•sēs•tēr´) *vn.* to coexist.

cofre (ko´fre) *m.* coffer, chest.

cogedor (ko•he•thor´) *m.* collector, gatherer; dustbin *(cajón)*; dustpan *(cucharón)*.

coger (ko•her´) *va.* to catch, to get hold of, to grab *(asir)*; to occupy *(ocupar)*; to gather *(recoger)*; to catch by surprise *(sorprender)*.

cogote (ko•go´te) *m.* nape of the neck.

coheredero, ra (ko•e•re•the´ro, râ) *n.* joint heir or heiress.

coherencia (ko•e•ren´syâ) *f.* coherence.

coherente (ko•e•ren´te) *adj.* coherent; cohesive *(cohesivo)*.

cohesión (ko•e•syon´) *f.* cohesion.

cohete (ko•e´te) *m.* skyrocket *(artificio de fuego)*; rocket; — **espacial,** space rocket.

cohibir (ko•ē•vēr´) *va.* to restrain, to curb.

cohorte (ko•or´te) *f.* cohort; — **de males,** series of misfortunes, streak of bad luck.

coincidencia (ko•ēn•sē•then´syâ) *f.* coincidence.

coincidente (ko•ēn•sē•then´te) *adj.* coincident.

coincidir (ko•ēn•sē•thēr´) *vn.* to coincide.

coito (ko´ē•to) *m.* coitus.

cojear (ko•he•âr´) *vn.* to halt, to limp; to wobble *(un mueble)*; (coll.) to get off the straight and narrow.

cojera (ko•he´râ) *f.* lameness, limping.

cojín (ko•hēn´) *m.* cushion.

cojinete (ko•hē•ne´te) *m.* (mech.) bearing; small cushion; — **de bolas,** ball bearing; — **de rodillos,** roller bearing.

col (kol) *f.* cabbage.

cola (ko´lâ) *f.* tail; train *(de vestido)*; line *(hilera de personas)*; glue *(pasta)* **a la —,** behind; **hacer —,** to stand in line.

colaboración (ko•lâ•vo•râ•syon´) *f.* collaboration.

colaborar (ko•lâ•vo•râr´) *vn.* to collaborate.

coladera (ko•lâ•the´râ) *f.* strainer, colander.

colador (ko•lâ•thor´) *m.* colander, strainer.

colapso (ko•lâp´so) *m.* (med.) prostration, collapse.

colar* (ko•lâr´) *va.* to strain; to confer *(beneficio o grado)*; to pass off *(en virtud de engaño)*; **—,** *vi.* to squeeze through; **—se,**

to crash, to sneak in.

colateral (ko•lâ•te•râl´) *adj.* collateral.

colcha (kol´châ) *f.* bedspread, quilt.

colchón (kol•chon´) *m.* mattress; — **de muelles,** spring mattress; — **de pluma,** feather mattress; — **de viento,** air mattress.

colección (kol•lek•syon´) *f.* collection.

colecta (ko•lek´tâ) *f.* assessment *(de tributos);* offering *(caritativa);* collect *(oración).*

colectar (ko•lek•târ´) *va.* to collect.

colectividad (ko•lek•tē•vē•thâth´) *f.* collectivity.

colectivo, va (ko•lek•tē´vo, vâ) *adj.* collective, aggregated; **con- trato —,** group contract; **socie- dad —va,** general partner- ship.

colector (ko•lek•tor´) *m.* collec- tor, gatherer.

colega (ko•le´gâ) *m.* and *f.* col- league.

colegial (ko•le•hyâl´) *m.* colle- gian, student; —, *adj.* colle- giate, college.

colegiala (ko•le•hyâ´lâ) *f.* woman collegian.

colegio (ko•le´hyo) *m.* college; private school, academy *(escuela).*

cólera (ko´le•râ) *f.* anger, rage,

fury; **montar en —,** to fly into a rage; —, *m.* (med.) cholera.

colérico, ca (ko•le´rē•ko, kâ) *adj.* choleric; suffering from cholera *(enfermo de cólera).*

colesterol (ko•les•te•rol´) *m.* (med.) cholesterol.

colgadero (kol•gâ•the´ro) *m.* hook; clothesline

colgante (kol•gân´te) *adj.* sus- pended, hanging; **puente —,** suspension bridge.

colgar* (kol•gâr´) *va.* to hang, to suspend; to decorate with han- gings *(adornar);* —, *vn.* to be suspended.

colibrí (ko•lē•vrē´) *m.* humming- bird.

cólico (ko´lē•ko) *m.* colic.

coliflor (ko•lē•flor´) *f.* cauliflower.

colilla (ko•lē´yâ) *f.* cigarette butt.

colina (ko•lē´nâ) *f.* hill.

coliseo (ko•lē•se´o) *m.* coliseum.

colmar (kol•mâr´) *va.* to heap up, to fill up; — **con,** (fig.) to shower with.

colmillo (kol•mē´yo) *m.* eyetooth; tusk *(del elefante);* **tener—,** to be sly.

colocación (ko•lo•kâ•syon´) *f.* placement *(acción);* situation, position.

colocar (ko•lo•kâr´) *va.* to situa- te, to place; — **dinero,** to invest money.

colon (ko´lon) *m.* (anat.) colon,

large intestine.

Colón (ko•lon´) Columbus.

colón (ko•lon´) *m.* monetary unit of Costa Rica and El Salvador.

colonia (ko•lo´nyâ) *f.* colony; (Cuba) sugar-cane field *(de azúcar);* (Mex.) subdivision, neighborhood *(barrio).*

colonial (ko•lo•nyâl´) *adj.* colonial.

colonización (ko•lo•nē•sâ•syon´) *f.* colonization.

colonizar (ko•lo•nē•sâr´) *va.* to colonize.

coloquio (ko•lo´kyo) *m.* colloquy; chat, conversation *(plática).*

color (ko•lor´) *m.* color; rouge *(colorete);* **este — destiñe,** this color fades.

colorado,da (ko•lo•râ´tho, thâ)*adj.* ruddy, red.

colorante (ko•lo•rân´te) *m.* coloring.

colorar (ko•lo•râr´) *va.* to color; to tint, to dye *(teñir).*

colorear (ko•lo•re•âr´) *va.* to color; (fig.) to palliate, to cover up *(disimular);* **—,** *vn.* to grow red.

colorido (ko•lo•rē´tho) *m.* coloring; pretext, pretense *(pretexto).*

colosal (ko•lo•sâl´) *adj.* colossal, great.

coloso (ko•lo´so) *m.* colossus.

columna (ko•lūm´nâ) *f.* column.

columnata (ko•lūm•na´tâ) *f.* colonnade.

columpiarse (ko•lūm•pyâr´se) *vr.* to swing.

columpio (ko•lūm´pyo) *m.* swing.

collar (ko•yâr´) *m.* necklace *(adorno);* collar.

coma (ko´mâ) *f.* comma; **—,** *m.* (med.) coma.

comadre (ko•mâ´thre) *f.* midwife *(partera);* godmother of one's child *(madrina);* close friend, crony *(amiga).*

comadreja (ko•mâ•thre´hâ) *f.* weasel.

comadrona (ko•mâ•thro´nâ) *f.* midwife.

comandancia (ko•mân•dân´syâ) *f.* command.

comandante (ko•mân•dân´te) *m.* commander, chief; major *(de batallón).*

comandar (ko•mân•dâr´) *va.* (mil.) to command.

comando (ko•mân´do) *m.* (mil.) commando.

comarca (ko•mâr´kâ) *f.* territory, district, region.

comatoso, sa (ko•mâ•to´so, sâ) *adj.* (med.) comatose.

combate (kom•bâ´te) *m.* combat, struggle; (fig.) conflict; **fuera de —,** out of action; (fig.) out of the running; **aeroplano de—,** fighter plane.

combatidor (kom•bâ•tē•thor´) *m.*

combatant.

combatiente (kom•bâ•tyen´te) *m.* combatant; **no —,** non-combatant.

combatir (kom•bâ•tēr´) *va.* and *vn.* to combat, to struggle, to fight.

combinación (kom•bē•nâ•syon´) *f.* combination.

combinar (kom•bē•nâr´) *va.* and *vr.* to combine.

combustible (kom•būs•tē´vle) *adj.* combustible; **—,** *m.* fuel.

combustión (kom•būs•tyon´) *f.* combustion.

comedia (ko•me´thyâ) *f.* comedy, play.

comediante, ta (ko•me•thyân´te, tâ) *n.* actor, comedian.

comedido, da (ko•me•thē´tho, thâ) *adj.* polite, courteous.

comedor, ra (ko•me•thor´, râ) *n.* eater; **—,** *m.* dining room.

comentador, ra (ko•men•tâ•thor´, râ) *n.* commentator.

comentar (ko•men•târ´) *va.* to comment on, to remark, to speak of.

comentario (ko•men•tâ´ryo) *m.* comment, commentary.

comenzar* (ko•men•sâr´) *va.* and *vn.* to commence, to begin.

comer (ko•mer´) *va.* to eat; to eat away, to consume *(gastar);* to take *(ajedrez y damas);* **—,** *vn.*

to have dinner; **dar de —,** to feed; **—se,** to skip over, to jump.

comercial (ko•mer•syâl´) *adj.* commercial.

comerciante (ko•mer•syân´te) *m.* trader, merchant, tradesman.

comerciar (ko•mer•syâr´) *va.* to trade, to do business, to have dealings; **— en,** to deal in.

comercio (ko•mer´syo) *m.* trade, commerce, business; communication, inter-course *(comunicación);* **en el —,** in the shops; **junta de —,** board of trade.

comestible (ko•mes•tē´vle) *adj.* edible; **—s,** *m. pl.* foodstuffs, groceries, food; **tienda de —s,** grocery store.

cometa (ko•me´tâ) *m.* comet; **—,** *f.* kite.

cometer (ko•me•ter´) *va.* to commit; to entrust, to charge *(encargar).*

comezón (ko•me•son´) *f.* itch; (fig.) burning desire, fervent wish.

comicios (ko•mē´syos) *m. pl.* election, voting.

cómico, ca (ko´mē•ko, kâ) *adj.* comic, comical, funny; **—,** *m.* actor, comedian; **—,** *f.* actress, comedienne.

comida (ko•mē´thâ) *f.* eating; food *(alimento);* meal *(habitual);* dinner *(principal);* **—**

chatarra, junk food;— **para llevar,** take-out;— **rápida,** fast food.

comienzo (ko•myen´so) *m.* beginning.

comillas (ko•mē´yâs) *f. pl.* quotation marks; **entre —,** in quotation marks.

comino (ko•mē´no) *m.* cumin; **no valer un —,** to be absolutely worthless.

comisaría (ko•mē•sâ•rē´â) *f.* commissariat *(oficina);* commissioner´s duties.

comisario (ko•mē•sâ´ryo) *m.* commissary, deputy, commissioner; (Sp. Am.) police inspector *(de policía).*

comisión (ko•mē•syon´) *f.* commission; errand *(encargo);* **—,** on commission.

comisionado (ko•mē•syo•nâ´tho) *m.* commissioner.

comisionar (ko•mē•syo•nâr´) *va.* to commission.

comisionista (ko•mē•syo•nēs´tâ) *m.* commission agent, salesman on commission.

comité (ko•mē•te´) *m.* committee.

comitiva (ko•mē•tē´va) *f.* suite, retinue, cortege, followers.

como (ko´mo) *adv.* and *conj.* (*interr.* **cómo**) as *(lo mismo que);* such as, like *(tal como);* almost *(casi);* how *(de qué manera);* why *(por qué);* — **quiera que,** whereas, inasmuch as; however, no matter how; **¿a cómo estamos?** what is the date?

cómoda (ko´mo•thâ) *f.* chest of drawers.

comodidad (ko•mo•thē•thâth´) *f.* comfort, ease, convenience; profit, interest *(interés).*

cómodo, da (ko´mo•tho, thâ) *adj.* convenient, commodious, comfortable.

compacto, ta (kom•pâk´to, tâ) *adj.* compact, close; (fig.) thick, dense *(apiñado).*

compadecer* (kom•pâ•the•ser´) *va.* to pity, to sympathize with; **—se de,** to take pity on.

compadre (kom•pâ´thre) *m.* godfather of one´s child *(padrino);* close friend, crony *(amigo).*

compaginar (kom•pâ•hē•nâr´) *va.* (print.) to page; to put in order *(ordenar).*

compañero, ra (kom•pâ•nye´ro, râ) *n.* companion, comrade; fellow, mate; **— de cuarto** roommate; **— de destierro,** fellow exile; **— de viaje,** traveling companion.

compañía (kom•pâ•nyē´â) *f.* company.

comparable (kom•pâ•râ´vle) *adj.* comparable.

comparación (kom•pâ•râ•syon´)

f. comparison.

comparar (kom•pâ•râr´) *va.* to compare.

comparecer* (kom•pâ•re•ser´) *vn.* to appear.

compartir (kom•pâr•tēr´) *va.* to divide, to share.

compás (kom•pâs´) *m.* pair of compasses; calipers; (mus.) measure, time; (naut.) compass; (fig.) rule, guide.

compasión (kom•pâ•syon´) *f.* compassion, pity.

compasivo, va (kom•pâ•sē´vo, va) *adj.* compassionate.

compatible (kom•pâ•tē´vle) *adj.* compatible.

compatriota (kom•pâ•tryo´tâ) *m.* and *f.* fellow countryman, compatriot.

compeler (kom•pe•ler´) *va.* to compel, to constrain.

compendiar (kom•pen•dyâr´) *va.* to summarize.

compendio (kom•pen´dyo) *m.* summary, compendium.

compensación (kom•pen•sâ•syon´) *f.* compensation, recompense; **casa de —,** clearing house.

compensar (kom•pen•sâr´) *va.* and *vn.* to compensate, to make amends, to recompense.

competencia (kom•pe•ten´syâ) *f.* competition, rivalry; competence *(aptitud).*

competente (kom•pe•ten´te) *adj.* competent; sufficient, adequate, just *(propio).*

competer (kom•pe•ter´) *vn.* to be one´s due, to be incumbent on one, to be in one´s competence.

competir* (kom•pe•tēr´) *vn.* to vie, to contend, to compete, to rival.

compilar (kom•pē•lâr´) *va.* to compile.

compinche (kom•pēn´che) *m.* (coll.) comrade, confidant, crony.

complacer* (kom•plâ•ser´) *va.* to please; **—se,** to be pleased, to be happy.

complejidad (kom•ple•hē•thâth´) *f.* complexity.

complejo (kom•ple´ho) *m.* complex; **—, ja,** *adj.* complex, intricate.

complementario, ria (kom•ple•men•tâ•ryo, ryâ) *adj.* complementary.

complemento (kom•ple•men´to) *m.* complement; completion *(plenitud);* (gram.) object.

completar (kom•ple•tar´) *va.* to complete.

completo, ta (kom•ple´to, tâ) *adj.* complete; perfect, all-round *(acabado);* **por —to,** completely.

complexión (kom•plek•syon´) *f.* constitution, physique.

complicar (kom•plē•kâr´) *va.* to

complicate.

cómplice (kom′plē•se) *m.* and *f.* accomplice.

complicidad (kom•plē•sē•thâth′) *f.* complicity.

complot (kom•plot′) *m.* plot, conspiracy.

componer* (kom•po•ner′) *va.* to compose; (math.) to compound; to form, to make up *(formar);* to mend, to repair *(reparar);* to strengthen, to restore *(restaurar);* to prepare, to mix *(aderezar);* to adjust, to settle, to reconcile *(reconciliar);* to calm *(moderar);* **—se,** to make up, to put on makeup; **—se de,** to be composed of.

composición (kom•po•sē•syon′) *f.* composition; composure *(mesura);* adjustment, agreement *(ajuste).*

compositor, ra (kom•po•sē•tor′, râ) *n.* composer.

compostura (kom•pos•tū′râ) *f.* composition *(construcción);* mending, repair *(reparo);* neatness *(aseo);* agreement, adjustment *(convenio);* composure, circumspection *(mesura).*

compra (kom′ prâ) *f.* purchase; day′s shopping *(para el gasto diario);* **—s,** *pl.* purchases; **—s al contado,** cash purchases; **ir de —s,** to go shopping.

comprador, ra (kom•prâ•thor′, râ) *n.* buyer, purchaser.

comprar (kom•prâr′) *va.* to buy, to purchase; **— al contado,** to buy for cash; **— al crédito** or **al fiado,** to buy on credit; **— al por mayor (menor),** to buy at wholesale (retail); **— de ocasión,** to buy secondhand.

comprender (kom•pren•der′) *va.* to include, to contain, to comprise *(contener);* to comprehend, to understand *(entender).*

comprensión (kom•pren•syon′) *f.* comprehension, understanding.

comprensivo, va (kom•pren•sē′vo, vâ) *adj.* comprehensive.

compresión (kom•pre•syon′) *f.* compression, pressure.

comprimir (kom•prē•mēr′) *va.* to compress, to condense; to repress, to restrain *(reprimir);* **—se,** to restrain oneself, to control oneself.

comprobante (kom•pro•vân′te) *adj.* proving; **—,** *m.* voucher, receipt.

comprobar* (kom•pro•vâr′) *va.* to verify, to check, to confirm, to prove.

compromiso (kom•pro•mē′so) *m.* engagement *(esponsales);* compromise *(convenio);* pledge, commitment *(obligación);* compromising position *(embarazo).*

compuerta (kom•pwer′tâ) *f.* floodgate, half door *(media puerta).*

compuesto (kom•pwes′to) *m.* compound; —, **ta,** *adj.* compound, composed.

compulsión (kom•pūl•syon′) *f.* compulsion.

compulsivo, va (kom•pūl•sē′vo, vâ) *adj.* compulsive.

compulsorio, ria (kom•pūl•so′ryo, ryâ) *adj.* compulsory.

computación (kom•pū•tâ•syon′) *f.* computation.

computador, ra (kom•pu•tâ•thor′, râ) *n.* computer; —**ra digital,** digital computer.

computar (kom•pū•târ′) *va.* to compute.

cómputo (kom′pū•to) *m.* computation, calculation.

comulgar (ko•mūl•gâr′) *va.* to administer Communion to; —, *vn.* to take Communion.

común (ko•mūn′) *adj.* common; **acciones en** —, common stock; **de** — **acuerdo,** by mutual consent; **en** —, jointly; **poco** —, unusual; **por lo** —, in general, generally; —, *m.* community, people; water-closet *(retrete).*

comuna (ko•mū′nâ) *f.* town hall, municipality.

comunal (ko•mū•nâl′) *m.* commonalty, common people; —, *adj.* community, communal.

comunicación (ko•mū•nē•kâ•syon′) *f.* communication, message; — **radioeléctrica,** radio message.

comunicar (ko•mū•nē•kâr′) *va.* and *vr.* to communicate.

comunicativo, va (ko•mū•nē•kâ•te′vo, vâ) *adj.* communicative.

comunidad (ko•mū•nē•thâth′) *f.* community.

comunión (ko•mū•nyon′) (eccl.) Communion; communication, intercourse.

comunismo (ko•mū•nēz′mo) *m.* communism.

comunista (ko•mū•nēs′tâ) *m.* and *f.* communist.

con (kon) *prep.* with; despite *(a pesar de);* — **que,** then, therefore; — **tal que,** on condition that; **dar** —, to find; **tratar** —, to do business with, to deal with.

concavidad (kong•kâ•vē•thâth′) *f.* concavity.

cóncavo, va (kong′kâ•vo, va) *adj.* concave.

concebir* (kon•se•vēr′) *va.* and *vn.* to conceive.

conceder (kon•se•ther′) *va.* to grant, to concede.

concejal (kon•se•hâl′) *m.* councilman, councilor.

concejo (kon•se′ho) *m.* town council.

concentración (kon•sen•trâ•syon′) *f.* concentration; **campo de —,** concentration camp.

concentrado, da (kon•sen•trâ′tho, thâ) *adj.* concentrated.

concentrar (kon•sen•trâr′) *va.* and vr. to concentrate.

concepción (kon•sep•syon′) *f.* conception *(acción);* idea, concept *(producto).*

concepto (kon•sep′to) *m.* concept, idea thought; judgment, opinion *(juicio);* witticism *(agudeza);* reason *(motivo);* **por todos —s,** by and large.

concerniente (kon•ser•nyen′te) *adj.* concerning, relating.

concernir* (kon•ser•nēr′) *vn.* to regard, to concern.

concertar* (kon•ser•târ′) *va.* to concert; (mus.) to harmonize; to arrange, to settle on *(un negocio);* to reconcile *(intenciones);* to set *(un hueso);* — *vn.* to agree, to be in accord.

concesión (kon•se•syon′) *f.* concession; grant *(otorgamiento).*

conciencia (kon•syen′syâ) *f.* conscience; awareness *(conocimiento).*

concienzudo, da

(kon•syen•sū′tho, thâ) *adj.* conscientious.

concierto (kon•syer′to) *m.* concert, agreement; (mus.) concert; **de —,** with one accord, in concert.

conciliación (kon•sē•lyâ•syon′) *f.* conciliation, reconciliation.

conciliar (kon•sē•lyâr′) *va.* to conciliate. to reconcile; —, *adj.* conciliar, council.

concilio (kon•sē′lyo) *m.* (eccl.) council.

conciso, sa (kon•sē′so, sâ) *adj.* concise, brief.

conciudadano, na (kon•syū•thâ•thâ′no, nâ) *n.* fellow citizen, fellow countryman.

cónclave (kong′klâ•ve) or **conclave** (kong•klâ′ve) *m.* conclave.

concluir* (kong•klwēr′) *va.* to conclude; to convince *(convencer).*

conclusión (kong•klū•syon′) *f.* conclusion.

concluso, sa (kong•klū′so, sâ) *adj.* closed, concluded.

concluyente (kong•klū•yente) *adj.* conclusive.

concordancia (kong•kor•thân′s-yâ) *f.* (gram.) agreement; (mus.) harmony; concord; —s, *pl.* concordance.

concordar* (kong•kor•thâr′) *va.* to accord; —, *vn.* to agree.

concretar (kong•kre•târ´) *va.* to combine, to unite; to make concrete, to reduce to essentials *(reducir);* **—se,** to limit oneself.

concreto, ta (kong•kre´to, tâ) *adj.* concrete, definite; **en —to,** in short.

concubina (kong•kū•vē´nâ) *f.* concubine, mistress.

concurrencia (kong•kū•rren´syâ) concurrence; coincidence *(simultaneidad);* gathering *(junta).*

concurrir (kong•kū•rrēr´) *vn.* to concur; to assemble, to gather *(juntarse).*

concurso (kong•kūr´so) *m.* concourse, crowd, assembly; help, aid *(ayuda);* presence *(asistencia);* contest *(competencia);* — **de belleza,** beauty contest; — **deportivo,** athletic meet.

concusión (kong•kū•syon´) *f.* (med.) concussion; shake, shock.

concha (kon´châ) *f.* shell; tortoise shell *(carey);* (theat.) prompter´s box.

condado (kon•dâ´tho) *m.* earldom, county.

conde (kon´de) *m.* earl, count; gypsy chief *(de los gitanos).*

condecorar (kon•de•ko•râr´) *va.* to decorate, to award a decoration.

condenable (kon•de•nâ´vle) *adj.* condemnable.

condena (kon•de´nâ) *f.* condemnation.

condenar (kon•de•nâr´) *va.* to condemn; to sentence *(pronunciar sentencia);* (eccl.) to damn; to board up, to close up *(cerrar);* **—se,** (eccl.) to be damned.

condensación (kon•den•sâ•syon´) *f.* condensation.

condensar (kon•den•sâr´) *va.* and *vr.* to condense.

condesa (kon•de´sâ) *f.* countess.

condescendencia, (kon•des•sen•d en´syâ) *f.* affability, complaisance.

condescender* (kon•des•sen•der´) *vn.* to consent, to agree.

condescendiente (kon•des•sen•dyen´te) *adj.* complaisant, obliging.

condición (kon•dē•syon´) *f.* condition; quality *(calidad);* basis *(base);* station, position *(posición);* character, nature *(carácter).*

condicional (kon•dē•syo•nâl´) *adj.* conditional.

condimentar (kon•dē•men•tar´) *va.* to season.

condimento (kon•dē•men´to) *m.* condiment, seasoning.

condiscípulo, la (kon•dēs•sē´pū•lo, lâ) *n.* fellow-student.

condolerse* (kon•do•ler´se) *vr.* to condole, to sympathize.

condominio (kon•do•mē´nyo) *m.* condominium.

condón (kon•don´) *m.* condom.

condonar (kon•do•nâr´) *va.* to pardon, to forgive, to condone.

cóndor (kon´dor) *m.* (orn.) condor.

conducción (kon•dūk•syon´) *f.* conduction; (auto.) driving; conducting, guiding *(de personas);* conveying, transport *(de mercancías).*

conducir* (kon•dū•sēr´) *va.* to transport, to convey *(cosas);* to conduct; to lead *(a personas);* — **un automóvil,** to drive an automobile; —**se** to conduct oneself, to behave oneself.

conducta (kon•dūk´tâ) *f.* leading. guiding *(conducción);* conduct, management *(gobierno);* behavior, conduct *(comportamiento).*

conductivo, va (kon•dūk•tē´vo, vâ) *adj.* conductive.

conducto (kon•dūk´to) *m.* conduit, tube; (anat.) channel, drain; **por — de,** through, by means of.

conductor, ra (kon•dūk•tor´, râ) *adj.* conductive; **hilo** or **alam-**bre —,** electric wire; —, *m.* conductor; (auto.) motorist, driver; (rail.) engineer.

condueño, ña (kon•dwe´nyo, nyâ) *n.* joint owner, partner.

conectar (ko•nek•târ´) *va.* to connect.

conejo, ja (ko•ne´ho, hâ) *n.* rabbit.

conejillo (ko•ne•hē´yo) *m.* small rabbit; — **de Indias,** guinea pig.

conexión (ko•nek•syon´) *f.* connection.

conexo, xa (ko•nek´so, sâ) *adj.* connected, united.

confeccionar (kom•fek•syo•nâr´) *va.* to make up, to put together; to prepare *(un medicamento).*

confederación (kom•fe•the•râ•syon´) *f.* confederacy, confederation.

confederado, da (kom•fe•the•râ´tho, thâ) *n.* and *adj.* confederate.

conferencia (kom•fe•ren´syâ) *f.* conference, talk *(plática);* lecture *(lección);* — **de larga distancia,** long-distance call.

conferencista (kom•fe•ren•sēs´tâ) *m.* and *f.* lecturer, speaker.

conferir* (kom•fe•rēr´) *va.* to confer, to grant.

confesar* (kom•fe•sâr´) *va.* to confess, to avow, to admit.

confesión (kom•fe•syon´) *f.* confession, avowal.

confesionario (kom•fe•syo•nâ´ryo) *m.* confessional; rules for the confessional *(reglas).*

confesor (kom•fe•sor´) *m.* confessor.

confeti (kom•fe´tē) *m.* confetti.

confiado da, (kom•fyâ´tho, thâ) *adj.* unsuspecting, credulous *(crédulo);* presumptuous.

confianza (kom•fyân´sâ) *f.* confidence, reliance *(seguridad);* self-reliance *(en si mismo).*

confiar (kom•fyâr´) *va.* to entrust, to confide *(encargar);* —, *vn.* to have faith, to rely.

confidencia (kom•fē•then´syâ) *f.* confidence.

confidencial (kom•fē•then•syâl´) *adj.* confidential.

confidente, ta (kom•fē•then´te, tâ) *n.* confidant; —, *adj.* faithful, trustworthy.

confín (kom•fēn´) *m.* limit, boundary.

confinar (kom•fē´nâr´) *va.* to confine; —, *vn.* to border.

confirmación (kom•fēr•mâ•syon´) *f.* confirmation.

confirmar (kom•fēr•mâr´) *va.* to confirm, to corroborate.

confiscación (kom•fēs•kâ•syon´) *f.* confiscation.

confiscar (kom•fēs•kâr´) *va.* to confiscate.

confitería (kom•fē•te•rē´â) *f.* confectioner´s shop.

conflicto (kom•flēk´to) *m.* conflict, fight, struggle.

confluir* (kom•flwēr´) *vn.* to join, to flow together (rim); to meet, to come together *(caminos);* to flock together, to crowd together *(gente).*

conformar (kom•for•mâr´) *va.* to conform, to make agree; —, *vn.* to conform, to agree; **—se,** to submit, to resign oneself.

conforme (kom•for´me) *adj.* conformable; **estar —,** to be in agreement; —, *adv.* according to.

conformidad (kom•for•mē•thâth´) *f.* conformity; patience, resignation *(tolerancia);* **de —,** by common consent; **de — con,** in accordance with.

confort (kom•fort´) *m.* comfort.

confortante (kom•for•tân´te) *adj.* comforting; —, *m.* sedative.

confortar (kom•for•târ´) *va.* to console, to comfort; to strengthen, to liven *(dar vigor).*

confrontar (kom•fron•târ´) *va.* to confront *(carear);* to compare *(cotejar).*

confundir (kom•fūn•dēr´) *va.* to confuse; to confound *(turbar).*

confusión (kom•fū•syon´) *f.* confusion; shame *(vergüenza).*

confuso, sa (kom•fū´so, sâ) *adj.* confused, confounded.

congelación (kon•he•lâ•syon´) *f.* freezing, — **rápida,** quick freezing.

congelador (kon•he•lâ•thor´) *m.* freezer.

congelar (kon•he•lâr´) *va.* and *vr.* to freeze, to congeal; (com.) to freeze, to immobilize.

congénito, ta (kon•he´nē•to, tâ) *adj.* congenital.

congestión (kon•hes•tyon´) *f.* (med.) congestion.

conglomerado (kong•glo•me•râ´-tho) *m.* conglomerate.

congoja (kong•go´hâ) *f.* anguish, grief, heartbreak.

congregación (kong•gre•gâ•syon´) *f.* congregation, assembly.

congregar (kong•gre•gâr´) *va.* to congregate, to assemble, to call together.

congreso (kong•gre´so) *m.* congress.

congruencia (kong•grwen´syâ) *f.* appropriateness, suitableness, congruity *(conveniencia):* congruence.

cónico, ca (ko´nē•ko, kâ) *adj.* conical.

conjetura (kon•he•tū´râ) *f.* conjecture.

conjeturar (kon•he•tū•râr´) *va.* to conjecture.

conjugación (kon•hū•gâ•syon´) *f.* (gram.) conjugation.

conjugar (kon•hū•gâr´) *va.* (gram.) to conjugate.

conjunción (kon•hūn•syon´) *f.* conjunction.

conjunto, ta (kon•hūn´to, tâ) *adj.* united, joint, conjunct; **el —,** the whole, the ensemble.

conllevar (kon•ye•vâr´) *va,* to stand, to put up with *(tolerar);* to help out with, to help bear *(ayudar).*

conmemoración (kon•me•mo•râ•syon´) *f.* commemoration.

conmemorar (kon•me•mo•râr´) *va.* to commemorate.

conmemorativo, va (kon•me•mo•râ•tē´vo, va) *adj.* memorial.

conmensurar (kon•men•sū•râr´) *va.* to commensurate.

conmiseración (kon•mē•se•râ•syon´) *f.* commiseration.

conmoción (kon•mo•syon´) *f.* tremor, quake *(sacudimiento);* shock *(del ánimo);* reaction, excitement, commotion *(tumulto).*

conmovedor, ra (kon•mo•ve•thor´, râ) *adj.* touching, moving; exciting, breath-taking, stirring.

conmover* (kon•mo•ver´) *va.* to touch, to move *(enternecer);* to stir, to excite *(inquietar).*

conmutar (kon•mū•târ´) *va.* to commute.

connatural (kon•nâ•tū•râl´) *adj.* inborn, ingrained, natural.

connivencia (kon•nē•ven´syâ) *f.* connivance.

connotación (kon•no•tâ•syon´) *f.* connotation; distant relationship *(parentesco).*

connotar (kon•no•târ´) *va.* to connote, to imply.

cono (ko´no) *m.* cone; — **de aire,** (avi.) air sleeve, air sock.

conocedor, ra (ko•no•se•thor´, râ) *n.* expert, connoisseur; —, *adj.* knowing, aware; — **de,** familiar with, expert in.

conocer* (ko•no•ser´) *va.* to know, to be acquainted with; to meet *(encontrar);* to recognize *(reconocer).*

conocido, da (ko•no•sē´tho, thâ) *n.* acquaintance; — *adj.* known.

conocimiento (ko•no•sē•myen´to) *m.* knowledge, understanding; consciousness *(facultad);* acquaintance *(conocido);* (com.) bill of lading; **poner en —,** to inform, to advise.

conquista (kong•kēs´tâ) *f.* conquest.

conquistador (kong•kēs•tâ•thor´) *m.* conqueror.

conquistar (kong•kēs•târ´) *va.* to conquer; (fig.) to convince, to win over.

consagración (kon•sâ•grâ•syon´) *f.* consecration.

consciente (kons•syen´te) *adj.* conscious.

conscripción (kons•krēp•syon´) *f.* conscription.

conscripto (kons•krep´to) *m.* draftee.

consecución (kon•se•kū•syon´) *f.* attainment.

consecuencia (kon•se•kwen´syâ) *f.* consequence, result; consistency *(correspondencia);* **como —,** in consequence, consequently; **en —,** therefore.

consecuente (kon•se•kwen´te) *m.* consequent; —, *adj.* consequent; consistent.

consecutivo, va (kon•se•kū•tē´vo, vâ) *adj.* consecutive.

conseguir* (kon•se•gēr´) *va.* to obtain, to get, to attain.

consejero, ra (kon•se•he´ro, râ) *n.* counselor, advisor; councilor *(de algún consejo).*

consejo (kon•se´ho) *m.* counsel, advice; council *(cuerpo);* — **de guerra,** courtmartial; — **directivo,** board of directors.

consenso (kon•sen´so) *m.* consensus.

consentimiento
(kon•sen•tē•myen´to) *m.* consent, assent; pampering, spoiling.

consentir* (kon•sen•tēr´) *va.* to consent to, to allow *(permitir);* to tolerate, to permit *(tolerar);* to spoil, to pamper *(mimar).*

conserje (kon•ser´he) *m.* concierge, janitor.

conserva (kon•ser´vâ) *f.* conserve, preserve; —s, *pl.* canned goods.

conservador (kon•ser•vâ•thor´) *m.* conservator, curator; (pol.) conservative; —, **ra,** *adj.* conservative.

conservar (kon•ser•vâr´) *va.* to can, to preserve *(hacer conservas);* to keep up, to maintain *(mantener);* to conserve *(cuidar de la permanencia de).*

conservatorio (kon•ser•vâ•to´ryo) *m.* conservatory; —, **ria,** *adj.* preservative.

considerable (kon•sē•the•râ´vle) *adj.* considerable; great, large *(muy grande).*

considerado, da
(kon•sē•the•râ´tho, thâ) *adj.* prudent considerate; esteemed, respected, highly considered *(respetado).*

considerar (kon•sē•the•râr´) *va.* to consider, to think over; to

respect, to think highly of *(respetar).*

consigna (kon•sēg´nâ) *f.* (mil.) watchword, countersign; (rail.) checkroom.

consigo (kon•se´go) *pron.* with oneself.

consiguiente (kon•sē•gyen´te) *adj.* consequent, resulting; —, *m.* consequence, effect; **por** —, consequently, as a result.

consistencia (kon•sēs•ten´syâ) *f.* consistence, consistency.

consola (kon•so´lâ) *f.* console table.

consolación (kon•so•lâ•syon´) *f.* consolation.

consolador, ra (kon•so•lâ•thor´, râ) *adj.* consoling, soothing; —, *n.* consoler.

consolar* (kon•so•lâr´) *va.* to console, to comfort, to soothe.

consolidación
(kon•so•lē•thâ•syon´) *f.* consolidation, merger.

consolidar (kon•so•lē•thâr´) *va.* to consolidate; (fig.) to cement, to assure; — **se,** to become consolidated.

consomé (kon•so•me´) *m.* consomme, broth.

consonante (kon•so•nân´te) *f.* (gram.) consonant; —, *m.* rhyme word; —, *adj.* consonant.

conspicuo, cua (kons•pē´kwo,

kwâ) *adj.* conspicuous, prominent, outstanding.

conspiración (kons•pē•râ•syon´) *f.* conspiracy, plot.

conspirador, ra (kons•pē•râ•thor´, râ) *n.* conspirator, plotter.

conspirar (kons•pē•râr´) *vn.* to conspire, to plot.

constancia (kons•tân´syâ) *f.* constancy, perseverance; proof *(prueba);* certainty *(certeza);* **dejar — de,** to establish, to prove.

constante (kons•tân´te) *adj.* persevering, constant; certain, sure *(cierto).*

constelación (kons•te•lâ•syon´) *f.* constellation.

consternación (kons•ter•nâ•syon´) *f.* consternation.

consternar (kons•ter•nâr´) *va.* to dismay, to consternate.

constipación (kons•tē•pâ•syon´) *f.* cold, head cold; **— de vientre,** constipation.

constipado (kons•tē•pâ´tho) *m.* cold in the head; **—do, da,** *adj.* having a head cold.

constiparse (kons•tē•pâr´se) *vr.* to catch cold.

constitución (kons•tē•tū•syon´) *f.* constitution.

constitucional (kons•tē•tū•syo•nâl´) *adj.* constitutional.

constituir* (kons•tē•twēr´) *va.* to constitute.

constituyente (kons•tē•tū•yen´te) *n.* and *adj.* constituent.

constreñimiento (kons•tre•nyē•myen´to) *m.* constraint.

constreñir* (kons•tre•nyēr´) *va.* to constrain, to force; (med.) to constipate.

construcción (kons•trūk•syon´) *f.* construction; building, structure *(obra construida).*

constructor, ra (kons•trūk•tor´, râ) *n.* builder; **—,** *adj.* building.

construir* (kons•trwēr´) *va.* to build, to construct; (gram.) to construe.

consuelo (kon•swe´lo) *m.* consolation, comfort; joy, merriment *(alegría).*

cónsul (kon´sūl) *m.* consul.

consulado (kon•sū•lâ´tho) *m.* consulate.

consulta (kon•sūl´tâ) *f.* consultation; opinion, appraisal *(opinión).*

consultar (kon•sūl•târ´) *va.* to consult; to discuss, to deal with *(deliberar).*

consultorio (kon•sūl•to´ryo) *m.* consultant´s office; clinic *(de médico).*

consumación (kon•sū•mâ•syon´)

f. consummation; termination, extinction *(acabamiento).*

consumar (kon•sū•mâr´) *va.* to consummate, to perfect.

consumidor, ra (kon•sū•mē•thor´ râ) *n.* consumer; —, *adj.* consuming.

consumir (kon•sū•mēr´) *va.* to consume, to use up; to consume, to destroy *(destruir);* —se, to waste away, to languish.

consumo (kon•sū´mo) *m.* consumption.

contabilidad (kon•tâ•vē•lē•thâth´) *f.* accounting, bookkeeping.

contacto (kon•tâk´to) *m.* contact, touch; —del magneto, (avi.) ignition switch.

contado, da (kon•tâ´tho, thâ) *adj.* scarce, rare; de —do, instantly; in hand; al —do, in cash, in ready money; $50 al —do, $50 down; tanto al —do, so much down.

contador (kon•tâ•thor´) *m.* accountant, bookkeeper; meter, gauge *(aparato);* — Geiger, Geiger counter.

contaduría (kon•tâ•thū•rē´â) *f.* accounting *(contabilidad);* accountancy *(oficio).*

contagiar (kon•tâ•hyâr´) *va.* to infect; —se, to become infected.

contagio (kon•tâ´hyo) *m.* contagion.

contagioso, sa (kon•tâ•hyo´so, sâ) *adj.* contagious, catching.

contaminación (kon•tâ•mē•nâ•syon´) *f.* contamination; (fig.) defilement, corruption.

contaminar (kon•tâ•mē•nâr´) *va.* to contaminate; (fig.) to defile, to corrupt.

contar* (kon•târ´) *va.* to count; to charge, to debit *(meter en cuenta);* to relate, to tell *(referir);* — con, to rely upon, to count on.

contemplación (kon•tem•plâ•syon´) *f.* contemplation.

contemplar (kon•tem•plâr´) *va.* to contemplate, to meditate; to indulge, to be lenient with *(complacer).*

contemplativo, va (kon•tem•plâ•tē´vo, vâ) *adj.* contemplative.

contemporáneo, nea (kon•tem•po•râ´ne•o, ne•â) *n.* and *adj.* contemporary.

contender* (kon•ten•der´) *vn.* to struggle, to contend; (fig.) to compete, to vie.

contendiente (kon•ten•dyen´te) *m.* and *f.* competitor, contender.

contener* (kon•te•ner´) *va.* to contain, to be comprised of; to hold back, to restrain *(repri-*

mir).

contenido, da (kon•te•nē´tho, thâ) *adj.* moderate, restrained; —, *m.* contents.

contentar (kon•ten•târ´) *va.* to content, to satisfy, to please; — **se,** to be pleased or satisfied.

contento, ta (kon•ten´to, tâ) *adj.* glad, pleased, content; —, *m.* contentment.

conteo (kon•te´o) *m.* (coll.) count, counting; — **regresivo,** countdown.

contestar (kon•tes•târ´) *va.* to answer; to confirm, to substantiate *(atestiguar); vn.* to agree, to be in accord.

contienda (kon•tyen´dâ) *f.* contest, dispute, struggle, fight.

contiguo, gua (kon•tē´gwo, gwâ) *adj.* contiguous, bordering.

continencia (kon•tē•nen´syâ) *f.* continence, moderation.

continental (kon•tē•nen•tâl´) *adj.* continental.

continente (kon•tē•nen´te) *m.* continent; mien, bearing *(aspecto);* container *(cosa que contiene);* —, *adj.* abstinent, moderate.

contingencia (kon•tēn•hen´syâ) *f.* contingency, contingence; risk *(riesgo).*

continuación (kon•tē•nwâ•syon´) *f.* continuation, continuance *(acción);* continuity *(efecto);* **a**

—, below, hereafter.

continuadamente (kon•tē•nwâ•thâ•men´te) *adv.* continuously.

continuar (kon•tē•nwâr´) *va.* and *vn.* to continue.

continuidad (kon•tē•nwē•thâth´) *f.* continuity.

continuo, nua (kon•tē´nwo, nwâ) *adj.* continuous, continual, ceaseless; **de —nuo,** continually.

contorcerse* (kon•tor•ser´se) *vr.* to writhe.

contorno (kon•tor´no) *m.* environs; contour, outline *(de una figura);* **en —,** round about; **cultivo en —,** contour plowing.

contorsión (kon•tor•syon´) *f.* contortion.

contra (kon´trâ) *prep.* against; facing *(enfrente);* **seguro — incendio,** fire insurance; **ir en —,** to go against.

contraataque (kon•trâ•â•tâ´ke) *m.* counterattack.

contrabandista (kon•trâ•vân•dēs´tâ) *m.* and *f.* smuggler, dealer in contraband.

contrabando (kon•trâ•vân´do) *m.* contraband, smuggling.

contracción (kon•trâk•syon´) *f.* contraction; — **económica,** recession.

contraceptivo (kon•trâ•sep•tē´vo)

m. contraceptive; — **bucal,** oral contraceptive.

contracorriente
(kon•trâ•ko•rryen´te) *f.* countercurrent, backwater.

contradecir* (kon•trâ•the•sēr´) *va.* to contradict, to gainsay.

contradicción
(kon•trâ•thēk•syon´) *f.* contradiction.

contradictorio, ria
(kon•trâ•thēk•to´ryo, ryâ) *adj.* contradictory, opposite.

contraer* (kon•trâ•er´) *va.* to catch *(una enfermedad);* to acquire *(una costumbre);* to limit, to restrict *(reducir).*

contrafuerte (kon•trâ•fwer´te) *m.* counterfort, buttress.

contrahecho, cha
(kon•trâ•e´cho, châ) *adj.* deformed, humpbacked *(deforme);* counterfeit *(falsificado).*

contralor (kon•trâ•lor´) *m.* controller, inspector.

contramarcha (kon•trâ•mâr´châ) *f.* (mil.) countermarch; (auto.) reverse; going back, return over the same route.

contraorden (kon•trâ•or´then) *f.* countermand.

contrapaso (kon•trâ•pâ´so) *m.* back step; (mus.) countermelody.

contrapeso (kon•trâ•pe´so) *m.* counterbalance; counterweight;

tightrope walker´s pole *(balancín);* (Chile) uneasiness *(inquietud);* **hacer — a,** to counterbalance, to offset.

contraposición
(kon•trâ•po•sē•syon´) *f.* contrast.

contrapunto (kon•trâ•pūn´to) *m.* (mus.) counterpoint.

contrariar (kon•trâ•ryâr´) *va.* to oppose *(oponerse a);* to annoy *(enfadar);* to resist *(estorbar).*

contrariedad (kon•trâ•rye•thâth´) *f.* opposition, resistance; vexation, annoyance.

contrario, ria (kon•trâ´ryo, ryâ) *n.* opponent, antagonist; **llevar la —,** to take the opposite side; **—,** *adj.* contrary, opposite; adverse, hostile *(adverso);* **al — rio,** on the contrary.

contrarrevolución
(kon•trâ•rre•vo•lū•syon´) counterrevolution.

contraseña (kon•trâ•se´nyâ) *f.* countersign; (mil.) watchword, password.

contrastar (kon•trâs•târ´) *va.* to face, to resist *(hacer frente);* to assay, to analyze *(moneda);* to verify, to check *(pesas);* **—,** *vn.* to contrast.

contraste (kon•trâs´te) *m.* contrast; opposition, resistance.

contratación (kon•trâ•tâ•syon´) *f.* trade, dealings *(acción);* business transaction, deal *(efecto)*.

contratante (kon•trâ•tân´te) *adj.* contracting; —, *m.* contractor.

contratar (kon•trâ•târ´) *va.* to contract, to hire *(un servicio);* to negotiate, to agree on, to contract for.

contratiempo (kon•trâ•tyem´po) *m.* mishap, accident, misfortune.

contrato (kon•trâ´to) *m.* contract; **celebrar un** —, to draw up a contract.

contraveneno (kon•trâ•ve•ne´no) *m.* antidote.

contravenir* (kon•trâ•ve•nēr´) *va.* to contravene, to go against.

contribución (kon•trē•vū•syon´) *f.* contribution; tax *(impuesto).*

contribuir* (kon•trē•vwēr´) *va.* to contribute.

contribuyente (kon•trē•vū•yen´te) *adj.* contributing, contributory; —, *m.* and *f.* contributor; taxpayer.

contrincante (kon•trēng•kân´te) *m.* competitor, opponent.

contrito, ta (kon•trē´to, tâ) *adj.* contrite, penitent.

control (kon•trol´)*m.* control, check; — **remoto,** remote control.

controlar (kon•tro•lâr´) *va.* to control.

controversia (kon•tro•ver´syâ) *f.*

controversy, dispute.

contusión (kon•tū•syon´) *f.* contusion, bruise.

convalecencia (kom•bâ•le•sen´syâ) *f.* convalescence.

convalecer* (kom•bâ•le•ser´) *vn.* to convalesce; (fig.) to be out of danger, to be out of harm's way.

convaleciente (kom•bâ•le•syen´te) *adj.* convalescing; —, *m.* and *f.* convalescent.

convecino, na (kom•be•sē´no, nâ) *adj.* neighboring.

convencer (kom•ben•ser´) *va.* to convince.

convencimiento (kom•ben•sē•myen´tō) *m.* conviction.

convención (kom•ben•syon´) *f.* convention; agreement *(conveniencia).*

convencional (kom•ben•syo•nâl´) *adj.* conventional.

convenido, da (kom•be•nē´tho, thâ) *adj.* agreed, decided.

conveniencia (kom•be•nyen´syâ) *f.* advantage, profit *(utilidad);* convenience, ease, comfort *(comodidad);* agreement *(convenio);* suitability *(conformidad).*

conveniente (kom•be•nyen´te) *adj.* profitable, advantageous; convenient, easy; suitable; advisable, desirable *(oportuno).*

convenio (kom•be´nyo) *m.* compact, covenant; (com.) bankruptcy settlement.

convenir* (kom•be•nēr´) *vn.* to agree, to be in agreement *(estar de acuerdo);* to convene, to assemble *(juntarse);* to be suitable, to be becoming *(corresponder);* to be important, to be desirable *(ser a propósito).*

convento (kom•ben´to) *m.* convent *(de religiosas);* monastery *(de religiosos).*

conversación (kom•ber•sâ•syon´) *f.* conversation; **amigo de la —,** given to good conversation.

conversar (kom•ber•sâr´) *vn.* to converse; cope to live, to dwell *(habitar);* to deal, to have to do *(comunicar).*

conversión (kom•ber•syon´) *f.* conversion.

convertible (kom•ber•tē´vle) *adj.* and *m.* convertible.

convertir* (kom•ber•tēr´) *va.* to convert; to change, to transform *(mudar);* **—se,** to become, to change.

convexo, xa (kom•bek´so, sâ) *adj.* convex.

convicción (kom•bēk•syon´) *f.* conviction.

convicto, ta (kom•bēk´to, tâ) *adj.* convicted, found guilty; **—,** *n.* convict.

convidar (kom•bē•thâr´) *va.* to invite; (fig.) to urge, to entreat; **— a uno con,** to treat someone to **—se,** to offer one's services.

convincente (kom•bēn•sen´te) *adj.* convincing.

convocar (kom•bo•kâr´) *va.* to convoke, to assemble.

convocatoria (kom•bo•kâ•to´ryâ) *f.* notification, notice of a meeting.

convoy (kom•bo´ē) *m.* convoy; (coll.) retinue, following *(séquito);* (fig.) table cruets *(taller).*

convulsión (kom•būl•syon´) *f.* convulsion.

conyugal (kon•yū•gâl´) *adj.* conjugal.

cónyuges, (kón•yū•hes) *m. pl.* married couple, husband and wife.

coñac (ko•nyâk´) *m.* cognac.

cooperación (ko•o•pe•râ•syon´) *f.* cooperation.

cooperar (ko•o•pe•râr´) *vn.* to cooperate.

cooperativo, va (ko•o•pe•râ•tē´vo, vâ) *adj.* cooperative; **—,** *f.* cooperative.

coordinación (ko•or•thē•nâ•syon´) *f.* coordination.

coordinar (ko•or•thē•nâr´) *va.* to harmonize, to coordinate.

copa (ko´pâ) *f.* goblet, glass, wineglass; treetop *(del árbol);* crown *(del sombrero);* **—s,** *pl.*

hearts; **tomar una —,** to have a drink.

copia (ko´pyâ) *f.* plenty, abundance *(muchedumbre);* copy.

copiar, (ko•pyâr´) *va.* to copy.

copioso, sa (ko•pyo´so, sâ) *adj.* copious, abundant.

copla (ko´plâ) *f.* ballad, popular song; stanza *(estrofa);* couplet *(pareja).*

copo (ko´po) *m.* snowflake.

coqueta (ko•ke´tâ) *f.* coquette, flirt.

coquetear (ko•ke•te•âr´) *vn.* to coquet, to flirt.

coraje (ko•râ´he) *m.* courage *(valor);* anger *(ira).*

coral (ko•râl´) *m.* coral; **—es,** *pl.* coral necklace, coral beads; **—,** *adj.* choral.

coraza (ko•râ´sâ) *f.* cuirass; (naut.) armor; (zool.) shell.

corazón (ko•râ•son´) *m.* heart; **de —,** wholeheartedly, with all one´s heart; **enfermedad del —,** heart trouble.

corazonada (ko•râ•so•nâ´thâ) *f.* feeling *(presentimiento);* rash impulse, thoughtless move *(impulso).*

corbata (kor•vâ´tâ) *f.* cravat, necktie.

corcova (kor•ko´vâ) *f.* hump, protuberance.

corcovado, da (kor•ko•vâ´tho, thâ) *adj.* humpbacked, hunch-backed.

corchete (kor•che´te) *m.* clasp *(broche);* bench hook *(de carpintero);* bracket *(signo);* (coll.) constable.

corcho (kor´cho) *m.* cork; beehive *(colmena).*

cordel (kor•thel´) *m.* string, cord.

cordero (kor•the´ro) *m.* lamb; lambskin *(piel).*

cordial (kor•thyâl´) *adj.* cordial, hearty, affectionate; **—,** *m.* cordial.

cordialidad (kor•thyâ•lē•thâth´) *f.* cordiality.

cordillera (kor•the•ye´râ) *f.* range of mountains.

córdoba (kor´tho•vâ) *m.* monetary unit of Nicaragua.

cordón (kor•thon´) *m.* cord, string; cordon *(de personas).*

cordura (kor•thū´râ) *f.* prudence, wisdom, judgment.

coreografía (ko•re•o•grâ•fē´â) *f.* choreography.

corista (ko•rēs´tâ) *m.* (eccl.) choir brother; **—,** *m.* and *f.* (theat.) member of the chorus; **—,** *f.* chorine, chorus girl.

cornamenta (kor•nâ•men´tâ) *f.* horns; antlers *(del venado).*

córnea (kor´ne•â) *f.* cornea.

cornear (kor•ne•âr´) *va.* to butt, to gore.

corneta (kor•ne´tâ) *f.* cornet; hunting horn *(de caza);* (mil.)

bugle; pennant *(banderita);* —,
m. bugler.

cornisa (kor•nē´sâ) *f.* cornice,
molding.

cornucopia (kor•nū•ko´pyâ) *f.*
cornucopia, horn of plenty;
ornate mirror with candelabra
(espejo).

cornudo, da (kor•nū´tho, thâ)
adj. horned.

coro (ko´ro) *m.* (eccl.) choir; chorus; **en** —, all together, in unison.

corona (ko•ro´nâ) *f.* crown;
(eccl.) tonsure; (ast.) corona.

coronación (ko•ro•nâ•syon´) *f.*
coronation.

coronar (ko•ro•nâr´) *va.* to
crown; to reward *(premiar);* to
climax, to culminate *(perfeccionar).*

coronario, ria (ko•ro•nâ´ryo, ryâ)
adj. relating to the crown;
(med.) coronary

coronel (ko•ro•nel´) *m.* (mil.)
colonel.

coronilla (ko•ro•nē´yâ) *f.* crown
of the head.

corporación (kor•po•râ•syon´) *f.*
corporation, society.

corporal (kor•po•râl´) *adj.* corporal, bodfly; —, *m.* (eccl.) corporal.

corpóreo, rea (kor•po´re•o, re•â)
adj. corporeal.

corpulencia (kor•pū•len´syâ) *f.*

corpulence.

corpulento, ta (kor•pū•len´to, tâ)
adj. corpulent, bulky.

corpuscular (kor•pūs•kū•lâr´)
adj. corpuscular.

corral (ko•rrâl´) *m.* yard; court
theater *(de comedias);* **corral**
(en el campo); **aves de** —, poultry; **hacer** —**es**, (coll.) to play
hooky.

corrección (ko•rrek•syon´) *f.*
correction; correctness *(calidad);* refinement *(urbanidad).*

correcto, ta (ko•rrek´to, tâ) *adj.*
correct; refined, proper *(fino).*

corrector, ra (ko•rrek•tor´, râ) *n.*
corrector; (print.) proofreader.

corredizo, za (ko•rre•thē´so, sâ)
adj. easily untied; **nudo** —,
slipknot; **puerta** —, sliding
door.

corredor, ra (ko•rre•thor´, râ)
adj. running; —, *n.* runner; —,
m. (com.) broker; (mil.) scout;
corridor, hall *(pasillo):* track-
man *(de pista y campo);* —**s**, *f.
pl.* (orn.) flightless birds.

corregir* (ko•rre•hēr´) *va.* to correct; to punish *(castigar);* to
lessen, to mitigate *(disminuir).*

correlación (ko•rre•lâ•syon´) *f.*
correlation.

correlacionar
(ko•rre•lâ•syo•nâr´) *va.* to
correlate.

correo (ko•rre´o) *m.* mail; postman, mail-man *(cartero)*; post office *(casa)*; accomplice *(responsable)*; **a vuelta de —,** by return mail.

correr (ko•rrer´) *vn.* to run, to race; to flow *(el agua)*; to blow *(el viento)*.

correría (ko•rre•rē´â) *f.* excursion; (mil.) raid, incursion; **—s,** youthful escapades.

correspondencia (ko•rres•pon•den´syâ) *f.* correspondence; relationship, harmony *(relación)*; communication, contact *(comunicación)*; mail *(correo)*; transfer, connection *(entre vehículos)*; **estar en — con,** to correspond with; **llevar la —,** to be in charge of the correspondence.

corresponder (ko•rres•pon•der´) *vn.* to correspond; to be connected, communicate *(habitaciones)*; to repay, reciprocate *(recompensar)*; to concern *(tocar)*; **— con,** to repay for; **—se con,** to correspond with.

correspondiente (ko•rres•pon•dyen´te) *adj.* corresponding; **—,** *m.* and *f.* correspondent.

corresponsal (ko•rres•pon•sâl´) *m.* correspondent.

corretear (ko•rre•te•âr´) *vn.* (coll.) to rove, to wander; to run back and forth, to run about

(jugando); to pursue.

corrida (ko•rrē´thâ) *f.* race; **— de toros,** bullfight; **de —,** at full speed.

corriente (ko•rryen´te) *f.* current; stream, flow, course, progression *(curso)*.

corroborar (ko•rro•vo•râr´) *va.* to corroborate; to strengthen *(fortificar)*.

corroer (ko•rro•er´) *va.* to corrode.

corromper (ko•rrom•per´) *va.* (fig.) to corrupt; to spoil, to ruin *(echar a perder)*; to seduce *(seducir)*; **—,** *vn.* to smell bad; **—se,** to rot, to spoil.

corrosión (ko•rro•syon´) *f.* corrosion.

corrupción (ko•rrūp•syon´) *f.* corruption; putrefaction, spoilage; seduction.

corruptivo, va (ko•rrūp•tē´vo, vâ) *adj.* corruptive.

corruptor, ra (ko•rrūp•tor´, râ) *n.* corrupter; **—.** *adj.* corrupting.

cortacircuitos (kor•tâ•sēr•kwē´- tos) *m.* (elec.) circuit breaker.

cortado, da (kor•tâ´tho, thâ) *adj.* disconnected, choppy *(estilo)*; adapted, proportioned *(ajustado)*.

cortar (kor•târ´) *va.* to cut; to cut off *(separar)*; to cut out *(suprimir)*; to interrupt, to

break into *(una conversacíon);*
—se, to stop short, to be at a
loss for words; to coagulate
(coagularse).

cortaúñas (kor•tâ•ū´nyâs) *m.*
nail clippers.

corte (kor´te) *m.* edge, cutting
edge *(filo);* cross section *(de un
edificio);* material *(para una
prenda);* cut *(lesión);* edge *(de
libro);* cutting down, felling *(de
árboles);* cut, cutting; **—,** *f.*
court; court-yard *(patio);* **hacer
la —,** to court, to woo.

cortejar (kor•te•hâr´) *va.* to woo,
to court *(a una mujer);* to fete,
to treat royally.

cortejo (kor•te´ho) *m.* courtship,
wooing; gift, present *(regalo);*
entourage *(comitiva).*

Cortes (kor´tes) *f. pl.* Spanish
Parliament.

cortés (kor•tes´) *adj.* courteous,
genteel, polite.

cortesano, na (kor•te•sâ´no, nâ)
adj. court, of the court; courteous, urbane *(cortés);* **—,** *m.*
courtier; **—,** *f.* courtesan.

cortesía (kor•te•sē´â) *f.* courtesy,
politeness *(cortesanía);* (com.)
days of grace; expression of
respect *(tratamiento);* gift, present *(regalo).*

corteza (kor•te´sâ) *f.* (anat.) cortex; bark *(de árbol);* peel *(de
fruta);* crust *(de pan);* (fig.) outward appearance; grossness,
roughness *(grosería).*

cortina (kor•tē´nâ) *f.* curtain; **—
de hieno,** iron curtain; **— de
humo,** smoke screen.

corto, ta (kor´to, tâ) *adj.* short;
scanty *(escaso);* small *(pequeño);* limited, lacking in ability
(de escaso talento); shy, timid
(tímido) **a la —ta o a la larga,**
sooner or later.

cortocircuito (kor•to•sēr•kwē´to)
m. (elec). short circuit.

corva (kor´vâ) *f.* hollow of the
knee, ham.

corvadura (kor•vâ•thū´râ) *f.* curvature; (arch.) bend of an arch.

cosa (ko´sâ) *f.* thing; **no hay tal
—,** there is no such thing; **otra
—,** something else; **ninguna —,**
nothing; **— de cajón,** matter of
course, routine.

cosecha (ko•se´châ) *f.* harvest,
crop; harvest time *(tiempo);* **de
su —,** of one's own invention.

cosechar (ko•se•châr´) *va.* to
reap, to harvest.

coser (ko•ser´) *va.* to sew; (fig.)
to join *(unir);* **máquina de —,**
sewing machine.

cosmético (koz•me´tē•ko) *m.* cosmetic.

cósmico, ca (koz´mē•ko, kâ) *adj.*
cosmic.

cosmopolita (koz•mo•po•lē´tâ)
m. and *f.* cosmopolite; **—,** *adj.*

cosmopolitan.

cosquillas (kos•kē´yâs) *f. pl.* tickling; **hacer —,** to tickle.

cosquillear (kos•kē•ye•âr´) *va.* to tickle.

cosquilloso, sa (kos•kē•yo´so, sâ) *adj.* ticklish.

costa (kos´tâ) *f.* cost, price; coast, shore *(litoral);* **a toda —,** at any cost; **a lo largo de la —,** coastwise.

costado (kos•tâ´tho) *m.* side; (mil.) flank; (naut.) ship´s side.

costal (kos•tâl´) *m.* sack, large bag; tamper *(pisón); —, adj.* (anat.) costal.

costanero, ra (kos•tâ•ne´ro, râ) *adj.* coastal; sloping *(en cuesta).*

costar* (kos•târ´) *vn.* to cost; **—,** *vt.* to cause, to give.

costarricense, (kos•tâ•rrē•sen´se) *m. and f.* and *adj.* Costa Rican.

costear (kos•te•âr´) *va.* to pay the cost of; *vn.* to sail along the coast.

costero, ra (kos•te´ro, râ) *adj.* coastal; **—,** *f.* hill, slope; **—,** *n.* coastal inhabitant.

costilla (kos•tē´yâ) *f.* rib; rung *(de silla);* stave *(de barril).*

costo (kos´to) *m.* cost, expense; **— de fabricación,** production cost.

costoso, sa (kos•to´so, sâ) *adj.* costly, dear, expensive.

costumbre (kos•tūm´bre) *f.* custom, habit; **de —,** usually; **tener por —,** to be in the habit of.

costura (kos•tū´râ) *f.* sewing; seam *(sutura);* (naut.) splice.

costurera (kos•tū•re´râ) *f.* seamstress, dressmaker.

costurero (kos•tū•re´ro) *m.* sewing room *(cuarto);* sewing box *(cajón).*

cotidiano na, (ko•tē•thyâ´no, nâ) *adj.* daily.

cotización (ko•tē•sâ•syon´) *f.* (com.) quotation.

cotizar (ko•tē•sâr´) *va.* (com.) to quote.

coyote (ko•yo´te) *m.* coyote.

coyuntura (ko•yūn•tū´râ) *f.* (anat.) joint, articulation; occasion, moment *(oportunidad);* economic picture *(estado económico).*

cráneo (krâ´ne•o) *m.* skull, cranium.

cráter (krâ´ter) *m.* crater.

crátera (krâ´te•râ) *f.* krater.

creación (kre•â•syon´) *f.* creation.

Creador (kre•â•thor´) *m.* Creator, Maker.

creador, ra (kre•â•thor´, râ) *adj.* creative; **—,** *n.* originator, creator.

crear (kre•âr´) *va.* to create, to

originate; to establish, to found
(fundar).

crecer* (kre•ser') vn. to grow; to
increase to swell (por nueva
materia).

creces (kre'ses) f. pl. augmenta-
tion, increase; **pagar con —,** to
pay back generously, to pay
more than is due.

crecido, da (kre•se'tho, thâ) adj.
grown, increased, large.

creciente (kre•syen'te) f. swell,
floodtide (crecida); crescent (de
la luna); **—,** adj. growing, swelling.

crecimiento (kre•se•myen'to) m.
increase; growth.

credencial (kre•then•syâl') f. cre-
dential.

credibilidad (kre•thē•vē•lē•thâ-
th') f. credibility.

crédito (kre'thē•to) m. credit; **—
mercantil,** good will; **a —,** on
credit; **—s activos,** assets; **—s
pasivos,** liabilities.

credo (kre'tho) m. creed; **en
menos de un —,** in less than a
jiffy.

credulidad (kre•thū•lē•thâth') f.
credulity.

crédulo, la (kre'thū•lo, lâ) adj.
credulous.

creencia (kre•en'syâ) f. creden-
ce; belief (opinión); faith, religious persuasion (fe religioso).

creer* (kre•er') va. to believe; to

think (tener por probable); **¡ya
lo creo!** I should say so! you
bet! of course!

creíble (kre•ē'vle) adj. credible,
believable.

crema (kre'mâ) f. cream; skin
cream (para el cutis); **— batida,**
whipped cream; **— de afeitar,**
shaving cream.

cremación (kre•mâ•syon') f. cremation.

crémor (kre'mor) or **crémor tártaro** (kre'mor târ'tâ•ro) m.
cream of tartar.

crencha (kren'châ) f. part of
one's hair.

crepuscular (kre•pūs•kū•lâr')
adj. twilight.

crepúsculo (kre•pūs'kū•lo) m.
twilight.

crespo, pa (kres'po, pâ) adj.
crisp (hojas); curly (cabello);
(fig.) bombastic, turgid (estilo);
(fig.) upset, angry (alterado); **—,**
m. curl.

cresta (kres'tâ) f. crest; **— de
gallo,** cockscomb.

creyente (kre•yen'te) adj. believ-
ing; **—,** m. and f. believer.

cría (krē'â) f. raising; breeding
(de animales); offspring, young
(conjunto).

criada (kryâ'thâ) f. maid.

criadero (kryâ•the'ro) m. tree
nursery (de arbolillos); breeding ground (de animales); **—,**

ra, *adj.* prolific, productive.

criado (kryâ´tho) *m.* servant; —, **da,** *adj.* bred, brought up.

criador (kryâ•thor´) *m.* creator; breeder; —, **ra,** *adj.* nourishing; creating, creative; fruitful.

crianza (kryân´sâ) *f.* raising, rearing *(acción);* breeding *(efecto);* nursing *(lactancia);* **dar —,** to bring up, to rear.

criar (kryâr´) *va.* to create *(dar motivo);* to produce *(producir);* to breed, to rear *(animales);* to nurse, to suckle *(nutrir):* to raise, to bring up *(a los niños).*

criatura (kryâ•tū´râ) *f.* creation, work, thing created *(cosa criada);* small child, baby *(niño);* creature *(hechura).*

crimen (krē´men) *m.* crime.

criminal (krē•mē•nâl´) *m.* and *f.* and *adj.* criminal.

criminalista (krē•mē•nâ•lēs´tâ) *adj.* pertaining to criminal law; **abogado —,** criminal lawyer.

criminología (krē•mē•no•lo•hē´â) *f.* criminology.

crin (krēn) *f.* mane.

criollo, lla (kryo´yo, yâ) *n.* and *adj.* Creole *(de padres europeos);* —, *adj.* native, indigenous.

cripta (krēp´tâ) *f.* crypt.

crisantemo (krē•sân•te´mo) *m.* chrysanthemum.

crisis (krē´sēs) *f.* crisis; attack *(ataque);* mature decision *(juicio).*

crispar (krēs•pâr´) *va.* to contract, to twitch; (coll.) to put on edge, to make nervous.

cristal (krēs•tâl´) *m.* crystal; pane of glass *(hoja de vidrio);* — **tallado,** cut crystal.

cristalería (krēs•tâ•le•rē´â) *f.* glassware.

cristalino, na (krēs•tâ•lē´no, nâ) *adj.* crystalline, clear.

cristalización (krēs•tâ•lē•sâ•syon´) *f.* crystallization.

cristalizar (krēs•tâ•lē•sâr´) *va.* to crystallize.

cristiandad (krēs•tyân•dâth´) *f.* Christianity, Christendom.

cristianismo (krēs•tyâ•nēz´mo) *m.* Christianity, Christendom.

cristiano, na (krēs•tyâ´no, nâ) *n.* and *adj.* Christian.

Cristo (krēs´to) *m.* Christ.

criterio (krē•te´ryo) *m.* criterion *(regla);* judgment *(juicio).*

crítica (krē´tē•kâ) *f.* criticism.

criticable (krē•tē•kâ´vle) *adj.* open to criticism.

criticar (krē•tē•kâr´) *va.* to criticize, to find fault with; to evaluate *(analizar).*

crítico (krē´tē•ko) *m.* critic; —, **ca,** *adj.* critical.

cromo (kro´mo) *m.* chromium, chrome.

cromosoma (kro•mo•so´mâ) *m.*

(biol.) chromosome.

crónica (kro´nē•kâ) *f.* chronicle; news feature, news story *(de prensa).*

crónico, ca (kro´nē•ko, kâ) *adj.* chronic.

cronista (kro•nēs´tâ) *m.* and *f.* chronicler; news writer, feature writer.

cronología (kro•no•lo•hē´â) *f.* chronology.

cronológicamente (kro•no•lo•hē•kâ men´te) *adv.* chronologically.

cronológico, ca (kro•no•lo´hē•kō, kâ) *adj.* chronological.

cruce (krū´se) *m.* crossing; intersection *(punto).*

crucero (krū•se´ro) *m.* cruise.

crucial (krū•syâl´) *adj.* crucial, critical.

crucificar (krū•sē•fē•kâr´) *va.* to crucify; (fig.) to torment.

crucifijo (krū•sē•fē´ho) *m.* crucifix.

crucigrama (krū•sē•grâ´mâ) *m.* crossword puzzle.

crudeza (krū•the´sâ) *f.* crudeness.

crudo, da (krū´tho, thâ) *adj.* raw *(sin cocer);* green, unripe *(no maduro);* unprocessed, crude *(sin preparación);* hard *(agua);* raw, cold *(tiempo);* (fig.) harsh, sharp *(áspero);* (coll.) hung over *(tras una borrachera);* hard to

digest *(de difícil digestión).*

cruel (krwel) *adj.* cruel, heartless *(despiadado);* savage, bloodthirsty *(sanguinario);* intense, bitter *(riguroso).*

crueldad (krwel•dâth´) *f.* cruelty; savageness; intensity.

cruento, ta (krwen´to, tâ) *adj.* bloody, savage.

crujía (krū•hē´â) *f.* corridor, passageway; — **de hospital,** hospital ward.

crujido (krū•hē´tho) *m.* crack; crackling, crunch; chattering; rustling.

crujir (krū•hēr´) *vn.* to crack *(la madera);* to crackle, to crunch *(hojas secas);* to chatter *(los dientes);* to rustle *(la seda).*

cruz (krūs) *f.* cross; tail, reverse *(de una moneda).*

cruzada (krū•sâ´thâ) *f.* crusade.

cruzado, da (krū•sâ´tho, thâ) *adj.* crossed; mixed-breed *(animal);* double-breasted *(saco);* —, *m.* crusader.

cruzamiento (krū•sâ•myen´to) *m.* crossing; — **de calle,** street crossing; — **de vía,** (rail.) junction.

cruzar (krū•sâr´) *va.* to cross; to come across *(encontrar);* (naut.) to cruise.

cuaderno (kwâ•ther´no) *m.* notebook.

cuadra (kwâ´thrâ) *f.* city block.

cuadrado, da (kwâ•thrâ´tho, thâ) *adj.* square; (fig.) perfect, flawless *(cabal); m.* (math.) square.

cuadragésimo, ma (kwâ•thrâ•he´sē•mo, ma) *adj.* fortieth.

cuadrangular (kwâ•thrâng•gū•lâr´) *adj.* quadrangular; —, *m.* home run.

cuadrángulo (kwâ•thrâng´gū•lo) *m.* quadrangle.

cuadrante (kwâ•thrân´te), *m.* quadrant; face *(del reloj).*

cuadrar (kwâ•thrâr´) *va.* to square; to rule in squares *(cuadricular);* —, *vi.* to agree, to measure up *(conformarse);* to please, to be fine *(agradar);* to come out right *(cuentas);* —**se,** to square one´s shoulders.

cuadricular (kwâ•thrē•kū•lâr´) *vt.* to mark off in squares, to rule in squares.

cuadrilátero, ra (kwâ•thrē•lâ´te•ro, râ) *adj.* and *m.* quadrilateral.

cuadrilongo, ga (kwâ•thrē•long´go, gâ) *adj.* oblong, rectangular.

cuadro (kwâ´thro) *m.* square; picture, painting *(pintura);* frame *(marco);* (theat.) scene; (mil.) cadre; (naut.) ward-room; — **de control,** (elec.) switchboard.

cuadrúpedo, da

(kwâ•thrū´pe•tho, thâ) *adj.* quadruped.

cuajada (kwa•hâ´thâ) *f.* curd; cottage cheese *(requesón).*

cuajar (kwâ•hâr´) *va.* to coagulate, to curdle; —, *vn.* to jell, to come through *(lograr);* to suit, to please *(gustar);* —**se,** to coagulate, to curdle; to fill up *(llenarse).*

cual (kwâl) *pron.* which, which one; just as, like *(usado con tal);* —, *adv.* such as, according to how.

cuál (kwâl) *interr. pron.* which one, which; some *(disyuntivo);* —, *adv.* how.

cualidad (kwâ•lē•thâth´) *f.* quality.

cualquier (kwâl•kyer´) *adj. any.*

cualquiera (kwâl•kye´râ) *adj.* any; —, *pron.* anyone, someone, anybody, somebody.

cuan (kwân´) *adv.* as.

cuán (kwân) *adv.* how; — **grande es Dios!** how great is God!

cuando (kwân´do) (*interr.* **cuándo**) *adv.* when; in case, if *(en caso de que);* —, *conj.* even if, although even though; since *(puesto que)*

cuantía (kwân•tē´â) *f.* quantity; rank, distinction *(importancia).*

cuantioso, sa (kwân•tyo´so, sâ) *adj.* numerous, abundant.

cuanto, ta (kwân´to, tâ) *adj.* as

much as, all, whatever.

cuanto (kwân´to) *adv.* as soon as; **— antes,** at once; **— más,** the more; all the more; **en —,** as soon as; while *(mientras);* **en — a,** with regard to; **por —,** inasmuch as.

cuánto, ta (kwân´to, tâ) *interr. adj.* how much.

cuánto (kwân´to) *adv.* how much; how, to what degree *(de qué manera).*

cuarenta (kwâ•ren´tâ) *adj.* forty.

cuarentena (kwâ•ren•te´nâ) *f.* Lent; quarantine.

cuaresma (kwâ•rez´mâ) *f.* Lent.

cuarta (kwâr´tâ) *f.* quarter; run of four cards *(de naipes);* (naut.) rhumb, point.

cuartear (kwâr•te•âr´) *va.* to quarter; to divide up *(dividir);* to make the fourth for *(un juego);* to drive from side to side *(un carruaje);* **—se,** to split, to crack.

cuartel (kwâr•tel´) *m.* quarter, fourth; district, section *(barrio);* (mil.) quarters; plot *(de terreno);* quarter, mercy *(gracia);* (naut.) hatch; **— general,** headquarters.

cuarteto (kwâr•te´to) *m.* quartet.

cuartilla (kwâr•tē´yâ) *f.* fourth part of an **arroba;** quarter sheet of paper *(de un pliego);* pastern *(de caballería).*

cuarto (kwâr´to) *m.* fourth part, quarter; room *(aposento).*

cuarzo (kwâr´so) *m.* quartz.

cuate, ta (kwâ´te, tâ) or **coate, ta,** *n.* and *adj.* (Mex.) twin; **—,** *n.* chum, pal, close friend.

cuatro (kwâ´tro) *adj.* four; **—,** *m.* figure four; **las —,** four o´clock.

cubano, na (kū•vâ´no, nâ) *adj.* and *n.* Cuban.

cubeta (kū•ve´tâ) *f.* bucket; (phot.) tray.

cúbico, ca (kū´vē•ko, kâ) *adj.* cubic.

cubierta (kū•vyer´tâ) *f.* cover; envelope *(sobre);* dust jacket *(de libro);* pretext; (naut.) deck.

cubierto (kū•vyer´to) *m.* protection, shelter *(abrigo);* setting, cover *(servicio de mesa).*

cubil (kū•vēl´) *m.* den, lair, cave.

cubilete (kū•vē•le´te) *m.* copper pan; dice box *(para dados);* (Sp. Am.) high hat *(sombrero).*

cubo (kū´vo) *m.* (math.) cube; millpond *(estanque);* pail *(balde);* socket *(de candelero);* hub *(de rueda).*

cubrecama (kū•vre•kâ´mâ) *f.* bedspread.

cubrir* (kū•vrēr´) *va.* to cover; (fig.) to drown out *(ahogar);* to cover up, to hide *(disimular);* **— una cuenta,** to balance an account; **—se,** to put on one´s hat.

cucaña (kū•kâ´nyâ) *f.* greased pole; (coll.) snap, cinch, cake-walk *(ganga).*

cucaracha (kū•kâ•râ´châ) *f.* cockroach.

cuclillo (kū•klē´yo) *m.* cuckoo; (fig.) cuckold.

cuco, ca (kū´ko, kâ) *adj.* (coll.) pretty, nice; sly, crafty *(taimado);* —, *m.* cuckoo.

cuchara (kū•châ´râ) *f.* spoon.

cucharada (kū•châ•râ´thâ) *f.* spoonful.

cucharita (kū•châ•rē´tâ) *f.* teaspoon.

cucharón (kū•châ•ron´) *m.* soup ladle, soup spoon.

cuchicheo (kū•chē•che´o) *m.* whispering.

cuchilla (kū•chē´yâ) *f.* large knife; cleaver *(de carnicero);* blade *(de la hoja de afeitar).*

cuchillada (kū•chē•yâ´thâ) *f.* knife cut, gash; slash *(en un vestido);* —s, *pl.* wrangle, quarrel.

cuchillo (kū•chē´yo) *m.* knife; gusset, gore *(de una prenda).*

cueca (kwe´kâ) *f.* popular Chilean dance.

cuello (kwe´yo) *m.* neck; collar *(de una prenda);* **levantar el** —, (coll.) to have one's head above water, to see one's way clear.

cuenca (kweng´kâ) *f.* wooden bowl; (geog.) valley, river basin; (anat.) eye socket.

cuenta (kwen´tâ) *f.* account; calculation, count *(cálculo);* (com.) bill; bead *(del rosario);* **abonar en** —, to credit with; **adeudar en** —, to charge to one's account; **caer en la** —, to become aware, to realize; — **abierta** or **corriente,** checking account; — **pendiente,** account due; **dar** — **de,** to report on; **darse** —, to realize; **llevar** —s, to keep accounts; **tener en** —, to take into account, to bear in mind; **tomar por su** —, to assume responsibility for.

cuentagotas (kwen•tâ•go´tâs) *m.* medicine dropper.

cuentista, (kwen•tēs´tâ) *m.* and *f.* storyteller; talebearer, gossip *(chismoso).*

cuento (kwen´to) *m.* story, account *(relato);* count *(cómputo);* tale, story *(chisme);* — **de viejas,** old wives' tale.

cuerda (kwer´thâ) *f.* (mus.) string; mainspring *(del reloj);* (math.) chord; rope, cord; — **vocal,** vocal chord; **bajo** —, underhandedly; **dar** —, to wind; (fig.) to give free rein to; **sin** —, unwound.

cuerdo, da (kwer´tho, thâ) *adj.* sane; prudent, wise *(sabio).*

cuerno (kwer´no) *m.* horn; — **de abundancia,** horn of plenty;

levantar hasta los —s de la luna, to praise to the skies.

cuero (kwe´ro) *m.* hide, skin; leather *(curtido y preparado);* **— cabelludo,** scalp; **en —s,** stark naked.

cuerpo (kwer´po) *m.* body; cadaver, corpse; build, physique *(talle);* section, part *(parte);* (mil.) corps; **— de aviación,** air corps; **— a —,** hand to hand.

cuervo (kwer´vo) *m.* (orn.) crow, raven.

cuesta (kwes´tâ) *f.* hill, slope, decline; **a —s,** on one's shoulders; **ir — abajo,** to go downhill, to be on the decline; **hacérsele — arriba,** to be hard to do for, to be distasteful to.

cuestión (kwes•tyon´) *f.* question, matter; problem *(punto dudoso);* argument, quarrel *(riña).*

cuestionar (kwes•tyo•nâr´) *va.* to question, to dispute.

cuestionario (kwes•tyo•nâ´ryo) *m.* questionnaire.

cueva (kwe´vâ) *f.* cave, cavern; cellar *(sótano).*

cuidado (kwē•thâ´tho) *m.* care *(esmero);* concern, problem *(a cargo de uno);* anxiety, worry *(recelo);* **estar con —,** to be worried.

cuidadosamente (kwē•thâ•tho•sâ•men´te) *adv.* carefully.

cuidadoso, sa (kwē•thâ•tho´so, sâ) *adj.* careful; observant, watchful *(vigilante).*

cuidaniños (kwē•thâ•nē´nyos) *m.* and *f.* baby-sitter.

cuidar (kwē•thâr´) *va.* to take care of, to look after *(asistir);* to be careful with (of) *(poner cuidado);* **—se,** to be careful of one's health.

cuita (kwē´tâ) *f.* grief, sorrow, suffering.

cuitado, da (kwē•tâ´tho, thâ) *adj.* griefstricken, sorrowful; (fig.) cowardly, irresolute *(apocado).*

culantro (kū•lân´tro) or **cilantro** (sē•lân´tro) *m.* (bot.) coriander.

culebra (kū•le´vrâ) *f.* snake; **— de cascabel,** rattlesnake.

culminación (kūl•mē•nâ•syon´) *f.* culmination.

culminante (kūl•mē•nân´te) *adj.* predominant; **punto —,** high point, high-water mark.

culpa (kūl´pâ) *f.* wrong, fault, defect *(falta);* guilt, blame *(responsabilidad);* **tener la —,** to be at fault, to be to blame.

culpabilidad (kūl•pâ•vē•lē•thâth´) *f.* guiltiness.

culpable (kūl•pâ´vle) *adj.* guilty, at fault.

culpar (kūl•pâr´) *va.* to accuse,

to blame.

cultivado, da (kul•tē•vâ′tho, thâ) *adj.* cultivated, cultured; **perlas —s**, cultured pearls.

cultivar (kūl•tē•vâr′) *va.* to cultivate; to grow *(plantar).*

cultivo (kūl•tē′vo) *m.* cultivation; culture *(de microbios).*

culto, ta (kūl′to, tâ) *adj.* cultured, cultivated; affected, overly refined *(culterano);* **—,** *m.* veneration, worship *(homenaje);* religion, form of worship *(religión);* (fig.) cult *(admiración).*

cultura (kūl•tū′râ) *f.* cultivation, culture.

cumbre (kūm′bre) *f.* summit, peak; highpoint, height *(punto culminante).*

cumpleaños (kūm•ple•â′nyos′) *m.* birthday.

cumplido, da (kūm•plē′tho, thâ) *adj.* full, complete; long, full *(vestido);* courteous *(cortés);* **—,** *m.* courtesy, attention.

cumplimiento (kūm•plē•myen′to) *m.* compliment *(parabién);* accomplishment, fulfillment; expiration *(vencimiento).*

cumplir (kūm•plēr′) *va.* to execute, to fulfill, to carry out *(ejecutar);* **— años,** to have a birthday; **—,** *vn.* to fall due, to expire *(vencer);* to be fitting, to be proper *(convenir).*

cúmulo (kū′mū•lo) *m.* heap, pile *(montón);* (fig) lot, great deal; cumulus cloud *(nube).*

cuna (kū′nâ) *f.* cradle; homeland *(patria);* birthplace *(lugar de nacimiento);* foundling home *(de expósitos);* source, cause *(origen);* **de humilde —,** of lowly birth.

cuña (kū′nyâ) *f.* wedge; (coll.) support, backing *(apoyo).*

cuñada (kū•nyâ′thâ) *f.* sister-in-law.

cuñado (kū•nyâ′tho) *m.* brother-in-law.

cuociente (kwo•syen′te) *m.* quotient.

cuota (kwo′tâ) *f.* quota, share.

cupo (kū′po) *m.* quota, share.

cupón (kū•pon′) *m.* (com.) coupon.

cúpula (kū′pū•lâ) *f.* cupola, dome; **—geodésica,** geodesic dome.

cuquillo (kū•kē′yo) *m.* (orn.) cuckoo.

cura (kū′•râ) *m.* parish priest; **—, f.** healing *(curación);* cure, remedy *(método curativo).*

curable (kū•râ′vle) *adj.* curable.

curandero (kū•rân•de′ro) *m.* quack, medicaster: medicine man.

curar (kū•râr′) *va.* to cure, to heal; **—se,** to be cured, to recover.

curativo, va (kū•râ•tē′vo, vâ)

adj. curative, healing.

curato (kū•râ´to) *m.* parish (*parroquia*); pastorate, ministry (*cargo de cura*).

curio (kū´ryo) *m.* curite.

curiosear (kū•ryo•se•âr´) *vn.* to pry, to snoop, to meddle.

curiosidad (kū•ryo•sē•thâth´) *f.* curiosity; neatness (*aseo*); object of curiosity, rarity (*cosa curiosa*).

curioso, sa (kū•ryo´so; sâ) *adj.* curious; tidy, neat; careful (*cuidadoso*).

cursado, da (kū•sâ´tho, thâ) *adj.* skilled, versed.

cursar (kū•sâr´) *va.* to take, to study (*una materia*); to haunt, to frequent (*un paraje*); to engage in frequently (*una cosa*); to follow through with (*una solicitud*).

cursi (kūr´sē) *adj.* tawdry, cheap, in bad taste.

cursivo, va (kūr•sē´vo, vâ) *adj.* cursive; **letra —,** cursive.

curso (kūr´so) *m.* course; circulation, currency (*de una moneda*); **— de repaso,** refresher course; **— de verano,** summer course.

curtidor, (kūr•tē•thor´) *m.* tan-

ner.

curtir (kūr•tēr´) *va.* to tan (*las pieles*); to sunburn, to tan (*el cutis*); to inure, to harden (*acostumbrar a la vida dura*).

curucú (kū•rū•kū´) *m.* quetzal.

curva (kūr´vâ) *f.* curve

curvatura (kūr•vâ•tū´râ) *f.* curvature.

curvear (kūr ve•âr´) *vn.* to curve.

curvilíneo, nea (kūr•vē•lē´ne•o, ne•â) *adj.* curvilinear.

curvo, va (kūr´vo, vâ) *adj.* curved, bent.

cúspide (kūs´pē•the) *f.* cusp (*de diente*); peak (*de montaña*); (math.) apex.

custodia (kūs•to´thyâ) *f.* custody; custodian (*persona*); (eccl.) monstrance.

custodiar (kūs•to•thyâr´) *va.* to guard, to keep in custody.

cutáneo, nea (kū•tâ´ne•o, ne•â) *adj.* cutaneous.

cúter, (kū´ter) *m.* (naut.) cutter.

cutícula (kū•tē´kū•lâ) *f.* cuticle.

cutis, (kū´tēs) *m.* or *f.* skin, complexion.

cuyo, ya (kū´yo, yâ) *pron.* of which, of whom, whose.

czar (sâr) **= zar.**

CH

cháchara (châ´châ•râ) *f.* (coll.) chitchat, chatter, idle talk; —, *pl.* trinkets, trifles.

chal (châl) *m.* shawl.

chalán, ana (châ•lân´, â´nâ) *f.* horsetrader, shrewd businessman; —, *adj.* shrewd.

chaleco (châ•le´ko) *m.* waistcoat, vest.

chamaco, ca (châ•mâ´ko, kâ) *n.* (Mex.) youngster, kid.

chamarra (châ•mâ´rrâ) *f.* jacket.

champaña (châm•pâ´nyâ) *m.* champagne.

champiñones (châm•pē•nyo´nes) *m. pl.* mushrooms.

champú (châm•pū´) *m.* shampoo.

chamuscar (châ•mūs•kâr´) *va.* to singe.

chancla (châng´klâ) *f.* old shoe.

chancleta (châng•kle´tâ) *f.* house slipper.

chanclo (châng´klo) *m.* patten; rubber, overshoe *(zapato de goma).*

chantaje (chân•tâ´he) *m.* blackmail.

chantajista (chân•tâ•hēs´tâ) *m. and f.* blackmailer.

chanza (chân´sâ) *f.* joke, jest, fun.

chapa (châ´pâ) *f.* thin sheet *(hoja);* color, flush *(del rostro);* veneer *(de madera).*

chaparreras (châ•pâ•rre´râs) *f.*

pl. (Mex.) chaps.

chaparro (châ•pâ´rro) *m.* dwarf evergreen oak; —, **rra,** *adj.* short and stocky.

chapear (châ•pe•âr´) *va.* to sheet, to plate; to veneer; **—se,** (Chile) to feather one´s nest.

chapitel (châ•pē•tel´) *m.* (arch.) capital.

chapotear (châ•po•te•âr´) *va.* to sponge down, to wet down; —, *vn.* to splash in the water; to splash *(sonar el agua batida).*

chapucear (châ•pū•se•âr´) *va.* to botch.

chapucero (châ•pū•se´ro) *m.* blacksmith *(herrero);* poor craftsman; **—, ra,** *adj.* rough, clumsy, bungling.

chapulín (châ•pū•lēn´) *m.* grasshopper.

chaqueta (châ•ke´tâ) *f.* jacket, coat.

chaquetear (châ•ke•te•âr´) *vn.* to turn tail; to change camps, to change viewpoints *(de opiniones).*

charada (châ•râ´thâ) *f.* charade.

charanga (châ•râng´gâ) *f.* brass band.

charca (châr´kâ) *f.* pool, pond.

charco (châr´ko) *m.* puddle; **cruzar el —,** (coll.) to cross the pond.

charla (châr´lâ) *f.* idle chitchat, chatter; conversation, chatting;

informal talk *(conferencia)*.

charlador, ra (châr•lâ•thor´, râ) *n*. chatterbox, great talker; —, *adj*. talkative.

charlar (châr•lâr´) *vn*. to chatter, to chitchat; to chat, to talk *(conversar)*.

charlatán, ana (châr•lâ•tân´, â´nâ) *n*. windbag; gossip, idle talker *(indiscreto)*; charlatan, medicine man, quack *(curandero)*.

charnela (châr•ne´lâ) *f*. hinge.

charol (châ•rol´) *m*. lacquer, enamel; patent leather *(cuero)*.

charro (châ´rro) *m*. Mexican horseman in fancy dress; —, **rra,** *adj*. gaudy, overdone, in poor taste *(de mal gusto)*; boorish, uncouth *(rústico)*.

chasco (chisto) *m*. joke, prank *(broma)*; disappointment; **llevarse —,** to be disappointed.

chasquear (châs•ke•âr´) *va*. to crack to snap *(el látigo)*; to play a joke on *(burlarse)*; to fail, to disappoint *(faltar)*; —, *vn*. to crack, to snap.

chasquido (châs•ke´tho) *m*. snap, crack.

chato, ta (châ´to, tâ) *adj*. flat; pugnosed *(de nariz)*.

chaveta (châ•ve´tâ) *f*. pin, cotter pin; **perder la —,** (fig.) to go out of one´s head, to go off the deep end.

checoslovaco, ca (che•koz•lo•vâ´ko, kâ) *adj*. and *n*. Czechoslovakian.

cheque (che´ke) *m*. (corn.) check; **— al portador,** check to bearer; **— de caja,** cashier´s check; **— de viajeros,** traveler´s check.

chicle (chē´kle) *m*. chicle; chewing gum *(goma de masticar)*.

chico, ca (chē´ko, kâ) *adj*. little, small; *n*. child; (coll.) young person *(joven)*.

chicoria (chē•ko´ryâ) *f*. chicory.

chícharo (chē´châ•ro) *m*. pea.

chicharra (chē•châ´rrâ) *f*. cicada.

chicharrón (chē•châ•rron´) *m*. food burned to a crisp *(manjar requemado)*; cracklings *(del cerdo)*.

chiflar (chē•flâr´) *vn*. to whistle; —, *va*. to boo, to jeer; **—se,** to go half out of one´s mind; **—se con,** to be enfatuated with, to be mad about.

chiflido (chē•flē´tho) *m*. whistle; boo.

chile (chē´le) *m*. (bot.) chili, red pepper.

chileno, na (chē•le´no, nâ) *n*. and *adj*. Chilean.

chillar (chē•yâr´) *vn*. to scream, to shriek, to howl, to sob.

chillido (chē•yē´tho) *m*. scream, shriek; **dar un —,** to utter a shriek, scream.

chillón, ona (chē•yon´, o´nâ) *adj*.

screachy, shrill *(sonido);* loud, flashy, showy *(color);* n. bawler, screamer; —, *m.* nail.

chimenea (chē•me•ne´â) *f.* chimney; (naut.) funnel.

chimpancé (chēm•pân•se´) *m.* chimpanzee.

china (chē´nâ) *f.* pebble; (Cuba and P.R.) orange; — **poblana,** national costume of Mexico; **la C —,** China.

chinche (chēn´che) *f.* bedbug; thumbtack *(clavito);* —, *m.* and *f.* pill, boring person.

chino, na (chē´no, nâ) *n.* and *adj.* Chinese; —, *m.* Chinese language.

chiquillo, lla (che•kē´yo, yâ) *n.* child, youngster.

chiquito, ta (chē•kē´to, tâ) *adj.* little, small; —, *m.* little boy; —, *f.* little girl.

chirinola (chē•rē•no´lâ) *f.* trifle, mere nothing.

chirla (chēr´lâ) *f.* mussel.

chirriar (chē•rryâr´) *vn.* to sizzle *(de un calor);* to squeak, to creak *(al ludir);* to chirp *(los pájaros).*

chirrido (chē•rrē´tho) *m.* chirping; sizzling; creaking, squeaking.

chisme (chēz´me) *m.* gossip.

chismear (chēz•me•âr´) *vn.* to carry tales, to gossip.

chismoso, sa (chēz•mo´so, sâ) *adj.* gossipy, talebearing; —, *n.* gossip, talebearer.

chispa (chēs´pâ) *f.* spark; tiny diamond *(diamante);* tiny bit, little bit *(partícula);* liveliness, sparkle *(viveza);* tipsiness *(borrachera);* **echar —s,** to be furious, to rant and rave.

chispeante (chēs•pe•ân´te) *adj.* sparkling; witty, bright.

chispear (chēs•pe•âr´) *vn.* to spark *(echar chispas),* to glitter, to sparkle *(relucir);* to sprinkle *(llover).*

chistar (chēs•târ´) *vn.* to open one´s mouth, to say a word; **sin — ni mistar,** (coll.) without saying boo.

chiste (chēs´te) *m.* joke, funny story; humor *(gracia).*

chistoso, sa (chēs•to´so, sâ) *adj.* funny, comical, humorous.

chivo, va (chē´vo, vâ) *n.* kid, young goat.

chocante (cho•kân´te) *adj.* shocking, offensive.

chocar (cho•kâr´) *vn.* to smash, to crash; (fig.) to collide, to clash *(pelear); to* shock, to upset *(irritar).*

chocolate (cho•ko•lâ´te) *m.* chocolate.

chofer (cho•fer) or **chófer** (cho´fer) *m.* chauffeur, driver.

choque (cho´ke) *m.* collision, crash *(impacto);* (mil.) clash,

encounter; conflict, dispute
(contienda); shock *(conmoción)*.

chorizo (cho•rē′so) *m.* pork
sausage.

chorrear (cho•rre•âr′) *vn.* to
gush, to pour out; to drip
(goteando); (fig.) to flow steadily.

chorrillo (cho•rrē′yo) *m.* steady
stream, continual flow.

chorro (cho′rro) *m.* gush, flow;
jet *(de vapor);* **a —s,** heavily,
copiously.

choza (cho′sâ) *f.* hut, cabin.

chubasco (chū•vâs′ko) *m.* rain-
squall, rainstorm.

chuleta (chū•le′tâ) *f.* chop; **— de
cordero,** lamb chop; **— de
puerco,** pork chop; **— de terne-**

ra, veal chop.

chupador (chū•pâ•thor′) *m.* teething ring.

chupar (chū•pâr′) *va.* to suck;
(fig.) to sponge on, to drain, to
sap *(quitar a uno);* **—se** to grow
weak and thin.

chupón (chū•pon′) *m.* (bot.) sucker; (mech.) piston, sucker; **—,
ona,** *n.* swindler; drain; **—,** *adj.*
fond of sucking.

churrasco (chū•rrâs′ko) *m.*
charcoal broiled meat.

chus ni mus (chūs nē mūs)
(coll.) **no decir —,** not to say a
word.

chusma (chūz′mâ) *f.* rabble,
mob.

D

dable (dâ′vle) *adj.* feasible, possible.

dádiva (dâ′thē•vâ) *f.* gift, present.

dadivoso, sa (dâ•thē•vo′so, sâ)
adj. generous, open-handed.

dado (dâ′tho) *m.* die; **—s,** *pl.*
dice; **—, —da,** *adj.* given; **—do
que** or **—do caso que,** on condition that, provided that.

dador, ra (da•thor′, râ) *n.* giver,
donator; (com.) endorser; bearer *(portador);* **— de sangre,**

blood donor.

daga (dâ′gâ) *f.* dagger.

dalia (dâ′lyâ) *f.* (bot.) dahlia.

daltoniano, na (dâl•to•nyâ′no,
nâ) *adj.* color-blind.

daltonismo (dâl•to•nēz′mo) *m.*
color blindness.

dama (dâ′mâ) *f.* lady; mistress
(manceba); king *(en damas);*
queen *(en ajedrez);* (theat.) leading lady; **—s,** *pl.* checkers.

damisela (dâ•mē•se′lâ) *f.* sweet
young thing, young lady.

damnificar (dâm•ne•fe•kâr´) *va.* to hurt, to damage, to harm.

danés, esa (dâ•nes´, e´sâ) *adj.* Danish; —, *n.* Dane.

Danubio (dâ•nū´vyo) *m.* Danube.

danza (dân´sâ) *f.* dance.

danzante (dân•sân´te) *m.* dancer; giddy, lightheaded individual *(atolondrado).*

danzar (dân•sâr´) *va.* to dance; —, *vn.* (coll.) to meddle, to butt in.

dañar (dâ•nyâr´) *va.* to damage, to injure; to spoil, to ruin *(echar a perder).*

dañino, na (dâ•nye´no, nâ) *adj.* harmful, dangerous.

daño (dâ´nyo) *m.* damage, injury; ruin; —s y perjuicios, damages; **hacer** —, to hurt, to injure.

dañoso, sa (dâ•nyo´so, sâ) *adj.* injurious, harmful, detrimental.

dar* (dâr) *va.* to give; to consider *(considerar);* to strike *(la hora);* —, *vn.* to matter *(importar);* to fall *(caer);* to insist *(empeñarse);* to arise *(ocurrir);* to tell *(presagiar).*

dardo (dâr´tho) *m.* dart, arrow.

data (dâ´tâ) *f.* date; (com.) item.

datar (dâ•târ´) *va.* to date.

dátil (dâ´tel) *m.* (bot.) date.

dato (da´to) *m.* datum; —s, *pl.* data, information.

D. de J.C.: después de Jesucristo, A.D. after Christ.

de (de) *prep,* of *(posesión);* from *(origen);* for *(para);* by *(por);* with *(con).*

debajo (de•vâ´ho) *adv.* underneath, below; — **de,** beneath, under.

debate (de•vâ´te) *m.* debate, discussion; contest, struggle *(contienda).*

debatir (de•vâ•ter´) *va.* to debate, to discuss; to contest, to struggle for *(combatir).*

debe (de´ve) *m.* (com.) debits.

deber (de•ver´) *m.* obligation, duty; —, *va.* to owe.

debidamente (de•ve•thâ•men´te) *adv.* duly, properly.

debido, da (de•ve´tho, thâ) *adj.* due, proper, just.

débil (de´vel) *adj.* weak.

debilidad (de•ve•le•thâth´) *f.* weakness.

debilitar (de•ve•le•târ´) *va.* to debilitate, to weaken; —**se,** to become weak.

debitar (de•ve•târ´) *va.* (com.) to debit.

débito (de´ve•to) *m.* debt.

debut (de•vūt´) *m.* debut.

debutar (de•vū•târ´) *vn.* to make one´s debut.

década (de´kâ•thâ) *f.* decade.

decadencia (de•kâ•then´syâ) *f.*

decline, decadence.

decadente (de•kâ•then′te) *adj.* decadent, declining.

decaer* (de•kâ•er′) *vn.* to decline, to fail, to decay.

decaído, da (de•kâ•ē′tho, thâ) *adj.* decadent, in decline; weakened, spiritless *(abatido)*.

decaimiento (de•kâē•myen′to) *m.* decay, decline; lack of vitality *(desaliento)*.

decapitar (de•kâ•pē•târ′) *va.* to behead.

decasílabo, ba (de•kâ•sē′lâ•vo, vâ) *adj.* decasyllabic; —, *m.* decasyllable.

deceleración (de•se•le•râ•syon′) *f.* deceleration.

decencia (de•sen′syâ) *f.* decency.

decentar* (de•sen•târ′) *va.* to cut the first piece of; — **la salud,** to begin to lose one′s health; — **se,** to get bedsores.

decente, (de•sen′te) *adj.* decent; appropriate, proper *(conveniente);* neat, tidy *(aseado)*.

decepción (de•sep•syon′) *f.* disappointment *(desengaño);* deception *(engaño)*.

decible (de•sē′vle) *adj.* expressible.

decidido, da (de•sē•thē′tho, thâ) *adj.* determined, resolute, energetic.

decidir (de•sē•thēr′) *va.* to decide, to determine; to make deci-

de, to cause to make a decision *(mover a decidirse);* —**se,** to decide, to make a decision.

decigramo (de•sē•grâ′mo) *m.* decigram.

decimal (de•sē•mâl′) *adj.* decimal; (eccl.) tithing.

décimo, ma (de′sē•mo, mâ) *adj.* and *m.* tenth.

decimoctavo, va (de•sē•mok•tâ′vo, vâ) *m.* and *adj.* eighteenth.

decimonono, na (de•sē•mo•no′no, nâ) or **decimonoveno, na** (de•sē•mo•no ve′no, nâ) *m.* and *adj.* nineteenth.

decimoquinto, ta (de•sē•mo•kēn′to, tâ) *m.* and *adj.* fifteenth.

decimoséptimo, ma (de•sē•mo•sep′tē•mo, ma) *m.* and *adj.* seventeenth.

decimotercio, cia (de•sē•mo•ter′syo, syâ) or **decimotercero, ra** (de•sē•mo•ter•se′ro, râ) *m.* and *adj.* thirteenth.

decir* (de•sēr′) *va.* to say; to tell *(relatar);* to talk *(hablar); to* call *(nombrar);* to mean *(significar);* **querer** —, to mean; **por lo así,** as it were; —, *m.* familiar saying.

decisión (de•sē•syon′) *f.* decision; determination *(ánimo)*.

decisivo, va (de•sē•sē′vo, vâ) *adj.* decisive.

declamación (de•klâ•mâ•syon′) *f.* elocution, public speaking *(arte);* (fig.) wordiness, rhetoric.

declamar (de•klâ•mâr′) *va.* to declaim, to deliver; —, *vn.* to harangue, to rail.

declaración (de•klâ•râ•syon′) declaration; testimony, evidence *(del testigo).*

declarar (de•klâ•râr′) *va.* to declare; —, vi. to give evidence, to give testimony; —**se,** to break out, to take place *(manifestarse);* to declare oneself.

declinar (de•klē•nâr′) *vn.* to decline; to bend, to slope *(inclinarse);* —, *va.* (gram.) to decline; to refute.

declive (de•klē′ve) *m.* declivity, slope.

decomisar (de•ko•mē•sâr′) *va.* to confiscate.

decomiso (de•ko•mē′so) *m.* confiscation.

decoración (de•ko•râ•syon′) *f.* decoration; (theat.) setting, stage set; decorating *(arte);* memorizing *(de memoria).*

decorado (de•ko•râ′tho) *m.* decoration; stage set; decorating.

decorador, ra (de•ko•râ•thor′, râ) *n.* decorator; —, *adj.* decorating.

decorar (de•ko•râr′) *va.* to decorate; to memorize, to learn by heart.

decoro (de•ko′ro) *m.* honor, respect; decorum *(recato).*

decremento (de•kre•men′to) *m.* decrease, diminution.

decrépito, ta (de•kre′pē•to, tâ) *adj.* decrepit.

decrepitud (de•kre•pē•tūth′) *f.* decrepitude.

decretar (de•kre•târ′) *va.* to decree.

decreto (de•kre′to) *m.* decree.

dedal (de•thâl′) *m.* thimble.

dedicación (de•thē•kâ•syon′) *f.* dedication.

dedicado, da (de•thē•kâ′tho, thâ) *adj.* dedicated; devoted.

dedicar (de•thē•kâr′) *va.* to dedicate; to devote, to apply *(emplear).*

dedicatoria (de•thē•kâ•to′ryâ) *f.* dedication.

dedo (de′tho) *m.* finger *(de la mano);* toe *(del pie);* finger′s breadth *(medida);* — **indice,** index finger; — **meñique,** little finger; — **pulgar,** thumb; — **del corazón,** middle finger; — **anular,** ring finger.

deducción (de•thūk•syon′) *f.* deduction; derivation, source *(derivación).*

deducir* (de•thū•ser′) *va.* to deduce; to deduct *(rebajar).*

defectivo, va (de•fek•tē′vo, vâ)

adj. defective.

defecto (de. fek´to) *m.* defect; lack *(carencia)*.

defectuoso, sa (de•fek•two´so, sâ) *adj.* defective.

defender* (de•fen•der´) *va.* to defend; to protect *(proteger)*.

defensa (de•fen´sâ) *f.* defense; protection; tusk *(colmillo); , m.* linebacker; — **civil,** civil defense.

defensivo, va (de•fen•sē´vo, vâ) *adj.* defensive.

defensor, ra (de•fen•sor´, râ) *n.* defender, supporter; —, *m.* lawyer for the defense.

deferencia (de•fe•ren´syâ) *f.* deference.

deferente (de•fe•ren´te) *adj.* deferential; deferent *(que lleva fuera)*.

deficiencia (de•fē•syen´syâ) *f.* deficiency.

deficiente (de•fē•syen´te) *adj.* deficient.

déficit (de´fē•sēt) *m.* deficit.

definición (de•fē•nē•syon´) *f.* definition; decision, finding *(determinación)*.

definido, da (de•fē•ne´tho, thâ) *adj.* definite.

definir (de•fē•nēr´) *va.* to define; to decide, to find on; to finish *(una obra)*.

definitivo, va (de•fē•nē•tē´vo, vâ) *adj.* definitive; **en —va,** defini-

tely, decisively.

deformado, da (de•for•mâ´tho, thâ) *adj.* deformed.

deformar (de•for•mar´) *va.* to deform; (fig.) to distort *(alterar)*.

deformidad (de•for•mē•thâth´) *f.* deformity; gross blunder *(error)*.

defraudar (de•frâu•thâr´) *va.* to defraud, to cheat; (fig.) to ruin, to spoil *(frustrar)*.

defunción (de•fūn•syon´) *f.* demise, passing.

degenerado, da (de•he•ne•râ´tho, thâ) *adj.* degenerated; —, *n.* and *adj.* degenerate.

degenerar (de•he•ne•râr´) *vn.* to degenerate.

degollar* (de•go•yâr´) *va.* to behead; (fig.) to ruin, to destroy *(destruir)*.

degradar (de•grâ•thâr) *va.* to degrade, to demean; to demote *(a un militar);* to tone down *(color);* to scale down *(tamaño)*.

dehesa (de•e´sâ) *f.* pasture, grazing land.

deidad (deē•thâth´) *f.* deity; divinity *(esencia divina)*.

deificar (deē•fē•kâr´) *va.* to deify.

deísta (de•ēs´tâ) *m.* deist.

dejadez (de•hâ•thes´) *f.* negligence, carelessness.

dejado, da (de•hâ´tho, thâ) *adj.* careless, negligent; dejected, spiritless *(abatido)*.

dejar (de•hâr´) *va.* to leave; to let, to allow, to permit *(consentir);* to loan, to let have *(prestar);* to stop *(cesar);* — **atrás,** to leave behind, to excel, to surpass; — **de,** to fail to; —**se,** to abandon oneself, to give oneself over.

dejo (de´ho) *m.* end, termination; negligence, carelessness *(descuido);* aftertaste *(gustillo);* aftereffect *(sentimiento).*

del (del) of the.

delantal (de•lân•tâl´) *m.* apron.

delante (de•lân´te) *adv.* ahead; — **de,** in front of.

delantero, ra (de•lân•te´ro, râ) *adj.* foremost, first; —, *m.* front mule runner; —, *f.* front part; lead, advantage *(distancia);* (theat.) first row; **tomar la** —, to get ahead, to take the lead.

delatar (de•lâ•târ´) *va.* to accuse, to denounce.

delator, ra (de•lâ•tor´, râ) *n.* accuser, denouncer.

delectación (de•lek•tâ•syon´) *f.* pleasure, delight.

delegación (de•le•gâ•syon´) *f.* delegation.

delegado, da (de•le•gâ´tho, thâ) *n.* delegate.

delegar (de•le•gâr´) *va.* to delegate.

deleitar (de•leē•tar´) *va.* to delight.

deleite (de•le´ē•te) *m.* pleasure, delight.

deletrear (de•le•tre•âr´) *va.* and *vn.* to spell; to decipher, to interpret *(adivinar).*

deletreo (de•le•tre´o) *m.* spelling.

delfín (del•fēn´) *m.* dauphin; (zool.) dolphin.

delgado, da (del•gâ´tho, thâ) *adj.* thin, slender, lean; sharp, acute *(agudo);* fine, thin *(tenue).*

deliberación (de•lē•ve•râ•syon´) *f.* deliberation; resolution, decision *(resolución).*

deliberadamente (de•lē•ve•râ•thâ•men´•te) *adv.* deliberately, willfully.

deliberar (de•lē•ve•râr´) *vn.* to deliberate, to consider carefully; —, *va.* to resolve, to decide.

delicadeza (de•lē•kâ•the´sâ) *f.* delicacy; scrupulousness, exactitude *(escrupulosidad).*

delicado, da (de•lē•kâ´tho, thâ) *adj.* delicate; keen, quick *(ingenioso);* scrupulous.

delicia (de•lē´syâ) *f.* delight, pleasure.

delicioso, sa (de•lē•syo´so, sâ) *adj.* delicious *(placer sensual);* delightful.

delimitar (de•lē•mē•târ´) *va.* to delimit, to define.

delincuencia (de•lēng•kwen´syâ) *f.* delinquency.

delincuente (de•lēng•kwen´te) *m.* and *f.* and *adj.* delinquent, criminal.

delineación (de•lē•ne•â•syon´) *f.* delineation, sketch, portrayal.

delineamiento (de•lē•ne•â•myen´to) *m.* delineation.

delinear (de•lē•ne•âr´) *va.* to delineate, to sketch, to portray.

delirar (de•lē•râr´) *vn.* to be delirious, to rant; (fig.) to talk out of one´s head, to talk foolishness.

delirio (de•lē´ryo) *m.* delirium; nonsense *(disparate).*

delito (de•lē´to) *m.* crime, infraction.

delta (del´tâ) *f.* delta.

delusorio, ria (de•lū•so´ryo ryâ) *adj.* deceiving, deceptive, misleading.

demacrado, da (de•mâ•krâ´tho, thâ) *adj.* emaciated.

demacrarse (de•mâ•krâr´se) *vr.* to waste away, to become emaciated.

demanda (de•mân´dâ) *f.* (com.) demand; endeavor *(empresa);* request, petition *(súplica);* charge, complaint *(del litigante)* **oferta y —,** supply and demand.

demandado, da (de•man´dâ´tho, thâ) *n.* defendant.

demandante (de•mân•dân´te) *m.* and *f.* plaintiff.

demandar (de•mân•dâr´) *va.* to request, to petition; to bring charges against, to lodge a complaint against *(ante el juez).*

demarcar (de•mâr•kâr´) *va.* to mark off the limits of, to demarcate.

demás (de•mâs´) *adj.* other, remainder of the; **los** or **las —,** the rest, the others; **—** *adv.* besides; **y —,** and so forth, and so on; **estar —,** to be more than needed, to be superfluous; **por —,** in vain, to no purpose; excessively, too much *(en demasía).*

demasiado, da (de•mâ•syâ´tho, thâ) *adj.* excessive, too much; **—do,** *adv.* too much, excessively.

demencia (de•men´syâ) *f.* madness, insanity, dementia.

demente (de•men´te) *adj.* mad, insane, demented.

demérito (de•me´rē•to) *m.* demerit.

democracia (de•mo•krâ´syâ) *f.* democracy.

demócrata (de•mo´krâ•tâ) *m.* and *f.* democrat.

democrático, ca (de•mo•krâ´tē•ko, kâ) *adj.* democratic.

democratizar
(de•mo•krâ•tē•sâr´) va. to
democratize.

demoler* (de•mo•ler´) va. to
demolish, to destroy, to tear
down.

demonio (de•mo´nyo) m. devil,
demon; ¡—¡ interj. darn it!

demora (de•mo´râ) f. delay.

demorar (de•mo•râr´) vn. to
delay, to tarry; —, va. to delay,
to slow up.

demostración (de•mos•trâ•syon´)
f. demonstration; display, show
(manifestación).

demostrar* (de•mos•trâr´) va. to
prove, to demonstrate.

demostrativo, va
(de•mos•trâ•tē´vo, vâ) adj.
demonstrative.

denegar* (de•ne•gâr) va. to deny,
to re
fuse.

denigración (de•nē•grâ•syon´) f.
defamation, maligning..

denigrante (de•nē•grân´te) adj.
defamatory.

denigrar (de•nē•grâr´) va. to
malign, to defame.

denominación
(de•no•mē•nâ•syon´) f. denomination.

denominador
(de•no•mē•nâ•thor´) m. (math.)
denominator.

denominar (de•no•mē•nâr´) va.

to name, to mention.

denotar (de•no•târ´) va. to denote, to indicate.

densidad (den•sē•thâth´) f. density; — **específica,** specific gravity.

denso, sa (den´so, sâ) adj.
dense.

dentadura (den•tâ•thū´râ) f. set
of teeth; denture, false teeth (la
postiza).

dental (den•tâl´) m. (agr.) plowshare beam (del arado); metal
tooth (del trillo); —, adj. dental;
pasta —, toothpaste.

dentellada (den•te•yâ´thâ) f.
gnashing (sin mascar nada);
tooth mark (huella); bite
(acción); **a —s,** with one´s
teeth.

dentífrico (den•tē´frē•ko) m. den-
tifrice; — **ca,** adj. for cleaning
the teeth; **polvo —,** tooth powder; **pasta —,** toothpaste.

dentista (den•tēs´tâ) m. and f.
dentist.

dentistería (den•tēs•te•rē´â) f.
dentistry.

dentro (den´tro) adv. within,
inside; — **de,** inside of; — **de
poco,** shortly; **hacia —,** in,
inward, inside; **por —,** on the
inside, within.

denuncia (de•nūn´syâ) f. denunciation; announcement.

denunciación

(de•nūn•syâ•syon´) *f.* denunciation, denouncement.

denunciador, ra (de•nūn•syâ•thor´, râ) *n.* denouncer.

denunciar (de•nūn•syâr´) *va.* to announce, to declare *(declarar);* to denounce *(acusar);* to predict, to foretell *(pronosticar).*

deparar (de•pâ•râr´) *va.* to furnish, to provide *(proporcionar);* to afford, to present *(poner delante).*

departamental (de•pâr•tâ•men•tâl´) *adj.* departmental.

departamento (de•pâr•tâ•men´- to) *m.* department; compartment *(compartimiento);* apartment *(apartamento);* administrative divisions of a territory; province *(en algunos paises de latinoamérica).*

dependencia (de•pen•den´syâ) *f.* dependency; relationship, connection *(relación);* business, affair *(negocio).*

depender (de•pen•der´) *vn.* to depend, to be dependent; — **de,** to be contingent on, to depend on.

dependiente (de•pen•dyen´te) *m.* dependent; employee, clerk *(empleado);* —, *adj.* dependent.

deplorable (de•plo•râ´vle) *adj.* deplorable, regrettable.

deplorar (de•plo•râr´) *va.* to deplore, to regret.

deportación (de•por•tâ•syon´) *f.* deportation.

deportar (de•por•târ´) *va.* to deport.

deporte (de•por´te) *m.* sport.

deportivo, va (de•por•tē´vo, vâ) *adj.* sport, sporting; **club —vo,** athletic club.

deposición (de•po•sē•syon´) *f.* deposition; movement *(del vientre);* deposal *(privación).*

depositar (de•po•sē•tar´) *va.* to deposit; (fig.) to confide, to entrust *(encomendar).*

depósito (de•po´sē•to) *m.* deposit, depository.

depravación (de•prâ•vâ•syon´) *f.* depravity.

depravar (de•prâ•vâr´) *va.* to deprave, to corrupt.

deprecar (de•pre•kâr´) *va.* to beg, to implore.

depreciación (de•pre•syâ•syon´) *f.* depreciation.

depreciar (de•pre•syâr´) *va.* to depreciate.

depresión (de•pre•syon´) *f.* depression.

deprimente (de•prē•men´te) *adj.* depressing.

deprimir (de•prē•mēr´) *va.* to depress; to compress *(reducir el volumen);* to weaken *(quitar las fuerzas);* to disparage, to belittle *(humillar)*.

depurador (de•pū•râ•thor´) *m.* purifier.

depurar (de•pū•râr´) *va.* to purify.

derecha (de•re´châ) *f.* right hand *(mano);* right side *(lado);* (pol.) right wing; **a**—**s,** properly, correctly; **a la** —, to the right.

derechista (de•re•chēs´tâ) *m.* and *f.* (pol.) conservative.

derecho cha (de•re´cho, châ) *adj.* right; straight *(recto o vertical);* just, legitimate, right *(justo);* — **cho,** *adv.* straight ahead; —, *m.* law *(leyes);* right *(facultad);* right side *(lado labrado);* **dar** — **cho,** to entitle; —**os consulares,** consular fees; —**os de aduana** or **arancelarios,** customs duties; —**os de entrada,** import duties; —**os de autor,** royalties; — **humanos,** human rights, — **os reservados,** all rights reserved; **facultad de** —**cho,** law school.

deriva (de•rē´vâ) *f.* drift; **a la** —, drifting.

derivación (de•rē•vâ•syon´) *f.* derivation.

derivado (de•rē•vâ´tho) *m.* by-product; (gram.) derivative; —, **da,** *adj.* derived.

derivar (de•rē•vâr´) *va.* to derive; to direct, to focus *(encaminar);* —, *vn.* (naut.) to drift; to

derive, to be derived.

dermatología (der•mâ•to•lo•hē´â) *f.* dermatology.

derramamiento (de•rrâ•mâ•myen´to) *m.* overflow; scattering; outpour; — **de sangre,** bloodshed.

derramar (de•rrâ•mâr´) *va.* to pour, to splash *(un líquido);* to scatter *(cosas menudas);* to spread *(una noticia);* — **se,** to run over, to overflow *(un líquido);* to scatter, to fan out *(desparramarse).*

derrame (de•rrâ´me) *m.* loss, waste; leak-age *(del recipiente);* — **cerebral,** (med.) stroke.

derrelicto, ta (de•rre•lēk´to, tâ) *adj.* and *m.* derelict.

derretimiento (de•rre•tē•myen´to) *m.* melting.

derretir* (de•rre•tēr´) *va.* to melt *(liquidar);* (fig.) to run through, to burn up *(gastar);* —**se,** to fall hard, to fall head over heels *(enamorarse);* to fall apart, to be all broken up *(deshacerse).*

derribar (de•rre•vâr´) *va.* to knock down *(un edificio);* to throw down *(a una persona);* to overthrow *(trastornar);* —**se,** to throw oneself on the ground.

derribo (de•rre´vo) *m.* demolition, knocking down; overthrow; rubble, debris *(materiales).*

derrocar (de•rro•kâr´) va. to hurl, to dash (despeñar); (fig.) to tear down, to demolish (derribar); to unseat, to pull down (a uno en poder).

derrochar (de•rro•châr´) va. to squander, to waste.

derroche (de•rro´che) m. squandering, waste.

derrota (de•rro´tâ) f. (mil.) defeat, rout; road, path (camino).

derrotar (de•rro•târ´) va. (naut.) to throw off course; (mil.) to defeat; to ruin (destruir).

derrotero (de•rro•te´ro) m. (naut.) course (ruta); (naut.) chart book (libro); (fig.) plan of action (modo de obrar).

derrotista (de•rro•tēs´tâ) m. and f. defeatist.

derruir* (de•rrwēr´) va. to demolish, to tear down, to wreck.

derrumbar (de•rrūm•bâr´) va. to throw headlong, to dash; (Sp. Am.) to knock down, to throw down (derribar); —se, to cave in, to collapse.

derrumbe (de•rrūm´be) m. collapse, cave-in.

desabotonar (de•sâ•vo•to•nâr´) va. to unbutton; —, vn. to blossom.

desabrigado, da (de•sâ•vrē•gâ´tho, thâ) adj. without one´s coat; (fig.) shelterless (desamparado).

desabrochar (de•sâ•vro•châr´) va. to unbutton, to unfasten; —se con, to confide in.

desacertado, da (de•sâ•ser•tâ´tho, thâ) adj. mistaken, wrong, in error.

desacierto (de•sâ•syer´to) m. error, mistake, blunder.

desacomodado, da (de•sâ•ko•mo•thâ´•tho, thâ) adj. unemployed, out of work (sin acomodo); uncomfortable (incómodo); without means, in want (sin medios).

desacomodar (de•sâ•ko•mo•thâr´) va. to inconvenience; to discharge (quitar el empleo); —se, to lose one´s job.

desacordado, da (de•sâ•kor´thâ´tho, thâ) adj. poorly matched, unharmonious.

desacorde (de•sâ´kor´the) adj. discordant, inharmonious.

desacostumbrarse (de•sâ•kos•tūm•brâr´se) vr. to become unaccustomed.

desacreditar (de•sâ•kre•thē•târ´) va. to discredit.

desactivar (de•sâk•tē•vâr´) va. to deactivate.

desacuerdo (de•sâ•kwer´tho) m. disagreement, discord; failure to remember (falta de memoria).

desafecto (de•sâ fek´to) m. disaffection, ill will, enmity.

desafiar (de•sâ•fyâr´) *va.* to challenge; (fig.) to defy, to brave
(oponerse).

desafinar (de•sâ•fē•nâr´) *vn.* and
vr. to be off key *(la voz);* to be
out of tune *(un instrumento);*
(fig.) to talk out of turn.

desafio (de•sâ•fē´o) *m.* challenge
(acción); duel *(efecto);* rivalry,
contest *(competencia).*

desaforado, da (de•sâ•fo•râ´tho,
thâ) *adj.* lawless, heedless *(sin
ley);* unearthly, extraordinary
(excesivo).

desaforar* (de•sâ•fo•râr´) *va.* to
violate the rights of; **—se,** to
get beside oneself, to go to pieces.

desafortunado, da
(de•sâ•for•tū•nâ´tho, thâ) *adj.*
unfortunate.

desagradable (de•sâ•grâ•thâ´vle)
adj. disagreeable, unpleasant.

desagradar (de•sâ•grâ•thâr´) *va.*
to displease, to offend.

desagradecido, da
(de•sâ•grâ•the•sē´tho, tha) *adj.*
ungrateful; **—,** *n.* ingrate.

desagrado (de•sâ•grâ´tho) *m.*
displeasure.

desagraviar (de•sâ•grâ•vyâr´) *va.*
to make amends for.

desagravio (de•sâ•grâ´vyo) *m.*
satisfaction, amends.

desaguar (de•sâ•gwâr´) *va.* and

vn. to drain.

desagüe (de•sâ´gwe) *m.* draining,
drainage; drain pipe, drain
(conducto).

desahogado, da (de•sâ•o•gâ´tho,
thâ) *adj.* impudent *(descarado);*
comfortable *(cómodo).*

desahogar (de•sâ•o•gâr´) *va.* to
ease, to relieve *(aliviar);* to give
free rein to *(dar rienda suelta);*
—se, to get relief; to unburden
oneself, to get a problem off
one´s chest *(expansionarse).*

desahogo (de•sâ•o´go) *m.* relief
(alivio); relaxation *(ensanche);*
ease, comfort *(comodidad);* freedom, lack of restraint *(libertad).*

desairar (de•sâē•râr´) *va.* to disregard to rebuff *(rechazar);* to
slight, to offend *(desatender);*
to detract from *(deslucir).*

desajuste (de•sâ•hūs´te) *m.* breakdown, collapse.

desalentar* (de•sâ•len•târ´) *va.*
to wind *(dificultar el aliento);*
(fig.) to discourage; **—se,** to lose
hope, to be discouraged.

desaliento (de•sâ•lyen´to) *m.* dis-
pair, discouragement, dejec-
tion.

desaliñar (de•sâ•lē•nyâr´) *va.* to
disarrange, to mess up.

desalmado, da (de•sâl•mâ´tho,
thâ) *adj.* cruel, inhuman, heartless.

desalojar (de•sâ•lo•hâr′) *va.* to dislodge; to abandon, to evacuate *(abandonar);* to displace *(desplazar);* —, *vn.* to move out.

desamarrar (de•sâ•mâ•rrâr′) *va.* to unmoor; (fig.) to let loose of *(desasir).*

desamparar (de•sâm•pâ•râr′) *va.* to forsake, to abandon; to relinquish *(con renuncia de derecho).*

desamparo (de•sâm•pâ′ro) *m.* abandonment, forlornness, desolation; relinquishment.

desandar* (de•sân•dâr′) *va.* to retrace, to go back over.

desangrar (de• sâng•grâr′) *va.* to remove a large amount of blood from; (fig.) to drain *(un estanque);* to impoverish slowly *(empobrecer).*

desanimado, da (de•sâ•nē•mâ′-tho, thâ) *adj.* downhearted; dull, spiritless *(poco animado).*

desanimar (de•sâ•nē•mâr′) *va.* to discourage; —**se,** to become discouraged.

desanudar (de•sâ•nū•thâr′) *va.* to untie; (fig.) to disentangle, to unravel *(disolver).*

desapacible (de•sâ•pâ•sē′vle) *adj.* disagreeable, unpleasant.

desaparecer* (de•sâ•pâ•re•ser′) *va.* to whisk out of sight; —, *vn.* to disappear.

desaparejar (de•sâ•pâ•re•hâr′) *va.* to un-harness *(una caballería);* (naut.) to unrig.

desaparición (de•sâ•pâ•rē•syon′) *f.* disappearance.

desapasionar (de•sâ•pâ•syo•nâr′) *va.* to make objective, to remove one′s prejudice *(volver imparcial);* to root out one′s passion.

desapercibido, da (de•sâ•per•sē•vē′tho, thâ) *adj.* unprepared, not ready.

desaplicado, da (de•sâ•plē•kâ′-tho, thâ) *adj.* careless, lazy, indifferent.

desaprobación (de•sâ•pro•vâ•syon′) *f.* disapproval.

desaprobar* (de•sâ •pro•vâr′) *va.* to disapprove of.

desaprovechado, da (de•sâ•pro•ve•châ′tho, thâ) *adj.* lacking drive, lacking ambition, indifferent *(persona);* wasted, untapped, unused.

desaprovechar (de•sâ•pro•vechâr′) *va.* to misuse, to waste.

desarmar (de •sâr•mâr′) *va.* to disarm; to take apart, to dismount, to disassemble *(desmontar);* (naut.) to unrig; (mil.) to disband; (fig.) to pacify, to assuage *(templar).*

desarme (de• sâr′me) *m.* disarmament, disassembly; pacifying.

desarraigar (de•sâ• rrâē• gâr´)
va. to uproot; (fig.) to root out,
to eradicate.

desarraigo (de•sâ•rrâ´ē•go) *m.*
(fig.) eradication; uprooting.

desarreglado, da (de•sâ•rre•glâ´-
tho, thâ) *adj.* immoderate,
intemperate; disorderly (desordenado).

desarreglar (de•sâ•rre•glâr´) *va.*
to put out of order, to upset.

desarreglo (de•sâ•rre´glo) *m.*
disorder.

desarrollar (de•sâ•rro•yâr´) *va.*
to unroll, to unwrap; (fig.) to
develop (acrecentar).

desarrollo (de•sâ•rro´yo) *m.*
development, growth.

desarropar (de• sâ•rro•pâr´) *va.*
to undress.

desarrugar (de•sâ•rrū•gâr´) *va.*
to take out the wrinkles from.

desasir* (de• sâ•sēr´) *va.* to let
loose of, to let go of; —se de, to
get rid of.

desasosiego (de•sâ•so•sye´go) *m.*
restlessness, uneasiness.

desastre (de• sâs´tre) *m.* disaster, misfortune.

desastroso sa, (de •sâs•tro´so,
sâ) *adj.* disastrous.

desatar (de•sâ•târ´) *va.* to untie,
to loosen (deshacer); to figure
out, to clear up (aclarar); —se,
to break out (descomedirse); to

come out of one's shell (perder
la timidez).

desatascar (de•sâ•tâs•kâr´) *va.*
to pull out of the mud; to
unplug (una cañería); (fig.) to
get out of a jam (de un apuro).

desatender* (de•sâ•ten• der´) *va.*
to pay no attention to, to disregard, to neglect, to slight.

desatento, ta (de• sâ•ten´to, tâ)
adj. inattentive, careless; rude,
uncivil (descortés).

desatinado, da (de•sâ•tē •nâ´-
tho, thâ) *adj.* senseless, foolish;
off-the-mark.

desatinar (de•sâ•tē•nâr´) *va.* to
drive out of one's mind, to
drive to distraction; —, *vn.* to
talk nonsense.

desatino (de•sâ•tē´no) *m.* foolishness, nonsense.

desatornillar (de•sâ•tor•nē•yâr´)
va. to unscrew.

desavenir* (de• sâ•ve•nēr´) *va.* to
put at odds, to make disagree.

desayuno (de•sâ´yū´no) *m.* breakfast.

desazón (de• sâ•son´) *f.* taste-
lessness; poor quality (de las
tierras); (fig.) trouble, bad time
(molestia); queasiness, upset
(de salud).

desazonado, da (de• sâ•so
•nâ´tho, thâ) *adj.* queasy; poor;
upset, bothered.

desazonar (de•sâ•so•nâr´) *va.* to

take away the taste of; (fig.) to upset, to bother *(molestar);* — **se,** to feel indisposed.

desbandarse (dez•vân•dâr´se) *vr.* to disband, to disperse.

desbaratado, da (dez•vâ•râ•tâ´tho, thâ) *adj.* broken; upset.

desbaratar (dez•vâ•râ•târ´) *va.* to break, to ruin *(arruinar);* to run through, to waste *(disipar);* (fig.) to spoil, to upset *(estorbar);* (mil.) to rout; —, *vn.* to talk nonsense.

desbordar (dez •vor•thâr´) *vn.* to overflow, to spill over, to run over; (fig.) to know no bounds *(rebosar).*

desbordamiento (dez•vor•thâ•myen´to) *m.* overflowing.

descabellado da (des•kâ•ve•yâ´-tho,thâ) *adj.* disorderly, unruly, unrestrained.

descabellar (des• kâ•ve•yâr´) *va.* to muss.

descabezado, da (des•kâ•ve•sâ´tho, thâ) *adj.* (fig.) out of one´s head; headless.

descabezar (des•kâ•ve•sâr´) *va.* to behead; to lop off the top of *(un árbol);* —**se,** to rack one´s brains.

descabullirse* (des•kâ• vū•yēr´se) *vr.* to escape, to get

away; (fig.) to get oneself off the hook.

descalabrar (des•kâ•lâ•vrâr´) *va.* to injure in the head; to hurt, to injure *(herir).*

descalificar (des•kâ•lē •fē•kâr´) *va.* to disqualify.

descalzar (des•kâl•sâr´) *va.* to pull off, to take off; to take off one´s shoes *(quitar el calzado).*

descalzo, za (des•kâl´so, sâ) *adj.* barefooted.

descaminar (des• kâ•mē•nâr´) *va.* to misguide, to lead astray, to mislead.

descansado, da (des•kân•sâ´tho, thâ) *adj.* peaceful, quiet, restful.

descansar (des•kân•sâr´) *va.* to rest *(apoyar);* to spell, to relieve *(ayudar);* *vn.* to rest.

descanso (des•kân´so) *m.* rest, repose.

descarado, da (des•kâ•râ´tho, thâ) *adj.* impudent, barefaced, cheeky.

descarga (des•kâr´gâ) *f.* unloading; (mil.) volley; discharge, firing.

descargadero (des•kâr•gâ•the´ro) *m.* wharf, dock.

descargar (des•kâr•gâr´) *va.* to unload *(la carga);* to discharge, to fire *(un arma);* to free, to relieve *(de una obligación);* to let go with, to let have *(un* *golpe);* —**se,** to be cleared of the charges, to be acquitted.

descargo (des• kâr´go) *m.* discharge; acquittal; unloading.

descaro (des•kâ´ro) *m.* impudence, audacity.

descarrilar (des•kâ•rrē •lâr´) *vn.* (rail.) to jump the track, to derail.

descartar (des•kâr•târ´) *va.* to cast aside, to throw off *(apartar);* to count out, to leave out *(de un proyecto);* to discard *(un naipe).*

descasar (des•kâr´sâr) *va.* to separate; to annul the marriage of *(anular el matrimonio);* to throw out of balance *(cosas que casaban bien).*

descascarar (des•kâs•kâ•râr´) *va.* to skin *(una manzana);* to peel *(una naranja);* to shell *(una nuez);* to shuck, to husk *(la espiga).*

descendencia (des•sen•den´syâ) *f.* descent *(linaje);* descendants.

descendente (des•sen•den´te) *adj.* descending.

descender* (des•sen•der´) *vn.* to descend; to derive, to originate *(derivarse);* —, *va.* to lower, to take down.

descendiente (des•sen•dyen´te) *adj.* descending; —, *m.* descendant.

descendimiento

(des•sen•dē•myen´to) *m.* descent; lowering.

descenso (des•sen´so) *m.* descent; (fig.) degradation.

descentralización (des•sen•trâ• lē•sâ• syon´) *f.* decentralization.

descentralizar (des•sen•trâ•lē•sâr´) *va.* to decentralize.

descentrar (des•sen•trâr´) *va.* to put off center; —**se,** to be off center.

descifrar (des•sē• frâr´) *va.* to decipher, to decode.

descobijar (des•ko•vē•hâr´) *va.* to uncover, to remove the blankets from.

descolgar* (des• kol•gâr´) *va.* to take down *(algo colgado);* to lower with a rope *(bajar);* to take down the hangings from *(una iglesia);* to take down the draperies from *(una casa);* —**se,** to slide down a rope; (fig.) to slip down, to descend.

descolorar (des•ko•lo•râr´) *va.* to discolor.

descolorido, da (des•ko•lo•rē´-tho, thâ) *adj.* faded, discolored.

descollar* (des•ko•yâr´) *vn.* to excel, to be outstanding.

descomedido, da (des •ko•me•thē´tho, thâ) *adj.* excessive, out of proportion *(excesivo);* rude, disrespectful *(descortés).*

descomedirse*
(des•ko•me•thēr´se) *vr.* to be rude, to be disrespectful.

descomponer* (des•kom•po•ner´) *va.* (chem.) to decompose, to break down; to put out of order *(desordenar);* to put at odds, to hurt the friendship of (dos *personas);* —se, to decompose, to rot *(corromperse);* to lose one's composure *(perder la serenidad).*

descomposición
(des•kom•po•sē•syon´) *f.* falling out; (chem.) decomposition, breakdown; decay, rotting; loss of composure.

descompuesto, ta
(des•kom•pwes´to, tâ) *adj.* decomposed rotten; out of order; distorted *(alterado);* (fig.) discourteous, insolent *(descortés).*

desconcertado, da
(des•kon•ser•tâ´tho, thâ) *adj.* disconcerted; dislocated; out of order; (fig.) evil *(de mala vida).*

desconcertar* (des• kon•ser•târ´) *va.* to put out of order *(desordenar);* to dislocate *(un hueso);* to disconcert *(con-fundir);* —se, to have a falling out *(enemistarse);* (fig.) to be rude, to be disrespectful.

desconectar (des•ko•nek•târ´) *va.* (elec.) to disconnect; (fig.) to detach, to separate *(desunir).*

desconfiado, da (des•kom•fyâ´-tho, thâ) *adj.* suspicious, distrustful.

desconfianza (des•kom•fyân´sâ) *f.* distrust, lack of confidence, mistrust.

desconfiar (des•kom•fyâr´) *vn.* to lack confidence, to be distrustful; — de, to mistrust, to distrust.

desconforme (des•kom•for´me) *adj.* in disagreement; unresigned, dissatisfied *(no satisfecho).*

desconformidad
(des•kom•for•mē•thâth´) *f.* disagreement *(desacuerdo);* impatience, dissatisfaction.

descongelar (des•kon•he•lâr´) *va.* to defrost.

desconocer* (des•ko•no•ser´) *va.* to disown, to disavow *(rechazar);* not to know *(no conocer);* not to recognize *(no reconocer);* to have forgotten *(no recordar);* to pretend unawareness of *(darse por desentendido).*

desconocido, da (des•ko•no•sē´-tho, thâ) *adj.* ungrateful *(ingrato);* unknown, foreign *(ignorado);* unrecognizable *(muy cambiado);* —, *n.* stranger.

desconsiderado, da
(des•kon•sē•the•râ´tho, thâ)

adj. inconsiderate.

desconsolado, da
(des•kon•so•lâ´tho, thâ) *adj.*
disconsolate, grieving.

desconsolar* (des•kon•so•lâr´)
va. to grieve, to hurt, to pain.

desconsuelo (des•kon•swe´lo) *m.*
dejection, grief, suffering.

descontar* (des•kon•târ´) *va.* to
discount; to grant, to assume
to be true *(dar por cierto);* to
deduct *(rebajar).*

descontentar (des•kon•ten•târ´)
va. to displease, to dissatisfy.

descontento (des•kon•ten´to) *m.*
discontent, dissatisfaction, displeasure; —, **ta,** *adj.* dissatisfied, discontented, displeased.

descontinuar (des•kon•tē•nwâr´)
va. to discontinue.

descorazonado, da
(des•ko•râ•so•nâ´tho, thâ) *adj.*
depressed, in low spirits, glum.

descorrer (des•ko•rrer´) *vn.* to
run, to flow; —, *va.* to retravel,
to go back over; — **la cortina,**
to draw open the curtain.

descortés (des•kor•tes´) *adj.*
impolite, discourteous.

descortesía (des•kor•te•sē´â) *f.*
discourtesy, impoliteness.

descoser (des•ko•ser´) *va.* to rip,
to unstitch; **—se,** (fig.) to let
slip out, to let out of the bag.

descosido (des•ko•sē´tho) *m.*
ripped seam, rip; — **da,** *adj.*

ripped, unstitched; indiscreet,
given to revealing confidences
(imprudente).

descrédito (des•kre´thē•to) *m.*
discredit.

descreer* (des•kre•er´) *va.* to
disbelieve, to fail to believe.

describir* (des•krē•vēr´) *va.* to
describe.

descripción (des•krēp•syon´) *f.*
description

descriptivo, va (des•krēp•tē´vo,
vâ) *adj.* descriptive.

descrito, ta (des•krē´to, tâ) *adj.*
described.

descuartizar (des•kwâr•tē•sâr´)
va, to quarter; (coll.) to divide
up, to split up *(hacer pedazos).*

descubierto, ta (des•kū•vyer´to,
tâ) *adj.* uncovered.

descubridor, ra
(des•kū•vrē•thor´, râ) *n.* disco-
verer; —, *m.* (mil.) scout.

descubrimiento
(des•kū•vrē•myen´to) *m.* discovery.

descubrir* (des•kū•vrēr´) *va.* to
uncover (destapar); to disclose
(manifestar); to discover *(lo
ignorado);* ; to invent *(inventar);*
to make out, to have a view of
(alcanzar a ver); **—se,** to take
off one's hat.

descuento (des•kwen´to) *m.* discount; deduction.

descuidar (des•kwē•thâr´) *va.* to

relieve, to free *(de una obligación);* to distract *(distraer);* to neglect, to be careless of *(no cuidar de).*

descuido (des•kwē'tho) *m.* carelessness, neglect; slip, oversight *(desliz).*

desde (dez'the) *prep.* since *(de tiempo);* from *(de espacio);* — **luego,** of course, — **entonces,** since then; — **que,** since; — **ahora,** from now on; — **un principio,** from the beginning.

desdecir* (dez•the•sēr') *vn.* to go counter, to be out of keeping *(no corresponder);* —**se,** to retract a remark, to take back what one has said.

desdén (dez•then') *m.* disdain, contempt.

desdentado da (dez•then•tâ'tho, thâ) *adj.* toothless.

desdeñar (dez•the•nyâr') *va.* to disdain, to look down on; —**se,** to be disdainful.

desdicha (dez•thē'châ) *f.* misfortune; dire poverty *(pobreza).*

desdoblar (dez•tho•vlâr') *va.* to unfold, to spread out.

deseable (de•se•â'vle) *adj.* desirable.

desear (de•se•âr') *va.* to desire, to wish; — **saber,** to wonder.

desecar (de•se•kâr') *va.* to dry; (fig.) to harden.

desechable (de•se•châ'vle) *adj.*

disposable.

desechar (de•se•châr') *va.* to reject *(rechazar);* to throw out *(arrojar);* to depreciate, to underrate *(menospreciar);* to cast off (apartar de sí).

desecho (de•se'cho) *m.* residue, remainder *(residuo);* discard, castoff *(cosa que no sirve);* low opinion, low regard *(menosprecio).*

desembarazar (de•sem•bâ•râ•sâr') *va.* to clear, to disencumber; to clear out, to empty *(desocupar).*

desembarcadero (de•sem•bâr•kâ•the'ro) *m.* landing place.

desembarcar (de•sem•bâr•kâr') *va.* to unload; —, *vn.* to disembark, to land.

desembarco (de•sem•bâr'ko) *m.* landing, disembarkment.

desembarque (de•sem•bâr'ke) *m.* landing, unloading.

desembocar (de•sem•bo•car') *vn.* to run, to end *(una calle);* to flow, to empty *(un río).*

desembolsar (de•sem•bol•sâr') *va.* to empty out from a purse; (fig.) to expend, to disburse.

desemejante (de•se•me•hân'te) *adj.* dissimilar, different, unlike.

desemejanza (de•se•me•hân'sâ) *f.* dissimilarity, difference, unlikeness.

desempacar (de•sem•pâ•kâr´)
va. to unpack, to unwrap.

desempaquetar
(de•sem•pâ•ke•târ´) *va.* to
unpack, to unwrap.

desempatar (de•sem•pâ•târ´) *va.*
to break the tie in.

desempeñar (de•sem•pe•nyâr´)
va. to redeem *(una garantía);* to
get out of debt *(librar de deudas);* to play *(un papel);* to fulfill, to carry out *(cumplir);* to
get out of a difficult situation
(sacar airoso).

desempeño (de•sem•pe´nyo) *m.*
redeeming; fulfillment, performance.

desempleado, da
(de•sem•ple•â´tho, thâ) *adj.*
unemployed.

desempleo (de•sem•ple´o) *m.*
unemployment.

desempolvar (de•sem•pol•vâr´)
va. to dust off; to brush up on
(traer a la memoria); —**se,** to
brush up.

desencadenar
(de•seng•kâ•the•nâr´) *va.* to
unchain; (fig.) to unleash, to
set abroad; —**se,** to break out,
to be unleashed.

desencajar (de•seng•kâ•hâr´) *va.*
to pull out of place, to pull
from its socket or fitting; —**se,**
to become contorted.

desencantar (de•seng•kân•târ´)
va. to disenchant, to disillusion.

desencanto (de•seng•kân´to) *m.*
disenchantment, disillusion.

desenconar (de•seng•ko•nâr··´)
va. to reduce *(la inflamación);*
to appease, to calm *(el ánimo);*
—**se,** to abate, to sub-side.

desencordar* (de•seng•kor•thâr´)
va. to unstring.

desencorvar (de•seng•kor•vâr´)
va. to straighten.

desenfadar (de•sem•fâ•thâr´) *va.*
to calm the anger of, to
appease.

desenfrenado, da
(de•sem•fre•nâ´tho, thâ) *adj.*
wanton, unbridled; debauched.

desenfrenar (de•sem•fre•nâr´)
va. to unbridle; —**se,** to become
completely debauched; to be
unleashed *(los elementos).*

desenfreno (de•sem•fre´no) *m.*
debauchery *(libertinaje);*
unbridling; unleashing.

desengañar (de˙seng•gâ•nyâr´)
va. to open one´s eyes to, to
undeceive; to disillusion, to
disappoint *(quitar ilusiones).*

desengaño (de•seng•gâ´nyo) *m.*
disillusionment, disappointment; naked truth, fact of the
matter *(claridad).*

desenlace (de•sen•lâ´se) *m.*
denouement, outcome.

desenlazar (de•sen•lâ•sâr´) *va.* to untie; (fig.) to unravel, to resolve, to clear up *(solucionar)*.

desenmascarar (de•sen•mâs•kâ•râr´) *va.* to unmask; (fig.) to expose, to reveal; —**se,** to unmask.

desenojo (de•se•no´ho) *m.* calming down, quieting down.

desenredar (de•sen•rre•thâr´) *va.* to disentangle; —**se,** to extricate oneself, to free oneself.

desenrollar (de•sen•rro•yâr´) *va.* to unroll.

desensartar (de•sen•sâr•târ´) *va.* to unthread.

desensillar (de•sen•sē•yâr´) *va.* to unsaddle.

desentenderse* (de•sen•ten•der´se) *vr.* to pretend ignorance, to pretend not to notice; — **de,** to disregard, to ignore; to have nothing to do with *(prescindir de).*

desentendido, da (de•sen•ten•dē´tho, thâ) *adj.* unmindful; **hacerse el** — or **la** — to feign ignorance, to pretend to be unaware.

desenterrar* (de•sen•te•rrâr´) *va.* to disinter, to dig up.

desentono (de•sen•to´no) *m.* poor tone; (fig.) rude tone of voice.

desenvoltura (de•sem•bol•tū´râ) *f.* ease, effortlessness, self-assurance, freedom; articulateness *(de elocución).*

desenvolver* (de•sem•bol•ver´) *va.* to unwrap, to unroll *(desarrollar);* to clear up, to unravel *(desenredar);* to develop *(acrecentar);* —**se**, to act with assurance, to get along well.

desenvuelto, ta (de• sem•bwel´-to, tâ) *adj.* poised self-assured; articulate.

deseo (de•se´o) *m.* desire, wish.

deseoso, sa (de•se•o´so, sa) *adj.* desirous.

desequilibrio (de•se•kē•lē´vryo) *m.* unsteadiness, lack of balance.

deserción (de•ser•syon´) *f.* desertion.

desertar (de•ser•târ´) *va.* to desert; to withdraw, to abandon *(la apelación).*

desertor (de•ser•tor´) *m.* deserter.

desesperación (de•ses•pe•râ•syon´) *f.* despair, desperation; anger, fury *(cólera).*

desesperado, da (de•ses•pe•râ´-tho, thâ) *adj.* desperate, hopeless.

desesperar (de•ses•pe•râr´) *va.* to make desperate; (coll.) to annoy, to get on one s nerves *(impacientar);* **—se,** to grow desperate.

desfalcar (des•fâl•kâr´) *va.* to embezzle.

desfalco (des• fâl´ko) *m.* embezzlement.

desfallecer* (des•fâ•ye•ser´) *vn.* to weaken, to fall away; to faint *(desmayarse);* —, *va.* to weaken; — **de hambre,** to starve, to weaken by lack of food.

desfallecido, da (des•fâ•ye•sē´tho, thâ) *adj.* weak, faint; unconscious.

desfallecimiento (des•fâ•ye•sē•myen´to) *m.* weakening, faintness; swoon, fainting *(desmayo).*

desfavorable (des•fâ•vo•râ´vle) *adj.* unfavorable.

desfavorecer* (des•fâ•vo•re•ser´) *va.* to disfavor.

desfigurar (des•fē•gū•râr´) *va.* to disfigure, to deform; to cover, to disguise *(disimular);* to distort *(alterar);* **—se,** to become disfigured; to be distorted.

desfigurado, da (des•fē•gū•râ´tho, thâ) *adj.* deformed, disfigured; hidden, covered; distorted.

desfilar (des•fē•lâr´) *vn.* to march, to parade; (coll.) to troop out, to file out *(salir uno tras otro);* (mil.) to march in review.

desfile (des•fē´le) *m.* parade.

desganado, da (dez•gâ•nâ´tho, thâ) *adj.* having no appetite; without will.

desgano (dez•gâ´no) *m.* lack of appetite *(inapetencia);* lack of interest *(tedio).*

desgarrador, ra (dez•gâ•rrâ•thor´, râ) *adj.* piercing; (fig.) heartrending.

desgarrar (dez•gâ•rrâr´) *va.* to tear, to rip; to rend, to hurt deeply *(los sentimientos);* **—se,** to tear oneself away.

desgastar (dez•gâs•târ´) *va.* to consume, to wear away slowly; (fig.) to ruin, to spoil *(echar a perder);* **—se** (fig.) to lose one´s vigor, to lose one´s verve.

desgaste (dez•gâs´te) *m.* wearing away, eating away.

desgobierno (dez•go•vyer´no) *m.* misgovernment, mismanagement.

desgracia (dez•grâ´syâ) *f.* misfortune, mishap *(acontecimiento);* disgrace *(pérdida de favor);* bad luck, adversity *(mala suerte);* sharpness, disagreeableness *(aspereza);* **por —,** unfortunately.

desgraciado, da (dez•grâ•syâ´tho, thâ) *adj.* unfortunate; out of favor *(desfavorecido);* disagreeable, unpleasant *(desagradable).*

desgranar (dez•grâ•nâr´) *va.* to remove the kernels from *(el maíz)* ; to seed *(las uvas);* to remove the grains from *(el trigo).*

desgrasar (dez•grâ•sâr´) *va.* to remove the grease from.

desguarnecer* (dez•gwâr•ne•ser´) *va.* to strip of adornments, to remove the trimmings from; (mech.) to strip down; to disarm *(una plaza).*

deshabitado, da (de•sâ•vĕ•tâ´-tho, thâ) *adj.* deserted, desolate.

deshabitar (de•sâ•vē•tar´) *va.* to move out of *(una casa);* to depopulate *(un territorio).*

deshacer* (de•sâ•ser´) *va.* to undo; to rout, to defeat *(derrotar);* to take apart *(despedazar);* to dissolve *(liquidar);* to break up *(descomponer);* —**se,** to break, to be smashed; to be on edge, to be on pins and needles *(estar inquieto);* to outdo oneself *(trabajar mucho);* to injure, to damage *(maltratarse);* to wear oneself out, to overwork *(extenuarse);* —**se en,** to break into; —**se de,** to get rid of.

deshebrar (de•se•vrâr´) *va.* to unravel; (fig.) to shred, to make mincemeat of.

deshecho, cha (de•se´cho, châ) *adj.* undone; broken; enormous; torrential; routed; **borrasca —,** violent storm.

deshelar* (de•se•lâr´) *va.* to thaw; —**se,** to thaw, to melt.

desheredar (de•se•re•thâr´) *va.* to disinherit; —**se,** to be a black sheep; to get away from one´s family.

desherrar* (de•se•rrâr´) *va.* to unchain; to unshoe *(la caballería).*

deshielo (de•sye´lo) *m.* thaw.

deshilachar (de•sē•lâ•châr´) *va.* to unravel.

deshinchar (de•sēn•châr´) *va.* to reduce the swelling on; (fig.) to appease, to calm down; —**se,** to go down, to be reduced; (fig.) to come down a notch, to have one´s pride deflated.

deshonesto, ta (de•so•nes´to, tâ) *adj.* indecent, lewd.

deshonor (de•so•nor´) *m.* disgrace, shame.

deshonrar (de•son•rrâr´) *va.* to disgrace, to dishonor *(hacer perder la honra);* to affront, to insult *(injuriar).*

deshonroso, sa (de•son•rro´so, sâ) *adj.* dishonorable, vile, infamous.

deshora (de•so´râ) *f.* inopportune moment, wrong time.

deshuesar (de•swe•sâr´) *va.* to bone *(la carne);* to pit *(un* *fruto).*

deshumedecer*
(de•su•me•the•ser´) *va.* to
dehumidify.

desierto, ta (de•syer´to, tâ) *adj.*
deserted, solitary; —, *m.*
desert, wilderness; **predicar en
el —,** to be a voice crying in the
wilderness.

designación (de•sēg•nâ•syon´) *f.*
designation.

designar (de•sēg•nâr´) *va.* to
designate; to plan, to project
(formar designio).

desigual (de•sē•gwâl´) *adj.*
unequal, unlike; uneven, rough
(barrancoso); difficult, thorny
(arduo); changeable *(vario).*

desigualar (de•sē•gwâ•lâr´) *va.*
to make unequal; **—se,** to surpass, to excel.

desigualdad (de•sē•gwâl•dâth´) *f.*
unlikeness, unequalness;
unevenness, roughness *(de un
terreno);* (math.) inequality.

desilusión (de•sē•lū•syon´) *f.*
disillusion.

desilusionar (de•sē•lū•syo•nâr´)
va. to disillusion; **—se,** to
become disillusioned.

desinfectante (de•sēm
•fek•tân´te) *m.* disinfectant.

desinfectar (de•sēm•fek•târ´) *va.*
to disinfect.

desinflable (de•sēm•flâ´vle) *adj.*
deflatable.

desinflación (de•sēm•flâ•syon´) *f.*
deflation.

desinflamar (de•sēm•flâ•mâr´)
va. to soothe the inflammation
in.

desinflar (de•sēm•flâr´) *va.* to
deflate.

desintegración
(de•sēn•te•grâ•syon´) *f.* disintegration.

desintegrar (de•sēn•te•grâr´) *va.*
and *vn.* to disintegrate.

desinterés (de•sēn•te•res´) *m.*
unselfishness, disinterested-
ness.

desistir (de•sēs•tēr´) *vn.* to
desist, to cease, to stop.

deslave (dez•lâ´ve) *m.* washout,
landslide.

desleal (dez•le•âl´) *adj.* disloyal.

deslealtad (dez•le•âl•tâth´) *f.* disloyalty, breach of faith.

desleír* (dez •le•ēr´) *va.* to dilute,
to dissolve.

desligar (dez•lē•gâr´) *va.* to
loosen, to unbind; (fig.) to
untangle, to clear up
(desenredar).

deslinde (dez•lēn´de) *m.* demar-
cation.

desliz (dez•lēs´) *m.* slip, sliding;
(fig.) slip, mistake, false step
(falta).

deslizamiento (dez•lē •sâ•myen´-
to) *m.* slide, slip.

deslizar (dez•lē•sâr´) *va.* to slide;

to do without thinking *(por descuido);* —, *vn.* to slip, to slide; —**se,** to scurry away, to slip away; (fig.) to make a false step.

deslucir* (dez•lū•sēr´) *va.* to offset, to spoil, to ruin the effect of *(quitar la gracia);* to discredit, to ruin the reputation of *(desacreditar).*

deslumbrante (dez•lūm•brân´te) *adj.* dazzling.

deslumbrar (dez•lūm•brâr´) *va.* to dazzle; (fig.) to puzzle, to perplex *(dejar en la incertidumbre);* to overwhelm *(producir una impresión excesiva).*

deslustre (dez•lūs´tre) *m.* tarnish; (fig.) stain, discredit blemish *(descrédito).*

desmantelar (dez•mân•te•lâr´) *va.* to dismantle, to tear down *(derribar);* (fig.) to abandon, to desert; (naut.) to dismast.

desmayar (dez•mâ•yâr´) *va.* to daunt, to dishearten, to dismay; —, *vn.* (fig.) to fail, to falter; —**se,** to faint.

desmayo (dez•mâ´yo) *m.* disheartenment, dismay; failure, faltering *(desfallecimiento);* faint.

desmedido, da (dez•me•thē´tho, thâ) *adj.* out of proportion, excessive.

desmejorado, da (dez•me•ho•râ´-

tho, thâ) *adj.* sickly, wan.

desmejorar (dez•me•ho•râr´) *va.* to worsen, to deteriorate; —, *vn.* to lose one´s health.

desmembrar* (dez•mem•brâr´) *va.* to dismember, to cut up.

desmemoriado, da (dez•me•mo•ryâ´tho, thâ) *adj.* forgetful.

desmentir* (dez• men•tēr´) *va.* to contradict *(contradecir);* to give the lie to.

desmenuzar (dez•me•nū•sâr´) *va.* to tear into small pieces, to shred; (fig.) to pick to pieces *(criticar severamente).*

desmerecer* (dez•me•re•ser´) *va.* to be unworthy of; —, *vn.* to compare unfavorably.

desmesurado, da (dez•me•sū•râ´tho, thâ) *adj.* excessive, unwarranted; discourteous *(insolente).*

desmontar (dez •mon•târ´) *va.* to clear *(los árboles);* to level *(el terreno);* to clear away *(un montón);* to take down, to dismantle *(una máquina);* to dismount *(al jinete);* —, *vn.* and *vr.* to dismount, to alight.

desmoralizar (dez•mo•râ •lē•sâr´) *va.* to demoralize.

desmoronar (dez•mo•ro•nâr´) *va.* to chip away, to wear away; —se, to decay, to crumble.

desmovilizar (dez•mo•vē•lē•sâr´)

va. to demobilize.

desnatado, da (dez•nâ•tâ´tho, thâ) *adj.* skimmed.

desnatar (dez•nâ•târ´) *va.* to skim; to take the flower of *(sacar lo mejor).*

desnaturalizado, da (dez•nâ•tū•râ•lē•sâ´tho, thâ) *adj.* unnatural, inhuman.

desnaturalizar (dez•nâ•tū•râ•lē•sâr´) *va.* to denaturalize; to twist, to give a false slant, to misconstrue *(desfigurar).*

desnivel (dez•nē•vel´) *m.* unevenness *(falta de nivel);* difference in elevation *(entre dos puntos);* **paso a —,** under-pass.

desnucar (dez•nū•kâr´) *va.* and *vr.* to break one´s neck.

desnudar (dez•nū•thâr´) *va.* to strip; (fig.) to denude, to strip bare.

desnudez (dez•nū•thes´) *f.* nakedness, bareness.

desnudo, da (dez•nū´tho, thâ) *adj.* naked, bare; (fig.) lacking *(falto de);* half naked, destitute *(muy pobre);* plain, unadulterated *(sin rebozo).*

desnutrición (dez•nū•trē•syon´) *f.* malnutrition.

desnutrido, da (dez•nū•trē´tho, thâ) *adj.* suffering from malnutrition.

desobedecer* (de•so•ve•the•ser´)

va. to disobey.

desobediencia (de·so•ve•thyen´s-yâ) *f.* disobedience; — **civil,** civil disobedience.

desobediente (de•so•ve•thyen´te) *adj.* disobedient.

desocupar (de•so•kū•pâr´) *va.* to empty, to clear out; **—se,** to get out, to be freed.

desodorante (de •so •tho•rân´te) *m.* deodorant.

desolación (de•so•lâ •syon´) *f.* desolation.

desolar* (de•so•lâr´) *va.* to desolate; **—se,** (fig.) to become overwrought, to get very upset.

desollar* (de•so•yâr´) *va.* to skin; (fig.) to fleece, to take to the cleaners.

desorden (de•sor´then) *m.* disorder.

desordenado, da (de•sor•the•nâ´tho, thâ) *adj.* disorderly, unruly.

desordenar (de •sor•the •nâr´) *va.* to disarrange, to put out of order; **—se,** to live a disorderly life.

desorganización (de•sor•gâ•nē•sâ•syon´) *f.* disorganization.

desorganizar (dâ•sor•gâ•nē•sâr´) *va.* to disorganize.

desorientado, da (de•so•ryen•tâ´tho, thâ) *adj.* having lost one's bearings; (fig.)

confused, disconcerted.

despacio (des•pâ´syo) *adv.* slowly; ¡—! *interj.* slow up! hold on there!

despachar (des•pâ•châr´) *va.* to dispatch; to sell *(mercaderías)*; to take care of, to wait on *(a los compradores)*; to send away *(despedir);* **—se,** to hurry up; ⁻**se uno a su gusto,** (coll.) to say whatever one pleases.

despacho (des•pâ´cho) *m.* dispatch; dismissal *(despedida);* store *(tienda);* office *(oficina).*

desparramar (des•pâ•rrâ•mâr´) *va.* to scatter, to spread out; (fig.) to squander, to waste *(el caudal);* **—se,** to lead a reckless life.

despavorido, da (des•pâ•vo•rē´tho, thâ) *adj.* frightened, terrified.

despecho (des•pe´cho) *m.* rancor, resentment, bitterness *(disgusto);* despair, desperation *(desesperación);* **a — de,** in spite of.

despedazar (des•pe•thâ•sâr´) *va.* to tear into pieces; (fig.) to break, to shatter; **—se de risa,** to burst into fits of laughter.

despedida (des•pe•thē´thâ) *f.* good-bye, leave-taking; giving off; dismissal; discharge; loosening.

despedir* (des•pe•thēr´) *va.* to loosen, to free *(soltar);* to discharge, to fire *(quitar el empleo);* to dismiss, to send away *(apartar de sí);* to give off, to emit *(esparcir);* to say goodbye to *(acompañar al que se va);* **—se,** to take one's leave, to say good-bye.

despegar (des•pe•gâr´) *va.* to unglue; **—,** *vn.* (avi.) to take off; **—se,** to come unstuck; not to go well, to be unbecoming *(caer mal).*

despego (des•pe´go) *m.* (fig.) coolness, indifference, detachment.

despegue (des•pe´ge) *m.* takeoff; blast-off *(de un cohete);* **— de emergencia,** (avi.) emergency take-off.

despeinado (des•pe͞e•nâ´tho, thâ) *adj.* uncombed, unkempt, tousled.

despeinar (des•pe͞e•nâr´) *va.* to mess up one's hairdo.

despejado, da (des•pe•hâ´tho, thâ) *adj.* quick, able *(listo);* clear, cloudless *(libre* de *nubes);* bright, ready *(inteligente);* broad, roomy *(espacioso).*

despejar (des•pe•hâr´) *va.* to clear *(desocupar);* (math.) to solve; (fig.) to clear up, to clarify *(aclarar);* **—se,** to be at ease; to clear up *(el tiempo).*

despellejar (des•pe•ye•hâr´) *va.* to skin.

despensa (des•pen´sâ) *f.* pantry; provisions, food supply *(provisiones)*.

despeñadero (des•pe•nyâ•the´ro) *m.* precipice; (fig.) great danger, risky undertaking.

despeñar (des•pe•nyâr´) *va.* to cast, to throw, to hurl; —**se,** to fall headlong, to hurtle.

desperdiciar (des•per•thē•syâr´) *va.* to squander, to waste, to lose.

desperdicio (des•per•thē´syo) *m.* waste loss, squandering; —**s,** *pl.* waste, odd bits.

despertador (des•per•tâ•thor´) *m.* alarm clock.

despertar* (des•per•târ´) *va.* to wake, to awake; (fig.) to awaken; —**se,** to wake up, to waken.

despiadado, da (des•pyâ•thâ´tho, thâ) or **desapiadado, da** (de•sâ•pyâ•thâ´tho, thâ) *adj.* pitiless, merciless, inhuman.

despierto, ta (des•pyer´to, tâ) *adj.* awake; (fig.) quick, alert (vivo).

despilfarro (des•pēl•fâ´rro) *m.* wastefulness, mismanagement *(descuido);* reckless expense *(gasto).*

despintar (des•pēn•târ´) *va.* to wash the paint from; (fig.) to ruin, to alter *(desfigurar);* —, *vn.* not to take after one´s family; —**se,** to become discolored, to fade.

desplantar (des•plân•târ´) *va.* to uproot *(desarraigar);* —**se,** to lose one´s stance.

desplante (des•plân´te) *m.* poor stance; (fig.) impropriety, insolence *(descaro).*

desplazado, da (des•plâ•sâ´tho, thâ) *adj.* displaced; **persona** —, displaced person.

desplazar (des•plâ•sâr´) *va.* to displace.

desplazamiento (des•plâ•sâ•myen´to) *m.* displacement.

desplegar* (des•ple•gâr´) *va.* to unfold; (fig.) to display *(hacer alarde);* to explain *(aclarar);* to unfurl *(una bandera);* (mil.) to deploy.

desplomar (des•plo•mâr´) *va.* to knock over; —**se,** to fall over, to collapse; to plummet to the ground, to plunge to the ground *(caer a plomo).*

desplumar (des•plū•mâr´) *va.* to deplume, to pluck; (fig.) to fleece.

despoblado (des•po•vlâ´tho) *m.* uninhabited region.

despoblar* (des•po•vlâr´) *va.* to depopulate; (fig.) to lay waste, to strip.

despojar (des•po•hâr´) va. to strip, to rob; to remove from, to take off *(quitar);* **—se,** to strip; to give up, to renounce *(voluntariamente).*

desposeer* (des•po•se•er´) va. to dispossess; **—se,** to renounce one´s possessions.

déspota (des´po•tâ) m. despot; (fig.) tyrant.

despotismo (des•po•tēz´mo) m. despotism.

despreciable (des•pre•syâ´vle) adj. contemptible, despicable.

despreciar (des•pre•syâr´) va. to despise, to scorn.

desprecio (des•pre´syo) m. scorn, contempt.

desprender (des•pren•der´) va. to unfasten, to loosen; **—se,** to come loose, to come unfastened; to be shown, to be manifest *(inferirse).*

desprendimiento (des•pren•dē•myen´to) m. unloosening, unfastening; disinterest, coolness *(desapego);* (fig.) generosity *(largueza).*

despreocuparse (des•pre•o•kū•pâr´se) vr. to forget one´s worries; to lose one´s interest *(desentenderse).*

desprestigiar (des•pres•tē•hyâr´) va. to discredit, to bring into disrepute, to lose one´s reputation.

desprestigio (des•pres•tē´hyo) m. loss of prestige, discredit, disrepute.

desprevenido, da (des•pre•ve•nē´tho, thâ) adj. unprepared, unaware.

desproporción (des•pro•por•syon´) f. disproportion.

después (des•pwes´) adv. afterward, later; **— de** after.

despuntar (des•pūn•târ´) va. to blunt; (naut.) to round; **—,** vn. to sprout *(las plantas);* to sparkle, to show wit *(una persona);* to start, to begin *(empezar);* **al — del día,** at break of day.

desquitar (des•kē•târ´) va. to recoup *(una pérdida);* to avenge *(un disgusto);* **—se,** to recoup one´s losses; to take revenge.

desquite (des•kē´te) m. revenge; recoup.

desrielarse (dez•rrye•lâr´se) vr. (Sp. Am.) to jump the track, to derail.

destacar (des•ta•kâr´) va. to make stand out, to highlight; (mil.) to detach; **—se,** to be prominent, to stand out.

destapar (des•tâ•pâr´) va. to uncover; **—se,** (fig.) to unburden oneself; **—se con,** to confide in.

destello (des•te´yo) m. gleam,

glimmer, flash.

destemplado, da (des•tem•plâ´tho, thâ) *adj.* (mus.) out of tune; intemperate.

destemplanza (des•tem•plân´sâ) *f.* intemperateness; (med.) slight fever.

desteñir* (des•te•nyēr´) *va.* to discolor, to fade.

desterrado, da (des•te•rrâ´tho, thâ) *n.* exile; —, *adj.* exiled, banished.

desterrar* (des•te•rrâr´) *va.* to banish, to exile; (fig.) to expel, to drive away *(alejar);* to remove the earth from *(quitar la tierra).*

destierro (des•tye´rro) *m.* exile, banishment.

destilación (des•tē•lâ•syon´) *f.* distillation.

destilar (des•tē•lâr´) *va.* and *vn.* to distil.

destinar (des•tē•nâr´) *va.* to destine, to intend; to send *(enviar).*

destinatario, ria (des•tē•nâ•tâ´-ryo, ryâ) *n.* addressee.

destino (des•tē´no) *m.* destiny, fate; destination *(destinación);* post, position *(empleo);* **con —a,** bound for.

destitución (des•tē•tū•syon´) *f.* destitution, abandonment.

destituir* (des•tē•twēr´) *va.* to deprive *(privar);* to dismiss

from office *(de un cargo).*

destornillador (des•tor•nē•yâ•thor´) *m.* screwdriver.

destornillar (des•tor•nē•yâr´) *va.* to unscrew; **—se,** (fig.) to go off the deep end, to lose one's head.

destreza (des•tre´sâ) *f.* dexterity, skill, ability.

destronar (des•tro•nâr´) *va.* to dethrone; (fig.) to depose.

destroncar (des•trong•kâr´) *va.* to lop off the top of, to cut short *(un árbol);* (fig.) to mutilate *(el cuerpo);* to wear out, to bush *(cansar);* to ruin *(en los negocios).*

destrozar (des•tro•sâr´) *va.* to destroy, to rip to pieces; (fig.) to ruin; (mil.) to crush.

destrozo (des•tro´so) *m.* destruction, ripping to pieces; (mil) rout, severe defeat.

destrucción (des•trūk•syon´) *f.* destruction, ruin.

destructivo, va (des•trūk•tē´vo, vâ) *adj.* destructive.

destructor (des•trūk•tor´) *m.* (naut.) destroyer; —, **ra,** *adj.* destroying, destructive.

destruir* (des•trwēr´) *va.* to destroy, to ruin; **—se,** (math.) to cancel out.

desunir (de•sū•nēr´) *va.* to separate; (fig.) to disunite.

desusar (de•sū•sâr´) *va.* to drop from use, to stop using.

desuso (de•sū´so) *m.* disuse, obsoleteness.

desvalido, da (dez•vâ•lē´tho, thâ) *adj.* helpless, destitute.

desvalorizar (dez•vâ•lo•rē•sâr´) *va.* to devaluate.

desvanecer* (dez•vâ•ne•ser´) *va.* to dispel; —**se,** to evaporate, to be dissipated; to lose one´s senses, to black out, to faint *(desmayarse);* to grow proud, to become haughty *(envanecerse).*

desvarío (dez•vâ•rē´o) *m.* delirium; (fig.) aberration.

desvelar (dez•ve•lâr´) *va.* to keep awake; —**se,** (fig.) to make great sacrifices, to go out of one´s way.

desvelo (dez•ve´lo) *m.* keeping awake; staying awake *(acción de desvelarse);* great pains, sacrifices *(solicitud).*

desventaja (dez•ven•tâ´hâ) *f.* disadvantage.

desventura (dez•ven•tū´râ) *f.* misfortune, bad luck.

desventurado, da (dez•ven•tū•râ´tho, thâ) *adj.* unfortunate.

desvergonzado, da (dez•ver•gon•sâ´tho, thâ) *adj.* shameless, insolent, cheeky.

desvergüenza (dez•ver•gwen´sâ) *f.* shamelessness, cheek, effrontery.

desviación (dez•vyâ•syon´) *f.* deviation, diversion; (auto.) detour.

desviar (dez•vyâr´) *va.* to divert; (fig.) to draw away, to separate *(apartar);* —**se,** to deviate, to change direction.

desvío (dez•vē´o) *m.* deviation, diversion; (auto.) bypass, detour; (fig.) indifference, aversion *(desapego).*

detallar (de•tâ•yâr´) *va.* to detail.

detalle (de•tâ´ye) *m.* detail; (com.) retail; **vender al —,** to retail.

detective (de•tek•tē´ve) *m.* detective.

detector, (de•tek•tor´) *m.* detector.

detener* (de•te•ner´) *va.* to stop, to arrest; to retain, to keep *(guardar);* —**se,** to stop; to delay, to go slowly *(retardarse).*

detenido, da (de•te•nē´tho thâ) *adj.* sparing, scant *(escaso);* careful, painstaking *(minucioso);* under arrest *(preso).*

detenimiento (de•te•nē•myen´to) *m.* thoroughness, care *(cuidado);* detainment.

detergente (de•ter•hen´te) *m.* and *adj.* detergent.

deteriorar (de•te•ryo•râr´) *va.* and *vr.* to deteriorate.

deterioro (de•te•ryo´ro) *m.* deterioration.

determinación
(de•ter•mē•nâ•syon´) *f.* determination; resolution, boldness *(osadía);* **tomar la —,** to make the decision.

determinado, da (de•ter•mē•nâ´-tho, thâ) *adj.* bold, resolute *(atrevido);* definite, specific *(preciso);* **artículo —,** definite article.

determinar (de•ter•mē•nâr´) *va.* to determine; to fix, to decide on *(señalar).*

detestable (de•tes•tâ´vle) *adj.* detestable; frightful, beastly *(muy malo).*

detestar (de•tes•târ´) *va.* to detest.

detonación (de•to•nâ•syon´) *f.* detonation.

detractor (de•trâk•tor´) *m.* slanderer.

detrás (de•trâs´) *adv.* behind; (fig.) behind one´s back, in one´s absence; **por —,** from behind; **— de,** in back of, behind.

detrimento (de•trē•men´to) *m.* detriment, damage.

deuda (de´ū•thâ) *f.* debt; fault, offense *(falta).*

deudor, ra (deū•thor´, râ) *n.* debtor.

devaneo (de•vâ•ne´o) *m.* delirium; idle pursuit, frivolous pas-

time *(distracción);* crush *(amorío).*

devastación (de•vâs•tâ•syon´) *f.* devastation.

devastador, ra (de•vâs•tâ•thor´, râ) *n.* devastator, ravager; **—,** *adj.* devastating, ravaging.

devastar (de•vâs•târ´) *va.* to devastate, to ravage.

devoción (de•vo•syon´) *f.* devotion; special fondness *(afición);* wont, habit *(costumbre);* **estar a la — de,** to be under the thumb of.

devolución (de•vo•lū•syon´) *f.* return, restitution.

devolutivo, va (de•vo•lū•tē´vo, vâ) *adj.* to be returned; **con carácter —vo,** on a loan basis.

devolver* (de•vol•ver´) *va.* to return *(al dueño);* to restore *(al estado primitivo);* (coll.) to throw up *(vomitar).*

devorar (de•vo•râr´) *va.* to devour; **— sus lágrimas,** to hold back one´s tears.

devoto, ta (de•vo´to, tâ) *adj.* devout; devoted *(a una persona);* devotional *(que mueve a devoción).*

D.F.: Distrito Federal Federal District.

día (dē´â) *m.* day; **al otro —,** on the following day; **— de trabajo,** workday, working day; **al —,** up to date; **a treinta —s vista,**

at thirty days´ sight; — **quebra-do,** half holiday; — **feriado,** — **festivo or** — **de fiesta,** holiday; **dentro de ocho** —**as,** within a week; **de hoy en ocho** —**s,** a week from today; **el** — **siguiente,** the next day.

diabetes (dyâ•vetes) *f.* diabetes.

diabético, ca (dyâ•ve´tē•ko, kâ) *adj.* diabetic.

diablo (dyâ´vlo) *m.* devil; **más sabe el** — **por viejo que por** —, experience is the best teacher.

diabólico, ca (dyâ•vo´lē•ko, kâ) *adj.* diabolical, devilish.

diáfano, na (dyâ´fâ•no, nâ) *adj.* diaphanous.

diagnosticar (dyâg•nos•tē•kâr´) *va.* to diagnose.

diagnóstico (dyâg•nos´tē•ko) *m.* diagnosis; —, **ca,** *adj.* diagnostic.

diagonal (dyâ•go•nâl´) *adj.* oblique.

diagrama (dyâ•grâ´mâ) *m.* diagram, graph.

dialéctica (dyâ•lek´tē•kâ) *f.* dialectic.

dialecto (dyâ•lek´to) *m.* dialect.

diálogo (dyâ´lo•go) *m.* dialogue.

diamante, (dyâ•mân´te) *m.* diamond; — **en bruto,** rough diamond.

diametral (dyâ•me•trâl) *adj.* diametrical.

diámetro (dyâ´me•tro) *m.* diame-

ter.

diario (dyâ´ryo) *m.* daily *(publicación);* diary *(relación);* daily earnings *(ganancia);* daily expenses *(gasto);* — **hablado,** news report; —, **ria,** *adj.* daily.

diarrea (dyâ•rre´â) *f.* diarrhea.

dibujante (dē•vū•hân´te) *m.* draftsman.

dibujar (dē•vū•hâr´) *va.* to draw; (fig.) to sketch, to indicate.

dibujo (dē•vū´ho) *m.* drawing; (fig.) sketch, outline; —**s animados,** animated cartoon; **no meterse en** —**s** , not to get off the track.

dicción (dēk•syon´) *f.* diction; expression, word *(palabra).*

diccionario (dēk•syo•nâ´ryo) *m.* dictionary.

diciembre (dē•syem´ bre) *m.* December.

dictado (dēk•tâ´tho) *m.* dictation; title *(título);* —**s** , *pl.* dictates.

dictador (dēk•tâ•thor´) *m.* dictator.

dictadura (dēk•tâ•thū´râ) *f.* dictatorship.

dictar (dēk•târ´) *va.* to dictate.

dicha (dē´châ) *f.* happiness, good fortune; **por** —, luckily, fortunately.

dicho (dē´cho) *m.* saying; remark *(ocurrencia);* testimony *(del testigo);* —, **cha,** *adj.* said; **dejar** —

cho, to leave word.

dichoso, sa (dē´cho´so, sâ) *adj.*
happy, joyful.

diecinueve or **diez y nueve**
(dye•sē•nwe´ve) *m.* and *adj.*
nineteen.

dieciocho or **diez y ocho**
(dye•syo´cho) *m.* and *adj.*
eighteen.

dieciséis or **diez y seis**
(dye•sē•se´ēs) *m.* and *adj.* sixteen.

diecisiete or **diez y siete**
(dye•sē•sye´te) *m.* and *adj.*
seventeen.

diente (dyen´te) *m.* tooth; (arch.)
projection; **—s postizos,** false
teeth; **hablar** or **decir entre —s**
, to mumble, to mutter.

diestro tra (dyes´tro, trâ) *adj.*
right; skillful, expert *(hábil);* a
—o y siniestro higgledy-pig-
gledy, haphazardly; **—,** *m.*
matador.

dieta (dye´tâ) *f.* diet.

diez (dyes´) *adj.* and *m.* ten.

diezmar (dyez•mâr´) *va.* to deci-
mate.

diezmo (dyez´mo) *m.* tithe; **—,
ma,** *adj.* tenth.

difamación (dē•fâ•mâ•syon´) *f.*
defamation.

difamar (dē•fâ•mâr´) *va.* to defame, to libel.

diferencia (dē•fe•ren´syâ) *f.* difference; **a — de,** unlike.

diferenciar (dē•fe•ren•syâr´) *va.*
to differentiate; to change, to
vary *(variar);* **—,** *vn.* to differ; **—
se,** to stand out, to distinguish
oneself.

diferente (dē•fe•ren´te) *adj.* different, unlike.

diferir* (dē•fe•rēr´) *va.* to defer,
to put off; **—,** *vn.* to differ.

dificil (dē•fē´sēl) *adj.* difficult;
unlikely *(improbable).*

dificilmente (dē•fē•sēl•men´te)
adv. with difficulty.

dificultar (dē•fē•kūl•târ´) *va.* to
make difficult; **—se,** to become
difficult.

dificultoso, sa (dē•fē•kūl•to´so,
sâ) *adj.* difficult.

difundido, da (dē•fūn•dē´tho,
thâ) *adj.* spread, diffused.

difundir (dē•fūn•dēr´) *va.* to
spread, to diffuse.

difunto, ta (dē•fūn´to, tâ) *adj.*
dead, deceased; **—,** *n.*
deceased, dead person.

difusión (dē•fū•syon´) *f.* diffu-
sion.

difusivo, va (dē•fū•sē´vo, vâ) *adj.*
diffusive.

difuso, sa (dē•fū´so, sâ) *adj.* diffuse; **orador —so,** long-winded
speaker.

difusora (dē•fū•so´râ) *f.* broadcasting station.

digerible (dē•he•rē´vle) *adj.*
digestible.

digerir* (dē•he•rēr´) *va.* to digest; (fig.) to swallow, to take *(sobrellevar).*

digestión (dē•hes•tyon´) *f.* digestion.

digestivo, va (dē•hes•tē´vo, vâ) *adj.* digestive.

digesto (dē•hes´to) *m.* digest.

digital (dē•hē•tâl´) *f.* —, *adj.* digital; **impresiones** or **huellas —es,** fingerprints.

dignarse (dēg•nâr´se) *vr.* to condescend, to deign.

dignatario (dēg•nâ•tâ´ryo) *m.* dignitary, high official.

dignidad (dēg•nē•thâth´) *f.* dignity.

digno, na (dēg´no, nâ) *adj.* worthy; — **de confianza,** trustworthy, dependable, reliable.

digresión (dē•gre•syon´) *f.* digression.

dilapidar (dē•lâ•pē•thâr´) *va.* to dilapidate.

dilatación (dē•lâ•tâ•syon´) *f.* expansion, dilation; (fig.) calmness under stress *(serenidad).*

dilatado, da (dē•lâ•tâ´tho, thâ) *adj.* extensive, numerous.

dilatar (dē•lâ•târ´) *va.* to expand, to dilate; (fig.) to delay *(retrasar);* to spread *(propagar);* **—se,** to talk at great length, to be long-winded.

dilema (dē•le´mâ) *m.* dilemma.

diligencia (dē•lē•hen´syâ) *f.*
effort, care *(esmero);* speed *(prisa);* (coll.) matter, job *(negocio).*

diligente (dē•lē•hen´te) *adj.* diligent; prompt, swift *(pronto).*

dilucidación (dē•lū•sē•thâ•syon´) *f.* explanation.

dilucidar (dē•lū•sē•thâr´) *va.* to elucidate, to explain.

diluir* (dē•lwēr´) *va.* and *vr.* to dilute.

diluvio (dē•lū´vyo) *m.* deluge.

dimensión (dē•men•syon´) *f.* dimension; dimensions *(tamaño).*

dimes (dē´mes) *m. pl.* **andar en — y diretes.** (coll.) to contend, to argue back and forth.

diminución (dē•mē•nū•syon´) *f.* diminution, decrease.

diminutivo, va (dē•mē•nū•tē´vo, vâ) *m.* and *adj.* (gram.) diminutive.

diminuto, ta (dē•mē•nū´to, tâ) *adj.* defective, faulty; diminutive, very tiny *(muy pequeño).*

dimitir (dē•mē•tēr´) *va.* and *vn.* to resign.

Dinamarca (dē•nâ•mâr´kâ) *f.* Denmark.

dinámica (dē•nâ´mē•kâ) *f.* dynamics.

dinámico, ca (dē•nâ´mē•ko, kâ) *adj.* dynamic.

dinamismo (dē•nâ•mēz´mo) *m.* dynamism; (fig.) energy, vigor.

dinamita (dē•nâ•mē′tâ) *f.* dynamite.

dinastía (dē•nâs•tē′â) *f.* dynasty.

dineral (dē•ne•râl′) *m.* large sum of money; **costar un —,** to cost a fortune.

dinero (dē•ne′ro) *m.* money; — **contante y sonante,** ready money, cash.

dinosaurio (dē•no•sâ′ū•ryo) *m.* dinosaur.

dintel (dēn•tel′) *m.* transverse, lintel.

diócesis (dyo′se•sēs) *f.* diocese.

diorama (dyo•râ′mâ) *m.* diorama.

Dios (dyos) *m.* God; — **es grande,** let us trust in God, God will help us; — **mediante,** with the help of God; — **quiera,** — **lo permita,** God grant.

dios (dyos) *m.* god, deity.

diosa (dyo′sâ) *f.* goddess, female deity.

dióxido de carbono (dyok′sē•tho•the•kar•vo′no) *m.* carbon dioxide.

diploma (dē•plo′mâ) *m.* diploma *(título);* license, certificate.

diplomacia (dē•plo•mâ′syâ) or **diplomática** (dē•plo•mâ′tē•kâ) *f.* diplomacy.

diplomático, ca (dē•plo•mâ′tē•ko, kâ) *adj.* diplomatic; —, *m.* diplomat.

diptongo (dēp•tong′go) *m.* diphthong.

diputación (dē•pū•tâ•syon′) *f.* delegation.

diputado (dē•pū•tâ′tho) *m.* delegate, deputy.

diputar (dē•pū•târ′) *va.* to delegate.

dique (dē′ke) *m.* dike; — **de carena,** dry dock; — **flotante,** floating dock.

dirección (dē•rek•syon′) *f.* direction, directorship *(cargo);* directorate, board of directors *(junta);* address *(morada);* — **telegráfica** or **cablegráfica,** cable address; **de dos —ones,** two-way.

directivo, va (dē•rek•tē′vo, vâ) *adj.* managing; —, *f.* directive; board of directors *(junta).*

directo, ta (dē•rek′to, tâ) *adj.* direct; —, *m.* straight *(blow).*

director, ra (dē•rek•tor′, râ) *adj.* directing, directive; —, *n.* director; principal *(de escuela);* — **de escena,** stage manager;— **ejecutivo,** chief executive officer.

directorio, ria (dē•rek•to′ryo, ryâ) *adj.* directory; —, *m.* directory, guide; board, directorate *(junta).*

dirigente (dē•rē•hen′te) *adj.* leading.

dirigible (dē•rē•hē′vle) *m.* dirigible; —, *adj.* controllable.

dirigir (dē•rē•hēr′) *va.* to direct;

to address *(una carta);* to dedicate *(una obra);* — **la palabra,** to address; —**se,** to go; —**se a,** to speak to, to address.

discerniente (dēs•ser•nyen´te) *adj.* discerning.

discernimiento (dēs•ser•nē•myen´to) *m.* discernment; appointment as guardian.

discernir* (dēs•ser•nēr´) *va.* to discern; to appoint as guardian *(encargar la tutela).*

disciplina (dēs•sē•plē´nâ) *f.* discipline.

disciplinar (dēs•sē•plē•nâr´) *va.* to discipline.

discípulo, la (dēs•sē´pū•lo, lâ) *n.* disciple; pupil *(alumno).*

disco (dēs´ko) *m.* disk; record *(grabación);* discus *(atlético).*

discordancia (dēs•kor•thân´syâ) *f.* difference.

discordante (dēs•kor•thân´te) *adj.* discordant, different.

discordar* (dēs•kor•thâr´) *vn.* to be at variance, to disagree; (mus.) to be out of harmony.

discorde (dēs•kor´the) *adj.* in disagreement, at variance; (mus.) out of harmony.

discordia (dēs•kor´thyâ) *f.* discord; **manzana de la —,** bone of contention.

discreción (dēs•kre•syon´) *f.* discretion; quick mind, ready wit

(agudeza); **a —,** at discretion, as much as one thinks best.

discrepancia (dēs•kre´pân´syâ) *f.* discrepancy.

discreto, ta (dēs•kre´to, tâ) *adj.* discreet; discrete *(discontinuo);* witty *(agudo).*

disculpa (dēs•kūl´pâ) *f.* apology, excuse.

disculpar (dēs•kūl•pâr´) *va.* to excuse, to pardon; — **se,** to apologize, to excuse oneself.

discurrir (dēs•kū•rrēr´) *vn.* to ramble about *(andar);* to flow *(fluir),* to pass *(transcurrir);* to ponder *(reflexionar);* —**,** *va.* to figure out; to draw *(inferir).*

discurso (dēs•kūr´so) *m.* reasoning power *(facultad);* speech *(charla);* sentence *(oración);* **hilo del —,** train of thought.

discusión (dēs•kū•syon´) *f.* discussion.

discutible (dēs•kū•tē´vle) *adj.* debatable.

discutir (dēs•kū•tēr´) *va.* and *vn.* to discuss, to argue.

disecar (dē•se•kâr´) *va.* to dissect.

disección (dē•sek•syon´) *f.* dissection.

diseminación (dē•se•mē•nâ•syon´) *f.* dissemination.

diseminar (dē•se•mē•nâr´) *va.* to disseminate.

disentería (dē•sen•te•rē´â) *f.* dysentery.

disentir* (dē•sen•tēr´) *vn.* to dissent, to disagree.

diseñar (dē•se•nyâr´) *va.* to draw, to design.

diseño (dē•se´nyo) *m.* design, drawing; description, word portrayal *(descripción)*.

disertación (dē•ser•tâ•syon´) *f.* dissertation.

disertar (dē•ser•târ´) *vn.* to dissertate.

disfraz (dēs•frâs´) *m.* disguise.

disfrazar (dēs•frâ•sâr´) *va.* to disguise.

disfrutar (dēs•frū•târ´) *va.* to enjoy *(gozar de);* to have the use of, to make use of *(aprovechar).*

disgregación (dēz•gre•gâ•syon´) *f.* disintegration.

disgregar, (dēz•gre•gâr´) *va.* to disintegrate.

disgustar (dēz•gūs•târ´) *va.* to displease, to bother; **—se con,** to quarrel with, to have a falling out with.

disgusto (dēz•gūs´to) *m.* displeasure, bother *(molestia);* quarrel *(disputa);* worry *(inquietud);* **a —,** against one's will; **llevarse un —,** to be disappointed.

disimetría (dē•sē•me•trē´â) *f.* lack of symmetry.

disímil (dē•sē´mēl) *adj.* dissimilar.

disimuladamente (dē•sē•mū•lâ•thâ men´te) *adv.* pretending ignorance; on the sly *(a hurtadillas).*

disimular (dē•sē•mū•lâr´) *va.* to hide, to cover up; to pretend to know nothing about *(desentenderse de);* **—,** *vn.* to dissemble.

disimulo (dē•sē•mū´lo) *m.* hiding, covering up; pretense.

disipación (dē•sē•pâ•syon´) *f.* dissipation.

disipado, da (dē•sē•pâ´tho, thâ) *adj.* dissipated, prodigal.

disipar (dē•sē•pâr´) *va.* to dissipate.

dislocación (dēz•lo•kâ•syon´) *f.* dislocation.

dislocar (dēz•lo•kâr´) *va.* to dislocate; to break up *(dispersar);* (fig.) to carve up *(dismembrar).*

disminuir (dēz•mē•nwēr´) *va.* to diminish.

disolución (dē•so•lū•syon´) *f.* dissolution; dissoluteness *(desenfreno).*

disoluto, ta (dē•so•lū´to, tâ) *adj.* dissolute, licentious.

disolver* (dē•sol•ver´) *va.* to dissolve; **—se,** to dissolve, to break up.

disonante (dē•so•nân´te) *adj.* dissonant, inharmonious.

disonar* (dē•so•nâr´) *vn.* to be in

discord, to be dissonant.

disparar (dēs•pâ•râr´) *va.* to throw hard, to heave *(arrojar);* to fire *(una escopeta);* —**se,** to dart off, to rush off.

disparatado, da (dēs•pâ•râ•tâ´-tho, thâ) *adj.* absurd, nonsensical; (coll.) huge, enormous *(excesivo).*

disparate (dēs•pâ•râ´te) *m.* nonsense, absurdity; (coll.) excess, enormity.

disparejo, ja (dēs•pâ•re´ho, hâ) *adj.* unequal, uneven.

disparidad (dēs•pâ•rē•thâth´) *f.* disparity.

disparo (dēs•pâ´ro) *m.* shot.

dispensar (dēs•pen•sâr´) *va.* to dispense *(administrar);* to exempt, to excuse *(eximir);* to forgive, to excuse *(absolver).*

dispersar, (dēs•per•sâr´) *va.* and *vr.* to scatter, to disperse.

disperso, sa (dēs•per´so, sâ) *adj.* dispersed, scattered.

displicencia (dēs•plē•sen´syâ) *f.* displeasure, disdain *(desagrado);* slacking off, slowing up *(desaliento).*

disponer* (dēs•po•ner´) *va.* to dispose *(prevenir);* to ready, to make ready *(preparar);* to determine, to decide *(determinar);* — **de,** to have at one´s disposal, to have the use of; —**se,** to get ready, to prepare.

disponible (dēs•po•nē´vle) *adj.* available.

disponibilidad (dēs•po•nē•vē•lē•thâth´) *f.* availability.

disposición (dēs•po•sē•syon´) *f.* disposition; disposal; plan, arrangement *(arreglo);* preparation *(preparativo).*

dispuesto, ta (dēs•pwes´to, tâ) *adj.* disposed, fit, ready; **bien** —, favorably inclined; **mal** —, unfavorably disposed.

disputa (dēs•pū´tâ)*f.* dispute, controversy.

disputar (dēs•pū•tar´) *va.* to dispute, to argue; —, *vn.* to quarrel.

disquete (dēs•ke´te) *m.* diskette.

distancia (dēs•tân´syâ) *f.* distance; (fig.) difference.

distante (dēs•tân´te) *adj.* removed, at a distance; far-off, distant, remote *(remoto).*

distender* (dēs•ten•der´) *va.* and *vr. to* distend.

distinción (dēs•tēn•syon´) *f.* distinction; division *(separación).*

distinguido, da (dēs•tēng•gē´tho, thâ) *adj.* distinguished.

distinguir (dēs•tēng•gēr´) *va.* to distinguish; to honor *(otorgar).*

distintivo, va (dēs•tēn•tē´vo, vâ) *adj.* distinctive; —, *m.* distinction, distinguishing feature; insignia, mark, badge *(marca).*

distinto, ta (dēs•tēn′to, tâ) *adj.* distinct; different *(diferente).*

distracción (dēs•trâk•syon′) *f.* distraction.

distraer* (dēs•trâ•er′) *va.* to distract; to misappropriate *(malversar);* —**se,** to enjoy oneself, to have fun.

distraído, da (dēs•trâ•ē′tho, thâ) *adj.* distracted; dissolute *(licencioso).*

distribución (dēs•trē•vū•syon′) *f.* distribution; arrangement *(arreglo).*

distribuidor (dēs•trē•vwē•thor′) *m.* (auto.) distributor; — **automático,** vending machine.

distribuir*, (dēs•trē•vwēr′) *va.* to distribute; to lay out, to arrange *(disponer).*

distrito (dēs•trē′to) *m.* district.

distrofia (dēs•tro′fyâ) *f.* distrophy; — **muscular,** muscular distrophy.

disturbar (dēs•tūr•vâr′) *va.* to bother, to disturb.

disturbio (dēs•tūr′vyo) *m.* disturbance, interruption, bother.

disuadir (dē•swâ•thēr′) *va.* to dissuade.

diurético, ca (dyū•re′tē•ko, kâ) *adj.* diuretic; —, *m.* diuretic.

diurno, na, (dyūr′no, nâ) *adj.* diurnal.

diva (dē′vâ) *f.* prima donna, diva.

divagación (dē•vâ•gâ•syon′) *f.* wandering; digression, rambling.

divagar (dē•vâ•gâr′) *vn.* to digress, to ramble; to wander *(vagar a la ventura).*

diván (dē•vân′) *m.* sofa.

divergencia (dē•ver•hen′syâ) *f.* divergence.

diversidad (dē•ver•sē•thâth′) *f.* diversity, variety.

diversificar (dē•ver•sē•fē•kâr′) *va.* to diversify, to vary.

diversión (dē•ver•syon′) *f.* diversion.

diverso, sa (dē•ver′so, sâ) *adj.* diverse, different.

divertido, da (dē•ver•tē′tho, thâ) *adj.* amusing, enjoyable.

divertir* (dē•ver•tēr′) *va.* to amuse, to entertain; to divert *(apartar);* —**se,** to have a good time, to enjoy oneself.

dividendo (dē•vē•then′do) *m.* (math. and com.) dividend.

dividir (dē•vē•thēr′) *va.* to divide; —**se,** to part company, to separate.

divinidad (dē•vē•nē•thâth′) *f.* divinity; (fig.) exceptional beauty *(persona).*

divino, na (dē•vē′no, nâ) *adj.* divine.

divisa (dē•vē′sâ) *f.* motto *(lema);* badge *(señal);* foreign currency *(papel moneda).*

división (dē•vē•syon´) *f.* division.

divisorio, ria (dē•vē•so´ryo, ryâ) *adj.* dividing.

divorciar (dē•vor•syâr´) *va.* to divorce; **—se,** to get a divorce.

divorcio (dē•vor´syo) *m.* divorce; (fig.) divorcement.

divulgación (dē•vūl•gâ•syon´) *f.* divulgence; spreading, circulation.

divulgar (dē•vūl•gâr´) *va.* to divulge *(un secreto);* to spread, to circulate *(una noticia).*

dizque (dēs´ke) *m.* (Sp. Am.) hearsay, gossip; **—,** *adv.* possibly, they say that.

doblado (do•vlâ´tho) *m.* dubbing of a film; **—, da,** *adj.* wiry, strong *(recio);* uneven broken *(quebrado);* folded *(plegado);* (fig.) double-dealing, artful *(taimado).*

doblar (do•vlâr´) *va.* to double *(aumentar);* to fold up *(un mantel);* to bend *(torcer);* to round *(un cabo);* to dub *(una película);* to sway *(inclinar a una persona);* **—,** *vn.* to toll.

doble (do´vle) *adj.* double; brawny, tough *(fornido);* two-faced *(disimulado);* **—,** *m.* crease, fold *(doblez);* tolling *(de campanas);* copy *(reproducción);* (theat.) double.

doblez (do•vles´) *m.* crease, fold; **—,** *m.* or *f.* duplicity *(disimulo).*

doce (do´se) *adj.* and *m.* twelve.

docena (do•se´nâ) *f.* dozen; **— del fraile,** (coll.) baker´s dozen.

doceno, na (do•se´no, nâ) *adj.* twelfth.

docente (do•sen´te) *adj.* teaching; **personal —,** teaching staff.

dócil (do´sēl) *adj.* docile, obedient; malleable, tractable *(dúctil).*

docilidad (do•sē•lē•thâth´) *f.* docility, obedience.

docto, ta (dok´to, tâ) *adj.* learned.

doctor (dok•tor´) *m.* doctor.

doctorado (dok•to•râ´tho) *m.* doctorate.

documentación (do•kū•men•tâ•syon´) *f.* documentation.

documental (do•kū•men•tâl´) *adj.* and documentary.

documento (do•kū•men´to) *m.* document.

dólar (do´lâr) *m.* dollar.

dolencia (do•len´syâ) *f.* affliction, sickness.

doler* (do•ler´) *vn.* to hurt, to ache; to grieve, to pain *(causar disgusto);* **—se,** to regret, to be sorry; to complain *(quejarse).*

dolor (do•lor´) *m.* ache, pain; regret *(arrepentimiento).*

dolorido, da (do•lo•rē´tho, thâ) *adj.* painful sore; grieving, bereaved *(desconsolado).*

doloroso, sa (do•lo•ro´so, sâ) *adj.* lamentable, regrettable *(lastimoso);* painful *(que causa dolor).*

domable (do•mâ´vle) *adj.* tamable.

domador, ra (do•mâ•thor´, râ) *n.* Animal tamer; horsebreaker, bronco buster.

domar (do•mâr´) *va.* to tame; (fig.) to subdue, to master *(vencer);* **sin —,** untamed, unbroken.

domesticar (do•mes•tē•kâr´) *va.* to domesticate.

domesticidad (do•mes•tē•sē•thâth´) *f.* domesticity.

doméstico, ca (do•mes´tē•ko, kâ) *adj.* and *m.* domestic.

domicilio (do•mē•sē´lyo) *m.* domicile, home.

dominador, ra (do•mē•nâ•thor´, râ) *adj.* dominating; **—,** *n.* dominator.

dominante (do•mē•nân´te) *adj.* dominant; domineering *(avasallador).*

dominar (do•mē•nâr´) *va.* to dominate; **—se,** to control oneself.

domingo (do•mēng´go) *m.* Sunday.

dominicano, na (do•mē•nē•kâ´no, nâ) *adj.* and *n.* Dominican.

dominio (do•mē´nyo) *m.* dominance; domain, dominion *(territorio).*

dominó (do•mē•no´) *m.* domino; dominoes *(juego).*

don (don) *m.* gift, quality; Don *(título);* **— de la palabra,** ability with words; **— de gentes,** ability to get along.

donación (do•nâ syon´) *f.* donation, giving.

donador, ra (do•nâ•thor´, râ) *n.* giver, donor; **— de sangre,** blood donor.

donante (do•nân´te) *m.* and *f.* donor, giver.

donar (do•nâr´) *va.* to donate.

donativo (do•nâ•tē´vo) *m.* donation.

doncella (don•se´yâ) *f.* virgin, maiden.

donde (don´de) *adv.* where; which *(lo cual).*

dónde (don´de) *adv.* where?¿por **—?** with what reason?

dondequiera (don•de•kye´râ) *adv.* anywhere, wherever.

doña (do´nyâ) *f.* Doña.

dorado, da (do•râ´tho, thâ) *adj.* gilded; **—,** *m.* gilding.

dorar (do•râr´) *va.* to gild; (fig.) to sugarcoat *(paliar);* to brown lightly *(tostar).*

dormido, da (dor•mē´tho, thâ) *adj.* asleep.

dormir* (dor•mēr´) *vn.* to sleep;

—se, to fall asleep; **hacer —,** to put to sleep.

dormitar (dor•mē•tär´) *vn.* to doze, to be half asleep.

dormitorio (dor•mē•to´ryo) *m.* bedroom.

dorsal (dor•säl´) *adj.* dorsal; **espina —,** spinal column, backbone.

dorso (dor´so) *m.* back.

dos (dos) *adj.* and *m.* two; **de — en —,** two abreast, two by two.

doscientos, tas (dos•syen´tos, täs) *m.* and *adj.* two hundred.

dosis (do´sēs) *f.* dose, (fig.) some, degree.

dotación (do•tä•syon´) *f.* endowment; (naut.) complement; staff, crew *(personal).*

dotar (do•tär´) *va.* to endow; (fig.) to staff, to provide *(asignar).*

dote (do´te) *m.* and *f.* dower, dowry; **llevarse —,** to receive a dowry; **—,** *f.* quality, good point.

dragón (drä•gon´) *m.* dragon; (mil.) dragoon.

drama (drä´mä) *m.* drama.

dramático, ca (drä•mä´tē•ko, kä) *adj.* dramatic.

dramatizar (drä•mä•tē•sär´) *va.* to dramatize.

dramaturgo (drä•mä•tūr´go) *m.* dramatist, playwright.

drástico, ca (dräs´tē•ko, kä) *adj.* drastic.

drenaje (dre•nä´he) *m.* (med.) drainage.

droga (dro´gä) *f.* drug; (fig.) trick, ruse *(embuste);* nuisance, pill *(cosa molesta);* (Mex.) debt.

droguería (dro•ge•rē´ä) *f.* drugstore.

droguero (dro•ge´ro) *m.* druggist.

ducho, cha (dū´cho, chä) *adj.* dexterous, accomplished; **—,** *f.* shower.

duda (dū´thä) *f.* doubt; **poner en —,** to question; **no cabe —,** there is no doubt; **en la — vale más abstenerse,** when in doubt, don´t.

dudar (dū•thär´) *va.* to doubt; **—,** *vn.* to be undecided, not to know.

dudoso, sa (dū•tho´so, sä) *adj.* doubtful, dubious.

duelo (dwe´lo) *m.* duel *(combate);* suffering, woe, grief *(aflicción);* mourning *(por la muerte de uno);* mourners *(los que asisten a los funerales).*

duende (dwen´de) *m.* elf, goblin.

dueño, ña (dwe´nyo, nyä) *n.* owner, proprietor.

dueto (dwe´to) *m.* duet.

dulce (dūl´se) *adj.* sweet; malleable *(dúctil);* fresh *(agua);* **—,** *m.* piece of candy.

dulcería (dūl•se•rē´ä) *f.* candy shop.

dulcificante (dūl•sē•fē•kân´te) *m.* sweetener.

dulcificar (dūl•sē•fē•kâr´) *va.* to sweeten.

dulzura,(dūl•sū´râ) *f.* sweetness; gentleness, mildness *(suavidad).*

dúo (dū´o) *m.* (mus.) duo, duet.

duodécimo, ma (dwo•the´sē•mo, mâ) *adj.* twelfth.

duplicación (dū•plē•kâ•syon´) *f.* duplication; doubling.

duplicado (dū•plē•kâ´tho) *m.* duplicate.

duplicar (dū•plē•kâr´) *va.* to duplicate; to double *(multiplicar por dos).*

duplicidad (dū•plē•sē•thâth´) *f.* duplicity, falseness.

duque (dū´ke) *m.* duke.

duquesa (dū•ke´sâ) *f.* duchess.

durabilidad (dū•râ•vē•lē•thâth´) *f.* durability.

duración (dū•râ•syon´) *f.* duration.

duradero, ra (dū•râ•the´ro, râ) *adj.* lasting, durable.

durante (dū•rân´te) *adv.* during.

durar (dū•râr´) *vn.* to last, to endure; to remain *(subsistir);* to wear well (la *ropa).*

durazn, (dū•râz´no) *m.* peach; peach tree *(árbol).*

dureza (dū•re´sâ) *f.* hardness; (med.) hardening.

durmiente (dūr•myen´te) *adj.* sleeping; —, *m.* (arch.) sleeper, stringer; (rail.) crosstie.

duro, ra (dū´ro, râ) *adj.* hard; strong, vigorous *(resistente);* rough, cruel *(violento);* harsh *(áspero);* —**ro**, *adv.* hard; —, *m.* dollar, peso.

E

e (e) *conj.* and.

ébano (e´vâ•no) *m.* ebony.

ebriedad (e•vrye•thâth´) *f.* intoxication, drunkenness.

ebrio, bria (e´vryo, vryâ) *adj.* intoxicated, drunk; (fig.) blind.

ebullición (e•vū•yē•syon´) *f.* boiling; (fig.) turmoil, ferment, frenzy.

eclesiástico (e•kle•syâs´tē•ko) *m.* clergyman, ecclesiastic; —, **ca,** *adj.* ecclesiastical.

eclipsar (e•klēp•sâr´) *va.* (ast.) to eclipse; to blot out, to hide *(ocultar);* —**se,** to drop out of sight.

eclipse (e•klēp´se) *m.* eclipse.

eco (e´ko) *m.* echo.

ecología (e•ko•lo•hē´â) ecology.

economía (e•ko•no•mē´â) *f.* economy; — **política,** economics, political economy; — **domésti-ca,** home economics, domestic science.

económico, ca (e•ko•noˊmē•ko, kâ) *adj.* economic; economical, saving *(ahorrador).*

economista (e•ko•no•mēsˊtâ) *m.* economist.

economizar (e•ko•no•mē•sârˊ) *va.* to save, to economize.

ecoturismo (e•ko•tū•rēzˊmo) *m.* ecotourism.

ectoplasma (ek•to•plâzˊmâ) *m.* ectoplasm.

ecuación (e•kwâ•syonˊ) *f.* equation.

ecuador (e•kwâ•thorˊ) *m.* equator; **E—,** Ecuador.

ecuatorial (e•kwâ•to•ryâlˊ) *adj.* equatorial.

ecuatoriano, na (e•kwâ•to•ryâ-no, nâ) *n.* Ecuadorian; —, *adj.* from Ecuador.

ecuestre (e•kwesˊtre) *adj.* equestrian.

eczema (ek•seˊmâ) *f.* eczema.

echar (e•chârˊ) *va.* to throw *(echar);* to discharge *(despedir);* to throw out *(arrojar);* to attribute *(imponer);* to go *(ir);* — **a correr,** to start running; — **a perder,** to ruin, to spoil; — **a pique,** to scuttle; — **de menos,** to miss; — **de ver,** to notice; — **la de,** to pride oneself on being;

— **raíces,** to take root; — **las cartas en el correo,** to mail the letters; —**se,** to throw oneself; to stretch out *(acostarse);* —**se para atrás,** to jump back;, (fig.) to go back on oneˊs word.

edad (e•thâthˊ) *f.* age; time *(época);* — **media,** Middle Ages; **ser mayor de —,** to be of age; **ser menor de —** to be a minor.

edición (e•thē•syonˊ) *f.* edition; publication *(impresión).*

edicto (e•thēkˊto) *m.* edict.

edificar (e•thē•fē•kârˊ) *va.* to build, to construct; to set up *(fundar);* (fig.) to edify, to set an example for.

edificio (e•thē•fēˊsyo) *m.* building, structure.

editor, ra (e•thē•torˊ, râ) *n.* publisher; editorial writer *(que escribe editoriales);* —, *adj.* publishing; **casa —ra,** publishing house.

editorial (e•thē•to•ryâlˊ) *adj.* publishing; *m.* editorial; —, *f.* publishing house.

educación (e•thū•kâ•syonˊ) *f.* education, upbringing, rearing.

educado, da (e•thū•kâˊtho, thâ) *adj.* wellmannered, refined.

educar (e•thū•kârˊ) *va.* to educate, to instruct, to rear, to bring up.

educativo, va (e•thū•kâ•tēˊvo, vâ) *adj.* educational.

EE. UU. or **E.U.A.: Estados Unidos, Estados Unidos de América** U.S. or U. S. A. United States of America.

efectivamente (e•fek•tē•vâ•men´te) *adv.* actually, really, certainly.

efectividad (e•fek•tē•vē•thâth´) *f.* reality, truth, certainty.

efectivo, va (e•fek•tē´vo, vâ) *adj.* true, real, actual; —, *m.* cash, specie; **hacer —vo,** to cash; **valor —vo,** real value.

efecto (e•fek´to) *m.* effect, result; piece of merchandise (artículo); purpose, end (fin); **—s,** *pl.* goods, belongings; **en —to,** in fact, in truth.

efectuar (e•fek•twâr´) *va.* to effect, to produce, to accomplish; **— un pago,** to make a payment.

efervescencia (e•fer•ves•sen´syâ) *f.* effervescence; (fig.) fervor, unrest.

eficaz (e•fē•kâs´) *adj.* effective.

efigie (e•fē´hye) *f.* effigy; image (en una moneda); (fig.) personification.

efímero, ra (e•fē´me•ro, râ) *adj.* ephemeral, short-lived.

efusión (e•fū•syon´) *f.* effusion, gush.

efusivo, va (e•fū•sē´vo, vâ) *adj.* effusive, gushing.

egipcio, cia (e•hēp´syo, syâ) *n.*

and *adj.* Egyptian.

Egipto (e•hēp´to) *m.* Egypt.

egoísmo (e•go•ēz´mo) *m.* selfishness, egoism.

egoísta (e•go•ēs´tâ) *adj.* egoistic, selfish, self-centered; —, *m.* and *f.* egoist, self-seeker.

eje, (e´he) *m.* axle (barra); axis.

ejecución (e•he•kū•syon´) *f.* execution.

ejecutante (e•he•kū•tân´te) *m.* and *f.* performer.

ejecutar (e•he•kū•târ´) *va.* to execute; to distrain (por via legal); to play (tocar).

ejecutivo, va (e•he•kū•tē´vo, vâ) *adj.* demanding (apremiante); executive; —, *n.* executive; —, *f.* board of directors.

ejemplar (e•hem•plâr´) *m.* copy; pattern, original (normal); —, *adj.* exemplary.

ejemplificar (e•hem•plē•fē•kâr´) *va.* to exemplify.

ejemplo (e•hem´plo) *m.* example; **— casero,** everyday example; **por —,** for instance.

ejercer (e•her•ser´) *va.* to exercise, to perform (una facultad); to practice (una profesión); **— la medicina,** to practice medicine.

ejercicio (e•her•sē´syo) *m.* exercise, practice; (mil.) drill; **— de tiro,** target practice.

ejército (e•her´sē•to) *m.* army.

ejido (e•hē´tho) *m.* common land; (Mex.) communal farm.

ejote (e•ho´te) *m.* (Mex.) string bean. **el—,** (el) art. (m. sing.) the.

él (el) pron. he; him (con preposición), it (cosa o animal). — **mismo,** he himself.

elaboración (e•lâ•vo•râ•syon´) *f.* elaboration.

elaborado, da (e•lâ•vo•râ´tho, thâ) *adj.* processed, worked.

elaborar (e•lâ•vo•râr´) *va.* to elaborate; to work, to process (preparar).

elasticidad (e•lâs•tē•sē•thâth´) *f.* elastic- ity; (fig.) laxity.

elección (e•lek•syon´) *f.* freedom of action; (pol.) election; selection (escogido).

electo, ta (e•lek´to, tâ) *n.* and *adj.* elect.

electorado (e•lek•to•râ´tho) *m.* electorate.

electoral (e•lek•to•râl´) *adj.* electoral.

electricidad (e•lek•trē•sē•thâth´) *f.* electricity.

electricista (e•lek•trē•sēs´tâ) *m.* electrician.

eléctrico, ca (e•lek´trē•ko, kâ) *adj.* electric, electrical.

electrificar (e•lek•trē•fē•kâr´) *va.* to electrify.

electrizar (e•lek•trē•sâr´) *va.* to electrify.

electrocardiógrafo (e•lek•tro•kar•thyo´ grâ•fo) *m.* electrocardiograph.

electrocardiograma (e•lek•tro•kâr•thyo•grâ´ mâ) *m.* electrocardiogram.

electrocución (e•lek•tro•kū•syon´) *f.* electrocution.

electrodo (e•lek•tro´tho) *m.* electrode.

electromagnético, ca (e•lek•tro•mâg•ne´ tē•ko, kâ) *adj.* electromagnetic.

electromotriz (e•lek•tro•mo•trēs´) *f. adj.* electromotive.

electrón (e•lek•tron´) *m.* electron.

electrónica, (e•lek•tro´nē•kâ) *f.* electronics.

electrónico, ca (e•lek•tro´nē•ko, kâ) *adj.* electronic.

electrotecnia (e•lek•tro•teg´nyâ) *f.* electrical engineering.

elefante (e•le•fân´te) *m.* elephant.

elegancia (e•le•gân´syâ) *f.* elegance.

elegía (e•le•jē´â) *f.* elegy.

elegible (e•le•hē´vle) *adj.* eligible.

elegir* (e•le•hēr´) *va.* to elect; to choose (escoger).

elementa, (e•le•men•tâl´) *adj.* elemental; elementary (fundamental).

elemento (e•le•men´to) *m.* element; integral part *(fundamento)*.

elevación (e•le•va•syon´) *f.* raising; (fig.) elevation; (geog.) height; (fig.) ecstasy, rapture *(enajenamiento)*.

elevado da (e•le•vâ´tho, thâ) *adj.* high, tall; (fig.) lofty, elevated.

elevador (e•le•vâ•thor´) *m.* hoist, lift; (Sp. Am.) elevator *(ascensor)*.

eliminación (e•lē•mē•nâ•syon´) *f.* elimination.

eliminar (e•lē•mē•nâr´) *va.* to eliminate.

elipse (e•lēp´se) *f.* (math.) ellipse.

elixir (e•lēk´sēr) or **elixir** (e•lēk•sēr´) *m.* elixir.

elocución (e•lo•kū•syon´) *f.* elocution *(parte de la retórica)*; speaking style, self-expression.

elocuente (e•lo•kwen´te) *adj.* eloquent.

elogiar (e•lo•hyâr´) *va.* to eulogize, to extol.

elogio (e•lo´hyo) *m.* eulogy, extolling.

eludir (e•lū•thēr) *va.* to elude, to avoid.

ella (e´yâ) *pron.* she; her *(con preposición)*; it *(cosa o animal)*; — **misma,** she herself.

ello (e´yo) *pron.* it, that.

ellos, ellas (e´yos, e´yâs) *pron. pl.* they.

emanación (e•mâ•nâ•syon´) *f.* emanation; (fig.) indication, expression.

emanar (e•mâ•nâr´) *vn.* to emanate.

emancipación (e•mân•sē•pâ•syon´) *f.* emancipation.

emancipar (e•mân•sē•pâr´) *va.* to emancipate, to set free.

embajada (em•bâ•hâ´thâ) *f.* embassy.

embajador (em•bâ•hâ•thor´) *m.* ambassador.

embaldosar (em•bâl•do•sâr´) *va.* to tile, to floor with tiles.

embalsamar (em•bâl•sâ•mar´) *va.* to embalm; to perfume *(perfumar)*.

embarazada (em•bâ•râ•sâ´thâ) *f. adj.* pregnant; —, *f.* pregnant woman.

embarazo (em•bâ•râ´so) *m.* obstruction; pregnancy; awkwardness, embarrassment *(falta de soltura)*.

embarazoso, sa (em•bâ•râ•so´so, sâ) *adj.* awkward, troublesome, hindering.

embarcación (em•bâr•kâ•syon´) *f.* vessel, ship; embarkation *(embarco)*.

embarcadero (em•bâr•kâ•the´ro) *m.* wharf, dock, pier; (rail.) platform.

embargo (em•bâr´go) *m.* embargo; bother, trouble; attachment; **sin —,** nevertheless, however.

embarque (em•bâr´ke) *m.* shipment, embarkment.

embarrar (em•bâ•rrâr´) *va.* to daub with mud, to muddy *(de barro);* to smear, to daub.

embeber (em•be•ver´) *va.* to absorb, to soak up *(absorber);* to contain, to hold *(contener);* to shorten (recoger); to soak *(empapar);* to insert *(encajar);* **—,** *vn.* to shrink; **—se,** to be wrapped up, to be absorbed.

embellecer* (em•be•ye•ser´) *va.* to embellish, to beautify.

embestida (em•bes•tē´thâ) *f.* assault, violent attack.

embestir* (em•bes•tēr´) *va.* to attack, to assault.

emblandecer* (em•blân•de•ser´) *va.* to soften, to make tender; **—se,** to be moved to pity, to soften.

emblanquecer (em•blâng•ke•ser´) *va.* to whiten, to turn white.

emblema (em•ble´mâ) *m.* emblem.

embobecer* (em•bo•ve•ser´) *va.* to stupefy, to benumb.

embocadura (em•bo•kâ•thū´râ) *f.* mouthpiece; mouth *(de río);* taste *(de vino);* squeezing in, forcing through *(acción),* (coll.) **tomar la —,** to get the hang of

it, to catch on.

embolsar (em•bol•sâr´) *va.* to take in, to make *(cobrar);* to put in one's purse.

emborrachar (em•bo•rrâ•châr´) *va.* to intoxicate, to make drunk; **—se,** to get drunk, to become intoxicated.

emboscada (em•bos•kâ´thâ) *f.* ambush.

embotado, da (em•bo•tâ´tho, thâ) *adj.* dull, blunt.

embotar (em•bo•târ´) *va.* to blunt; (fig.) to dull, to weaken; **—se,** to wear boots.

embotellar (em•bo•te•yâr´) *va.* to bottle.

embragar (em•brâ•gâr´) *vn.* to let out or release the clutch pedal; (auto.) to put in gear; (mech.) to engage.

embrague (em•brâ´ge) *m.* clutch *(mecanismo);* letting out the clutch *(acción).*

embriagar (em•bryâ•gâr´) *va.* to intoxicate, to make drunk; (fig.) to enrapture, to carry away.

embriaguez (em•bryâ•ges´) *f.* intoxication, drunkenness; (fig.) rapture, bliss.

embrión (em•bryon´) *m.* embryo.

embrionario, ria (em•bryo•nâ´r-yo, ryâ) *adj.* embryonic.

embrollar (em•bro´yâr´) *va.* to entangle, to confuse.

embrollo (em•bro´yo) *m.* tangle,

confusion; trick, ruse
(embuste); (fig.) tight spot.

embrujar (em•brū•hâr´) *va.* to
bewitch.

embudo (em•bū´tho) *m.* funnel
(instrumento); trap, trick
(trampa).

embuste (em•būs´te) *m.* trick,
wile, artifice; **—s,** *pl.* gewgaws,
trinkets.

embustero, ra (em•bus•te´ro, râ)
n. cheat, liar, trickster; — *adj.*
tricky, deceitful.

emergencia (e•mer•hen´syâ) *f.*
emergency *(urgencia);* emergence *(salida);* **campo de —,** (avi.)
emergency landing field; **sala de
—,** emergency room.

emérito (e•me´rē•to) *adj.* emeritus.

emersión (e•mer•syon´) *f.* emer-
sion.

emigración (e•mē•grâ•syon´) *f.*
emigration.

emigrante (e•mē•grân´te) *m.* and
f. emigrant.

emigrar (e•mē•grâr´) *vn.* to emigrate.

eminente (e•mē•nen´te) *adj.* eminent.

emisario (e•mē•sâ´ryo) *m.* emissary.

emisora (e•mē•so´râ) *f.* broadcasting station.

emitir (e•mē•tēr´) *va.* to issue
(poner en circulación); to emit,

to give off *(arrojar);* (rad. and
T.V.) to transmit, to broadcast;
to give out, to express *(manifestar).*

emoción (e•mo•syon´) *f.* emotion,
feeling.

emocionante (e•mo•syo•nân´te)
adj. thrilling, exciting.

emocionar (e•mo•syo•nâr´) *va.* to
excite, to thrill, to affect.

emotivo, va (e•mo•tē´vo, vâ) *adj.*
emotional, emotive.

empacar (em•pâ•kâr´) *va.* to
pack.

empadronamiento
(em•pâ•thro•nâ•myen´to) *m.*
census.

empadronar (em•pâ•thro•nâr´)
va. to take a census of.

empalago (em•pâ•lâ´go) *m.*
stuffed feeling; disgust.

empalagoso, sa (em•pâ•lâ•go´so,
sâ) *adj.* cloying, sickeningly
sweet *(meloso);* wearisome,
troublesome *(pesado).*

empalmar (em•pâl•mâr´) *va.* to
splice; (fig.) to hook up, to connect *(unir);* —, *vi.* to join, to
hook up; to follow right after
(suceder a continuación).

empalme (em•pâl´me) *m.* (rail.)
junction; (rad.) hookup.

empanada (em•pâ•nâ´thâ) *f.*
meat pie.

empantanar (em•pân•tâ•nâr´)
va. to swamp *(inundar);* (fig.) to

bog down, to block.

empañar (em•pâ•nyâr´) *va.* to swaddle, to wrap *(a las criaturas);* to blur, to cloud *(oscurecer);* (fig.) to tarnish, to sully *(manchar).*

empapar (em•pâ•pâr´) *va.* to saturate, to soak, to drench *(remojar);* to absorb *(absorber);* **—se,** to become thoroughly grounded, to go into deeply.

empaque (em•pâ´ke) *m.* packing.

empaquetar (em•pâ•ke•târ´) *va.* to pack, to package.

emparedado (em•pâ•re•thâ´tho) *m.* sandwich; **—, da,** *adj.* walled-in, secluded.

emparejar (em•pâ•re•hâr´) *va.* to match *(formar, pareja);* to level, to equalize *(poner al nivel);* **—,** *vn.* to be level, to catch up.

emparentar* (em•pâ•ren•târ´) *vn.* to become related by marriage.

empastar (em•pâs•târ´) *va.* to fill with dough, to cover with paste; to fill *(un diente);* to hard-bind *(un libro).*

empatar (em•pâ•târ´) *va.* to tie; to tie up, to delay *(estorbar).*

empate (em•pâ´te) *m.* tie; delay, tie-up.

empedernir* (em•pe•ther•nēr´) *va.* to harden; **—se,** to become insensitive, to become hard-

ened.

empedrado (em•pe•thrâ´tho) *m.* stone pavement.

empedrar* (em•pe•thrâr´) *va.* to pave with stones.

empellón (em•pe•yon´) *m.* forceful push, heavy shove; **a — ones,** roughly, violently.

empeñar (em•pe•nyâr´) *va.* to pawn *(dar en prenda);* to obligate, to pledge *(poner por empeño);* to compel, to require *(precisar);* **—se,** to insist, to persist, to go into debt *(endeudarse).*

empeño (em•pe´nyo) *m.* determination, resolve *(deseo vehemente);* obligation, pledge *(obligación);* backer *(padrino);* (Mex.). pawn shop.

empeorar (em•pe•o•râr´) *va.* to make worse, to worsen, **—,** *vn.* to grow worse, to worsen, to deteriorate.

empequeñecer* (em•pe•ke•nye•ser´) *va.* to belittle, to minimize.

emperador (em•pe•râ•thor´) *m.* emperor.

emperatriz (em•pe•râ•trēs´) *f.* empress.

empero (em•pe´ro) *conj.* however, nevertheless.

empezar* (em•pe•sâr´) *va.* to begin, to commence.

empinar (em•pē•nâr´) *va.* to

raise, to lift; —**se,** to stand on tiptoe; (fig.) to tower.

empírico (em•pē´rē•ko) *m.* empiric, empiricist; —, **ca,** *adj.* empirical.

emplastar (em•plâs•târ´) *va.* (med.) to put a plaster on; (fig.) to put makeup on; to delay, to foul up *(un negocio);* —**se,** to get all sticky, to get messed up.

emplasto (em•plâs´to) *m.* plaster.

emplazamiento (em•plâ•sâ•myen´to) *m.* site, location; summons, citation *(cita).*

emplazar (em•plâ•sâr´) *va.* to summon; to place, to locate *(colocar).*

empleado, da (em•ple•â´tho, thâ) *n.* employee.

empleo (em•ple´o) *m.* employment, occupation.

emplumar (em•plū•mâr´) *va.* to feather, to put feathers on; to tar and feather *(a una persona);* —**se,** to grow feathers.

emplumecer* (em•plū•me•ser´) *vn.* to grow feathers.

empobrecer* (em•po•vre•ser´) *va.* to impoverish, to reduce to poverty; —**se,** to grow poor.

empobrecimiento (em•po•vre•sē•myen´to) *m.* impoverishing.

empolvado, da (em•pol•vâ´tho, thâ) *adj.* powdered; dusty;

(Mex.) out of practice, rusty.

empolvar (em•pol•vâr´) *va.* to powder *(el rostro);* to cover with dust; —**se,** to become dusty; (Mex.) to be out of practice *(perder la práctica).*

emprendedor, ra (em•pren•de•thor´, râ) *adj.* enterprising.

emprender (em•pren•der´) *va.* to initiate, to undertake.

empresa (em•pre´sâ) *f.* enterprise, undertaking; symbol, motto *(lema);* company, firm *(sociedad);* **libre** —, free enterprise.

empresario (em•pre•sâ´ryo) *m.* contractor *(por contrata);* (theat.) impresario, manager.

empujar (em•pū•hâr´) *va.* to push, to shove; to press *(hacer presión);* (fig.) to oust, to remove.

empuje (em•pū´he) *m.* push, shove; (avi.) thrust; (fig.) drive, energy.

empujón (em•pū•hon´) *m.* shove, forceful push; rapid strides *(avance rápido);* **a** — **ones,** roughly, carelessly.

empuñar (em•pū•nyâr´) *va.* to grasp, to clutch, to grip *(por el puño);* to hold, to take hold of *(con la mano).*

emulsión (e•mūl•syon´) *f.* emulsion.

en (en) *prep.* at, in; on *(encima de);* — **adelante,** in the future; — **cuanto,** as soon as; — **cuanto a,** as to, in regard to; — **domingo,** on Sunday; — **casa,** at home; — **la clase,** in class.

enajenamiento (e•nâ•he•nâ•myen′to) *m.* alienation; (fig.) lack of attention, absentmindedness.

enaltecer* (e•nâl•te•ser′) *va.* to praise, to exalt.

enamoradizo, za (e•nâ•mo•râ•thē′so, sâ) *adj.* inclined to falling in love easily.

enamoramiento (e•nâ•mo•râ•myen′to) *m.* falling in love.

enamorar (e•nâ•mo•râr′) *va.* to enamor, to inspire love in; to court, to woo *(decir requiebros);* —**se,** to fall in love.

enano, na (e•nâ′no, nâ) *adj.* dwarfish; —, *n.* dwarf, midget.

enarbolar (e•nâr•vo•lâr′) *va.* to hoist, to raise; —**se,** to become angry, to lose one′s temper.

enardecer* (e•nâr•the•ser′) *va.* to inflame, to kindle, to excite.

encabezamiento, (eng•kâ•ve•sâ•myen′to) *m.* census *(registro);* heading *(de una carta);* foreword, preface *(de un libro).*

encabezar (eng•kâ•ve•sâr′) *va.* to make a census of; to put a heading on; to write a preface to; (fig.) to lead, to head up.

encadenamiento (eng•kâ•the•nâ•myen′to) *m.* linking together; chaining together; connecting.

encadenar (eng•kâ•the•nâr′) *va.* to chain; (fig.) to link together, to connect.

encajonar (eng•kâ•ho•nâr′) *va.* to box, to case; to squeeze *(estrechar);* (fig.) to put in close quarters.

encalvecer* (eng•kâl•ve•ser′) *vn.* to get bald, to lose one′s hair.

encaminar (eng•kâ•mē•nâr′) *va.* to show the way, to start out; to direct *(dirigir);* —**se,** to start out; to be on the way.

encandecer* (eng•kân•de•ser′) *va.* to bring to a white heat, to make red-hot.

encandilar (eng•kân•dē•lâr′) *va.* to dazzle, to daze; (fig.) to confuse, to perplex; —**se,** to become bloodshot.

encanecer* (eng•kâ•ne•ser′) *vn.* to turn gray; (fig.) to grow old.

encantador, ra (eng•kân•tâ•thor′, râ) *adj.* charming, delightful, enchanting; —, *m.* enchanter, sorcerer, magician; —, *f.* sorceress, enchantress.

encantar (eng•kân•târ′) *va.* to enchant, to cast a spell on;

(fig.) to charm, to captivate.

encanto (eng•kân´to) *m.* enchantment, spell; (fig.) charm, delightfulness.

encapotar (eng•kâ•po•târ´) *va.* to cloak; —**se,** to put on one´s cape; (fig.) to cloud over, to become overcast *(el cielo);* to grow sullen, to frown *(una persona).*

encapricharse (eng•kâ•prē•châr´se) *vr.* to be stubborn, to persist.

encapuchar (eng•kâ•pū•châr´) *va.* to put a hood on.

encarar (eng•kâ•râr´) *va.* to aim at *(apuntar);* to face, to come face to face with.

encarcelar (eng•kâr•se•lâr´) *va.* to imprison.

encarecer* (eng•kâ•re•ser´) *va.* to raise the price of; (fig.) to praise, to rate highly *(alabar);* to urge, to recommend strongly *(recomendar).*

encargar (eng•kâr•gâr´) *va.* to give the job, to entrust; —**se de,** to take upon oneself, to take charge of, to take care of.

encargo (eng•kâr´go) *m.* entrusting, giving the job *(acción);* job, responsibility; position *(empleo).*

encariñar (eng•kâ•rē•nyâr´)*va.* to inspire affection in; —**se con,**to become fond of.

encarnación (eng•kâr•nâ•syon´) *f.* incarnation.

encarnar (eng•kâr•nâr´) *vn.* to become incarnate; to grow new flesh *(una herida);* (fig.) to make a tremendous impression; —, *vt.* to embody, to personify; —**se,** to mix, to fuse.

encarnizar (eng•kâr•nē•sâr´) *va.* to flesh; (fig.) to make bloodthirsty, to brutalize; —**se,** to become bloodthirsty; to take out one´s wrath *(una persona).*

encarrilar (eng•kâ•rrē•lâr´) *va.* to channel, to direct; (fig.) to put to rights, to set right.

encasillado (eng•kâ•sē•yâ´tho) *m.* set of pigeonholes; (poi.) slate of candidates.

encasillar (eng•kâ•sē•yâr´) *va.* to pigeonhole; to classify, to sort out *(clasificar).*

encastillar (eng•kâs•tē•yâr´) *va.* to fortify with castles; to stack up *(apilar).*

encausar (eng•kâū•sâr´) *va.* to indict, to prosecute.

encauzar (eng•kâū•sâr´) *vt.* to channel, to direct.

encenagarse (en•se•nâ•gâr´se) *vr.* to get covered with mud; (fig.) to wallow in vice.

encendedor (en•sen•de•thor´) *m.* lighter; — **de cigarrillos,** cigarette lighter.

encender* (en•sen•der´) *va.* to

light *(pegar fuego);* to ignite, to set on fire *(incendiar);* to turn on, to switch on *(la luz);* (fig.) to kindle, to inflame *(excitar);* **—se**, to blush, to turn red.

encerar (en•se•râr´) *vn.* to wax.

encerrar* (en•se•rrâr´) *va.* to shut up, to confine, to lock up; to hold, to contain *(contener);* **—se,** to go into seclusion.

encía (en•sē´â) *f.* (anat.) gum.

enciclopedia (en•sē•klo•pe´thyâ) *f.* encyclopedia.

enciclopédico, ca (en•se•klo•pe´thē•ko, kâ) *adj.* encyclopedic.

encierro (en•sye´rro) *m.* confinement, locking up; enclosure *(lugar);* seclusion, retirement *(clausura);* narrow cell *(prisión);* pen for fighting bulls *(toril).*

encima (en•sē´mâ) *adv.* above, over; on top *(en la parte superior);* as well, morever *(además);* **—** **de,** on top of, on; **por — de,** over.

encina (en•sē´nâ) *f.* holm oak, ilex.

enclaustrado, da (eng•klāūs•trâ´tho, thâ) *adj.* cloistered; (fig.) hidden away.

enclavar (eng•klâ•vâr´) *va.* to nail.

enclavijar (eng•klâ•vē•hâr´) *va.* to pin, to join with dowels;

(mus.) to peg.

encoger (eng•ko•her´) *va.* to draw back, to pull back; (fig.) to make timid, to impede, to hold back: **—se,** to shrink; **—se de hombros,** to shrug one´s shoulders.

encolerizar (eng•ko•le•rē•sar´) *va.* to anger, to infuriate.

encomendar* (eng•ko•men•dâr´) *va.* to recommend, to entrust; **—se,** to commit oneself, to rely.

encomiar (eng•ko•myâr´) *va.* to praise.

encomienda (eng•ko•myen´dâ) *f.* commission, trust *(encargo);* (Sp. Am.) package by mail *(envío);* praise *(elogio);* — **postal,** parcel post.

encono (eng•ko´no) *m.* malevolence, rancor, ill-will.

encontrar* (eng•kon•trâr´) *va.* to meet by chance, to come upon *(tropezar con);* to find, to locate *(hallar);* **—se,** to run into each other; to meet *(concurrir);* to clash,to be at odds *(las opiniones);* to be, to find oneself *(estar);* **—se con,** to meet.

encopetado, da (eng•ko•pe•tâ´tho, thâ) *adj.* presumptuous, boastful.

encorchar (eng•kor•châr´) *va.* to hive *(las abejas);* to cork *(una botella).*

encorvar (eng•kor•vâr´) *va.* to

bend, to curve.

encrucijada (en•krū•sē•hä´thä) *f.* crossroads *(de caminos);* intersection *(de calles).*

encrudecer* (eng•krū•the•ser´) *va.* to make rough and raw; (fig.) to rub the wrong way, to exasperate *(irritar).*

encuadernar (eng•kwâ•ther•när´) *va.* to bind.

encuadrar (eng•kwâ•thrär´) *va.* to frame; to insert, to fit *(encajar).*

encubrir (eng•kū•vrēr´) *va.* to hide, to conceal.

encuentro (eng•kwen´tro) *m.* collision, crash *(choque);* meeting, encounter *(acto de encontrarse);* disagreement, opposition *(en el parecer);* match, game *(deportivo);* (mil.) encounter, clash; find (*hallazgo);* **salir a —,** to go out to meet; to face *(hacer)*

encuesta (eng•kwes´tâ) *f.* investigation, poll.

encumbrar (eng•kūm•brär´) *va.* to raise, to elevate; to reach the top of *(un monte);* **—se,** to grow vain, to swell with pride *(envanecerse);* to tower, to loom.

encurtido (eng•kūr•tē´tho) *m.* pickle; **— con eneldo,** dill pickle.

enchilada (en•chē•lâ´thâ) *f.* (Mex.) tortilla seasoned with chili and stuffed with cheese and meat.

enchufe (en•chū´fe) *m.* (elec.) outlet *(conexión);* plug *(aparato);* connection *(de cañerías);* **tener —,** (coll.) to have pull.

endemoniado, da (en•de•mo•nyâ´tho, thâ) *adj.* possessed, bedeviled; (coll.) devilish, fiendish.

enderezamiento (en•de•re•sâ•myen´to) *m.* straightening.

enderezar (en•de•re•sâr´) *va.* to straighten; to rectify *(enmendar);* to direct, to send straight *(encaminar).*

endeudarse (en•deū•thâr´se) *vr.* to get into debt.

endiosar (en•dyo•sâr´) *va.* to deify; **—se,** (fig.) to puff up with pride *(engreírse);* to be absorbed, to be deeply engrossed *(enajenarse).*

endorso (en•dor´so) *m.* endorsement.

endosante (en•do•sân´te) *m.* endorser.

endosar (en•do•sâr´) *va.* to endorse; (fig.) to load with, to throw on *(una carga).*

endulzar (en•dūl•sâr´) *va.* to sweeten *(dulcificar);* to soften *(suavizar).*

endurecer* (en•dū•re•ser´) *va.* to harden; —**se,** to become cruel, to grow hard.

endurecido, da (en•dū•re•sē´tho, thâ) *adj.* hardened.

endurecimiento (en•dū•re•sē•myen´to) *m.* hardening; (fig.) obstinacy *(obstinación).*

enemigo, ga (e•ne•mē´go, gâ) *adj.* unfriendly, hostile; —, *n.* enemy.

enemistad (e•ne•mēs•tâth´) *f.* enmity, hatred.

enemistar (e•ne•mēs•târ´) *va.* to estrange, to make enemies; —se, to become enemies.

energía (e•ner•hē´â) *f.* power, force *(potencia);* strength *(eficacia);* (phy.) energy; — **atómica,** atomic energy; —**nuclear** or **nuclearia,** nuclear power; — **solar,** solar power.

enérgico, ca (e•ner´hē•ko, kâ) *adj.* energetic; powerful, strong *(eficaz).*

enero (e•ne´ro) *m.* January.

enfadado, da (em•fâ•thâ´tho, thâ) *adj.* angry, irate; annoyed, vexed.

enfadar (em•fâ•thâr´) *va.* to anger, to make angry; to annoy, to vex *(fastidiar);* —se, to get angry; to be annoyed.

enfado (em•fâ´tho) *m.* vexation, annoyance; anger, ire *(enojo).*

énfasis (em´fâ•sēs) *m.* emphasis.

enfático, at (em•fâ´tē•ko, kâ) *adj.* emphatic.

enfermar (em•fer•mar´) *va.* to sicken, to make sick; (fig.) to weaken *(debilitar);* —, *vn.* to get sick ; —se, (Sp. Am.) to get sick.

enfermedad (em•fer•me•thâth´) *f.* illness, sickness, disease.

enfermería (em•fer•me•rē´â) *f.* infirmary.

enfermero, ra (em•fer•me´ro, râ) *n.* nurse.

enfermo, ma (em•fer´mo, ma) *adj.* sick; diseased *(atacado);* —, *n.* sick person, patient; **ponerse** —, to get sick.

enfilar (em•fē•lâr´) *va.* to line up; to string *(ensartar);* to follow the course of *(seguir).*

enflaquecer* (em•flâ•ke•ser´) *va.* to make lose weight; (fig.) to weaken *(enervar);* —se, to lose weight, to get thin.

enfoque (em•fo´ke) *m.* focus.

enfrenar (em•fre•nâr´) *va.* to bridle *(el caballo);* (mech.) to brake; (fig.) to curb, to check.

enfrentar (em•fren•târ´) *va.* to bring face to face, to confront *(poner frente a frente);* to face *(hacer frente).*

enfrente (em•fren´te) *adv.* across, opposite; in front;

opposed *(en contra).*

enfriamiento (em•fryâ•myen´to) *m.* refrigeration, cooling; (med.) chill; — **por aire,** air-cooling.

enfriar (em•fryâr´) *va.* to cool, to refrigerate; (fig.) to chill, to dampen *(amortiguar);* —, *vn.* to cool off.

enfurecer* (em•fū•re•ser´) *va.* to infuriate, to enrage; —**se,** to grow furious; (fig.) to get rough, to become wild *(alborotarse).*

engalanar (eng•gâ•lâ•nâr´) *va.* to adorn, to deck out.

enganchar (eng•gân•châr´) *va.* to hook, to connect; to hang *(en una percha);* to hitch *(la caballería);* (mil.) to recruit; (coll.) to hook, to trap *(obligar con maña).*

enganche (eng•gân´che) *m.* connection, hook; (Mex.) down payment.

engañar (eng•gâ•nyâr´) *va.* to deceive, to cheat; to mislead, to take advantage of *(abusar de);* to wile away, to pass *(entretener);* —**se,** to be mistaken, to be wrong.

engaño (eng•gâ´nyo) *m.* mistake; deceit *(trampa).*

engañoso, sa (eng•gâ•nyo´so, sâ) *adj.* deceitful, misleading.

engarzar (eng•gâr•sâr´) *va.* to curl *(rizar);* to thread, to wire *(reunir con un hilo).*

engastar (eng•gâs•târ´) *va.* to enchase, to mount.

engaste (eng•gâs´te) *m.* setting, mounting.

engazar (eng•gâ•sâr´) *va.* to curl *(rizar);* to thread, to wire *(unir);* to dye after weaving *(un paño).*

engendrar (en•hen•drâr´) *va.* to engender, to beget.

englobar (eng•glo•vâr´) *va.* to lump together.

engolfar (eng•gol•fâr´) *vn.* to go far out to sea; —**se,** to throw oneself heart and soul, to devote all one´s time.

engranaje (eng•grâ•nâ´he) *m.* gear, gears; meshing *(acción).*

engranar (eng•grâ•nâr´) *vn.* to mesh, to gear.

engrandecer* (eng•grân•de•ser´) *va.* to increase, to augment; to aggrandize, to extol *(alabar).*

engrasar (eng•grâ•sâr´) *va.* to grease, to oil.

engreir* (eng•gre•ēr´) *va.* to make vain, to make proud; (Sp. Ant) to spoil, to overindulge *(mimar).*

engrosar* (eng•gro•sâr´) *va.* to thicken; (fig.) to swell; —, *vn.* to put on weight.

engullir* (eng•gū•yēr´) *va.* to gobble up, to gulp down.

enhebrar (e•ne•vrâr´) *va.* to thread.

enigma (e•nēg´mâ) *m.* riddle,

enigma.

enigmático, ca (e•nēg•mâ´tē•ko, kâ) *adj.* enigmatical.

enjabonar (en•hâ•vo•nâr´) *va.* to soap, to lather.

enjambre (en•hâm´bre) *m.* swarm of bees; (fig.) throng, swarm *(multitud).*

enjaretar (en•hâ•re•târ´) *va.* to run through the hem; (fig.) to reel off, to dash off *(decir atropelladamente);* to palm off, to fob off *(encajar).*

enjaular (en•hâū•lâr´) *va.* to cage; (coll.) to jail.

enjoyar (en•ho•yâr´) *va.* to put jewels on; (fig.) to embellish.

enjuagar (en•hwâ•gar´) *va.* to rinse, to rinse out.

enjuague (en•hwâ´ge) *m.* rinse, rinsing; mouthwash *(para la boca).*

enjuiciar (en•hwē•syâr´) *va.* to pass judgment on; to try *(instruir);* to sue, to bring to trial *(sujetar a juicio).*

enjuto, ta (en•hū´to, tâ) *adj.* dry *(seco);* skinny, sparse *(flaco).*

enlace (en•lâ´se) *m.* connection, link *(conexión);* relationship *(parentesco);* (rail.) junction; wedding *(casamiento).*

enlatado, da (en•lâ•tâ´tho, thâ) *adj.* canned, preserved; **productos —s,** canned goods.

enlatar (en•lâ•târ´) *va.* to can, to tin.

enloquecer* (en•lo•ke•ser´) *va.* to madden, to drive mad; **—se,** to go mad; (fig.) to be mad, to be wild.

enloquecido, da (en•lo•ke•sē´-tho, thâ) *adj.* deranged, mad.

enloquecimiento (en•lo•ke•sē•myen´to) *m.* madness, insanity.

enlosar (en•lo•sâr´) *va.* to set flagstones on, to lay with flagstone.

enlutar (en•lū•târ´) *va.* to dress in mourning; **—se,** to go into mourning.

enmarañar (en•mâ•râ•nyâr´) *va.* to entangle, to snarl up (fig.) to confuse, to mix up.

enmarcar (en•mâr•kâr´) *va.* to frame.

enmascarar (en•mâs•kâ•râr´) *va.* to mask.

enmendar* (en•men•dâr´) *va.* to amend, to correct *(corregir);* to make restitution for *(subsanar);* to revise *(una sentencia).*

enmienda (en•myen´dâ) *f.* correction; revision, amendment; restitution.

enmohecer* (en•mo•e•ser´) *va.* to mold; to rust *(herrumbrar);* **—se,** to grow moldly; to rust, to get rusty.

enmudecer* (en•mū•the•ser´) *va.* to silence, to keep silent; **—,**

vn. to lose one's speech; *(fig.)* to keep quiet, to say nothing *(callarse).*

ennegrecer* (en•ne•gre•ser´) *va.* to blacken.

ennoblecer* (en•no•vle•ser´) *va.* to ennoble.

enojado, da (e•no•hâ´tho, thâ) *adj.* angry, cross.

enojar (e•no•hâr´) *va.* to anger, to make angry; to peeve, to irritate *(desazonar);* —**se,** to get angry.

enojo (e•no´ho) *m.* anger; irritation, bother *(molestia).*

enojón, ona (e•no•hon´, o´nâ) *adj.* (Sp. Am.) quick-tempered, irritable.

enorgullecer* (e•nor•gū•ye• ser´) *va.* to fill with pride; —**se,** to swell with pride.

enorme (e•nor´me) *adj.* enormous, huge; —**mente,** *adv.* enormously.

enormidad (e•nor•mē•thâth´) *f.* enormity.

enramada (en•rrâ•mâ´thâ) *f.* boughs *(ramaje);* bower, leafy retreat *(cobertizo).*

enredar (en•rre•thâr´) *va.* to net *(prender con red);* to twist up, to tangle *(enmarañar);* to stir up, to start *(discordia);* to mix up, to entangle *(en un mal negocio);* —**se,** to have an affair *(amancebarse);* to present

problems, to run afoul *(un negocio).*

enredo (en•rre´tho) *m.* tangle, snarl *(maraña);* prank *(travesura);* trick, trap *(engaño);* problem, difficulty *(complicación);* plot *(trama).*

enrejado (en•rre•hâ´tho) *m.* grillwork, grating; openwork *(labor de mano).*

enrevesado, da (en•rre•ve•sâ´-tho, thâ) *adj.* intricate, complicated; *(fig.)* contrary, headstrong *(travieso).*

enriquecer* (en•rrē•ke•ser´) *va.* to enrich; —, *vn.* to grow rich.

enriscar (en•rrēs•kâr´) *va.* (fig.) to elevate, to raise, —**se,** to take refuge among the rocks.

enrizar (en•rrē•sâr´) *va.* to curl.

enrojecer* (en•rro•he•ser´) *va.* to make red-hot *(en el fuego);* to redden, to make red; —**se,** to blush, to redden.

enrollar (en•rro•yâr´) *va.* to wind, to roll.

enronquecer* (en•rrong•ke•ser´) *va.* to make hoarse; —, *vn.* to grow hoarse.

ensalada (en•sâ•lâ´thâ) *f.* salad; *(fig.)* hodgepodge.

ensalzar (en•sâl•sâr´) *va.* to exalt, to praise; —**se,** to boast, to make much of oneself.

ensamblar (en•sâm•blâr´) *va.* to assemble, to fit together.

ensanchar (en•sân•chär´) *va.* to widen, to enlarge; **—se,** to assume an air of importance.

ensangrentar* (en•sâng•gren•târ´) *va.* to bloody, to make bloody; **—se,** (fig.) to rage, to seethe; **—se con,** to take out one's wrath on.

ensañar (en•sâ•nyâr´) *va.* to enrage, to infuriate; **—se en** to vent one's rage on, to do unnecessary violence.

ensartar (en•sâr•târ´) *va.* to string; to stick, to drive *(introducir).*

ensayar (en•sâ•yâr´) *va.* to experiment with, to try out *(probar);* to teach, to train *(adiestrar);* (theat.) to rehearse.

ensayo (en•sâ´yo) *m.* trying out, experiment; essay *(escrito);* (theat.) rehearsal; assay; **— general,** dress rehearsal.

ensenada (en•se•nâ´thâ) *f.* cove, small bay.

enseña (en•se´nyâ) *f.* standard, ensign, colors.

enseñanza (en•se•nyân´sâ) *f.* teaching, instruction; **primera —,** primary grades; **segunda —,** high school grades.

enseñar (en•se•nyâr´) *va.* to teach, to instruct *(instruir);* to show *(mostrar);* to point out *(indicar).*

ensillar (en•sē•yâr´) *va.* to saddle.

ensimismarse (en•sē•mēz•mâr´se) *vr.* to be lost in thought *(absorberse);* to be stuck on oneself *(engreírse).*

ensordecer* (en•sor•the•ser´) *va.* to deafen; **—,** *vn.* to grow deaf; to keep quiet, not to answer *(enmudecer).*

ensuciar (en•sū•syâr´) *va.* to dirty, to soil; (fig.) to tarnish, to stain *(deslustrar);* **—se,** (fig.) to accept bribes, to be able to be bought.

ensueño (en•swe´nyo) *m.* dream, reverie, illusion.

entablado, da (en•tâ•vlâ´tho, thâ) *adj.* boarded, made of boards; **—,** *m.* wooden flooring.

entablar (en•tâ•vlâr´) *va.* to board over; to splint *(entabillar);* to broach *(comenzar).*

entalladura (en•tâ•yâ•thū´râ) *f.* carving; tap, notch *(en el árbol);* groove *(en las maderas).*

entallar (en•tâ•yâr´) *va.* to carve; to tap, to notch; to groove; **—,** *vn.* to fit.

entender* (en•ten•der´) *va.* to understand *(comprender);* to know *(conocer);.* to intend, to mean *(querer);* to believe *(creer).*

entendimiento (en•ten•dē•myen´to) *m.* understanding; good judgment (juicio).

enterar (en•te•râr´) va. to inform, to notify, to let know; **—se de,** to find out about, to be informed of.

entereza (en•te•re´sâ) f. entirety, perfection; (fig.) perseverance, steadfastness (fortaleza).

enternecer* (en•ter•ne•ser´) va. to soften; (fig.) to affect, to move (conmover); **—se,** to be touched, to be moved.

enternecimiento (en•ter•ne•sē•myen´to) m. compassion, pity.

entero, ra (en•te´ro, râ) adj. whole, entire; (fig.) just, upstanding (recto); resolute (firme); virtuous honest (incorruptible); **por —ro,** entirely, completely.

enterrar* (en•te•rrâr´) va. to bury.

entibiar (en•tē•vyâr´) va. to cool.

entidad (en•tē•thâth´) f. entity, being; importance, value (valor).

entierro (en•tye´rro) m. burial.

entomología (en•to•mo•lo•hē´â) f. entomology.

entonación (en•to•nâ•syon´) f. intonation; (fig.) presumption, airs (presunción).

entonar (en•to•nâr´) va. to intone; to sing in tune (afinando la voz); (med.) to tone up; to harmonize (armonizar).

entontecer* (en•ton•te•ser´) va. to stupefy, to dull; **—se,** to grow stupid.

entornar (en•tor•nâr´) va. to leave ajar, to leave half-open.

entorpecer* (en•tor•pe•ser´) va. to stupefy, to dull; (fig.) to block, to hinder (estorbar).

entrada (en•trâ´thâ) f. entry (acción); entrance (sitio); attendance (concurrencia); admission, ticket (billete); beginning (principio); first course (de una comida); (com.) receipt; ear, access (favor).

entrambos, bas (en•trâm´bos, bâs) adj. pl. both.

entrante (en•trân´te) adj. next, incoming, coming.

entrañable (en•trâ•nyâ´vle) adj. intimate, very dear.

entrañas (en•trâ´nyâs) f. pl. intestines; (fig.) bowels (lo más oculto); very heart, life blood (lo más íntimo).

entrar (en•trâr´) vn. to enter; to pierce, to penetrate (penetrar); to fit (caber); to be used (emplearse); to start up (manifestarse); **—,** va. to bring in (introducir); to get through to (pegar).

entre (en´tre) prep. between; among (en medio de); within *(dentro);* — **manos,** at hand, on hand.

entreabierto, ta (en•tre•â•vyer´-to, tâ) *adj.* ajar, half-open.

entreabrir* (en•tre•â•vrēr´) *va.* to open half-way, to leave ajar.

entreacto (en•tre•âk´to) *n.* (theat.) intermission.

entrecoger (en•tre•ko•her´) *va.* to catch, to intercept, to grab hold of.

entrecortado, da (en•tre•kor•tâ´-tho, thâ) *adj.* faltering, intermittent, broken.

entrega (en•tre´gâ) *f.* delivery, handing over; surrender; — **inmediata,** special delivery.

entregar (en•tre•gâr´) *va.* to deliver, to hand over; —**se,** to surrender, to give up; to devote oneself, to give oneself over *(dedicarse).*

entrelazado, da (en•tre•lâ•sâ´-tho, thâ) *adj.* interlaced, entwined.

entrelazar (en•tre•lâ•sâr´) *va.* to interlace, to entwine.

entremés (en•tre•mes´) *m.* (theat.) scene of comic relief; appetizer *(en la comida).*

entremetido, da (en•tre•me•tē´-tho, thâ) *n.* meddler; —, **da,** *adj.* meddling, meddlesome.

entrenador (en•tre•nâ•thor´) *m.* trainer, coach.

entrenar (en•tre•nâr´) *va.* to

train, to coach.

entreoir* (en•tre•o•ēr´) *va.* to barely hear, to catch snatches of.

entretanto (en•tre•tân´to) *adv.* meanwhile.

entretejer (en•tre•te•her´) *va.* to interweave.

entretener* (en•tre•te•ner´) *va.* to entertain, to amuse *(divertir);* to delay to put off *(demorar);* to allay *(hacer más llevadero).*

entretenido, da (en•tre•te•nē´-tho, thâ) *adj.* pleasant, amusing.

entretenimiento (en•tre•te•nē•myen´to) *m.* amusement, entertainment.

entrevenado, da (en•tre•ve•nâ´-tho, thâ) *adj.* intravenous.

entrevenarse (en•tre•ve•nâr´se) *vr.* to spread through the veins.

entrever* (en•tre•ver´) *va.* to catch a glimpse of, to barely see.

entrevista (en•tre•vēs´tâ) *f.* interview.

entristecer* (en•trēs•te•ser´) *va.* to sadden, to grieve; —**se,** to grieve, to be sad.

entronar (en•tro•nâr´) *va.* to enthrone.

entronque (en•trong´ke) *m.* (rail.) junction; common ancestry, relationship.

entubar (en•tū•vâr´) *va.* to pipe.

entumecer* (en•tū•me•ser´) *va.* to numb, to make numb; **—se,** (fig.) to swell, to rise *(hincharse).*

entumecimiento (en•tū•me•sē•myen´to) *m.* numbness; numbing *(acción).*

enturbiar (en•tūr•vyâr´) *va.* to muddy, to stir up; (fig.) to spoil, to upset *(turbar).*

entusiasmar (en•tū•syâz•mâr´) *va.* to enthuse, to make enthusiastic; **—se,** to enthuse.

entusiasta (en•tū•syâs´tâ) *m.* and *f.* enthusiast, fan; **—,** *adj.* enthusiastic.

enumeración (e•nū•me•râ•syon´) *f.* enumeration.

enumerar (e•nū•me•râr´) *va.* to enumerate.

enunciación (e•nūn•syâ•syon´) *f.* enunciation, declaration, clear statement.

enunciar (e•nūn•syâr´) *va.* to enunciate, to declare, to state clearly.

envainar (em•bâē•nâr´) *va.* to sheathe.

envanecer* (em•bâ•ne•ser´) *va.* to make vain, to swell up, to puff up; **—se,** to become vain.

envasar (em•bâ•sâr´) *va.* to bottle *(en vasijas);* to package; to drink too much *(beber con exceso).*

envase (em•bâ´se) *m.* bottling; packaging; container *(recipiente).*

envejecer* (em•be•he•ser´) *va.* to age; **—,** *vn.* to age, to grow older.

envejecimiento (em•be•he•sē•myen´to) *m.* aging.

envenenamiento (em•be•ne•nâ•myen´to) *m.* poisoning.

envenenar (em•be•ne•nâr´) *va.* to poison.

envestir* (em•bes•tēr´) *va.* to invest.

enviado (em•byâ´tho) *m.* envoy, messenger.

enviar (em•byâr´) *va.* to send.

enviciar (em•bē•syâr´) *va.* to vitiate, to corrupt; **—se en** to spend too much time at, to go overboard on.

envidia (em•bē´thyâ) *f.* envy; desire *(emulación).*

envidiable (em•bē•thyyâ´vle) *adj.* enviable.

envidiar (em•bē•thyâr´) *vn.* to envy; to wish one had, to long for *(desear).*

envidioso, sa (em•bē•thyo´so, sâ) *adj.* envious.

envilecer* (em•bē•le•ser´) *va.* to degrade, to debase; **—se,** to degrade oneself, to be debased.

envío (em•bē´o) *m.* shipment,

remittance.

enviudar (em•byū•thâr´) *vn.* to be widowed; to be left a widower *(quedarse viudo).*

envoltura (em•bol•tū´râ) *f.* covering, wrapping; swaddling clothes *(del niño).*

envolver* (em•bol•ver´) *va.* to wrap, to cover, to involve *(mezclar);* to swaddle *(al niño);* to complicate to hide *(ocultar);* —**se,** to have an affair.

enyesar (en•ye•sâr´) *va.* to plaster; (med.) to put in a cast.

enzima (en•sē´mâ) *f.* (biol.) enzyme.

eón (e•on´) *m.* aeon.

epicentro (e•pē•sen´tro) *m.* epicenter.

épico, ca (e´pē•ko, kâ) *adj.* epic.

epidemia (e•pē•the´myâ) *f.* epidemic.

epidermis (e•pē•ther´mēs) *f.* epidermis.

epígrafe (e•pē´grâ•fe) *m.* epigraph.

epilepsia (e•pē•lep´syâ) *f.* epilepsy.

epílogo (e•pē´lo•go) *m.* epilogue.

episcopado (e•pēs•ko•pâ´tho) *m.* bishopric; episcopate *(conjunto de obispos).*

episodio (e•pē•so´thyo) *m.* episode.

epístola (e•pēs´to•lâ) *f.* epistle; (eccl.) Epistle.

epistolar (e•pēs•to•lâr´) *adj.* epistolary.

epitafio (e•pē•tâ´fyo) *m.* epitaph.

epíteto (e•pē´te•to) *m.* epithet.

época (e´po•kâ) *f.* epoch, age, era, period.

epopeya (e•po•pe´yâ) *f.* epic poem; (fig.) saga, epic.

equidad (e•kē•thâth´) *f.* equity; moderation *(templanza).*

equilátero, ra (e•kē•lâ´te•ro, râ) *adj.* equilateral.

equilibrar (e•kē•lē•vrâr´) *va.* to balance, to equilibrate.

equilibrio (e•kē•lē´vryo) *m.* equilibrium, balance; (fig.) poise *(ecuanimidad);* — **político,** balance of power.

equipaje (e•kē•pâ´he) *m.* baggage, luggage; (naut.) crew; **coche de —,** baggage car; — **de mano,** hand baggage, carry-on.

equipar (e•kē•pâr´) *va.* to fit out, to equip, to furnish.

equipo (e•kē´po) *m.* equipment, outfit, team *(grupo).*

equis (e´kēs) *f.* name of the letter x.

equitativo, va (e•kē•tâ•tē´vo, va) *adj.* equitable, just; **trato —,** square deal.

equivalente (e•kē•vâ•len´te) *adj.* equivalent.

equivaler* (e•kē•vâ•ler´) *vn.* to be of equal value, to have the same value.

equivocación (e•kē•vo•kâ•syon´) *f.* error, misunderstanding.

equivocar (e•kē•vo•kâr´) *va.* to mistake; **—se,** to be mistaken.

era (e´râ) *f.* era *(época);* plot, patch *(de hortalizas);* threshing floor *(para la trilla).*

erección (e•rek•syon´) *f.* erection; foundation, establishment *(fundación).*

eremita (e•re•mē´tâ) *m.* hermit.

erguir* (er•gēr´) *va.* to raise, to straighten up; **—se,** (fig.) to be puffed up, to become haughty.

erigir (e•rē•hēr´) *va.* to erect, to build *(construir);* to found, to establish *(instituir);* to elevate, to raise *(elevar).*

ermita (er•mēta) *f.* hermitage.

ermitaño (er•mē•tâ´nyo) *m.* hermit *(eremita);* hermit crab *(crustáceo).*

erosión (e•ro•syon´) *f.* erosion; abrasion, scrape *(abrasión).*

erótico, ca (e•ro´tē•ko, kâ) *adj.* erotic.

erradicación (e•rrâ•thē•kâ•syon´) *f.* eradication.

erradicar (e•rrâ•thē•kâr´) *va.* to eradicate.

errante (e•rrân´te) *adj.* errant, wandering, roving.

errar* (e•rrâr´) *va.* to miss, to fall short of; **—,** *vn.* to wander, to rove; **— el blanco,** to miss the mark.

erre (e´rre) *f.* name of the double letter rr and of the single letter r when initial in a word or following l, n, or s.

error (e•rror´) *m.* error, mistake.

eructo (e•rūk´to) *m.* belch.

erudición (e•rū•thē•syon´) *f.* erudition, learning.

erudito, ta (e•rū•thē´to, tâ) *adj.* learned, erudite; **—,** *m.* scholar, man of erudition.

erupción (e•rūp•syon´) *f.* eruption.

erutar (e•rū•târh)
eruto, (e•rū´to)= **eructar, eructo.**

esbelto, ta (ez•vel´to, tâ) *adj.* slender, graceful.

esbozar (ez•vo•sâr´) *va.* to sketch, to out-line.

esbozo (ez•vo´so) *m.* outline, sketch.

escabeche (es•kâ•ve´che) *m.* pickle; **pescado en —,** pickled fish.

escabullirse* (es•kâ•vū•yēr´se) *vr.* to escape, to get away.

escafandra (es•kâ•fân´drâ) *f.* diving suit; **— espacial,** spacesuit; **— autónoma,** Scuba.

escala (es•kâ´lâ) *f.* ladder *(escalera);* scale *(sucesión);* (mus.) scale; (naut.) port of call; **hacer — en,** to stop at, to call at.

escalar (es•kâ •lâr´) *va.* to climb, to scale.

escalafón (es•kâ•lâ•fon´) *m.*

seniority scale, grade scale.

escaldar (es•kâl•dâr´) *va.* to scald.

escalera (es•kâ•le´râ) *f.* stairs, stairway; run *(de naipes);* — **de mano** stepladder; — **mecánica** escalator.

escalofrío (es•kâ•lo•frē´o) *m.* chill.

escalón (es•kâ•lon´) *m.* step, tread *(peldaño);* (fig.) grade, rank; (mil.) echelon.

escalonar (es•kâ•lo•nâr´) *va.* to stagger *(en tiempos sucesivos);* to space out, to place at intervals *(de trecho en trecho).*

escama (es•kâ´mâ) *f.* scale; (fig.) resentment *(desazón).*

escamar (es•kâ•mâr´) *va.* to scale; (fig.) to make wary, to teach; —**se,** to become wary, to learn from experience.

escampar (es•kâm•pâr´) *vn.* to stop rain.

escandalizar (es•kân•dâ•lē•sâr´) *va.* to scandalize, to shock; —**se,** to be scandalized, to be outraged.

escándalo (es•kân´dâ•lo) *m.* scandal; (fig.) uproar *(alboroto).*

escandaloso, sa (es•kân•dâ•lo´so, sâ) *adj.* scandalous; boisterous *(revoltoso)*

escapada (es•kâ•pâ´thâ) *f.* escape, flight.

escapar (es•kâ•pâr´) *va.* to race,

to run at high speed; —, *vn.* to escape; to flee *(salir a todo escape);* —**se,** to escape, to get free; to run out, to escape *(un liquido).*

escaparate (es•kâ•pâ•râ´te) *m.* show window *(en la fachada);* display cabinet, showcase *(alacena).*

escape (es•kâ´pe) *m.* escape, flight *(fuga);* leak *(de un líquido);* (mech.) exhaust; escapement, *(del reloj);* **a todo** —, at top space.

escapismo (es•kâ•pēz´mo) *m.* escapism.

escarabajo (es•kâ•râ•vâ´ho) *m.* dung beetle, scarab; (coll.) twerp.

escaramuza (es•kâ•râ•mū´sâ) *f.* skirmish.

escaramuzar (es•kâ•râ•mū•sâr´) *vn.* to skirmish.

escarbar (es•kâr•vâr´) *va.* to scratch; to clean, to pick *(los dientes);* to stir, to poke *(la lumbre);* (fig.) to sift through, to dig into *(inquirir).*

escarcha (es•kâr´châ) *f.* hoarfrost.

escarchar (es •kâr•châr´) *va.* to sugar; —, *vn.* to be frost.

escarmentar* (es•kâr•men•târ´) *vn.* to profit by experience, to take warning; —, *va.* to punish severely.

escarmiento (es•kâr•myen´to) *m.* caution, profit from experience *(cautela);* punishment *(castigo).*

escarnecer* (es•kâr•ne•ser´) *va.* to mock, to ridicule, to scoff at.

escarpado, da (es•kâr•pâ´tho, thâ) *adj.* sloping steeply; steep *(empinado).*

escarpia (es•kâr´pyâ) *f.* hook.

escasear (es•kâ•se•âr´) *va.* to skimp on, to spare, to give grudgingly; —, *vn.* to be scarce, to be in short supply.

escasez (es•kâ•ses´) *f. shortage (poca cantidad).*

escaso, sa (es•kâ´so, sâ) *adj.* limited, in short supply, scanty *(poco abundante);* stingy, niggardly *(mezquino).*

escena, (es•se´na) *f.* stage *(escenario);* scene; **poner en —,** to stage.

escenario (es•se•nâ´ryo) *m.* stage.

escepticismo (es•sep•tē•sēz´mo) *m.* skepticism.

esclarecer* (es•klâ•re•ser´) *va.* to illuminate, to light up; (fig.) to ennoble *(ilustrar);* to clear up, to explain *(dilucidar);* —, *vn.* to begin to dawn.

esclarecido, da (es•klâ•re•sē´tho, thâ) *adj.* illustrious, noble.

esclavitud (es•klâ•vē•tūth´) *f.* slavery.

esclavizar (es•klâ•vē•sâr´) *va.* to enslave.

esclavo, va (es•klâ´vo, vâ) *n.* slave, captive.

esclerosis (es•kle•ro´sēs) *f.* (med.) sclerosis; — **múltiple,** multiple sclerosis.

escoba (es•ko´vâ) *f.* broom.

escocés, esa (es•ko•ses´, e´sâ) *n.* Scot; —, *adj.* Scotch, Scottish.

escoger (es•ko•her´) *va.* to choose, to select.

escogido, da (es•ko•hē´tho, thâ) *adj.* chosen, selected *(selecto);* choice *(excelente).*

escolar (es•ko•lâr´) *m.* pupil, student; —, *adj.* student, scholastic; **sistema —,** school system.

escolástico, ca (es•ko•lâs´tē•ko, kâ) *adj.* scholastic.

escolta (es•kol´tâ) *f.* escort.

escoltar (es•kol•târ´) *va.* to escort.

escombro (es•kom´bro) *m.* rubble, debris; (ichth.) mackerel.

esconder (es•kon•der´) *va.* to hide, to conceal.

escondidas (es•kon•dē´thâs) or **escondidillas** (es•kon•dē•thē´yas) a secretly; **a — de,** without the knowledge of.

escondido, da (es•kon•dē´tho, thâ) *adj.* hidden.

escondite (es•kon•dē´te) *m.* hiding place; hide-and-seek *(juego).*

escopeta (es•ko•pe′tâ) *f.* shotgun; **a tiro de —,** within gunshot; **aquí te quiero —,** this is it! it′s now or never!

escoplo (es•ko′plo) *m.* chisel.

escorpión (es•kor•pyon′) *m.* scorpion.

escotado, da (es•ko•tâ′tho, thâ) *adj.* lownecked, décolleté.

escote (es•ko′te) *m.* décolletage; share, part *(de un gasto común).*

escozor (es•ko•sor′) *m.* smart, sting; (fig.) grief, pain.

escribano (es•krē•vâ′no) *m.* clerk.

escribir* (es•krē•vēr′) *va.* to write; to spell *(ortografiar);* — **a máquina,** to typewrite.

escrito (es•krē′to) *m.* writing; written document *(papel manuscrito);* **por —,** in writing; —, **ta,** *adj.* written.

escritor, ra (es•krē•tor′, râ) *n.* writer.

escritorio (es•krē•to′ryo) *m.* writing desk *(mueble);* office; desktop *(computación).*

escritura (es•krē•tū′râ) *f.* penmanship, handwriting *(caligrafía);* writing *(acción);* document *(escrito);* script, alphabet *(caracteres);* deed *(instrumento público).*

escrúpulo (es•krū′pū•lo) *m.* scruple.

escrutinio (es•krū•tē′nyo) *m.* scrutiny; polling and counting votes *(en las elecciones).*

escuálido, da (es•kwâ′lē•tho, thâ) *adj.* squalid.

escuchar (es•kū•châr′) *va.* to listen to.

escudar (es•kū•thâr′) *va.* to shield.

escudo (es•kū′tho) *m.* shield; escutcheon, coat of arms *(cuerpo de blasón).*

escudriñar (es•kū•thrē•nyâr′) *va.* to scrutinize.

escuela (es•kwe′lâ) *f.* school; — **de párvulos,** kindergarten; — **dominical,** Sunday school; — **para externos,** day school; — **para internos,** boarding school.

escueto, ta (es•kwe′to, tâ) *adj.* unadorned, plain, bare.

esculpir (es•kūl•pēr′) *va.* to sculpture, to sculpt; to engrave *(grabar).*

escultor (es•kūl•tor′) *m.* sculptor.

escultura (es•kūl•tū′râ) *f.* sculpture.

escupir (es•kū•pēr′) *va.* to spit; (fig.) to cast off *(echar de sí).*

escurrimiento (es•kū•rrē•myen′-to) *m.* run-off, dripping, flow.

escurrir (es•kū•rrēr′) *va.* to drain; to let drain *(los platos fregados);* —, *vn.* to drip *(caer* *gota a gota);* to slip *(deslizar);* —**se,** to slip.

ese, sa (e´se, sâ) *adj.* **ése, sa,** *pron.* that; —**sos, sas,** *pl.* those.

esencia, (e•sen´syâ) *f.* essence.

esencial (e•sen•syâl´) *adj.* essential.

esfera (es•fe´râ) *f.* sphere; dial *(del reloj).*

esférico, ca (es•fe´rē•ko, kâ) *adj.* spherical.

esforzado, da (es•for•sâ´tho, thâ) *adj.* strong, vigorous.

esforzar* (es•for•sâr´) *va.* to strengthen; to encourage *(alentar);* —**se,** to exert oneself, to make an effort.

esfuerzo (es•fuer´so) *m.* effort; spirit, vigor, courage *(vigor).*

esfumarse (es•fū•mâr´se) *vr.* to disappear, to vanish.

esgrima (ez•grē´mâ) *f.* fencing.

eslabón (ez•lâ•von´) *m.* link.

esmaltar (ez•mâl•târ´) *va.* to enamel; (fig.) to adorn, to brighten.

esmalte (ez•mâl´te) *m.* enamel; — **para las uñas,** nail polish.

esmerado, da (ez•me•râ´tho, thâ) *adj.* painstaking, careful.

esmeralda (ez•me•râl´dâ) *f.* emerald.

esmerar (ez•me•râr´) *va.* to polish; —**se,** to do one's best, to take pains.

esmero (ez•me´ro) *m.* great care, pains-taking.

esmoquin (ez•mo•kēn) tuxedo; dinner jacket.

esnobismo (ez•no•vēz´mo) *m.* snobbery.

eso (e´so) *pron.* that, that matter; — **de,** that matter of; **a** — **de,** about; **por** —, for that reason, therefore; **nada de** —, not at all, absolutely not.

esófago (e•so´fâ•go) *m.* esophagus.

espacial (es•pâ•syâl´) *adj.* spatial; **cápsula** —, space capsule.

espacio (es•pâ´syo) *m.* space; period *(de tiempo);* piece *(de terreno);* slowness *(lentitud).*

espacioso, sa (es•pâ•syo´so, sâ) *adj.* spacious, roomy.

espada (es•pâ´thâ) *f.* sword; spade *(de naipes);* swordsman *(persona);* —, *m.* matador.

espalda (es•pâl´dâ) *f.* back; backstroke *(en la natación);* —**s,** *pl.* back, shoulders; **a** —**s,** behind one's back; **cargo de** —**s,** round-shouldered; **dar la** —, to turn one's back on.

espaldilla (es•pal•dē´yâ) *f.* shoulder blade.

espantadizo, za (es•pân•tâ•thē´so, sâ) *adj.* skittish *(caballo);* easily frightened.

espantamoscas (es•pân•tâ•mos´kâs) *m.* fly swatter.

espantapájaros
(es•pân•tâ•pâ´hâ•ros) *m.* scarecrow.

espantar (es•pân•târ´) *va.* to
frighten, to terrify; to frighten
away, to chase away *(ahuyentar).*

espanto (es•pân´to) *m.* fright,
terror *(terror);* menace, threat
(amenaza); specter *(fantasma).*

España (es•pâ´nyâ) *f.* Spain.

español, la (es•pâ•nyol´, lâ) *adj.*
Spanish; —, *n.* Spaniard; —,
m. Spanish language.

esparcir (es•pâr•sēr´) *va.* to scatter, to spread out *(derramar);*
to spread *(divulgar);* —**se,** to
open up, to enjoy oneself.

espárrago (es•pâ´rrâ•go) *m.*
asparagus.

espasmo (es•pâz´mo) *m.* spasm.

espástico, ca (es•pâs´tē•ko, kâ)
adj. spastic.

espátula (es•pâ´tū•lâ) *f.* spatula.

especias (es•pe´syâs) *f. pl.* spi-
ces.

especial (e•spe•syâl´) *adj.* special, particular; **en** —, specially.

especialidad (es•pe•syâ•lē•thâ•
th´) *f.* specialty.

especialista (es•pe•syâ•lēs´tâ) *m.*
and *f.* specialist.

especializarse (es•pe•syâ•lē•sâr´-
se) *vr.* to specialize.

especialmente (es•pe•syâl•men´-

te) *adv.* specially.

especie (es•pe´sye) *f.* species;
kind, quality *(calidad);* (fig.)
case, instance *(caso).*

especificación
(es•pe•sē•fē•kâ•syon´) *f.* specification.

especificar (es•pe•s•fē•kâr´) *va.*
to specify.

específico, ca (es•pe•sē´fē•ko,
kâ) *adj.* specific; —, *m.* patent
medicine.

espécimen (es•pe´sē•men) *m.*
specimen.

espectacular (es•pek•tâ•kū•lâr´)
adj. spectacular.

espectáculo (es•pek•tâ´kū•lo) *m.*
show, public amusement; spectacle, display *(lo que atrae la
atención).*

espectador, ra (es•pek•tâ•thor´,
râ) *n.* spectator, onlooker.

espectral (es•pek•trâl´) *adj.*
spectral, ghostly.

espectro (es•pek´tro) *m.* specter,
ghost; (phy.) spectrum.

especulación (es•pe•kū•lâ•syon´)
f. speculation.

especular (es•pe•kū•lâr´) *va.* to
speculate on; —, *vn.* to speculate.

especulativo, va
(es•pe•kū•lâ•tē´vo, vâ) *adj.* speculative.

espejismo (es•pe•hēz´mo) *m.*
mirage.

espejo (es•pe´ho) *m.* mirror; — **de retrovisión,** rearview mirror.

espeluznante (es•pe•luz•nân´te) *adj.* hair-raising.

espera (es•pe´râ) *f.* wait; stay, delay *(jurídica);* patience, restraint *(paciencia);* **sala de —,** waiting room.

esperanza (es•pe•rân´sâ) *f.* hope, expectation; **áncora de —,** (naut.) sheet anchor.

esperanzar (es•pe•rân•sâr´) *va.* to give hope.

esperar (es•pe•râr´) *va.* to hope for, to wait for, to await *(aguardar);* to expect *(creer).*

esperma (es•per´mâ) *f.* sperm.

espesar (es•pe•sâr´) *va.* to thicken; to close up, to tighten *(apretar).*

espeso, sa (es•pe´so, sâ) *adj.* thick, dense.

espía (es•pē´â) *m.* and *f.* spy.

espiar (es•pyâr´) *va.* to spy on, to observe carefully.

espiga (es•pē´gâ) *f.* ear *(del trigo);* peg *(clavo);* fuse *(espoleta).*

espigón (es•pē•gon´) *m.* ear of corn *(mazorca);* sting *(aguijón);* point *(punta).*

espina (es•pē´nâ) *f.* (bot.) thorn; sliver *(astilla);* (ichth.) bone; (anat.) spine; (fig.) thorn in one's side *(pesar);* **estar en —s,** to be on needles and pins.

espinaca (es•pē•nâ´kâ) *f.* (bot.) spinach.

espinar (es•pē•nâr´) *va.* to prick; —, *m.* brier patch; (fig.) rub, difficulty *(enredo).*

espinazo (es•pē•nâ´so) *m.* spine, backbone.

espinilla (es•pē•nē´yâ) *f.* shinbone; pimple *(barrillo).*

espinoso, sa (es•pē•no´so, sâ) *adj.* spiny; thorny; (fig.) tricky, complicated *(enredado).*

espiral (es•pē•râl´) *adj.* spiral; —, *f.* spiral; —, *m.* spiral spring.

espiritismo (es•pē•rē•tēz´mo) *m.* spiritualism, spiritism.

espíritu (es•pē´rē•tū) *m.* spirit.

espiritual (es•pē•rē•twâl´) *adj.* spiritual.

espiritualidad (es•pē•rē•twâ•lē´-thâth´) *f.* spirituality.

espléndido, da (es•plen´dē•tho, thâ) *adj.* splendid, magnificent; brilliant, bright *(resplandeciente).*

esplendor (es•plen•dor´) *m.* radiance, splendor.

esponja (es•pon´hâ) *f.* sponge.

esponjar (es•pon•hâr´) *va.* to make spongy, to fluff up; **—se,** to puff up with pride.

esponjoso, sa (es•pon•ho´so, sâ) *adj.* spongy.

espontaneidad (es•pon•tâ•nee•thâth´) *f.* spontaneity.

espontáneo, nea (es•pon•tâ′ne•o, ne•â) *adj.* spontaneous.

esposa (es•po′sâ) *f.* wife; **—s,** *pl.* manacles, handcuffs.

esposo (es•poso) *m.* husband; **—s,** *pl.* married couple.

espuela (es•pwe′lâ) *f.* spur; (bot.) larkspur.

espuma (es•pū′mâ) *f.* foam, froth; (fig.) cream *(flor);* **hule —,** foam rubber.

espumoso, sa (es•pū•mo′so, sâ) *adj.* frothy, foamy.

espurio, ria (es•pū′ryo, ryâ) *adj.* spurious, adulterated.

esqueleto (es•ke•le′to) *m.* skeleton.

esquema (es•ke′mâ) *m.* diagram, outline.

esquí (es•kē′) *m.* ski.

esquiador, ra (es•kyâ•thor′, râ) *n.* skier.

esquiar (es•kyâr′) *vn.* to ski.

esquilar (es•kē•lâr′) *va.* to shear.

esquimal (es•kē•mâl′) *adj.* and *n.* Eskimo.

esquina (es•kē′nâ) *f.* corner; **doblar la —,** to turn the corner; **hacer —,** to be on the corner.

esquivar (es•kē•vâr′) *va.* to avoid, to dodge; **—se,** to get out, to retract.

esquivo, va (es•kē′vo, vâ) *adj.* diffident, aloof.

estabilidad (es•tâ•vē • lē• thâth′) *f.* stability.

estabilización (es•tâ•vē•lē•sâ•syon′) *f.* stabilization.

estabilizador (es•tâ•vē•lē•sâ•thor′) *m.* stabilizer.

estabilizar (es•tâ•vē•lē•sâr′) *va.* to stabilize.

estable (es•tâ′vle) *adj.* stable.

establecer* (es•tâ•vle•ser′) *va.* to establish; **—se,** to settle, to establish oneself.

establecimiento (es•tâ•vle•sē•myen′to) *m.* establishment; statute *(ley).*

establo (es•tâ′vlo) *m.* stable.

estación (es•tâ•syon′) *f.* station; residence *(morada);* stay, stopover *(paraje);* season *(temporada).*

estacionamiento (es•tâ•syo•nâ•myen′to) *m.* (auto.) parking.

estacionar (es•tâ•syo•nâr′) *va.* (auto.) to park; to position, to station *(colocar).*

estacionario, ria (es•tâ•syo•nâ′ryo, ryâ) *adj.* stationary.

estadio (es•tâ′thyo) *m.* stadium; furlong *(medida);* phase, period *(fase).*

estadística (es•tâ•thēs′tē•kâ) *f.* statistics; **— demográfica,** vital statistics.

estadístico (es•tâ•thēs′tē•ko) *m.*

statistician; —, **ca,** *adj.* statistical.

estado (es•tâ´tho) *m.* state; statement *(cuenta);* — **de cuenta,** statement of account; — **de guerra,** martial law; — **de sitio,** state of siege; — **mayor,** military staff; **hombre de —,** statesman; — **protector,** welfare state; **ministro de E —,** Secretary of State.

Estados Unidos de América (es•tâ´thos ū•nē´thoz the â•me´rē•kâ) *m. pl.* United States of America.

estadounidense (es•tâ•tho•ū•nē•then´se) or **estadunidense** (es•tâ•thū•nē•then´se) *adj.* American, United States; —, *m.* and *f.* American, United States resident.

estafa (es•tâ´fâ) *f.* swindle.

estafador, ra (es•tâ•fâ•thor´, râ) *n.* swindler.

estafar (es•tâ•fâr´) *va.* to swindle.

estallar (es•tâ•yâr´) *vn.* to blow up *(reventar);* to crack *(el látigo);* (fig.) to break out *(un incendio, la guerra).*

estallido (es•tâ•yē´tho) *m.* crack; report *(explosión);* outbreak *(de la guerra);* blowing up.

estambre (es•tâm´bre) *m.* wool yarn; (bot.) stamen; — **de la**

vida, (fig.) fabric of life.

estampa (es•tâm´pâ) *f.* printed image; (fig.) looks, appearance *(aspecto);* press *(imprenta);* mark *(huella).*

estampar (es•tâm•pâr´) *va.* to print, to stamp; to press, to imprint *(una medalla);* (coll.) to throw, to dash *(arrojar).*

estampida (es•tâm•pē´thâ) *f.* stampede.

estampilla (es•tâm•pē´yâ) *f.* signet, seal (Sp. Am.) postage stamp.

estancamiento (es•tâng•kâ•myen´to) *m.* standstill; delay.

estancar (es•tâng•kâr´) *va.* to stem, to hold back *(detener);* to hold up, to delay *(suspender la marcha).*

estancia (es•tân´syâ) *f.* stay, sojourn; (Sp. Am.) ranch, country estate *(finca).*

estanciero, ra (es•tân•sye´ro, râ) *n.* farmer, rancher.

estandardización (es•tân•dâr•thē•sâ syon´) *f.* standardization.

estandarte (es•tân•dâr´te) *m.* banner, standard.

estanque (es•tâng´ke) *m.* reservoir, pond.

estante (es•tân´te) *m.* bookcase.

estaño (es•tâ´nyo) *m.* (chem.) tin.

estaquilla (es•tâ•kē´yâ) *f.* cleat; spike *(estaca).*

estar* (es•tar´) *vn.* to be; — **de prisa,** to be in a hurry; — **sobre sí,** to be cautious, to be alert; — **por,** to be in favor of; **¿estamos?** agreed? is that alright? — **bien,** to be well; — **de,** to be in the middle of; — **de pie,** to be standing; — **mal,** to be ill; — **en sí,** to be fully aware of one´s actions; — **para,** to be about to; — **de receso,** to be adjourned.

estarcido (es•târ•sē´tho) *m.* stencil.

estarcir (es•târ•sēr´) *va.* to stencil.

estática (es•tâ´tē•kâ) *f.* statics.

estático, ca (es•tâ´tē•ko, kâ) *adj.* static.

estatua (es•tâ´twâ) *f.* statue.

estatura (es•tâ•tū´râ) *f.* stature.

estatuto (es•tâ•tū´to) *m.* statute.

este (es´te) *m.* east.

este, ta (es´te, tâ) *adj.* éste, ta, *pron.* this; the latter; —**ta noche,** tonight; —**tos, tas,** *pl.* these.

estela (es•te´lâ) *f.* wake *(de buque de vapor);* trail *(de estrella).*

estera (es•te´râ) *f.* matting.

estereotipar (es•te•re•o•tē•pâr´) *va.* to stereotype.

estéril (es•te´rēl) *adj.* sterile, barren.

esterilidad (es•te•rē•lē•thâth´) *f.* sterility, barrenness.

esterilización (es•te•rē•lē•sâ•syon´) *f.* sterilization.

esterilizador (es•te•rē•lē•sâ•thor´) *m.* sterilizer; —, **ra,** *adj.* sterilizing.

esterilizar (es•te•rē•lē•sâr´) *va.* to sterilize.

esterlina (es•ter•lē´nâ) *adj.* sterling; **libra —,** pound sterling.

esteroide (es•te•ro´ē•the) *m.* steroid.

estética (es•te´tē•kâ) *f.* aesthetics.

estetoscopio (es•te•tos•ko´pyo) *m.* stethoscope.

estiércol (es•tyer´kol) *m.* manure.

estigma (es•tēg´mâ) *m.* stigma; —**s,** *pl.* stigmata.

estilo (es•tē´lo) *m.* style; stylus *(para escribir);* **por el —,** like that, of that kind.

estima (es•tē´mâ) *f.* esteem.

estimar (es•tē•mâr´) *va.* to esteem, to value; to estimate *(evaluar).*

estimulante (es•tē•mū•lân´te) *m.* stimulant; —, *adj.* stimulating.

estimular (es•tē•mū•lâr´) *va.* to stimulate.

estímulo (es•tē´mū•lo) *m.* stimulus; (fig.) impulse, motivation.

estipendio (es•tē•pen´dyo) *m.* stipend.

estipulación (es•te•pū•lâ•syon´) *f.* stipulation.

estirador (es•tē râ•thor´) *m.* stretcher.

estirar (es•tē•râr´) *va.* to stretch out, to pull out; (fig.) to stretch to the limit, to draw out; — **la pata,** (coll.) to kick the bucket.

estirón (es•tē•ron´) *m.* pull, jerk; **dar un —,** to grow rapidly, to shoot up.

estirpe (es•tēr´pe) *f.* origin, stock, family.

esto (es´to) *pron.* this, this matter; **a —,** hereto; **con —,** herewith; **en —,** at that moment; **por —,** for this reason; **— es,** that is, that is to say.

estofado, da (es•to•fâ´tho, thâ) *adj.* quilted; stewed.

estofar (es•to•fâr´) *va.* to quilt *(bordar);* to stew *(guisar).*

estola (es•to´lâ) *f.* stole.

estólido, da (es•to´lē•tho, thâ) *adj.* stupid, dense.

estomacal (es•to•mâ•kâl´) *adj.* stomachic, stomach; **malestar —,** upset stomach.

estómago (es•to´mâ•go) *m.* stomach.

estorbar (es•tor•vâr´) *va.* to hinder, to obstruct; (fig.) to bother, to annoy *(incomodar).*

estorbo (es•tor•vo) *m.* hindrance, obstruction; bother, annoyance.

estornudar (es•tor•nū•thâr´) *vn.* to sneeze.

estornudo (es•tor•nū´tho) *m.* sneeze.

estrafalario, ria (es•trâ•fâ•lâ´ryo, ryâ) *adj.* slovenly, unkempt; (fig.) outlandish, weird.

estrago (es•trâ´go) *m.* ravage, havoc.

estrangulación (es•trâng•gū•lâ•syon´) *f.* strangulation.

estrangulador, ra (es•trâng•gū•lâ•thor´, râ) *adj.* choking, strangling.

estrangular (es•trâng•gū•1âr´) *va.* to choke, to strangle; (med.) to strangulate.

estratagema (es•trâ•tâ•he´mâ) *f.* stratagem; (fig.) trickiness, craftiness *(astucia).*

estrategia (es•trâ•te´hyâ) *f.* strategy.

estratégico, ca (es•trâ•te´hē•ko, kâ) *adj.* strategic.

estrechar (es•tre•châr´) *va.* to tighten, to narrow; (fig.) to press, to close in on *(apretar).*

estrecho (es•tre´cho) *m.* (geog.) straits; period of want *(escasez);* —, **cha,** narrow *(angosto);* tight *(apretado);* (fig.) narrow, mean *(apocado);* close *(íntimo);* severe, harsh *(rígido).*

estregar* (es•tre•gâr´) *va.* to rub.

estrella (es•tre´yâ) *f.* star.

estrellado, da (es•tre•yâ´tho, thâ) *adj.* starry; dashed to pieces; **huevos —s**, fried eggs.

estrellar (es•tre•yâr´) *va.* to dash to pieces, to smash to bits; to fry *(los huevos);* **—se**, to smash, to crash; (fig.) to fail *(fracasar);* to fill with stars *(el cielo).*

estremecer* (es•tre•me•ser´) *va.* to jolt, to shake; **—se,** to quake, to shake, to tremble.

estrenar (es•tre•nâr´) *va.* to inaugurate; to use for the first time *(una prenda);* to premiere *(una comedia);* **—se**, to make one´s debut; to premiere.

estreno (es•tre´no) *m.* inauguration; first time in use; premiere; debut.

estrenuo, nua (es•tre´nwo, nwâ) *adj.* strenuous, rigorous.

estreñimiento (es•tre•nyē•myen´to) *m.* constipation.

estreñir* (es•tre•nyēr´) *va.* to constipate; **—se,** to become constipated.

estrépito (es•tre´pē•to) *m.* crash, loud noise; show, splash *(ostentación).*

estría (es•trē´â) *f.* groove.

estribar (es•trē•vâr´) *vn.* to rest, to lie; **— en,** to be supported

by, to be grounded on.

estribillo (es•trē•vē´yo) *m.* refrain; (fig.) favorite word.

estribo (es•trē´vo) *m.* (arch.) buttress; running board *(del coche);* stirrup; **perder los—s**, to act foolishly, to lose one´s head.

estricto, ta (es•trēk´to, tâ) *adj.* strict.

estridente (es•trē•then´te) *adj.* strident, piercing *(agudo);* clamorous, noisy *(ruidoso).*

estrofa (es•tro´fâ) *f.* stanza; strophe *(del canto griego).*

estrógeno (es•tro´he•no) *m.* estrogen.

estropear (es•tro•pe•âr´) *va.* to cripple *(dejar lisiado);* to misuse, to abuse *(maltratar);* to spoil, to ruin *(echar a perder).*

estructura (es•trūk•tū´râ) *f.* structure.

estruendo (es•trwen´do) *m.* blast, din *(ruido);* confusion, hullabaloo, uproar *(alboroto);* great pomp and circumstance *(pompa).*

estuco (es•tū´ko) *m.* stucco.

estuche (es•tū´che) *m.* kit; **ser un —,** (coll.) to be handy, to be very versatile.

estudiantado (es•tū•thyân•ta´-tho) *m.* student body.

estudiante (es•tū•thyân´te) *m.* student.

estudiantil (es•tū•thyân•tēl´) *adj.* student, scholastic.

estudiar (es•tū•thyâr´) *va.* to study.

estudio (es•tū´thyo) *m.* study; studio *(aposento).*

estufa (es•tū´fâ) *f.* stove *(fogón);* heater *(calorífero);* greenhouse *(invernáculo).*

estupefacción (es´tū´pe•fâk•syon´) *f.* astonishment, great surprise, amazement.

estupefacto, ta (es•tū•pe•fâk´to, tâ) *adj.* amazed, astonished.

estupendo, da (es•tū•pen´do,dâ) *adj.* stupendous, marvelous.

estupidez (es•tū•pē•thes´) *f.* stupidity.

estúpido, da (es•tū´pē•tho, thâ) *adj.* stupid.

estupor (es•tū•por´) *m.* stupor; (fig.) daze.

etapa (e•tâ´pâ) *f.* phase, stage *(fase);* leg *(distancia entre altos);* stop, pause *(escala);* (mil.) ration.

etéreo, rea (e•te´re•o, re•â) *adj.* ethereal.

eternidad (e•ter•nē•thâth´) *f.* eternity.

eterno, na (e•ter´no, nâ) *adj.* eternal.

ética (e´tē•kâ) *f.* ethics.

ético, ca (e´tē•ko, kâ´) *adj.* ethical.

etileno (e•tē•le´no) *m.* (chem.) ethylene.

etilo (e•tē´lo) *m.* ethyl.

etimología (e•tē•mo•lo•hē´â) *f.* etymology.

etiope (e•tyo´pe) *n.* and *adj.* Ethiopian.

etiqueta (e• tē• ke´ tâ) *f.* etiquette; formality *(ceremonia);* tag, label *(marbete);* **de —,** in formal dress.

étnico, ca (eth´nē•ko, kâ) *adj.* ethnic.

etnógrafo (eth•no´grâ•fo) *m.* ethnographer.

etnológico, ca (eth•no•lo´hē•ko, kâ) *adj.* ethnological.

etnólogo (eth•no´lo•go) *m.* ethnologist.

etrusco, ca (e•trūs´ko , kâ) *n.* and *adj.* Etruscan.

E.U.A.: Estados Unidos de América U.S.A. United States of America.

eucalipto (eū•kâ•lēp´to) *m.* eucalyptus.

Europa (eū•ro´pâ) *f.* Europe.

europeo, pea (eū•ro•pe´o, pe´â) *n.* and *adj.* European.

eutanasia (eū•tâ•nâ´syâ) *f.* euthanasia.

evacuación (e•vâ•kwâ•syon´) *f.* evacuation; carrying out; emptying; movement.

evacuar (e•vâ•kwâr´) *va.* to evacuate; to empty *(desocupar);* to carry out *(cumplir).*

evadir (e•vâ•thēr´) *va.* to evade, to avoid; —**se**, to flee, to escape.

evaluación (e•vâ•lwâ•syon´) *f.* evaluation.

evaluar (e•vâ•lwâr´) *va.* to evaluate.

evangélico, ca (e•vân•he´lē•ko, kâ) *adj.* evangelical.

evangelio (e•vân•he´lyo) *m.* Gospel.

evangelista (e•vân•he•lēs´tâ) *m.* Evangelist; (Mex.) public letter writer, scribe.

evaporar (e•vâ•po•râr´) *va.* and *vr.* To evaporate.

evasión (e•vâ•syon´) *f.* evasion, escape *(fuga);* subterfuge *(evasiva).*

evasivo, va (e•vâ•sē´vo, vâ) *adj.* evasive, elusive.

eventual (e•ven•twâl´) *adj.* possible, contingent; fringe *(emolumento).*

evidencia (e•vē•then´syâ) *f.* evidence, manifestation; **poner en** —, to make clear, to demonstrate.

evidente (e•vē•then´te) *adj.* evident, clear, manifest.

evitable (e•vē•tâ´vle) *adj.* avoidable.

evitar (e•vē•târ´) *va.* to avoid.

evocación (e•vo•kâ•syon´) *f.* evocation.

evocar (e•vo•kâr´) *va.* to evoke.

evolución (e•vo•lū•syon´) *f.* evolution; change *(mudanza).*

evolucionar (e•vo•lū•syo•nâr´) *vn.* to evolve, to undergo evolution.

exacerbar (ek•sâ•ser•vâr´) *va.* to exasperate, to irritate.

exactitud (ek•sâk•tē•tūth´) *f.* exactness.

exacto, ta (ek•sâk´to, tâ) *adj.* exact; ¡—! *interj.* fine! perfect!

exageración (ek•sâ•he•râ•syon´) *f.* exaggeration.

exaltación (ek•sâl•tâ•syon´) *f.* exaltation.

exaltado, da (ek•sâl•tâ´tho, thâ) *adj.* hotheaded, fanatic.

exaltar (ek•sâl•târ´) *va.* to exalt; —**se,** to become highly excited, to get carried away.

examen (ek•sâ´men) *m.* examination.

examinar (ek•sâ•mē•nâr´) *va.* to examine.

exánime (ek•sâ´nē•me) *adj.* lifeless; faint *(desmayado).*

exasperar (ek•sâs•pe•râr´) *va.* to exasperate; —**se,** to become intense *(un dolor).*

excavación (es•kâ•vâ•syon´) *f.* excavation.

excavadora (es•kâ•vâ•tho´râ) *f.* power shovel.

excavar (es•kâ•vâr´) *va.* to excavate.

exceder (ek•se•ther´) *va.* to excede; **—se,** to overdo, to overstep the limit, to go too far.

excelencia (ek•se•len´syâ) *f.* excellence; **E—,** Excellency *(tratamiento).*

excelente (ek•se•len´te) *adj.* excellent.

excentricidad (ek•sen•trē•sē•thâth´) *f.* eccentricity.

excéntrico, ca (ek•sen´trē•ko, kâ) *adj.* eccentric.

excepción (ek•sep•syon´) *f.* exception.

excepcional (ek•sep´syo•nâl´) *adj.* exceptional.

excepto (ek•sep´to) *adv.* with the exception of.

excesivo, va (ek•se•sē´vo, vâ) *adj.* excessive.

exceso (ek•se´so) *m.* excess; **— de peso** or **de equipaje,** excess baggage.

excitación (ek•sē•tâ•syon´) *f.* excitement.

excitante (ek•sē•tân´te) *adj.* exciting; (med.) stimulating; **—,** *m.* stimulant.

excitar (ek•sē•târ´) *va.* to excite; to stimulate.

exclamación (es•klâ•mâ•syon´) *f.* exclamation.

exclamar (es•klâ•mâr´) *vn.* to exclaim.

excluir* (es•klwēr´) *va.* to exclu-de.

exclusión (es•klū•syon´) *f.* exclusion.

exclusivamente (es•klū•sē•vâ•men´te) *adv.* exclusively.

exclusivo, va (es•klū•sē´vo, vâ) *adj.* exclusive; **—,** *f.* (com.) exclusive rights, sole dealership.

excomulgar (es•ko•mūl•gâr´) *va.* to excommunicate.

excomunión (es•ko•mū•nyon´) *f.* excommunication.

excremento (es•kre•men´to) *m.* excrement.

excretar (es•kre•târ´) *va.* to excrete.

excursión (es•kūr•syon´) *f.* excursion.

excusa (es•kū´sâ) *f.* excuse.

excusable (es•kū•sâ´vle) *adj.* excusable.

excusado, da (es•kū•sâ´tho, thâ) *adj.* exempt *(por privilegio);* unnecessary *(superfluo);* private *(reservado);* **—,** *m.* washroom, lavatory, toilet.

excusar (es•kū•sâr´) *va.* to excuse; to avoid *(evitar);* to exempt *(eximir).*

execrar (ek•se•krâr´) *va.* to execrate.

exención (ek•sen•syon´) *f.* exemption.

exento, ta (ek•sen´to, tâ) *adj.*

exempt, free.

exhalar (ek•sâ•lâr´) *va.* to exhale; to emit *(un suspiro).*

exhausto, ta (ek•sâ´ūs•to, tâ) *adj.* exhausted, depleted.

exhibición (ek•sē•vē•syon´) *f.* exhibition.

exhibicionista (ek•sē•vē•syo•nēs´tâ) *m. and f.* exhibitionist.

exhibir (ek•sē•vēr´) *va.* to exhibit.

exhortar (ek•sor•târ´) *va.* to exhort.

exhumar (ek•sū•mâr´) *va.* to exhume.

exigencia (ek•sē•hen´syâ) *f.* demand.

exigente (ek•sē•hen´te) *adj.* exacting, demanding, exigent.

exigir (ek•sē•hēr´) *va.* to demand, to necessitate; to exact, to collect *(percibir).*

exiliado, da (ek•sē•lyâ´tho, thâ) *n.* exile.

exiliar (ek•sē•lyâr´) *va.* to exile.

eximio, mia (ek•sē´myo, myâ) *adj.* superior, choice.

existencia (ek•sēs•ten´syâ) *f.* existence, being; **en —,** in stock; **—s,** *pl.* stock on hand.

existencialismo (ek•sēs•ten•syâ•lēz´mo) *m.* existentialism.

existente (ek•sēs•ten´te) *adj.* existent.

existir (ek•sēs•tēr´) *vn.* to exist; to be in existence *(durar).*

éxito (ek´sē•to) *m.* result, outcome *(fin);* success *(resultado feliz).*

éxodo (ek´so•tho) *m.* exodus.

exoneración (ek•so•ne•râ•syon´) *f.* exoneration.

exonerar (ek•so•ne•râr´) *va.* to exonerate; to dismiss, to relieve *(de un empleo).*

exorbitante (ek•sor•vē•tân´te) *adj.* exorbitant, excessive.

exótico, ca (ek•so´tē•ko, kâ) *adj.* exotic.

expansión (es•pân•syon´) *f.* expansion; expansiveness *(manifestación efusiva).*

expansivo, va (es•pân•sē´vo, vâ) *adj.* expansive.

expatriación (es•pâ•tryâ•syon´) *f.* expatriation.

expectación (es•pek•tâ•syon´) *f.* expectation.

expectativa (es•pek•tâ•tē´vâ) *f.* expectancy.

expedición (es•pe•thē•syon´) expedition; promptness *(prontitud);* (*com.*) shipment; **gastos de —,** shipping expenses.

expedicionario, ria (es•pe•thē•syo•nâ´ryo, ryâ) *adj.* expeditionary.

expedidor (es•pe•thē•thor´) *m.* shipper.

expediente (es•pe•thyen´te) *m.*

expedient *(pretexto);* file, dossier *(conjunto de papeles);* dispatch, ease *(prontitud).*

expedir* (es•pe•thēr´) *va.* to expedite; to issue *(un documento);* to dispatch, to ship *(enviar).*

expeler (es•pe•ler´) *va.* to expel.

expensas (es•pen´sâs) *f. pl.* expenses, charges; **a — de,** at the expense of.

experiencia (es•pe•ryen´•syâ) *f.* experience.

experimentado, da (es•pe•rē•men•tâ´tho, thâ) *adj.* experienced.

experimental (es•pe•rē•men•tal´) *adj.* experimental.

experimentar (es•pe•rē•men•târ´) *va.* to experience; to try out, to experiment with *(probar).*

experimento (es•pe•rē•men´to) *m.* experiment.

experto, ta (es•per´to, tâ) *n.* and *adj.* expert.

expirar (es•pē•râr´) *vn.* to expire.

explanada (es•plâ•nâ´thâ) *f.* esplanade.

explicable (es•plē•kâ´vle) *adj.* explainable.

explicación (es•plē•kâ•syon´) *f.* explanation.

explícito, ta (es•plē´sē•to, tâ) *adj.* explicit.

exploración (es•plo•râ•syon´) *f.*

exploration.

explorador, ra (es•plo•râ thor´, râ) *n.* explorer;—, *adj.* exploratory; **niño —,** boy scout.

explorar (es•plo•râr´) *va.* to explore.

explosión (es•plo•syon´) *f.* explosion.

explosivo, va (es•plo•se´vo, vâ) *adj.* and *m.* explosive.

explotación (es•plo•tâ•syon´) *f.* exploitation.

explotar (es•plo•târ´) *va.* to exploit; —, *vn.* to explode.

exponente (es•po•nen´te) *m.* and *f.* exponent; —, *m.* (math.) exponent.

exponer* (es•po•ner´) *va.* to expose; to exhibit *(un cuadro);* to risk *(poner en peligro).*

exportación (es•por•tâ•syon´) *f.* exportation, export.

exportador, ra (es•por•tâ•thor´, râ) *adj.* exporting; **casa —,** export company; —, exporter.

exposición (es•po•sē•syon´) *f.* exposition; exposure *(orientación);* danger, exposure to risk *(riesgo).*

expositor, ra (es•po•sē•tor´, râ) *n.* expositor; exhibitor *(en una exposición pública).*

expresar, (es•pre•sâr´) *va.* to express.

expresión (es•pre•syon´) *f.* expression.

expresivo, va (es•pre•sē′vo, vâ) *adj.* expressive; affectionate, demonstrative *(afectuoso)*.

expreso, sa (es•pre′so, sâ) *adj.* and *m.* express; — **aéreo,** air express.

exprimir (es•prē•mēr′) *va.* to squeeze out; (fig.) to drain, to wring out *(agotar);* to express clearly, to make clear *(expresar)*.

expuesto, ta (es•pwes′to, tâ) *adj.* dangerous; **lo —to,** what has been said.

expulsar (es•pūl•sâr′) *va.* to expel, to expulse.

expulsión (es•pūl•syon′) *f.* expulsion.

exquisito, ta (es•kē•sē′to, tâ) *adj.* exquisite.

éxtasis (es′tâ•sēs) *m.* ecstasy.

extático, ca (es•tâ′tē•ko, kâ) *adj.* ecstatic.

extender* (es•ten•der′) *va.* to extend, to spread; to draw up, to make out *(un documento);* **—se,** to spread *(propagarse);* to reach *(alcanzar)*.

extensión (es•ten•syon′) *f.* extension; extent *(importancia)*.

extensivo, va (es•ten•sē′vo, vâ) *adj.* extensive; **sentido —,** extended meaning.

extenuar (es•te•nwâr′) *va.* to debilitate, to weaken.

exterior (es•te•ryor′) *adj.* exte-

rior, outer; overseas, foreign *(con el extranjero);* —, *m.* outward look, appearance; abroad *(países extranjeros)*.

exterioridad (es•te•ryo•rē•thâth′) *f.* outer appearance *(apariencia);* outer show, hollow demonstration *(pompa)*.

exteriorizar (es•te•ryo•rē•sâr′) *va.* to externalize, to express.

exterminador (es•ter•mē•nâ•thor′) *m.* exterminator.

exterminar (es•ter•mē•nâr′) *va.* to exterminate.

externo, na (es•ter′no, nâ) *adj.* external; —, *n.* day pupil.

extinción (es•tēn•syon′) *f.* extinction.

extinguir (es•tēng•gēr′) *va.* to extinguish.

extinto, ta (es•tēn′to, tâ) *adj.* extinguished, extinct; (Sp. Am.) passed on, dead.

extirpar (es•tēr•pâr′) *va.* to root out, to uproot; (fig.) to extirpate.

extorsión (es•tor•syon′) *f.* obtaining by force, wresting; (fig.) turmoil, upset *(daño)*.

extra (es′trâ) *adj.* special, superior; —, *m.* and *f.* (theat.) extra; —, *m.* extra edition *(de periódico);* bonus, added payment *(gaje);* — **de,** (coll.) in addition to, besides.

extracción (es•trâk•syon´) *f.* extraction.

extracto (es•trâk´to) *m.* extract.

extraer* (es•trâ•er´) *va.* to extract.

extranjero, ra (es•trân•he´ro, râ) *adj.* foreign; **cambio —,** foreign exchange; **—,** *n.* foreigner; **—,** *m.* foreign lands; **ir al —ro,** to go abroad.

extrañar (es•trâ•nyâr´) *va.* to be lonesome for, to miss *(echar de menos);* to exile *(desterrar);* to estrange *(privar del trato);* to be surprised by *(notar con extrañeza);* to find hard to get used to *(sentir la novedad de);* to surprise *(causar sorpresa);* **—se de,** to be surprised at.

extraño, ña (es•trâ´nyo, nyâ) *n.* stranger; **—,** *adj.* strange; not a party, disassociated *(que no tiene que ver).*

extraoficial (es•trâ•o•fē•syâl´) *adj.* unofficial, off the record.

extraordinario, ria (es•trâ•or•thē•nâ´ryo, ryâ) *adj.* extraordinary; **—,** *m.* specialty *(manjar);* special edition *(de un periódico).*

extrasensorio, ria (es•trâ•sen•so´ryo, ryâ) *adj.* extrasensory.

extraterrestre (es•trâ•te•rres´tre) *adj.* from outer space.

extravagancia (es•trâ•vâ•gân´s-yâ) *f.* eccentricity.

extravagante, (es•trâ•vâ•gân´te) *adj.* eccentric.

extravertido, da (es•trâ•ver•tē´-tho, thâ) *n.* extrovert; **—,** *adj.* extroverted.

extraviar (es•trâ•vyâr´) *va.* to mislead, to lead astray; to misplace, to mislay *(una cosa);* **—se,** (fig.) to stray from the straight and narrow.

extravío (es•trâ•vē´o) *m.* misleading; misplacing; (fig.) bad habits, going astray; (coll.) trouble, bother *(molestia).*

extremado, da (es•tre•mâ´tho, thâ) *adj.* extreme.

extremidad (es•tre•mē•thâth´) *f.* extremity.

extremista (es•tre•mēs´tâ) *m.* and *f.* and *adj.* extremist.

extremo, ma (es•tre´mo, ma) *adj.* extreme, last; **—,** *m.* end, tip; extreme *(grado último);* great care *(esmero);* **de —mo a —mo,** from one end to the other; **en —mo, por —mo,** extremely.

F

fábrica (fâ′vrē•kâ) *f.* factory, mill; manufacture *(fabricación);* construction *(edificio).*

fabricación (fâ•vrē•kâ•syon′) *f.* manufacture.

fabricante (fâ•vrē•kân′te) *m.* manufacturer; factory owner *(dueño).*

fabricar (fâ•vrē•kâr′) *va.* to manufacture, to produce; to construct *(construir);* (fig.) to fabricate, to create.

fábula (fâ•vū′lâ) *f.* fable; gossip, hearsay *(hablilla).*

fabuloso, sa (fâ•vū•lo′so, sâ) *adj.* fabulous.

facción (fâk•syon′) *f.* faction; (mil.) action; **—ones,** *pl.* features.

faceta (fâ•se′tâ) *f.* facet *(cara);* phase, aspect *(aspecto).*

facial (fâ•syâl′) *adj.* facial.

fácil (fâ′sēl) *adj.* easy; likely *(probable).*

facilidad (fâ•sē•lē•thath′) *f.* facility, ability *(destreza);* easiness *(calidad de fácil);* overindulgence *(complacencia);* **—es,** *pl.* advantages, convenience.

facilitar (fâ•sē•lē•târ′) *va.* to facilitate; to supply, to provide with *(proporcionar).*

fácilmente (fâ•sēl•men′te) *adv.* easily.

facsímile (fâk•sē′mē•le) *m.* facsimile.

factor (fâk•tor′) *m.* factor; (rail.) shipping agent; **— Rh,** Rh factor, **— de seguridad,** safety factor.

factura (fâk•tū′râ) *f.* invoice, bill.

facturar (fâk•tū•râr′) *va.* to invoice; (rail.) to check.

facultad (fa•kūl•tâth′) *f.* faculty; property *(propiedad);* school *(de una universidad);* authority *(derecho).*

facha (fâ′châ) *f.* appearance, aspect, mien; **ponerse en —** to dress shabbily.

fachada (fa•châ′thâ) *f.* facade.

faisán (fâē•sân′) *m.* pheasant.

faja (fâ′hâ) *f.* band, strip; sash *(ceñidor).*

fajar (fâ•hâr′) *va.* to wrap, to bandage; to put a sash on *(ceñir).*

fajo (fâ′ho) *m.* bundle.

falacia (fâ•lâ′syâ) *f.* trickery, deceit.

falange (fâ•lân′he) *f.* phalanx.

falda (fâl′dâ) *f.* skirt; lap *(regazo);* lower slope, foothill *(de un monte);* **perrillo de —,** lap dog.

faldero, ra (fâl•de′ro, râ) *adj.* (fig.) fond of women′s company; **perro —,** lap dog.

falsear (fâl•se•âr′) *va.* to falsify; to pierce *(la armadura);* to force, to break open *(una cerradura);* **—,** *vn.* to be off tune *(disonar)* to weaken *(flaquear).*

falsedad (fâl•se•thâth´) *f.* falsehood, untruth.

falsete (fâl•se´te) *m.* falsetto; plug *(corcho).*

falsificación (fâl•sē•fē•kâ•syon´) *f.* falsification.

falso, sa (fâl´so, sâ) *adj.* false; counterfeit; unsteady, unstable *(caballo);* **en —so,** falsely.

falta (fâl´tâ) *f.* lack, want *(privación);* mistake, error *(equivocación);* breach, infraction *(en el obrar);* **— de pago,** non-payment; **hacer —,** to be necessary, to be needed; **poner —s,** to find fault; **a — de,** by lack of, by want of; **sin —,** without fail.

faltar (fâl•tar´) *vn.* to be lacking; to run short, to run out *(acabar);* to fail to show up *(a una cita);* to fail, to fall short *(no cumplir);* to be absent, to be missing *(estar ausente);* **¡no faltaba más!** (coll.) not on your life! that´s the last straw!

falto, ta (fâl´to, tâ) *adj.* wanting, lacking, short.

fallar (fâ•yâr´) *va.* to decide, to find on, to judge *(un proceso);* to trump *(poner triunfo);* **—,** *vn.* to fail, to fall through *(frustrarse);* to weaken *(flaquear).*

fallecer* (fâ•ye•ser´) *vn.* to die, to pass on.

fallo (fâ´yo) *m.* finding, verdict; lack of a suit *(en los juegos);* **—, lla,** *adj.* out of, lacking.

fama (fâ´ma) *f.* reputation *(reputación);* fame *(celebridad);* talk, rumor *(voz pública);* **es —,** they say, it´s said.

familia (fâ•mē´lya) *f.* family; servants *(servidumbre).*

familiar (fâ•mē•lyâr´) *adj.* familiar; colloquial *(corriente);* **—,** *m.* relative, relation *(miembro de la familia);* familiar.

familiarizar (fâ•mē•lyâ•rē•sâr´) *va.* to familiarize; **—se,** to become familiar, to acquaint oneself.

famoso, sa (fâ•mo´so, sâ) *adj.* famous; (coll.) first-rate, excellent, top-notch.

fanal (fâ•nâl´) *m.* lighthouse; bell jar *(campana de cristal).*

fanático, ca (fâ•nâ´tē•ko, kâ) *adj.* fanatic.

fanatismo (fâ•nâ•tēz´mo) *m.* fanaticism.

fandango (fan•dâng´go) *m.,* fandango; (coll.) mess, muddle *(lío).*

fanfarrón, ona (fan•fâ•rron´, o´nâ) *adj.* boasting, bragging; **—,** *n.* braggart, boaster.

fango (fâng´go) *m.* mire, mud.

fangoso, sa (fang•go´so, sâ) *adj.* muddy, miry.

fantasear (fan•tâ•se•âr´) *vn.* to daydream, to let one´s mind wander.

fantasia (fân•tâ•sē´â) *f.* fantasy; fancy *(imaginación).*

fantasma,(fân•tâz´mâ) *m.* phantom; (fig.) stuffed shirt *(persona entonada).*

fantástico ca, (fân•tâs´tē•ko, kâ) *adj.* fantastic; (fig.) stuffy *(presuntuoso).*

farándula (fâ•rân´dū•lâ) *f.* profession of the farceur; hocus-pocus, rigmarole *(faramalla.)*

Faraón (fâ•râ•on´) *m.* Pharoah; f—, faro.

faringe (fâ•rēn´he) *f.* (anat.) pharynx.

fariseo (fa•rē•se´o) *m.* Pharisee; pharisee *(hipócrita).*

farmacéutico, ca (fâr•mâ•se´ū•tē•ko, kâ) *adj.* pharmaceutical; —, *m.* pharmacist.

farmacia (fâr•mâ´syâ) *f.* pharmacy.

faro (fâ´ro) *m.* lighthouse; (fig.) beacon; (auto.) headlight.

farol (fâ•rol´) *m.* lantern; (naut.) light.

farola (fâ•ro´lâ) *f.* street light.

farsa (fâr´sâ) *f.* farce; company of farceurs *(compañía)*

farsante (fâr•sân´te) *m.* and *f.* farceur; —, *m.* and *f.* and *adj.* humbug.

fascinación (fâs•sē•nâ•syon´) *f.* fascination.

fascismo (fâs•sēz´mo) *m.* fascism.

fascista (fâs•sēs´tâ) *m.* and *f.* fascist.

fase (fa´se) *f.* phase, aspect.

fastidiar (fâs•tē•thyâr´) *va.* (fig.) to annoy, to bother, to bore.

fastidio (fas•tē´thyo) *m.* annoyance, boredom, bother.

fastidioso, sa (fas•tē•thyo´so, sâ) *adj.* annoying, boring, bothersome.

fatal (fâ•tâl´) *adj.* fatal; terrible, very bad *(malo).*

fatalidad (fâ•tâ•lē•thâth´) *f.* fate; disaster, misfortune *(desgracia).*

fatalismo (fâ•tâ•lēz´mo) *f.* fatalism.

fatalista (fâ•tâ•lēs´tâ) *m.* and *f.* fatalist; —, *adj.* fatalistic.

fatiga (fâ•tē´gâ) *f.* fatigue; toil, labor *(trabajo);* difficulty in breathing *(respiración dificultosa);* nausea.

fatigar (fâ•tē•gâr´) *va.* to tire, to wear out.

fatigoso, sa (fâ•tē•go´so, sâ) *adj.* weary-some, tiresome.

fauna (fâ´ū•nâ) *f.* fauna.

favor (fâ•vor´) *m.* favor; **a — de,** by means of, due to *(por medio de);* in favor of.

favorable (fâ•vo•râ´vle) *adj.* favorable.

favorecer* (fâ•vo•re•ser´) *va.* to

favor; to help *(amparar)*.

favoritismo (fâ•vo•rē•tēz´mo) *m.* favo-ritism.

favorito, ta (fâ•vo•rē´to, tâ) *adj.* favorite.

faz (fâs´) *f.* face; side *(lado)*.

fe (fe) *f.* faith; faithfulness *(fidelidad)*; testimony *(testimonio)*; **a — mía,** on my honor; **dar —,** to certify, to testify.

fealdad (fe•âl•dâth´) *f.* ugliness.

febrero (fe•vre´ro) *m.* February.

febril (fe•vrēl´) *adj.* feverish.

fecal (fe•kâl´) *adj.* (med.) fecal.

fecundar (fe•kūn•dâr´) *va.* (biol.) to fertilize; to make fertile, to make fruitful.

fecundidad (fe•kūn•dē•thâth´) *f.* fecundity, prolificness.

fecundo, da (fe•kūn´do, dâ) *adj.* fruitful, prolific *(productivo)*; fertile.

fecha (fe´châ) *f.* date; day *(día transcurrido)*; **a treinta días —,** at thirty days' sight; **hasta la —,** to date; **con —,** under date.

fechoría (fe•cho•rē´â) *f.* misdeed, villainy.

federación (fe•the•râ•syon´) *f.* federation.

federal (fe•the•râl´) *adj.* federal.

fehaciente (fe•â•syen´te) *adj.* authentic.

felicidad (fe•lē•sē•thâth´) *f.* happiness.

felicitación (fe•lē•sē•tâ•syon´) *f.* congratulation.

felicitar (fe•lē•sē•târ´) *va.* to congratulate, to felicitate.

feligrés, esa (fe•lē•gres´, e´sâ) *n.* parishioner.

felino, na (fe•lē´no, nâ) *adj.* feline.

feliz (fe•lēs´) *adj.* happy, fortunate.

felpa (fel´pâ) *f.* plush; (coll.) good drubbing, beating.

femenino, na (fe•me•nē´no, nâ) *adj.* feminine; (biol.) female.

feminista, (fe•mē•nēs´tâ) *m.* and *f.* feminist.

fémur (fe´mūr) *m.* femur, thighbone.

fenomenal (fe•no•me•nâl´) *adj.* phenomenal.

fenómeno (fe•no´me•no) *m.* phenomenon; (coll.) freak *(monstruo)*.

feo, fea (fe´o, fe´â) *adj.* ugly.

féretro (fe´re•tro) *m.* coffin.

feria (fe´ryâ) *f.* weekday fair *(mercado)*; day off *(suspensión del trabajo)*.

feriado, da (fe•ryâ´tho, thâ) *adj.* off, free; **día —do,** holiday, day off.

feriar (fe•ryâr´) *va.* to buy at the fair; to treat to *(regalar)*; **—,** *vn.* to suspend work.

fermentación (fer•men•tâ•syon´) *f.* fermentation.

ferocidad (fe•ro•sē•thâth´) *f.*

ferocity, ferociousness.

feroz (fe•ros´) *adj.* ferocious.

ferretería (fe•rre•te•rē´â) *f.* hardware store.

ferrocarril (fe•rro•kâ•rrēl´) *m.* railroad; — **de cable,** cable railroad; — **subterráneo,** subway; **por —,** by rail.

ferrocarrilero, ra (fe•rro•kâ•rrē•le´ro, râ) *adj.* (Sp. Am.) railroad; —, *m.* railroad man.

ferroviario, ria (fe•rro•vyâ´ryo, ryâ) *adj.* railroad.

fértil (fer´tēl) *adj.* fertile, fruitful.

fertilidad (fer•tē•lē•thâth´) *f.* fertility, fruitfulness.

fertilización (fer•tē•lē•sâ•syon´) *f.* fertilization.

fertilizante (fer•tē•lē•sân´te) *m.* fertilizer.

fertilizar (fer•tē•lē•sâr´) *va.* to fertilize.

férvido, da (fer´vē•tho, thâ) *adj.* fervent, ardent.

ferviente (fer•vyen´te) *adj.* fervent.

fervor, (fer•vor´) *m.* fervor.

fervoroso, sa (fer•vo•ro´so, sâ) *adj.* fervent, ardent, eager.

festejar (fes•te•hâr´) *va.* to celebrate, to entertain *(agasajar);* to court, to woo *(galantear);* to court.

festejo (fes•te´ho) *m.* fete, entertainment; courtship, wooing.

festividad (fes•tē•vē•thath´) *f.* festivity.

festivo, va (fes•tē´vo, vâ) *adj.* festive; **día —vo,** holiday.

fetiche (fe•tē´che) *m.* fetish.

fétido, da (fe´tē•tho, thâ) *adj.* fetid, stinking.

feto (fe´to) *m.* fetus.

feúcho, cha (fe•ū´cho, châ) *adj.* frightfully ugly.

feudal (feū•thâl´) *adj.* feudal.

fiable (fyâ´vle) *adj.* responsible, trustworthy.

fiado, da (fyâ´tho, thâ) *adj.* on trust; **al —do,** on credit charged.

fiambre (fyâm´bre) *adj.* cold, served cold; —**s,** *pl.* cold cuts.

fianza (fyân´sâ) *f.* surety, guarantee; bond *(prenda);* **dar** or **prestar —,** to go good for.

fiar (fyâr´) *va.* to go good for; to sell on credit *(vender a crédito);* to trust with *(dar en confianza);* —, *vn.* to trust.

fiasco (fyâs´ko) *m.* failure.

fibra (fē´vrâ) *f.* fiber; grain *(de madera);* (fig.) vigor, toughness *(energía).*

fibroso, sa (fē•vro´so, sâ) *adj.* fibrous.

ficción (fēk•syon´) *f.* fiction.

ficticio, cia (fēk•tē´syo, syâ) *adj.* fictitious.

ficha (fē´châ) *f.* chip *(en el juego);* token *(en substitución* *de moneda);* index card *(cédula).*

fichero (fē•che´ro) *m.* card index, card file.

fidedigno, na (fē•the•thēg´no, nâ) *adj.* trustworthy, believable.

fidelidad (fē•the•lē•thâth´) *f.* fidelity; accuracy, care *(exactitud).*

fiebre (fye´vre) *f.* fever; — **amarilla,** yellow fever; — **cerebral,** brain fever, meningitis; — **aftosa,** hoof-and-mouth disease.

fiel (fyel´) *adj.* faithful.

fiera (fye´râ) *f.* beast, wild animal; (fig.) fiend, monster *(persona).*

fiero, ra (fye´ro, râ) *adj.* bestial; hard, cruel *(duro);* huge, monstrous *(excesivo)* (fig.) horrible, frightful.

fiesta (fyes´tâ) *f.* (eccl.) feast, festival; holiday *(día sagrado);* party, festivity *(regocijo);* **aguar la —,** (fig.) to spoil the fun; **no estar para —s,** (coll.) to be in no mood for jokes.

figura (fē•gū´râ) *f.* figure; countenance, face *(rostro);* representation *(símbolo);* face card *(naipe);* (mus.) note.

figurado, da (fē•gū•râ´tho, thâ) *adj.* figurative.

figurar (fe•gū•râr´) *va.* to por-

tray, to figure; to feign, to pretend *(fingir);* —, *vn.* to figure, to be counted; —**se,** to imagine.

fijar (fē•hâr´) *va.* to fix, to fasten; (fig.) to determine, to fix *(precisar);* (phot.) to fix; —**se,** to notice, to take notice; **se prohibe — carteles** post no bills.

fijeza (fē•he´sâ) *f.* firmness, stability; persistence *(continuidad).*

fijo, ja (fē´ho, hâ) *adj.* fixed; **de —jo,** certainly, surely.

fila (fē´lâ) *f.* row, line.

filantropía (fē•lân•tro•pē´â) *f.* philanthrophy.

filantrópico, ca (fe•lân•tro´pē•ko, kâ) *adj.* philanthropic.

filántropo (fē•lân´tro•po) *m.* philanthropist.

filarmónico, ca (fē•lâr•mo´nē•ko, kâ) *adj.* philharmonic.

filete (fē•le´te) *m.* fillet; small spit *(asador).*

filiación (fē•lyâ•syon´) *f.* filiation; description *(señas personales).*

filial (fē•lyâl´) *adj.* filial.

filipino, na (fē•lē•pē´no, nâ) *n.* and *adj.* Filipino; —, *adj.* Philippine.

filisteo, tea (fē•lēs•te´o, te´â) *n.* and *adj.* Philistine.

filmar (fēl•mâr´) *va.* to film.

filme (fēl´me) *m.* film.

filmoteca (fēl•mo•te´kâ) *f.* film library.

filo (fē´lo) *m.* cutting edge; dividing line, division *(línea).*

filosofar, (fe•lo•so•fâr´) *vn.* to philosophize.

filosofía (fe•lo•so•fē´â) *f.* philosophy.

filósofo (fē•lo´so•fo) *m.* philosopher.

filtrar (fēl•trâr´) *va.* to filter; — **se,** to filter, to seep.

filtro (fēl´tro) *m.* filter; love potion *(bebida);* — **de vacío,** vacuum filter.

fin (fēn) *m.* end; **al —,** at last; **en —,** in conclusion, in short; **sin —** endless number.

finado, da (fē•nâ´tho, thâ) *n.* dead, deceased.

final (fē•nâl´) *adj.* final; **—,** *m.* end; **—,** *f.* finals, main event.

finalidad (fē•nâ•lē•thâth´) *f.* end, purpose.

finalista (fē•nâ•lēs´tâ) *m.* and *f.* finalist.

finalizar (fē•nâ•lē•sâr´) *va.* to finish, to conclude.

finalmente (fē•nâl•men´te) *adv.* finally, at last.

financiamiento (fē•nân•syâ•myen´to) *m.* financing.

financiar (fē•nân•syâr´) *va.* to finance.

financiero, ra (fē•nân•sye´ro, râ) *adj.* financial; **—,** *n.* financeer.

finca (fēng´kâ) *f.* piece of land, property; (Sp. Am.) ranch, country place.

fineza (fē•ne´sâ) *f.* fineness; token of friendship *(dádiva);* refinement *(delicadeza);* good turn *(acción amistosa).*

fingido, da (fēn•hē´tho, thâ) *adj.* false, feigned, not genuine.

fingimiento (fēn•hē•myen´to) *m.* feigning, pretense.

fingir (fēn•hēr´) *va.* to feign, to fake, to pretend; **—se,** to pretend to be.

fino, na (fē´no, nâ) *adj.* fine; polite, courteous *(cortés);* true *(fiel);* cunning *(astuto).*

finura (fē•nū´râ) *f.* delicacy *(delicadeza);* excellence *(primor);* courtesy, politeness.

firma (fēr´mâ) *f.* signature; company, firm *(razón social);* signing *(acto de firmar).*

firmamento (fēr•mâ•men´to) *m.* firmament.

firmar (fēr•mâr´) *va.* to sign.

firme (fēr´me) *adj.* firm stable.

firmeza (fēr•me´sâ) *f.* firmness, stability.

fiscal (fēs•kâl´) *m.* public prosecutor, district attorney; treasurer *(agente del fisco);* **—,** *adj.* fiscal.

fiscalizar (fēs•kâ•lē•sâr´) *va. (fig.)* to meddle in, to pry into.

fisco (fēs´ko) *m.* treasury department.

física (fē´sē•kâ) *f.* physics.

físico, ca (fē′sē•ko, kâ) *adj.*
physical; —, *m.* physicist; outward appearance, looks *(de
una persona)*.

fisiología (fē•syo•lo•hē′â) *f.* physiology.

fisión (fē•syon′) *f.* fission; —
nuclear, nuclear fission.

fisonomía (fē•so•no•mē′â) *f.*
look, countenance, features.

flaco, ca (flâ′ko, kâ) *adj.* thin;
(fig.) feeble.

flagrante (flâ•grân′te) *adj.* flagrant; **en —,** in the act red-
handed.

flamante (fla•mân′te) *adj.* flaming, bright; brand-new *(nuevo)*.

flamenco, ca (flâ•meng′ko, kâ) *n.*
and *adj.* Flemish; **baile —co,**
Andalusian gypsy dance; —, *m.*
flamingo.

flan (flân) *m.* custard.

flanco (flâng′ko) *m.* flank, side.

flanquear (flâng•ke•âr′) *va.* (mil.)
to flank, to outflank.

flaquear (flâ•ke•âr′) *vn.* to flag,
to weaken, to lose spirit, to
slacken.

flaqueza (flâ•ke′sâ) *f.* leanness
(delgadez); meagerness
(pobreza); feebleness, weakness
(debilidad); failing *(fragilidad)*.

flatulento, ta (flâ•tū•len′to, tâ)
adj. flatulent.

flauta (flâ′ū•tâ) *f.* (mus.) flute.

flautista (flâū•tēs′tâ) *m.* and *f.*

flutist, flautist.

flecha (fle′châ)

flema (fle′mâ) *f.* phlegm; (fig.)
apathy.

flemático, ca (fle•mâ′tē•ko, kâ)
adj. phlegmatic.

flequillo (fle•kē′yo) *m.* bangs.

fletar (fle•târ′) *va.* to freight, to
load *(embarcar);* to charter
(alquilar).

flete (fle′te) *m.* freight; — **aéreo,**
air-freight.

flexibilidad (flek•sē•vē•lē•thâth′)
f. flexibility, mobility.

flexible (flek•sē′vle) *adj.* flexible.

flojera (flo•he′râ) *f.* laziness,
slackness.

flojo, ja (flo′ho, hâ) *adj.* loose,
slack; weak *(sin fuerza ;* (fig.)
lazy, idle *(perezoso)*.

flor (flor) *f.* flower; **echar —es,** to
compliment, to flatter; — **de la
edad,** prime of life.

flora, (flo′râ) *f.* (bot.) flora.

florear (flo•re•âr′) *va.* to take the
best part of; —, *vn.* to be
always paying compliments.

florecer* (flo•re•ser′) *vn.* to blossom, to flower, to bloom; (fig.)
to flourish.

floreciente (flo•re•syen′te) *adj.* in
bloom, flowering; (fig.) flourish-
ing *(próspero)*.

Florencia (flo•ren′syâ) *f.*
Florence.

florentino, na (flo•ren•tē′no, nâ)

n. and *adj.* Florentine.

florero (flo•re′ro) *m.* vase for flowers.

florete (flo•re′te) *m.* foil.

floricultura (flo•rē•kūl•tū′râ) *f.* floriculture.

florido, da (flo•rē′tho, thâ) *adj.* florid, flowery; choice, select *(selecto)*.

flota (flo′tâ) *f.* fleet; — **aérea,** air fleet.

flotación (flo•tâ•syon′) *f.* floating.

flotar (flo•târ′) *vn.* to float.

flote (flo′te) *m.* floating; **a —,** buoyant, afloat.

fluctuación (flūk•twâ•syon′) *f.* fluctuation.

fluidez (flwē•thes′) *f.* fluidity; (fig.) fluency.

fluido, da (flwē′tho, thâ) *adj.* fluid; (fig.) fluent; —, *m.* fluid.

fluir* (flwēr) *vn.* to flow, to run.

flujo (flū′ho) *m.* flow.

fluorescencia (flwo•res•sen′syâ) *f.* fluorescence.

fluorescente (flwo•res•sen′te) *adj.* fluorescent.

fluvial (flū•vyâl′) *adj.* fluvial; **vías —es,** waterways.

foca (fo′kâ) *f.* (zool.) seal; **piel de —,** sealskin.

focal (fo•kâl′) *adj.* focal.

foco (fo′ko) *m.* focus; lightbulb.

fofo, fa (fo′fo, fâ) *adj.* soft, fluffy.

fogón, (fo•gon′) *m.* stove; vent *(en el arma de fuego).*

foliación (fo•lyâ•syon′) *f.* foliation.

folklore (fol•klor′) *m.* folklore.

folklórico, ca (fol•klo′rē•ko, kâ) *adj.* folkloric.

folklorista (fol•klo•rēs′tâ) *m.* student of folklore.

follaje (fo•yâ′he) *m.* foliage.

folleto (fo•ye′to) *m.* pamphlet.

fomentar (fo•men•târ′) *va.* to heat, to warm; (fig.) to incite, to foment *(excitar);* to promote, to further *(dar auxilio).*

fomento (fo•men′to) *m.* heat, warmth; (fig.) promotion, foment.

fonda (fon′dâ) *f.* inn.

fondo (fon′do) *m.* bottom *(parte más baja);* depth *(hondura);* back, back part *(de un salón);* background *(campo);* fund *(caudal);* qualities *(índole);* — **doble,** false bottom; **artículo de —,** editorial; **dar —,** to cast anchor; **a —,** completely, fully.

fonética (fo•ne′tē•kâ) *f.* phonetics.

fonético, ca (fo•ne′tē•ko, kâ) *adj.* phonetic.

forajido, da (fo•râ•hē′tho, thâ) *n.* outlaw, highwayman.

foráneo, nea (fo•râ′ne•o, ne•â) *adj.* foreign, strange.

forastero, ra (fo•ras•te′ro, râ) *adj.* strange; —, *n.* stranger.

fórceps (for′seps) *m.* forceps.

forense (fo•ren´se) *adj.* forensic.

forestal (fo•res•tâl´) *adj.* forest.

forjador (for•hâ•thor´) *m.* smith; (fig.) inventor, fabricator.

forjadura (for•hâ•thū´râ) *f.* forging; (fig.) fabrication.

forjar (for•hâr´) *va.* to forge, to work; (fig.) to invent, to coin, to fabricate.

forma (for´mâ) *f.* form, shape ; way *(modo de proceder);* (print.) format.

formación (for•mâ•syon´) *f.* formation.

formal (for•mâl´) *adj.* formal; reliable, serious *(cumplido).*

formalidad (for•mâ•lē•thâth´) *f.* formality; reliability, seriousness *(exactitud).*

formalizar (for•mâ•lē•sâr´) *va.* to formalize; —se, to grow stiff, to get very formal *(darse por ofendido);* to become serious, to grow up.

formar (for•mâr´) *va.* to form, to shape; — **causa,** to bring suit.

formativo, va (for•mâ•tē´vo, vâ) *adj.* formative.

formato (for•mâ´to) *m.* (print.) format.

formidable (for•mē•thâ´vle) *adj.* formidable, terrific.

fórmula (for´mū•lâ) *f.* formula.

formular (for•mū•lâr´) *va.* to formulate.

formulario (for•mū•lâ´ryo) *m.*

form, blank.

foro (fo´ro) *m.* forum; bar *(jurisprudencia);* (theat.) back of the stage.

forraje (fo•rrâ´he) *m.* forage, fodder.

forrar (fo•rrâr´) *va.* to line; to cover *(cubrir).*

fortalecer* (for•tâ•le•ser´) *va.* to fortify, to strengthen.

fortaleza, (for•tâ•le´sâ) *f.* fortitude; fortress *(recinto fortificado).*

fortificación (for•tē•fē•kâ•syon´) *f.* fortification.

fortificar (for•tē•fē•kâr´) *va.* to fortify.

fortín (for•tēn´) *m.* small fort; bunker *(en los atrincheramientos).*

fortuito, ta (for•twē´to, tâ) *adj.* fortuitous, unforseen.

fortuna (for•tū´nâ) *f.* fortunes *(azar);* luck *(buena suerte);* fortune *(hacienda);* storm *(tempestad);* **por —,** luckily, fortunately.

forzado, da (for•sâ´tho, thâ) *adj.* forced, compelled; —, *m.* convict.

forzar* (for•sâr´) *va.* to force; to ravish *(una mujer);* to force one´s way in, to storm *(entrar por violencia).*

forzoso, sa (for•so´so, sâ) *adj.* unavoidable.

fosa (fo´sâ) *f.* grave; (anat.) cavity.

fosfato (fos•fâ´to) *m.* phosphate.

fosforescente (fos•fo•res•sen´te) *adj.* phosphorescent.

fosfórico, ca (fos•fo´rē•ko, kâ) *adj.* phosphoric.

fósforo (fos´fo•ro) *m.* phosphorus; match *(cerillo).*

fósil (fo´sēl) *adj.* and *m.* fossil.

foso (fo´so) *m.* pit; (mil.) moat, trench; (auto.) grease pit.

fotocopiar (fo•to•ko•pyâr´) *va.* xerox, copy.

fotograbado (fo•to•grâ•vâ´tho) *m.* photoengraving, photogravure.

fotografia (fo•to•grâ•fē´â) *f.* photograph *(reproducción);* photography *(arte);* — **aérea,** aerial photography.

fotografiar (fo•to•gra•fyâr´) *va.* to photograph.

fotógrafo (fo•to´grâ•fo) *m.* photographer.

fotómetro (fo•to´me•tro) *m.* photometer; (phot.) light meter.

fotón (fo•ton´) *m.* photon.

fotosíntesis (fo•to•sēn´te•sēs) *f.* (chem.) photosynthesis.

fotostático, ca (fo•tos•tâ´tē•ko, kâ) *adj.* photostatic.

fracasar (frâ•kâ•sâr´) *vn.* to be wrecked, to be dashed.

fracaso (frâ•kâ´so) *m.* collapse, ruin; fiasco *(malogro).*

fracción (frâk•syon´) *f.* fraction; division, cutting up *(división).*

fraccionario, ria (frâk•syo•nâ´r-yo, ryâ) *adj.* fractional.

fractura (frâk•tū´râ) *f.* fracture *(de un hueso);* break, rupture.

fracturar (frâk•tū•râr´) *va.* to fracture; to break open, to smash.

fragancia (fra•gân´syâ) *f.* fragrance, perfume.

fragante (frâ•gân´te) *adj.* fragrant; flagrant *(flagrante).*

fragata (fra•gâ´tâ) *f.* (naut.) frigate.

frágil (frâ´hēl) *adj.* fragile; (fig.) weak, frail.

fragilidad (frâ•hē•lē•thâth´) *f.* fragility; (fig.) frailty.

fragmento (frâg•men´to) *m.* fragment.

fragua (frâ´gwâ) *f.* forge.

fraguar (frâ•gwâr´) *va.* to forge; to contrive *(idear);* —, *vn.* to solidify, to harden.

fraile (frâ´ē•le) *m.* friar.

frambuesa (frâm•bwe´sâ) *f.* raspberry.

francés, esa (frân•ses´, e´sa) *adj.* French; —, *m.* French language *(idioma);* Frenchman; —, *f.* French woman.

Francia (frân´syâ) *f.* France.

franco, ca (frâng´ko, kâ) *adj.* free *(exento);* liberal, generous *(dadivoso);* frank, open *(sincero);* — **a bordo,** free on

board; —, *m.* franc; —, *n.*
Frank.

franela (frâ•ne´lâ) *f.* flannel.

franja (frân´hâ) *f.* fringe; strip,
band *(lista)*.

franqueza (frâng•ke´sâ) *f.* frankness *(sinceridad);* liberty, freedom *(exención);* liberality *(generosidad)*.

franquicia (frâng•kē´syâ) *f.*
immunity from customs pay-
ments; franchise; free mailing
privileges *(de correo)*.

frasco (frâs´ko) *m.* flask; powder
horn *(para la pólvora)*.

frase (frâ´se) *f.* phrase; sentence
(oración); — **en sentido figurado,** figure of speech.

fraternal (frâ•ter•nâl´) *adj.* fraternal, brotherly.

fraternidad (frâ•ter•nē•thâth´) *f.*
fraternity, brotherhood.

fraude (fra´ū•the) *m.* fraud,
cheating.

fraudulento, ta (frâū•thū•len´to,
tâ) *adj.* fraudulent.

fray (frâ´ē) *m.* friar.

frazada (frâ•sâ´thâ) *f.* blanket.

frecuencia (fre•kwen´syâ) *f.* frequency; **con —,** frequently.

fregadero (fre•gâ•the´ro) *m.*
kitchen sink.

fregado (fre•gâ´tho) *m.* scouring,
washing; scrubbing.

fregar* (fre•gâr´) *va.* to scrub
(estregar); to scour, to wash

(los platos); (coll.) to rub the
wrong way, to annoy *(fastidiar)*.

freir* (fre•ēr´) *va.* to fry.

fréjol (fre´hol) *m.* kidney bean.

frenar (fre•nâr´) *va.* to brake.

frenesí (fre•ne•sē´) *m.* frenzy.

frenético, ca (fre•ne´tē•ko, kâ)
adj. frenzied.

freno (fre´no) *m.* bridle; (mech.)
brake; — **de aire,** air brake; —
s, braces *(odontología)*.

frente (fren´te) *f.* forehead; (fig.)
face; — **a —,** face to face; —,
m. front; **en —.** in front; — **a,**
in front of; **hacer —,** to face, to
stand up to.

fresa (fre´sâ) *f.* strawberry.

fresco, ca (fres´ko, kâ) *adj.* cool;
fresh *(reciente);* (fig.) healthy,
ruddy *(de buen color);* unruf-
fled *(sereno);* (coll.) fresh,
cheeky *(descarado)*.

frescura (fres•kū´râ) *f.* freshness; coolness; calmness,
steadiness *(desenfado);* smart
remark, jibe *(chanza);* (fig.)
carelessness *(descuido)*.

fresno (frez´no) *m.* ash tree.

frialdad (fryâl•dâth´) *f.* coldness;
indifference *(indiferencia);*
(med.) frigidity; (fig) stupidity
(necedad).

fricción (frēk•syon´) *f.* friction.

friega (frye´gâ) *f.* massage; whipping.

frígido, da (frē´hē•tho, thâ) *adj.*

frigid.

frijol (frē•hol´) *m.* kidney bean.

frío, fria (frē´o, frē´â) *adj.* and *m.* cold; **hacer** — or **tener** —, to be cold.

fritada (frē•tâ´thâ) *f.* fry.

frito, ta (frē´to, tâ) *adj.* fried.

fritura (frē•tū´râ) *f.* fry.

frivolidad (frē•vo•lē•thâth´) *f.* frivolity.

frívolo, la (frē´vo•lo, lâ) *adj.* frivolous.

frondosidad (fron•do•sē•thâth´) *f.* thick foliage.

frontera (fron•te´râ) *f.* frontier, border.

fronterizo, za (fron•te•rē´so, sâ) *adj.* frontier, border; opposite, on the other side *(que está en frente).*

frontón (fron•ton´) *m.* pelota court *(cancha);* court wall *(pared);* (arch.) pediment.

frotar (fro•târ´) *va.* to rub.

fructífero, ra (frūk•tē´fe•ro, râ) *adj.* fruitful.

fructuoso, sa (fruk•two´so, sâ) *adj.* fruitful.

frugal (frū•gâl´) *adj.* frugal, sparing.

frugalidad (frū•gâ•lē•thâth´) *f.* frugality.

fruncimiento (frūn•sē•myen´to) *m.* gathering, ruffling; (fig.) ruse, trick *(embuste).*

fruncir (frūn•sēr´) *va.* to gather,

to ruffle *(una tela);* (fig.) to press together *(recoger);* — **las cejas,** to knit one's eyebrows, to frown; — **los labios,** to purse one's lips; — **el ceño,** to frown.

frustrar (frūs•trâr´) *va.* to frustrate, to thwart; to fail in the attempt of *(un delito);* —**se,** to miscarry, to fall through.

fruta (frū´tâ) *f.* fruit.

fruto (frū´to) *m.* fruit.

fuego (fwe´go) *m.* fire; burning sensation *(picazón);* dwelling *(hogar);* —**s artificiales,** fireworks.

fuente (fwen´te) *f.* fountain *(construcción);* source *(principio);* spring *(manantial);* platter *(plato).*

fuera (fwe´râ) *adv.* without, outside; — **de,** outside of; over and above *(además de);* — **de sí,** frantic, beside oneself; — **de alcance,** beyond reach; — **de ley,** lawless, outside the law; ¡—! *interj.* out of the way! make way!

fuerte (fwer´te) *m.* small fortification; —, *adj.* strong; considerable *(grande);* —, *adv.* loud; hard (con fuerza).

fuerza (fwer´sâ) *f.* force; strength *(solidez);* power *(poderío);* **a — de,** by dint of; — **electromotriz,** electromotive force; — **mayor,** act of God; —**s,** *pl.* (mil.) forces.

fuete (fwe´te) *m.* (Sp. Am.) horse-whip.

fuga (fū´gâ) *f.* flight; exuberance *(ardor);* leak, escape *(de un liquido);* (mus.) fugue.

fugarse (fū•gâr´se) *vr.* to escape, to flee.

fugaz (fū•gâs´) *adj.* fleeting, momentary.

fugitivo, va (fū•hē•tē´vo, va) *adj.* and *n.* fugitive.

fulgor (fūl•gor´) *m.* glow, brilliance, splendor.

fulgurar (fūl•gū•râr´) *vn.* to flash, to shine brilliantly.

fulminar (fūl•mē•nâr´) *va.* to strike dead; to throw off *(arrojar)* ; (fig.) to thunder *(dictar);* —, *vn.* to fulminate.

fumada (fū•mâ´thâ) *f.* puff.

fumador, ra (fū•mâ•thor´, râ) *n.* smoker, —, *adj.* given to smoking.

fumar (fū•mâr´) *va.* and *vn.* to smoke.

fumigación (fū•mē•gâ•syon´) *f.* fumigation.

función (fūn•syon´) *f.* function; (theat.) performance; (mil.) engagement.

funcionamiento (fūn•syo•nâ•myen´to) *m.* performance, function, running.

funcionar (fūn•syo•nâr´) *vn.* to function, to work, to run.

funcionario (fūn•syo•nâ´ryo) *m.* official, functionary.

funda (fūn´dâ) *f.* case, cover; slip cover *(de butaca);* — **de almohada,** pillowcase.

fundación (fūn•dâ•syon´) *f.* foundation.

fundador, ra (fūn•dâ•thor´, râ) *n.* founder.

fundamental (fūn•dâ•men•tâl´) *adj.* fundamental.

fundamento (fūn•dâ•men´to) *m.* foundation, base; seriousness, levelheadedness *(formalidad);* grounds *(motivo).*

fundar (fūn•dâr´) *va.* to found, to establish.

fundición (fūn•dē•syon´) *f.* melting, fusion; founding, casting.

fundir (fūn•dēr´) *va.* to found, to cast *(un objeto);* to fuse, to melt; —se, (fig.) to fuse, to join.

fúnebre (fū´ne•vre) *adj.* funeral, funereal.

funeral (fū•ne•râl´) *adj.* funereal; —es, *m. pl.* funeral.

funesto, ta (fū•nes´to, tâ) *adj.* mournful, dismal; ill-fated, disastrous *(fatal).*

furia (fū´ryâ) *f.* fury, rage; (fig.) haste *(prisa);* **a toda —,** with the utmost speed.

furor (fū•ror´) *m.* fury.

furtivo, va (fūr•tē´vo, vâ) *adj.* furtive, sly; **cazador —vo,** poacher.

fuselaje (fū•se•lâ´he) *m.* fuselage.

fusible (fū•sē´vle) *m.* (elec.) fuse;
caja de —s, fuse box.

fusil (fū•sēl´) *m.* rifle.

fusilar (fū•sē•lâr´) *va.* to shoot,
to execute; (coll.) to plagiarize,
to steal.

fusilazo (fū•sē•lâ´so) *m.* rifle
shot.

fusión (fū•syon´) *f.* fusion.

fustigar (fūs•tē•gâr´) *va.* to lash;
(fig.) to rake over the coals
(criticar).

fútbol (fūt´bol) *m.* soccer; football *(de Estados Unidos).*

fútil (fū´tēl) *adj.* useless, trifling,
unimportant.

futuro, ra (fū•tū´ro, râ) *adj.* and
m. future; **en un — próximo,** in
the near future.

G

gabán (gâ•vân´) *m.* overcoat.

gabardina (gâ•vâr•thē´nâ) *f.*
gabardine *(tela);* trench coat
(abrigo).

gabinete (gâ•vē•ne´te) *m.* (poi.)
cabinet; study *(aposento);* exhibition hall, exhibit *(colección).*

gacela (gâ•se´lâ) *f.* gazelle.

gaceta (gâ•se´tâ) *f.* newspaper.

gacho, cha (gâ´cho, châ) *adj.*
curved down, bent down.

gafa (gâ´fâ) *f.* hook; **—s,** *pl.* spectacles, glasses.

gaita (gâ´ē•tâ) *f.* bagpipe.

gala (gâ´lâ) *f.* finery, elegant
dress; grace, refinement
(garbo); pride *(lo más selecto);*
hacer —, to glory in.

galán (gâ•lân´) *m.* gallant, suit-
or, swain *(novio);* dandy, swell;
primer —, (theat.) leading man.

galante (gâ•lân´te) *adj.* gallant;

coquettish *(mujer).*

galantería (gâ•lân•te•rē´â) *f.*
gallantry, elegance *(elegancia);*
liberality, generosity *(liberalidad).*

galápago (gâ•lâ´pâ•go) *m.* sea
turtle; light saddle *(silla).*

galardón (gâ•lâr•thon´) *m.*
reward, recompense.

galeón (gâ•le•on´) *m.* (naut.) gal-
leon.

galera (gâ•le´râ) *f.* (naut.) galley;
covered wagon *(carro);* wom-
en´s prison *(cárcel);* (print.) galley.

galería (gâ•le•rē´â) *f.* gallery.

Gales (ga´les) *m.* Wales.

galgo (gâl´go) *m.* greyhound.

galón (gâ•lon´) *m.* braid; gallon
(medida).

galopar (gâ•lo•pâr´) *vn.* to gallop.

galope (gâ•lo´pe) *m.* gallop; **a —,**

in a hurry, in great haste.

galopear (gâ•lo•pe•âr´) = **galopar.**

gallardete (gâ•yâr•the´te) *m.* pennant, streamer.

gallardía (gâ•yâr•thē´â) *f.* grace ease, effortlessness *(gracia);* resourcefulness, spirit *(ánimo).*

gallardo, da (gâ•yâr´tho, thâ) *adj.* graceful, elegant; spirited, resourceful; (fig.) splendid *(hermoso).*

gallego, ga (gâ•ye´go, gâ) *n.* and *adj.* Galician.

galleta (gâ•ye´tâ) *f.* hardtack, sea biscuit; cracker *(bizcocho seco).*

gallina (gâ•yē´nâ) *f.* hen.

gallinazo (gâ•yē•nâ´so) *m.* (zool.) turkey buzzard.

gallinero, ra (gâ•yē•ne´ro, râ) *n.* poulterer; —, *m.* chicken coop; (theat.) peanut gallery; (coll.) bedlam, madhouse *(gritería).*

gallo (gâ´yo) *m.* cock; **misa de —,** midnight mass.

gama (gâ´mâ) *f. (mus.)* gamut; (zool.) doe.

gamuza (gâ•mū´sâ) *f.* chamois.

gana (gâ´nâ) *f.* desire, wish; **tener —s de,** to feel like; **de buena —,** with pleasure, willingly, gladly; **de mala —,** unwillingly, with reluctance.

ganadería (gâ•nâ•the•rē´â) *f.* cattle raising *(cría);* stock cattle *(ganado).*

ganadero, ra (gâ•nâ•the´ro, râ) *n.* cattle dealer, cattle raiser; —, *adj.* cattle, livestock.

ganado (gâ•nâ´tho) *m.* cattle, livestock.

ganador, ra (gâ•nâ•thor´, râ) *n.* winner; earner; —, *adj.* winning; earning.

ganancia (gâ•nân´syâ) *f.* gain, profit, earnings.

ganar (gâ•nâr´) *va.* to earn; to win *(por lucha o casualidad);* to reach *(alcanzar);* to win over *(captar la voluntad);* to be ahead of *(aventajar);* to deserve, to earn *(merecer);* —, *vn.* to improve.

gancho (gan´cho) *m.* hook; wheedler, coaxer *(que solicita con maña);* charm, allure *(atractivo).*

ganga (gâng´gâ) *f.* (orn.) European sand grouse; bargain; windfall *(ventaja inesperada).*

gangoso, sa (gâng•go´so, sâ) *adj.* snuffling, sniveling.

gangrena (gâng•gre´nâ) *f.* gangrene.

ganso, sa (gân´so, sâ) *n.* goose; —, *m.* gander.

garabatear (gâ•râ•vâ•te•âr´) *va.* to hook; to scrawl, to scribble *(garrapatear).*

garabato (gâ•râ•vâ´to) *m.* hook, scrawl, scribbling; —s, *pl.* fidgeting of the hands.

garaje (gâ•râ´he) *m.* garage.

garante (ga•rân´te) *m.* guarantor.

garantía (gâ•ran•tē´â) *f.* guarantee,
pledge.

garantizar (gâ•rân•tē•sâr´) *va.* to
guarantee.

garapiña (gâ•râ•pē´nyâ) *f.* sugar-
coating, icing, frosting.

garapiñado, da
(gâ•râ•pē•nyâ´tho, thâ) *adj.*
candied, frosted, glace; **almendras —s,** sugar-coated
almonds.

garbanzo (gâr•vân´so) *m.* chick-
pea.

garbo (gâr´vo) *m.* gracefulness,
elegance, grace; gallantry, generous nature *(desinterés).*

gardenia (gâr•the´nyâ) *f.* (bot.)
gardenia.

gargajo (gâr•gâ´ho) *m.* phlegm,
spittle.

garganta (gâr•gân´tâ) *f.* throat;
instep *(del pie);* neck *(de una
botella);* narrows *(de un río);*
narrow pass *(entre montañas).*

gárgara (gâr´gâ•râ) *f.* gargle;
hacer —s, to gargle.

gárgola (gâr´go•lâ) *f.* gargoyle.

garita (gâ•rē´tâ) *f.* sentry box;
(rail.) line-man´s box; (auto.)
cab.

garra (gâ´rrâ) *f.* claws; (orn.)
talons; **caer en las —s de,** to
fall in the clutches of.

garrafa (gâ•rrâ´fâ) *f.* decanter,
carafe.

garrafón (gâ•rrâ•fon´) *m.* demijohn, large water jar.

garrapata (gâ•rrâ•pâ´tâ) *f.* (ent.)
tick.

garrapato (gâ•rrâ•pâ´to) *m.*
scrawl, doodle.

garza (gâr´sâ) *f.* heron.

gas (gâs) *m.* gas; **— lacrimógeno,**
tear gas.

gasa (ga´sâ) *f.* gauze, chiffon.

gaseoso, sa (gâ•se•o´so, sâ) *adj.*
gaseous; **—,** *f.* soft drink, soda
water.

gasolina (gâ•so•lē´nâ) *f.* gasoline;
tanque de —, gasoline tank.

gasolinera (gâ•so•lē•ne´râ) *f.*
(naut.) motor launch; (auto.)
gas station.

gastado, da (gâs•tâ´tho, thâ) *adj.*
wornout, tired out; worn down
(borrado); used up, spent *(desgastado).*

gastar (gâs•târ´) *va.* to spend *(el
dinero);* to use up, to go
through *(consumir);* to lay
waste *(un territorio);* to waste
(echar a perder); to have
always *(tener habitualmente);*
to use *(usar);* **—las,** (coll.) to
behave, to act.

gasto (gâs´to) *m.* expense, cost;
waste; consumption.

gata (gâ´tâ) *f.* she-cat, tabby; **a —s,** on all fours.

gatear (gâ•te•âr´) *vn.* to creep, to go on all fours *(andar a gatas)*; to climb up, to clamber up *(trepar)*; —, *va.* to scratch; (coll.) to snatch, to pilfer *(hurtar)*.

gatillo (gâ•tē´yo) *m.* pincers, tooth extractor; trigger *(del arma de fuego)*.

gato (gâ´to) *m.* cat, tomcat; car jack, lifting jack *(enganche)*; hooking tong *(garfio)*; (fig.) sneak thief *(ladrón)*; — **montés,** wildcat.

gaucho (gâ´ū•cho) *m.* Argentine cowboy.

gaveta (gâ•ve´tâ) *f.* desk drawer.

gavilán (gâ•vē•lân´) *m.* (orn.) sparrow hawk.

gaviota (gâ•vyo´tâ) *f.* (orn.) gull, sea gull.

gaznate (gâz•nâ´te) *m.* throttle, windpipe.

gelatina (he•lâ•tē´nâ) *f.* gelatine.

gema (he´mâ) *f.* gem, precious stone.

gemelo, la (he•me´lo, lâ) *n.* twin; **—s,** *m. pl.* cuff links *(juego de botones)*; opera glasses *(de teatro)*; binoculars *(prismáticos)*.

gemido (he•mē´tho) *m.* groan, moan, wail; **dar —s,** to groan.

gemir* (he•mēr´) *vn.* to groan, to moan, to wail.

gen, (hen) *m.* gene.

gendarme (hen•dâr´me) *m.* gendarme.

genealogía (he•ne•â•lo•hē´â) *f.* genealogy.

generación (he•ne•râ•syon´) *f.* generation.

generador (he•ne•râ•thor´) *m.* generator.

general (he•ne•râl´) *m.* general; —, *adj.* general, usual; **en —,** generally, in general; **por lo —,** as a rule; **cuartel —,** headquarters; **procurador —,** Attorney General.

generalizar (he•ne•râ•lē•sâr´) *va.* to generalize; to spread, to make common *(hacer público)*.

genérico, ca (he•ne´rē•ko, kâ) *adj.* generic.

género (he´ne•ro) *m.* (biol.) genus; kind, sort *(clase)*; (gram.) gender; — **humano,** mankind.

generosidad (he•ne•ro•sē•thâth´) *f.* generosity.

generoso sa, (he•ne•ro´so, sâ) *adj.* generous.

Génesis (he´ne•sēs) *m.* Genesis; **g—,** *f.* genesis, origin.

genética (he•ne´tē•kâ) *f.* genetics.

genio (he´nyo) *m.* sort, kind *(índole)*; temper, disposition *(inclinación)*; genius *(talento)*.

genital (he•ne•tâl´) *adj.* genital.

genocidio (he•no•se´thyo) *m.*
genocide.

gente (hen´te) *f.* people; **— bien,**
well-to do; **ser buena —,** (Sp.
Am.) to be likable, to be nice.

gentil (hen•tēl´) *m.* and *f.* and
adj. pagan; **—,** *adj.* refined,
genteel *(gracioso);* obvious, evident *(notable).*

gentileza (hen•tē•le´sâ) *f.* gentility, elegance; kindness *(amabilidad).*

gentilicio, cia (hen•tē•lē´syo, syâ)
adj. national; family
(perteneciente al linaje).

gentío (hen•tē´o) *m.* crowd, multitude.

gentuza (hen•tū´sâ) *f.* rabble,
mob.

genuino, na (he•nwē´no, nâ) *adj.*
genuine, pure.

geofísico, ca (he•o•fē´sē•ko, kâ)
adj. geophysical; **año —,**
geophysical year.

geofísica (he•o•fē´sē•kâ) *f.*
geophysics.

geografía, (he•o•grâ•fē´â) *f.* geography.

geográfico ca (he•o•grâ´fē•ko,
kâ) *adj.* geographical.

geógrafo (he•o´grâ•fo) *m.* geographer.

geología (he•o•lo•hē´â) *f.* geology.

geólogo (he•o´lo•go) *m.* geologist.

geometría (he•o•me•trē´a) *f.* geometry.

geométrico, ca (he•o•me´trē•ko,
kâ) *adj.* geometrical, geometric.

gerencia (he•ren´syâ) *f.* management, administration.

gerente (he•ren´te) *m.* manager.

germen (her´men) *m.* germ; origin, source *(principio).*

germicida (her•mē•sē´thâ) *adj.*
germicidal.

germinar (her•mē•nâr´) *vn.* to
germinate.

gerundio (he•rūn´dyo) *m.* (gram.)
present participle.

gestación (hes•tâ•syon´) *f.* gestation.

gesticular (hes•tē•kū•lâr´) *vn.* to
gesticulate.

gestión (hes•tyon´) *f.* management; effort, measure *(diligencia).*

gestionar (hes•tyo•nâr´) *va.* to
carry out, to implement.

gesto (hes´to) *m.* face *(semblante)* look, expression *(expresión);* movement, gesture
(ademán).

gigante (hē•gân´te) *m.* giant; **—,**
adj. gigantic.

gigantesco, ca (hē•gân•tes´ko,
kâ) *adj.* gigantic, huge.

gimnasia (hēm•nâ´syâ) *f.* gymnastics.

gimnasio (hēm•nâ´syo) *m.* gymnasium.

gimnasta (hēm•nâs´tâ) *m.* and *f.*
gymnast.

gimnástica (hēm•nâs´tē•kâ) *f.* gymnastics.

gimnástico, ca (hēm•nâs´tē•ko, kâ) *adj.* gymnastic.

ginebra (hē•ne´vrâ) *f.* gin; (fig.) confusion, bedlam *(confusión)*.

ginecología (hē•ne•ko•lo•hē´â) *f.* (med.) gynecology.

gingivitis (hēn•hē•vē´tēs) *f.* (med.) gingivitis.

gira (hē´râ) = **jira.**

girafa (hē•râ´fâ) *f.* giraffe.

girar (hē•râr´) *vn.* to rotate, to revolve; to turn, to revolve *(desarrollarse);* to turn *(desviarse);* —, *va.* (com.) to draw; — **contra,** to draw on.

girasol (hē•râ•sol´) *m.* sunflower.

giro (hē´ro) *m.* rotation, revolution; turn, tack *(de un asunto);* (com.) draft; — **a la vista,** sight draft; — **postal,** money order.

gitanesco, ca (hē•tâ•nes´ko, kâ) *adj.* gypsy-like.

gitano, na (hē•tâ´no, nâ) *n.* gypsy; —, *adj.* fawning, sly, tricky.

glacial (glâ´syâl) *adj.* glacial.

glaciar (glâ•syâr´) *m.* glacier.

gladiador, (glâ•thyâ•thor´) or **gladiator** (glâ•thyâ•tor´) *m.* gladiator.

glándula (glân´dū•lâ) *f.* gland.

glaucoma (glâū•ko´mâ) *f.* (med.) glaucoma.

glicerina (glē•se•rē´nâ) *f.* glyceri-ne.

global (glo•vâl´) *adj.* total, lump, all-inclusive.

globalización (glo•vâ•lē•sâ•syon´), *f.* globalization.

globo (glo´vo) *m.* globe, sphere; **en —,** as a whole, in a lump sum; — **del ojo,** eyeball.

glóbulo (glo´vū•lo) *m.* globule; — **s rojos,** red blood corpuscles; **—s blancos,** white blood corpuscles.

gloria (glo´ryâ) *f.* glory; **saber a —,** to taste delicious; **oler a —,** to smell delightful.

glorieta (glo•rye´tâ) *f.* bower, arbor; circle *(en una encrucijada).*

glorificación (glo•rē•fē•kâ•syon´) *f.* glorification.

glorificar (glo•rē•fē•kâr´) *va.* to glorify; **—se,** to boast, to vaunt.

glorioso, sa (glo•ryo´so, sâ) *adj.* glorious.

glosa (glo´sâ) *f.* gloss, commentary.

glosar (glo•sâr´) *va.* to gloss, to comment on; (fig.) to find fault with.

glosario (glo•sâ´ryo) *m.* glossary.

glotón, ona (glo•ton´, o´nâ) *n.* glutton; —, *adj.* gluttonous.

glotonería (glo•to•ne•rē´â) *f.* gluttony.

glucosa (glū•ko´sâ) *f.* glucose.

gobernación (go•ver•nâ•syon´) *f.* government, governing.

gobernador, ra (go•ver•nâ•thor´, râ) *adj.* governing; —, *m.* governor; —, *f.* governor´s wife.

gobernante (go•ver•nân´te) *m.* governor; (coll.) self-appointed authority; —, *adj.* governing.

gobernar* (go•ver•nâr´) *va.* to govern; to guide, to direct *(guiar);* (naut.) to steer; —, *vn.* to steer.

gobierno (go•vyer´no) *m.* government; direction; (naut.) helm.

goce (go´se) *m.* enjoyment, possession.

gol (gol) *m.* goal.

golf (golf) *m.* golf; **campo de —,** golf course, links.

golfo (gol´fo) *m.* gulf.

golondrina (go•lon•drē´nâ) *f.* (orn.) swallow.

golosina (go•lo•sē´nâ) *f.* tidbit, delicacy; (fig.) frill, trifle *(chuchería).*

goloso, sa (go•lo´so, sâ) *adj.* gluttonous.

golpe (gol´pe) *m.* blow; large quantity *(copia);* beat *(del corazón);* flap *(del bolsillo);* blow, calamity *(desgracia);* shock, surprise *(admiración):* **de —,** all at once.

golpear (gol•pe•âr´) *va.* to beat, to hit.

goma (go´mâ) *f.* gum, rubber; —

de mascar, chewing gum; — **laca,** shellac; — **para borrar,** eraser.

gomoso, sa (go•mo´so, sâ) *adj.* gummy.

góndola (gon´do•lâ) *f.* gondola.

gordo, da (gor´tho, thâ) *adj.* fat; stocky *(muy abultado).*

gordura (gor•thū´râ) *f.* grease *(grasa);* fatness *(corpulencia).*

gorila (go•rē´lâ) *m.* (zool.) gorilla.

gorjeo (gor•he´o) *m.* trilling, warbling.

gorra (go´rrâ) *f.* cap; **de —,** (coll.)at others´expense, by sponging.

gorrión (go•rryon´) *m.* sparrow.

gorro (go´rro) *m.* cap.

gota (go´tâ) *f.* drop; (med.) gout.

gotear (go•te•âr´) *vn.* to drip; to trickle.

gotera (go•te´râ) *f.* leak *(hendedura);* dripping water; water stains *(señal).*

gozar (go•sâr´) *va.* to enjoy; — **de,** to possess; **—se,** to enjoy, to have fun.

gozne (goz´ne) *m.* hinge.

gozo (go´so) *m.* joy, pleasure, delight.

gozoso, sa (go•so´so, sâ) *adj.* joyful, cheerful.

grabación (grâ•vâ•syon´) *f.* recording, cutting; — **en cinta,** tape recording.

grabado (grâ•vâ´tho) *m.* engrav-

ing; print, picture *(estampa);* —
al agua fuerte, etching.

grabador (grâ•vâ•thor´) *m.*
engraver; recorder *(de discos).*

grabadora (grâ•vâ•tho´râ) *f.* tape
recorder.

grabar (grâ•vâr´) *va.* to engrave;
to record, to cut *(un disco);*
(fig.) to etch, to impress; — **al
agua fuerte,** to etch.

gracia (grâ´syâ) *f.* grace *(garbo);*
boon *(beneficio);* pardon
(perdón); witty remark *(chiste);*
name *(nombre);* **hacer —,** to
amuse, to strike as funny;
tener —, to be amusing; **—s,**
pl. thanks; **dar —s,** to thank.

gracioso, sa (grâ•syo´so, sâ) *adj.*
graceful, charming *(garboso);*
funny, witty; gratuitous *(gratuito);* —, *n.* comic.

grada (gra´thâ) *f.* step *(peldaño);*
row, tier *(de anfiteatro);* (agr.)
harrow; **—s,** *pl.* steps.

grado (grâ´tho) *m.* degree; grade
(sección de escuela); step
(grada).

graduación (grâ•thwâ•syon´) *f.*
graduation; *(mil.)* rank, grade.

graduado, da (grâ•thwâ´tho, thâ)
n. graduate, alumnus; —, *adj.*
graduated.

gradual (gra•thwâl´) *adj.* gradual.

graduar (grâ•thwâr´) *va.* to graduate; to classify *(clasificar);* —

se, to graduate, to be graduated.

gráfico, ca (grâ´fē•ko, kâ) *adj.*
graphic; —, *m.* (math.) graph;
—, *f.* scale, graph.

gramática (grâ•mâ´tē•kâ) *f.*
grammar.

gramatical (grâ•mâ•tē•kâl´) *adj.*
grammatical.

gramático (grâ•mâ´tē•ko) *m.*
grammarian.

gramo (grâ´mo) *m.* gram.

gran (gran) *adj.* apocope of
grande, great; large, big.

granada (grâ•nâ´thâ) *f.* (mil.)
grenade; pomegranate; — **de
metralla,** shrapnel.

granadero (grâ•nâ•the´ro) *m.*
(mil.) grenadier.

granadilla (grâ•nâ•thē´yâ) *f.* passion flower; passion fruit
(fruto).

granado, da (grâ•nâ´tho, thâ)
adj. select, illustrious; experienced, mature *(experto);* —,
m. pomegranate tree.

granar (grâ•nâr´) *vn.* to go to
seed, to seed.

Gran Bretaña (grâm•bre•tâ´nyâ)
f. Great Britain.

grande (grân´de) *adj.* large, big;
great *(notable);* —, *m.* grandee.

grandiosidad
(grân•dyo•sē•thâth´) *f.* splendor, magnificence.

grandioso, sa (grân•dyo´so, sâ)

adj. magnificent, splendid.

granero (grâ•ne′ro) *m.* granary.

granito (grâ•nē′to) *m.* granite.

granizada (grâ•nē•sâ′thâ) *f.* hailstorm; (fig.) downpour, torrent.

granizar (grâ•nē•sâr′) *vn.* to hail.

granizo (grâ•nē′so) *m.* hail.

granja (grân′hâ) *f.* grange, farm; country home *(quinta de recreo).*

granjear (grân•he•âr′) *va.* to earn; to win *(la voluntad).*

grano (grâ′no) *m.* grain; (med.) pimple; **ir al —,** to get to the point.

grapa (grâ′pâ) *f.* staple.

grapador (grâ•pâ•thor′) *m.* stapler.

grasa (grâ′sâ) *f.* fat; grease *(manteca);* dirt *(mugre);* **— de ballena,** whale blubber.

grasiento, ta (grâ•syen′to, tâ) *adj.* greasy.

gratificación (grâ•tē•fē•kâ•syon′) *f.* gratification; bonus *(de servicio extraordinario);* gratuity *(propina).*

gratificar (grâ•tē•fē•kâr′) *va.* to reward, to recompense *(recompensar);* to gratify, to please *(agradar).*

gratis (grâ′tēs) *adv.* gratis, free.

gratitud (grâ•tē•tūth′) *f.* gratitude, grate-fulness.

grato, ta (grâ′to, tâ) *adj.* pleasant, pleasing.

gratuito, ta (grâ•twē′to, tâ) *adj.* gratuitous; unwarranted *(arbitrario).*

gravar (grâ•vâr′) *va.* to burden, to oppress; to encumber *(un inmueble).*

grave (grâ′ve) *adj.* heavy; grave *(serio);* weighty *(importante);* (gram.) grave; very sick *(enfermo).*

gravedad (grâ•ve•thâth′) *f.* gravity; seriousness *(importancia);* **fuerza de —,** force of gravity; **ausencia de —,** weightlessness.

gravitación (grâ•vē•tâ•syon′) *f.* gravitation.

gravitar (grâ•vē•târ′) *vn.* to gravitate.

graznar (grâz•nâr′) *vn.* to cackle, to caw.

Grecia (gre′syâ) *f.* Greece.

gremio (gre′myo) *m.* guild, union, society.

greña (gre′nyâ) *f.* matted hair, snarled hair; (fig.) tangle, snarl *(maraña).*

greñudo, da (gre•nyū′tho, thâ) *adj.* with one′s hair in snarls.

grey (gre′ē) *f.* flock.

griego, ga (grye′go, gâ) *n.* and *adj.* Greek.

grieta (grye′ta) *f.* crack, chink.

grifo, fa (grē′fo, fâ) *adj.* kinky, curly; **—,** *m.* griffin; faucet *(llave).*

grillo (grē′yo) *m.* cricket; **—s,** *pl.*

fetters, irons.

gringo, ga (gring´go, gâ) *n.* (Sp. Am.) Yankee.

gripe (grē´pe) *f.* grippe.

gris (grēs´) *adj.* gray; —, *m.* (coll.) cold, sharp wind.

gritar (grē•târ´) *vn.* to cry out, to shout, to scream.

grito (grē´to) *m.* shout, outcry, scream.

Groenlandia (gro•en•lân´dyâ) *f.* Greenland.

grosería (gro•se•rē´â) *f.* coarseness, illbreeding.

grosero, ra (gro•se´ro, râ) *adj.* coarse, rude, unpolished.

grotesco, ca (gro•tes´ko, kâ) *adj.* grotesque.

grúa (grū´â) *f.* crane, derrick.

gruesa (grwe´sa) *f.* gross.

grueso, sa (grwe´so, sâ) *adj.* thick; large *(abultado);* dense *(de entendimiento);* —, *m.* heaviness; thickness *(espesor).*

grulla (grū´yâ) *f.* (orn.) crane.

gruñido (grū•nyē´tho) *m.* grunt; grumble; creak.

gruñir* (grū•nyēr´) *vn.* to grunt; to grumble *(murmurar);* to creak *(chirriar).*

grupo (grū´po) *m.* group.

gruta (grū´tâ) *f.* grotto.

guacamayo, ya (gwâ•ka•mâ´yo, yâ) *n.* macaw.

guachinango (gwâ•chē•nâng´go)

m. (ichth). red snapper.

guajolote (gwâ•ho•lo´te) *m.* (Mex.) turkey.

guanaco (gwâ•nâ´ko) *m.* (zool.) guanaco.

guano (gwâ´no) *m.* guano.

guante (gwân´te) *m.* glove; —s, *pl.* tip.

guapo, pa (gwâ´po, pâ) *adj.* good-looking, handsome *(bien parecido);* stouthearted, brave *(valiente);* showy *(ostentoso);* —, *m.* bully, tough guy; beau, gallant *(galán).*

guarapo (gwâ•râ´po) *m.* sugarcane juice.

guarda (gwâr´thâ) *m.* and *f.* custodian; —, *f.* custody, care; endpaper *(de libro).*

guardabrisa (gwâr•thâ•vrē´sâ) *m.* windshield.

guardacostas (gwâr•thâ•kos´tâs) *m.* coast guard cutter.

guardaespaldas (gwâr•thâ•es•pâl´dâs) *m.* bodyguard.

guardapolvo (gwâr•thâ•pol´vo) *m.* dust cover *(cubierta);* duster, smock *(vestido).*

guardar (gwâr•thâr´) *va.* to keep; to guard *(vigilar);* to protect *(preservar de daño);* —se, to avoid *(evitar);* to protect oneself *(preservarse);* — **rencor,** to hold a grudge.

guardarropa (gwâr•thâ•rro´pâ)

m. ward-robe; checkroom *(en local público),* —, *f* (theat.) wardrobe mistress; check girl.

guardavidas (gwâr•thâ•vē´thâs) *m.* lifeguard.

guardería (guar•the•rē´â) *f.* day nursery.

guardia (guâr´thyâ) *f.* guard; keeping, care *(custodia);* (naut.) watch; —, *m.* guardsman; — **civil,** national guardsman.

guardián, ana (gwâr•thyân´, â´nâ) *n.* keeper, guardian.

guarida (gwâ•rē´thâ) *f.* den, lair; refuge, shelter *(amparo).*

guarnecer* (gwâr•ne•ser´) *va.* to set *(engastar);* to garnish, to decorate *(adornar);* (mil.) to garrison; to provide, to supply *(suministrar).*

guarnición (gwâr•nē•syon´) *f.* setting; decoration, garnishment; (mil.) garrison.

guasa (gwâ´sâ) *f.* (ichth.) jewfish; (coll.) stupidity, dullness *(pesadez)*; fun, jest *(broma).*

guasón, ona (gwâ•son´, o´na) *adj.* (coll.) dull, boring *(soso);* humorous, witty, sharp, fond of jokes *(bromista);* —, *n.* joker.

guatemalteco, ca (gwâ•te•mâl•te´ko, kâ) *n.* and *adj.* Guatemalan.

guayaba (gwâ•yâ´vâ) *f.* guava.

guayabo (gwâ•yâ´vo) *m.* guava tree.

gubernamental (gū•ver•na•men•tâl´) *adj.* governmental.

gubernativo, va (gū•ver•nâ•tē´vo, vâ) *adj.* governmental.

güero, ra (gwe´ro, râ) *adj.* (Mex.) blond, fair-haired; —, *n.* towhead; light-skinned.

guerra (ge´rrâ) *f.* war; hostility *(discordia);* —**fría,** cold war; — **nuclear,** nuclear war; — **química,** chemical warfare; — **de guerrillas,** guerrilla warfare; **hacer la —,** to wage war; **dar —,** to cause trouble, to be a nuisance.

guerrero (ge•rre´ro) *m.* warrior; —, **ra,** *adj.* martial, warlike.

guerrilla (ge•rrē´yâ) *f.* guerilla warfare; guerrilla party *(partida).*

guía (gē´â) *m.* and *f.* guide; —, *f.* guide; guidebook *(libro).*

guiar (gyâr) *va.* to guide, to lead; (auto.) to drive.

guiñada (gē•nyâ´thâ) *f.* wink.

guiñapo (gē•nyâ´po) *m.* tatter, rag.

guiñar (gē•nyâr´) *va.* to wink.

guión (gyon) *m.* banner, standard; (fig.) leader *(guía);* outline *(escrito breve);* script *(argumento);* (gram.) hyphen.

guirnalda (gēr•nâl´dâ) *f.* garland, wreath.

guisado (gē•sâ´tho) *m.* meat

stew *(de carne);* stew.

guisar (gē•sär´) *va.* to cook, to stew; (fig.) to prepare, to ready *(aderezar).*

guiso (gē´so) *m.* stewed dish, stew.

guitarra (gē•tâ´rrâ) *f.* guitar.

guitarrista (gē•tâ•rrēs´tâ) *m.* and *f.* guitar player.

gula (gū´lâ) *f.* gluttony.

gusano (gū•sâ´no) *m.* worm; — **de luz,** glowworm, — **de seda,** silkworm.

gustación (gūs•tâ•syon´) *f.* tast-

ing.

gustar (gūs•tär´) *va.* to taste; —, *vn.* to be pleasing, to be enjoyable; — **de,** to have a liking for, to take pleasure in.

gusto (gūs´to) *m.* taste; pleasure, delight *(placer);* decision, choice *(voluntad);* **a —,** to one´s liking, however one wishes; **tener — en,** to be glad to; **tanto —,** glad to meet you.

gutural (gū•tū•râl´) *adj.* guttural.

H

haba (â´vâ) *f.* (bot.) broad bean.

Habana (â•vâ´nâ) *f.* Havana.

habanero, ra (â•vâ•ne´ro, râ) *n.* and *adj.* Havanan; —, *f.* habanera.

habano (â•vâ´no) *m.* Havana cigar.

haber* (â•ver´) *va.* to get hold of; —, *v. auxiliary* to have; —, *vn.* there to be; **va a —,** there is going to be; — **de** to have to; —, *m.* (com.) credit side; —**es,** *pl.* property, goods; **hay,** there is, there are.

habichuela (â•vē•chwe´lâ) *f.* kidney bean; — **verde,** string bean.

hábil (â´vēl) *adj.* capable, quali-

fied *(capaz);* skillful, clever *(ingenioso).*

habilidad (â•vē•lē•thâth´) *f.* qualification, capacity; aptitude, skillfulness, ability.

habilitado, da (â•vē•lē•tâ´tho, thâ) *adj.* qualified; —, *m.* paymaster.

habilitar (â•vē•lē•târ´) *va.* to qualify, to enable; to equip, to furnish *(proveer).*

habitación (â•vē•tâ•syon´) *f.* dwelling, residence *(domicilio);* room *(aposento);* (zool.) habitat.

habitante (â•vē•tân´te) *m.* and *f.* inhabitant.

habitar (â•vē•târ´) *va.* to inhabit, to live in.

hábito (a´vē•to) *m.* dress *(vestido);* custom, habit *(costumbre).*

habitual (â•vē•twâl´) *adj.* habitual, customary, usual.

habituar (â•vē•twâr´) *va.* to accustom; **—se,** to accustom oneself, to get used.

habla (â´vlâ) *f.* speech; **sin —,** speechless.

hablador, ra (â•vlâ•thor´, râ) *n.* chatterbox *(parlanchín);* gossip *(murmurador);* **—,** *adj.* talkative; gossipy.

hablar (a•vlâr´) *vn.* to talk; to speak *(conversar);* **—,** *va.* to say *(decir);* to speak *(un idioma).*

hacedor, ra (â•se•thor´, râ) *n.* maker, creator; manager *(de una hacienda).*

hacendado (â •sen•dâ´tho) *m.* landowner, property owner; (Sp. Am.) rancher; **—, da,** *adj.* landed.

hacendoso, sa (a•sen•do´so, sâ) *adj.* domestic, good around the house.

hacer* (â•ser´) *va.* to make *(crear);* to work *(obrar);* to make up *(arreglar);* to contain *(contener);* to get used *(acostumbrar);* to do *(ocuparse en);* to make *(obligar);* to play *(aparentar);* **—,** *vn.* to matter; **— alarde,** to boast; **— alto,** to halt; **— burla,** to poke fun at;

— calor, to be warm.

hacia (â´syâ) *prep.* toward; about *(cerca de);* **— acá,** this way, over here; **— atrás,** backward; **— abajo,** down, downward; **— arriba,** up, upward.

hacienda (â•syen´dâ) *f.* holdings, possessions *(fortuna);* farm, country place *(finca).*

hacina, (â•sē•nâr´) *va.* to stack up, to pile up.

hacha (â´châ) *f.* ax *(herramienta);* torch *(tea de esparto).*

hada (â´thâ) *f.* fairy; **cuento de —s,** fairy tale.

haitiano, na (âē•tyâ´no, nâ) *n.* and *adj.* Haitian.

halagar (â•lâ•gâr´) *va.* to please; to cajole, to flatter *(lisonjear).*

halago (â•lâ´go) *m.* pleasure, appeal *(agrado);* flattery *(lisonja).*

halagüeño, ña (a•lâ•gwe´nyo, nyâ) *adj.* pleasing, appealing; flattering.

halcón (âl•kon´) *m.* falcon, hawk.

hálito (â´lē•to) *m.* breath; (poet.) gentle breeze.

halo (â´lo) *m.* halo.

haltera (âl•te´râ) *f.* barbell, weight.

hallazgo (â•yâz´go) *m.* finding, location *(acción);* find, discovery *(cosa hallada);* reward *(recompensa).*

hamaca (â•mâ′kâ) *f.* hammock.

hambre (âm′bre) *f.* hunger; famine *(escasez);* **tener —,** to be hungry; **matar el —,** to satisfy one's hunger.

hambriento, ta (âm•bryen′to, tâ) *adj.* hungry.

hamburguesa (âm•būr•ge′sâ) *f.* hamburger.

hangar (âng•gâr′) *m.* hangar.

haragán, ana (â•râ•gân′, â′nâ) *n.* idler, loafer, good-for-nothing; **—,** *adj.* lazy, idle.

harapiento, ta (â•râ•pyen′to, tâ) *adj.* ragged, in tatters.

harapo (â•râ′po) *m.* rag, tatter.

haraposo, sa (â•râ•po′so, sâ) *adj.* ragged.

harén (â•ren′) *m.* harem.

harina (â•rē′nâ) *f.* flour; fine powder *(polvo menudo);* **— de maíz,** corn meal.

harinero (â•rē•ne′ro) *m.* flour dealer; **—, ra,** *adj.* flour.

harmonía (âr•mo•nē′â) *f.* harmony.

hartar (ar•târ′) *va.* to stuff, to satiate *(saciar);* (fig.) to satisfy, to appease *(satisfacer);* to bore, to tire *(molestar);* **—se,** to be fed up.

harto, ta (âr′to, tâ) *adj.* satiated; sufficient *(bastante);* **—to,** *adv.* enough.

hasta (âs′tâ) *prep.* until, till *(tiempo);* as far as *(espacio);* as much as *(cantidad);* **— ahora** or **— aquí,** till now; **— luego** or **— después,** see you later; **— no más,** to the very limit; **— la vista,** I'll be seeing you; **—** *conj.* even.

hastío (âs•tē′o) *m.* aversion, disgust.

haya (â′yâ) *f.* beech tree.

haz (âs) *m.* bundle; beam *(de rayos);* **—,** *f.* face; (fig.) surface *(de una tela).*

hazaña (â•sâ′nyâ) *f.* exploit, achievement, feat.

he (e) *adv.* **— allí,** there is; **— aquí,** here is; **—me aquí,** here I am.

hebilla (e•vē′yâ) *f.* buckle.

hebraico, ca (e•vrâ′ē•ko, kâ) *adj.* Hebraic.

hebreo, ea (e•vre′o, e′â) *n.* and *adj.* Hebrew; **—,** *m.* Hebrew language.

hectárea (ek•tâ′re•â) *f.* hectare.

hechicería (e •chē•se•rē′â) *f.* witchcraft; enchantment *(encanto).*

hechicero, ra (e•chē•se′ro, râ) *adj.* bewitching; **—,** *f.* witch, sorceress; **—,** *m.* warlock, sorcerer.

hechizar (e•chē•sâr′) *va.* to bewitch, to enchant.

hechizo (e•chē′so) *m.* enchantment, spell.

hecho, cha (e′cho, châ.) *adj.*

made, done; used, accustomed *(acostumbrado);* **bien —,** well done; **mal —,** poorly done; **—,** *m.* happening *(acontecimiento);* matter *(asunto);* act *(acción).*

hechura (e•chū´râ) *f.* construction, workmanship *(composición);* creature, creation *(criatura);* shape, appearance *(forma);* making *(acción).*

heder* (e•ther´) *vn.* to stink, to smell bad.

hediondo, da (e•thyon´do, dâ) *adj.* fetid, stinking, malodorous.

heladería (e•lâ•the•rē´â) *f.* ice-cream parlor.

helado, da (e •lâ´tho, thâ) *adj.* freezing, like ice; (fig.) cold *(desdeñoso);* astounded, thunderstruck *(atónito);* **—,** *m.* ice cream.

helar* (e•lâr´) *va.* to freeze; (fig.) to strike *(dejar suspenso);* to discourage *(desanimar);* **—se,** to freeze.

helecho (e•le´cho) *m.* (bot.) fern.

hélice (e´lē•se) *f.* helix; (avi.) propeller.

helicóptero (e•lē•kop´te•ro) *m.* helicopter.

helio (e´lyo) *m.* helium.

hembra (em´brâ) *f.* female; eye *(de un corchete);* nut *(de tornillo).*

hemisferio (e•mēs•fe´ryo) *m.* hemisphere.

hemoglobina (e•mo•glo•vē´nâ) *f.* (med.) hemoglobin.

hemorragia (e•mo•rrâ´hyâ) *f.* (med.) hemorrhage.

hemorroides (e•mo•rro´ē•thes) *f. pl.* piles, hemorrhoids.

henchir* (en•chēr´) *va.* to fill, to stuff; **—se,** to overeat, to stuff oneself.

hendedura (en•de•thū´râ) = **hendidura.**

hender* (en•der´) *va.* to split; to cut one´s way through *(abrirse paso).*

hendidura (en•dē•thū´ra) *f.* crack, split.

heno (e´no) *m.* hay.

hepatitis (e•pâ•tē´tēs) *f.* (med.) hepatitis.

heraldo (e•râl´do) *m.* herald.

herbaje (er•vâ´he) *m.* herbage, pasture.

hercúleo, ea (er•kū´le•o, e•â) *adj.* herculean.

heredar (e•re•thâr´) *va.* to inherit.

hereditario, ria (e•re•thē•tâ´ryo, ryâ) *adj.* hereditary.

heredero, ra (e•re•the´ro, râ) *n.* heir; heiress.

hereje (e•re´he) *m. and f.* heretic.

herejía (e•re•hē´â) *f.* heresy.

herencia (e•ren´syâ) *f.* inheritance, heritage; (biol.) heredity.

herético, ca (e•re′tē•ko, kâ) *adj.* heretic.

herida (e•rē′thâ) *f.* wound, injury.

herido, da (e•rē′tho, thâ) *adj.* wounded, injured.

herir* (e•rēr′) *va.* to wound, to injure; (fig.) to hurt; to touch *(el corazón).*

hermafrodita (er•mâ•fro•thē′tâ) *adj.* hermaphrodite.

hermanastra (er•mâ•nâs′trâ) *f.* stepsister, half sister.

hermanastro (er•mâ•nâs′tro) *m.* stepbrother, half brother.

hermandad (er•man•dâth′) *f.* fraternity, brotherhood; (fig.) affinity, likeness *(correspondencia).*

hermano, na (er•mâ′no, nâ) *n.* brother; sister; mate *(de cosas);* **primo —** or **prima —,** first cousin; **—na de la Caridad,** Sister of Charity.

hermético, ca (er•me′tē•ko, kâ) *adj.* hermetic, airtight.

hermosear (er•mo•se•âr′) *va.* to beautify, to make handsome.

hermoso (er•mo′so, sâ) *adj.* beautiful, handsome.

hermosura (er•mo•sū′râ) *f.* beauty.

hernia (er′nyâ) *f.* hernia.

héroe (e′ro•e) *m.* hero.

heroicidad (e•roē•sē•thâth′) *f.* heroism.

heroico, ca (e•ro′ē•ko, kâ) *adj.* heroics.

heroísmo (e•ro•ēz′mo) *m.* heroism.

herradura (e•rrâ•thū′râ) *f.* horseshoe.

herramienta (e•rrâ•myen′tâ) *f.* tool, implement *(instrumento);* set of tools *(conjunto);* (coll.) choppers, grinders *(dentadura).*

herrar* (e•rrâr′) *va.* to shoe; to brand *(marcar).*

herrero (e•rre′ro) *m.* blacksmith.

herrumbre (e•rrūm′bre) *f.* rust, rustiness.

hervidero (er•vē•the′ro) *m.* boiling, bubbling; (fig.) bubbling spring *(manantial);* rattle, wheeze *(del pecho);* swarm, throng *(muchedumbre).*

hervir* (er•vēr′) *vn.* to boil; (fig.) to be teeming *(abundar).*

hervor (er•vor′) *m.* boiling, boil; (fig.) fire, spirit *(ardor).*

heterogéneo, nea (e•te•ro•he′ne•o, ne•â) *adj.* heterogeneous.

hexágono (ek•sâ′go•no) *m.* hexagon.

hexámetro (ek•sâ′me•tro) *m.* hexameter.

híbrido, da (e′vrē•tho, thâ) *adj.* and *n.* hybrid.

hidalgo, ga (ē•thâl′go, gâ) **—,** *adj.* noble, illustrious; **—,** *m.* nobleman; **—,** *f.* noblewoman.

hidratación (ē•thrâ•tâ•syon´) *f.* hydration.

hidráulico, ca (ē•thrâ´ū•lē•ko, kâ) *adj.* hydraulic.

hidroeléctrico, ca (ē•thro•e•lek´trē•ko, kâ) *adj.* hydroelectric.

hidrofobia (ē•thro•fo´vyâ) *f.* hydrophobia, rabies.

hidrógeno (ē•thro´he•no) *m.* (chem.) hydrogen; **— líquido,** liquid hydrogen.

hiedra (ye´thrâ) *f.* ivy.

hiel (yel´) *f.* gall, bile.

hielo (ye´lo) *m.* ice; (fig.) coldness *(frialdad);* **— seco,** dry ice.

hiena (ye´nâ) *f.* hyena.

hierba (yer´vâ) *f.* grass; **— mate,** (bot.) maté; **— medecinal,** herb.

hierbabuena (yer•vâ•vwe´nâ) *f.* (bot.) mint.

hierro (ye´rro) *m.* iron; brand *(marca);* **—s,** *pl.* fetters; **— colado** or **de fundición,** or **fundido,** cast iron; **— forjado** or **de fragua,** wrought iron.

hígado (ē´gâ•tho) *m.* liver; (coll.) guts, courage *(valentía).*

higiene (ē•hye´ne) *f.* hygiene.

higiénico, ca (ē•hye´nē•ko, kâ) *adj.* hygienic, sanitary; **papel — co,** toilet paper, bathroom tissue.

higo (ē´go) *m.* fig.

higuera (ē•ge´râ) *f.* fig tree.

hijastro, tra (ē•hâs´tro, trâ) *n.* stepchild.

hijo, ja (ē´ho, hâ) *n.* child, offspring *(de un animal);* brainchild *(obra);* **—,** *m.* son; **—,** *f.* daughter.

hilacha (ē•lâ´châ) *f.* ravel, shred.

hilado (ē•lâ´tho) *m.* spinning; thread, yarn *(producto).*

hilador, ra (ē•la•thor´, râ) *n.* spinner; **—,** *adj.* spinning.

hilar (ē•lâr´) *va.* to spin.

hilera (ē•le´râ) *f.* row, line, file.

hilo (ē´lo) *m.* thread *(hebra);* linen *(tela);* wire *(alambre);* thin stream, trickle *(chorro);* thread *(del discurso);* **cortar el —,** (fig.) to interrupt; **al —,** with the grain.

hilvanar (ēl•vâ•nâr´) *va.* to baste; (fig.) to tie together *(enlazar);* (coll.) to throw together.

himno (ēm´no) *m.* hymn; anthem *(canto nacional).*

hincapié (ēng•kâ•pye´) *m.* getting a foot-hold, taking a firm stance; **hacer — en,** to stress, to emphasize, to underline.

hincar (ēng•kâr´) *va.* to thrust in, to drive in; **— el diente,** to bite; **—se,** to kneel down.

hinchar (ēn•châr´) *va.* to swell; (fig.) to puff up *(exagerar);* **—se,** to swell up; to puff up *(envanecerse).*

hinchazón (ēn•châ•son´) *f.*

swelling; ostentation, vanity
(ostentación).

hindú (ēn´dū´) *m.* and *f.* and
adj. Hindu.

hipérbole (ē•per´vo•le) *f.* hyperbole.

hipersónico, ca (ē•per•so´nē•ko,
kâ) *adj.* hypersonic.

hipertensión (ē•per•ten•syon´) *f.*
hypertension.

hipnótico, ca (ēp•no´tē•ko, kâ)
adj. hypnotic.

hipnotismo (ēp•no•tēz´mo) *m.*
hypnotism.

hipnotizar (ēp•no•tē•sâr´) *va.* to
hypnotize.

hipo (ē´po) *m.* hiccough.

hipocondría (ē•po•kon•drē´â) *f.*
hypochondria.

hipocresía (ē•po•kre•sē´â) *f.*
hypocrisy.

hipócrita (ē•po´krē•tâ) *adj.* hypocritical; —, *m.* and *f.* hypocrite.

hipodérmico, ca
(ē•po•ther´mē•ko, kâ) *adj.*
hypodermic.

hipódromo, (ē•po´thro•mo) *m.*
race track.

hipopótamo (ē•po•po´tâ•mo) *m.*
hippopotamus.

hipoteca (ē•po•te´kâ) *f.* mortgage.

hipotecar (ē•po•te•kâr´) *va.* to
mortgage.

hipotecario, ria (ē•po•te•kâ´ryo,
ryâ) *adj.* mortgage; **juicio —,**

mortgage foreclosure.

hipotensión (ē•po•ten•syon´) *f.*
hypotension.

hipótesis (ē•po´te•sēs) *f.* hypothesis.

hipotético, ca (ē•po•te´tē•ko, kâ)
adj. hypothetical.

hirviente (ēr•vyen´te) *adj.* boiling.

hispano, na (ēs•pâ´no, nâ) *adj.*
Hispanic.

Hispanoamérica
(ēs•pâ•no•â•me´rē•kâ) *f.*
Spanish America.

hispanoamericano, na
(ēs•pâ•no•â•me•rē•kâ´no, nâ)
adj. and *n.* Spanish American.

histamina (ēs•tâ•mē´nâ) *f.* hista-
mine.

histérico, ca (ēs•te´rē•ko, kâ)
adj. hysterical.

histerismo (ēs•te•rēz´mo) *m.*
hysteria.

historia (ēs•to´ryâ) *f.* history;
tale, story *(cuento)*.

historiador, ra (ēs•to•ryâ•thor´,
râ) *n.* historian.

historial (ēs•to•ryâl´) *adj.* historical; —, *m.* background.

histórico, ca (ēs•to´rē•ko, kâ)
adj. historical, historic.

historieta (ēs•to•rye´tâ) *f.* short
story, anecdote; — **cómica,**
comic strip.

hito (ē´to) *m.* landmark, guidepost; (fig.) target *(blanco)*; **a —,**

fixedly; **mirar de — en —,** to stare at, to fix one's gaze on.

hocico (o•sē´ko) *m.* snout, muzzle; (coll.) face; **meter el — en todo,** (coll.) to stick one's nose into everything.

hogar (o•gâr´) *m.* hearth, fireplace; home *(casa).*

hogareño, ña (o•gâ•re´nyo, nyâ) *adj.* home-loving.

hoguera (o•ge´râ) *f.* bonfire, huge blaze.

hoja (o´hâ) *f.* leaf; blade *(cuchilla);* sheet hoja *(de papel);* **— de afeitar,** razor blade; **— de apunte,** tally sheet; **— de cálculo,** spreadsheet; **— de lata,** tin; **— de ruta,** (avi.) flight plan; **— en blanco,** blank sheet.

hojalata (o•hâ•lâ´tâ) *f.* tinplate, tin.

hojaldre (o•hâl´dre) *f.* puff paste.

hojarasca (o•hâ•râs´kâ) *f.* dead leaves; excess leafage *(de un árbol);* (fig.) dross, froth.

hojear (o•he•âr´) *va.* to skim through, to scan.

¡hola! (o´lâ) *interj.* hello! hi!

Holanda (o•lân´dâ) *f.* Holland.

holandés, esa (o•lân•des´, e´sâ) *adj.* Dutch.

holgado, da (ol•gâ´tho, thâ) *adj.* unoccupied, idle; roomy, ample, wide *(ancho);* (fig.) leisurely, worry-free.

holganza (ol•gân´sâ) *f.* leisure, relaxation; laziness *(pereza);* pleasure, joy *(placer).*

holgar* (ol•gâr´) *vn.* to rest *(descansar);* to be useless *(ser inútil);* **—se,** to amuse oneself.

holgazán, ana (ol•gâ•sân´, â´nâ) *n.* idler, loafer; **—,** *adj.* lazy, do-nothing.

holgazanear (ol•gâ•sâ•ne•âr´) *vn.* to idle, to loaf.

holgura (ol•gū´râ) *f.* frolic, merrymaking; roominess *(anchura);* ease, comfort *(bienestar).*

holocausto (o•lo•kâ´ūs•to) *m.* holocaust.

hollar* (o•yâr´) *va.* to trample, to tread upon.

hombre (om´bre) *m.* man; omber *(juego de naipes);* **— de bien,** honorable man; **— de negocios,** businessman; **— de letras,** literary man; **— de Estado,** statesman; **— de ciencia,** scientist; **— rana,** frogman.

hombría (om•brē´â) *f.* manhood.

hombro (om´bro) *m.* shoulder.

homenaje (o•me•nâ´he) *m.* homage, tribute; **rendir —,** to pay homage, to honor.

homeopatía (o•me•o•pâ•tē´â) *f.* (med.) homeopathy.

homicida (o•mē•sē´thâ) *m.* and *f.* homicide; **—,** *adj.* homicidal.

homicidio (o•mē•sē´thyo) *m.* homicide.

homogéneo, nea (o•mo•he´ne•o, ne•â) *adj.* homogeneous.

homogenizar (o•mo•he•nē•sâr´) *va.* to homogenize.

honda (on´dâ) *f.* slingshot.

hondear (on•de•âr´) *va.* (naut.) to sound.

hondo, da (on´do, dâ) *adj.* deep; (fig.) profound.

hondura (on•dū´râ) *f.* depth, profundity; **meterse en —s,** (coll.) to get into deep water, to go over one´s head.

hondureño, ña (on•dū•re´nyo, nyâ) *n.* and *adj.* Honduran.

honestidad (o•nes•tē•thâth´) *f.* integrity, decency; politeness, decorum *(urbanidad).*

honesto, ta (o•nes´to, tâ) *adj.* decent; polite, polished, refined.

hongo (ong´go) *m.* mushroom; fungus; derby *(sombrero).*

honor (o•nor´) *m.* honor.

honorable (o•no•râ´vle) *adj.* honorable.

honorífico, ca (o•no•rē´fē•ko, kâ) *adj.* honorable; **mención —ca,** honorable mention.

honra (on´rrâ) *f.* honor, self-respect; repute, acclaim *(buena fama).*

honradez (on•rrâ•thes´) *f.* honesty.

honrado, da (on•rrâ´tho, thâ) *adj.* honest.

honra, (on•rrâr´) *va.* to honor; **—se,** to deem it an honor.

honroso, sa (on•rro´so, sâ) *adj.* honorable.

hora (o´râ) *f.* hour; time *(momento de terminado);* **— de comer,** mealtime; **media —,** half an hour.

horadar (o•râ•thâr´) *va.* to drill a hole through.

horario, ria (o•râ´ryo, ryâ) *adj.* hourly; **—,** *m.* hour hand *(de reloj);* timetable, schedule.

horca (or´kâ) *f.* gallows; (agr.) pitchfork.

horchata (or•châ´tâ) *f.* orgeat.

horizontal (o•rē•son•tâl´) *adj.* horizontal.

horizonte (o•rē•son´te) *m.* horizon.

horma (or´mâ) *f.* mold, form; **— de zapatos,** shoe last.

hormiga (or•mē´gâ) *f.* ant.

hormiguear (or•mē•ge•âr´) *vn.* to itch, to crawl *(picar);* (fig.) to swarm, to flock.

hormiguero (or•mē•ge´ro) *m.* anthill.

hormona (or•mo´nâ) *f.* hormone.

hornada (or•nâ´thâ) *f.* batch.

hornear (or•ne•âr´) *va.* to bake; **—,** *vn.* to be a baker.

hornilla (or•nē´yâ) *f.* burner.

horno (or´no) *m.* oven; **alto —,** blast furnace; **— de ladrillo,** brick kiln.

horóscopo (o•ros´ko•po) *m.* horoscope.

horrendo, da (o•rren´do, dâ) *adj.* horrible, hideous.

horrible (o•rrē´vle) *adj.* horrid, horrible.

horror (o•rror´) *m.* horror.

horrorizar (o•rro•rē•sâr´) *va.* to horrify.

horroroso, sa (o•rro•ro´so, sâ) *adj.* horrible, hideous.

hortaliza (or•tâ•lē´sâ) *f.* vegetable.

horticultura (or•tē•kūl•tū´râ) *f.* horticulture.

hosco, ca (os´ko, kâ) *adj.* dark *(oscuro);* sullen, gloomy *(severo).*

hospedaje (os•pe•thâ´he) *m.* lodging.

hospedar (os•pe•thâr´) *va.* to lodge, to put up; **—se en,** to lodge at, to put up at.

hospicio (os•pē´syo) *m.* home, asylum; **— de huérfanos,** orphanage.

hospital (os•pē•tâl´) *m.* hospital.

hospitalidad (os•pē•tâ•lē•thâth´) *f.* hospitality

hospitalización (os•pē•tâ•lē•sâ•syon´) *f.* hospitalization.

hostería (os•te•rē´â) *f.* inn.

hostia (os´tyâ) *f.* wafer; (eccl.) Host.

hostigar (os•tē•gâr´) *va.* to whip *(azotar);* to harass, to keep after *(acosar).*

hostil (os•tēl´) *adj.* hostile, adverse.

hostilidad (os•tē•lē•thâth´) *f.* hostility, enmity.

hostilizar (os•tē•lē•sâr´) *va.* to inflict damage on, to make telling inroads on.

hotel (o•tel´) *m.* hotel.

hotelero, ra (o•te•le´ro, râ) *n.* innkeeper; **—,** *adj.* hotel; **industria —,** hotel industry.

hoy (o´ē) *adv.* today; **de — en adelante,** henceforth, from now on; **— día,** nowadays.

hoyo (o´yo) *m.* hole; pit *(en una superficie);* grave *(tumba).*

hoz (os) *f.* sickle.

huarache (wâ•râ´che) *m.* (Mex.) sandal.

hueco, ca (we´ko, kâ) *adj.* hollow; deep *(voz);* fluffy, soft *(mullido);* pretentious *(afectado);* **—,** *m.* hollow; space *(intervalo);* (coll.) opening *(empleo vacante).*

huelga (wel´gâ) *f.* strike; **— de brazos caídos,** sit-down strike.

huella (we´yâ) *f.* track, trace; **—s digitales,** fingerprints.

huérfano, na (wer´fâ•no, nâ) *n.* and *adj.* orphan.

huerta (wer´tâ) *f.* large orchard; vast irrigated area *(terreno de regadío).*

huerto (wer´to) *m.* vegetable garden, kitchen garden; orchard *(de árboles frutales).*

hueso (we´so) *m.* bone; stone *(del fruto);* (fig.) hard job *(cosa dificultosa).*

huésped, da (wes´peth, thâ) *n.* innkeeper *(mesonero);* guest, roomer, boarder *(persona alojada);* (biol.) host, —, *m.* host; —, *f.* hostess.

huesudo, da (we•sū´tho, thâ) *adj.* bony. —, *f.* (orn.) oviduct.

huevo (we´vo) *m.* egg; (biol.) ovum; — **cocido,** hard-boiled egg; — **condimentado con picantes,** deviled egg; — **frito** or — **estrellado,** fried egg; — **pasado por agua,** or — **tibio,** soft-boiled egg; —**s revueltos,** scrambled eggs.

huida (wē´thâ) *f.* flight, escape.

huir* (wēr) *vn.* to flee, to escape.

hule (ū´le) *m.* rubber; oilcloth *(tela);* — **espuma,** foam rubber.

humanidad (ū•mâ•nē•thâth´) *f.* humanity.

humanitario, ria (ū•mâ•nē•tâ´ryo, ryâ) *n.* and *adj.* humanitarian.

humano, na (ū•mâ´no, nâ) *adj.* human; humane, kind *(bondadoso).*

humeante (ū•me•ân´te) *adj.* smoking; steaming.

humear (ū•me•âr´) *vn.* to smoke; to steam *(despedir vapor).*

humedad (ū•me•thâth´) *f.* humidity, moisture.

humedecedor (ū•me•the•se•thor´) *m.* humidifier.

humedecer* (ū•me•the• ser´) *va.* to moisten, to wet.

húmedo, da (ū´me•tho, thâ) *adj.* humid, damp, moist; wet *(cargado de líquido).*

humildad (ū•mēl•dâth´) *f.* humility; humbleness *(sumisión).*

humilde (ū•mēl´de) *adj.* humble; **de — cuna,** of humble birth.

humillación (ū•mē•yâ•syon´) *f.* humiliation.

humillar (ū•mē•yâr´) *va.* to humble, to humiliate; to bend down, to bow down *(doblar);* — **se,** to humble oneself.

humo (ū´mo) *m.* smoke; fume, steam *(vapor).*

humor (ū•mor´) *m.* humor; **buen** —, good humor; **mal** —, moodiness; **estar de buen** —, to be in good spirits, to be in a good mood.

humorismo (ū•mo•rēz´mo) *m.* humor.

humorista (ū•mo•rēs´tâ) *m.* and *f.* humorist.

hundimiento (ūn•dē•myen´to) *m.* sinking.

hundir (ūn•dēr´) *vn.* to sink;

(fig.) to stump *(confundir)*; to ruin, to defeat *(abrumar)*; **—se,** (fig.) to be wrecked, to be ruined; (coll.) to drop out of sight *(desaparecer)*.

húngaro, ra (ūng′gâ•ro, râ) *adj.* and *n.* Hungarian.

Hungría (ūng•grē′â) *f.* Hungary.

huracán (ū•râ′•kân′) *m.* hurricane.

hurgón (ūr•gon′) *m.* poker.

hurtadillas (ūr•tâ•thē′yâs) **a —,** stealthily.

hurtar (ūr•târ′) *va.* to steal; (fig.) to move aside *(apartar)*.

husmear (ūz•me•âr′) *va.* to scent; to pry into, to poke into *(averiguar)*.

husmeo (ūz•me′o) *m.* prying.

huso (ū′so) *m.* spindle.

I

ibérico, ca (ē•ve′rē•ko, kâ) *adj.* Iberian.

iberoamericano, na (ē•ve•ro•â•me•rē•kâ′no, nâ) *adj.* and *n.* Ibero-American.

ictericia (ēk•te•rē′syâ) *f.* jaundice.

ida (ē′thâ) *f.* going; (fig.) dash, start *(ímpetu)*; **—s y venidas,** comings and goings; **billete** or **boleto de — y vuelta,** round-trip ticket.

idea (ē•the′â) *f.* idea; **cambiar de —,** to change one's mind.

ideal (ē•the•âl′) *m.* and *adj.* ideal.

idealismo (ē•the•â•lēz′mo) *m.* idealism.

idealista (ē•the•â•lēs′tâ) *m.* and *f.* idealist; **—,** *adj.* idealistic.

idealización (ē•the•â•lē•sâ•syon′) *f.* idealization.

idear (ē•the•âr′) *va.* to think up, to plan.

idéntico, ca (ē•then′tē•ko, kâ) *adj.* identical.

identidad (ē•then•tē•thâth′) *f.* identity; **cédula de —,** identification card.

identificar (ē•then•tē•fē•kâr′) *va.* to identify; **—se,** to identify oneself.

ideología (ē•the•o•lo•hē′â) *f.* ideology.

ideológico, ca (ē•the•o•lo′ hē•ko, kâ) *adj.* ideological.

idioma (ē•thyo′mâ) *m.* language.

idiomático, ca (ē•thyo•mâ′tē•ko, kâ) *adj.* idiomatic.

idiosincrasia (ē•thyo•sēng•krâ′syâ) *f.* individual temperament, own ways, idiosyncrasy.

idiota (ē•thyoʹtâ) *m.* and *f.* idiot;
—, *adj.* idiotic.

idiotez (ē•thyo•tesʹ) *f.* idiocy.

idólatra (ē•thoʹlâ•trâ) *m.* and *f.*
idolater.

idolatrar (ē•tho•lâ•trârʹ) *va.* to
idolize.

idolatría (ē•tho•lâ•trēʹâ) *f.* idolatry.

ídolo (ēʹtho•lo) *m.* idol.

iglesia (ē•gleʹsyâ) *f.* church.

ignición (ēg•nē•syonʹ) *f.* ignition.

ignorancia (ēg•no•rânʹsyâ) *f.*
ignorance.

ignorante (ēg•no•rânʹte) *adj.*
ignorant.

ignorar (ēg•no•rârʹ) *va.* to be
unaware of, not to know.

igual (ē•gwâlʹ) *adj.* equal; like
(muy parecido); the same (de la
misma clase); constant *(que no
varía);* smooth *(liso).*

igualar (ē•gwâ•larʹ) *va.* to
smooth out *(allanar);* to equalize, to make equal *(hacer
igual);* (fig.) to equate *(juzgar
igual);* —, *vn.* to be equal.

igualdad (ē•gwâl•dâthʹ) *f.* equality.

iguana (ē•gwâʹnâ) *f.* iguana.

ilegal (ē•le•gâlʹ) *adj.* illegal,
unlawful.

ilegítimo, ma (ē•le•hēʹtē•mo, mâ)
adj. illegitimate.

ileso, sa (ē•leʹso, sâ) *adj.*
unhurt.

ilícito, ta (ē•lēʹsē•to, tâ) *adj.* illicit, unlawful.

ilimitado, da (ē•lē•mē•tâʹtho,
thâ) *adj.* unlimited, boundless.

ilógico, ca (ē•loʹhē•ko, kâ) *adj.*
illogical.

iluminación (ē•lū•mē•nâ•syonʹ)
f. illumination.

iluminar (ē•lū•mē•nârʹ) *va.* to
illuminate.

ilusión (ē•lū•syonʹ) *f.* illusion.

ilusionarse (ē•lū•syo•nârʹse) *vr.*
to daydream, to indulge in
wishful thinking.

iluso, sa (ē•lūʹso, sâ) *adj.* delud-
ed; visionary *(soñador).*

ilusorio, ria (ē•lū•soʹryo, ryâ)
adj. illusory.

ilustración (ē•lūs•trâ•syonʹ) *f.*
illustration *(grabado);* enlightenment *(movimiento);* learning
(instrucción).

ilustrar (ē•lūs•trârʹ) *va.* to illustrate; to enlighten *(instruir).*

ilustre (ē•lūsʹtre) *adj.* illustrious,
eminent.

imagen (ē•mâʹhen) *f.* image.

imaginación (ē•mâʹ•hē•nâ•syonʹ)
f. imagination; fancy, figment
(cosa imaginada).

imaginar (ē•mâ•hē•nârʹ) *va.* to
imagine.

imaginario, ria (ē•mâ•hē•nâʹryo,
ryâ) *adj.* imaginary.

imán (ē•mânʹ) *m.* magnet.

imbécil (ēm•be´sēl) *m.* and *f.* imbecile; —, *adj.* imbecilic; idiotic, foolish *(tonto).*

imbuir* (ēm•bwēr´) *va.* to imbue.

imitación (ē•mē•tâ•syon´) *f.* imitation.

imitador, ra (e•mē•tâ•thor´, râ) *n.* imitator; —, *adj.* imitative.

imitar (ē•mē•târ´) *va.* to imitate.

impaciencia (ēm•pâ•syen´syâ) *f.* impatience.

impaciente (ēm•pâ•syen´te) *adj.* impatient.

impacto, (ēm•pâk´to) *m.* impact.

impar (ēm•pâr´) *adj.* odd, uneven *(número);* unmatched.

imparcial (ēm•pâr•syâl´) *adj.* impartial.

imparcialidad (ēm•pâr•syâ•lē•thâth´) *f.* impartiality.

impartir (ēm•pâr•tēr´) *va.* to impart.

impasible (ēm•pâ•sē´vle) *adj.* impassible; impassive *(insensible).*

impávido, da (ēm•pâ´vē•tho, thâ) *adj.* fearless, intrepid.

impecable (ēm•pe•kâ´vle) *adj.* impeccable.

impedimento (ēm•pe•thē•men´to) *m.* impediment.

impedir* (ēm•pe•thēr´) *va.* to impede.

impenetrable (ēm•pe•ne•trâ´vle) *adj.* impenetrable.

imperar (ēm•pe•râr´) *vn.* to reign.

imperativo, va (ēm•pe•râ•tē´vo, vâ) *adj.* and *m.* imperative.

imperceptible (ēm•per•sep•tē´vle) *adj.* imperceptible.

imperdonable (ēm•per•tho•nâ´vle) *adj.* unpardonable.

imperfección (ēm•per•fek•syon´) *f.* imperfection.

imperfecto, ta (ēm•per•fek´to, tâ) *adj.* imperfect.

imperial (ēm•pe•ryâl´) *adj.* imperial.

imperialismo (ēm•pe•ryâ•lēz´mo) *m.* imperialism.

imperialista (ēm•pe•ryâ•lēs´tâ) *adj.* imperialistic.

imperio (ēm•pe´ryo) *m.* empire.

impermeable (ēm•per•me•â´vle) *adj.* impermeable, waterproof; —, *m.* raincoat.

impersonal (ēm•per•so•nâl´) *adj.* impersonal.

impertinencia (ēm•per•tē•nen´syâ) *f.* impertinence.

impertinente (ēm•per•tē•nen´te) *adj.* impertinent.

imperturbable (ēm•per•tūr•vâ´vle) *adj.* imperturbable.

ímpetu (ēm´pe•tū) *m.* impetus; impetuousness *(violencia).*

impetuoso, sa (ēm•pe•two´so, sâ) *adj.* impetuous.

impío, pía (ēm•pē´o, pē´â) *adj.* impious.

implacable (ēm•plâ•kâ´vle) *adj.* implacable.

implicación(ēm•plē•kâ•syon´) *f.* implication.

implícito, ta (ēm•plē´sē•to, tâ) *adj.* implicit.

implorar (ēm•plo•râr´) *va.* to implore.

impolítico, ca (ēm•po•lē´tē•ko, kâ) *adj.* impolite.

imponente (ēm•po•nen´te) *adj.* imposing.

imponer* (ēm•po•ner´) *va.* to impose; to deposit *(poner a rédito);* to instruct *(instruir);* to charge falsely with *(atribuir falsamente).*

importación (ēm•por•tâ•syon´) *f.* importation.

importador, ra (ēm•por•tâ•thor´, râ) *n.* importer; —, *adj.* importing

importancia (ēm•por•tân´sya) *f.* importance.

importante (ēm•por•tân´te) *adj.* important.

importar (ēm•por•târ´) *vn.* to be important, to matter; to import *(géneros);* **no —,** not to matter.

importe (ēm•por´te) *m.* amount.

imposibilidad (ēm•po•sē•vē•lē•thâth´) *f.* impossibility.

imposibilitar (ēm•po•sē•vē•lē•târ´) *va.* to make impossible; **—se,** to become crippled.

imposible (ēm•po•sē´vle) *adj.* impossible.

imposición (ēm•po•sē•syon´) *f.* imposition.

impostor, ra (ēm•pos•tor´, râ) *n.* impostor, fraud.

impotencia (ēm•po•ten´syâ) *f.* impotence.

impotente (ēm•po•ten´te) *adj.* impotent.

impracticable (ēm•prâk•tē•kâ´vle) *adj.* impracticable.

imprecar (ēm•pre•kâr´) *va.* to imprecate, to curse.

impregnarse (ēm•preg•nâr´se) *vr.* to become impregnated.

imprenta (ēm•pren´tâ) *f.* printing *(arte);* printing office *(edificio);* (fig.) press.

imprescindible (ēm•pres•sēn•dē´vle) *adj.* indispensable, essential.

impresión (ēm•pre•syon´) *f.* printing *(acción);* presswork *(calidad del impreso);* impression *(huella);* **— digital,** fingerprint.

impresionable (ēm•pre•syo•nâ´vle) *adj.* impressionable.

impresionar (ēm•pre•syo•nâr´) *va.* to impress.

impreso (ēm•pre´so) *m.* printed

matter; —, **sa,** *adj.* printed.

impresor, ra (ēm•pre•sôr´, râ) *n.*
printer.

imprevisto, ta (ēm•pre•vēs´to, tâ)
adj. unforeseen,
unexpected,unprovided-for.

imprimir (ēm•prē•mēr´) *va.* to
press, to imprint *(huellas);* to
print *(un libro);* (fig.) to impart.

improbable (ēm´pro•vâ•vle) *adj.*
improbable, unlikely.

improductivo, va
(ēm•pro´thūk•tē´vo, vâ) *adj.*
unproductive.

impropio, pia (ēm•pro´pyo, pyâ)
adj. improper, unfit.

improvisación
(em•pro•vē•sâ•syon´) *f.* improvisation.

improvisar (ēm•pro•vē•sâr´) *va.*
to improvise.

imprudente (ēm•prū•then´te)
adj. imprudent, unwise.

impudente (ēm•pū•then´te) *adj.*
impudent, shameless.

impuesto (ēm•pwes´to) *m.* tax;
cobrar —s, to tax.

impugnar (ēm•pūg•nâr´) *va.* to
impugn, to oppose.

impulsar (ēm•pūl•sâr´) *va.* to
drive, to propel.

impulsivo, va (ēm•pūl•sē´vo, vâ)
adj. impulsive.

impulso (ēm•pūl´so) *m.* impulse.

impune (ēm•pū´ne) *adj.* unpunished.

impunidad (ēm•pū•nē•thâth´) *f.*
impunity.

impureza, (ēm•pū•re´sâ) *f.* impurity.

impuro, ra (ēm•pū´ro, râ) *adj.*
impure.

inaccesible (ē•nâk•se•sē´vle) *adj.*
inaccessible; (fig.) incomprehensible.

inaceptable (ē•nâ•sep•tâ´vle) *adj.*
unacceptable.

inactividad (ē•nâk•tē•vē•thâth´)
f. inactivity.

inadaptable (e•nâ•thâp•tâ´vle)
adj. unadaptable.

inadecuado, da (ē•nâ•the•kwâ´-
tho, thâ) *adj.* inadequate.

inadmisible (ē•nâth•mē•sē´vle)
adj. inadmissible.

inadvertencia (ē•nâth•ver•ten´s-
yâ) *f.* oversight.

inajenable (ē•nâ•he•nâ´vle) *adj.*
inalienable.

inalámbrico, ca
(ē•nâ•lâm´brē•ko, kâ) *adj.* wireless.

inalterable (ē•nâl•te•râ´vle) *adj.*
unalterable.

inanimado, da (ē•nâ•nē•mâ´tho,
thâ) *adj.* lifeless, inanimate.

inastillable (ē•nâs•tē•yâ´vle) *adj.*
shatter-proof.

inaudito, ta (ē•nâū•thē´to, tâ)
adj. unheard-of.

inauguración
(ē•nâū•gū•râ•syon´) *f.* inaugu-

ration.

inaugurar (ē•nâū•gū•râr´) *va.* to inaugurate.

inca (ēng´kâ) *m.* Inca.

incansable (ēng•kân•sâ´vle) *adj.* tireless, indefatigable.

incapacidad (ēng•kâ•pâ•sē•thâth´) *f.* incapacity; (fig.) lack of ability, stupidity *(rudeza).*

incapacitar (ēng•kâ•pâ•sē•tar´) *va.* to incapacitate.

incapaz (ēng•kâ•pâz´) *adj.* incapable; (fig.) incompetent *(falto de talento).*

incauto, ta (ēng•kâ´ū•to, ta) *adj.* incautious, unwary.

incendiar (ēn•sen•dyâr´) *va.* to set on fire; **—se,** to catch fire.

incendio (ēn•sen´dyo) *m.* fire.

incentivo (ēn•sen•tē´vo) *m.* inducement, incentive.

incertidumbre (ēn•ser•tē•thūm´bre) *f.* uncertainty.

incesante (ēn•se•sân´te) *adj.* incessant, unceasing.

incesto (ēn•ses´to) *m.* incest.

incidencia (ēn•sē•then´syâ) *f.* incidence; (fig.) incident *(lo que sobreviene);* **por —,** by chance, accidentally.

incidente (ēn•sē•then´te) *m.* incident, event.

incidir (ēn•sē•thēr´) *vn.* to fall into, to run into; (med.) to make an incision.

incienso (ēn•syen´so) *m.* incense.

incierto, ta (ēn•syer´to, tâ) *adj.* uncertain, doubtful.

incinerador (ēn•sē•ne•râ•thor´) *m.* incinerator.

incinerar (ēn•sē•ne•râr´) *va.* to incinerate.

incisión (ēn•sē•syon´) *f.* incision.

incisivo, va (ēn•sē•sē´vo, vâ) *adj.* incisive.

inciso (ēn•sē´so) *m.* clause.

incitar (ēn•sē•târ´) *va.* to incite.

incivil (ēn•sē•vēl´) *adj.* uncivil.

inclemencia (ēng•kle•men´syâ) *f.* inclemency, seventy; **a la —,** exposed, without shelter.

inclinación (ēng•klē•nâ•syon´) *f.* inclination.

inclinar (ēng•klē•nâr´) *va.* to incline; **—se,** to be inclined.

incluir* (ēng•klwēr´) *va.* to include.

inclusión (ēng•klū•syon´) *f.* inclusion.

incluso, sa (ēng•klū´so, sâ) *adj.* enclosed.

incoherente (ēng•ko•e•ren´te) *adj.* incoherent.

incomodar (ēng•ko•mo•thâr´) *va.* to inconvenience, to bother, to annoy.

incomodidad (ēng•ko•mo•thē•thâth´) *f.* inconvenience, annoyance, discomfort.

incómodo, da (ēng•ko´mo•tho, thâ) *adj.* uncomfortable, inconvenient.

incomparable (ēng•kom•pâ•râ´vle) *adj.* incomparable, matchless.

incompatibilidad (ēng•kôm•pâ•tē•vē•lē• thâth´) *f.* incompatibility.

incompatible (ēng•kom•pâ•tē´vle) *adj.* incompatible.

incompetencia (ēng•kom•pe•ten´syâ) *f.* incompetency.

incompleto, ta (ēng•kom•ple´to, tâ) *adj.* incomplete.

incomprensible (ēng•kom•pren•sē´vle) *adj.* incomprehensible.

inconcebible (ēng•kon•se•vē´vle) *adj.* inconceivable.

inconforme (ēng•kom•for´me) *adj.* in disagreement; unsatisfied.

incongelable (ēng•kon•he•lâ´vle) *adj.* **solución —,** antifreeze.

incongruencia (ēng•kong•grwen´syâ) *f.* incongruity.

incongruo, grua (ēng•kong´grwo, grwâ) *adj.* incongruous.

inconsciencia (eng•kons•syen´syâ) *f.* unconsciousness.

inconsciente (ēng•kons•syen´te) *adj.* unconscious.

inconsecuencia (ēng•kon•se•kwen´syâ) *f.* inconsistency, illogic.

inconsiderado, da (ēng•kon•se•the•râ tho, thâ) *adj.* inconsiderate.

inconsolable (en•kon•so•lâ´vle) *adj.* inconsolable.

inconstante (ēng•kons•tân´te) *adj.* inconstant, variable.

inconstitucional (ēng•kons•tē•tū•syo•nâl´) *adj.* unconstitutional.

inconveniencia (ēng•kom•be•nyen´syâ) *f.* inconvenience *(descomodidad);* unsuitability.

inconveniente (ēng•kom•be•nyen´te) *adj.* inconvenient; unsuitable; **—,** *m.* objection, disadvantage *(impedimento);* resulting damage, harm done *(daño).*

incorporación (ēng•kor•po•râ•syon´) *f.* incorporation; joining.

incorporar (ēng•kor•po•râr´) *va.* to incorporate; to sit up, to straighten up *(el cuerpo);* **—se,** to join; to sit up, to straighten up.

incorrecto, ta (eng•ko•rrek´to, tâ) *adj.* incorrect.

incorruptible (ēng•ko•rrūp•tē´vle) *adj.* incorruptible.

incredulidad
(ēng•kre•thū•lē•thâth´) *f.*
incredulity.

incrédulo, la (ēng•krē´thū•lo, lâ)
adj. incredulous.

increíble (ēng•kre•ē´vle) *adj.*
incredible.

incremento (ēng•kre•men´to) *m.*
increment.

incubación (ēng•kū•vâ•syon´) *f.*
incubation, hatching.

incubadora (ēng•kū•vâ•tho´râ) *f.*
incubator.

incubar (ēng•kū•vâr´) *va.* to
hatch, to incubate.

inculcar (ēng•kūl•kâr´) *va.* to
inculcate.

inculpar (ēng•kūl•pâr´) *va.* to
accuse.

inculto, ta (ēng•kūl´to, tâ) *adj.*
uncultivated.

incumplido, da (ēng•kūm•plē´-
tho, thâ) *adj.* unreliable.

incurable (ēng•kū•râ´vle) *adj.*
incurable.

incurrir (ēng•kū•rrēr´) *vn.* to
incur.

incursión (ēng•kūr•syon´) *f.*
incursion; —**aérea,** air raid.

indebido, da (ēn•de•vē´tho, thâ)
adj. undue; illegal, unlawful
(ilícito).

indecencia (ēn•de•sen´syâ) *f.*
indecency.

indecente (ēn•de•sen´te) *adj.*
indecent.

indecisión (ēn•de•sē•syon´) *f.*
irresolution, indecision.

indeciso, sa (en•de•sē´so, sâ)
adj. irresolute, undecided;
vague, imprecise *(vago).*

indefenso, sa (ēn•de•fen´so, sâ)
adj. defenseless.

indefinible (ēn•de•fē•nē´vle) *adj.*
indefinable.

indefinido, da (ēn•de•fē•nē´tho,
thâ) *adj.* indefinite.

indemnización
(ēn•dem•nē•sâ•syon´) *f.* indemnity, compensation.

indemnizar (ēn•dem•nē•sâr´) *va.*
to indemnify.

independencia
(ēn•de•pen•den´syâ) *f.* independence.

independiente (ēn•de•pen•dyen´-
te) *adj.* independent.

indescriptible (ēn•des•krēp•tē´-
vle) *adj.* indescribable.

indestructible
(ēn•des•trūk•tē´vle) *adj.* indestructible.

indeterminado, da
(ēn•de•ter•mē•nâ´tho, thâ) *adj.*
undetermined; irresolute,
undecided *(indeciso).*

Indias Occidentales (ēn´dyâs
ok•sē•then• tâ´les) *f. pl.* West
Indies.

Indias Orientales (ēn´dyâs
o•ryen•tâ´les) *f. pl.* East Indies.

indicación (ēn•dē•kâ•syon´) *f.*

indication.

indicador (ēn•dē•kâ•thor´) *m.*
indicator.

indicar (ēn•dē•kâr´) *va.* to indicate.

índice (ēn´dē•se) *m.* index; hand
(del reloj); index finger *(dedo);*
table of contents *(de capítulos).*

indicio (en•dē´syo) *m.* indication,
sign.

índico, ca (ēn´dē•ko, kâ) *adj.*
East Indian; **Océano I—,** Indian
Ocean.

indiferencia (ēn•dē•fe•ren´syâ) *f.*
indifference, unconcern.

indiferente (ēn•dē•fe•ren´te) *adj.*
indifferent.

indígena (ēn•dē´he•nâ) *adj.*
indigenous, native; **—,** *m.* and
f. native.

indigestión (ēn•dē•hes•tyon´) *f.*
indigestion.

indigesto, ta (ēn•dē•hes´to, tâ)
adj. indigestible; undigested
(sin digerir).

indignación (ēn•dēg•nâ•syon´) *f.*
indignation.

indignado, da (ēn•dēg•nâ´tho,
thâ) *adj.* indignant.

indigno, na (ēn•dēg´no, nâ) *adj.*
unworthy, undeserving; disgraceful, contemptible *(ruin).*

indio, dia (ēn´dyo, dyâ) *n.* and
adj. Indian, native.

indirecto, ta (ēn•dē•rek´to, tâ)
adj. indirect.

indisciplinado, da
(ēn•dēs•sē•plē•nâ´tho, thâ) *adj.*
undisciplined.

indiscreción (ēn•dēs•kre•syon´)
f. indiscretion.

indiscutible (ēn•dēs•kū•tē´vle)
adj. unquestionable.

indisoluble (ēn•dē•so•lū´vle) *adj.*
indissoluble.

indispensable
(ēn•dēs•pen•sâ´vle) *adj.* indispensable.

indisponer* (ēn•dēs•po•ner´) *va.*
to make feel under the weather
(alterar la salud); to put at
odds *(malquistar);* to indispose.

indisposición
(ēn•dēs•po•sē•syon´) *f.* indisposition; unwillingness *(para una
cosa).*

individual (ēn•dē•vē•thwâl´) *adj.*
individual.

individualizar
(ēn•dē•vē•thwâ•lē•sâr) *va.* to
individualize.

individuo (ēn•dē•vē´thwo) *m.*
individual.

indivisible (ēn•dē•vē•sē´vle) *adj.*
indivisible.

índole (ēn´do•le) *f.* temperament,
inclination *(genio);* class, kind,
nature *(clase).*

indomable (ēn•do•mâ´vle) *adj.*
untamable, wild.

inducción (ēn•dūk•syon´) *f.*
induction.

inducir* (ēn•dū•sēr´) *va.* to induce.

indudable (ēn•dū•thâ´vle) *adj.* unquestionable, certain.

indulgencia (ēn•dūl•hen´syâ) *f.* indulgence.

indulgente (ēn•dūl•hen´te) *adj.* indulgent.

indumentaria (ēn•dū•men•tâ´ryâ) *f.* clothing, attire.

industria (ēn•dūs´tryâ) *f.* industry; ability, knack *(destreza).*

industrial (ēn•dūs•tryâl´) *adj.* industrial.

inédito, ta (ē•ne´thē•to, tâ) *adj.* unpublished.

ineficacia (ē•ne•fē•kâ´syâ) *f.* inefficacy.

ineptitud (ē•nep•tē•tūth´) *f.* ineptitude.

inepto, ta (ē•nep´to, tâ) *adj.* inept, unfit; stupid *(necio).*

inequívoco, ca (ē•ne•kē´vo•ko, kâ) *adj.* unmistakable.

inercia (ē•ner´syâ) *f.* inertia.

inerte (ē•ner´te) *adj.* inert; (fig.) dull, sluggish.

inesperado, da (ē•nes•pe•râ´tho, thâ) *adj.* unexpected, unforeseen.

inevitable (ē•ne•vē•tâ´vle) *adj.* unavoidable, inevitable.

inexacto, ta (ē•nek•sâk´to, tâ) *adj.* inaccurate, inexact.

inexcusable (ē•nes•kū•sâ´vle) *adj.* inexcusable, unpardonable.

inexperto, ta (ē•nes•per´to, tâ) *adj.* inexperienced; —, *n.* novice.

inexplicable, (ē•nes•plē•kâ´vle) *adj.* inexplicable.

infalible (ēm•fâ•lē´vle) *adj.* infallible.

infame (ēm•fâ´me) *adj.* infamous; terrible *(vil);* —, *m.* and *f.* wretch, scoundrel.

infamia (ēm•fâ´myâ) *f.* infamy.

infancia (ēm•fân´syâ) *f.* early childhood, infancy.

infanta (ēm•fân´tâ) *f.* infanta; little girl *(niña pequeña).*

infante (ēm•fân´te) *m.* (mil.) infantryman; infante; little boy *(niño pequeño).*

infantería (ēm•fân•te•rē´â) *f.* infantry; — **de marina,** marines.

infanticidio (ēm•fân•tē•sē´thyo) *m.* infanticide.

infantil (ēm•fân•tēl´) *adj.* infantile.

infarto (ēm•fâr´to) *m.* (med.) infarct, heart attack.

infección (ēm•fek•syon´) *f.* infection.

infectar (ēm•fek•târ´) *va.* to infect.

infeliz (ēm•fe•lēs´) *adj.* unhappy, unfortunate.

inferior (ēm•fe•ryor´) *adj.* lower

(colocado debajo); (fig.) inferior.

inferioridad
(ēm•fe•ryo•rē•thâth´) *f.* inferiority; **complejo de —,** inferiority complex.

inferir* (ēm•fe•rēr´) *va.* to infer; to cause, to bring about *(ocasionar).*

infernal (ēm•fer•nâl´) *adj.* infernal.

infestar (ēm•fes•târ´) *va.* to infest.

infidelidad (ēm•fē•the•lē•thâth´) *f.* infidelity.

infiel (ēm•fyel´) *adj.* unfaithful; inaccurate *(falto de exactitud).*

infierno (ēm•fyer´no) *m.* hell.

infiltración (ēm•fēl•trâ•syon´) *f.* infiltration.

infiltrar (ēm•fēl•trâr´) *va.* and *vr.* to infiltrate.

ínfimo, ma (ēm´fē•mo,mâ) *adj.* lowest, most abject.

infinitivo (ēm•fē•nē•tē´vo) *m.* (gram.) infinitive.

infinito, ta (ēm•fē•nē´to, tâ) *adj.* infinite; **—to,** *adv.* a great deal; immensely; **—,** *m.* (math. and phot.) infinity.

inflación (ēm•flâ•syon´) *f.* inflation.

inflamable (ēm•flâ•mâ´vle) *adj.* inflammable.

inflamación (ēm•flâ•mâ•syon´) *f.* inflammation.

inflamar (ēm•flâ•mâr´) *va.* to set fire to *(encender);* (fig.) to inflame *(el ánimo);* **—se,** to catch fire.

inflar (ēm•flâr´) *va.* to inflate.

inflexible (ēm•flek•sē´vle) *adj.* inflexible.

influencia (ēm•flwen´syâ) *f.* influence.

influenza (ēm•flwen´sa) *f.* influenza.

influir* (ēm•flwēr´) *vn.* to influence.

influyente (ēm•flū•yen´te) *adj.* influential.

información (ēm•for•mâ•syon´) *f.* information; inquiry, investigation *(averiguación).*

informal (ēm•for•mâl´) *adj.* informal; unreliable *(falto de seriedad).*

informalidad
(ēm•for•ma•lē•thâth´) *f.* unreliability; informality.

informante (ēm•for•mân´te) *m.* and *f.* informer, informant.

informar (ēm•for•mâr´) *va.* to inform, to report.

informe (ēm•for´me) *m.* report, account *(acción de informar);* piece of information *(noticia);* **—,** *adj.* shapeless.

infortunio (ēm•for•tū´nyo) *m.* misfortune.

infracción (ēm•frâk•syon´) *f.* infraction, violation; **— de tránsito,** traffic violation.

infrarrojo, ja (ēm•frâ•rro´ho, hâ) *adj.* infrared.

infrecuente (ēm•fre•kwen´te) *adj.* infrequent, unusual.

infructuoso, sa (ēm•frŭk•two´so, sâ) *adj.* fruitless, unproductive, unprofitable.

infundir (ēm•fŭn•dēr´) *va.* to infuse, to instill.

infusión (ēm•fŭ•syon´) *f.* infusion.

ingeniar (ēn•he•nyâr´) *va.* to conceive, to contrive; —**se,** to contrive a way, to manage.

ingeniero (ēn•he•nye´ro) *m.* engineer.

ingenioso, sa (ēn•he•nyo´so, sâ) *adj.* ingenious; talented; creative; clever.

ingenuidad (ēn•he•nwē•thâth´) *f.* ingenuousness.

ingenuo, nua, (ēn•he´nwo, nwâ) *adj.* ingenuous.

ingerencia (ēn•he•ren´syâ) *f.* interference, meddling.

ingerir* (ēn•he•rēr´) *va.* to ingest; — **se,** to mix, to meddle.

Inglaterra (ēng•glâ•te´rrâ) *f.* England.

inglés, esa (ēng•gles´, e´sâ) *adj.* English; —, *n.* Briton; —, *m.* Englishman; —, *f.* Englishwoman; —, *m.* English language.

ingratitud (ēng•grâ•tē•tūth´) *f.* ingratitude.

ingrato, ta (ēng•grâ´to, tâ) *adj.* ungrateful *(desagradecido);* disagreeable, unpleasant *(áspero);* unproductive, unrewarding.

ingrediente (ēng•gre•thyen´te) *m.* ingredient.

inhabilitar (ē•nâ•vē•lē•târ´) *va.* to disqualify.

inhabitable (ē•nâ•vē•tâ´vle) *adj.* uninhabitable.

inhalador (ē•nâ•lâ•thor´) *m.* inhaler.

inherente (ē•ne•ren´te) *adj.* inherent.

inhibición (ē•nē•vē•syon´) *f.* inhibition.

inhumano, na (ē•nū•mâ´no, nâ) *adj.* inhuman, cruel.

inicial (ē•nē•syâl´) *f.* and *adj.* initial.

iniciar (ē•nē•syâr´) *va.* to initiate, to begin; —**se,** to be initiated; (eccl.) to receive one´s first orders.

iniciativo, va (ē•nē•syâ•tē´vo, vâ) *adj.* first, preliminary; —, *f.* initiative.

inicuo, cua (ē•nē´kwo, kwâ) *adj.* iniquitous; unjust *(falto de equidad).*

inigualado, da (ē•nē•gwâ•lâ´tho, thâ) *adj.* unequaled.

iniquidad (ē•nē•kē•thâth´) *f.* iniquity; injustice.

injertar, (ēn•her•târ´) *va.* to graft.

injerto (ēn•her´to) *m.* graft; grafting *(acción).*

injuria (ēn•hū´ryâ) *f.* offense, insult; harm, damage *(daño).*

injuriar (ēn•kū•ryâr´) *va.* to insult; to harm *(dañar).*

injusticia (ēn•hūs•tē´syâ) *f.* injustice.

injusto, ta (ēn•hūs´to, ta) *adj.* unjust.

inmaculado, da (ēn•mâ•kū•lâ´tho, thâ) *adj.* immaculate.

inmaduro, ra (ēn•mâ•thū´ro, râ) *adj.* immature.

inmediato, ta (ēn•me•thyâ´to, tâ) *adj.* immediate; **de —to,** immediately.

inmensidad (ēn•men•sē•thâth´) *f.* immensity.

inmenso, sa (ēn•men´so, sâ) *adj.* immense.

inmersión (ēn•mer•syon´) *f.* immersion.

inmigración (ēn•mē•grâ•syon´) *f.* immigration.

inmigrar (ēn•mē•grâr´) *vn.* to immigrate.

inminente (ēn•mē•nen´te) *adj.* imminent.

inmoderado, da (ēn•mo•the•râ´tho, thâ) *adj.* immoderate.

inmoral (ēn•mo•râl´) *adj.* immoral.

inmoralidad (ēn•mo•râ•lē•thâth´) *f.* immorality.

inmortal (ēn•mor•tâl´) *adj.* immortal.

inmortalidad (ēn•mor•tâ•lē•thâth´) *f.* immortality.

inmóvil (ēn•mo´vēl) *adj.* immovable; motionless *(que no se mueve);* firm, resolute *(constante).*

inmueble (ēn•mwe´vle) *adj.* real; **bienes —s,** real estate, immovables.

inmundicia (ēn•mūn•dē´syâ) *f.* dirt, filth; (fig.) indecency.

inmune (ēn•mū´ne) *adj.* immune.

inmunidad (ēn•mū•nē•thâth´) *f.* immunity.

inmunizar (ēn•mū•nē•sâr´) *va.* to immunize.

inmutar (ēn•mū•târ´) *va.* to change; **—se,** to change countenance.

innato, ta (ēn•nâ´to, tâ) *adj.* inborn, innate.

innecesario, ria (ēn•ne•se•sâ´ryo, ryâ) *adj.* unnecessary.

innovación (ēn•no•vâ•syon´) *f.* innovation.

innovar (ēn•no•vâr´) *va.* to innovate.

innumerable (ēn•nū•me•râ´vle) *adj.* innumerable.

inocencia (ē•no•sen´syâ) *f.* innocence.

inocente (ē•no•sen´te) *adj.* innocent.

inocuo, cua (ē•no′kwo, kwâ) *adj.* harmless.

inodoro, ra (ē•no•tho′ro, râ) *adj.* odorless; —, *m.* water closet.

inofensivo, va (ē•no•fen•sē′vo, vâ) *adj.* inoffensive, harmless.

inolvidable (ē•nol•vē•thâ′vle) *adj.* unforgettable.

inoxidable, (ē•nok•sē•thâ′vle) *adj.* rustproof; **acero —,** stainless steel.

inquebrantable (ēng•ke•vrân•tâ′vle) *adj.* unbreakable; (fig.) unswerving, unshakable.

inquietar, (ēng•kye•târ′) va. to disturb, to concern, to worry.

inquieto, ta (ēng•kye′to, tâ) *adj.* restless, anxious, uneasy.

inquilino, na (ēng•kē•lē′no, nâ) *n.* tenant, renter.

inquirir* (ēng•kē•rēr′) *va.* to inquire into, to investigate.

inquisición (ēng•kē•sē•syon′) *f.* (eccl.) inquisition; inquiry, investigation.

insaciable (ēn•sâ•syâ′vle) *adj.* insatiable.

insano, na, (ēn•sâ′no, nâ) *adj.* insane, mad.

inscribir* (ēns•krē•vēr′) *va.* to inscribe; **—se,** to register.

inscripción (ēns•krēp•syon′) *f.* inscription; registration.

insecticida (ēn•sek•tē•sē′thâ) *m.* insecticide.

insecto (ēn•sek′to) *m.* insect.

inseguridad (ēn•se•gū•rē•thâth′) *f.* insecurity; uncertainty *(incertidumbre).*

inseguro, ra (ēn•se•gū′ro, râ) *adj.* uncertain; unsteady, insecure *(inestable).*

insensatez (ēn•sen•sâ•tes′) *f.* stupidity, folly.

insensible (ēn•sen•sē′vle) *adj.* insensible; (fig.) insensitive *(impasible);* imperceptible.

inseparable (ēn•se•pâ•râ′vle) *adj.* inseparable.

insertar (ēn•ser•târ′) *va.* to insert.

insignia (ēn•sēg′nyâ) *f.* badge; **—s,** *pl.* insignia.

insignificancia (ēn•sēg•nē•fē•kân′syâ) *f.* insignificance.

insignificante (ēn•sēg•nē•fē•kân′te) *adj.* insignificant.

insinuación (ēn•sē•nwâ•syon′) *f.* insinuation, hint.

insinuar (ēn•sē•nwâr′) *va.* to insinuate, to imply, to hint; **—se,** to steal, to slip, to creep.

insipidez (ēn•sē•pē•thes′) *f.* insipidity.

insípido, da, (ēn•sē′pē•tho, thâ) *adj.* insipid.

insistir (ēn•sēs•tēr′) *vn.* to insist; to rest, to lie *(descansar).*

insolente (ēn•so•len´te) *adj.* insolent.

insólito, ta (ēn•so´lē•to, tâ) *adj.* unusual, uncommon.

insoluble (ēn•so•lū´vle) *adj.* insoluble.

insomnio (ēn•som´nyo) *m.* insomnia.

inspección (ēns•pek•syon´) *f.* inspection.

inspeccionar (ēns•pek•syo•nâr´) *va.* to inspect, to examine.

inspector (ēns•pek•tor´) *m.* inspector.

inspiración (ēns•pē•râ•syon´) *f.* inspiration.

instalación (ēns•tâ•lâ•syon´) *f.* installation.

instalar (ēns•tâ•lâr´) *va.* to install; — **de nuevo,** to reinstate.

instancia (ēns•tân´syâ) *f.* entreaty, request.

instantáneo, nea (ēns•tân•thâ´ne•o, ne•â) *adj.* instantaneous; —, *f.* snapshot.

instante (ēns•tân´te) *m.* instant; **al —,** immediately.

instar (ēns•târ´) *va.* to press, to urge; —, *vn.* to be urgent.

instigar (ēns•tē•gâr´) *va.* to instigate.

instintivo, va (ēns•tēn•tē´vo, vâ) *adj.* instinctive.

instinto (ēns•tēn´to) *m.* instinct; — **de conservación,** instinct of self-preservation.

institución (ēns•tē•tū•syon´) *f.* institution.

instituir* (ēns•tē•twēr´) *va.* to institute, to establish.

instituto (ēns•tē•tū´to) *m.* institute.

instrucción (ēns´trūk•syon´) *f.* instruction; education *(enseñanza).*

instructivo, va (ēns•trūk•tē´vo, vâ) *adj.* instructive.

instructor (ēns•trūk•tor´) *m.* instructor, teacher.

instruido, da (ēns•trwē´tho, thâ) *adj.* well-educated; well-informed.

instruir* (ēns•trwēr´) *va.* to instruct, to teach; to let know, to inform *(informar).*

instrumento (ēns•trū•men´to) *m.* implement *(herramienta);* instrument; — **de viento,** wind instrument; — **de cuerda,** string instrument.

insubordinado, da (ēn•sū•vor•thē•nâ´tho, thâ) *adj.* insubordinate.

insubordinar (ēn•sū•vor•thē•nâr´) *va.* to incite to insubordination; **—se,** to rebel.

insuficiencia (ēn•sū•fē•syen´syâ) *f.* insufficiency, inadequacy.

insuficiente (ēn•sū•fē•syen´te) *adj.* insufficient, inadequate.

insulina (ēn•sū•lē´nâ) *f.* insulin.

insulso, sa 284

insulso, sa (ēn•sūl′so, sâ) *adj.* insipid, tasteless.

insultar (ēn•sūl•târ′) *va.* to insult.

insulto (ēn•sūl′to) *m.* insult, offense.

insuperable (ēn•sū•pe•râ′vle) *adj.* insurmountable.

insurrección (ēn•sū•rrek•syon′) *f.* insurrection.

insustituible (ēn•sūs•tē•twē′vle) *adj.* irreplaceable.

intacto, ta (ēn•tâk′to, tâ) *adj.* intact, whole.

intachable (ēn•tâ•châ′vle) *adj.* blameless, irreproachable.

integración (ēn•te•grâ•syon′) *f.* integration.

integral (ēn•te•grâl′) *adj.* integral, whole.

integridad (ēn•te•grē•thâth′) *f.* integrity; virginity *(virginidad)*.

íntegro, gra (ēn′te•gro, grâ) *adj.* integral, whole; (fig.) honest, upright *(probo)*.

intelectual (ēn•te•lek•twâl′) *adj.* intellectual.

inteligencia (ēn•te•lē•hen′syâ) *f.* intelligence, understanding.

inteligente (ēn•te•lē•hen′te) *adj.* intelligent.

intemperie (ēn•tem•pe′rye) *f.* rough weather; **a la —,** outdoors.

intempestivo, va (ēn•tem•pes•tē′vo, vâ) *adj.* inopportune, badly timed.

intención (ēn•ten•syon′) *f.* intention, wish; caution *(cautela);* (fig.) dangerousness *(de un animal);* **con —,** on purpose.

intencionadamente (ēn•ten•syo•nâ•thâ•men′te) *adv.* intentionally.

intencionado, da (ēn•ten•syo•nâ′tho, thâ) *adj.* inclined, disposed.

intensidad (ēn•ten•sē•thâth′) *f.* intensity.

intensificar (ēn•ten•sē•fē•kâr′) *va.* to intensify.

intensivo, va (ēn•ten•sē′vo, vâ) *adj.* intensive.

intenso, sa (ēn•ten′so, sâ) *adj.* intense.

intentar (ēn•ten•târ′) *va.* to try, to attempt *(procurar);* to intend.

intento (ēn•ten′to) *m.* intent, purpose.

interamericano, na (ēn•te•râ•me•rē•kâ′no, nâ) *adj.* interamerican.

intercambio (ēn•ter•kâm′byo) *m.* interchange.

interceder (ēn•ter•se•ther′) *vn.* to intercede.

interceptar (ēn•ter•sep•târ′) *va.* to intercept.

interés (ēn•te•res′) *m.* interest; **tipo de —,** rate of interest.

interesante (ēn•te•re•sân′te) *adj.*

interesting.

interesar (ēn•te•re•sâr´) to interest; to involve *(obligar);* **—se,** to become interested.

interferencia (ēn•ter•fe•ren´syâ) *f.* interference.

interior (ēn•te•ryôr´) *adj.* inner; internal *(propio de la nación);* **ropa —,** underwear; **—,** *m.* interior, **—es,** *pl.* entrails, internal parts.

interjección (ēn•ter•hek•syon´) *f.* (gram.) interjection.

interlocutor, ra (ēn•ter•lo•kū•tor´, râ) *n.* speaker.

interludio (ēn•ter•lū´thyo) *m.* interlude.

intermediar (ēn•ter•me•thyâr´) *va.* to interpose, to intervene, to mediate.

intermedio, dia (ēn•ter•me´thyo, thyâ) *adj.* intermediate; **—,** *m.* interval; (theat.) intermission; **por —dio de,** through, by means of.

interminable (ēn•ter•mē•nâ´vle) *adj.* interminable, endless.

intermitente (ēn•ter•mē•ten´te) *adj.* intermittent.

internacional (ēn•ter•nâ•syo•nâl´) *adj.* international.

internado, da (ēn•ter•nâ´tho thâ) *adj.* interned; **—,** *m.* boarding school; student body *(conjunto de alumnos).*

internar (ēn•ter•nâr´) *va.* to take inland; to intern *(encerrar);* **— se,** to penetrate; to curry favor *(ganarse la amistad).*

interno, na (ēn•ter´no, nâ) *adj.* internal; boarding *(alumno);* **—,** *n.* boarding school student.

interponer* (ēn•ter•po•ner´) *va.* to interpose.

interpretación (ēn•ter•pre•tâ•syon´) *f.* interpretation.

interpretar (ēn•ter•pre•târ´) *va.* to interpret.

intérprete (ēn•ter´pre•te) *m.* and *f.* interpreter.

interrogante (ēn•te•rro•gân´te) *adj.* interrogative; **—,** *m.* and *f.* questioner.

interrogativo, va (ēn•te•rro•gâ•tē´vo, vâ) *adj.* interrogative.

interrogatorio (ēn•te´rro•gâ•to´r-yo) *m.* questioning.

interrumpir (ēn•te•rrūm•pēr´) *va.* to interrupt.

interrupción (ēn•te•rrūp•syon´) *f.* interruption.

intersección (ēn•ter•sek•syon´) *f.* intersection.

intervalo (ēn•ter•vâ´lo) *m.* interval.

intervención (ēn•ter•ven•syon´) *f.* intervention; (med.) operation.

intervenir* (ēn•ter•ve•nēr´) *vn.* to happen *(acontecer);* to take part *(tomar parte);* to intervene, to intercede; —, *va.* to audit; (med.) to operate on.

intestino, na (ēn•tes•tē´no, nâ) *adj.* internal; —, *m.* intestine.

intimar (ēn•tē•mâr´) *va.* to intimate, to declare; —, *vn.* to become intimate.

intimidación (ēn•tē•mē•thâ•syon´) *f.* intimidation.

intimidad (ēn•tē•mē•thâth´) *f.* intimacy.

intimidar (ēn•tē•mē•thâr´) *va.* to intimidate; —se, to lose courage.

intocable (ēn•to•kâ´vle) *adj.* untouchable.

intolerable (ēn•to•le•râ´vle) *adj.* intolerable, insufferable.

intolerante (ēn•to•le•rân´te) *adj.* intolerant.

intoxicación (ēn•tok•sē•kâ•syon´) *f.* intoxication.

intranquilo, la (ēn•trâng•kē´lo, lâ) *adj.* restless, uneasy.

intransitable (ēn•trân•sē•tâ´vle) *adj.* impassable.

intravenoso, sa (ēn•trâ•ve•no´so, sâ) *adj.* intravenous.

intrépido, da (ēn•tre´pē•tho, thâ) *adj.* intrepid, daring.

intrigar (ēn•trē•gâr´) *va.* and *vn.* to intrigue.

intrínseco, ca (ēn•trēn´se•ko, kâ) *adj.* intrinsic.

introducción (ēn•tro•thūk•syon´) *f.* introduction.

introducir* (ēn•tro•thū•sēr´) *va.* to introduce; to show in *(dar entrada);* to insert *(meter).*

introductorio, ria (ēn•tro•thūk•to´ryo•ryâ) *adj.* introductory.

introspección (ēn•tros•pek•syon´) *f.* introspection.

introspectivo, va (ēn•tros•pek•tē´vo, vâ) *adj.* introspective.

intruso, sa (ēn•trū´so, sâ) *adj.* intrusive; —, *n.* intruder.

intuición (ēn•twē•syon´) *f.* intuition.

inundación (ē•nūn•dâ•syon´) *f.* inundation; (fig.) deluge, flood.

inundar (ē•nūn•dâr´) *va.* to inundate, to overflow.

inútil (ē•nū´tēl) *adj.* useless, needless.

inutilidad (ē•nū•tē•lē•thâth´) *f.* uselessness.

inútilmente (ē•nū•tēl•men´te) *adv.* uselessly.

invadir (ēm•bâ•thēr´) *va.* to invade.

invalidar (ēm•bâ•lē•thâr´) *va.* to invalidate.

inválido, da (ēm•bâ´lē•tho, thâ)

adj. invalid, null; —, *n.* invalid.

invasión (ēm•bâ•syon´) *f.* invasion.

invasor, ra (ēm•bâ•sor, râ) *n.* invader; —, *adj.* invading.

invencible (ēm•ben•sē´vle) *adj.* invincible.

invención (ēm•ben•syon´) *f.* invention.

inventar (ēm•ben•târ´) *va.* to invent.

inventario (ēm•ben•tâ´ryo) *m.* inventory.

invento (ēm•ben´to) *m.* invention.

inventor, ra (ēm•ben•tor´, râ) *n.* inventor.

invernadero (ēm•ber•nâ•the´ro) *m.* greenhouse.

inverosímil (ēm•be•ro•sē´mēl) *adj.* unlikely, improbable.

inversión (ēm•ber•syon´) *f.* inversion; (com.) investment.

inversionista (ēm•ber•syo•nēs´tâ) *m.* and *f.* investor.

inverso, sa (ēm•ber´so, sâ) *adj.* inverted, inverse; opposite *(contrario).*

invertebrado, da (ēm•ber•te•vrâ´tho, thâ) *adj.* and *m.* invertebrate.

invertir* (ēm•ber•tēr´) *va.* to invert; (com.) to invest; to spend *(el tiempo).*

investigación

(ēm•bes•tē•gâ•syon´) *f.* investigation.

investigar (ēm•bes•tē•gâr´) *va.* to investigate.

investir* (ēm•bes•tēr´) *va.* to invest, to endow.

invierno (ēm•byer´no) *m.* winter; **en pleno** —, in the dead of winter.

invisible (ēm•bē•sē´vle) *adj.* invisible.

invitación (ēm•bē•tâ•syon´) *f.* invitation.

invitado, da (ēm•bē•tâ´tho, thâ) *n.* guest.

invocación (ēm•bo•kâ•syon´) *f.* invocation.

involuntario, ria (ēm•bo•lūn•tâ´ryo, ryâ) *adj.* involuntary.

invulnerable (ēm•būl•ne•râ´vle) *adj.* invulnerable.

inyección (ēn•yek•syon´) *f.* injection; (coll.) shot; — **estimulante,** (med.) booster shot.

inyectar (ēn•yek•târ´) *va.* to inject.

inyector (ēn•yek•tor´) *m.* (mech.) injector.

ion (yon) *m.* ion.

ir* (ēr) *vn.* to go; to be *(estar);* to be diferent *(distinguirse);* to proceed *(proceder);* to become, to be fitting *(sentar);* — **adelante,** to get ahead, to progress; — **y venir,** to go back and forth; — **a lo largo de,** to go along; —**se,** to leak *(rezumarse);* to slip *(deslizarse);* to pass on *(morirse);* to go away, to leave *(moverse).*

ira (ēʹrâ) *f.* anger, wrath.

iris (ēʹrēs) *m.* rainbow; (anat.) iris.

Irlanda (ēr•lânʹdâ) *f.* Ireland.

irlandés, esa (ēr•lân•desʹ eʹsâ) *adj.* Irish; —, *m.* Irishman; —, *f.* Irishwoman.

ironía (ē•ro•nēʹâ) *f.* irony.

irónico, ca (ē•roʹnē•ko, kâ) *adj.* ironical, ironic.

irracional (ē•rrâ•syo•nâlʹ) *adj.* irrational.

irradiación (ē•rrâ•thyâ•syonʹ) *f.* irradiation.

irrazonable (ē•rrâ•so•nâʹvle) *adj.* unreasonable.

irrefutable (ē•rre•fū•tâʹvle) *adj.* irrefutable.

irregular (ē•rre•gū•lârʹ) *adj.* irregular.

irreparable (ē•rre•pâ•râʹvle) *adj.* irreparable.

irresistible (ē•rre•sēs•tēʹvle) *adj.* irresistible.

irresponsable (ē•rres•pon•sâʹvle) *adj.* irresponsible.

irrevocable (ē•rre•vo•kâʹvle) *adj.* irrevocable.

irrigación (ē•rre•gâ•syonʹ) *f.* irrigation.

irritación (ē•rrē•tâ•syonʹ) *f.* irritation.

irritado, da (ē•rrē•tâʹtho, thâ) *adj.* irritated.

irritar (ē•rrē•târʹ) *va.* to irritate; (fig.) to fan, to stir up *(aumentar).*

irrompible (ē•rrom•pēʹvle) *adj.* unbreakable.

irrupción (ē•rrūp•syonʹ) *f.* violent attack; invasion *(invasión).*

isla (ēz•lâ) *f.* isle, island.

israelí (ēz•rrâ•e•lēʹ) *m. and f.* and *adj.* Israeli.

israelita (ēz•rrâ•e•lēʹtâ) *m. and f.* and *adj.* Israelite.

istmo (ēzʹmo) *m.* isthmus.

Italia (ē•tâʹlyâ) *f.* Italy.

italiano, na (ē•tâ•lyâʹno nâ) *n.* and *adj.* Italian; —, *m.* Italian language.

itinerario, ria (ē•tē•ne•râʹryo, ryâ) *adj. and m.* itinerary.

izquierdista (ēs•kyer•thēsʹtâ) *m. and f.* (pol.) leftist.

izquierdo, da (ēs•kyerʹtho, thâ) *adj.* left; left-handed *(zurdo);* —, *f.* left; left hand.

J

jabalí, (hâ•vâ•lē′) *m.* wild boar.

jabalina (hâ•vâ•lē′nâ) *f.* wild sow; javelin *(arma).*

jabón (hâ•von′) *m.* soap.

jabonadura (hâ•vo•nâ•thū′râ) *f.* soaping, lathering; —s, *pl.* soapsuds, sudsy water.

jacal (hâ•kâl′) *m.* (Mex) hut, shack.

jacarandá (hâ•kâ•rân•dâ′) *m.* (bot.) jacaranda.

jactancia (hâk•tân′syâ) *f.* boasting.

jactancioso, sa (hâk•tân•syo′so, sâ′) *adj.* boastful.

jade (hâ′the) *m.* jade.

jadeante (hâ•the•ân′te) *adj.* out of breath, panting.

jadear (hâ•the•âr′) *vn.* to pant.

jaguar (hâ•gwâr′) *m.* jaguar.

jaiba (hâ′ē•vâ) *f.* (Sp. Am.) crab.

jalea (hâ•le′â) *f.* jelly.

jamás (ha•mas′) *adv.* never; para siempre —, for ever and ever; nunca —, never again.

jamón (hâ•mon′) *m.* ham.

Japón (hâ•pon′) *m.* Japan.

japonés, esa (hâ•po•nes′, e′sâ) *adj.* and *n.* Japanese; —, *m.* Japanese language.

jaqueca (hâ•ke′kâ) *f.* headache.

jarabe (hâ•râ′ve) *m.* sirup; — tapatío, Mexican national dance.

jardín (hâr•thēn′) *m.* garden; — de la infancia, kindergarten.

jardinería (hâr•thē•ne•rē′â) *f.* gardening.

jaripeo (hâ•rē•pe′o) *m.* (Sp. Am.) rodeo.

jarra (hâ′rrâ) *f.* jug, jar, pitcher; en —s, with one′s arms akimbo.

jarro (hâ′rro) *m.* pitcher.

jarrón (hâ•rron′) *m.* large urn.

jaula (hâ′ū•lâ) cage.

jazz (yâs) *m.* jazz.

jefatura (he•fâ•tū′râ) *f.* headquarters; leadership *(dirección);* — de policía, police headquarters.

jefe (he′fe) *m.* chief, head, leader, boss.

jengibre (hen•hē′vre) *m.* (bot.) ginger.

jerarquía (he•râr•kē′â) *f.* hierarchy.

jerez (he•res′) *m.* sherry.

jeringa (he•rēng′gâ) *f.* syringe; — hipodérmica, hypodermic syringe.

jeroglífico, ca (he•ro•glē′fē•ko, kâ) *adj.* and *m.* hieroglyphic.

Jesucristo (he•sū•krēs′to) *m.* Jesus Christ.

jesuita (he•swē′tâ) *m.* and *adj.* Jesuit.

Jesús (he•sūs′) *m.* Jesus; ¡—! *interj.* good night!

jilguero (hēl•ge′ro) *m.* linnet.

jinete (hē•ne′te) *m.* horseman, rider.

jira (hē´râ) *f.* excursion, tour; — **campestre,** picnic; — **comercial,** business trip.

jirafa (hē•râ´fâ) *f.* giraffe.

jirón (hē•ron´) *m.* shred, piece.

jitomate (hē•to•mâ´te) *m.* (Mex.) tomato.

jonrón (hon•rron´) *m.* home run.

jornada (hor•nâ´thâ) *f.* day´s journey; trip, journey *(todo el viaje);* (mil.) foray; (fig.) lifespan *(vida);* (theat.) act; scene *(episodio).*

jornalero (hor•nâ•le´ro) *m.* day laborer.

joroba (ho•ro´vâ) *f.* hump; (fig.) nuisance, bother.

jorobado, da (ho•ro•vâ´tho, thâ) *adj.* hunchbacked.

jota (ho´ta) *f.* j. *(letra).*

joven (ho´ven) *adj.* young; —, *m.* young man; —, *f.* young woman.

jovial (ho•vyâl´) *adj.* jovial.

joya (ho´yâ) *f.* jewel *(adorno);* present, gift *(regalo).*

joyeria (ho•ye•rē´â) *f.* jewelry store.

joyero (ho•ye´ro) *m.* jeweler; jewel case *(estuche).*

jubilación (hū•vē•lâ•syon´) *f.* retirement; pension *(renta);* happiness *(alegría).*

jubilar (hū•vē•lâr´) *va.* to retire, to pension; (coll.) to get rid of, to cast off *(desechar);* —, *vn.* to

retire; to be glad *(alegrarse).*

júbilo (hū´vē•lo) *m.* merriment; jubilation.

judaico, ca (hū•thâ´ē•ko, kâ) *adj.* Judaic.

judía (hū•thē´â) *f.* kidney bean.

judicial (hū•thē•syâl´) *adj.* judicial.

judío, día (hū•thē´o, thē´â) *adj.* Jewish; —, *n.* Jew.

juego (hwe´go) *m.* game; play *(acción de jugar);* set *(conjunto);* — **de damas,** checkers.

jueves (hwe´ves) *m.* Thursday.

juez (hwes) *m.* judge.

jugada (hū•gâ´thâ) *f.* play, move; **mala** —, (fig.) dirty deal, underhanded thing to do.

jugador, ra (hū•gâ•thor´, râ) *n.* player.

jugar* (hū•gâr´) *vn.* to play; to move *(moverse);* to match *(hacer juego);* to become involved *(intervenir);* —, *va.* to wield *(una arma);* to risk, to gamble *(arriesgar).*

jugo (hū´go) *m.* juice; (fig.) meat *(lo más sustancial).*

jugoso, sa (hū•go´so, sâ) *adj.* juicy, succulent.

juguete (hū•ge´te) *m.* toy, plaything.

juguetear (hū•ge•te•âr´) *vn.* to fool around, to play, to romp.

juicio (hwē´syo) *m.* judgment; right mind *(sana razón);* trial *(proceso).*

juicioso, sa (hwē•syo´so, sâ) *adj.* judicious.

julio (hū´lyo) *m.* July.

junco (hung´ko) *m.* (bot.) rush; Chinese junk.

junio (hū´nyo) *m.* June.

junta (hūn´tâ) *f.* meeting *(reunión);* board *(de directores);* seam, joint *(juntura);* connection *(unión);* — **directiva,** board of directors.

juntar (hūn•târ´) *va.* to join, to unite *(unir);* to collect, to gather *(amontonar);* —**se,** to assemble, to gather.

junto (hūn´to) *adv.* near, close; — **a,** close to; —, **ta,** *adj.* united, joined.

juntura (hūn•tū´râ) *f.* joint seam.

jura (hū´râ) *f.* pledge of allegiance; oath *(juramento).*

jurado (hū•râ´tho) *m.* juror, juryman; jury *(tribunal).*

juramentar (hū•râ•men•târ´) *va.* to swear in.

juramento (hū•râ•men´to) *m.* oath; **prestar** —, to take oath.

jurar (hū•râr´) *va.* to swear; to swear loyalty to *(un país);* —, *vn.* to swear.

jurídico, ca (hū•rē´thē•ko, kâ) *adj.* lawful, legal, juridical.

jurisdicción (hū•rēz•thēk•syon´) *f.* jurisdiction.

jurista (hū•rēs´tâ) *m.* jurist.

justicia (hūs•tē´syâ) *f.* justice; rightness *(calidad de justo);* execution *(castigo).*

justificación (hūs•tē•fē•kâ•syon´) *f.* justification.

justificar (hūs•tē•fē•kâr´) *va.* to justify.

justo, ta (hūs´to, tâ) *adj.* just; exact, perfect *(exacto);* —, *n.* righteous person.

juvenil (hū•ve•nēl´) *adj.* youthful.

juventud (hū•ven•tūth´) *f.* youth.

juzgado (hūz•gâ´tho) *m.* tribunal, court.

juzgar (hūz•gâr´) *va.* and *vn.* to judge.

K

kaki (kâ´kē) *m.* and *adj.* khaki.

kaleidoscopio (kâ•leē•thos•ko´pyo) *m.* kaleidoscope.

kermés (ker•mez´) *f.* bazaar; charity fair; potluck.

kilo (kē´lo) *m.* kilo, kilogram.

kilogramo (kē•lo•grâ´mo) *m.* kilogram.

kilometraje (kē•lo•me•trâ´he) *m.*

mileage.

kilométrico, ca (kē•lo•me′trē•ko, kâ) *adj.* kilometric; (coll.) too long; **billete —co,** mileage ticket; **discurso —,** very long speech.

kilómetro (kē•lo′me•tro) *m.* kilometer.

kilotón (kē•lo•ton′) *m.* kiloton.

kilotonelada (kē•lo•to•ne•lâ′thâ) *f.* kiloton.

kilovatio (kē•lo•vâ′tyo) *m.* kilowatt.

kilovoltio (kē•lo•vol′tyo) *m.* kilovolt.

kimono (kē•mo′no) *m.* kimono.

kiosco (kyos′ko) = **quiosco.**

L

la (lâ) *art. (f. sing.)* the, as **la señora, la casa; —,** *pron. (accusative f. sing.)* her, it, as **la vio,** he saw her, **la compré,** I bought it **(casa).**

laberinto (lâ•ve•rēn′to) *m.* labyrinth, maze.

labio (lâ′vyo) *m.* lip.

labor (lâ•vor′) *f.* labor, task *(trabajo);* needlework *(adorno);* tilling, working *(aradura).*

laboratorio (lâ•vo•râ•to′ryo) *m.* laboratory.

laborioso, sa (lâ•vo•ryo′so, sâ) *adj.* laborious, industrious.

labrado, da (lâ•vrâ′tho, thâ) *adj.* worked; finely carved or wrought; **—,** *m.* cultivated land.

labrador, ra (la•vrâ•thor′,râ) *n.* laborer; farmer, farmhand.

labranza (lâ•vrân′sâ) *f.* farming, agriculture *(cultivo);* landhold-

ing, farm *(hacienda).*

labrar (lâ•vrâr′) *va.* to work *(trabajar);* to labor, to cultivate *(arar);* to cause, bring about.

labriego, ga (lâ•vrye′go, gâ) *n.* peasant.

laca (lâ′ka) *f.* lac *(resina);* lacquer *(pintura).*

lacio, cia (lâ′syo, syâ) *adj.* faded, withered *(marchito);* languid *(flojo);* straight *(cabello).*

lacra (lâ′krâ) *f.* mark left by an illness *(enfermedad);* fault, vice *(defecto).*

lacrar (lâ•krâr′) *va.* to damage the health of *(salud);* to hurt financially *(negocios);* to seal with sealing wax *(lacre).*

lacre (lâ′kre) *m.* sealing wax.

lactancia (lâk•tân′syâ) *f.* time of suckling.

lácteo, tea (lâk′te•o, te•â) *adj.* lactic, lacteous, milky; **ácido —**

, (chem.) lactic acid; **Via —,** Milky Way.

lactosa (lâk•to´sâ) *f.* (chem.) lactose.

lado (lâ´tho) *m.* side; facet, aspect; **al otro —,** on the other side; **al — de,** by the side of; near to; **— superior,** upper side; **por otro —,** on the other hand; **¡a un —!** to one side, clear the way!

ladrar (lâ•thrâr´) *vn.* to bark.

ladrillo (lâ•thrē´yo) *m.* brick.

ladrón (lâ•thron´) *m.* thief, robber, highwayman.

lagartija (lâ•gâr•tē´hâ) *f.* (zool.) small lizard.

lagarto (lâ•gâr´to) *m.* lizard; alligator *(caimán).*

lago (lâ´go) *m.* lake.

lágrima (lâ´grē•mâ) *f.* tear.

lagrimoso, sa (lâ•grē•mo´so, sâ) *adj.* weeping, shedding tears.

laguna (lâ•gū´nâ) *f.* lagoon, pond *(lago);* blank space, hiatus *(hueco en blanco);* gap, deficiency *(vacío).*

laico, ca (lâ´ē•ko, kâ) *adj.* lay, laic.

lamentable (lâ•men•tâ´vle) *adj.* lamentable, deplorable, pitiable.

lamentar (lâ•men•târ´) *va.* to lament, to regret; **—,** *vn.* and *vr.* to lament, to mourn.

lamento (lâ•men´to) *m.* lamenta-tion, lament, mourning.

lamer (lâ•mer´) *va.* to lick, to lap.

lámina (lâ´mē•nâ) *f.* plate, sheet of metal *(plancha);* copper plate, engraving *(grabado);* print picture *(estampa).*

laminar (lâ•mē•nâr´) *va.* to laminate.

lámpara (lâm´pâ•râ) *f.* lamp.

lampiño, ña (lâm•pē´nyo, nyâ) *adj.* beardless.

lana (lâ´nâ) *f.* wool; (Mex. coll.) money, cash.

lancha (lân´châ) *f.* barge, lighter *(de carga);* launch; **— de carrera,** speedboat; **— de salvavidas,** lifeboat.

langosta (lâng•gos´tâ) *f.* (ent.) locust; lobster *(crustáceo);* swindler *(estafador).*

languidecer* (lâng•gē•the•ser´) *vn.* to droop, to languish.

lánguido, da (lâng´gē•tho, thâ) *adj.* languid, faint, weak *(flaco);* languorous, languishing *(abatido).*

lanolina (lâ•no•lē´nâ) *f.* lanolin.

lanudo, da (lâ•nū´tho, thâ) *adj.* woolly, fleecy.

lanza (lân´sâ) *f.* lance, spear *(arma);* tongue, pole *(palo);* nozzle *(tubo).*

lanzacohetes (lân•sâ•ko•e´tes) *m.* rocket launcher.

lanzador (lân•sâ•thor´) *m.* pitcher (in baseball).

lanzamiento (lân•sâ•myen´to) *m.* launching.

lanzar (lân•sâr´) *va.* to throw, to dart, to launch, to fling; to eject *(despojar);* —**se,** to throw oneself forward or downward.

lapicero (lâ•pē•se´ro) *m.* pencil holder; lead pencil.

lápida (lâ´pē•thâ) *f.* tombstone.

lápiz (la´pēs) *m.* lead pencil; (min.) black lead; — **de labios** or **labial,** lipstick.

larga (lâr´gâ) *f.* delay, adjournment; **a la —,** in the long run.

largo, ga (lâr´go, gâ) *adj.* long; (coll.) generous, liberal; copious *(abundante);* **de —gometraje,** full-length (applied to films); —, *m.* length; **todo lo o de,** the full length of; **a lo —go,** lengthwise.

laringe (lâ•rēn´he) *f.* larynx.

laringitis (lâ•rēn•hē´tēs) *f.* (med.) laryngitis.

larva (lâr´vâ) *f.* (zool.) lar*va.*

lascivo, va (lâs•sē´vo, vâ) *adj.* lascivious, lewd.

lástima (lâs´tē´mâ) *f.* compassion, pity; object of pity *(cosa).*

lastimar (lâs•tē•mâr´) *va.* to hurt, to wound *(herir);* to grieve, to sadden *(agraviar).*

lastimoso, sa (lâs•tē•mo´so, sâ) *adj.* grievous, mournful.

lata (lâ´tâ) *f.* tin can *(bote);* (coll.) nuisance, annoyance *(fastidio);*

dar —, to annoy, to be a nuisance; **productos en —,** canned goods.

latente (lâ•ten´te) *adj.* dormant, concealed.

lateral (lâ•te•râl´) *adj.* lateral.

latido (lâ•tē´tho) *m.* throbbing, palpitation *(del corazón);* yelping of dogs *(ladrido)..*

látigo(lâ´tē•go) *m.* whip.

latín (lâ•tēn´) *m.* Latin language.

latino, na (lâ•tē´no, nâ) *adj.* and *n.* Latin.

Latinoamérica (lâ•tē•no•â•me´rē•kâ) *f.* Latin America.

latinoamericano, na (lâ•tē•no•â•me•rē• kâ´no, nâ) *n.* and *adj.* Latin American.

latir (lâ•tēr´) vn. to palpitate; to howl, to yelp *(ladrar).*

latitud (lâ•tē•tūth´) *f.* breadth, width *(ancho);* (fig.) latitude.

latón (lâ•ton´) *m.* brass.

latoso, sa (lâ•to´so, sâ) *adj.* annoying, boring.

laudable (lâū•thâ´vle) *adj.* laudable, praiseworthy.

laurel (lâū•rel´) *m.* (bot.) laurel; laurel crown.

lavabo (lâ•vâ´vo) *m.* washbowl; sink.

lavado (lâ•vâ´tho) *m.* washing, wash.

lavadora (lâ•vâ•tho´râ) *f.* washing machine.

lavandera (lâ•vân•de′râ) *f* . laundress.

lavandería (lâ•vân•de•rē′â) *f.* laundry; —**automática,** laundromat.

lavaplatos (lâ•vâ•plâ′tos) *m.* or *f.* dishwasher; —, *f.* dishwashing machine.

lavar (lâ•vâr′) *va.* to wash; to tint, to give a wash to *(dibujo).*

laxante (lâk•sân′te) *m.* and *adj.* (med.) laxative.

lazo (lâ′so) *m.* lasso; slipk not *(nudo);* snare, trick *(ardid);* tie, bond *(vínculo);* bow; — **de zapato,** shoestring.

le (le) *pron. (dative sing.)* to him, to her, to it.

leal (le•âl′) *adj.* loyal, faithful.

lealtad (le•âl•tâth′) *f.* loyalty.

lección (lek•syon′) *f.* lesson.

lector, ra (lek•tor′, râ) *adj.* reading; —, *n.* reader; — **de pruebas,** copyreader.

lectura (lek•tū′ra) *f.* reading.

leche (le′che) *f.* milk.

lechón, ona (le•chon′, o′nâ) *n.* sucking pig.

lechuga (le•chū′gâ) *f.* lettuce.

lechuza (le•chū′sâ) *f.* owl.

leer* (le•er′) *va.* to read; to lecture on *(enseñar).*

legal (le•gâl′) *adj.* legal, lawful.

legalidad (le•gâ•lē•thâth′) *f.* legality, fidelity.

legalizar (le•gâ•lē•sâr′) *va.* to legalize.

legañoso, sa (le•gâ•nyo′so, sâ) *adj.* bleary, blear-eyed.

legendario, ria (le•hen•dâ′ryo, ryâ) *adj.* legendary.

legible (le•hē′vle) *adj.* legible.

legión (le•hyon′) *f.* legion.

legislación (le•hēz•lâ•syon′) *f.* legislation.

legislar (le•hēz•lâr′) *vn.* to legislate.

legislativo, va (le•hēz•lâ•tē′vo, vâ) *adj.* legislative.

legislatura (le•hez•lâ•tū′râ) *f.* legislature.

legitimar (le•hē•tē•mar′) *va.* to legitimate, to make lawful.

legítimo, ma (le•hē′tē•mo, mâ) *adj.* legitimate, lawful.

legua (le′gwâ) *f.* league (measure of length); **a —s,** very distant.

legumbre (le•gūm′bre) *f.* vegetable.

leído, da (le•ē′tho, thâ) *adj.* well-read.

lejanía (le•hâ•nē′â) *f.* distance, remoteness.

lejano, na (le•hâ′no, nâ) *adj.* distant, remote, far; **en un futuro no —,** in the near future.

lejos (le′hos) *adv.* at a great distance, far off.

lema (le′mâ) *m.* motto, slogan *(mote);* theme of a literary composition *(tema);* (math.) lemma.

lencería (len•se•rē′â) *f.* linen

goods; linen shop *(estableci-miento).*

lengua (leng´gwâ) *f.* tongue; language, tongue *(idioma).*

lenguaje (leng•gwâ´he) *m.* language, style, choice of words.

lente (len´te) *m.* lens; —**s,** *m. pl.* eye-glasses; reading glasses; —**s de contacto,** contact lenses.

lenteja (len•te´hâ) *f.* (bot.) lentil.

lentitud (len•tē•tūth´) *f.* slowness.

lento, ta (len´to, tâ) *adj.* slow, tardy, lazy.

leña (le´nyâ) *f.* firewood.

leñador, ra (le•nyâ•thor´, râ) *n.* wood-man, woodcutter.

León (le•on´) *m.* Leo, Leon.

león (le•on´) *m.* lion; — **marino,** sea lion.

leona (le•o´nâ) *f.* lioness.

leopardo (le•o•pâr´tho) *m.* leopard.

lesión (le•syon´) *f.* damage *(daño);* wound, injury.

lesionar (le•syo•nâr´) *va.* to injure.

letanía *f.* litany.

letárgico, ca (le•târ´hē•ko, kâ) *adj.* lethargic.

letargo (le•târ´go) *m.* lethargy; drowsiness *(modorra).*

letra (le´trâ) *f.* letter *(carácter);* handwriting *(escritura);* printing type *(tipo);* (com.) draft; words to a song; **buena —,**

good handwriting; **al pie de la —,** literally.

letrado, da (le•trâ´tho, thâ) *adj.* learned, lettered; —, *m.* lawyer.

letrero (le•tre´ro) *m.* inscription, label *(etiqueta);* notice, poster, sign.

leucocitos (leū•ko•sē´tos) *m. pl.* leucocytes, white corpuscles.

levadura (le•vâ•thū´râ) *f.* yeast, leaven, ferment.

levantamiento (le•vân•tâ•myen´to) *m.* elevation; insurrection, uprising *(motín).*

levantar (le•vân•târ´) *va.* to raise, to lift *(alzar);* to build, to construct *(fabricar);* to impute falsely; to promote, to cause *(producir);* — **el campo,** to break camp; —**se,** to rise; to get up from bed; to stand up.

leve (le´ve) *adj.* light trifling.

ley (le´ē) *f.* law; loyalty, obligation, devotion *(fidelidad);* **proyecto de —,** proposed bill; **fuera de —,** lawless.

leyenda (le•yen´dâ) *f.* inscription; legend.

libélula (lē•ve´lū•lâ) *f.* dragonfly.

liberal (lē•ve•râl´) *adj.* liberal, generous.

liberar (lē•ve•râr´) *va.* to free, to release.

liberalizar (lē•ve•râ•lē•sâr´) *va.* to liberalize.

libertad (lē•ver•tâth´) *f.* liberty,

freedom, independence.

libertador, ra (lē•ver•tâ•thor´, râ) *n.* deliverer, liberator.

libertar (lē•ver•târ´) *va.* to free, to set at liberty; to exempt, to clear *(eximir).*

libertinaje (lē•ver•tē•nâ´he) *m.* licentiousness.

libra (lē´vrâ) *f.* pound (weight).

librar (lē•vrâr´) *va.* to free, to rid, to deliver; (corn.) to give order for payment of, to draw; to put, to place *(confianza);* **—bien** or **— mal,** to come off or acquit oneself well or badly; **—se de,** to rid oneself of, to be rid of.

libre (lē´vre) *adj.* free; exempt; — **empresa,** free enterprise; — **pensador, ra,** freethinker; **—,** *m.* (Mex.) taxicab.

librepensador (lē•vre•pen•sâ•thor´) *m.* freethinker.

librería (lē•vre•rē´â) *f.* bookstore.

librero (lē•vre´ro) *m.* bookseller; (Mex.) bookcase.

libreta (lē•vre´tâ) *f.* notebook.

libreto (lē•vre´to) *m.* (rad.) script.

libro (lē´vro) *m.* book.

licencia (lē•sen´syâ) *f.* permission, license; **—para manejar,** driver´s license.

licenciado (lē•sen•syâ´tho) *m.* holder of a master´s degree; (Sp. Am.) lawyer.

licito, ta (lē´sē•to, tâ) *adj.* lawful.

licor (lē•kor´) *m.* liquor *(bebida);* liquid.

licuar (lē•kwâr´) *va.* to liquefy.

líder (lē´ther) *m.* and *f.* leader.

liderear (lē•the•re•âr´) *va.* (Sp. Am.) to lead, to be the leader of, to command.

lidiar (lē•thyâr´) *vn.* to fight, to struggle; **—con,** to contend, to put up with.

liebre (lye´vre) *f.* hare.

lienzo (lyen´so) *m.* linen; canvas, painting *(pintura).*

liga (lē´gâ) *f.* garter; birdlime *(visco);* coalition; (met) alloy; rubber band.

ligar (lē•gâr´) *va.* to tie, to bind, to fasten; to alloy *(alear);* to confederate *(confederar);* **—se,** to league; to be allied; to bind oneself to a contract.

ligereza (lē•he•re´sâ) *f.* lightness; fickleness; swiftness.

ligero, ra (lē•he´ro, râ) *adj.* light; swift, rapid *(rápido);* fickle *(inconstante).*

lijar (lē•hâr´) *va.* to smooth, to polish.

lila (lē´lâ) lilac bush; lilac *(flor).*

lima (lē´mâ) *f.* file.

limar (lē•mâr´) *va.* to file; to polish *(pulir).*

limbo (lēm´bo) *m.* limbo.

limeño, ña (lē•me´nyo nyâ) *n.* native of Lima; **—,** *adj.* from Lima, of Lima.

limitación (lē•mē•tâ•syon´) *f.* limitation, restriction.

limitar (lē•mē•târ´) *va.* to limit; to restrain *(moderar)*.

límite (lē´mē•te) *m.* limit, boundary; — **de velocidad,** speed limit.

limón (lē•mon´) *m.* lemon.

limonada (lē•mo•nâ´thâ) *f.* lemonade.

limosna (lē•môz´nâ) *f.* alms, charity.

limosnero, ra (lē•môz•ne´ro, râ) *adj.* charitable; —, *n.* beggar *(pordiosero);* alms giver *(donador).*

limpiador (lēm•pyâ•thor´) *m.* cleanser, scourer.

limpiaparabrisas (lem•pyâ•pâ•râ•vrē´sâs) *m.* windshield wiper.

limpiar (lēm•pyâr´) *va.* to clean, to cleanse.

límpido, da (lēm´pē•tho, thâ) *adj.* clear, limpid.

limpieza (lēm•pye´sâ) *f.* cleanliness, neatness *(aseo);* chastity, purity *(pureza);* precision, exactness *(destreza).*

limpio, pia (lēm´pyo, pyâ) *adj.* clean, neat; pure; exact, precise.

linaje (lē•nâ´he) *m.* lineage, descent.

linaza (lē•nâ´sâ) *f.* linseed; **aceite de —,** linseed oil.

lince (lēn´se) *m.* lynx; (fig.) keen person, fox; — *adj.* sharp-eyed, keen-sighted.

linchar (lēn•châr´) *va.* to lynch.

lindar (lēn•dâr´) *vn.* to be contiguous.

lindero (lēn•de´ro) *m.* boundary, edge.

lindo, da (lēn´do, dâ) *adj.* handsome, pretty; wonderful, perfect *(exquisito)*

línea (lē´ne•â) *f.* line; (fig.) boundary, limit.

lineal (lē•ne•âl´) *adj.* lineal, linear.

linfático, ca (lēm•fâ´tē•ko, kâ) *adj.* lymphatic.

lingüística (lēng•gwēs´tē•kâ) *f.* linguistics.

lino (lē´no) *m.* flax; linen *(textil);* **semilla de —,** flaxseed.

linóleo (lē•no´le•o) *m.* linoleum.

linterna (lēn•ter´nâ) *f.* lantern; — **de bolsillo,** flashlight; — **delantera,** head-light; — **trasera** or — **de cola,** taillight.

liquidación (lē•kē•thâ•syon´) *f.* liquidation, settlement; clearance sale *(venta).*

liquidar (lē•kē•thâr´) *va.* to liquefy, to melt, to liquidate, to dissolve *(disolver);* to settle, to clear *(ajustar).*

líquido, da (lē´kē´•tho, thâ) *adj.* liquid.

lira (lē´râ) *f.* lyre.

lírico, ca (lē′rē•ko, kâ) *adj.* lyrical, lyric.

lirio (lē′ryo) *m.* iris; — **blanco,** lily.

Lisboa (lēz•vo′â) *f.* Lisbon.

liso, sa (lē′so, sâ) *adj.* plain, even, flat, smooth.

lisonjear (lē•son•he•âr′) *va.* to flatter; to charm, to delight (*deleitar*).

lista (lēs′tâ) *f.* slip, narrow strip (*tira*); list, catalogue (*catálogo*); colored stripe (*de tejidos*).

listo, ta (lēs′to, tâ) *adj.* ready, prepared (*apercibido*); prompt, quick (*pronto*); clever (*sagaz*).

listón (lēs•ton′) *m.* ribbon; tape.

litera (lē•te′râ) *f.* litter; berth (*camarote*); —**s,** *pl.* bunk beds.

literal (lē•te•râl′) *adj.* literal.

literario, ria (lē•te•râ′•ryo, ryâ) *adj.* literary.

literatura (lē•te•râ•tū′râ) *f.* literature.

litigar (lē•tē•gâr′) *va.* to litigate, to take to court.

litigio (lē•tē′hyo) *m.* lawsuit.

litoral (lē•to•râl′) *m.* littoral, coast; —, *adj.* littoral, coastal.

litro (lē′tro) *m.* liter.

litúrgico, ca (lē•tūr′hē•ko, kâ) *adj.* liturgical.

liviano, na (lē•vyâ′no, nâ) *adj.* light; fickle (*inconstante*); lewd (*lascivo*).

lívido, da (lē′vē•tho, thâ) *adj.* livid, pale.

lo (lo) *pron.* (*accusative m.* and *neuter sing.*) him, it; —, *art.* (*neuter sing.*) the (used before a masculine adjective with noun force); — **bueno,** the good thing.

loable (lo•â′vle) *adj.* laudable.

lobo (lo′vo) *m.* wolf.

lóbrego, ga (lo′vre•go, gâ) *adj.* murky, obscure; (fig.) sad, gloomy, glum.

lóbulo (lo′vū•lo) *m.* lobe.

local (lo•kâl′) *adj.* local: —, *m.* place.

localización (lo•kâ•lē•sâ•syon′) *f.* placing, location.

localizar (lo•kâ•lē•sâr′) *va.* to localize; to locate (*encontrar*).

loción (lo•syon′) *f.* lotion.

loco, ca (lo′ko, kâ) *adj.* mad, crazy, insane; **casa de —cos,** insane asylum; — **rematado,** stark raving mad; **volverse** —, to go mad.

locomoción (lo•ko•mo•syon′) *f.* locomotion.

locomotora (lo•ko•mo•to′râ) *f.* locomotive.

locura (lo•kū′râ) *f.* madness, insanity; passion, frenzy (*exaltación*); folly, foolishness (*desacierto*).

locutor, ra (lo•kū•tor′, râ) *n.* announcer; —**de radio** or **de televisión,** radio or T.V.

announcer or commentator.

lodo (lo´tho) *m.* mud, mire.

logaritmo (lo•gâ•rēth´mo) *m.* logarithm.

logia (lo´hyâ) *f.* lodge, secret society.

lógica (lo´hē•kâ) *f.* logic.

lógico, ca (lo´hē•ko, kâ) *adj.* logical, reasonable; — *m.* logician.

logística (lo•hēs´tē•kâ) *f.* logistics.

lograr (lo•grâr´) *va.* to gain, to obtain, to succeed in, to attain.

logro (lo´gro) *m.* gaining, attainment, accomplishment.

loma (lo´mâ) *f.* hillock.

lombriz (lom•brēs´) *f.* earthworm; — **solitaria,** tapeworm.

lomo (lo´mo) *m.* (anat.) loin; back, spine *(de libro);* crease *(de tejido);* ridge *(entre surcos);* **llevar a** or **traer a —,** to carry on one´s back.

lona (lo´nâ) *f.* canvas.

londinense (lon•dē•nen´se) *m.* and *f.* and *adj.* Londoner, from London.

Londres (lon´dres) *m.* London.

longaniza (long•gâ•nē´sâ) *f.* long, narrow pork sausage.

longevidad s (lôn•he•vē•thâth´) *f.* longevity.

longitud (lon•hē•tūth´) *f.* length; (geog.) longitude; — **de onda,** (rad.) wavelength.

lonja (lon´hâ) *f.* (com.) exchange; grocery store, delicatessen *(tienda);* warehouse *(almacén);* slice *(tira);* (Mex. Coll.) roll of fat, love-handle.

loro (lo´ro) *m.* parrot.

losa (lo´sâ) *f.* flagstone, slab.

lote (lo´te) *m.* lot, share.

lotería (lo•te•rē´â) *f.* lottery; lotto *(juego).*

loza (lo´sâ) *f.* porcelain, chinaware.

lubricación (lū•vrē•kâ•syon´) *f.* lubrication.

lubricante (lū•vre•kân´te) *adj.* lubricating; —, *m.* lubricant.

lubricar (lū•vrē•kâr´) **lubrificar,** (lū•vrē•fē•kâr´) *va.* to lubricate.

lucero (lū•se´ro) *m.* morning star, day star.

lucidez (lū•sē•thes´) *f.* brilliance, splendor.

luciente (lū•syen´te) *adj.* bright, shining.

luciérnaga (lū•syer´nâ•gâ) *f.* glowworm, firefly.

lucir* (lū•sēr´) *vn.* to shine, to be brilliant; (fig.) to be of benefit, to be useful; to excel, to do well *(sobresalir);* —, *va.* to light up, to illuminate; to sport, to show off *(alardear);* —**se,** to dress up, to put on one´s Sunday best.

lucrativo, va (lū•krâ•tē´vo, vâ) *adj.* lucrative.

lucha (lū´châ) *f.* struggle, strife; wrestling *(deporte).*

luchador, ra (lū•châ•thor´, râ) *n.* wrestler; fighter, contender.

luchar (lū•châr´) *vn.* to wrestle; to struggle, to fight.

luego (lwe´go) *adv.* at once, immediately *(prontamente);* then, afterwards, later *(después);* **desde —,** of course; **hasta —,** good-by; **— que,** as soon as.

lugar (lū•gâr´) *m.* place; village *(aldea);* employment, office *(empleo);* cause, motive *(motivo).*

lugarteniente (lū•gâr•te•nyen´te) *m.* deputy, lieutenant.

lujo (lū´ho) *m.* luxury, elegant.

lujuria (lū•hū´ryâ) *f.* lewdness; (fig.) excess, excessiveness.

lumbre (lūm´bre) *f.* light; (fig.) brilliance, brightness.

luna (lū´nâ) *f.* moon; plate glass *(cristal);* **— de miel,** honey-moon.

lunar (lū•nâr´) *m.* mole, skin blemish; **—,** *adj.* lunar.

lunático, ca (lū•nâ´tē•ko, kâ) *adj.* lunatic, moonstruck.

lunes (lū´nes) *m.* Monday.

lustrar (lūs•trâr´) *va.* to shine, to polish.

lustre (lūs´tre) *m.* gloss, luster; (fig.) splendor, glory.

lustroso, sa (lūs•tro´so, sâ) *adj.* bright, brilliant.

luterano, na (lū•te•râ´no, nâ) *n.* and *adj.* Lutheran.

luto (lū´to) *m.* mourning; bereavement *(duelo);* **de —,** in mourning.

luz (lūs) *f.* light; news, information *(aviso);* guide, example *(modelo);* **dar a —,** to give birth; **— de la luna,** moonlight; **— solar,** sunlight; **— diurna, — del día,** daylight.

LL

llaga (yâ´gâ) *f.* wound, sore.

llama (yâ´mâ) *f.* flame; (zool.) llama.

llamada (yâ•mâ´thâ) *f.* call; (mil.) summons; **— de incendios,** fire alarm; **— de larga distancia,** long-distance call.

llamado, da (yâ•mâ´tho, thâ) *adj.* so-called, by the name of.

llamar (yâ•mar´) *va.* to call; to summon, to cite *(convocar);* to call on, to invoke *(invocar);* **—,** *vn.* to knock; **— con señas,** to motion to, to signal; **¿cómo se llama Ud.?** what is your name?

llaneza (yâ•ne´sâ) *f.* simplicity, sincerity, openness.

llano, na (yâ´no, nâ) *adj.* plain,

even, smooth; unassuming, simple *(sencillo);* evident *(claro);* —, *m.* plain, prairie.

llanta (yân´tâ) *f.* rim *(de rueda);* tire *(neumático).*

llanto (yân´to) *m.* flood of tears, weeping.

llanura (yâ•nū´râ) *f.* evenness, level *(calidad);* plain *(superficie).*

llave (yâ´ve) *f.* key; hammer *(de arma de fuego);* **ama de —s,** housekeeper; **cerrar con —,** to lock; **— inglesa,** monkey wrench; **— maestra,** master key.

llavero (yâ•ve´ro) *m.* keeper of the keys; key ring, key chain *(anillo).*

llegada (ye•gâ´thâ) *f.* arrival, coming.

llegar (ye•gâr´) *vn.* to arrive, to reach; **— a ser,** to become.

llenar (ye•nâr´) *va.* to fill; to fulfill, to meet *(cumplir);* to fill out *(un formulario).*

lleno, na (ye´no, nâ) *adj.* full; **de —no,** entirely, fully.

llevar (ye•vâr´) *va.* to carry, to bear, to take; to lead, to take *(conducir);* to wear *(vestir);* to receive, to obtain *(lograr);* to win over, to persuade *(persuadir);* **— puesto,** to be wearing, to have on; **—se,** to take away; **—se bien,** to get along well together; **—se chasco,** to be disappointed.

llorar (yo•râr´) *va.* and *vn.* to weep, to cry; (fig.) to bewail, to mourn, to feel deeply.

lloriqueo (yo•rē•ke´o) *m.* whining, crying.

llover* (yo•ver´) *vn.* to rain.

lloviznar (yo•vēz•nâr´) *vn.* to drizzle.

lluvia (yū´vyâ) *f.* rain.

lluvioso, sa (yū•vyo´so, sâ) *adj.* rainy.

M

M.ª: María Mary.

macabro, bra (mâ•kâ´vro, vrâ) *adj.* macabre, hideous.

macarrones (mâ•kâ•rro´nes) *m. pl.* macaroni.

maceta (mâ•se´tâ) *f.* flowerpot.

macizo, za (mâ•sē´so, sâ) *adj.* massive, solid.

machacar (mâ•châ•kâr´) *va.* to pound, to crush; —, *vn.* to harp on the same thing, to dwell monotonously on one subject.

machete (mâ•che´te) *m.*

machete, heavy knife.

macho (mâ´cho) *m.* male animal; hook *(del corchete);* (mech.) male part; —, *adj.* male; masculine, manly, virile (robusto).

machucar (mâ•chū•kâr´) va. to pound, to crush.

madera (mâ•the´râ) f. timber, wood.

madero (mâ•the´ro) m. beam of timber; piece of lumber.

madrastra (mâ•thrâs´trâ) f. stepmother.

madre (mâ´thre) f. mother; riverbed (del río); main sewer line (alcantarilla).

madrileño ña, (mâ•thrē•le´nyo, nyâ) n. inhabitant of Madrid; —, adj. from Madrid, of Madrid.

madrina (mâ•thrē´nâ) f. godmother.

madrugada (mâ•thrū•gâ´thâ) f. dawn; **de** —, at break of day.

madrugar (mâ•thrū•gâr´) vn. to get up early; (fig.) to be ahead of the game, to be ready ahead of time.

madurar (mâ•thū•râr´) va. to ripen; —, vn. to ripen, to grow ripe; (fig.) to arrive at maturity, to mature.

madurez (mâ•thū•res´) f. maturity; prudence, wisdom (juicio).

maestra (mâ•es´trâ) f. schoolmistress, woman teacher.

maestría (mâ•es•trē´â) *f.* skill, mastery.

maestro (mâ•es´tro) *m.* master, expert; teacher; (mus.) maestro; —, **tra,** *adj.* masterly; **obra** —, masterpiece.

magia (mâ´hya) f. magic.

mágico, ca (mâ´hē•ko, kâ) *adj.* magical; —, *m.* magician.

magistrado (ma•hēs•trâ´tho) *m.* magistrate.

magistral (mâ•hēs•trâl´) *adj.* magisterial; masterful, definitive *(soberano).*

magnesia (mâg•ne´syâ) *f.* magnesia.

magnético, ca (mâg•ne´tē•ko, kâ) *adj.* magnetic.

magnetismo (mâg•ne•tēz´mo) *m.* magnetism.

magneto (mâg•ne´to) *m.* magneto.

magnificar (mâg•nē•fē•kâr´) *va.* to exalt, to magnify.

magnificencia, (mâg•nē•fē•sen´syâ) *f.* magnificence, splendor.

magnífico, ca (mâg•nē´fē•ko, kâ) *adj.* magnificent, splendid.

magnitud (mâg•nē•tūth´) *f.* magnitude, grandeur.

magnolia (mâg•no´lyâ) *f.* (bot.) magnolia.

mago (mâ´go) *n.* magician, wizard.

magro, gra (mâ´gro, grâ) *adj.*

meager, thin.

maguey (mâ•ge´ē) *m.* (bot.) maguey, century plant.

magullar (mâ•gū•yâr´) *va.* to bruise.

maíz (mâ•ēs´) *m.* corn, maize; — **machacado** or **molido,** hominy; **palomitas de —,** (Mex.) popcorn.

majadero, ra (mâ•hâ•the´ro, râ) *adj.* dull, silly, foolish; annoying, bothersome *(pesado);* —, *n.* pest, bore; —, *m.* pestle.

majestad (mâ•hes•tâth´) *f.* majesty.

majestuoso, sa (mâ•hes•two´so, sa) *adj.* majestic, sublime.

mal (mâl) *m.* evil, bad; pain, ache *(dolencia);* illness *(enfermedad),* misfortune, bad luck *(desgracia);* injury, damage *(daño);* — **de garganta,** sore throat; —, *adj.* (used only before masculine nouns) bad; **ir, caer** or **venir —,** to be unbecoming or displeasing.

malabarista (mâ•lâ•vâ•rēs´tâ) *m.* or *f.* juggler.

malacate (mâ•lâ•kâ´te) *m.* hoist.

malagradecido, da (mâ•lâ•grâ•the•sē´tho, thâ) *adj.* ungrateful.

malaria (mâ•lâ´ryâ) *f.* malaria.

malaventurado, da (mâ•lâ•ven•tū•râ´tho, thâ) *adj.* unfortunate.

malcriado, da (mâl•kryâ´tho, thâ) *adj.* illbred, ill-behaved.

maldad (mâl•dâth´) *f.* wickedness.

maldecir* (mâl•de•sēr´) *va.* to curse.

maldición (mâl•dē•syon´) *f.* malediction, curse, cursing.

maldito, ta (mâl•dē´to, tâ) *adj.* perverse, wicked; damned, cursed *(condenado);* ¡— **sea!** *interj.* damn it!

malecón (mâ•le•kon´) *m.* sea wall, breakwater *(de mar);* levee, dike.

malentendido (mâ•len•ten•dē´tho) or **mal entendimiento** (mâl•en•ten•dē•myen´to) *m.* misunderstanding.

malestar (mâ•les•târ´)*m.* (med.) queasiness, indisposition; uneasiness, anxiety.

maleta (mâ•le´tâ) *f.* suitcase.

malevolencia (mâ•1e•vo•len´syâ) *f.* malevolence.

malévolo, la (mâ•le´vo•lo, lâ) *adj.* malevolent.

malgastar (mâl•gâs•târ´) *va.* to waste, to misuse.

malhecho (mâ•le´cho) *m.* evil act, wrong; —, **cha,** *adj.* malformed, deformed.

malhumorado, da (mâ•lū•mo•râ´tho, thâ) *adj.* peevish, ill-humored.

malicia (mâ•lē´syâ) *f.* malice,

perversity; suspicion *(recelo);* cunning, artifice *(maña);* **tener —,** to suspect.

malicioso, sa (mâ•lē•syo′so, sâ) *adj.* malicious, wicked.

malignidad (mâ•lēg•nē•thâth′) *f.* malignity, malice, evildoing.

maligno, na (mâ•lēg′no, nâ) *adj.* malignant, malicious.

malintencionado, da (mâ•lēn•ten•syo•nâ′tho, thâ) *adj.* ill-disposed.

malnutrido, da (mâl•nū•trē′tho, thâ) *adj.* undernourished.

malo, la (mâ′lo, lâ) *adj.* bad, wicked; sickly, sick, ill *(de salud).*

malograr (mâ•lo•grâr′) *va.* to waste, not to take advantage of, to miss; **—se,** to fail, to fall through.

malquerer* (mâl•ke•rer′) *va.* to have a grudge against.

malquisto, ta (mâl•kēs′to, tâ) *adj.* hated, detested.

maltratar (mâl•trâ•târ′) *va.* to treat badly, to abuse, to mistreat.

malvado, da (mâl•va′tho, thâ) *adj* wicked, perverse; **—,** *n:* wrongdoer, villain.

malla (ma′yâ) *f.* mesh *(de red);* mail *(de cota);* tights *(de gimnasta);* (Sp. Am.) bathing suit.

mamá (mâ•mâ′) *f.* mamma.

mamar (mâ•mâr′) *va.* and *vn.* to suck.

mamarracho (mâ•mâ•rrâ′cho) *m.* white elephant, piece of junk.

mamey (mâ•me′ē) *m.* (bot.) mamey, mammee.

mamífero, ra (mâ•mē′fe•ro, râ) *adj.* mammalian; **—,** *m.* mammal.

mampara (mâm•pâ′râ) *f.* screen.

maná (ma•nâ′) *m.* manna.

manada (mâ•nâ′thâ) *f.* flock, drove, herd: (coll.) crowd, pack; **— de lobos,** wolf pack.

manantial (mâ•nân•tyâl′) *m.* spring; (fig.) origin, source.

manar (mâ•nâr′) *vn.* to spring, to issue, to flow out; to distill *(destilar);* to abound, to be teeming *(abundar).*

mancebo (mân•se′vo) *m.* youth, young man; salesclerk *(dependiente).*

mancuerna (mâng•kwer′nâ) *f.* pair tied together; **—s,** cuff links.

mancha (mân′châ) *f.* stain, spot, blot.

manchego, ga (mân•che′go, gâ) *n.* a native of La Mancha, Spain; **queso —,** cheese from La Mancha.

mandado (mân•dâ′tho) *m.* mandate; errand *(recado);* message *(mensaje).*

mandar (mân•dâr′) *va.* to command, to order; to will, to bequeath *(legar);* to send *(enviar);* —, vn. to rule, to govern, to give the orders.

mandatario (mân•dâ•tâ´ryo) *m.* mandatory; (Sp. Am) director.

mandato (mân•dâ´to) *m.* mandate, order.

mandíbula (man•dē´vū•lâ) *f.* jawbone, jaw.

mando (mân´do) *m.* command, authority, power.

mandolin (mân•do•lēn´) *m.* or **mandolina** (mân•do•lē´nâ) *f.* mandolin.

mandón, ona (mân•don´, o´nâ) *adj.* imperious, domineering; —, *n.* imperious, haughty person.

mandril (mân•drēl´) *m.* (zool.) baboon.

manejable (mâ•ne•hâ´vle) *adj.* manageable.

manejar (mâ•ne•hâr´) *va.* to manage, to handle; to drive *(un coche);* **—se,** to behave.

manera (mâ•ne´râ) *f.* manner, way; kind *(especie);* **de ninguna** —, not at all.

manga (mâng´gâ) *f.* sleeve; waterspout *(de agua);* hose *(tubo);* **— de aire,** (avi.) jet stream.

mango (mâng´go) *m.* handle, haft; (bot.) mango.

manguera (mâng•ge´râ) *f.* hose for sprinkling.

maní (mâ•nē´) *m.* (Cuba) peanut.

manía (mâ•nē´â) *f.* frenzy, madness.

maniático, ca (mâ•nyâ´tē•ko, kâ) *adj.* maniac, mad, frantic.

manicomio (mâ•nē•ko´myo) *m.* insane asylum.

manicurista (mâ•nē•kū•rēs´tâ) *m.* and *f.* manicurist.

manifestación (mâ•nē•fes•tâ•syon´) *f.* manifestation, demonstration, declaration, statement.

manifestar* (mâ•nē•fes•târ´) *va.* to manifest, to show.

manifiesto, ta (mâ•nē•fyes´to, tâ) *adj.* manifest, open; manifesto.

manija (mâ•nē´hâ) *f.* handle, crank, hand lever.

manipular (mâ•nē•pū•lâr´) *va.* to manipulate, to manage.

maniquí (mâ•nē•kē´) *m.* mannikin.

manjar (mân•hâr´) *m.* choice food, specialty food.

mano (mâ´no) *f.* hand; coat, layer *(de pintura);* , **a** —, at hand; **a —s llenas,** liberally, abundantly; **tener buena** —, to be skillful; **— de obra,** labor, construction work; **de propia** —, with one´s own hand; **venir a las —s,** to come to blows; **¡—s a la obra!** let´s get started! let´s get going!

manojo (mâ•no′ho) *m.* handful, bundle.

manosear (mâ•no•se•âr′) *va.* to handle.

manotear (mâ•no•te•âr′) *vn.* to gesture with the hands; — *va.* to slap.

mansión (mân•syon′) *f.* sojourn, residence *(detención);* abode, home *(morada);* mansion.

manso, sa (mân′so, sâ) *adj.* tame, gentle, mild.

manta (mân′tâ) *f.* blanket: — **de cielo,** cheesecloth.

manteca (mân•te′kâ) *f.* lard.

mantel (mân•tel′) *m.* tablecloth.

mantener* (mân•te•ner′) *va.* to maintain, to support.

mantenimiento (mân•te•nē•mye-n′to) *m.* maintenance, support.

mantequilla (mân•te•kē′yâ) *f.* butter.

manto (mân′to) *m.* mantle, cloak, robe.

mantón (mân•ton′) *m.* shawl; — **de Manila,** Spanish shawl.

manual (mâ•nwâl′) *adj.* manual; handy. easy to handle *(manuable);* —, *m.* manual.

manufactura (mâ•nū•fâk•tū′râ) *f.* manufacture.

manufacturar (mâ•nū•fâk•tū•râr′) *va.* to manufacture.

manuscrito (mâ•nūs•krē′to) *m.* manuscript; —, **ta,** *adj.* hand-written.

manutención (mâ•nū•ten•syon′) *f.* maintaining; maintenance *(efecto).*

manzana (mân•sâ′nâ) *f.* apple; block *(de casas).*

manzano (mân•sâ′no) *m.* apple tree.

maña (mâ′nyâ) *f.* dexterity, skill, cleverness, ability *(destreza);* artifice, cunning, trickery *(astucia);* evil way, vice, bad habit *(vicio).*

mañana (mâ•nyâ′nâ) *f.* morning; —, *adv.* tomorrow; **pasado** —, day after tomorrow.

mañanear (mâ•nyâ•ne•âr′) *vn.* to be an early riser, to have the habit of getting up early.

mapa (ma′pa) *m.* map.

mapache (mâ•pâ′che) *m.* (zool.) raccoon.

maqueta (mâ•ke′tâ) *f.* mock-up, scale model.

maquiavélico, ca (mâ•kyâ•ve′lē•ko, kâ) *adj.* Machiavelian.

maquillaje (mâ•kē•yâ′he) *m.* makeup.

maquillar (mâ•kē•yâr′) *va.* to make up; —**se,** to put on one′s makeup.

máquina (mâ′kē•nâ) *f.* machine, engine; — **de calcular,** calculating machine; — **de coser,** sewing machine; — **de escribir,**

typewriter;— **de vapor,** steam engine.

maquinación (mâ′kē•nâ•syon′) *f.* machination.

maquinaria (mâ•kē•nâ′ryâ) *f.* machinery.

maquinista (mâ•kē•nēs′tâ) *m.* machinist, mechanician; driver, engineer *(conductor).*

mar (mâr) *m.* or *f.* sea; **en alta —** , on the high seas.

maravilla (mâ•râ•vē′yâ) *f.* wonder; **a las mil —s,** uncommonly well, exquisitely; **a —,** marvelously.

maravilloso, sa (mâ•râ•vē•yo′so, sâ) *adj.* wonderful, marvelous.

marca (mâr′kâ) *f.* mark, sign; **— de fábrica,** trademark, brand name.

marcial (mâr•syâl′) *adj.* martial, warlike.

marco (mâr′ko) *m.* frame; mark *(moneda).*

marcha (mar′châ) *f.* march; (fig.) course, development; **ponerse en —,** to proceed, to start off; **reducir** or **acortar la —,** to slow down.

marchitar (mâr•chē•târ′) *va.* to wither; to fade *(desteñir);* (fig.) to deprive of vigor, to devitalize.

marchito, ta (mâr•chē′to, tâ) *adj.* faded; withered.

marea (mâ•re′â) *f.* tide; **— alta,** high tide; **— menguante,** ebb tide.

mareado, da (mâ•re•â′tho, thâ) *adj.* dizzy; (naut.) seasick.

marearse (mâ•re•âr′se) *vr.* to get seasick: to get dizzy; (fig.) to have success go to one's head.

mareo (mâ•re′o) *m.* seasickness.

marfil (mâr•fēl′) *m.* ivory.

margarina (mâr•gâ•rē′nâ) *f.* margarine.

margarita (mâr•gâ•rē′tâ) *f.* daisy.

margen (mâr′hen) *m.* or *f.* margin, border; marginal note *(apostilla).*

mariachi (mâ•ryâ′chē) *m.* (Mex.) street band, mariachi; musician in a mariachi.

marido (mâ•rē′tho) *m.* husband.

marina (mâ•rē′nâ) *f.* navy; (com.) shipping fleet.

marinero (mâ•rē•ne′ro) *m.* sailor.

marino, na (mâ•rē′no, nâ) *adj.* marine; **—,** *m.* mariner, seaman.

mariposa (mâ•rē•po′sâ) *f.* butterfly.

mariscal (mâ•rēs•kâl′) *m.* marshal; horseshoer, blacksmith *(herrador);* **— de campo,** field marshal.

marisco (mâ•rēs′ko) *m.* shellfish.

marital (mâ•re•tâl′) *adj.* marital.

marítimo, ma (mâ•rē′tē•mo, mâ) *adj.* maritime, marine.

marmita (mâr•mē´tâ) f. kettle, pot.

mármol (mâr´mol) m. marble.

marmota (mâr•mo´tâ) f. marmot; (Sp. Am.) woodchuck, groundhog.

maroma (mâ•ro´mâ) f. rope; (Sp. Am.) feat, stunt.

marqués (mâr•kes´) m. marquis.

marquesa (mâr•ke´sâ) f. marchioness.

marquesina (mâr•ke•sē´nâ) f. marquee, canopy.

marrano (mâ•rrâ´no) m. pig, hog; (fig.) sloppy, unkempt person.

marroquí (mâ•rro•kē´) m. and f. and adj. Moroccan; —, m. morocco leather.

marsellés, esa (mâr•se•yes´, e´sâ) n. and adj. native of Marseilles; of Marseilles; la M— the Marseillaise, French national anthem.

martes (mâr´tes) m. Tuesday.

martillar (mâr•tē•yâr´) va. to hammer.

martillo (mâr•tē´yo) m. hammer.

mártir (mâr´tēr) m. or f. martyr.

martirio (mâr•tē´ryo) m. martyrdom; (fig.) torture.

martirizar (mâr•tē•rē•zâr´) va. to martyr; to torture, to wrack.

marzo (mâr´so) m. March.

mas (mâs) conj. but, yet.

más (mâs) adv. more; a —, besides, moreover; — o menos, more or less; a — tardar, at latest; sin — ni —, without more ado; — frío, colder; — caliente, hotter; lo —, the most; — allá, farther; tanto —, so much more; —, adj. more — alimento, more food.

masa (mâ´sâ) f. dough, paste (pasta); mass.

masaje (mâ•sâ´he) m. massage.

mascar (mâs•kâr´) va. to chew.

máscara (mâs´kâ•râ) m. or f. masquerader; —, f. mask; baile de —s, masquerade ball.

mascota (mâs•ko´tâ) f. mascot.

masculino, na (mâs•kū•lē´no, nâ) adj, masculine, male.

masticar (mâs•tē•kâr´) va. to masticate, to chew.

mástil (mâs´tēl) m. (naut.) topmast; pylon.

mata (mâ´tâ) f. plant, shrub.

matadero (mâ•tâ•the´ro) m. slaughter-house.

matamoscas (mâ•tâ•mos´kâs) m. flyswatter.

matanza (mâ•tân´sâ) f. slaughtering; massacre (mortandad).

matar (mâ•târ´) va. to kill; —se, to commit suicide; to be killed.

mate (mâ´te) m. checkmate (del ajedrez); maté.

matemática (mâ•te•mâ´tē•kâ) f. mathematics.

matemático, ca (ma•te•mâ´tē•ko,

kâ) *adj.* mathematical; —, *m.* mathematician.

materia (mâ•te´ryâ) *f.* matter, material; (fig.) subject, topic, matter; (med.) pus; — **prima,** raw material.

material (mâ•te•ryâl´) *adj.* material, corporal; (fig.) rude, uncouth; —, *m.* ingredients, materials.

materialismo (mâ•te•ryâ•lēz´mo) *m.* materialism.

maternal (mâ•ter•nâl´) *adj.* maternal, motherly.

maternidad (mâ•ter•nē•thâth´) *f.* motherhood, motherliness.

matiné (mâ•tē•ne´) *f.* matinée.

matiz (mâ•tēs´) *m.* shade, nuance.

matizar (mâ•tē•sâr´) *va.* to mix well, to blend, to shade.

matón (mâ•ton´) *m.* bully.

matorral (mâ •to•rrâl´) *m.* brambles, thicket, dense underbrush.

matraca (mâ•trâ´kâ) *f.* rattle; **dar** —, to annoy, to tease.

matricidio (mâ•trē•sē´thyo) *m.* matricide.

matrícula (mâ•trē´kū•lâ) *f.* register, list; license plate *(placa);* registration, number registered *(conjunto).*

matricular (ma•trē•kū•lâr´) *va.* to matriculate; —**se,** to register.

matrimonial (mâ•trē•mo•nyâl´) *adj.* matrimonial.

matrimonio (mâ•trē•mo´nyo) *m.* marriage, matrimony.

matriz (mâ•trēs´) *f.* uterus, womb; mold; —, *adj.* main, parent.

matrona (mâ•tro´nâ) *f.* matron.

matutino, na (mâ•tū•tē´no, nâ) *adj.* morning, in the morning.

maullar (mâū•yâr´) *vn.* to mew, to meow.

máxima (mâk´sē•mâ) *f.* maxim, rule.

máxime (mâk´sē•me) *adv.* principally.

máximo, ma (mâk´sē•mo, mâ) *adj.* maximum, chief, principal; —, *m.* maximum.

mayo (mâ´yo) *m.* May.

mayonesa (mâ•yo•ne´sâ) *f.* and *adj.* mayonnaise.

mayor (mâ•yor´) *adj.* greater, larger; elder *(edad);* — **de edad,** of age; —, *m.* superior; (mil.) major; **al por** —, wholesale.

mayorista (mâ•yo•rēs´tâ) *m.* wholesaler.

mayoría (mâ•yo•rē´â) *f.* majority.

mayúscula (mâ•yūs´kū•lâ) *f.* capital letter.

mazorca (mâ•sor´kâ) *f.* ear of corn.

me (me) *pron.* me, to me; me *(acusativo).*

mear (me•âr´) *vn.* to urinate.

mecánicamente

(me•kâ•nē•kâ•men´te) *adv.* mechanically, automatically.

mecánica (me•kâ´nē•kâ) *f.* mechanics.

mecánico, ca (me•kâ´nē•ko, kâ) *adj.* mechanical; —, *m.* mechanic.

mecanismo (me•kâ•nēz´mo) *m.* mechanism.

mecanizar (me•kâ•nē•sâr´) *va.* to mechanize.

mecanografía (me•kâ•no•grâ•fē´â) *f.* typewriting, typing.

mecedora (me•se•tho´râ) *f.* rocking chair, rocker.

mecer (me•ser´) *va.* to swing, to rock.

mecha (me´châ) *f.* wick; fuse *(cuerda);* match *(fósforo).*

medalla (me•thâ´yâ) *f.* medal.

medallón (me•thâ•yon´) *m.* medallion; locket *(relicario).*

media (me´thyâ) *f.* stocking.

mediación (me•thyâ•syon´) *f.* mediation, intervention.

mediador (me•thyâ•thor´) *m.* mediator, go-between.

mediano, na (me•thyâ´no, nâ) *adj.* moderate, average, medium; mediocre, passable.

medianoche (me•thyâ•no´che) *f.* midnight.

mediante (me•thyân´te) *adv.* by means of, through; **Dios —,** God willing.

mediar (me•thyâr´) *vn.* to be in the middle; to intercede, to mediate *(interceder).*

medicamento (me•thē•kâ•men´to) *m.* medicine.

medicina (me•thē•sē´nâ) *f.* medicine; — **espacial,** space medicine.

medicinal (me•thē•sē•nâl´) *adj.* medicinal.

médico (me´thē•ko) *m.* physician; —, **ca,** *adj.* medical.

medida (me•thē´thâ) *f.* measure; **a la —,** made-to-measure, tailor-made; **a — que,** at the same time that, in proportion as.

medidor (me•thē•thor´) *m.* meter, gauge; —, **ra,** *n.* measurer.

medieval (me•thye•vâl´) *adj.* medieval.

medio, dia (me´thyo, thyâ) *adj.* half; halfway *(moderado);* middle, average *(usual);* mean, average *(de promedio);* **a — asta,** at halfmast; **a —dias,** by halves; **de peso —,** middle weight; — **hora,** half an hour; **—dia noche,** midnight; **la Edad M—,** the Middle Ages.

mediocre (me•thyo´kre) *adj.* middling, mediocre.

mediocridad (me•thyo•krē•thâth´) *f.* mediocrity.

mediodía (me•thyo•thē´â) *m.*

noon, midday; south *(sur).*

medir* (me•thēr´) *va.* to measure; —**se,** to act with moderation.

meditación (me•thē•tâ •syon´) *f.* meditation.

meditar (me•thē•târ´) *va.* and *vn.* to meditate, to consider.

Mediterráneo (me•thē•te•rrá´-ne•o) *m.* Mediterranean.

medroso, sa (me•thro´so, sâ) *adj.* fearful, *(temeroso);* terrible, frightful.

medula (me•thū´lâ) or **médula** (me´thū lâ) *f.* marrow; (fig.) essence, pith, main part.

megáfono (me•gá´fo•no) *m.* megaphone.

mejicano, na (me•hē•ká´no, nâ) = **mexicano, na.**

mejilla (me•hē´yâ) *f.* cheek.

mejor (me•hor´) *adj.* and *adv.* better, best; — **dicho,** rather, more properly; **a lo —,** when least expected.

mejora (me•ho´râ) *f.* improvement.

mejoramiento (me•ho•râ•myen´-to) *m.* improvement, enhancement.

mejorar (me•ho•râr´) *va.* to improve, to cultivate; to heighten *(realzar);* to mend *(componer);* —, *vn.* to recover, to get over a disease; —**se,** to improve, to get better.

mejoría (me•ho•rē´â) *f.* improvement; (med.) recovery; advantage *(ventaja).*

melancolía (me•lâng•ko•lē´â) *f.* melancholy.

melaza (me•lâ´sâ) *f.* molasses.

melena (me•le´nâ) *f.* long, bushy hair; mane *(del león).*

melocotón (me•lo•ko•ton´) *m.* (bot.) peach.

melodía (me•lo•thē´â) *f.* melody.

melodrama (me•lo•thrâ´mâ) *m.* melodrama.

melón (me•lon´) *m.* melon; — **de verano,** cantaloupe.

meloso, sa (me•lo´so, sâ) *adj.* like honey; sweet, mellow *(dulce).*

mellizo, za (me•yē´so, sâ) *n.* and *adj.* twin.

membrana (mem•brâ´nâ) *f.* membrane.

membrillo (mem•brē´yo) *m.* quince; quince tree *(arbusto).*

memorable (me•mo•râ´vle) *adj.* memorable.

memorándum (me•mo•rân´dun) *m.* memorandum; notebook *(librito).*

memoria (me•mo´ryâ) *f.* memory; account, report *(relación);* **de —, by heart, from memory; —s,** *pl.* compliments, regards; memoirs *(de acontecimientos).*

memorial (me•mo•ryâl´) *m.* memorandum book; memorial,

brief *(relación)*.

mencionar (men•syo•när´) *va.* to mention.

mendigar (men•dē•gär´) *va.* to ask for charity, to beg.

mendigo (men•dē´go) *m.* beggar.

menear (me•ne•är´) *va.* to stir, to agitate *(un líquido);* to wiggle, to wag; —**se,** to wag, to wiggle; (fig.) to bustle about, to bestir oneself.

menester (me•nes•ter´) *m.* necessity, want; **ser** —, to be necessary; —**es,** *pl.* bodily needs, bare necessities.

menguar (meng•gwär´) *vn.* to decay, to fall off; to decrease, to diminish *(disminuir);* to fail *(faltar).*

meningitis (me•nēn•hē´tēs) *f.* (med.) meningitis.

menor (me•nor´) *m.* and *f.* minor, person under age; —, *adj.* less, smaller; younger *(edad);* **por** —, (com.) retail; minutely, detailedly.

menos (me´nos) *adv.* less; with the exception of *(excepto);* **a lo** —, or **por lo** —, at least, in any event; **lo** — **posible,** the least possible; **venir a** —, to decline, to lessen; **a** — **que,** unless; **echar de** —, to miss.

menoscabar (me•nos•kä•vär´) *va.* to lessen; to worsen, to make worse *(empeorar);* to

reduce *(reducir).*

menospreciar (me•nos•pre•syär´) *va.* to undervalue, to underestimate; to despise, to contemn *(desdeñar).*

mensaje (men•sä´he) *m.* message, errand; — **s no deseados,** junk mail, SPAM.

mensajero, ra (men•sä•he´ro, rä) *n.* messenger.

menstruación (mens•trwä•syon´) *f.* menstruation.

mensual (men•swäl´) *adj.* monthly; —**mente,** *adv.* monthly.

mensualidad (men•swä•lē•thäth´) *f.* monthly payment.

menta (men´tä) *f.* (bot.) mint.

mental (men•täl´) *adj.* mental, intellectual.

mentalidad (men•tä•lē•thäth´) *f.* mentality.

mentalmente (men•täl•men´te) *adv.* mentally.

mentar* (men•tär´) *va.* to mention.

mente (men´te) *f.* mind, understanding.

mentir* (men•tēr´) *vn.* to lie, to tell falsehoods.

mentira (men•tē´rä) *f.* lie, falsehood; **decir** —, to lie; **parecer** —, to seem impossible.

mentiroso, sa (men•tē•ro´so, sä) *adj.* lying, deceitful; —, *n.* liar.

mentón (men•ton´) *m.* chin.

menú (me•nū´) *m.* menu, bill of fare.

menudeo (me•nū•the´o) *m.* retail; **al —,** at retail.

menudo, da (me•nū´tho, thâ) *adj.* small, minute; **a —do,** repeatedly, often; **—, *m.*** change, silver; tripe, entrails *(de res);* tripe soup.

meñique (me•nyē´ke) *m.* little finger.

mercadería (mer•kâ•the•rē´â) *f.* commodity, merchandise.

mercado (mer•kâ´tho) *m.* market; market place *(sitio);* **— de valores,** stock market.

mercadotecnia (mer•kâ•tho•teg´nyâ) *f.* marketing.

mercancía (mer•kân´sē´â) *f.* trade, traffic *(trato);* goods, merchandise.

mercante (mer•kân´te) *adj.* merchant.

mercantil (mer•kân•tēl´) *adj.* commercial, mercantile.

merced (mer•seth´) *f.* favor, grace; mercy, will, pleasure *(voluntad);* **estar a — de otro,** to be at another's mercy.

mercenario (mer•se•nâ´ryo) *m.* day laborer; (mil.) mercenary; **—, ria,** *adj.* mercenary.

mercurio (mer•kū´ryo) *m.* mercury, quicksilver.

merecedor, ra (me•re•se•thor´, râ) *adj.* deserving, worthy.

merecer* (me•re•ser´) *va.* to deserve, to merit; **—,** *vn.* to be deserving.

merecido, da (me•re•sē´tho, thâ) *adj.* deserved; **bien** or **mal —,** well- or ill-deserved; **—,** *m.* just punishment, just deserts.

merecimiento (me•re•sē•myen´-to) *m.* merit, desert.

merendar* (me•ren•dâr´) *vn.* to have a snack.

merengue (me•reng´ge) *m.* meringue, typical dance of the Dominican Republic.

meridiano (me•rē•thyâ´no) *m.* meridian; **pasado —,** afternoon; **—, na,** *adj.* meridional.

merienda (me•ryen´dâ) *f.* light lunch, snack; **— campestre,** picnic lunch.

mérito (me´rē•to) *m.* merit, desert.

meritorio, ria (me•rē•to´ryo, ryâ) *adj.* meritorious, laudable.

mermelada (mer•me•lâ´thâ) *f.* marmalade.

mero (me´ro) *m.* (ichth). pollack; **—, ra,** *adj.* mere, pure; (Mex. coll.) real, actual; **—ro,** *adv.* (Mex. coll.) almost.

mes (mes) *m.* month.

mesa (me´sâ) *f.* table; **— redonda,** round table; **poner la —,** to set the table; **quitar la —,** to clear the table.

mesada (me•sâ´thâ) *f.* monthly payment.

meseta (me•se´tâ) *f.* landing *(de escalera);* plateau.

Mesías (me•sē´âs) *m.* Messiah.

mesón (me•son´) *m.* inn, hostelry.

mestizo, za (mes•tē´so, sâ) *n.* half-breed; —, *adj.* of mixed blood.

mesura (me•sū´râ) *f.* grave deportment, dignity, politeness *(educación);* moderation *(moderación).*

meta (me´tâ) *f.* goal, finish line; (fig.) end, goal.

metabolismo (me•tâ•vo•lēz´mo) *m.* metabolism.

metafísica (me•tâ•fē´sē•kâ) *f.* metaphysics.

metáfora (me•tâ´fo•râ) *f.* metaphor.

metafórico, ca (me•tâ•fo´rē•ko, kâ) *adj.* metaphorical.

metal (me•tâl´) *m.* metal; brass *(latón);* tone, timbre *(de la voz).*

metálico, ca (me•tâ´lē•ko, kâ) *adj.* metallic, metal.

metalurgia (me•tâ•lūr´hyâ) *f.* metallurgy.

metamorfosis (me•tâ•mor•fo´sēs) *f.* metamorphosis.

meteoro (me•te•o´ro) *m.* meteor.

meteorología (me•te•o•ro•lo•hē´â) *f.* meteoro-

logy.

meter (me•ter´) *va.* to place in, to put in, to insert; to cause, to start *(promover);* to smuggle *(contrabandear);* —se, to meddle, to interfere.

meticuloso, sa (me•tē•kū•lo´so, sâ) *adj.* conscientious, meticulous.

metódico, ca (me•to´thē•ko, kâ) *adj.* methodical, systematic.

metodista (me•to•thēs´tâ) *m.* and *f.* and *adj.* Methodist.

método (me´to•tho) *m.* method.

metraje (me•trâ´he) *m.* length in meters; **de largo —,** full length (film).

métrico, ca (me´trē•ko, kâ) *adj.* metrical.

metro (me´tro) *m.* meter; (coll.) subway.

metrópoli (me•tro´po•lē) *f.* metropolis.

metropolitano, na (me•tro•po•lē•tâ´no, nâ) *adj.* metropolitan; —, *m.* subway.

mexicano, na (me•hē•kâ´no, nâ) or **mejicano, na,** *n.* and *adj.* Mexican.

mezcla (mes´klâ) *f.* mixture, medley.

mezclar (mes•klâr´) *va.* to mix, to mingle; —se, to mix, to take part.

mezclilla (mes•kle´yâ) *f.* denim.

mezcolanza or **mescolanza**

(mes•ko•lân´• sâ) *f.* hodgepodge.

mezquindad (mes•kēn•dâth´) *f.* penury, poverty; avarice, stinginess *(avaricia);* trifle *(pequeñez).*

mezquino, na (mes•kē´no, nâ) *adj.* poor, indigent; avaricious, covetous; mean, petty.

mezquita (mes•kē´tâ) *f.* mosque.

mi (mē) *pron.* my; —, *m.* (mus.) mi.

mi (mē) *pron. (object of prep.)* me.

microbio (mē•kro´vyo) *m.* microbe, germ.

microbiólogo (mē•kro•vyo´lo•go) *m.* microbiologist.

microcircuito (mē•kro•sēr•kwē´to) *m.* microcircuit.

microfilme (mē•kro•fēl´me) *m.* microfilm.

micrófono (mē•kro´fo•no) *m.* microphone; receiver *(del teléfono).*

micrómetro (mē•kro´me•tro) *m.* micrometer.

microonda (mē•kro•on´dâ) *f.* microwave.

microscopio (mē•kros•ko´pyo) *m.* microscope.

miedo (mye´tho) *m.* fear, dread; **tener** —, to be afraid.

miedoso, sa (mye•tho´so, sâ) *adj.* afraid, fearful.

miel (myel) *f.* honey; **luna de** —, honeymoon.

miembro (myem´bro) *m.* member; (anat.) limb.

mientras (myen´trâs) *adv.* while; — **tanto,** meanwhile, in the meantime.

miércoles (myer´ko•les) *m.* Wednesday; **M— de Ceniza,** Ash Wednesday.

miga (mē´gâ) crumb.

migaja (mē•gâ´hâ) *f.* scrap, crumb, small particle.

migración (mē•grâ•syon´) *f.* migration.

mil (mēl) *m.* one thousand; **por** —, per thousand; — **millones,** one thousand million; one billion in U.S.A.

milagro (mē•lâ´gro) *m.* miracle, wonder; ex-voto *(presentalla).*

milagroso, sa (mē•lâ•gro´so, sâ) *adj.* miraculous.

milenario, ria (mē•le•nâ´ryo, ryâ) *adj.* millenary; —, *m.* millennium.

milésimo, ma (mē•le´sē•mo, mâ) *adj.* thousandth.

milicia (mē•lē´syâ) *f.* militia.

miligramo (mē•lē•grâ´mo) *m.* milligram.

milímetro (mē•lē´me•tro) *m.* millimeter.

militar (mē•lē•târ´) *adj.* military; —, *vn.* to serve in the army.

milpa (mēl´pâ) *f.* (Sp. Am.) cornfield.

milla (mē´ya) *f.* mile.

millar (mē•yâr´) *m.* thousand.

millón (mē•yon´) *m.* million.

millonario, ria (mē•yo•nâ´ryo, ryâ) *n.* millionaire.

mimar (mē•mâr´) *va.* to indulge, to cater to, to spoil *(consentir);* to treat with affection; to gratify.

mímica (mē´mē•kâ) *f.* mimicry.

mimo (mē´mo) *m.* mime, mimic *(actor);* mimicry, satire *(representación);* gratification, affection; indulgence, spoiling *(del niño).*

mina (mē´nâ) *f.* mine; (fig.) wealth, goldmine, trove; **— terrestre,** land mine.

minar (mē•nâr´) *va.* to mine; to undermine *(destruir);* (fig.) to work hard at, to pursue diligently.

mineral (mē•ne•râl´) *m.* mineral; fountainhead, wellspring *(de una fuente);* —, *adj.* mineral.

minero (mē•ne´ro) *m.* miner; —, **ra,** *adj.* mining.

miniatura (mē•nyâ•tū´râ) *f.* miniature.

mínimo, ma (mē´nē•mo, mâ) *adj.* least, slightest.

ministerio (mē•nēs•te´ryo) *m.* ministry, department; function, position *(empleo);* cabinet *(cuerpo).*

ministro (mē•nēs´tro) *m.* minister; (pol.) secretary, minister; **M— de Estado,** Secretary of State.

minoría (mē•no•rē´â) **minoridad,** (mē• no•rē•thâth´) *f.* minority.

minucioso, sa (mē•nū•syo´so, sâ) *adj.* minute, very exact.

minúscula (mē•nūs´kū•lâ) *adj.* small, lower-case; —, *f.* lower-case letter.

minuto (mē•nū´to) *m.* minute.

mío (mē´o) **mía,** (mē´â) *pron.* mine; —, *adj.* of mine.

miope (myo´pe) *adj.* nearsighted; —, *m.* and *f.* nearsighted person.

miopía (myo•pē´â) *f.* nearsightedness.

mira (mē´râ) *f.* gunsight; purpose, intention *(propósito);* care *(interés);* **estar a la —,** to be on the lookout, to be on the alert.

mirada (mē•râ´thâ) *f.* glance *(vistazo);* gaze; **clavar la —,** to peer, to stare.

mirador, ra (mē•râ•thor´, râ) *n.* spectator, onlooker; —, *m.* enclosed porch *(balcón);* belvedere.

mirar (mē•râr´) *va.* to behold, to look at, to observe; to spy on *(espiar);* to face, to look over *(estar situado).*

mirasol (mē•râ•sol´) *m.* (bot.) sunflower.

mirlo (mēr´lo) *m.* blackbird.

mirto (mēr´to) *m.* myrtle.

misa (mē´sâ) *f.* mass; **— del gallo,** midnight mass **cantar —,** to say mass.

misántropo (mē•sân´tro•po) *m.* misanthrope, misanthropist.

misceláneo, nea (mēs•se•lâ´ne•o, ne•â) *adj.* miscellaneous.

miserable (mē•se•râ´vle) *adj.* miserable, wretched; stingy, avaricious *(avariento).*

miseria (mē•se´ryâ) *f.* misery; niggardliness *(tacañería)* ; trifle *(pequeñez).*

misericordia (mē•se•rē•kor´thyâ) *f.* mercy, clemency, pity.

mísero, ra (mē´se•ro, râ) *adj.* miserable, poor, wretched.

misión (mē•syon´) *f.* mission.

misionero, ra (mē•syo•ne´ro, râ) *n.* missionary.

mismo, ma (mēz´mo, mâ) *adj.* same; **ahora —mo,** just now; **yo —,** I myself; **él —,** he himself; **usted —,** you yourself; **el** or **la —,** the same; **ella —,** she herself; **ellos —s,** they themselves.

misterio (mēs•te´ryo) *m.* mystery.

misterioso, sa (mēs•te•ryo´so, sâ) *adj.* mysterious.

mística (mēs´tē•kâ) *f.* mysticism.

místico, ca (mēs´tē•ko, kâ) *adj.* mystic, mystical.

mitad (mē•tâth´) *f.* half; middle *(medio).*

mítico, ca (mē´tē•ko, kâ) *adj.* mythical.

mitigación (mē•tē•gâ•syon´) *f.* mitigation.

mitin (mē´tēn) *m.* meeting.

mito (mē´to) *m.* myth.

mitología (mē•to•lo•hē´â) *f.* mythology.

mixto, ta (mēs´to, tâ) *adj.* mixed, mingled.

mixtura (mēs•tū´râ) *f.* mixture.

mobiliario (mo•vē•lyâ´ryo) *m.* furniture; chattels *(enseres).*

moco (mo´ko) *m.* mucus.

mocosidad (mo•ko•sē•thâth´) *f.* mucosity.

mocoso, sa (mo•ko´so, sâ) *adj.* sniveling, mucous; **—,** *n.* brat.

mochila (mo•chē´lâ) *f.* knapsack.

mocho, cha (mo´cho, châ) *adj.* hornless; shaved *(pelado);* maimed *(mutilado).*

moda (mo´thâ) *f.* fashion, mode; **a la —,** in style; **de —,** fashionable; **última —,** latest fashion.

modales (mo•thâ´les) *m. pl.* manners, breeding, bearing.

modalidad (mo•thâ•lē•thâth´) *f.* nature, character, quality.

modelar (mo•the•lâr´) *va.* to model, to form.

modelo (mo•the´lo) *m.* model, pattern.

moderación (mo•the•râ•syon´) *f.* moderation, temperance.

moderado, da (mo•the•râ´tho, thâ) *adj.* moderate, temperate.

modernismo (mo•ther•nēz´mo) *m.* modernism.

modernista (mo•ther•nēs´tâ) *adj.* modernistic.

modernización (mo•ther•nē•sâ•syon´) *f.* modernization.

modernizar (mo•ther•nē•sâr´) *va.* to modernize.

moderno, na (mo•ther´no, nâ) *adj.* modern

modestia (mo•thes´tyâ) *f.* humility, diffidence.

modesto, ta (mo•thes´to, tâ) *adj.* unassuming, modest, unpretentious.

modificación (mo•thē•fē•kâ•syon´) *f.* modification.

modificador (mo•thē•fē•kâ•thor´) *m.* modifier.

modificar (mo•thē•fē•kâr´) *va.* to modify.

modismo (mo•thēz´mo) *m.* idiom, idiomatic expression.

modo (mo´tho) *m.* mode, method, manner; moderation *(templanza);* (gram.) mood; **de — que,** so that; **de ningún —,** by no means; **de todos —s,** by all means.

modorra (mo•tho´rrâ) *f.* drowsiness.

modulación (mo•thū•lâ•syon´) *f.* modulation.

modular (mo•thū•lâr´) *va.* to modulate.

moho (mo´o) *m.* (bot.) mold; rust.

mohoso, sa (mo•o´so, sa) *adj.* moldy, musty; rusty.

moisés (moē•ses´) *m.* bassinet.

mojar (mo•hâr´) *va.* to wet, to moisten; **—se,** to get wet.

molde (mol´de) *m.* mold, matrix *(el hueco);* pattern; (fig.) example, model.

moldura (mol•dū´râ) *f.* molding.

mole (mo´le) *adj.* soft, mild; **—,** *f.* mass, bulk; **—,** *m.* (Mex.) kind of spicy sauce for fowl and meat stews.

molécula (mo•le´kū•lâ) *f.* molecule.

moler* (mo•ler´) *va.* to grind, to pound; (fig.) to vex, to annoy.

molestar (mo•les•târ´) *va.* to annoy, to trouble.

molestia (mo•les´tyâ) *f.* disturbance, annoyance *(fastidio);* discomfort *(incomodidad);* indisposition, ailment *(desazón).*

molesto, ta (mo•les´to, tâ) *adj.* troublesome.

molestoso, sa (mo•les•to´so, sâ) *adj.* annoying, bothersome.

molienda (mo•lyen´dâ) *f.* grinding, pounding.

molino (mo•lē´no) *m.* mill; **— de**

viento, windmill.

mollera (mo•ye´râ) *f.* crown of head; **ser duro de —,** to be headstrong or hardheaded *(testarudo);* to be dense or dull *(duro).*

momentáneo, nea (mo•men•tâ´ne•o, ne•â) *adj.* momentary.

momento (mo•men´to) *m.* moment.

momia (mo´myâ) *f.* mummy.

mona (mo´nâ) *f.* female monkey; (fig.) copycat, imitator; drunkenness *(borrachera);* drunkard *(ebrio).*

monaguillo (mo•nâ•gē´yo) *m.* acolyte, altar boy.

monarca (mo•nâr´kâ) *m.* monarch.

monarquía (mo•nâr•kē´â) *f.* monarchy.

monasterio (mo•nâs•te´ryo) *m.* monastery, cloister.

mondongo (mon•dong´go) *m.* animal intestines.

moneda (mo•ne´thâ) *f.* money, coinage, currency; **— corriente,** currency; **— falsa,** counterfeit money; **— legal,** legal tender; **casa de —,** mint; **papel —,** paper money.

monedero (mo•ne•the´ro) *m.* coiner; coin purse *(portamonedas).*

monetario, ria (mo•ne•tâ´ryo,

ryâ) *adj.* monetary.

mongoloide (mon•go•lo´ē•the) *adj.* Mongoloid.

monigote (mo•nē•go´te) *m.* lay brother; (coll.) bumpkin, dolt, lout *(torpe);* (coll.) poor painting *(pintura);* badly done statue *(estatua).*

monitor (mo•nē•tor´) *m.* monitor.

monja (mon´hâ) *f.* nun.

monje (mon´he) *m.* monk.

mono, na (mo´no, nâ) *adj.* (coll.) pretty, cute; **—,** *m.* monkey; ape *(antropomorfo).*

monogamia (mo•no•gâ´myâ) *f.* monogamy.

monograma (mo•no•grâ´mâ) *m.* monogram.

monolito (mo•no•lē´to) *m.* monolith.

monólogo (mo•no´lo•go) *m.* monologue.

monopolio (mo•no•po´lyo) *m.* monopoly.

monorriel (mo•no•rryel´) *m.* monorail.

monosílabo, ba (mo•no•sē´lâ•vo, vâ) *adj.* monosyllabic; **—,** *m.* monosyllable.

monotonía (mo•no•to•nē´â) *f.* monotony.

monótono, na (mo•no´to•no, nâ) *adj.* monotonous.

monstruo (mons´trwo) *m.* monster.

monstruosidad (mons•trwo•sē•thâth´) *f.* monstrosity.

monstruoso, sa (mons•trwo´so, sâ) *adj.* monstrous, freakish.

montaje (mon•tâ´he) *m.* assembly, setting up, putting up, mounting *(armado);* editing *(de un filme);* —s, *pl.* artillery carriage.

montaña (mon•tâ´nyâ) *f.* mountain.

montañoso, sa (mon•tâ•nyo´so, sâ) *adj.* mountainous.

montar (mon•târ´) *vn.* to climb up, to get up; to mount *(en una cabalgadura);* to ride horseback *(cabalgar);* —, *vt.* to set up, to put together *(armar);* to amount to, to come to *(una cantidad);* to edit *(un filme).*

monte (mon´te) *m.* mountain; wilds, brush *(sin roturar);* (fig.) stumbling block, obstacle.

monto (mon´to) *m.* amount, sum.

montón (mon•ton´) *m.* heap, pile, mass, cluster; **a —ones,** abundantly, in great quantities.

montura (mon•tū´râ) *f.* mount *(cabalgadura);* saddle trappings *(de caballería);* mounting, framework *(armazón).*

monumental (mo•nū•men•tâl´) *adj.* monumental.

monumento (mo•nū•men´to) *m.* monument.

moño (mo´nyo) *m.* topknot, loop *(del pelo);* (orn.) tuft, crest.

mora (mo´râ) *f.* blackberry, mulberry.

morado, da (mo•râ´tho, thâ) *adj.* violet, purple.

moral (mo•râl´) *m.* mulberry tree; —, *f.* morals, ethics; —, *adj.* moral.

moraleja (mo•râ•le´hâ) *f.* moral, moral lesson.

moralidad (mo•râ•lē•thâth´) *f.* morality, morals.

morar (mo•râr´) *vn.* to inhabit, to dwell.

moratoria (mo•râ•to´ryâ) *f.* moratorium.

mórbido, da (mor´vē•tho, thâ) *adj.* diseased, morbid.

morcilla (mor•sē´yâ) *f.* blood sausage.

mordaz (mor•thâs´) *adj.* biting, sarcastic.

mordaza (mor•thâ´sâ) *f.* gag.

mordedura (mor•the•thū´râ) *f.* bite.

morder* (mor•ther´) *va.* to bite.

mordisco (mor•thēs´ko) or **mordiscón** (mor•thēs•kon´) *m.* bite.

morena (mo•re´nâ) *f.* (ichth.) moray eel; brunette *(mujer).*

moreno, na (mo•re´no, nâ) *adj.* swarthy, dark brown.

morfina (mor•fē´nâ) *f.* morphine.

moribundo, da (mo•rē•vūn´do, dâ) *adj.* dying.

morir* (mo•rēr´) *vn.* to die, to expire; —**se,** to go out, to be extinguished.

moro, ra (mo´ro, râ) *adj.* Moorish; —, *n.* Moor; Moslem *(mahometano).*

morral (mo•rrâl´) *m.* feed bag, nose bag *(para pienso);* sack, provisions sack.

mortal (mor•tâl´) *adj.* mortal, fatal, deadly; mortal *(sujeto a la muerte).*

mortalidad (mor•tâ•lē•thâth´) *f.* mortality; death rate *(cantidad).*

mortero (mor•te´ro) *m.* mortar.

mortificar (mor•tē•fē•kâr´) *va.* to mortify; to afflict, to vex *(afligir).*

mortuorio (mor•two´ryo) *m.* burial, funeral; —, rite, *adj.* mortuary.

mosaico (mo•sâ´ē•ko) *m.* mosaic.

mosca (mos´kâ) *f.* fly.

moscarda (mos•kâr´thâ) *f.* horsefly.

Moscú (mos•kū´) *m.* Moscow.

mosquetero (mos•ke•te´ro) *m.* musketeer.

mosquitero (mos•kē•te´ro) *m.* mosquito net.

mosquito (mos•kē´to) *m.* mosquito.

mostacho (mos•tâ´cho) *m.* mustache.

mostaza (mos•tâ´sâ) *f.* mustard; mustard seed *(semilla).*

mostrador (mos•trâ•thor´) *m.* shop counter.

mostrar* (mos•trâr´) *va.* to show, to exhibit; —**se,** to appear, to show oneself.

mota (mo´tâ) *f.* burl *(del paño);* speck.

motín (mo•tēn´) *m.* mutiny, riot.

motivar (mo•tē•vâr´) *va.* to motivate, to give a motive for; to justify, to explain the reason for *(explicar).*

motivo (mo•tē´vo) *m.* motive, cause, reason; **con este** —, therefore; **con** — **de,** by reason of.

motocicleta (mo•to•sē•kle´tâ) *f.* motorcycle.

motor, ra (mo•tor´, râ) *adj.* moving, motor; —, *m.* motor, engine; — **de búsqueda,** search engine; **poner en marcha el** —, to start the motor.

motriz (mo•trēs´) *f. adj.* motor, moving.

movedizo, za (mo•ve•thē´so, sâ) *adj.* moving, movable.

mover* (mo•ver´) *va.* to move; to stir up, to cause *(suscitar).*

movible (mo•vē´•vle) *adj.* movable.

móvil (mo´•vēl) *adj.* movable; —,

m. motive, incentive.

movilización (mo•vē•lē•sâ•syon´)
f. mobilization.

movilizar (mo•vē•lē•sâr´) *va.* to
mobilize.

movimiento (mo•vē•myen´•to) *m.*
movement.

moza (mo´•sâ) *f.* girl; maidservant *(sirvienta).*

mozo, za (mo´•so, sâ) *adj.*
young; —, *m.* youth, lad;
manservant *(sirviente);* waiter
(camarero).

muchacha (mū•châ´•châ) *f.* girl,
lass, young woman.

muchacho (mū•châ´•cho) *m.*
boy, young man; —, **cha,** *adj.*
boyish; girlish.

muchedumbre
(mū•che•thūm´•bre) *f.* crowd,
multitude.

mucho, cha (mū´•cho, châ) *adj.*
much, abundant; — **tiempo,** a
long time; **hay —s,** there are
many; **—cho** *adv.* much.

mudanza (mū•thân´•sâ) *f.*
change; mutation; inconstancy
(inconstancia); **estoy de —,** I
am moving.

mudar (mū•thâr´) *va.* to change;
to molt; **—se de casa,** to move,
to move into a new home.

mudo, da (mū´•tho, thâ) *adj.*
dumb; silent, mute *(callado).*

mueble (mwe´•vle) *m.* piece of
furniture; **—s,** *pl.* furniture.

mueblería (mwe•vle•rē´•â) *f.* furniture store.

mueca (mwe´•kâ) *f.* grimace, wry
face.

muela (mwe´•lâ) *f.* molar tooth;
— **cordal** or **del juicio,** wisdom
tooth.

muelle (mwe´•ye) *adj.* tender,
delicate, soft; —, *m.* spring
(resorte); (naut.) dock, quay,
wharf; (rail.) freight dock.

muérdago (mwer´•thâ•go) *m.*
mistletoe.

muerte (mwer´•te) *f.* death.

muerto (mwer´•to) *m.* corpse; —,
ta, *adj.* dead.

muestra (mwes´•trâ) *f.* sample
(de mercancía); sign *(de tienda);* pattern, model *(modelo);*
(mil.) muster, inspection; face,
dial *(del reloj);* indication, sample, example *(señal).*

mugido (mū•hē´•tho) *m.* lowing,
bellowing.

mugir (mū•hēr´) *vn.* to low, to
bellow.

mugre (mū´•gre) *f.* dirt, grease.

mujer (mū•her´) *f.* woman; wife
(casada).

muladar (mū•lâ•thâr´) *m.* trash
heap.

mulato, ta (mū•lâ´•to, tâ) *n.* and
adj. mulatto.

muleta (mū•le´•tâ) *f.* crutch.

multa (mūl´•tâ) *f.* fine, penalty.

multar (mūl•târ´) *va.* to impose

a penalty on, to penalize, to fine.

multifacético, ca (mūl•tē•fâ•se´•tē•ko, kâ) *adj.* multiphase.

multimillonario, ria (mūl•tē•mē•yo•nâ´•ryo, ryâ) *adj.* and *n.* multimillionaire.

múltiple (mūl´•tē•ple) *adj.* multiple, manifold.

multiplicador, ra (mūl•tē•plē•kâ•thor´, râ) *n.* multiplier; —, *m.* (math.) multiplier.

multiplicar (mūl•tē•plē•kâr´) *va.* to multiply.

multiplicidad (mūl•tē•plē•sē•thâth´) *f.* multiplicity.

multitud (mūl•tē•tūth´) *f.* multitude, crowd.

mullir* (mū•yēr´) *va.* to shake up, to fluff up.

mundano, na (mūn•dâ´•no, nâ) *adj.* mundane, worldly.

mundial (mūn•dyâl´) *adj.* worldwide, world.

mundo (mūn´•do) *m.* world; **todo el —,** everybody.

munición (mū•nē•syon´) *f.* ammunition.

municipal (mū•nē•sē•pâl´) *adj.* municipal.

municipio (mū•nē•sē´•pyo) *m.* city council.

muñeca (mū•nye´•kâ) *f.* (anat.)

wrist; doll *(juguete)*.

muñeco (mū•nye´•ko) *m.* figurine, statuette.

mural (mū•râl´) *m.* and *adj.* mural.

muralla (mū•râ´•yâ) *f.* rampart, wall.

murciélago (mūr•sye´•lâ•go) *m.* (zool.) bat. **murmuración** (mūr•mū•râ•syon´) *f.* backbiting, gossip.

murmurar (mūr•mū•râr´) *vn.* to murmur; to backbite, to gossip *(chismear)*.

muro (mū´•ro) *m.* wall.

musa (mū´•sâ) *f.* Muse.

muscular (mūs•kū•lâr´) *adj.* muscular.

músculo (mūs´•kū•lo) *m.* muscle.

museo (mū•se´•o) *m.* museum.

musgo (mūz´•go) *m.* moss.

música (mū´•sē•kâ) *f.* music; **— de cámara,** chamber music; **— sagrada,** church music.

musical (mū•sē•kâl´) *adj.* musical.

músico (mū´•sē•ko) *m.* musician.

muslo (muz´•lo) *m.* thigh.

mustio, tia (mūs´•tyo, tyâ) *adj.* withered *(marchito);* sad, sorrowful *(triste)*.

musulmán, na (mū•sūl•mâ´n, nâ) *adj.* and *n.* Mohammedan.

mutación (mū•tâ•syon´) *f.* mutation, change.

mutilación (mū•tē•lâ•syon´) *f.*
mutilation.

mutilar (mū•tē•lâr´) *va.* to mutilate, to maim.

mutismo (mū•tēz´•mo) *m.* mute-

ness.

mutual (mū•twâl´) *adj.* mutual.

mutuo, tua (mū´•two, twâ) *adj.*
mutual, reciprocal.

muy (mwē) *adv.* very; greatly
(altamente).

N

naba (nâ´•vâ) *f.* rutabaga,
Swedish turnip.

nabo (nâ´•vo) *m.* turnip.

nácar (nâ´•kâr) *m.* mother-of-
pearl.

nacer* (nâ•ser´) *vn.* to be born;
(bot.) to bud, to germinate.

nacido, da (nâ•sē´•tho, thâ) *adj.*
born.

naciente (nâ•syen´•te) *adj.* rising; **el sol —,** the rising sun.

nacimiento (nâ•sē•myen´•to) *m.*
birth; Nativity *(de Jesucristo);*
manger *(belén).*

nación (nâ•syon´) *f.* nation.

nacional (nâ•syo•nâl´) *adj.* national.

nacionalidad (nâ•syo•nâ•lē•thâ-
th´) *f.* nationality.

nacionalismo
(nâ•syo•nâ•lēz´•mo) *m.* nationalism.

nacionalista (nâ•syo•nâ•lēs´•tâ)
m. and *f.* nationalist.

Naciones Unidas (nâ•syo´•nes
ū•nē´•thâs) *f. pl.* United

Nations.

nada (nâ´•thâ) *f.* nothing; **de —,**
don´t mention it, you´re wel-
come; **— de eso,** of course not,
not at all; **—,** *adv.* in no way,
by no means.

nadador, ra (nâ•thâ•thor´, râ) *n.*
swimmer; **—,** *adj.* swimming.

nadar (nâ•thâr´) *vn.* to swim.

nadie (nâ´•thye) *pron.* nobody,
no one.

naipe (nâ´•ē•pe) *m.* playing card.

nalga (nâl´•gâ) *f.* buttock; **—s,**
pl. rump.

nana (nâ´•nâ) *f.* (Mex.) nursemaid.

Nápoles (na´•po•les) *f.* Naples.

naranja (nâ•rân´•hâ) *f.* orange;
jugo de —, orange juice.

naranjado, da (nâ•rân•ha´•tho,
thâ) *adj.* orange-colored.

naranjo (nâ•rân´•ho) *m.* orange
tree.

narciso (nâr•sē´•so) *m.* (bot.)
narcissus; narcissist.

narcótico, ca (nâr•ko´•tē•ko, kâ)

adj. and *m.* narcotic.

narigón, ona (nâ•rē•gon´•, o´•nâ) or **narigudo, da** (nâ•rē•gū´•tho, thâ) *adj.* big-nosed.

nariz (nâ•rēs´) *f.* nose; sense of smell *(olfato);* nostril *(ventana).*

narración (nâ•rrâ•syon´) *f.* narration, account.

narrador, ra (nâ•rrâ•thor´•, râ) *n.* narrator.

narrar (nâ•rrâr´) *va.* to narrate, to tell.

nasal (nâ•sâl´) *adj.* nasal.

natación (nâ•tâ•syon´) *f.* swimming.

natal (nâ•tâl´) *adj.* natal, native; **pueblo —,** home town; **ciudad —,** native city.

natalidad (nâ•tâ•lē•thâth´) *f.* birth rate.

natalicio (nâ•tâ•lē´•syo) *m.* birthday.

natilla (nâ•tē´•yâ) *f.* custard.

natividad (nâ•tē•vē•thâth´) *f.* nativity.

nativo, va (nâ•tē´•vo, vâ) *adj.* native.

natural (nâ•tū•râl´) *adj.* natural; native *(originario);* natural, unaffected *(ingenuo);* **al —,** unaffectedly; **del —,** from life.

naturaleza (nâ•tū•râ•le´•sâ) *f.* nature.

naturalista (nâ•tū•râ•lēs´•tâ) *m.* naturalist.

naufragar (nâū•frâ•gâr´) *vn.* to

be shipwrecked; (fig.) to fail, to be ruined.

naufragio (nâū•frâ´•hyo) *m.* shipwreck.

náufrago, ga (nâ´•ū•frâ•go, gâ) *n.* shipwrecked person.

náusea (nâ´•ū•se•â) *f.* nausea.

náutica (nâ´•ū•tē•kâ) *f.* navigation, nautical science.

náutico, ca (nâ´•ū•tē•ko, kâ) *adj.* nautical.

navaja (nâ•vâ´•hâ) *f.* pocketknife; **— de afeitar,** razor.

naval (nâ•vâl´) *adj.* naval.

nave (nâ´•ve) *f.* ship; (arch.) nave; **— espacial,** spacecraft, spaceship.

navegación (nâ•ve•gâ•syon´) *f.* navigation, shipping.

navegante (nâ•ve•gân´•te) *m.* navigator, seafarer.

Navidad (nâ•vē•thâth´) *f.* Christmas.

navideño, ña (nâ•vē•the´•nyo, nyâ) *adj.* pertaining to Christmas; **espíritu —ño,** Christmas spirit.

neblina (ne•vlē´•nâ) *f.* mist.

nebuloso, sa (ne•vū•lo´•so, sâ) *adj.* cloudy; (fig.) nebulous, foggy, hazy.

necedad (ne•se•thâth´) *f.* gross ignorance; stupidity *(tontería);* nonsense *(disparate).*

necesario (ne•se•sâ´•ryo, ryâ) *adj.* necessary.

necesidad (ne•se•sē•thâth´) *f.* necessity, need, want.

necesitado, da (ne•se•sē•tâ´•tho, thâ) *adj.* needy, indigent.

necio, cia (ne´•syo, syâ) *adj.* ignorant, stupid, foolish.

néctar (nek´•târ) *m.* nectar.

nefasto, ta (ne•fâs´•to, tâ) *adj.* unlucky, ill-fated.

negar* (ne•gâr´) *va.* to deny; —se, to refuse, to decline.

negativo, va (ne•gâ•tē´•vo, vâ) *adj.* negative; —, *f.* refusal, denial; (phot.) negative.

negligencia (ne•glē•hen´•syâ) *f.* negligence.

negligente (ne•glē•hen´•te) *adj.* careless, heedless.

negociación (ne•go•syâ•syon´) *f.* negotiation; (com.) transaction, business deal, affair.

negociante (ne•go•syân´•te) *m.* and *f.* trader, dealer, merchant.

negociar (ne•go•syâr´) *va.* to negotiate; —, *vn.* to trade, to deal.

negocio (ne•go´•syo) *m.* business; **hombre de —s,** businessman.

negro, gra (ne´•gro, grâ) *adj.* black.

nene, na (ne´•ne, nâ) *n.* baby.

neón (ne•on´) *m.* neon; **alumbrado de —,** neon lighting.

neoyorquino, na (ne•o•yor•kē´•no, nâ) *n.* New

Yorker; —, *adj.* from New York, of New York.

nepotismo (ne•po•tēz´•mo) *m.* nepotism.

nervio (ner´•vyo) *m.* nerve.

nervioso, sa (ner•vyo´•so, sâ) *adj.* nervous.

neto, ta (ne´•to, tâ) *adj.* net.

neumático (neū•mâ´•tē•ko) *m.* tire; **— desinflado,** deflated tire; **— de repuesto,** spare tire; **—, ca,** *adj.* pneumatic.

neumonía (neū•mo•nē´•â) *f.* pneumonia.

neurosis (neū•ro´•sēs) *f.* neurosis.

neurótico, ca (neū•ro´•tē•ko, kâ) *adj.* neurotic.

neutral (neū•trâl´) *adj.* neutral.

neutralizar (neū•trâ•lē•sâr´) *va.* (chem.) to neutralize.

neutrón (neū•tron´) *m.* neutron.

nevada (ne•vâ´•thâ) *f.* snowfall.

nevado, da (ne•vâ´•tho, thâ) *adj.* snow-covered, snow-capped.

nevar* (ne•vâr´) *vn.* to snow.

nevería (ne•ve•rē´•â) *f.* ice cream store.

ni (nē) *conj.* neither, nor; **— el uno — el otro,** neither one nor the other.

nicaragüense (nē•kâ•ra•gwen´•se) *m.* and *f.* and *adj.* Nicaraguan.

nicotina (nē•ko•tē´•na) *f.* nicotine.

nicho (nē´•cho) *m.* niche.

nido (nē´•tho) *m.* nest; den, hangout *(de bribones)*.

niebla (nye´•vlâ) *f.* fog.

nieta (nye´•tâ) *f.* granddaughter.

nieto (nye´•to) *m.* grandson.

nieve (nye´•ve) *f.* snow.

Nilo (nē´•lo) *m.* Nile.

ninfa (nēm´•fâ) *f.* nymph.

ningún (nēng•gūn´) *adj.* (apocope of ninguno), no, not any (used only before masculine nouns); **de — modo,** in no way, by no means.

ninguno, na (nēng•gū´•no, nâ) *adj.* none, not one, neither; **en —na parte,** no place; nowhere.

niña (nē´•nyâ) *f.* little girl; **— del ojo,** pupil of the eye; **— de los ojos,** (coll.) apple of one's eye.

niñera (nē•nye´•râ) *f.* nursemaid; babysitter *(por horas)*.

niñez (nē•nyes´) *f.* childhood.

niño, ña (ne´•nyo, nyâ) *adj.* childish; **—,** *n.* child, infant; **desde —,** from infancy, since childhood.

níquel (nē´•kel) *m.* nickel.

nítido, da (nē´•tē•tho, thâ) *adj.* (poet.) bright, pure, shining.

nitrato (nē•trâ´•to) *m.* (chem.) nitrate, saltpeter.

nitrógeno (nē•tro´•he•no) *m.* nitrogen.

nivel (nē•vel´) *m.* level, plane; **a —,** perfectly level.

nivelación (nē•ve•lâ•syon´) *f.* grading, leveling.

nivelar (nē•ve•lâr´) *va.* to level.

no (no) *adv.* no *(uso absoluto);* not.

noble (no´•vle) *adj.* noble, illustrious.

nobleza (no•vle´•sâ) *f.* nobleness; nobility *(de título)*.

noción (no•syon´) *f.* notion, idea.

nocivo, va (no•sē´•vo, vâ) *adj.* injurious.

nocturno, na (nok•tūr´•no, nâ) *adj.* (zool.) nocturnal; nightly; **—,** *m.* nocturn; (mus.) nocturne.

noche (no´•che) *f.* night; **esta —,** tonight, this evening; **de —,** at night; **media —,** midnight; **N— Buena,** Christmas Eve; **cada —, todas las —s,** every night; **buenas —s,** good evening; good night *(despedida)*.

nogal (no•gâl´) *m.* walnut tree; walnut *(madera)*.

nómada (no´•mâ•thâ) or **nómade** (no´•mâ• the) *adj.* nomad, nomadic.

nombramiento (nom•brâ•myen´•to) *m.* nomination, appointment *(elección);* mention, naming.

nombrar (nom•brâr´) *va.* to name; to nominate *(nominar);* to appoint *(señalar)*.

nombre (nom´•bre) *m.* name *(de*

persona); title; reputation *(fama).*

nómina (no´•mē•nâ) *f.* catalogue; pay roll *(de paga);* membership list *(de socios).*

nominal (no•mē•nâl´) *adj.* nominal.

nonagenario, ria (no•nâ•he•nâ´•ryo, ryâ) *adj..* ninety years old; —, *n.* nonagenarian.

nonagésimo, ma (no•nâ•he´•sē•mo, mâ) *adj.* ninetieth.

nono, na (no´•no, nâ) *adj.* ninth.

nordeste (nor•thes´•te) *m.* northeast.

nórdico, ca (nor´•thē•ko, kâ) *adj.* and *n.* Nordic.

norma (nor´•mâ) *f.* norm, standard, model; square *(escuadra).*

normal (nor•mâl´) *adj.* normal.

noroeste (no•ro•es´•te) *m.* northwest.

norte (nor´•te) *m.* north; (fig.) rule, guide.

Norte América (nor´•te•â•me´•rē•kâ) *f.* North America.

norteamericano, na (nor•te•â•me•rē•kâ´• no, nâ) *n.* and *adj.* North American; a native of U.S.A. *(estadounidense).*

Noruega (no•rwe´•gâ) *f.* Norway.

noruego, ga (no•rwe´•go, gâ) *n.*

and *adj.* Norwegian.

nos (nos) *pron.* us, to us.

nosotros, tras (no•so´•tros, trâs) *pron.* we; us *(con preposición).*

nostalgia (nos•tâl´•hyâ) *f.* homesickness *(de la patria);* nostalgia.

nota (no´•tâ) *f.* note; grade *(calificación);* — **bene,** n. B. take notice; — **de entrega,** delivery order; — **musical,** musical note.

notable (no•tâ´•vle) *adj.* notable, remarkable, distinguished.

notación (no•tâ•syon´) *f.* notation.

notar (no•târ´) *va.* to note, to mark; to remark, to observe *(reparar).*

notario (no•tâ´•ryo) *m.* notary public.

noticia (no•tē´•syâ) *f.* notice; knowledge, information *(conocimiento);* piece of news *(novedad);* **en espera de sus —s,** (com.) awaiting your reply.

noticiero, ra (no•tē•sye´•ro, râ) *n.* newscaster, news commentator.

notificación (no•tē•fē•kâ•syon´) *f.* notification.

notificar (no•tē•fē•kâr´) *va.* to notify, to inform.

notoriedad (no•to•rye•thâth´) *f.* notoriety.

notorio, ria (no•to´•ryo, ryâ) *adj.*

well-known, known to all.

novato, ta (no•vâ´•to, tâ) *adj.*
new; —, *n.* novice, greenhorn.
freshman.

novecientos, tas
(no•ve•syen´•tos, tâs) *adj.* and
m. nine hundred.

novedad (no•ve•thâth´) *f.*
novelty, newness; change *(cambio); news (noticias);* —**es,** *pl.*
notions.

novela (no•ve´•lâ) *f.* novel; (fig.)
he, tale.

novelesco, ca (no•ve•les´•ko, kâ)
adj. novelesque.

novelista (no•ve•lês´•tâ) *m.* and
f. novelist.

noveno, na (no•ve´•no, nâ) *adj.*
ninth.

noventa (no•ven´•tâ) *m.* and *adj.*
ninety.

novia (no´•vyâ) *f.* newlywed;
fiancée, betrothed woman
(prometida); sweetheart, girl-
friend *(querida).*

noviazgo (no•vyâz´•go) *m.*
courtship.

novicio, cia (no•ve´•syo, syâ) *n.*
novice.

noviembre (no•vyem´•bre) *m.*
November.

novio (no´•vyo) *m.* fiancé; sweetheart, boyfriend; newlywed
(recién casado). **viaje de** —**s,**
honeymoon trip.

nube (nū´•ve) *f.* cloud.

nublado, da (nū•vlâ´•tho, thâ)
adj. cloudy.

nublarse (nū•vlâr´•se) *vr.* to
cloud over, to become cloudy.

nuca (nū´•kâ) *f.* nape.

nuclear (nū•kle•âr´) *adj.*
nuclear; **desintegración** —,
nuclear fission; **física** —,
nuclear physics.

nucleario, ria (nū•kle•â´•ryo,
ryâ) nuclear.

núcleo (nū´•kle•o) *m.* nucleus
(del átomo); core *(del fruto).*

nudillo (nū•thē´•yo) *m.* knuckle
(artejo); small knot.

nudo (nū´•tho) *m.* knot; (bot.)
knot, gnarl; — **corredizo,** slipknot.

nuera (nwe´•râ) *f.* daughter-in-
law.

nuestro, tra (nwes´•tro, trâ) *adj.*
our; —, *pron.* ours.

nueve (nwe´•ve) *m.* and *adj.*
nine.

nuevo, va (nwe´•vo, vâ) *adj.* new;
another *(otro);* **de** —**vo,** once
more, again; **¿qué hay de** —**vo?**
is there any news? what's
new?

nuez (nwes) *f.* nut; walnut *(del
nogal);* (anat.) Adam's apple; —
moscada or **de especia,** nutmeg.

nulidad (nū•lē•thâth´) *f.* nullity,
nonentity.

nulo, la (nū´•lo, lâ) *adj.* null,

void.

numeración (nū•me•râ•syon´) *f.* numeration, numbering.

numerador (nū•me•râ•thor´) *m.* numerator.

numeral (nū•me•râl´) *adj.* numeral.

numerar (nū•me•râr´) *va.* to number *(marcar);* to numerate, to count.

numérico, ca (nū•me´•rē•ko, kâ) *adj.* numerical.

número (nū´•me•ro) *m.* number.

numeroso, sa (nū•me•ro´•so, sâ) *adj.* numerous.

nunca (nūng´•kâ) *adv.* never.

nupcial (nūp•syâl´) *adj.* nuptial.

nupcias (nūp´•syâs) *f. pl.* nuptials, wedding.

nutrición (nū•trē•syon´) *f.* nutrition; feeding *(acción).*

nutrir (nū•trēr´) *va.* to nourish.

nutritivo, va (nū•trē•tē´•vo, vâ) *adj.* nutritive, nourishing.

nylon (nâ´•ē•lon) *m.* nylon.

Ñ

ñame (nyâ´•me) *m.* (bot.) tropical yam.

ñapa (nyâ´•pâ) *f.* (Sp. Am.) lagniappe.

O

o (o) (ó when between numbers) *conj.* or; **el uno — el otro,** either one or the other.

oasis (o•â´•sēs) *m.* oasis.

obedecer* (o•ve•the•ser´) *va.* to obey.

obediencia (o•ve•thyen´•syâ) *f.* obedience.

obediente (o•ve•thyen´•te) *adj.* obedient.

obertura (o•ver•tū´•râ) *f.* (mus.) overture.

obesidad (o•ve•sē•thâth´) *f.* obe-sity.

obeso, sa (o•ve´so, sâ) *adj.* obese.

obispo (o•vēs´po) *m.* bishop; (ichth.) ray.

obituario (o•vē•twâ´ryo) *m.* obi-tuary.

objeción (ov•he•syon´) *f.* objec-tion; **poner —,** to raise an objection.

objetivo, va (ov•he•tē´vo, vâ) *adj.* objective; **—,** *m,* objective, pur-pose; lens *(lente).*

objeto (ov•he′to) *m.* object; subject *(asunto).*

oblicuo, cua (o•vlē′kwo, kwâ) *adj.* oblique.

obligación (o•vlē•gâ•syon′) *f.* obligation, duty; debt *(deuda).*

obligado, da (o•vlē•gâ′tho, thâ) *adj.* obliged, obligated, beholden.

obligar (o•vlē•gâr′) *va.* to oblige, to force.

obligatorio, ria (o•vlē•gâ•to′ryo, ryâ) *adj.* compulsory, obligatory.

oboe (o•vo′e) *m.* (mus.) oboe.

obra (o′vrâ) *f.* work; construction *(edificio);* virtue, power *(medio);* — **maestra,** masterpiece; **manos a la —,** let′s get started.

obrar (o•vrâr′) *va.* to work; to do, to execute *(hacer);* to build *(edificar);* —, *vn.* to be; to have a bowel movement *(del vientre).*

obrero, ra (o•vre′ro, râ) *n.* worker; (eccl.) churchwarden.

obscenidad (ovs•se•nē•thâth′) *f.* obscenity.

obsceno, na (ovs•se′no, nâ) *adj.* obscene.

obsequiar (ov•se•kyâr′) *va.* to court; to give *(regalar);* to shower with attention *(agasajar).*

obsequio (ov•se′kyo) *m.* gift; attention, kindness *(agasajo).*

observación (ov•ser•vâ•syon′) *f.* observation.

observador, ra (ov•ser•vâ•thor′, râ) *n.* observer; —, *adj.* observant.

observar (ov•ser•vâr′) *va.* to observe.

observatorio (ov•ser•vâ•to′ryo) *m.* observatory.

obsesión (ov•se•syon′) *f.* obsession.

obstáculo (ovs•tâ′kū•lo) *m.* obstacle, bar, impediment.

obstante (ovs•tân′te) *adj.* in the way; **no —,** notwithstanding, nevertheless.

obstetricia (ovs•te•trē′syâ) *f.* obstetrics.

obstinación (ovs•tē•nâ•syon′) *f.* obstinacy, stubbornness.

obstrucción (ovs•trūk•syon′) *f.* obstruction.

obstruir* (ovs•trwēr) *va.* to obstruct; **—se,** to get blocked up, to get stopped up.

obtener* (ov•te•ner′) *va.* to obtain, to get; to retain, to maintain *(conservar).*

obtuso, sa (ov•tū′so, sâ) *adj.* obtuse, blunt; (fig.) slow, dense.

obvio, via (ov′vyo, vyâ) *adj.* obvious, evident.

ocasión (o•kâ•syon′) *f.* occasion; danger, risk *(peligro);* **de —,** used, secondhand.

ocasional (o•kâ•syo•nâl′) *adj.*

occasional; causative, causal
(que ocasiona).

ocasionar (o•kâ•syo•når´) *va.* to
cause, to occasion; to move, to
motivate *(mover);* to endanger
(poner en peligro).

ocaso (o•kâ´so) *m.* occident;
decline *(bajada);* sunset *(puesta
del sol).*

occidente (ok•sē•then´te) *m.*
occident, west.

océano (o•se´â•no) *m.* ocean.

ocio (o´syo) *m.* leisure; pastime
(pasatiempo); idleness *(holgaza-
nería).*

ociosidad (o•syo•sē•thâth´) *f.*
idleness, laziness.

ocre (o´kre) *m.* ochre.

octágono (ok•tâ´go•no) *m.* octagon.

octava (ok•tâ´vâ) *f.* octave.

octavo, va (ok•tâ´vo, vâ) *adj.*
eighth.

octubre (ok•tū´vre) *m.* October.

ocular (o•kū•lâr´) *adj.* ocular; —,
m. eye-piece, ocular.

ocultar (o•kūl•târ´) *va.* to hide,
to conceal.

oculto, ta (o•kūl´to, tâ) *adj.* hidden, concealed.

ocupación (o•kū•pâ•syon´) *f.*
occupation; employment
(empleo).

ocupado, da (o•kū•pâ´tho, thâ)
adj. busy, occupied.

ocupar (o•kū•pâr´) *va.* to occu-

py; to bother *(estorbar);* to
attract the attention of *(llamar
la atención);* **—se en** to give
one´s attention to.

ocurrencia (o•kū•rren´syâ) *f.*
occurrence, event, incident;
brainstorm *(pensamiento);* witticism *(dicho agudo).*

ocurrir (o•kū•rrēr´) *vn.* to occur,
to happen *(suceder);* to occur
(a la mente); **— a,** to have
recourse to.

ochenta (o•chen´tâ) *adj.* and *m.*
eighty.

ocho (o´cho) *m.* and *adj.* eight.

ochocientos (o•cho•syen´tos) *m.*
and *adj.* eight hundred.

odiar (o•thyâr´) *va.* to hate.

odio (o´thyo) *m.* hatred.

odisea (o•thē•se´â) *f.* odyssey.

odontología (o•thon•to•lo•hē´â) *f.*
odontology.

odorífero, ra (o•tho•rē´fe•ro, râ)
adj. fragrant.

oeste (o•es´te) *m.* west; west
wind *(viento).*

ofender (o•fen•der´) *va.* to
offend; to injure *(maltratar);* to
bother, to annoy *(fastidiar);* **—
se,** to get angry, to take
offense.

ofensa (o•fen´sâ) *f.* offense;
injury *(herida);* annoyance *(fastidio).*

ofensivo, va (o•fen•sē´vo, vâ) *adj.*
offensive.

oferta (o•fer´tâ) *f.* offer; offering, gift *(don);* — **y demanda,** supply and demand.

oficial (o•fē•syâl´) *adj.* official; —, *m.* officer, official; journeyman *(obrero);* clerk *(empleado);* (mil.) officer.

oficina (o•fē•sē´nâ) *f.* office; workshop *(taller);* laboratory *(laboratorio).*

oficio (o•fē´syo) *m.* occupation; office *(cargo);* trade *(de artes mecánicas);* official letter *(comunicación).*

ofrecer* (o•fre•ser´) *va.* to offer; —**se,** to occur, to happen.

ofrecimiento (o•fre•sē•myen´to) *m.* offer.

ofrenda (o•fren´dâ) *f.* offering.

ofuscar (o•fūs•kâr´) *va.* to darken, to obscure; to confuse *(confundir);* —**se,** to get confused.

oído (o•ē´tho) *m.* hearing; (anat.) ear; **hablar al** —, to whisper.

oir* (o•ēr´) *va.* to hear; to listen to *(atender);* to understand *(entender);* to attend *(asistir).*

ojeada (o•he•â´thâ). *f.* glance, look.

ojear (o•he•âr´) *va.* to eye, to look at, to stare at; to give the evil eye to *(aojar);* to raise *(la caza);* (fig.) to frighten.

ojera (o•he´râ) *f.* eye cup; —**s,** *pl.* dark rings under the eyes.

ojo (o´ho) *m.* eye; spring *(de agua);* hole *(del pan);* span *(de un puente);* (print.) type size; attention *(atención);* note *(señal);* scrubbing *(mano de jabón);* **en un abrir y cerrar de** —**s**, in the twinkling of an eye, in a second.

ola (o´lâ) *f.* wave; (fig.) wave, surge.

oleaje (o•le•â´he) *m.* running sea, sea swell.

óleo (o´le•o) *m.* oil; olive oil *(de oliva).*

oler* (o•ler´) *va.* to smell; (fig.) to ferret out; —, *vn.* to smell; to smack *(tener señas).*

olfato (ol•fâ´to) *m.* sense of smell, smell; (fig.) a keen nose, acumen.

oligarquía (o•lē•gâr•kē´â) *f.* oligarchy.

Olimpiada (o•lēm•pyâ´thâ) *f.* Olympics.

olímpico, ca (o•lēm´pē•ko, kâ) *adj.* Olympic; Olympian *(soberbia).*

oliva (o•lē´vâ) *f.* olive; olive tree *(árbol);* owl *(lechuza);* (fig.) peace.

olivo (o•lē´vo) *m.* olive tree; olive wood *(madera).*

olmo (ol´mo) *m.* elm tree.

olor (o•lor´) *m.* odor, scent, smell; hope *(esperanza);* (fig.) reputation.

oloroso, sa (o•lo•ro´so, sâ) *adj.*

fragrant, odorous.

olvidadizo, za (ol•vē•thâ•thē´so, sâ) *adj.* forgetful, absent-minded; ungrateful *(desagradecido).*

olvidar (ol•vē•thâr´) *va.* and *vr.* to forget.

olvido (ol•vē´tho) *m.* forgetfulness; **dar al —, echar al —,** to forget completely, to bury.

olla (o´yâ) *f.* pot, kettle; stew *(guisado);* eddy *(remolino);* **—a presión,** pressure cooker; **— express,** (Mex.) pressure cooker; **— podrida,** potpourri.

ombligo (om•blē´go) *m.* navel; umbilical cord *(cordón).*

omisión (o•mē•syon´) *f.* omission; neglect, remissness *(descuido).*

omitir (o•mē•tēr´) *va.* to omit; to overlook *(pasar en silencio).*

ómnibus (om´nē•vūs) *m.* omnibus, bus.

omnipotencia (om•nē•po•ten´s-yâ) *f.* omnipotence.

omnipotente (om•nē•po•ten´te) *adj.* omnipotent, almighty.

once (on´se) *m.* and *adj.* eleven.

onceno, na (on•se´no, nâ) *adj.* eleventh; elevenman team.

onda (on´dâ) *f.* wave; scallop *(guarnición);* flicker *(de la llama);* (rad.) wave length— **sonora,** sound wave.

ondeado, da (on•de•â´tho ,thâ)

adj. wavy.

ondulación (on•dū•lâ•syon´) *f.* undulation, wave.

ondulado, da (on•dū•lâ´tho, thâ) *adj.* wavy, rippled; rolling *(terreno).*

ondular (on•dū•lâr´) *vn.* to undulate; — *va.* to wave, to make wavy.

oneroso, sa (o•ne•ro´ so, sâ) *adj.* onerous.

onza, (on´sâ) *f.* ounce.

onzavo, va (on•sâ´vo, vâ) *m.* and *adj.* eleventh.

opaco, ca (o•pâ´ko, kâ) *adj.* opaque; dark, somber *(oscuro);* melancholy, gloomy *(triste).*

ópalo (o´pâ•lo) *m.* opal.

opción (op•syon´) *f.* option.

ópera (o´pe•râ) *f.* opera.

operación (o•pe•râ•syon´) *f.* operation; — **cesárea,** Caesarean section.

operar (o•pe•râr´) *va.* to operate on; —, *vn.* to take effect; to operate *(maniobrar);* — **se,** to have an operation.

operario, ria (o•pe•râ´ryo, ryâ) *n.* laborer, workman.

opinar (o•pē•nâr´) *vn.* to express an opinion.

opinión (o•pē•nyon´) *f.* opinion.

opio (o´pyo) *m.* opium.

oponer* (o•po•ner´) *va.* to oppose, to put up; — **se a,** to oppose; to compete for *(pre-*

tender un cargo).

oportunidad (o•por•tū•nē•thâ-th´) *f.* right moment, opportunity; opportuneness *(calidad de oportuno).*

oportuno, na (o•por•tū´no, nâ) *adj.* opportune, timely; witty *(ocurrente).*

oposición (o•po•sē•syon´) *f.* opposition; competition *(concurso).*

opositor, ra (o•po•sē•tor´, râ) *n.* opponent.

opresión (o•pre•syon´) *f.* oppression.

opresor, ra (o•pre•sor´, râ) *n.* oppressor.

oprimir (o•prē•mēr´) *va.* (fig.) to oppress *(sujetar);* to press, to squeeze.

optar (op•târ´) *va.* to choose, to select.

óptico, ca (op´tē•ko, kâ) *adj.* optic, optical; —, *m.* optician.

optimismo (op•tē•mēz´mo) *m.* optimism.

óptimo, ma (op´tē•mo, mâ) *adj.* best.

optómetra (op•to´me•trâ) *m.* optometrist.

optometría (op•to•me•trē´â) *f.* optometry.

opuesto, ta (o•pwes´to, tâ) *adj.* opposite, contrary.

opulencia (o•pū•len´syâ) *f.* opulence, wealth, riches.

oración (o•ra•syon´) *f.* oration, speech; prayer *(rezo);* (gram.) sentence.

oráculo (o•râ´kū•lo) *m.* oracle.

orador, ra (o´•râ•thor´, râ) *n.* orator, speaker; petitioner *(que pide);* —, *m.* preacher.

oral (o•râl´) *adj.* oral.

orangután (o•râng•gū•tân´) *m.* (zool.) orangutan.

orar (o•râr´) *vn.* to make a speech, to speak; to pray *(rezar);* —, *vt.* to beg, to supplicate.

oratoria (o•râ•to´ryâ) *f.* oratory, rhetoric.

oratorio (o•râ•to´ryo) *m.* oratory; oratorio *(composición);* —, **ria,** *adj.* rhetorical, oratorical.

orbe (or´ve) *m.* orb; world, sphere *(mundo);* (ichth.) globefish.

órbita (or´ve•ta) *f.* orbit.

orden (or´then) *m.* order; (eccl.) Holy Orders; — **del día,** (mil.) order of the day; —, *f.* order, command; (eccl.) order; **a sus órdenes,** at your service.

ordenado, da (or•the•nâ´tho, thâ) *adj.* neat, orderly.

ordenador (or•the•nâ•thor´) *m.* computer.

ordenanza (or•the•nân´sâ) *f.* order; command *(mandato);* method, system *(arreglo);* ordinance *(regla);* —, *m.* (mil.)

orderly.

ordenar (or•the•nâr´) *va.* to arrange, to put in order *(arreglar);* to order, to command *(mandar);* (eccl.) to ordain; —**se,** to become ordained.

ordeñar (or•the•nyâr´) *va.* to milk.

ordinal (or•the•nâl´) *adj.* ordinal.

ordinario, ria (or•thē•nâ´ryo, ryâ) *adj.* ordinary; daily *(diario);* **de** —**rio,** usually, ordinarily; —, *m.* ordinary.

orégano (o•re´gâ•no) *m.* (bot.) oregano, wild marjoram.

oreja (o•re´hâ) *f.* ear; hearing *(sentido);* outer ear *(ternilla);* flap *(del zapato);* (fig.) gossip.

orejera (o•re•he´râ) *f.* ear muff; moldboard *(del arado).*

orfandad (or•fân•dâth´) *f.* orphanage; (fig.) neglect, desertion.

orfebre (or•fe´vre) *m.* goldsmith; silversmith *(platero).*

orgánico, ca (or•gâ´nē•ko, kâ) *adj.* organic.

organismo (or•gâ•nēz´mo) *m.* organization; organism *(conjunto de órganos).*

organización (or•gâ•nē•sâ•syon´) *f.* organization.

organizador, ra (or•gâ•nē•sâ•thor´, râ) *n.* organizer; —, *adj.* organizing.

organizar (or•gâ•nē•sâr´) *va.* to organize.

órgano (or´gâ•no) *m.* organ; — **de cañones** pipe organ.

orgullo (or•gū´yo) *m.* pride; haughtiness *(altivez).*

orgulloso, sa (or•gū•yo´so, sâ) *adj.* proud; haughty.

orientación (o•ryen•tâ•syon´) *f.* orientation; (naut.) trimming; — **por inercia,** (avi.) inertial guidance; — **vocacional,** vocational guidance.

oriental (o•ryen•tâl´) *adj.* (geog.) Oriental; eastern.

orientar (o•ryen•târ´) *va.* to orient; (naut.) to trim; —**se,** to get one´s bearings, to orient oneself.

oriente (o•ryen´te) *m.* orient, east; (geog.) Orient.

origen (o•rē´hen) *m.* origin; descent *(ascendencia).*

original (o•rē•hē•nâl´) *adj.* original; eccentric, odd *(extraño);* —, *m.* original, first copy; oddball *(persona extravagante).*

originar (o•rē•hē•nâr´) *va.* to cause, to be the origin of; —**se,** to originate.

originario, ria (o•rē•hē•nâ´ryo, ryâ) *adj.* native, originating; being the cause *(que da origen);* — **de Inglaterra,** native of England.

orilla (o•rē´yâ) *f.* border, margin

(margen); edge *(de tela);* sidewalk *(acera);* shore *(ribera);* fresh breeze *(vientecillo).*

orina (o•rē´nâ) *f.* urine.

orinar (o•rē•nâr´) *vn.* to urinate.

oriol (o•ryol´) *m.* (orn.) oriole.

oriundo, da (o•ryūn´do, dâ) *adj.* native.

ornamento (or•nâ•men´to) *m.* ornament, embellishment; (fig.) virtue, asset; —**s**, *pl.* (eccl.) vestments.

ornar (or•nâr) *va.* to trim, to adorn.

oro (o´ro) *m.* gold; (fig.) wealth, riches; **de** —, golden.

orquesta (or•kes´tâ) *f.* orchestra.

orquídea (or•kē´the•â) *f.* orchid.

ortiga (or•tē´gâ) *f.* (bot.) nettle.

ortodóntico (or•to•thon´tē•ko) *m.* orthodontist.

ortodoxo, xa (or•to•thok´so, sâ) *adj.* orthodox.

ortografia (or•to•grâ•fē´â) *f.* orthography.

ortopédico, ca (or•to•pe´thē•ko, kâ) *adj.* orthopedic; —, *n.* orthopedist.

oruga (o•rū´gâ) *f.* (bot.) rocket; (ent. and mech.) caterpillar.

os (os) *pron.* you; to you *(dativo).*

osa (o´sâ) *f.* she-bear; **O—Mayor,** (ast.) Great Bear.

osadía (o•sâ•the´â) *f.* boldness, courage.

osar (o•sâr´) *vn.* to dare, to venture.

oscilar (os•sē´lâr´) *vn.* to oscillate; (fig.) to vacillate.

oscurecer* (os•kū•re•ser´) *va.* to darken; (fig.) to obscure; (fig.) to confuse *(confundir);* to shade *(pintura);* —, *vi.* to darken, to grow dark; —**se,** to get cloudy, to cloud over; (fig.) to vanish into thin air.

oscuridad (os•kū•rē•thâth´) *f.* darkness; (fig.) obscurity; confusion.

oscuro, ra (os•kū´ro, râ) *adj.* dark; (fig.) obscure; **a —as,** in the dark.

óseo, sea (o´se•o, se•â) *adj.* bony.

oso (o´so) *m.* bear; — **pardo,** brown bear; — **hormiguero,** anteater.

ostentación (os•ten•tâ•syon´) *f.* displaying, showing; great display, ostentation *(vanagloria);* pomp *(magnificencia).*

ostentar (os•ten•târ´) *va.* to show, to display; to show off *(hacer gala de).*

ostentoso, sa (os•ten•to´so, sâ) *adj.* sumptuous, magnificent.

ostra (os´trâ) *f.* oyster.

ostracismo (os•trâ•sēz´mo) *m.* ostracism.

otoñal (o•to•nyâl´) *adj.* autumnal.

otoño (o•to´nyo) *m.* autumn, fall.

otorgamiento (o•tor•gâ•myen´to) *m.* grant; consent, approval *(aprobación);* closing *(de un contrato).*

otorgar (o•tor•gâr´) *va.* to consent to *(consentir);* to grant *(conceder).*

otro, otra (o´tro, o´trâ) *adj.* another, other; **al — lado,** on the other side; **—a vez,** once more, again; **el uno al —,** one to the other, to each other; **el uno o el —,** one or the other; **ni el uno ni el —,** neither one nor the other, neither one; **por —a parte,** on the other hand; **en alguna — parte,** somewhere else.

ovación (o•vâ•syon´) *f.* ovation.

ovalado, da (o•vâ•lâ´tho, thâ) *adj.* oval.

óvalo (o´vâ•lo) *m.* oval.

ovario (o•vâ´ryo) *m.* ovary.

oveja (o•ve´hâ) *f.* sheep.

ovillo (o•vē´yo) *m.* ball of yarn; (fig.) snarl, tangle, confused mess *(enredo).*

ovíparo, ra (o•vē´pâ•ro, râ) *adj.* oviparous.

oxidar (ok•sē•thâr´) *va.* to oxidize; **—se,** to rust, to get rusty.

óxido (ok´sē•tho) *m.* (chem.) oxide; **— de cinc,** zinc oxide.

oxígeno (ok•sē´he•no) *m.* (chem.) oxygen.

oyente (o•yen´te) *m.* and *f.* listener; auditor *(alumno);* **—s,** *pl.* audience.

P

pabellón (pâ•ve•yon´) *m.* pavilion; flag *(bandera);* stack *(armas);* bell *(de un instrumento);* protection *(protección).*

paciencia (pâ•syen´syâ) *f.* patience.

paciente (pâ•syen´te) *adj.* and *m.* and *f.* patient.

pacificar (pâ•sē•fē•kâr´) *va.* to pacify, to make peaceful; **—,** *vn.* to negotiate for peace; **—se,** to become peaceful.

pacifico, ca (pâ•sē´fe•ko, kâ) *adj.* pacific, peaceful.

pacifista (pâ•sē•fēs´tâ) *n.* and *adj.* pacifist.

pactar (pâk•târ´) *va.* to agree on, to agree to.

pacto (pâk´to) *m.* pact, agreement.

padecer* (pâ•the•ser´) *va.* to suffer.

padecimiento (pa•the•sē•myen´to) *m.* suffering.

padrastro (pâ•thrâs´tro) *m.* stepfather; bad father *(mal padre);*

obstacle *(obstáculo);* hangnail *(pellejo).*

padre (pâ´thre) *m.* father; sire, stud *(del ganado);* —**s,** *pl.* parents; forefathers *(antepasados).*

padrino (pâ•thrē´no) *m.* godfather; second *(que acompaña);* sponsor *(que favorece);* — **de boda,** groomsman.

paella (pâ•e´yâ) *f.* paella.

paga (pâ´gâ) *f.* payment; satisfaction *(satisfacción);* fee, wage *(sueldo);* requital *(correspondencia).*

pagador, ra (pâ•gâ•thor´, râ) *n.* payer.

pagano (pâ•gâ´no) *m.* heathen, pagan; (coll.) dupe, easy mark *(de quien se abusa);* —, **na,** *adj.* heathen, pagan.

pagar (pâ•gâr´) *va.* to pay, to pay for; to repay, to return *(corresponder);* —**se de,** to be pleased with; to boast about *(jactarse).*

página (pa´hē•nâ) *f.* page;— **inicial,** home page.

pago (pâ´go) *m.* pay, payment; satisfaction, recompense *(recompensa);* region *(distrito);* village *(aldea).*

pagoda (pâ•go´thâ) *f.* pagoda.

país (pa•ēs´) *m.* country, land; landscape (*pintura).*

paisaje (pâē•sâ´he) *m.* landscape.

paisano, na (pâē•sâ´no, nâ) *adj.*

of the same country; —, *n.* countryman, compatriot; rustic *(campesino);* civilian *(que no es militar).*

paja (pâ´hâ) *f.* straw.

pajar (pâ•hâr´) *m.* hayloft.

pajarera (pâ•hâ•re´râ) *f.* bird cage.

pájaro (pâ´hâ•ro) *m.* bird; (fig.) fox; (fig.) specialist *(especialista);* **vista de —,** bird´s-eye view; — **carpintero,** woodpecker.

pala (pâ´la) *f.* shovel; blade *(parte ancha);* racket *(raqueta);* setting *(de las joyas);* (fig.) guile, cunning; vamp *(de un zapato).*

palabra (pâ•lâ´vrâ) *f.* word; speech *(facultad);* gift of oratory *(oratoria);* floor *(turno);* **de —,** by word of mouth; **dirigir la —,** to address; **libertad de —,** freedom of speech; **pedir la —,** to ask for the floor; **tener la —,** to have the floor; — **por —,** literally, word for word.

palabrota (pâ•lâ•vro´tâ) *f.* vulgarity; harsh word *(ofensiva).*

palacio (pâ´•lâ´syo) *m.* palace.

palada (pâ•lâ´thâ) *f.* shovelful; stroke *(de un remo).*

paladar (pâ•lâ•thâr´) *m.* palate; taste *(sabor);* fig.) feeling, sensitivity *(gusto).*

palanca (pâ•lâng´kâ) *f.* lever;

pole *(pértiga)*; influence, pull *(influencia)*.

paleontología (pâ•le•on•to•lo•hē´â) *f.* paleontology.

paleta (pâ•le´tâ) *f.* fire shovel; palette *(del pintor)*; trowel *(llana)*; shoulder blade *(omóplato)*; lollipop *(dulce)*; blade *(álabe)* serving knife *(espátula)*.

palidecer* (pâ•lē•the•ser´) *vn.* to turn pale, to pale.

palidez (pâ•lē•thes´) *f.* paleness, wanness.

palillo (pâ•lē´yo) *m.* bobbin *(bolillo)*; toothpick *(de dientes)*; drumstick *(para tocar)*; stem *(del tabaco)*; (fig.) chit-chat.

paliza (pâ•lē´sâ) *f.* beating, drubbing.

palma (pal´mâ) *f.* palm; (fig.) victory, triumph; sole *(de un caballo)*; **—s,** *pl.* applause; **batir —s,** to clap hands.

palmada (pâl•mâ´thâ) *f.* slap *(golpe)*; clap; **—s,** *pl.* clapping.

palmera (pâl•me´râ) *f.* palm tree.

palmo (pâl´mo) *m.* palm; **— a —,** inch by inch.

palmotear (pâl•mo•te•âr´) *vn.* to applaud.

palmoteo (pâl•mo•te´o) *m.* clapping; lick, rap *(palmetazo)*.

palo (pâ´lo) *m.* stick; (naut.) mast; blow *(golpe)*; hook *(de letra)*; handle *(mango)*; suit *(de la baraja)*.

paloma (pâ•lo´mâ) *f.* dove, pigeon; (fig.) lamb; high collar *(cuello)*; **— viajera** or **mensajera,** homing pigeon, carrier pigeon.

palomino (pa•lo•mē´no) *m.* young pigeon; whippersnapper, stripling *(joven)*.

palomita (pâ•lo•mē´tâ) *f.* squab; **—s de maíz,** popcorn.

palomo (pâ•lo´mo) *m.* cock pigeon.

palpable (pâl•pâ´vle) *adj.* palpable; evident.

palpar (pâl•pâr) *va.* to feel, to touch; to grope through *(andar a tientas)*; to be certain of *(conocer)*.

palpitación (pâl•pē•tâ•syon´) *f.* palpitation.

palpitante (pâl•pē•tân´te) *adj.* palpitating.

palpitar (pâl•pē•târ´) *vn.* to palpitate, to beat, to throb.

paludismo (pâ•lū•thēz´mo) *m.* malaria.

pampa (pâm´pâ) *f.* pampa, plain.

pan (pân) *m.* bread; loaf of bread; dough *(masa sobada)*; food *(alimento)*; (fig.) wheat *(trigo)*; foil *(hoja de oro)*.

panacea (pâ•nâ•se´â) *f.* panacea, cure-all.

panadería (pâ•nâ•the•rē´â) *f.* baking trade *(oficio)*; bakery.

panadero, ra (pâ•nâ•the´ro, râ)

n. baker.

panameño, ña (pâ•nâ•me´nyo, nyâ) *n.* and *adj.* Panamenian.

páncreas (pâng´kre•âs) *m.* pancreas.

panda (pân´dâ) *m.* (zool.) panda.

pandemónium (pân•de•mo´nyūn) *m.* pandemonium.

pandilla (pân•dē´yâ) *f.* gang; gathering, group *(que va al campo).*

pánico (pâ´nē•ko) *m.* panic, terror.

panorama (pâ•no•râ´mâ) *m.* panorama.

pantalones (pân•tâ•lo´nes) *m. pl.* trousers, pants.

pantalla (pân•tâ´yâ) *f.* screen; lamp shade *(para la luz);* screen *(telón);* (fig.) blind, front.

pantano (pân•tâ´no) *m.* swamp, marsh, bog; (fig.) quagmire, morass.

pantanoso, sa (pân•tâ•no´so, sâ) *adj.* marshy, fenny, boggy; (fig.) sticky, messy.

panteón (pân•te•on´) *m.* pantheon; cemetery *(cementerio).*

pantera (pân•te´râ) *f.* panther.

pantomima (pân•to•mē´mâ) *f.* pantomime.

pantorrilla (pân•to•rrē´yâ) *f.* calf.

pantufla (pân•tū´flâ) *f.* slipper.

panza (pân´sâ) *f.* belly, paunch; belly, bulge *(de vasija).*

pañal (pâ•nyâl´) *m.* diaper; shirt-tail *(de camisa);* —**es,** *pl.* infancy *(niñez);* first stages *(principios).*

paño (pâ´nyo) *m.* cloth; breadth of cloth *(ancho);* tapestry *(tapiz);* growth over eye *(del ojo);* spot *(mancha);* defect *(defecto);* coating, film *(que disminuye el brillo).*

pañuelo (pâ•nywe´lo) *m.* handkerchief.

papa (pâ´pâ) *m.* Pope; (coll.) papa *(papá);* —, *f.* potato; —**s,** *f. pl.* food, grub.

papá (pâ•pâ´) *m.* papa, dad.

papada (pâ•pâ´thâ) *f.* double chin; dewlap *(de animales).*

papado (pâ•pâ´tho) *m.* papacy.

papal (pâ•pâl´) *adj.* papal.

papalote (pâ•pâ•lo´te) *m.* kite.

papaya (pâ•pâ´yâ) *f.* (hot.) papaya.

papel (pâ•pel´) *m.* paper; sheet of paper *(hoja);* role, part *(de una obra dramática);* — **encerado,** waxed paper; — **de entapizar,** wallpaper; — **de escribir,** writing paper; — **de estraza,** brown paper; — **de excusado,** — **higiénico,** toilet paper; — **de lija,** sandpaper; — **de seda,** tissue paper; — **moneda,** paper money; — **sellado,** official document paper.

papeleo (pâ•pe•le´o) *m.* red tape;

leafing through papers *(acción de revolver papeles)*.

papelería (pâ•pe•le•rē´â) *f.* stationery store *(tienda);* bunch of papers.

papera (pâ•pe´râ) *f.* goiter; mumps *(parótida);* —**s,** *pl.* (med.) scrofula.

paquete (pâ•ke´te) *m.* package, packet, bundle; (naut.) packet boat.

par (pâr) *adj.* similar, equal, alike; (math.) even; **sin —,** peerless, matchless; —**es o nones,** even or odd; —, *f.* par; —, *m.* pair; peer *(título)*.

para (pa´râ) *prep.* for, to, in order to; toward *(hacia);* good for *(capacidad);* **estar —,** to be about to; — **que,** so that, in order that.

parábola (pâ•râ´vo•lâ) *f.* parable; parabola *(curva)*.

parabrisa (pâ•râ•vrē´sâ) *m.* windshield.

paracaídas (pâ•râ•kâ•ē´thâs) *m.* parachute.

paracaidista (pâ•râ•kâē•thēs´tâ) *m.* parachutist; (Mex. coll.) party crasher; —**s,** *pl.* paratroops.

parachoques (pâ•râ•cho´kes) *m.* (rail.) buffer, bumper; (auto.) bumper.

parada (pâ•râ´thâ) *f.* (mil.) parade; (mus.) pause; stop *(del*

autobus); end *(fin);* stall *(de res);* dam *(presa);* stake, bet *(en el juego)*.

parado, da (pâ•râ´tho, thâ) *adj.* stopped; unemployed *(desocupado)* (Sp. Am.) standing up.

paradoja (pâ•râ•tho´hâ) *f.* paradox.

parador (pâ•râ•thor´) *m.* catcher; inn, hostelry *(mesón);* — **para turistas,** tourist court, motel.

parafina (pâ•râ•fē´nâ) *f.* paraffin.

parafrasear (pâ•râ•frâ•se•âr´) *va.* to paraphrase.

paraguas (pâ•râ´gwâs) *m.* umbrella.

paraíso (pâ•râ•ē´so) *m.* paradise.

paralelo, la (pâ•râ•le´lo, lâ) *adj.* and *n.* parallel.

paralelogramo (pâ•râ•le•lo•grâ´mo) *m.* parallelogram.

parálisis (pâ•râ´lē•sēs) *f.* (med.) paralysis.

paralítico, ca (pâ•râ•lē´tē•ko, kâ) *adj.* paralytic.

paramilitar (pâ•râ•mē•lē•târ´) *adj.* paramilitary.

páramo (pâ´râ•mo) *m.* highland desert, wasteland, paramo.

parapeto (pâ•râ•pe´to) *m.* parapet.

parapléjico, ca (pâ•râ•ple´hē•ko, kâ) paraplegic.

parar (pâ•râr´) *vn.* to stop, to halt; to end *(terminar);* to come into the possession of *(propiedad);* to end up *(reducirse);* to stay *(hospedarse);* —, *vt.* to detain, to impede *(detener).*

pararrayo (pâ•râ•rrâ´yo) *m.* lightning rod.

parásito (pâ•râ´sē•to) *m.* parasite.

parcial (pâr•syâl´) *adj.* partial.

parcialidad (pâr•syâ•lē•thâth´) *f.* partiality; faction *(confederación);* circle, group *(facción);* friendliness *(amistad);* partisanship *(falta de neutralidad).*

parcialmente (pâr•syâl•men´te) *adv.* partially, in part; passionately *(apasionadamente).*

parco, ca (pâr´ko, kâ) *adj.* sparing, frugal; temperate, moderate *(sobrio).*

parche (pâr´che) *m.* patch; plaster *(para heridas);* drumhead *(piel);* (fig.) drum *(tambor);* (fig.) splotch *(en la pintura).*

pardo, da (pâr´tho, thâ) *adj.* brown, dun; cloudy *(nublado);* flat *(de la voz);* mulatto *(mulato);* —, *m.* leopard.

pardusco, ca (pâr•thūs´ko, kâ) *adj.* grayish, grizzly.

parecer (pâ•re•ser´) *m.* opinion, judgment; mien; demeanor *(aspecto);* al —, apparently; —*, *vn.* to appear; to show up *(lo perdido);* —se a, to look like, to

resemble.

parecido, da (pâ•re•sē´tho, thâ) *adj.* similar, like; —, *m.* resemblance.

pared (pâ•reth´) *f.* wall.

pareja (pâ•re´ha) *f.* pair, couple.

parentela (pâ•ren•te´lâ) *f.* relatives, kin.

parentesco (pâ•ren•tes´ko) *m.* relationship.

paréntesis (pâ•ren´te•sēs) *m.* parenthesis.

pariente, ta (pâ•ryen´te, tâ) *n.* relative; (coll.) mate.

parir (pâ•rēr´) *va.* to give birth to; (fig.) to bring forth, to cause; —, *vn.* to give birth.

parisiense (pâ•rē•syen´se) *m.* and *f.* and *adj.* Parisian.

parlamentario, ria (pâr•lâ•men•tâ´ryo, ryâ) *adj.* parliamentary; —, *m.* member of Parliament.

parlamento (pâr•lâ•men´to) *m.* harangue *(arenga);* oration; (pol.) parliament.

parlotear (pâr•lo•te•âr´) *vn.* to babble.

parmesano, na (pâr•me•sâ´no, nâ) *adj.* Parmesan; **queso —,** Parmesan cheese.

paro (pâ´ro) *m.* lockout *(cierre patronal);* work stoppage; — **forzoso,** unemployment, layoff.

parodia (pâ•ro´thyâ) *f.* parody.

paroxismo (pâ•rok•sēz´mo) *m.*

paroxysm, fit.

parpadear (pâr•pâ•the•âr´) *vn.* to blink.

párpado (pâr´pâ•tho) *m.* eyelid.

parque (pâr´ke) *m.* park; (auto.) parking lot;— **de diversiones,** theme park.

parra (pâ´rrâ) *f.* grapevine; **subirse a la —,** (coll.) to lose one´s temper.

párrafo (pâ´rrâ•fo) *m.* paragraph; paragraph mark *(punto y aparte).*

parral (pâ•rrâl´) *m.* vine arbor; wild vineyard *(viña);* earthen jar *(vaso).*

parranda (pâ•rrân´dâ) *f.* carousal, spree; **andar de —,** to go out on the town, to make the rounds.

parrandear (pâ•rrân•de•âr´) *vn.* to go on a spree, to go out on the town.

parrilla (pâ•rrē´yâ) *f.* grill; grillroom *(comedor).*

párroco (pâ´rro•ko) *m.* parson.

parroquia (pâ•rro´kyâ) *f.* (eccl.) parish; parish priest *(cura);* trade, clientele, customers *(clientela).*

parte (pâr´te) *f.* part; side *(lado);* party *(persona);* **por otra —,** on the other hand, besides; **en —,** partly, in part; **en alguna —,** somewhere; **en alguna otra —,** somewhere else; **en ninguna —**, no place; **en todas —s,** everywhere; **de — de,** from, by order of; **¿de — de quién?** who is calling?; **tomar —,** to take part; **por una —,** on the one hand; **por mi —,** as concerns me; **de mi —,** from me; **— superior,** upper side. top; **— inferior,** lower side, bottom.

partera (pâr•te´râ) *f.* midwife.

partero (pâr•te´ro) *m.* obstetrician.

participación (pâr•tē•sē•pâ•syon´) *f.* participation; communication *(aviso).*

participante (pâr•tē•sē•pân´te) *m.* and *f.* participant; notifier *(que avisa).*

participar (pâr•tē•sē•pâr´) *vn.* to participate; **—,** *va.* to inform of, to communicate.

participio (pâr•tē•sē´pyo) *m.* participle.

partícula (pâr•tē´kū•1â) *f.* particle.

particular (pâr•tē•kū•lâr´) *adj.* particular; special *(especial);* private *(no público);* **—** *m.* private citizen; point, matter *(asunto).*

partida (pâr•tē´thâ) *f.* departure; (mil.) party of soldiers; game, round *(juego);* shipment, consignment *(cantidad);* item, entry *(asiento);* copy *(copia).*

partidario, ria (pâr•tē•thâ´ryo,

ryâ) *adj.* partisan, adherent; —, *n.* partisan, advocate.

partido (pâr•tē´tho) *m.* (pol.) party; advantage *(ventaja);* help *(amparo);* match *(deportivo);* agreement *(convenio);* measures, means *(medio);* district *(región);* **sacarle — a,** to take advantage of.

partir (pâr•tēr´) *va.* to divide; to split, to break *(hender);* to separate *(separar);* —, *vn.* to depart; to make up one´s mind *(resolverse);* **a — de,** beginning with, starting with, as of.

partitura (pâr•tē•tū´râ) *f.* (mus.) score.

parto (pâr´to) *m.* childbirth; infant *(niño);* (fig.) production *(producción);* (fig.) creation *(creación);* expectation *(expectación).*

párvulo, la (pâr´vū•lo, lâ) *adj.* very small; gullible *(inocente);* humble *(humilde);* —, *n.* child; **escuela de —los,** kindergarten.

pasa (pâ´sâ) *f.* raisin; **ciruela —,** prune.

pasada (pâ•sâ´thâ) *f.* passage, passing; (coll.) misbehavior; **de —,** on the way, in passing.

pasadizo (pâ•sâ•thē´so) *m.* narrow passage, alley, lane.

pasado (pâ•sâ´tho) *m.* past; (mil.) traitor; (gram.) past tense; **—s,** *pl.* ancestors; —,

adj. past; **— mañana,** day after tomorrow; **en tiempos —s,** in former times.

pasaje (pâ•sâ´he) *m.* passage; fare *(precio).*

pasajero, ra (pâ•sâ•he´ro, râ) *adj.* fleeting, transitory; well-traveled *(sitio);* —, *n.* passenger.

pasamano (pâ•sâ•mâ´no) *m.* railing, handrail, banister; lace, braid, cord *(guarnición).*

pasante (pâ•sân´te) *m.* or *f.* assistant; tutor *(profesor).*

pasaporte (pâ•sâ•por´te) *m.* passport.

pasar (pâ•sâr´) *vt.* to transport *(conducir);* to pass; to send *(enviar);* to cross, to cross over *(atravesar);* to smuggle *(meter de contrabando);* to strain *(colar);* to swallow *(tragar);* to surpass *(exceder);* to overlook *(tolerar);* to undergo, to suffer *(sufrir);* to tutor *(explicar);* to assist *(asistir); to* review *(repasar);* to dry *(desecar);* —, *vn.* to pass; to happen *(suceder);* to last *(durar);* to get along *(tener lo necesario);* to spend *(tiempo);* to pass away *(morir);* to value, to cost *(valer);* to blow over *(cesar);* to happen; **— por alto,** to overlook, to omit.

pasatiempo (pâ•sâ•tyem´po) *m.* pastime, amusement, diversion.

Pascua (pâs´kwâ) *f.* Passover; Easter *(de flores);* **—s,** Christmastide.

pase (pâ´se) *m.* permit; pass *(en el juego).*

pasear (pâ•se•âr´) *vn.* to take a walk, *to* walk; to go for a ride, to take a ride *(en vehículo);* walk; **—,** *vt.* to walk *(un caballo);* to show around *(hacer ver);* **—se,** (fig.) to ramble on; to loaf, to loiter *(estar ocioso).*

paseo (pâ•se´o) *m.* walk, stroll *(a pie);* ride *(en vehículo);* promenade; **— en el campo,** hiking; **ir de —** or **dar un —,** to go out walking or driving; **echar de —,** to get rid of.

pasillo (pâ•se´yo) *m.* corridor, hallway; stitch *(puntada);* short step *(paso).*

pasión (pâ•syon´) *f.* passion; suffering *(sufrimiento).*

pasivo, va (pâ•se´vo, vâ) *adj.* passive; inactive *(inactivo);* pensionary *(de un pensión);* **—,** *m.* liabilities.

pasmar (pâz•mâr´) *va.* to cause a spasm; to stun, to stupefy *(entumecer);* to chill *(enfriar);* to freeze *(helar);* to astonish, to astound *(asombrar);* **—se,** to suffer spasms *(enfermedad);* to be astonished; to dull *(una pintura).*

pasmo (pâz´mo) *m.* cold; tetanus, lockjaw *(tétanos);* amazement *(asombro);* wonder *(causa).*

paso (pâ´so) *m.* step (espacio); pace (movimiento); passing (acto de pasar); passage (lugar); footprint, track (huella); pass (licencia); stitch (puntada); migration (de las aves); strait (estrecho); event, happening (suceso).

pasta (pâs´tâ) *f.* pasta; dough; unworked metal *(metal);* cardboard *(cartón);* pulp *(para papel);* bookbinding *(encuadernación);* **de buena —,** goodnatured; **— de dientes,** toothpaste.

pastar (pâs•târ´) *vn.* to pasture, to graze; **—,** *va.* to lead to graze.

pastel (pâs•tel´) *m.* pastry, cake.

pastelería (pâs•te•le•rē´â) *f.* pastry shop; pastry *(conjunto);* pastry making *(fabricación).*

pasterizar (pâs•te•rē•sâr´) *va.* to pasteurize.

pastilla (pâs•tē´yâ) *f.* tablet, lozenge *(medicina);* drop.

pasto (pâs´to) *m.* pasture, grazing *(acción de pastar);* fodder *(alimento);* grass;(fig.) fuel, food.

pastor (pas•tor´) *m.* shepherd; (eccl.) pastor; **— protestante,**

minister; — **alemán,** German shepherd dog.

pata (pâ′tâ) *f.* foot, leg, paw; foot *(base);* duck *(ave);* (coll.) leg; pocket flap *(cartera);* **—s arriba,** topsy-turvy, upside down.

patada (pâ•tâ′thâ) *f.* kick; (coll.) step; (fig.) footprint *(huella).*

pataleo (pâ•tâ•le′o) *m.* foot stamping.

patán (pâ•tân′) *m.* yokel, hick; rustic, peasant *(rústico).*

patata (pâ•tâ′tâ) *f.* potato.

patear (pâ•te•âr′) *va.* to kick; (coll.) to light into *(maltratar);* **—,** *vn.* to stamp the feet *(dar patadas);* (coll.) to run from pillar to post *(andar mucho);* (fig.) to be furious *(estar enfadado).*

patente (pâ•ten′te) *adj.* patent, manifest, evident; **—,** *f.* permit, warrant, certificate; **— de invención,** patent.

paternal (pâ•ter•nâl′) *adj.* paternal, fatherly.

paternidad (pâ•ter•nē•thâth′) *f.* paternity *(lazo jurídico);* fatherhood.

paterno, na (pâ•ter′no, nâ) *adj.* paternal, fatherly.

patético, ca (pâ•te′tē•ko, kâ) *adj.* pathetic.

patín (pâ•tēn′) *m.* skate; **— de hielo,** ice skate; **— de ruedas,** roller skate.

patinador, ra (pâ•tē•na•thor′, râ) *n.* skater.

patinar (pâ•tē•nâr′) *vn.* to skate *(en patines);* to skid.

patio (pâ′tyo) *m.* patio; (theat.) pit; (Sp. Am.) yard *(corral).*

pato, ta (pâ′to, tâ) *n.* duck.

patología (pâ•to•lo•hē′â) *f.* pathology.

patológico, ca (pâ•to•lo′hē•ko, kâ) *adj.* pathological.

patólogo (pâ•to′lo•go) *m.* pathologist.

patria (pâ′tryâ) *f.* native country, fatherland.

patriarca (pâ•tryâr′kâ) *m.* patriarch.

patriarcal (pâ•tryâr kâl′) *adj.* patriarchal.

patrimonio (pâ•trē•mo′nyo) *m.* patrimony, inheritance.

patriota (pâ•tryo′tâ) *m. and f.* patriot.

patriótico, ca (pâ•tryo′tē•ko, kâ) *adj.* patriotic.

patriotismo (pâ•tryo•tēz′mo) *m.* patriotism.

patrocinar (pâ•tro•sē•nâr′) *va.* to patronize, to favor; to protect *(proteger).*

patrocinio (pâ•tro•sē′nyo) *m.* protection *(protección);* patronage.

patrón (pâ•tron′) *m.* patron; captain *(de un buque);* landlord *(dueño);* boss, employer *(amo);* patron saint *(santo);* pattern *(dechado);* standard *(metal);* stock *(planta);* — **oro,** gold standard.

patrona (pâ•tro´nâ) *f.* patroness; landlady *(dueña);* patron saint *(santa).*

patrulla (pâ•trū´yâ) *f.* (mil.) patrol, squad; gang *(pandilla).*

paupérrimo, ma (pâū•pe´rrē•mo, mâ) *adj.* exceedingly poor, poverty-stricken.

pausa (pâ´ū•sâ) *f.* pause; slowness, deliberation *(lentitud);* (mus.) rest.

pausar (pâū•sâr´) *vn.* to pause.

pauta (pâ´ū•tâ) *f.* ruler; ruled lines *(rayas);* standard, model *(dechado);* (mus.) staff.

pavimentar (pâ•vē•men•târ´) *va.* to pave.

pavimento (pâ•vē•men´to) *m.* pavement.

pavo (pâ´vo) *m.* turkey; (fig.) dimwit; — **real,** peacock.

pavor (pâ•vor´) *m.* terror, horror.

pavoroso, sa (pâ•vo•ro´so, sâ) *adj.* terrible, horrible.

payaso (pâ•yâ´so) *m.* clown.

paz (pâs) *f.* peace; tranquillity *(tranquilidad);* (eccl.) kiss of peace.

peaje (pe•â´he) *m.* toll.

peatón (pe•â•ton´) *m.* pedestrian; route mailman *(cartero).*

peca (pe´kâ) *f.* freckle, spot.

pecado (pe•kâ´tho) *m.* sin; (coll.) devil.

pecador, ra (pe•kâ•thor´, râ) *n.* sinner; —, *f.* (coll.) prostitute.

pecar (pe•kâr´) *vn.* to sin; to go wrong, to make a mistake *(errar).*

pecoso, sa (pe•ko´so, sâ) *adj.* freckled.

peculiar (pe•kū•lyâr´) *adj.* peculiar, individual.

pecuniario, ria (pe•kū•nyâ´ryo, ryâ) *adj.* pecuniary.

pecho (pe´cho) *m.* breast; chest; teat *(mama);* hillock *(cuesta);* bosom, heart *(interior);* courage, valor *(valor);* voice *(voz);* tax, tribute *(tributo);* **dar el —,** to suckle; **tomar a —,** to take to heart.

pechuga (pe•chū´gâ) *f.* breast; (fig.) bosom.

pedagogía (pe•thâ•go•hē´â) *f.* pedagogy.

pedagogo (pe•thâ•go´go) *m.* pedagogue, teacher; mentor, vergil *(mentor).*

pedal (pe•thâl´) *m.* (mus.) pedal; (mech.) treadle, pedal.

pedantería (pe•thân•te•rē´â) *f.* pedantry.

pedazo (pe•thâ´so) *m.* piece, bit; **hacer —s,** to break to pieces, to shatter.

pedernal (pe•ther•nâl´) *m.* flint; (fig.) flintiness.

pedestal (pe•thes•tâl´) *m.*

pedestal; (fig.) basis.

pediatra (pe•thyâ´trâ) *m.* pediatrician.

pediatría (pe•thyâ•trē´â) *f.* pediatrics.

pedido (pe•thē´tho) *m.* request; (com.) order; — **de ensayo,** trial order.

pedir* (pe•thēr´) *va.* to ask, to ask for; to solicit, to petition *(solicitar);* to demand *(reclamar);* to crave, to desire *(anhelar);* to ask someone's hand in marriage *(para casarse);* — **cuenta,** to bring a person to account; — **prestado,** to borrow.

pedrada (pe•thrâ´thâ) *f.* stoning; mark, bruise *(señal);* hairbow *(lazo);* (fig.) taunt, gibe.

pedregoso, sa (pe•thre•go´so, sâ) *adj.* stony, rocky; afflicted by gallstones *(mal de piedra).*

pegadizo, za (pe•gâ•thē´so, sâ) *adj.* sticky, gluey; contagious *(contagioso);* mooching, parasitic *(parásito);* false, artificial *(falso).*

pegadura (pe•gâ•thū´râ) *f.* sticking *(acción);* patch.

pegajoso, sa (pe•gâ•ho´so, sâ) *adj.* sticky; attractive, alluring *(atractivo);* contagious *(contagioso);* (fig.) soft, smooth *(suave).*

pegar (pe•gâr´) *va.* to cement, to stick, to paste, to glue; to join, to attach *(juntar);* to strike, to beat *(golpear);* to communicate *(comunicar).*

peinado (peē•nâ´tho) *m.* coiffure, hairdo.

peinador (peē•nâ•thor´) *m.* hairdresser.

peinadora (peē•nâ•tho´râ) *f.* hairdresser.

peinar (peē•nâr´) *va.* to comb; — **se,** to comb one's hair.

peine (pe´ē•ne) *m.* comb; card *(carda);* instep *(empeine);* (fig.) sly devil, sly one *(púa).*

pelado, da (pe•lâ´tho, thâ) *n.* (Mex.) peasant; —, *adj.* bald *(calvo);* peeled, pared *(sin piel);* bare *(desnudo);* poor *(pobre);* shameless *(desvergonzado);* even *(número).*

pelar (pe•lâr´) *va.* to pull out one's hair; to pluck *(desplumar);* to peel, to pare *(mondar);* (fig.) to snatch, to grab *(despojar);* to clean out *(ganar).*

peldaño (pel•dâ´nyo) *m.* step.

pelea (pe•le´â) *f.* battle, fight; quarrel *(disputa);* (fig.) diligence *(diligencia).*

pelear (pe•le•âr´) *vn.* to fight, to battle; to quarrel *(reñir);* —**se,** to fight; (fig.) to split up, to break up *(separarse).*

pelícano (pe•lē´kâ•no) *m.* pelican; pincers *(gatillo).*

película (pe•lē´kū•lâ) *f.* film;
rollo de —s, film roll.

peligrar (pe•lē•grâr´) *vn.* to be in
danger.

peligro (pe•lē´gro) *m.* danger,
risk, peril.

peligroso, sa (pe•lē•gro´so, sâ)
adj. dangerous, perilous.

pelirrojo, ja (pe•lē•rro´ho, hâ)
adj. and *n.* redhead.

pelo (pe´lo) *m.* hair *(cabello);* pile
(de un tejido); flaw *(en una
joya);* hairspring *(muelle);* fuzz,
down *(vello);* raw silk *(seda);*
vein *(grieta);* grain *(de madera);*
(fig.) trifle; **a —,** to the purpose,
timely; **tomar el —,** to tease, to
kid.

pelota (pe•lo´tâ) *f.* ball; ball
game *(juego).*

peltre (pel´tre) *m.* pewter.

peluca (pe•lū´kâ) *f.* wig; (coll.)
bawling out, dressing down.

peludo, da (pe•lū´tho, thâ) *adj.*
hairy.

peluquería (pe•lū•ke•rē´â) *f.* barbershop *(de hombres);* beauty
parlor.

pelusa (pe•lū´sâ) *f.* fuzz, down
(vello); nap; (fig.) childish envy.

pelvis (pel´vēs) *f.* pelvis.

pellejo (pe•ye´ho) *m.* skin; hide;
pelt *(de animal);* wineskin
(odre); (coll.) drunk, lush.

pellizcar (pe•yēs•kâr´) *va.* to

pinch; to graze, to nip *(herir);*
to take a speck of *(tomar
pequeña cantidad);* **—se,** (fig.)
to yearn, to pine.

pellizco (pe•yēs´ko) *m.* pinch;
graze, nip *(herida);* smidgen,
pinch *(corta cantidad).*

pena (pe´nâ) *f.* pain; sadness,
shame; punishment *(castigo);*
trouble, difficulty *(dificultad);*
pendant *(pendiente);* (orn.)
penna; **a duras —s,** with difficulty; **merecer** or **valer la —,** to
be worthwhile; **so — de,** under
penalty of.

penacho (pe•nâ´cho) *m.* (orn.)
crest; plumes *(adorno);* (fig.)
pride, haughtiness.

penal (pe•nâl´) *adj.* penal; **—,** *m.*
penitentiary.

penar (pe•nâr´) *vn.* to suffer; **—,**
va. to penalize, to punish.

pendencia (pen•den´syâ) *f.* quarrel, dispute; litigation *(litis-
pendencia).*

pendiente (pen•dyen´te) *adj.*
hanging; pending *(que está por
resolverse);* **— de pago,** pending
payment, unpaid; **—,** *m.* pendant; earring, eardrop *(arete);*
—, *f.* slope, grade, incline; **—
arriba,** uphill slope.

péndola (pen´do•lâ) *f.* pendulum;
pendulum clock *(reloj);* suspension *(varilla).*

pendón (pen•don´) *m.* standard,

banner, pennon; shoot *(vásta-go);* (coll.) frump *(mujer desali-ñada);* (coll.) rake, libertine *(libertino).*

péndulo, la (pen´dū•lo, lâ) *adj.* pendent, hanging; —, *m.* pen-dulum.

pene (pe´ne) *m.* (anat.) penis.

penetración (pe•ne•trâ•syon´) *f.* penetration.

penetrante (pe•ne•trân´te) *adj.* penetrating.

penetrar (pe•ne•trâr´) *va.* to pen-etrate; (fig.) to fathom, to com-prehend.

penicilina (pe•nē•sē•lē´nâ) *f.* penicillin.

peninsula (pe•nēn´sū•lâ) *f.* peninsula.

peninsular (pe•nēn•sū•lâr´) *adj.* peninsular; —, *m.* (Sp. Am.) Spaniard.

penitencia (pe•nē•ten´syâ) *f.* penitence, repentance; penance *(sacramento).*

penitenciaría (pe•nē ten•syâ•rē´â) *f.* penitentiary.

penoso, sa (pe•no´so sâ) *adj.* hard, difficult *(trabajoso);* suf-fering, afflicted *(afligido);* (coll.) conceited, vain *(presumido).*

pensamiento (pen•sâ•myen´to) *m.* thought; suspicion *(sospecha);* (bot.) pansy.

pensar* (pen•sâr´) *vn.* to think; to intend *(proponerse).*

pensativo, va (pen•sâ•tē´vo, vâ) *adj.* pensive, thoughtful.

pensión (pen•syon´) *f.* pension, annuity; allowance *(asi-gnación);* board *(pupilaje);* grant *(para estudios);* board-inghouse, pension *(casa).*

pensionado, da (pen•syo•nâ´tho, thâ) *adj.* pensioned; —, *n.* pen-sioner; —, *m.* boarding school.

pensionar (pen•syo•nâr´) *va.* to award a pension to.

pentágono (pen•tâ´go•no) *m.* pentagon.

pentagrama (pen•tâ•grâ´mâ) *m.* (mus.) staff

penumbra (pe•nūm´brâ) *f.* penumbra.

penuria (pe•nū´ryâ) *f.* penury, poverty, indigence, need, want.

peña (pe´nyâ) *f.* rock, boulder; rocky peak *(monte);* friends, comrades *(amigos).*

peñasco (pē•nyâs´ko) *m.* crag, peak; (zool.) murex.

peñón (pe•nyon´) *m.* rocky peak *(monte);* boulder; **P— de Gibraltar,** Rock of Gibraltar.

peón (pe•ôn´) *f.* pedestrian; labo-rer *(jornalero);* foot soldier *(sol-dado);* top *(juguete);* pawn *(del ajedrez);* checker *(del juego de damas);* axle *(árbol);* beehive *(colmena).*

peor (pe•or´) *adj.* and *adv.* worse; **tanto —,** so much the worse; **de mal en —,** from bad to worse.

pepino (pe•pē′no) *m.* cucumber.

pepita (pe•pē′tâ) *f.* seed; pip *(enfermedad);* nugget *(metal).*

pequeño, ña (pe•ke′nyo, nyâ) *adj.* little, small; young *(joven);* lowly, humble *(humilde);* (fig.) trifling.

pera (pe′râ) *f.* pear; (fig.) goatee *(barba);* (fig.) plum *(destino lucrativo).*

percance (per•kân′se) *m.* perquisite; bad luck, misfortune *(infortunio).*

percepción (per•sep•syon′) *f.* perception; idea *(idea).*

perceptible (per•sep•tē′vle) *adj.* perceptible, perceivable; receivable, collectible.

percibir (per•sē•vēr′) *va.* to collect, to receive *(recibir);* to perceive; to comprehend *(comprender).*

percusión (per•kū•syon′) *f.* percussion; **instrumento de —,** percussion instrument.

perder* (per•ther′) *va.* to lose; to waste *(malgastar);* to miss *(un tren);* to fail, to flunk *(no aprobar);* to spoil *(dañar);* to ruin *(arruinar);* —, *vn.* to lose; to fade *(desteñirse);* **echar a —,** to ruin; **—se,** to get lost, to go astray.

pérdida (per′thē•thâ) *f.* loss; damage *(daño).*

perdido, da (per•thē′tho, thâ) *adj.* lost.

perdiz (per•thēs′) *f.* partridge.

perdón (per•thon′) *m.* pardon; forgiveness, remission *(indulgencia);* (coll.) hot drop of oil or wax *(gota).*

perdonable (per•tho•nâ′vle) *adj.* pardonable.

perdonar (per•tho•nâr′) *va.* to pardon; to excuse *(exceptuar);* (fig.) to renounce *(renunciar).*

perdurable (per•thū•râ′vle) *adj.* perpetual, everlasting; durable, long-lasting *(durable).*

perecedero, ra (pe•re•se•the′ro, râ) *adj.* perishable; —, *m.* necessity, want.

perecer* (pe•re•ser′) *vn.* to perish, to die *(morir);* to suffer *(padecer);* to be poverty-stricken *(tener pobreza);* **—se,** (fig.) to yearn, to pine; (fig.) to anguish *(padecer).*

peregrinación (pe•re•grē′nâ•syon′) *f.* pilgrimage.

peregrino, na (pe•re•grē′no, nâ) *adj.* traveling; foreign *(extranjero);* migratory *(de aves);* strange, rare *(raro);* elegant *(elegante);* mortal *(mortal);* —, *n.* pilgrim.

perejil (pe•re•hēl′) *m.* parsley; (fig.) frilliness, gaudiness.

perenne (pe•ren´ne) *adj.* continuous, incessant; (bot.) perennial.

pereza (pe•re´sâ) *f.* laziness; negligence, carelessness *(descuido).*

perezoso, sa (pe•re•so´so, sâ) *adj.* lazy; negligent, careless *(descuidado);* —, *m.* sloth.

perfección (per•fek•syon´) *f.* perfection.

perfeccionar (per•fek•syo•nâr´) *va.* to perfect, to give the finishing touches.

perfecto, ta (per•fek´to, tâ) *adj.* perfect.

perfil (per•fēl´) *m.* profile; edging *(adorno);* sketch, outline *(de la pintura).*

perfilar (per•fē•lâr´) *va.* to profile, to out-line; (fig.) to perfect, to refine; —**se,** to be outlined.

perforación (per•fo•râ•syon´) *f.* perforation, puncture.

perforar (per•fo•râr´) *va.* to perforate, to puncture.

perfumar (per•fū•mâr´) *va.* to perfume.

perfume (per•fū´me) *m.* perfume.

pericia (pe•rē´syâ) *f.* skill, ability.

perico (pe•rē´ko) *m.* periwig, peruke; parakeet *(ave);* large fan *(abanico);* giant asparagus *(espárrago);* (coll.) chamber pot *(sillico);* (Mex.) chatter-box.

periferia (pe•rē•fe´ryâ) *f.* periphery.

perilla (pe•rē´yâ) *f.* small pear; pearshaped ornament *(adorno);* pommel *(de una silla de montar);* goatee *(barba);* earlobe *(de la oreja).*

perímetro (pe•rē´me•tro) *m.* perimeter.

periódico, ca (pe•ryo´thē•ko, kâ) *adj.* periodical; —, *m.* newspaper.

periodismo (pe•ryo•thēz´mo) *m.* journalism.

periodista (pe•ryo•thēs´tâ) *m.* and *f.* journalist.

período (pe•rē´o•tho) or **periodo,** (pē•ryo´tho) *m.* (gram.) periodic sentence; period; cycle *(ciclo).*

perito, ta (pe•rē´to, tâ) *adj.* expert, skilled; —, *m.* expert.

perjudicar (per•hū•thē•kâr´) *va.* to harm, to damage.

perjudicial (per•hū•thē•syâl´) *adj.* damaging, harmful, injurious.

perjuicio (per•hwē´syo) *m.* injury, harm, damage.

perjurar (per•hū•râr´) *vn.* to commit perjury; to swear *(jurar);* —**se,** to commit perjury *(jurar en falso);* to perjure oneself.

perjurio (per•hu´ryo) *m.* perjury.

perla (per´lâ) *f.* pearl; **de —s,** just right; —**s cultivadas,** cultured pearls.

permanecer* (per•mâ•ne•ser´) vn. to remain, to stay.

permanente (per•mâ•nen´te) adj. permanent; —, m. permanent wave.

permiso (per•mē´so) m. permission, authorization; deviation (en las monedas).

permitido, da (per•mē•tē´tho, thâ) adj. allowed, permitted; **no está —do,** it is not allowed.

permitir (per•mē•tēr´) va. to permit, to allow; **—se,** to take the liberty, to permit oneself; **Dios lo permita,** God willing.

permutar (per•mu•târ´) va. to exchange; to change (variar).

pernicioso, sa (per•nē•syo´so, sâ) adj. pernicious, destructive.

pero (pe´ro) conj. but; yet (sino); —, m. defect, fault; objection (objeción); **poner —s,** to find fault.

perorar (pe•ro•râr´) vn. to make a speech; (fig.) to nag, to hound (pedir).

perorata (pe•ro•râ´tâ) harangue, speech.

peróxido (pe•rok´sē•tho) m. peroxide.

perpendicular (per•pen•dē•kū•lâr´) adj. perpendicular.

perpetrar (per•pe•trâr´) va. to perpetrate, to commit.

perpetuar (per•pe•twâr´) va. to perpetuate.

perpetuo, tua (per•pe´two, twâ) adj. perpetual.

perplejidad (per•ple•hē•thâth´) f. perplexity.

perplejo, ja (per•ple´ho, hâ) adj. perplexed.

perra (pe´rrâ) f. female dog, bitch; drunkenness, intoxication (borrachera); (coll.) childish anger.

perro (pe´rro) m. dog.

persa (per´sâ) n. and adj. Persian.

perseguir* (per•se•gēr´) va. to pursue; (fig.) to persecute; to dun, to hound (importunar).

perseverancia (per•se•ve•rân´syâ) f. perseverance, persistency.

perseverante (per•se•ve•rân´te) adj. perseverant.

perseverar (per•se•ve•râr´) vn. to persevere, to persist.

persiana (per•syâ´nâ) f. window blind, Venetian blind.

persignarse (per•sēg•nâr´se) vr. to make the sign of the cross, to bless oneself; (coll.) to begin the day´s selling.

persistencia (per•sēs•ten´syâ) f. persistence, persistency.

persistente (per•sēs•ten´te) adj. persistent, tenacious.

persistir (per•sēs•tēr´) vn. to persist.

persona (per•so´nâ) *f.* person; personage *(persona importante);* character *(de una obra literaria);* **por —,** per capita; **— desplazada,** displaced person.

personaje (per•so•nâ´he) *m.* personage; character *(obra literaria).*

personal (per•so•nâl´) *adj.* personal; **—,** *m.* personnel, staff; staff expenses *(gastos).*

personalidad (per•so•nâ•lē•thâth´) *f.* personality.

personificar (per•so•nē•fē•kâr´) *va.* to personify.

perspectiva (pers•pek•tē´vâ) *f.* perspective; false representation *(representación falsa);* prospect *(expectiva).*

perspicacia (pers•pē•kâ´syâ) *f.* clear-sightedness; perspicacity *(entendimiento).*

persuadir (per•swâ•thēr´) *va.* to persuade, to convince.

persuasión (per•swâ•syon´) *f.* persuasion.

persuasivo, va (per•swâ•sē´vo, vâ) *adj.* persuasive.

pertenecer* (per•te•ne•ser´) *vn.* to belong; to pertain, to concern, to have to do *(concernir).*

perteneciente (per•te•ne•syen´te) *adj.* belonging, pertaining.

pertenencia (per•te•nen´syâ) *f.* right of property; territory, domain *(territorio);* appurtenance, adjunct *(accesorio).*

pertinaz (per•tē•nâs´) *adj.* pertinacious, obstinate.

pertinencia (per•tē•nen´syâ) *f.* relevance, pertinence.

pertrechos (per•tre´chos) *m. pl.* ordnance *(de guerra);* tools, instruments.

perturbación (per•tūr•vâ•syon´) *f.* disturbance, perturbation.

perturbar (per•tūr•vâr´) *va.* to perturb, to disturb, to trouble; to confuse, to mix up *(un discurso).*

peruano, na (pe•rwâ´no, nâ) *adj.* and *n.* Peruvian.

perversión (per•ver•syon´) *f.* perversion, depravation, corruption.

perverso, sa (per•ver´so, sâ) *adj.* perverse.

pervertir* (per•ver•tēr´) *va.* to pervert, to corrupt.

pesa (pe´sâ) *f.* weight; **—s y medidas,** weights and measures.

pesadilla (pe•sâ•thē´yâ) *f.* nightmare.

pesado, da (pe•sâ´tho, thâ) *adj.* heavy; slow *(lento);* tiresome, tedious *(molesto);* harmful, injurious *(sensible);* harsh, hard *(áspero);* **sueño —,** profound sleep.

pesadumbre (pe•sâ•thūm´bre) *f.*

heaviness; injury, offense *(injuria);* gravity *(pesantez);* quarrel, dispute *(riña);* grief, sorrow *(tristeza).*

pésame (pe´sâ•me) *m.* condolence, sympathy.

pesar (pe•sâr´) *m.* sorrow, grief; regret, repentance *(arrepentimiento);* **a — de,** in spite of, notwithstanding; —**,** *vn.* to weigh, to have weight; to be heavy *(pesar mucho);* to be valuable *(valer);* —**,** *va.* to weigh; (fig.) to weigh down, to grieve.

pesca (pes´kâ) *f.* fishing; — **con arpón,** spear fishing.

pescadería (pes•kâ•the•rē´â) *f.* fish market.

pescado (pes•kâ´tho) *m.* fish; salted codfish *(abadejo).*

pescador, ra (pes•kâ•thor´, râ) *n.* fisherman; —**,** *m.* (ichth.) angler.

pescar (pes•kâr´) *va.* to fish; to catch *(peces);* (coll.) to get hold of, to latch onto *(coger);* to catch, to surprise *(sorprender).*

pescuezo (pes•kwe´so) *m.* neck; (fig.) haughtiness, pride.

pesebre (pe•se´vre) *m.* manger.

pesimista (pe•sē•mēs´tâ) *m.* and *f.* pessimist; —**,** *adj.* pessimistic.

pésimo, ma (pe´sē•mo, mâ) *adj.* very bad, abominable.

peso (pe´so) *m.* peso *(moneda);* gravity *(pesantez);* weight; balance *(balanza);* — **atómico,** atomic weight.

pesquisa (pes•kē´sâ) *f.* inquiry, investigation.

pestaña (pes•tâ´nyâ) *f.* eyelash; edge, edging *(ceja);* (bot.) cilium.

peste (pes´te) *f.* pest, plague; stench, stink *(mal olor);* (fig.) corruption *(corrupción);* (coll.) epidemic *(abundancia).*

pestilencia (pes•tē•len´syâ) *f.* pestilence, plague.

petaca (pe•tâ´kâ) *f.* leather chest *(arca);* cigar box *(estuche).*

pétalo (pe´tâ•lo) *m.* petal.

petardo (pe•tar´tho) *m.* petard; bomb *(bomba);* cheat, fraud *(engaño).*

petición (pe•tē•syon´) *f.* petition, request; plea.

petirrojo (pe•tē•rro´ho) *m.* robin red-breast.

pétreo, trea (pe´tre•o, tre•â) *adj.* stony.

petrificar (pe•trē•fē•kâr´) *va.* and *vr.* to petrify.

petróleo (pe•tro´le•o) *m.* petroleum, oil.

petrolero, ra (pe•tro•le´ro, râ) *adj.* pertaining to oil; arsonistic *(incendiario).*

petrolífero, ra (pe•tro•lē´fe•ro, râ) *adj.* oil producing; **campos**

—s, oil fields.

pez (pes) *m.* fish; long pile *(montón);* (fig.) fruit of one's labors *(resultado);* **peces de colores,** goldfish; —, *f.* pitch, tar; — **griega,** rosin.

pezuña (pe•sū´nyâ) *f.* hoof.

piadoso, sa (pyâ•tho´so sâ) *adj.* pious; merciful, benevolent *(benigno).*

pianista (pyâ•nēs´tâ) *m.* and *f.* pianist.

piano (pyâ´no) *m.* piano; — **de cola,** grand piano.

pianoforte (pyâ•no•for´te) *m.* pianoforte.

picadillo (pē•kâ•thē´yo) *m.* mincemeat; hash *(guisado).*

picado, da (pē•kâ´tho, thâ) *adj.* perforated; piqued *(enojado);* —, *m.* hash; (avi.) dive.

picador (pē•kâ•thor´) *m.* picador; trainer *(de caballos);* cutting board *(tajo);* lock-breaker *(ladrón).*

picadura (pē•kâ•thū´râ) *f.* prick, puncture *(picotazo);* bite; cut, slit *(cisura);* cut tobacco *(tobaco);* cavity *(caries).*

picaflor (pē•kâ•flor´) *m.* (orn.) hummingbird; flirt *(tenorio).*

picamaderos (pē•kâ•mâ•the´ros) *m.* (orn.) woodpecker.

picante (pē•kân´te) *adj.* stinging, pricking; hot, highly seasoned; (fig.) spicy.

picahielo (pē•kâ•ye´lo) *m.* ice pick.

picar (pē•kâr´) *va.* to prick, to puncture; to jab, to goad *(al toro);* to prick, to bite *(morder);* to chop up, to mince *(dividir);* to peck *(de las aves);* to take the bait *(morder el cebo);* to itch *(escozor);* to burn *(enardecer).*

picardía (pē•kâr•thē´â) *f.* knavery, roguery; deceit, trickery *(engaño);* mischievousness *(travesura);* bunch of rascals *(junta).*

picaresco, ca (pē•kâ•res´ko, kâ) *adj.* roguish, knavish; picaresque *(de la literatura).*

pícaro, ra (pē´kâ•ro, râ) *adj.* roguish; sly, rascally, tricky *(astuto);* (fig.) mischievous *(travieso);* —, *m.* rogue; rascal; mischief.

picazón (pē•kâ•son´) *f.* itching, itch; (fig.) displeasure *(disgusto).*

pico (pē´ko) *m.* beak, bill; peak *(de montaña);* spout *(de vasija);* corner *(de pañuelo);* loquacity *(habladuría);* **perder por el —,** to miss out by not knowing when to keep one's mouth shut; **cien dólares y —,** a little more than one hundred dollars; **la una y —,** a little after one o'clock.

picoso, sa (pē•ko′so, sâ) *adj.* pitted with small pox; (Mex. coll.) hot, highly seasoned.

picudo, da (pē•kū′tho, thâ) *adj.* beaked; sharp-pointed *(puntiagudo); (fig.)* talkative; —, *m.* spit.

pie (pye) *m.* foot; base *(base);* basis *(origen);* trunk *(de árbol);* — **cuadrado,** square foot; **al — de la letra,** literally; **a —,** on foot; **dar —,** to give occasion; **estar de —,** to be standing; **ponerse de —,** to stand up; **dedo del —,** toe; — **de atleta,** (med.) athlete′s foot; **de —s a cabeza,** from head to toe.

piedad (pye•thâth′) *f.* piety; mercy, pity *(misericordia).*

piedra (pye′thrâ) *f.* stone; gem *(preciosa);* hail *(granizo);* — **angular,** cornerstone; **—de afilar,** whetstone.

piel (pyel) *f.* skin; hide, pelt *(cuero curtido);* leather *(sin pelo).*

pierna (pyer′nâ) *f.* leg.

pieza (pye′sâ) *f.* piece; play *(obra dramática);* room *(habitación).*

pigmeo, mea (pēg•me′o, me′â) *n.* and *adj.* pygmy.

pijama (pē•hâ′mâ) *m.* pajamas.

pila (pē′lâ) *f.* trough; (eccl.) font; pile *(montón);* (elec.) battery; — **de agua bendita,** holy-water font; **nombre de —,** Christian name; — **seca,** dry battery.

pilar (pē•lâr′) *m.* basin *(de fuente);* milestone *(hito);* (arch.) pillar; —, *va.* to pound, to crush.

pilastra (pē•lâs′trâ) *f.* pilaster.

píldora (pēl′do•râ) *f.* pill.

piloto (pē•lo′to) *m.* pilot; first mate *(segundo);* — **automático,** auto pilot; — **de prueba,** test pilot.

pillaje (pē•yâ′he) *m.* pillage, plunder.

pillar (pē•yâr′) *va.* to pillage, to plunder; to seize, to grab, to snatch *(agarrar).*

pilluelo (pē•ywe′lo) *m.* urchin, scamp.

pimentero (pē•men•te′ro) *m.* pepper shaker; pepper plant *(mata).*

pimentón (pē•men•ton′) *m.* paprika; red pepper *(colorado).*

pimienta (pē•myen′tâ) *f.* pepper.

pimiento (pē•myen′to) *m.* pepper; red pepper *(colorado).*

pináculo (pē•nâ′kū•lo) *m.* pinnacle.

pincel (pēn•sel′) *m.* brush.

pincelada (pēn•se•lâ′thâ) *f.* brushstroke.

pinchar (pēn•châr′) *va.* to prick.

pinchazo (pēn•châ′so) *m.* prick; puncture *(en un neumático).*

pingüe (pēn′gwe) *adj.* fat, greasy; rich, fertile *(fecundo).*

pingüino (pēn•gwē´no) *m.* penguin.

pino, na (pē´no, nâ) *adj.* steep; —, *m.* (bot.) pine.

pinta (pēn´tâ) *f.* spot, mark; sign, mark *(señal);* pint *(medida).*

pintar (pēn•târ´) *va.* to paint; to picture, to describe *(describir);* to exaggerate *(exagerar);* —, *vn.* to begin to ripen; (coll.) to show up, to crop out *(mostrarse);* —se, to put on one's make-up.

pintor, ra (pen•tor´, râ) *n.* painter, artist.

pintoresco, ca (pēn•to•res´ko, kâ) *adj.* picturesque.

pintura (pēn•tū´râ) *f.* painting, picture *(cuadro);* paint.

pinzas (pēn´sâs) *f. pl.* pincers; (med.) forceps.

piña (pē´nyâ) *f.* pineapple; fir cone *(del abeto).*

piñata (pē•nyâ´tâ) *f.* piñata, decorated jar filled with candy and toys.

piojo (pyo´ho) *m.* louse.

piojoso, sa (pyo•ho´so, sâ) *adj.* full of lice, lousy.

pipa (pē´pâ) *f.* pipe; fuse *(espoleta);* cask *(barrica).*

piquete (pē•ke´te) *m.* prick, jab; picket *(estaca);* (mil.) picket.

pirámide (pē•ra´mē•the) *f.* pyramid.

pirata (pē•râ´tâ) *m.* pirate; (fig.)

cruel wretch.

piromanía (pē•ro•mâ•nē´â) *f.* pyromania.

piropo (pē•ro´po) *m.* compliment, flattery.

pirotecnia (pē•ro•teg´nyâ) *f.* pyrotechnics.

pirueta (pē•rwe´ tâ) *f.* pirouette.

pisada (pē•sâ´thâ) *f.* footstep; footprint *(huella).*

pisar (pē•sâr´) *va.* to step on, to tread on; to tramp, to stamp down *(apretar);* (fig.) to mistreat.

piscina (pēs•sē´nâ) *f.* fishpond *(de peces);* swimming pool.

piso (pē´so) *m.* story; floor *(suelo);* flat, apartment *(vivienda);* — **bajo,** ground floor; **casa de tres —s,** three-story house.

pisotear (pē•so•te•âr´) *va.* to trample on, to tread under foot.

pista (pēs´tâ) *f.* trace, footprint *(huella);* track; — **y campo,** track and field; — **de aterrizaje,** landing strip, landing field; — **de despegue,** runway.

pistacho (pēs•tâ´cho) *m.* pistachio, pistachio nut.

pistola (pēs•to´lâ) *f.* pistol.

pistón (pēs•ton´) *m.* piston *(émbolo);* percussion cap.

pitazo (pē•tâ´so) *m.* whistle; (auto.) honk.

pitillo (pē•tē´yo) *m.* cigarette.

pito (pē´to) *m.* whistle; **no me importa un —,** I don´t give a hang.

pituitario, ria (pē•twē•tâ´ryo, ryâ) *adj.* pituitary.

pizarra (pē•sâ´rrâ) *f.* blackboard, chalkboard *(pizarrón).*

pizarrón (pē•sâ•rron´) *m.* blackboard, chalkboard.

pizca (pēs´kâ) *f.* pinch, bit; **ni—,** not a bit.

placa (plâ´kâ) *f.* plaque; sheet, plate *(plancha);* (auto.) license plate.

placentero, ra (plâ•sen•te´ro, râ) *adj.* pleasant, agreeable.

placer (plâ•ser´) *m.* pleasure, delight; (min.) placer; **—*,** *vn.* to please.

plaga (plâ´gâ) *f.* plague.

plagar (plâ•gâr´) *va.* to plague, to torment.

plagio (plâ´hyo) *m.* plagiarism.

plácido, da (plâ´sē•tho, thâ) *adj.* placid, quiet.

plan (plân) *m.* plan, design, project.

plana (plâ´nâ) *f.* trowel; page *(de libro);* level *(llanura).*

plancha (plân´châ) *f.* plate, sheet; flatiron *(utensilio).*

planchado, da (plân•châ´tho, thâ) *adj.* ironed; **—,** *m.* ironing.

planchar (plân•châr´) *va.* to iron, to mangle.

planear (plâ•ne•âr´) *vn.* to glide;

—, *va.* to plan, to organize.

planeta (plâ•ne´tâ) *m.* planet.

planicie (plâ•nē´sye) *f.* plain, prairie.

planificar (plâ•nē•fē•kâr´) *va.* to make a plan for, to plan.

plano, na (plâ´no, nâ) *adj.* level, flat; **—,** *m.* plan; (math.) plane; **de —no,** right out, directly, flatly; **primer —no,** foreground.

planta (plân´tâ) *f.* plant; sole *(del pie);* floor plan *(de edificio);* **— baja,** ground floor.

plantación (plân•tâ•syon´) *f.* plantation; planting *(acción).*

plantar (plân•târ´) *va.* to plant; to fix upright, to stick *(hincar);* to put, to place *(colocar);* to found, to establish *(plantear);* (coll.) to jilt *(burlar);* to give *(un golpe);* **—se,** to stand firm.

plantear (plân•te•âr´) *va.* to lay out, to plan *(tantear);* to found *(establecer);* to propose, to offer *(proponer).*

plantel (plân•tel´) *m.* (bot.) nursery; plant, establishment *(de educación).*

plañir* (plâ•nyēr´) *vn.* to lament, to grieve, to wail.

plasma (plâz´mâ) *m.* (biol.) plasma; (min.) plasm.

plástico, ca (plâs´tē•ko, kâ) *adj.* and *m.* plastic.

plata (plâ´tâ) *f.* silver; (fig.) money; **en —,** briefly, to the point; — **labrada,** silverware.

plataforma (plâ•tâ•for´mâ) *f.* platform.

plátano (plâ´tâ•no) *m.* plantain, banana; plane tree *(árbol).*

plateado, da (plâ•te•â´tho, thâ) *adj.* silvery; silver-plated.

platear (plâ•te•âr´) *va.* to coat with silver.

platero (plâ•te´ro) *m.* silversmith.

plática (plâ´tē•kâ) *f.* conversation, chat.

platicar (plâ•tē•kâr´) *vn.* to converse, to chat.

platillo (plâ•tē´yo) *m.* saucer; (mus.) cymbal; — **volador,** flying saucer.

platino (plâ•tē´no) *m.* platinum.

plato (plâ´to) *m.* dish, plate; dish *(vianda);* **lista de —s,** bill of fare, menu.

platónico, ca (plâ•to´nē•ko, kâ) *adj.* Platonic.

plausible (plâū•sē´vle) *adj.* plausible.

playa (plâ´yâ) *f.* beach, strand.

plaza (plâ´sâ) *f.* square: market place *(mercado);* (mil.) fortified city; place; employment *(empleo);* sentar (mil.) to enlist; — **de toros,** bull ring.

plazo (plâ´so) *m.* term, date of payment; **a —,** on credit, on time; **a corto —,** short-term; **a — fijo,** for a fixed period.

plegable (ple•gâ´vle) *adj.* pliable; foldable *(doblegable).*

plegadizo, za (ple•gâ•thē´so, sâ) *adj.* folding, collapsible.

plegar* (ple•gâr´) *va.* to fold *(doblegar);* to pleat; —**se,** to submit.

plegaria (ple•gâ´ryâ) *f.* prayer.

pleito (ple´ē•to) *m.* dispute, controversy, quarrel *(disputa);* lawsuit, litigation.

plenamente (ple•nâ•men´te) *adv.* fully, completely.

plenitud (ple•nē•tuth´) *f.* fullness, plenitude.

pleno, na (ple´no, nâ) *adj.* full; **en — invierno,** in the dead of winter.

pleonasmo (ple•o•nâz´mo) *m.* pleonasm.

pliego (plye´go) *m.* sheet *(de papel);* folder *(doblado);* sealed document.

pliegue (plye´ge) *m.* fold; pleat.

plomero (plo•me´ro) *m.* plumber.

plomo (plo´mo) *m.* lead; — **derretido,** melted lead.

pluma (plū´mâ) *f.* feather; plume *(adorno);* pen *(para escribir);* — **estilográfica,** — **fuente,** fountain pen.

plumaje (plū•mâ´he) *m.* plumage; feathers *(adorno).*

plural (plū•ral´) *adj.* (gram.) plural.

pluralidad (plū•râ•lē•thâth´) *f.*

plurality; numerousness *(multiplicidad)*.

plutonio (plū•to´nyo) *m.* plutonium.

población (po•vlâ•syon´) *f.* population;

poblado (po•vlâ´tho) *m.* town, village, hamlet.

poblar* (po•vlâr´) *va.* to populate, to people; —, *vn.* to procreate; —**se,** to bud.

pobre (po´vre) *adj.* poor.

pobreza (po•vre´sâ) *f.* poverty, poorness; (fig.) sterility, barrenness.

pocilga (po•sēl´gâ) *f.* pigsty.

poción (po•syon´) *f.* potion.

poco, ca (po´ko, kâ) *adj.* little; —**s,** *pl.* few; —**o,** *adv.* little; — **a** —, gradually, little by little; **hace** —, a short time ago, a little while ago; **a** —, shortly after, very soon; **tan** — **como,** as little as; — **común,** unusual; — **bondadoso,** unkind; **por** —, almost; —, *m.* small part; **un** —, a little.

poda (po´thâ) *f.* pruning.

podar (po•thâr´) *va.* to prune.

podenco (po•theng´ko) *m.* hound.

poder (po•ther´) *m.* power; possession *(posesión);* proxy *(instrumento);* — **adquisitivo,** purchasing power; **en** — **de,** in the hands of; **por** —, by proxy;

a más no —, to the limit, to the utmost; —*, *vn.* to be able; to be possible *(ser contingente).*

poderoso, sa (po•the•ro´so, sâ) *adj.* powerful; eminent *(eminente).*

podredumbre (po•thre•thūm´bre) *f.* putrid matter; (fig.) grief.

podrir* (po•thrēr´) = **pudrir.**

poema (po•e´mâ) *m.* poem.

poesía (po•e•sē´â) *f.* poetry.

poeta (po•e´tâ) *m.* poet.

poético, ca (po•e´tē•ko, kâ) *adj.* poetic.

polaco, ca (po•lâ´ko, kâ) *adj.* Polish; —, *n.* Pole; —, *m.* Polish language.

polar (po•lâr´) *adj.* polar.

polca (pol´kâ) *f.* polka.

polémica (po•le´mē•kâ) *f.* polemics; polemic *(controversia).*

polen (po´len) *m.* (bot.) pollen.

policía (po•lē•sē´â) *f.* police; **vigilante de** —, patrolman; —, *m.* policeman.

policiaco, ca (po•lē•syâ´ko, kâ) *adj.* police; **novela** —, detective story, whodunit.

policromo, ma (po•lē•kro´mo, mâ) *adj.* multicolored.

polifacético, ca (po•lē•fâ•se´tē•ko, kâ) *adj.* of many aspects, many-sided.

poligamia (po•lē•gâ´myâ) *f.* polygamy.

polígamo, ma (po•lē´gâ•mo, mâ) *n.* polygamist; —, *adj.* polygamous.

polígono (po•lē´go•no) *m.* polygon.

polilla (po•lē´yâ) *f.* moth.

polímero (po•lē´me•ro) *m.* polymer.

política (po•lē´tē•kâ) *f.* politics; policy *(programa)*; manners, tact *(cortesía)*.

póliza (po´lē•sâ) *f.* policy; — **de seguro,** insurance policy.

polo (po´lo) *m.* (geog. and elec.) pole; polo.

polonesa (po•lo•ne´sâ) *f. (mus.)* polonaise.

Polonia (po•lo´nyâ) *f.* Poland.

poltrón, ona (pol•tron´, o´nâ) *adj.* idle, lazy; **silla —,** armchair; —, *n.* poltroon, coward.

poluto, ta (po•lū´to, tâ) *adj.* filthy, dirty.

polvera (pol•ve´râ) *f.* compact.

polvo (pol´vo) *m.* powder; dust *(tierra menuda);* — **dentífrico,** tooth powder; — **de hornear,** baking powder; — **de talco,** talcum powder; **en —,** powdered.

pólvora (pol´vo•râ) *f.* gunpowder; fireworks *(fuegos artificiales).*

polvoriento, ta (pol•vo•ryen´to, tâ) *adj.* dusty.

polvoroso, sa (pol•vo•ro´so, sâ) *adj.* dusty.

pollo (po´yo) *m.* young chick.

pomada (po•mâ´thâ) *f.* pomade.

pomerano, na (po•me•ra´no, nâ) *adj.* and *n.* Pomeranian.

pomo (po´mo) *m.* (bot.) pome; pommel.

pompa (pom´pâ) *f.* pomp, grandeur; bubble *(esfera).*

pomposo, sa (pom•po´so, sâ) *adj.* pompous, ostentatious; magnificent *(magnifico).*

pómulo (po´mū•lo) *m.* cheekbone.

ponche (pon´che) *m.* punch; eggnog *(de huevo).*

ponchera (pon•che´râ) *f.* punchbowl.

poncho (pon´cho) *m.* (Sp. Am.) poncho.

ponderación (pon•de•râ•syon´) *f.* ponderation, consideration; exaggeration *(exageración).*

ponderar (pon•de•râr´) *va.* to weigh, to consider; to extol *(encarecer).*

poner* (po•ner´) *va.* to put, to place; to set *(preparar);* to suppose, to assume *(suponer);* to take *(tardar);* (theat.) to put on; to instill *(causar);* to lay *(huevos).*

poniente (po•nyen´te) *m.* west; west wind *(viento).*

pontífice (pon•tē´fē•se) *m.* pontiff.

ponzoñoso, sa (pon•so•nyo´so, sâ) *adj.* poisonous.

popa (po´pâ) *f.* (naut.) poop, stern.

popote (po•po´te), *m.* (Mex.) drinking straw.

populacho (po•pū•lâ´cho) *m.* populace, mob, rabble.

popular (po•pū•lâr´) *adj.* popular.

popularidad (po•pū•lâ•rē•thâth´) *f.* popularity.

popurrí (po•pū•rre´) *m.* potpourri, medley.

póquer (po´ker) *m.* poker.

poquito, ta (po•kē´to, tâ) *adj.* very little; —, *m.* a very little; —to a —to, little by little, bit by bit.

por (por) *prep.* by *(causa);* over, through *(a través de);* as *(como);* through, by means of *(manera);* for; around, about *(aproximación);* ¿— qué? why?; — lo tanto, as a result.

porcelana (por•se•lâ´nâ) *f.* porcelain.

porcentaje (por•sen•tâ´he) *m.* percentage.

porción (por•syon´) *f.* portion.

pormenor (por•me•nor´) *m.* detail.

poro (po´ro) *m.* pore.

poroso, sa (po•ro´so, sâ) *adj.* porous.

porque (por´ke) *conj.* because; so that, in order that *(para que).*

porqué (por•ke´) *m.* cause, reason; (coll.) amount.

porquería (por•ke•rē´â) *f.* nastiness, foulness; trifle *(bagatela);* vile action *(acción).*

porra (po´rrâ) *f.* club; (coll.) last *(en un juego);* bore *(sujeto pesado);* (Mex.) rooters, backers.

portaaviones (por•tâ•â•vyo´nes) *m.* aircraft carrier, flattop.

portada (por•tâ´thâ) *f.* title page; cover *(de revista);* facade *(de edificio).*

portador, ra (por•tâ•thor´, râ) *n.* carrier, bearer; porter *(porteador).*

portaestandarte (por•tâ•es•tân•dâr´te) *m.* (mil.) standard bearer.

portal (por•tâl´) *m.* vestibule *(zaguán);* portico, porch *(pórtico);* creche(*belén).*

portamonedas (por•tâ•mo•ne´-thas) *m.* purse, pocketbook, coin purse.

portar (por•târ´) *va.* to carry, to bear; —se, to behave, to conduct oneself.

portátil (por•tâ´tēl) *adj.* portable.

portavoz (por•tâ•vos´) *m.* megaphone; (fig.) mouthpiece, spokesman.

portazo (por•tâ´so) *m.* bang of a door, slam of a door.

porte (por´te) *m.* freight, postage

(costo); conduct, bearing, carriage *(presencia);* — **a cobrar,** charges collect; — **pagado** or **cobrado,** charges prepaid.

portentoso, sa (por•ten•to′so, sâ) *adj.* prodigious, marvelous.

portero, ra (por•te′ro, râ) *n.* porter, janitor; —, *m.* goal keeper.

pórtico (por′te•ko) *m.* portico, porch.

portón (por•ton′) *m.* gate, entrance.

portugués, esa (por•tū•ges′, e′sa) *n.* and *adj.* Portuguese; —, *m.* Portuguese language.

porvenir (por•ve•nēr′) *m.* future.

pos (pos) **en** —, after, behind.

posada (po•sâ′thâ) *f.* boarding-house, inn *(albergue);* lodging; (Mex.) Christmas party.

posdata (poz•thâ′tâ) *f.* postscript.

poseedor, ra (po•se•e•thor′, râ) *n.* owner, possessor; —, *adj.* possessing, owning.

poseer* (po•se•er′) *va.* to hold, to possess, to own.

poseído, da, (po•se•e′tho, thâ) *adj.* possessed.

posesión (po•se•syon′) *f.* possession.

posesivo, va (po•se•se′vo, vâ) *adj.* (gram.) possessive.

posibilidad (po•sē•vē•lē•thâth′) *f.* possibility.

posible (po•se′vle) *adj.* possible;

hacer lo —, to do one's best; **lo más pronto** —, as soon as possible.

posición (po•sē•syon′) *f.* position.

positivo, va (po•sē•tē′vo, vâ) *adj.* positive.

posponer* (pos•po•ner′) *va.* to postpone, to defer, to put off.

postal (pos•tâl′) *adj.* postal; **paquete** —, parcel post.

poste (pos′te) *m.* post, pillar.

postergar (pos•ter•gâr′) *va.* to defer, to delay.

posterior (pos•te•ryor′) *adj.* posterior, back, rear.

posteriormente (pos•te•ryor•men′te) *adv.* later, subsequently.

postizo, za (pos•tē′so, sâ) *adj.* artificial, false; **dientes** —**zos,** false teeth.

postración (pos•trâ•syon′) *f.* prostration.

postrar (pos•trâr′) *va.* to humble, to humiliate; (fig.) to weaken; —**se,** to prostrate oneself; to kneel down (arrodillarse).

postre (pos′tre) *adj.* last in order; **a la** —, at last; —, *m.* dessert.

postrer (pos•trer′) or **postrero, ra** (pos•tre′ro, râ) *adj.* last.

postular (pos•tū•lâr′) *va.* to postulate, to seek.

póstumo, ma (pos′tū•mo, mâ)

adj. posthumous.

postura (pos•tū´râ) *f.* posture, position; price offered (oferta); bet, wager (apuesta).

potaje (po•tâ´he) *m.* pottage; (fig.) hodgepodge.

potasio (po•tâ´syo) *m.* potassium.

pote (po´te) *m.* pot, jar.

potencia (po•ten´syâ) *f.* power; potential (posibilidad); **las grandes —s,** the great powers.

potencial (po•ten•syâl´) *m.* (elec.) potential.

potente (po•ten´te) *adj.* potent, powerful.

potestad (po•tes•tâth´) *f.* power, dominion, jurisdiction.

potro (po´tro) *m.* colt, foal; rack (caballete); (fig.) cross, burden.

pozo (po´so) *m.* well; (min.) shaft.

práctica (prâk´tē•kâ) *f.* practice; skill (destreza).

practicante (prâk•tē•kân´te) *m.* and *f.* (med.) intern.

practicar (prâk•tē•kâr´) *va.* to ractice; to exercise, to make use of (ejercer).

práctico, ca (prâk´tē•ko, kâ) *adj.* practical; skillful (diestro).

pradera (prâ•the´râ) *f.* meadowland.

prado (prâ´tho) *m.* meadow.

preámbulo (pre•âm´bū•lo) *m.* preamble; dodge, evasion (rodeo).

precario, ria (pre•kâ´ryo, ryâ) *adj.* precarious.

precaución (pre•kâū•syon´) *f.* precaution.

precaver (pre•kâ•ver´) *va.* to prevent, to guard against.

precedente (pre•se•then´te) *adj.* precedent, foregoing; **—, *m.*** precedent; **sin —,** unequalled, unexcelled, all-time.

preceder (pre•se•ther´) *va.* to precede, to go before.

precepto (pre•sep´to) *m.* precept; order (mandato).

preceptor (pre•sep•tor´) *m.* teacher; preceptor (ayo).

preciar (pre•syâr´) *va.* to value, to appraise; **—se de,** to take pride in, to boast.

precio (pre´syo) *m.* price; value (valor).

precioso, sa (pre•syo´so, sâ) *adj.* precious; (coll.) beautiful (bello); **piedra —,** gem.

precipicio (pre•cē•pē´syo) *m.* precipice, cliff; violent fall (caída); (fig.) ruin, disaster.

precipitación (pre•se•pē•tâ•syon´) *f.* precipitation.

precipitar (pre•sē•pē•târ´) *va.* to precipitate; to dash, to cast (lanzar); **—se,** to run headlong, to rush.

precisar (pre•sē•sâr´) *va.* to compel, to oblige *(obligar)*; to necessitate *(necesitar)*; to state *(explicar)*; —, *vn.* to be necessary.

precisión (pre•sē•syon´) *f.* precision; necessity *(obligación)*; **con toda** —, on time, very promptly.

preciso, sa (pre•sē´so, sâ) *adj.* necessary, requisite; precise, exact *(exacto)*.

precoz (pre•kos´) *adj.* precocious.

precursor, ra (pre•kūr•sor´, râ) *n.* forerunner; —, *adj.* preceding.

predecesor, ra (pre•the•se•sor´, râ) *n.* predecessor, forerunner.

predecir* (pre•the•sēr´) *va.* to foretell, to predict.

predestinación (pre•thes•tē•nâ•syon´) *f.* predestination.

predeterminar (pre•the•ter•mē•nâr´) *va.* to predetermine.

predicador (pre•thē•kâ•thor´) *m.* preacher.

predicar (pre•thē•kâr´) *va.* to preach; to praise to the skies *(alabar)*; to advise, to counsel *(amonestar)*.

predicción (pre•thēk•syon´) *f.* prediction.

predilección (pre•thē•lek•syon´) *f.* predilection, preference.

predilecto, ta (pre•thē•lek´to, tâ) *adj.* darling, favorite; preferred *(preferido)*.

predio (pre´thyo) *m.* landed property, estate.

predisponer* (pre•thēs•po•ner´) *va.* to predispose.

predominante (pre•tho•mē•nan´-te) *adj.* predominating, predominant.

predominar (pre•tho•mē•nâr´) *va.* and *vn.* to predominate.

preeminencia (pre•e•mē•nen´syâ) *f.* preeminence.

prefabricar (pre•fâ•vrē•kâr´) *vt.* to prefabricate.

prefacio (pre•fâ´syo) *m.* preface.

preferencia (pre•fe•ren´syâ) *f.* preference; **de** —, preferably.

preferente (pre•fe•ren´te) *adj.* preferred, preferable.

preferible (pre•fe•rē´vle) *adj.* preferable.

preferir* (pre•fe•rēr´) *va.* to prefer.

pregonar (pre•go•nâr´) *va.* to proclaim, to announce; to peddle, to hawk *(una mercancía)*.

pregunta (pre•gūn´tâ) *f.* question; **hacer una** —, to ask a question.

preguntar (pre•gūn•târ´) *va.* to question, to ask; —**se,** to wonder.

preguntón, ona (pre•gūn•ton´, o´nâ) *n.* inquisitive person; —, *adj.* inquisitive.

prehistórico, ca (preēs•to´rē•ko, kâ) *adj.* prehistoric.

prejuicio (pre•hwē´syo) *m.* prejudice.

preliminar (pre•lē•mē•nâr´) *adj.* preliminary; **—es,** *m. pl.* preliminaries, preliminary steps.

preludio (pre•lū´thyo) *m.* prelude.

prematuro, ra (pre•mâ•tū´ro, râ) *adj.* premature.

premeditación (pre•me•thē•tâ•syon´) *f.* premeditation.

premeditar (pre•me•thē•târ´) *va.* to premeditate.

premiar (pre•myâr´) *va.* to reward, to remunerate.

premio (pre´myo) *m.* reward, prize; (com.) premium.

premisa (pre•mē´sâ) *f.* premise.

premura (pre•mū´râ) *f.* haste, hurry, urgency *(instancia);* difficult situation *(apuro).*

prenatal (pre•nâ•tâl´) *adj.* prenatal.

prenda (pren´dâ) *f.* pledge *(prueba);* pawn *(seguridad);* piece of jewelry *(alhaja);* trait, quality *(cualidad);* loved one; **— de vestir,** article of clothing; **—s,** *pl.* accomplishments, talents.

prendar (pren•dâr´) *va.* to pledge; to ingratiate oneself *(ganar la voluntad);* **—se de,** to take a fancy to, to be charmed by.

prender (pren•der´) *va.* to seize, to catch *(asir);* to imprison *(aprisionar);* to pin on *(clavar);* (P.R.) to kindle *(encender);* **—,** *vn.* to catch fire *(encenderse);* to take root *(arraigar);* **—se,** to get dressed up.

prensa (pren´sâ) *f,* press; **dar a la —,** to have published; **P— Asociada,** Associated Press.

prensar (pren•sâr) *va.* to press.

preñado, da (pre•nyâ´tho, thâ) *adj.* pregnant; (fig.) full *(lleno).*

preocupación (pre•o•kū•pâ•syon´) *f.* care, preoccupation; bias, prejudice *(prejuicio).*

preocupar (pre•o•kū•pâr´) *va.* to worry, to preoccupy; **—se por,** to care about, to worry about.

preparación (pre•pâ•râ•syon´) *f.* preparation.

preparar (pre•pâ•râr´) *va.* to prepare; **—se,** to get ready.

preparativos (pre•pâ•râ•tē´vos) *m. pl.* preparations, preliminary steps.

preponderancia (pre•pon•de•rân´syâ) *f.* preponderance.

preponderar (pre•pon•de•râr´) *vn.* to prevail.

preposición (pre•po•sē•syon´) *f.*

(gram.) preposition.

prerrogativa (pre•rro•gâ•tē´vä) *f.* prerogative.

presa (pre´sâ) *f.* capture, seizure; prey, catch *(cosa apresada);* dam *(en un río);* hold *(en la lucha);* —**s**, *pl.* tusks *(colmillos);* claws *(uñas).*

presagio (pre•sâ´hyo) *m.* presage, omen.

prescindir (pres•sēn•dēr´) *vn.* —**de,** to disregard, to dispense with; to do without *(privarse).*

prescribir* (pres•krē•vēr´) *va.* to prescribe.

prescripción (pres•krēp•syon´) *f.* prescription.

presencia (pre•sen´syâ) *f.* presence; appearance *(aspecto).*

presenciar (pre•sen•syâr´) *va.* to witness, to see.

presentación (pre•sen•tâ•syon´) *f.* presentation; introduction; **a** —, (com.) at sight.

presentar (pre•sen•târ´) *va.* to present, to introduce *(introducir);* —**se,** to appear; to introduce oneself.

presente (pre•sen´te) *adj.* present; —, *m.* present, gift; **al** —, at present, at the moment; **el 20 del** —, the 20th of the current month; **hacer** —, to call attention; **tener** —, to keep in mind.

presentimiento

(pre•sen•tē•myen´to) *m.* presentiment, premonition.

presentir* (pre•sen•tēr´) *va.* to have a premonition of.

preservación (pre•ser•vâ•syon´) *f.* preservation, protection.

preservar (pre•ser•vâr´) *va.* to preserve, to protect.

presidencia (pre•sē•then´syâ) *f.* presidency.

presidencial (pre•sē•then•syal´) *adj.* presidential.

presidente (pre•sē•then´te) *m.* president; chairman *(de un comité).*

presidio (pre•sē´thyo) *m.* penitentiary, prison; (mil.) garrison.

presidir (pre•sē•thēr´) *va.* to preside over.

presión (pre•syon´) *f.* pressure; — **arterial,** — **sanguínea,** blood pressure.

preso, sa (pre´so, sâ) *n.* prisoner; —, *adj.* imprisoned.

prestamista (pres•tâ•mēs´tâ) *m.* and *f.* moneylender.

préstamo (pres´tâ•mo) *m.* loan.

prestar (pres•târ´) *va.* to lend, to loan; **pedir prestado,** to borrow.

presteza (pres•te´sâ) *f.* quickness, haste, speed.

prestigio (pres•tē´hyo) *m.* prestige; illusion *(engaño).*

presto, ta (pres´to, tâ) *adj.* quick, prompt, ready; —**to,** *adv.* quickly, in a hurry.

presumido, da (pre•sū•mē´tho, thâ) *adj.* presumptuous, arrogant; vain, prideful *(vanidoso).*

presumir (pre•sū•mēr´) *va.* to presume; —, *vn.* to boast, to have a high opinion of oneself.

presunción (pre•sūn•syon´) *f.* presumption; conceit *(amor propio).*

presunto, ta (pre•sūn´to, tâ) *adj.* presumed, presumptive; — **heredero,** heir apparent.

presuntuoso, sa (pre•sūn•two´- so, sâ) *adj.* presumptuous, vain.

presuponer* (pre•sū•po•ner´) *va.* to presuppose; to budget *(hacer un presupuesto).*

presupuesto (pre•sū•pwes´to) *m.* budget; reason *(motivo).*

presuroso, sa (pre•sū•ro´so, sâ) *adj.* hasty, prompt, quick.

pretender (pre•ten•der´) *va.* to pretend to, to claim; to try, to attempt *(intentar);* to maintain, to contend *(sostener).*

pretendiente (pre•ten•dyen´te) *m.* suitor *(novio);* candidate, office seeker *(candidato).*

pretensión (pre•ten•syon´) *f.* pretension; effort *(empeño).*

pretérito, ta (pre•te´rē•to, tâ) *adj.* preterit, past; —, *m.* (gram.) past tense.

pretexto (pre•tes´to) *m.* pretext, pretense.

prevalecer* (pre•vâ•le•ser´) *vn.* to prevail; to take root *(arraigar).*

prevención (pre•ven•syon´) *f.* prevention; preparation *(preparación);* —**ones,** *pl.* provisions.

prevenido, da (pre•ve•nē´tho, thâ) *adj.* prepared, provided *(provisto);* well-stocked, stocked, abundant *(abundante);* provident, careful, cautious, foresighted *(providente).*

prevenir* (pre•ve•nēr´) *va.* to prepare *(preparar);* to foresee, to foreknow *(prever);* to prevent *(impedir);* to advise, to warn *(advertir);* —**se,** to get ready.

preventivo, va (pre•ven•tē´vo, vâ) *m.* and *adj.* preventive.

prever* (pre•ver´) *va.* to foresee, to forecast.

previo, via (pre´vyo, vyâ) *adj.* previous, former.

previsión (pre•vē•syon´) *f.* foresight, prevision, forecast.

prieto, ta (prye´to, tâ) *adj.* blackish, very dark; compact, tight *(apretado);* —, *n.* very dark-complexioned person.

prima (prē´mâ) *f.* prime; (mus.) treble; (com.) premium.

primario, ria (prē•mâ´ryo, ryâ) *adj.* primary; **escuela** —, elementary school.

primavera (prē•mâ•ve´râ) *f.* spring.

primaveral (prē•mâ•ve•râl´) *adj.* spring-like.

primer (prē•mer´) *adj.* (apocope of primero) first; **en — lugar,** in the first place.

primero, ra (prē•me´ro, râ) *adj.* first; prior, former *(antiguo);* **—s auxilios,** first aid; **— enseñanza,** primary education; **por —ra vez,** for the first time; **—ro,** *adv.* rather, sooner.

primitivo, va (prē•mē•tē´vo, vâ) *adj.* primitive.

primo, ma (prē´mo, mâ) *adj.* first; **—,** *n.* cousin.

primor (prē•mor´) *m.* beauty; dexterity, ability *(habilidad).*

primoroso, sa (prē•mo•ro´so, sâ) *adj.* elegant, fine, excellent; able, accomplished *(diestro).*

princesa (prēn•se´sâ) *f.* princess.

principal (prēn•sē•pâl´) *adj.* principal, chief, main.

principalmente (prēn•sē•pâl•men´te) *adv.* mainly, principally, for the most part.

príncipe (prēn´sē•pe) *m.* prince.

principiante (prēn•sē•pyân´te) *m.* and *f.* beginner; learner.

principio (prēn•sē´pyo) *m.* beginning, commencement; principle *(fundamento);* **en —,** essentially; **al —,** at the beginning; **desde un —,** from the beginning.

prioridad (pryo•rē•thâth´) *f.* priority.

prisa (prē´sâ) *f.* hurry, haste; **a toda —,** at full speed; **darse —,** to hurry; **tener —,** to be in a hurry; **con —,** in a hurry.

prisión (prē•syon´) *f.* seizure, capture; prison *(cárcel);* **—ones,** *pl.* fetters.

prisionero, ra (prē•syo•ne´ro, râ) *n.* prisoner; (fig.) captive, slave.

prisma (prēz´mâ) *m.* prism.

privado, da (prē•vâ´tho, thâ) *adj.* private; devoid *(careciente).*

privar (prē•vâr´) *va.* to deprive; to prohibit *(prohibir);* **—se,** to deprive oneself.

privilegiado, da (prē•vē•le•hyâ´tho, thâ) *adj.* privileged, favorite.

privilegio (prē•vē•le´hyo) *m.* privilege.

pro (pro) *m.* or *f.* profit, benefit, advantage; **en — de,** in behalf of; **el — y el contra,** the pros and cons.

proa (pro´â) *f.* (naut.) prow.

probabilidad (pro•vâ•vē•lē•thâth´) *f.* probability, likelihood; **ley de —es,** law of averages.

probable (pro•vâ´vle) *adj.* probable, likely.

probado, da (pro•vâ´tho, thâ) *adj.* proved, tried.

probar* (pro•vâr´) *va.* to try; to

prove *(comprobar);* to taste *(saborear);* to examine, to test *(examinar);* to justify *(justificar);* —, *vn.* to suit, to agree; —se, to try on.

probeta (pro•ve′tâ) *f.* test tube.

problema (pro•vle′mâ) *m.* problem.

problemático, ca (pro•vle•mâ′tē•ko, kâ) *adj.* problematical.

procedencia (pro•se•then′syâ) *f.* origin, source.

procedente (pro•se•then′te) *adj.* coming, proceeding, originating.

proceder (pro•se•ther′) *m.* procedure, behavior; —, *vn.* to proceed; to be wise *(convenir).*

procedimiento (pro•se•thē•myen′to) *m.* procedure.

procesar (pro•se•sâr′) *va.* to sue, to prosecute; to indict *(acusar).*

procesión (pro•se•syon′) *f.* procession; parade *(desfile).*

proceso (pro•se′so) *m.* process, lawsuit; en — de quiebra, in a state of bankruptcy, in the hands of the receivers.

proclama (pro•klâ′mâ) *f.* proclamation.

proclamación (pro•klâ•mâ•syon′) *f.* proclamation; acclamation *(alabanza pública).*

proclamar (pro•klâ•mâr′) *va.* to proclaim.

procrear (pro•kre•âr) *va.* to procreate.

procurador (pro•kū•râ•thor′) *m.* attorney; — público, attorney at law; P— General, Attorney General.

procurar (pro•kū•râr′) *va.* to act as attorney for; to try, to attempt *(intentar).*

prodigalidad (pro•thē•gâ•lē•thâth′) *f.* prodigality.

prodigar (pro•thē•gâr′) *va.*to waste, to lavish

prodigio (pro•thē′hyo) *m.* prodigy, marvel, wonder.

prodigioso, sa (pro•thē•hyo′so, sâ) *adj.* prodigious; excellent, fine *(admirable).*

pródigo, ga (pro′thē•go, gâ) *adj.* prodigal; lavish *(dadivoso).*

producción (pro•thū•syon′) *f.* production; — en serie, mass production.

producir* (pro•thū•sēr′) *va.* to produce.

productivo, va (pro•thūk•tē′vo, vâ) *adj.* productive.

producto (pro•thū′to) *m.* product; proceeds, receipts *(beneficio).*

proeza (pro•e′sâ) *f.* prowess, exploit.

profanación (pro•fâ•nâ•syon′) *f.* profanation.

profanar (pro•fâ•nâr′) *va.* to profane, to desecrate.

profano, na (pro•fâ′no, nâ) *adj.*
profane.

profecía (pro•fe•se′â) *f.* prophecy.

proferir* (pro•fe•rēr′) *va.* to
utter, to exclaim.

profesar (pro•fe•sâr′) *va.* to profess; —, *vn.* (eccl.) to take one′s
vows, to enter a religious order.

profesión (pro•fe•syon′) *f.* profession.

profesional (pro•fe•syo•nâl′) *adj.*
and *m.* and *f.* professional.

profesor, ra (pro•fe•sor′, râ) *n.*
professor *(catedrático);* teacher.

profesorado (pro•fe•so•râ′tho) *m.*
teachers, faculty; professorship
(cargo).

profeta (pro•fe′tâ) *m.* prophet.

profético, ca (pro•fe′tē•ko, kâ)
adj. prophetic.

profetizar (pro•fe•tē•sâr′) *va.* to
prophesy.

prófugo, ga (pro′fū•go, gâ) *adj.*
fugitive.

profundidad (pro•fūn•dē•thâth′)
f. profoundness, depth.

profundizar (pro•fūn•dē•sâr′) *va.*
deepen; (fig.) to penetrate into,
to go into.

profundo, da (pro•fūn′do, dâ)
adj. profound, deep.

profusión (pro•fū•syon′) *f.* profusion.

programa (pro•grâ′mâ) *m.* pro-

gram; — **de estudios,** curriculum.

programación
(pro•grâ•mâ•syon′) *f.* programming.

progresar (pro•gre•sâr′) *vn.* to
progress, to improve.

progresión (pro•gre•syon′) *f.* progression.

progresista (pro•gre•sēs′tâ) *adj.*
progressive.

progresivo, va (pro•gre•sē′vo, vâ)
adj. progressive.

progreso (pro•gre′so) *m.*
progress, advancement.

prohibición (proē•vē•syon′) *f.*
prohibition.

prohibido, da (proē•vē′tho, thâ)
adj. forbidden.

prohibir (proē•vēr′) *va.* to prohibit, to forbid.

prohibitivo, va (proē•vē•tē′vo, vâ)
adj. prohibitive.

prolijo, ja (pro•lē′ho, hâ) *adj.*
tedious, overly long, drawn-
out.

prólogo (pro′lo•go) *m.* prologue.

prolongado, da (pro•long•gâ′tho,
thâ) *adj.* prolonged, extended.

prolongar (pro•long•gâr′) *va.* to
prolong.

promedio (pro•me′thyo) *m.* average, median; middle *(de una
cosa).*

promesa (pro•me′sâ) *f.* promise.

prometedor, ra (pro•me•te•thor′,

râ) *adj.* promising.

prometer (pro•me•ter´) *va.* to promise; —, *vn.* to be promising; —**se,** to get engaged.

prometido, da (pro•me•tē´tho, thâ) *adj.* engaged; —, *f.* fiancée; —, *m.* fiancé.

prominencia (pro•mē•nen´syâ) *f.* prominence.

promoción (pro•mo•syon´) *f.* promotion.

promotor, ra (pro•mo•tor´, râ) *n.* promoter.

promover* (pro•mo•ver´) *va.* to promote, to further.

pronombre (pro•nom´bre) *m.* pronoun.

pronosticar (pro•nos•tē•kâr´) *va.* to prognosticate, to predict, to forecast.

pronóstico (pro•nos´tē•ko) *m.* prognosis, forecast; almanac *(calendario).*

prontitud (pron•tē•tūth´) *f.* promptness, speed.

pronto, ta (pron´to, tâ) *adj.* prompt, speedy; —**to,** *adv.* soon, promptly; **tan —to como,** as soon as; **de —to,** all of a sudden; **por lo —to,** temporarily.

pronunciación (pro•nūn•syâ•syon´) *f.* pronunciation.

pronunciamiento (pro•nūn•syâ•myen´to) *m.*

decree, pronouncement; military uprising *(rebelión).*

pronunciar (pro•nūn•syâr´) *va.* to pronounce; — **un discurso,** to make a speech; —**se,** to rebel.

propaganda (pro•pâ•gân´dâ) *f.* propaganda; advertising media *(comercial).*

propagandista (pro•pâ•gân•dēs´tâ) *m.* and *f.* and *adj.* propagandist.

propensión (pro•pen•syon´) *f.* propensity, inclination.

propenso, sa (pro•pen´so, sâ) *adj.* prone, inclined; — **a accidentes,** accident-prone.

propiedad (pro•pye•thâth´) *f.* ownership *(dominio);* property.

propietario, ria (pro•pye•tâ´ryo, ryâ) *n.* proprietor.

propina (pro•pē´nâ) *f.* tip, gratuity.

propio, pia (pro´pyo, pyâ) *adj.* proper; own *(de la misma persona);* characteristic *(distintivo);* selfsame, very *(mismo);* —, *m.* messenger.

proponer* (pro•po•ner´) *va.* to propose, to suggest; —**se,** to intend, to plan, to be determined.

proporción (pro•por•syon´) *f.* proportion; occasion, opportunity *(coyuntura).*

proporcionado, da

(pro•por•syo•na´tho, thâ) *adj.* proportionate; fit *(idóneo)*.

proporcionar (pro•por•syo•nâr´) *va.* to proportion; to adjust, to adapt *(arreglar);* to provide, to afford, to supply *(suministrar)*.

proposición (pro•po•sē•syon´) *f.* proposition.

propósito (pro•po´sē•to) *m.* purpose, intention; **a —,** to the point, by the way; **de —,** on purpose, purposely; **fuera de —** , untimely, beside the point; **a — de,** with regard to, apropos of.

propuesta (pro•pwes´tâ) *f.* proposal, proposition.

propulsión (pro•pūl•syon´) *f.* propulsion.

propulsor, ra (pro•pūl•sor´, râ) *adj.* propulsive.

prórroga (pro´rro•gâ) *f.* extension, renewal.

prorrogar (pro•rro•gâr´) *va.* to put off, to delay, to postpone.

prosa (pro´sâ) *f.* prose.

proscribir* (pros•krē•vēr´) *va.* to exile *(desterrar);* to outlaw.

proscripción (pros•krēp•syon´) *f.* ban, proscription.

proscripto (pros•krēp´to) *m.* outlaw; exile *(desterrado)*.

prosecución (pro•se•kū•syon´) *f.* prosecution; pursuit *(perseguimiento)*.

proseguir* (pro•se•gēr´) *va.* to

pursue, to continue, to carry on.

prosperar (pros•pe•râr´) *va.* to favor; **—,** *vn.* to prosper, to thrive.

prosperidad (pros•pe•rē•thâth´) *f.* prosperity.

próspero, ra (pros´pe•ro, râ) *adj.* prosperous.

próstata (pros´tâ•tâ) *f.* prostate gland.

protagonista (pro•tâ go•nēs´tâ) *m.* and *f.* protagonist.

protección (pro•tek•syon´) *f.* protection.

protector, ra (pro•tek•tor´, râ) *n.* protector, patron; **—,** *adj.* protective.

proteger (pro•te•her´) *va.* to protect, to defend.

protegido, da (pro•te•hē´tho, thâ) *adj.* protected.

proteína (pro•te•ē´nâ) *f.* protein.

protesta (pro•tes´tâ) *f.* protest.

protestante (pro•tes•tân´te) *m.* and *f.* and *adj.* Protestant.

protestar (pro•tes•târ´) *va.* to profess, to affirm; **—,** *vn.* to protest, to oppose; **— contra,** to object to, to oppose.

protocolo (pro•to•ko´lo) *m.* protocol.

protoplasma (pro•to•plâz ´mâ) *m.* protoplasm.

prototipo (pro•to•tē´po) *m.* prototype.

protuberancia
(pro•tū•ve•rân´syâ) *f.* protuberance.

provecho (pro•ve´cho) *m.* profit
benefit, advantage; usefulness
(utilidad).

provechoso, sa (pro•ve•cho´so,
sâ) *adj.* profitable, beneficial,
favorable.

proveer* (pro•ve•er´) *va.* to provide, to provision; **—se de,** to
provide oneself with.

provenir* (pro•ve•nēr´) *vn.* to
proceed, to arise, to originate.

proverbial (pro•ver•vyâl´) *adj.*
proverbial.

proverbio (pro•ver´vyo) *m.* proverb.

providencia (pro•vē•then´syâ) *f.*
providence, foresight; (eccl.)
divine providence.

providencial (pro•vē•then•syâl´)
adj. providential.

provinciano, na (pro•vēn•syâ´no,
nâ) *adj.* and *n.* provincial.

provisión (pro•vē•syon´) *f.* provision, supply, stock.

provisional (pro•vē•syo•nâl´)
adj. pro-visional, temporary.

provocación (pro•vo•kâ•syon´) *f.*
provocation.

provocar (pro•vo•kâr´) *va.* to
provoke; to further *(facilitar).*

provocativo, va (pro•vo•kâ•tē´vo,
vâ) *adj.* provocative.

próximamente
(prok•sē•mâ•men´te) *adv.* very
soon, shortly.

proximidad (prok•sē•mē•thâth´)
f. proximity.

próximo, ma (prok´sē•mo, mâ)
adj. next, nearest, following;
pariente —, close relative.

proyección (pro•yek•syon´) *f.*
projection.

proyectar (pro•yek•târ´) *va.* to
protect; to plan *(preparar).*

proyectil (pro•yek•tēl´) *m.* missile, projectile.

proyecto (pro•yek´to) *m.* project,
plan; **— del gobierno,** government project; **— de ley,** proposed bill.

proyector (pro•yek•tor´) *m.* projector; searchlight *(reflector).*

prudencia (prū•then´syâ) *f.* prudence, wisdom.

prudente (prū•then´te) *adj.* prudent, cautious.

prueba (prwe´vâ) *f.* proof; trial,
test, experiment *(examen);*
trial, attempt *(tentativa);* token,
sample *(muestra);* (phot. and
print.) proof; **a — de agua,**
waterproof; **a — de bala,** bulletproof; **a — de bomba,**
bombproof.

pseudónimo (pseū•tho´nē•mo) =
seudónimo.

psicoanálisis
(psē•ko•â•nâ´lē•sēs) = **sicoanálisis.**

psicología (psē•ko•lo•hē´â) =
sicología.

psicológico (psē•ko•lo´hē•ko) =
sicológico.

psicólogo (psē•ko´lo•go) = sicólogo.

psicosis (psē•ko´sēs) = sicosis.

psicosomático
(psē•ko•so•mâ´tē•ko) = sicoso-
mático.

psiquiatra (psē•kyâ´trâ) =
siquiatra.

psíquico (psē´kē•ko) = síquico.

púa (pū´â) f. sharp point; graft
(vástago); tooth (de peine);
(zool.) barb; (mus.) plectrum;
(fig.) remorse, anguish; alambre de —, barbed wire.

publicación (pū•vlē•kâ•syon´) f.
publication.

publicar (pū•vlē•kâr´) va. to
publish; to publicize (hacer
público).

publicidad (pū•vlē•sē•thâth´) f.
publicity.

público, ca (pū´vlē•ko, kâ) adj.
public; —, m. attendance,
audience.

puchero (pū•che´ro) m. pot;
meat stew (guisado); pout, grimace (mueca); hacer —s, to
pout.

pudiente (pū•thyen´te) adj. rich;
powerful (poderoso).

pudor (pū•thor´) m. bashfulness,
modesty, decorum.

pudrir* (pū•thrēr´) va. to make
putrid, to putrefy; (fig.) to consume, to worry; —se, to rot.

pueblo (pwe´vlo) m. town, village; country, people (nación);
— natal, hometown, native
town.

puente (pwen´te) m. bridge; —
colgante, suspension bridge; —
levadizo, drawbridge.

puerca (pwer´kâ) f. sow.

puerco, ca (pwer´ko, kâ) adj.
nasty, filthy, dirty; rude
(grosero); —, m. hog, pig; carne
de —co, pork; —co espín, porcupine.

pueril (pwe•rēl´) adj. childish,
puerile.

puerta (pwer´tâ) f. door; doorway
(entrada); (fig.) gateway; —
corrediza, sliding door; — de
entrada, front door; — trasera,
back door.

puerto (pwer´to) m. port, harbor;
narrow pass, defile (des-
filadero); — aéreo, airport; —
franco, free port.

pues (pwes) conj. since, inasmuch as; —, adv. then, therefore; ¡—! interj. well then!

puesta (pwes´tâ) f. (ast.) set, setting; stake (en el juego); — de
sol, sunset.

puesto (pwes´to) m. place, particular spot; job, position,
employment (empleo); (mil.)

encampment; booth, stand *(tiendecilla)*; blind *(de caza)*; —, **ta,** *adj.* put, set, placed; **—to que,** since.

pugna (pūg′nâ) *f.* combat, battle, struggle.

pugnar (pūg•nâr′) *vn.* to fight, to struggle; *(fig.)* to strive earnestly, to work doggedly.

pujante (pū•hân′te) *adj.* powerful, strong, robust, strapping.

pujar (pū•hâr′) *va.* to push ahead, to push through *(mejorar)*; —, *vn.* to hesitate, to falter; *(fig.)* to pout.

pulcritud (pūl•krē•tūth′) *f.* neatness, tidiness.

pulcro, era (pūl′kro, krâ) *adj.* neat, tidy, clean.

pulga (pūl′gâ) *f.* flea.

pulgada (pūl•gâ′thâ) *f.* inch.

pulgar (pūl•gâr′) *m.* thumb.

pulido, da (pū•lē′tho, thâ) *adj.* neat, nice *(nítido)*; polished.

pulir (pū•lēr′) *va.* to polish, to burnish; to put the finishing touches on *(perfeccionar)*; **—se,** to get all dressed up.

pulmón (pūl•mon′) *m.* lung; **— acuático,** aqualung; **— de acero,** iron lung.

pulmonía (pūl•mo•nē′â) *f.* pneumonia.

púlpito (pūl′pē•to) *m.* pulpit.

pulpo (pūl′po) *m.* octopus.

pulsar (pūl•sâr′) *va.* to touch; *(med.)* to take one′s pulse; to explore, to try *(tantear)*; —, *vn.* to pulse, to throb.

pulsera (pūl•se′râ) *f.* bracelet; *(med.)* wrist bandage.

pulso (pūl′so) *m.* pulse.

pulverizar (pūl•ve•rē•sâr′) *va.* to pulverize; to atomize, to spray *(un líquido)*.

puma (pū′mâ) *m.* (zool.) puma, cougar.

punta (pūn′tâ) *f.* point, tip.

puntada (pūn•tâ′thâ) *f.* stitch.

puntapié (pūn•ta•pye′) *m.* kick.

puntería (pūn•te•rē′â) *f.* aim; marksmanship *(habilidad)*.

puntiagudo, da (pūn•tyâ•gū′tho, thâ) *adj.* sharp-pointed.

puntilla (pūn•tē′yâ) *f.* brad, tack; narrow lace edging *(encaje)*; **de —s,** on tiptoe.

puntillo (pūn•tē′yo) *m.* small point; (mus.) dot.

punto (pūn′to) *m.* period *(punto redondo)*; point, matter *(asunto)*; hole, notch *(de correa)*; dot *(de la i)*; point of honor *(pundonor)*; goal, point *(de tanteo)*; mesh *(malla)*; moment, time, point *(oportunidad)*; **al —,** instantly; **estar a — de,** to be about to; **hasta cierto —,** in some measure, to some degree; **— de partida,** or **de arranque,** starting point; **— de ebullición,** boiling point; **— de vista,** point of view; **son las dos en —,** it is exactly two o′clock; **— y coma,** semicolon.

puntuación (pūn•twâ•syon′) *f.* punctuation; score *(tanteo).*

puntual (pūn•twâl′) *adj.* punctual, exact; sure, certain *(seguro).*

puntualidad (pūn•twâ•lē•thâth′) *f.* punctuality, exactness; certainty.

puntualizar (pūn•twâ•lē•sâr′) *va.* to fix in one′s mind, to retain in one′s memory; to accomplish *(acabar).*

punzada (pūn•sâ′thâ) *f.* prick, sting; (fig.) pain, anguish.

punzar (pūn•sâr′) *va.* to prick, to sting, to throb; (fig.) to hurt, to wound.

punzón (pūn•son′) *m.* punch; burin *(buril).*

puñado (pū•nyâ′tho) *m.* handful.

puñal (pū•nyâl′) *m.* dagger.

puñalada (pū•nyâ•lâ′thâ) *f.* stab with a dagger.

puñetazo (pū•nye•tâ′so) *m.* blow with the fist.

puño (pū′nyo) *m.* fist; handful, fistful *(manojo);* wristband, cuff *(bocamanga);* handle *(mango);* hilt *(de arma blanca).*

pupila (pū•pē′lâ) *f.* (anat.) pupil.

pupilo, la (pū•pē′lo, lâ) *n.* boarder; day student *(mediopension-*

ista); orphan, ward *(huérfano).*

pupitre (pū•pē′tre) *m.* desk, writing desk.

puramente (pū•râ•men′te) *adv.* purely.

puré (pū•re′) *m.* thick soup, purée; **— de papas,** or **de patatas,** mashed potatoes.

pureza (pū•re′zâ) *f.* purity, chastity.

purga (pūr′gâ) *f.* physic; (fig.) purge.

purgante (pūr•gân′te) *m.* purgative, physic.

purgar (pūr•gâr′) *va.* to purge, to purify; to clear up *(sospechas);* to expiate *(un delito).*

purgatorio (pūr•gâ•to′ryo) *m.* purgatory.

purificación (pū•rē•fē•kâ•syon′) *f.* purification.

purificar (pū•rē•fē•kâr′) *va.* to purify; **—se,** to be purified, to be cleansed.

purista (pū•rēs′tâ) *m.* and *f.* purist.

puritano, na (pū•rē•tâ′no, nâ) *adj.* puritanical; **—,** *n.* Puritan.

puro, ra (pū′ro, râ) *adj.* pure; (fig.) flawless, perfect; outright, absolute *(mero);* **a —,** by dint of; **—,** *m.* cigar.

púrpura (pūr′pū•râ) *f.* purple.

purpúreo, rea (pūr•pū′re•o, re•â) *adj.* purple.

pus (pūs) *m.* pus.

putrefacción (pū•tre•fâk•syon´) *f.* putrefaction.

pútrido, da (pū´trē•tho, thâ) *adj.* putrid, rotten.

puya (pū´yâ) *f.* goad.

Q

que (ke) *pron.* that, which, who, whom; —, *conj.* that; and (y); since *(pues);* whether (o); without *(sin que);* **than** *(comparativo);* **a menos** —, unless; **con tal** —, provided that.

qué (ke) *interr. pron.* which? what?; **sin** — **ni para** —, without rhyme or reason; **no hay de** —, don´t mention it.

quebrada (ke•vrâ´thâ) *f.* gorge, defile; (Sp. Am.) brook.

quebradizo, za (ke•vrâ•thē´so, sâ) *adj.* brittle; (fig.) fragile; quavering (voz).

quebrado (ke•vrâ´tho) *m.* (math.) fraction; —, **da,** broken; (com.) bankrupt; faded, washed out *(de colores);* (med.) ruptured.

quebrantar (ke•vrân•târ´) *va.* to break, to crack, to burst *(hendir);* to shatter *(estrellar);* to pound, to grind *(moler);* (fig.) to violate, to break; —**se,** to break down, to crack due to strain.

quebranto (ke•vrân´to) *m.* breakage; (fig.) great loss, reversal *(gran pérdida);* breakdown, collapse *(de fuerzas).*

quebrar* (ke•vrâr´) *va.* to break; (fig.) to upset, to interrupt *(interrumpir);* to soften *(suavizar);* to trouble *(molestar);*to break one´s heart *(mover a lástima);* —**se,** to break down.

queda (ke´thâ) *f.* curfew.

quedar (ke•thâr´) *vn.* to remain; to stop, to stay *(detenerse);* to be *(estar);* to be left, to be left over *(restar);* — **bien,** to fit well; to come out well *(salir bien);* — **en,** to agree to; —**se con,** to keep; (fig.) to deceive *(engañar);* —**se a oscuras,** to be left in the dark.

quedo, da (ke´tho, thâ) *adj.* quiet, still; —**do,** *adv.* softly, quietly.

quehacer (ke•â•ser´) *m.* task, job, chore; —**es de la casa,** household duties.

queja (ke´hâ) *f.* complaint, gripe; moan.

quejarse (ke•hâr´se) *vr.* to complain, to gripe; to moan, to wail *(gemir).*

quejido (ke•hē´tho) *m.* groan, moan.

quemadura (ke•mâ•thū´râ) *f.* burn, burning.

quemar (ke•mâr´) *va.* to burn; to scorch *(el sol);* to freeze *(el hielo);* —, *vn.* to be hot, to burn.

quemazón (ke•mâ•son´) *f.* burn; intense heat *(calor);* smarting, burning sensation *(comezón).*

querella (ke•re´yâ) *f.* complaint; quarrel, dispute *(discordia).*

querer* (ke•rer´) *va.* to wish, to want; to like, to be fond of *(tener cariño);* to love *(amar);* to resolve, to decide *(resolver);* — **decir,** to mean, to signify; **sin** —, unintentionally, unwillingly; **como quiera,** anyhow, anyway; **cuando quiera,** at any time; **donde quiera,** anywhere; **Dios quiera,** God willing; **quiera o no quiera,** whether or not; — **más,** to prefer.

querido, da (ke•rē´tho, thâ) *adj.* dear, beloved; —, *n.* dear, darling.

querosina (ke•ro•sē´nâ) *f.* kerosene.

querubín (ke•rū•vēn´) *m.* cherub.

quesadilla (ke•sâ•thē´yâ) *f.* cheesecake; pastry *(pastecillo);* (Mex.) fried tortilla filled with cheese.

queso (ke´so) *m.* cheese; — **Gruyére,** Swiss cheese.

quetzal (ket•sâl´) *m.* (orn.) quetzal; monetary unit of Guatemala.

quicio (kē´syo) *m.* pivot hole; **estar fuera de** —, to be out of order, not to be working properly.

quiebra (kye´vrâ) *f.* crack, fissure *(hendedura);* loss *(pérdida);* damage *(menoscabo);* (com.) bankruptcy; decision to liquidate *(juicio);* **en** —, in bankruptcy; bankrupt.

quien (kyen) *pron.* who, whom; whoever *(la persona que).*

quién (kyen) *interr. pron.* who? whom?

quienquiera (kyeng•kye´râ) *pron.* whosoever, whoever, anyone, anybody.

quieto, ta (kye´to, tâ) *adj.* quiet, still, tranquil; (fig.) clean-living *(virtuoso).*

quietud (kye•tūth´) *f.* quietness, peace, tranquillity; (fig.) rest, repose.

quijada (kē•hâ´thâ) *f.* jaw, jawbone.

quijote (kē•ho´te) *m.* quixote, quixotic person, impractical idealist.

quilatar (kē•lâ•târ´) *va.* to assay; to purify *(purificar).*

quilate (kē•lâ´te) *m.* carat.

quimera (kē•me′râ) *f.* chimera;
quarrel *(riña).*

quimérico, ca (kē•me′rē•ko, kâ)
adj. chimerical, imaginary.

química (kē′mē•kâ) *f.* chemistry.

químico (kē′mē•ko) *m.* chemist;
—, **ca,** *adj.* chemical.

quimioterapia (kē•myo•te•râ′p-
yâ) *f.* chemotherapy.

quince (kēn′se) *adj.* and *m.* fifteen.

quincena (kēn•se′nâ) *f.* two
weeks, fortnight; semimonthly
pay *(paga).*

quincuagésimo, ma
(kēng•kwâ•he′sē•mo, mâ) *m.*
and *adj.* fiftieth.

quinientos, tas (kē•nyen′tos,
tâs) *adj.* and *m.* five hundred.

quinta (kēn′tâ) *f.* country house;
(mil.) conscription, draft; five of
a kind *(en los naipes);* (mus.)
fifth.

quintaesencia (kēn•tâ•e•sen′syâ)
f. quintessence.

quintal (kēn•tâl′) *m.* quintal,
hundredweight.

quinteto (kēn•te′to) *m.* quintette.

quinto (kēn′to) *m.* fifth; —, **ta,**
adj. fifth.

quintuples (kēn′tū•ples) *m.* or *f.*
pl. quintuplets.

quíntuplo, pia (kēn′tū•plo, plâ)
adj. quintuple, fivefold.

quiosco (kyos′ko) *m.* kiosk; — **de
periódicos,** newsstand.

quirúrgico, ca (kē•rūr′hē•ko, kâ)
adj. surgical.

quisquilloso, sa (kēs•kē•yo′so,
sâ) *adj.* trifling, hairsplitting;
touchy, peevish, irritable *(coji-
joso).*

quiste (kēs′te) *m.* cyst.

quitamanchas (kē•tâ•mân′châs)
m. spot remover.

quitapón (kē•tâ•pon′) *m.* headstall; **de** —, removable, detachable.

quitar (kē•târ′) *va.* to take away;
to remove *(remover);* to abrogate, to annul *(abolir);* to prevent, to hinder *(impedir);* to
free, to exempt *(libertar);* to
parry *(parar);* — **la mesa,** to
clear the table; —**se,** to get rid
of *(deshacerse de);* to take off;
to leave *(irse).*

quita y pon (kē′tâ ē pon′) **de** —,
detachable, removable.

quizá, quizás (kē•sâ′, kē•sâs′)
adv. perhaps.

R

rábano (rrâ′vâ•no) *m.* radish; —
picante, horseradish.

rabí (rrâ•vē´) *m.* rabbi.

rabia (rrâ´vyâ) *f.* rage, fury; rabies *(enfermedad).*

rabiar (rrâ•vyâr´) *vn.* to storm, to rage; to be in agony *(padecer dolor);* to have rabies *(enfermedad);* **a —,** like the devil.

rabieta (rrâ•vye´tâ) *f.* fit, temper tantrum.

rabino (rrâ•vē´no) *m.* rabbi.

rabioso, sa (rrâ•vyo´so, sâ) *adj.* rabid; furious *(airoso);* vehement, violent *(vehemente).*

rabo (rrâ´vo) *m.* tail; stem *(pecíolo).*

racimo (rrâ•sē´mo) *m.* bunch, cluster.

raciocinar (rrâ•syo•sē•nâr´) *vn.* to reason, to ratiocinate.

raciocinio (rrâ•syo•sē´nyo) *m.* reason; ratiocination *(raciocinación);* argument *(argumento).*

ración (rrâ•syon´) *f.* ration; portion *(porción).*

racional (rrâ•syo•nâl´) *adj.* rational; reasonable *(razonable).*

racionamiento (rrâ•syo•nâ•myen´to) *m.* rationing.

racionar (rrâ•syo•nâr´) *va.* to ration.

racismo (rrâ•sēz´mo) *m.* racism.

racista (rrâ•sēs´tâ) *m.* and *f.* racist.

radar (rrâ•thâr´) *m.* radar.

radiación (rrâ•thyâ•syon´) *f.* radiation.

radiactividad (rrâ•thyâk•tē•vē•thâth´) *f.* radioactivity.

radiactivo, va (rrâ•thyâk•tē´vo, vâ) *adj.* radioactive.

radiador (rrâ•thyâ•thor´) *m.* radiator.

radiante (rrâ•thyân´te) *adj.* radiant.

radiar (rrâ•thyâr´) *va.* to broadcast *(al público);* to radio; **—,** *vn.* to radiate.

radical (rrâ•thē•kâl´) *adj.* radical; **—,** *m.* radical.

radicar (rrâ•thē•kâr´) *vn.* to take root; to be found, to be located *(estar);* **—se,** to take root *(arraigar);* to settle down, to establish oneself *(establecerse);* to reside, to dwell *(morar).*

radio (rrâ´thyo) *m.* or *f.* radio; **—,** *m.* (math. and anat.) radius; (chem.) radium.

radioactividad (rrâ•thyo•âk•tē•vē•thâth´) *f.* radioactivity.

radioactivo, va (rrâ•thyo•ak•tē´vo, vâ) *adj.* radioactive.

radiocomunicación (rrâ•thyo•ko•mū• nē•kâ•syon´) *f.* radio communication.

radiodifundir (rrâ•thyo•thē•fūn•dēr´) *va.* to broadcast.

radiodifusión

(rrâ•thyo•thē•fū•syon´) *f.* broadcast, radiobroadcast.

radiodifusora
(rrâ•thyo•thē•fū•so´râ) *f.*
broadcasting station.

radioemisión
(rrâ•thyo•e•mē•syon´) *f.* transmission.

radioemisor, ra
(rrâ•thyo•e•mē•sor´, râ) *adj.*
broadcasting.

radiografía (rrâ•thyo•grâ•fē´â) *f.*
X ray.

radiotrasmisor
(rrâ•thyo•trâz•mē•sor´) *m.*
radio transmitter.

radioyente (rrâ•thyo•yen´te) *m.*
and *f.* radio listener.

ráfaga (rrâ´fâ•gâ) *f.* gust of wind;
cloud *(nube);* (mil.) burst of
gunfire; flash of light *(luz).*

raíz (rrâ•ēs´) *f.* root; — **cuadrada,** square root; **bienes raíces,**
landed property.

raja (rrâ´hâ) *f.* splinter, chip;
slice *(rebanada);* chink, fissure,
crack *(hendedura).*

rajá (rrâ•hâ´) *m.* rajah.

rajar (rrâ•hâr´) *va.* to split, to
crack *(agrietar);* to chop, to
slice *(dividir);* —, *vn.* (fig, and
coll.) to tell fish stories *(mentir);* to chatter, to jabber
(hablar); —**se,** (coll.) to back
out.

rama (rrâ´mâ) branch.

ramaje (rrâ•mâ´he) *m.* foliage;
branches *(ramas).*

ramificación
(rrâ•mē•fē•kâ•syon´) *f.* ramification.

ramificarse (rrâ•mē•fē•kâr´se)
vr. to ramify, to branch out.

ramillete (rrâ•mē•ye´te) *m.*
nosegay, bouquet; (fig.) center-
piece *(adorno);* (fig.) collection
(colección); (bot.) cluster.

ramo (rrâ´mo) *m.* branch;
bunch, bouquet *(de flores);*
(fig.) touch *(enfermedad).*

rampa (rrâm´pâ) *f.* ramp; cramp
(calambre).

rana (rrâ´nâ) *f.* frog; **hombre —,**
frogman.

rancio, cia (rrân´syo, syâ) *adj.*
rancid, rank; (fig.) old-fashioned.

ranchero (rrân•che´ro) *m.* rancher; cook *(que guisa).*

rancho (rrân´cho) *m.* mess;
messmates *(que comen juntos);*
camp *(campamento);* (fig.) get-
together; ranch *(granja);* (Sp.
Am.) hut; (naut.) command.

rango (rrâng´go) *m.* class, category; (Sp. Am.) class.

ranura (rrâ•nū´râ) *f.* groove.

rapidez (rrâ•pē•thes´) *f.* speed,
swiftness.

rápido, da (rrâ´pē•tho, thâ) *adj.*
fast, swift, rapid, speedy.

rapto (rrâp´to) *m.* abduction,

carrying off; ecstasy, rapture *(éxtasis);* (med.) faint, loss of consciousness.

raqueta (rrâ•ke′tâ) *f.* racket; badminton *(juego);* rake *(de la casa de juego);* — **de nieve,** snowshoe.

rareza (rrâ•re′sâ) *f.* rarity *(cosa);* rareness; idiosyncrasy *(acción).*

raro, ra (rrâ′ro, râ) *adj.* rare; eccentric *(extravagante).*

ras (rrâs) *m.* levelness, evenness.

rascacielos (rrâs•kâ•sye′los) *m.* skyscraper.

rascar (rrâs•kâr′) *va.* to scratch *(arañar);* to scrape.

rasgado, da (rrâz•gâ′tho, thâ) *adj.* torn; wide *(grande);* —, *m.* rip, tear; **boca** —, wide mouth; **ojos** —**s,** wide eyes.

rasgar (rrâz•gâr′) *va.* to tear, to rip; to strum *(rasguear).*

rasgo (rrâz′go) *m.* dash, stroke, flourish; (fig.) deed, action *(acción);* characteristic, feature *(característica);* —**s,** *pl.* (anat.) features.

rasguear (rrâz•ge•âr′) *vn.* to make flourishes; (mus.) to strum.

rasgueo (rrâz•ge′o) *m.* strumming.

rasguño (rrâz•gū′nyo) *m.* scratch; sketch *(dibujo).*

raso (rrâ′so) *m.* satin, sateen; —,

sa, *adj.* smooth, flat *(plano);* backless; common, undistinguished *(no distinguido);* clear *(de la atmósfera);* **al** —**so,** in the open air.

raspadura (rrâs•pâ•thū′râ) *f.* scraping; erasure *(de papel).*

raspar (rrâs•pâr′) *va.* to scrape, to rasp; to burn *(picar);* to steal *(hurtar);* to graze *(rasar).*

rastra (rrâs′trâ) *f.* rake *(rastro);* sign *(vestigio);* sledge *(narria);* **caminar a** —**s,** to crawl.

rastrear (rrâs•tre•âr′) *va.* to trace, to inquire into, to investigate; to trawl *(pesca);* —, *vn.* to skim along close to the ground.

rastreo (rrâs•tre′o) *m.* trawling; tracing.

rastro (rrâs′tro) *m.* track *(señal);* slaughterhouse *(matadero);* rake *(instrumento);* (fig.) sign, trail.

rastrojo (rrâs•tro′ho) *m.* stubble.

rasurar (rra•sū•râr′) *va.* to shave.

rata (rrâ′tâ) *f.* (zool.) rat.

ratear, (rrâ•te•âr′) *va.* to snatch *(hurtar).*

ratería (rrâ•te•rē′â) *f.* petty theft; (fig.) meanness.

ratero, ra (rrâ•te′ro, râ) *adj.* mean, vile; —, *n.* pickpocket, sneak thief.

ratificar (rrâ•tē•fē•kâr′) *va.* to

ratify.

rato (rrâ´to) *m.* while, moment; **al poco —,** shortly, in a short while; **a —s,** occasionally; **pasar el —,** to while away the time.

ratón (rrâ•ton´) *m.* mouse; mouse *(computación).*

ratonera (rrâ•to•ne´râ) *f.* mousetrap; place where rats breed *(madriguera).*

raudal (rrâū•thâl´) *m.* torrent, stream; (fig.) abundance, flood.

raya (rrâ´yâ) *f.* stripe, line; end, limit *(término);* (gram.) dash; **a —,** within bounds; **—,** *m.* (ichth.) ray.

rayado, da (rrâ•yâ´tho, thâ) *adj.* striped.

rayar (rrâ•yâr´) *va.* to draw lines on, to rule; to stripe; to underline *(subrayar);* to cross out *(borrar);* (Mex.) to pay; **— en,** to border on.

rayo (rrâ´yo) *m.* ray, beam; flash of lightning *(relámpago);* spoke *(de rueda).*

raza (rrâ´sâ) *f.* race, lineage; (fig.) strain, breed.

razón (rrâ•son´) *f.* reason, cause, motive; (math.) ratio; rate *(cómputo);* **— social,** firm name; **a — de,** at the rate of; **dar —,** to inform, to give account; **dar la —,** to agree with; **perder la —,** to go insane;

tener —, to be right; **no tener —,** to be wrong.

razonable (rrâ•so•nâ´vle) *adj.* reasonable.

razonado, da (rrâ•so•nâ´tho, thâ) *adj.* rational, prudent.

razonamiento (rrâ•so•nâ•myen´-to) *m.* reasoning.

razonar (rrâ•so•nâr´) *vn.* to reason; **—,** *va.* to reason out.

reacción (rre•âk•syon´) *f.* reaction; **— en cadena,** chain reaction.

reaccionar (rre•âk•syo•nâr´) *vn.* to react.

reaccionario, ria (rre•âk•syo•nâ´ryo, ryâ) *adj.* reactionary.

reactivar (rre•âk•tē•vâr´) *vt.* to reactivate.

reactor (rre•âk•tor´) *m.* reactor.

reajuste (rre•â•hūs´te) *m.* readjustment.

real (rre•âl´) *adj.* real, actual; royal *(del rey);* **pavo —,** peacock; **—,** *m.* real.

realce (rre•âl´se) *m.* embossing, raised work; (fig.) luster, splendor, enhancement; **dar —,** to build up, to highlight, to give importance to.

realeza (rre•â•le´sâ) *f.* royalty.

realidad (rre•â•lē•thâth´) *f.* reality, fact; truthfulness, sincerity *(ingenuidad);* **en —,** truly, really.

realismo (rre•â•lēz´mo) *m.* realism.

realista (rre•â•lēs´tâ) *m. and f.* royalist *(de la monarquía);* realist.

realización (rre•â•lē•sâ•syon´) *f.* realization, fulfillment.

realizar (rre•â•lē•sâr´) *va.* to realize, to fulfill.

realmente (rre•âl•men´te) *adv.* really.

realzar (rre•âl•sâr´) *va.* to raise, to elevate; to emboss *(labrar);* (fig.) to heighten.

reanudar (rre•â•nū•thâr´) *va.* to renew, to resume.

reaparecer* (rre•â•pâ•re•ser´) *vn.* to re-appear.

rebaja (rre•vâ´hâ) *f.* reduction, rebate.

rebasar (rre•vâ•sâr´) *va.* to lessen, to diminish; (com.) to reduce, to give a rebate on; — **se** to humble oneself.

rebanada (rre•vâ•nâ´thâ) *f.* slice.

rebaño (rre•vâ´nyo) *m.* flock.

rebasar (rre•vâ•sâr´) *va.* to go beyond, to exceed; to pass *(un coche).*

rebelarse (rre•ve•lâr´se) *vr.* to revolt, to rebel; (fig.) to resist, to oppose.

rebelde (rre•vel´de) *m.* rebel; —, *adj.* rebellious.

rebeldía (rre•vel•dē´â) *f.* rebelliousness, disobedience.

rebelión (rre•ve•lyon´) *f.* rebellion, revolt.

rebosar (rre•vo•sâr´) *vn.* to run over, to overflow; (fig.) to abound, to be abundant.

rebotar (rre•vo•târ´) *va.* to repel; —, *vn.* to rebound.

rebote (rre•vo´te) *m.* rebound; **de** —, indirectly, on the rebound.

rebozo (rre•vo´so) *m.* shawl; (fig.) pretext; **de** —, secretly; **sin** —, frankly, openly.

rebuscado, da (rre•vūs•kâ´tho, thâ) *adj.* affected, stilted.

rebuznar (rre•vūz•nâr´) *vn.* to bray.

rebuzno (rre•vūz´no) *m.* braying.

recado (rre•kâ´tho) *m.* message; gift *(regalo);* regards *(recuerdo).*

recaer* (rre•kâ•er´) *vn.* to fall back, to fall again; (med.) to have a relapse; to fall, to come *(parar en uno).*

recaída (rre•kâ•ē´thâ) *f.* relapse.

recalentar* (rre•kâ•len•târ´) *va.* to reheat.

recámara (rre•kâ´mâ•râ) *f.* dressing room; (Mex.) bedroom; chamber *(del arma);* (fig.) circumspection.

recamarera (rre•kâ•mâ•re´râ) *f.* (Sp. Am.) chambermaid.

recapacitar (rre•kâ•pâ•sē•tar´) *va.* to recall to mind, to run over.

recapitular (rre•kâ•pē•tū•lâr´)

va. to recapitulate.

recargar (rre•kâr•gâr´) *va.* to reload; to overload *(aumentar la carga);* (fig.) to overdress, to overdecorate; to increase *(agravar).*

recatado, da (rre•kâ•tâ´tho, thâ) *adj.* prudent, circumspect.

recato (rre•kâ´to) *m.* caution, circumspection *(cautela);* modesty, reserve.

recaudar (rre•kâū•thâr´) *va.* to take in, to collect *(caudales);* to take charge of, to keep under surveillance.

recelo (rre•se´lo) *m.* dread, suspicion, mistrust.

recepción (rre•sep•syon´) *f.* reception; acceptance *(admisión).*

receptor (rre•sep•tor´) *m.* receiver; — **de cabeza,** headset.

receso (rre•se´so) *m.* withdrawal, separation; (Mex.) recess; **estar de —,** to be adjourned.

receta (rre•se´tâ) *f.* recipe; prescription *(de un medicamento).*

recetar (rre•se•târ´) *va.* to prescribe.

recibir (rre•sē•vēr´) *va.* to receive; to approve, to accept *(aprobar);* to let in *(admitir);* to go to meet *(salir al encuentro de);* —**se,** to receive one's degree.

recibo (rre•sē´vo) *m.* receipt,

voucher.

recién (rre•syen´) *adv.* recently, lately; — **casado, da,** newlywed.

reciente (rre•syen´te) *adj.* late, recent.

recientemente (rre•syen•te•men´te) *adv.* recently, lately.

recinto (rre•sēn´to) *m.* area, space.

recio, cia (rre´syo, syâ) *adj.* stout, strong; coarse, heavy, thick *(abultado);* rude, sharp *(áspero);* arduous, rough *(vigoroso);* —**cio,** *adv.* strongly, stoutly; **hablar —cio,** to talk loudly.

recipiente (rre•sē•pyen´te) *m.* recipient, container.

reciprocidad (rre•sē•pro•sē•thâth´) *f.* reciprocity.

reciproco, ca (rre•sē´pro•ko, kâ) *adj.* reciprocal.

recitación (rre•sē•tâ•syon´) *f.* recitation.

recitar (rre•sē•tar´) *va.* to recite.

reclamación (rre•klâ•mâ•syon´) *f.* claim, demand; reclaim; complaint.

reclamar (rre•klâ•mâr´) *va.* to claim, to demand; to reclaim *(reivindicar);* to call for, to beg for *(implorar);* to lure *(las aves);* —, *vn.* to complain.

reclinar (rre•klē•nâr´) *va.* and *vr.* to recline, to lean.

recluir* (rre•klwēr´) *va.* to shut in, to seclude; —**se,** to go into seclusion.

recluta (rre•klū´tā) *f.* recruiting; —, *m.* recruit.

reclutamiento (rre•klū•tā•myen´-to) *m.* recruiting.

reclutar (rre•klū•tār´) *va.* to recruit.

recobrar (rre•ko•vrār´) *va.* to recover; —**se,** to recover.

recogedor, ra (rre•ko•he•thor´, râ) *n.* harborer, shelterer *(que da acogida);* gatherer; —, *m.* scraper; — **de basura,** dustpan.

recoger (rre•ko•her´) *va.* to take back; to gather, to collect, to pick up *(reunir);* to shelter *(abrigar);* to compile *(compilar);* —**se,** to take shelter, to take refuge; to retire *(a dormir);* (fig.) to withdraw from the world.

recogimiento (rre•ko•hē•myen´-to) *m.* gathering, collecting; sheltering; retiring.

recomendación (rre•ko•men•dâ•syon´) *f.* recommendation.

recomendar* (rre•ko•men•dâr´) *va.* to recommend.

recompensa (rre•kom•pen´sâ) *f.* recompense, reward; **en —,** as a reward.

recompensar (rre•kom•pen•sâr´) *va.* to recompense, to reward.

reconciliación (rre•kon•sē•lyâ•syon´) *f.* reconciliation.

reconciliar (rre•kon•sē•lyâr´) *va.* to reconcile; —**se,** to become reconciled.

reconocer* (re•ko•no•ser´) *va.* to examine closely; to acknowledge, to be aware of *(admitir);* to confess, to admit *(confesar);* to recognize *(distinguir);* to consider *(contemplar);* —**se,** to know oneself.

reconocido, da (re•ko•no•sē´tho, thâ) *adj.* grateful.

reconocimiento (re•ko•no•sē•myen´to) *m.* recognition; acknowledgement; gratitude *(agradecimiento);* confession; examination, inquiry *(examen).*

reconstruir* (re•kons•trwēr´) *va.* to reconstruct.

reconvenir* (re•kom•be•nēr´) *va.* to retort with, to recriminate with.

recopilación (re•ko•pē•lâ•syon´) *f.* sumary, abridgement.

recopilar (re•ko•pē•lâr´) *va.* to compile.

recordar* (re•kor•thâr´) *va.* to remind of *(avisar);* to remember, to recall; —, *vn.* to remember.

recorrer (rre•ko•rrer´) *va.* to travel, to travel over *(caminar);*

to repair *(reparar);* to run over, to go over *(repasar);* to peruse, to examine *(registrar).*

recortar (rre•kor•târ´) *va.* to cut away, to
trim off; to cut out *(figuras).*

recorte (rre•kor´te) *m.* cutting, clipping; **—de periódico,** newspaper clipping.

recostar* (rre•kos•târ´) *va.* to lean, to recline.

recrear (rre•kre•âr´) *va.* to amuse, to recreate; to re-create *(crear de nuevo);* **—se,** to enjoy oneself, to have some recreation.

recreativo, va (rre•kre•â•tē´vo, vâ) *adj.* recreative, diverting.

recriminación (rre•krē•mē•nâ•syon´) *f.* recrimination.

recriminar (rre•krē•mē•nar´) *va.* to recriminate.

rectamente (rrek•tâ•mente) *adv.* justly, rightly.

rectangular (rrek•tâng•gū•lâr´) *adj.* rectangular.

rectángulo (rrek•tâng´gū•lo) *m.* rectangle.

rectificar (rrek•tē•fē•kâr´) *va.* to rectify, to correct.

rectilíneo, nea (rrek•tē•lē´ne•o, ne•â) *adj.* rectilinear.

rectitud (rrek•tē•tūth´) *f.* straightness; (fig.) rectitude.

recto, ta (rrek´to, tâ) *adj.*

straight; (fig.) just, upright *(justo);* literal *(sentido primitivo).*

recubrir* (rre•kū•vrēr´) *va.* to cover; to recover *(cubrir de nuevo);* to recap *(una llanta).*

recuento (rre•kwen´to) *m.* inventory *(inventario);* count *(enumeración);* recount *(segunda cuenta).*

recuerdo (rre•kwer´tho) *m.* remembrance, memory, impression; souvenir, reminder *(cosa que recuerda);* souvenir, remembrance *(regalo).*

recuperación (rre•kū•pe•râ•syon´) *f.* recovery; recuperation.

recuperar (rre•kū•pe•râr´) *va.* to recover, to regain; **—se,** to recuperate.

recurrir (rre•kū•rrēr´) *vn.* to resort, to have recourse, to turn.

recurso (rre•kūr´so) *m.* resorting, having recourse *(acción);* request *(solicitud);* recourse, resort *(medio).*

rechazar (rre•châ•sâr´) *va.* to repel, to repulse *(resistir);* to reject *(no aceptar);* to resist *(no ceder a).*

rechazo (rre•châ´so) *m.* rejection *(negativa);* recoil, rebound *(rebote).*

rechinar (rre•chē•nâr´) *vn.* to

gnash *(los dientes);* to grind, to creak; (fig.) to do begrudgingly, to balk *(refunfuñar).*

rechoncho, cha (rre•chon´cho, châ) *adj.* (coll.) chubby.

red (reth) *f.* net; mesh, netting *(tejido);* (fig.) trap *(ardid);* network *(sistema).*

redacción (rre•thâk•syon´) *f.* editing; editorial offices *(lugar);* editorial staff *(personal).*

redactar (rre•thâk•târ´) *va.* to edit, to word, to write up.

redactor, ra (rre•thâk•tor, râ) *n.* editor.

redecilla (rre•the•sē´yâ) *f.* hairnet.

redentor, ra (rre•then•tor´, râ) *n.* redeemer; —, *adj.* redeeming.

redil (rre•thēl´) *m.* sheepfold; **volver al** —, (fig.) to get back on the straight and narrow.

redimible (rre•thē•mē´vle) *adj.* redeemable.

redimir (rre•thē•mēr´) *va.* to ransom *(al cautivo);* to redeem *(lo empeñado); to* exempt *(en un censo);* to buy back *(lo vendido).*

redoblar (rre•tho•vlâr´) *va.* to double; to bend back *(un clavo);* to go over, to do again *(repetir).*

redonda (rre•thon´dâ) *f.* (mus.) whole note; region, area *(comarca).*

redondear (rre•thon•de•âr´) *va.* to round off; to clear *(sanear).*

redondez (rre•thon•des´) *f.* roundness.

redondo, da (rre•thon´do, dâ) *adj.* round; **a la —,** round-about, around.

reducción (rre•thūk•syon´) *f.* reduction; subjugation *(sometimiento);* (Sp.Am.) village of Indian converts.

reducir* (rre•thū•sēr´) *va.* to reduce; to subjugate *(someter);* — **la marcha,** to slow down; **—se,** to cut down, to make ends meet; **—se a,** to resolve to, to be obliged to.

redundante (rre•thūn•dân´te), *adj.* redundant, superfluous.

redundar (rre•thūn•dâr´) *vn.* to overflow, to spill over *(rebosar).*

reelección (rre•e•lek•syon´) *f.* reelection.

reelegir* (rre•e•le•hēr´) *va.* to reelect.

reembolsar (rre•em•bol•sâr´) = **rembolsar.**

reembolso (rre•em•bol´so) = **rembolso.**

reemplazar (rre•em•plâ•sâr´) = **remplazar.**

reemplazo (rre•em•plâ´so) = **remplazo.**

reencarnación (rre•eng•kâr•nâ•syon´) *f.* reincarnation.

refacción (rre•fâk•syon´) *f.* snack, light lunch *(merienda);* (Sp. Am.) repair *(reparación);* (coll.) bonus *(añadidura);* **pie-zas de —,** spare parts.

referencia (rre•fe•ren´syâ) *f.* refe-rence.

referente (rre•fe•ren´te) *adj.* related, connected.

referir* (rre•fe•rēr´) *va.* to relate *(contar);* to refer *(encaminar);* to relate *(relacionar);* **—se,** to refer *(remitirse);* to relate.

refinado, da (rre•fē•nâ´tho, thâ) *adj.* refined; (fig.) outstanding, distinguished *(sobresaliente);* clever, shrewd *(astuto).*

refinamiento (rre•fē•nâ•myen´to) *m.* good taste, care, refinement.

refinar (rre•fē•nâr´) *va.* to refine.

reflejar (rre•fle•hâr´) *va.* to reflect.

reflejo (rre•fle´ho) *m.* reflection; reflex *(movimiento reflejo);* immediate reaction *(reacción rápida);* —. **ja,** *adj.* reflected; (gram.) reflexive; reflex *(incons-ciente).*

reflexión (rre•flek•syon´) *f.* reflection.

reflexionar (rre•flek•syo•nâr´) *vn.* to reflect, to meditate, to con-sider.

reflexivo, va (rre•flek•se´vo, vâ) *adj.* (gram.) reflexive; thought-ful, considerate *(que obra con reflexión);* reflecting.

reforma (rre•for´mâ) *f.* reform; **R—,** (eccl.) Reformation.

reformación (rre•for•mâ•syon´) *f.* reform.

reformar (rre•for•mâr´) *va.* to reform.

reformatorio (rre•for•mâ•to´ryo) *m.* reformatory.

reforzado, da (rre•for•sâ´tho, thâ) *adj.* reinforced; strength-ened.

reforzar* (rre•for•sâr´) *va.* to strengthen; to reinforce *(dar mayor solidez);* (fig.) to encour-age *(animar).*

refrán (rre•frân´) *m.* proverb, saying.

refrenar (rre•fre•nâr´) *va.* to rein; (fig.) to check, to curb.

refrescante (rre•fres•kân´te) *adj.* refreshing.

refrescar (rre•fres•kâr´) *va.* to cool off; to renew *(renovar);* to refresh *(un recuerdo);* —, *vn.* to refresh oneself; to cool off *(el tiempo).*

refresco (rre•fres´ko) *m.* refres-hment.

refrigerador (rre•frē•he•râ•thor´) *m.* refrigerator.

refrigerar (rre•frē•he•râr´) *va.* to refrigerate.

refuerzo (rre•fwer´so) *m.* reinfor-cement.

refugiado, da (ree•fū•hyâ´tho,

thâ) *n.* refugee.

refugiar (rre•fū•hyâr´) *va.* to shelter; **—se,** to take refuge.

refugio (rre•fū´hyo) *m.* refuge; shelter *(asilo).*

refulgente (rre•fūl•hen´te) *adj.* radiant, shining.

refunfuñar (rre•fūm•fū•nyâr´) *vn.* to growl, to grumble.

refutar (rre•fū•târ´) *va.* to refute.

regadera (rre•gâ•the´râ) *f.* sprinkling can; irrigation canal *(reguera).*

regalar (rre•gâ•lâr´) *va.* to make a gift of; to regale *(halagar);* —se, not to spare oneself anything.

regalo (rre•gâ´lo) *m.* gift; pleasure *(gusto);* repast *(comida);* ease *(comodidad).*

regañar (rre•gâ•nyâr´) *va.* (coll.) to scold, to nag, to reprimand; —, *vn.* to snarl; to grumble *(enfadarse).*

regañón, ona (rre•gâ•nyon´ o´nâ) *adj.* snarling; grumbling; scolding, nagging.

regar* (rre•gâr´) *va.* to sprinkle *(esparcir agua);* to water; to flow through *(atravesar);* to spread *(derramar).*

regatear (rre•gâ•te•âr´) *va.* to haggle over; —, *vn.* to jockey for position.

regateo (rre•gâ•te´o) *m.* bargaining, haggling; (naut.) regatta.

regazo (rre•gâ´so) *m.* lap; (fig.) fold, lap.

regeneración (re•he•ne•râ•syon´) *f.* regeneration.

regenerar (rre•he•ne•râr´) *va.* to regenerate.

regente (rre•hen´te) *m.* regent.

régimen (rre´hē•men) *m.* regime; (med.) regimen, diet; period *(periodo);* (gram.) government.

regimiento (rre•hē•myen´to) *m.* administration, direction; aldermen, councilmen, council *(conjunto de regidores);* (mil.) regiment.

regio, gia (rre´hyo, hyâ) *adj.* royal, regal.

región (rre•hyon´) *f.* region.

regionalismo (rre•hyo•nâ•lēz´mo) *m.* regionalism.

regir* (rre•hēr´) *va.* to rule, to govern; to administrate, to direct *(guiar);*—, *vn.* to be in force.

registrador, ra (rre•hēs•trâ•thor´, râ) *adj.* registering; **caja** —, cash register.

registrar (rre•hēs•trâr´) *va.* to inspect, to examine *(examinar);* to search *(buscar);* to enter, to record, to register *(transcribir);* to mark *(anotar);* —se, to register.

registro (rre•hēs´tro) *m.* register; registry office *(lugar);* bookmark *(de libro);* record, entry *(asiento);* regulator *(del reloj);* check point *(de lo empotrado).*

regla (rre´glâ) *f.* ruler *(instrumento);* rule; order *(disciplina);* — **áurea,** golden rule.

reglamento (rreg•lâ•men´to) *m.* bylaws.

regocijar (rre•go•sē•hâr´) *va.* to gladden, to delight; —**se por,** to rejoice at.

regocijo (rre•go•sē´ho) *m.* joy, rejoicing, happiness.

regresar (rre•gre•sâr´) *vn.* to return, to come back.

regreso (rre•gre´so) *m.* return; **de** —, on the way back.

regulador, ra (rre•gū•lâ•thor´, râ) *adj.* regulating; —, *m.* regulator.

regular (rre•gū•lâr´) *va.* to regulate, to adjust; —, *adj.* regular; average *(mediano).*

regularidad (rre•gū•lâ•rē•thâth´) *f.* regularity.

rehabilitación (rre•â•vē•lē•tâ•syon´) *f.* rehabilitation.

rehabilitar (rre•â•vē•lē•târ´) *va.* to rehabilitate.

rehacer* (rre•â•ser´) *va.* to redo, to re-make; to repair *(reparar);* —**se,** to rally one´s forces; to compose oneself *(serenarse).*

rehén (rre•en´) *m.* hostage.

rehusar (rre•ū•sâr´) *va.* to refuse, to decline.

reimpresión (rreēm•pre•syon´) *f.* reprint.

reimprimir (rreēm•prē•mēr´) *va.* to reprint.

reina (rre´ē•nâ) *f.* queen.

reinado (rreē•nâ´tho) *m.* reign.

reinar (rreē•nâr´) *va.* to reign; to prevail *(prevalecer).*

reincidir (rreēn•sē•thēr´) *vn.* to relapse, to fall back; — **en un error,** to repeat an error.

reino (rre´ē•no) *m.* kingdom.

Reino Unido (rre´ē•no ū•nē´tho) *m.* United Kingdom.

reintegración (rreēn•te•grâ•syon´) *f.* reintegration, restoration.

reintegrar (rreēn•te•grâr´) *va.* to reintegrate; to restore *(reconstituir);* —**se,** to recoup one´s losses.

reintegro (rreēn•te´gro) *m.* reintegration; restoration.

reir* (rre•ēr´) *vn.* to laugh; —, *vt.* to laugh at; **reírse de,** to laugh at.

reiterar (rreē•te•râr´) *va.* to reiterate, to repeat.

reja (rre´hâ) *f.* plowshare *(del arado);* grille, grillwork.

rejuvenecer* (rre•hū•ve•ne•ser´) *va.* to rejuvenate.

relación (rre•lâ•syon´) *f.* relationship *(conexión);* dealing *(trato);* account *(narración);* —**ones,** *pl.* courtship.

relacionado, da (rre•lâ•syo•nâ´-tho, thâ) *adj.* related, connected.

relacionar (rre•lâ•syo•nâr´) *va.* to relate; **—se,** to become acquainted.

relajar (rre•lâ•hâr´) *va.* to relax.

relámpago (rre•lâm´pâ•go) *m.* lightning flash; **cierre —,** zipper.

relampaguear (rre•lâm•pâ•ge•âr´) *vn.* to lightning; (fig.) to flash, to sparkle *(centellar).*

relatar (rre•lâ•târ´) *va.* to relate.

relatividad (rre•lâ•tē•vē•thâth´) *f.* relativity.

relativo, va (rre•lâ•tē´vo, vâ) *adj.* relative; **—vo a,** with regard to, as concerns.

relato (rre•lâ´to) *m.* statement, account.

relevante (rre•le•vân´te) *adj.* eminent, outstanding.

relevar (rre•le•vâr´) *va.* to put into relief; to free, to relieve *(exonerar);* to replace *(sustituir);* **—,** *vn.* to stand out; **—se,** to take turns.

relevo (rre•le´vo) *m.* (mil.) relief; relieving, freeing; **carrera de —s,** relay race.

relieve (rre•lye´ve) *m.* relief; **bajo —,** basrelief; **dar —,** to emphasize, to highlight.

religión (rre•lē•hyon´) *f.* religion.

religioso, sa (rre•lē•hyo´so, sâ) *adj.* religious; **—,** *m.* monk, brother; **—,** *f.* nun, sister.

reliquia (rre•lē´kyâ) *f.* relic.

reloj (rre•lo´) *m.* clock; **— de pulsera,** wrist watch; **— de arena,** hourglass; **— de bolsillo,** pocket watch.

relojería (rre•lo•he•rē´â) *f.* watchmaking *(arte);* watch shop *(taller).*

reluciente (rre•lū•syen´te) *adj.* resplendent, glittering.

relucir* (rre•lū•sēr´) *vn.* to shine.

rellenar (rre•ye•nâr´) *va.* to refill; to stuff *(henchir).*

relleno (rre•ye´no) *m.* filling, stuffing, padding, packing; **—, na,** *adj.* chock-full, stuffed.

remanente (rre•mâ•nen´te) *m.* residue, remains, remnant.

remar (rre•mâr´) *vn.* to row.

rematado, da (rre•mâ•tâ´tho, thâ) *adj.* utter, absolute, hopeless, incurable; **loco —,** stark raving mad.

rematar (rre•mâ•târ´) *va.* to auction off *(subastar);* to complete, to finish *(acabar);* to kill off, to finish off *(matar);* **—,** *vn.* to end; **—se,** to be utterly ruined.

remate (rre•mâ´te) *m.* end, completion; winning bid *(en una subasta);* **por —,** finally; **de —,** absolutely, hopelessly, incurably.

rembolsar (rrem•bol•sâr´) *va.* to reimburse.

rembolso (rrem•bol´so) *m,* reimbursement.

remediable (rre•me•thyâ´vle) *adj.* remediable, curable.

remediar (rre•me•thyâr´) *va.* to remedy; to free from risk *(librar de riesgo);* to prevent, to avoid *(estorbar).*

remedio (rre•me´thyo) *m.* remedy; re-course *(recurso);* **sin —,** helpless, unavoidable: **no tener —,** to be beyond help; **no tiene —,** it can´t be helped.

remendar* (rre•men•dâr´) *va.* to mend, to repair.

remero (rre•me´ro) *m.* rower, oarsman.

remesa (rre•me´sâ) *f.* remittance *(de dinero);* shipment, sending.

reminiscencia (rre•mē•nēs•sen´syâ) *f.* reminiscence.

remisión (rre•mē•syon´) *f.* remission *(suspensión);* shipment *(envío);* forgiveness *(perdón);* reference *(referencia);* remittance *(de dinero).*

remitente (rre•mē•ten´te) *m.* and *f.* remitter, sender; **—,** *adj.* remittent.

remitir (rre•mē•tēr´) *va.* to remit; to send *(enviar);* to refer to *(indicar);* to reduce, to slacken *(disminuir);* **—,** *vn.* to abate, to lose force; **—se a,** to refer to, to cite.

remojar (rre•mo•hâr´) *va.* to soak, to steep; (fig.) to celebrate.

remolacha (rre•mo•lâ´châ) *f.* beet.

remolcador (rre•mol•kâ•thor´) *m.* tug boat.

remolcar (rre•mol•kâr´) *va.* to tow.

remolino (rre•mo•lē´no) *m.* whirl.

remolón, ona (rre•mo•lon´, o´nâ) *adj.* slow, lazy; laggard; **—,** *m.* upper tusk.

remolque (rre•mol´ke) *m.* towing, tow; tow line *(cabo);* trailer *(vehículo remolcado);* **llevar a —,** to tow along.

remordimiento (rre•mor•thē•myen´to) *m.* remorse.

remoto, ta (rre•mo´to, tâ) *adj.* remote, distant, far.

remover* (rre•mo•ver´) *va.* to remove *(quitar);* to change around *(cambiar);* to dismiss *(deponer);* to stir, to stir up *(agitar);* **—se,** to get upset.

remplazar (rrem•plâ•sâr´) *va.* to replace.

remplazo (rrem•plâ´so) *m.* replacement, substitute.

renacer* (rre•nâ•ser´) *vn.* (eccl.) to be born again; to come to life again; (fig.) to feel as good as new.

renacimiento (rre•nâ•se•myen´- to) *m.* renascence, rebirth; **R—,** Renaissance.

rencor (rreng•kor´) *m.* rancor, grudge, ill will; **guardar —,** to bear a grudge.

rendición (rren•de•syon´) *f.* surrender; profit, yield (réditos); rendition (interpretación).

rendido, da (rren•de´tho, thâ) *adj.* worn-out, fatigued (cansado); submissive (sumiso).

rendija (rren•de´hâ) *f.* crevice, crack.

rendimiento (rren•de•myen´to) *m.* weariness (fatiga); submissiveness (sumisión); output, yield (utilidad).

rendir* (rren•der´) *va.* to overcome (vencer); to deliver over (entregar); to subdue (sujetar); to produce, to yield (producir); **—se,** to surrender (entregarse); to wear oneself out (fatigarse).

renegado, da (rre•ne•gâ´tho, thâ) *n.* apostate, renegade; **—,** *adj.* (coll.) surly.

renegar* (rre•ne•gâr´) *va.* to deny, to disown (negar); to nag; to detest, to abhor (abominar); **—,** *vn.* to abandon Christianity; to blaspheme, to curse (blasfemar).

renglón (rreng•glon´) *m.* line.

reno (rre´no) *m.* reindeer.

renombrado, da (rre•nom•brâ´tho, thâ) *adj.* renowned.

renombre (rre•nom´bre) *m.* renown.

renovación (rre•no•vâ•syon´) *f.* renovation, renewal.

renovar* (rre•no•vâr´) *va.* to renovate; to replace (sustituir); to repeat (reiterar).

renta (rren´tâ) *f.* rent, income.

renuente (rre•nwen´te) *adj.* reluctant, unwilling.

renuncia (rre•nûn´syâ) *f.* refusal; resignation.

renunciar (rre•nûn•syâr´) *va.* to renounce; to refuse (no aceptar); to resign from (un empleo).

reñido, da (rre•nyē´tho, thâ) *adj.* at loggerheads, at odds (enemistado); hard-fought.

reñir* (rre•nyēr´) *vn.* to wrangle, to quarrel, to fight; to have a falling out, to become enemies (enemistarse); **—,** *va.* to fight (un desafío); to scold (regañar).

reo (rre´o) *m. and f.* offender, criminal.

reojo (rre•o´ho) **mirar de —,** to look out of the corner of one´s eye; (coll.) to look at contemptuously, to look askance at (con desprecio).

reparable (rre•pâ•râ´vle) *adj.* reparable, remediable; noteworthy *(notable)*.

reparación (rre•pâ•râ´•syon´) *f.* reparation, repair.

reparar (rre•pâ•râr´) *va.* to repair, to mend *(componer);* to parry *(evitar);* to note, to observe *(notar);* to make amends for *(remediar)*.

reparo (rre•pâ´•ro) *m.* repair, reparation; remark, observation *(observación);* warning, notice *(advertencia);* defense *(defensa);* obstacle, difficulty *(dificultad);* **poner —,** to object.

repartición (rre•pâr•tê•syon´) *f.* distribution, division.

repartir (rre•pâr•têr´) *va.* to distribute, to divide up.

reparto (rre•pâr´•to) *m.* distribution; allotment *(asignación);* assessment *(contribución);* (theat.) cast of characters; (Sp. Am.) subdivision.

repasar (rre•pâ•sâr´) *va.* to review *(recorrer);* to revise *(corregir);* to look over *(examinar);* to repass, to retrace *(desandar)*.

repaso (rre•pâ´•so) *m.* review; revision.

repatriación (rre•pâ•tryâ•syon´) *f.* repatriation.

repatriado, da (rre•pâ•tryâ´•tho, thâ) *adj.* repatriated; **—,** *n.* repatriate.

repeler (rre•pe•ler´) *va.* to repel, to reject.

repelón (rre•pe•lon´) *m.* pull on one´s hair; snag *(en las medias);* tiny bit *(porción):* bolt, dash *(del caballo);* **a —ones,** little by little, bit by bit; **de —,** quickly.

repente (rre•pen´•te) *m.* (coll.) burst, start; **de —,** suddenly.

repentino, na (rre•pen•tê´•no, nâ) *adj.* sudden, unforeseen.

repercusión (rre•per•kū•syon´) *f.* reverberation, repercussion: bouncing off.

repercutir (rre•per•kū•têr´) *vn.* to reverberate; to be deflected, to rebound, to bounce off *(un cuerpo)*.

repertorio (rre•per•to´•ryo) *m.* repertory.

repetición (rre•pe•tê•syon´) *f.* repetition; (mus.) repeat.

repetir* (rre•pe•têr´) *va.* to repeat.

repisa (rre•pê´•sâ) *f.* stand.

repleto, ta (rre•ple´•to, tâ) *adj.* replete, full, loaded.

réplica (rre´•plê•kâ) *f.* answer, retort; replica *(copia)*.

replicar (rre•plê•kâr´) *vn.* to reply, to retort; to answer back, to argue *(poner objeciones)*.

reponer* (rre•po•ner´) *va.* to put back, to replace; to revive *(una obra dramática);* to retort, to reply *(replicar);* to reinstate, to provide *(remplazar);* —**se,** to calm down *(serenarse);* to recover.

reportar (rre•por•târ´) *va.* to refrain, to hold back *(refrenar);* to obtain, to reach, to attain *(lograr);* to carry, to bring *(llevar).*

reportero, ra (rre•por•te´ro, râ) *n.* reporter; —, *adj.* reporting.

reposado, da (rre•po•sâ´tho, thâ) *adj.* quiet, peaceful; settled *(un liquido).*

reposar (rre•po•sâr´) *vn.* to rest; —**se,** to settle.

reposo (rre•po´so) *m.* rest, repose.

repostería (rre•pos•te•rē´â) *f.* pastry shop *(tienda).*

reprender (rre•pren•der´) *va.* to reprimand, to scold, to blame.

reprensión (rre•pren•syôn´) *f.* reprimand, scolding, blame.

represalia (rre•pre•sâ´lyâ) *f.* reprisal, retaliation.

representación (rre•pre•sen•tâ•syon´) *f.* representation; authority *(autoridad);* (theat.) performance.

representante (rre•pre•sen•tân´te) *m. and f.* representative; (theat.) actor.

representar (rre•pre•sen•târ´) *va.* to represent; (theat.) to perform, to present.

representativo, va (rre•pre•sen•tâ•tē´vo, vâ) *adj.* representative.

represión (rre•pre•syon´) *f.* repression.

reprimenda (rre•prē•men´dâ) *f.* reprimand.

reprimir (rre•prē•mēr´) *va.* to repress.

reprobable (rre•pro•vâ´vle) *adj.* reprehensible.

reprobación (rre•pro•vâ•syon´) *f.* reprobation, condemnation; failing, flunking *(en una prueba).*

reprobar* (rre•pro•vâr´) *va.* to reprove; to condemn; to fail, to flunk.

reprochar (rre•pro•châr´) *va.* to reproach.

reproche (rre•pro´che) *m.* reproach.

reproducción (rre•pro•thūk•syon´) *f.* reproduction.

reproducir* (rre•pro•thū•sēr´) *va.* to reproduce.

reptil (rrep•tēl´) *m.* reptile.

república (rre•pū´vlē•kâ) *f.* republic.

República Sudafricana, (rre•pū´vlē•kâ sū´• thâ•frē•kâ´nâ) *f.* South African Republic.

republicano, na (rre•pū•vlē•kâ´no, nâ) *adj. and n.* republican.

repudiar (rre•pū•thyâr´) *va.* to

repudiate.

repuesto (rre•pwes´to) *m.* replacement; **piezas de —,** spare parts; **llanta** or **neumático de —,** spare tire.

repugnancia (rre•pūg•nân´syâ) *f.* repugnance, contradiction.

repugnante (rre•pūg•nân´te) *adj.* repugnant, disgusting.

repugnar (rre•pūg•nâr´) *va.* to contradict *(ser opuesto);* to do with reluctance, to be against *(hacer de mala gana);* **—,** *vn.* to be repugnant.

repulsión (rre•pūl•syon´) *f.* repulsion.

reputación (rre•pū•tâ•syon´) *f.* reputation, renown.

reputar (rre•pū•târ´) *va.* to repute; to esteem *(apreciar).*

requerimiento (rre•ke•rē•myen´-to) *m.* notification; requiring; examination.

requerir* (rre•ke•rēr´) *va.* to notify *(avisar);* to require *(necesitar);* to examine *(examinar);* to persuade *(inducir);* to court *(amorosamente).*

requesón (rre•ke•son´) *m.* cottage cheese; curds *(residuos).*

requisito (rre•kē•sē´to) *m.* requisite, requirement.

res (rres) *f.* head of cattle; wild animal *(salvaje);* **carne de —,** beef.

resaca (rre•sâ´kâ) *f.* undertow; (coll.) hangover *(malestar).*

resaltar (rre•sâl•târ) *vn.* to rebound; to project *(sobresalir);* (fig.) to stand out *(destacarse).*

resbaladizo, za (rrez•vâ•lâ•thē´-so, sâ) *adj.* slippery; (fig.) tricky, deceptive.

resbalar (rrez•vâ•lâr´) *vn.* and *vr.* to slip, to slide; (fig.) to trip up, to make a mistake.

resbalón (rrez•vâ•lon´) *m.* slip, sliding; (fig.) slip, error.

resbaloso, sa (rrez•vâ•lo´so, sâ) *adj.* slippery.

rescatar (rres•kâ•târ´) *va.* to ransom *(a un cautivo);* to redeem.

rescate (rres•kâ´te) *m.* ransom; redemption price.

resecar (rre•se•kâr´) *va.* to dry out, to dry thoroughly.

resentido, da (rre•sen•tē´tho, thâ) *adj.* resentful, angry, hurt, offended.

resentimiento (rre•sen•tē•myen´-to) *m.* resentment.

resentirse* (rre•sen•tēr´se) *vr.* to begin to give way, to weaken *(flaquear);* to feel resentment, to be hurt *(enojarse).*

reseña (rre•se´nyâ) *f.* review; personal description *(de una persona).*

reseñar (rre•se•nyâr´) *va.* to review; to describe *(describir).*

reserva (rre•ser´vâ) *f.* reserve;

reservation *(excepción);* **con** or **bajo la mayor —,** in strictest confidence; **de —,** spare, extra; **sin —,** frankly, openly.

reservado, da (rre•ser•vâ´tho, thâ) *adj.* reserved; cautious *(cauteloso);* circumspect *(discreto);* **—,** *m.* booth.

reservar (rre•ser•vâr´) *va.* to reserve; to retain, to keep back *(retener);* to conceal, to hide *(ocultar);* to postpone *(aplazar);* **—se,** to beware, to be on one´s guard.

resfriado (rres•fryâ´tho) *m.* cold.

resfriarse (rres•fryâr´se) *vr.* to catch cold.

resfrío (rres•frē´o) *m.* cold.

resguardar (rrez•gwâr•thâr´) *va.* to preserve, to defend; **—se,** to be on one´s guard.

resguardo (rez•gwar´tho) *m.* defense, protection *(defensa);* voucher *(cédula).*

residencia (rre•sē•then´syâ) *f.* residence.

residencial (rre•sē•then•syâl´) *adj.* residential.

residente (rre•sē•then´te) *adj.* residing; **—,** *m.* and *f.* resident, inhabitant.

residir (rre•sē•ther´) *vn.* to reside, to dwell.

residuo (rre•sē´thwo) *m.* residue.

resignación (rre•sēg•nâ•syon´) *f.* resignation.

resignado, da (rre•sēg•nâ´tho, thâ) *adj.* resigned.

resignarse (rre•sēg•nâr´se) *vr.* to be resigned, to resign oneself.

resina (rre•sē´nâ) *f.* resin, rosin.

resistencia (rre•sēs•ten´syâ) *f.* resistance.

resistente (rre•sēs•ten´te) *adj.* resistant.

resistible (rre•sēs•tē´vle) *adj.* resistible.

resistir (rre•sēs•tēr´) *va.* to stand, to bear *(tolerar);* to resist *(rechazar);* **—,** *vn.* to resist; **—se,** to struggle.

resolución (rre•so•lū•syon´) *f.* resolution.

resoluto, ta (rre•so•lū´to, tâ) *adj.* resolute, resolved.

resolver* (rre•sol•ver´) *va.* to resolve, to solve; to decide on *(determinar);* to dissolve *(disolver);* to break down, to analyze *(analizar);* **—se,** to resolve, to determine, to make up one´s mind.

resonancia (rre•so•nân´syâ) *f.* resonance.

resonar* (rre•so•nâr´) *vn.* to resound; (fig.) to have repercussions.

resorte (rre•sor´te) *m.* spring; (fig.) spring-board *(medio).*

respaldar (rres•pâl•dâr´) *va.* (fig.) to indorse, to back; **—,** *m.* backrest.

respaldo (rres•pâl′do) *m.* back-rest; (fig.) backing, indorsement.

respectivo, va (rres•pek•tē′vo, vâ) *adj.* respective.

respecto (rres•pek′to) *m.* relation, respect; **al —,** in this regard; **— a** or **con — a,** in regard to, relative to.

respetable (rres•pe•tâ′vle) *adj.* respectable, honorable.

respetar (rres•pe•târ′) *va.* to respect.

respeto (rres•pe′to) *m.* respect, regard, consideration.

respetuoso, sa (rres•pe•two′so, sâ) *adj.* respectful.

respiración (rres•pē•râ•syon′) *f.* respiration, breathing; circulation *(en un aposento).*

respirar (rres•pē•râr′) *vn.* and *va.* to breathe.

respiro (rres•pē′ro) *m.* breathing.

resplandecer* (rres•plân•de•ser′) *vn.* To shine, to glitter; (fig.) to excel, to stand out.

resplandeciente (rres•plân•de•syen′te) *adj.* resplendent, brilliant, radiant.

resplandor (rres•plân•dor′) *m.* brilliance, radiance.

responder (rres•pon•der′) *va.* to answer; **—,** *vn.* to respond; to answer back *(ser respondón);* to be answerable, to be respon-sible *(ser responsable).*

responsabilidad (rres•pon•sâ•vē•lē•thâth′) *f.* responsibility.

responsable (rres•pon•sâ′vle) *adj.* responsible, accountable.

respuesta (rres•pwes′tâ) *f.* answer, reply.

resquebrar* (rres′ke•vrâr′) *va.* to start to break, to open cracks.

resta (rres′tâ) *f.* (math.) subtraction; remainder *(residuo).*

restablecer* (rres•tâ•vle•ser′) *va.* to reestablish, to restore; **—se,** to recover.

restablecimiento (rres•tâ•vle•sē•myen′to) *m.* reestablishment; recovery *(convalecencia).*

restante (rres•tân′te) *m.* rest, remainder; **—,** *adj.* remaining.

restar (rres•târ′) *va.* to subtract; **—,** *vn.* to be left, to remain.

restauración (rres•tâū•râ•syon′) *f.* restoration.

restaurante (rres•tâū•rân′te) *m.* restaurant.

restaurar (rres•tâū•rar′) *va.* to restore.

restituir* (rres•tē•twēr′) *va.* to restore; **—se,** to return, to go back.

resto (rres′to) *m.* remainder, rest.

restregar* (rres•tre•gâr′) *va.* to scrub hard.

restricción (rres•trēk•syon´) *f.* restriction, limitation.

restringir (rres•trēn•hēr´) *va.* to limit, to restrict.

restriñir* (rres•trē•nyēr´) *va.* to constrict,

resucitar (rre•sū•sē•târ´) *va.* to resuscitate; to resurrect *(volver la vida).*

resuelto, ta (rre•swel´to, tâ) *adj.* resolved, determined; rapid, diligent *(pronto).*

resultado (rre•sūl•tâ´tho) *m.* result, consequence, outcome.

resultar (rre•sūl•târ´) *vn.* to result; to turn out *(salir).*

resumen (rre•sū´men) *m.* summary.

resumir (rre•sū•mēr´) *va.* to abridge, to summarize.

resurgir (rre•sūr•hēr´) *vn.* to reappear.

resurrección (rre•sū•rrek•syon´) *f.* resurrection.

retaguardia (rre•tâ•gwâr´thyâ) *f.* rear guard.

retar (rre•târ´) *va.* to challenge; (coll.) to call down *(reprender.)*

retardar (rre•târ•thâr´) *va.* to retard, to delay.

retardo (rre•tar´tho) *m.* delay.

retazo (rre•tâ´so) *m.* remnant, scrap; —s, *pl.* odds and ends.

retención (rre•ten•syon´) *f.* retention.

retener* (rre•te•ner´) *va.* to retain.

reticente (rre•tē•sen´te) *adj.* reticent.

retina (rre•tē´nâ) *f.* retina.

retirada (rre•tē•râ´thâ) *f.* withdrawal; retreat *(lugar).*

retirado, da (rre•tē•râ´tho, thâ) *adj.* retired.

retirar (rre•tē•râr´) *va.* to withdraw; (mil.) to retire; to take away *(guitar);* —**se,** to retire *(irse);* to go into seclusion.

retiro (rre•tē´ro) *m.* retirement.

reto (rre´to) *m.* challenge; threat *(amenaza).*

retocar (rre•to•kâr´) *va.* to retouch; to put the finishing touches on *(dar la última mano).*

retoque (rre•to´ke) *m.* retouching; slight touch *(de una enfermedad).*

retorcer* (rre•tor•ser´) *va.* to twist.

retorcimiento (rre•tor•sē•myen´to) *m.* twisting.

retórica (rre•to´rē•ka) *f.* rhetoric.

retórico, ca (rre•to´rē•ko, kâ), *adj.* rhetorical.

retornar (rre•tor•nâr´) *va.* to return, to give back; —, *vn.* to return, to go back.

retorno (rre•tor´no) *m.* return; barter, ex-change (trueque).

retortijón (rre•tor•tē•hon´) *m.* twisting; — de tripas, cramp.

retractar (rre•trâk•târ´) *va.* to retract.

retraer* (rre•trâ•er´) *va.* to bring back; to dissuade (disuadir); —se, to take refuge (refugiarse); to back off, to retreat (retirarse).

retraído, da (rre•trâ•ē´tho, thâ) *adj.* reserved, shy.

retraimiento (rre•trâē•myen´to) *m.* retreat, asylum, seclusion; aloofness, reserve (reserva).

retrasar (rre•trâ•sâr´) *va.* to defer, to put off; —, *vn.* to lag, to decline; to be slow (el reloj); —se, to be delayed.

retraso (rre•trâ´so) *m.* delay, slowness.

retratar (rre•trâ•târ´) *va.* to portray; to photograph (fotografiar); —se, to sit for a portrait.

retrato (rre•trâ´to) *m.* portrait; photograph; **vivo** —, very image.

retribución (rre•trē•vū•syon´) *f.* retribution.

retribuir* (rre•trē•vwēr´) *va.* to repay.

retroactivo, va (rre•tro•âk•tē´vo, vâ) *adj.* retroactive.

retroceder (rre•tro•se•ther´) *vn.* to back up, to go backward.

retroceso (rre•tro•se´so) *m.* retrocession.

retrógrado, da (rre•tro´grâ•tho, thâ) *adj.* retrograde; (fig.) back-ward.

retroimpulso (rre•troēm•pūl´so) *m.* jet propulsion.

retrospectivo, va (rre•tros•pek tē´vo, vâ) *adj.* retrospective, backward; **en** —a, in retrospect.

reuma (rre´ū•mâ) *f.* (med.) rheumatism.

reumático, ca (rreū•mâ´tē•ko, kâ´) *adj.* rheumatic.

reumatismo (rreū•mâ•tēz´mo) *m.* rheumatism.

reunión (rreū•nyon´) *f.* reunion, meeting, gathering; reuniting *(acción).*

reunir (rreū•nēr´) *va.* to bring together, to reunite; to gather together *(juntar);* —se, to meet, to rendezvous.

revalidar (rre•vâ•lē•thâr´) *va.* to revalidate; —se, to take one's qualifying exams for a degree.

revelación (rre•ve•lâ•syon´) *f.* revelation, disclosure; (phot.) development.

revelar (rre•ve•lâr´) *va.* to reveal, to disclose; (phot.) to develop.

revendedor (rre•ven•de•thor´) *m.* reseller.

revender (rre•ven•der´) *va.* to resell.

reventa (rre•ven´tâ) *m.* resale.

reventar* (rre•ven•târ´) *vn.* to blow out *(un neumático);* to break *(las olas);* to burst out *(brotar);* to explode *(por impulso interior);* to be dying, to be itching *(con ansias);* —, *va.* to smash; to annoy *(molestar);* (fig.) to break, to ruin.

reverberar (rre•âr•ve•râr´) *va.* to reverberate.

reverdecer* (rre•ver•the•ser´) *vn.* to grow green again; (fig.) to get back one´s pep.

reverencia (rre•ve•ren´syâ) *f.* reverence; bow, curtsy *(inclinación).*

reverenciar (rre•ve•ren•syâr´) *va.* to venerate, to revere.

reverendo, da (rre•ve•ren´do, dâ) *adj.* reverent; (eccl.) reverend.

reverente (rre•ve•ren´te) *adj.* respectful, reverent.

reverso (rre•ver´so) *m.* reverse; **el — de la medalla,** the exact opposite.

revés (rre•ves´) *m.* reverse, wrong side; misfortune *(desgracia);* **al —,** back-wards; inside out *(invertido).*

revestir* (rre•ves•tēr´) *va.* to put on, to don *(vestir);* to cover *(cubrir);* to assume, to present *(un aspecto);* **—se,** to grow proud *(engreírse); to* be swayed *(imbuirse);* to gird oneself.

revisar (rre•vē•sâr´) *va.* to revise; to check *(controlar).*

revisión (rre•vē•syon´) *f.* revision; checking.

revisor, ra (rre•vē•sor´, râ) *n.* checker, examiner; (rail.) conductor; —, *adj.* examining.

revista (rre•vēs´tâ) *f.* review; magazine, review *(publicación).*

revivir (rre•vē•vēr´) *vn.* to revive.

revocable (rre•vo•kâ´vle) *adj.* revocable.

revocación (rre•vo•kâ•syon´) *f.* revocation.

revocar (rre•vo•kâr´) *va.* to revoke; to drive back *(hacer retroceder).*

revolcarse* (rre•vol•kâr´se) *vr.* to wallow, to roll around.

revolotear (rre•vo•lo•te•âr´) *vn.* to flutter.

revoltoso, sa (rre•vol•to´so, sâ) *adj.* seditious, riotous; wild, noisy *(turbulento).*

revolución (rre•vo•lū•syon´) *f.* revolution.

revolucionar (rre•vo•lū•syo•nâr´) *va. to* revolutionize.

revolucionario, ria (rre•vo•lū•syo•nâ´ryo, ryâ) *adj.* revolutionary.

revolver* (rre•vol•ver´) *va.* to stir, to shake *(menear);* to involve *(enredar);* to upset *(producir náuseas);* to look through, to go through *(registrar);* to go over *(discurrir);* to stir up *(alborotar);* to rotate, to revolve *(hacer dar vueltas).*

revólver (rre•vol´ver) *m.* revolver.

revuelta (rre•vwel′tâ) *f.* revolt, uprising; turn *(cambio de dirección).*

revuelto, ta (rre•vwel′to, tâ) *adj.* in disorder, confused, mixed up; boisterous, restless *(turbulento).*

rey (rre′ē) *m.* king; **los Reyes Magos,** the three Wise Men.

rezagado, da (rre•sâ•gâ′tho, thâ) *adj.* left behind.

rezagar (rre•sâ•gâr′) *va.* to leave behind; to defer *(diferir);* **—se,** to remain behind, to lag behind.

rezar (rre•sâr′) *va.* to pray.

rezo (rre′so) *m.* praying, prayers; daily devotions *(oficio religioso).*

ricino (rre•sē′no) *m.* castor oil plant; **aceite de —** castor oil.

rico, ca (rrē′ko, kâ) *adj.* rich; delicious *(delicioso).*

ridiculez (rre•thē•kū•les′) *f.* ridiculous thing, stupid thing.

ridículo, la (rre•thē′kū•lo, lâ) *adj.* ridiculous; **poner en —,** to make a fool of.

riego (rrye′go) *m.* watering; sprinkling *(esparcimiento);* water supply *(agua disponible).*

riel (rryel) *m.* rail.

rienda (rryen′dâ) *f.* rein; **a — suelta,** with free rein.

riesgo (rryez′go) *m.* danger, risk.

rifa (rrē′fâ) *f.* raffle, lottery *(sorteo);* scuffle, dispute *(disputa).*

rifar (rre•fâr′) *va.* to raffle.

rigidez (rrē•hē•thes′) *f.* rigidity, stiffness.

rígido, da (rrē′hē•tho, thâ) *adj.* rigid.

rigor (rrē•gor′) *m.* rigor.

riguroso, sa (rrē•gū•ro′so, sâ) *adj.* rigorous.

rima (rrē′mâ) *f.* rhyme.

rimar (rrē•mâr′) *va.* and *vn.* to rhyme.

rincón (rrēng•kon′) *m.* corner.

rinoceronte (rrē•no•se•ron′te) *m.* rhinoceros.

riña (rrē′nyâ) *f.* quarrel.

riñón (rrē•nyon′) *m.* kidney.

río (rrē′o) *m.* river.

riqueza (rrē•ke′sâ) *f.* riches, wealth.

risa (rrē′sâ) *f.* laugh, laughter.

risco (rrēs′ko) *m.* cliff.

risueño, ña (rrē•swe′nyo, nyâ) *adj.* smiling, pleasant.

rítmico, ca (rrēth′mē•ko, kâ) *adj.* rhythmical.

ritmo (rrēth′mo) *m.* rhythm.

rito (rrē′to) *m.* rite, ceremony.

ritual (rrē•twâl′) *adj.* and *m.* ritual.

rival (rrē•vâl′) *m.* and *f.* rival, competitor.

rivalidad (rrē•vâ•lē•thâth′) *f.* rivalry.

rivalizar (rrē•vâ•lē•sâr′) *vn.* to rival, to vie.

rizado, da (rre•sâ′tho, thâ) *adj.*

curly; rippled.

rizar (rrē•sâr´) va. to curl *(el pelo);* to ripple *(el agua);* to fold into strips *(el papel).*

rizo (rrē´so) *m.* curl.

róbalo (rro´vâ•lo) or **robalo** (rro•vâ´lo) *m.* (zool.) bass.

robar (rro•vâr´) va. to steal, to rob; to abduct, to kidnap *(raptar).*

roble (rro´vle) *m.* oak tree.

robo (rro´vo) *m.* robbery, theft; abduction.

robustecer* (rro•vūs•te•ser´) va. to strengthen, to invigorate.

robusto, ta (rro•vūs´to, tâ) *adj.* robust, vigorous.

roca (rro´kâ) *f.* rock.

roce (rro´se) *m.* rubbing; clearing of underbrush; (fig.) rubbing elbows *(trato).*

rociar (rro•syâr´) va. to sprinkle; (fig.) to scatter about; —, vn. to be dew.

rocín (rro•sēn´) *m.* hack; (fig.) clod, lout.

rocinante (rro•sē•nân´te) *m.* nag, hack.

rocío (rro•sē´o) *m.* dew.

rocoso, sa (rro•ko´so, sâ) *adj.* rocky.

rodaje (rro•thâ´he) *m.* wheels, workings; — **de una película**, shooting of a film.

rodar* (rro•thâr´) vn. to roll; to roll down *(caer);* to rotate

(alrededor de un eje).

rodear (rro•the•âr´) vn. to go around; to go a roundabout way *(dar un rodeo);* —, va. to encircle, to surround.

rodeo (rro•the´o) *m.* going around; round-about way *(camino más largo);* dodge *(regate);* roundup *(del ganado);* (fig.) hedging, beating around the bush.

rodilla (rro•thē´yâ) *f.* knee; **de —s,** on one´s knees, kneeling down; **hincar la —,** (fig.) to bend the knee.

rodillo, (rro•thē´yo) *m.* roller, cylinder; rolling pin *(de cocina).*

roedor, ra (rro•e•thor´, râ) *adj.* gnawing; —, *m.* rodent.

roer* (rro•er´) va. to gnaw; (fig.) to corrode.

rogar* (rro•gâr´) va. to entreat, to beg, to implore.

rojizo, za (rro•hē´so, sâ) *adj.* reddish.

rojo, ja (rro´ho, hâ) *adj.* red; —, *n.* (poi.) Red.

rollo (rro´yo) *m.* roller *(rodillo);* roll.

Roma (rro´mâ) *f.* Rome.

romance (rro•mân´se) *adj.* Romance; —. *m.* Spanish language *(idioma);* ballad *(poema);* novel of chivalry *(novela);* **hablar en —,** to speak plainly.

romano, na (rro•mâ´no, nâ) *adj.*

and *n.* Roman.

romanticismo (rro•mân•tē•sēz´-mo) *m.* romanticism.

romántico, ca (rro•mân´tē•ko, kâ) *adj.* romantic; —, *m.* romanticist.

rombo (rrom´bo) *m.* rhombus.

rompecabezas (rrom•pe•kâ•ve´-sâs) *m.* riddle, puzzle; jigsaw puzzle *(juego)*.

rompehielos (rrom•pe•ye´los) *m.* icebreaker.

rompenueces (rrom•pe•nwe´ses) *m.* nutcracker.

romper* (rrom•per´) *va.* to tear up *(desgarrar);* to break *(quebrar);* to ruin *(destrozar);* (fig.) to shatter, to disrupt, to interrupt; —, *vn.* to break; to break out *(prorrumpir).*

rompimiento (rrom•pē•myen´to) *m.* breaking; tearing; crack *(abertura);* (fig.) falling out *(riña);* disruption.

rompope (rrom•po´pe) *m.* (Mex.) eggnog.

ron (rron) *m.* rum.

roncar (rrong•kâr´) *vn.* to snore; (fig.) to roar, to howl.

ronco, ca (rrong´ko, kâ) *adj.* hoarse, husky.

roncha (rron´châ) *f.* welt.

rondar (rron•dâr´) *vn.* to patrol, to make one´s rounds; to roam around *(paseando);* —, *va.* to circle around.

ronquido (rrong•kē´tho) *m.* snore; (fig.) roar, howl.

ropa (rro´pâ) *f.* clothing, clothes: material *(tela);* — **blanca,** household linen; — **hecha,** ready-made clothes; — **interior** or — **íntima,** underwear, lingerie.

ropero (rro•pe´ro) *m.* wardrobe; —, **ra,** *n.* clothier.

rosa (rro´sâ) *f.* rose; **color de** —, rose color, pink.

rosado, da (rro•sâ´tho, thâ) *adj.* rose-colored, rosy.

rosario (rro•sâ´ryo) *m.* rosary; (mech.) chain pump.

rosquilla (rros•kē´yâ) *f.* roll, bun.

rostro (rros´tro) *m.* countenance, face; **hacer** —. to face, to resist.

rotación (rro•tâ•syon´) *f.* rotation.

rotativo, va (rro•tâ•tē´vo, vâ) *adj.* revolving, rotary.

rotatorio, ria (rro•tâ•to´ryo, ryâ) *adj.* rotatory.

roto, ta (rro´to, tâ) *adj.* broken, destroyed; tattered, ragged *(andrajoso);* (fig.) corrupt, debauched *(licencioso).*

rótula (rro´tū•lâ) *f.* kneecap.

rótulo (rro´tū•lo) *m.* label; poster *(letrero).*

rotundo, da (rro•tūn´do, dâ) *adj.* (fig.) rotund, sonorous; absolute, final *(terminante);* **éxito** —, complete success.

rozadura (rro•sâ•thū´râ) *f.*
(med.) scrape; rubbing, friction.

rozar (rro•sâr´) *va.* to clear *(el
terreno);* to graze on *(las bestias);* to rub, to scrape *(raer);* —
, *vn.* to graze, to touch slightly;
—se, to be very close.

rubéola (rrū•ve´o•lâ) *f.* German
measles.

rubí (rrū•vē´) *m.* ruby.

rubio, bia (rrū´vyo, vyâ) *adj.*
blond.

rubor (rrū•vor´) *m.* blush; bashfulness *(timidez).*

ruborizarse (rrū•vo•rē•sâr´se) *vr.*
to blush, to flush.

rúbrica (rrū´vrē•kâ) *f.* (eccl.)
rubric; flourish *(después de la
firma);* heading *(título);* **ser de
—,** to be of long standing.

rudeza (rrū•the´sâ) *f.* roughness,
crudeness; stupidity; (fig.)
rudeness.

rudimentos (rrū•thē•men´tos) *m.
pl.* rudiments.

rudo, da (rrū´tho, thâ) *adj.*
rough, crude, coarse; stupid
(torpe); (fig.) rude *(áspero).*

rueda (rrwe´thâ) *f.* wheel; turn
(turno); slice *(rebanada);* —
libre, freewheeling; **— de la fortuna,** wheel of fortune; **— del
timón,** (naut.) helm, wheel.

ruego (rrwe´go) *m.* request,
entreaty, plea. **rufián** (rrū•fyân´)
m. pander; (fig.) lowlife,

scoundrel.

rugido (rrū•hē´tho) *m.* roaring;
bellowing.

rugir (rrū•hēr´) *vn.* to roar; (fig.)
to bellow.

ruido (rrwē´tho) *m.* noise.

ruidoso, sa (rrwē•tho´so, sâ) *adj.*
noisy, clamorous, loud.

ruin (rrwēn´) *adj.* mean, vile,
despicable; avaricious, penny-
pinching *(avaro).*

ruina (rrwē´nâ) *f.* ruin.

ruindad (rrwēn•dâth´) *f.* meanness, baseness; avarice.

ruinoso, sa (rrwē•no´so, sâ) *adj.*
ruinous.

ruiseñor (rrwē•se•nyor´) *m.*
nightingale.

ruleta (rrū•le´tâ) *f.* roulette.

rumano, na (rrū•mâ´no, nâ) *n.*
and *adj.* Romanian.

rumbo (rrūm´bo) *m.* (naut.)
bearing, course, direction;
route, way *(camino);* (coll.)
pomp, show; **con — a,** bound
for.

rumiar (rrū•myâr´) *va.* to ruminate.

rumor (rrū•mor´) *m.* buzzing *(de
voces);* rumor, gossip *(voz);*
noise, din.

rupestre (rrū•pes´tre) *adj.* rock;
arte —, cave painting.

ruptura (rrūp•tū´râ) *f.* rupture,
break.

rural (rrū•râl´) *adj.* rural.

Rusia (rrū´syâ) *f.* Russia.

ruso, sa (rrū´so, sâ) *n.* and *adj.* Russian.

rústico, ca (rrūs´tē•ko, kâ) *adj.* rustic; **en —ca** or **a la —,** paperback; **—,** *m.* rustic, pea-

sant.

ruta (rrū´tâ) *f.* route.

rutina (rrū•tē´nâ) *f.* routine.

rutinario, ria (rrū•tē•nâ´ryo, ryâ) *adj.* routine.

S

sábado (sâ´vâ•tho) *m.* Saturday; Sabbath *(de los judíos)*

sabana (sâ•vâ´nâ) *f.* savanna.

sábana (sâ´vâ•nâ) *f.* bed sheet.

sabelotodo (sâ•ve•lo•to´tho) *m.* know-it-all.

saber* (sâ•ver´) *va.* to know, to find out *(conocer);* to be able to, to know how to *(ser diestro);* **— a,** to taste of; **—,** *m.* learning, knowledge; **a —,** namely, as follows; **es de —,** it is to be noted; **sin —lo,** unwittingly; **— de,** to know about; to hear from *(tener noticias de).*

sabiduría (sâ•vē•thū•rē´â) *f.* knowledge, wisdom.

sabiendas (sâ•vyen´dâs) **a —,** knowingly, consciously, deliberately.

sabio, bia (sâ´vyo, vyâ) *adj.* sage, wise; **—,** *n.* sage, scholar.

sabor (sâ•vor´) *m.* taste.

saborear (sâ•vo•re•âr´) *va.* to enjoy, to relish *(paladear);* to give a taste, to give zest

(sazonar); **—se,** to savor slowly, to enjoy keenly.

sabotaje (sâ•vo•tâ´he) *m.* sabotage.

sabotear (sâ•vo•te•âr´) *va.* to sabotage.

sabroso, sa (sâ•vro´so, sâ) *adj.* savory, delicious *(gustoso);* appetizing *(apetitoso);* (coll.) salty.

sabueso (sâ•vwe´so) *m.* bloodhound.

sacapuntas (sâ•kâ•pūn´tâs) *m.* pencil sharpener.

sacar (sâ•kâr´) *va.* to take out *(extraer);* to release *(librar);* to figure out *(averiguar);* to get *(obtener).*

sacarina (sâ•kâ•rē´nâ) *f.* saccharine.

sacerdote (sâ•ser•tho´te) *m.* priest.

saciar (sâ•syâr´) *va.* to satiate.

saciedad (sâ•sye•thâth´) *f.* satiety.

saco (sâ´ko) *m.* sack, bag

(bolsa); sackful, bagful (con-tenido); pillage (saqueo); coat (chaqueta); — **de yute,** gunny sack; **no echar en — roto,** not to forget, not to fail to keep in mind.

sacramental (sâ•krâ•men•tal´) adj. sacra-mental.

sacramento (sâ•krâ•men´to) m. sacrament.

sacrificar (sâ•krē•fē•kâr´) va. to sacrifice: to slaughter (las reses).

sacrificio (sâ•krē•fē´syo) m. sac-rifice.

sacrilegio (sâ•krē•le´hyo) m. sac-rilege.

sacro, cra (sâ´kro, krâ) adj. holy, sacred.

sacudida (sâ•kū•thē´thâ) f. shake, jerk, jolt.

sacudir (sâ•kū•thēr´) va. to shake, to jerk; to beat (gol-pear); to shake off (arrojar); — **se.** (coll.) to cough up (dinero): to dismiss brusquely (una per-sona).

saeta (sâ•e´tâ) f. arrow, dart (flecha); religious couplet, usu-ally sung (copla).

sagacidad (sâ•gâ•sē•thâth´) f. sagacity, shrewdness.

sainete (sâē•ne´te) m. farce, comedy (farsa); sauce (salsa); (fig.) zest, gusto.

sal (sal) f. salt (condimento); wit (ingenio); grace, charm (donai-re).

sala (sâ´lâ) f. hall; parlor, living room (de la casa); — **de clase,** classroom;— **chat,** chat room (internet); — **de espera,** waiting room; — **de hospital,** hospital ward; — **de muestras,** show-room; — **de recreo,** rumpus room.

salado, da (sâ•lâ´tho, thâ) adj. salted, salty (sabroso); graceful (gracioso); witty (chistoso).

salar (sâ•lâr´) va. to salt.

salario (sâ•lâ´ryo) m. salary.

salchicha (sâl´ chē´châ) f. small sausage; (mil.) long, narrow fuse.

salchichón (sal•chē•chon´) m. salami.

saldo (sâl´do) m. balance; sale items, remainders (mercancías).

salero (sâ•le´ro) m. salt shaker (vasito); salthouse (salín); (coll.) gracefulness.

salida (sâ•lē´thâ) f. leaving, departure (partida); environs (alrededores); projection (pro-yección); outcome, result (resultado); exit; (fig.) recourse, pretext (recurso); escape (esca-patoria); (mil.) sortie; golf tee; — **de sol,** sunrise; — **de teatro,** light wrap; (fig.) **tener buenas —s,** to be witty.

salino, na (sâ•lē′no, nâ) *adj.* saline.

salir* (sâ•lēr′) *vn.* to depart, to leave, to go out *(partir);* to free oneself *(librarse);* to appear, to come out *(aparecer);* to sprout *(brotar);* to come out *(una mancha);* to stick out *(sobresalir);* to turn out *(resultar);* to proceed, to come from *(proceder);* to begin, to start *(empezar);* to get rid of *(deshacerse de).*

salitre (sâ•lē′tre) *m.* saltpeter.

saliva (sâ•lē′vâ) *f.* saliva.

salmo (sâl′mo) *m.* psalm.

salmón (sâl•mon′) *m.* salmon.

salobre (sâ•lo′vre) *adj.* brackish, salty.

salón (sâ•lon′) *m.* salon; large hall *(sala grande);* — **de baile,** ballroom; — **de belleza,** beauty parlor.

salpicadura (sal•pē•kâ•thū′râ) *f.* splash, sprinkling.

salpicar (sâl•pē•kâr′) *va.* to splash; to sprinkle; (fig.) to punctuate, to sprinkle *(esparcir);* to skip around in, to jump around in *(la lectura).*

salpullido (sâl•pū•yē′tho) *m.* (med.) rash, prickly heat *(erupción);* flea bite *(de pulga).*

salsa (sâl′sâ) *f.* sauce, gravy, dressing; — **francesa,** French dressing; — **de to-mate,** tomato sauce, ketchup, catsup; —

inglesa, Worcestershire sauce; **estar en su** —, (fig.) to be right in one′s element.

salsera (sâl•se′râ) *f.* gravy boat.

saltar (sâl•târ′) *vn.* to skip *(cabriolar);* to jump *(brincar);* to bounce *(rebotar);* to fly *(volar);* to spurt *(surgir);* to break, to explode *(estallar);* to fall *(desprenderse);* (fig.) to stand out *(notarse);* to come out with *(disparar);* to flash in one′s mind *(recordar);* —, *va.* to leap, to jump *(atravesar);* to skip over *(omitir);* — **a los ojos,** to be obvious, to stand out.

salto (sâl′to) *m.* leap, jump, spring *(cabriola);* leapfrog *(juego);* abyss, chasm *(sima);* omission *(descuido);* palpitation *(del corazón);* — **de agua,** waterfall; **dar —s,** to jump; — **de altura, high** jump; — **mortal,** somersault; **en un —,** quickly.

saltón (sal•ton′) *m.* grasshopper; —, **ona,** *adj.* hopping, jumping; bulging *(protuberante).*

salubridad (sâ•lū•vrē•thâth′) *f.* healthfulness; **Departamento de S—,** Public Health Department.

salud (sâ•lūth′) *f.* health; salvation *(salvación);* **estar bien de** —, to be in good health; **estar mal de** —, to be in poor health;

¡—! to your health!

saludable (sâ•lū•thâ´vle) *adj.* wholesome, healthful; beneficial *(provechoso).*

saludar (sâ•lū•thâr´) *va.* to greet; (mil.) to salute; to hail, to acclaim *(aclamar).*

saludo (sâ•lū´tho) *m.* (mil.) salute; greeting.

salvación (sâl•vâ•syon´) *f.* salvation, deliverance.

salvado (sâl•vâ´tho) *m.* bran.

salvador, ra (sâl•vâ•thor´, râ) *adj.* saving; —, *n.* saver, savior.

salvadoreño, ña (sâl•vâ•tho•re´nyo, nyâ) *n.* and *adj.* Salvadorean.

salvaguardia (sâl•vâ•gwâr´thyâ) *m.* guard, watchman; —, *f.* safe-conduct; (fig.) protection, safeguard *(amparo).*

salvaje (sâl•vâ´he) *adj.* savage, wild.

salvajismo (sâl•va•hēz´mo) *m.* savagery.

salvamento (sâl•vâ•men´to) *m.* safety, safe place *(lugar);* rescue *(libramiento);* **escalera de** —, fire escape.

salvar (sâl•vâr´) *va.* to save, to rescue *(librar);* to avoid *(evitar);* to exclude *(excluir);* to jump *(saltar);* to cover, to pass over *(recorrer);* —**se,** to be saved.

salvavidas (sâl•vâ•vē´thâs) *m.* life pre-server.

salvo, va (sâl´vo, vâ) *adj.* saved, safe *(ileso);* omitted *(omitido);* **sano y —vo,** safe and sound; **estar a** —, to be safe; —**vo,** *adv.* except.

salvoconducto (sâl•vo•kon•dūk´to) *m.* safe-conduct.

samba (sâm´bâ) *f.* samba.

san (sân) *adj.* saint.

sanalotodo (sâ•nâ•lo•to´tho) *m.* panacea, cure-all.

sanar (sâ•nâr´) *va.* to heal; —, *vn.* to heal; to recover *(recobrar la salud).*

sanatorio (sâ•nâ•to´ryo) *m.* sanatorium, sanitarium.

sanción (sân•syon´) *f.* sanction.

sancionar (sân•syo•nâr´) *va.* to sanction.

sandalia (sân•dâ´lyâ) *f.* sandal.

sandez (sân•des´) *f.* folly, stupidity.

sandía (sân•dē´â) *f.* watermelon.

saneamiento (sâ•ne•â•myen´to) *m.* indemnification, going good; sanitation, making sanitary.

sangrar (sâng•râr´) *va.* to bleed; (fig.) to drain *(dar salida);* (coll.) to bleed white.

sangre (sâng´gre) *f.* blood; **a — fria,** in cold blood; **banco de** —, blood bank; **donador or donante de** —, blood donor; **tener** —, to be resolute, to have spirit.

sangría (sâng•grē´â) *f.* bleeding; tap *(en un árbol);* drain.

sangriento, ta (sâng•gryen´to, tâ) *adj.* bloody; bloodthirsty *(sanguinario).*

sanguijuela (sâng•gē•hwe´lâ) *f.* leech.

sanidad (sâ•nē•thâth´) *f.* healthiness; healthfulness *(salubridad);* **patente de —,** bill of health.

sanitario, ria (sâ•nē•tâ´ryo, ryâ) *adj.* sanitary.

sano, na (sâ´no, nâ) *adj.* healthy, sound; healthful *(saludable);* intact, complete *(sin daño);* sound *(sensato).*

sánscrito, ta (sâns´krē•to, tâ) *adj.* Sanskrit.

santidad (sân•tē•thâth´) *f.* sanctity, holiness.

santificación (sân•tē•fē•kâ•syon´) *f.* sanctification.

santificar (sân•tē•fē•kâr´) *va.* to sanctify; (coll.) to excuse.

santiguar (sân•tē•gwâr´) *va.* to make the sign of the cross over; (coll.) to whack *(abofetear);* **—se,** to cross oneself.

santísimo, ma (sân•tē´sē•mo, ma) *adj.* most holy.

santo, ta (sân´to, tâ) *adj.* holy; **—,** *n.* saint.

santuario (sân•twâ´ryo) *m.* sanc-tuary.

saña (sâ´nyâ) *f.* blind fury, rage.

sapo (sâ´po) *m.* toad.

saquear (sâ•ke•âr´) *va.* to sack, to pillage.

saqueo (sâ•ke´o) *m.* pillage, sacking.

sarampión (sâ•râm•pyon´) *m.* measles.

sarcasmo (sâr•kâz´mo) *m.* sarcasm.

sarcástico, ca (sâr•kâs´tē•ko, kâ) *adj.* sarcastic.

sardina (sâr•thē´nâ) *f.* sardine.

sargento (sâr•hen´to) *m.* sergeant.

sarpullido (sâr•pū•yē´tho) = **salpullido.**

sarro (sâ´rro) *m.* incrustation; tartar *(en los dientes).*

sartén (sâr•ten´) *f.* frying pan.

sastre (sâs´tre) *m.* tailor.

sastrería (sâs•tre•rē´â) *f.* tailor´s shop.

satélite (sâ•te´lē•te) *m.* satellite; (coll.) bailiff, constable *(alguacil);* (fig.) satellite, follower *(partidario).*

sátira (sâ´tē•râ) *f.* satire.

satírico, ca (sâ•tē´rē•ko, kâ) *adj.* satirical.

sátiro (sâ´tē•ro) *m.* satyr

satisfacción (sâ•tēs•fâk•syon´) *f.* satisfaction.

satisfacer* (sâ•tēs•fâ•ser´) *va.* to satisfy; **—se,** to get satisfaction.

satisfactorio, ria
(sâ•tēs•fâk•to´ryo, ryâ) *adj.* satisfactory.

satisfecho, cha (sâ•tēs•fe´cho, châ) *adj.* satisfied, content; self-satisfied *(presumido)*.

saturación (sâ•tū•râ•syon´) *f.* (chem.) saturation.

sauce (sâ´ū•se) *m.* (bot.) willow.

sazón (sâ•son´) *f.* maturity *(madurez);* time, season *(ocasión);* taste, flavor; **en —,** at the right time, opportunely; **a la —,** then, at that time.

sazonado, da (sâ•so•nâ´tho, thâ) *adj.* seasoned; (fig.) expressive, clever.

sazonar (sâ•so•nâr´) *va.* to season; **—se,** to ripen.

se (se) *pron.* himself (él); herself *(ella);* itself *(ello);* yourself *(usted);* themselves *(ellos, ellas);* yourselves *(ustedes);* each other *(idea recíproca);* — **dice,** it is said, one says, they say; — **resolvió el problema,** the problem was solved.

sebo (se´vo) *m.* tallow *(de herbívoro);* fat, grease.

seboso, sa (se•vo´so, sâ) *adj.* fat, greasy.

seca (se´kâ) *f.* drought, dry weather *(sequía);* sandbank *(secano);* (med.) swelling.

secador, ra (se•kâ•thor´) *m.* o *f.* dryer;— **de pelo,** blow-dryer.

secar (se•kâr´) *va.* to dry; (fig.) to annoy, to bother *(fastidiar);* — **se,** to dry out; to dry up *(un río);* to wither *(una planta);* to grow wizened *(enflaquecerse);* (fig.) to grow hard.

sección (sek•syon´) *f.* section; cross section *(perfil).*

secesión (se•se•syon´) *f.* secession.

seco, ca (se´ko, kâ) *adj.* dry; arid, barren *(árido);* lean *(flaco);* withered dead *(muerto);* (fig.) harsh, sharp *(áspero);* indifferent *(indiferente);* **en — co,** high and dry.

secretaría (se•kre•tâ•rē´â) *f.* secretaryship *(cargo);* secretariat *(oficina).*

secretario, ria (se•kre•tâ´ryo, ryâ) *n.* secretary; scribe *(escribano);* — **particular,** private secretary.

secreción (se•kre•syon´) *f.* secretion.

secreto, ta (se•kre´to, tâ) *adj.* secret; secretive *(callado);* —, *m.* secret; secrecy *(sigilio);* hiding place *(lugar);* **de — inviolable,** top-secret; **en —to,** in secret, in private.

secta (sek´tâ) *f.* sect; doctrine *(doctrina).*

secuela (se•kwe´lâ) *f.* sequel, result.

secuestrar (se•kwes•trâr´) *va.* to

abduct, to kidnap; to sequester *(confiscar).*

secuestro (se•kwes´tro) *m.* kidnapping.

secular (se•kū•lâr´) *adj.* secular; longseated, deep-rooted *(muy viejo).*

secundario, ria (se•kūn•dâ´ryo, ryâ) *adj.* secondary; **escuela —,** high school.

sed (seth) *f.* thirst; **tener —,** to be thirsty.

seda (se´thâ) *f.* silk.

sedante (se•thân´te) *m.* sedative, tranquilizer.

sedativo, va (se•thâ•tē´vo, vâ) *adj.* sedative.

sede (se´the) *f.* seat, headquarters *(residencia).*

sedentario, ria (se•then•tâ´ryo, ryâ) *adj.* sedentary.

sediento, ta (se•thyen´to, tâ) *adj.* dry, thirsty; eager, anxious *(ansioso).*

sedimento (se•thē•men´to) *m.* sediment.

seducción (se•thūk•syon´) *f.* seduction.

seducir* (se•thū•sēr´) *va.* to seduce; to bribe *(sobornar);* to attract, to charm, to captivate *(encantar).*

seductor, ra (se•thūk•tor´, râ) *adj.* attractive, fascinating, charming; seductive.

segar* (se•gar´) *va.* to reap, to mow, to harvest *(cosechar);* to cut *(cortar);* (fig.) to cut down, to restrict.

segmento (seg•men´to) *m.* segment.

segregación (se•gre•gâ•syon´) *f.* segregation; secretion.

segregar (se•gre•gâr´) *va.* to segregate; to secrete *(secretar).*

seguida (se•gē´thâ) *f.* series, succession; **en —,** immediately, at once; **de —,** consecutively, continuously.

seguido, da (se•gē´tho, thâ) *adj.* successive, in a row; straight *(en línea recta);* **todo —do,** straight ahead.

seguir* (se•gēr´) *va.* to follow *(ir detrás de);* to pursue *(perseguir);* to continue; to accompany *(acompañar);* to exercise, to profess *(ejercer);* to imitate *(imitar);* **—se,** to ensue, to result; (fig.) to originate, to proceed.

según (se•gūn´) *prep.* according to; **—,** *adv.* depending on how; **— aviso,** per advice; **— y como,** it depends.

segundo, da (se•gūn´do, dâ) *adj.* second; **en —do lugar,** secondly; **de —da mano,** secondhand; **—,** *m.* second.

seguridad (se•gū•rē•thâth´) *f.* security; surety *(fianza);* assurance, certainty *(certeza);*

safety *(fuera de peligro);* **caja de —,** safety deposit box; **fiador de —,** safety catch.

seguro, ra (se•gū′ro, râ) *adj.* secure, safe *(salvo);* certain, sure *(cierto);* firm, constant *(constante);* unsuspecting *(desprevenido);* **—,** *m.* insurance *(aseguración);* leave, safe-conduct *(salvoconducto);* certainty, assurance *(seguridad);* safety lock *(del fusil).*

seis (se′ēs) *adj.* and *m.* six.

selección (se•lek•syon′) *f.* selection, choice.

selecto, ta (se•lek′to, tâ) *adj.* select, choice.

selva (sel′vâ) *f.* forest.

sellar (se•yâr′) *va.* to seal; (fig.) to stamp *(estampar);* to finish up *(concluir).*

sello (se′yo) *m.* seal; stamp *(timbre);* (med.) wafer; **— de correo,** postage stamp; **poner el — a,** to finish up, to put the finishing touch on.

semáforo (se•mâ′fo•ro) *m.* traffic light *(de tránsito).*

semana (se•mâ′nâ) *f.* week.

semanal (se•mâ•nâl′) *adj.* weekly.

semanalmente (se•mâ•nâl•men′te) *adv.* weekly, every week.

semblante (sem•blân′te) *m.* face, countenance *(cara);* aspect *(apariencia).*

sembrado (sem•brâ′tho) *m.* cultivated field.

sembrador, ra (sem•brâ•thor′, râ) *n.* sower, planter.

sembrar* (sem•brâr′) *va.* to sow, to plant; (fig.) to scatter.

semejante (se•me•hân′te) *adj.* similar, like; **—,** *m.* fellowman.

semejanza (se•me•hân′sâ) *f.* resemblance, likeness.

semejar (se•me•hâr′) *vn.* to resemble.

sementar* (se•men•târ′) *va.* to seed, to plant.

semestral (se•mes•trâl′) *adj.* semiyearly, semiannual.

semestre (se•mes′tre) *m.* semester.

semianual (se•myâ•nwâl′) *adj.* semiannual.

semicírculo (se•mē•sēr′kū•lo) *m.* semicircle.

semifinal (se•mē•fē•nâl′) *adj.* and *f.* semifinal.

semilla (se•mē′yâ) *f.* seed.

senado (se•nâ′tho) *m.* senate.

senador (se•nâ•thor′) *m.* senator.

sencillez (sen•sē•yes′) *f.* simplicity; (fig.) candor, naiveté.

sencillo, lla (sen•sē′yo, yâ) *adj.* simple; lightweight *(ligero);* (fig.) candid, simple; **—,** *m.* change.

senda (sen′dâ) *f.* path, footpath.

sendero (sen•de′ro) *m.* path, trail.

senil (se•nēl´) *adj.* senile.

sensación (sen•sâ•syon´) *f.* sensation, feeling.

sensatez (sen•sâ•tes´) *f.* reasonableness, good sense.

sensato, ta (sen•sâ´to, tâ) *adj.* reasonable, sensible.

sensibilidad (sen•sē•vē•lē•thâth´) *f.* sensibility; sensitivity *(emotividad).*

sensible (sen•sē´vle) *adj.* sensible; sensitive *(susceptible);* marked *(perceptible);* regrettable, deep-felt.

sensitivo, va (sen•sē•tē´vo, vâ) *adj.* sensitive.

sentado, da (sen•tâ´tho, thâ) *adj.* seated; - **dar por —do,** to take for granted.

sentar* (sen•târ´) *va.* to seat; **—,** *vn.* to agree with *(un alimento);* to be becoming, to look good *(una prenda);* to be fitting *(convenir);* to please *(agradar);* **— bien,** to do good; **— mal,** to do harm; **—se,** to sit down.

sentencia (sen•ten´syâ) *f.* sentence; decision, judgment *(decisión).*

sentenciar (sen•ten•syâr´) *va.* to sentence; (fig.) to pass judgment on, to give one´s opinion of.

sentido (sen•tē´tho) *m.* sense; meaning *(significado);* feeling *(conocimiento);* direction *(direc-*

ción); **— práctico,** common sense; **—, da,** *adj.* sensitive.

sentimental (sen•tē•men•tâl´) *adj.* sentimental.

sentimiento (sen•tē•myen´to) *m.* sentiment; feeling *(impresión);* sorrow *(aflicción).*

sentir* (sen•tēr´) *va.* to feel; to regret, to be sorry about *(lamentar);* to hear *(oir);* to read well *(el verso);* to feel about *(juzgar);* to sense *(prever);* **—se,** to feel; to feel hurt *(formar queja).*

seña (se´nyâ) *f.* sign, mark, token; (mil.) password; **—s,** *pl.* address; **hacer —s,** to hail, to wave at.

señal (se•nyâl´) *f.* mark; trace *(vestigio);* sign *(de tránsito);* **— de alto** or **de parada,** stop sign.

señalar (se•nyâ•lâr´) *va.* to mark; to indicate, to point out *(indicar);* to deter-mine, to designate *(determinar);* **—se,** to excel.

señor (se•nyor´) *m.* owner, master *(dueño);* lord *(de un feudo);* gentleman; sir *(de cortesía);* Mr., Mister *(con el apellido).*

señora (se•nyo´râ) *f.* owner, mistress *(dueña);* lady; madam *(de cortesía);* Mrs. *(con el apellido);* wife *(esposa).*

señoría (se•nyo•rē´â) *f.* lordship.

señorío (se•nyo•rē´o) *m.* self-control, dignity *(gravedad);* sway, dominion *(dominio).*

señorita (se•nyo•rē′tä) *f.* young lady; Miss *(con el apellido);* (coll.) mistress of the house.

señuelo (se•nywe′lo) *m.* lure, enticement.

separable (se•pâ•râ′vle) *adj.* separable.

separación (se•pâ•râ•syon′) *f.* separation.

separado, da (se•pâ•râ′tho, thâ) *adj.* separate; **por —do,** under separate cover.

separar (se•pâ•râr′) *va.* to separate; to discharge *(de un empleo);* **—se,** to separate; to retire, to withdraw *(retirarse).*

sepelio (se•pe′lyo) *m.* burial.

septicemia (sep•tē•se′myâ) *f.* (med.) septicemia, blood poisoning.

septiembre (sep•tyem′bre) *m.* September.

séptimo, ma (sep′tē•mo, mâ) *m.* and *adj.* seventh.

septuagésimo, ma (sep•twâ•he′sē•mo, mâ) *adj.* seventieth.

sepulcro (se•pūl′kro) *m.* sepulcher, grave, tomb.

sepultar (se•pūl•târ′) *va.* to bury, to inter.

sepultura (se•pūl•tū′râ) *f.* sepulture, grave; burial.

sepulturero (se•pūl•tū•re′ro) *m.*

gravedigger.

sequedad (se•ke•thâth′) *f.* dryness; (fig.) curtness, sharpness.

sequía (se•kē′â) *f.* drought; (Sp. Am.) thirst, dryness *(sed).*

séquito (se′kē•to) *m.* retinue, suite, following.

ser* (ser) *vn.* to be; **llegar a —,** to become; **— de,** to be from; **—, m.** being, life.

serenata (se•re•nâ′tâ) *f.* serenade.

serenidad (se•re•nē•thâth′) *f.* serenity, quiet.

sereno (se•re′no) *m.* night air *(humedad);* night watchman *(vigilante);* **—, na,** *adj.* serene, calm, quiet; cloudless *(sin nubes).*

serie (se′rye) *f.* series.

seriedad (se•rye•thâth′) *f.* seriousness; sternness, gravity.

serio, ria (se′ryo, ryâ) *adj.* serious; stern, grave *(severo).*

sermón (ser•mon′) *m.* sermon.

serpentina (ser•pen•tē′nâ) *f.* streamer; (min.) serpentine.

serpiente (ser•pyen′te) *f.* serpent, snake.

serranía (se•rrâ•nē′â) *f.* mountainous region.

serrano, na (se•rrâ′no, nâ) *adj.* mountain; **—, n.** mountaineer.

serrucho (se•rrū′cho) *m.* handsaw.

servicial (ser•vē•syâl′) *adj.* compliant, accommodating.

servicio (ser•vē´syo) *m.* service; wear *(utilidad);* good turn *(favor);* worship *(culto);* table-ware *(vajilla);* chamber pot *(ori-nal);* — **diurno,** day service; — **nocturno,** night service.

servidor, ra (ser•vē•thor´, râ) *n.* servant; **su** —, your servant, at your service.

servidumbre (ser•vē•thūm´bre) *f.* servitude *(esclavitud);* staff of servants *(conjunto de criados);* *(fig.)* compulsion, drive *(de una pasión).*

servil (ser•vēl´) *adj.* servile.

servilleta (ser•vē•ye´tâ) *f.* nap-kin.

servir* (ser•vēr´) *va.* to serve; to wait on *(al que come);* —, *vn.* to serve; (mil.) to be on active duty; to be of use *(ser útil);* — **se,** to deign, to please; —**se de,** to make use of.

sesenta (se•sen´tâ) *m.* and *adj.* sixty.

sesgado, da (sez•gâ´tho, thâ) *adj.* oblique, slanting.

sesgar (sez•gâr´) *va.* to twist *(torcer);* to cut on the bias *(cor-tar).*

sesión (se•syon´) *f.* session; show, showing *(de una pelícu-la).*

seso (se´so) *m.* brain.

setecientos, tas (se•te•syen´tos, tâs) *m.* and *adj.* seven hun-dred.

setenta (se•ten´tâ) *m.* and *adj.* seventy.

seto (se´to) *m.* fence, enclosure; — **vivo,** hedge.

seudónimo (seū•tho´nē•mo) *m.* pseudonym.

severidad (se•ve•rē•thâth´) *f.* severity *(rigor);* strictness *(exactitud);* seriousness *(seriedad).*

severo, ra (se•ve´ro, râ) *adj.* severe; strict; serious.

sevillano, na (se•vē•yâ´no, nâ) *n.* and *adj.* Sevillian.

sexagésimo, ma (sek•sâ•he´sē•mo, mâ) *m.* and *adj.* sixtieth.

sexto, ta (ses´to, tâ) *m.* and *adj.* sixth.

si (sē) *conj.* if; even though, although *(aunque);* whether *(caso dudoso);* — **acaso,** or **por** — **acaso,** just in case; — **no,** if not; —, *m.* (mus.) si.

sí (sē´) *adv.* yes; **él** — **lo hizo,** he did do it; —, *m.* yes, assent; —, *pron.* himself (Al); herself *(ella);* itself *(ello);* yourself *(usted);* themselves *(ellos, ellas);* your-selves *(ustedes);* each other *(idea recíproca);* **de** —, in him-self; **de por** —, on his own, alone; **para** —, to himself; **dar de** —, to extend, to stretch;

volver en —, to come to, to recover one's senses.

siamés, esa (syâ•mes´, e´sâ) *adj.* and *n.* Siamese.

sicoanálisis (sē•ko•â•nâ´lē•sēs) *m.* or *f.* psychoanalysis.

sicología (sē•ko•lo•hē´â) *f.* psychology.

sicológico, ca (sē•ko•lo´hē•ko, kâ) *adj.* psychological.

sicólogo, ga (sē•ko´lo•go, gâ) *n.* psychologist.

sicosis (sē•ko´sēs) *f.* psychosis.

S.I.D.A.: síndrome de inmunodeficiencia adquirida A.I.D.S., acquired immunodeficiency syndrome.

siembra (syem´brâ) *f.* seedtime *(tiempo);* sowing, seeding *(acto);* sown field *(campo sembrado).*

siempre (syem´pre) *adv.* always; in any event *(en todo caso);* — **jamás,** for ever and ever.

siempreviva (syem•pre•vē´vâ) *f.* (bat.) everlasting.

sien (syen) *f.* temple.

sierpe (syer´pe) *f.* serpent, snake.

sierra (sye´rrâ) *f.* saw; mountain range *(cordillera).*

siete (sye´te) *m.* and *adj.* seven.

sigilo (sē•hē´lo) *m.* seal *(sello);* secret, reserve *(secreto).*

sigiloso, sa (sē•hē•lo´so, sâ) *adj.* reserved, silent.

sigla (sē´glâ) *f.* initial *(letra inicial);* abbreviation *(abreviatura).*

siglo (sē´glo) *m.* century.

significación (sēg•nē•fē•kâ•syon´) *f.* significance.

significado (sēg•nē•fē•kâ´tho) *m.* meaning.

significar (sēg•nē•fē•kâr´) *va.* to signify, to mean; to make known *(hacer saber).*

significativo, va (sēg•nē•fē•kâ•tē´vo, va) *adj.* significant, meaningful.

signo (sēg´no) *m.* sign *(señal);* mark *(de escritura).*

siguiente (sē•gyen´te) *adj.* following, successive; **al día —,** on the following day, next day.

sílaba (sē´lâ•vâ) *f.* syllable.

silbar (sēl•vâr´) *va.* to hiss; —, *vn.* to whistle.

silbato (sēl•vâ´to) *m.* whistle.

silbido (sēl•vē´tho) *m.* whistle; hissing *(burla);* whistling.

silenciador (sē•len•syâ•thor´) *m.* silencer; (auto.) muffler.

silencio (sē•len´syo) *m.* silence; ¡—! *interj.* quiet! hush!

silencioso, sa (sē•len•syo´so, sâ) *adj.* silent.

silueta (sē•lwe´tâ) *f.* silhouette, outline.

silvestre (sēl•ves´tre) *adj.* wild.

silla (sē´yâ) *f.* chair; saddle *(de*

montar).

sillón (sē•yon´) *m.* easy chair, overstuffed chair; sidesaddle *(de montar).*

simbólico, ca (sēm•bo´lē•ko, kâ) *adj.* symbolical.

simbolismo (sēm•bo•lēz´mo) *m.* symbolism.

simbolizar (sēm•bo•lē•sâr´) *va.* to symbolize.

símbolo (sēm´bo•lo) *m.* symbol; adage *(dicho).*

simetría (sē•me•trē´â) *f.* symmetry.

simétrico, ca (sē•me´trē•ko, kâ) *adj.* symmetrical.

simiente (sē•myen´te) *f.* seed *(semilla).*

símil (sē´mēl) *m.* resemblance; (rhet.) simile; —, *adj.* similar.

similar (sē•mē•lâr´) *adj.* similar.

similitud (sē•mē•lē•tūth´) *f.* similitude, similarity.

simpatía (sēm•pâ•tē´â) *f.* sympathy, empathy; charm *(encanto);* liking *(cariño);* affinity *(afinidad);* **tener — por,** to like, to find pleasant and congenial.

simpático, ca (sēm•pâ´tē•ko, kâ) *adj.* sympathetic *(compasivo);* likable, pleasant, nice *(agradable).*

simpatizar (sēm•pâ•tē•sâr´) *vn.* to get along well; — **con,** to feel at home with, to feel kindly toward.

simple (sēm´ple) *adj.* simple; single *(sin duplicar);* pure *(puro);* insipid *(insípido);* —, *m.* and *f.* simpleton.

simpleza (sēm•ple´sâ) *f.* foolishness, stupidity.

simplicidad (sēm•plē•sē•thâth´) *f.* simplicity.

simplificar (sēm•plē•fē•kâr´) *va.* to simplify.

simulación (sē•mū•lâ•syon´) *f.* simulation.

simulacro (sē•mū•lâ´kro) *m.* simulacrum, image *(imagen);* phantasm, apparition *(aparición);* simulation, pretense *(simulación);* (mil.) maneuvers, war games.

simular (sē•mū•lâr´) *va.* to simulate, to feign, to pretend.

simultáneo, nea (sē•mūl•tâ´ne•o, ne•â) *adj.* simultaneous.

sin (sēn) *prep.* without; not counting *(aparte de);* — **embargo,** notwithstanding, nevertheless; — **duda,** doubtlessly; — **reserva,** without reservation; — **saberlo,** unawares, without knowing it; — **noticia de,** without news from; — **valor,** of no value, without value; — **piedad,** without pity, pitiless; — **nombre,** nameless, without a name; **telegrafía — hilos,** wireless telegraphy.

sinagoga (sē•nâ•goˊgâ) *f.* synagogue.

sinceridad (sēn•se•rē•thâthˊ) *f.* sincerity.

sincero, ra (sēn•seˊro, râ) *adj.* sincere.

sincronizar (sēng•kro•nē•sârˊ) *va.* to synchronize.

sindicar (sēn•dē•kârˊ) *va.* to accuse *(acusar);* to inform on *(informar contra);* to unionize *(agremiar);* to syndicate *(de dinero o valores);* —**se,** to become unionized.

sindicato (sēn•dē•kâˊto) *m.* syndicate; — **de obreros,** labor union.

sinfonía (sēm•fo•nēˊâ) *f.* symphony.

singular (sēng•gū•lârˊ) *adj.* singular.

singularizar (sēng•gū•lâ•rē•sârˊ) *va.* to distinguish; (gram.) to singularize; —**se,** to distinguish oneself.

siniestra (sē•nyesˊtrâ) *f.* left hand; left side, left.

siniestro, tra (sē•nyesˊtro, trâ) *adj.* left; (fig.) sinister; —, *m.* loss.

sinnúmero (sēn•nūˊme•ro) *m.* endless amount, great many, no end.

sino (sēˊno) *conj.* but, but rather; except *(menos).*

sinónimo, ma (sē•noˊnē•mo, mâ) *adj.* synonymous; —, *m.* synonym.

sinopsis (sē•nopˊsēs) *f.* synopsis.

sinrazón (sēn•rrâ•sonˊ) *f.* injustice, wrong.

sinsonte (sēn•sonˊte) *m.* mockingbird.

sintaxis (sēn•tâkˊsēs) *f.* syntax.

síntesis (sēnˊte•sēs) *f.* synthesis.

sintético, ca (sēn•teˊtē•ko, kâ) *adj.* synthetic.

síntoma (sēnˊto•mâ) *m.* symptom.

sintonización (sēn•to•nē•sâ•syonˊ) *f.* (rad.) tuning in.

sintonizar (sēn•to•nē•sârˊ) *va.* (rad.) to tune in.

sinvergüenza (sēm•ber•gwenˊsâ) *adj.* roguish, rascally; —, *m.* and *f.* scoundrel.

siquiatra (sē•kyâˊtrâ) *m.* psychiatrist.

síquico, ca (sēˊkē•ko, kâ) *adj.* psychic.

siquiera (sē•kyeˊrâ) *conj.* even if, although; —, *adv.* at least *(al menos);* even; **ni** —, not even.

sirena (sē•reˊnâ) *f.* siren; mermaid *(ninfa marina);* (fig.) vamp, siren.

sirviente, ta (sēr•vyenˊte, tâ) *n.* servant.

sísmico, ca (sēzˊmē•ko, kâ) *adj.* seismic; **movimiento** —, earthquake.

sismógrafo (sēz•mo´grâ•fo) *m.* seismograph.

sistema (sēs•te´mâ) *m.* system; — **escolar,** school system.

sistemático, ca (sēs•te•mâ´tē•ko, kâ) *adj.* systematic.

sitio (sē´tyo) *m.* place; country home *(hacienda);* — **web,** web site.

situación (sē•twâ•syon´) *f.* position, situation.

situado, da (sē•twâ´tho, thâ) *adj.* situated, located.

situar (sē•twâr´) *va.* to place, to situate; to assign *(fondos).*

sobar (so•vâr´) *va.* to knead, to soften*(ablandar);* to handle, to paw *(manosear);* to pummel, to beat *(pegar);* to annoy *(molestar).*

soberanía (so•ve•râ•nē´â) *f.* sovereignty.

soberano, na (so•ve•râ´no, nâ) *adj.* and *n.* sovereign.

soberbia (so•ver´vyâ) *f.* pride, haughtiness; magnificence, splendor *(de un edificio);* anger, wrath *(cólera).*

soberbio, bia (so•ver´vyo, vyâ) *adj.* proud, haughty; superb, magnificent; wrathful, angry.

sobornar (so•vor•nâr´) *va.* to bribe.

soborno (so•vor´no) *m.* bribe.

sobra (so´vrâ) *f.* excess, surplus; —**s,** pl. leftovers; waste *(dese-*

chos); **de** —, more than enough.

sobrante (so•vrân´te) *m.* residue, surplus; *adj.* leftover, excess.

sobrar (so•vrâr´) *vn.* to be too much, to be unnecessary *(estar de más);* to be more than enough *(haber más que lo necesario);* to remain, to be left over *(quedar);* —, *va.* to outdo.

sobre (so´vre) *prep.* on *(encima de);* about *(acerca de);* in addition to *(además de);* —**cero,** above zero; — **todo,** above all; —**lo cual,** on which, about which; —, *m.* envelope.

sobrecarga (so•vre•kâr´gâ) *f.* surcharge *(cobro);* extra load, overload *(carga);*packing cord *soga); fig.)* added annoyance *(molestia).*

sobrecargar (so•vre•kâr•gâr´) *va.* to overload; to fell *(una costura).*

sobreexcitar (so•vre´ek•sē•târ´) *va.* to overexcite.

sobrehumano, na (sov•reū•mâ´no, nâ) *adj.* superhuman.

sobrellevar (so•vre•ye•vâr´) *va.* to ease, to help with; (fig.) to put up with, to tolerate *(soportar).*

sobremanera (so•vre•mâ•ne´râ) *adv.* exceedingly.

sobrenatural (so•vre•nâ•tū•râl´)

adj. supernatural.

sobrenombre (so•vre•nom´bre) *m.* nickname.

sobrentender* (so•vren•ten•der´) *va.* to understand, to deduce; —**se,** to go without saying.

sobrepasar (so•vre•pâ•sâr´) *va.* to surpass.

sobrepeso (so•vre•pe´so) *m.* overweight.

sobreponer* (so•vre•po•ner´) *va.* to superimpose, to put on top of; —**se,** to master the situation, to win out, to prevail.

sobreproducción (so•vre•pro•thūk•syon´) *f.* overproduction.

sobresaliente (so•vre•sâ•lyen´te) *adj.* projecting; (fig.) outstanding; —, *m.* and *f.* substitute, understudy; —, *m.* excellent.

sobresalir* (so•vre•sâ•ler´) *vn.* to project, to stick out; (fig.) to excel, to stand out.

sobresaltado, da (so•vre•sâl•tâ´tho, thâ) *adj.* frightened, startled.

sobresalto (so•vre•sâl´to) *m.* fright, scare, start; **de** —, suddenly, unexpectedly.

sobrevenir* (so•vre•ve•ner´) *vn.* to come immediately afterward *(después);* to happen unexpectedly *(improvisamente);* to come at the same time *(al mismo tiempo);* — **a,** to come right on top of.

sobreviviente (so•vre•vē•vyen´te) *m.* and *f.* survivor; —, *adj.* surviving.

sobrevivir (so•vre•vē•vēr´) *vn.* to survive; — **a,** to outlive, to survive.

sobriedad (so•vrye•thâth´) *f.* sobriety, temperance.

sobrina (so•vrē´nâ) *f.* niece.

sobrino (so•vrē´no) *m.* nephew.

sobrio, bria (so´vryo, vryâ) *adj.* sober, temperate, moderate.

socavar (so•kâ•vâr´) *va.* to undermine, to weaken.

sociabilidad (so•syâ•vē•lē•thâth´) *f.* sociability.

sociable (so•syâ´vle) *adj.* sociable.

social (so•syâl´) *adj.* social.

socialismo (so•syâ•lēz´mo) *m.* socialism.

socialista (so•syâ•lēs´tâ) *m.* and *f.* socialist; —, *adj.* socialistic, socialist.

socializar (so•syâ•lē•sâr´) *va.* to socialize.

sociedad (so•sye•thâth´) *f.* society; (com.)company; — **anónima,** corporation; —**benéfica,** charity, welfare organization.

socio, cia (so´syo, syâ) *n.* associate, partner; member *(miembro);* (coll.) fellow, guy.

sociología (so•syo•lo•hē´â) *f.* sociology.

sociólogo (so•syo´lo•go) *m.* sociologist.

socorrer (so•ko•rrer´) *va.* to aid, to help; to pay in part, to pay on account *(pagar)*.

socorro (so•ko´rro) *m.* help, aid.

sodio (so´thyo) *m.* sodium.

soez (so•es´) *adj.* mean, vile.

sofá (so•fâ´) *m.* sofa, couch, lounge.

sofocación (so•fo•kâ•syon´) *f.* suffocation, smothering.

sofocante (so•fo•kân´te) *adj.* suffocating, stifling.

sofocar (so•fo•kâr´) *va.* to suffocate *(ahogar)*; to put out, to extinguish *(apagar)*; to harass *(importunar)*; to inflame *(inquietar)*; to embarrass *(avergonzar)*.

soga (so´gâ) *f.* rope.

soja (so´hâ) *f.* (bot.) soybean.

sojuzgar (so•hūz•gâr´) *va.* to conquer, to subdue.

sol (sol) *m.* sun; sunlight *(luz)*; day *(día)*; monetary unit of Peru; (mus.) sol; **hace—,** it is sunny; **puesta del —,** sunset; **rayo de —,** sunbeam; **salida del —,** sunrise.

solapa (so•lâ´pâ) *f.* lapel *(del vestido)*; pretense, cover, pretext *(ficción)*.

solapado, da (so•lâ•pâ´tho, thâ) *adj.* cunning, crafty, artful.

solapar (so•lâ•pâr´) *va.* to put lapels on *(un vestido)*; to conceal, to hide; —, *vn.* to drape.

solaz (so•lâs´) *m.* solace, consolation, change; **a —,** gladly.

solazar (so•lâ•sâr´) *va.* to solace, to comfort.

soldado (sol•dâ´tho) *m.* soldier; **— de a caballo,** cavalryman; **— de marina,** marine; **— de reserva,** reservist.

soldadura (sol•dâ•thū´râ) *f.* soldering; solder *(materia)*.

soldar* (sol•dâr´) *va.* to solder; (fig.) to connect *(unir)*; to right, to make amends for *(enmendar)*; **—se,** to stick together.

soleado, da (so•le•â´tho, thâ) *adj.* sunny.

soledad (so•le•thâth´) *f.* solitude; lonely place *(sitio)*; loneliness *(melancolía)*.

solemne (so•lem´ne) *adj.* solemn; (coll.)awful, real, absolute.

solemnidad (so•lem•nē•thâth´) *f.* solemnity; formality *(formalidad)*.

solemnizar (so•lem•nē•sâr´) *va.* to solemnize.

soler* (so•ler´) *vn.* to be accustomed to, to be in the habit of; to be customary for *(ser frecuente)*.

solicitante (so•lē•sē•tân´te) *m.* and *f.* applicant.

solicitar (so•lē•sē•târ´) *va.* to try for *(pretender)*; to apply for *(gestionar);* (fig.) to attract.

solícito, ta (so•lē´sē•to, tâ) *adj.* solicitous, careful.

solicitud (so•lē•sē•tūth´) *f.* solicitude; application, request, petition *(memorial);* **a —,** on request.

solidaridad (so•lē•thâ•rē•thâth´) *f.* solidarity.

solidez (so•lē•thes´) *f.* solidity; volume *(volumen).*

sólido, da (so´lē•tho, thâ) *adj.* solid; strong, robust *(vigoroso);* **—,** *m.* solid.

soliloquio (so•lē•lo´kyo) *m.* soliloquy.

solista (so•lēs´tâ) *m.* and *f.* soloist.

solitaria (so•lē•tâ´ryâ) *f.* tapeworm.

solitario, ria (so•lē•tâ´ryo, ryâ) *adj.* solitary, lonely; **—,** *m.* solitaire; hermit *(ermitaño).*

solo (so´lo) *m.* (mus.) solo; **—, la,** *adj.* alone; only, sole *(único);* **a —las,** alone, unaided.

sólo (so´lo) *adv.* only.

solomillo (so•lo•mē´yo) or **solomo** (so•lo´mō) *m.* sirloin.

soltar* (sol•târ´) *va.* to untie, to loosen *(desatar);* to free *(dar libertad a);* to let go of *(desasir);* to release, to let out *(dar salida a);* to explain *(explicar);* to resolve *(resolver);* to come out with *(decir);* **—se,**

to become adept *(adquirir agilidad);* to loosen up, to unwind *(relajar);* to begin *(empezar).*

soltero, ra (sol•te´ro, râ) *adj.* unmarried, single; **—,** *m.* bachelor; **—,** *f.* bachelor girl.

solterón, ona (sol•te•ron´, o´nâ) *adj.* old and still single; **—,** *f.* old maid, spinster; **—,** *m.* old bachelor.

soltura (sol•tū´râ) *f.* loosening; explanation; freedom, agility *(en los movimientos);* openness, frankness *(desvergüenza);* fluency *(de dicción);* release, freeing *(de un preso).*

soluble (so•lū´vle) *adj.* soluble.

solución (so•lū•syon´) *f.* solution.

solucionar (so•lū•syo•nâr´) *va.* to settle, to resolve.

solvencia (sol•ven´syâ) *f.* solvency.

solventar (sol•ven•târ´) *va.* to settle, to liquidate.

sollozar (so•yo•sâr´) *vn.* to sob.

sollozo (so•yo´so) *m.* sob.

sombra (som´brâ) *f.* shade, shadow *(proyección);* darkness *(oscuridad);* shade, spirit *(fantasma);* favor *(asilo);* **hacer —,** to be shady; **tener buena —,** to be pleasant, to be nice; **esto no tiene — de verdad,** there´s not a trace of truth in this.

sombrear (som•bre•âr´) *va.* to

shade.

sombrero (som•bre′ro) *m.* hat.

sombrilla (som•bre′yâ) *f.* parasol.

sombrío, bría (som•bre′o, bre′â) *adj.* shady, shaded; (fig.) gloomy, bleak *(tétrico).*

someter (so•me•ter′) *va.* to subject, to subdue *(sujetar);* to conquer, to vanquish *(conquistar);* to submit *(encomendar);* —**se,** to humble oneself, to submit.

somnolencia (som•no•len′syâ) *f.* sleepiness, drowsiness.

son (son) *m.* music, soft notes; news *(noticia);* pretext *(pretexto);* manner *(modo);* **a — de,** at the sound of; **en —de,** as, like, in the manner of; **en — de burla,** in the mocking way, mockingly.

sonámbulo, la (so•nâm′bū•lo, lâ) *n.* and *adj.* somnambulist.

sonar* (so•nâr′) *va.* to play *(un instrumento);* to sound; to blow *(las narices);* —, *vn.* to sound: to sound right, to sound familiar *(ofrecerse al recuerdo);* to seem *(parecer).*

sonata (so•nâ′tâ) *f.* (mus.) sonata.

sondeo (son•de′o) *m.* sounding; probing.

soneto (so•ne′to) *m.* sonnet.

sónico, ca (so′ne•ko, kâ) *adj.*

sonic.

sonido (so•ne′tho) *m.* sound; (fig.) news *(noticia).*

sonoro, ra (so•no′ro, râ) *adj.* sonorous.

sonreir (son•rre•er′) *vn.* and *vr.* to smile; — **burlonamente,** to snicker, to smile sarcastically.

sonriente (son•rryen′te) *adj.* smiling.

sonrisa (son•rre′sâ) smile.

sonrojar (son•rro•hâr′) *va.* to make blush; —**se,** to blush.

sonrojo (son•rro′ho) *m.* blush; impropriety *(improperio).*

sonrosado, da (son•rro•sâ′tho, thâ) *adj.* pink.

sonsacar (son•sâ•kâr′) *va.* to make off with.

soñador, ra (so•nyâ•thor′, râ) *n.* dreamer.

soñar* (so•nyâr′) *va.* and *vn.* to dream; — **despierto,** to daydream; — **con,** to dream of; ¡ni —lo! I wouldn't dream of it!

soñoliento, ta (so•nyo•lyen′to, tâ) *adj.* sleepy, drowsy; soporific *(soporífero);* (fig.) dull, lazy *(tardo).*

sopa (so′pâ) *f.* soup; **estar hecho una —,** to be sopping wet.

soplar (so•plâr′) *vn.* to blow; —, *va.* to blow away: to steal *(robar);* to blow up, to inflate *(inflar);* to inspire *(inspirar);* to whisper *(apuntar);* (fig.) to squeal on *(delatar)*.

soplete (so•ple´te) *m.* blowtorch.

soplo (so´plo) *m.* blowing; gust *(del viento);* (fig.) moment *(instante);* (coll.) piece of advice, tip *(aviso);* tale *(delación)*.

sopor (so•por´) *m.* drowsiness, sleepiness; stupor *(estado morboso)*.

soporte (so•por´te) *m.* support.

soportar (so•por•târ´) *va.* to support, to bear, to hold up *(cargar);* (fig.) to tolerate, to endure *(tolerar)*.

soprano (so•prâ´no) *f.* (mus.) soprano.

sorber* (sor•ver´) *va.* to sip, to suck; to draw in, to soak up; to absorb *(atraer);* to swallow up *(absorber)*.

sorbete (sor•ve´te) *m.* sherbet.

sorbo (sor´vo) *m.* sipping; sip, taste *(líquido);* **tomar a —s,** to sip.

sordera (sor•the´râ) *f.* deafness.

sordo, da (sor´tho, thâ) *adj.* deaf; silent, mute *(callado);* muffled *(no claro);* (gram.) voiceless.

sordomudo, da (sor•tho•mū´tho, thâ) *adj.* deaf and dumb; —, *n.* deafmute.

sorprendente (sor•pren•den´te) *adj.* surprising.

sorprender (sor•pren•der´) *va.* to surprise.

sorpresa (sor•pre´sâ) *f.* surprise; **de —,** unawares.

sortear (sor•te•âr´) *va.* to draw lots for; to dodge, to sidestep *(evitar);* to maneuver with *(al toro)*.

sorteo (sor•te´o) *m.* drawing lots; dodging.

sortija (sor•tē´hâ) *f.* ring; ringlet.

sortilegio (sor•tē•le´hyo) *m.* sorcery, witchcraft.

sosegado, da (so•se•gâ´tho, thâ) *adj.* quiet, peaceful, composed.

sosegar* (so•se•gâr´) *va.* to calm, to quiet; —, *vn.* to rest, to quiet down; **—se,** to calm down.

sosiego (so•sye´go) *m.* tranquillity, serenity, calm.

soslayo, ya (soz•lâ´yo, yâ) *adj.* oblique; **al —yo,** obliquely, on a slant; **de —yo,** sideways, sidelong; **mirar de —yo,** to look askance at.

sospecha (sos•pe´châ) *f.* suspicion.

sospechar (sos•pe•châr´) *va.* and *vn.* to suspect.

sospechoso, sa (sos•pe•cho´so, sâ) *adj.* suspicious.

sostén (sos•ten´) *m.* support *(apoyo);* brassiere *(prenda);* steadiness *(del buque)*.

sostener* (sos•te•ner´) *va.* to support, to sustain, to hold up; (fig.) to back, to uphold *(apoyar);* to bear, to endure *(toler-*

ar); to maintain, to provide for *(mantener);* —**se** to support oneself.

sostenido, da (sos•te•ne̅´tho, thâ) *adj.* sustained; —, *m.* (mus.) sharp.

sostenimiento (sos•te•ne̅•myen´- to) *m.* sustenance, support.

sotana (so•tâ´nâ) *f.* cassock; (coll.) beating, drubbing *(pal- iza).*

sótano (so´tâ•no) *m.* basement, cellar.

soya (so´yâ) *f.* soybean.

su (su̅) *pron.* his *(de él);* her *(de ella);* its; one´s *(de uno).*

suave (swâ´ve) *adj.* smooth, soft, suave *(blando);* gentle, mild *(tranquilo).*

suavidad (swâ•ve•thâth´) *f.* soft- ness, suaveness, smoothness; gentleness.

suavizar (swâ•ve•sâr´) *va.* to soften; to mollify, to pacify *(apaciguar);* —**se,** to calm down.

subalterno, na (su̅•vâl•ter´no, nâ) *adj.* inferior, subordinate.

subarrendar* (su̅•vâ•rren•dâr´) *va.* to sublet, to sublease.

subasta (su̅•vâs´tâ) *f.* auction; open bid-ding *(de contrata).*

subconsciente (su̅v•kon•syen´te) *adj.* subconscious.

subdesarrollado, da (suv•the•sâ•rro•yâ´ tho, thâ)

adj. underdeveloped.

súbdito, ta (su̅v´the̅•to, tâ) *n.* and *adj.* subject.

subdividir (su̅v•the̅•ve̅•the̅r´) *va.* to subdivide.

subdivisión (su̅v•the̅•ve̅•syon´) *f.* subdivision.

subgerente (su̅v•he•ren´te) *m.* assistant manager.

subida (su̅•ve̅´thâ) *f.* climb, ascent.

subido, da (su̅•ve̅´tho, thâ) *adj.* intense, penetrating *(fuerte);* fine, excellent *(fino);* very high *(elevado).*

subir (su̅•ve̅r´) *vn.* to climb up, to go up; to come to, to amount to *(importar);* to rise, to swell *(crecer);* (fig.) to get worse *(agravarse):* to progress, to advance *(ascender).*

súbitamente (su̅•ve̅•tâ•men´te) *adv.* suddenly.

súbito, ta (su̅´ve̅•to, tâ) *adj.* sud- den, hasty; unforeseen *(impre- visto);* **de —,** suddenly.

subjuntivo (su̅v•hu̅n•te̅´vo) *m.* (gram.) subjunctive.

sublevación (su̅•vle•vâ•syon´) *f.* revolt, rebellion.

sublevar (su̅•vle•vâr´) *va.* to excite to rebellion; —, *vn.* to revolt, to rebel.

sublime (su̅•vle̅´me) *adj.* sub- lime, exalted.

submarino (su̅v•mâ•re̅´no) *m.*

submarine.

subnormal (sūv•nor•mâl´) *adj.* subnormal.

subordinado, da (sū•vor•thē•nâ´tho, thâ) *n.* and *adj.* subordinate.

subordinar (sū•vor•thē•nâr´) *va.* to subordinate.

subrayar (sū•vrâ•yâr´) va. to underline, to underscore.

subscribir (sūvs•krē•vēr´) = **suscribir.**

subscripción (sūvs•krēp•syon´) = **suscripción.**

subscrito (sūvs•krē´to) = **suscrito.**

subsecretario, ria (sūv•se•kre•tâ´ryo, ryâ) *n.* undersecretary, assistant secretary.

subsecuente (sūv•se•kwen´te) *adj.* subsequent, following.

subsidiario, ria (sūv•sē•thyâ´ryo, ryâ) *adj.* subsidiary.

subsidio (sūv•sē´thyo) *m.* subsidy.

subsiguiente (sūv•sē•gyen´te) *adj.* subsequent, following.

subsistencia (sūv•sēs•ten´syâ) *f.* subsistence.

subsistir (sūv•sēs•tēr´) *vn.* to subsist.

substancia (sūvs•tân´syâ) = **sustancia.**

substancial (sūvs•tân•syâl´) = **sustancial.**

substancioso (sūvs•tân•syo´so)=**sustancioso.**

substitución(sūvs•tē•tū•syon´)=**sustitución.**

substituir (sūvs•tē•twēr´) = **sustituir.**

substituto (sūvs•tē•tū´to) = **sustituto.**

substracción (sūvs•trâk•syon´) =**sustracción.**

substraer (sūvs•trâ•er´) = **sustraer.**

subteniente (sūv•te•nyen´te) *m.* second lieutenant.

subterráneo, nea (sūv•te•rrâ´-ne•o, ne•â) *adj.* subterraneous, subterranean.

subtitulo (sūv•tē´tū•lo) *m.* subtitle.

suburbano, na (sū•vūr•vâ´no, nâ) *adj.* suburban; —, *n.* suburbanite.

suburbio (sū•vūr´vyo) *m.* suburb.

subvención (sūv•ven•syon´) *f.* subsidy, endowment.

subversión (sūv•ver•syon´) *f.* subversion, overthrow.

subversivo, va (sūv•ver•sē´vo, vâ) *adj.* subversive.

subyugar (sūv•yū•gâr´) *va.* to subdue, to subjugate.

succión (sūk•syon´) *f.* suction.

suceder (sū•se•ther´) *vn.* to happen *(ocurrir);* to follow, to succeed *(seguir);* to inherit *(heredar).*

sucesión (sū•se•syon´) *f.* succession; issue, offspring *(prole).*

sucesivo, va (sū•se•sē´vo, vâ) *adj.* successive; **en lo —vo,** from now on, in the future.

suceso, (sū•se´so) *m.* event *(acontecimiento);* outcome *(resultado);* success *(buen éxito).*

suciedad (sū•sye•thâth´) *f.* filth, dirt *(inmundicia);* dirtiness, filthiness *(calidad de sucio);* (fig.) dirty remark.

sucio, cia (sū´syo, syâ) *adj.* dirty, filthy.

suculento, ta (sū•kū•len´to, *adj.* subtropical.

suburbano, na (sū•vūr•vâ´no, nâ) *adj.* suburban; —, *n.* suburbanite.

suburbio (sū•vūr´vyo) *m.* suburb.

subvención (sūv•ven•syon´) *f.* subsidy, endowment.

subversión (sūv•ver•syon´) *f.* subversion, overthrow.

subversivo, va (sūv•ver•sē´vo, vâ) *adj.* subversive.

subyugar (sūv•yū•gâr´) *va.* to subdue, to subjugate.

succión (sūk•syon´) *f.* suction.

suceder (sū•se•ther´) *vn.* to happen *(ocurrir);* to follow, to succeed *(seguir);* to inherit *(heredar).*

sucesión (sū•se•syon´) *f.* succession; issue, offspring *(prole).*

sucesivo, va (sū•se•sē´vo, vâ) *adj.* successive; **en lo —vo,** from now on, in the future.

suceso (sū•se´so) *m.* event *(acontecimiento);* outcome *(resultado);* success *(buen éxito).*

sucesor, ra (sū•se•sor´, râ) *n.* successor; heir *(heredero).*

suciedad (sū•sye•thâth´) *f.* filth, dirt *(inmundicia);* dirtiness, filthiness *(calidad de sucio);* (fig.) dirty remark.

sucinto, ta (sū•sēn´to, tâ) *adj.* succinct.

sucio, cia (sū´syo, syâ) *adj.* dirty, filthy.

suculento, ta (sū•kū•len´to, tâ) *adj.* succulent.

sucumbir (sū•kūm•bēr´) *vn.* to succumb.

sucursal (sū•kūr•sâl´) *adj.* subsidiary; —, *f.* branch, subsidiary.

sud (sūth) *m.* south.

sudafricano, na (sū•thâ•frē•kâ´no, nâ) *n.* and *adj.* South African.

sudamericano, na (sū•thâ•me•rē•kâ´no,nâ) *n.* and *adj.* South American.

sudar (sū•thâr´) *va.* and *vn.* to sweat.

sudeste (sū•thes´te) *m.* southeast.

sudoeste (sū•tho•es´te) *m.* southwest.

sudor (sū•thor´) *m.* sweat.

Suecia (swe´syâ) *f.* Sweden.

sueco, ca (swe´ko, kâ) *adj.* Swedish; — *n.* Swede.

suegra (swe´grâ) *f.* mother-in-law.

suegro (swe´gro) *m.* father-in-law.

suela (swe´lâ) *f.* sole.

sueldo (swel´do) *m.* salary, pay.

suelo (swe´lo) *m.* ground; soil *(terreno);* floor *(piso);* bottom *(superficie inferior).*

suelto, ta (swel´to, tâ) *adj.* loose; rapid,quick *(veloz);* bold *(atrevido);* loose *(disgregado);* single *(separado).*

sueño (swe´nyo) *m.* sleep; dream *(fantasía);* **tener —,** to be sleepy; **no dormir —,** not to sleep a wink; **conciliar el —,** to manage to get to sleep; **entre — s,** dozing.

suero (swe´ro) *m.* serum.

suerte (swer´te) *f.* luck, fortune; fate *(destino);* kind, sort *(género);* **tener —,** to be lucky; **echar —s,** to draw lots.

suficiencia (sū•fe•syen´syâ) *f.* sufficiency, adequacy; **a —,** sufficient, enough.

suficiente (sū•fe•syen´te) *adj.* sufficient, enough *(bastante);*

fit, apt *(apto).*

sufijo (sū•fe´ho) *m.* suffix.

sufragio (sū•frâ´hyo) *m.* vote, suffrage *(voto);* aid, assistance *(ayuda).*

sufrimiento (sū•fre•myen´to) *m.* patience, endurance.

sufrir (sū•frer´) *va.* to suffer *(padecer);* to endure, to tolerate, to bear *(sostener).*

sugerencia (sū•he•ren´syâ) *f.* suggestion.

sugerir* (sū•he•rer´) *va.* to suggest.

sugestión (sū•hes•tyon´) *f.* suggestion.

suicida (swe•se´thâ) *m.* and *f.* suicide.

suicidarse (swe•se•thâr´se) *vr.* to commit suicide.

suicidio (swe•se•´thyo) *m.* suicide.

Suiza (swe´sâ) *f.* Switzerland.

suizo, za (swe´so, sâ) *n.* and *adj.* Swiss; *f.* dispute, row.

sujeción (sū•he•syon´) *f.* subjection, control; fastening, holding; **con — a,** subject to.

sujetar (sū•he•tar´) *va.* to subject *(someter);* to hold, to fasten *(afirmar).*

sujeto, ta (sū•he´to, tâ) *adj.* subject; fastened; **estar — a,** to be subject to; —, *m.* subject.

sulfato (sūl•fâ´to) *m.* (chem.) sulphate.

sulfonamida (sūl•fo•nä•mē´thâ) *f.* sulfonamide.

sulfúrico (sūl•fū´rē•ko) *adj.* sulphuric.

sultán (sūl•tân´) *m.* sultan.

suma (sū´mä) *f.* addition *(acción);* sum, amount *(total);* essence *(lo más importante);* summary *(compendio);* **en —,** in short.

sumamente (sū•mä•men´te) *adv.* exceedingly.

sumar (sū•mâr´) *va.* to add; to summarize, to sum up *(compendiar);* to amount to *(componer).*

sumergir (sū•mer•hēr´) *va.* and *vr.* to submerge, to sink.

sumersión (sū•mer•syon´) *f.* submersion.

suministrador, ra (sū•mē•nēs•trä•thor´, râ) *n.* provider.

suministrar (sū•mē•nēs•trâr´) *va.* to supply, to furnish.

suministro (sū•mē•nēs´tro) *m.* provision, supply; **—s,** pl. (mil.) supplies.

sumir (sū•mēr´) *va.* to sink, to lower; **—se,** to be sunken in; (fig.) to wallow *(abismarse).*

sumisión (sū•mē•syon´) *f.* submission.

sumiso, sa (sū•mē´so sâ) *adj.* submissive.

sumo, ma (sū´mo, mâ) *adj.*

supreme; **a lo—mo,** at most; **de —mo,** completely.

suntuoso, sa (sūn•two´so, sâ) *adj.* sumptuous.

superable (sū•pe•râ´vle) *adj.* surmountable, superable.

superar (sū•pe•râr´) *va.* to surpass, to excel *(exceder);* to overcome, to surmount *(sobrepujar).*

superficial (sū•per•fē•syâl´) *adj.* superficial; surface.

superficie (sū•per•fē´sye) *f.* surface; (math.) area.

superfluo, flua (sū•per´flwo, flwâ) *adj.* superfluous.

superhombre (sū•pe•rom´bre) *m.* superman.

superintendente (sū•pe•rēn•ten•den´te) *m.* superintendent, director.

superior (sū•pe•ryor´) *adj.* (fig.) superior; upper *(más alto);* higher *(más elevado);* **parte —,** topside; **—,** *m.* superior.

superioridad (sū•pe•ryo•rē•thâth´) *f.* superiority; **complejo de —,** superiority complex.

supermercado (sū•per•mer•kâ´tho) *m.* supermarket.

supersónico, ca (sū•per•so´nē•ko, kâ) *adj.* supersonic; **velocidad —ca,** supersonic speed.

superstición (sū•pers•tē•syon´) *f.*

superstition.

supersticioso, sa
(sū•pers•tē•syo′so, sâ) *adj.*
superstitious.

supervivencia
(sū•per•vē•ven′syâ) *f.* survival;
survivorship *(de una renta);* —
del más apto. survival of the
fittest.

superviviente (sū•per•vē•vyen′te)
m. and *f.* survivor; —, *adj.* surviving.

suplemento (sū•ple•men′to) *m.*
supplement.

suplente (sū•plen′te) *adj.* and *m.*
substitute, alternate.

súplica (sū′plē•kâ) *f.* petition,
request *(escrito);* entreaty.

suplicar (sū•plē•kâr′) *va.* to
entreat, to beg, to implore
(rogar); to petition *(ante el tribunal).*

suplicio (sū•plē′syo) *m.* punishment *(castigo);* (fig.) anguish,
suffering, torment.

suplir, (sū•plēr′) *va.* to make up,
to supply; to replace, to take
the place of *(remplazar);* to
make up for *(remediar).*

suponer* (sū•po•ner′) *va.* to
suppose; to imply, to call for
(importar); —, *vn.* to carry
weight.

suposición (sū•po•sē•syon′) *f.*
supposition; weight, importance *(autoridad);* falsehood
(impostura).

supremacía (sū•pre•mâ•sē′â) *f.*
supremacy.

supremo, ma (sū•pre′mo, mâ)
adj. supreme.

supresión (sū•pre•syon′) *f.* suppression.

suprimir (sū•prē•mēr′) *va.* to
suppress; to omit, to leave out
(omitir).

sur (sūr) *m.* south; south wind
(viento).

surcar (sūr•kâr′) *va.* to furrow.

surco (sūr′ko) *m.* furrow.

surgir (sūr•hēr′) *vn.* to gush out,
to spurt *(surtir);* to arise, to
spring up, to emerge *(manifestarse);* (naut.) to anchor.

suroeste (sū•ro•es′te) = **sudoeste.**

surrealismo (sū•rre•â•lēz′mo) *m.*
surrealism.

surtido (sūr•tē′tho) *m.* assortment, supply.

surtir (sūr•tēr′) *va.* to supply, to
furnish, to fit out; —, *vn.* to
gush out, to jet, to spout.

sus (sūs) *pron,* their; your *(de
usted).*

susceptible (sūs•sep•tē′vle) *adj.*
susceptible; touchy *(picajoso).*

suscitar (sūs•sē•târ′) *va.* to
excite, to stir up.

suscribir (sūs•krē•vēr′) *va.* to
subscribe; to subscribe to *(convenir con);* —**se a,** to subscribe

to.

suscripción (sūs•krēp•syon´) *f.* subscription.

suscriptor, ra (sūs•krēp•tor´, râ) *n.* subscriber.

suspender (sūs•pen•der´) *va.* to suspend; to amaze *(causar admiración);* to fail *(al examinando);* to fire, to discharge *(destituir).*

suspensión (sūs•pen•syon´) *f.* suspension; amazement.

suspicacia (sūs•pē•kâ´syâ) *f.* suspiciousness, distrust.

suspicaz (sūs•pē•kâs´) *adj.* suspicious, distrustful.

suspirar (sūs•pē•râr´) *vn.* to sigh; — **por,** to long for.

suspiro (sūs•pē´ro) *m.* sigh; (P.R.) meringue.

sustancia (sūs•tân´syâ) *f.* substance.

sustancial (sūs•tân•syâl´) *adj.* substantial.

sustancioso, sa (sūs•tân•syo´so, sâ) *adj.* substantial; nutritious, nourishing *(nutritivo).*

sustantivo, va (sūs•tân•tē´vo, vâ) *adj.* and *m.* (gram.) substantive, noun.

sustentar (sūs•ten•târ´) *va.* to sustain, to support, to maintain.

sustento (sūs•ten´to) *m.* sustenance, support.

sustitución (sūs•tē•tū•syon´) *f.* substitution.

sustituir* (sūs•tē•twēr´) *va.* to replace, to substitute for.

sustituto, ta (sūs•tē•tū´to, tâ) *adj.* and *n.* substitute.

susto (sūs´to) *m.* fright, scare; (fig.) dread *(preocupación);* **llevarse un —,** to get a good scare.

sustracción (sūs•trâk•syon´) *f.* subtraction.

sustraer* (sūs•trâ•er´) *va.* to remove, to take away; (math.) to subtract; to steal *(robar);* — **se,** to withdraw, to get out.

susurrar (sū•sū•rrâr´) *vn.* to whisper; to be whispered about *(una cosa secreta);* to rustle *(el viento);* to murmur *(el agua).*

susurro (sū•sū´rro) *m.* whisper; murmur; rustle.

sutil (sū•tēl´) *adj.* fine, thin *(tenue);* (fig.) subtle.

sutileza (sū•tē le´sâ) *f.* fineness; subtlety.

suyo, ya (sū´yo, yâ) *pron.* his *(de él);* hers *(de ella);* theirs *(de ellos);* one's *(de uno);* yours *(de usted);* —, *adj.* his; her; their; your; **de —yo,** on one's own; in itself *(propiamente).*

T

tabaco (tâ•vâ´ko) *m.* tobacco.

tábano (tâ´vâ•no) *m.* horsefly.

tabaquería (tâ•vâ•ke•rē´a) *f.* cigar store *(tienda)*; cigar factory *(fábrica).*

taberna (tâ•ver´nâ) *f.* tavern, saloon.

tabernáculo (tâ•ver•nâ´kū•lo) *m.* tabernacle.

tabique (tâ•vē´ke) *m.* partition.

tabla (tâ´vlâ) *f.* board *(madera)*; slab *(losa)*; butcher's block *(de carnicería)*; index *(índice)*; (math.) table; bed of earth *(tierra)*; pleat *(pliegue)*; catalogue *(catálogo)*; **—s,** *pl.* tie, draw; stage *(escenario).*

tablero (tâ•vle´ro) *m.* board; chessboard *(de ajedrez)*; checkerboard *(de damas)*; stock of a crossbow *(de una ballesta)*; cutting board *(de la sastrería)*; counter *(mostrador)*; blackboard *(pizarrón)*; (orn.) petrel.

tableta (tâ•vle´tâ) *f.* tablet; small chocolate cake *(pastilla)*; pill *(píldora).*

tabú (tâ•vū´) *m.* taboo.

tacaño, ña (tâ•kâ´nyo, nyâ) *adj.* artful, knavish *(astuto)*; miserly, stingy *(mezquino).*

taciturno, na (tâ•sē•tūr´no, nâ) *adj.* taciturn, silent *(callado)*; melancholy *(triste).*

taco (tâ´ko) *m.* stopper, stopple; wad *(cilindro)*; rammer *(baqueta)*; billiard cue *(del billar)*; snack *(bocado)*; swallow of wine *(trago)*; oath *(grosería)*; (Mex.) stuffed rolled tortilla.

tacón (tâ•kon´) *m.* heel; **— de goma** or **de caucho,** rubber heel.

táctico, ca (tâk´tē•ko, kâ) *adj.* tactical; **—,** *m.* tactician.

tacto (tâk´to) *m.* touch, feeling; tact *(diplomacia)*; knack *(tino).*

tacha (tâ´châ) *f.* fault, defect; large tack *(clavo)*; **sin —,** perfect.

tachar (tâ•châr´) *va.* to find fault with *(poner falta)*; to reprehend *(censurar)*; to erase, to efface *(borrar)*; to challenge *(al testigo).*

tachuela (tâ•chwe´lâ) *f.* tack, nail.

tafetán (tâ•fe•tân´) *m.* taffeta.

tahúr (tâ•ūr´) *m.* gambler, gamester.

taimado, da (tâē•mâ´tho, thâ) *adj.* sly, cunning, crafty.

tajar (tâ•hâr´) *va.* to cut, to chop, to slice, to carve.

tal (tâl) *adj.* such, such a; **con — que,** provided that; **no hay —,** no such thing; **¿qué —?** how goes it? how are you getting along? **— vez,** perhaps.

taladrar (tâ•lâ•thrâr´) *va.* to bore, to pierce, to drill; to pierce one s ears *(de un ruido);* to get to the root of *(de un problema).*

taladro (tâ•lâ´thro) *m.* borer, gimlet,auger, drill; drill hole *(agujero).*

tálamo (tâ´lâ•mo) *m.* bridal bed; (bot.) thalamus.

talar (tâ•lâr´) *va.* to fell *(árboles);* to desolate, to raise havoc in *(arruinar).*

talco (tâl´ko) *m.* talc *(silicato);* tinsel *(lámina);* **polvo de —,** talcum powder.

talento (tâ•len´to) *m.* talent.

talentoso, sa (tâ•len•to´so, sâ) *adj.* talented.

talón (tâ•lon´) *m.* heel; check, stub, coupon *(comprobante).*

talla (tâ´yâ) *f.* engraving *(grabado);* sculpture *(escultura);* stature *(estatura);* size *(tamaño);* height scale *(instrumento);* reward *(premio);* hand *(en las cartas).*

tallado, da (tâ•yâ´tho, thâ) *adj.* cut, carved, engraved; **buen —,** well-formed; *m.* carving; engraving.

tallador (tâ•yâ•thor´) *m.* engraver.

tallar (tâ•yâr´) *va.* to cut *(una piedra);* to carve *(madera);* to engrave; to appraise *(apreciar);* to measure *(medir);* **—,** *vi.* to discourse *(discurrir);* to talk of love *(del amor);* **—,** *adj.* ready to be cut or carved.

tallarín (tâ•yâ•rēn´) *m.* noodle; **sopa de—ines,** noodle soup.

talle (tâ´ye) *m.* shape, size, proportion *(proporción);* waist *(cintura);* appearance *(apariencia).*

taller (tâ•yer´) *m.* workshop; **— de reparaciones,** repair shop.

tallo (tâ´yo) *m.* shoot, sprout *(renuevo);* stem; (coll.) cabbage.

tamal (tâ•mâl´) *m.* tamale.

tamaño (tâ•mâ´nyo) *m.* size; **—, ña,** *adj.* so small *(tan pequeño);* so large *(tan grande);* very small *(muy pequeño);* very large *(muy grande).*

tamarindo (tâ•mâ•rēn´do) *m.* tamarind.

tambalear (tâm•bâ•le•âr´) *vn.* and *vr.* to stagger, to totter.

tambaleo (tâm•bâ•le´o) *m.* staggering, reeling.

también (tâm•byen´) *adv.* also, too, likewise, as well.

tambor (tâm•bor´) *m.* drum; drummer *(persona);* drum *(barril);* coffee roaster *(asador);* reel *(para arrollar);* tambour frame (aro); eardrum (tímpano).

tamboril (tâm•bo•rēl´) m. tabor, small drum.

tamborilero (tâm•bo•rē•le´ro) or **tamboritero** (tam•bo•rē•te´ro) m. tabor player, drummer.

tampoco (tâm•po´ko) adv. neither, not either.

tan (tan) m. boom, drum beat; —,adv. so; as (equivalencia); — **pronto como,** as soon as.

tándem (tân´den) m. tandem.

tangente (tân•hen´te) f. (math.) tangent; **salir por la —,** to evade the issue.

Tánger (tân´her), f. Tangier.

tangible (tân•hē´vle) adj. tangible.

tango (tâng´go) m. tango.

tanque (tâng´ke) m. tank; beeswax (propóleos); water tank (de agua); dipper (cazo); pool (estanque).

tanto (tân´to) m. certain sum, a quantity; copy (copia); chip, marker (para tantear); —, **ta,** adj. so much, as much (tan grande); very great (muy grande); —**to,** adv. so, that way (de tal modo); so much, so long (en tal grado); **mientras —,** meanwhile; **por lo —,** therefore; — **como,** as much as; — **más,** so much more (cantidad); especially, particularly (especialmente); —**s,** m. pl. score,

points.

tapa (tâ´pâ) f. lid, cover (tapadera); book cover (de un libro); snack served with wine (bocado).

tapar (tâ•pâr´) va. to cover, to close (cubrir); to bundle up (abrigar); to conceal, to hide (ocultar).

tapete (tâ•pe´te) m. small carpet (alfombra); runner (de mesa).

tapia (tâ´pyâ) f. adobe wall (pared); enclosure (cerca); **sordo como una —,** stone deaf.

tapiar (tâ•pyâr´) va. to wall up (cerrar con tapias); to stop up, to close up (cerrar un hueco).

tapicería (tâ•pē•se•rē´â) f. tapestry; upholstery.

tapicero (tâ•pē•se´ro) m. tapestry maker; upholsterer (de muebles).

tapioca (tâ•pyo´kâ) f. tapioca.

tapiz (tâ•pēs´) m. tapestry; **papel —,** wallpaper.

tapizar (tâ•pē•sâr´) va. to cover with tapestry (de tapiz); to cover with rugs (de alfombras); to upholster (de muebles).

tapón (tâ•pon´) m. cork, plug, stopper; (med.) tampon.

taquilla (tâ•kē´yâ) f. file cabinet (armario); box office, ticket office, ticket window (de billetes); box-office take, receipts (cantidad recaudada).

taquillero (tâ•kē•ye′ro) *m.* ticket seller; —, **ra,** *adj.* (Mex.) successful at the box office; popular.

tara (tâ′râ) *f.* tare *(de peso);* tally *(tarja);* (med.) defect.

tarántula (tâ•rân′tū•lâ) *f.* tarantula.

tararear (tâ•râ•re•âr′) *va.* to hum.

tardanza (târ•thân′sâ) *f.* tardiness, delay.

tardar (târ•thâr′) *vn.* to be long, to spend time; to take one, to spend *(emplear tiempo);* **a más** —, at the latest.

tarde (târ′the) *f.* afternoon; dusk, early evening *(anochecer);* **buenas** —**s,** good afternoon; —, *adv.* late; **más** —, later.

tardío, día (târ•thē′o, thē′â) *adj.* late, slow, tardy.

tardo, da (târ′tho, thâ) *adj.* sluggish *(perezoso);* late *(tardío);* slow, dense *(torpe).*

tarea (tâ•re′â) *f.* task; trouble, worry *(penalidad);* obsession, same old thing *(afán).*

tarifa (tâ•rē′fâ) *f.* tariff, charge, rate, fare; price list *(catálogo).*

tarima (tâ•rē′mâ) *f.* platform, stand *(entablado);* low bench *(banco).*

tarjeta (târ•he′tâ) *f.* card; imprint *(impresión);* — **de cré-**

dito, credit card; — **postal,** postcard.

tartamudear (târ•tâ•mū•the•âr′) *vn.* to stutter, to stammer.

tartamudo, da (târ•tâ•mū′tho, thâ) *n.* stammerer, stutterer; —, *adj.* stammering, stuttering.

tártaro (târ′tâ•ro) *m.* cream of tartar; tartar *(de los dientes).*

tarugo (tâ•rū′go) *m.* peg *(clavija);* chunk, hunk *(zoquete);* block *(para pavimentar);* (coll.) cheat *(embustero);* dunce *(tonto).*

tasa (tâ′sâ) *f.* rate, value, assize; fixed price *(precio fijo);* measure, rule *(medida);* regulation *(regulación).*

tasajo (tâ•sâ′ho) *m.* jerked beef.

tatuaje (tâ•twâ′he) *m.* tattoo; tattooing *(acto).*

taxi (tâk′sē) *m.* taxicab.

taza (tâ′sâ) *f.* cup; cupful *(contenido);* bowl *(tazón);* basin *(de una fuente);* cup guard *(de una espada).*

te (te) *pron.* you; to you *(dativo)*

té (te) *m.* tea.

teatral (te•â•trâl′) *adj.* theatrical.

teatro (te•â′tro) *m.* theater, playhouse; stage *(escenario);* theater *(arte).*

tecla (te′klâ) *f.* key; (fig.) delicate matter.

teclado (te•klâ′tho) *m.* keyboard.

técnico, ca (teg′nē•ko, kâ) *adj.* technical; —, *f.* technique; —, *m:* technician.

tecnicolor (teg•nē•ko•lor´) *m.* technicolor.

tecnológico, ca (teg•no•lo´hē•ko, kâ) *adj.* technological.

tecolote (te•ko•lo´te) *m.* (Mex.) owl.

techo (te´cho) *m.* roof; ceiling *(parte interior);* house *(casa);* **bajo —,** indoors.

tedio (te´thyo) *m.* tedium, boredom.

teja (te´hâ) *f.* roof tile; linden *(árbol).*

tejado (te•hâ´tho) *m.* tiled roof.

tejar (te•hâr´) *m.* tileworks; —, *va.* to tile.

tejedor, ra (te•he•thor´, râ) *n.* weaver; intriguer *(intrigante).*

tejer (te•her´) *va.* to weave; to braid *(entrelazar);* to knit *(hacer puntos);* (fig.) to contrive.

tejido (te•hē´tho) *m.* texture, web; textile, fabric *(cosa tejida);* (anat.) tissue.

tela (te´lâ) *f.* cloth, fabric; membrane, tissue *(membrana);* scum *(nata);* web *(de araña);* — **de hilo,** linen cloth; — **adhesiva,** adhesive tape; — **aisladora,** (elec.) insulating tape; **en — de juicio,** in doubt, under consideration.

telar (te•lâr´) *m.* loom.

telaraña (te•lâ•râ´nyâ) *f.* cobweb, spider web; will-o'-the-wisp *(cosa sutil);* trifle (bagatela).

telefonear (te•le•fo•ne•âr´) *va.* and *vn.* to telephone.

teléfono (te•le´fo•no) *m.* telephone;— **celular,** cell phone.

telegrafiar (te•le•grâ•fyâr´) *va.* and *vn.* to telegraph.

telégrafo (te•le´grâ•fo) *m.* telegraph.

teleguiado, da (te•le•gyâ´tho, thâ) *adj.*remote-control.

telenovela (te•le•no•ve´lâ) *f.* soap opera, television serial.

telerreceptor (te•le•rre•sep•tor´) *m.* television set.

telescopio (te•les•ko´pyo) *m.* telescope.

teletipo (te•le•tē´po) *m.* teletype.

televidente (te•le•vē•then´te) *m.* and *f.* televiewer, television viewer.

televisión (te•le•vē•syon´) *f.* television.

televisor (te•le•vē•sor´) *m.* television set.

telón (te•lon´) *m.* drop, curtain; — **de boca,** front curtain.

tema (te´mâ) *m.* theme *(proposición);* subject *(asunto);* (mus.) theme; —, *f.* obstinacy *(porfía);* contentiousness *(oposición);* mania, obsession *(idea fija).*

temblar* (tem•blâr´) *vn.* to tremble to quiver *(agitarse);* to waver *(vacilar);* (fig.) to be terrified.

temblor (tem•blor´) *m.* trembling, tremor; earthquake *(terremoto)*.

tembloroso, sa (tem•blo•ro´so, sâ) *adj.* trembling, shaky.

temer (te•mer´) *va.* to fear; — *vi.* to be afraid.

temerario, ria (te•me•râ´ryo, ryâ) *adj.* rash, reckless, brash; —, *n.* daredevil.

temeridad (te•me•rē•thâth´) *f.* rashness, recklessness *(calidad);* folly, foolishness *(acto);* rash judgment *(juicio).*

temeroso, sa (te•me•ro´so, sâ) *adj.* timid.

temible (te•mē´vle) *adj.* dreadful, terrible.

temor (te•mor´) *m.* dread, fear; suspicion *(sospecha);* misgiving *(recelo).*

témpano (tem´pâ•no) *m.* kettle drum; drumhead *(piel);* side of bacon *(tocino);* block *(pedazo);* — **de hielo,** iceberg.

temperamento (tem•pe•râ•men´to) *m.* weather; temperament, nature, temper *(estado fisiológico);* conciliation *(arbitrio).*

temperatura (tem•pe•râ•tū´râ) *f.* temperature; weather *(temperie).*

tempestad (tem•pes•tâth´) *f.* storm; rough seas *(del mar);* (fig.) agitation, upheaval.

tempestuoso, sa (tem•pes•two´so, sâ) *adj.* tempestuous, stormy.

templado, da (tem•plâ´tho, thâ) *adj.* temperate, moderate; lukewarm *(tibio);* average *(del estilo).*

templar (tem•plâr´) *va.* to moderate; to heat *(calentar);* to temper *(metal);* to dilute *(mezclar);* to relieve *(sosegar);* (mus.) to tune; —**se,** to be moderate.

templo (tem´plo) *m.* temple.

temporada (tem•po•râ´thâ) *f.* time, period; season *(habitual).*

temporal (tern•po•râl´) *adj.* temporary; temporal *(secular);* —, *m.* tempest, storm *(tempestad);* weather *(temperie).*

temprano, na (tem•prâ´no, nâ) *adj.* early; —**no,** *adv.* early.

tenacidad (te•nâ•sē•thâth´) *f.* tenacity.

tenaz (te•nâs´) *adj.* tenacious.

tenazas (te•nâ´sâs) *f. pl.* tongs, pincers, pliers.

tendedero (ten•de•the´ro) *m.* clothesline.

tendencia (ten•den´syâ) *f.* tendency.

tender* (ten•der´) *va.* to stretch out, to unfold, to spread out; to hang out *(para secar);* to extend *(extender);* —, *vn.* to tend; —**se,** to stretch out.

tendido (ten•dē´tho) *m.* extending, spreading out; lower deck seats *(galería);* wash *(ropa);* batch of bread *(pan).*

tendón (ten•don´) *m.* tendon; — **de Aquiles,** Achilles´ tendon.

tenebroso, sa (te•ne•vro´so, sâ) *adj.* dark, shadowy, gloomy; (fig.) obscure.

tenedor (te•ne•thor´) *m.* holder; fork *(utensilio);* — **de libros,** bookkeeper, accountant.

tener* (te´ner´) *va.* to have, to hold, to possess; to maintain *(mantener);* to consist of, to contain *(comprender);* to dominate, to subject *(sujetar);* to finish, to stop *(parar);* to keep, to fulfill *(cumplir);* to spend, to pass *(pasar).*

teniente (te•nyen´te) *m.* deputy *(sustituto);* lieutenant.

tenis (te´nēs) *m.* tennis; tennis court *(sitio);* — **de mesa,** ping pong, table tennis.

tenor (te•nor´) *m.* condition, nature; contents *(contenido);* (mus.) tenor.

tensión (ten•syon´) *f.* tension; — **arterial,** blood pressure.

tentación (ten•tâ•syon´) *f.* temptation.

tentáculo (ten•tâ´kū•lo) *m.* tentacle.

tentador, ra (ten•tâ•thor´, râ) *adj.* attractive, tempting; —, *n.*

tempter; —, *m.* devil.

tentar* (ten•târ´) *va.* to touch; to test *(probar);* to grope through *(andar a tientas);* to tempt *(instigar);* to try, to attempt *(intentar).*

tentativo, va (ten•tâ•tē´vo, vâ) *adj.* tentative; —, *f.* attempt, try.

tentempié (ten•tem•pye´) *m.* snack, bite.

tenue (te´nwe) *adj.* tenuous, delicate; unimportant, trivial *(de poca importancia).*

teñir* (te•nyēr´) *va.* to tint, to dye; to tone down *(de la pintura).*

teología (te•o•lo•hē´â) *f.* theology.

teológico, ca (te•o•lo´hē•ko, kâ) *adj.* theological.

teorema (te•o•re´mâ) *m.* theorem.

teoría (te•o•rē´â) or **teórica** (te•o´rē•kâ) *f.* theory.

teórico, ca (te•o´rē•ko, kâ) *adj.* theoretical.

tequila (te•kē´lâ) *m.* tequila.

terapéutico, ca (te•râ•pe´ū•tē•ko, kâ) *adj.* therapeutic; —, *f.* therapeutics.

tercero, ra (ter•se´ro, râ) *adj.* third; —, *m.* third party; pander *(alcahuete).*

terceto (ter•se´to) *m.* tercet; (mus.) trio.

tercia (ter′syâ) *f.* third.

terciar (ter•syâr′) *va.* to place crosswise, to put on the bias; to cut in three *(dividir).*

tercio, cia (ter′syo, syâ) *adj.* third; —, *m.* third; load *(fardo);* (mil.) corps; **hacer buen —cio,** to help, to do a good turn.

terciopelado, da (ter•syo•pe•lâ′-tho, thâ) *adj.*velvety.

terciopelo (ter•syo•pe′lo) *m.* velvet.

terco, ca (ter′ko, kâ) *adj.*obstinate, stubborn; very hard, resistant *(difícil de labrar).*

termal (ter•mâl′) *adj.* thermal.

termas (ter′mâs) *f. pl.* hot baths, hot springs; public baths *(de los romanos).*

térmico, ca (ter′mē•ko, kâ) *adj.*thermal, thermic.

terminal (ter•mē•nâl′) *adj.* terminal, final; —, *m.* terminal.

terminante (ter•mē•nân′te) *adj.* final, decisive, conclusive; **orden —,** strict order.

terminar (ter•mē•nâr′) *va.* to terminate, to end, to finish; —, *vn.* to end; **—se,** to be leading, to be pointing.

término (ter′mē•no) *m.* term; termination, end; boundary *(línea divisoria);* limit *(límite);* term *(tiempo);* object, purpose *(objeto);* situation *(situación);* demeanor *(modo de portarse);*

— medio, compromise.

terminología (ter•mē•no•lo•hē′â) *f.* terminology.

termodinámica (ter•mo•thē•nâ′mē•kâ) *f.* thermodynamics.

termómetro (ter•mo′me•tro) *m.* thermometer.

termonuclear (ter•mo•nū•kle•âr′) *adj.* thermonuclear.

termos (ter′mos) *m.* thermos bottle.

termostato (ter•mos•tâ′to) *m.* thermostat.

ternero, ra (ter•ne′ro, râ) *n.* calf; —, *f.* veal.

ternura (ter•nū′râ) *f.* tenderness, affection.

terquedad (ter•ke•thâth′) *f.* stubbornness, obstinacy.

terraplén (te•rrâ•plen′) *m.* fill *(para rellenar);* embankment; rampart *(defensa);* terrace, platform *(plataforma).*

terraza (te•rrâ′sâ) *f.* terrace, veranda; flat roof (terrado); sidewalk cafe (café); garden plot *(era);* glazed jar *(jarra).*

terremoto (te•rre•mo′to) *m.* earthquake.

terreno, na (te•rre′no, nâ) *adj.* earthly, terrestrial; —, *m.* land, ground, terrain; (fig.) proving ground.

terrestre (te•rres′tre) *adj.* terrestrial, earthly.

terrible (te•rrē´vle) *adj.* terrible, dreadful; surly, gruff *(áspero de genio)*; extraordinary, immeasurable *(extraordinario)*.

territorial (te•rrē•to•ryâl´) *adj.* territorial.

territorio (te•rrē•to´ryo) *m.* territory.

terror (te•rror´) *m.* terror, dread, fear.

terrorismo (te•rro•rēz´mo) *m.* terrorism.

terso, sa (ter´so, sâ) *adj.* smooth, glossy; terse *(del lenguaje)*.

tesis (te´sēs) *f.* thesis.

tesorería (te•so•re•rē´â) *f.* treasury.

tesorero, ra (te•so•re´ro, râ) *n.* treasurer.

tesoro (te•so´ro) *m.* treasure; treasury *(erario)*; treasure room; treasure house *(lugar)*; *(fig.)* thesaurus.

testamento (tes•tâ•men´to) *m.* will, testament.

testar (tes•târ´) *vn.* to make out one's will; —, *va.* to erase.

testarudo, da (tes•tâ•rū´tho, thâ) *adj.* obstinate, bullheaded.

testículo (tes•tē´kū•lo) *m.* testicle.

testificar (tes•tē•fē•kâr´) *vn.* to attest, to testify; —, *va.* to witness.

testigo (tes•tē´go) *m.* witness.

testimoniar (tes•tē•mo•nyâr´) *va.* to attest to, to bear witness to.

testimonio (tes•tē•mo´nyo) *m.* testimony.

tétano (te´tâ•no) *m.* (med.) tetanus, lockjaw.

tetera (te•te´râ) *f.* teapot, teakettle.

tétrico, ca (te´trē•ko, kâ) *adj.* gloomy, sad, melancholy.

textil (tes•tēl´) *adj.* and *m.* textile.

texto (tes´to) *m.* text; passage *(pasaje)*; **libro de —,** text book.

textual (tes•twâl´) *adj.* textual.

tez (tes) *f.* surface; skin, complexion *(del rostro humano)*.

ti (tē) *pron.* you; **para —,** for you.

tía (tē´â) *f.* aunt.

tibia (tē´vyâ) *f.* shinbone.

tibio, bia (tē´vyo, vyâ) *adj.* lukewarm; careless, remiss *(descuidado)*.

tiburón (tē•vū•ron´) *m.* shark.

tictac (tēk•tâk´) *m.* ticktock.

tiempo (tyem´po) *m.* time; season *(estación)*; weather *(temperie)*; (mus.) tempo; (gram.) tense; **— atrás,** some time ago; **— desocupado,** spare time; **a —**, in time; **a —s,** at times; **a su — debido,** in due time; **a un —,** at once, at the same time; **hacer buen —,** to be good weather; **más —,** longer;

tomarse —, to take one´s time; **en un** —, formerly; **hace mucho** —, a long time ago; **en** —**s pasados,** in former times.

tienda (tyen´dâ) *f.* tent; (naut.) awning; (com.) store, shop;— **de conveniencia,** convenience store.

tierno, na (tyer´no, nâ) *adj.* tender, delicate, soft *(delicado);* new *(recién);* childlike, young *(de la niñez);* teary, tearful *(propenso al llanto);* affectionate, loving *(cariñoso).*

tierra (tye´rrâ) *f.* earth; soil *(materia);* land *(terreno);* homeland *(patria);* ground *(suelo);* **echar por** —, to destroy, to ruin; **echar** — **a,** to cover up, to hide.

tieso, sa (tye´so, sâ) *adj.* stiff, hard, firm; tense, taut *(tenso);* robust *(robusto);* valiant *(valiente);* stubborn *(terco);* pompous *(afectadamente grave).*

tifoideo, dea (tē•foē•the´o, the´â) *adj.* typhoid; —, *f.* typhoid fever.

tifus (tē´fūs) *m.* (med.) typhus.

tigre (tē´gre) *m.* tiger; savage *(persona brutal).*

tijeras (tē•he´râs) *f. pl.* scissors.

tildar (tēl•dâr´) *va.* to erase; to brand, to stigmatize *(señalar);* to put a tilde over *(poner tilde).*

tilde (tēl´de) *f.* tilde; censure, criticism *(tacha);* iota *(cosa mínima).*

timar (tē•mâr´) *va.* to swindle; to deceive *(engañar);* —**se,** to make eyes.

timbal (tēm•bâl´) *m.* kettledrum.

timbrazo (tēm•brâ´so) *n.* clang.

timbre (tēm´bre) *m.* postage stamp *(de correo);* seal, stamp; electric bell *(aparato);* crest *(insignia);* (fig.) glorious deed.

timidez (tē•mē•thes´) *f.* timidity, shyness.

tímido, da (tē´mē•tho, thâ) *adj.* timid, shy.

timo (tē´mo) *m.* swindle; gag, joke *(broma);* **dar un** —, to swindle; to deceive *(engañar).* helm; — **de dirección,** rudder.

tímpano (tēm´pâ•no) *m.* kettledrum; (anat.) tympanum, eardrum.

tina (tē´nâ) *f.* earthen jar *(de barro);* tub; — **de baño,** bathtub.

tinaja (tē•nâ´hâ) *f.* large earthen jar.

tiniebla (tē•nye´vlâ) *f.* darkness, obscurity; —**s,** *pl.* utter darkness; gross ignorance *(ignorancia).*

tino (tē´no) *m.* skill, deftness; marksmanship *(para dar en el blanco);* judgment, prudence *(juicio).*

tinta (tēn´tâ) *f.* tint; ink *(para escribir);* **saber algo de buena —,** to know something on good authority; **—s,** *pl.* shades, hues.

tinte (tēn´te) *m.* tint, dye; dyeing *(acto);* dyer´s shop *(tienda).*

tintinear (tēn•tē•ne•âr´) *vn.* to tinkle.

tinto, ta (tēn´to, tâ) *adj.*red; **vino —,** red wine.

tintorería (tēn•to•re•rē´â) *f.* dry cleaning shop.

tintura (tēn•tū´râ) *f.* dye.

tío (tē´o) *m.* uncle; (coll.) old man *(viejo);* guy *(sujeto);* **— abuelo,** great uncle.

típico, ca (tē´pē•ko, kâ) *adj.* characteristic, typical.

tipo (tē´po) *m.* type, model; standard pattern *(norma);* type *(letra);* figure, build *(figura);* rate *(razón);* **— de cambio,** rate of exchange; **— de descuento,** rate of discount; **— de interés,** rate of interest.

tira (tē´râ) *f.* strip; **—s,** *pl.* rags.

tirada (te• râ´thâ) *f.* cast, throw; distance *(distancia);* length of time *(tiempo);* (print.) run; stroke *(en el golf);* edition, issue *(edición);* **— aparte,** reprint.

tiranía (tē•râ•nē´â) *f.* tyranny.

tiránico, ca (tē•râ´nē•ko, kâ) *adj.* tyrannical.

tirano, na (tē•râ´no, nâ) *adj.* tyrannical;**—,** *n.* tyrant.

tirante (tē•rân´te) *m.* beam *(de un tejado);* trace *(de las caballerías);* brace; **—s,** *pl.* suspenders; **—,** *adj.*tense, taut, drawn; (fig.) strained, forced.

tirar (tē•râr´) *va.* to throw, to toss, to cast; to tear down *(derribar);* to stretch *(estirar);* to pull; to draw *(trazar);* to fire, to shoot *(disparar);* to throw away, to waste *(malgastar);* **—,** *vn.* to attract *(atraer).*

tiritar (tē•rē•târ´) *vn.* to shiver.

tiro (tē´ro) *m.* throw, cast; mark *(impresión);* charge *(carga);* shot *(disparo);* report *(estampido);* round *(cantidad);* range *(alcance);* rifle range *(lugar).*

tiroides (tē•ro´ē•thes) *adj.* and *f.* (anat.) thyroid.

tirón (tē•ron´) *m.* pull, haul, tug; apprentice, novice *(aprendiz);* **de un —,** all at once, at one stroke.

tiroteo (tē•ro•te´o) *m.* random shooting.

tísico, ca (tē´sē•ko, kâ) *adj.* tubercular, consumptive.

tisis (tē´sēs) *f,* consumption, tuberculosis.

titánico, ca (tē•tâ´nē•ko, kâ) *adj.* titanic, colossal.

títere (tē´te•re) *m.* puppet; pipsqueak *(su jeto ridículo);*

obsession *(idea fija);* —**s,** *pl.* puppet show.

titiritero (tē•tē•rē•te´ro) *m.* puppeteer.

titubear (tē•tū•ve•âr´) *vn.* to stammer, to hesitate; to totter *(perder la estabilidad);* to be perplexed *(sentir perplejidad).*

titubeo (tē•tū•ve´o) *m.* hesitation, stammering; tottering; perplexity.

titular (tē•tū•lâr´) *va.* to title; —, *vn.* to obtain a title; —, *adj.* and *m.* titular.

título (tē´tū•lo) *m.* title; headline *(letrero);* document, deed *(documento);* diploma *(testimonio);* nobility *(dignidad).*

tiza (tē´sâ) *f.* chalk.

tiznar (tēz•nâr´) *va.* to cover with soot; (fig.) to tarnish, to stain.

tizne (tez´ne) *m.* soot; partly burned stick *(madera).*

toalla (to•â´yâ) *f.* towel; pillow cover *(cubierta);* — **sin fin,** roller towel.

toallero (to•â•ye´ro) *m.* towel rack.

tobillo (to•vē´yo) *m.* ankle.

tocadiscos (to•kâ•thēs´kos) *m.* record player.

tocado (to•kâ´tho) *m.* headdress *(prenda);* hairdo *(peinado);* —, **da,** *adj.* touched, crazy.

tocador (to•kâ•thor´) *m.* dressing table; boudoir *(aposento);* —,

ra, *n.* player.

tocante (to•kân´te) *adj.* touching; — **a,** concerning, relating to.

tocar (to•kâr´) *va.* to touch, to feel; (mus.) to play; to call *(avisar);* to strike, to bump *(tropezar);* to strike *(herir);* to learn, to experience *(conocer);* to be time to *(momento oportuno);* to touch on *(tratar de);* to touch up *(pintar);* to comb *(el pelo).*

tocino (to•sē´no) *m.* bacon *(lardo);* salt pork.

todavía (to•thâ•vē´â) *adv.* yet, still; even *(aun).*

todo, da (to´tho, thâ) *adj.* all; every *(cada);* whole *(entero);* — **el año,** all year around; —**dos los dias,** every day; —**das las noches,** every night; **en** —**das partes,** everywhere; — **el mundo,** everybody; **de** —**s modos,** anyhow, anyway; —, *m.* whole, entirety; —**do,** *adv.* entirely, completely; **ante** —**do,** first of all; **con** —**do,** still, nevertheless; **sobre** —**do,** above all, especially.

todopoderoso (to•tho•po•the•ro´so) *adj.* almighty.

toga (to´gâ) *f.* toga.

tolerable (to•le•râ´vle) *adj.* tolerable, bearable.

tolerancia (to•le•rân´syâ) *f.* tolerance;consent, permission *(permiso).*

tolerar (to•le•râr´) *va.* to tolerate; to endure, to bear *(soportar).*

tolvanera (tol•vâ•ne´râ) *f.* dust storm.

toma (to´mâ) *f.* taking; capture, seizure *(conquista);* portion *(porción);* water faucet *(grifo);* — **de posesión,** inauguration.

tomar (to•mar´) *va.* to take *(coger);* to seize, to grasp; to receive, to accept *(recibir);* to understand, to interpret, to perceive *(entender);* to eat *(comer);* to drink *(beber);* to rent *(alquilar);* to acquire *(adquirir);* to contract, to hire *(contratar).*

tomate (to•mâ´te) *m.* tomato.

tomillo (to•mē´yo) *m.* (bot.) thyme.

tomo (to´mo) *m.* bulk *(grueso);* tome, volume; (fig.) importance, value.

ton (ton) *m.* tone; **sin — ni son,** without rhyme or reason.

tonada (to•nâ´thâ) *f.* tune, melody, air.

tonel (to•nel´) *m.* cask, barrel.

tonelada (to•ne•lâ´thâ) *f.* ton; casks *(tonelería);* (naut.) tonnage duty.

tonelaje (to•ne•lâ´he) *m.* tonnage.

tono (to´no) *m.* tone.

tonsilitis (ton•sē•lē´tēs) *f.* tonsilitis.

tontería (ton•te•rē´â) *f.* foolishness, nonsense.

tonto, ta (ton´to, tâ) *adj.* stupid, foolish; —, *n.* fool, dunce; — **útil,** dupe, tool.

topacio (to•pâ´syo) *m.* topaz.

topar (to•pâr´) *va.* to bump into; to come across *(hallar);* to find *(encontrar);* *vn.* to butt, to bump *(topetar);* to lie, to consist *(consistir).*

tope (to´pe) *m.* bumper; brake *(para detener);* obstacle *(tropiezo);* blow *(golpe);* (rail.) buffers; **precio —,** ceiling price.

tópico, ca (to´pē•ko, kâ) *adj.* topical; —, *m.* topic, subject.

topo (to´po) *m.* (zool.) mole; (coll.) lummox.

topografía (to•po•grâ•fē´â) *f.* topography.

topográfico, ca (to•po•grâ´fē•ko, kâ) *adj.* topographical.

tórax (to´râks) *m.* (anat.) thorax.

torbellino (tor•ve•yē´no) *m.* whirlwind.

torcedura (tor•se•thū´râ) *f.* twisting, wrenching; twist; weak wine *(aguapié).*

torcer* (tor•ser´) *va.* to twist; to double, to curve *(encorvar);* to turn *(cambiar de dirección);* to screw up *(el semblante);* to distort *(tergiversar);* to pervert *(desviar);* —**se,** to go astray; to turn sour *(agriarse).*

torcido, da (tor sē´tho, thâ) *adj.* twisted, curved; crooked, dishonest *(no honrado).*

tordo (tor´tho) *m.* thrush; —, — **da,** *adj.* dappled.

torear (to•re•âr´) *vn.* to fight bulls; —, *vt.* to tease.

toreo (to•re´o) *m.* bullfighting.

torero (to•re´ro) *m.* bullfighter.

tormenta (tor•men´tâ) *f.* storm, thundershower, thunderstorm; adversity, misfortune *(adversidad);* (fig.) turmoil, unrest.

tormento (tor•men´to) *m.* torment, pain; torture *(tortura);* (fig.) anguish, torment.

tornado (tor•nâ´tho) *m.* tornado.

tornar (tor•nâr´) *va.* to return, to restore; to make *(mudar);* —, *vn.* to return.

tornasol (tor•nâ•sol´) *m.* (bot.) sunflower, heliotrope; iridescence *(reflejo);* (chem.) litmus.

torneo (tor•ne´o) *m.* tournament.

tornillo (tor•nē´yo) *m.* screw *(clavo);* vise *(prensa);* bolt.

torniquete (tor•nē•ke´te) *m.* turnstile; (med.) tourniquet.

torno (tor´no) *m.* wheel *(rueda);* lathe; winch, windlass *(armazón);* brake *(freno);* turn *(vuelta);* vise *(prensa);* **en — de,** around.

toro (to´ro) *m.* bull; **corrida de —s,** bullfight.

toronja (to•ron´hâ) *f.* grapefruit.

torpe (tor´pe) *adj.* slow, heavy *(tardo);* stupid, dull *(tonto);* clumsy, awkward *(desmañado).*

torpedero (tor•pe•the´ro) *m.* torpedo boat.

torpedo (tor•pe´tho) *m.* torpedo.

torpeza (tor•pe´sâ) *f.* slowness, heaviness, torpor *(pesadez);* stupidity, dullness *(estupidez);* clumsiness *(desmaña).*

torre (to´rre) *f.* tower, turret; steeple *(de una iglesia);* country house *(casa de campo);* rook *(en el ajedrez).*

torrente (to•rren´te) *m.* torrent; (fig.) crowd, mob.

torreón (to•rre•on´) *m.* fortified tower.

tórrido, da (to´rrē•tho, thâ) *adj.* torrid.

torso (tor´so) *m.* trunk, torso.

torta (tor´tâ) *f.* cake; (coll.) punch *(golpe);* — **compuesta,** (Mex.) stuffed bun sandwich.

tortilla (tor•tē´yâ) *f.* omelet; (Mex.) tortilla.

tórtola (tor´to•lâ) *f.* turtledove.

tortuga (tor•tū´gâ) *f.* tortoise *(de tierra);* turtle.

tortuoso, sa (tor•two´so, sâ) *adj.* tortuous, twisting; (fig.) devious.

torturar (tor•tū•râr´) *va.* to torture.

tos (tos) *f.* cough.

tosco, ca (tos´ko, kâ) *adj.* coarse, ill-bred; (fig.) uncultured, ignorant.

toser (to•ser´) *vn.* to cough.

tostada (tos•tâ´thâ) *f.* slice of toast; (fig.) bother, nuisance; (Mex.) meat tart *(torta de carne).*

tostado, da (tos•tâ´tho, thâ) *adj.* tanned; sunburned *(quemado del sol);* light brown *(marrón);* toasted *(cocido).*

tostador (tos•ta•thor´) *m.* toaster.

tostar* (tos•târ´) *va.* to toast; to heat too much *(calentar demasiado);* **—se al sol,** to sunbathe.

total (to•tal´) *m.* whole, totality; **—,** *adj.* total, entire.

totalidad (to•tâ•lē•thâth´) *f.* totality, whole.

totalitario, ria (to•tâ•lē•tâ´ryo, ryâ) *adj.* totalitarian.

totalmente (to•tâl•men´te) *adv.* totally, entirely.

tóxico, ca (tok´sē•ko, kâ) *adj.* toxic.

toxina (tok•sē´nâ) *f.* (med.) toxin.

traba (trâ´vâ) *f.* obstacle, impediment; hobble *(para atar caballos);* trammel, restraint *(para sujetar).*

trabajador, ra (trâ•vâ•hâ•thor´, râ) *n.* worker, laborer; **—,** *adj.* hard-working, industrious.

trabajar (trâ•vâ•hâr´) *vn.* to work; (fig.) to bend *(torcerse);* to strain *(afanarse);* **—,** *va.* to work.

trabajo (trâ•vâ´ho) *m.* work; workmanship *(destreza);* difficulty, trouble *(dificultad);* **—s forzados,** hard labor; **costar —,** to be difficult; **—s,** *pl.* straits, misery.

trabalenguas (tra•vâ•leng´gwâs) *m.* tongue twister.

tracción (trâk•syon´) *f.* traction.

tractor (trâk•tor´) *m.* tractor; **— de orugas,** caterpillar tractor.

tradición (trâ•thē•syon´) *f.* tradition; delivery *(entrega).*

tradicional (trâ•thē•syo•nâl´) *adj.* traditional.

traducción (trâ•thūk•syon´) *f.* translation; interpretation *(interpretación).*

traducir* (trâ•thū•sēr´) *va.* to translate.

traductor, ra (trâ•thūk•tor´, râ) *n.* translator.

traer* (trâ•er´) *va.* to bring, to carry; to attract *(atraer);* to cause *(causar);* to have *(tener);* to wear *(llevar);* to cite, to adduce *(citar);* to make, to oblige *(obligar);* to persuade *(persuadir);* **—se,** to dress.

traficante (trâ•fē•kân´te) *m.* merchant, dealer.

traficar (trâ•fē•kâr´) *vn.* to do business, to deal; to travel *(correr).*

tráfico (trâ´fē•ko) *m.* traffic, trade; traffic *(tránsito).*

tragaluz (trâ•gâ•lūs´) *m.* skylight.

tragar (trâ•gâr´) *va.* to swallow; to glut *(comer mucho);* to swallow up *(abismar);* —**se,** to play dumb *(disimular);* to swallow; to stand, to put up with *(soportar).*

tragedia (trâ•he´thyâ) *f.* tragedy.

trágico, ca (trâ´hē•ko, kâ) *adj.* tragic.

trago (trâ´go) *m.* swallow; adversity, misfortune *(adversidad);* **a** —**s,** by degrees, little by little.

traición (trâē•syon´) *f.* treason; **a** —, deceitfully.

traicionar (trâē•syo•nâr´) *va.* to betray.

traidor, ra (trâē•thor´, râ) *n.* traitor; —, *adj.* treacherous.

traje (trâ´he) *m.* dress *(vestido);* suit; native dress *(vestido peculiar);* (Sp. Am.) mask *(máscara);* — **a la medida,** suit made to order; — **de etiqueta,** evening clothes, dress suit.

trama (trâ´mâ) *f.* weave; plot, scheme *(artificio);* plot *(de una obra literaria);* blossom *(de los árboles).*

tramar (trâ•mâr´) *va.* to weave; to plot, to scheme *(maquinar);* —, *vn.* to blossom.

tramitación (trâ•mē•tâ•syon´) *f.* transaction; steps *(serie de trámites).*

trámite (trâ´mē•te) *m.* passage *(paso);* step, requirement.

tramo (trâ´mo) *m.* tract, lot *(de tierra);* flight *(de escalones);* span *(de un puente);* passage *(pasaje);* length *(de piscina).*

trampa (trâm´pâ) *f.* trap, snare; trapdoor *(puerta);* sliding door *(de un mostrador);* trick *(ardid);* fly *(portañuela);* bad debt *(deuda);* bunker *(en el golf);* **hacer** —, to cheat.

trampolín (trâm•po•lēn´) *m.* springboard.

tramposo, sa (trâm•po´so, sâ) *adj.* deceitful, swindling; cheating *(en el juego).*

tranca (trâng´kâ) *f.* beam; crossbar, crossbeam *(para seguridad).*

trancar (trâng•kâr´) *va.* to bar.

trance (trân´se) *m.* critical moment *(apuro);* writ of payment *(judicial);* last stage *(de la vida);* **a todo** —, at all costs.

tranquilidad (trâng•kē•lē•thâth´) *f.* tranquility, quiet.

tranquilizar (trâng•kē•lē•sâr´) *va.* to soothe, to quiet.

tranquilo, la (trâng•kē´lo, lâ) *adj.*

tranquil, calm, quiet.

transacción (tran•sâk•syon´) *f.* compromise, concession *(componenda);* adjustment *(ajustamiento);* transaction *(negocio).*

transatlántico (trân•sâth•lân´tē•ko) = **trasatlántico.**

transbordar (trânz•vor•thâr´) = **trasbordar.**

transcendencia (trâns•sen•den´syâ) = **trascendencia.**

transcendental (trans•sen•den•tâl´) = **trascendental.**

transcender (trâns•sen•der´) = **trascender.**

transcribir (trâns•krē•vēr´) = **trascribir.**

transcurrir (trâns•kū•rrēr´) = **trascurrir.**

transcurso (trâns•kūr´so) = **trascurso.**

transeúnte (trân•se•ūn´te) *adj.* transitory; —, *m.* and *f.* passer-by; transient *(que reside poco).*

transferir (trâns•fe•rēr´) = **trasferir.**

transfigurarse (trâns•fē•gū•râr´-se) = **trasfigurarse.**

transformación (trâns•for•mâ•syon´) = **trasformación.**

transformador (trâns•for•mâ•thor´) = **trasformador.**

transformar (trâns•for•mâr´) = **trasformar.**

transfusión (trâns•fū•syon´) = **trasfusión.**

transgresor (trânz•gre•sor´) = **trasgresor.**

transición (trân•sē•syon´) *f.* transition.

transistor (trân•sēs•tor´) *m.* transistor.

transitar (trân•sē•târ´) *vn.* to pass by, to pass through; to travel *(viajar).*

tránsito (trân´sē•to) *m.* transit; transition *(transición);* stop *(parada);* passage *(paso);* death *(de un santo);* traffic *(tráfico);* **señal de** —, traffic sign.

transitorio, ria (trân•sē•to´ryo, ryâ) *adj.* transitory.

transmisión (trânz•mē•syon´) = **trasmisión.**

transmitir (trânz•mē•tēr´) = **trasmitir.**

transparente (trâns•pâ•ren´te) = **trasparente.**

transpirar (trâns•pē•râr´) = **traspirar.**

transplantar (trâns•plân•târ´) = **trasplantar.**

transponer (trâns•po•ner´) = **trasponer.**

transportar (trâns•por•târ´) = **trasportar.**

transporte (trâns•por´te) = **tras-**

porte.

transposición
(trans•po•sē•syon´) = **trasposi-
ción**

transversal (trânz•ver•sâl´) =
trasversal.

tranvía (trâm•bē´â) *m.* streetcar.

trapo (trâ´po) *m.* rag, tatter;
cape *(de torero);* — **de limpiar,**
cleaning rag; —**s,** *pl.* (coll.)
duds, clothes.

tráquea (trâ´ke•â) *f.* (med.) trachea, windpipe.

traqueo (trâ•ke´o))*m.* popping,
crack; shaking *(agitación);* jolt
(sacudida).

tras (trâs) *prep.* after, behind;
after *(en busca de);* behind, in
back of *(detrás de);* — **de,**
besides, in addition to; —, *m.*
behind; —, — bang, bang.

trasatlántico, ca
(trâ•sâth•lân´tē•ko, kâ) *adj.*
transatlantic; —, *m.* transatlantic liner.

trasbordar (trâz•vor•thâr´) *va.* to
transfer.

trascendencia (trâs•sen•den´syâ)
f. penetration *(penetración);*
importance, consequence *(con-
sequencia);* transcendence *(filosofía).*

trascendental (trâs•sen•den•tâl´)
adj. extensive, important,
serious *(importante);* transcendental *(filosofía).*

trascender* (trâs•sen•der´) *vn.*
to come to light *(empezar a ser
conocido);* to transmit, to
spread *(comunicarse);* to be
fragrant *(exhalar olor);* to transcend *(filosofía);* —, *vt.* to dig
into.

trascribir* (trâs•krē•vēr´) *va.* to
transcribe; to copy *(copiar).*

trascurrir (trâs•kū•rrēr´) *vn.* to
pass, to go by.

trascurso (trâs•kūr´so) *m.*
course, passing.

trasero, ra (trâ•se´ro, râ) *adj.*
back, rear, hind; **asiento** —,
back seat; —, *m.* buttock.

trasferir* (trâs•fe•rēr´) *va.* to
transfer; to postpone, to put off
(diferir).

trasfigurarse (trâs•fē•gū•râr´se)
vr. to be transfigured.

trasformación
(trâs•for•mâ•syon´) *f.* transformation.

trasformador (trâs•for•mâ•thor´)
m. transformer, converter.

trasformar (trâs•for•mâr´) *va.
and vr.* to transform, to
change.

trasfusión (trâs•fū•syon´) *f.*
transfusion.

trasgresor (trâz•gre•sor´) *m.*
transgressor, lawbreaker.

trasladar (trâz•lâ•thâr´) *va.* to
move, to change; to transfer *(a
un funcionario);* to translate

(traducir); to postpone *(diferir);* to copy, to transcribe *(copiar).*

traslado (trâz•lâ´tho) *m.* copy, transcript *(copia);* transfer; notification *(jurídico).*

traslucirse* (trâz•lū•sēr´se) *vr.* to be transparent; to be inferred *(deducirse).*

trasmisión (trâz•mē•syon´) *f.* transmission.

trasmisor (trâz•mē•sor´) *m.* transmitter.

trasmitir (trâz•mē•tēr´) *va.* to transmit, to transfer.

trasnochar (trâz•no•châr´) *vn.* to stay up all night; —, *vt.* to sleep on.

trasparente (trâs•pâ•ren´te) *adj.* transparent.

traspasar (trâs•pâ•sâr´) *va.* to transport *(llevar);* to cross, to cross over *(pasar);* to transfer *(trasferir);* to pass through again *(repasar);* to transgress *(transgredir);* to trespass *(exceder);* (fig.) to distress, to grieve.

traspirar (trâs•pē•râr´) *vn.* to transpire; to perspire *(sudar).*

trasplantar (trâs•plân•târ´) *va.* to transplant; —**se,** to emigrate.

trasponer* (trâs•po•ner´) *va.* to transpose, to transfer, to transport; —**se,** to detour; to be half asleep *(quedarse algo dormido).*

trasportar (trâs•por•târ´) *va.* to transport, to convey; (mus.) to transpose; —**se,** to get carried away.

trasporte (trâs•por´te) *m.* transportation, transport, conveyance; transport ship *(buque);* rapture, ecstasy *(efusión).*

traste (trâs´te) *m.* (mus.) fret; **dar al — con,** to ruin, to spoil.

trastienda (tras•tyen´dâ) *f.* back room *(de una tienda);* shrewdness, astuteness *(astucia).*

trasto (trâs´to) *m.* piece of junk *(mueble inútil);* piece of furniture *(mueble);* kitchen utensil *(utensilio);* good-for-nothing *(persona inútil);* (theat.) set piece.

trastornado, da (trâs•tor•nâ´tho, thâ) *adj.* unbalanced, crazy.

trastornar (trâs•tor•nâr´) *va.* to tip, to upset; to overturn, to turn upside-down *(volcar);* to mix up *(invertir el orden);* to disquiet, to disturb *(inquietar);* to go to one´s head *(perturbar el sentido);* to persuade *(persuadir).*

trastorno (trâs•tor´no) *m.* confusion, upset, mix-up.

trasversal (trâz•ver•sal´) *adj.* transverse; collateral *(de parientes);* **calle —,** crossroad.

tratable (trâ•tâ´vle) *adj.* tractable, compliant; courteous, sociable *(cortés)*.

tratado (trâ•tâ´tho) *m.* treaty, agreement; treatise *(escrito);* discourse *(discurso).*

tratamiento (trâ•tâ•myen´to) *m.* treatment; title *(título);* procedure *(procedimiento).*

tratar (trâ•târ´) *va.* to manage, to handle *(manejar);* to treat *(obrar con);* — **con,** to deal with; to have an affair with *(relaciones amorosas);* — **de,** to try to, to attempt to; to classify as *(calificar de).*

trato (trâ´to) *m.* treatment; title *(título);* contract *(contrato);* business dealings *(negocio);* agreement, deal *(tratado).*

trauma (trâ´ū•mâ) *m.* (med.) trauma.

través (trâ•ves´) *m.* bent, inclination *(inclinación);* misfortune, setback *(desgracia)*; **a — de,** across.

travesaño (trâ•ve•sâ´nyo) *m.* cross timber, crossbar, crossbeam; bolster *(almohada).*

travesía (trâ•ve•sē´â) *f.* side street *(callejuela);* crossing, voyage *(viaje);* distance *(distancia);* (naut.) side wind; through street *(carretera);* win *(cantidad de ganancia);* loss *(cantidad de pérdida);* pay *(de un marinero);* plain *(llanura).*

travesura (trâ•ve•sū´râ) *f.* mischief *(acción traviesa);* ingeniousness *(viveza de genio);* prank, smart trick *(acción culpable).*

travieso, sa (trâ•vye´so, sâ) *adj.* cross; mischievous *(pícaro);* ingenious, clever *(sagaz);* restless, uneasy, fidgety *(inquieto);* turbulent, rolling *(en movimiento continuo);* debauched *(distraído en vicios).*

trayectoria (trâ•yek•to´ryâ) *f.* trajectory.

traza (trâ´sâ) *f.* design *(diseño);* plan *(plan);* invention, scheme; *(invención):* appearance, looks *(apariencia);* —**s,** *pl.* (fig.) wits.

trazar (trâ•sâr´) *va.* to design *(diseñar);* to plan, to make plans for *(planear);* to draw, to trace *(delinear);* to outline, to sketch, to summarize *(bosquejar).*

trazo (trâ´so) *m.* plan, design; line *(línea);* stroke *(de la letra de mano).*

trébol (tre´vol) *m.* (bot.) clover; cloverleaf *(de una carretera).*

trece (tre´se) *m.* and *adj.* thirteen; **estarse en sus —,** to be persistent, to stick to one´s guns.

trecientos (tre•syen´tos) = **trescientos.**

trecho (tre´cho) *m.* stretch; well,

while *(de tiempo);* **a —s,** at intervals.

tregua (tre′gwâ) *f.* truce, armistice; rest, respite *(descanso);* **sin —,** unceasingly.

treinta (tre′ēn•tâ) *m.* and *adj.* thirty.

trémulo, la (tre′mū•lo, lâ) *adj.* tremulous, trembling.

tren (tren) *m.* train, retinue; show, ostentation *(ostentación);* (rail.) train; **— de aterrizaje,** landing gear; **— de ruedas,** running gear; **— elevado,** elevated train.

trenza (tren′sâ) *f.* braid *(del pelo);* braiding.

trenzar (tren•sâr′) *va.* to braid.

trepador, ra (tre•pâ•thor′, râ) *adj.* climbing.

trepar (tre•pâr′) *vn.* to climb; **—,** *vt.* to drill *(taladrar);* to put braiding on.

trepidación (tre•pē•thâ•syon′) *f.* vibration, trembling; trepidation *(miedo).*

tres (tres) *adj.* and *m.* three; **— veces,** thrice; three times.

trescientos, tas (tres•syen′tos, tâs) *m.* and *adj.* three hundred.

triangular (tryâng•gū•lâr′) *adj.* triangular; **—,** *va.* to triangulate.

triángulo (tryâng′gū•lo) *m.* triangle.

tribu (trē′vū) *f.* tribe.

tribulación (trē•vū•lâ•syon′) *f.* tribulation, affliction.

tribuna (trē•vū′nâ) *f.* tribune, platform.

tribunal (trē•vū•nâl′) *m.* tribunal, courthouse; court *(ministro o ministros de la justicia);* **T — supremo** Supreme Court.

tribuno (trē•vū′no) *m.* tribune; orator *(orador).*

tributario, ria (trē•vū•tâ′ryo, ryâ) *adj.* tributary.

tributo, (trē•vū′to) *m.* tribute; tax *(impuesto);* retribution *(retribución).*

triceps (trē′seps) *m.* (anat.) triceps.

triciclo (trē•sē′klo) *m.* tricycle.

tridente (trē•then′te) *adj.* three-pronged; **—,** *m.* trident.

trigésimo, ma (trē•he′sē•mo, mâ) *m.* and *adj.* thirtieth.

trigo (trē′go) *m.* wheat; money *(dinero).*

trigonometría (trē•go•no•me•trē′â) *f.* trigonometry.

trigueño, ña (trē•ge′nyo, nyâ) *adj.* brunet, brunette.

trilogía (trē•lo•hē′â) *f.* trilogy.

trillador, ra (trē•yâ•thor′, râ) *n.* thresher; threshing machine; **—,** *adj.* threshing; **máquina —,** threshing machine.

trillar (trē•yâr′) *va.* to thresh; (coll.) to hang around; to mistreat *(maltratar).*

trimestre (trē•mes´tre) *m.* space of three months.

trinchera (trēn•che´râ) *f.* trench, entrenchment.

trio (trē´o) *m.* (mus.) trio.

tripa (trē´pâ) *f.* gut, entrails, tripe, intestine; belly *(panza);* filling *(del cigarro);* —**s,** *pl.* insides; **hacer de —s corazón,** to pluck up courage.

triple (trē´ple) *adj.* triple.

triplicar (trē•plē•kâr´) *va.* to triple.

trípode (trē´po•the) *m.* or *f.* tripod.

tripulación (trē•pū•lâ•syon´) *f.* crew.

tripulado, da (trē•pū•lâ´tho, thâ) *adj.* manned.

tripular (trē•pū•lâr´) *va.* to man; to go on board *(ir a bordo).*

tris (trēs) *m.* tinkle; trice, instant *(instante);* **estar en un — que,** to be on the point of.

triste (trēs´te) *adj.* sad, mournful, melancholy.

tristeza (trēs•te´sâ) *f.* melancholy, sadness, gloom.

triturar (trē•tū•râr´) *va.* to crush, to grind, to pound; to chew, to crunch *(mascar);* (fig.) to abuse, to mistreat *(maltratar).*

triunfante (tryūm•fân´te) *adj.* triumphant, exultant.

triunfar (tryūm•fâr´) *vn.* to triumph; to trump *(en los naipes);* (fig.) to throw money around *(gastar).*

triunfo (tryūm´fo) *m.* triumph, victory; trump *(en los naipes)* heavy spending *(acto de gastar mucho).*

trivial (trē•vyâl´) *adj.* trivial, commonplace, trite.

trivialidad (trē•vyâ•lē•thâth´) *f.* trifle, triviality.

trocar* (tro•kâr´) *va.* to exchange; to change, to vary *(cambiar);* to vomit *(vomitar);* to confuse, to mix up *(equivocar);* —**se,** to change; to change seats *(permutar el asiento).*

trofeo (tro•fe´o) *m.* trophy; booty, plunder *(despojo);* (fig.) victory *(victoria).*

trolebús (tro•le•vūs´) *m.* trolley bus.

tromba (trom´bâ) *f.* waterspout; tornado *(terrestre).*

trombón (trom•bon´) *m.* (mus.) trombone.

trompa (trom´bâ) *f.* trumpet, horn; trunk *(de los elefantes);* proboscis *(de insectos).*

trompeta (trom•pe´tâ) *f.* trumpet, horn; —, *m.* trumpeter.

trompetero (trom•pe•te´ro) *m.* trumpeter; trumpet maker *(fabricante).*

tronar* (tro•nâr´) *vn.* to thunder;

(fig.) to go bankrupt *(arruinarse);* to harangue, to thunder *(hablar o escribir).*

troncar (trong•kâr´) = **truncar.**

tronco (trong´ko) *m.* trunk; team *(de caballos);* log *(leño);* stock, lineage *(linaje);* (fig.) thickhead *(persona).*

trono (tro´no) *m.* throne.

tronzar (tron•sâr´) *va.* to shatter, to break; to pleat *(hacer pliegues);* (fig.) to tire out, to wear out.

tropa (tro´pâ) *f.* troop; plebeians *(gentecilla);* mob, crowd *(muchedumbre);* —**s de asalto,** storm troops; — **de línea,** regular army.

tropezar* (tro•pe•sâr´) *vn.* to stumble, to trip; to be detained, to be obstructed, to be held up *(detenerse);* to go wrong, to slip up *(deslizarse en un error);* (fig.) to oppose, to dispute *(oponerse);* to quarrel *(reñir);* (fig.) to bump into *(hallar).*

tropical (tro•pē•kâl´) *adj.* tropical.

trópico (tro´pē•ko) *m.* tropic; —, **ca,** *adj.* tropical.

tropiezo (tro•pye´so) *m.* obstacle; stumble, trip *(tropezón);* slip, fault, mistake *(yerro);* quarrel, argument, *(riña).*

tropo (tro´po) *m.* figure of speech.

trotamundos (tro•tâ•mūn´dos) *m.* and *f.* globetrotter.

trotar (tro•târ´) *vn.* to trot.

trote (tro´te) *m.* trot; fix, jam *(apuro);*
a —, hastily, hurriedly.

trovador, ra (tro•vâ•thor´, râ) *n.* minstrel, troubadour.

trozo (tro´so) *m.* piece, bit, part, fragment; selection *(selección);* (rail.) section of a line.

trucha (trū´châ) *f.* trout; crane *(cabria).*

trueno (trwe´no) *m.* thunderclap; shot, report *(del tiro).*

trueque (trwe´ke) *m.* exchange; —**s,** *pl.* change.

truhán, ana (trū•ân´, â´nâ) *n.* buffoon, clown; cheat, crook *(sinverguenza);* —, *adj.* cheating, thieving.

truhanería (trwâ•ne•rē´â) *f.* buffoonery.

truncar (trūng•kâr´) *va.* to cut off; to behead, to decapitate *(cortar la cabeza);* to leave out *(omitir);* to weaken; — **la carrera,** to ruin one´s hopes for a career.

tu (tū) *adj.* your.

tú (tū) *pron.* you.

tuba (tū´vâ) *f.* tuba.

tuberculosis (tū•ver•kū•lo´sēs) *f.* (med.) tuberculosis.

tubería (tū•ve•rē´â) *f.* pipeline;

tubing, piping *(conjunto de tubos).*

tubo (tū′vo) *m.* tube, pipe, duct; — **de escape,** exhaust pipe.

tuerca (twer′kâ) *f.* screw.

tuerto, ta (twer′to, tâ) *adj.* twisted, crooked; one-eyed *(de un ojo).*

tuétano (twe′tâ•no) *m.* marrow.

tulipán (tū•lē•pân′) *m.* tulip.

tumba (tūm′bâ) *f.* tomb, grave; tumble, fall *(caída).*

tumbar (tūm•bâr′) *va.* to tip over, to knock down; (coll.) to stun; —, *vn.* to fall down, to take a fall.

tumefacto, ta (tū•me•fak′to, tâ) *adj.* tumescent.

tumor (tū•mor′) *m.* tumor.

tumulto (tū•mūl′to) *m.* tumult, uproar.

tuna (tū′nâ) *f.* prickly pear; wandering, loafing *(vida vagabunda).*

tunante (tū•nân′te) *adj.* astute, cunning *(taimado);* vagabond; —, *m.* vagabond; rascal, hooligan *(bribón).*

túnel (tū′nel) *m.* tunnel.

túnica (tū′nē•kâ) *f.* tunic; membrane *(membrana).*

turba (tūr′vâ) *f.* crowd, mob *(gentío);* turf, sod, peat.

turbación (tūr•vâ•syon′) *f.* confusion, disorder.

turbar (tūr•vâr′) *va.* to disturb, to upset; to stir up *(enturbiar).*

turbina (tūr•vē′nâ) *f.* turbine.

turbio, bia (tūr′vyo, vyâ) *adj.* muddy, turbid; (fig.) confused *(confuso);* turbulent, upset *(agitado).*

turbulencia (tūr•vū•len′syâ) *f.* turbulence; confusion, disorder *(confusión).*

turbulento, ta (tūr•vū•len′to, tâ) *adj.* turbulent.

turco, ca (tūr′ko, kâ) *adj.* Turkish; —, *n.* Turk.

turismo (tū•rēz′mo) *m.* tourism.

turista (tū•rēs′tâ) *m.* and *f.* tourist.

turnar (tūr•nâr′) *vn.* to alternate.

turno (tūr′no) *m.* turn, shift; **por** —, in turn; — **diurno,** day shift.

turquesa (tūr•ke′sâ) *f.* turquoise.

turquí (tūr•kē′) *adj.* turquoise blue.

Turquía (tūr•kē′â) *f.* Turkey.

tutear (tū•te•âr′) *va.* to address as tú instead of usted.

tutela (tū•te′lâ) *f.* guardianship, tutelage.

tutelar (tū•te•lâr′) *adj.* protective, guardian.

tutor, ra (tū•tor′, râ) *n.* guardian.

tuyo, ya (tū′yo, yâ) *adj.* your; —, *pron.* yours.

U

u (ū) *conj.* or.

ubicación (ū•vē•kâ•syon´) *f.* location, situation.

ubicar (ū•vē•kâr´) *vn.* and *vr.* to be located, to be situated; — *va.* (Sp. Am.) to locate, to find.

ufanarse (ū•fâ•nâr´se) *vr.* to boast.

ufano, na (ū•fâ´no, nâ) *adj.* haughty, arrogant; (fig.) satisfied, content *(satisfecho)*.

ujier (ū•hyer´) *m.* usher, doorman.

úlcera (ūl´se•râ) *f.* ulcer.

ulceroso, sa (ūl•se•ro´so, sâ) *adj.* ulcerous.

ulterior (ūl•te•ryor´) *adj.* ulterior; later *(posterior)*.

últimamente (ūl•tē•mâ•men´te) *adv.* lately; finally *(finalmente)*.

ultimátum (ūl•tē•mâ´tūn) *m.* ultimatum.

último, ma (ūl´tē•mo, ma) *adj.* last, latest, farthest *(más remoto)*; best, superior *(superior)*; last, final *(final)*; **a —mos del mes, de la semana,** at the end of the month, week; **por —mo,** lastly, finally.

ultrajar (ūl•trâ•hâr´) *va.* to outrage, to insult; to abuse, to mistreat *(maltratar)*.

ultraje (ūl•trâ´he) *m.* abuse, outrage.

ultramoderno, na (ūl•trâ•mo•ther´no, nâ) *adj.* ultramodern.

ultrasónico, ca (ūl•trâ•so´nē•ko, kâ) *adj.* ultrasonic.

ultravioleta (ūl•trâ•vyo•le´tâ) *adj.* ultra-violet.

umbilical (ūm•bē•lē•kâl´) *adj.* umbilical.

umbral (ūm•brâl´) *m.* threshold, door-step; (fig.) threshold.

un, una (ūn, ū´nâ) *adj.* one; —, *art.* a, an; **una vez,** once.

unánime (ū•nâ´nē•me) *adj.* unanimous.

unanimidad (ū•nâ•nē•mē•thâ-th´) *f.* unanimity.

uncir (ūn•sēr´) *va.* to yoke.

undécimo, ma (ūn•de´sē•mo, mâ) *adj.* eleventh.

ungir (ūn•hēr´) *va.* to anoint.

ungüento (ūn•gwen´to) *m.* unguent, ointment; (fig.) balm.

único, ca (ū´nē•ko, kâ) *adj.* sole, only; (fig.) unique, unusual.

unidad (ū•nē•thâth´) *f.* unity *(cualidad)*; unit.

unificación (ū•nē•fē•kâ•syon´) *f.* unification.

uniforme (ū•nē•for´me) *adj.* and

m. uniform.

uniformidad (ū•nē•for•mē•thâth´) *f.* uniformity.

unilateral (ū•nē•lâ•te•râl´) *adj.* unilateral.

unión (ū•nyon´) *f.* union;

unir (ū•nēr´) *va.* to join, to unite.

unísono, na (ū•nē´so•no, nâ) *adj.* unison.

universal (ū•nē•ver•sâl´) *adj.* universal.

universidad (ū•nē•ver•sē•thâth´) *f.* university *(instituto).*

universo (ū•nē•ver´so) *m.* universe.

uno (ū´no) *m.* one; —, **na,** *pron.* one; —, *adj.* sole, the same; — **a otro,** one an-other; **cada —,** each one; everyone; — **a —,** one by one.

unos, nas (ū´nos, nâs) *pron.* and *adj. pl.* some.

untar (ūn•târ´) *va.* to oil, to grease; (fig.) to grease one´s palm, to bribe.

unto (ūn´to) *m.*grease; fat *(del animal).*

uña (ū´nyâ) *f.* nail; hoof *(casco);* claw, talon *(garra);* stinger *(del alacrán);* thorn *(espina);* scab *(costra);* hook *(garfio);* **ser — y carne,** to be very close friends.

uranio (ū•râ´nyo) *m.* uranium.

urbanización

(ūr•vâ•nē•sâ•syon´) *f.* urbanization.

urbanizar (ūr•vâ•nē•sâr´) *va* to urbanize.

urbano, na (ūr•vâ´no, nâ) *adj.* polite, well-bred *(cortesano);* urban.

urbe (ūr´ve) *f.* metropolis, city.

urgencia (ūr•hen´syâ) *f.* urgency; emergency *(necesidad).*

urgente (ūr•hen´te) *adj.* pressing, urgent.

urgir (ūr•hēr´) *vn.* to be urgent.

urna (ūr´nâ) *f.* urn; — **electoral,** ballot box.

urticaria (ūr•tē•kâ´ryâ) *f.* (med.) hives.

uruguayo, ya (ū•rū•gwâ´yo, yâ) *n.* and *adj.* Uruguayan.

usado, da (ū•sâ´tho, thâ) *adj.* used, worn; used, accustomed *(habituado).*

usar (ū•sâr´) *va.* to use, to make use of; to practice, to follow *(un empleo);* —, *vn.* to be used to.

uso (ū´so) *m.* use; style, custom *(modo).*

usted (ūs•teth´) *pron.* you; — **mismo,** you yourself.

ustedes (ūs•te´thes) pron *pl.* you.

usual (ū•swâl´) *adj.* usual, customary.

usufructo (ū•sū•frūk´to) *m.* profit, benefit; usufruct *(derecho)*

usurpación (ū•sūr•pâ•syon´) *f.*

usurpation, seizure.

usurpar (ū•sūr•pâr´) *va.* to usurp, to seize.

utensilio (ū•ten•sē´lyo) *m.* utensil.

uterino, na (ū•te•rē´no, nâ) *adj.* uterine.

útero (ū´te•ro) *m.* uterus, womb.

útil (ū´tēl) *adj.* useful; **—es,** *m.pl.* utensils, tools; **—es de escritorio,** stationery.

utilidad (ū•tē•lē•thâth´) *f.* utility; profit *(provecho).*

utilizable (ū•tē•lē•sâ´vle) *adj.* usable.

utilizar (ū•tē•lē•sâr´) *va.* to make use of, to utilize.

utopia (ū•to•pē´â) *f.* Utopia or utopia.

uva (ū´vâ) *f.* grape; barberry *(berberí).*

V

vaca (bâ´kâ) *f.* cow; pool *(dinero).*

vacaciones (bâ•kâ•syo´nes) *f. pl.* holidays, vacation.

vacante (bâ•kân´te) *adj.* vacant; **—,** *f.* vacancy.

vaciar (bâ•syâr´) *va.* to empty; to drain *(beber);* to cast *(metales).*

vacilación (bâ•sē•lâ•syon´) *f.* vacillation; wobbling, shaking.

vacilante (bâ•sē•lân´te) *adj.* vacillating; unsteady, wobbling.

vacilar (bâ•sē•1âr´) *vn.* to be unsteady, to totter, to wobble *(tambalearse);* to waver, to flicker *(temblar);* (fig.) to vacillate, to hesitate, to doubt *(titubear).*

vacío, cía (bâ•sē´o, sē´â) *adj.* empty; (fig.) void, devoid *(falto);* (fig.) vain *(presuntuoso);* **—,** *m.* (phy.) vacuum; hole *(hueco);* (fig.) void.

vacuna (bâ•kū´nâ) *f.* vaccine.

vacunar (bâ•kū•nâr´) *va.* to vaccinate.

vagabundo, da (bâ•gâ•vūn´do, dâ) *adj.* vagabond.

vagar (bâ•gâr´) *vn.* to rove, to wander; **—,** *m.* leisure *(tiempo libre);* slowness.

vagina (bâ•hē´nâ) *f.* (anat.) vagina.

vago, ga (bâ´go, gâ) *adj.* vagrant, wandering; vague *(indeciso);* **—,** *n.* vagrant; **en —go,** unsteadily; in vain *(en vano).*

vagón (bâ•gon´) *m.* railroad car; **— cama,** sleeping car.

vahído (bâ•ē´tho) *m.* vertigo, dizziness.

vaho (bâ´o) *m.* steam, vapor.

vaina (bâ´ē•nâ) *f.* pod, husk

(cáscara).

vainilla (bâe•nē′yâ) *f.* vanilla.

vaivén (bâe•ven′) *m.* movement to and fro; (fig.) fluctuation; risk, danger *(riesgo).*

vajilla (bâ•hē′yâ) *f.* table service, set of dishes; — **de plata,** silverware.

vale (bâ′le) *m.* promissory note, I•O•U. *(pagaré);* voucher.

valenciano, na (bâ•len•syâ′no, nâ) *adj.* and *n.* Valencian.

valentía (bâ•len•tē′â) *f.* valor, courage; bragging, boasting *(jactancia).*

valer* (bâ•ler′) *vn.* to be valuable; to be important *(tener autoridad);* to be valid *(de monedas);* to prevail *(prevalecer);* to avail *(servir);* (fig.) to have influence, to have pull; —, *va.* to protect, to favor *(amparar);* to result in *(redituar);* to be worth *(equivaler);* — **la pena,** to be worthwhile; —**se,** to use; to resort to *(recurrir);* —**se por sí mismo,** to be selfreliant.

validar (bâ•le•thâr′) *va.* to validate.

validez (bâ•le•thes′) *f.* validity; strength *(fuerza).*

válido, da (bâ′le•tho, thâ) *adj.* valid; sound, strong.

valiente (bâ•lyen′te) *adj.* valiant, brave, courageous; vigorous *(activo);* first-rate *(excelente);*

(fig.) extreme.

valioso, sa (bâ•lyo′so, sâ) *adj.* valuable; rich, wealthy *(rico).*

valor (bâ•lor′) *m.* value, worth; force, power *(fuerza);* equivalence *(equivalencia);* courage, valor *(calidad del alma);* cheek *(osadía);* **sin —,** worthless.

valorar (bâ•lo•râr′) or **valorear** (bâ•lo•re•âr′) *va.* to value; to use *(utilizar);* to increase the value of *(aumentar),*

vals (bâls) *m.* waltz.

valuar (bâ•lwâr′) *va.* to evaluate, to estimate.

válvula (bâl′vū•lâ) *f.* valve.

valla (bâ′yâ) *f.* barricade, fence; (fig.) obstacle, impediment.

valle (bâ′ye) *m.* valley.

vandalismo (bân•dâ•lēz′mo) *m.* vandalism.

vanguardia (bâng•gwâr′dyâ) *f.* vanguard, van.

vanidad (bâ•nē•thâth′) *f.* vanity.

vanidoso, sa (bâ•nē•tho′so, sâ) *adj.* vain.

vano, na (bâ′no, nâ) *adj.* vain; —, *m.* hollow; **en —no,** in vain.

vapor (bâ•por′) *m.* vapor, steam; (naut.) steamer, steamship.

vaquero (bâ•ke′ro) *m.* cowboy; —, **ra,** *adj.* cowboy, ranch.

vara (bâ′râ) *f.* twig, branch *(rama);* rod, pole *(palo);* staff *(de mando);* — **alta,** upper hand.

variable (bâ•rya´vle) *adj.* and *f.* variable.

variación (bâ•ryâ•syon´) *f.* variation.

variado, da (bâ•ryâ´tho, thâ) *adj.* variegated *(colores);* varied, diverse.

variante, (bâ•ryân´te) *adj.* and *f.* variant; —, *adj.* varying.

variar (bâ•ryâr´) *va.* to vary, to change; —, *vn.* to vary.

varicela (bâ•rē•se´lâ) *f.* (med.) chicken pox.

varicoso, sa (bâ•rē•ko´so, sâ) *adj.* varicose.

variedad (bâ•rye•thâth´) *f.* variety, diversity *(diversidad);* inconstancy, instability; change, alteration *(mudanza);* variation *(variación).*

vario (bâ´ryo, ryâ) *adj.* varied, various; (fig.) fickle, inconstant.

varón (bâ•ron´) *m.* male; man *(adulto);* man of standing *(hombre respetable).*

varonil (bâ•ro•nēl´) *adj.* male; (fig.) manly, virile.

vaselina (bâ•se•lē´nâ) *f.* vaseline, petroleum jelly.

vasija (bâ•sē´hâ) *f.* vessel, dish.

vaso (bâ´so) *m.* glass *(para beber);* vase.

vástago (bâs´tâ•go) *m.* bud, shoot; (fig.) offshoot, descendant; rod, bar *(barra).*

vasto, ta (bâs´to, tâ) *adj.* vast, huge.

Vaticano (bâ•tē•kâ´no) *m.* Vatican.

vaticinar (bâ•tē•sē•nâr´) *va.* to divine, to foretell.

vaticinio (bâ•tē•sē´nyo) *m.* foretelling, prediction, forecast.

vatio (bâ´tyo) *m.* watt

véase (be´â•se) see, refer to.

vecindario (be•sēn•dâ´ryo) *m.* neighborhood, district.

vecino, na (be•sē´no, nâ) *adj.* neighboring, near; —, *n.* neighbor; inhabitant *(habitante).*

vector (bek•tor´) *m.* (avi.) vector.

vedar (be•thâr´) *va.* to prohibit, to forbid *(prohibir);* to impede *(impedir).*

vegetación (be•he•tâ•syon´) *f.* vegetation.

vegetal (be•he•tâl´) *adj.* and *m.* vegetable.

vegetariano, na (be•he•tâ•ryâ´no, nâ) *adj.* and *m.* vegetarian.

vehemencia (be•e•men´syâ) *f.* vehemence.

vehemente (be•e•men´te) *adj.* vehement.

vehículo (be•ē´kū•lo) *m.* vehicle.

veinte (be´ēn•te) *adj.* and *m.* twenty.

veintena (beēn•te´nâ) *f.* score, twenty.

veinteno, na (beēn•te´no, nâ) *adj.* twentieth.

veintiuno, na (beēn•tyū´no, nâ) *adj.* twenty-one.

vejez (be•hes´) *f.* old age; (fig.) old story.

vejiga (be•hē´gâ) *f.* bladder; blister *(ampolla)*.

vela (be´lâ) *f.* watch, vigil; night work *(trabajo)*; pilgrimage *(romería)*; guard *(centinela)*; candle *(para alumbrar)*.

velación (be•lâ•syon´) *f.* watch, watching.

velador (be•lâ•thor´) *m.* watchman, caretaker *(guardia)*; wooden candlestick *(candelero)*; lamp stand *(mesita)*.

velar (be•lâr´) *vn.* to stay awake; to work nights *(trabajar)*; (fig.) to take care, to watch; —, *va.* to look after *(asistir)*; (fig.) to observe closely.

velero, ra (be•le´ro, râ) *adj.* swift-sailing; —, *m.* sailboat.

velo (be´lo) *m.* veil; (fig.) pretext.

velocidad (be•lo•sē•thâth´) *f.* velocity, speed; **a toda —,** at full speed; **cambio de —,** gear shift; **— aérea,** air speed; **— máxima,** speed limit.

veloz (be•los´) *adj.* swift, quick.

vello (be´yo) *m.* down, fuzz.

vellocino (be•yo•sē´no) *m.* fleece.

velloso, sa (be•yo´so, sâ) *adj.* downy, fuzzy.

velludo, da (be•yū´tho, thâ) *adj.* shaggy, woolly, hairy; —, *m.*

velvet.

vena (be´nâ) *f.* vein; (fig.) inspiration; **estar en —,** to feel in the mood.

venado (be•nâ´tho) *m.* deer.

vencedor, ra (ben•se•thor´, râ) *n.* conqueror, victor; —, *adj.* victorious.

vencer (ben•ser´) *va.* to conquer; to excede, to surpass *(exceder)*; to prevail over *(prevalecer)*; to suffer *(sufrir)*; to twist, to bend *(torcer)*; —, *vn.* to fall due; to expire, to run out *(terminar)*; **— se,** to control oneself.

vencido, da (ben•sē´tho, thâ) *adj.* conquered; due *(debido)*; **darse por —,** to give up, to yield.

vencimiento (ben•sē•myen´to) *m.* victory; (com.) expiration.

venda (ben´dâ) *f.* bandage; blindfold *(sobre los ojos)*.

vendaje (ben•dâ´he) *m.* bandage, dressing.

vendar (ben•dâr´) *va.* to bandage; to blindfold; (fig.) to blind *(cegar)*.

vendedor, ra (ben•de•thor´, râ) *n.* seller; —, *m.* salesman; —, *f.* saleswoman.

vender (ben•der´) *va.* to sell; to sell out, to betray *(traicionar)*; **— al por menor,** to sell retail; **— al por mayor,** to sell wholesale.

vendible (ben•dē´vle) *adj.* salable, marketable.

veneciano, na (be•ne•syâ´ no, nâ) *adj.* and *n.* Venetian.

veneno (be•ne´no) *m.* poison, venom.

venenoso, sa (be•ne•no´so, sâ) *adj.* venomous, poisonous.

veneración (be•ne•râ•syon´) *f.* veneration, worship.

venerar (be•ne•râr´) *va.* to venerate, to worship.

venezolano, na (be•ne•so•lâ´no, nâ) *n.* and *adj.* Venezuelan.

venganza (beng•gân´sâ) *f.* revenge, vengeance.

vengar (beng•gâr´) *va.* to revenge, to avenge; **—se de,** to take revenge for.

vengativo, va (beng•ga•tē´vo, vâ) *adj.* revengeful, vindictive.

venida (be•nē´thâ) *f.* arrival; return *(regreso);* (fig.) impetuosity.

venidero, ra (be•nē•the´ro, râ) *adj.* coming, next, approaching; **el próximo —,** the coming month; **—s,** *m. pl.* posterity.

venir* (be•nēr´) *vn.* to come, to arrive; to agree to *(conformarse);* to fit, to suit *(ajustarse);* **— a menos,** to decay, to decline; **¿a qué viene eso?** to what purpose is that? **el mes que viene,** next month; **—de,** to come from: **ir y —,** to go back

asid forth; **— de perillas, — como anillo al dedo,** to be very opportune, to be in the nick of time.

venta (ben´tâ) *f.* sale; roadside inn *(mesón).*

ventaja (ben•tâ´hâ) *f.* advantage; **con — recíproca,** to mutual advantage; **llevar —,** to have the advantage over.

ventajoso, sa (ben•tâ•ho´so, sâ) *adj.* advantageous.

ventana (ben•tâ´nâ) *f.* window; **repisa de —,** windowsill; **vidrio de —,** windowpane.

ventanilla (ben•tâ•nē´yâ) *f.* small window; peephole *(abertura).*

ventilación (ben•tē•lâ•syon´) *f.* ventilation; discussion *(discusión).*

ventilador (ben•tē•lâ•thor´) *m.* ventilator, fan.

ventilar (ben•tē•lâr´) *va.* and *vr.* to ventilate, to air; to discuss *(discutir).*

ventrículo (ben•trē´kū•lo) *m.* (anat.) ventricle.

ventrílocuo (ben•trē´lo•kwo) *m.* ventriloquist.

ventura (ben•tū´râ) *f.* luck, chance, fortune; risk, danger *(riesgo);* **por —,** perhaps.

venturoso, sa (ben•tū•ro´so, sâ) *adj.* lucky, fortunate, happy.

ver* (ber) *va.* to see; to look at; to note, to observe *(observar);*

to understand *(comprender);* to consider, to reflect *(considerar);* to predict *(prevenir);* **vamos a —,** let's see; **veremos,** we'll see, maybe; **hacer —,** to claim, to make believe; **ser de —,** to be worthy of attention; **—se,** to find oneself; **—se en apuros,** to be in trouble; **—se bien,** to look well; **—,** *m.* sight, appearance, aspect; **a mi —,** in my opinion, to my way of thinking.

veranear (be•râ•ne•âr´) *vn.* to spend the summer, to vacation.

verano (be•râ´no) *m.* summer.

veras (be´râs) *f. pl.* truth, sincerity; **de —,** in truth, really.

veraz (be•râs´) *adj.* veracious, truthful, sincere.

verbal (ber•vâl´) *adj.* verbal, oral.

verbo (ber´vo) *m.* word, term; (gram.) verb.

verdad (ber•thâth´) *f.* truth; **en —,** really, indeed; **ser hombre de —,** to be a man of his word; **decir a un cuatro —es,** to tell someone off.

verdaderamente (ber•thâ•the•râ•men´te) *adv.* truly, in fact.

verdadero, ra (ber•thâ•the´ro, râ) *adj.* true, real; sincere *(sincero).*

verde (ber´the) *adj.* green; fresh, vigorous *(vigoroso);* (fig.) young,

inexperienced *(joven);* off-color *(desvergonzado);* **—,** *m.* fodder; bitterness *(del vino).*

verdor (ber•thor´) *m.* verdure, greenness; (fig.) youth, vigor.

verdoso, sa (ber•tho´so, sâ) *adj.* greenish.

verdugo (ber•thū´go) *m.* young shoot; whip *(azote);* welt *(roncha);* (orn.) shrike; hangman *(ejecutor);* (fig.) savage, brute; (fig.) torment, plague *(azote).*

verdura (ber•thū´râ) *f.* verdure; vegetables, greens *(hortaliza).*

vereda (be•re´thâ) *f.* path, trail.

veredicto (be•re•thēk´to) *m.* verdict.

vergel (ber•hel´) *m.* flower garden.

vergonzante (ber•gon•sân´te) *adj.* shameful, shamefaced.

vergonzoso, sa (ber•gon•so´so, sâ) *adj.* bashful, shy; shameful *(bochornoso).*

vergüenza (ber•gwen´sâ) *f.* shame; bashfulness *(timidez);* confusion *(confusión);* **tener —,** to be ashamed; to have dignity, to be honorable *(tener pundonor).*

verídico ca (be•re´the•ko, kâ) *adj.* truthful.

verificar (be•re•fe•kâr´) *va.* to verify, to prove; to check *(examinar);* **—se,** to be verified, to turn out true; to take place *(realizarse).*

verja (ber´hâ) *f.* grate, lattice; iron fence *(cerca).*

vermut (ber•mūt´) *m.* vermouth.

verosímil (be•ro•sē´mēl) *adj.* plausible, credible.

verraco (be•rrâ´ko) *m.* boar.

verruga (be•rrū´gâ) *f.* wart; (coll.) nuisance; (coll.) defect *(tacha).*

verrugoso, sa (be•rrū•go´so, sâ) *adj.* warty.

versar (ber•sâr´) *vn.* to turn, to go around; (Cuba) to versify; — **sobre,** to deal with; —**se** to become skillful.

versátil (ber•sâ´tēl) *adj.* versatile; (fig.) fickle.

versículo (ber•sē´kū•lo) *m.* versicle; verse *(de la Biblia).*

versión (ber•syon´) *f.* translation *(traducción);* version, interpretation.

verso (ber´so) *m.* verse, stanza; — **blanco,** —**suelto,** blank verse; — **libre,** free verse.

vértebra (ber´te•vrâ) *f.* vertebra.

vertebrado, da (ber•te•vrâ´tho, thâ) *m.* and *adj.* vertebrate.

vertedero (ber•te•the´ro) *m.* drain, sewer.

verter* (ber•ter´) *va* and *vr.* to spill, to empty, to pour *(derramar);* to translate *(traducir);* —, *vn.* to flow.

vertical (ber•tē•kâl´) *adj.* vertical, upright.

vértice (ber´tē•se) *m.* vertex; (fig.) crown *(de la cabeza).*

vertiente (ber•tyen´te) *adj.* sloping; —, *m.* or *f.* slope.

vértigo (ber´tē•go) *m.* dizziness, vertigo; (fig.) giddiness.

vespertino, na (bes•per•tē´no, nâ) *adj.* evening.

vestíbulo (bes•tē´vū•lo) *m.* vestibule; (theat.) lobby.

vestido (bes•tē´tho) *m.* suit; dress *(de mujer).*

vestidura (bes•tē thū´râ) *f.* dress, wearing apparel.

vestigio (bes•tē´hyo) *m.* vestige, trace; footprint *(huella).*

vestir* (bes•tēr´) *va.* to clothe, to dress; to furnish *(guarnecer);* (fig.) to decorate; (fig.) to cloak, to disguise *(disfrazar);* **de** —, dressy, elegant; —**se,** to get dressed.

vestuario (bes•twâ´ryo) *m.* apparel, wardrobe; (mil.) uniform; (theat.) dressing room.

veterano, na (be•te•râ´no, nâ) *adj.* experienced, practiced; —, *m.* veteran.

veterinario (be•te•rē•nâ´ryo) *m.* veterinary.

vez (bes) *f.* time; turn *(turno);* **a la** —, at the same time; **a la — que,** while; **a veces, algunas veces,** sometimes; **en — de,** instead of; **otra** —, again; **varias veces,** several times; **tal**

—, ´perhaps; **una —,** once; **dos veces,** twice; **a su —,** in turn; **cada —,** each time, every time; **rara —,** seldom; **por primera —**, for the first time; **algunas veces,** sometimes; **de — en cuando,** from time to time; **toda — que,** whenever; **cada — más,** more and more.

vía (bē´â) *f.* way, road, route; mode, manner, method *(modo);* track *(carril);* **— férrea,** railway; **— marítima,** waterway; **— láctea,** Milky Way; **—s respiratorias,** respiratory tract.

viaducto (byâ•thūk´to) *m.* viaduct, underpass.

viajar (byâ•hâr´) *vn.* to travel.

viaje (byâ´he) *m.* journey, voyage, trip; water main *(de agua);* **— sencillo,** one-way trip; **— redondo** or **de ida y vuelta,** round trip; **gastos de —,** traveling expenses; **ir de —,** to go on a trip.

viajero, ra (byâ•he´ro, râ) *n.* traveler.

vialidad (byâ•lē•thâth´) *f.* road system, highway service, communication.

vianda (byân´dâ) *f.* food.

víbora (bē´vo•râ) *f.* viper.

vibración (bē•vrâ•syon´) *f.* vibration.

vibrador (bē•vrâ•thor´) *m.* vibrator.

vibrar (bē•vrâr´) *va.* to vibrate, to quiver; to throw, to hurl *(arrojar);* **—,** *vn.* to vibrate.

vicepresidente (bē•se•pre•sē•then´te) *m.* vice-president; vice-chairman *(de un comité).*

viceversa (bē•se•ver´sâ) *adv.* vice versa.

vicio (bē´syo) *m.* vice; overgrowth *(de árboles);* **de —,** without reason.

vicioso, sa (bē•syo´so, sâ) *adj.* vicious; defective *(defectuoso);* excessive *(excesivo).*

vicisitud (bē•sē•sē•tūth´) *f.* vicissitude.

víctima (bēk´tē•mâ) *f.* victim.

victoria (bēk•to´ryâ) *f.* victory.

victorioso, sa (bēk•to•ryo´so, sâ) *adj.* victorious.

vid (bēth) *f.* (bot.) vine.

vida (bē´thâ) *f.* life; **— media,** (chem.) half-life; **ganarse la —,** to earn a living.

video (bē´the•o), *m.* video; **— cámara,** video camera.

vidriera (bē•thrye´râ) *f.* show case *(vitrina);* shop window *(escaparate);* leaded window *(ventana).*

vidrio (bē´thryo) *m.* glass; pane of glass *(de ventana);* piece of glassware; **— inastillable,** shatter-proof glass; **— soplado,** blown glass.

viejo, ja (bye´ho, hâ) *adj.* old,

aged; wornout *(usado)*; — **amigo,** former friend

vienés, esa (bye•nes´, e´sâ) *adj.* and *n.* Viennese.

viento (byen´to) *m.* wind; air *(aire)*; scent *(olor)*; (fig.) vanity; **hace —,** it is windy; **molino de —,** windmill.

vientre (byen´tre) *m.* stomach; belly *(panza)*.

viernes (byer´nes) *m.* Friday.

viga (bē´gâ) *f.* beam.

vigente (bē•hen´te) *adj.* in force.

vigésimo, ma (bē•he´sē•mo, mâ) *m.* and *adj.* twentieth.

vigía (bē•hē´â) *f.* watchtower; (naut.) shoal, rock; —, *m.* lookout, watch.

vigilancia (bē•hē•lân´syâ) *f.* vigilance, watchfulness; care *(cuidado)*.

vigilante (bē•hē•lân´te) *adj.* vigilant, alert; —, *m.* guard, caretaker; policeman *(de policía)*.

vigilar (bē•hē•lâr´) *va.* to watch over, to look after; to observe *(observar)*.

vigilia (bē•hē´lyâ) *f.* vigil, watch; watchfulness, alertness *(vela)*; eve *(víspera)*.

vigor (bē•gor´) *m.* vigor; **entrar en —,** to go into effect.

vigorizar (bē•go•rē•sâr´) *va.* to strengthen, to invigorate.

vigoroso, sa (bē•go•ro´so, sâ) *adj.* vigorous, hardy.

vil (bēl) *adj.* mean, sordid, low *(bajo)*; worthless *(sin valor)*; ungrateful *(ingrato)*.

vileza (bē•le´sâ) *f.* meanness, lowness *(bajeza)*; abjectness *(miseria)*.

villa (bē´yâ) *f.* village, small town; villa *(casa)*.

villancico (bē•yân•sē´ko) *m.* Christmas carol.

vinagre (bē•nâ´gre) *m.* vinegar.

vincular (bēng•kū•lâr´) *va.* to entail *(los bienes)*; (fig.) to link, to secure, to fasten.

vínculo (bēng´kū•lo) *m.* tie, bond; entail.

vindicación (bēn•dē•kâ•syon´) *f.* vindication.

vindicar (bēn•dē•kâr´) *va.* to vindicate, to avenge.

vindicativo, va (bēn•dē•kâ•tē´vo, vâ) *adj.* vindictive, vengeful.

vinilo (bē•nē´lo) *m.* vinyl.

vino (bē´no) *m.* wine; — **añejo,** aged wine; — **tinto,** red wine.

viña (bē´nyâ) *f.* vineyard.

viola (byo´lâ) *f.* viola.

violáceo, cea (byo•lâ´se•o, se•â) *adj.* violet-colored.

violación (byo•lâ•syon´) *f.* violation.

violado, da (byo•lâ´tho, thâ) *adj.* violet-colored *(color)*; violated.

violar (byo•lâr´) *va.* to violate, to break; to ravish *(forzar)*; to profane, to desecrate *(profanar)*.

violencia (byo•len´syâ) *f.* violence.

violento, ta (byo•len´to, tâ) *adj.* violent.

violeta (byo•le´tâ) *f.* (bot.) violet; —, *adj.* violet.

violin (byo•lēn´) *m.* violin.

violinista (byo•lē•nēs´tâ) *m.* and *f.* violinist.

violón (byo•lon´) *m.* bass viol.

violonchelo (byo•lon•che´lo) *m.* violoncello.

viperino, na (bē•pē•rē´no, nâ) *adj.* viperous; **lengua —,** venomous tongue.

virar (bē•râr´) *va.* (naut.) to veer; —, vn. to turn.

virgen (bēr´hen) *adj.* and *f.* virgin.

virginal (bēr•hē•nâl´) *arj.* virginal.

virginidad (bēr•hē•nē•thath´) *f.* virginity; (fig.) purity, candor.

viril (bē•rēl´) *adj.* virile, manly.

virilidad (bē•rē•lē•thâth´) *f.* virility.

virreinato (bē•rreē•nâ´to) *m.* viceroyship.

virrey (bē•rre´ē) *m.* viceroy.

virtud (bēr•tūth´) *f.* virtue; efficacy *(eficacia);* vigor, courage *(vigor).*

virtuoso, sa (bēr•two´so, sâ) *adj.* virtuous.

viruela (bē•rwe´lâ) *f.* smallpox; **—s locas,** chicken pox.

virulento, ta (bē•rū•len´to, tâ) *adj.* virulent.

virus (bē´rūs) *m.* (med.) virus.

visa (bē´sâ) *f.* visa.

viscosidad (bēs•ko•sē•thâth´) *f.* viscosity.

visible (bē•sē´vle) *adj.* visible; (fig.) apparent, conspicuous.

visión (bē•syon´) *f.* vision; sight *(persona ridícula).*

visionario, ria (bē•syo•nâ´ryo, ryâ) *adj.* visionary.

visita (bē•sē´tâ) *f.* visit; visitor, guest *(huésped);* **hacer —s,** to pay visits; **— de cumplimiento,** courtesy call.

visitar (bē•sē•târ´) *va.* to visit; **—se,** to be on visiting terms.

vislumbrar (bēz•lūm•brâr´) *va.* to catch a glimpse of, to perceive indistinctly; (fig) to have an inkling of, to conjecture *(conjeturar).*

visón (bē•son´) *m.* mink; **abrigo de —,** mink coat.

víspera (bēs´pe•râ) *f.* eve, day before; **— de Año Nuevo,** New Year´s Eve.

vista (bēs´tâ) *f.* sight, eyesight; appearance, aspect *(aspecto);* view, vista *(paisaje);* glance *(vistazo);* purpose, intent *(intento);* trial *(ante el tribunal);* **—s,** windows *(ventanas);* collar and cuffs; —, *m.* customs officer; **— de pájaro,**

bird's-eye view.

vistazo (bēs•tä´so) *m.* glance.

visto (bēs´to) *adj.* obvious; — **que,** considering that; **por lo —**, apparently; — **bueno,** O.K.; **dar el — bueno,** to give one's approval.

visual (bē•swäl´) *adj.* visual.

vital (bē•täl´) *adj.* vital, essential.

vitalidad (bē•tä•lē•thäth´)*f.* vitality.

vitamina (bē•tä•mē´nä) *f.* vitamin.

vitorear (bē•to•re•är´) *va.* to cheer, to applaud.

vitrina (bē•trē´nä) *f.* showcase.

viuda, (byū´thä) *f.* widow.

viudez (byū•thes´) *f.* widowhood.

viudo (byū´tho) *m.* widower.

¡viva! (bē´vä) *interj.* hurrah! hail!

vivacidad (bē•vä•sē•thäth´) *f.* vivacity, liveliness.

víveres (bē´ve•res) *m. pl.* provisions.

vivero (bē•ve´ro) *m.* (bot.) nursery; fish hatchery *(de peces).*

viveza (bē•ve´sä) *f.* liveliness; keenness *(ardor);* quickness *(agudeza).*

vivienda (bē•vyen´dä) *f.* dwelling, house; manner of living *(modo de vivir).*

viviente (bē•vyen´te) *adj.* alive, living.

vivificar (bē•vē•fē•kär´) *va.* to vivify, to enliven.

vivir (bē•vēr´) *vn.* to live; to last *(durar);* — **de,** to live on.

vivo, va (bē´vo, vä) *adj.* living, alive; intense, sharp *(intenso);* lively *(que concibe pronto);* ingenious, sharp *(sutil);* bright *(brillante);* active, lively *(activo).*

vocablo (bo•kä´vlo) *m.* word.

vocabulario (bo•kä•vū•lä´ryo) *m.* vocabulary; dictionary *(diccionario).*

vocación (bo•kä•syon´) *f.* vocation, calling.

vocacional (bo•kä•syo•näl´) *adj.* vocational; **escuela —,** vocational school.

vocal (bo•käl´) *f.* vowel; —, *adj.* vocal, oral.

vocalización (bo•kä•lē•sä•syon´) *f.* (mus.) vocalization.

vocear (bo•se•är´) *vn.* to cry, to shout; to proclaim *(publicar a voces);* to calf *(llamar);* to acclaim *(aclamar).*

volador, ra (bo•lä•thor´, rä) *adj.* flying; hanging *(pendiente);* speedy, fast *(que corre con ligereza);* —, *m.* (ichth.) flying fish; rocket.

volante (bo•län´te) *adj.* flying; unsettled *(que no tiene asiento fijo);* portable *(de quita y pon);* —, *m.* shuttlecock; steering wheel *(rueda);* minting press *(prensa);* note, memorandum *(papel);* ruffle *(guarnición).*

volar (bo•lâr´) *vn.* to fly; to project, to stick out *(sobresalir);* to do right away *(hacer);* to disappear *(desaparecer);* to spread *(propagarse);* —, *va.* to blow up, to detonate; to irritate, to anger *(irritar);* to rouse *(de la caza);* —**se,** to get angry.

volátil (bo•lâ´tēl) *adj.* volatile; flying *(que vuela).*

volcán (bol•kân´) *m.* volcano.

volcar* (bol•kâr´) *va.* to tip, to tip over, to upset; to make dizzy *(turbar la cabeza);* to change one´s mind *(hacer mudar de parecer);* to exasperate *(irritar);* —, *vn.* to turn over.

voltaje (bol•tâ´he) *m.* (elec.) voltage, tension.

voltear (bol•te•âr´) *va.* to turn over; to reverse *(poner al revés);* to move *(trastrocar);* to build *(construir);* —, *vn.* to tumble.

volteo (bol•te´o) *m.* reversal *(inversión);* overturning; tumbling *(acción de voltearse).*

voltio (bol´tyo) *m.* (elec.) volt.

voluble (bo•lū´vle) *adj.* voluble; (fig.) inconstant, fickle.

volumen (bo•lū´men) *m.* volume.

voluminoso, sa (bo•lū•mē•no´so, sâ) *adj.* voluminous.

voluntad (bo•lūn•tâth´) *f.* will; free will *(libre albedrío);* good

will *(benevolencia);* **a —,** at will; **de buena —,** willingly, with pleasure.

voluntario, ria (bo•lūn•tâ´ryo, ryâ) *adj.* voluntary; —, *n.* volunteer.

voluptuoso, sa (bo•lūp•two´so, sâ) *adj.* voluptuous; voluptuary *(dado a los placeres).*

volver* (bol•ver´) *vt.* to turn; to translate *(traducir);* to return, to restore *(devolver);* to change, to transform *(mudar);* —**se,** to become; to turn sour *(agriarse).*

vomitar (bo•mē•târ´) *va.* to vomit.

vómito (bo´mē•to) *m.* vomiting, vomit.

voracidad (bo•râ•sē•thâth´) *f.* voracity.

vorágine (bo•râ´hē•ne) *f.* whirlpool, vortex.

voraz (bo•râs´) *adj.* voracious.

vórtice (bor´tē•se) *m.* vortex, whirlpool; eye *(de un ciclón).*

vos (bos) *pron.* you.

vosotros, tras (bo•so´tros, trâs) *pron. pl.* you.

votación (bo•tâ•syon´) *f.* voting.

votante (bo•tân´te) *m. and f.* voter.

votar (bo•târ´) *va. and vn.* to vow *(echar votos);* to swear; to vote.

voto (bo´to) *m.* vow; vote *(parecer);* wish *(deseo);* votive offering *(ruego);* voter *(persona);*

curse *(juramento);* **hacer —s,** to wish well.

voz (bos) *f.* voice; sound *(sonido);* noise *(ruido);* shout *(grito);* word.

vuelo (bwe′lo) *m.* flight; wing *(ala);* width, fullness *(amplitud);* ruffle, frill *(adorno);* woodland *(arbolado).*

vuelta (bwel′tâ) *f.* turn, revolution; curve *(curvatura);* return *(regreso, devolución);* beating *(zurra);* harshness *(aspereza);* repetition *(repetición);* reverse, other side *(otro lado);* ruffle *(adorno);* **a — de correo,** by return mail; **viaje de —,** return trip; **dar la —,** to turn around; to take a walk *(a pie);* to take a ride *(en vehículo).*

vuelto (bwel′to) *m.* (Sp. Am.) change; **dar el —,** to give back one′s change.

vuestro, tra (bwes′tro, trâ) *pron.* yours; *adj.* your.

vulcanización (būl•kâ•nē•sâ•syon′) *f.* vulcanization.

vulcanizar (būl•kâ•nē•sâr′) *va.* to vulcanize.

vulgar (būl•gâr′) *adj.* vulgar, common, ordinary; vernacular *(de las lenguas).*

vulgaridad (būl•gâ•rē•thâth′) *f.* vulgarity.

vulgo (būl′go) *m.* common people; **—,** *adv.* commonly, vulgarly.

vulnerar (būl•ne•râr′) *va.* to injure, to damage.

W

whisky (wēs′kē) *m.* whiskey.

whist (wēst) *m.* whist

X

xenón (kse•non′) *m.* xenon.

xilófono (ksē•lo′fo•no) *m.* (mus.) xylophone.

Y

y (ē) *conj.* and.

ya (yâ) *adv.* already; now *(ahora);* presently, soon *(más adelante);* immediately, right now *(en seguida);* finally *(finalmente);* — **no,** no longer; — **que,** since, seeing that; ¡—! *interj.* enough *(basta)!* I see! that's right!

yacer* (yâ•ser´) *vn.* to lie, to lie down; to be buried *(estar enterrado);* to be located, to lie *(estar).*

yanqui (yâng´kē) *adj.* and *m.* Yankee.

yarda (yâr´thâ) *f.* yard.

yate (yâ´te) *m.* yacht.

ye (ye) *f.* name of the letter y.

yedra (ye´thrâ) = **hiedra.**

yegua (ye´gwâ) *f.* mare.

yelmo (yel´mo) *m.* helmet.

yema (ye´mâ) *f.* bud; yolk *(de los huevos);* (fig.) best, cream; — **del dedo,** tip of the finger.

yerba (yer´vâ) *f.* grass; **mala** —, marijuana (Coll.); — **buena,** mint; — **mate,** Paraguay tea; —

s, *pl.* grass, pasture.

yermo (yer´mo) *m.* desert, wasteland; —, **ma,** *adj.* uncultivated; uninhabited, deserted *(inhabitado).*

yerno (yer´no) *m.* son-in-law.

yerto, ta (yer´to, tâ) *adj.* stiff, inflexible; rigid.

yeso (ye´so) *m.* gypsum; plaster *(mezclado con agua);* plaster cast *(obra de escultura).*

yo (yo) *pron.* I; — **mismo,** I myself.

yodo (yo´tho) *m.* iodine.

yodoformo (yo•tho•for´mo) *m.* (chem.) iodoform.

yuca (yū´kâ) *f.* (bot.) yucca.

yugo (yū´go) *m.* yoke; (naut.) transom.

yugoslavo, va (yū•goz•lâ´vo, vâ) *n.* and *adj.* Yugoslavian.

yugular (yū•gū•lâr´) *adj.* jugular; **vena** —, jugular vein.

yunque (yūng´ke) *m.* anvil; (fig.) long-suffering person; tool *(que trabaja mucho).*

yunta (yūn´tâ) *f.* team, yoke.

Z

zacate (sâ•kâ´te) *m.* (Mex.) hay, grass.

zafar (sâ•fâr´) *va.* (naut.) to untie, to loosen; to adorn, to garnish; —**se,** to evade

(escaparse); (fig.) to get out of *(librarse).*

zafir (sâ•fēr´) or **zafiro** (sâ•fē´ro) *m.* sapphire.

zaguán (sâ•gwân´) *m.* hall,

vestibule.

zamarra (sâ•mä´rrâ) *f.* sheep-skin; sheepskin jacket *(chaqueta).*

zambo, ba (sâm´bo, bâ) *adj.* knock-kneed.

zambullida (sâm•bū•yē´thâ) *f.* dipping, dunking.

zambullirse* (sâm•bū•yēr´se) *vr.* to plunge, to dive, to jump; to hide *(esconderse).*

zanahoria (sâ•nâ•o´ryâ) *f.* carrot.

zanca (sâng´kâ) *f.* shank.

zancada (sâng•kâ´thâ) *f.* stride, long step.

zancadilla (sâng•kâ•thē´yâ) *f.* trip; (fig.) trick, deceit.

zanco (sâng´ko) *m.* stilt.

zancudo, da (sâng•kū´tho, thâ) *adj.* long-legged; (orn.) wading; —, *m.* (Sp. Am.) mosquito.

zángano (sâng´gâ•no) *m.* drone; sponger *(que vive de gorra);* lazy lout *(ocioso).*

zanja (sân´hâ) *f.* ditch, trench.

zapa (sâ´pâ) *f.* spade.

zapatazo (sâ•pâ•tâ´so) *m.* blow with a shoe.

zapatería (sâ•pâ•te•rē´â) *f.* shoe store.

zapatero (sâ•pâ•te´ro) *m.* shoe-maker; shoe seller *(vendedor).*

zapatilla (sâ•pâ•tē´yâ) *f.* pump; slipper *(de comodidad).*

zapato (sâ•pâ´to) *m.* shoe; **—s de goma** or **de hule,** rubbers.

zapote (sâ•po´te) *m.* (bot.) sapota.

zar (sr) *m.* czar.

zarigüeya (sâ•rē•gwe´yâ) *f.* opossum.

zarpa (sâr´pâ) *f.* claw; (naut.) weighing anchor.

zarpar (sâr•pâr´) *vn.* to weigh anchor, to set sail.

zarpazo (sâr•pâ´so) *m.* thud, thump *(batacazo);* clawing.

zarza (sâr´sâ) *f.* bramblebush, blackberry bush.

zarzal (sâr•sâl´) *m.* brambles, blackberry patch.

zarzamora (sâr•sâ•mo´râ) *f.* bramble-berry, blackberry.

zarzo (sâr´so) *m.* wattle, trellis.

zepelín (se•pe•lēn´) *m.* (avi.) blimp, zeppelin, dirigible.

zeta (se´tâ) *f.* name of the letter z.

zigzag (sēg•sâg´) *m.* zigzag.

zirconio (sēr•ko´nyo) *m.* zircon.

zócalo (so´kâ•lo) *m.* (arch.) socle; (Mex.) plaza, square.

zodiaco (so•thyâ´ko) or **zodíaco** (so•the´â•ko) *m.* zodiac.

zona (so´nâ) *f.* zone; belt *(faja);* — **de marcha lenta,** slow-driving zone; — **de peligro,** danger zone; — **de tránsito,** traffic lane.

zoología (so•o•lo•hē´â) *f.* zoology.

zoológico, ca (so•o•lo´hē•ko, kâ) *adj.* zoological.

zorra (so´rrâ) *f.* fox.

zorrería (so•rre•rē´â) *f.* cunning, craft.

zorrillo (so•rrē´yo) *m.* skunk.

zorro (so´rro) *m.* fox.

zorzal (sor•sâl´) *m.* (orn.) thrush.

zote (so´te) *m.* dolt, lout, lug.

zozobra (so•so´vrâ) *f.* foundering; (fig.) uneasiness, anxiety.

zueco (swe´ko) *m.* wooden shoe; galosh *(de goma)*.

zumba (sūm´bâ) *f.* cow bell *(cencerro)*; whistle *(bramadera)*; (fig.) joke, trick *(raya)*; flogging, whipping.

zumbar (sūm•bâr´) *vn.* to hum; to buzz; to ring *(los oídos)*; to jest, to joke *(dar chasco)*.

zumbido (sūm•bē´tho) *m.* humming; buzzing.

zumo (sū´mo) *m.* juice; (fig.) advantage; — **de limón,** lemon juice.

zurcir (sūr•sēr´) *va.* to darn, to mend; to join, to unite *(unir)*; (coll.) to weave, to hatch *(mentiras)*.

zurdo, da (sūr´tho, thâ) *adj.* left; lefthanded *(de la mano izquierda)*.

zurrapa (sū•rrâ´pâ) *f.* lees, dregs; (coll.) scum, garbage.

zurrar (sū•rrâr´) *va.* to curry, to dress; to whip, to lash *(castigar)*; to bawl out *(censurar)*; to get the best of *(vencer)*.

Part II

ENGLISH - SPANISH

INGLÉS - ESPAÑOL

ABBREVIATURAS

adj.	adjective, *adjetivo*
adv.	adverb, *adverbio*
avi.	aviation, *aviación*
agr.	agriculture, *agricultura*
anat.	anatomy, *anatomía*
arch,	architecture, *arquitectura*
Arg.	Argentina, *Argentina*
art.	article, *artículo*
ast.	astronomy, *astronomía*
auto.	automobile, *automóvil*
biol.	biology, *biología*
Bol.	Bolivia, *Bolivia*
Bot.	botany, *botánica*
chem.	chemistry, *química*
Col.	Columbia, *Colombia*
coll.	colloquial, *familiar*
com.	commerce, *comercio*
conj.	conjunction, *conjunción*
dent.	dentistry, *dentistería*
eccl.	ecclesiastic, *eclesiástico*
Ecu.	Ecuador, *Ecuador*
elec.	electricity, *electricidad*
ent.	entomology, *entomología*
f.	feminine, *femenino*
fig.	figurative(ly), *figurado*
geog.	geography, *geografía*
geol.	geology, *geología*
gram.	grammar, *gramática*
Guat.	Guatemala, *Guatemala*
ichth.	ichthyology, *ictiología*
inter/.	interjection, *interjección*
interr.	interrogative, *interrogativo*
m.	masculine, *masculino*

math.	mathematics, *matemáticas*
mech.	mechanics, *mecánica*
med.	medicine, *medicina*
Mex.	Mexico, *Méjico*
mil.	military art, *milicia*
min.	mining, *minería*
mus,	music, *música*
n.	noun, *sustantivo*
naut.	nautical, *náutico* or *marino*
orn.	ornithology, *ornitología*
phot.	photography, *fotografía*
phy.	physics, *física*
pl.	plural, *plural*
poet.	poetry, *poética*
pol.	politics, *política*
p.p.	past participle, *participio pasado*
P.R.	Puerto Rico, *Puerto Rico*
prep.	preposition, *preposición*
print.	printing, *imprenta*
pron.	pronoun, *pronombre*
rad.	radio, *radiocomunación*
rail.	railway, *ferrocarril*
rhet.	rhetoric, *retórica*
sing.	singular, *singular*
Sp.Am	Spanish America, *Hispanoamérica*
theat.	theater, *teatro*
TV.	television, *televisión*
Urug.	Uruguay, *Uruguay*
v.	verb, *verbo*
va.	transitive verb, *verbo activo*
Ven.	Venezuela, *Venezuela*
vet.	veterinary, *veterinaria*
vi., vn.	intransitive verb, *verbo neutro*
vr.	reflexive verb, *verbo reflexivo*
vt.	transitive verb, *verbo activo*
zool.	zoology, *zoología*

English - Spanish

A

a [ei] *art.* un, uno, una; —, *prep.* a, al, en, por ej. **abed,** en cama, **aloud,** en voz alta.

aback [a-bák] *adv.* detrás, atrás; (naut.) en facha; **to be taken —** , quedar desconcertado.

abacus [á-ba-kus] *n.* ábaco, *m.*

abandon [a-bán-don] *vt.* abandonar, dejar.

abase [a-bash] *vt.* rebajar (en rango, puesto, estimación, etc.); degradar.

abate [a-béit] *vt.* minorar, disminuir, rebajar; —, *vi.* disminuirse.

abbey [a-bi] *n.* abadía, *f.;* monasterio, *m.*

abbreviate [a-bri-viéit] *vt.* abreviar, acortar, compendiar.

abbreviation [a-bri-viéi-shon] *n.* abreviación, abreviatura, *f.*

ABC's [ei-bi-sis] *n. pl.* abecé, abecedario, *m.*

abdicate [áb-di-keit] *vt.* abdicar, renunciar.

abdication [ab-di-kéi-shon] *n.* abdicación, renuncia, *f.;* dimisión, f.

abdomen [ab-dó-men] *n.* abdomen, vientre, *m.;* barriga, *f*

abduct [ab-dákt] *vt.* secuestrar.

aberration [a-be-réi-shon] *n.* desvío, extravío, *m.,* aberración, *f.*

abet [a-bét] *vt.* favorecer, patrocinar, sostener; excitar, animar.

abhor [a-bór] *vt.* aborrecer, detestar.

abide [a-báid] *vi.* habitar, morar; permanecer; —, *vt.* soportar, sufrir; defender, sostener; **to — by,** cumplir con, sostenerse en.

ability [a-bí-li-ti] *n.* potencia, habilidad, capacidad, aptitud *f.;* facilidad, *f.*

abject [ab-yékt] *adj.* vil, despreciable, bajo; desanimado; **—ly,** *adv.* abyectamente.

ablaze [a-bléis] *adj.* en llamas.

able [éi-bol] *adj.* fuerte, capaz, hábil; **to be — to,** saber; poder.

able-bodied [ei-bol-bó-did] *adj.* robusto, vigoroso.

ably [éi-bli] *adv.* con habilidad.

abnormal [ab-nór-mal] *adj.*

anormal; deforme.

aboard [a-bord] *adv.* a bordo; **to go —**, embarcarse; **all —!** señores viajeros al tren!

abode [a-bóud] *n.* domicilio, *m.*, habitación, *f.*

abolish [a-bó-lish] *vt.* abolir, anular, suprimir; destruir o dar fin a alguna cosa; revocar.

abominable [a-bó-mi-na-bol] *adj.* abominable, detestable.

aboriginal [a-bo-rí-yi-nal] *adj.* aborigen, primitivo, originario.

abound [a-báund] *vi.* abundar.

about [a-báut] *prep.* cerca de, por ahí, hacia; sobre; acerca; tocante a; **—,** *adv.* en contorno, aquí y allá; aproximadamente, cerca de; **to go —,** andar acá y acullá; **it is — twelve,** son aproximadamente las doce; **all —,** en todo lugar; en todas partes; **to be —,** tratar de.

above [a-bóuf] *prep.* encima, sobre, superior, más alto (en cuanto a situación, dignidad, etc.); **—,** *adv.* arriba; **— all,** sobre todo, principalmente; **— mentioned,** ya mencionado, susodicho, sobredicho.

abrasion [a-bréi-shon] *n.* raspadura, *f.*; rozamiento, *m.*; fricción, *f.*; desgaste por rozamiento o fricción.

abrasive [á-bre-sif] *adj.* raspante, abrasivo; **—s,** *n. pl.* abrasi-

vos, *m. pl.*

abreast [a-brést] *adv.* de costado; **to be — of the** news, estar al corriente.

abridge [a-brích] *vt.* abreviar, compendiar; acortar.

abroad [a-bróud] *adv.* fuera de casa o del país; **to go —,** salir, ir al extranjero.

abrupt [a-brapt] *adj.* quebrado, desigual; precipitado, repentino; bronco, rudo.

abscess [a-bsés] *n.* absceso, *m.*, postema, *f.*

absence [áb-sens] *n.* ausencia, *f.*; falta, *f.*; abstracción, *f.*; **leave of —,** licencia, *f.*

absent [áb-sent] *adj.* ausente; fuera de sí; distraído.

absentee [áb-sen-ti] *n.* el que está ausente de su empleo, etc.

absent-minded [áb-sent-mainded] *adj.* distraído, inatento.

absolute [áb-so-lut] *adj.* absoluto; categórico; positivo; arbitrario; completo; puro.

absolve [ab-sólv] *vt.* absolver, dispensar, exentar.

absorb [ab-sérb] *vt.* absorber.

absorbent [ab-sér-bent] *n. y adj.* (med.) absorbente, *m.*

absorption [ab-sór-shon] *n.* absorción, *f.*

abstain [abs-téin] *vi.* abstenerse, privarse.

abstract [abs-trákt] *vt.* abstraer;

compendiar; —, *adj.* abstracto; —, *n.* extracto, *m.;* sumario, compendio, m.

abstraction [abs-trák-shon] *n.* abstracción, *f.;* distracción, *f.*

absurd [ab-sérd] *adj.* absurdo.

absurdity [ab-sér-di-ti] *n.* absurdo, *m.;* ridiculez, *f.*

abundance [ab-sérd-nis] *n.* abundancia, copia, plenitud, *f.;* raudal, *m.;* **in —,** a rodo.

abundant [a-bán-dant] *adj.* abundante; sobrado.

abuse [a-bíus] *vt.* abusar; engañar; maltratar, violar; —, *n.* abuso, engaño, *m.;* corruptela, seducción, *f.;* injuria, afrenta, *f.*

abusive [a-bíusif] *adj.* abusivo, injurioso.

academic, academical [a-ca-dé-mik], [a-ca-dé-mi-kal] *adj.* académico.

academy [a-cá-de-mi] *n.* academia, *f.,* colegio, *m.*

accede [ak-síd] *vi.* acceder, convenir en alguna cosa, asentir.

accelerate [ak-sé-le-reit] *vt.* acelerar.

acceleration [ak-se-le-réi-shon] *n.* aceleración, prisa, *f.,* apremio, *m.*

accelerator [ak-se-le-réi-ta] *n.* acelerador, *m.*

accent [ák-sent] *n.* acento, *m.,* modulación, *f.,* tono, *m.;* —, *vt.*

acentuar, colocar los acentos; intensificar.

accentuate [ak-sén-tueit] *vt.* acentuar; intensificar.

accept [ak-sépt] *vt.* aceptar; admitir; recibir favorablemente.

acceptable [ak-sép-ta-bol] *adj.* aceptable, grato, digno de aceptación.

acceptance [ak-sép-tans] *n.* aceptación, recepción, *f.;* recibimiento, *m.*

access [ak-sés] *n.* acceso, *m.;* entrada, *f.;* aumento, *m.*

accessory [ak-sé-so-ri] *adj.* accesorio; concomitante; casual; —, *n.* cómplice, *m.* y *f.*

accident [ák-si-dent] *n.* accidente, *m.;* casualidad, *f.;* suceso imprevisto, lance (funesto), *m.;* **— insurance,** seguro contra accidentes.

accidental [ak-si-dén-tal] *adj.* accidental, casual, contingente.

acclaim [a-kléim] *vt.* aclamar, aplaudir, vitorear.

acclamation [a-kla-méi-shon] *n.* aclamación, *f.,* aplauso, *m.*

acclimate [á-kli-meit] *vt.* aclimatar.

acclimated [-akli-méi-tid] *adj.* aclimatado.

accolade [á-ko-leid] *n.* elogio, *m.;* premio, *m.;* reconocimiento de méritos.

accommodate [a-kó-mo-deit] *vt.*

acomodar, ajustar; —, *vi.* adaptarse, conformarse.

accommodating [a-ko-mo-déitin] *adj.* servicial, complaciente; obsequioso.

accommodation [a-ko-mo-déishon] *n.* comodidad, *f.;* localidad, *f.;* habitación, *f.;* cabida, *f.;* cuarto, *m.;* —s, localidades, *f. pl.;* facilidades de alojamiento.

accompaniment [a-kom-pá-niment] *n.* (mus.) acompañamiento, *m.*

accompany [a-kóm-pa-ni] *vt.* acompañar.

accomplice [a-kóm-plis] *n.* cómplice, *m. y f.*

accomplish [a-kóm-plish] *vt.* efectuar, llevar a cabo, realizar, lograr, conseguir; cumplir.

accomplished [a-kóm-plishd] *adj.* perfecto; completo; capaz, bien preparado.

accomplishment [a-kóm-plishment] *n.* realización, *f.,* cumplimiento entero de alguna cosa; —s, *n. pl.* habilidades, *f. pl.;* conocimientos, *m. pl.;* prendas, *f. pl.*

accord [a-kórd] *n.* acuerdo, convenio, *m.;* armonía, *f.;* simetría, *f.;* **of one's own —,** espontáneamente; **with one —,** unánimemente; —, *vt.* acordar; —, *vi.* estar de acuerdo.

accordance [a-kór-dans] *n.* conformidad, *f.,* acuerdo, *m.*

according [a-kór-din] *adj.* conforme; **— to,** según; **—ly,** *adv.* consecuentemente, por consiguiente.

accordion [a-kór-dion] *n.* acordeón, *m.*

account [a-káunt] *n.* cuenta, *f.,* cálculo, *m.,* estimación, *f.* ; aprecio, *m.;* narración, *f.;* relación, *f.;* motivo, *m.;* **for my —, on my —,** a mi cuenta; **on — of,** a causa de, a cargo de, por motivo de; **on no —,** de ninguna manera; **to be of no —,** ser un cero a la izquierda; **to bring (a person) to —,** pedir cuentas (a una persona); **to charge to one's —,** adeudar en cuenta; **to keep an —,** llevar cuenta; **unsettled —,** cuenta pendiente; **to take into —,** tomar en cuenta.

accountable [a-káun-ta-bol] *adj.* responsable.

accountant [a-káun-tant] *n.* contador, *m.,* tenedor de libros.

accounting [akáuntin] *n.* contabilidad, *f.*

accredit [a-kré-dit] *vt.* acreditar, patrocinar.

accredited [a-kré-di-tid] *adj.* autorizado.

accrue [akrú] *vi.* resultar, provenir.

accumulate [a-kiú-mu-leit] *vt.* acumular; amontonar; —, *vi.* crecer, aumentarse.

accuracy [a-kiú-ra-si] *n.* exactitud, precisión, *f.;* esmero, cuidado, *m.*

accurate [a-kiú-reit] *adj.* exacto, puntual; certero (de un tiro o un tirador); atinado (en un cálculo, etc.).

accursed [a-kér-sid] *adj.* maldito, maldecido; execrable; excomulgado; **— be!** ¡mal haya!

accusation [a-kiu-séi-shon] *n.* acusación, *f.;* cargo, *m.*

accuse [a-kiús] *vt.* acusar; culpar; formar causa.

accustom [a-kás-tom] *vt.* acostumbrar, avezar; **— oneself,** familiarizarse.

ace [éis] *n.* as (de naipe), *m.;* aviador sobresaliente; migaja, partícula, *f.*

acetone [á-si-toun] *n.* (chem.) acetona, *f.*

ache [éik] *n.* dolor continuo, mal, *m.;* —, *vi.* doler.

achieve [a-chíf] *vt.* ejecutar, perfeccionar; ganar, obtener; lograr, realizar.

achievement [a-chíf-ment] *n.* ejecución, *f.;* acción heroica; hazaña, *f.;* logro, *m.*

Achilles tendon [a-kí-lis-ten-don] *n.* tendón de Aquiles.

aching [éi-kin] *adj.* doliente.

acid [á-sid] *adj.* ácido, agrio, acedo; —, *n.* ácido, *m.*

acidity [a-sí-di-ti] *n.* agrura, acedía, acidez, acritud, *f.*

acknowledgment [ak-nó-lichment] *n.* reconocimiento, *m.;* gratitud, *f.;* concesión, *f.*

acne [ak-ní] *n.* (med.) acné, *f.*

acoustics [a-kás-tiks] *n.* acústica, *f.*

acquaint [a-kuéint] *vt.* advertir, avisar, enterar, familiarizar, informar; **to be —ed with,** conocer.

acquaintance [a-kuéin-tans] *n.* conocimiento, *m.;* familiaridad, *f.;* conocido, *m.,* conocida, *f.*

acquiesce [a-kuis] *vi.* consentir, asentir.

acquiescence [a-kui-sens] *n.* asenso, consentimiento, *m.,* sumisión, *f.*

acquire [a-kuálar] *vt.* adquirir, obtener.

acquisition [a-kui-sí-shon] *n.* adquisición, obtención, *f.*

acquit [a-kuít] *vt.* libertar, absolver; pagar.

acre [éi-kar] *n.* acre (medida de tierra que equivale a 40 áreas), *m.*

acreage [éi-krich] *n.* número de acres.

acrid [á-krid] *adj.* acre mordaz.

acrobat [a-kro-bá-tik] *n.* acróbata, *m.* y *f.,* volatinero, *m.*

acrobatics [a-kro-bá-tiks] *n.* acrobacia, *f.*

across [a-krós] *adv.* de través de una parte a otra; —, *prep.* a través de, por.

act [ákt] *vt.* representar; obrar; —, *vi.* hacer, efectuar; —, *n.* acto, hecho, *m.;* acción, *f.;* efecto, *m.;* acto (de una comedia, etc.), *m.*

acting [ák-tin] *n.* representación, *f.;* —, *adj.* interino, suplente.

action [ák-shon] *n.* acción, operación, *f.;* batalla, *f.;* gesticulación, *f.;* proceso, *m.;* actividad, *f.;* funcionamiento, *m.;* hecho, *m.;* gestión, *f.;* —s, conducta, *f.,* comportamiento, *m.*

activate [ák-ti-veit] *vt.* activar.

active [ak-tíf] *adj.* activo; eficaz, ocupado; ágil.

activity [ak-tív-li] *n.* agilidad, actividad, *f.;* prontitud, *f.;* vivacidad, *f.*

actor [ák-tar] *n.* actor, ejecutante, *m.;* agente, *m.;* cómico, actor (en los teatros), *m.*

actress [ák-tres] *n.* actriz, cómica, *f.*

actual [ák-chual] *adj.* cierto, real; efectivo.

acute [a-kiút] *adj.* agudo; ingenioso; —ly, *adv.* con agudeza.

A.D. [ei-di] (in the year of our Lord) D. de J. C. (después de J.C.).

ad [ád] *n.* anuncio, *m.*

adage [á-dich] *n.* proverbio, *m.;* refrán, *m.*

adamant [á-da-mant] *adj.* firme, tenaz, inflexible.

adapt [a-dápt] *vt.* adaptar; ajustar.

adaptability [a-dap-ta-bí-li-ti] *n.* adaptabilidad, *f.*

add [ad] *vt.* juntar; sumar; agregar, añadir.

addicted [a-dík-tid] *adj.* adicto; — to, apasionado por, adicto a.

addition [a-dí-shon] *n.* adición, *f.*

additional [a-dí-sho-nal] *adj.* adicional; —ly, *adv.* en o por adición, además.

address [á-dres] *vt.* hablar, dirigir la palabra; —, *n.* oración, *f.,* discurso, *m.;* señas, *f. pl.,* dirección, *f.*

addressee [a-dre-sí] *n.* destinatario, ria.

adept [a-dép'] *adj.* adepto, sabio, experto; —, *n.* sabio, bia, experto, ta.

adequate [á-di-kueit] *adj.* adecuado, proporcionado; suficiente; a propósito.

adhere [a-díar] *vi.* adherir; aficionarse; pegarse.

adherent [a-día-rant] *adj.* pegajoso; tenaz; adherente; —, *n.* adherente, *m.,* partidario, ria.

adhesion [a-dí-shon] *n.* adhesión, *f.;* adherencia, *f.*

adhesive [a-dí-sif] *adj.* pegajoso, tenaz; — **plaster,** — **tape,** esparadrapo, *m.,* cinta adhesiva.

adjacent [ad-já-sent] *adj.* adyacente, contiguo; colindante.

adjective [ad-jéck-tif] *n.* adjetivo, *m.*

adjoin [ad-jóin] *vt.* juntar; unir; —, *vi.* estar contiguo.

adjoining [ad-jói-nin] *adj.* contiguo, siguiente.

adjourn [ad-jén] *vt.* y *vi.* diferir, aplazar; suspender, clausurar (una reunión, etc.).

adjournment [ad-jérn-ment] *n.* prórroga, *f.;* aplazamiento, *m.;* clausura (de una reunión, etc.).

adjust [ad-yást] *vt.* ajustar. acomodar.

adjuster [ad-yás-tar] *n.* mediador, ajustador, *m.*

adjustment [ad-yást-ment] *n.* ajustamiento, ajuste, arreglo, *m.*

administer [ad-mí-nis-tar] *vt.* administrar, gobernar; desempeñar; dar, surtir, proveer.

administration [ad-mi-nis-tréi-shon] *n.* administración, *f.;* gobierno, *m.;* dirección, *f.;* gerencia, *f.*

admirable [ád-mi-ra-bol] *adj.* admirable.

admiral [ád-mi-ral] *n.* almirante, *m.*

admiration [ad-mi-réi-shon] *n.* admiración, *f.*

admire [ad-maiar] *vt.* admirar; estimar; contemplar.

admirer [ad-mai-rar] *n.* admirador, *m.;* amante, pretendiente, *m.*

admiringly [ad-mai-rin-li] *adv.* con admiración.

admission [ad-mí-shon] *n.* admisión, recepción, entrada, *f.;* concesión, *f* ; ingreso, *m.*

admit [ad-mít] *vt.* admitir, dar entrada; recibir, conceder, permitir; confesar; reconocer.

admittance [ád-mi-tans] *n.* entrada, admisión, *f.;* **no** —, se prohibe la entrada.

adobe [a-dóu-bi] *n.* adobe, *m.*

adolescence [a-dó-le-sens] *n.* adolescencia, *f.*

adolescent [a-dó-le-sent] *adj.* y *n.* adolescente, *m.* y *f.*

adopt [a-dópt] *vt.* adoptar, prohijar.

adoption [a-dóp-shon] *n.* adopción, *f.*

adoration [a-do-réi-shon] *n.* adoración, *f.*

adore [a-dór] *vt.* adorar.

adorn [a-dórn] *vt.* adornar; ornar; **to** — **oneself,** prenderse, adornarse.

adornment [a-dórn-ment] *n.* adorno, atavío, *m.*

adrenalin [a-drí-na-lin] *n.* adrenalina, *f.*

adrift [a-dríft] *adj.* y *adv.* flotante, a merced de las olas; al
garete.

adult [á-dalt] *adj.* y *n.* adulto, ta.

advance [ad-váns] *vt.* avanzar;
promover; pagar adelantado; —
, *vi.* hacer progresos; —, *n.*
avance, *m.;* adelanto, *m.;* **in —,**
con anticipación, por adelantado.

advanced [ad-vánsd] *adj.* adelantado, avanzado.

advancement [ad-váns-ment] *n.*
adelantamiento, *m.;* progreso,
m.; promoción, *f.*

advantage [ad-ván-tich] *n.* ventaja, superioridad, *f.;* provecho,
beneficio, *m.;* delantera, *f.;* **to
take — of,** aprovecharse de,
sacarle partido a.

advantageous [ad-van-tí-chos]
adj. ventajoso, útil; **—ly,** *adv.*
ventajosamente.

adventure [ad-ván-chuar] *n.*
aventura, *f.;* riesgo, *m.;* —, *vi.*
osar, emprender; —, *vt.* aventurar.

adventurer [ad-ván-chu-rar] *n.*
aventurero, *m.*

adventuresome, adventurous,
[ad-vén-cha-som], [ad-vén-chu-
ros] *adj.* intrépido; atrevido;
aventurero; valeroso.

adverb [ad-vérb] *n.* adverbio, *m.*

adverbial [ad-vér-bial] *adj.*
adverbial.

adversary [ad-vér-sa-ri] *n.* adversario, ria, enemigo, ga.

adverse [ad-vérs] *adj.* adverso,
contrario.

adversity [ad-vér-si-ti] *n.* adversidad, calamidad, *f.;* infortunio,
m.

advertise [ád-ver-tais] *vt.* anunciar, hacerle propaganda (a
algo).

advertisement [ad-vér-tis-ment]
n. aviso, *m.;* anuncio, *m.*

advertiser [ad-ve-tái-sar] *n.*
anunciante, *m.*

advertising [ad-ver-tái-sin] *n.*
propaganda, *f.;* publicidad, *f.*

advice [ad-váis] *n.* consejo, *m.;*
parecer, *m.*

advisability [ad-vai-sa-bí-li-ti] *n.*
prudencia, conveniencia, propiedad, *f.*

advisable [adváisebol] *adj.* prudente, conveniente, aconsejable.

advise [ad-váis] *vt.* aconsejar;
avisar; —, *vi.* consultar, aconsejarse.

adviser, advisor [ad-vái-sar] *n.*
consejero, consultor, *m.*

advisory [ad-vái-so-ri] *adj.* con-
sultivo.

advocate [ád-vo-keit] *n.* abogado,
m.; protector, *m.;* partidario,
m.; —, *vt.* defender; apoyar.

aerial [é-rial] *adj.* aéreo; —, *n.*
(rad.) antena, *f.*

aerodynamics [ea-ro-dai-ná-miks] *n.* aerodinámica, *f.*

aeronautics [ea-ro-nó-tik] *n.* aeronáutica, *f.*

aeroplane [é-ro-plein] *n.* aeroplano, avión, *m.*

aerosol [é-ro-sol] *n.* aerosol, *m.*

aesthetics [e-ros-tá-tik] *n.* estética, *f.*

afar [afár] *adv.* lejos, distante; **from** —, de algún lugar distante, desde lejos.

affable [á-fe-bol] *adj.* afable, complaciente.

affair [a-féar] *n.* asunto, *m.;* negocio, *m.;* lance, duelo, *m.;* **love** —, amorío, *m.*

affect [a-fék] *vt.* conmover; afectar; hacer mella.

affected [a-fék-ted] *adj.* afectado; remilgado, lleno de afectación; —**ly**, *adv.* con afectación.

affection [a-fék-shon] *n.* amor, afecto, *m.;* afección, *f.*

affectionate [a-fék-sho-net] *adj.* afectuoso, benévolo; cariñoso; —**ly**, *adv.* cariñosamente.

affiliate [a-fí-lieit] *vt.* ahijar; afiliar.

affiliation [a-fi-liéi-shon] *n.* afiliación, *f.*

affirm [a-férm] *vt.* afirmar, declarar, confirmar, ratificar, aprobar.

affirmation [a-fer-méi-shon] *n.* afirmación, *f.*

affirmative [a-fír-ma-tif] *adj.* afirmativo.

affix [a-fíks] *vt.* anexar, añadir, fijar; —, *n.* (gram.) afijo, *m.*

afflict [a-flíkt] *vt.* afligir; atormentar.

affliction [aflík-shon] *n.* aflicción, *f.;* dolor, *m.;* pena, *f.*

affluence [á-fluens] *n.* copia, abundancia, *f.*

affluent [á-fluent] *adj.* afluente, opulento, rico.

afford [a-fórd] *vt.* dar; proveer; producir; proporcionar; facilitar; tener los medios, tener los recursos.

affront [a-frónt] *n.* afrenta, injuria, *f.;* —, *vt.* afrentar, insultar, ultrajar.

afraid [a-fréid] *adj.* temeroso, espantado, tímido, miedoso; **to be** —, temer, tener miedo.

afresh [a-frésh] *adv.* de nuevo, otra vez.

after [áf-tar] *prep.* después de, detrás; según; tras de; **day** — **tomorrow,** pasado mañana; —, *adv.* después.

aftereffect [af-tar-e-fékt] *n.* resultado, *m.,* efecto resultante.

afterlife [áf-tar-laif] *n.* vida venidera.

aftermath [áf-tar-maz] *n.* retoño, *m.,* segunda cosecha; consecuencias (generalmente desastrosas), *f. pl.*

afternoon [áf-tar-nun] *n.* tarde *f.;* pasado meridiano.

afterthought [áf-tar-zót] *n.* reflexión posterior.

afterward, afterwards [áf-tar-uard], [áf-tar-uards] *adv.* después, en seguida, luego.

again [e-géin] *adv.* otra vez; — **and** —, muchas veces, repetidas veces.

against [a-géinst] *prep.* contra; enfrente.

age [éich] *n.* edad, *f.;* siglo, *m.;* vejez, *f.;* época, *f.;* **of** —, mayor de edad; —, *vi.* envejecer.

aged [éi-chid] *adj.* anciano; añejo.

agency [éi-chen-si] *n.* agencia, *f.,* medio, *m.*

agent [éi-chant] *n.* agente, *m.;* asistente, *m.;* casero, *m.;* **insurance** —, agente de seguros.

aggravate [á-gra-veit] *vt.* agravar; empeorar; intensificar.

aggravating [a-gra-véi-tin] *adj.* agravante; irritante.

aggravation [a-gra-véi-shon] *n.* agravación, *f.,* agravamiento, *m.*

aggregate [á-gre-gueit] *n.* agregado, *m.;* unión, *f.;* —, *vt.* juntar, reunir.

aggregation [a-gri-guéi-shon] *n.* agregación, *f.*

aggression [a-gré-shon] *n.* agre-sión, *f.;* ataque, asalto, *m.*

aggressive [a-gré-sif] *adj.* agresivo, ofensivo.

aggressor [a-gré-sar] *n.* agresor, *m.*

aghast [a-gást] *adj.* horrorizado.

agile [á-chail] *adj.* ágil; vivo, diestro.

agitate [á-chi-teit] *vt.* agitar; discutir con ahínco; —*vi.* excitar los ánimos, alborotar opiniones.

agitation [a-chi-téi-shon] *n.* agitación, *f.;* perturbación, *f.*

agitator [a-chi-téi-tar] *n.* agitador, incitador, *m.*

aglow [a-glóu] *adj.* fulgurante, ardiente; radiante.

ago [e-góu] *adv.* atrás; hace; **long**—, hace mucho; **a few days** —, hace unos días.

agonizing [a-go-nái-sin] *adj.* agonizante.

agony [á-go-ni] *n.* agonía, *f.;* angustia extrema.

agrarian [a-gréa-rian] *adj.* agrario.

agree [a-grí] *vi.* concordar, convenir; consentir; **to** — **with**, dar la razón a, estar de acuerdo con.

agreeable [a-gria-bí-li-ti] *adj.* conveniente, agradable; amable; — **with**, según, conforme a.

agreed [a-gríid] *adj.* establecido,

convenido; —! *interj.* ¡de acuerdo!

agreement [a-grí-ment] *n.* acuerdo, *m.;* conformidad, *f.;* unión, *f.;* pacto, *m.;* **by** —, de acuerdo; **general** —, consenso, *m.;* **to reach an** —, ponerse de acuerdo.

agricultural [a-gri-kál-chu-ral] *adj.* agrario, agrícola.

agriculture [a-gri-kál-char] *n.* agricultura, *f.*

ahead [a-jéd] *adv.* más allá, delante de otro; en adelante; enfrente; **to go** —, continuar, seguir.

aid [éid] *vt.* ayudar, socorrer; conllevar; —, *n.* ayuda, *f.;* auxilio, socorro, *m.*

aide [éid] *n.* ayudante, *m.*

ail [éil] *vt.* afligir, molestar; **what** **—s you?** ¿qué le duele a Ud.?

ailing [éi-lin] *adj.* doliente, enfermizo, achacoso.

ailment [éil-ment] *n.* dolencia, indisposición, *f.*

aim [éim] *vt.* apuntar, dirigir el tiro con el ojo; aspirar a; intentar; —, *n.* designio, intento, punto, *m.;* mira, *f.;* puntería, *f.;* blanco, *m.*

aimless [éim-les] *adj.* sin designio, sin dirección, sin objeto.

ain't [éint] *contracción familiar* de **am not, is not, are not,** no estar, no ser.

air [éa] *n.* aire, *m.;* (mus.) tonada, *f.;* semblante, *m.;* —, *adj.* de aire; aéreo; — **chamber,** cámara de aire; —**conditioned,** con aire acondicionado; — **line,** línea aérea; — **liner,** avión de pasajeros; — **mail,** correo aéreo, correspondencia aérea, vía aérea; —, *vt.* airear; secar; ventilar.

airborne [éa-born] *adj.* aéreo, trasportado por aire.

air-condition [éa-kon-dí-shon] *vt.* acondicionar el clima interior.

air conditioning [ea-kon-dí-shonin] *n.* acondicionamiento del aire, aire acondicionado; ventilación, *f.*

aircraft [éa-kraf] *n.* aeronave, *f.,* avión, *m.;* — **carrier,** portaaviones, *m.*

airlift [éa-lif] *n.* puente aéreo; ayuda aérea

airmail [éa-meil] *adj.* aeropostal; — **letter,** carta aérea, carta por avión; —, *vt.* enviar por correo aéreo.

airplane [éa-plein] *n.* aeroplano, avión, *m.;* — **carrier,** portaaviones, *m.*

airport [éa-port] *n.* aeropuerto, aeródromo, *m.*

airsickness [ea-sík-nes] *n.* mareo en un viaje aéreo.

airstrip [éa-strip] *n.* pista de aterrizaje.

airtight [éa-tait] *adj.* herméticamente cerrado, hermético, a prueba de aire.

airy [éa-ri] *adj.* aéreo; etéreo; alegre; lleno de aire.

aisle [áil] *n.* nave de una iglesia; pasillo, *m.*, crujía, *f.; pasadizo, m.*

ajar [á-yar] *adj.* entreabierto.

akin [a-kín] *adj.* consanguíneo, emparentado; análogo, semejante.

alacrity [a-lá-kri-ti] *n.* alacridad, presteza, *f.*

alarm [a-lárm] *n.* alarma, *f.;* rebato, *m.;* — **clock,** despertador, reloj despertador; **burglar** —, alarma contra ladrones; **fire** —, alarma contra incendios, **to sound the** —, dar la alarma; —, *vt.* alarmar, inquietar.

alarming [a-lár-min] *adj.* alarmante; sorprendente.

alarmist [á-lar-mist] *n.* alarmista, *m. y f.*

alas [ál-as] *interj.* ¡ay! ¡ay de mí!

albino [al-bí-nou] *n. y adj.* albino, na.

album [ál-bom] *n.* álbum, *m.*

alcohol [al-ko-jol] *n.* alcohol, *m.*

alcoholic [al-ko-jó-lik] *adj.* alcohólico.

ale [éil] *n.* variedad de cerveza.

alert [á-lert] *adj.* alerto, vivo.

alertness [a-lért-nis] *n.* cuidado,

m.; vigilancia, *f.;* viveza, actividad, *f.*

alga [ál-ga] *n.* alga (planta del mar), *f.*

algebra [ál-che-bra] *n.* álgebra, *f.*

alias [éi-lias] *adv.* alias, de otra manera.

alibi [á-li-bai] *n.* (leyes) coartada, *f.*

alien [éi-lian] *adj.* extraño; — , *n.* forastero, ra; extranjero, ra; extraterrestre, *m.*

alienate [éi-lia-neit] *vt.* enajenar; malquistar, indisponer.

align [a-láin] *vt.* alinear.

alignment [a-láin-ment] *n.* alineación, *f.*

alike [a-láik] *adj.* semejante, igual; — , *adv.* igualmente.

alimentary [a-li-mén-ta-ri] *adj.* alimenticio; alimentario.

alive [a-láif] *adj.* vivo, viviente; activo.

alkali [ál-ka-li] *n.* álcali, *m.*

alkaline [ál-ka-lain] *adj.* alcalino.

all [ol] *adj.* todo; — , *adv.* enteramente; — **at once,** — **of a sudden,** de repente, de un tirón; — **the better,** tanto mejor; **not at** — , de ninguna manera; no hay de qué; **once and for** — , una vez por todas; — **right,** bueno; satisfactorio; — **year round,** todo el año; — , *n.* todo, *m.*

allay [á-lei] *vt.* aliviar, apaciguar.

allege [a-léch] *vt.* alegar; declarar.

allegiance [al-lí-gians] *n.* lealtad, fidelidad, *f.*; **pledge of —** , jura a la bandera.

allegorical [a-li-gí-ri-kal] *adj.* alegórico.

allegory [a-lí-go-ri] *n.* alegoría, *f.*

allergic [a-lér-chik] *adj.* alérgico.

allergy [a-lér-chi] *n.* alergia, *f.*

alleviate [á-li-viéit] *vt.* aliviar, aligerar.

alley [á-li] *n.* paseo arbolado; callejuela, *f.*, pasadizo, *m.*, callejón, *m.*

alliance [a-lái-ans] *n.* alianza, *f.*; parentela, *f.*

allied [a-láid] *adj.* aliado, confederado.

alligator [a-li-géi-tar] *n.* lagarto, caimán, *m.*

allocate [á-lo-keit] *vt.* asignar, distribuir.

allocation [a-lo-kéi-shon] *n.* distribución, colocación, asignación, fijación, *f.*

allot [á-lot] *vt.* distribuir por suerte; asignar, repartir.

allotment [a-lót-ment] *n.* asignación, *f.*; repartimiento, *m.*; lote, *m.*, parte, porción, *f.*

allow [a-láu] *vt.* conceder, aprobar; permitir; dar, pagar; **— ing that,** supuesto que.

allowable [a-láua-bol] *adj.* admisible, permitido, justo.

allowance [a-láuans] *n.* concesión, *f*; licencia, *f.;* bonificación, *f*; (naut.) ración, *f.,* alimentos, *m. pl.;* mesada, *f.*

alloy [a-lói] *vt.* ligar, mezclar un metal con otro; aquilatar oro;— ,*n.* liga, aleación, mezcla, *f.*

all-round [ól-raund] *adj.* completo; por todas partes, en todas formas.

all-time [ól-taim] *adj.* inigualado hasta ahora.

allude [a-liúd] *vi.* aludir.

allure [a-liúar] *vt.* alucinar; cebar; fascinar; — *n.* seducción, *f.*

alluring [a-liúa-rin] *adj.* seductor.

allusion [a-liúa-shon] *n.* alusión, *f.*

ally [al-i] *n.* aliado, da; asociado, da; — , *vt.* hacer alianza; vincular.

almanac [ál-ma-nak] *n.* almanaque, *m.*

almighty [al-mái-ti] *adj.* omnipotente, todopoderoso.

almond [ál-mond] *n.* almendra, *f.;* — **tree,** almendro, *m.*

almost [ól-moust] *adv.* casi, cerca de.

alms [áms] *n.* limosna, *f.*

aloft [a-lóft] *prep.* arriba, sobre.

alone [a-lóun] *adj.* solo; — , *adv.* solamente, sólo; a solas; **to let**

— , dejar en paz.

along [a-lóng] *adv.* a lo largo; adelante; junto con; **to get — with,** llevarse bien (con alguien).

alongside [a-lóng-said] *adv.* y *prep.* al lado.

aloof [a-lúf] *adv.* lejos, de lejos, a lo largo; — , *adj.* reservado, apartado.

aloud [a-láud] *adv.* en voz alta.

alphabet [ál-fa-bet] *n.* alfabeto, *m.*

alphabetical [al-fa-bé-ti-kal] *adj.* alfabético.

alphabetically [al-fa-bé-ti-ka-li] *adv.* alfabéticamente, por orden alfabético.

Alps [álps] Alpes, *m. pl.*

already [ol-ré-di] *adv.* ya.

also [ól-sou] *adv.* también, igualmente, además.

alter [ál-tar] *vt.* alterar, mudar, modificar.

alteration [al-te-réi-shon] *n.* alteración, *f.*; cambio, *m.*

alternate [ál-ter-neit] *adj.* alternativo, recíproco; — , *vt.* alternar, variar; — , *n.* suplente, *m.*

alternating [al-ter-néi-tin] *adj.* alterno, alternativo; — **current,** corriente alterna.

alternative [al-tér-na-tif] *n.* alternativa, disyuntiva, *f.*; — , *adj.* alternativo.

although [ól-do] *conj.* aunque, no obstante, bien que; si.

altitude [al-ti-tiud] *n.* altitud, altura, *f.*; (avi.) elevación, *f.*

alto [al-tou] *n.* y *adj.* contralto, *f.*

altogether [al-to-gé-dar] *adv.* del todo, enteramente.

altruism [al-tru-ísem] *n.* altruismo, *m.*

aluminum [a-liú-mi-nom] *n.* (chem.) aluminio, *m.*

alumnus [a-liúm-na] *n.* *(pl. alumni)* ex alumno, persona graduada de una escuela o universidad.

always [ól-ueis] *adv.* siempre, constantemente, en todo tiempo, sin cesar.

A.M., a.m. [ei-em] : **before noon** A.M. antemeridiano.

am [am] (1ª persona del singular de indicativo del verbo to be) soy; estoy.

amalgamate [a-mal-ga-meit] *vt.* y *vi.* amalgamar.

amass [a-mas] *vt.* acumular, amontonar.

amateur [a-ma-ter] *n.* aficionado, da, novato, ta, principiante.

amateurish [a-ma-té-rish] *adj.* novato; superficial, como un aficionado o principiante.

amaze [a-méis] *vt.* sorprender, asombrar.

amazement [a-méis-ment] *n.* asombro, pasmo, *m.*

amazing [a-méi-sin] *adj.* extraño, pasmoso, asombroso.

Amazon [a-má-son] Amazonas, *m.*

ambassador [am-bá-sa-dor] *n.* embajador, *m.*

amber [ám-bar] *n.* ámbar, *m.;* — , *adj.* ambarino.

ambiguity [am-bí-güi-ti] *n.* ambigüedad, duda, *f.;* equívoco, *m.*

ambiguous [am-bí-guos] *adj.* ambiguo.

ambition [am-bí-shon] *n.* ambición, *f.*

ambitious [am-bí-shos] *adj.* ambicioso.

amble [am-bol] *n.* paso de andadura del caballo; — , *vi.* amblar.

ambulance [ám-biu-lans] *n.* ambulancia, *f.*

ambush [am-búsh] *n.* emboscada, celada, *f.;* sorpresa, *f.;* — , *vt.* emboscar.

ameba [a-mí-ba] *n.* amiba, *f.*

ameliorate [a-mí-lio-reit] *vt.* mejorar.

amen [a-men] *interj.* amén.

amenable [a-mí-na-bol] *adj.* responsable; sujeto, ta.

amend [a-ménd] *vt.* enmendar; — , *vi.* enmendarse, reformarse, restablecerse.

amendment [a-ménd-ment] *n.* enmienda, reforma, *f.;* remedio, *m.*

amends [a-ménds] *n. sing.* y *pl.* recompensa, compensación, *f.;* satisfacción, *f.;* **to make** — , reparar.

American [a-mé-ri-kan] *n.* y *adj.* americano, na.

Americanized [a-me-ri-ka-naisd] *adj.* americanizado.

amethyst [a-mé-cist] *n.* amatista, *f.*

amiable [ei-mi-abol] *adj.* amable, amigable.

amicable [a-mí-ka-bol] *adj.* amigable, amistoso.

amid, amidst [a-mid], [a-mist] *prep.* entre, en medio de.

amino acid [a-mi-nou-á-sid] *n.* aminoácido, *m.*

amiss [a-mis] *adj.* importuno, impropio; — , *adv.* fuera de lugar.

ammonia [a-mou-nia] *n.* amoniaco, *m.*

ammunition [a-miu-ní-shon] *n.* munición, *f.;* pertrechos, *m. pl.*

amnesty [am-né-si-ti] *n.* amnistía, *f.,* indulto, *m.*

amoeba = [a-mí-ba] **ameba.**

among, amongst [a-móng], [a-óngst] *prep.* entre, mezclado con, en medio de.

amorous [á-mo-ros] *adj.* amoroso.

amount [a-máunt] *n.* importe, *m.;* cantidad, *f.;* suma, *f.;* monto, *m.;* producto, *m.;*

(com.) montante, *m.*; — , *vi.* montar, importar, subir, ascender; **to — to,** arrojar; llegar a ser.

amphibious [am-fí-bios] *adj.* anfibio.

amphitheater [am-fí-zi-á-tar] *n.* anfiteatro, *m.*

ample [ámpl] *adj.* amplio, vasto.

amplification [am-pli-fi-kéi-shon] *n.* amplificación, *f.;* extensión, *f.*

amplifier [am-pli-fáiar] *n.* amplificador, *m.*

amplif [ám-pli-fai] *vt.* ampliar, extender; — , *vi.* extenderse.

amplitude [ám-pli-tiud] *n.* amplitud, extensión, *f.;* abundancia, *f.*.

amply [ám-pli] *adv.* ampliamente, copiosamente.

amputate [ám-piu-teit] *vt.* amputar.

amputation [am-piu-téi-shon] *n.* amputación, *f.;* corte, *m.*

amputee [ám-piu-ti]*n.* persona que ha sufrido una amputación.

amulet [á-miu-leit] *n.* amuleto, *m.*

amuse [a-miús] *vt.* entretener, divertir.

amusement [a-miús-ment] *n.* diversión, *f.*, pasatiempo, entretenimiento, *m.*; — **park,** parque de diversiones.

amusing [a-miú-sin] *adj.* divertido; **to be — ,** tener gracia; ser divertido; — **ly**, *adv.* entretenidamente.

an [an] *art.* un, uno, una.

analogy [a-ná-lo-chi] *n.* analogía, conformidad, *f.*

analysis [a-ná-lai-sis] *n.* análisis, *m.* y *f.*

analytical [a-na-lí-ti-kal] *adj.* analítico.

analyze [á-na-lais] *vt.* analizar.

anarchy [á-nar-ki] *n.* anarquía, *f.*

anatomical [a-na-tó-mi-kal] *adj.* anatómico.

anatomy [a-na-to-mi] *n.* anatomía, *f.*

ancestor [an-sís-tar] *n.* abuelo, *m.;* — **s**, *pl.* antepasados, *m. pl.*

ancestry [an-ses-tri] *n.* linaje de antepasados; raza, estirpe, prosapia, *f.*

anchor [an-kar] *n.* ancla, áncora, *f.;* — , *vi.* ancorar, echar las anclas; surgir; **to cast — ,** dar fondo; — , *vt.* (naut.) sujetar con el ancla.

anchovy [an-chó-vi] *n.* anchoa, *f.*

ancient [éin-shant] *adj.* antiguo, anciano.

and [and] *conj.* y; e (antes de palabras que empiezan con **i** o **hi**, con excepción de **hie**); — **so on,** y así sucesivamente.

Andalusian [an-da-lú-sian] *n. y adj.* andaluz, za.

anecdote [a-nik-dout] *n.* anécdota, *f.*

anemia [a-ní-mia] *n.* anemia, *f.*

anemic [a-ní-mik] *adj.* anémico.

anesthesia [a-nis-zí-sia] *n.* anestesia, *f.*

anesthetic [a-nis-zé-tik] *adj.* anestésico.

anew [a-niu] *adv.* de nuevo, nuevamente, otra vez.

angel [éin-chel] *n.* ángel *m.*

angelic, angelical [ein-ché-lik], [an-ché-li-kal] *adj.* angélico, angelical.

anger [án-gar] *n.* ira, cólera, *f.;* — , *vt.* enojar, irritar, encolerizar.

angle [ángel] *n.* ángulo, *m.;* punto de vista; — , *vt.* pescar con caña; halagar.

angler [án-glar] *n.* pescador de caña, cañero, *m.*

Anglo-Saxon [an-glou-sák-son] *n. y adj.* anglosajón, ona.

Angora [an-go-ra] *n.* Angora; — **cat,** gato de Angora.

angry [an-gri] *adj.* colérico, irritado, enojado, indignado, resentido.

anguish [an-güish] *n.* ansia, pena, angustia, *f.*

angular [an-giu-lar] *adj.* angular.

animal [a-ni-mal] *n. y adj.* animal, *m.*

animate [á-ni-meit] *vt.* animar; alentar; — , *adj.* viviente, animado.

animated [a-ni-méi-tid] *adj.* animado, lleno de vida; — **cartoon,** caricatura animada.

animation [a-ni-mei-shon] *n.* animación, *f.*

animosity [a-ni-mó-si-ti] *n.* animosidad, *f.*

anise [a-nis] *n.* anís, *m.*

ankle [án-kel] *n.* tobillo, *m.*

annex [á-neks] *vt.* anexar; apropiarse piarse de — , *n.* anexo, *m.;* sucursal,

annihilate [a-náia-leit] *vt.* aniquilar.

anniversary [a-ni-vér-sa-ri] *n.* aniversario, *m.*

annotation [a-no-téi-shon] *n.* anotación, *f.*

announce [a-náuns] *vt.* anunciar, publicar; notificar, avisar.

announcement [a-náuns-ment] *n.* advertencia, *f.;* aviso, anuncio, *m.;* notificación, *f.*

announcer [a-náunsar] *n.* anunciador, ra; locutor, ra; notificador, ra.

annoy [a-noi] *vt.* molestar; fastidiar.

annoyance [a-nóians] *n.* molestia, *f.;* fastidio, *m.;* (coll.) lata, *f.*

annoying [a-nói-in] *adj.* molestoso.

annual [á-nual] *adj.* anual.

anonymous [a-nó-ni-mos] *adj.* anónimo.

another [a-nó-dar] *adj.* otro, diferente; **one —** , uno a otro.

answer [án-sar] *vi.* responder, contestar, replicar; corresponder; **—** , *vt.* refutar; contestar; satisfacer; surtir efecto; **—** *n.* respuesta, contestación, réplica, *f.*

answerable [án-sa-ra-bol] *adj.* responsable; conforme; discutible.

ant [ant] *n.* hormiga, *f.*

antagonism [an-ta-go-nísem] *n.* antagonismo, *m.;* rivalidad, *f.*

antagonist [an-ta-go-nist] *n.* antagonista, *m. y f.;* contrario, ria.

antagonistic [an-ta-go-nís-tik] *adj.* antagónico.

antagonize [an-ta-go-nais] *vt.* contrariar, oponerse a.

antarctic [an-tár-tik] *adj.* antártico.

anteater [ant-ítar] *n.* oso hormiguero.

antecedent [an-tí-si-dant] *adj.* antecedente; **— s**, *n. pl.* antecedentes, *m. pl.*

antelope [an-tí-loup] *n.* antílope, *m.*

antenna [an-te-na] *n.* (zool. y rad.) antena, *f.*

anthem [án-zem] *n.* himno, *m.;*

national — , himno nacional.

anthology [an-zó-lo-chi] *n.* antología, *f.*

anthropology [an-zro-pó-lo-chi] *n.* antropología, *f.*

antibiotic [an-ti-bió-tik] *n. y adj.* antibiótico, *m.*

antibody [an-ti-bo-di] *n.* anticuerpo, *m.*

antics [án-tiks] *n. pl.* travesuras, gracias, *f. pl.*

anticipate [an-tí-si-peit] *vt.* anticipar, prevenir.

anticipation [an-ti-si-péi-shon] *n.* anticipación, *f* .

antidote [an-ti-dout] *n.* antídoto, contraveneno, *m.*

antifreeze [an-ti-frís] *n.* solución incongelable.

antihistamine [an-ti-jís-ta-min] *n.* antihistamina, *f.*

antiquated [an-ti-kuéi-tid] *adj.* anticuado.

antique [án-tik] *adj.* antiguo; **—** , *n.* antigüedad, *f.*

antiquity [an-ti-kui-ti] *n.* antigüedad, *f.;* ancianidad, *f.*

antiseptic [an-ti-sep-tik] *adj.* antiséptico.

antisocial [an-ti-sóu-shal] *adj.* antisocial.

antithesis [an-ti-zí-sis] *n.* antítesis, *f.*

antonym [an-tó-nim] *n.* antónimo, *m.*

Antwerp [an-tuárp] *n.* Amberes,

f.

anxiety [ánk-saia-ti] *n.* ansiedad, ansia, *f.;* afán, *m.;* cuidado, *m.*

anxious [ank-shos] *adj.* ansioso; inquieto.

any [é-ni] *adj.* y *pron.* cualquier, cualquiera, alguno, alguna, todo; — **more,** más.

anybody [éni-badi] *pron.* alguno, alguien; cualquiera.

anyhow [éni-jau] *adv.* de cualquier modo; de todos modos.

anyone [éni-uan] *pron.* alguno, cualquiera.

anything [éni-zin] *pron.* algo.

anyway [éni-uei] *adv.* como quiera; de todos modos.

anywhere [éni-uear] *adv.* en cualquier lugar, dondequiera.

apart [a-párt] *adv.* aparte; separadamente; — , *adj.* separado.

apartment [a-párt-ment] *n.* departamento, apartamiento, piso, *m.;* — **house,** edificio de departamentos.

apathy [á-pa-zi] *n.* apatía, *f.*

ape [éip] *n.* mono, *m.;* simio, *m.;* —,*vt.* remedar, imitar.

aperture [a-pér-chuar] *n.* abertura, *f.*

apex [éi-peks] *n.* ápice, *m.,* cúspide, *f.;* colmo, *m.;* cima, *f.*

apiece [a-pís] *adv.* por cabeza, por persona.

apologetic, apological [a-po-lou-yé-tik], [a-po-lou-yé-ti-kal]

adj. apologético; que se disculpa.

apologize [a-pó-lo-chais] *vi.* disculparse, pedir excusas.

apology [a-pó-lo-chi] *n.* apología, defensa, *f.;* satisfacción, disculpa, *f.*

apostrophe [a-pos-tro-fi] *n.* apóstrofe, *f.,* dicterio, *m.;* (gram.) apóstrofo, *m.*

appall [a-pól] *vt.* espantar, aterrar; deprimir, abatir.

appalling [a-pó-lin] *adj.* aterrador, espantoso.

apparatus [a-pa-réi-tas] *n.* aparato, aparejo, *m.*

apparel [a-pa-rel] *n.* traje, vestido, *m.;* ropa, *f.;* **wearing** — , vestuario, *m.;* — , *vt.* vestir, trajear; adornar.

apparent [a-pa-rent] *adj.* evidente, aparente; —**ly**, *adv.* claramente, al parecer, por lo visto.

apparition [a-pa-rí-shon] *n.* aparición, visión, *f.*

appeal [a-píl] *vi.* apelar; recurrir; interesar; atraer; suplicar; — , *n.* súplica, *f.;* exhortación, *f.;* (leyes) apelación, *f.;* incentivo, estímulo, *m.;* simpatía, atracción, *f.*

appear [a-píar] *vi.* aparecer, manifestar; ser evidente; salir, parecer; tener cara de.

appearance [a-pía-rans] *n.* apariencia, *f.,* aspecto, *m.;* vista, *f.;*

aparición, f.

appease [a-pís] vt. apaciguar,
aplacar, reconciliar.

appeasement [a-pís-ment] n.
apaciguamiento, m.

append [a-pen] vt. añadir,
anexar.

appendage [a-pen-dich] n. cosa
accesoria; apéndice, m; dependencia, f.

appendicitis [a-pen-di-sái-tis] n.
apendicitis, f.

appendix [a-pen-diks] n.
apéndice, m.

appetite [a-pi-tait] n. apetito, m.

appetizer [a-pi-tái-sar] n. aperitivo, m.

appetizing [a-pi-tai-sin] adj.
apetitoso.

applaud [a-plód] vt. aplaudir;
alabar, palmear; aclamar, palmotear.

applause [a-plós] n. aplauso, m.

apple [ápel] n. manzana, f.; —
orchard, manzanal, manzanar,
m.; — **pie,** — **tart,** pastel o
pastelillo de manzanas; —
tree, manzano, m.

applesauce [ápel-saus] n. puré
de manzana.

appliance [a-plians] n. utensilio,
instrumento, aparato, m.;
herramienta, f.

applicable [a-plí-ka-bol] adj.
aplicable, apto; conforme.

applicant [á-pli-kant] n. aspirante, solicitante, m. y f. candidato, ta.

application [a-pli-kéi-shon] n.
solicitud f.; aplicación, f.

applied [a-plaid] adj. aplicado,
adaptado.

apply [a-plái] vt. aplicar, acomodar; **to — for,** solicitar; — , vi.
dirigirse a, recurrir a.

appoint [a-point] vt. señalar,
determinar, decretar; nombrar,
designar.

appointment [a-point-ment] n.
estipulación, f ; decreto, mandato, m., orden, f.; nombramiento, m.; cita, f., compromiso, m.; designación, f .

appreciable [a-prí-sha-bol] adj.
apreciable; sensible, perceptible.

appreciate [a-prí-shieit] vt.
apreciar; estimar; valuar.

appreciation [a-pri-shi-éi-shon]
n. aprecio, m.; tasa, f.

appreciative [a-pri-jén-sif] adj.
apreciativo; agradecido.

apprehend [a-pri-jend] vt. aprehender, prender; concebir,
comprender; temer.

apprehension [a-pri-jén-shon] n.
aprehensión, f.; recelo, m;
presa, captura, f.

apprehensive [a-pri-jén-sif] adj.
aprehensivo, tímido; perspicaz;
to become — , sobrecogerse.

apprentice [a-pren-tis] n. aprendiz, *m.;* — , *vt.* poner a alguno de aprendiz.

approach [a-prouch] *vt.* y *vi.* abordar, aproximar, acercar, aproximarse; — , *n.* acceso, *m.;* acercamiento, *m.;* proximidad, *f.*

appropriate [a-pro-prieit] *vt.* apropiar, adaptar; (com.) asignar (una partida); — , *adj.* apropiado; particular, peculiar.

appropriation [a-pro-pri-éishon] *n.* apropiación, *f.;* partida asignada para algún propósito.

approval [a-pru-val] *n.* aprobación, *f.;* **on** — , a prueba, a vistas.

approve [a-prúf] *vt.* aprobar; dar la razón.

approximate [a-prok-si-meit] *vt.* y *vi.* acercar, acercarse; — , *adj.* aproximado.

apricot [éi-pri-kot] *n.* albaricoque, *m.;* (Mex.) chabacano, *m.*

April [éi-pril] *n.* abril, *m.*

apron [éi-pron] *n.* delantal, *m.*

apt [apt] *adj.* apto, idóneo.

aptitude, aptness [ap-ti-tiud], [ap-nis] *n.* aptitud, *f.;* disposición natural.

aquamarine [a-kua-ma-rin] *n.* aguamarina, *f.*

aquarium [a-kua-rium] *n.* acuario, *m.;* pecera, *f.*

aquatic [a-kua-tik] *adj.* acuático.

aqueduct [a-kui-dakt] *n.* acue-ducto, *m.*

aqueous [éi-kuos] *adj.* acuoso.

aquiline [a-kui-lain] *adj.* aguileño.

Arab, Arabian [a-rab], [a-rei-bian] *n.* y *adj.* árabe, *m.* y *f.,* arábigo ga.

Arabic [a-ra-bik] *adj.* árabe, arábigo, arábico.

arable [a-rabol] *adj.* labrantío, cultivable.

arbitrary [ar-bí-tra-ri] *adj.* arbitrario, despótico.

arbitrate [ár-bi-treit] *vt.* y *vi.* arbitrar, juzgar como árbitro.

arbitration [ar-bi-tréi-shon] *n.* arbitrio, arbitraje, *m.*

arbitrator [ar-bi-tréi-tar] *n.* arbitrador, árbitro, *m.*

arc [árk] *n.* arco, *m.;* — **lamp,** — **light,** lámpara de arco; — **weld,** — **welding,** soldadura eléctrica o de arco.

arcade [ar-keid] *n.* arcada, bóveda, *f.*

arch [arch] *n.* arco (de círculo, de puente, etc.), *m.;* **straight** — , arco adintelado; — , *vt.* cubrir con arcos; — , *adj.* principal, insigne; grande; infame; artero, bellaco (se usa en composición como aumentativo) .

archaeological o **archeological** [ar-kio-ló-chi-kal] *adj.* arqueológico.

archaic [ar-keik] *adj.* arcaico.

arched [archt] *adj.* arqueado, abovedado.

archer [ár-char] *n.* arquero, *m.*

archery [ár-che-ri] *n.* ballestería, *f.*

archipelago [ar-ki-ple-li-gou] *n.* archipiélago, *m.*

architect [ar-ki-tect] *n.* arquitecto, *m.*

architectural [ar-ki-ték-cha-ral] *adj.* arquitectónico.

architecture [ar-ki-ték-char] *n.* arquitectura, *f.*

archives [ar-kaif] *n. pl.* archivos, *m. pl.*

archway [arch-uei] *n.* arcada, bóveda, *f.*

arctic [ark-tik] *adj.* ártico.

ardent [ar-dant] *adj.* ardiente; apasionado.

ardor [ar-dar] *n.* ardor, *m.;* vehemencia, *f.;* pasión, *f.*

arduous [ar-dos] *adj.* arduo; laborioso; difícil.

are [ar] *plural y 2ª persona del singular de indicativo* del verbo **to be.**

area [ea-ria] *n.* área, *f.;* espacio, *m.;* superficie, *f.*

arena [a-ri-na] *n.* palenque, *m.;* arena, pista, *f.*

argue [ar-guiu] *vi.* disputar, discutir, argüir; replicar; discurrir; — , *vt.* probar con argumentos.

argument [ar-guiu-ment] *n.* argumento, *m.,* controversia, *f.*

arid [a-rid] *adj.* árido, seco, estéril.

arise [a-rais] *vi.* levantarse; nacer, provenir.

aristocracy [a-ris-to-kra-si] *n.* aristocracia, *f.*

aristocrat [a-ris-to-krat] *n.* aristócrata, *m.* y *f.*

aristocratic [a-ris-to-kra-tik] *adj.* aristocrático.

arithmetic [a-riz-me-tik] *n.* aritmética, *f.*

arithmetical [a-riz-me-ti-kal] *adj.* aritmético.

ark [ark] *n.* arca, *f.*

arm [arm] *n.* brazo, *m.;* rama de árbol; poder, *m.;* arma, *f.;* — **in** — , de bracete.

armadillo [ar-ma-di-lou] *n.* armadillo, *m.*

armament [ar-ma-ment] *n.* (naut.) armamento de navíos; (mil.) armamento, *m.*

armchair [arm-chear] *n.* silla de brazos, poltrona, butaca, *f.*

armor [ar-mor] *n.* armadura, *f.;* (mil.) fuerzas y vehículos blindados; — **plate,** coraza, *f.*

armored [ar-mort] *adj.* blindado, acorazado.

armpit [arm-pit] *n.* axila, *f.*

army [ar-mi] *n.* ejército, *m.;* tropas, *f. pl.*

aroma [a-rou-ma] *n.* aroma, *m.*

aromatic [a-rou-ma-tik] *adj.* aromático, oloroso.

around [a-raund] *prep.* alrededor de; — , *adv.* alrededor; en o al derredor; en torno.

arouse [a-rous] *vt.* despertar; excitar; sublevar.

arrange [a-reinch] *vt.* colocar, poner en orden, arreglar.

arrangement [a-reinch-ment] *n.* colocación, *f.;* orden, arreglo, *m.;* **flower** — , arreglo floral.

array [a-rei] *n.* adorno, vestido, atavío, *m.;* orden de batalla; serie imponente de cosas; — , *vt.* colocar; vestir, adornar.

arrest [a-rest] *n.* arresto, *m.;* detención, *f.;* — , *vt.* arrestar, prender; atraer (la atención).

arrival [a-rai-val] *n.* arribo, *m.;* llegada, venida, *f.*

arrive [a-raiv] *vi.* arribar; llegar; venir.

arrogance [a-ro-gans] *n.* arrogancia, presunción, *f.*

arrogant [a-ro-gant] *adj.* arrogante, presuntuoso.

arrow [a-rou] *n.* flecha, saeta, *f.,* dardo, *m.*

arrowhead [a-rou-jed] *n.* casquillo, *m.;* punta de flecha.

arsenal [ar-si-nal] *n.* (mil.) arsenal, *m.;* (naut.) atarazana, armería, *f.*

arson [ar-son] *n.* incendio provocado intencional-mente.

art [art] *n.* arte, *m.* y *f.;* indus-

tria, *f.;* ciencia, *f.;* **the fine** — **s,** las bellas artes.

artery [ar-te-ri] *n.* arteria, *f.*

artful [art-ful] *adj.* artificioso; diestro.

arthritic [ar-zri-tik] *adj.* artrítico.

arthritis [ar-zrai-tis] *n.* (med.) artritis, *f.;* **rheumatoid** — ,artritis reumatoidea.

article [ar-ti-kel] *n.* artículo, *m.*

articulate [ar-ti-kiu-lit] *adj.* articulado; claro, distinto; — , *vt.* articular, pronunciar distintamente.

articulation [ar-ti-kiu-léishon] *n.* articulación, *f.;* pronunciación, *f.*

artichoke [ar-ti-chouk] *n.* (bot.) alcachofa, *f.*

artifact [ar-ti-fakt] *n.* artefacto, *m.*

artifice [ar-ti-fis] *n.* artificio, fraude, *m.*

artificial [ar-ti-fi-shal] *adj.* artificial; artificioso; sintético.

artillery [ar-ti-le-ri] *n.* artillería, *f.*

artisan [ar-ti-san] *n.* mecánico, artesano, *m.*

artist [ar-tist] *n.* artista, *m.* y *f.,* pintor, ra.

artistic [ar-tis-tik] *adj.* artístico.

as [as] *conj.* y *adv.* como; mientras; también; pues; en son de; visto que, pues que; — **much,** tanto; — **far** — , hasta; — **it**

were, por decirlo así; — **for,** — **to,** en cuanto a.

ascend [a-send] *vi.* ascender, subir.

ascendancy [a-sen-dan-si] *n.* ascendiente, influjo, poder, *m.*

ascension [a-sen-shon] *n.* ascensión, *f.*

ascent [a-sent] *n.* subida, *f.;* eminencia, *f.;* altura, *f.*

ascertain [a-ser-tein] *vt.* indagar, averiguar.

ash [ash] *n.* (bot.) fresno, *m.;* — **es,** *pl.* ceniza, *f.;* reliquias de un cadáver; — **tray,** cenicero, *m.*

ashamed [a-sheimd] *adj.* avergonzado; **to be** — **,** tener vergüenza.

ashen [ashn] *adj.* ceniciento, pálido.

ashore [a-shor] *adv.* en tierra, a tierra.

Asiatic [ei-sha-tik] *n.* y *adj.* asiático, ca.

aside [a-said] *adv.* al lado, aparte.

ask [ask] *vt.* y *vi.* preguntar; pedir, rogar; **to** — **a question,** hacer una pregunta; **to** — **for,** pedir.

askance [as-kans] *adv.* al sesgo, oblicuamente; de refilón; sospechosamente.

aslant [as-lant] *adv.* oblicuamente.

asleep [as-líp] *adj.* dormido; **to fall** — **,** dormirse.

asparagus [as-pa-ra-gos] *n.* espárrago, *m.*

aspect [as-pekt] *n.* aspecto, *m.;* vista, *f.;* aire, *m.;* semblante, *m.*

asphalt [as-falt] *n.* asfalto, *m.*

asphyxiate [as-fik-sieit] *vt.* asfixiar.

asphyxiation [as-fik-siei-shon] *n.* asfixia, *f.*

aspiration [as-pi-rei-shon] *n.* aspiración, *f.*

aspire [as-paiar] *vi.* aspirar, desear.

aspirin [as-pi-rin] *n.* aspirina, *f.*

ass [as] asno, *m.*

assail [a-seil] *vt.* asaltar, atacar, acometer.

assassin [a-sa-sin] *n.* asesino, na.

assassinate [a-sa-si-neit] *vt.* asesinar, matar.

assassination [a-sa-si-nei-shon] *n.* asesinato, *m.*

assault [a-solt] *n.* asalto, *m.;* insulto, *m.;* — **,** *vt.* acometer, asaltar.

assemblage [a-sem-blich] *n.* multitud, *f.;* ensambladura, *f.,* empalme, *m.*

assemble [a-sem-bol] *vt.* congregar, convocar; afluir; ensamblar, armar; — **,** *vi.* juntarse.

assembling [a-sem-blin] *adj.* de

ensamble.

assembly [a-sem-bli] *n.* asamblea, junta, *f.;* congreso, *m.;* montaje, *m.;* concurso, *m.;* concurrencia, *f.;* — **line,** línea de montaje.

assent [a-sent] *n.* asenso, *m.;* aprobación, *f.,* consentimiento, *m.;* — , *vi.* asentir, aprobar.

assert [a-sert] *vt.* sostener, mantener; afirmar.

assertion [a-sershon] *n.* aserción, *f.*

assess [a-ses] *vt.* amillarar, imponer (contribuciones) .

assessment [a-ses-ment] *n.* amillaramiento, impuesto, *m.;* catastro, *m.*

asset [a-set] *n.* algo de valor; ventaja, *f.;* — **s,** *pl.* (com.) haber, activo, capital, *m.*

assiduous [a-si-duos] *adj.* asiduo, aplicado, constante; — **ly,** *adv.* constantemente; diligentemente.

assign [a-sain] *vt.* asignar, destinar, fijar.

assignment [a-sain-ment] *n.* asignación, *f.;* cesión, *f.;* señalamiento, *m;* tarea escolar.

assimilate [a-si-mi-leit] *vt.* asimilar; asemejar.

assimilation [a-si-miu-lei-shon] *n.* asimilación, *f.*

assist [a-sist] *vt.* asistir, ayudar, socorrer.

assistance [a-sis-tans] *n.* asistencia, *f.;* socorro, *m.;* colaboración, *f.*

assistant [a-sis-tant] *n.* asistente, ayudante, *m.*

associate [a-sou-shiet] *vt.* asociar; **to** — **with,** acompañar, frecuentar; — , *adj.* asociado; — , *n.* socio, compañero, *m.*

association [a-sou-si-ei-shon] *n.* asociación, unión, sociedad, agrupación, *f.;* club, *m.*

assorted [a-sor-tid] *adj.* clasificado; — **goods,** artículos variados.

assortment [a-sort-ment] *n.* surtido, *m.;* variedad, *f.*

assuage [a-sueich] *vt.* mitigar, suavizar.

assume [a-siúm] *vt.* arrogar, apropiar, presumir; — , *vi.* arrogarse.

assumption [a-siúm-shon] *n.* presunción, suposición, *f.*

assurance [a-shua-rans] *n.* seguridad, certeza, convicción, *f.;* fianza, *f.;* confianza, *f.;* seguro, *m.*

assure [a-shuar] *vt.* asegurar, afirmar; prometer.

asterisk [as-te-risk] *n.* asterisco, *m.*

asthma [as-ma] *n.* asma, *f.*

asthmatic [as-ma-tik] *adj.* asmático.

astigmatism [as-tig-ma-tí-sem]

n. (med.) astigmatismo, *m.*

astonish [as-to-nish] *vt.* pasmar, sorprender.

astonishing [as-to-ni-shin] *adj.* asombroso.

astonishment [as-to-nish-ment] *n.* pasmo, asombro, *m.; *sorpresa, *f.*

astound [as-taund] *vt.* consternar, aterrar, pasmar.

astounding [as-taun-din] *adj.* asombroso.

astray [as-trei] *adj.* y *adv.* extraviado, descaminado; en forma descaminada; **to lead** — , desviar, seducir; **to go** — , ir por mal camino.

astringent [as-trin-chent] *n.* **y** *adj.* astringente, *m.*

astrology [as-tro-lo-chi] *n.* astrología, *f.*

astronaut [as-tro-not] *n.* astronauta, *m.*

astronomer [as-tro-no-mar] *n.* astrónomo, *m.*

astronomy [as-tro-no-mi] *n.* astronomía, *f.*

astrophysics [as-tro-fi-siks] *n.* astrofísica, *f.*

astute [as-tiút] *adj.* astuto; aleve.

asunder [a-sán-dar] *adv.* separadamente, en pedazos.

asylum [a-sái-lam] *n.* asilo, refugio, *m.; *seno, *m.; **insane** — , casa de locos, manicomio, *m.*

at [at] *prep.* a, en; — **once,** al instante; en seguida; — **all,** nada; siempre; — **first**, al principio; — **large,** en libertad; — **last,** al fin, por último; — **your service,** su servidor o servidora, a sus órdenes.

ate [eit] *pretérito* del verbo **eat.**

atheist [ei-ti-ist] *n.* ateo, atea.

athlete [a-zlí-tik] *n.* atleta, *m.* y *f.; *—' **s foot,** (med.).

athletic [a-zlí-tik] *adj.* atlético, deportista; robusto, vigoroso.

athletics [a-zlí-tiks] *n. pl.* deportes, *m. pl.*

Atlantic [at-lán-tik] *n.* y *adj.* Atlántico, *m.*

atlas [at-las] *n.* atlas, *m.*

A.T.M. [ei-ti-em] : **automatic teller machine** cajero automático.

atmosphere [at-mos-fíar] *n.* atmósfera, *f.*, ambiente, *m.*

atom [a-tom] *n.* átomo, *m.; *— **bomb,** bomba atómica.

atomic [a-to-mik] *adj.* atómico; — **energy,** energía atómica.

atonement [a-ton-ment] *n.* expiación, propiciación, *f.*

atop [a-top] *prep.* encima de; sobre.

atrocious [a-tro-shos] *adj.* atroz; enorme; odioso.

atrocity [a-tro-si-ti] *n.* atrocidad, enormidad, *f.*

attach [a-tach] *vt.* pegar, sujetar,

fijar; atar, ligar; (leyes) embargar.

attachment [a-tach-ment] *n.* adherencia, *f.*; afecto, *m.*; (leyes) embargo, secuestro, *m.*; aditamento, anexo, *m*; adjunto *(en una comunicación), m.*

attack [a-tak] *vt.* atacar; acometer; — , *n.* ataque, *m.*

attain [a-tein] *vt.* ganar, conseguir, obtener, alcanzar.

attainable [a-tei-na-bol] *adj.* asequible.

attainment [a-tein-ment] *n.* logro, *m.*; realización, *f.*; consecución de lo que se pretende; — s, *pl.* conocimientos, *m. pl*; logros, *m. pl.*

attempt [a-tempt] *vt.* intentar, probar, experimentar; procurar; — , *n.* empresa, *f.*; experimento infructuoso; tentativa, *f.*; prueba, *f.*

attend [a-tend] *vt.* servir, asistir; acompañar; — , *vi.* prestar atención.

attendance [a-ten-dans] *n.* concurrencia, asistencia, *f.*; tren, séquito, *m.*; servicio, *m.*; cuidado, *m.*

attendant [a-ten-dant] *n.* sirviente, *m.*; cortejo, *m.*

attention [a-ten-shon] *n.* atención, *f.*; cuidado, *m.*; **to attract** — , llamar la atención; **to call** — , hacer presente; **to give** —

to, ocuparse en o de; **to pay** — , hacer caso, prestar o poner atención; **to pay no** — , no hacer caso.

attentive [a-ten-tif] *adj.* atento; cuidadoso; — **ly**, *adv.* con atención.

attest [a-test] *vt.* atestiguar; dar fe.

attic [a-tik] *n.* desván, *m.*; guardilla, *f.*

attire [a-taiar] *n.* atavío, *m.*; — , *vt.* adornar, ataviar.

attitude [a-ti-tiud] *n.* actitud, *f.*, manera de ser; postura, *f.*

attorney [a-ter-ni] *n.* procurador, abogado, *m.*; (leyes) mandatario, *m.*

attract [a-trakt] *vt.* atraer, persuadir; seducir; **to — attention,** llamar la atención.

attraction [a-trak-shon] *n.* atracción, *f.*; atractivo, *m.*

attractive [a-trak-tif] *adj.* atractivo, simpático; seductor.

attribute [a-tri-biut] *vt.* atribuir; — , *n.* atributo, *m.*

attune [a-triún] *vt.* acordar; armonizar.

auburn [o-bern] *n. y adj.* castaño rojizo.

auction [auk-shon] *n.* venta pública, subasta, *f.*, remate, *m.*

auctioneer [auk-sho-niar] *n.* rematador, subastador, martillero, *m.*

audacious [au-dei-shos] *adj.* audaz, temerario; — **ly,** *adv.* atrevidamente.

audacity [au-da-si-ti] *n.* audacia, osadía *f.*

audible [o-di-bol] *adj.* perceptible al oído; — **bly,** *adv.* alto, de modo que se pueda oír.

audience [o-dians] *n.* audiencia, *f.;* auditorio, *m.;* concurrencia, *f.* oyentes, *m. pl.;* circunstantes, *m.* pl.

audiovisual [ou-dio-vi-shual] *adj.* audiovisual.

audit [o-dit] *n.* remate de una cuenta; auditoría contable; — , *vt.* rematar una cuenta, examinar; pelotear.

audition [o-di-shon] *n.* audición, *f.;* — , *vt.* conceder audición; — , *vi.* presentar audición.

auditor [o-di-tor] *n.* contador, *m.;* oidor, *m.*

auditorium [o-di-to-rium] *n.* anfiteatro, *m.;* teatro, *m.;* auditorio, *m.;* sala de conferencias o diversiones; salón de actos.

augment [og-ment] *vt.* aumentar, acrecentar; — , *vi.* crecer.

August [o-gast] *n.* agosto *(mes)* , *m.*

aunt [ant] *n.* tía, *f.*

aurora [o-roks] *n.* aurora, *f.;* — **borealis,** aurora boreal.

auspices [os-pais] *n. pl.* **auspicios,** *m. pl.;* protección, *f.*

auspicious [os-pi-shos] *adj.* próspero, favorable; propicio; — **ly,** *adv.* prósperamente.

austere [os-tíar] *adj.* austero, severo, rígido.

austerity [os-teriti] *n.* austeridad, *f.;* mortificación, *f.;* severidad, *f.*

authentic [o-zen-tik] *adj.* auténtico.

authenticity [o-zen-ti-si-ti] *n.* autenticidad, *f* .

author [o-zar] *n.* autor, escritor, *m.*

authoritative [o-zo-ri-ta-tif] *adj.* autoritativo.

authority [o-zo-ri-ti] *n.* autoridad *f.;* férula, *f.*

authorization [o-zo-ri-séi-shon] *n.* autorización, *f.,* permiso, *m.*

authorize [o-zo-rais] *vt.* autorizar; — **d,** *adj.* autorizado.

autobiography [o-to-bai-ou-gra-fi] *n.* autobiografía, *f.*

auto [o-tou] *n.* coche, carro, automóvil, *m.*

autograph [o-to-graf] *n.* y *adj.* autógrafo, *m.;* — , *vt.* autografiar.

automatic [o-to-ma-tik] *adj.* automático.

automation [o-to-méi-shon] *n.* automatización, *f.*

automobile [o-to-mo-bil] *n.* automóvil, *m.*

automotive [o-to-mou-tif] *adj.*

automotor, automotriz.

autonomous [o-to-no-mos] *adj.* autónomo.

autonomy [o-to-no-mi] *n.* autonomía, *f.*

autopilot [o-to-pái-lot] *n.* piloto automático.

autopsy [o-top-si] *n.* autopsia.

autumn [o-tom] *n.* otoño, *m.*

autumnal [o-tom-nal] *adj.* otoñal.

auxiliary [ok-si-lia-ri] *adj.* auxiliar, asistente.

avail [a-véil] *vt.* aprovechar; — , *vi.* servir, ser ventajoso; — , *n.* provecho, *m.;* ventaja, *f.;* **to no** — , en vano, sin éxito; — **one-self of,** aprovecharse de.

available [a-véi-la-bol] *adj.* accesible; disponible.

avalanche [a-va-lanch] *n.* avalancha, *f.;* alud, lurte, *m.;* torrente, *m.*

avarice [a-va-ris] *n.* avaricia, *f.*

avaricious [a-va-ri-shos] *adj.* avaro.

avenge [a-vench] *vt.* y *vi.* vengarse, castigar; vindicar.

avenger [a-ven-char] *n.* vengador, ra.

avenue [a-ven-niu] *n.* avenida, *f.*

average [a-ve-rich] *vt.* tomar un término medio; promediar; — , *n.* término medio, promedio, *m.;* **law of** — **s,** ley de probabilidades, *f.;* — , *adj.* medio.

aversion [a-vér-shon] *n.* aversión, *f.,* disgusto, *m.*

avert [a-vért] *vt.* desviar, apartar; evitar.

aviary [éi-via-ri] *n.* avería, pajarera, *f.*

aviation [ei-vi-éi-shon] *n.* aviación, *f.*

aviator [ei-vi-éi-tar] *n.* aviador, *m.*

avid [á-vid] *adj.* ávido, codicioso, voraz.

avidity [á-vi-di-ti] *n.* codicia, avidez, *f.*

avocado [a-vo-ka-dou] *n.* aguacate, *m.*

avoid [a-void] *vt.* evitar, escapar, huir; (leyes) anular.

avoidable [a-voi-da-bol] *adj.* evitable.

avoidance [a-voi-dans] *n.* evitación, *f.;* anulación, *f.*

avow [a-vou] *vt.* confesar, declarar.

await [a-uéit]*vt.* aguardar; — **ing your reply,** en espera de sus noticias.

awake [a-uéik] *vt.* y *vi.* despertar; — , *adj.* despierto; **wide** — , alerta; completamente despierto.

award [a-uárd] *vt.* juzgar; otorgar, adjudicar; conceder; — , *n.* sentencia, decisión, *f.;* premio, *m.,* adjudicación, *f.*

aware [a-uéar] *adj.* cauto, vigilante; sabedor; enterado; consciente.

away [a-uéi] *adv.* ausente, fuera; *interj.* ¡fuera! ¡quita de ahí! **far and** —, de mucho, con mucho.

awe [óu] *n.* miedo, pavor, *m.,* temor reverencial; —, *vt.* infundir miedo o temor reverencial, pasmar.

awe-inspiring [ou-ins-páia-rin] *adj.* imponente.

awe-struck [ou-strák] *adj.* aterrado, espantado; embargado por el respeto.

awful [ou-fol] *adj.* tremendo; funesto; horroroso; — **ly**, *adv.* con respeto y veneración; (coll.) muy, excesivamente.

awhile [a-uáil] *adv.* por un rato, por algún tiempo.

awkward [óuk-uard] *adj.* tosco, inculto, rudo; torpe, poco diestro.

ax, axe [aks] *n.* hacha, *f.;* —, *vt.* cortar con hacha; (fig.) eliminar.

axiom [ak-siom] *n.* axioma, *m.*

axis [ak-sis] *n.* eje, *m.;* alianza, *f.*

axle [aksl] *n.* eje de una rueda; — **box,** buje, *m.*

aye, ay [ai] *adv.* sí; —, *n.* voto afirmativo.

azalea [a-sei-lia] *n.* (bot.) azalea, *f.*

Aztec [as-tek] *n.* y *adj.* azteca.

B

babble [babel] *vi.* charlar, parlotear; — **o babbling,** *n.* charla, *f.;* murmullo (de un arroyo), *m.*

babe [béib] *n.* niño pequeño, nene, infante, bebé, *m.*

baby [bei-bi] *n.* niño pequeño, nene, infante, *m.;* — **boy,** nene, *m.;* — **girl,** nena, *f.*

babyish [bei-bi-ish] *adj.* pueril, infantil, como niño chiquito.

baby-sit [bei-bi-sit] *vi.* cuidar niños ocasionalmente, servir de niñera.

baby-sitter [bei-bi-si-tar] *n.* cui-

daniños, *m.* o *f.,* persona que cuida niños ajenos mientras los padres van de visita, al cine, etc.

baccalaureate [ba-ka-lo-ri-it] *n.* bachillerato, *m.*

bachelor [ba-che-lor] *n.* soltero, *m.;* bachiller, *m.*

back [bak] *n.* dorso, *m.;* espalda, *f.;* lomo, *m.;* revés (de la mano), *m.;* — **of a book,** lomo, *m.;* **to turn one's** —, dar la espalda; —, *adj.* posterior; — **seat,** asiento trasero; —, *vt.* sostener, apoyar, favorecer, *adv.* atrás, detrás; **to come —** , regresar; **a few years —** , hace algunos años; **to fall —** , hacerse atrás; **to go — to,** remontar a; **— of,** detrás, tras de.

backbone [bak-boun] *n.* hueso dorsal, espinazo, *m.,* espina, *f.;* (fig.) firmeza, decisión, *f.*

backdoor [bak-doar] *n.* puerta trasera.

backer [ba-kar] *n.* partidario, sostenedor, *m.*

backgammon [bak-ga-mon] *n.* juego de chaquete o tablas.

background [bak-graund] *n.* fondo, *m.;* ambiente, *m.;* antecedentes, *m. pl.,* educación, *f.*

backlog [bak-log] *n.* tronco trasero en una hoguera; (com.) reserva de pedidos pendientes.

backstage [bak-steich] *n.* (theat.) parte detrás del telón o detrás de bastidores.

backward [bak-uod] *adj.* opuesto; retrógrado; retrospectivo; tardo, lento; **to be —** , ser tímido; **— s,** *adv.* de espaldas, hacia atrás.

bacon [bei-kon] *n.* tocino, *m.*

bacteria [bak-ti-ria] *n. pl.* bacterias, *f. pl.*

bacteriology [bak-ti-ri-o-lo-yi] *n.* bacteriología, *f.*

bad [bad] *adj.* mal, malo; perverso; infeliz; dañoso; indispuesto;

vicioso; **to look —** , tener mala cara.

badge [bach] *n.* señal, *f.;* símbolo, *m.;* divisa, *f.*

badger [ba-char] *n.* tejón, *m.;* — , *vt.* fatigar; cansar, atormentar; **to — with questions,** importunar con preguntas.

bad-tempered [bad-tem-ped] *adj.* de mal humor, de mal carácter.

baffle [ba-fol] *vt.* eludir; confundir, hundir.

bag [bag] *n.* saco, *m.;* bolsa, *f.;* talego, *m.*

baggage [ba-geich] *n.* equipaje, *m.;* **— check,** talón, *m.;* **— room,** sala de equipajes.

bagpipe [bag-paips] *n.* (mus.) gaita, *f.*

bail [beil] *n.* fianza, caución (juratoria) , *f.;* fiador, *m.;* recaudo, *m.;* **to go — for,** salir fiador; — , *vt.* caucionar, fiar; salir fiador, dar fianza; **to give —** , sanear; **on —,** bajo fianza; **to — out,** vaciar; (avi.) descender en paracaídas.

bailiff [bei-lif] *n.* alguacil, *m.;* mayordomo, *m.*

bait [beit] *vt.* cebar; azuzar; atraer; — , *n.* cebo, *m.;* anzuelo, *m.;* carnada, *f.*

bake [beik] *vt.* cocer en horno.

baker [bei-kar] *n.* hornero, panadero, *m.*

bakery [bei-ka-ri] *n.* panadería,

f.

baking [bei-kin] *n.* hornada, *f.;*
— **powder,** polvo de hornear;
— **soda,** bicarbonato de sosa.

balance [ba-lans] *n.* balanza, *f.;*
equilibrio, *m.;* resto, *m.;* balance, *m.;* saldo de una cuenta; **to
lose one's** — , caerse, perder el
equilibrio; — , *vt.* pesar en
balanza; contrapesar; saldar;
considerar; examinar; **to** — **an
account,** cubrir una cuenta.

balcony [bal-ko-ni] *n.* balcón,
m.; galería, *f.;* anfiteatro, *m.*

bald [bold] *adj.* calvo; simple,
desabrido.

baldness [bold-nes] *n.* calvicie, *f.*

balk [bolk] *vi.* rebelarse (un
caballo, etc.); resistirse.

ball [bol] *n.* bola, *f.;* pelota, *f.;*
bala, *f.;* baile, *m.;* — **bearing,**
cojinete de bolas; — **point pen,**
pluma atómica, bolígrafo, *m.*

ballad [ba-lad] *n.* balada, *f.;*
romance *m.*

ballerina [ba-le-ri-na] *n.* bailarina, *f.*

ballet [ba-lei] *n.* ballet, *m.*

ballot [ba-lot] *n.* cédula para
votar; boleto electoral; escrutinio, *m.;* papeleta, balota, *f.;* —
vi. votar con balotas; — **box,**
urna electoral.

ballplayer [bol-ple-yar] *n.* jugador de pelota.

ballroom [bol-rum] *n.* salón de

baile.

balm [balm] *n.* bálsamo, *m.*

balmy [bal-mi] *adj.* balsámico;
fragante; suave, agradable.

bamboo [bam-bu] *n.* bambú, *m.*

bamboozle [bam-bu-sel] *vt.*
(coll.) engañar, embaucar.

ban [ban] *n.* bando, anuncio,
m.; excomunión, *f.;* proclama,
f.; prohibición, *f.;* — , *vt.* prohibir, vedar; excomulgar; malde-
cir.

banana [ba-na-na] *n.* plátano,
m., banana, *f.,* banano, guineo,
cambur, *m.*

band [band] *n.* venda, faja, *f.;*
unión, *f.;* charanga, banda (de
soldados), *f.;* orquesta, *f.;* — ,
vt. unir, juntar; vendar.

bandage [ban-deich] *n.* venda,
faja, *f.;* vendaje, *m.;* — , *vt.*
vendar, fajar.

bandanna [ban-da-na] *n.* paño-
leta, *f.,* pañuelo grande de colores.

bandit [ban-dit] *n.* bandido, da.

bandstand [band-stand] *n.* plataforma de banda, quiosco de
música.

bandwagon [band-va-gon] *n.*
vehículo para banda de música; **to get on the** — , (pol.)
adherirse a una candidatura
probablemente triunfante;
unirse a un grupo.

bane [bein] *n.* destrucción, *f.;*

azote, *m.*

bang [bang] *n.* puñada, *f.;* puñetazo, *m.;* ruido de un golpe; —
s, flequillo (del cabello), *m.;* — ,
vt. dar puñadas, sacudir;
cerrar con violencia; — ! *interj.*
¡ pum!

bangle [ban-guel] *n.* brazalete,
m., ajorca, *f.*

banish [ba-nish] *vt.* desterrar,
echar fuera, proscribir, expa-
triar.

banishment [ba-nish-ment] *n.*
destierro, *m.*

banister [ba-nis-tar] *n.* pasamano, *m.,* baranda, *f.*

banjo [ban-yo] *n.* banjo (variedad de guitarrilla), *m.*

bank [bank] *n.* orilla (de río),
ribera, *f.;* montón de tierra;
banco, cambio, *m.;* dique, *m.;*
escollo, *m.;* — **balance,** saldo
bancario; — **book,** libreta de
banco o de depósitos; **blood** —
, banco de sangre; **savings**— ,
banco de ahorros; — , *vt.* poner
dinero en un banco; detener el
agua con diques; (avi.) ban-
quear; escorar.

banker [ban-kar] *n.* banquero,
m.

banking [ban-king] *n.* banca, *f.;*
— , *adj.* bancario; — **house,**
casa de banca.

bankrupt [bank-rapt] *adj.* insol-
vente; quebrado, en bancarro-
ta; — , *n.* fallido, *m.,* persona
en bancarrota.

bankruptcy [bank-rapt-si] *n.*
bancarrota, quiebra, *f.*

banner [ba-nar] *n.* bandera, *f.;*
estandarte, *m.*

banquet [ban-kuit] *n.* banquete,
m., comida suntuosa; — , *vt.* y
vi. banquetear.

banter [ban-tar] *vt.* zumbar;
divertirse a costa de alguno; —
, *n.* zumba, burla, *f.*

baptism [bap-tisem] *n.* bautismo, bautizo, *m.*

baptize [bap-tais] *vt.* bautizar.

bar [bar] *n.* barra, *f.;* tranca, *f.;*
obstáculo, *m.;* (leyes) estrados,
m. pl.; aparador, *m.;* cantina,
f.; barrera, *f.;* palanca, *f.;* — **s,**
pl. rejas, *f. pl.;* **in** — **s,** en barra
o en barras; — , *vt.* barrear;
cerrar con barras; impedir;
prohibir; excluir; — , *prep.*
excepto; — **none,** sin excluir a
nadie.

barb [barb] *n.* púa, *f.*

barbarian [bar-ba-rian] *n.* hombre bárbaro; — , *adj.* bárbaro,
cruel.

barbarism [bar-ba-ri-sem] *n.*
(gram.) barbarismo, *m.;* crueldad, *f.;* barbaridad, *f.*

barbarous [bar-ba-ros] *adj.* bárbaro, cruel.

barbecue [bar-bi-kiu] *n.* barbacoa, *f.;* — **pit,** asador, *m.*

barbed [barbd] *adj.* barbado; — **wire**, alambre de púas.

barber [bar-bar] *n.* barbero, *m.*

barbershop [bar-bi-tal] *n.* peluquería, barbería, *f.*

bare [bear] *adj.* desnudo, descubierto; simple; pobre; puro; — , *vt.* desnudar; descubrir.

barefoot, barefooted [bear-fut], [bear-futid] *adj.* descalzo, sin zapatos.

barelegged [bear-le-gid] *adj.* con las piernas desnudas, sin medias.

barely [bear-li] *adv.* apenas, solamente; pobremente.

bargain [bar-guein] *n.* contrato, pacto, *m.;* ganga, *f.;* — , *vi.* pactar, negociar; regatear.

baritone [ba-ri-toun] *n.* (mus.) barítono, *m.*

barium [ba-riom] *n.* (chem.) bario, *m.*

bark [bark] *n.* corteza, *f.;* ladrido (del perro), *m.;* — , *vi.* ladrar.

barley [bar-li] *n.* cebada, *f.*

barn [barn] *n.* granero, pajar, *m.;* establo, *m.*

barnyard [barn-yard] *n.* patio de granja, corral, *m.*

barometer [ba-ro-mi-tar] *n.* barómetro, *m.*

baron [ba-ron] *n.* barón, *m.;* (coll.) poderoso industrial.

baroness [ba-ro-nes] *n.* baronesa, *f.*

baroque [ba-rok] *adj.* (arch.) barroco.

barrack [ba-rak] *n.* cuartel, *m.;* barraca, *f.*

barrel [ba-ral] *n.* barril, *m.;* cañón de escopeta; cilindro, *m.;* — , *vt.* embarrilar.

barren [ba-ren] *adj.* estéril, infructuoso; seco.

barricade [ba-ri-keid] *n.* barricada, *f.;* estacada, *f.;* barrera, *f.;* — , *vt.* cerrar con barreras, empalizar; atrincherar.

barrier [ba-riar] *n.* barrera, *f.;* obstáculo, *m.;* **sound** — , barrera sónica.

bartender [bar-ten-dar] *n.* tabernero, cantinero, *m.*

barter [bar-tar] *vi.* permutar, traficar; — , *vt.* cambiar, trocar; — , *n.* cambio, trueque, *m.*

base [beis] *n.* fondo, *m.;* basa, base, *f.;* pedestal, *m.;* contrabajo, *m.;* pie, *m.;* — , *vt.* apoyar; basar; — , *adj.* bajo, vil.

baseball [beis-bol] *n.* béisbol, *m.;* pelota de béisbol; juego de béisbol.

baseboard [beis-bord] *n.* tabla que sirve de base; friso, *m.*

baseless [beis-les] *adj.* sin fondo o base.

basement [beis-ment] *n.* sótano, *m.*

baseness [beis-nes] *n.* bajeza, vileza, *f.;* ilegitimidad de nacimiento; mezquindad, *f.*

bashful [bash-ful] *adj.* vergonzo-so, modesto, tímido.

bashfulness [bash-ful-nes] *n.* vergüenza, modestia, timidez, cortedad, esquivez, *f.*

basic [bei-sik] *adj.* fundamental, básico.

basin [beisn] *n.* palangana, vasi-ja, *f.;* cuenca (de un río), *f.*

basis [bei-sis] *n.* base, *f.;* funda-mento, *m.,* suposición, *f.;* pie, *m.*

bask [bask] *vi.* exponerse (al sol); **to — in the sunshine,** ponerse a tomar el sol.

basket [bas-kit] *n.* cesta, canas-ta.

basketball [bas-kit-bol] *n.* bás-quetbol , baloncesto, *m.*

Basque [bask] *n. y adj.* vasco, ca.

bass [bas] *n.* estera, *f.;* esparto, *m.;* (ichth.) lobina, *f.,* róbalo o robalo, *m.*

bass [bas] *n.* (mus.) bajo, *m.;* tono bajo y profundo; — , *adj.* (mus.) bajo; — **drum,** bombo, *m.;* — **horn,** tuba, *f.;* — **viol,** violón, contrabajo, *m.*

bassinet [ba-si-net] *n.* cesta cuna, cuna, *f.;* (Mex.) moisés, *m.*

bassoon [ba-sun] *n.* (mus.) bajón, *m.*

bastard [bas-tard] *n. y adj.* bas-

tardo, da.

baste [beist] *vt.* pringar la carne en el asador; hilvanar; bastear.

bat [bat] *n.* bate, garrote, palo, *m.;* murciélago, *m.;* — , *vt.* batear, golpear a la pelota.

batch [bach] *n.* hornada, *f.;* can-tidad de cosas producidas a un tiempo; pilada, *f.;* carga, *f.;* colada, *f.;* (Arg.) past n, *m.;* (Cuba) templa, *f.;* (Mex.) turno de colada.

bath [baz] *n.* baño, *m.*

bathe [beiz] *vt. y vi.* bañar, bañarse.

bathhouse [baz-jaus] *n.* baln-eario, *m.*

bathing [ba-zing] *n.* baño, *m.*

bathrobe [baz-roub] *n.* peinador, *m.,* bata, *f.*

bathroom [baz-rum] *n.* cuarto de baño, *m.*

bathtub [baz-tab] *n.* bañera, tina de baño, *f.*

baton [ba-ton] *n.* batuta, *f.*

battalion [ba-ta-lion] *n.* (mil.) batallón, *m.*

batter [ba-tar] *n.* batido, *m.;* pasta culinaria; bateador, vole-ador (de la pelota), *m.;* — , *vt.* apalear; batir; cañonear; demo-ler.

battery [ba-te-ri] *n.* acumulador, *m.;* batería.

battle [ba-tel] *n.* batalla, *f.;* com-bate, *m.;* — **front,** frente de

combate; — **ground,** campo de
batalla.

battlefield [ba-tel-fild] *n.* campo
de batalla.

battleship [ba-tel-ship] *n.* acorazado, *m.*

bawl [bol] *vi.* gritar, vocear;
ladrar.

bay [bei] *n.* bahía, *f.;* laurel,
lauro, *m.;* — , *vi.* ladrar; balar;
— , *adj.* bayo; **to keep at** — ,
tener a raya.

bayonet [ba-yo-net] *n.* bayoneta,
f.; — , *vt.* traspasar con la
bayoneta.

bazaar [ba-sar] *n.* bazar, *m.*

bazooka [ba-sú-ka] *n.* cañón
portátil contra tanques.

B.C. [bi-si] : **Before Christ** A. de
J.C. antes de Jesucristo.

be [bi] *vi.* ser; estar; quedar; **to**
— **ill,** estar malo, estar enfermo; **to** — **in a hurry,** estar de
prisa; **to** — **right,** tener razón;
to — **well,** estar bien o bueno.

beach [bich] *n.* costa, ribera, orilla, playa, *f.;* — **comber,** vagabundo de las playas, *m.;* — ,
vt. y vi. (naut.) encallar.

beacon [bi-kon] *n.* fanal, faro, *m.*

bead [bid] *n.* cuenta, chaquira,
f.; — **s,** *n. pl.* rosario, *m.*

beaded [bid-ed] *adj.* adornado
con cuentas o chaquiras.

beagle [bigel] *n.* sabueso, *m.*

beak [bik] *n.* pico, *m.;* espolón

de navío.

beam [bim] *n.* viga, *f.;* rayo de
luz; volante, *m.;* brazos de
balanza; — **of timber,** madero,
m.; — , *vi.* emitir rayos, brillar.

beaming [bi-min] *adj.* radiante.

bean [bin] *n.* (bot.) haba, habichuela, *f.;* frijol, *m.;* **kidney** —
s, frijoles rojos o colorados;
navy — **s,** frijoles blancos.

bear [bear] *n.* oso, *m.;* bajista
(en la bolsa), *m.;* **she** — , osa,
f.; — , *vt.* llevar alguna cosa
como carga; sostener; apoyar;
soportar; producir; parir; conllevar, portar; — , *vi.* sufrir
(algún dolor); tolerar; — , *vt. y
vi.* resistir; **to** — **a grudge,**
guardar rencor; **to** — **in mind,**
tener presente, tener en cuenta.

beard [bíard] *n.* barba, *f.;* arista
de espiga; — , *vt.* desafiar.

bearded [bíarded] *adj.* barbado;
barbudo.

bearer [bearar] *n.* portador, ra;
árbol fructífero.

bearing [bea-rin] *n.* situación, *f.
;* comportamiento, *m.;* relación,
f.; sufrimiento, *m.,* paciencia,
f.; (mech.) cojinete, *m.*

beast [bist] *n.* bestia, *f.;* bruto,
m.; res, *f.;* hombre brutal; —
of burden, acémila, *f.*

beastly [bistli] *adj.* bestial, brutal; — , *adv.* brutalmente.

beat [bit] *vt.* golpear; batir; tocar (un tambor); pisar; abatir; ganar (en un juego) ; — , *vi.* pulsar, palpitar; — , *n.* golpe, *m.;* pulsación, *f.;* ronda, *f.*

beater [bitar] *n.* batidor, *m.,* batidora, *f.*

beating [bi-tin] *n.* paliza, zurra, *f.;* pulsación, *f.*

beau [bou] *n.* petimetre, currutaco, *m.;* novio, pretendiente, *m.*

beautiful [biu-ti-ful] *adj.* hermoso, bello; precioso; — **ly**, *adv.* con belleza o perfección.

beautify [biu-ti-fai] *vt.* hermosear, embellecer; adornar; — , *vi.* hermosearse.

beauty [biu-ti] *n.* hermosura, belleza, *f.;* preciosidad, *f.;* — **parlor,** — **salon,** salón de belleza; — **spot,** lunar (que embellece), *m.*

beaver [bi-var] *n.* castor, *m.*

becalm [bi-kalm] *vt.* serenar, sosegar.

because [bi-kos] *conj.* porque; pues; que; — **of,** a causa de.

beckon [be-kon] *vi.* hacer seña con la cabeza o la mano, llamar con señas.

become [bi-kam] *vt.* sentar, quedar bien; — , *vi.* hacerse, convertirse; ponerse; llegar a ser.

becoming [bi-ka-min] *adj.* conveniente; que le queda bien a

uno.

bed [bed] *n.* cama, *f.;* (geol.) yacimiento, *m.*

bedding [be-din] *n.* ropa de cama; accesorios de cama.

bedlam [bed-lam] *n.* belén, *m.,* algarabía, *f.;* confusión, *f.*

bedpost [bed-poust] *n.* pilar de cama.

bedroom [bed-rum] *n.* alcoba, *f.,* cuarto de dormir, dormitorio, *m.,* recámara, *f.*

bedside [bed-said] *n.* lado de la cama; cabecera, *f.*

bedspread [bed-spred] *n.* colcha, sobrecama, *f.*

bedspring [bed-sprin] *n.* colchón de muelles.

bedtime [bed-taim] *n.* hora de acostarse.

bee [bí] *n.* abeja, *f.*

beech [bích] *n.* (bot.) haya, *f.*

beechnut [bích-nat] *n.* hayuco, *m.*

beef [bíf] *n.* buey, toro, *m.;* vaca, *f.;* carne de res o de vaca.

beefsteak [bíf-steik] *n.* bistec, *m.*

been [bín] *p.p.* del verbo **be.**

beer [bíar] *n.* cerveza, *f.*

beeswax [bís-uaks] *n.* cera de abejas.

beet [bít] *n.* remolacha, betarraga, *f.;* (Mex.) betabel, *m.;* — **root,** betarraga, *f.;* — **sugar,** azúcar de remolacha.

beetle [bí-tel] *n.* escarabajo, *m.;*

pisón, *m.*

befall [bi-fol] *vi.* suceder, acontecer, sobrevenir.

before [bi-for] *adv.* más adelante; delante, enfrente; ante, antes de; — , *prep.* antes de, ante; delante de, enfrente de; — , *conj.* antes que.

beforehand [bi-for-jand] *adv.* de antemano, con anterioridad, anticipadamente.

befriend [bi-frend] *vt.* favorecer, proteger, amparar.

beg [beg] *vt.* mendigar, rogar; suplicar; pedir; — , *vi.* vivir de limosna.

began [bi-gan] *pretérito* del verbo **begin.**

beggar [be-gar] *n.* mendigo, ga; limosnero, ra.

beggarly [be-gar-li] *adj.* pobre, miserable; despreciable.

begin [bi-guin] *vt.* y *vi.* comenzar, principiar.

beginner [bi-gui-nar] *n.* principiante, *m.* y *f.*, novicio, cia.

beginning [bi-gui-nin] *n.* principio, comienzo, *m.*; origen, *m.*; — s, *pl.* rudimentos, *m. pl.*; **at the** — , al principio; — **with,** a partir de.

behave [bi-jeiv] *vi.* comportarse, portarse (bien o mal), manejarse.

behavior [bi-jei-vior] *n.* conducta, *f.*; proceder, *m.*; comporta-

miento, *m.*

behead [bi-jed] *vt.* decapitar; descabezar.

behind [bi-jaind] *prep.* detrás de, tras; en zaga a, inferior a; **from** — , por detrás; — , *adv.* detrás, atrás; atrasadamente.

behold [bi-jold] *vt.* ver, contemplar, observar; — !*interj.* ¡he aquí! ¡mira!

beige [beish] *n.* color entre rojo y amarillo o entre gris y pardo, color arena.

being [bí-ing] *n.* existencia, *f.*; estado, *m.*; persona, *f.*

belated [bi-lei-tid] *adj.* demorado, atrasado.

belch [belch] *vi.* vomitar; — , *n.* eructo, *m.*, eructación, *f.*

Belgian [bel-chan] *n.* y *adj.* belga, *m.* y *f.*

Belgium [bel-yam] Bélgica, *f.*

belie [bi-lai] *vt.* desmentir; desdecir, contrastar con.

belief [bi-líf] *n.* fe, creencia, *f.*; opinión, *f.*; credo, *m.*

believable [bi-lí-va-bol] *adj.* creíble.

believe [bi-lív] *vt.* creer; — , *vi.* pensar, imaginar.

believer [bi-lí-var] *n.* creyente, fiel, cristiano, *m.*

belittle [bi-li-tel] *vt.* dar poca importancia (a algo).

bell [bel] *n.* campana, *f.*; bronce, *m.*; — **ringer,** campanero, *m.*;

call — , timbre, *m.*

bellboy [bel-boi] *n.* botones, *m.*, mozo de hotel.

bellhop = **bellboy.**

belligerent [bi-li-che-rent] *adj.* beligerante.

bellow [be-lou] *vi.* bramar; rugir; vociferar; — , *n.* bramido, *m.*

bellowing [be-louin] *adj.* rugiente.

belly [be-li] *n.* vientre, *m.;* panza, barriga, *f.*

belong [bi-lon] *vi.* pertenecer, tocar a, concernir.

belongings [bi-lon-guings] *n. pl.* propiedad, *f.;* efectos, anexos, *m. pl.*

beloved [bi-la-vid] *adj.* querido, amado.

below [bi-lou] *adv. y prep.* debajo, inferior; abajo.

belt [belt] *n.* cinturón, cinto, *m.;* correa, *f.;* cintura, *f.;* **to hit below the** — , (boxeo) dar un golpe bajo; (fig.) herir con saña; **to tighten one's** — , tomar aliento, soportar.

bench [bench] *n.* banco, *m.;* tribunal, *m.*

bend [bend] *vt.* encorvar, inclinar, plegar; hacer una reverencia; — , *vi.* encorvarse; cimbrarse; inclinarse; — , *n.* , encorvadura, *f.;* codo, *m.;* giro, *m.*

beneath [bi-níz] *adv. y prep.* debajo, abajo; de lo más hondo.

benediction [be-ni-dik-shon] *n.* bendición, *f.*

benefactor [be-ni-fak-tor] *n.* bienhechor, ra.

beneficent [bi-ni-fi-sent] *adj.* benéfico.

beneficial [be-ni-fi-shal] *adj.* beneficioso, provechoso, útil.

beneficiary [be-ni-fi-sha-ri] *n.* beneficiario, ria.

benefit [be-ni-fit] *n.* beneficio, *m.;* utilidad, *f.;* provecho, *m.;* bien, *m.;* **for the** — **of,** a beneficio de; — , *vt.* beneficiar; — , *vi.* beneficiarse; prevalerse.

benevolence [bi-ne-vo-lans] *n.* benevolencia, gracia, *f.*

benevolent [bi-ne-vo-lent] *adj.* benévolo; — **society,** sociedad benéfica.

benign [bi-nain] *adj.* benigno; afable; liberal.

bent [bent] *n.* inclinación, tendencia, *f.*

benzene [ben-sín] *n.* (chem.) bencina, *f.*

bequeath [bi-kuiz] *vt.* legar en testamento.

berate [bi-reit] *vt.* regañar con vehemencia.

bereave [bi-rív] *vt.* despojar, privar.

bereavement [bi-rív-ment] *n.* despojo, *m.;* luto, duelo, *m.*

bereft [bi-reft] *adj.* despojado, privado.

beret [be-rei] *n.* boina, *f.*

berry [be-ri] *n.* baya, *f.*

berth [berz] *n.* litera, *f.;* camarote, *m.*

beseech [bi-sich] *vt.* suplicar, implorar, conjurar, rogar.

beset [bi-set] *vt.* sitiar; cercar; perseguir; acosar; aturdir, confundir.

besetting [bi-se-tin] *adj.* habitual (aplícase al peligro o al pecado).

beside [bi-said] *prep.* al lado de; cerca de, junto a; en comparación con; — **oneself,** fuera de sí, trastornado.

besides [bi-saids] *adv.* por otra parte, además; — , *prep.* además de.

best [best] *adj.* mejor; — **man,** padrino de boda; — **seller,** éxito de librería; — , *n.* lo mejor; **to do one's** — , hacer todo lo posible.

bestial [bes-tial] *adj.* bestial, brutal.

bestow [bis-tou] *vt.* dar, conferir; otorgar; dar en matrimonio; regalar; dedicar; — **upon,** deparar.

bet [bet] *n.* apuesta, *f.;* — , *vt.* apostar.

betray [bi-trei] *vt.* hacer traición, traicionar; divulgar algún secreto.

betrayal [bi-treial] *n.* traición, *f.*

betrothed [bi-throzd] *adj.* comprometido, prometido; — , *n.* prometido, da.

better [be-tar] *adj. y adv.* mejor; más bien; — **half,** cara mitad; **so much the** — , tanto mejor; — **s,** *n. pl.* superiores, *m. pl.;* — , *vt.* mejorar, reformar.

bettor, better [be-tar] *n.* apostador, ra.

between [bi-tuin] *prep.* entre, en medio de.

beverage [be-va-rich] *n.* bebida, *f.*

bewail [bi-ueil] *vt. y vi.* lamentar, deplorar.

beware [bi-uear] *vi.* tener cuidado, guardarse; — ! *interj.* ¡cuidado! ¡mira!

bewilder [bi-uil-dar] *vt.* descaminar; pasmar; — , *vi.* extraviarse; confundirse.

bewilderment [bi-uil-der-ment] *n.* extravío, *m.;* confusión, *f.*

bewitch [bi-uich] *vt.* encantar, hechizar.

bewitching [bi-ui-chin] *adj.* encantador, cautivador.

beyond [bi-yond] *prep.* más allá, más adelante, fuera de.

biannual [bai-a-niual] *adj.* semestral, semianual.

bias [baias] *n.* propensión, inclinación, parcialidad, *f.;* preocupación, *f.*; sesgo, *m.*;objeto, fin, *m.*; **on the —** , al sesgo; **to cut on the —** , sesear; **—** , *vt.* inclinar; preocupar; predisponer.

biased [baiast] *adj.* predispuesto.

bib [bib] *n.* babero *m.*

Bible [bai-bol] *n.* Biblia (la sagrada escritura), *f.*

Biblical [bi-bli-kal] *adj.* bíblico.

bibliography [bi-blio-gra-fi] *n.* bibliografía, *f.*

bicarbonate [bai-kar-bo-neit] *n.* bicarbonato, *m.*

biceps [bai-seps] *n.* bíceps, *m.*

bicker [bi-kar] *vi.* reñir, disputar.

bicycle [bai-si-kol] *n.* bicicleta, *f.*; **to ride a —** , montar en bicicleta.

bicycling [bai-si-klin] *n.* ciclismo, *m.*

bid [bid] *vt.* convidar; mandar; envidar; ofrecer; **— adieu to,** despedirse; **—** , *n.* oferta, *f.*

big [big] *adj.* grande, lleno; inflado; **B— Dipper,** (ast.) Osa Mayor, *f.*

bigness [big-nes] *n.* grandeza, *f.*

bigot [bi-got] *n.* persona fanática; hipócrita, *m.* y *f.*

bigoted [bi-go-tid] *adj.* santurrón, intolerante.

bigotry [bi-go-tri] *n.* fanatismo, *m.*; intolerancia, *f.*

bile [bail] *n.* bilis, *f.*; cólera, *f.*

bilingual [bai-lin-gual] *adj.* bilingüe.

bill [bil] *n.* pico de ave; cédula, *f.*; cuenta, factura, *f.*; **—** , *vt.* enviar una cuenta, facturar.

billboard [bil-bord] *n.* cartelera, *f.*

billiards [bi-liards] *n.* billar, *m.*

billion [bi-lion] *n.* billón, *m.*, millón de millones (en España, Inglaterra, y Alemania); mil millones (en Francia y los Estados Unidos).

billionaire [bi-lio-niar] *n.* billonario, ria.

bimonthly [bai-monzli] *adj.* bimestral.

bin [bin] *n.* artesón, *m.*; armario, *m.*, despensa, *f.*

bind [baind] *vt.* atar; unir; encuadernar; obligar, constreñir; impedir; poner a uno a servir; **—** , *vi.* ser obligatorio.

binder [bain-dar] *n.* encuadernador, *m.*

binding [bain-din] *n.* venda, faja, *f.*; encuadernación, *f.*; pasta (para libros), *f.*

bingo [bin-gou] *n.* variedad de lotería de cartones.

binocular [bi-no-kiu-lar] *adj.* binocular; **— s**, *n. pl.*gemelos, lentes, binóculos, *m. pl.*

biochemistry [baiou-ke-mis-tri] *n.* bioquímica, *f.*

biographical [baiou-gra-fi-kal]

adj. biográfico.

biography [baiou-gra-fi] *n.* biografía, *f.*

biological [baio-lo-chik] *adj.* biológico.

biology [baio-lo-chi] *n.* biología, *f.*

bipartisan [bai-par-ti-san] *adj.* representativo de dos partidos políticos.

birch [berch] *n.* (bot.) abedul, *m.*

bird [berd] *n.* ave, *f.;* pájaro, *m.;* — **of prey,** ave de rapiña.

bird's-eye view [berds-ai-viu] *n.* vista a vuelo de pájaro.

birth [berz] *n.* nacimiento, *m.;* origen, *m.;* parto, *m.;* linaje, *m.;* — **certificate,** certificado o acta de nacimiento, f.; to give — , dar a luz, parir.

birthday [berzdei] *n.* cumpleaños, natalicio, *m.;* **to have a —** , cumplir años.

birthmark [berz-mark] *n.* lunar, *m.,* marca de nacimiento.

birthplace [berz-pleis] *n.* suelo nativo, lugar de nacimiento.

Biscay [bis-kei] Vizcaya, *f.*

biscuit [bis-kit] *n.* bizcocho, bollo, *m.;* galleta, *f.*

bisect [bai-sekt] *vt.* bisecar, dividir en dos partes; — , *vi.* bifurcarse.

bishop [bi-shop] *n.* obispo, *m.;* alfil (en el ajedrez) , *m.*

bison [bai-son] *n.* bisonte, búfalo, *m.*

bit [bit] *n.* bocado, *m.;* pedacito, *m.;* pizca, *f.;* brote, *m.;* trozo, *m.;* **two — s** (coll. E.U.A.) 25ā (moneda de E.U.A.) ; — , *vt.* refrenar; — , *pretérito* del verbo **bite.**

bite [bait] *vt.* morder; punzar, picar; satirizar; engañar; — **the dust,** caer muerto; (fig.) quedar totalmente derrotado; — , *n.* tentempié, *m.*

biting [bai-tin] *adj.* mordaz, acre, picante.

bitten [bi-ten] *p.p.* del verbo **bite.**

bitterness [bi-ter-nes] *n.* amargor, *m.;* amargura, *f.;* rencor, *m.;* pena, *f.;* dolor, *m.*

bizarre [bi-zar] *adj.* raro, extravagante.

blab [blab] *vt.* parlar, charlar, divulgar; — , *vi.* chismear; — , *n.* chismoso, sa.

black [blak] *adj.* negro, oscuro; tétrico, malvado; funesto **widow,** araña americana, capulina; — , *n.* color negro; — , *vt.* teñir de negro, negrecer; limpiar (las botas).

blackball [blak-bol] *vt.* excluir a uno votando con una bolita negra; jugar la suerte con una bola negra; votar en contra.

blackberry [blak-be-ri] *n.* zarzamora, mora, *f* .

blackbird [blak-berd] *n.* mirlo,

m.

blackboard [blak-bord] *n.* pizarra, *f.*, pizarrón, tablero, *m.*

blacken [blaken] *vt.* teñir de negro; ennegrecer.

blackhead [blak-jed] *n.* espinilla, *f.*

blackmail [blak-meil] *n.* chantaje, *m.;* —, *vt.* chantajear, amenazar con chantaje.

blackout [blak-aut] *n.* oscurecimiento, *m.*

blacksmith [blak-smiz] *n.* herrero, *m.*

bladder [bla-dar] *n.* vejiga, *f.*

blade [bleid] *n.* brizna, hoja, *f.;* pala (de remo), *f.;* valentón, *m.;* — **of a propeller,** aleta, *f.*

blame [bleim] *vt.* vituperar; culpar; achacar; —, *n.* culpa, vituperación, imputación, *f.*

blameless [bleim-les] *adj.* inocente, irreprensible, intachable, puro.

blameworthy [bleim-uer-zi] *adj.* culpable.

blanch [blanch] *vt.* blanquear; mondar, pelar; hacer pálido.

bland [bland] *adj.* blando, suave, dulce, apacible, gentil, agradable, sutil.

blank [blank] *adj.* blanco; pálido; confuso; vacío, sin interés; **verse,** verso sin rima; —, *n.* blanco, *m.*, espacio en blanco.

blanket [blan-ket] *n.* cubierta de cama, frazada, manta, *f.*, cobertor, *m;* —, *adj.* general.

blare [blar] *vt.* proclamar ruidosamente.

blaspheme [blas-fim] *vt. y vi.* blasfemar; jurar.

blasphemy [blas-fi-mi] *n.* blasfemia, *f.*, reniego, *m.*

blast [blast] *n.* ráfaga, *f.;* — **furnace,** horno alto; —, *vt.* marchitar, secar; arruinar; volar con pólvora.

blast-off [blast-of] *n.* despegue, *m.*

blatant [blei-tant] *adj.* vocinglero.

blaze [bleis] *n.* llama, *f.;* hoguera, *f.;* mancha blanca en la frente de los animales; señal de guía hecha en los troncos de los árboles; —, *vi.* encenderse en llama; brillar, resplandecer; —, *vt.* inflamar; flamear; llamear.

bleach [blich] *vt. y vi.* blanquear al sol; blanquear.

bleachers [blich-ers] *n. pl.* gradas al aire libre.

bleak [blík] *adj.* pálido, descolorido; frío, helado; sombrío.

blear, bleared, blear-eyed, bleary [blíar], [blíad], [blíad-aid], [blíari] *adj.* legañoso o lagañoso.

bleat [blít] *n.* balido, *m.;* —, *vi.* balar.

bled [bled] *pretérito y p.p.* del

verbo **bleed.**

bleed [blíd] *vt.* sacar sangre; (print.) sangrar.

blemish [ble-mish] *vt.* manchar, ensuciar; infamar; — , *n.* tacha, *f.;* deshonra, infamia, *f.;* lunar, *m.*

blend [blend] *vt.* mezclar, combinar; — , *vi.* armonizar; — , *n.* mezcla, *f.;* armonía, *f.*

blender [blen-dar] *n.* mezclador, *m.;* licuadora, *f.*

bless [bles] *vt.* bendecir, alabar; (coll.) santiguar.

blessed [ble-sid] *adj.* bendito; afortunado.

blessing [ble-sin] *n.* bendición, *f.*

blight [blait] *n.* tizón, *m.;* pulgón, *m.;* plaga, *f.;* daño, *m.;* — , *vi.* agostarse, perjudicarse.

blind [blaind] *adj.* ciego; oculto; oscuro; — **alley,** callejón sin salida; — **person,** ciego, ga; — , *vt.* cegar; deslumbrar; — , *n.* velo, *m.;* subterfugio, *m.;* emboscada, *f.;* **Venetian — s,** persianas, *f. pl.*

blindfold [blaind-foul] *vt.* vendar los ojos; — , *adj.* con los ojos vendados.

blindly [blaind-li] *adv.* ciegamente, a ciegas.

blindness [blain-nes] *n.* ceguera, *f.*

blink [blink] *vi.* guiñar, parpadear.

blissful [blis-ful] *adj.* feliz en sumo grado; beato, bienaventurado; — **ly,** *adv.* embelesadamente.

blister [blis-tar] *n.* vejiga, ampolla, *f.;* — , *vi.* ampollarse.

blithe [blaiz] *adj.* alegre, contento, gozoso.

blizzard [bli-sard] *n.* tormenta de nieve.

bloat [blout] *vt.* hinchar; — , *vi.* entumecerse; abotagarse.

block [blok] *n.* zoquete, *m.;* horma (de sombrero), *f.;* bloque, *m.;* cuadernal, *m.;* témpano, *m.;* obstáculo, *m.;* manzana, cuadra (de una calle), — **and tackle,** polea con aparejo; — , *vt.* bloquear.

blockade [blo-keid] *n.* bloqueo, *m.;* cerco, *m.;* **to run a — ,** romper el bloqueo; — , *vt.* bloquear.

blockhead [blok-jed] *n.* bruto, necio, zopenco, *m.*

blog [blog] sitio web fácil de usar en el cual puede expresar rápidamente sus opiniones e interactuar con otros usuarios.

blond, blonde [blond] *n. y adj.* rubio, bia, (Mex.) güero, ra.

blood [blad] *n.* sangre, *f.;* linaje, parentesco, *m.;* ira, cólera, *f.;* apetito animal; — **bank,** banco de sangre; — **clot,** embolia, *f.;* — **donor,** donante o donador de sangre; — **poisoning,** septicemia, *f.*; — **pressure,** presión arterial; — **vessel,** vena, *f.*; — **plasma,** plasma, *m.*; — **count,** cuenta de los glóbulos de la sangre; **in cold** — , en sangre fría; — **test,** análisis de la sangre; — **transfusion,** trasfusión de sangre.

bloodhound [blad-jaund] *n.* sabueso, *m.*

bloodshed [blad-shed] *n.* matanza, *f.,* derramamiento de sangre.

bloodshot [blad-shot] *adj.* ensangrentado (aplícase a los ojos).

bloody [bladi] *adj.* sangriento, ensangrentado; cruel.

bloom [blúm] *n.* flor, *f.*; florecimiento, *m.*; — , *vi.* florecer.

blossom [blo-som] *n.* flor, *f.*; capullo, botón, *m.*; — , *vi.* florecer.

blot [blot] *vt.* manchar (lo escrito); cancelar; denigrar; — , *n.* mancha, *f.*

blotch [bloch] *n.* roncha, *f.*; mancha, *f.*

blouse [blaus] *n.* blusa (de mujer), *f.*

blow [blou] *n.* golpe, *m.*; pedrada, *f.*; — , *vi.* soplar, sonar; **to** — **(one's nose),** sonarse (las narices); **to** — **up,** volar o volarse por medio de pólvora; ventear; (print.) ampliar mediante proyección; —, *vt.* soplar; inflar.

blow-dryer [blou-draier] *n.* secador de pelo, *m,* secadora de pelo, *f.*

blown [bloun] *adj.* soplado; — , *p.p.* del verbo **blow.**

blowout [blou-aut] *n.* reventazón, *f.*; ruptura de neumático o llanta.

blowpipe [blou-paip] *n.* soplete, *m.*; cerbatana, *f.*

blowtorch [blou-torch] *n.* soplete para soldar.

blubber [bla-bar] *n.* grasa de ballena; — , *vi.* llorar hasta hincharse los carrillos; gimotear.

blue [blú] *adj.* azul, cerúleo.

blueberry [blu-be-ri] *n.* baya comestible de color azul.

bluebird [blú-berd] *n.* (orn.) azulejo, *m;* pájaro azul; pájaro cantor.

bluejay *n.* variedad de pájaro azul con copete.

blueprint [blu-print] *n.* heliografía, *f.,* heliógrafo, *m.*

blues [blús] *n. pl.* (coll.) melancolía, *f.*; hipocondria, *f.*; tipo de jazz melancólico.

bluff [blaf] *n.* risco escarpado, morro, *m.*; fanfarronada, *f.*; — , *adj.* rústico, rudo, francote; — , *vt.* impedir con pretextos de valentía o de recursos; — , *vi.*

baladronear; engañar, hacer alarde.

bluish [bluish] *adj.* azulado.

blunder [blan-dar] *n.* desatino, *m.;* error craso; atolondramiento, *m.;* disparate, *m.;* — , *vt. y vi.* confundir; desatinar.

blunt [blant] *adj.* obtuso, boto; lerdo; bronco; grosero; — , *vt.* embotar; enervar; calmar (un dolor).

blur [blar] *n.* mancha, *f.;* — , *vt.* manchar; infamar.

blush [blash] *n.* rubor, *m.;* sonrojo, *m.;* — , *vi.* ruborizarse; sonrojarse.

boa [bo] *n.* boa (serpiente), *f.;* boa (cuello de pieles), *f.*

boar [bor] *n.* verraco, *m.;* **wild —** , jabalí, *m.*

board [bord] *n.* tabla, *f.;* mesa, *f.;* tribunal, consejo, *m.;* junta, *f.;* (naut.) bordo, *m.;* **— of directors,** consejo directivo, directorio, *m.,* junta directiva; **— of trustees,** junta directiva; cartulina, *f.;* **free on —** , franco a bordo; **on —** , (naut.) a bordo; — , *vt.* abordar; hospedar, alojar; subir a; — , *vi.* hospedarse; **to — up,** entablar.

boarder [bor-dar] *n.* pensionista, *m. y f.,* pupilo, *m.*

boarding school [bor-din-skúl] *n.* colegio para internos.

boardinghouse [bor-din-jaus] *n.* casa de pupilos; casa de huéspedes; posada, pensión, *f.*

boardwalk [bord-uok] *n.* paseo entablado a la orilla del mar, malecón, *m.*

boast [boust] *n.* jactancia, ostentación, *f.;* — , *vi.* presumir; jactarse, hacer alarde, hacer gala; preciarse de; — , *vt.* blasonar; **to — about,** jactarse de.

boastful [boust-ful] *adj.* jactancioso.

boat [bout] *n.* bote, *m.;* barca, chalupa, *f.;* buque, barco, *m.;* **tug —** , remolcador, *m.;* **in the same —** , en una misma situación, en un mismo caso.

bob [bob] *n.* meneo, vaivén, *m.;* melena (corte de pelo corto de las mujeres), *f.;* — , *vt. y vi.* menear o mover la cabeza, bambolear; cortar corto el cabello.

bobby pin [bo-bi-pin] *n.* pasador, *m.,* horquilla corrugada para el pelo.

bobcat [bob-kat] *n.* variedad de lince.

bobsled [bob-sled] *n.* trineo de dos rastras.

bode [boud] *vt. y vi.* presagiar, pronosticar; **to — ill,** ser de mal agüero; **to — well,** prometer bien.

bodily [bo-di-li] *adj.* corpóreo, físico; — , *adv.* en peso; conjuntamente.

body [bo-di] *n.* cuerpo, *m.;* caja o carrocería de un coche; individuo, *m.;* gremio, *m.;* consistencia, *f.;* **any—** , cualquiera; **every—** , cada uno, todos.

bodyguard [bo-di-gard] *n.* (mil.) guardaespaldas, *m.*

bog [bog] *n.* pantano, *m.;* — , *vt.* y *vi.* (a veces con down), hundir, hundirse.

bogus [bo-gus] *adj.* fingido, falso.

boil [boil] *vi.* hervir, bullir, hervirle a uno la sangre; — , *vt.* cocer.

boiler [boi-lar] *n.* caldera, *f.;* hervidor, *m.*

boiling [boi-lin] *adj.* hirviendo, hirviente; — **point,** punto de ebullición.

boisterous [bois-te-ros] *adj.* borrascoso, tempestuoso; violento; ruidoso.

bold [bould] *adj.* atrevido; valiente; audaz; temerario; imprudente; — **face,** (print.) letra negrilla; — **ly,** *adv.* descaradamente; atrevidamente.

boldness [bould-nes] *n.* intrepidez, *f.;* valentía, *f.;* osadía, *f.;* confianza, *f.*

bolero [bo-le-rou] *n.* bolero (baile andaluz), *m.;* bolero, *m.,* chaqueta corta.

boll [bol] *n.* cápsula (de lino o cáñamo), *f.;* — **weevil,** picudo, *m.,* gorgojo del algodón.

bolster [bouls-tar] *n.* travesero, *m.;* cabezal, cojín, *m.;* cabecera, *f.;* — , *vt.* apoyar, auxiliar;— **up,** sostener, apoyar; alentar.

bolt [boult] *n.* dardo, *m.;* flecha, *f ;* cerrojo, *m.;* chaveta, *f.;* tornillo, *m.;* **door —** , pasador, *m.;* — , *vt.* cerrar con cerrojo; — , *vi.* desbocarse (un caballo).

bomb [bom] *n.* (mil.) bomba, *f.;* **atomic —** , bomba atómica; **hydrogen —** , bomba de hidrógeno.

bombard [bom-bard] *vt.* bombardear.

bombardment [bom-bard-ment] *n.* bombardeo, *m.*

bomber [bom-bar] *n.* bombardero, *m.,* avión de bombardeo.

bombproof [bomb-prúf] *adj.* a prueba de bombas.

bombshell [bomb-shel] *n.* bomba, granada, *f.*

bona fide [bouna-faidi] *adj.* de buena fe.

bonbon [bon-bon] *n.* confite, bombón, *m.*

bond [bond] *n.* ligadura, *f.;* vínculo, lazo, *m.;* vale, *m.;* obligación, *f.;* (com.) bono, *m.;* **in —** , bajo fianza; — , *vt.* poner en depósito.

bondage [bon-dich] *n.* esclavitud, servidumbre, *f.*

bone [boun] *n.* hueso, *m.;* — , *vt.* desosar.

boneless [boun-les] *adj.* sin huesos, desosado.

bonfire [bon-faiar] *n.* hoguera, fogata, *f.*

bonnet [bo-nit] *n.* gorra, *f.;* bonete, *m.;* sombrero, *m.*

bonus [bo-nos] *n.* prima, *f.;* bonificación, gratificación, *f.*

bony [bou-ni] *adj.* huesudo.

boob, booby [búb], [bú-bi] *n.* zote, *m.,* persona boba; **booby trap,** (mil.) granada o mina disimulada que estalla al moverse el objeto que la oculta.

book [buk] *n.* libro, *m.;* — , *vt.* asentar en un libro; inscribir; contratar (a un artista, etc.); fichar (al acusado).

bookcase [buk-keis] *n.* armario para libros, estante, *m.;* (Mex.) librero, *m.*

bookie [bu-ki] *n.* (coll.) persona cuyo negocio es apostar a las carreras de caballos.

booking [bu-kin] *n.* registro, *m.;* — **office,** oficina de reservaciones (de pasajes).

bookkeeper [buk-kí-par] *n.* tenedor de libros.

bookkeeping [buk-kí-pin] *n.* teneduría de libros, contabilidad, *f.*

booklet *n.* folleto, *m.*

bookmark [buk-mei-kar] *n.* marcador de libro.

bookseller [buk-se-lar] *n.* librero, *m.,* vendedor de libros.

bookstand [buk-stand] *n.* puesto de libros.

bookstore [buk-stor] *n.* librería, *f.*

bookworm [buk-uerm] *n.* polilla que roe los libros; (fig.) ratón de biblioteca.

boom [bum] *n.* (naut.) botalón, *m.;* bonanza, *f.,*repentina prosperidad; rugido seco, estampido, *m.;* — , *vi.* zumbar.

boomerang [bu-me-ran] *n.* bumerang, *m.*

boon [bun] *n.* presente, regalo, *m.;* favor, *m.,* gracia, *f.;* — , *adj.* alegre, festivo; generoso.

boost [bust] *vt.* levantar o empujar hacia arriba; asistir; — , *vi.* aprobar con entusiasmo; — , *n.* ayuda, *f.,* aumento, *m.*

boot [but] *n.* bota, *f.;* **riding** — , bota de montar; **to** — , además, por añadidura.

booth [buz] *n.* barraca, cabaña, *f.;* puesto, *m.;* reservado (en una heladería, etc.), *m.;* casilla, *f.;* caseta, *f.*

bootleg [but-leg] *vt.* y *vi.* contrabandear (usualmente en licores).

bootlegger [but-legar] *n.* contrabandista (usualmente de licores), *m.*

booty [bu-ti] *n.* botín, *m.; presa, f.;* saqueo, despojo, *m.*

booze [bus] *vi.* (coll.) emborracharse; — , *n.* (coll.) bebida alcohólica.

border [bor-dar] *n.* orilla, *f.;* borde, *m.;* vera, *f.,* margen, *m.;* frontera, *f.;* — , *vi.* confinar; bordear; — , *vt.* limitar; **to — on,** rayar en.

bordering [bor-de-rin] *adj.* contiguo, colindante; — **on,** rayando en.

borderland [bor-der-land] *n.* frontera, *f.,* confín, *m.*

borderline [bor-der-lain] *n.* límite, *m.,* orilla, *f.;* — , *adj.* incierto; — **case,** caso en los límites de lo anormal.

bore [bor] *vt.* taladrar, horadar, perforar, barrenar; fastidiar; — , *pretérito* del verbo **bear;** — , *n.* taladro, *m.;* calibre, *m.;* perforación, *f.;* latoso, sa, majadero, ra.

boredom [bor-dom] *n.* tedio, fastidio, *m.*

boric [bo-rik] *adj.* bórico; — **acid,** ácido bórico.

boring [bo-rin] *adj.* fastidioso, aburridor, aburrido.

born [born] *adj.* nacido; destinado; **to be —,** nacer.

borne [born] *p.p.* del verbo **bear.**

borrow [bo-rou] *vt.* pedir presta-do.

borrower [bo-rouar] *n.* prestatario, ia.

boss [bos] *n.* clavo *m.;* protuberancia, *f.;* (coll.) cacique, jefe, *m.*

botanical [bo-ta-nikl] *adj.* botánico.

botany [bo-ta-ni] *n.* botánica, *f.*

botch [boch] *n.* remiendo chapucero; roncha, *f.;* — , *vt.* remendar, chapucear.

both [bouz] *pron. y adj.* ambos, ambas, los dos, las dos; — , *conj.* tanto como.

bother [bo-zar] *vt.* aturrullar; confundir, molestar; incomodar; — , *n.* estorbo, *m.;* mortificación, *f.*

bottle [botel] *n.* botella, *f.;* — , *vt.* embotellar; — **up,** embotellar; (fig.) ahogar, reprimir.

bottleneck [botel-nek] *n.* cuello de botella; (fig.) obstáculo, impedimento, *m.;* cuello de estrangulación.

bottom [bo-tom] *n.* fondo, *m.;* fundamento, *m.;* valle, *m.;* buque, *m.;* **false — ,** fondo doble; **at — ,** en el fondo, realmente; — , *adj.* fundamental; mínimo.

bottomless [bo-tom-les] *adj.* insondable; sin fondo.

bough [bo] *n.* rama (de un árbol), *f.*

bought [bot] *pretérito y p.p.* del verbo **buy.**

boulder [boul-dar] *n.* canto rodado; china, peña, *f.;* guijarro, *m.;* peña desprendida de una masa de roca.

boulevard [bu-le-var] *n.* avenida, *f.,* paseo, bulevar, *m.*

bounce [bauns] *vi.* arremeter, brincar; saltar; — , *n.* golpazo brinco, *m.;* bravata, *f.*

bouncing [baun-sin] *adj.* fuerte, bien formado, robusto.

bound [baund] *n.* límite, *m.;* salto, *m.;* repercusión, *f.;* **within** — **s,** a raya; — , *vt.* confinar, limitar; destinar; obligar; reprimir; — , *vi.* resaltar, brincar; — , *pretérito y p.p.* del verbo **bind;** — , *adj.* destinado; — **for,** con rumbo a, con destino a.

boundary [baun-de-ri] *n.* límite, *m.;* frontera, *f.;* meta, línea, *f.;* aledaño, *m.*

boundless [baund-les] *adj.* ilimitado, infinito.

bounteous, bountiful [baun-tios], [baun-ti-ful] *adj.* liberal, generoso, bienhechor.

bounty [baun-ti] *n.* liberalidad, bondad, *f.*

bouquet [bu-kei] *n.* ramillete de flores, ramo, *m.;* aroma, olor, *m.*

bourgeois [bur-yua] *adj.* bur-gués.

bout [baut] *n.* turno, *m.;* encuentro, combate, *m.*

bow [bau] *vt.* encorvar, doblar, oprimir; — , *vi.* encorvarse; saludar; hacer reverencia; — , *n.* reverencia, inclinación, *f.;* (naut.) proa, *f.*

bow [bau] *n.* arco, *m.;* lazo (de cinta, etc.), *m.*

bowels [bauals] *n. pl.* intestinos, *m. pl.;* entrañas, *f. pl.*

bower [bauar] *n.* enramada de jardín; bóveda, *f.;* aposento retirado.

bowl [boul] *n.* taza, *f.;* **wash** — , jofaina, *f.,* lavamanos, *m.;* — , *vi.* jugar boliche o bolos, jugar a las bochas.

bowlegged [bou-legd] *adj.* patizambo, patiestevado.

bowling [bou-lin] *n.* juego de bolos, juego de boliche; — **alley,** bolera, *f.,* mesa de boliche; — **pin,** bolo, *m.*

box [boks] *n.* caja, cajita, *f.;* cofre, *m.;* **axle** — , buje, *m.;* — **office,** taquilla, *f.;* — **on the ear,** bofetada, *f.;* — **seat,** asiento en palco; — , *vt.* meter alguna cosa en una caja; apuñetear; — , *vi.* combatir a puñadas, boxear.

boxer [bok-sar] *n.* boxeador, *m.*

boxing [bok-sin] *n.* boxeo, *m.*

boy [boi] *n.* muchacho, *m.;* niño,

m.; criado, lacayo, *m.;* zagal, *m.;* — **friend,** amigo predilecto, novio potencial; — **scout,** muchacho explorador.

boycott [boi-kot] *vt.* boicotear; —, *n.* boicoteo, boicot, *m.*

boyhood [boi-jud] *n.* niñez, *f.*

boyish [boi-ish] *adj.* pueril, propio de un niño varón; frívolo.

bra [bra] *n.* brassiere, sostén, corpiño, soporte (para senos), *m.*

brace [breis] *n.* abrazadera, *f.;* manija, *f.;* —, *vt.* apoyar, reforzar.

bracelet [breis-let] *n.* brazalete, *m.,* pulsera, *f.*

bracing [brei-sin] *n.* refuerzo, *m.;* —, *adj.* fortificante, tónico.

bracket [bra-ket] *n.* puntal, *m.;* rinconera, *f.;* consola, *f.;* —s, *pl.* (print.) corchetes, *m. pl.*

brag [brag] *n.* jactancia, *f.;* —, *vi.* jactarse, fanfarronear.

braid [breid] *n.* trenza, *f.;* pasamano, *m.,* trencilla, *f.;* —, *vt.* trenzar.

braille [breil] *n.* escritura en relieve para uso de los ciegos.

brain [brein] *n.* cerebro, *m.;* seso, juicio, *m.*

brainless [brein-les] *adj.* insensato, estúpido.

brainwashing [brein-uoshin] *n.* lavado cerebral.

brake [breik] *n.* freno, *m.;* **to apply the** —s, frenar; **to release the** —s, quitar el freno.

bramble [bram-bol] *n.* zarza, espina, *f.*

bran [bran] *n.* salvado, afrecho, *m.*

branch [branch] *n.* rama (de árbol), *f.;* brazo, *m.;* ramal, *m.;* sucursal, *f.;* ramo (de la ciencia, el arte, etc.), *m.;* —, *vt.* y *vi.* ramificar, ramificarse; — **out,** ramificarse.

brand [brand] *n.* tizón, *m.;* hierro, *m.;* marca, *f.;* nota de infamia; marca de fábrica.

brandish [bran-dish] *vt.* blandir, ondear.

brand-new [brand-niu] *adj.* flamante, enteramente nuevo.

brandy [bran-di] *n.* aguardiente, *m.;* coñac, *m.*

brass [bras] *n.* bronce, *m.;* desvergüenza, *f.;* — **band,** charanga, *f.*

brassiere [brasiar] *n.* brassiere, soporte (para senos), *m.;* corpiño, sostén, *m.*

brat [brat] *n.* rapaz, chiquillo, *m.* (se usa en forma despectiva).

brave [breiv] *adj.* bravo, valiente, atrevido; —, *vt.* combatir, desafiar.

bravery [breiv-li] *n.* valor, *m.;* braveza, *f.*

brawl [brol] *n.* quimera, disputa, camorra, pelotera, *f.;* —, *vi.*

alborotar; vocinglear.

bray [brei] *vi.* rebuznar; —, *n.* rebuzno (del asno), *m.*; ruido bronco.

brazen [breisn] *adj.* de bronce; caradura, desvergonzado; imprudente; —, *vi.* encararse con desfachatez.

Brazil [bra-sil] Brasil, *m.*

Brazilian [bra-si-lian] *n.* y *adj.* brasileño, ña.

breach [brích] *n.* rotura, *f.*; brecha, *f.*; violación, *f.*; **— of trust, — of faith,** abuso de confianza; **— of promise,** falta de palabra.

bread [bred] *n.* pan, *m.*; (fig.) sustento, *m.*; **— line,** fila de los que esperan la gratuita distribución de pan; **brown —, whole-wheat —,** pan moreno, pan negro o de centeno.

breadth [bredz] *n.* anchura, *f.*

break [breik] *vt.* y *vi.* quebrar; vencer; quebrantar; violar; domar; arruinar; partir; interrumpir, romperse; reventarse algún tumor; separarse; (com.) quebrar; **to — out,** abrirse salida; estallar; **to — to pieces,** hacer pedazos; —, *n.* rotura, *f.*; rompimiento, *m.*; ruptura, *f.*; interrupción, *f.*; **— of day,** aurora, *f.*

breakable [breik-abol] *adj.* frágil, rompible.

breakdown [breik-daun] *n.* des-

calabro, *m.*; avería repentina; decadencia, *f.*, decaimiento (de salud, de ánimo), *m.*; desarreglo, *m.*; interrupción, *f.*; postración, *f.*

breakfast [brek-fast] *n.* desayuno, *m.*; —, *vi.* desayunarse.

breaking [breikin] *n.* rompimiento, *m.*; fractura, *f.*

breakwater [breik-uotar] *n.* muelle, *m.*; dique, *m.*; escollera, *f.*

breast [brest] *n.* pecho, seno, *m.*; corazón, *m.*; **—stroke** (natación), braza, *f.*; —, *vt.* acometer; resistir; arrostrar valerosamente.

breath [brez] *n.* aliento, *m.*, respiración, *f.*; soplo de aire; momento, *m.*; **out of —,** jadeante, sin aliento.

breathe [bríz] *vt.* y *vi.* respirar; exhalar.

breathing [brí-zin] *n.* aspiración, *f.*; respiración, *f.*

breathless [brezles] *adj.* falto de aliento; desalentado.

breath-taking [brez-tei-kin] *adj.* conmovedor, excitante.

bred [bred] *pretérito* y *p.p.* del verbo **breed; ill—,** malcriado; **well—,** bien educado.

breech [brích] *n.* trasero, *m.*

breeches [brí-ches] *n. pl.* calzones, *m. pl.*

breed [brid] *n.* casta, raza, *f.*; —, *vt.* procrear, engendrar; criar;

educar; —, *vi.* parir; multiplicarse.

breeding [brídin] *n.* crianza, *f.;*
buena educación; modales, *m.*
pl.

breeze [brís] *n.* brisa, *f.,* céfiro,
m.

breezy [brí-si] *adj.* refrescado
con brisas.

brevity [bre-vi-ti] *n.* brevedad,
concisión, *f.*

brew [brú] *vt.* tramar, maquinar,
mezclar; —, *vi.* **hacer cerveza;**
—, *n.* calderada de cerveza.

brewery [brúeri] *n.* cervecería, *f.*

bribe [braib] *n.* cohecho, soborno, *m.;* —, *vt.* cohechar,
corromper, sobornar.

bribery [brai-be-ri] *n.* soborno,
m.

brick [brik] *n.* ladrillo, *m.*

bricklayer [brik-leiar] *n.* albañil,
m.

bridal [braidal] *adj.* nupcial.

bride [braid] *n.* novia, desposa-
da, *f.*

bridegroom [braid-grum] *n.*
novio, desposado, *m.*

bridesmaid [braids-meid] *n.*
dama, *f.,* madrina de boda.

bridge [brich] *n.* puente, *m.;*
suspension —, puente colgante; —, *vt.* construir un puente;
salvar un obstáculo.

bridle [brai-dol] *n.* brida, *f.,*
freno, *m.;* —, *vt.* embridar;

reprimir, refrenar.

brief [bríf] *adj.* breve, conciso,
sucinto; —, *n.* compendio, *m.;*
breve, *m.;* (leyes) escrito, *m.;* —
case, cartera, *f.;* portadocu-
mentos, portapapeles, *m.;* **in —**
, en pocas palabras, en breve;
—, *vt.* hacer un resumen.

briefing [brífin] *n.* instrucciones
(a aviadores militares, etc.), *f.*
pl.

bright [brait] *adj.* claro, luciente,
brillante; luminoso; vivo.

brighten [brai-ten] *vt.* pulir, dar
lustre; ilustrar; —, *vi.* aclarar.

brightness [braitnis] *n.* esplendor, *m.,* brillantez, *f.;* agudeza,
f.; claridad, *f.;* lucimiento, *m.*

brilliance, brilliancy [bri-lians],
[bri-liansi] *n.* brillantez, *f.,* resplandor, brillo, esplendor, fulgor, *m.*

brilliant [bri-liant] *adj.* brillante;
luminoso; resplandeciente; —,
n. brillante (diamante abrillan-
tado), *m.*

brim [brim] *n.* borde, extremo,
m.; orilla, *f.;* ala (de sombrero),
f.; —, *vt.* llenar hasta el borde;
—, *vi.* estar lleno.

brimstone [brim-stoun] *n.* azufre, *m.*

brine [brain] *n.* salmuera, *f.*

bring [brin] *vt.* llevar, traer; conducir; inducir; persuadir; **to —**
about, efectuar; **to —forth,** pro-

ducir; parir; **to — up,** educar;
to — to pass, efectuar, realizar.
brink [brink] *n.* orilla, *f.;* margen, *m.* y *f.,* borde, *m.*
brisk [brisk] *adj.* vivo, alegre,
jovial; fresco.
British Columbia [bri-tish-ko-
lum-bia] Colombia Británica.
brittle [bri-tol] *adj.* quebradizo,
frágil.
broach [brouch] *vt.* iniciar, entablar.
broad [broud] *adj.* ancho; abierto; extenso.
broadcast [broud-kast] *n.* radiodifusión, *f.;* —, *vt.* radiodifundir.
broadcasting [broud-kastin] *n.*
radiodifusión, *f.;* audición, *f.;*
perifonía, *f.;* **— station,** emisora, radiodifusora, *f.;* —, *adj.*
radioemisor.
broaden [brouden] *vt.* y *vi.*
ensanchar, ensancharse.
broad-minded [broud-maindid]
adj. tolerante, de ideas liberales.
broccoli [bro-ko-li] *n.* (bot.) bróculi, brécol, *m.*
brochure [brou-shiuar] *n.* folleto,
m.
broil [broil] *vt.* asar a la parrilla.
broiler [broilar] *n.* parrilla, *f.*
broke [brouk] *pretérito* del
verbo **break.**
broken [brouken] *adj.* roto, que-

brado; interrumpido; —
English, inglés mal articulado;
—, *p.p.* del verbo **break.**
broken-down [brouken-daun]
adj. afligido, abatido; descompuesto.
broken-hearted [brouken-jartid]
adj. triste, abatido, acongojado,
con el corazón hecho trizas.
bromide [bro-maid] *n.* bromuro,
m.
bronchial [bron-kial] *adj.* bron-
quial; **— tube,** bronquio, *m.*
bronchitis [bron-kai-tis] *n.* bronquitis, *f.*
bronze [bronz] *n.* bronce, *m.;* —,
vt. broncear.
brooch [brouch] *n.* broche, *m.*
brood [brúd] *vi.* cobijar; pensar
alguna cosa con cuidado,
madurar; —, *n.* raza, *f.;* nidada, *f.*
brook [bruk] *n.* arroyo, *m.;* (Sp.
Am.) quebrada, *f.;* —, *vt.* sufrir,
tolerar.
broom [brum] *n.* escoba, *f.*
broomstick [brum-stik] *n.* palo
de escoba.
broth [broz] *n.* caldo, *m.*
brother [bro-dar] *n.* hermano, *m.*
brotherhood [broder-jud] *n.* hermandad, fraternidad, *f.*
brother-in-law [bro-dar-in-loa] *n.*
cuñado, *m.,* hermano político.
brotherly [bro-der-li] *adj.* fraternal.

brought [brot] *pretérito* y *p.p.* del verbo bring.

brow [brau] *n.* ceja, *f.;* frente, *f.;* cima, *f.*

brown [braun] *adj.* bruno, moreno; castaño; pardo; **—paper,** papel de estraza, *m.;* **— sugar,** azúcar morena; —, *vt.* dorar, tostar.

brownies [braunis] *n. pl.* duendes de los cuentos de hadas; pastelitos de chocolate y nueces.

browse [braus] *vt.* y *vi.* ramonear, pacer; **to —over a book,** hojear, leer un libro.

bruise [brus] *vt.* magullar, machacar, abollar, majar; pulverizar; —, *n.* magulladura, contusión, *f.*

brunette [bru-net] *n.* y *adj.* morena, trigueña, *f.*

brunt [brant] *n.* choque, *m.;* esfuerzo, *m.*

brush [brash] *n.* bruza, *f.;* brocha, *f.;* cepillo, *m.;* encuentro, *m.,* escaramuza, *f.;* **artist's —,** pincel, *m.;* —, *vt.* cepillar; **to — off,** despedir con brusquedad; —, *vi.* mover apresuradamente; pasar ligeramente.

brushwood [brash-vud] *n.* breñal, zarzal, *m.*

brusque [brask] *adj.* brusco, rudo, descortés.

Brussels sprouts [bra-sels-sprauts] *n. pl.* (bot.) colecitas de Bruselas.

brutal [bru-tal] *adj.* brutal, bruto.

brute [brut] *n.* bruto, *m.;* —, *adj.* feroz, bestial; irracional.

bubble [babel] *n.* burbuja, *f.;* bagatela, *f.;* —, *vi.* burbujear, bullir; **— over,** estar en efervescencia; borbotar; hervir.

buck [bak] *n.* gamo, *m.;* macho (de algunos animales), *m.*

bucket [ba-ket] *n.* cubo, pozal, *m.;* cangilón, *m.;* cucharón, *m.*

buckle [bakel] *n.* hebilla, *f.;* —, *vt.* abrochar con hebilla; afianzar; **— down to,** dedicarse (a algo) con empeño; —, *vi.* encorvarse.

buckwheat [bak-uit] *n.* trigo sarraceno.

bud [bad] *n.* botón, *m.;* capullo, *m.;* —, *vi.* florecer, brotar; —, *vt.* injertar.

buddy [bad] *n.* hermano, camarada, compañero, *m.*

budge [badch] *vi.* moverse, menearse.

budget [bachet] *n.* presupuesto, *m.*

buff [baf] *n.* pulidor, *m.;* aficionado, da; color amarillo rojizo; —, *adj.* de color amarillo rojizo; —, *vt.* lustrar, dar lustre; pulir.

buffalo [ba-fa-lou] *n.* búfalo, *m.*

buffoon [ba-fun] *n.* bufón, gracioso, *m.*

bug [bag] *n.* chinche, *f.;* insecto,
bicho, *m.*

buggy [ba-gui] *n.* calesa, *f.;* **baby
—**, cochecito de niño; **—**, *adj.*
chinchoso; con bichos.

bugle [baguel] *n.* clarín, *m.;* corneta, *f.*

bugler [biu-glar] *n.* corneta,
trompetero, *m.*

build [bild] *vt.* edificar; construir.

builder [bil-dar] *n.* arquitecto,
m.; constructor, *m.*

building [bild-in] *n.* edificio, *m.;*
construcción, *f.*

bulb [balb] *n.* bulbo, *m.;* cebolla,
f.; **electric light —**, foco de luz
eléctrica.

bulk [balk] *n.* masa, *f.;* volumen,
m.; grosura, *f.;* mayor parte;
capacidad de un buque.

bulky [balki] *adj.* macizo, grueso, grande.

bull [bul] *n.* toro, *m.;* disparate,
m.; bula *f.,* breve pontificio;
dicho absurdo; **— ring**, plaza
de toros; **—'s eye**, centro de
blanco; (naut.) claraboya, *f.*

bulldozer [bul-dou-sar] *n.* nive-
ladora, *f.,* abrebrechas, *m.*

bullet [bulit] *n.* bala, *f.*

bulletin [bu-li-tin] *n.* boletín, *m.;*
— board, tablero para avisos.

bulletproof [bu-let-pruf] *adj.* a
prueba de bala.

bullfight [bulfait] *n.* corrida de
toros.

bullfighter [bul-fai-tar] *n.* torero,
m.

bullfrog [bul-frog] *n.* rana grande.

bully [buli] *n.* espadachín, *m.;*
valentón, *m.;* rufián, *m.;* (coll.)
gallito, *m.;* **—**, *vi.* fanfarronear.

bulwark [bul-uork] *n.* baluarte,
m.; **—**, *vt.* fortificar con baluar-
tes.

bum [bum] *n.* holgazán, bribón,
m.

bumblebee [bam-bol-bi] *n.* abejón, abejorro, zángano, *m.*

bump [bamp] *n.* hinchazón, *f.;*
giba, *f.;* golpe, *m.;* **—**, *vt.* y *vi.*
chocar contra.

bumper [bam-par] *n.* parachoques o paragolpes de un auto,
defensa, *f;* **—**, *adj.* (coll.) excelente; abundante; **— crop**,
cosecha abundante.

bun [ban] *n.* bollo (de pan, etc.),
m.

bunch [banch] *n.* montón, *m.;*
manojo, *m.;* ramo, racimo, *m.;*
—, *vt.* y *vi.* agrupar, amontonar; poner en racimo.

bungalow [ban-ga-lou] *n.* casa
de un piso.

bungle [bangl] *vt.* y *vi.* chapucear, chafallar; hacer algo cha-
bacanamente; **—**, *n.* chabaca-

nería, *f.*

bunk [bank] *n.* camarote, *m.;* — **beds,** literas, *f. pl.*

bunker [ban-kar] *n.* (golf) trampa, *f.*

buoy [buoi] *n.* (naut.) boya, *f.;* —, *vt.* boyar; —**up,** apoyar, sostener.

buoyant [boiant] *adj.* boyante.

burden [ber-den] *n.* carga, *f.,* cargo, *m.;* —, *vt.* cargar; gravar.

bureau [biua-rou] *n.* armario,. *m.;* tocador, *m.,* cómoda, *f.;* escritorio, *m.;* oficina, *f.;* departamento, *m.,* división, *f.*

bureaucracy [biua-rou-kra-si] *n.* burocracia, *f.*

burglar [ber-glar] *n.* salteador, ladrón, *m.;* — **alarm,** alarma contra ladrones.

burglary [ber-gla-ri] *n.* asalto, robo, *m.*

burial [berial] *n.* entierro, enterramiento, *m.*

burlesque [ber-lesk] *adj.* burlesco; —, *n.*función teatral de género festivo y picaresco; —, *vt. y vi.* burlarse; parodiar.

burly [ber-li] *adj.* voluminoso; vigoroso; turbulento.

burn [bern] *vt.* quemar, abrasar o herir, incendiar; —, *vi.* arder; —, *n.* quemadura, *f.*

burnish [ber-nish] *vt.* bruñir, dar lustre.

burst [berst] *vi.* reventar; abrirse; **to** — **out laughing,** soltar una carcajada; —, *n.* reventón, *m.;* rebosadura, *f.*

bury [be-ri] *vt.* enterrar, sepultar; esconder.

bus [bas] *n.* autobús, ómnibus, camión, *m.*

bush [bash] *n.* arbusto, *m.;* cola de zorra; **to beat around the** —, acercarse indirectamente a una cosa, andar con rodeos.

bushy [bashi] *adj.* espeso, lleno de arbustos; lanudo.

busily [bi-si-li] *adv.* solícitamente, diligentemente.

business [bis-nes] *n.* empleo, *m.,* ocupación, *f.;* negocio, *m.;* quehacer, *m.;* — **house,** casa de comercio; — **man,** hombre de negocios; — **transaction.** negociación, operación, *f.;* **to do** — **with,** tratar con.

businessman [bis-nes-man] *n.* comerciante, *m.*

bust [bast] *n.* busto, *m.*

bustle [ba-sel] *n.* confusión, *f.,* ruido, *m.;* polisón, *m.;* —, *vi.* apurarse con estrépito; menearse.

busy [bi-si] *adj.* ocupado; atareado; entremetido; —, *vt.* ocupar.

busybody [bi-si-bo-di] *n.* entremetido, da; (coll.) camasquince, *m. y f.*

but [bat] *prep.* excepto; —, *conj. y adv.* menos; pero; solamente.

butcher [bu-char] *n.* carnicero, *m.;* —'s **shop,** carnicería, *f.;* —, *vt.* matar atrozmente.

butler [batlar] *n.* mayordomo, *m.*

butt [bat] *n.* culata, *f.;* blanco, hito, *m.;* bota, *f.,* cuba para guardar vino, etc.; persona a quien se ridiculiza; cabezada (golpe de la cabeza), *f.;* —, *vt.* topar.

butter [ba-tar] *n.* mantequilla, manteca, *f.*

buttercup [bater-kap] *n.* (bot.) ranúnculo, *m.*

butterfly [ba-tar-flai] *n.* mariposa, *f.*

buttermilk [ba-tar-milk] *n.* suero de mantequilla; (Mex.) jocoqui, *m.*

buttock [ba-tok] *n.* nalga, *f.;* anca, grupa, *f.*

button [baton] *n.* botón, *m.;* **call** —, botón de llamada; **push** —, botón de contacto; —, *vt.* abotonar.

buttress [ba-tres] *n.* contrafuerte, *m.;* sostén, apoyo, *m.;* —, *vt.* suministrar un sostén; afianzar.

buy [bai] *vt.* comprar; **to — at retail,** comprar al por menor; **to — at wholesale,** comprar al por mayor; **to — for cash,** comprar al contado; **to — on credit,** comprar al crédito o fiado.

buyer [baiar] *n.* comprador, *m.,* compradora, *f.*

buzz [bas] *n.* susurro, soplo, *m.;* —, *vi.* zumbar; cuchichear.

by [bai] *prep.* por; a, en; de; con; al lado de, cerca de; —, *adv.* cerca; a un lado; **— all means,** de todos modos, cueste lo que cueste; **— and —,** dentro de poco, luego; **— much,** con mucho;**— the way,** de paso, a propósito.

bygone [bai-goun] *adj.* pasado; —, *n.* lo pasado.

bylaws [bai-lo] *n. pl.* estatutos, *m. pl.,* reglamento, *m.*

by-pass [bai-pas] *n.* desvío, *m.;* —, *vt.* desviar.

by-product [bai-pro-dukt] *n.* derivado, subproducto, *m.*

bystander [bai-stan-dar] *n.* circunstante, *m.* y *f.,* espectador, ra.

Byzantine [bai-sen-tain] *n.* y *adj.* bizantino, na.

C

cab [kab] *n.* coche de alquiler, taxi, *m.*

cabana [ka-ba-na] *n.* cabaña, caseta, *f.*

cabaret [ka-ba-rei] *n.* cabaret, *m.*

cabbage [ka-beich] *n.* repollo, *m.*; berza, col. *f.*

cabin [ka-bin] *n.* cabaña, cabina, barraca, *f ;* choza, *f.;* camarote, *m.;* — **steward,** mayordomo, *m.*

cabinet [ka-bi-net] *n.* gabinete, *m.;* escritorio, *m.;* ministerio, *m.;* — **council,** consejo de ministros.

cable [kei-bol] *n.* cable, — **car,** ferrocarril funicular; vehículo manejado por un cable; —, *adj.* cablegráfico; — **television,** televisión por cable, cablevisión, *f.*

cabman [kab-man] *n.* chofer de taxi.

cackle [kakol] *vi.* cacarear, graznar; —, *n.* cacareo, *m.;* charla, *f.*

cactus [kak-tus] *n.* (bot.) cacto, *m.*

cadaver [ka-dei-var] *n.* cadáver, cuerpo, *m.*

cadence [keidans] *n.* (mus.) cadencia, *f.*

cadet [ka-det] *n.* cadete, *m.*

Caesarean [si-sa-rian] *adj.* cesáreo; — **section,** operación cesárea.

café [ka-fei] *n.* café, restaurante, *m.,* cantina, *f.*

cafeteria [ka-fi-tia-ria] *n.* cafetería, *f.,* restaurante en donde se sirve uno mismo.

cage [keidch] *n.* jaula, *f ;* alambrera, *f.;* prisión, *f.;* —, *vt.* enjaular.

cake [keik] *n.* torta, *f.;* bizcocho, pastel, *m.;*—, *vi.* endurecerse, coagularse.

calamity [ka-la-mi-ti] *n.* calamidad, miseria, *f.*

calcium [kal-siom] *n.* calcio, *m.*

calculate [kal-kiu-leit] *vt.* calcular, contar.

calculating [kal-kiu-lei-tin] *adj.* calculador; de calcular; — **machine,** máquina de calcular.

calculation [kal-kiu-lei-shon] *n.* calculación, cuenta, *f.;* cálculo, *m.*

calculator [kal-kiu-lei-tor] *n.* calculadora, *f.*

calculus [kal-kiu-los] *n.* cálculo, *m.*

calendar [ka-len-dar] *n.* calendario, almanaque, *m.*

calf [kalf] *n.* ternero, ra; cuero de ternero; (anat.) pantorrilla, *f.*

caliber [ka-li-ber] *n.* calibre, *m.*

calibration [ka-li-brei-shon] *n.* calibración, *f.*

calico [ka-li-kou] *n.* percal, *m.,* zaraza, *f.*

calipers [ka-li-pars] *n. pl.* compás de calibres; compás de espesores.

call [kol] *vt.* llamar, nombrar; convocar, citar; apelar; denominar; **to — for,** ir por (algo o alguien) ; **to — names,** injuriar; **to — the roll,** pasar lista; **to — to order,** llamar al orden, abrir la sesión; **to — on,** visitar; —, *n.* llamada, *f.;* instancia, *f ;* invitación, *f ;* urgencia, *f.;* vocación, profesión, *f.;* empleo, *m.;* grito, *m.;* (naut.) pito, *m.;* (mil.) toque, *m.;* **to have a close —,** salvarse en una tablita.

calla lily [ka-la-li-li] *n.* lirio, *m.;* (Mex.) alcatraz, *f*

calling [ko-lin] *n.* profesión, vocación, *f.*

callous [ka-los] *adj.* calloso, endurecido; insensible.

calm [kalm] *n.* calma, tranquilidad, *f.;* —, *adj.* quieto, tranquilo; —, *vt.* calmar, aplacar, aquietar; **to — down,** serenarse.

calorie [ka-lo-ri] *n.* caloría, *f.*

calves [kalvs] *n. pl.* de **calf.**

calyx [ka-liks] *n.* (bot.) cáliz, *m.*

came [keim] *pretérito* del verbo **come.**

camel [ka-mel] *n.* camello, *m.*

camera [ka-me-ra] *n.* cámara, *f.;* **— man,** camarógrara, *f.;* **digital—,** cámara digital;

camouflage [ka-mu-flash] *n.* (mil.) camuflaje, *m.,* simulación, *f.,* fingimiento, engaño, *m.;* disfraz, *m.*

camp [kamp] *n.* (mil.) campo, *m.;* **army —,** campamento del ejército; **to break —,** levantar el campo; **—** *adj.* campal; —, *vi.* acampar.

campaign [kam-pein] *n.* campaña, *f.;* —, *vi.* hacer campaña; hacerle propaganda (a algún candidato) .

campfire [kamp-faia] *n.* hoguera en el campo.

camphor [kam-for] *n.* alcanfor, *m.*

campus [kam-pus] *n.* patio o terrenos de una universidad, un colegio, un instituto, etc.

can [kan] *vi.* poder, saber; —, *vt.* envasar en latas; —, *n.* lata, *f.,* bote, *m.;* **—opener,** abrelatas, *m.,* abridor de latas.

Canada [ka-na-da] Canadá, *m.*

Canadian [ka-nei-dian] *n.* y *adj.* canadiense, *m.* y *f.*

canal [ka-nal] *n.* canal, *m.*

Canaries, Canary Islands [ka-na-ris], [ka-na-ri-ai-lands] Las Canarias, Islas Canarias.

canary [ka-na-ri] *n.* canario, *m.*

canasta [ka-nas-ta] *n.* canasta (juego de naipes), *f.*

cancel [kan-sel] *vt.* cancelar, borrar; anular, invalidar;

barrear.

cancellation [kan-se-lei-shon] *n.* cancelación, *f.*

cancer [kan-sar] *n.* (med.) cáncer, *m.*

cancerous [kan-se-rous] *adj.* canceroso.

candid [kan-ded] *adj.* cándido, sencillo, ingenuo, sincero.

candidate [kan-di-deit] *n.* candidato, ta, aspirante (a un puesto, cargo, etc.), *m. y f.*

candied [kan-did] *adj.* garapiñado, en almíbar.

candle [kan-dol] *n.* candela, vela, bujía, *f.*

candlestick [kan-del-stik] *n.* candelero, *m.*

candor [kan-dor] *n.* candor, *m.;* sinceridad, ingenuidad, *f.*

candy [kan-di] *vt.* confitar; garapiñar; —, *n.* bombón, dulce, *m.*

cane [kein] *n.* caña, *f.;* bastón, *m.;* — **plantation,** cañal, cañaveral, *m.*

canine [ka-nain] *adj.* canino, perruno,

canker [kan-kar] *n.* llaga ulcerosa; —, *vt.* roer, corromper; —, *vi.* corromperse, roerse.

cannibal [ka-ni-bal] *n.* caníbal, *m.,* antropófago, ga.

cannon [ka-non] *n.* cañón, *m.*

canoe [ka-nu] *n.* canoa, *f.;* bote, *m.;* (Mex.) chalupa, *f.;* piragua, *f.*

canon [ka-non] *n.* canon, *m.,* regla, *f.;* (eccl.) canónigo, *m.;* — **law,** derecho canónico.

canonize [ka-no-nais] *vt.* canonizar.

cantaloupe, cantaloup [kan-ta-lup] *n.* melón de verano.

canteen [kan-tin] *n.* (mil.) cantina, *f.,* tienda de provisiones para soldados; vasija en que los soldados, viajeros, etc. llevan agua.

canter [kan-ter] *n.* medio galope, *m.*

canvas [kan-vas] *n.* cañamazo, *m.;* lona, *f.*

canyon [ka-nion] *n.* desfiladero, cañón, *m.*

cap [kap] *n.* gorra, *f.;* birrete, *m.;* cachucha, *f.;* — **and gown,** traje académico o toga y birrete; —. *vt.* poner remate a; **to** — **the climax,** llegar al colmo; **percussion** —, cápsula fulminante.

capability [ka-pa-bi-li-ti] *n.* capacidad, aptitud, habilidad, *f.*

capable [kei-pa-bol] *adj.* capaz, idóneo.

capacity [ka-pa-si-ti] *n.* capacidad, *f.;* inteligencia, habilidad, *f.;* calidad, *f.;* **seating** —, cabida, *f.*

cape [keip] *n.* cabo, promontorio, *m.;* capa, *f.;* capota, *f.;* capote, *m.*

capillary [ka-pi-la-ri] *adj.* capilar.

capital [ka-pi-tal] *adj.* capital, excelente; principal;— **punishment,** pena de muerte; —, *n.* (arch.) capitel, *m.;* capital (la ciudad principal), *f.;* capital, *m.;* mayúscula, *f.;* **to invest —.** colocar un capital.

capitalist [ka-pi-ta-list] *n.* capitalista, *m.* y *f.*

capitalize [ka-pi-ta-lais] *vt.* capitalizar.

Capitol [ka-pi-tol] *n.* Capitolio, *m.*

capricious [ka-pri-shos] *adj.* caprichoso.

capsize [kap-sais] *vt.* y *vr.* (naut.) volcar, volcarse.

capsule [kap-siul] *n.* cápsula, *f.*

captain [kap-tein] *n.* capitán, *m.*

caption [kap-shon] *n.* presa, captura, *f.;* (print.) título, subtítulos pie de grabado.

captivate [kap-ti-veit] *vt.* cautivar; esclavizar.

captive [kap-tiv] *n.* cautivo, va; esclavo, *va.*

captivity [kap-ti-vi-ti] *n.* cautividad, esclavitud, *f.;* cautiverio, *m.*

captor [kap-tor] *n.* apresador, *m.*

capture [kap-char] *n.* captura, *f.;* presa, *f.;* toma, *f.;* —, *vt.* apresar; capturar.

car [kar] *n.* carreta, *f.;* carro, *m.;*

coche, auto-móvil, *m.*

caramel [ka-ra-mel] *n.* caramelo, *m.*

carat [ka-rat] *n.* quilate, *m.*

caravan [ka-ra-van] *n.* caravana, *f.*

carbohydrate [kar-bou-hai-dreit] *n.* carbohidrato, *m.*

carbon [kar-bon] *n.* carbón, *m.;* — **copy,** copia al carbón, copia en papel carbón; réplica, *f.;* — **paper,** papel carbón.

carbonic [kar-bo-nik] *adj.* carbónico; — **acid,** ácido carbónico.

carburetor [kar-biu-re-tar] *n.* carburador, *m.*

carcass [kar-kas] *n.* animal muerto; casco, *m.;* armazón, *f.*

card [kard] *n.* naipe, *m.,* carta, *f.;* tarjeta, *f.;* carda (para cardar lana), *f.;* — **catalogue,** catálogo de fichas; — **index,** fichero, *m.;* —, *vt.* cardar (lana).

cardboard [kard-bord] *n.* cartón, *m.*

cardigan [kar-di-gan] *n.* suéter o chaqueta tejida con botonadura al frente.

cardinal [kar-di-nal] *adj.* cardinal, principal; rojo, purpurado; — **points,** puntos cardinales; —, *n.* cardenal, *m.;* (orn.) cardenal, *m.*

cardiogram [kar-dio-gram] *n.* (med.) cardiograma, *m.*

care [kear] *n.* cuidado, esmero,

m.; solicitud, *f.;* cargo, *m.;* vigilancia, *f.;* **to take — of,** cuidar de; —, *vi.* cuidar, tener cuidado; inquietarse; estimar, apreciar.

career [ka-riar] *n.* carrera, profesión, *f.;* curso, *m.*

carefree [kea-fri] *adj.* libre, sin cuidados.

careful [kea-ful] *adj.* cuidadoso, ansioso, prudente, solícito; **to be —,** tener cuidado.

careless [kea-les] *adj.* descuidado, negligente; indolente; **—ly,** *adv.* descuidadamente.

carelessness [kea-lis-nes] *n.* descuido, *m.,* negligencia, *f.*

caress [ka-res] *n.* caricia, *f.;* —, *vt.* acariciar, halagar.

cargo [kar-gou] *n.* cargamento de navío; carga, *f.;* consignación, *f.*

caricature [ka-ri-ka-chuar] *n.* caricatura, *f.;* —, *vt.* hacer caricaturas; ridiculizar.

carnal [kar-nal] *adj.* carnal; sensual.

carnation [kar-nei-shon] *n.* (bot.) clavel, *m.*

carnival [kar-ni-val] *n.* carnaval, *m.*

carnivorous [kar-ni-vo-ros] *adj.* carnívoro.

carol [ka-rol] *n.* villancico, *m.;* **Christmas —,** villancico o canción de Navidad.

carp [karp] *n.* carpa, *f;* —, *vi.* censurar, criticar, reprobar.

carpenter [kar-pen-tar] *n.* carpintero, *m.*

carpet [kar-pet] *n.* alfombra, *f.;* tapete, *m.;* tapiz, *m.;* **— sweeper,** barredor de alfombra; —, *vt.* cubrir con alfombras, tapizar.

carpeting [kar-pe-tin] *n.* material para tapices; tapicería, *f.*

carpool [kar-pul] *n.* cooperación para compartir los gastos de trasporte en automóvil.

carriage [ka-rich] *n.* porte, talante, *m.;* coche, *m.,* carroza, *f.;* carruaje, *m.* vehículo, *m.;* carga, *f.*

carrier [ka-riar] *n.* portador, carretero, *m.;* trasportador, *m.;* **aircraft —,** (naut.) portaaviones, *m.;* **— pigeon,** paloma mensajera.

carrion [ka-rion] *n.* carroña, *f.*

carrot [ka-rot] *n.* zanahoria, *f.*

carry [ka-ri] *vt.* llevar, conducir; portar; lograr; cargar; **to — on,** continuar; **to — out,** cumplir, llevar a cabo, realizar.

cart [kart] *n.* carro, *m.;* carreta, *f.;* —, *vt.* acarrear.

cartel [kar-tel] *n.* cartel, *m.*

cartilage [kar-ti-leich] *n.* cartílago, *m.*

carton [kar-ton] *n.* caja de cartón.

cartoon [kar-tún] *n.* caricatura, *f.;* boceto, *m.;* **animated —,** caricatura animada; —, *vt.* y *vi.* caricaturizar; bosquejar.

cartoonist [kar-tú-nist] *n.* caricaturista, *m.* y *f.*

cartridge [kar-tridch] *n.* cartucho, *m.;* **blank —,** cartucho en blanco; **— shell,** cápsula, *f.*

carve [karv] *vt.* cincelar; tajar; grabar.

carving [kar-vin] *n.* escultura, entalladura, *f.;* **—knife,** tajador, *m.,* cuchillo de tajar.

cascade [kas-keid] *n.* cascada, *f.;* salto de agua.

case [keis] *n.* estado, *m.;* situación, *f.;* causa, *f.;* bolsa, *f.;* caso, *m.;* estuche, *m.;* vaina, *f.;* caja, *f.;* (gram.) caso, *m.;* **in —,** si acaso, caso que; **in the — of,** en caso de.

cash [kash] *n.* dinero contante o efectivo, caja, *f.;* **— and carry,** compra al contado en que el comprador se lleva él mismo la mercancía.

cashew [ka-shu] *n.* anacardo, *m.;* **— nut,** nuez de la India.

cashier [ka-shiar] *n.* cajero, ra; **—'s check,** cheque de caja.

cashmere [kash-miar] *n.* casimir (tela) *m.*

cask [kask] *n.* barril, tonel, *m.*

casket [kas-ket] *n* ataúd, *m.*

casserole [kas-seroul] *n.* cacerola, *f.;* **— dish,** guiso al horno de una combinación de ingredientes en una cacerola.

cast [kast] *vt.* tirar, lanzar; echar; modelar; **to—lots,** echar suertes; —, *vi.* amoldarse; —, *n.* tiro, golpe, *m.;* forma, *f ;* matiz, *m.;* (theat.) reparto, elenco artístico; —, *adj.* fundido; **— iron,** hierro colado; **— steel,** acero, fundido.

castanets [kas-ta-nets] *n. pl.* castañuelas, *f. pl.*

castaway [kas-ta-uei] *n.* réprobo, *m.;* náufrago, ga.

caste [kast] *n.* casta, *f.,* clase social; **to lose —,** perder la posición social.

Castile [kas-til] Castilla, *f.*

Castilian [kas-ti-lian] *n.* y *adj.* castellano, na.

casting [kas-tin] *n.* tiro, *m.;* vaciado, *m.;* (theat.) distribución de papeles a los actores.

castle [ka-sel] *n.* castillo, *m.;* fortaleza, *f.;* —, *vt.* encastillar; **to — one's king,** enrocar (en el juego de ajedrez).

castoff [kast-of] *adj.* descartado; **— clothes,** ropa de desecho; **— iron,** hierro de desecho.

castor [kas-tor] *n.* castor, *m.;* sombrero castor;**— oil,** aceite de ricino, de castor o de palmacristi.

casual [ka-shiual] *adj.* casual,

fortuito; — **clothing,** ropa sencilla, ropa de calle o para deportes.

casualty [ka-shiual-ti] *n.* accidente, *m.;* caso, *m.;* —**ties,** *n. pl.* víctimas de accidentes o de guerra, etc.

cat [kat] *n.* gato, *m.,* gata, *f.;* **to let the — out of the bag,** revelar un secreto.

cataclysm [ka-ta-kli-sem] *n.* cataclismo, diluvio, *m.*

catalogue [ka-ta-log] *n.* catálogo, *m.;* rol, lista, f.

Catalonia [ka-ta-lou-nia] Cataluña, f.

Catalonian [ka-ta-lou-nian] *n. y adj.* catalán, ana.

catapult [ka-ta-palt] *n.* catapulta, f.

cataract [ka-ta-rakt] *n.* cascada, catarata, *f.;* (med.) catarata, f.

catastrophe [ka-tas-tro-fi] *n.* catástrofe, f.

catch [kach] *vt.* coger, agarrar, asir; atrapar; pillar; sorprender; —, *vi.* pegarse, ser contagioso; prender; **to — cold,** resfriarse; **to — fire,** encenderse; —, *n.* botín, *m.,* presa, *f.;* captura, *f.;* trampa, *f.;* buen partido; acto de parar la pelota.

catcher [ka-char] *n.* cogedor, ra; parador de la pelota (en el béisbol).

catchy [ka-chi] *adj.* atrayente,

agradable; engañoso.

catechism [ka-ti-kisem] *n.* catecismo, *m.*

categorical [ka-ti-go-ri-kal] *adj.* categórico.

category [ka-ti-go-ri] *n.* categoría, f.

cater [kei-tar] *vi.* abastecer, proveer; halagar, complacer.

caterer [kei-ta-rar] *n.* proveedor, ra, abastecedor, ra; persona que proporciona lo que se ha de comer en una cena, banquete, etc.

caterpillar [keita-pi-lar] *n.* oruga, *f.;* — **tractor,** tractor de oruga.

catfish [kat-fish] *n.* (ichth.) barbo, *m.*

cathartic [ka-zar-tik] *adj.* (med.) catártico; —, *n.* purgante, laxante, *m.*

cathedral [ka-zi-dral] *n.* catedral, f.

cathode, cathodic [ka-zoud], [ka-zo-dik] *adj.* catódico; — **ray tube,** tubo de rayos catódicos.

catholic [ka-zo-lik] *n. y adj.* católico, ca.

catholicism [ka-zo-li-si-zem] *n.* catolicismo, *m.*

cattle [katel] *n.* ganado, *m.,* ganado vacuno.

cattleman [katel-men] *n.* ganadero, *m.,* criador de ganado.

caucus [kou-kos] *n.* junta electoral.

caught [kout] *pretérito y p.p.* del verbo **catch.**

cauliflower [kou-li-flauar] *n.* coliflor, *f.*

cause [kous] *n.* causa, *f.;* razón, *f.;* motivo, lugar, *m.;* proceso, *m.;* —, *vt.* motivar, causar.

caustic [kous-tik] *n. y adj.* cáustico, *m.*

caution [kau-shon] *n.* prudencia, precaución, *f.;* aviso *m.;* —, *vt.* avisar, amonestar, advertir.

cautionary [kau-shoneri] *adj.* de índole preventiva; dado a tomar precauciones.

cautious [kau-shos] *adj.* cauteloso, prudente, circunspecto, cauto; **to be** —, estar sobre sí, ser cauteloso.

cavalcade [ka-val-keid] *n.* cabalgata, cabalgada, *f.*

cavalier [ka-va-lier] *n.* jinete, *m.;* caballero, *m.*

cavalry [ka-val-ri] *n.* caballería, *f.*

cavalryman [ka-val-ri-man] *n.* soldado de a caballo; soldado de caballería.

cave [keiv] *n.* cueva, caverna, *f.*

cavern [ka-vern] *n.* caverna, *f.;* antro, *m.*

caviar [ka-viar] *n.* caviar, *m.*

cavity [ka-vi-ti] *n.* hueco, *m.,* cavidad, *f.;* seno, *m.*

caw [ko] *vi.* graznar.

C.D. [si-di] : **compact disc** disco compacto, m; — **player,** reproductor de CD, m.

cease [sis] *vt.* parar suspender, cesar, dejar de; —, *vi.* desistir.

ceaseless [sis-les] *adj.* incesante, continuo.

cedar [si-dar] *n.* cedro, *m.*

cede [sid] *vt.* ceder, trasferir.

ceiling [si-lin] *n.* techo o cielo raso de una habitación; (avi.) cielo máximo; —, *adj.* máximo.

celebrate [se-li-breit] *vt.* celebrar; elogiar.

celebration [se-li-brei-shon] *n.* celebración, *f.;* alabanza, *f.*

celebrity [se-li-bri-ti] *n.* celebridad, fama, *f.;* persona célebre.

celery [se-le-ri] *n.* apio, *m.*

celestial [si-les-tial] *adj.* celeste, divino, celestial.

celibate [se-li-beit] *n. y adj.* soltero, ra, célibe, *m. y f.*

cell [sel] *n.* celda, *f.;* cueva, *f.;* célula, *f.*

cellar [se-lar] *n.* sótano, *m.,* bodega, *f.*

cello [che-lou] *n.* violonchelo, *m.*

cellophane [se-lo-fein] *n.* celofán, *m.*

cellular [se-liu-lar] *adj.* celular;— **phone,** teléfono celular, *m.*

celluloid [se-liu-loid] *n.* celuloide, *m.*

cellulose [se-liu-lous] *n.* (chem.) celulosa, *f.*

cement [se-ment] *n*. argamasa, *f*.; cemento, *m*.; —, *vt*. pesar con cemento, conglutinar; —, *vi*. unirse.

cemetery [se-mi-tri] *n*. cementerio, *m*.

censor [sen-sar] *n*. censor, *m*.; crítico, *m*.

censorship [sen-sorg-ship] *n*. censura, *f*.

censure [sen-shar] *n*. censura, reprensión, *f*.; *vt*. censurar, reprender; criticar.

census [sen-sas] *n*. censo, encabezamiento, empadronamiento, *m*.

cent [sent] *n*. centavo, *m*.; céntimo, *m*.; **per** —, por ciento.

centennial [sen-te-nial] *n*. y *adj*. centenario, *m*.

center [sen-tar] *n*. centro, *m*.; (fútbol) centro, *m*.; —, *vt*. colocar en un centro; reconcentrar; —, *vi*. colocarse en el centro, reconcentrarse.

centigrade [sen-ti-greid] *n*. y *adj*. centígrado, *m*.

centigram [sen-ti-gram] *n*. centigramo, *m*.

centimeter [sen-ti-mi-tar] *n*. centímetro, *m*.

centipede [sen-ti-pid] *n*. ciempiés, *m*.

central [sen-tral] *adj*. central; céntrico.

Central America [sen-tral-a-me-ri-ka] América Central, *f*.

centralization [sen-tra-lai-sei-shon] *n*. centralización, *f*,

centralize [sen-tra-lais] *vt*. centralizar.

century [sen-tiu-ri] *n*. siglo, *m*.

ceramics [se-ra-miks] *n*. cerámica, *f*.

cereal [si-rial] *n*. cereal, *m*.

cerebral [sen-tral] *adj*. cerebral; — **palsy,** parálisis cerebral, diplegia espástica.

cerebrum [se-ri-brum] *n*. cerebro, *m*.

ceremonial [se-ri-mou-nial] *adj*. ceremonial; —, *n*. ceremonial, *m*., rito externo.

ceremonious [se-ri-mou-nios] *adj*. ceremonioso.

ceremony [se-ri-mo-ni] *n*. ceremonia, *f*.

certain [ser-tein] *adj*. cierto, evidente; **seguro,** certero, indudable; efectivo; — **sum,** —**quantity,** un tanto.

certainty, certitude [ser-tein-ti], [ser-ti-tiud] *n*. certeza, *f*.; seguridad, *f*.; certidumbre, *f*.; **with** —, a ciencia cierta.

certificate [ser-ti-fi-ket] *n*. certificado; testimonio, *m*.; (com.) bono, *m*.; certificación, *f*.; **birth** —, acta de nacimiento.

certified [ser-ti-faid] *adj*. certificado; — **public accountant,** contador público titulado.

certify [ser-ti-fai] *vt.* certificar, afirmar; dar fe.

cessation [se-sei-shon] *n.* cesación *f.*

cesspool [ses-pul] *n.* cloaca, *f.;* sumidero, *m.*

chafe [cheif] *vt.* frotar, irritar.

chagrin [sha-grin] *n.* mortificación, *f.;* disgusto, *m.*

chain [chein] *n.* cadena, *f.;* serie, sucesión, *f.;* —**gang,** gavilla de malhechores encadenados juntos, collera, *f.;* — **reaction,** reacción en cadena; — **store,** tienda de una serie que pertenece a una misma empresa; —**s,** *n. pl.* esclavitud, *f.;* —, *vt.* encadenar, atar con cadena.

chair [chear] *n.* silla, *f.;* **easy** —, silla poltrona; **folding** —, silla plegadiza; **swivel** —, silla giratoria; **wheel** —, silla de ruedas; —, *vt.* entronizar; colocar en un cargo público.

chairman [chear-man] *n.* presidente (de una reunión o junta), *m.*

chalice [cha-lis] *n.* cáliz, *m.*

chalk [chok] *n.* tiza, *f.;* gis, *m.;* yeso, *m.;* —, *vt.* dibujar con yeso o tiza; bosquejar, lapizar; **to — up,** aumentar un precio; ganar puntos.

challenge [cha-lendch] *n.* desafío, cartel, *m.;* pretensión, *f.;* recusación, *f.;* —, *vt.* desafiar; retar; provocar, reclamar.

challenger [cha-len-yer] *n.* desafiador, ra, retador, ra.

chamber [cheim-bar] *n.* cámara, *f.;* aposento, *m.;* (mil.) cámara de mina; **air** —, cámara de aire; — **music,** música de cámara;— **of commerce,** cámara de comercio, *f.*

chamberlain [cheim-ba-lin] *n.* camarero, *m.;* chambelán, *m.*

chamber maid [cheim-ba-meid] *n.* moza de cámara, camarera, *f.*

chameleon [ca-mi-lion] *n.* camaleón, *m.*

chamois [sha-mua] *n.* gamuza, *f.*

champ [champ] *vt.* morder, mascar; —, *n.* (coll.) campeón, ona.

champagne [sham-pein] *n.* champaña, *m.,* (coll.) champán, *m.*

champion [cham-pion] *n.* campeón, ona; paladín, *m.;* —, *vt.* defender, respaldar, apoyar.

championship [cham-pion-ship] *n.* campeonato, *m.*

chance [chans] *n.* ventura, suerte, ocasión, oportunidad, casualidad, *f.,* acaso, *m.;* riesgo, *m.;* **by** —, por casualidad, —, *vi.* acaecer, acontecer; —, *adj.* fortuito, casual.

chancellor [chan-se-lor] *n.* canciller, *m.;* rector, *m.*

chandelier [shan-de-liar] *n.*

araña de luces.

change [chinch] *vt.* cambiar; trasmutar; variar; **to — cars,** trasbordar; **to — one's clothes,** mudar de ropa; — *vi.* riar, alterarse; revolverse (el tiempo); —, *n.* mudanza, variedad, *f.;* vicisitud, *f.;* cambio, *m.;* variación, *f.;* suelto (moneda), *m.;* **to make —,** cambiar (moneda).

changeable [chein-cha-bol] *adj.* variable, inconstante; mudable, cambiante.

channel [cha-nel] *n.* canal, *m.;* conducto, *m.;* **TV —,** canal de televisión; —, *vt.* acanalar, estriar.

chant [chant] *n.* sonsonete, *m.;* —, *vt.* cantar; repetir algo monótonamente.

chaos [keios] *n.* caos, *m.,* confusión, *f.*

chaotic [keio-tik] *adj.* confuso, caótico.

chap [chap] *vi.* rajarse, henderse, agrietarse; —, *n.* rendija, *f ;* mandíbula (de animal, etc.), *f.;* (coll.) mozo, chico, *m.;* tipo, *m.*

chapel [cha-pel] *n.* capilla, *f.*

chaperon [sha-pe-roun] *n.* señora o señor de compañía; escolta, *f.;* —, *vt.* acompañar; escoltar.

chaplain [chaplin] *n.* capellán, *m.*

chaps [chaps] *n. pl.* zahones, *m.*

pl. chaparreras, *f. pl.*

chapter [chap-tar] *n.* capítulo, *m.;* cabildo, *m.;* filial de una confraternidad.

char [char] *vt.* hacer carbón de leña; carbonizar.

character [ca-rak-tar] *n.* carácter, *m.;* señal, *f.;* distintivo, *m.;* letra, *f.;* calidad, *f.;* (theat.) parte, *f.;* papel, *m.;* personaje, *m.;* modalidad, *f.;* (coll.) persona rara o excéntrica.

characteristic [ka-rak-te-ris-tik] *adj.* característico; típico;—, *n.* rasgo, *m.,* peculiaridad, *f.*

characterize [ka-rak-te-rais] *vt.* caracterizar, imprimir, calificar.

charade [sha-rad] *n.* charada, *f.*

charcoal [kar-koul] *n.* carbón, *m.;* carbón vegetal; carbón de leña.

charge [charch] *vt.* encargar, comisionar; cobrar; cargar; acusar, imputar; **to — to account,** adeudar en cuenta, cargar en cuenta; —, *n.* cargo, cuidado, *m.;* mandato, *m.;* acusación, *f.;* tarifa, *f ;* (mil.) ataque, *m.;* carga, *f.;* **— collect,** porte debido, porte por cobrar; **— prepaid,** porte pagado o cobrado; **extra —,** gasto adicional; **— account,** cuenta abierta; **in — of,** a cargo de.

charitable [cha-ri-ta-bol] *adj.* caritativo, limosnero, benévolo;

benigno, clemente.

charity [cha-ri-ti] *n.* caridad, benevolencia, *f.;* limosna, *f.;* beneficencia, *f.*

charlatan [shar-la-tan] *n.* charlatán, curandero, *m.*

charm [charm] *n.* encanto, *m.;* atractivo, *m.;* simpatía, *f.;* —, *vt.* encantar, embelesar, atraer; seducir.

charming [char-min] *adj.* seductor; simpático; encantador.

chart. [chart] *n.* carta de navegar; (avi.) carta, *f.;* hoja de información gráfica; cuadro, *m.;* —, *vt.* marcar en un cuadro; **to — a course,** marcar un derrotero.

charter [char-tar] *n.* carta constitucional: letra patente; privilegio, *m.;* carta, *f.;* cédula, *f.;* —, *vt.* fletar (un barco, etc.); estatuir; — **member,** miembro o socio fundador.

chase [cheis] *vt.* cazar; perseguir; acosar; cincelar; —, *n.* caza, *f.;* **to give —,** corretear, perseguir.

chasm [kasem] *n.* hendidura, *f.;* vacío, *m.;* abismo, *m.*

chaste [cheist] *adj.* casto; puro; honesto; púdico.

chasten [chei-sen] *vt.* corregir, castigar.

chastise [chas-tis] *vt.* castigar, reformar, corregir.

chastity [chas-ti-ti] *n.* castidad, pureza, *f.*

chat [chat] *vi.* charlar, platicar; —, *n.* plática, charla, conversación, *f;* — **room,** (internet) sala de chat, *f.*

chatter [cha-tar] *vi.* cotorrear; charlar; castañetear; —, *n.* chirrido, *m.;* charla, *f.*

chatty [cha-ti] *adj.* locuaz, parlanchín.

chauffeur [sho-far] *n.* chófer, *m.*

cheap [chip] *adj.* barato; —**ly,** *adv.* barato.

cheat [chit] *vt.* engañar, defraudar; hacer trampa; —, *n.* trampa, *f.;* fraude, engaño, *m.;* trampista, trápala, *m.* y *f.*

check [chek] *vt.* reprimir, refrenar; verificar, comprobar; examinar; mitigar; regañar; registrar, facturar; **to —,** tener a raya; **to — (baggage),** documentar, facturar (el equipaje) ; **to — in,** llegar (a un hotel); **to — out,** salirse (de un hotel) ; **to — off,** eliminar; —, *n.* restricción, *f ;* freno, *m.;* represión, *f.;* jaque, *m.;* libranza, *f.;* póliza, *f.;* cheque, *m.;* **cashier's —,** cheque de caja; **traveler's —,** cheque de viajero.

checkerboard [che-kar-bord] *n.* tablero de damas.

checkers [che-kars] *n.* juego de damas.

checking account [che-kin-a-kaunt] *n.* cuenta corriente, cuenta de cheques.

checkroom [chek-rum] *n.* consigna, guardarropía, *f., guarda-rropa, m.*

cheek [chík] *n.* cachete, carrillo, *m.,* mejilla, *f.;* (coll.) desvergüenza, *f.,* atrevimiento, *m.*

cheekbone [chík-boun] *n.* pómulo, *m.*

cheer [chiar] *n.* alegría, *f.;* buen humor; —, *vt.* animar, alentar; vitorear; —, *vi.* alegrarse, regocijarse; **to — up,** tomar ánimo; **— up!** ¡valor! ¡anímese!

cheerful [chiar-ful] *adj.* alegre, vivo, jovial; campechano, genial; **— mien,** buena cara.

cheerfulness [chiar-ful-nes] *n.* alegría, *f.;* buen humor, júbilo, *m.*

cheese [chís] *n.* queso, *m.;* **cottage —,** requesón, *m.*

cheeseburger [chís-ber-gar] *n.* hamburguesa con queso.

cheesecake [chís-keik] *n.* pastel de queso.

chef [shef] *n.* cocinero, *m.,* jefe de cocina.

chemical [ke-mi-kal] *adj.* químico; —, *n.* sustancia química; **— engineering,** ingeniería química; **— warfare,** guerra química.

chemist [kemist] *n.* químico, ca.

chemistry [ke-mis-tri] *n.* quími-ca, *f.*

cherish [che-rish] *vt.* mantener, fomentar, proteger; acariciar; estimar; **to — the hope,** abrigar la esperanza.

cherry [cherri] *n.* cereza, *f.;* —, *adj.* bermejo.

cherub [che-rab] *n.* querubín, *m.*

chess [ches] *n.* ajedrez, *m.*

chessboard [ches-bord] *n.* tablero de ajedrez.

chest [chest] *n.* pecho, *m.;* arca, *f.;* baúl, *m.;* cofre, *m.;* **— of drawers,** cómoda, *f.*

chestnut [ches-nat] *n.* castaña, *f.;* color de castaña; **— tree,** castaño, *m.;* —, *adj.* castaño.

chew [chu] *vt. y vi.* mascar, masticar; rumiar; meditar, reflexionar.

chewing gum [chuin-gam] *n.* chicle, *m.,* goma de mascar.

chick [chik] *n.* pollito, polluelo, *m.*

chicken [chi-ken] *n.* pollo, *m.;* (fig.) joven, *m.* y *f.;* **—pox,** viruelas locas; varicela, *f.;* **young —,** pollo, lla.

chide [chaid] *vt.* reprobar, regañar; —, *vi.* reñir, alborotar.

chief [chíf] *adj.* principal, capital; **— clerk,** oficial mayor; **commander in —,** generalísimo, *m.,* comandante en jefe; **— justice,** presidente de la corte suprema; **—of staff,** jefe de estado mayor.

chieftain, *n.* jefe, comandante, *m.*

chiffon [shi-fon] *n.* chifón, *m.,* gasa, *f.*

child [chaild] *n.* infante, *m.;* hijo, ja; niño, ña; párvulo, *m.;* **with —,** embarazada, encinta.

childbirth [chaild-berz] *n.* parto, alumbramiento, *m.*

childhood [chaild-jud] *n.* infancia, niñez, *f.*

childish [chail-dish] *adj.* frívolo, pueril; **—ly,** *adv.* puerilmente.

childless [chaild-les] *adj.* sin hijos.

childlike [chaild-laik] *adj.* pueril, infantil.

children [chil-dren] *n. pl.* niños, *m. pl.;* hijos, *m. pl.*

Chilean [chi-lian] *n. y adj.* chileno, na.

chili [chi-li] *n.* chile, *m.;* — **sauce,** salsa de chile o de ají.

chill [chil] *adj.* frío; **—,** *n.* frío, *m.;* escalofrío, *m.;* **—,** *vt.* enfriar; helar.

chime [chaim] *n.* armonía, *f.;* repique, *m.;* **—s,** *pl.* juego de campanas; **—,** *vi.* sonar con armonía; concordar; **—,** *vt.* repicar.

chimney [chim-ni] *n.* chimenea, *f.;* **— sweep,** limpiachimeneas, *m.*

chimpanzee [chim-pan-si] *n.* chimpancé, *m.*

chin [chin] *n.* barba, *f.,* mentón, *m.*

china, chinaware [chai-na], [chai-na-uear] *n.* porcelana, loza, *f.*

chink [chink] *n.* grieta, hendidura, *f.;* **—,** *vi.* henderse; resonar.

chip [chip] *vt.* desmenuzar, picar; **—,** *vi.* astillarse; **—,** *n.* brizna, astilla, *f.*

chipmunk [chip-mank] *n.* variedad de ardilla.

chiropodist [ki-ro-po-dist] *n.* pedicuro, *m.,* callista, *m.*

chiropractor [kai-rou-prak-tor] *n.* quiropráctico, *m.*

chirp [cherp] *vi.* chirriar, gorjear; **—,** *n.* gorjeo, chirrido, *m.*

chisel [chisol] *n.* escoplo, cincel, *m.;* **—,** *vt.* escoplear, cincelar, grabar; (coll.) estafar, engañar.

chivalrous, chivalric, [shi-valrous], [shi-val-rik] *adj.* caballeroso.

chivalry [shi-val-ri] *n.* caballería, *f.;* hazaña, *f.;* caballerosidad, *f.*

chives [chaivs] *n.* cebollino, *m.*

chloride [klo-raid] *n.* cloruro, *m.*

chlorine [klo-rin] *n.* cloro, *m.*

chloroform [klo-ro-form] *n.* cloroformo, *m.*

chlorophyll [klo-ro-fil] *n.* clorofila, *f.*

chock-full [chok-ful] *adj.* completamente lleno.

chocolate [choklit] *n.* chocolate,

m.

choice [chois] *n.* elección, selección, *f.;* preferencia, *f.;* opción, *f.;* —, *adj.* selecto, exquisito, excelente; escogido.

choir [kuaiar] *n.* coro, *m.*

choke [chouk] *vt.* sofocar; oprimir; tapar; —, *vi.* estrangularse; —, *n.* (auto.) regulador de aire, *m.*

choker [chou-kar] *n.* collar apretado.

cholera [ko-le-ra] *n.* cólera *m.*

cholesterol [ko-les-te-rol] *n.* colesterol, *m.*

choose [chus] *vt.* escoger, elegir, seleccionar.

chop [chop] *vt.* tajar, cortar; picar; —, *n.* chuleta, *f.;* **lamb —**, chuleta de cordero; **pork —**, chuleta de puerco; **veal —**, chuleta de ternera; **— suey,** olla china; **—s**, *n. pl.* quijadas, *f. pl.*

chopsticks [chop-stiks] *n. pl.* palillos (con que comen los chinos), *m. pl.*

choral [ko-ral] *adj.* coral.

chord [kord] *n.* (mus.) acorde, *m.;* cuerda, *f.;* —, *vt.* encordar.

chore [chor] *n.* tarea, *f.;* quehacer, *m.;* **—s**, *n. pl.* quehaceres de la casa.

chorus [ko-rus] *n.* coro, *m.*

chose [chous] *pretérito* del verbo **choose.**

chosen [chousen] *p.p.* del verbo **choose.**

chowder [chau-dar] *n.* sancocho (de pescado o almejas), *m.*

Christ [kraist] *n.* Jesucristo, Cristo, *m.*

christen [kr-isen] *vt.* cristianar, bautizar.

Christian [kris-tian] *n. y adj.* cristiano, na; **— name,** nombre de pila.

Christianity [kri-tia-ni-ti] *n.* cristianismo, *m.*, cristiandad, *f.*

Christmas [kris-mas] *n.* Navidad, Pascua, *f.;* **— gift,** aguinaldo, *m.;* **— carol,** villancico de Navidad; **— Eve,** víspera de Navidad, Nochebuena, *f.;* **to wish a Merry —,** desear felices Pascuas; **— tree,** árbol de Navidad; **— Day**, pascua de Navidad.

chrome [kroum] *n.* cromo, *m.*

chromium [kro-mium] *n.* cromo, *m.*

chromosome [krou-mo-soum] *n.* cromosoma, *m.*

chronic [kro-nik] *adj.* crónico.

chronicle [kro-nikl] *n.* crónica, *f.;* informe, *m.;* —, *vt.* hacer una crónica.

chronological [kro-no-lo-yi] *adj.* cronológico.

chronology [kro-no-lo-yi] *n.* cronología, *f.*

chrysalis [kri-sa-lis] *n.* crisálida,

.f.

chubby [cha-bi] *adj.* gordo, cariancho, rechoncho.

chuckle [cha-kel] *vi.* cloquear; reírse entre dientes.

chum [cham] *n.* camarada, *m. y f.*, compañero, ra, amigo íntimo, amiga íntima.

chump [champ] *n.* tajo, tronco, *m.;* (coll.) zopenco, ca, tonto, tonta.

chunk [chank] *n.* (coll.) tajo, tronco, *m.; (fig.)* cantidad suficiente.

church [cherch] *n.* iglesia, *f.;* templo, *m.;* — **music,** música sagrada.

churchgoer [cherch-gouar] *n.* devoto, ta, persona que asiste fielmente a la iglesia.

churchyard [cherch-yard] *n.* cementerio, *m.;* patio de la iglesia.

chute [shut] *n.* vertedor, *m.*

cider [sai-dar] *n.* sidra, *f.*

cigar [si-gar] *n.* cigarro, puro, *m.;* — **butt,** colilla, *f.;* — **box,** cigarrera, *f..*

cigarette [si-ga-ret] *n.* cigarrillo cigarro, *m.*, pitillo, *m.;* —**butt,** colilla, *f.;* —**case,** portacigarros, *m.*, pitillera, cigarrera, *f.;* — **holder,** boquilla, *f.;* — **lighter,** encendedor de cigarros, mechero, *m.*

cinch [sinch], *n.* cincha, *f.;* (coll.) algo muy fácil.

cinder [sin-dar] *n.* ceniza gruesa y caliente.

cinema [si-ne-ma] *n.* cinematógrafo, cine, *m.*

cinnamon [si-na-mon] *n.* canela, *f.*

circle [ser-kel] *n.* círculo, *m.;* corrillo, *m.;* asamblea, *f.;* rueda, *f.;* —, *vt.* circundar; cercar, ceñir; —, *vi.* circular.

circuit [ser-kit] *n.* ámbito, circuito, *m.;* vuelta, *f.*

circular [ser-kiu-lar] *adj.* circular, redondo; —, *n.* carta circular.

circulate [ser-kiu-leit] *vi.* circular; moverse alrededor.

circulating [ser-kiu-lei-tin] *adj.* circulante.

circulation [ser-kiu-lei-shon] *n.* circulación, *f.*

circumcise [ser-kum-sais] *vt.* circuncidar.

circumcision [ser-kum-si-son] *n.* circuncisión, *f.*

circumference [ser-kum-fe-rens] *n.* circunferencia, *f.;* circuito, *m.*

circumstance [ser-kum-stans] *n.* circunstancia, condición, *f.;* incidente, *m.;* —**s,** situación económica.

circumstantial [ser-kum-stan-shal] *adj.* accidental; indirecto; circunstancial; accesorio; —

evidence, evidencia circunstancial.

circumvent [ser-kum-vent] *vt.* embaucar, engañar con estratagema.

circus [ser-kus] *n.* circo, *m.;* arena, *f.;* hipódromo, *m.*

cistern [sis-tern] *n.* cisterna, *f.*

citadel [si-ta-del] *n.* ciudadela, fortaleza, *f.*

citation [sai-tei-shon] *n.* citación, mención, *f.*

cite [sait] *vt.* citar (a juicio); alegar; citar, referirse a.

citizen [si-tisen] *n.* ciudadano, na; **fellow —,** conciudadano, *m.*

citizenry [si-tisen-ri] *n.* masa de ciudadanos.

citizenship [si-tisen-ship] *n.* ciudadanía, *f.;* nacionalidad, *f.;* — **papers,** carta de ciudadanía.

citric [si-trik] *adj.* cítrico.

citrus [si-trus] *adj.* (bot.) cítrico.

city [si-ti] *n.* ciudad, *f.;* — **hall,** ayuntamiento, *m.;* palacio municipal.

civic [si-vik] *adj.* cívico; **—s,** *n.* instrucción cívica.

civil [si-vil] *adj.* civil, cortés; — **engineer,** ingeniero civil; — **service,** servicio civil.

civilian [si-vi-lian] *n.* paisano, na (persona no militar), particular, *m.;* jurisconsulto, *m.*

civilization [si-vi-lai-sei-shon] *n.* civilización, *f.*

civilize [si-vi-lais] *vt.* civilizar.

clad [klad] *adj.* vestido, cubierto.

claim [kleim] *vt.* pedir en juicio, reclamar, pretender como cosa debida; —, *n.* pretensión, *f ;* derecho, *m.;* reclamo, *m.;* reclamación, *f.;* **to enter a —,** demandar.

claimant [klei-mant] *n.* reclamante, *m. y f.;* demandador, ra.

clam [klam] *n.* almeja, *f.;* — **chowder,** sopa de almejas.

clamber [klam-bar] *vi.* gatear, trepar.

clammy [kla-mi] *adj.* viscoso; tenaz.

clamor [kla-mor] *n.* clamor, grito, *m.;* vocería, *f.;* —, *vi.* vociferar, gritar.

clamorous [kla-mo-ros] *adj.* clamoroso, tumultuoso, estrepitoso; **—ly,** *adv.* clamorosamente.

clamp [klamp] *n.* barrilete, *m.;* collar, *m.;* abrazadera, *f.;* manija, *f.;* collera, *f.;* tenazas, pinzas, *f. pl.;* grapa, laña, *f.;* sujetador, *m.;* —, *vt.* sujetar, afianzar; empalmar.

clan [klan] *n.* clan, *m.,* familia, tribu, raza, *f.*

clandestine [klan-des-tin] *adj.* clandestino, oculto.

clang [klang] *n.* rechino, sonido desapacible; —, *vi.* rechinar; sonar.

clank [klank] *vi.* rechinar; chillar; —, *n.* sonido estridente; retintín, *m.*

clansman [klans-man] *n.* miembro de un clan.

clap [klap] *vt.* batir; aplicar; palmear; —, *vi.* palmear, palmotear, aplaudir; **to — hands,** batir palmas; —, *n.* estrépito, *m.;* golpe, *m.;* trueno, *m.;* palmoteo, *m.*

clapping [kla-pin] *n.* palmada, *f.;* aplauso, palmoteo, *m.*

clarify [kla-ri-fai] *vt.* clarificar, aclarar; —, *vi.* aclararse.

clarinet [kla-ri-net] *n.* clarinete, *m.*

clarity [kla-ri-ti] *n.* claridad, *f.*

clash [klash] *vi.* encontrarse; chocar; contradecir; —, *vt.* batir, golpear; —, *n.* crujido, *m.;* estrépito, *m.;* disputa, *f ;* choque, *m.*

clasp [klasp] *n.* broche, *m.;* hebilla, *f.;* sujetador, *m.;* manija, *f.;* abrazo, *m.;* —, *vt.* abrochar; abrazar.

class [klas] *n.* clase, *f.;* género, *m.;* categoría, *f.;* —, *vt.* clasificar.

classic [kla-sik] *n.* y *adj.* clásico, *m.*

classical [kla-si-kal] *adj.* clásico.

classification [kla-si-fi-kei-shon] *n.* clasificación, *f.*

classify [kla-si-fai] *vt.* clasificar, graduar.

classmate [klas-meit] *n.* condiscípulo, la.

classroom [klas-rum] *n.* aula, *f.,* sala de clase.

clatter [kla-tar] *vi.* resonar; hacer ruido; —, *n.* ruido, alboroto, *m.*

clause [klos] *n.* cláusula, *f.;* artículo, *m.;* estipulación, *f.;* condición, *f.*

claustrophobia [klos-tro-fou-bia] *n.* claustrofobia, *f.*

claw [klo] *n.* garra, *f.;* garfa, *f.;* —, *vt.* desgarrar, arañar.

clay [klei] *n.* barro, *m.;* arcilla, *f.*

clean [klin] *adj.* limpio; casto; —, *adv.* enteramente; —, *vt.* limpiar.

clean-cut [klin-kat] *adj.* bien tallado; bien parecido; de buen carácter.

cleaner [kli-nar] *n.* limpiador, ra; sacamanchas, quitamanchas, *m.*

cleaning [kli-nin] *n.* limpieza, *f.*

cleanliness [klin-li-nes] *n.* limpieza, *f.;* aseo, *m.*

cleanse [klens] *vt.* limpiar, purificar; purgar.

clear [kliar] *adj.* claro, lucido; diáfano; neto; límpido; sereno; evidente; inocente; —, *vt.* clarificar, aclarar; justificar; absolver; **to — the table,** quitar la mesa; **to—up,** aclararse, despejarse (por ej. el cielo); —, *vi.* aclararse.

clearance [klia-rans] *n.* despejo, *m.;* (com.) despacho de aduana; utilidad líquida; (avi.) espacio, *m.;* (mech.) juego limpio (de una pieza, etc.) ; — **sale,** liquidación, *f.*

clear-cut [kliar-kat] *adj.* claro, bien definido.

clearing [klia-rin] *n.* espacio libre; aclaración, *f.* —**house,** casa de compensación.

clear-sighted [klia-sai-tid] *adj.* perspicaz, juicioso; clarividente.

cleave [kliv] *vt.* y *vi.* hender; partir; dividir; pegarse.

cleaver [kli-var] *n.* cuchillo de carnicero.

clef [klef] *n.* (mus.) clave, *f.*

cleft [kleft] *n.* hendidura, abertura, *f.*

clemency [kle-man-si] *n.* clemencia, *f.*

clench [klench] *vt.* cerrar, agarrar, asegurar.

clergy [kler-yi] *n.* clero, *m.*

clergyman [kler-yi-man] *n.* eclesiástico, clérigo, *m.*

cleric [kle-rik] *n.* clérigo, *m.*

clerical [kle-ri-kal] *adj.* clerical, eclesiástico; —, **work,** trabajo de oficina.

clerk [klerk] *n.* eclesiástico, clérigo; *m.;* dependiente, *m.;* **chief** —, oficial mayor.

clever [kle-ver] *adj.* diestro, hábil, mañoso; inteligente.

cleverness [kle-ver-nes] *n.* destreza, habilidad, *f.;* inteligencia, *f.*

clew [klú] *n.* ovillo de hilo; pista, *f.;* indicio, *m.;* —, *vt.* (naut.) cargar las velas.

click [klik] *vi.* sonar; (coll.) pegar, prosperar, gustar al público; —, *n.* ruidito (como de un reloj).

client [klaient] *n.* cliente, *m.* y *f.*

clientele [klian-tél] *n.* clientela, *f.*

cliff [klif] *n.* peñasco, asco, *m.;* precipicio, *m.,* barranca, *f.*

climate [klai-met] *n.* clima, *m.;* temperatura, *f.*

climax [klai-maks] *n.* colmo, *m.,* culminación, *f.;* clímax, *m.*

climb [klaim] *vt.* escalar, trepar; —, *vi.* subir.

climber [klaimar] *n.* trepador, ra; arribista, *m.* y *f.,* persona que aspira a escalas sociales más altas.

clinch [klinch] *vt.* empuñar, cerrar el puño; remachar un clavo; —, *vi.* agarrarse; —, *n.* agarro, agarrón, *m.*

cling [kling] *vi.* colgar, adherirse, pegarse.

clinic [kli-nik] *adj.* clínico; —, *n.* clínica, *f.;* consultorio, *m.;* clínica médica.

clinical [kli-ni-kal] *adj.* clínico.

clink [klink] *vt.* hacer resonar; —, *vi.* resonar; —, *n.* retintín, *m.*

clip [klip] *vt.* recortar; cortar a raíz; escatimar; —, *n.* tijeretada, *f.;* grapa, *f.;* gancho, *m.*

clipping [kli-pin] *n.* recorte, *m.*

clique [klik] *n.* camarilla, pandilla, *f.*

clock [klok] *n.* reloj, *m.* **alarm —,** despertador, *m.*

clockmaker [klok-mei-ker] *n.* relojero, *m.*

clockwise [klok-uais] *adj.* con movimiento circular a la derecha.

clockwork [klok-uek] *n.* mecanismo de un reloj; **like—,** sumamente exacto y puntual.

clog [klog] *n.* obstáculo, *m.;* galocha, *f.;* —, *vt.* obstruir; —, *vi.* coagularse.

cloister [klois-tar] *n.* claustro, monasterio, *m.*

close [klous] *vt.* cerrar, tapar; concluir, terminar; —, *vi.* cerrarse, unirse, convenirse; **to — (an account),** finiquitar (una cuenta); —, *n.* cercado, *m.;* fin, *m.;* conclusión, *f.;* cierre, *m.;* —, *adj.* cerrado; preso; estrecho, angosto; ajustado; avaro; — **fight,** combate reñido; — **quarters,** lugar estrecho, espacio limitado; —, *adv.* de cerca;

junto; estrechamente; secretamente; — **by,** muy cerca.

closed [kloust] *adj.* cerrado; — **shop,** contrato colectivo.

closed-circuit [klous-ser-kuit] *adj.* en circuito cerrado.

closeness [klous-nis] *n.* estrechez, espesura, reclusión, *f.*

closet [klo-sit] *n.* ropero, *m.;* gabinete, *m.;* **water—,** retrete, *m.;* —, *vt.* encerrar en un gabinete o en un ropero.

close-up [klous-ap] *n.* fotografía de cerca; algo visto muy de cerca.

closing [klousin]*n.* cierre, *m.;* conclusión, *f.;* clausura, *f.*

clot [klot] *n.* grumo, *m.,* coagulación, *f.;* **blood —,** embolia, *f.;* —, *vi.* cuajarse, coagularse.

cloth [kloz] *n.* paño, *m.;* mantel, *m.;* lienzo, *m.;* material, *m.;* — **binding,** encuadernación en tela.

clothe [klouz] *vt.* vestir, cubrir.

clothes [klouzs] *n. pl.* vestidura, *f.;* ropa, *f.;* — **closet,** ropero, *m.;* — **hanger,** percha, *f.;* colgador o gancho de ropa; **bed —,** ropa de cama.

clothesline [klouzs-lain] *n.* cuerda para tender la ropa, tendedero, *m.*

clothespin [klouzs-pin] *n.* gancho de tendedero, pinza para tender la ropa.

clothing [klou-zin] *n.* vestidos, *m. pl.;* ropa, *f.*

cloud [klaud] *n.* nube, *f.;* nublado, *m.;* (fig.) adversidad, *f.;* —, *vt.* anublar; oscurecer; —, *vi.* anublarse, nublarse; oscurecerse.

cloudy [klau-di] *adj.* nublado, nubloso; oscuro; sombrío, melancólico; pardo.

clove [klouv] *n.* (bot.) clavo, *m.*

clover [klo-ver] *n.* trébol, *m.*

cloverleaf [klauver-lif] *n.* hoja de trébol; trébol (en una carretera), *m.*

clown [klaun] *n.* payaso, sa.

club [klab] *n.* círculo, club, *m.;* garrote, *m.;* —, *vi.* unirse, formar un club; —, *vt.* golpear con un garrote; congregar; contribuir.

clue = [klu] **clew.**

clump [klamp] *n.* trozo sin forma; bosquecillo, *m.*

clumsiness [klam-si-nes] *n.* torpeza, desmaña, *f.*

clumsy [klam-si] *adj.* torpe, sin arte; desmañado.

clung [klang] *pretérito y p.p.* del verbo **cling.**

cluster [klas-tar] *n.* racimo, *m.;* manada, *f.;* pelotón, *m.;* —, *vt.* agrupar; —, *vi.* arracimarse; agruparse.

clutch [klach] *n.* (auto.) embrague, *m.;* garra, *f.;* acoplamiento, *m.;* — **pedal,** pedal del embrague; —, *vt.* embragar; empuñar, agarrar.

clutter [kla-tar] *vt.* poner en desorden; **to — up,** alborotar; —, *n.* confusión, *f.*

coach [kouch] *n.* coche, *m.;* carroza, *f ;* vagón, *m.;* entrenador (en un deporte), *m.;* —, *vt.* entrenar, preparar.

coachman [kouch-man] *n.* cochero, *m.*

coagulate [kou-a-guiu-leit] *vt.* coagular, cuajar; —, *vi.* coagularse, cuajarse, espesarse.

coal [koul] *n.* carbón, *m.;* — **dealer,** — **miner,** carbonero, m.; — **mine,** — **pit,** mina de carbón, carbonería, *f.; adj.* carbonero; carbonífero.

coalesce [kou-les] *vi.* juntarse, incorporarse.

coalition [koua-li-shon] *n.* coalición, confederación, *f.*

coarse [kors] *adj.* basto; ordinario; rústico; grueso.

coarseness [kor-se-nes] *n.* tosquedad, grosería, *f.*

coast [koust] *n.* costa, *f.;* litoral, *m.;* —, *adj.* litoral; — **guard,** guardacostas, *m.;* — **line,** litoral, *m.;* costa, *f.;* línea costanera; —, *vi.* costear; ir de bajada (en un vehículo) por impulso propio.

coastal [kous-tal] *adj.* costero,

costanero.

coaster [kous-tar] *n.* piloto, *m.;* buque costanero; —**brake,** freno de bicicleta.

coat [kout] *n.* saco, *m.;* chaqueta, americana, *f.;* abrigo, gabán, *m.;* capote, *m.;* — **of arms,** escudo de armas; — **of paint,** mano de pintura; —, *vt.* cubrir, vestir; bañar.

coating [kou-tin] *n.* revestimiento, *m.;* capa, *f.;* mano (de pintura, etc.), *f.*

coax [kouks] *vt.* instar, rogar con lisonja.

cob [kob] *n.* cisne macho; mazorca de maíz; jaca, *f.*

cobbler [koblar] *n.* zapatero remendón; zapatero, *m.*

cobweb [kob-ueb] *n.* telaraña, *f.;* (fig.) trama, *f.*

cocaine [ko-kein] *n.* cocaína, *f.*

cock [kok] *n.* gallo, *m.;* macho, *m.;* veleta, giraldilla, *f.;* grifo, *m.;* llave, *f.;* —, *vt.* montar (una escopeta); **to — the head,** erguir la cabeza.

cockfight, cockfighting [kok-fait], [kok-fai-tin] *n.* pelea de gallos.

cockpit [kok-pit] *n.* reñidero de gallos; (avi.) casilla o cámara de piloto; cabina, *f.;* (naut.) casilla, *f.*

cockroach [kokrouch] *n.* cucaracha, *f.*

cocktail [kok-teil] *n.* coctel, *m.*

cocoa [kou-kou] *n.* cacao, *m.;* chocolate, *m.*

coconut [ko-ko-nat] *n.* coco, *m.;* — **palm,** cocotero, *m.*

cocoon [ko-kun] *n.* capullo del gusano de seda.

cod [kod] *n.* bacalao, *m.;* merluza, *f.*

coddle [ko-del] *vt.* sancochar (huevos, etc.); acariciar; consentir; mimar, (Mex.) papachar.

code [koud] *n.* código, *m.;* clave, *f.*

codfish [kod-fish] *n.* bacalao, *m.*

coeducational [kou-e-diu-kei-sho-nal] *adj.* coeducativo.

coefficient [kou-i-fi-shient] *n.* coeficiente, *m.*

coerce [kou-ers] *vt.* obligar, forzar.

coercion [kou-ershon] *n.* coerción, *f.*

coexistence [kou-ik-sis-tans] *n.* coexistencia, *f.*

coffee [ko-fi] *n.* café, *m.;* — **break,** pausa en el trabajo para tomar café; — **plantation,** cafetal, *m.;* — **free,** cafeto, café, *m.*

coffeepot [ko-fi-pot] *n.* cafetera, *f.*

coffer [ko-fer] *n.* cofre, *m.,* caja, *f.*

coffin [ko-fin] *n.* féretro, ataúd, *m.;* caja, *f.*

cog [kog] *n.* diente (de rueda), *m.*

cogitate [ko-yi-teit] *vi.* pensar,

meditar.

cognac [kog-nak] *n.* coñac, *m.*

cognate [kog-neit] *adj.* consanguíneo; cognado, de origen
similar.

cogwheel [kog-uil] *n.* rueda den-
tada; rodezno, *m.*

coherence [kou-jia-rans] *n.*
coherencia, conexión, *f.*

coherent [kou-jia-rent] *adj.*
coherente, consistente, lógico.

cohesion [kou-ji-shon] *n.* coherencia, *f.;* cohesión, *f.*

cohesive [kou-ji-siv] *adj.* cohesivo.

cohort [kou-jort] *n.* cohorte, *f.;*
secuaz, partidario, *m.*

coiffure [koi-fiur] *n.* peinado,
tocado, *m.*

coil [koil] *vt.* recoger; enrollar; —
, *n.* (elec.) carrete, *m.;* bobina,
f.; espiral, *f.;* rollo, *m.*

coin [koin] *n.* cuña, *f.;* moneda, *f*
; dinero, *m.;* —, *vt.* acuñar
moneda; falsificar; inventar
(palabras, etc.).

coincide [kouin-said] *vi.* coincidir, concurrir, convenir.

coincidence [kouin-si-dans] *n.*
coincidencia, *f.;* casualidad, *f.*

coke [kouk] *n.* coque, *m.;* (coll.)
coca cola, *f.*

colander [kou-lander] *n.* coladera, *f.;* colador, *m.*

cold [kould] *adj.* frío; indiferente,
insensible; reservado; yerto; —

cream, crema para la cara; —
storage, conservación en cámara frigorífica; — **war,** guerra
fría; **to be** —, hacer frío; tener
frío; —, *n.* frío, *m.;* frialdad, *f.;*
(med.) catarro, resfriado; *m.;* **to
catch** —, constiparse, resfriarse.

cold-blooded [kould-bla-ded] *adj.*
impasible; cruel; en sangre fría.

coldness [kould-nes] *n.* frialdad,
f.; indiferencia, insensibilidad,
apatía, *f.*

coleslaw [kou-lis-loa] *n.* ensalada de col.

colic [ko-lik] *n.* cólico, *m.*

coliseum [ko-li-sium] *n.* coliseo,
anfiteatro, *m.*

colitis [ko-lai-tis] *n.* (med.) colitis, *f.*

collaborate [ko-la-bo-reit] *vt.*
cooperar; colaborar.

collaboration [ko-la-bo-rei-shon]
n. colaboración, *f.;* cooperación, *f.*

collaborator [ko-la-bo-rei-tar] *n.*
colaborador, ra.

collapse [ko-laps] *vi.* desplomar-
se; —, *n.* hundimiento, *m.;*
(med.) colapso, *m.;* derrumbe,
m.

collapsible [ko-lap-si-bol] *adj.*
plegadizo.

collar [ko-lar] *n.* collar, *m.;* collera, *f.;* —, *vt.* agarrar a uno por
el cuello.

collarbone [ko-lar-boun] *n.* clavícula, *f.*

collateral [ko-la-te-ral] *adj.* colateral; indirecto; —, *n.* aval, *m.*, garantía (en un préstamo),

colleague [ko-lig] *n.* colega, *m.* y *f.*, compañero, ra.

collect [ko-lekt] *vt.* recoger, colegir; cobrar; **to** — (taxes, etc.) recaudar (impuestos, etc.).

collection [ko-lek-shon] *n.* colecta, *f.*; colección, *f.*; compilación, *f.*; cobro, *m.*

collective [ko-lek-tiv] *adj.* colectivo, congregado; — **bargaining,** trato colectivo.

collector [ko-lek-tor] *n.* colector, *m.*; agente de cobros; — **of customs,** administrador de aduana.

college [ko-lech] *n.* universidad, *f.*, colegio universitario.

collegiate [ko-li-yieit] *adj.* colegial.

collide [ko-laid] *vi.* chocar, estrellarse.

collie [ko-li] *n.* perro pastor, *m.*

collision [ko-lu-shon] *n.* colisión, *f.*; choque, *m.*, atropello (de automóvil), *m.*

cologne [ko-loun] *n.* agua colonia, agua de Colonia.

colloquial [ko-lo-kial]*adj.* familiar, aceptable en conversación familiar.

colloquialism [ko-lo-kia-lisem] *n.* expresión familiar.

collusion [ko-lu-shon] *n.* colusión, *f.*

colon [kou-lon] *n.* (anat.) colon, *m.*; dos puntos (signo de puntuación).

colonel [ko-lo-nel] *n.* (mil.) coronel, *m.*

colonial [ko-lou-nial] *adj.* colonial.

colonize [ko-lo-nais] *vt.* colonizar.

colony [ko-lo-ni] *n.* colonia, *f.*

color [ko-lor] *n.* color *m.*; pretexto, *m.*; — **blindness,** daltonismo, *m.*; —**s,** *n. pl.* bandera, *f.*; —, *vt.* colorar; paliar; —, *vi.* enrojecerse, ponerse colorado.

color-blind [ko-lor-blaind] *adj.* daltoniano.

colored [ko-lord] *adj.* colorado, pintado, teñido; de raza negra; con prejuicio.

colorful [ko-lor-ful] *adj.* pintoresco, lleno de colorido.

coloring [ko-lo-rin] *n.* colorido, *m.*; colorante, *m.*

colorless [ko-lor-les] *adj.* descolorido, incoloro.

colossal [ko-lo-sal] *adj.* colosal.

colt [koult] *n.* potro, *m.*; muchacho sin juicio.

Columbus [ko-lom-bos] Colón.

column [ko-lum] *n.* columna, *f.*

columnist [ko-lum-nist] *n.* periodista encargado de una sección especial.

coma [kou-ma] *n.* (med.) coma, *f.,* letargo, *m.*

comb [koum] *n.* peine, *m.;* almohaza, *f.;* —, *vt.* peinar; almohazar; cardar (la lana) ; **to— one's hair,** peinarse.

combat [kom-bat] *n.* combate, *m.;* batalla, *f.;* —, *vt. y vi.* combatir; resistir.

combatant [kom-ba-tant] *n.* combatiente, *m. y f.*

combination [kom-bi-nei-shon] *n.* combinación, *f.*

combine [kom-bain] *vt.* combinar; —, *vi.* unirse; —, *n.* (agr.) máquina segadora, máquina trilladora; (coll.) combinación de personas u organizaciones para provecho comercial o político.

combustible [kom-bas-ti-bol] *adj.* combustible, inflamable.

combustion [kom-bas-chun] *n.* combustión, *f.;* incendio, *m.;* agitación violenta; — **chamber,** cámara de combustión.

come [kam] *vi.* venir, acontecer; originar; **to — back,** volver; **to — forward,** avanzar; **to — upon,** encontrarse con; **to — to,** volver en sí.

comeback [kam-bak] *n.* vuelta, *f.;* recobro, *m.;* rehabilitación, *f.;* recobranza, *f.;* réplica mordaz.

comedian [ko-mi-dian] *n.* comediante, *m. y f.,* cómico, ca.

comedy [ko-mi-di] *n.* comedia, *f.;* sainete, *m.*

comet [ko-mit] *n.* cometa, *m.*

comfort [kom-fort] *n.* consuelo, *m.;* comodidad, *f.;* bienestar, *m.;* —, *vt.* confortar; alentar, consolar.

comfortable [kom-for-ta-bol] *adj.* cómodo; consolatorio.

comforter [kom-for-tar] *n.* colcha, *f.;* consolador, ra.

comforting [kom-for-tin] *adj.* confortante, consolador.

comic [ko-mik] *adj.* cómico, burlesco; chistoso; — **opera,** ópera bufa; — **strip,** historieta cómica; **—s,** *n. pl.* historietas cómicas, (Mex.) montos, *m. pl.*

comical [ko-mi-kal] *adj.* chistoso, gracioso, bufo, burlesco.

coming [ka-min] *n.* venida, llegada, *f.;* —, *adj.* venidero, entrante; — **from,** procedente de.

comma [ko-ma] *n.* (gram.) coma, *f.*

command [ko-mand] *vt.* ordenar; mandar; —, *vi.* gobernar; imperar; mandar; —, *n.* orden, *f.,* comando, *m.;* señorío, *m.*

commandant [ko-man-der] *n.* comandante, *m.*

commander [ko-man-dar] *n.* jefe, *m.;* comandante, *m.;* capitán, *m.;* capitán de fragata; — **in**

chief, capitán general, generalísimo, *m.;* **lieutenant —,** capitán
de corbeta.

commandment [ko-mand-mant]
n. mandato, precepto, *m.;*
mandamiento, *m.*

commando [ko-man-dou] *n.*
comando, *m.,* incursión o expedición militar.

commemorate [ko-me-mo-reit]
vt. conmemorar; celebrar.

commemoration [ko-me-mo-reis-
hon] *n.* conmemoración, *f.*

commence [ko-mens] *vt. y vi.*
comenzar.

commencement [ko-mens-ment]
n. principio, *m.;* ejercicios de
graduación.

commend [ko-mend] *vt.* encomendar, encargar; alabar.

commendation [ko-men-dei-
shon] *n.* recomendación, *f.;*
encomio, *m.*

commensurate [ko-men-shu-reit]
adj. conmensurativo, en proporción.

comment [ko-ment] *n.* glosa, *f.;*
comentario, *m.;* —, *vt.* comentar, glosar.

commentary [ko-men-ta-ri] *n.*
comentario, *m.;* interpretación,
f.; glosa, *f.*

commentator [ko-men-tei-tor] *n.*
comentador, ra; (rad. y TV.)
locutor, ra.

commerce [ko-mers] *n.* comer-

cio, tráfico, trato, negocio, *m.;*
chamber of —, cámara de
comercio.

commercial [ko-mer-shal] *adj.*
comercial; —, *n.* comercial,
anuncio, *m.*

commercialize [ko-mer-sha-lais]
vt. comerciar, explotar un
negocio, poner un producto en
el mercado.

commiserate [ko-mi-se-reit] *vt.*
compadecer, tener compasión;
—, *vi.* compadecerse.

commissary [ko-mi-sa-ri] *n.*
comisario, *m.;* comisariato, *m.*

commission [ko-mi-shon] *n.*
comisión, *f.;* patente, *f.;* corre-
taje, *m.;* **out of —,** inutilizado,
gastado; **— merchant,** comisionista, *m.;* —, *vt.* comisionar;
encargar; apoderar. **commissio-
ned officer,** *n.* (mil.) oficial, *m.*

commissioner [ko-mi-sho-nar] *n.*
comisionado, delegado, *m.*

commit [ko-mit] *vt.* cometer;
depositar; encargar; **to — to
memory,** aprender de memoria.

commitment, commital [ko-mit-
ment], [ko-mi-tal] *n.* compromiso, *m.;* comisión, *f.;* (leyes) auto
de prisión.

committee [ko-mi-ti] *n.* comité,
m.; comisión, junta, *f.*

commodity [ko-mo-di-ti] *n.* artículo de consumo; mercadería,
f.

common [ko-mon] *adj.* común, público, general; ordinario; — **carrier,** portador, *m.;* — **law,** ley a fuerza de costumbre; — **people,** pueblo, *m.;* — **pleas,** (leyes) causas ajenas; — **sense,** sentido práctico; — **stock,** acciones comunes u ordinarias; —, *n.* lo usual; **in** —, en común.

commoner [ko-mo-nar] *n.* plebeyo, ya; miembro de la cámara baja (en Inglaterra) .

commonplace [ko-mon-pleis] *n.* lugar común; —, *adj.* trivial, banal.

commonwealth [ko-mon-uelz] *n.* república, *f.;* estado, *m.;* nación, *f.*

commotion [ko-mou-shon] *n.* tumulto, *m.;* perturbación del ánimo.

commune [ko-miun] *vi.* conversar; tener confidencias; comulgar; —, *n.* comuna, *f.,* menor división política de Francia, Italia, etc.; distrito municipal.

communicable [ko-miu-ni-ka-bol] *adj.* comunicable.

communicate [ko-miu-ni-keit] *vt.* comunicar, participar; —, *vi.* comunicarse.

communication [ko-miu-ni-kei-shon] *n.* comunicación, *f.;* participación, *f.;* escrito, *m.*

communicative [ko-miu-ni-ka-tiv] *adj.* comunicativo.

communion [ko-miu-nion] *n.* comunidad, *f.;* comunión, *f.;* **to take** —, comulgar.

communiqué [ko-miu-ni-kei] *n.* comunicación oficial.

communism [ko-miu-ni-sem] *n.* comunismo, *m.*

communist [ko-miu-nist] *n.* comunista, *m. y f.*

community [ko-miu-ni-ti] *n.* comunidad, *f.;* república, *f.;* común, *m.;* colectividad, *f.;* —, *adj.* comunal; — **chest,** caja de la comunidad, fondos benéficos de la comunidad.

commute [ko-miuti] *vt.* conmutar; —, *vi.* viajar diariamente.

commuter [ko-miu-tar] *n.* persona que viaja diariamente de una localidad a otra.

compact [kom-pakt] *adj.* compacto, sólido, denso; — **car,** automóvil pequeño; —, *n.* pacto, convenio, *m.;* neceser, *m.;* polvera, *f.;* —**ly,** *adv.* estrechamente; en pocas palabras.

companion [kom-pa-nion] *n.* compañero, ra; acompañante, *m. y f.*

companionship [kom-pa-nion-ship] *n.* camaradería, *f.;* compañerismo, *m.;* sociedad, compañía, *f.*

company [kom-pa-ni] *n.* compañía, sociedad, *f.;* compañía comercial; **to keep —,** hacer compañía a; tener relaciones con; **to part —** (with), separarse; **— union,** unión de los obreros de una empresa sin otras conexiones.

comparable [kom-pa-ra-bol] *adj.* comparable.

comparative [kom-pa-ra-tiv] *adj.* comparativo.

compare [kom-pear] *vt.* comparar, colacionar; confrontar; **—,** *n.* comparación, *f.;* **beyond —,** sin igual, sin comparación.

comparison [kom-pa-rison] *n.* comparación, *f.;* símil, *m.;* **in — with,** comparado con; **beyond —,** sin comparación, sin igual.

compartment [kom-part-ment] *n.* compartimiento, compartimento, *m.*

compass [kom-pas] *n.* alcance, *m.;* circunferencia, *f.;* compás, *m.;* brújula, *f.;* **—,** *vt.* circundar.

compassion [kom-pa-shon] *n.* compasión, piedad, *f.*

compatibility [kom-pa-te-bi-li-ti] *n.* compatibilidad, *f.*

compatible [kom-pa-ti-bol] *adj.* compatible.

compel [kom-pel] *vt.* compeler, obligar, constreñir.

compensate [kom-pen-seit] *vt.* y *vi.* compensar.

compensation [kom-pen-sei-shon] *n.* compensación, *f.;* resarcimiento, *m.*

compete [kom-pít] *vi.* competir.

competence [kom-pi-tens] *n.* competencia, *f.;* suficiencia, *f.*

competent [kom-pi-tent] *adj.* competente, capaz; adecuado; caracterizado.

competition [kom-pi-ti-shon] *n.* competencia, *f.;* concurso, *m.*

competitive [kom-pe-ti-tiv] *adj.* competidor.

compilation [kom-pi-lei-shon] *n.* compilación, *f.*

compile [kom-pail] *vt.* compilar.

complacence, complacency [kom-plei-sens] *n.* complacencia, *f.;* propia satisfacción.

complacent [kom-plei-sent] *adj.* complaciente, deseoso de servir; satisfecho de sí mismo.

complain [kom-plein] *vi.* quejarse, lamentarse; dolerse.

complaint [kom-pleint] *n.* queja, pena; *f.;* lamento, llanto, quejido, *m.;* reclamación, *f.;* **to file a —,** (leyes) quejarse, poner una queja.

complaisant [kom-plei-sant] *adj.* complaciente, cortés.

complement [kom-pli-ment] *n.* complemento, *m.;* **—,** *vt.* completar, complementar.

complementary [kom-pli-men-ta-ri] *adj.* complementario.

complete [kom-plít] *adj.* completo, cumplido, perfecto; —, *vt.* completar, acabar; llevar a cabo; rematar; **—ly,** *adv.* completamente, a fondo.

completion [kom-plí-shon] *n.* complemento, colmo, *m.*, terminación, *f.;* perfeccionamiento, *m.*

complex [kom-pleks] *adj.* complejo, compuesto; —, *n.* complejo, *m.;* **inferiority —,** complejo de inferioridad.

complexion [kom-plek-shon] *n.* cutis, *m.*, tez, *f.;* aspecto general.

compliance [kom-plaians] *n.* sumisión, condescendencia, *f.;* consentimiento, *m.;* **in — with,** de acuerdo con, accediendo (a sus deseos, etc.).

complicate [kom-pli-keit] *vt.* complicar.

complicated [kom-pli-kei-ted] *adj.* complicado, embrollado.

complicity [kom-pli-si-ti] *n.* complicidad, *f.*

compliment [kom-pli-ment] *n.* cumplido, *m.;* lisonja, *f.;* (coll.) piropo, *m.;* —, *vt.* echar flores; ensalzar, alabar.

complimentary [kom-pli-men-ta-ri] *adj.* ceremonioso; piropero; gratis, de cortesía.

comply [kom-plai] *vi.* cumplir; condescender, conformarse.

component [kom-pou-nent] *adj.* componente.

compose [kom-pous] *vt.* componer; sosegar; concertar, reglar, ordenar; **to — oneself,** serenarse.

composer [kom-pou-sar] *n.* autor, ra; compositor, ra; cajista, *m.* y *f.*

composite [kom-pou-sit] *n.* compuesto, *m.;* mezcla, *f.;* combinación de varias partes.

composition [kom-pou-si-shon] *n.* composición, *f.;* compuesto, *m.*

composure [kom-pou-shar] *n.* calma, *f.;* tranquilidad, *f.;* sangre fría; **to lose one's —,** perder la calma, perder la serenidad.

compound [kom-paund] *vt.* componer, combinar; —, *adj.* compuesto; —, *n.* compuesto, *m.;* (med.) confección, *f*.

comprehend [kom-pri-jend] *vt.* comprender, contener; entender, penetrar.

comprehensible [kom-pri-jen-si-bol] *adj.* comprensible, fácil de comprender, concebible.

comprehension [kom-pri-jen-shon] *n.* comprensión, *f.;* inteligencia, *f.*

compress [kom-pres] *vt.* comprimir, estrechar; —, *n.* cabezal, fomento, *m.*

compression [kom-pre-shon] *n.* compresión, *f.*

comprise [kom-prais] *vt.* comprender; incluir.

compromise [kom-pro-mais] *n.* transacción, *f.*, convenio, *m.*; —, *vi.* transigir.

compulsion [kom-pal-shon] *n.* compulsión, *f.*; apremio, *m.*

compulsive [kom-pal-siv-nes] *adj.* coactivo; obligatorio, compulsivo; —**ly,** *adv.* por fuerza.

compulsory [kom-pal-so-ri] *adj.* obligatorio, compulsivo.

computation [kom-piu-tei-shon] *n.* computación, cuenta, *f.*; cómputo, cálculo, *m.*

compute [kom-piut] *vt.* computar, calcular.

computer [kom-piu-tar] *n.* computadora, *f.*; ordenador, *m.*

comrade [kom-rid] *n.* camarada, *m.* y *f.*; compañero, ra.

comradeship [kom-rid-ship] *n.* camaradería, *f.*; compañerismo intimo.

concave [kon-keiv] *adj.* cóncavo.

conceal [kon-sil] *vt.* ocultar, esconder; —**ed,** *adj.* escondido, oculto; disimulado; secreto.

concede [kon-sid] *vt.* conceder, admitir; —, *vi.* asentir, acceder.

conceited [kon-si-ted] *adj.* afectado, vano, presumido.

conceivable [kon-si-va-bol] *adj.* concebible.

conceive [kon-siv] *vt.* concebir, comprender.

concentrate [kon-sen-treit] *vt.* y *vi.* concentrar, concentrarse.

concentration [kon-sen-trei-shon] *n.* concentración, *f.*; — **camp,** campo de concentración.

concentric, concentrical [kon-sen-trik] *adj.* concéntrico.

concept [kon-sept] *n.* concepto, *m.*

conception [kon-sep-shon] *n.* concepción, *f.*; concepto, *m.*

concern [kon-sern] *vt.* concernir, importar; pertenecer; —, *n.* negocio, *m.*; interés, *m.*; importancia, consecuencia, *f.*

concerning [kon-ser-nin] *prep.* tocante a, respecto a.

concert [kon-sert] *n.* concierto, *m.*; convenio, *m.*; —, *vt.* y *vi.* concertar, concertarse.

concerted [kon-ser-ted] *adj.* concertado, acordado, ajustado.

concession [kon-se-shon] *n.* concesión, cesión, *f.*; privilegio, *m.*

conciliate [kon-si-lieit] *vt.* conciliar; atraer.

conciliation [kon-si-liei-shon] *n.* conciliación, *f.*

concise [kon-sais] *adj.* conciso, sucinto.

conclude [kon-klud] *vt.* concluir; decidir; finalizar, terminar; epilogar.

conclusion [kon-klu-shon] *n.* conclusión, terminación, *f.*; fin, *m.*; clausura, *f.*; consecuencia,

f.

conclusive [kon-klu-siv] *adj.* decisivo, concluyente.

concourse [kon-kors] *n.* concurso, *m.*; reunión, *f.*; multitud, *f.*; gentío, *m.*

concrete [kon-krit] *n.* concreto, *m.*; cemento, *m.*; — **mixer,** mezcladora, *f.*; —, *adj.* concreto; —, *vt.* y *vi.* concretar.

concubine [kon-kiu-bain] *n.* concubina, *f.*

concur [kon-ker] *vi.* convenir, coincidir; acceder.

concussion [kon-ka-shon] *n.* concusión, *f.*

condemn [kon-dem] *vt.* condenar; desaprobar; vituperar.

condemnation [kon-dem-nei-shon] *n.* condenación, *f.*

condensation [kon-den-sei-shon] *n.* condensación, *f.*

condense [kon-dens] *vt.* condensar; comprimir.

condescend [kon-de-send] *vi.* condescender; consentir.

condescending [kon-de-sen-din] *adj.* complaciente, afable.

condescension [kon-de-sen-shon] *n.* condescendencia, *f.*

condiment [kon-di-ment] *n.* condimento, *m.*; salsa, *f.*

condition [kon-di-shon] *n.* situación, condición, *f.*; calidad, *f.*; requisito, *m.*; estado, *m.*; circunstancia, *f.*; **on — that,** con

tal que.

conditional [kon-di-sho-nal] *adj.* condicional, hipotético.

conditioned [kon-di-shond] *adj.* condicionado, acondicionado.

condolence [kon-dou-lens] *n.* pésame, *m.*, condolencia, *f.*

condom [kon-dom] *n.* condón.

condone [kon-doun] *vt.* condonar.

condor [kon-dor] *n.* (orn.) cóndor, *m.*

conduce [kon-dius] *vt.* conducir.

conduct [kon-dakt] *n.* conducta *f.*; manejo, proceder, *m.*; conducción (de tropas), *f.*; porte, *m.*; **safe —,** salvoconducto, *m.*

conduct [kon-dakt] *vt.* conducir, guiar.

conductor [kon-dak-tor] *n.* conductor, *m.*; guía, director, *m.*; conductor (de electricidad) *m.*

conduit [kon-dit] *n.* conducto, *m.*; caño, *m.*, cañería, *f.*

cone [koun] *n.* cono, *m.*; **paper —,** cucurucho, *m.*; **ice-cream —,** barquillo de mantecado, de nieve o de helados.

confederacy [kon-fe-de-ra-si] *n.* confederación, *f.*

confederate [kon-fe-de-rit] *vi.* confederarse; —, *adj.* confederado; —, *n.* confederado, *m.*

confederation [kon-fek-shon] *n.* federación, confederación, *f.*

conference [kon-fe-rens] *n.* conferencia, *f.;* sesión, junta, *f.*

confess [kon-fes] *vt.* y *vi.* confesar, confesarse.

confession [kon-fe-shon] *n.* confesión, *f.*

confessional [kon-fe-sho-nal] *n.* confesionario, *m.*

confessor [kon-fe-sor] *n.* confesor, *m.*

confetti [kon-fe-ti] *n.* confeti, *m.*

confidant, confidante [kon-fident], [kon-fi-dent] *n.* confidente, *m.,* confidenta, *f.*

confide [kon-faid] *vt.* y *vi.* confiar; fiarse.

confidence [kon-fi-dens] *n.* confianza, seguridad, *f.;* confidencia, *f.;* **in strictest —,** con o bajo la mayor reserva.

confident [kon-fi-dent] *adj.* cierto; fiado; seguro; confiado; —, *n.* confidente, *m.* y *f.;* **—ly,** *adv.* con seguridad.

confidential [kon-fi-den-shal] *adj.* confidencial; **—ly,** *adv.* en confianza, confidencialmente.

confiding [kon-fi-din] *adj.* fiel, seguro, confiado.

configuration [kon-fi-guiu-rei-shon] *n.* configuración, *f.*

confine [kon-fain] *n.* confín, límite, *m.;* —, *vt.* limitar; aprisionar; —; vi. confinar.

confinement [kon-fain-ment] *n.* prisión, *f.;* encierro, *m.*

confirm [kon-ferm] *vt.* confirmar; ratificar.

confirmation [kon-fer-mei-shon] *n.* confirmación, *f.;* ratificación, *f.;* prueba, *f.*

confiscate [kon-fis-keit] *vt.* confiscar, decomisar.

conflict [kon-flikt] *n.* conflicto, *m.;* combate, *m.;* pelea, *f.;* —, *vt.* contender; combatir; chocar; estar en conflicto.

conform [kon-form] *vt.* y *vi.* conformar, conformarse.

conformity [kon-for-mist] *n.* conformidad, *f.;* concordia, *f.*

confound [kon-faund] *vt.* turbar, confundir; destruir

confront [kon-front] *vt.* afrontar; confrontar, comparar.

confuse [kon-fius] *vt.* confundir; desordenar.

confused [kon-fiusd] *adj.* confuso, desorientado.

confusion [kon-fiu-shon] *n.* confusión, baraúnda, *f.;* desorden, *m.;* perturbación, *f.;* trápala, *f.;* trastorno, *m.*

congeal [kon-yil] *vt.* y vi. helar, congelar; congelarse.

congenital [kon-ye-ni-tal] *adj.* congénito.

congestion [kon-yes-chon] *n.* congestión, *f.*

conglomerate [kon-glo-me-reit] *vt.* conglomerar; aglomerar;—, *adj.* aglomerado; —, *n.* conglomerado, *m.*

conglomeration [kon-glo-me-rei-shon] *n.* aglomeración, *f.*

congregate [kon-gri-gueit] *vt.* congregar, reunir; —, *vi.* afluir; congregarse.

congregation [kon-gri-guei-shon] *n.* congregación, reunión, *f.*

congress [kon-gres] *n.* congreso, *m.;* conferencia, *f.*

congressional [kon-gre-sho-nal] *adj.* perteneciente o relativo al congreso.

congressman [kon-gres-man] *n.* diputado al congreso, congresista, *m.*

congresswoman [kon-gres-uo-man] *n.* diputada al congreso, congresista, *f.*

congruous [kon-gruos] *adj.* idóneo, congruente, congruo, apto.

conjecture [ko-yek-chuar] *n.* conjetura, suposición, *f.;* —, *vt.* conjeturar; pronosticar.

conjointly [ko-yoint-li] *adv.* conjuntamente, mancomunadamente.

conjugate [ko-yu-geuit] *vt.* (gram.) conjugar.

conjugation [ko-yu-guei-shon] *n.* (gram.) conjugación, *f.*

conjunction [ko-yank-shon] *n.* (gram.) conjunción, *f.;* unión, *f.*

conjure [ko-yuar] *vt.* rogar, pedir con instancia; —, *vi.* conjurar, encantar; hechizar.

connect [ko-nekt] *vt.* juntar, unir, enlazar; relacionar.

connection [ko-nek-shon] *n.* conexión, *f.;* —s, *n. pl.* relaciones, *f. pl.*

connivance [ko-nai-vans] *n.* connivencia, *f.*

connive [ko-naiv] *vi.* confabularse; fingir ignorancia; disimular.

connoisseur [ko-no-sir] *n.* perito, ta, conocedor, ra.

connotation [ko-nou-tei-shon] *n.* connotación, *f.*

connote [ko-nout] *vt.* connotar.

conquer [kon-ker] *vt.* conquistar; vencer.

conqueror [kon-ke-ror] *n.* vencedor, conquistador, *m.*

conquest [kon-kuest] *n.* conquista, *f.*

conscience [kon-sens] *n.* conciencia, *f.;* escrúpulo. *m.*

conscientious [kon-sen-shos] *adj.* concienzudo, escrupuloso; meticuloso; —ly, *adv.* según conciencia, concienzudamente.

conscious [kon-shos] *adj.* sabedor, convencido; consciente; —ly, *adv.* a sabiendas.

consciousness [kon-shos-nes] *n.* conocimiento, sentido, *m.*

conscript [kons-kript] *adj.* reclutado, seleccionado; —, *n.* conscripto, *m.,* recluta de servicio forzoso.

conscription [kons-krip-shon] *n.*

conscripción, *f.*, reclutamiento obligatorio.

consecration [kon-si-krei-shon] *n.* consagración, *f.*

consecutive [kon-se-kiu-tiv] *adj.* consecutivo, consiguiente.

consensus [kon-sen-sus] *n.* consenso, asenso, consentimiento, *m.*; opinión colectiva; consentimiento general.

consent [kon-sent] *n.* consentimiento, asenso, *m.*; aprobación, *f.*; —, *vi.* consentir; aprobar.

consequence [kon-si-kuens] *n.* consecuencia, *f.*; importancia, *f.*; efecto, *m.*

consequent [kon-si-kuet] *adj.* consiguiente.

conservative [kon-ser-va-tiv] *n.* y *adj.* conservador, ra.

conservatory [kon-ser-va-to-ri] *n.* conservatorio, *m.*

conserve [kon-serv] *vt.* conservar, cuidar; hacer conservas; —, *n.* conserva, *f.*

consider [kon-si-dar] *vt.* considerar, examinar; —, *vi.* pensar, deliberar; ponderar; reflexionar.

considerable [kon-si-de-ra-bol] *adj.* considerable; importante; bastante; —**bly,** *adv.* considerablemente.

considerate [kon-si-de-reit] *adj.* considerado, prudente, discre-

to; deferente.

consideration [kon-si-de-reishon] *n.* consideración, *f.*; deliberación, *f.*; importancia, *f.*; valor, mérito, *m.*

considering [kon-si-de-rin] *prep.* en atención a; en vista de; — **that,** en vista de que, considerando que.

consistence, consistency [kon-sis-tens], [kon-sis-ten-si] *n.* consistencia, *f.*

consistent [kon-sis-tent] *adj.* consistente; congruente; conveniente, conforme; sólido, estable.

consolation [kon-so-lei-shon] *n.* consolación, *f.*; consuelo, *m.*

console [kon-soul] *vt.* consolar; —, *n.* consola, *f.*

consolidate [kon-so-li-deit] *vt.* y *vi.* consolidar, consolidarse.

consolidation [kon-so-li-deishon] *n.* consolidación, *f.*

consommé [kon-so-mei] *n.* consomé, caldo, *m.*

consonant [kon-so-nant] *adj.* consonante, conforme; —, *n.* (gram.) consonante, *f.*

conspicuous [kons-pi-kuos] *adj.* conspicuo, aparente; notable; llamativo, sobresaliente; **to be** —, destacarse; —**ly,** *adv.* claramente, insignemente.

conspiracy [kons-pi-ra-si] *n.* conspiración, *f.*; trama, *f.*; complot, *m.;* lío, *m.*

conspirator [kons-pi-ra-tor] *n.* conspirador, ra.

conspire [kons-paiar] *vi.* conspirar, maquinar.

constancy [kons-tan-si] *n.* constancia, perseverancia, persistencia, *f.*

constant [kons-tant] *adj.* constante; seguro, firme; fiel; perseverante.

constellation [kons-te-lei-shon] *n.* constelación, *f.*

consternation [kons-ter-nei-shon] *n.* consternación, *f.;* terror, *m.*

constipation [kons-ti-pei-shon] *n.* estreñimiento, *m.*

constituency [kons-ti-tuen-si] *n.* junta electoral.

constitute [kons-ti-tiut] *vt.* constituir; establecer, diputar.

constitution [kons-ti-tiu-shon] *n.* constitución, *f.;* estado, *m.;* temperamento, *m.;* complexión *f.*

constitutional [kons-ti-tiu-sho-nal] *adj.* constitucional, legal.

constrain [kons-trein] *vt.* constreñir; forzar; restringir.

constraint [kons-treint] *n.* constreñimiento, *m.;* restricción, *f.*

constrict [kons-trikt] *vt.* constreñir, estrechar.

constriction [kons-trik-shon] *n.* constricción, contracción, *f.*

construct [kons-trakt] *vt.* construir, edificar.

construction [kons-trak-shon] *n.* construcción, *f.;* interpretación, *f.*

constructive [kons-trak-tive] *adj.* constructivo, constructor.

construe [kons-tru] *vt.* construir; interpretar.

consul [kon-sul] *n.* cónsul, *m.*

consular [kon-su-lar] *adj.* consular; — **corps,** cuerpo consular.

consulate [kon-su-leit] *n.* consulado, *m.*

consult [kon-sult] *vt.* y *vi.* consultar, consultarse; aconsejar; aconsejarse; — **together,** conferenciar.

consultation [kon-sul-tei-shon] *n.* consulta, deliberación, *f.*

consume [kon-sium] *vt.* consumir; disipar; destruir; desperdiciar; devorar (alimento); —, vi. consumirse.

consumer [kon-siu-mar] *n.* consumidor, ra.

consummate [kon-siu-mit] *vt.* consumar; acabar; —, *adj.* cumplido, consumado.

contact [kon-takt] *n.* contacto, *m.;* — **lenses,** lentes de contacto, pupilentes, *m. pl.;* —, *vt.* y *vi.* tocar; poner en contacto; ponerse en contacto.

contagion [kon-tei-chon] *n.* contagio, *m.;* infección, *f.*

contagious [kon-tei-chos] *adj.* contagioso.

contain [kon-tein] *vt.* contener, comprender; reprimir, refrenar.

container [kon-tei-nar] *n.* envase, *m.*, recipiente, *m.*

contaminate [kon-ta-mi-neit] *vt.* contaminar; corromper.

contemplate [kon-tem-pleit] *vt.* contemplar; —, vi. meditar, pensar.

contemplative [kon-tem-pla-tiv] *adj.* contemplativo.

contemporaneous, contemporary [kon-tem-po-rei-nios], [kon-tem-po-ra-ri] *adj.* contemporáneo.

contempt [kon-tempt] *n.* desprecio, desdén, *m.*

contemptible [kon-temp-ta-bol] *adj.* despreciable, vil.

contemptuous [kon-temp-tuos] *adj.* desdeñoso, insolente.

contend [kon-tend] vi. contender, disputar, afirmar; lidiar; competir.

content [kon-tent] *adj.* contento, satisfecho; —, *vt.* contentar, satisfacer; —, *n.* contento, *m.;* satisfacción, *f.;* **to one's heart's** —, a pedir de boca, a satisfacción perfecta.

content [kon-tent] *n.* contenido, *m.;* sustancia, esencia, significación (de un discurso, etc.), *f.;*

—**s**, *pl.* contenido *m.*

contention [kon-ten-shon] *n.* contención, altercación, *f.;* tema, *f.*

contentment [kon-tent-ment] *n.* contentamiento, placer, *m.*

contest [kon-test] *vt.* contestar, disputar, litigar; —, *n.* concurso, *m.;* competencia, *f.;* disputa, altercación, *f.*

contestant [kon-tes-tant] *adj.* contendiente, litigante; —, *n.* contendiente, litigante, *m.* y *f.;* concursante, *m.* y *f.*

context [kon-tekst] *n.* contexto, *m.;* contextura, *f.*

contiguous [kon-ti-guos-li] *adj.* contiguo, vecino.

continent [kon-ti-nent] *adj.* continente; —**ly,** *adv.* castamente; —, *n.* continente, *m.*

continental [kon-ti-nen-tal] *adj.* continental.

contingency [kon-tin-yens] *n.* contingencia, *f.;* acontecimiento, *m.;* eventualidad, *f.*

continuance [kon-ti-niuans] *n.* continuación, permanencia, *f.;* duración, *f.;* prolongación, *f.*

continuation [kon-ti-niu-ei-shon] *n.* continuación, *f.;* serie, *f.*

continue [kon-ti-niu] *vt.* continuar; —, vi. durar, perseverar, persistir.

continuity [kon-ti-nui-ti] *n.* continuidad, *f.*

continuous [kon-ti-niuos] *adj.* continuo.

contortion [kon-tor-shon] *n.* contorsión, *f.*

contour [kon-tuar] *n.* contorno, *m.; —* **plowing,** cultivo en contorno.

contraband [kon-tra-band] *n.* contrabando, *m.; —, adj.* prohibido, ilegal.

contraceptive [kon-tra-sep-tiv] *adj.* que evita la concepción; —, *n.* contraceptivo, anticonceptivo, *m.*

contract [kon-trakt] *vt.* contraer; abreviar; contratar; —, *vi.* contraerse; —, *n.* contrato, pacto, *m.*

contraction [kon-trak-shon] *n.* contracción, *f.;* abreviatura, *f.*

contradict [kon-tra-dikt] *vt.* contradecir.

contradiction [kon-tra-dik-shon] *n.* contradicción, oposición, *f.*

contradictory [kon-tra-dik-to-ri] *adj.* contradictorio.

contraption [kon-trap-shon] *n.* (coll.) dispositivo, artefacto, *m.*

contrary [kon-tra-ri] *adj.* contrario, opuesto; —, *n.* contrario, ria; **on the —,** al contrario, antes bien; **—rily,** *adv.* contrariamente.

contrast [kon-trast] *n.* contraste, *m.;* oposición, *f.; —, vt.* contrastar, oponer.

contribute [kon-tri-biut] *vt.* contribuir, ayudar.

contribution [kon-tri-biu-shon] *n.* contribución, *f.*

contributor [kon-tri-biu-tor] *n.* contribuidor, ra, contribuyente, *m.* y *f.*

contrite [kon-trait] *adj.* contrito, arrepentido.

contrivance [kon-trai-vans] *n.* designio, *m.;* invención, *f.*

contrive [kon-traiv] *vt.* inventar, trazar, maquinar; manejar; combinar.

control [kon-troul] *n.* control, *m.;* inspección, *f ;* conducción, *f.;* sujeción, *f.;* dirección, *f.,* mando, *m.;* gobierno, *m.; —* **tower,** torre de mando; —, *vt.* controlar, restringir; gobernar; refutar; registrar; criticar; **to — oneself,** contenerse; vencerse.

controller [kon-trou-lar] *n.* contralor, registrador, interventor, *m.*

controversial [kon-tro-ver-shal] *adj.* controvertible, discutible; sujeto a controversia.

controversy [kon-tro-ver-si] *n.* controversia, *f.*

contusion [kon-tiu-shon] *n.* contusión, *f.;* magullamiento, *m.*

conundrum [ko-nan-drom] *n.* adivinanza, *f.;* acertijo, *m.*

convalescence [kon-va-le-sens] *n.* convalecencia, *f.*

convalescent [kon-va-le-sent] *adj.* convaleciente.

convene [kon-vin] *vt.* convocar; juntar, unir; —, vi. convenir, juntarse.

convenience [kon-vi-niens] *n.* conveniencia, comodidad, *f.;* conformidad, *f.;* **at your —,** cuando le sea posible, cuando quiera; **— store,** tienda de conveniencia, *f.*

convenient [kon-vi-nient] *adj.* conveniente, apto, cómodo, propio.

convent [kon-vent] *n.* convento, claustro, monasterio, *m.*

convention [kon-ven-shon] *n.* convención, *f.;* convencionalismo, *m.*

conventional [kon-ven-sho-nal] *adj.* convencional; estipulado; tradicional.

converge [kon-verch] *vi.* convergir.

conversant [kon-ver-sant] *adj.* versado, familiarizado; **— with,** versado en.

conversation [kon-ver-sei-shon] *n.* conversación, plática, *f.;* tertulia, *f.*

conversational [kon-ver-sei-sho-nal] *adj.* de conversación.

converse [kon-vers] vi. conversar, platicar; —, *adj.* inverso; **—ly,** *adv.* a la inversa.

conversion [kon-ver-shon] *n.* conversión, trasmutación, *f.*

convert [kon-vert] *vt.* convertir, trasmutar; reducir; —, *vi.* convertirse; —, convertido, *m.;* catecúmeno, na.

convertible [kon-ver-ti-bol] *adj.* convertible, trasmutable; —, *n.* (auto.) convertible, *m.*

convex [kon-veks] *adj.* convexo.

convey [kon-vei] *vt.* trasportar; trasmitir, trasferir; conducir.

conveyance [kon-ve-yans] *n.* trasporte, *m.;* conducción, *f.;* vehículo, *m.*

conveyer, conveyor [kon-ve-yar] *n.* conductor, trasportador, *m.*

convict [kon-vikt] *vt.* probar la culpabilidad; condenar.

convict [kon-vikt] *n.* reo, convicto, *m.*

conviction [kon-vik-shon] *n.* convicción, *f.;* certidumbre, *f.;* condenación, *f.*

convince [kon-vins] *vt.* convencer, poner en evidencia; persuadir.

convincing [kon-vin-sin] *adj.* convincente, con convicción; **—ly,** *adv.* de una manera convincente.

convocation [kon-vo-kei-shon] *n.* convocación, *f.;* sínodo, *m.*

convoy [kon-voi] *vt.* convoyar; —, *n.* convoy, *m.;* escolta, *f.*

convulse [kon-vals] *vt.* conmover, trastornar.

convulsion [kon-val-shon] *n.* convulsión, *f.;* conmoción, *f.*

convulsive [kon-val-siv] *adj.* convulsivo.

cook [kuk] *n.* cocinero, ra; **pastry —,** repostero, ra; —, *vt.* cocinar, aderezar las viandas;—, vi. cocer, cocinar; guisar.

cookbook [kuk-buk] *n.* libro de cocina.

cooker [ku-kar] *n.* olla para cocinar; **pressure —,** olla a presión; (Mex.) olla express.

cookie [ku-ki] *n.* bollo, *m.;* galleta, galletita, *f.*

cooking [ku-kin] *n.* cocina, *f.;* arte culinario; —, *adj.* relativo a la cocina; **— range,** cocina económica; **— stove,** estufa, *f.,* cocina económica; **— utensils,** batería de cocina.

cool [kul] *adj.* fresco; indiferente; —, *vt.* enfriar, refrescar; **to — off,** aplacarse; refrescarse.

cooler [ku-lar] *n.* enfriadera, *f.;* enfriador, *m.;* (med.) refrigerante, *m.;* (coll.) prisión, cárcel, *f.*

coolness [kul-nes] *n.* fresco, *m.;* frialdad, frescura, *f.;* estolidez, *f.*

coop [kup] *n.* gallinero, *m.;* —, *vt.* enjaular, encarcelar.

cooperate [kou-o-pe-reit] vi. cooperar.

cooperation [kou-o-pe-rei-shon] *n.* cooperación, *f.*

cooperative [kou-o-pe-ra-tiv] *adj.* cooperativo, cooperador; **— apartment,** departamento de condominio.

coordinate [kou-or-di-neit] *vt.* coordinar.

coordination [kou-or-di-nei-shon] *n.* coordinación, *f.*

cop [kop] *n.* (coll.) policía, gendarme, *m.*

cope [koup] *n.* (eccl.) capa pluvial; arco, *m.,* bóveda, *f.;* albardilla, *f.;* —, *vi.* competir, lidiar con.

copious [kou-pios] *adj.* copioso, abundante;**— ly,** *adv.* en abundancia.

copper [ko-par] *n.* cobre, *m.;* cobre (color), *m.;* moneda de cobre; **— sulphate,** sulfato de cobre.

copy [ko-pi] *n.* copia, *f.;* original, *m.;* ejemplar, *m.;* —, *vt.* copiar; imitar.

copyright [ko-pi-rait] *n.* propiedad, derechos (de una obra literaria).

coquette [ko-ket] *n.* coqueta, *f.*

coquettish [ko-ke-tish] *adj.* coquetona, coqueta.

coral [ko-ral] *n.* coral, *m.;* —, *adj.* coralino, de coral; **— reef,** banco de coral.

cord [kord] *n.* cuerda, *f.;* cordel, *m.;* cuerda (medida para leña), *f.;* cordón, pasa-mano, *m.;* —, *vt.* encordelar.

cordial [kor-dial] *adj.* cordial, de corazón, amistoso; —, *n.* cordial (licor), *m.*

corduroy [kor-du-roi] *n.* pana, *f.*

core [kor] *n.* cuesco, *m.;* interior, centro, corazón, *m.;* cogollo, *m.;* núcleo, *m.*

cork [kork] *n.* corcho, *m.;* —, *vt.* tapar con corchos.

corn [korn] *n.* grano, *m.;* callo, *m.;* maíz, *m.;* — **meal,** harina de maíz; **sweet** —, maíz tierno; (Mex.) elote, *m.;* — **popper,** tostador de maíz; —, *vt.* salpresar; salar; granular.

cornea [kor-nia] *n.* (anat.) córnea, *f.*

corner [kor-nar] *n.* ángulo, *m.;* rincón, *m.;* esquina, *f.;* extremidad, *f.;* **to turn the** —, doblar la esquina; —, *vt.* acaparar.

cornered [kor-nerd] *adj.* anguloso; en aprieto.

cornerstone [kor-ner-uais] *n.* piedra angular.

cornice [kor-nis] *n.* cornisa, *f.*

cornstalk [korn-stalk] *n.* tallo de maíz.

cornstarch [korn-starch] *n.* maicena, *f.*

cornucopia [kor-niu-ko-pia] *n.* cornucopia, *f.*

corny [kor-ni] *adj.* (coll.) cursi.

corollary [ko-ro-la-ri] *n.* corola-

rio, *m.*

corona [ko-rou-na] *n.* (arch.) corona, *f.;* (astr.) halo, meteoro luminoso; (biol.) coronilla, *f.*

coronation [ko-ro-nei-shon] *n.* coronación, *f.*

coroner [ko-rou-nar] *n.* oficial que hace la inspección jurídica de los cadáveres.

corporal [kor-po-ral] *n.* (mil.) cabo, *m.;* —, *adj.* corpóreo, corporal; material, físico.

corporate [kor-po-reit] *adj.* formado en cuerpo o en comunidad; colectivo.

corporation [kor-po-rei-shon] *n.* corporación, *f.;* gremio, *m.;* sociedad anónima.

corps [korps] *n.* cuerpo de ejército; regimiento, *m.;* cuerpo, *m.;* **air** —, cuerpo de aviación.

corpse [kerps] *n.* cadáver, *m.*

corpuscular [ker-pus'-kiu-lar] *adj.* corpuscular.

corral [co-rral'] *n.* corral, *m.;* —, *vt.* acorralar.

correct [ker-rect'] *vt.* corregir, reprender, castigar; enmendar, amonestar; rectificar; —, *adj.* correcto, cierto; —**ly,** *adv.* correctamente.

correction [ker-rec'-shun] *n.* corrección, *f.;* castigo, *m.;* enmienda, *f.;* censura, *f.;* remedio, *m.*

correlate [ker'-e-lêt] *vt.* poner en

correlación.

correlation [ker-e-lê'-shun] *n.* correlación, *f.*

correspond [ker-es-pend'] *vi.* corresponder.

correspondence [ker-es-pend'-ens, i] *n.* correspondencia, *f.;* reciprocidad, *f.;* **to carry on the —,** llevar la correspondencia.

correspondent [ker-es-pend'-ent] *adj.* correspondiente; conforme; **—,** *n.* corresponsal, *m.*

corresponding [ker-es-pend'-in] *adj.* correspondiente; similar; congruente; **— secretary,** secretario encargado de la correspondencia.

corridor [ker'-i-dor] *n.* crujía, *f.;* pasillo, corredor, *m.*

corroborate [ker-reb'-o-rêt] *vt.* corroborar.

corrode [ker-rod'] *vt.* corroer.

corrosive [ke-ro'-siv] *adj.* corrosivo.

corrugate [ker-u-geit] *vt.* corrugar, arrugar.

corrugated [ker-u-geitd] *adj.* corrugado, acanalado, ondulado.

corrupt [ker-rupt'] *vt.* corromper; sobornar; infectar; **—,** *vi.* corromperse, pudrirse; **—,** *adj.* corrompido; depravado.

corruptible [ker-rupt-i-bl] *adj.* corruptible.

corruption [ker-rup-tiv] *n.* corrupción, perversión, *f.;* depravación, *f.;* impureza, *f.*

cortex [ker-tecs] *n.* corteza, *f.*

cosmetic [kes-me-tik] *n.* y *adj.* cosmético, *m.*

cosmic [kes-mik]] *adj.* cósmico; **— ray,** rayo cósmico.

cosmopolitan, cosmopolite [kes-mo-pel'-i-tan], [kes-mep'-o-lait] *n.* y *adj.* cosmopolita, *m.* y *f.*

Cossack [ko-sak]] *n.* y *adj.* cosaco, ca.

cost [kost] *n.* coste, costo, precio, *m.;* expensas, *f. pl.;* **at all —s,** a toda costa, a todo trance; **—,** *vi.* costar.

costly [kost-li] *adj.* costoso, suntuoso caro.

costume [kos-tum o kos-tium] *n.* traje, *m.;* ropa, *f.;* disfraz, *m.*

cot [kot] *n.* catre, *m.*

cottage [ko-tacg]] *n.* cabaña, casucha, *f.;* choza, *f.;* **— cheese,** requesón, *m.*

cotton [kotn] *n.* algodón, *m.;* **— flannel,** franela de algodón; **— goods,** tela de algodón; **spun —,** algodón hilado.

cottonseed [kotn-sid] *n.* semilla de algodón; **— oil,** aceite de semilla de algodón.

couch [cauch] *vi.* echarse; acostarse; **—,** *vt.* acostar; extender; esconder; expresar, manifestar; **—,** *n.* cama, *f.;* lecho, *m.;* canapé; sofa, m.

cough [kof] *n.* tos, *f.;* —, *vi.* toser; — **drop,** pastilla para la tos.

could [kud] *pretérito* del verbo **can.**

council [kaun-sil] *n.* concilio, concejo, *m.;* junta, *f.;* sínodo, *m.;* **town** —, cabildo, ayuntamiento, *m.*

councilor, councillor [kaun-si-lor] *n.* concejal, miembro del concejo.

counsel [kaun-sel] *n.* consejo, aviso, *m.;* abogado, *m.*

counselor, counsellor [kaun-se-lor] *n.* consejero, abogado, *m.*

count [kaunt] *vt.* contar, numerar; calcular; **to** — **on,** confiar, depender de; —, *n.* cuenta, *f.;* cálculo, *m.;* conde (título), *m.*

countdown [kaunt-daun] *n.* conteo regresivo.

countenance [kaun-ta-nans] *n.* rostro, *m.;* fisonomía, *f.;* aspecto, *m.;* semblante, *m.;* apoyo, *m.;* talante, *m.;* —, *vt.* proteger, ayudar, favorecer.

counter [kaun-tar] *n.* contador, *m.;* ficha, *f.;* mostrador, tablero, *m.;* **Geiger** —, contador Geiger, *m.;* —,*adv.* al revés; —, *adj.* contrario, adverso.

counteract [kaun-tar-akt] *vt.* contrariar, impedir, estorbar; frustrar.

counterattack [kaun-tar-a-tak] *n.* contraataque, *m.*

counterbalance [kaun-tar-ba-lans] *vt.* contrapesar; igualar; compensar; —, *n.* contrapeso, *m.*

counterclockwise [kaun-tar-klok-uais] *adj.* con movimiento circular a la izquierda.

counterfeit [kaun-ter-fit] *vt.* contrahacer, imitar, falsear.

counterfeiter [kaun-tar-fi-tar] *n.* falsificador, ra (de moneda, etc.).

counterpart [kaun-tar-part] *n.* complemento, *m.;* réplica, *f.;* persona que semeja mucho a otra.

counterpoint [kaun-tar-point] *n.* contrapunto, *m.*

countess [kaun-tes] *n.* condesa, *f.*

countless [kaunt-les] *adj.* innumerable.

country [ken-tri] *n.* país, *m.;* campo, *m.;* campiña, *f.;* región, *f.;* patria, *f.;* —, *adj.* rústico; campestre, rural; — **club,** club campestre; — **house,** casa de campo, granja, *f.*

countryman [ken-tri-man] *n.* paisano, compatriota, *m.*

countryside [ken-tri-said] *n.* campo, *m.,* región rural.

countrywoman [kaun-tri-uo-man] *n.* paisana, compatriota, *f.;* campesina, *f.*

county [kaun-ti] *n.* condado, *m.*

coup [ku] *n.* golpe maestro, golpe repentino; acción brillante; — **de grace,** golpe de gracia; — **d'état,** golpe de Estado.

couple [kapol] *n.* par, *m.;* pareja, *f.;* vínculo, *m.;* —, *vt.* unir, casar; —, vi. juntarse, unirse en un par.

coupling [ka-plin] *n.* acoplamiento, *m.;* unión, junta, *f.;* empalme, *m.;* —**s,** *n. pl.* (rail.) locomotoras acopladas.

coupon [ku-pon] *n.* cupón, talón, *m.*

courage [ka-rich] *n.* coraje, valor, *m.;* **to lose —,** intimidarse; **to take —,** cobrar ánimo.

courageous [ko-rei-chos] *adj.* valeroso, valiente. courier, *n.* correo, mensajero, *m.;* expreso, *m.*

course [kors] *n.* curso, *m.;* carrera, *f.;* camino, *m.;* ruta, *f.;* rumbo, *m.;* plato, *m.;* método, *m.;* entrada, *f ;* servicio, *m.;* asignatura, *f.;* — **(of time),** trascurso (del tiempo), *m.;* **of —,** naturalmente, por supuesto, desde luego; **in due —,** a su debido tiempo.

court [kort] *n.* corte, *f.;* palacio, *m.;* patio, *m.;* cortejo, *m.;* frontón, *m.;* — **of justice,** juzgado, *m.;* tribunal de justicia; —, *vt.* cortejar; solicitar; adular;

requerir, requebrar (una mujer).

courteous [kor-tios] *adj.* cortés; benévolo; caballeresco.

courtesy [ker-ti-si] *n.* cortesía *f.;* benignidad, *f.;* (Mex.) caravana, *f .*

courthouse [kort-jaus] *n.* foro, tribunal, *m.;* palacio de justicia.

court-martial [kort-mar-shal] *n.* (mil.) consejo militar, consejo de guerra.

courtroom [kort-rum] *n.* sala de justicia; tribunal, *m.*

courtship [kort-ship] *n.* cortejo, *m.;* galantería, *f.*

courtyard [kort-yard] *n.* patio, *m.*

cousin [ka-sin] *n.* primo, ma; **first —,** primo hermano, prima hermana.

cove [kav] *n.* (naut.) ensenada, cala, caleta, *f.*

covenant [ka-ve-nant] *n.* contrato, pacto, convenio, *m.;* —, vi. pactar, estipular.

cover [ka-var] *n.* cubierta, *f.;* abrigo, *m.;* pretexto, *m.;* **under separate —,** por separado; — **charge,** precio del cubierto (en un restaurante); —, *vt.* cubrir; tapar; ocultar; proteger; paliar.

covering [ka-ve-rin] *n.* ropa, *f.;* vestido, *m.;* cubierta, *f.*

covet [ka-vert] *vt.* codiciar, desear con ansia.

covetous [ka-vi-tos] *adj.* avariento, sórdido.

cow [kau] *n.* vaca, *f.;* —, *vt.* acobardar, intimidar.

coward [kaued] *n.* cobarde, *m.* y *f.*

cowardice [kaued-is] *n.* cobardía, timidez, *f.*

cowardly [kauedli] *adj.* cobarde.

cowboy [kau-boi] *n.* vaquero, gaucho, *m.*

cowherd [kau-jerd] *n.* vaquero, *m.*

cowhide [kau-jaid] *n.* cuero, *m.;* látigo, *m.*

co-worker [kau-uor-ker] *n.* colaborador, ra, compañero o compañera de trabajo.

coy [koi] *adj.* recatado, modesto; tímido; **—ly,** *adv.* con timidez.

coyote [koi-ou-ti] *n.* coyote, *m.*

cozy [kou-zi] *adj.* cómodo y agradable.

crab [krab] *n.* cangrejo, *m.;* jaiba, *f.;* persona de mal carácter; **— apple,** manzana silvestre.

crabbed, crabby [kra-bid], [krabi] *adj.* áspero, austero, bronco, tosco.

crack [krak] *n.* crujido, *m.;* raja, *f.;* quebraja, *f.;* —, *vt.* hender, rajar; romper; craquear (el petróleo); **to—down,** (coll.) compeler, obligar a obedecer; —, *vi.*

reventar; jactarse; —, *adj.* raro, fino, de superior calidad.

crackdown [krak-daun] *n.* (coll.) acción de aumentar la severidad de regulaciones o restricciones.

cracked [krakt] *adj.* quebrado, rajado; (coll.) demente; estúpido.

cracker [kra-kar] *n.* galleta, *f.;* cohete, *m.*

crackle [krakol] *vi.* crujir, chillar.

crackling [kra-klin] *n.* estallido, crujido, *m.*

cradle [kra-del] *n.* cuna, *f.;* —, *vt.* acunar.

craft [kraft] *n.* arte, *m.;* artificio, *m.;* astucia, *f.*

craftiness [kraf-ti-nes] *n.* astucia, estratagema, *f.*

craftsman [krafts-man] *n.* artífice, artesano, *m.*

crafty [kraf-it] *adj.* astuto, artificioso.

cramp [kramp] *n.* calambre, retortijón de tripas; *vt.* constreñir, apretar.

cranberry [kran-be-ri] *n.* arándano, *m.*

crane [krein] *n.* (orn.) grulla, *f.;* (mech.) grúa, *f.;* pescante, *m.*

cranium [kra-nium] *n.* cráneo, *m.*

crank [krank] *n.* manivela, *f.;* manija, *f.;* (coll.) maniático, ca; —, *vt.* poner en marcha un motor.

cranky [kran-ki] *adj.* malhumorado, excéntrico.

cranny [kra-ni] *n.* grieta, hendidura, *f.*

crash [krash] *vt.* y vi. estallar, rechinar; estrellar, estrellarse; chocar; **to — a party,** (coll.) concurrir a una fiesta sin invitación; —**,** *n.* estallido, fracaso, *m.;* choque, *m.;* —**,** *adj.* de socorro; — **landing,** aterrizaje accidentado o de emergencia.

crate [kreit] *n.* caja para embalar loza, etc.

crater [krei-tar] *n.* cráter, *m.*

crave [kreiv]*vt.* y *vi.* rogar, suplicar; apetecer; pedir; anhelar.

craving [kreiv] *adj.* insaciable, pedigüeño; —**,** *n.* deseo ardiente; antojo, *m.*

crawl [krol] *vi.* arrastrarse; caminar a rastras; —**,** *n.* crawl (en natación), *m.*

crayfish [krei-fish] *n.* cangrejo de río.

crayon [kre-yon] *n.* lápiz, pastel, *m.*

craze [kreis] *n.* locura, demencia, *f.;* antojo, capricho, *m.;* —**,** *vt.* enloquecer; —**,** *vi.* enloquecerse.

crazy [krei-si] *adj.* fatuo, simple; trastornado, loco.

creak [krik] *vi.* crujir, chirriar.

cream [krim] *n.* crema, *f.;* nata,

f.;—**,** crema batida.

creamy [kri-mi] *adj.* cremoso; lleno de nata o crema; parecido a la nata o la crema.

crease [kris] *n.* doblez, pliegue, *m.;* arruga, *f.;* — **resistant,** inarrugable; —**,** *vt.* arrugar, ajar, doblar.

create [kri-eit] *vt.* crear; causar.

creation [kri-ei-shon] *n.* creación, *f.;* obra creada.

creative [kri-ei-tiv] *adj.* creador, con habilidad o facultad para crear.

creator [kri-ei-tor] *n.* criador, ra; **the C—,** el Creador.

creature [kri-char] *n.* criatura, *f.*

credentials [kri-den-shals] *n. pl.* credenciales, *f. pl.*

credibility [kre-di-bi-li-ti] *n.* credibilidad, *f.*

credible [kre-di-bol] *adj.* creíble, verosímil.

credit [kre-dit] *n.* crédito, *m.;* reputación, *f.;* — **balance,** saldo acreedor; **blank —,** carta en blanco; **letter of —,** carta credencial o de crédito; **on —,** a crédito o fiado; —**,** *vt.* creer; fiar, acreditar; **to buy on —,** comprar a crédito; **to — with,** abonar en cuenta.

creditable [kre-di-ta-bol] *adj.* estimable, digno de encomio; — **bly,** *adv.* honorablemente; de manera encomiable.

credit card [kre-dit-kard] *n.* tarjeta de crédito.

creditor [kre-di-tor] *n.* acreedor, ra.

credulous [kre-diu-los] *adj.* crédulo; —ly, *adv.* con credulidad.

creed [krid] *n.* credo, *m.; profesión de fe.

creek [krik] *n.* riachuelo, arroyo, *m.*

creep [krip] *vi.* arrastrar, serpentear; gatear.

creepy [kri-pi] *adj.* pavoroso; que hormiguea.

cremate [kri-meit] *vt.* incinerar cadáveres.

cremation [kri-mei-shon] *n.* cremación, incineración (de cadáveres), *f.*

crescent [kresnt] *adj.* creciente; —, *n.* creciente (fase de la luna), *f.*

crestfallen [krest-fo-len] *adj.* acobardado, abatido de espíritu, decaído.

crevice [kri-vais] *n.* raja, hendidura *f.*

crew [kru] *n.* (naut.) tripulación, *f.*

crib [krib] *n.* pesebre, *m.;* cuna *f.; casucha, f.; (coll.) chuleta, f.; —, vi.* plagiar, hacer chuletas.

cribbage [kri-bich] *n.* variedad de juego de naipes.

cricket [kri-ket] *n.* (zool.) grillo, *m.;* vilorta (juego), *f.;* **field** —,

saltamontes, *m.;* caballeta, *f.*

crime [kraim] *n.* crimen, delito, *m.*

criminal [kri-mi-nal] *adj.* criminal, reo; —, *n.* reo convicto, criminal, *m.* y *f.*

criminology [kri-mi-no-lo-yi] *n.* criminología, *f.*

crimp [krimp] *n.* rizado (de cabello), *m.;* **to put a — in,** (coll.) poner un impedimento; —, *vt.* rizar, encrespar.

crimson [krim-son] *n.* carmesí, *m.;* —, *adj.* carmesí, bermejo.

cringe [krinch] *n.* bajeza, *f.;* servilismo, *m.;* —, *vi.* adular servilmente; encogerse, sobresaltarse.

crinkle [krin-kol] *n.* arruga, *f.;* —, *vt.* serpentear; arrugar.

crisis [krai-sis] *n.* crisis, *f.*

crisp [krisp] *adj.* crespo; frágil, quebradizo; fresco, terso, lozano (aplícase a la lechuga, el apio, etc.); claro, definido; —, *vt.* y *vi.* encrespar; ponerse crespo, rizarse.

crisscross [kris-kros] *adj.* entrelazado; —, *vt.* entrelazar, cruzar.

criterion [kri-te-rion] *n.* criterio, *m.*

critic [kri-tik] *n.* crítico, *m.*

critical [kri-ti-kal] *adj.* crítico; exacto; delicado; —ly, *adv.* en forma crítica.

criticism [kri-ti-si-zem] *n.* crítica, *f.;* censura, *f.*

criticize [kri-ti-sais] *vt.* criticar, censurar; **to give cause to —,** dar que decir.

critique [kri-tik] *n.* critica, *f.;* juicio crítico.

croak [krouk] *vi.* graznar, crascitar; croar.

crochet [krou-shei] *n.* tejido de gancho; —, *vt.* tejer con aguja de gancho.

crock [krok] *n.* cazuela, olla, *f.*

crocodile [kro-ko-dail] *n.* cocodrilo, *m.;* — **tears,** lágrimas de cocodrilo, dolor fingido.

crony [krou-ni] *n.* amigo (o conocido) antiguo; (coll.) compinche, *m.*

crook [kruk] *n.* gancho, *m.;* curva, *f.;* petardista, *m.* y *f.;* ladrón, ona; —, *vt.* encorvar, torcer; — *vi.* encorvarse.

crooked [kru-kid] *adj.* torcido, corvo; perverso; deshonesto, avieso; tortuoso; **to go —,** torcerse, desviarse del camino recto de la virtud.

croon [krun] *vt.* y *vi.* canturrear, cantar con melancolía exagerada.

crop [krop] *n.* cosecha, *f.;* mieses, *f. pl.;* producción, *f.;* buche de ave; cabello cortado corto; —, *vt.* segar, cosechar; cortar, desmochar.

cross [kros] *n.* cruz, *f.;* carga, *f.;* trabajo, *m.;* pena, aflicción, *f.;* tormento, *m.;* —, *adj.* contrario, opuesto, atravesado; enojado; mal humorado; — **reference,** contrarreferencia, comprobación, verificación, *f.;* — **section,** sección trasversal; sección representativa (de una población, etc.); —, *vt.* atravesar, cruzar; **to — off,** barrear; **to — over,** traspasar; — **ly,** *adv.* enojadamente, malhumoradamente.

crossbar, crossbeam [kros-bar] *n.* tranca, *f.;* travesaño, *m.*

crossbeam [kros-bim] *n.* viga trasversal.

crossbreed [kros-brid] *n.* raza cruzada.

crossed [krosd] *adj.* cruzado.

cross-examine [kros-ek-sa-min] *vt.* repreguntar; (fig.) acribillar a preguntas.

cross-eyed [kros-ai] *adj.* bizco, bisojo.

crossing [kro-sin] *n.* (rail.) cruzamiento de dos vías, cruce, *m.;* travesía, *f.;* **street —,** cruce de calle; **grade —,** paso o cruce a nivel.

crossroad [kros-roud] *n.* paso, cruce, *m.;* encrucijada, *f.*

cross-stitch [kros-stich] *n.* punto de cruz; —, *vt.* y *vi.* hacer puntos de cruz.

crossword puzzle [kros-ued-pasol] *n.* crucigrama, rompecabezas, *m.*

crotch [kroch] *n.* gancho, corchete, *m.;* bragadura, *f.;* bifurcación, *f.*

crouch [krouch] *vi.* agacharse, bajarse.

crow [krou] *n.* (orn.) cuervo, *m.;* barra, *f.;* canto del gallo; —, *vi.* cantar el gallo; alardearse.

crowbar [krou-bar] *n.* palanca de hierro; barreta, *f.;* pie de cabra.

crowd [kraud] *n.* tropel, *m.;* turba, muchedumbre, *f.;* multitud, *f.;* — **of people,** gentío, *m.;* —, *vt.* amontonar;—, *vi.* agruparse, amontonarse.

crowded [krau-ded] *adj.* lleno de gente.

crown [kraun] *n.* corona, *f.;* diadema, guirnalda, *f.;* rueda, *f.;* moneda de plata que vale cinco chelines; complemento, colmo, *m.;* —, *vt.* coronar, recompensar; dar cima; cubrir el peón que ha llegado a ser dama (en el juego de damas).

crucial [kru-shal] *adj.* crucial, decisivo, crítico.

crucifix [kru-si-fiks] *n.* crucifijo, *m.*

crucify [kru-si-fai] *vt.* crucificar; atormentar.

crude [krud] *adj.* crudo; inculto; tosco; — **(ore, oil, etc.),** (mineral, petróleo, etc.) bruto.

cruel [kruel] *adj.* cruel, inhumano.

cruelty [kruel-ti] *n.* crueldad, *f.;* barbarie, *f.*

cruise [krus] *n.* crucero, *m.;* viaje, *m.;* travesía, *f.;* excursión, *f.;* —, *vi.* navegar; viajar.

cruiser [kru-ser] *n.* crucero, *m.;* navegante, *m.;* acorazado, *m.*

crumb [kram] *n.* miga, *f.;* brote, *m.;* migaja (de pan, etc.), *f.*

crumble [kram-bel] desmenuzar; — **away,** derrumbarse; —, *vi.* desmigajarse; desmoronarse.

crumple [kram-pol] *vt.* arrugar, rabosear.

crunch [kranch] *vi.* crujir; —, *vt.* cascar con los dientes, mascar haciendo ruido.

crusade [kru-seid] *n.* cruzada, *f.*

crush [krash] *vt.* apretar, oprimir; aplastar, machacar.

crusty [kras-ti] *adj.* costroso; bronco, áspero.

crust [krast] *n.* costra, *f.;* corteza, *f.;* —, *vt.* encostrar; —, *vi.* encostrarse.

crutch [krach] *n.* muleta, *f.*

cry [krai] *vt.* y *vi.* gritar; pregonar; exclamar; llorar; —, *n.* grito, *m.;* llanto, *m.;* clamor, *m.;* **to — out,** dar gritos.

crying [krai-in] *adj.* lloroso; —, *n.* lloro, grito, *m.*

crypt [kript] *n.* cripta, *f.,* bóveda subterránea.

cryptic [krip-tik] *adj.* escondido, secreto.

crystal [kris-tal] *n.* cristal, *m.*

crystalline [kris-ta-lain] *adj.* cristalino; trasparente.

crystallize [kris-ta-lais] *vt.* cristalizar; —, *vi.* cristalizarse.

cub [kab] *n.* cachorro, *m.;* — **reporter,** aprendiz de reportero; — **scout,** cachorro, *m.*

Cuban [kiu-ban] *n. y adj.* cubano, na.

cubbyhole [ka-bi-joul] *n.* casilla, *f.,* casillero, *m.;* cualquier lugar pequeño y encerrado en forma de caverna.

cube [kiub] *n.* cubo, *m.;* **in —s,** cubicado.

cubic, cubical [kiu-bik] *adj.* cúbico.

cuckoo [ku-ku] *n.* cuclillo, cuco, *m.*

cucumber [ku-kam-bar] *n.* pepino, *m.*

cud [kad] *n.* panza, *f.;* primer estómago de los rumiantes; pasto contenido en la panza; **to chew the —,** rumiar; (fig.) reflexionar.

cuddle [kadol] *vt. y vi.* abrazar; acariciarse.

cue [kiu] *n.* cola, *f.;* apunte de comedia; indirecta, *f.;* taco (de billar), *m.*

cuff [kaf] *n.* puño de camisa o de vestido; — **links,** gemelos, *m. pl.,* mancuernillas, *f. pl.*

cul-de-sac [kal-de-sak] *n.* callejón sin salida.

culinary [ka-li-na-ri] *adj.* culinario, de la cocina.

culminate [kal-mi-neit] *vi.* culminar.

culmination [kal-mi-nei-shon] *n.* culminación, *f.*

culprit [kal-prit] *n.* reo, delincuente, *m.;* criminal, *m.*

cult [kalt] *n.* culto, *m.,* devoción, *f.*

cultivate [kal-ti-veit] *vi.* cultivar; mejorar; perfeccionar.

cultivated [kal-ti-vei-tid] *adj.* cultivado, labrado; culto.

cultivation [kal-ti-vei-shon] *n.* cultivación, *f.;* cultivo, *m.*

cultural [kal-chu-ral] *adj.* cultural.

culture [kal-char] *n.* cultura, *f.;* cultivo (de bacterias), *m.;* civilización, *f.*

cumbersome [kam-be-som] *adj.* engorroso, pesado, confuso.

cumulative [kiu-miu-la-tiv] *adj.* cumulativo.

cunning [ka-nin] *adj.* hábil; artificioso, astuto; intrigante; —, *n.* astucia, sutileza, .

cup [kap] *n.* taza, *f.;* (bot.) cáliz, *m.;* —, *vt.* aplicar ventosas; ahuecar en forma de taza.

cupboard [kap-bord] *n.* armario, aparador, *m.,* alacena, *f.;* rinconera, *f.*

cupcake [kap-keik] *n.* pastelito, bizcocho pequeño.

cupola [kiu-po-la] *n.* cúpula, *f.*

cur [ker] *n.* perro de la calle; villano, canalla, *m.*

curative [kiu-ra-tiv] *adj.* curativo; terapéutico.

curator [kiu-ra-tor] *n.* curador, *m.;* guardián, *m.;* curador (de un museo, etc.), *m.*

curb [kerb] *n.* barbada, *f.;* freno, *m.;* restricción, *f.;* orilla de la acera; —, *vt.* refrenar, contener, moderar.

curd [kerd] *n.* cuajada, *f.;* requesón, *m.;* —, *vt.* cuajar, coagular.

curdle [kerdl] *vt.* cuajar, coagular; —, *vi.* cuajarse, coagularse.

cure [kiuar] *n.* remedio, *m.;* curato, *m.;* —, *vt.* curar, sanar; **to — skins,** curar las pieles.

cure-all [kiua-rol] *n.* panacea, *f.*

curfew [ker-fiu] *n.* toque de queda.

curiosity [kiu-ri-o-si-ti] *n.* curiosidad, *f.;* rareza, *f.*

curious [kiu-rios] *adj.* curioso; raro, extraño.

curl [kerl] *n.* rizo de cabello; rizado, *m.;* —, *vt.* rizar, enrizar, enchinar; —, *vi.* rizarse.

curly [ker-li] *adj.* rizado.

currant [ka-rent] *n.* grosella, *f.*

currency [ka-ren-si] *n.* circulación, *f.;* moneda corriente; dinero, *m.;* **national —,** moneda nacional.

current [ka-rent] *adj.* corriente; del día; **— events,** sucesos del día; —, *n.* tendencia, *f.,* curso, *m.;* corriente, *f.;* corriente (eléctrica), *f.;* **—ly,** *adv.* actualmente.

curriculum [ka-ri-kiu-lom] *n.* programa de estudios.

curse [kers] *vt.* maldecir; —, *vi.* imprecar; blasfemar; —, *n.* maldición, *f.;* imprecación, *f.;* reniego, *m.*

cursed [kerst] *adj.* maldito; enfadoso.

cursory [ker-so-ri] *adj.* precipitado, inconsiderado.

curt [kert] *adj.* sucinto; brusco.

curtail [ker-teil] *vt.* cortar; mutilar; rebajar, reducir.

curtain [ker-ten] *n.* cortina, *f.;* telón (en los teatros), *m.*

curtsy [kert-si] *n.* reverencia, *f.,* saludo (de una mujer), *m.,* (Mex.) caravana, *f.;* —, *vt.* y *vi.* hacer una reverencia o caravana.

curvature [ker-va-chuar] *n.* curvatura, *f.*

curve [kerv] *vt.* encorvar; —, *adj.* corvo, torcido; —, *n.* curva, combadura, *f.*

cushion [ku-shion] *n.* cojín, *m.,* almohada, *f.*

custard [kas-tard] *n.* natillas, *f. pl.;* flan, *m.,* crema, *f.*

custodian [kas-to-dian] *n.* custodio, *m.*

custody [kas-to-di] *n.* custodia, *f.;* prisión, *f.;* cuidado, *m.*

custom [kas-tom] *n.* costumbre, *f.;* uso, *m.;* **—s collector,** administrador de aduana; **— duties,** derechos de aduana o arancelarios.

customary [kas-to-ma-ri] *adj.* usual, acostumbrado, ordinario.

customer [kas-to-mar] *n.* parroquiano, *m.;* cliente, *m.* y *f.;* comprador, ra.

custom-free [kas-tom-fri] *adj.* exento de derechos.

customhouse [kas-tom-jaus] *n.* aduana, *f.;* **— declaration,** manifiesto, *m.*

cut [kat] *vt.* cortar; separar; herir; dividir; alzar (los naipes); **to — short,** interrumpir; **—,** *n.* cortadura, *f.;* herida, *f.;* (print.) grabado, *m.;* clisé, *m.*

cute [kiut] *adj.* agradable, atractivo, gracioso; chistoso; (coll.) listo, inteligente.

cuticle [ka-ti-kel] *n.* epidermis, *f.;* lapa, *f.;* cutícula, *f.*

cutlet [kat-lit] *n.* costilla o chuleta para asar.

cutout [kat-aut] *n.* (elec.) desconectador, interruptor, *m.;* (auto.) silenciador, *m.;* recortado, recorte, *m.;* figura para recortar.

cutter [ka-tar] *n.* cortador, ra; (naut.) cúter, *m.*

cybernetics [sai-ba-ne-tiks] *n.* cibernética, *f.*

cycle [sai-kel] *n.* ciclo, *m.*

cyclist [sai-klist] *n.* ciclista, *m.* y *f.*

cyclone [sai-kloun] *n.* ciclón, huracán, *m.*

cylinder [si-lin-dar] *n.* cilindro, *m.;* rollo, *m.;* rodillo, *ni.;* **— head,** culata de cilindro.

cylindric, cylindrical [si-lin-drik] *adj.* cilíndrico.

cymbal [sim-bal] *n.* címbalo, platillo, *m.*

cynic, cynical [si-nik], [si-ni-kal]*adj.* cínico.

cynic [si-nik]*n.* cínico, *m.*

cynicism [si-ni-si-zem] *n.* cinismo, *m.*

cypress [sai-pris] *n.* ciprés, *m.;* **— nut,** piñuela, *f.* cyst, *n.* quiste, *m.;* lobanillo, *m.*

czar [zar] *n.* zar, *m.*

D

dab [dab] *vt.* frotar suavemente con algo blando o mojado; golpear suavemente; —, *n.* pedazo pequeño; salpicadura, *f.;* golpe blando; (ichth.) barbada, *f.*

dabble [da-bol] *vt.* rociar, salpicar; —, *vi.* chapotear; **to — in politics,** meterse en política (en forma superficial).

dachshund [dak-shund] *n.* perro de origen alemán, de cuerpo largo y patas muy cortas.

dad, daddy [dad], [da-di] *n.* papá, *m.*

daffodil [da-fo-dil] *n.* (bot.) narciso, *m.*

dagger [da-gar] *n.* puñal, *m.*

dahlia [da-lia] *n.* (bot.) dalia, *f.*

daily [dei-li] *adj.* diario, cotidiano; — *adv.* diariamente, cada día.

daintiness [dein-ti-nis] *n.* elegancia, *f.;* delicadeza, *f.*

dainty [dein-ti] *adj.* delicado; meticuloso, refinado; —, *n.* bocado exquisito.

dairy [dea-ri] *n.* lechería, quesería, *f.;* — **cattle,** vacas lecheras, vacas de leche.

daisy [dei-si] *n.* (bot.) margarita, maya, *f.*

dam [dam] *n.* madre, *f.* (aplícase especialmente a los animales cuadrúpedos); dique, *m.;* azud, *m.,* presa, *f.;* represa, *f.;* —, *vt.* represar; tapar.

damage [da-mich] *n.* daño, detrimento, *m.;* perjuicio, *m.;* —**s,** *n. pl.* daños y perjuicios, *m. pl.;* — *vt.* dañar.

dame [deim] *n.* dama, señora, *f.;* matrona, *f.*

damn [dam] *vt.* condenar; maldecir; —!, — **it!** *inter j.* ¡maldito sea!

damnable [dam-na-bol] *adj.* condenable; —**bly,** *adv.* de un modo condenable; horriblemente.

damnation [dam-nei-shon] *n.* condenación, maldición, *f.*

damned [damnd] *adj.* condenado.

damp [damp] *adj.* húmedo; —, *n.* humedad, *f.*

dampen [dam-pen] *vt.* humedecer; desanimar, abatir.

dampness [damp-nes] *n.* humedad, *f.*

damsel [dam-sel] *n.* damisela, señorita, *f.*

dance [dans] *n.* danza, *f.;* baile *m.;* — **hall,** salón de baile; —, *vi.* bailar.

dancer [dan-sar] *n.* danzarín, ina, bailarín, ina.

dandelion [dan-di-laion] *n.* (bot.) diente de león, amargón, *m.*

dandruff [dan-druf] *n.* caspa, *f.*

Dane [dein] *n.* danés, esa.

danger [dein-char] *n.* peligro, riesgo, escollo, *m.;* — **zone,** zona de peligro.

dangerous [dein-che-ros] *adj.* peligroso.

dangle [dan-gol] *vi.* fluctuar; estar colgado en el aire; colgar, columpiarse.

Danish [da-nish] *adj.* danés, dinamarqués.

dank [dank] *adj.* húmedo y desagradable.

dapple [dápel] *vt.* abigarrar; —, *adj.* vareteado; rayado; — **gray horse,** caballo rucio rodado.

dare [dear] *vi.* osar, atreverse, arriesgarse; —, *vt.* desafiar, provocar; —, *n.* reto, *m.*

daredevil [dear-de-vil] *n.* temerario, ria; calavera, *m.;* atrevido, da, valeroso, sa, valiente, *m. y f.;* persona que no teme a la muerte, que arriesga su vida.

daring [dea-rin] *n.* osadía, *f.;* — *adj.* osado, temerario; emprendedor.

dark [dark] *adj.* oscuro, opaco; ciego; ignorante, hosco, tétrico; moreno, trigueño; — **horse,** candidato incógnito que se postula en el momento más propicio; — , *n.* oscuridad, *f.;* ignorancia, *f.;* **in the** —, a oscuras.

darken [dar-ken] *vt.* oscurecer; —, *vi.* oscurecerse.

darkness [dark-nes] *n.* oscuridad, *f.;* tinieblas, *f. pl.*

darkroom [dark-rum] *n.* (phot.) cámara oscura, cuarto oscuro.

darling [dar-lin] *n.* predilecto, ta, favorito, ta; —, *adj.* querido, amado.

dart [dart] *n.* dardo, *m.*

dash [dash] *n.* arranque, *m.;* acometida, *f.;* raya, *f* ; donaire, *m.;* — *vt.* arrojar, tirar; chocar, estrellar, batir; **to** — **off,** bosquejar, escribir apresuradamente; **to** — **out,** salir precipitadamente.

dashboard [dash-bord] *n.* guardafango, paralodo, *m.;* tablero de instrumentos.

dashing [da-shin] *adj.* vistoso, brillante.

dastardly [das-tard-li] *adj.* cobarde, vil.

data [dei-ta] *n. pl.* datos, *m. pl;* — **base,** base de datos, *f.*

date [deit] *n.* data, fecha, *f.;* duración, *f.;* cita, *f.;* (bot.) dátil, *m.;* — **line,** límite fijado en el mapa para el cambio de fecha; **newspaper** — **line,** fecha en que se publica un periódico, una revista, etc.; **to —,** hasta la fecha; **out of —,** anticuado, fuera de moda; **under —,** con fecha; **up-to—** muy de moda, en boga; **what is the —?** ¿a cómo estamos? **—,** *vt.* datar; (coll.) **to — (some one),** salir de paseo (con un pretendiente o con una novia).

dated [dei-ted] *adj.* fechado.

daughter [do-tar] *n.* hija, *f.;* **— -in-law,** nuera, *f.*

daunt [dont] *vt.* intimidar, espantar.

dauntless [daunt-les] *adj.* intrépido, arrojado.

dawn [don] *n.* alba, *f.;* albor, *m.;* madrugada, *f.;* **—,** *vi.* amanecer.

day [dei] *n.* día, *m.;* periodo, *m.;* **by —,** de día; **— after tomorrow,** pasado mañana; **— before,** víspera, *f.;* **— by —,** día por día; **— laborer,** jornalero, *m.;* **— letter,** telegrama diurno; **— nursery,** guardería infantil; **— school,** escuela diurna; **— shift,** turno diurno; **— work,** trabajo diurno; **every —,** todos los días; **on the following —,** al otro día; **—s,** *n. pl.* tiempo, *m.;* vida, *f.;* **these —s,** hoy día; **thirty —s' sight,** treinta días vista o fecha.

daybreak [dei-breik] *n.* alba, *f.*

daydream [dei-drim] *n.* ilusión, fantasía, *f.;* ensueño, *m.;* qui-

mera, *f.;* castillos en el aire; **—,** *vi.* soñar despierto, hacerse ilusiones; estar en la luna.

daylight [dei-lait] *n.* día, *m.,* luz del día, luz natural; **— saving time,** hora oficial de verano.

daytime [dei-taim] *n.* tiempo del día.

daze [deis] *vt.* deslumbrar; ofuscar con luz demasiado viva.

dazed [deist] *adj.* aturdido, ofuscado.

dazzle [da-sel] *vt.* deslumbrar, ofuscar.

D.C.: District of Columbia D.C. Distrito de Columbia, E.U.A.

deactivate [di-ak-ti-veit] *vt.* desactivar.

dead [ded] *adj.* muerto, flojo, entorpecido; vacío; inútil; triste; apagado, sin espíritu; despoblado; evaporado; marchito; finado; **— center,** punto muerto; **— end,** callejón sin salida; **— heat,** corrida indecisa; **— letter,** carta no reclamada; **— silence,** silencio profundo; **— weight,** carga onerosa; peso propio de una máquina o vehículo; **the —,** los finados, los muertos; **— reckoning,** estima, *f.,* derrotero estimado.

deaden [de-den] *vt.* amortecer, amortiguar.

deadline [ded-lain] *n.* fecha fijada para la realización de una cosa, como la fecha de tirada de una revista, periódico, etc.

deadlock [ded-lok] *n.* estancamiento, *m.;* paro, *m.;* interrupción, *f.;* desacuerdo, *m.*

deadly [ded-li] *adj.* mortal; terrible, implacable.

deaf [def] *adj.* sordo; — **ears,** orejas de mercader; **to fall on** — **ears,** caer en saco roto.

deafen [de-fen] *vt.* ensordecer.

deaf-mute [def-miut] *n.* sordomudo, da.

deafness [def-nes] *n.* sordera, *f.;* desinclinación al oír.

deal [dil] *n.* negocio, convenio, *m.;* partida, porción, parte, *f.;* (com.) trato, *m.;* negociación, *f.;* mano (en el juego de naipes), *f.;* **square** —, trato equitativo; —, *vt.* distribuir; dar (las cartas); traficar; **to** — **in,** comerciar en; **to** — **with,** tratar de.

dealer [di-lar] *n.* negociante, distribuidor, *m.;* el que da las cartas en el juego de naipes.

dealing [di-lin] *n.* conducta, *f.;* trato, *m.;* tráfico, comercio, *m.;* —**s,** *n. pl.* transacciones, *f. pl.;* relaciones, *f. pl.*

dear [diar] *adj.* predilecto, amado; caro, costoso; querido; —**ly,** *adv.* caramente.

death [dez] *n.* muerte, *f.;* — **penalty,** pena de muerte, pena capital; — **rate,** mortalidad, *f.;*

— **warrant,** sentencia de muerte.

deathbed [dez-bed] *n.* lecho de muerte.

deathlike [dez-laik] *adj.* cadavérico; inmóvil.

deathly [dez-li] *adj.* cadavérico; mortal.

debase [di-beis] *vt.* humillar, envilecer; rebajar, deteriorar.

debate [di-beit] *n.* debate, *m.;* riña, disputa, *f.;* —, *vt.* discutir; ponderar; —, *vi.* deliberar; disputar.

debauch [di-boch] *n.* vida disoluta; exceso, libertinaje, *m.;* —, *vt.* depravar; corromper; —, *vi.* depravarse.

debit [de-bit] *n.* debe, cargo, *m.;* — **balance,** saldo deudor; —, *vt.* (com.) adeudar, cargar en una cuenta, debitar.

debris [de-bri] *n.* despojos, escombros, *m. pl.*

debt [debt] *n.* deuda, *f.;* débito, *m.;* obligación, *f.;* **floating** —, deuda flotante; **public** —, deuda pública; **to run into** —, adeudar, adeudarse, (Mex.) endrogarse.

debtor [deb-tar] *n.* deudor, ra.

debut [dei-bu] *n.* estreno, debut, *m.;* **to make one's** —, debutar.

debutante [dei-bu-tant] *n.* debutante, *f.,* señorita presentada por primera vez en sociedad.

decimeter dm. decímetro.

decade [di-keid] *n.* década, *f.*

decadence [de-ka-dens] *n.* decadencia, *f.*

decadent [de-ka-dent] *adj.* decadente.

decapitate [di-ka-pi-teit] *vt.* decapitar, degollar.

decay [di-kei] *vi.* decaer, descaecer, declinar; degenerar; venir a menos; —, *n.* descaecimiento, *m.;* decadencia, declinación, diminución, *f.;* (dent.) caries, *f.*

deceased [di-sist] *n.* y *adj.* finado, da, fallecido, da, muerto, ta, difunto, ta, extinto, ta.

deceit [di-sit] *n.* engaño, fraude, *m.;* impostura, *f.;* zancadilla, *f.*

deceitful [di-sit-ful] *adj.* fraudulento, engañoso.

deceive [di-siv] *vt.* engañar, defraudar, embaucar.

December [di-sem-bar] *n.* diciembre, *m.*

decency [di-sen-si] *n.* decencia, *f.;* modestia, *f.*

decent [di-sent] *adj.* decente, razonable; propio, conveniente; —ly, *adv.* decentemente.

deception [di-sepshon] *n.* decepción, impostura, *f.;* engaño, *m.;* trapisonda, *f.*

deceptive [di-sep-tiv] *adj.* falso, engañoso.

decide [di-said] *vt.* y *vi.* decidir, determinar, resolver, juzgar;

decretar.

deciduous [di-si-duos] *adj.* caedizo; temporáneo.

decimal [de-si-mal] *adj.* decimal; — **point,** punto decimal; — **fraction,** fracción decimal.

decipher [di-sai-far] *vt.* descifrar.

decision [di-si-shon] *n.* decisión, determinación, resolución, *f.*

decisive [di-sai-siv] *adj.* decisivo, terminante; —ly, *adv.* decisivamente.

deck [dek] *n.* (naut.) bordo, *m.,* cubierta, *f.;* baraja de naipes; — **chair,** silla de cubierta; — **hand,** marinero, estibador, *m.;* —, *vt.* adornar.

declaration [de-kla-rei-shon] *n.* declaración, manifestación, *f.;* explicación, *f.*

declare [di-klear] *vt.* declarar, manifestar.

decline [di-klain] *vt.* (gram.) declinar; rehusar; —, *vi.* decaer, desmejorar, venir a menos; inclinarse; —, *n.* declinación, *f.;* decadencia, *f.;* declive, *m.;* ocaso, *m.*

decode [di-koud] *vt.* descifrar (un cable, un escrito, etc.).

decompose [di-kom-pous] *vt.* descomponer; —, *vi.* pudrirse, descomponerse.

decorate [de-ko-reit] *vt.* decorar, adornar; condecorar.

decorator [de-ko-rei-tor] *n.* decorador, ra.

decorum [de-ko-rum] *n.* decoro, garbo, *m.;* decencia, *f.;* conveniencia, *f ;* pudor, *m.*

decoy [di-koi] *vt.* atraer (algún pájaro); embaucar, engañar; —, *n.* seducción, *f.;* reclamo, *m.;* lazo, ardid, *m.*

decrease [di-kris] *vt.* disminuir, reducir, minorar; —, *vi.* menguar; —, *n.* disminución, *f.*

decree [di-kri] *n.* decreto, edicto, *m.;* —, *vt.* decretar, ordenar.

decrepit [di-kre-pit] *adj.* decrépito.

dedicate [de-di-keit] *vt.* dedicar; consagrar.

dedication [de-di-kei-shon] *n.* dedicación, *f.;* dedicatoria, *f.*

deduce [di-dius] *vt.* deducir; derivar; inferir.

deduct [di-dakt] *vt.* deducir, sustraer.

deduction [di-dak-shon] *n.* deducción, rebaja, *f.;* descuento, *m.*

deed [did] *n.* acción, *f.;* hecho, *m.;* hazaña, *f.;* (law) escritura, *f.*

deem [dim] *vi.* juzgar, pensar, estimar.

deep [dip] *adj.* profundo; sagaz; grave; oscuro; taciturno; subido (aplícase al color); intenso; — **seated,** arraigado, profundo; **the —,** *n.* el piélago, la mar.

deepen [di-pen] *vt.* y *vi.* profundizar; oscurecer; intensificar.

deer [diar] *n. sing.* y *pl.* ciervo(s), venado(s), *m.*

deface [di-feis] *vt.* borrar, destruir; desfigurar, afear.

defame [di-feim] *vt.* difamar; calumniar.

default [di-folt] *n.* delito de omisión; morosidad en el pago de cuentas; defecto, *m.,* falta, *f.;* **to lose by —,** perder por ausencia, por no presentarse (a un torneo, a un juzgado, etc.); —, *vt.* y *vi.* faltar, delinquir.

defeat [di-fit] *n.* derrota, *f.;* vencimiento, *m.;* —, *vt.* derrotar; frustrar.

defeatist [di-fi-tist] *n.* pesimista, *m.* y *f.;* derrotista, abandonista, *m.* y *f.*

defect [di-fekt] *n.* defecto, *m.;* falta, *f.*

defection [di-fek-shon] *n.* defección, *f.;* fracaso, malogro, *m.*

defective [di-fek-tiv] *adj.* defectuoso, imperfecto.

defend [di-fend] *vt.* defender; proteger.

defendant [di-fen-dant] *adj.* defensivo; —, *n.* demandado, da, acusado, da.

defender [di-fen-dar] *n.* defensor, abogado, *m.*

defense [di-fens] *n.* defensa, *f.;* protección, *f.;* amparo, apoyo, sostén, *m.*

defenseless [di-fens-les-nes] *adj.* indefenso; impotente.

defensive [di-fen-siv] *adj.* defensivo; —**ly,** *adv.* de un modo defensivo.

defer [di-far] *vt.* diferir, retardar; posponer; postergar; —, *vi.* deferir.

deference [di-fe-rens] *n.* deferencia, *f.;* respeto, *m.;* consideración, *f.;* **in — to,** por consideración a.

deferential [de-fe-ren-shal] *adj.* respetuoso.

defiance [di-faians] *n.* desafío, *m.;* **in — of,** a despecho de.

deficiency [di-fi-shen-si] *n.* defecto, *m.;* imperfección, *f.;* falta, *f ;* insolvencia, *f.;* deficiencia, *f.*

deficient [di-fi-shent] *adj.* deficiente, pobre.

deficit [de-fi-sit] *n.* déficit, *m.*

defile [di-fail] *n.* desfiladero, *m.;* —, *vt.* corromper; deshonrar; ensuciar; —, *vi.* desfilar.

define [di-fain] *vt.* definir; limitar; determinar.

definite [de-fi-nit] *adj.* definido, exacto, preciso, limitado; cierto; concreto.

definition [de-fi-ni-shon] *n.* definición, *f.*

deflatable [di-flei-tabo] *adj.* desinflable.

deflate [di-fleit] *vt.* desinflar.

deflation [di-flei-shon] *n.* desinflación, *f.*

deflect [di-flekt] *vi.* desviarse; ladearse.

deform [di-form] *vt.* deformar, desfigurar.

deformity [di-for-mi-ti] *n.* deformidad, *f.*

defraud [di-frod] *vt.* defraudar frustrar.

defrost [di-frost] *vt.* descongelar, deshelar.

deft [deft] *adj.* despierto, despejado, diestro; —**ly,** *adv.* con ingenio y viveza.

defunct [di-fankt] *adj.* difunto, muerto; —, *n.* difunto, ta.

defy [di-fai] *vt.* desafiar, retar; despreciar; desdeñar.

degenerate [di-ye-ne-reit] *vi.* **degenerar;** —, *adj.* degenerado.

degrade [di-greid] *vt.* degradar; deshonrar, envilecer.

degree [di-gri] *n.* grado, *m.;* rango, *m.;* condición, *f.;* título universitario; **by —s,** gradualmente.

dehydrate [di-jai-dreit] *vt.* deshidratar.

deify [di-i-fai] *vt.* deificar; divinizar.

deign [dein] *vi.* dignarse; condescender.

deity [di-i-ti] *n.* deidad, divinidad, *f.*

deject [di-yekt] *vt.* abatir, desanimar.

dejected [di-yek-tid] *adj.* abatido.

dejection [di-yek-shon] *n.* decaimiento, *m.;* tristeza, aflicción, *f.;* (med.) evacuación, *f.*

delay [di-lei] *vt.* diferir; retardar; postergar; — *vi.* demorar; —, *n.* demora, *f.;* retardo, *m.;* retraso, *m.*

delectable [di-lek-ta-bol] *adj.* deleitoso, deleitable.

delegate [di-lek-ta-bol] *vt.* delegar, diputar; —, *n.* delegado, da, diputado, da.

delegation [de-le-guei-shon] *n.* delegación, diputación, comisión, *f.*

delete [di-lit] *vt.* suprimir, tachar.

deliberate [di-li-be-reit] *vt.* deliberar, considerar; —, *adj.* cauto; avisado, pensado, premeditado; —**ly**, *adv.* con premeditación, deliberadamente.

deliberation [di-li-be-rei-shon] *n.* deliberación, circunspección, *f.;* reflexión, *f.;* consulta, *f.*

delicacy [di-li-ka-si] *n.* delicadeza, *f.;* fragilidad, *f.;* escrupulosidad, *f.;* manjar, *m.*

delicate [de-li-keit] *adj.* delicado; exquisito; tierno; escrupuloso; —**ly**, *adv.* delicadamente.

delicious [di-li-shos] *adj.* delicioso; sabroso, exquisito.

delight [di-lait] *n.* delicia, *f.;* deleite, *m.;* placer, gozo, encanto, *m.;* **to take — in,** tener gusto en, estar encantado de; —, *vt.* deleitar; regocijar; —, *vi.* deleitarse.

delighted [di-lai-ted] *adj.* complacido, gozoso.

delightful [di-lait-ful] *adj.* delicioso; deleitable.

delineate [de-li-nieit] *vt.* delinear, diseñar.

delinquency [di-lin-kuen-si] *n.* delito, *m.;* culpa, *f.;* delincuencia, *f.;* **juvenile —,** delincuencia juvenil.

delinquent [di-lin-kuent] *n.* delincuente, *m.* y *f.*

delirious [di-li-rios] *adj.* desvariado; **to be —,** delirar.

delirium [di-li-riom] *n.* delirio, *m.;* **— tremens,** delírium tremens, *m.*

deliver [di-li-var] *vt.* entregar; dar; rendir; libertar; recitar, relatar; partear.

deliverance [di-li-ve-rans] *n.* libramiento, *m.;* salvación, *f.*

delivery [di-li-ve-ri] *n.* entrega, *f.;* liberación *f.;* alumbramiento, parto, *m.;* **general —** lista de correos, entrega general; **special —,** entrega inmediata.

delta [del-ta] *n.* delta, *f.*

delude *v*[di-lud] *t.* engañar, alucinar.

deluge [di-luch] *n.* inundación, *f.;* diluvio, *m.;* —, *vt.* inundar.

delusion [di-liu-shon] *n.* engaño, *m.;* ilusión, *f.*

delve [delv] *vt.* cavar; penetrar; sondear en busca de información.

demagogue [de-ma-gog] *n.* demagogo, *m.*

demand [di-mand] *n.* demanda, *f.;* petición jurídica (de una deuda); venta continuada; — **(for merchandise),** consumo (de mercancías), *m.;* —, *vt.* demandar, reclamar, pedir, requerir, exigir.

demeanor [di-mi-nor] *n.* porte, *m.;* conducta, *f.;* comportamiento, *m.;* **proper** —, corrección, *f.*

demented [di-men-tid] *adj.* demente, loco.

demerit [di-me-rit] *vt.* desmerecer.

demise [di-mais] *vt.* legar, dejar en testamento; ceder, arrendar; —, *n.* muerte, *f.;* óbito, *m.;* trasmisión de la corona por abdicación o muerte.

demobilize [di-mou-bi-lais] *vt.* desmovilizar.

democracy [de-mo-kra-si] *n.* democracia, *f.*

democrat [de-mo-krat] *n.* demócrata, *m.* y *f.*

democratic [de-mo-kra-tik] *adj.*
democrático, demócrata.

demolish [di-mo-lish] *vt.* demoler, arruinar; arrasar; batir.

demolition [di-mo-li-shon] *n.* demolición, *f* ; derribo, *m.;* — **bomb,** bomba de demolición.

demon [di-mon] *n.* demonio, diablo, *m* .

demonstrate [di-mons-treit] *vt.* demostrar, probar.

demonstration [de-mons-treit] *n.* demostración, *f.;* manifestación, *f.*

demonstrative [di-mons-tra-tiv] *adj.* demostrativo; expresivo; — **ly,** *adv.* demostrativamente.

demonstrator [de-mons-trei-tr] *n.* demostrador, ra.

demoralize [di-mo-ra-lais] *vt.* desmoralizar.

demote [di-mout] *vt.* degradar, rebajar en clase o en grado.

demotion [di-mou-shon] *n.* (mil.) degradación, *f.;* descenso de rango, categoría o empleo.

demure [di-miuar] *adj.* reservado; decoroso; grave, serio; —**ly,** *adv.* modestamente.

den [den] *n.* caverna, *f.;* antro, *m.;* estudio, *m.,* habitación para lectura o descanso.

deniable [di-naia-bol] *adj.* negable.

denial [di-naial] *n.* denegación, *f..*

denim [de-nim] *n.* mezclilla, *f* .,

tela de algodón basta y fuerte.

Denmark [de-mark] Dinamarca, f.

denomination [di-no-mi-nei-shon] n. denominación, f.; título, nombre, apelativo, m.

denominational [di-no-mi] adj. sectario.

denominator [di-no-mi-nei-tor] n. (math.) denominador, m.

denote [di-nout] vt. denotar, indicar.

denounce [di-nauns] vt. denunciar.

dense [dens] adj. denso, espeso; cerrado, estúpido; impenetrable.

density [den-si-ti] n. densidad, solidez, f.

dent [dent] n. abolladura, f.; mella, f.; —, vt. abollar.

dental [den-tal] adj. dental; — **clinic**, clínica dental; n. dental, f.

dentist [den-tist] n. dentista, m. y f.

dentistry [den-tis-tri] n. dentistería, f.

denture [den-char] n. dentadura postiza.

denunciation [di-nan-si-ei-shon] n. denunciación, f.

deny [di-nai] vt. negar, rehusar; renunciar; abjurar.

deodorant [di-ou-do-rant] n. y adj. desodorante, m.

deodorize [di-ou-do-rais] vt. quitar o disipar el mal olor (de algo).

depart [di-part] vi. partir; irse, salir; morir; desistir.

department [di-part-ment] n. departamento, m.; — **store**, bazar, m.; tienda dividida en secciones o departamentos.

departure [di-par-char] n. partida, salida, f.; desviación, f.

depend [di-pend] vi. depender; **it —s**, según y conforme, depende; **to — on, to — upon**, confiar en, contar con.

dependable [di-pen-da-bol] adj. digno de confianza.

dependence [di-pen-dans] n. dependencia, confianza, f.

dependency [di-pen-dan-si] n. dependencia, f.

dependent [di-pend] n. dependiente, m. y f., persona que depende de otra para su manutención; —, adj. dependiente, cifrado; — **upon**, cifrado en.

depict [di-pikt] vt. pintar, retratar; describir.

deplete [di-plit] vt. agotar, vaciar.

deplorable [di-plo-ra-bol] adj. deplorable, lamentable.

deplore [di-plor] vt. deplorar, lamentar.

deport [di-port] vt. deportar.

depose [di-pous] *vt.* deponer; destronar; testificar; **to — upon oath,** declarar bajo juramento.

deposit [di-po-sit] *vt.* depositar; **—,** *n.* depósito, *m.*

deposition [di-po-si-shon] *n.* deposición, *f.,* testimonio, *m.;* destitución, *f.*

depot [de-pau] *n.* depósito, almacén, *m.;* (rail.) estación, *f.,* paradero, *m.*

deprave [di-preiv] *vt.* depravar, corromper.

depravity [di-pra-vi-ti] *n.* depravación, *f.*

deprecate [de-pri-keit] *vt.* deprecar.

depreciate [di-pri-shieit] *vt.* depreciar.

depreciation [di-pri-shiei-shon] *n.* descrédito, *m.;* desestimación, *f.;* depreciación, *f.*

depress [di-pres] *vt.* deprimir, humillar.

depressed [di-prest] *adj.* desgraciado, deprimido; — (in spirit), descorazonado.

depression [di-pre-shon] *n.* depresión, *f.;* abatimiento, *m.;* contracción económica.

deprive [di-praiv] *vt.* privar, despojar, **to — of,** quitar.

depth [depz] *n.* profundidad, *f.;* abismo, *m.;* (fig.) seriedad, *f.;* oscuridad, *f.;* — **bomb,** bomba de profundidad; — **charge,** carga de profundidad.

deputy [de-piu-ti] *n.* diputado, delegado, *m.;* lugarteniente, *m.;* comisario, *m.*

derail [di-reil] *vt.* descarrilar.

derange [di-reinch] *vt.* desarreglar, desordenar; tras-tornar, volver loco.

derelict [de-ri-likt] *adj.* abandonado; infiel; descuidado; **—,** *n.* (naut.) derrelicto, *m.;* paria, *m.* y *f.*

derivation [de-ri-vei-shon] *n.* derivación, *f.*

derivative *n.* (gram.) derivado, *m.*

derive [di-raiv] *vt.* derivar; sacar; **—,** *vi.* derivarse, proceder.

dermatologist [der-ma-to-lo-yist] *n.* dermatólogo, *m.*

dermatology [der-ma-to-lo-yi] *n.* dermatología, *f.*

dermis *n.* (anat.) dermis, *f.,* cutis, *m.*

derogatory [di-ro-ga-to-ri] *adj.* derogatorio; despectivo.

descend [di-send] *vi.* descender.

descendant [di-send] *n.* vástago, *m.,* descendiente, *m.* y *f.*

descent [di-sent] *n.* descenso, *m.;* pendiente, *f.;* invasión, *f.;* descendencia, posteridad, *f.*

describe [dis-kraib] *vt.* describir, delinear; calificar; explicar.

description [dis-krip-shon] *n.* descripción, *f.;* **brief —,** reseña,

f.

descriptive [dis-krip-tiv] *adj.* descriptivo.

desecrate [de-si-kreit] *vt.* profanar.

desegregate [di-se-gre-geit] *vt.* integrar, suprimir la segregación (de razas).

desensitize [di-sen-sa-tais] *vt.* insensibilizar; (phot.) hacer insensible a la luz.

desert [di-sert] *n.* desierto, *m.*

desert [di-sert] *n.* mérito, *m.*; merecimiento, *m.*; —, *vt.* abandonar; —, *vi.* (mil.) desertar.

deserter [di-ser-tar] *n.* desertor, *m.*

desertion [di-ser-shon] *n.* deserción, *f.*

deserve [di-serv] *vt.* merecer; ser digno.

deserving [di-ser-vin] *adj.* meritorio; merecedor; **to be** —, valer, merecer.

design [di-sain] *vt.* designar, proyectar; tramar; diseñar; —, *n.* designio, intento, *m.*; diseño, plan, *m.*; dibujo, *m.*

designate [di-sai-nit] *vt.* designar; apuntar, señalar; distinguir.

designation [di-sai-nei-shon] *n.* designación, *f.*

designer [di-sai-nar] *n.* dibujante, proyectista, *m.* y *f.*; diseñador, ra; intrigante, *m.* y *f.*

desirability [di-sai-ra-bi-li-ti] *n.* ansia, *f.*; conveniencia, *f.*

desirable [di-saia-ra-bol] *adj.* deseable.

desire [di-saiar] *n.* deseo, *m.*; apetencia, *f.*; —, *vt.* desear, apetecer, querer, pedir.

desirous [di-saia-ros] *adj.* deseoso, ansioso.

desist [di-sist] *vi.* desistir.

desk [desk] *n.* escritorio, *m.*; papelera, *f.*; pupitre, *m.*; bufete, *m.*

desolation [de-so-li-shon] *n.* desolación, ruina, destrucción, *f.*

despair [dis-pear] *n.* desesperación, *f.*; —, *vi.* desesperar.

despairing [dis-pea-rin] *adj.* desesperado, sin esperanza.

desperate [des-pe-reit] *adj.* desesperado; furioso.

desperation [des-pa-rei-shon] *n.* desesperación, *f.*

despicable [des-pi-ka-bol] *adj.* vil, despreciable.

despise [des-pais] *vt.* despreciar; desdeñar. **despite**, *n.* despecho, *m.*;

despoil [des-poil] *vt.* despojar; privar.

despondent [des-pon-dent] *adj.* abatido, desalentado, desesperado, desanimado.

despot [des-pot] *n.* déspota, *m.* y *f.*

despotism [des-po-tísem] *n.* despotismo, *m.*

dessert [di-sert] *n.* postre, *m.*

destination [des-ti-nei-shon] *n.* destino, paradero, *m.*

destine [des-tin] *vt.* destinar, dedicar.

destiny [des-ti-ni] *n.* destino, sino, *m.*; suerte, *f.*

destitute [des-ti-tiut] *adj.* carente; en extrema necesidad.

destitution [des-ti-tiu-shon] *n.* destitución, privación, *f.*; abandono, *m.*

destroy [dis-troi] *vt.* destruir, arruinar; hacer pedazos.

destroyer [dis-troiar] *n.* destructor, ra; (naut.) destructor, *m.*, barco de guerra.

destruction [dis-trak-shon] *n.* destrucción, ruina, *f.*

destructive [dis-trak-tiv] *adj.* destructivo, ruinoso.

detach [di-tach] *vt.* separar, desprender; (mil.) destacar.

detachable [di-ta-cha-bol] *adj.* desmontable.

detail [di-teil] *n.* detalle, *m.*; particularidad, *f.*; circunstancia, *f.*; (mil.) destacamento, *m.*; **in —,** al por menor; detalladamente; **to go into —,** menudear; **—,** *vt.* detallar; referir con pormenores.

detain [di-tein] *vt.* retener, detener; impedir. detect, *vt.* descu-

brir; discernir.

detective [di-tek-tiv] *n.* detective, *m.*; **— story,** novela policiaca.

detector [di-tek-tor] *n.* descubridor, ra; detector, ra; indicador, *m.*

detention [de-ten-shon] *n.* detención, retención, *f.*; cautividad, *f.*; cautiverio, m.

deter [di-tar] *vt.* desanimar; disuadir.

detergent [di-ter-yent] *n.* y *adj.* detergente, *m.* deteriorate, *vt.* deteriorar.

deterioration [di-tia-rio-rei-shon] *n.* deterioración, *f.*, deterioro, *m.*

determination [di-ter-mi-nei-shon] *n.* determinación, *f.*; decisión, resolución, *f.*

determine [di-ter-min] *vt.* determinar, decidir; **—,** *vi.* decidir, resolver; **to be —d,** proponerse.

deterrent [di-te-rent] *adj.* disuasivo, desanimador; **—,** *n.* lo que desanima o disuade.

detest [di-test] *vt.* detestar, aborrecer.

detestable [di-tes-ta-bol] *adj.* detestable, abominable.

dethrone [di-zroun] *vt.* destronar.

detonation [de-to-nei-shon] *n.* detonación, fulminación, *f.*

detour [di-tuar] *n.* rodeo, *m.*; desvío, *m.*; desviación, *f.*; vuel-

ta, *f.;* —, *vt.* desviar (el tránsito) .

detract [di-trakt] *vt.* detractar,
retirar; disminuir; —, *vi.* denigrar.

detriment [de-tri-ment] *n.* detrimento, daño, perjuicio, *m.*

detrimental [de-tri-men-tal] *adj.*
perjudicial.

devaluate [de-vas-teit] *vt.* depreciar, rebajar el valor.

devastate [de-vas-teit] *vt.* devastar; robar.

devastation [de-vas-tei-shon] *n.*
devastación, ruina, *f.*

develop [di-ve-lop] *vt.* desenvolver; desarrollar; revelar (una
fotografía); —, *vi.* desarrollarse.

development [di-ve-lop-ment] *n.*
desarrollo, *m.*

deviate [di-vi-eit] *vi.* desviarse.

deviation [di-vi-ei-shon] *n.* desvío, *m.;* desviación, *f.*

device [di-vais] *n.* invento, *m.;*
aparato, mecanismo, artefacto,
m.; plan, ardid, *m.;* lema, *m.;*
proyecto, *m.;* artificio, *m.*

devil [de-vil] *n.* diablo, demonio,
m.

devious [di-vios] *adj.* desviado;
tortuoso.

devise [di-vais] *vt.* trazar; inventar; idear; legar; —, *n.* legado,
m.; donación testamentaria.

devitalize [di-vai-ta-lais] *vt.* restar vitalidad.

devoid [di-void] *adj.* vacío; carente.

devote [di-vout] *vt.* dedicar; consagrar; destinar; — **oneself,**
consagrarse.

devotion [di-vou-shon] *n.* devoción, *f.;* oración, *f.;* rezo, *m.;*
afición, *f.;* dedicación, *f.*

devour [di-vouar] *vt.* devorar.

devout [di-vout] *adj.* devoto,
piadoso.

dew [diu] *n.* rocío, *m.*

dewdrop [diu-drop] *n.* gota de
rocío.

dexterity [deks-te-ri-ti] *n.* destreza, *f.*

dexterous [deks-te-ros] *adj.* diestro, hábil.

dextrous [deks-trous] *adj.* diestro, experto.

diabetes [daia-bi-tis] *n.* diabetes,
f.

diabetic [daia-be-tik] *adj.* diabético.

diabolic diabolical [daia-bo-lik],
[daia-bo-li-kal] *adj.* diabólico.

diagnose [daiag-nous] *vt.* diagnosticar.

diagnosis [daiag-nou-sis] *n.*
(med.) diagnosis, *f.*

diagonal [dai-a-go-nal] *n.* y *adj.*
diagonal, *f.*

diagram [dai-a-gram] *n.* esquema, *m.;* diagrama, *m.;* gráfico,
m.

dial [daial] *n.* esfera de reloj;

cuadrante, reloj de sol; — **tele-phone,** teléfono automático **to — the number,** marcar el número.

dialing [daia-lin] *n.* acción de llamar por teléfono automático; sintonización, *f.*

dialect [daia-lekt] *n.* dialecto, *m.*

dialectics *n.* dialéctica, *f.*

dialogue [daia-log] *n.* diálogo, *m.*

diameter [daia-mi-tar] *n.* diáme-tro, *m.*

diamond [daia-mond] *n.* dia-mante, *m.;* brillante, *m.;* oro (de baraja), *m.;* — **cutter,** dia-mantista, *m.*

diaper [daia-par] *n.* pañal, *m.;* —, *vt.* proveer con pañales.

diaphragm [daia-fram] *n.* dia-fragma, *m.*

diarrhea [daia-ria] *n.* diarrea, *f.*

diary [daia-ri] *n.* diario, *m.*

dice [dais] *n. pl.* dados, *m. pl.*

dictate [dik-teit] *vt.* dictar; —, *n.* dictamen, *m.*

dictation [dik-tei-shon] *n.* dicta-do, *m.*

dictator [dik-tei-tor] *n.* caudillo, *m.;* dictador, *m.*

dictatorial [dik-ta-to-rial] *adj.* autoritativo, dictatorial, dicta-torio, imperioso.

dictatorship [dik-tei-tor-ship] *n.* dictadura, *f.*

diction [dik-shon] *n.* dicción, *f.;* estilo, *m.*

dictionary [dik-sho-na-ri] *n.* dic-cionario, léxico, *m.*

did [did] *pretérito* del verbo **do.**

die [dai] *vi.* morir, expirar; eva-porarse; desvanecerse; marchi-tarse; —, *n.* dado, *m.*

die-hard [dai-jard]*n.* persona intransigente y conservadora.

diesel [di-sel] *adj.* diesel; — **engine,** motor diesel.

diet [daiet] *n.* dieta, *f.;* régimen, *m.;* —, *vi.* estar a dieta.

dietician [daie-ti-shan] *n.* dietis-ta, *m.* y *f.*

differ [di-far] *vi.* diferenciarse; contradecir.

difference [di-frens] *n.* diferen-cia, disparidad, *f.;* variante, *f.*

different [di-ferent] *adj.* diferen-te; desemejante.

differential [di-fe-ren-shal] *n.* y *adj.* diferencial, *f.;* — **calculus,** (math.) cálculo diferencial.

differentiate [di-fe-ren-shieit] *vt.* diferenciar.

difficult [di-fi-kult] *adj.* difícil; áspero; enrevesado.

diffident [di-fi-dent] *adj.* tímido, modesto; falto de confianza en sí mismo.

diffuse [di-fius] *vt.* difundir, esparcir; —, *adj.* di-fundido, esparcido; prolijo.

dig [dig] *vt.* cavar, excavar; — **up,** desenterrar, desarraigar; —, *n.* (coll.) indirecta, *f.*

digest [dai-yest] *vt.* digerir; clasificar; asimilar mentalmente; —, *vi.* digerir; —, *n.* extracto, compendio, *m.*

digestible [di-yes-ti-bol] *adj.* digerible.

digestion [dai-yes-chon] *n.* digestión, *f.*

digestive [di-yes-tiv] *adj.* digestivo.

digger [di-gar] *n.* cavador, ra.

digging [di-gin] *n.* excavación, *f.;* —s, *n. pl.* lo excavado; lavaderos de arenas auríferas.

digit [di-yit] *n.* dígito, *m.*

dignified [dig-ni-faid] *adj.* altivo; serio, grave, con dignidad.

dignify [dig-ni-fai] *vt.* exaltar, elevar.

dignitary [dig-ni-ta-ri] *n.* dignatario, *m.*

dignity [dig-ni-ti] *n.* dignidad, *f.;* rango, *m.;* mesura, *f.*

digression [dai-gre-shon] *n.* digresión, *f.;* divagación, *f.;* desvío, *m.*

dike [daik] *n.* dique, canal, *m.*

dilapidate [di-la-pi-deit] *vt.* dilapidar.

dilapidated [di-la-pi-dei-ted] *adj.* arruinado; desvencijado.

dilate [dai-leit] *vt.* dilatar, extender; —, *vi.* dilatarse, extenderse.

dilated [dai-lei-tid] *adj.* dilatado, extendido; explayado, prolijo, difuso.

dilation [dai-lei-shon] *n.* dilatación, *f.*

dilemma [dai-le-ma] *n.* dilema, *m.*

dilettante [di-li-tan-ti] *n.* aficionado, da (de las bellas artes) .

diligence [di-li-yens] *n.* diligencia, *f.;* asiduidad, *f.*

diligent [di-li-yent] *adj.* diligente, asiduo; aplicado, hacendoso; —ly, *adv.* diligentemente.

dilute [dai-lut] *vt.* diluir.

dim [dim] *adj.* turbio de vista, oscuro; confuso; —, *vt.* ofuscar, oscurecer; eclipsar.

dime [daim] *n.* moneda de diez centavos en E.U.A.

dimension [di-men-shon] *n.* dimensión, medida, extensión, *f.*

diminish [di-mi-nish] *vt.* decrecer, disminuir; —, *vi.* ceder; menguar, disminuirse.

diminutive [di-mi-niu-tiv] *n.* y *adj.* diminutivo, *m.*

dimity [di-mi-ti] *n.* cotonía, *f.*

dimness [dim-nes] *n.* oscuridad, *f.;* opacidad, *f.*

din [din] *n.* ruido violento, alboroto, *m.;* —, *vt.* atolondrar.

dine [dain] *vt.* dar de comer o de cenar; —, *vi.* comer, cenar.

dingy [din-yi] *adj.* sucio; empañado.

dining [dai-nin] *adj.* comedor;

— car, coche comedor; **—
room,** comedor, *m.;* refectorio,
m.

dinner [di-nar] *n.* comida, cena,
f.

dinosaur [dai-na-sor] *n.* dinosaurio, *m.*

dint [dint] *n.* golpe, *m.;* **by — of,**
a fuerza de, a puro.

diocese [daio-sis] *n.* diócesis, *f.*

diorama [dai-o-ra-ma] *n.* diorama, *m.*

dip [dip] *vt.* remojar, sumergir;
—, *vi.* sumergirse; penetrar;
inclinarse; **—,** *n.* inmersión, *f.;*
inclinación, *f.*

diphtheria [dif-zia-ria] *n.* difteria,
f.

diphthong [dif-zong] *n.* diptongo,
m.

diploma [di-plou-ma] *n.* diploma,
m.

diplomacy [di-plou-ma-si] *n.*
diplomacia, *f.;* tacto, *m.*

diplomat [di-plou-mat] *n.* diplomático, *m.*

diplomatic [di-plou-ma-tik] *adj.*
diplomático; **— corps,** cuerpo
diplomático.

dipper [di-par] *n.* cucharón,
cazo, *m.;* **Big D—,** Osa Mayor.

dire [daiar] *adj.* horrendo, cruel;
deplorable.

direct [dai-rekt] *adj.* directo,
derecho, recto; claro; **—
current,** (elec.) corriente continua; **— hit,** blanco directo; **—,**
vt. dirigir, enderezar; ordenar.

direction [dai-rek-shon] *n.* dirección, *f.;* instrucción, *f.;* manejo,
m.; rumbo, curso, *m.*

director [dai-rek-tar] *n.* director,
m.; guía, *m.;* superintendente,
m.; **board of —s,** directorio, *m.,*
junta directiva.

directory [dai-rek-to-ri] *n.* directorio, *m.;* guía, *f.*

dirge [derch] *n.* canción lúgubre.

dirt [dert] *n.* suciedad, porquería, mugre, *f.*

dirty [der-ti] *adj.* puerco, sucio;
vil, bajo; **— trick,** mala partida,
mala broma; **—,** *vt.* ensuciar,
emporcar.

disability [di-sa-bi-li-ti] *n.* impotencia, *f.;* inhabilidad, incapacidad, *f.*

disable [di-sei-bol] *vt.* hacer
incapaz, incapacitar; (naut.)
desaparejar (un navío).

disablement [di-sei-bol-ment] *n.*
(leyes) impedimento, *m.;* (naut.)
desaparejo de una nave como
resultado de algún combate.

disadvantage [dis-ad-van-tich] *n.*
desventaja, *f.;* daño, *m.*

disagree [disa-gri] *vi.* desconve-
nir, discordar, no estar de
acuerdo.

disagreeable [disa-gri-a-bol] *adj.*
desagradable.

disagreement [disa-gri-ment] *n.*

desacuerdo, *m.*, discordia, *f.*; diferencia, *f.*; desconformidad, *f.*

disappear [di-sa-piar] *vi.* desaparecer; salir; esfumarse; ausentarse.

disappearance [di-sa-pia-rans] *n.* desaparición, *f.*

disappoint [di-sa-point] *vt.* frustrar, faltar a la palabra; decepcionar, engañar; **to be —ed,** llevarse chasco; estar decepcionado.

disappointment [di-sa-point-ment] *n.* chasco, *m.*; contratiempo, *m.*; decepción, *f.*

disapproval [di-sa-pru-val] *n.* desaprobación, censura, *f.*

disapprove [di-sa-pruv] *vt.* desaprobar.

disarm [dis-arm] *vt.* desarmar, privar de armas.

disarmament [dis-ar-ma-ment] *n.* desarme, *m.*

disarray [di-sa-rei] *n.* desarreglo, *m.*; —, *vt.* desnudar; desarreglar.

disassociate [di-sa-sou-shieit] *vt.* desasociar.

disaster [di-sas-tar] *n.* desastre, *m.*; infortunio, *m.*; catástrofe, *f.*

disastrous [di-sas-tros] *adj.* desastroso, infeliz; funesto.

disband [dis-band] *vt.* dividir, desunir; —, *vi.* dispersarse.

disbelief [dis-bi-lif] *n.* increduli-

dad, desconfianza, *f.*

disburse [dis-bers] *vt.* desembolsar, pagar.

discard [dis-kard] *vt.* descartar.

discern [di-sern] *vt. y vi.* discernir, percibir, distinguir.

discernible [di-ser-ni-bol] *adj.* perceptible.

discerning [di-ser-nin] *adj.* juicioso, perspicaz.

discernment [di-sern-ment] *n.* discernimiento, *m.*

discharge [di-charch] *vt.* descargar, pagar (una deuda, etc.); (mil.) licenciar; ejecutar, cumplir; descartar; despedir; —, *vi.* descargarse; —, *n.* descarga, *f.*; descargo, *m.*; finiquito, *m.*; dimisión, *f.*; absolución, *f.*

disciple [di-si-pol] *n.* discípulo, secuaz, *m.*

disciplinary [di-si-pli-na-ri] *adj.* disciplinario.

discipline [di-si-plin] *n.* disciplina, *f.*; enseñanza, *f.*; rigor, *m*; —, *vt.* disciplinar, instruir.

disclaim [dis-kleim] *vt.* negar, renunciar; repudiar, rechazar.

disclose [dis-klous] *vt.* descubrir, revelar.

disclosure [dis-klou-shar] *n.* descubrimiento, *m.*; revelación, *f.*

discolor [dis-ka-lor] *vt.* descolorar.

discoloration [dis-ka-lo-rei-shon]

n. descoloramiento, *m.;* mancha, *f.*

discomfort [dis-kom-fort] *n.* incomodidad, *f.;* aflicción, *f.;* molestia, *f.*

disconcert [dis-kon-sert] *vt.* desconcertar, confundir, turbar.

disconnect [dis-ko-nekt] *vt.* desconectar.

discontent [dis-kon-tent] *n.* descontento, *m.;* —, *adj.* descontento, disgustado; —, *vt.* descontentar.

discontented [dis-kon-ten-tid] *adj.* descontento.

discontinue [dis-kon-ti-niu] *vi.* descontinuar, interrumpir; cesar.

discord, discordance [dis-kord], [dis-kor-dans] *n.* discordia, *f.;* discordancia, disensión, *f.*

discordant [dis-kor-dant] *adj.* discorde; incongruo; —ly, *adv.* con discordancia.

discount [dis-kaunt] *n.* descuento, *m.;* rebaja, *f.;* **rate of** —, tipo de descuento; —, *vt.* descontar.

discourage [dis-kau-rich] *vt.* desalentar, desanimar.

discouragement [dis-kau-rich-ment] *n.* desaliento, *m.*

discourse [dis-kors] *n.* discurso, *m.;* tratado, *m.;* —, *vi.* conversar, discurrir, tratar (de).

discourteous [dis-kor-tos] *adj.* descortés, grosero.

discover [dis-ko-var] *vt.* descubrir; revelar; manifestar.

discovery [dis-ka-ve-ri] *n.* descubrimiento, *m.;* revelación, *f.*

discredit [dis-kre-dit] *n.* descrédito, deshonor, *m.;* —, *vt.* desacreditar, deshonrar.

discreet [dis-kriit] *adj.* discreto; circunspecto; callado.

discrepancy [dis-kre-pansi] *n.* discrepancia, diferencia, *f.;* variante, *f.*

discretion [dis-kre-shon] *n.* discreción, *f.*

discriminate [dis-kri-mi-neit] *vt.* discriminar.

discriminating [dis-kri-mi-nei-tin] *adj.* parcial, discerniente.

discrimination [dis-kri-mi-nei-shon] *n.* discriminación, *f.*

discuss [dis-kas] *vt.* discutir.

discussion [dis-ka-shon] *n.* discusión, *f.*

disdain [dis-dein] *vt.* desdeñar, despreciar; —, *n.* desdén, desprecio, *m.*

disease [di-sis] *n.* mal, *m.;* enfermedad, *f.;* **contagious** —, enfermedad contagiosa.

diseased [di-sist] *adj.* enfermo.

disembark [di-sim-bark] *vt. y vi.* desembarcar.

disengage [di-sin-gueich] *vt.* desenredar, librar; —, *vi.* libertarse de.

disfavor [dis-fei-var] *vt.* desfavo-

recer; —, *n.* disfavor, *m.;* desaprobación, *f.*

disfigure [dis-fi-gar] *vt.* desfigurar, afear.

disfigurement [dis-fi-ga-ment] *n.*
deformidad, *f.;* desfiguración, *f.*

disgrace [dis-greis] *n.* deshonra,
f.; desgracia, *f.;* —, *vt.* deshonrar; hacer caer en desgracia.

disgraceful [dis-greis-ful] *adj.*
deshonroso, ignominioso; **—ly,**
adv. vergonzosamente.

disguise [dis-gais] *vt.* disfrazar,
enmascarar; simular; —, *n.*
disfraz, *m.;* máscara, *f.*

disgust [dis-gast] *n.* disgusto,
m.; aversión, *f.;* fastidio, *m.;* **to
cause** —, repugnar; —, *vt.* disgustar, inspirar aversión.

dish [dish] *n.* fuente, *f.,* plato,
m.; taza, *f.;* **set of —es,** vajilla,
f.; —, *vt.* servir en un plato.

dishearten [dis-jar-ten] *vt.* desalentar.

dishonest [dis-ho-nest] *adj.* deshonesto; ignominioso.

dishonesty [dis-ho-nes-ti] *n.*
falta de honradez; deshonesti-
dad, impureza, *f.*

dishonor [dis-ho-nar] *n.* deshonra, ignominia, *f.;* —, *vt.* deshonrar, infamar.

dishonorable [dis-ho-no-ra-bol]
adj. deshonroso, afrentoso,
indecoroso; **—bly,** *adv.* ignominiosamente.

dishwasher [dish-ua-sher] *n.*
lavadora eléctrica de platos;
lavaplatos, *m.* o *f.*

disillusion [di-si-lu-shon] *n.* desengaño, *m.,* desilusión, *f.;* —,
vt. desengañar, desilusionar.

disinfect [di-sin-fekt] *vt.* desinfectar.

disinfectant [di-sin-fek-tant] *n.*
desinfectante, *m.*

disinherit [di-sin-je-rit] *vt.* desheredar.

disintegrate [dis-in-ti-greit] *vt.*
desintegrar; despedazar.

disintegration [dis-in-ti-grei-
shon] *n.* desintegración, *f.*

disjointed [dis-yoin-ted] *adj.* dislocado; **—ly,** *adv.* separadamente.

disk [disk] *n.* disco, *m.;* **— jockey,** (radio o TV.) anunciador
de programa con base en discos; D.J., tocadiscos.

diskette [dis-ket] *n.* disquete, *m.*

dislike [dis-laik] *n.* aversión,
repugnancia, *f.;* disgusto, *m.;*
—, *vt.* disgustar; desagradar.

dislocate [dis-lou-keit] *vt.* dislocar.

dislodge [dis-lodch] *vt.* y *vi.* desalojar.

disloyal [dis-loial] *adj.* desleal;
infiel.

disloyalty [dis-loial-ti] *n.* deslealtad, infidelidad, perfidia,

dismal [dis-mal] *adj.* triste,

funesto; horrendo.

dismantle [dis-man-tel] *vt.* (mil.) desmantelar (una plaza) ; desamueblar; (naut.) desaparejar.

dismay [dis-mei] *n.* consternación, *f.;* terror, *m.;* —, *vt.* y *vi.* consternar, consternarse, abatirse.

dismember [dis-mem-bar] *vt.* desmembrar.

dismiss [dis-mis] *vt.* despedir; echar; descartar.

dismissal, dismission [dis-mi-sal], [dis-mi-shon] *n.* despedida, *f.;* dimisión, *f.;* destitución, *f.*

dismount [dis-maunt] *vt.* desmontar, apearse (del caballo); —, *vi.* desmontar, descender.

disobedience [dis-o-bi-dians] *n.* desobediencia, *f.*

disobedient [dis-o-bi-dians] *adj.* desobediente.

disobey [dis-o-bei] *vt.* desobedecer.

disorder [dis-or-dar] *n.* desorden, *m.;* confusión, *f.;* indisposición, *f.;* desequilibrio, *m.;* —, *vt.* desordenar; perturbar.

disorderly [dis-or-der-li] *adj.* desarreglado, confuso.

disorganization [dis-or-ga-nai-sei-shon] *n.* desorganización, *f.*

disorganize [dis-or-ga-nais] *vt.* desorganizar.

disown [dis-oun] *vt.* negar, des-conocer; repudiar.

disparage [dis-pa-rich] *vt.* envilecer; mofar, menospreciar.

disparagement [dis-pa-rich-ment] *n.* menosprecio, desprecio, *m.;* insulto, *m.*

disparity [dis-pa-ri-ti] *n.* disparidad, *f.*

dispassionate [dis-pa-sho-nit] *adj.* sereno, desapasionado; templado.

dispatch [dis-pach] *n.* despacho, *m.;* embarque, *m.;* corn.) envío, *m.;* remisión, *f.;* —, *vt.* despachar; embarcar; remitir, enviar.

dispel [dis-pel] *vt.* disipar, dispersar.

dispense [dis-pens] *vt.* dispensar; distribuir; eximir.

disperse [dis-pers] *vt.* esparcir, disipar; dispersar.

displace [dis-pleis] *vt.* desplazar; dislocar, desordenar.

displaced [dis-pleist] *adj.* desplazado, dislocado; — **person,** persona desplazada.

displacement [dis-pleis-ment] *n.* cambio de situación, mudanza, *f.;* desalojamiento *m.;* (chem.) coladura, *f ;* (naut.) desplazamiento, *m.*

display [dis-plei] *vt.* desplegar; explicar; exponer; ostentar; —, *n.* ostentación, *f.;* despliegue, *m.;* exhibición, *f.*

displease [dis-plis] *vt.* disgustar;

ofender; desagradar; chocar.

displeasure [dis-pli-shar] *n.* disgusto, desagrado, *m.;* indignación, *f.*

disposable [dis-pou-sabl] *adj.* desechable.

disposal [dis-pou-sal] *n.* disposición, *f.*

dispose [dis-pous] *vt.* disponer; dar; arreglar; **to — of,** deshacerse de.

disposed [dis-poust] *adj.* dispuesto, inclinado; **well —,** bien dispuesto; **ill —,** mal dispuesto.

disposition [dis-po-si-shon] *n.* disposición, *f.;* índole, *f.;* inclinación, *f.;* carácter, *m.;* humor, *m.;* **good —,** buen humor, buen carácter.

dispossess [dis-po-ses] *vt.* desposeer; desalojar.

disproportion [dis-pro-por-shon] *n.* desproporción, *f.*

disproportionate [dis-pro-por-sho-nit] *adj.* desproporcionado.

disprove [dis-pruv] *vt.* confutar, refutar.

disputable [dis-piu-ta-bol] *adj.* disputable, contestable.

dispute [dis-piut] *n.* disputa, controversia, *f.;* **—,** *vt. y vi.* disputar, controvertir, argüir.

disqualify [dis-kuo-li-fai] *vt.* descalificar; inhabilitar.

disquiet [dis-kua-iet] *n.* inquietud, perturbación, *f.;* **—,** *vt.*

inquietar, turbar.

disregard [dis-ri-gard] *vt.* desatender, desdeñar; **—,** *n.* desatención, *f.;* desdén, *m.*

disreputable [dis-re-piu-tei-bol] *adj.* deshonroso; despreciable.

disrepute [dis-re-piut] *n.* descrédito, *m.;* mala fama; **to bring into —,** desacreditar, difamar, desprestigiar.

disrespect [dis-ris-pekt] *n.* irreverencia, falta de respeto.

disrespectful [dis-ris-pekt-ful] *adj.* irreverente, descortés.

disrupt [dis-rapt] *vt.* desbaratar, hacer pedazos; desorganizar, enredar.

disruption [dis-rap-tion] *n.* rompimiento, *m.;* fractura, *f.*

dissatisfaction [di-sa-tis-fak-shon] *n.* descontento, disgusto, *m.*

dissatisfied [di-sa-tis-faid] *adj.* descontento, no satisfecho.

dissatisfy [di-sa-tis-fai] *vt.* descontentar, desagradar.

dissect [di-sekt] *vt.* disecar.

dissection [di-sek-shon] *n.* disección, *f.*

dissemble [di-sem-bel] *vt. y vi.* disimular, fingir.

disseminate [di-se-mi-neit] *vt.* diseminar, sembrar, esparcir, propagar.

dissent [di-sent] *vi.* disentir, estar en desacuerdo; **—,** *n.*

disensión, *f.*

dissertation [di-ser-tei-shon] *n.* disertación, tesis, *f.*

dissimilar [di-si-mi-lar] *adj.* disímil.

dissipate [di-si-peit] *vt.* disipar.

dissipation [di-si-pei-shon] *n.* disipación, *f.;* libertinaje, *m.*

dissociate [di-sou-shieit] *vt.* disociar.

dissolve [di-solv] *vt.* disolver; —, *vi.* disolverse, derretirse.

dissonant [di-so-nant] *adj.* disonante; discordante; diferente.

dissuade [di-sueid] *vt.* disuadir.

distance [dis-tans] *n.* distancia, *f.;* lejanía, *f.;* respeto, *m.;* esquivez, *f.;* **at a —,** de lejos; **in the —,** a lo lejos; —, *vt.* apartar; sobrepasar; espaciar.

distant [dis-tant] *adj.* distante, lejano; esquivo; reservado; **very —,** a leguas, muy distante; muy esquivo.

distaste [dis-teist] *n.* hastío, disgusto, tedio, *m.*

distasteful [dis-teist-ful] *adj.* desabrido, desagradable; chocante; maligno.

distill [dis-til] *vt.* y *vi.* destilar; gotear.

distinct [dis-tinkt] *adj.* distinto, diferente; claro, sin confusión; **—ly,** *adv.* con claridad.

distinction [dis-tink-shon] *n.* distinción, diferencia, *f.;* **person**

of —, persona distinguida o eminente.

distinctive [dis-tink-tiv] *adj.* característico.

distinctness [dis-tinkt-nes] *n.* claridad, *f.*

distinguish [dis-tin-güish] *vt.* distinguir; discernir; **—ed,** *adj.* distinguido, caracterizado, señalado; eminente; notable, famoso, ilustre, considerado.

distort [dis-tort] *vt.* tergiversar, pervertir, torcer; disfrazar, falsear.

distortion [dis-tor-shon] *n.* contorsión, *f.;* torcimiento, *m.;* perversión, *f.*

distract [dis-trakt] *vt.* distraer; perturbar; **—ed,** *adj.* distraído; aturdido; perturbado.

distraction [dis-trak-shon] *n.* distracción, *f.;* confusión, *f.;* frenesí, *m,* locura, *f.*

distress [dis-tres] *n.* aflicción, *f.;* calamidad, miseria, *f.;* —, *vt.* angustiar, acongojar; (leyes) secuestrar, embargar.

distribute [dis-tri-biut] *vt.* distribuir, dividir, repartir.

distribution [dis-tri-biu-shon] *n.* distribución, *f.;* reparto, *m.*

distributor [dis-tri-biu-tar] *n.* distribuidor, ra.

district [dis-trikt] *n.* distrito, *m.;* región, *f.;* jurisdicción, *f.;* zona, *f.;* vecindario, *m.;* barrio (de una ciudad), *m.*

distrust [dis-trast] *vt.* desconfiar; —, *n.* desconfianza, sospecha, *f.;* suspicacia, *f.*

distrustful [dis-trast-ful] *adj.* desconfiado; sospechoso; suspicaz; —**ly,** *adv.* desconfiadamente.

disturb [dis-terb] *vt.* perturbar, estorbar.

disturbance [dis-ter-bans] *n.* disturbio, *m.;* confusión, *f.;* tumulto, *m.;* perturbación, *f.*

disuse [dis-ius] *n.* desuso, *m.;* —, *vt.* desusar.

ditch [dich] *n.* zanja, *f.;* foso, *m.;* cauce, *m.;* —, *vt.* abrir zanjas o fosos; (coll.) desembarazarse, dar calabazas.

diuretic [dai-ua-re-tik] *n.* y *adj.* diurético, *m.*

divan [di-van] *n.* diván, *m.*

dive [daiv] *vi.* sumergirse, zambullirse; bucear; (Mex.) echarse un clavado; —, *n.* zambullidura, *f.;* (Mex.) clavado, *m.;* (coll.) garito, *m.,* leonera, *f.;* — **bomber,** bombardero en picada.

diver [dai-var] *n.* buzo, *m.;* (orn.) somorgujo, *m.*

diverge [dai-verch] *vi.* divergir; divergirse; discrepar.

divergence [dai-ver-yens] *n.* divergencia, *f.*

divergent [dai-ver-yent] *adj.* divergente.

diverse [dai-vers] *adj.* diverso, diferente, variado.

diversify [dai-ver-si-fai] *vt.* diversificar.

diversion [dai-ver-shon] *n.* diversión, *f.;* pasatiempo, *m.*

diversity [dai-ver-si-ti] *n.* diversidad, *f.;* variedad, *f.*

divert [dai-vert] *vt.* desviar; divertir; recrear.

divide [di-vaid] *vt.* dividir, distribuir; repartir; partir; desunir; —, *vi.* desunirse, dividirse.

dividend [di-vi-dend] *n.* dividendo, *m.*

divider [di-vai-dar] *n.* (math.) divisor, *m.;* distribuidor, *m.;* compás de puntas.

divine [di-van] *adj.* divino, sublime, excelente; —, *n.* teólogo, *m.;* —, *vt.* conjeturar; —, *vi.* presentir; profetizar; adivinar.

diving [dai-vin] *n.* buceo, *m.;* —, *adj.* buceador; relativo al buceo; — **bell,** campana de bucear; — **suit,** escafandra, *f.*

divinity [di-vi-ni-ti] *n.* divinidad, *f.;* deidad, *f.;* teología, *f.*

divisibility [di-vi-si-bi-li-ti] *n.* divisibilidad, *f.*

divisible [di-vi-sa-bol] *adj.* divisible.

division [di-vi-shon] *n.* (math.) división, *f.;* desunión, *f.;* separación *f.*

divorce [di-vors] *n.* divorcio, *m.;*

—, *vt.* divorciar; divorciarse de.

divulge [dai-valch] *vt.* divulgar, publicar.

dizziness [di-si-nes] *n.* vértigo, *m.;* ligereza, *f.;* vahído, *m.;* vaivén, *m.;* mareo, *m.*

dizzy [di-si] *adj.* vertiginoso; mareado; (coll.) tonto, estúpido.

D.N.A.: deoxyribonucleic acid, A.D.N., ácido desoxirribonucleico.

do [du] *vt.* hacer, ejecutar, finalizar; despachar; —, *vi.* obrar; comportarse; prosperar; **to — away with,** suprimir, quitar; **how — you —?** ¿cómo está usted? **to — without,** pasarse sin, prescindir de.

docile [dou-sail] *adj.* dócil, apacible.

dock [dok] *n.* (naut.) muelle, desembarcadero, *m.;* **dry —,** astillero, *m.;* —, *vt.* descolar; entrar en muelle; cortar; descontar (parte del sueldo de alguien).

doctor [dok-tar] *n.* doctor, médico, *m.;* **D— of Law,** Doctor en Derecho; **D— of Philosophy,** Doctor en Filosofía; **—'s office,** consultorio de médico, gabinete, *m.;* —, *vt.* medicinar.

doctrine [dok-trin] *n.* doctrina, *f.;* erudición, *f.;* ciencia, *f.*

document [do-kiu-ment] *n.* documento, *m.;* precepto, *m.*

documentary [do-kiu-men-ta-ri] *n.* y *adj.* documental, *m.*

dodge [dodch] *vt.* evadir, esquivar.

doe [dou] *n.* (zool.) gama, *f.*

doer [douar] *n.* hacedor, actor, ejecutante, *m.*

does [das] 3ª persona del singular del verbo **do.**

dog [dog] *n.* perro, *m.;* **— days,** caniculares, *m. pl.;* **— fight,** pelea de perros, refriega, *f.;* (avi.) combate aéreo a muerte; **— kennel,** perrera, *f.;* **D— Star,** Sirio, Canícula; —, *vt.* espiar, perseguir.

doghouse [dog-jaus] *n.* perrera, casa de perro, *f.;* **to be in the —,** (coll.) estar castigado, estar en desgracia.

doings [duins] *n. pl.* hechos, *m. pl.;* acciones, *f. pl.;* eventos, *m. pl.*

doldrums [dol-drams] *n. pl.* fastidio, *m.;* abatimiento, *m.*

dole [doul] *n.* distribución, *f.;* porción, *f.;* limosna, *f.;* —, *vt.* repartir, distribuir.

doleful [doul-ful] *adj.* doloroso, lúgubre, triste.

doll [dol] *n.* muñeca, *f.;* **boy —,** muñeco, *m.*

dollar [do-lar] *n.* dólar, peso (moneda de E.U.A.), *m.;* **silver —,** peso fuerte.

dolly [do-li] *n.* muñequita, *f.;*

remachador, *m.;* (rail.) plataforma de tracción.

dolphin [dol-fin] *n.* delfín, *m.*

domain [dou-mein] *n.* dominio,
m.

dome [doum] *n.* cúpula, *f.;*
domo, *m.*

domestic [do-mes-tik] *adj.*
doméstico; interno; casero; —,
n. criado, da, sirviente, ta.

domesticate [do-mes-ti-keit] *vt.*
domesticar.

domicile [do-mi-sail] *n.* domicilio, *m.*

dominance [do-mi-nans] *n.* pre-
dominio, *m.*, ascendencia,
autoridad, *f.*

dominant [do-mi-nant] *adj.*
dominante.

dominate [do-mi-neit] *vt.* y *vi.*
dominar, predominar.

domination [do-mi-nei-shon] *n.*
dominación, *f.*

domineering [do-mi-nia-rin] *adj.*
tiránico, arrogante.

Dominican Republic [do-mi-ni-
kan-ri-pa-blik] República
Dominicana.

domino [do-mi-nou] *n.* dominó,
m.; traje de máscara; **—es,** *n.*
pl. dominó (juego), *m.*

donate [dou-neit] *vt.* donar, contribuir; obsequiar.

donation [dou-nei-shon] *n.*
donación, dádiva, contribución,
f.

done [dan] *adj.* hecho; cocido,
asado; **well —,** bien hecho; bien
cocido, bien asado; —, p.p. del
verbo **do.**

donkey [don-ki] *n.* burro, asno.

donor [do-nor] *n.* donador, ra.

doodle [du-del] *n.* garrapato, *m.;*
garabatos, *m. pl.;* —, *vt.* y *vi.*
garrapatear, hacer garabatos.

doom [dum] *n.* sentencia, *f.;*
condena, *f.;* suerte, *f.;* —, *vt.*
sentenciar, juzgar, condenar.

door [dor] *n.* puerta, *f.;* — **bolt,**
pasador, *m.;* — **knocker,** pica-
porte, llamador, *m.*, aldaba, *f.;*
front —, puerta de entrada;
within —s, en casa, bajo techo;
sliding —, puerta corrediza.

doorbell [dor-bel] *n.* timbre de
llamada.

doorhandle [dor-jan-dol] *n.* tirador para puertas.

doorkeeper [dor-ki-par] *n.*
portero, ujier, *m.*

doorknob [dor-nob] *n.* perilla, *f.*

doorman [dor-men] *n.* portero,
m.

doorstep[dor-step] *n.* umbral, *m.*

doorway [dor-uei] *n.* portada, *f.;*
portal, *m.;* puerta de entrada.

dope [doup] *n.* narcótico, *m.*,
droga heroica; (coll.) información, *f.;* (coll.) persona muy
estúpida; — **fiend,** morfinómano, na, persona adicta a las
drogas heroicas.

dormant [dor-mant] *adj.* durmiente; secreto; latente.

dormitory [dor-mi-to-ri] *n.* dormitorio, *m.*

dorsal [dor-sal] *adj.* dorsal.

dose [dous] *n.* dosis, porción, *f.;* —, *vt.* disponer la dosis de un remedio.

dot [dot] *n.* punto, *m.;* (mus.) puntillo, *m.;* —, *vt.* poner punto (a una letra).

double [da-bel] *adj.* doble, duplicado, duplo; falso, insincero; — **chin,** papada, *f.;* — **entry,** (com.) partida doble; — **play,** (béisbol) maniobra que pone fuera de juego a dos de los jugadores rivales; — **talk** (coll.) charla vacía de sentido aunque seria en apariencia; — **time,** paso doble o rápido; — **cross,** engañar; —, *n.* duplicado, *m.;* doble, *m.;* engaño, *m.;* artificio, *m.;* —, *vt.* doblar; duplicar; plegar.

double-breasted [da-bel-brestd] *adj.* con dos filas de botones (chaqueta o abrigo).

doubles [da-bels] *n. pl.* (tenis) juego de dobles.

doubt [daut] *n.* duda, sospecha, *f.;* **there is no —,** no cabe duda; **without —,** sin duda; —, *vt.* y *vi.* dudar; sospechar.

doubter [dau-tar] *n.* incrédulo, la.

doubtful [daut-ful] *adj.* dudoso; incierto.

doubtless [daut-les] *adj.* indudable; **—ly,** *adv.* sin duda, indudablemente.

dough [dau] *n.* masa, pasta, *f.;* (coll.) dinero, *m.*

doughnut [do-not] *n.* rosquilla, *f.,* variedad de buñuelo.

dour [dau] *adj.* torvo, austero.

douse [daus] *vt.* zambullir; empapar; —, *vi.* zambullirse; empaparse.

dove [dav] *n.* paloma, *f.;* **ring —,** paloma torcaz.

dowdy [dau-di] *adj.* desaliñado; —, *n.* mujer desaliñada.

dowel [dauel] *n.* tarugo, zoquete, *m.,* clavija de madera.

down [daun] *n.* plumón, flojel, *m.;* bozo, vello, *m.;* revés de fortuna; **ups and —s,** vaivenes, *m. pl.,* altas y bajas; —, *adj.* pendiente; —, *adv.* abajo; **so much —,** tanto al contado; —, *vt.* derribar; — **with!** ¡ abajo!

downcast [daun-kast] *adj.* apesadumbrado, cabizbajo.

downfall [daun-fol] *n.* ruina, decadencia, *f.;* desplome, *m.*

downgrade [daun-greid] *n.* cuesta abajo, bajada, *f.;* —, *vt.* rebajar en calidad; (mil.) degradar.

downhearted [daun-jar-ted] *adj.* abatido, desanimado.

downhill [daun-jil] *adj.* pendiente, hacia abajo; —, *adv.* cuesta abajo.

down payment [daun-pei-ment] *n.* pago inicial; (Mex.) enganche, *m.*

downpour [daun-por] *n.* aguacero, *m.;* chubasco.

downright [daun-rait] *adv.* sin ceremonias; de manera patente; por completo.

downstairs [daun-stears] *adv.* abajo de las escaleras; abajo; —, *n.* piso inferior.

downstream [daun-strim] *adv.* aguas abajo.

downtown [daun-taun] *n.* centro, *m.,* parte céntrica de una ciudad.

downward [daun-uard] *adj.* inclinado; —*s, adv.* hacia abajo.

dowry [dau-ri] *n.* dote, *m. o f.*

doze [dous] *n.* sueño ligero, siesta, *m.;* —, *vi.* dormitar.

dozen [dousen] *n.* docena, *f.*

Dr.: Doctor Dr. Doctor.

drab [drab] *n.* paño castaño; mujer desaliñada; prostituta, *f.;* color entre gris y café; —, *adj.* opaco; murrio; monótono.

draft [draft] *n.* dibujo, *m.;* (com.) giro, *m.,* letra de cambio, libranza, *f.;* corriente de aire; (mil.) leva, conscripción, *f.;* (naut.) calado, *m.;* — **board,** junta de conscripción; —**ing board,** tablero de dibujar, tabla para dibujo; **rough** —, borrador, *m.;* **sight** —, giro a la vista; **time** —, letra a plazo; **to honor a** —, dar acogida a una letra o un giro; —, *vt.* dibujar; redactar; reclutar forzosamente (en un ejército).

draftee [draf-ti] *n.* quinto, recluta, *m.*

draftsman [drafts-man] *n.* dibujante, *m.;* diseñador, *m.*

drag [drag] *vt.* arrastrar; tirar con fuerza; —, *vi.* arrastrarse por el suelo; —, *n.* rastro, *m.;* rémora, *f.;* (coll.) influencia, *f.*

dragon [dra-gon] *n.* dragón, *m.*

dragonfly [dra-gon-flai] *n.* libélula, *f.*

drain [drein] *vt.* desaguar; secar; sanear; —, (naut.) colador, *m.;* cauce, *m.;* cuneta, *f.;* sangradera, *f.*

drainage [drei-nich] *n.* desagüe, *m.;* saneamiento, *m.*

drainpipe [drein-paip] *n.* tubo de desagüe.

drama [dra-ma] *n.* drama, *m.*

dramatic, dramatical [dra-matik], [dra-ma-ti-kal] *adj.* dramático.

dramatics [dra-ma-tiks] *n. pl.* arte dramático; declamación, *f.*

dramatist [dra-ma-tist] *n.* dramaturgo, *m.*

dramatization [dra-ma-tai-sei-shon] *n.* versión dramatizada; representación o descripción dramática.

dramatize [dra-ma-tais] *vt.* dramatizar.

drank [drank] *pretérito* del verbo **drink.**

drape [dreip] *n.* cortina, colgadura, *f.; —, vt.* vestir, colgar decorativamente.

drapery [drei-pe-ri] *n.* ropaje, *m.;* cortinaje, *m.*

drastic [dras-tik] *adj.* drástico.

draught [draft] *n.* trago, *m.,* poción, *f.;* corriente de aire.

draw [dro] *vt.* tirar, traer; atraer; arrastrar; dibujar; librar una letra de cambio; **to — lots,** echar suertes; **to — nigh,** acercarse; **to — on,** librar a cargo de una persona; **to — out,** sacar; **to — up,** redactar, formular; —, *vi.* tirar, encogerse; moverse.

drawback [drou-bak] *n.* desventaja, *f.,* inconveniente, *m.*

drawer [drouar] *n.* cajón (de un mueble), *m.,* gaveta, *f.; —s, n. pl.* calzones, *m. pl.;* calzoncillos, *m. pl.*

drawing [droin] *n.* dibujo, *m.;* rifa, *f.; — room,* sala de recibo.

drawl [drol] *vi.* hablar con pesadez; —, *n.* enunciación penosa y lenta.

drawn [dron] *adj.* movido; halado; dibujado; desenvainado; estirado; —, p.p. del verbo **draw.**

dread [dred] *n.* miedo, terror, espanto, *m.; —, adj.* terrible; —, *vt.* y *vi.* temer.

dreadful [dred-ful] *adj.* terrible, espantoso; **—ly,** *adv.* terriblemente.

dream [drim] *n.* sueño, *m.;* fantasía, *f.;* ensueño, *m.; —, vi.* soñar; imaginarse.

dreamer [dri-mar] *n.* soñador, ra; visionario, ria.

dreary [dria-ri] *adj.* lúgubre, triste.

drench [drench] *vt.* empapar, mojar, humedecer; —, *n.* bebida purgante; empapada, *f.*

dress [dres] *n.* vestido, *m.;* atavío, tocado, *m.;* traje, *m.; —* **ball,** baile de etiqueta; — **goods,** tela para vestidos; — **rehearsal,** último ensayo (de una comedia, etc.); **—suit,** traje de etiqueta; **ready**-made **—,** traje hecho; —, *vt.* vestir, ataviar; revestir; curar las heridas; cocinar; —, *vi.* vestirse.

dresser [dre-sar] *n.* el que viste o adereza; tocador, *m.*

dressing [dre-sin] *n.* curación, *f.;* adorno, *m.;* salsa, *f.;* aderezo, *m.; —* **case,** neceser, *m.; —*

gown, peinador, *m.,* bata, *f.;* — **table,** tocador, *m.;* **French** —, salsa francesa, (para ensaladas), *f.*

dressy [dre-si] *adj.* vistoso; elegante.

drew [dru] *pretérito* del verbo draw.

dribble [dri-bol] *vt.* hacer caer gota a gota; —, *vi.* gotear.

drift [drift] *n.* impulso, *m.;* tempestad, *f.;* montón, *m.;* tendencia, *f.,* propósito, designio, *m.;* significado, *m.;* (naut.) deriva, *f.;* —, *vt.* impeler; amontonar; —, *vi.* formar en montones.

driftwood [drift-wud] *n.* leña acarreada por el agua.

drill [dril] *n.* taladro, *m.,* barrena, *f.;* (mil.) instrucción de reclutas; —, *vt.* taladrar; (mil.) disciplinar reclutas; —, *vi.* hacer el ejercicio.

drilling [dri-lin] *n.* perforación, *f.*

drink [drink] *vt.* y *vi.* beber, embeber, absorber; embriagarse; —, *n.* bebida, *f.*

drinker [drin-kar] *n.* bebedor, ra; borracho, cha.

drinking fountain [drin-kin-faun-tin]*n.* fuente pública para beber agua.

drip [drip] *vt.* despedir algún líquido a gotas; —, *vi.* gotear, destilar; —, *n.* gotera, *f.*

dripping [dri-pin] *n.* pringue, *m.*

o *f.;* chorreo, *m.;* —**s,** *n. pl.* pringue, *m.;* **bacon** —**s,** pringue, *m.* o *f.,* grasa de tocino.

drive [draiv] *n.* accionamiento, *m.;* paseo, *m.;* **to go out for a** —, ir de paseo, dar un paseo; —, *vt.* y *vi.* impeler; guiar, manejar, conducir; llevar; (mech.) impulsar; andar en coche; —**into,** hincar, forzar a; reducir a.

drive-in [draiv-in] *n.* restaurante en que el cliente es servido en su automóvil.

driven [driven] p.p. del verbo **drive.**

driver [drai-var] *n.* empujador, *m.;* cochero, *m.;* carretero, *m.;* conductor, *m.;* chófer *m.;* maquinista, *m.*

driveway [draiv-uei] *n.* calzada o entrada para coches.

driving [drai-vin] *adj.* motor; conductor; impulsor; —**license,** matrícula para conducir vehículos, licencia de conductor o de chófer; — **permit,** tarjeta de circulación; **to go out** —, ir de paseo, dar un paseo (en coche, etc.)

drizzle [dri-sel] *vi.* lloviznar; —, *n.* llovizna, *f.*

droll [droul] *adj.* jocoso, gracioso; —, *n.* bufón, *m.*

drone [droun] *n.* zángano de colmena, *m.;* haragán, *m.;* avión radioguiado; —, *vi.* zanganear; dar un sonido sordo.

drool [drul] *vi.* babear.

droop [drup] *vi.* inclinarse, colgar; desanimarse, desfallecer; —, *vt.* dejar caer.

drop [drop] *n.* gota, *f.;* pastilla, *f.;* pendiente, arete, *m.;* — **curtain,** telón de boca; **by** —**s,** gota a gota; **lemon** —, pastilla de limón; **letter** —, buzón, *m.;* —, *vt.* destilar, soltar; cesar; dejar; dejar caer; —, *vi.* gotear; desvanecerse; sobrevenir; languidecer; salirse; **to** — **dead,** caerse muerto.

drought [drout] *n.* seca, sequía, *f.;* sequedad, *f.;* sed, *f.*

drove [drouv] *n.* manada, *f.;* hato, *m.;* muchedumbre, *f.;* rebaño, *m.;* —, *pretérito* del verbo **drive.**

drown [draun] *vt.* sumergir; anegar; —, *vi.* anegarse; ahogarse.

drowse [draus] *vt.* y *vi.* adormecer, adormecerse.

drowsily [drau-si-li] *adv.* soñolientamente; lentamente.

drowsiness [drau-si-nes] *n.* somnolencia, pereza, *f.*

drowsy [drau-si] *adj.* soñoliento.

drudge [dradch] *vi.* trabajar ardua y monótonamente; —, *n.* ganapán, *m.;* yunque, esclavo, *m.*

drudgery [drad-che-ri] *n.* trabajo

arduo y monótono.

drug [drag] *n.* droga, *f.,* medicamento, *m.;* —**s,** *pl.* drogas, *f. pl.;* narcóticos, estupefacientes, *m. pl.;* —, *vt.* narcotizar.

druggist [dra-guist] *n.* farmacéutico, boticario, *m.*

drugstore [drag-stor] *n.* botica, farmacia, *f.*

drum [dram] *n.* tambor, *m.;* tímpano (del oído), *m.*

drummer [dra-mar] *n.* tambor, tamborilero, tamboritero, *m.;* (com.) viajante, *m.*

drumstick [dram-stik] *n.* palillo de tambor; pata (de ave cocida), *f.*

drunk [drank] *adj.* borracho, ebrio, embriagado; —, pp. del verbo drink.

drunken [dran-ken] *adj.* ebrio; — **revel,** orgía, *f.*

drunkenness [dran-ken-nes] *n.* embriaguez, borrachera, *f.*

dry [drai] *adj.* árido, seco; sediento; insípido; severo; — **battery,** pila seca, batería seca; — **cell,** pila seca; — **cleaning,** lavado en seco; —**cleaning shop,** tintorería, *f.;* — **dock,** dique de carena.

dryness [drai-nes] *n.* sequedad, *f.;* aridez de estilo.

dual [diual] *adj.* binario; — **control,** mando doble; mandos gemelos; — **personality,** doble personalidad.

dub [dab] *vt.* armar a alguno caballero; apellidar, poner apodo; doblar (películas).

dubious [da-bios] *adj.* dudoso.

duchess [da-chis] *n.* duquesa, *f..*

duck [dak] , *m. y f.;* pato, ta; tela fuerte más delgada que la lona; sumergida, *f.*

duct [dakt] *n.* canal, tubo, *m.;* conducto, *m.*

dud [dad] *n.* bomba que no estalla; (coll.) persona o cosa que resulta un fracaso; —s, *pl.* (coll.) ropa vieja.

duel [diuel] *n.* duelo, desafío, *m.;* —, *vi.* batirse en duelo.

duelist [daiu-deit] *n.* duelista, *m.*

duet [diu-et] *n.* (mus.) dúo, dueto, *m.*

dug [dag] *n.* teta, *f.;* —, *pretérito y p.p.* del verbo dig.

dugout [dag-aut] *n.* refugio subterráneo usado en casos de bombardeo; piragua, *f.*

duke [diuk] *n.* duque, *m.*

dull [dal] *adj.* lerdo, estúpido; insípido; obtuso; tosco; triste, murrio; opaco; — **of hearing,** algo sordo; —, *vt.* entontecer; obstruir; ofuscar.

dullness [dal-nes] *n.* estupidez, torpeza; *f.;* somnolencia, *f.;* pereza, *f.;* pesadez, *f.*

duly [diu-li] *adv.* debidamente; puntualmente.

dumb [dam] *adj.* mudo; (coll.) estúpido; —**ly**, *adv.* sin chistar, silenciosamente.

dumbbell *n.* (coll.) pesa, haltera, *f.;* persona estúpida.

dumfound [dam-faun] *vt. y vi.* confundir; enmudecer.

dummy [da-mi] *n.* mudo, da; estúpido, da; maniquí, *m.;* (print.) maqueta, *f.*

dump [damp] *n.* tristeza, *f;* vaciadero, depósito, basurero, *m.;* —**s**, *n. pl.* abatimiento, *m.,* murria, *f.;* — **truck,** carro de volteo; **to be in the** —**s,** tener melancolía.

dumping [dam-pin] *n.* vertimiento, *m.;* acto de arrojar, verter, descargar o volcar (basura, escombros, materiales de construcción, etc.); — **place,** — **ground,** lugar de descarga, vertedero, *m.*

dumpling [dam-plin] *n.* pastelito relleno con fruta o carne.

dumpy [dam-pi] *adj.* gordo, rollizo.

dunce [dans] *n.* zote, zopenco, *m.;* tonto, ta, bobo, ba, zonzo, za.

dune [diun] *n.* médano, *m.,* duna, *f.*

dung [dan] *n.* estiércol, *m.;* —, *vt.* estercolar.

dungeon [dan-yon] *n.* calabozo, *m.*

dupe [diup] *n.* bobo, ba; víctima, *f.;* tonto, ta; —, *vt.* engañar, embaucar.

duplex [diu-pleks] *adj.* duplo, gemelo, doble; — (apartment), departamento de dos pisos.

duplicate [diu-pli-keit] *n.* duplicado, *m.;* copia, *f.;* —, *vt.* duplicar.

duplicity [diu-pli-si-ti] *n.* duplicidad, *f.;* doblez, *m.* y *f.*

durability [diu-ra-bi-li-ti] *n.* duración, *f.;* estabilidad, *f.*

durable [diu-ra-bol] *adj.* duradero.

duration [diu-rei-shon] *n.* duración, *f.*

duress [diu-res] *n.* compulsión, *f.;* prisión, *f.*

during [diu-rin] *prep.* durante.

dusk [dask] *n.* crepúsculo, *m.;* —, *vi.* hacerse noche.

dusky [das-ki] *adj.* oscuro.

dust [dast] *n.* polvo, *m.;* —, *vt.* limpiar de polvo, desempolvar.

duster [das-tar] *n.* plumero, *m.;* persona o cosa que quita el polvo; guardapolvo, *m.*

dustpan [dast-pan] *n.* recogedor de basura, basurero, *m.*

dusty [das-ti] *adj.* polvoriento; empolvado.

Dutch [dach] *n.* y *adj.* holandés, esa.

dutiful [diu-ti-ful] *adj.* obediente, sumiso; respetuoso.

duty [diu-ti] *n.* deber, *m.;* obligación, *f.;* quehacer, *m.;* respeto, homenaje, *m.;* (mil.) facción, *f.;* derechos de aduana; **off** —, libre; **on** —, de servicio, de guardia.

dwarf [duorf] *n.* enano, na; —, *vt.* impedir que alguna cosa llegue a su tamaño natural; —, *vi.* empequeñecerse.

dwell [duel] *vi.* habitar, morar; dilatarse; — **upon,** explayarse.

dweller [due-lar] *n.* habitante, *m.* y *f.*.

dwelling [due-lin] *n.* habitación, residencia, *f.;* domicilio, *m.;* posada, *f.*

dwindle [duin-dol] *vi.* mermar, disminuirse; degenerar; consumirse.

dye [dai] *vt.* teñir, colorar; —, *n.* tinte, colorante, *m.*

dying [daiin] *adj.* agonizante, moribundo.

dynamic [dai-na-mik] *adj.* dinámico, enérgico; —s, *n. pl.* dinámica, *f.;* —ally, *adv.* con energía.

dynamite [dai-na-mait] *n.* dinamita, *f.*

dynasty [di-nas-ti] *n.* dinastía, *f.*

dysentery [di-sen-te-ri] *n.* disentería, *f.*

dystrophy [dis-tro-fi] *n.* distrofia, *f.*

E

each [ich] *adj.* cada; —, *pron.* cada uno, cada una, cada cual; — **other,** unos a otros, mutuamente.

eager [i-guar] *adj.* deseoso; fogoso; ardiente, vehemente; celoso, fervoroso.

eagerness [i-guer-nes] *n.* ansia, *f.;* anhelo, *m.;* vehemencia, *f.;* ardor, *m.*

eagle [i-guel] *n.* águila, *f.*

eagle-eyed [i-guel-aid] *adj.* de vista de lince, perspicaz.

ear [iar] *n.* oreja, *f.;* oído, *m.;* asa, *f.;* (bot.) espiga, *f.;* **by —,** de oído; — **of corn,** mazorca; *f.*

earache [iar-eik] *n.* dolor de oído.

eardrum [iar-dram] *n.* tímpano, *m.*

earl [erl] *n.* conde, *m.*

early [er-li] *adj.* temprano; primero; —, *adv.* temprano; — **bird,** madrugador, ra.

earmuff [ia-maf] *n.* orejera, *f.*

earn [ern] *vt.* ganar, obtener, conseguir.

earnest [er-nest] *adj.* ardiente, fervoroso, serio, importante; —, *n.* seriedad, *f.;* señal, *f.;* prueba, *f.;* **in good —,** de buena fe; —**ly,** *adv.* con ahínco.

earnestness [er-nest-nes] *n.* ansia, *f.;* ardor, celo, *m.;* seriedad, vehemencia, *f.;* **with —,** con ahínco.

earnings [er-nings] *n. pl.* ingresos, *m. pl.,* ganancias, *f. pl.*

earphone [iar-foun] *n.* audífono, auricular, *m.*

earring [iar-ring] *n.* arete, pendiente, *m.*

earshot [iar-shot] *n.* distancia a que se puede oír algo; **within —,** al alcance del oído.

earth [erz] *n.* tierra, *f.,* globo terráqueo; suelo, *m.*

earthen [er-zen] *adj.* terreno; hecho de tierra; de barro.

earthly [erz-li] *adj.* terrestre, mundano.

earthquake [erz-kueik] *n.* terremoto, *m.;* temblor de tierra.

earthworm [erz-uerm] *n.* lombriz de tierra.

earthy [erzi] *adj.* mundano, terrestre, terreno.

earwax [iar-uaks] *n.* cerumen, *m.*

ease [is] *n.* quietud, *f.;* reposo, ocio, *m.;* comodidad *f.;* facilidad, *f.;* **at —,** con desahogo; con soltura; —, *vt.* aliviar; mitigar.

easel [isel] *n.* caballete, *m.*

easily [isi-li] *adv.* fácilmente.

east [ist] *n.* oriente, este, *m.*

Easter [is-tar] *n.* Pascua de Resurrección; — **egg,** huevo real o de dulce dado como regalo para la Pascua florida.

easterly, eastern [is-ter-li], [is-tern] *adj.* oriental, del este.

eastward [ist-uard] *adv.* hacia el oriente, hacia el este.

easy [isi] *adj.* fácil; cortés, sociable; cómodo, pronto; libre; tranquilo; aliviado; — **chair,** silla poltrona; **on — street,** próspero; — **mark,** blanco, *m.,* víctima, *f.*

easygoing [isi-goin] *adj.* lento, tranquilo, bonazo; sereno; inalterable.

eat [it] *vt.* comer; roer; —, *vi.* alimentarse.

eaves [ivs] *n. pl.* socarrén *m.;* alero, *m.*

ebony [e-bo-ni] *n.* ébano, *m.*

eccentric [ik-sen-tric] *adj.* excéntrico.

eccentricity [ik-sen-tri-si-ti] *n.* excentricidad, *f.*

ecclesiastic [i-kle-si-as-tic] *n.* y *adj.* eclesiástico, *m.*

echo [e-kou] *n.* eco, *m.;* —, *vi.* resonar, repercutir (la voz) ; —, *vt.* hacer eco.

eclipse [i-klips] *n.* eclipse, *m.;* —, *vt.* eclipsar.

economic, economical [i-ko-no-mik] *adj.* económico, frugal, parco, moderado.

economics [i-ko-no-miks] *n.* economía, *f.*

economist [i-ko-no-mist] *n.* economista, *m.*

economize [i-ko-no-mais] *vt.* y *vi.* economizar; ser económico.

economy [i-ko-no-mi] *n.* economía, *f.;* frugalidad, *f.*

ecotourism [i-ko-tu-rism] *n.* ecoturismo, *m.*

ecstasy [eks-ta-si] *n.* éxtasis, *m.*

ecstatic [eks-ta-tik] *adj.* extático; —**ally,** *adv.* en éxtasis.

edge [ech] *n.* filo, borde, *m.;* orilla, *f.;* vera, *f.;* punta, *f.;* esquina, *f.;* margen, *in.* y *f.;* **on —,** impaciente, nervioso; —, *vt.* afilar; introducir; — *vi.* avanzar poco a poco escurriéndose; — **away,** alejarse.

edgewise [ech-uais] *adv.* de canto, de lado.

edging [ed-chin] *n.* orla, orilla, *f.*

edible [e-di-bol] *adj.* comedero, comestible.

edict [i-dikt] *n.* edicto, mandato, *m.*

edifice [e-di-fis] *n.* edificio, *m.;* fábrica, *f.*

edify [e-di-fai] *vt.* edificar.

edit [e-dit] *vt.* redactar; dirigir (una publicación); revisar o corregir (un artículo, etc.).

edition [i-di-shon] *n.* edición, *f.;* publicación, *f.;* impresión, *f.;* tirada, *f.*

editor [e-di-tor] *n.* director, redactor, editor (de una publicación), *m.;* persona que corrige o revisa (un artículo, etc.).

editorial [e-di-to-rial] *n.* editorial, *m.;* artículo de fondo; — **staff,** redacción, *f.,* cuerpo de redacción.

educate [e-diu-keit] *vt.* educar; enseñar.

educated [e-diu-kei-tid] *adj.* educado, instruido.

education [e-diu-kei-shon] *n.* educación, *f.;* crianza, *f.*

educational [e-diu-kei-sho-nal] *adj.* educativo.

educator [e-diu-kei-tor] *n.* pedagogo, educador, maestro, *m.*

eel [il] *n.* anguila, *f.*

eerie [ia-ri] *adj.* que infunde terror, como un fantasma; asustado; horripilante.

effect [i-fekt] *n.* efecto, *m.;* realidad, *f.;* **to take** —, entrar en vigor; —**s,** *n. pl.* efectos, bienes, *m. pl.;* —, *vt.* efectuar, ejecutar.

effective [i-fek-tiv] *adj.* eficaz; efectivo; real; —, *n.* soldado disponible para la guerra.

effeminate [i-fe-mi-neit] *vt.* afeminar, debilitar; —, *vi.* afeminarse, enervarse; —, *adj.* afe-

minado; — **man,** marica, maricón, hombre afeminado.

effervescent [e-fer-ve-sent] *adj.* efervescente.

efficacious [e-fi-kei-shos] *adj.* eficaz.

efficiency [e-fi-shens] *n.* eficiencia, virtud, *f.,* rendimiento (de una máquina), *m.*

effigy [e-fi-yi] *n.* efigie, imagen, *f.;* retrato, *m.*

effort [e-fort] *n.* esfuerzo, empeño, *m.,* gestión, *f.*

effusion [e-fiu-shon] *n.* efusión, *f.*

effusive [e-fiu-siv] *adj.* expansivo, efusivo.

e.g.: for example p.ej. por ejemplo, vg. verbigracia.

egg [eg] *n.* huevo, *m.;* — **beater,** batidor de huevos; — **cell,** célula embrionaria; — **white,** clara de huevo; **deviled** —, huevo relleno; **fried** —, huevo frito o estrellado; **hard-boiled** —, huevo cocido o duro; **poached** —, huevo escalfado; **scrambled** —, huevo revuelto; **soft-boiled** —, huevo tibio o pasado por agua; —, *vt.* mezclar con huevos; **to** — **on,** incitar, hurgar, azuzar.

eggnog [eg-nog] *n.* yema mejida, ponche de huevo, (Mex.) rompope, *m.*

eggplant [eg-plant] *n.* (bot.)

berenjena, *f.*

eggshell [eg-shel] *n.* cascarón de huevo.

egg yolk [eg-youlk] *n.* yema de huevo.

ego [i-gou] *n.* ego, yo, *m.*

egoism, egotism [e-gou-isem], [e-gou-tisem] *n.* egoísmo, *m.*

egoistical, egotistical [e-gou-tis-ti-kal], [e-gou-is-ti-kal] *adj.* egoísta.

Egypt [i-yipt] Egipto, *m.*

Egyptian [i-yip-shan] *n.* y *adj.* egipcio, cia.

eight [eit] *n.* y *adj.* ocho, *m.*

eighteen [ei-tin] *n.* y *adj.* dieciocho o diez y ocho, *m.*

eighteenth [ei-tinz] *n.* y *adj.* decimoctavo, dieciocheno, *m.*

eighth [eiz] *n.* y *adj.* octavo, *m.*

eightieth [ei-tiez] *n.* y *adj.* octogésimo, *m.*

eighty [ei-ti] *n.* y *adj.* ochenta, *m.*

either [ai-dar] *pron.* y *adj.* cualquiera, uno de dos; —, *conj.* o, sea, ya, ora.

ejaculation [i-ya-kiu-lei-shon] *n.* eyaculación, *f.*

eject [i-yekt] *vt.* expeler, desechar.

ejection [i-yek-shon] *n.* expulsión, *f.;* (med.) evacuación, *f.;* — **seat,** asiento expulsor.

elaborate [i-la-bo-reit] *vt.* elaborar; —, *adj.* trabajado, primoro-

so.

elapse [i-laps] *vi.* pasar, correr, trascurrir (el tiempo) .

elastic [i-las-tik] *n.* goma, *f.;* —, *adj.* repercusivo.

elation [i-lei-shon] *n.* júbilo, *m.*

elbow [el-bou] *n.* codo, *m.;* —, *vt.* y *vi.* dar codazos, empujar con el codo; codearse.

elbowroom [el-bou-rum] *n.* anchura, *f.;* espacio suficiente; (fig.) libertad, latitud, *f.*

elder [el-dar] *adj.* que tiene más edad, mayor; —, *n.* anciano, antepasado, *m.;* eclesiástico, *m.;* jefe de una tribu; (bot.) saúco, *m.*

elderly [el-de-li] *adj.* de edad madura, anciano.

eldest [el-dest] *adj.* mayor, más anciano.

elect [i-lekt] *vt.* elegir; —, *adj.* elegido, electo, escogido.

election [i-lek-shon] *n.* elección, *f.;* —**s,** comicios, *m. pl.*

electoral [i-lek-to-ral] *adj.* electoral; — **college,** colegio electoral.

electorate [i-lek-to-reit] *n.* electorado, *m.*

electric [i-lek-trik] *adj.* eléctrico; — **bulb,** bombilla eléctrica, foco; — **cable,** cable conductor; — **chair,** silla eléctrica; — **fixtures,** instalación eléctrica; — **lamp,** lámpara eléctrica; — **meter,** contador electrómetro;

— **motor,** electromotor, *m.*; — **plant,** planta eléctrica; — **switch,** conmutador, *m.*; — **wire,** hilo o alambre conductor.

electrical [i-lek-tri-kal] *adj.* eléctrico; — **engineering,** electrotecnia, ingeniería eléctrica; — **transcription,** (radio y TV.) trascripción mediante cinta magnética.

electrician [i-lek-tri-shan] *n.* electricista, *m.*

electricity [i-lek-tri-si-ti] *n.* electricidad, *f.*

electrify [i-lek-tri-fai] *vt.* electrizar.

electrocardiogram [i-lek-tro-kardio-gram] *n.* electrocardiograma, *m.*

electrocute [i-lek-tro-kiut] *vt.* electrocutar.

electrocution [i-lek-tro-kiu-shon] *n.* electrocución, *f.*

electrolyte [i-lek-tro-lait] *n.* electrólito, *m.*

electrochemistry [i-lek-tro-ke-mis-tri] *n.* electroquímica, *f.*

electromagnet [i-lek-tro-mag-net] *n.* electroimán, *m.*

electromagnetic [i-lek-tro-magne-tik] *adj.* electromagnético; —**field,** campo electromagnético.

electromotive [i-lek-tro-mo-tiv] *adj.* electromotor, electromotriz; — **force,** fuerza electromo-triz.

electron [i-lek-tron] *n.* electrón, *m.*

electronics [i-lek-tro-niks] *n.* electrónica, *f.*

elegance [e-li-gans] *n.* elegancia, *f.*

elegant [e-li-gant] *adj.* elegante, delicado; lujoso.

elegy [e-li-chi] *n.* elegía, *f.*

element [e-li-ment] *n.* elemento, *m.*; fundamento, *m.*; —**s,** *n. pl.* elementos, *m. pl.*; principios, *m. pl.*; bases, *f. pl.*; elementos atmosféricos.

elemental [e-li-men-tal] *adj.* elemental, simple, inicial.

elementary [e-li-men-ta-ri] *adj.* elemental, simple, inicial; — **school,** escuela primaria.

elephant [e-li-fant] *n.* elefante, *m.*

elevate [e-li-veit] *vt.* alzar, exaltar.

elevated [e-li-vei-ted] *adj.* elevado; — **railroad,** ferrocarril elevado; — **train,** tren elevado.

elevation [e-li-vei-shon] *n.* elevación, *f.*; altura, *f.*; alteza (de pensamientos), *f.*

elevator [e-li-vei-tar] *n.* ascensor, elevador, *m.*

eleven [i-le-ven] *n. y adj.* once, *m.*; oncena, *f.*

eleventh [i-le-venz] *n. y adj.* onceno, undécimo, *m.*

elf [elf] *n.* duende, *m.; persona* traviesa.

elicit [i-li-sit] *vt.* incitar; educir; sacar; atraer.

eligible [e-li-yi-bol] *adj.* elegible; deseable.

eliminate [i-li-mi-neit] *vt.* eliminar, descartar.

elk [elk] *n.* alce, *m.,* anta, *f.*

elliptic, elliptical [i-lip-tik], [i-lip-ti-kal]*adj.* elíptico.

elm [elm] *n.* olmo, *m.*

elocution [e-lo-kiu-shon] *n.* elocución, *f.; declamación, f.*

elongate [i-lon-gueit] *vt.* y *vi.* alargar, extender.

elope [i-loup] *vi.* escapar, huir; fugarse con un amante.

elopement [i-loup-ment] *n.* fuga con un amante; huida, *f.*

eloquent [e-lo-kuent] *adj.* elocuente.

else [els] *adj.* otro; más; —, *adv.* si no; de otro modo; **nothing** —, nada más; **somewhere** —, en alguna otra parte.

elsewhere [els-uear] *adv.* en otra parte.

elucidate [e-lu-si-deit] *vt.* dilucidar, explicar.

elude [e-lud] *vt.* eludir, evadir.

elusive, elusory [i-lu-siv-nes], [i-lu-so-ri] *adj.* artificioso, falaz; evasivo.

emaciate [i-mei-sieit] *vt.* extenuar, adelgazar.

emaciated [i-mei-si-eited]*adj.* demacrado; chupado; **to become** —, demacrarse.

e-mail [i-meil] *n.* correo electrónico, *m.*

emanate [i-ma-neit] *vi.* emanar.

emanation [i-ma-nei-shon] *n.* emanación, *f.; origen, m.*

emancipate [i-man-si-peit] *vt.* emancipar; dar libertad.

emancipation [i-man-si-pei-shon] *n.* emancipación, *f.*

emancipator [i-man-si-pei-tar] *n.* libertador, *m.*

embalm [im-balm] *vt.* embalsamar.

embank [im-bank] *vt.* terraplenar; represar.

embankment [im-bank-ment] *n.* encajonamiento, *m.;* malecón, dique, *m.,* presa, *f.;* terraplén, *m.*

embargo [im-bar-gou] *n.* embargo, *m.;* detención, *f.;* comiso, *m.;* —, *vt.* embargar.

embarrass [im-ba-ras] *vt.* avergonzar, desconcertar, turbar.

embarrassed [im-ba-rast] *adj.* avergonzado, cortado.

embarrassing [im-ba-rasin]*adj.* penoso, vergonzoso.

embarrassment [im-ba-ras-ment] *n.* turbación, *f.;* bochorno, *m.;* vergüenza, pena, *f.*

embassy [em-ba-si] *n.* embajada, *f.*

embellish [em-be-lish] vt. hermosear, adornar.

ember [em-ber]n. ascua, f.

embezzle [em-be-zel] vt. desfalcar.

embezzlement [em-be-zel-ment] n. hurto, m.; desfalco, m.

embezzler [em-bez-lar] n. desfalcador, ra.

embitter [em-bi-tar] vt. amargar, agriar.

emblazon [em-bla-son] vt. blasonar.

emblem [em-blem] n. emblema, m.

embody [im-bo-di] vt. encarnar, incluir.

emboss [im-bos] vt. realzar, imprimir en relieve.

embrace [im-breis] vt. abrazar; contener; —, n. abrazo, m.

embroider [em-broi-dar] vt. bordar.

embroidery [im-broi-de-ri] n. bordado, m.

embroil [im-broil] vt. embrollar; confundir.

embryo [em-briou] n. embrión, m.

emerald [e-me-rald] n. esmeralda, f.

emerge [i-merch] vi. surgir; emerger.

emergence [i-mer-chens] n. emergencia, aparición, f.

emergency [i-mer-chen-si] n.

aprieto, m.; emergencia, f ; necesidad urgente; — landing field, (avi.) campo de aterrizaje de emergencia; in case of —, en caso de necesidad o de emergencia; — room, sala de emergencia, f.

emeritus [i-mi-ri-tus] adj. emérito, retirado.

emigrant [e-mi-grant] n. y adj. emigrante, m. y f.

emigrate [e-mi-greit] vi. emigrar.

emigration [e-mi-grei-shon] n. emigración, f.

eminent [e-mi-nent] adj. eminente, elevado; distinguido; relevante.

emissary [e-mi-sa-ri] n. emisario, m.; espía, m. y f.

emit [i-mit] vt. emitir, echar de sí; arrojar, despedir.

emotion [i-mou-shon] n. emoción, f.; conmoción, f.

emotional [i-mou-sho-nal] adj. emocional; sensible, impresionable.

emperor [em-pe-rar] n. emperador, m.

emphasis [em-fa-sis] n. énfasis, m. y f.

emphasize [em-fa-sais] vt. hablar con énfasis; acentuar; hacer hincapié; recalcar.

emphatic [em-fa-tik] adj. enfático.

empire [em-paiar] n. imperio, m.

employee [em-ploi-yi] *n.* empleado, da.

employer [im-ploiar] *n.* dueño,
patrón, *m.*

employment [im-ploi-ment] *n.*
empleo, *m.;* ocupación, *f.;*
cargo, *m.;* **to give — to,** colocar,
emplear.

emporium [em-po-rium] *n.*
emporio, *m.*

empower [im-pauar] *vt.* autorizar, dar poder, facultar.

empress [em-pris] *n.* emperatriz
f

emptiness [emp-ti-nes] *n.* vacui-
dad, *f.,* vacío, *m.;* futilidad, *f.*

empty [emp-ti] *adj.* vacío; vano;
ignorante; —, *vt.* vaciar, evacuar, verter.

empty-handed [emp-ti-janded]
adj. manivacío, con las manos
vacías.

emulate [e-miu-leit] *vt.* emular,
competir con; imitar.

emulsify [e-mal-si-fai] *vt.* emul-
sionar.

emulsion [e-mal-shon] *n.* emulsión, *f.*

enable [i-nei-bol] *vt.* habilitar;
poner en estado de.

enact [i-nakt] *vt.* establecer,
decretar; efectuar.

enamel [i-na-mel] *n.* esmalte,
m.; —, *vt.* esmaltar.

encampment [in-kamp-ment] *n.*
campamento, *m.*

encase [in-keis] *vt.* encajar,
encajonar, incluir.

enchant [in-chant] *vt.* encantar.

enchanting [in-chan-tin] *adj.*
encantador.

enchantment [in-chant-ment] *n.*
encanto, *m.*

enchantress [in-chan-tres] *n.*
encantadora, *f.;* mujer seducto-
ra.

enclose [in-klous] *vt.* cercar, cir-
cunvalar, circundar; incluir;
encerrar.

enclosure [in-klo-shar] *n.* cercamiento, *m.;* cercado, *m.;* caja
(de engranaje, etc.), *f.;* anexo
(en una carta), *m.*

encompass [in-kam-pas] *vt.* circundar; cercar; circuir.

encore [an-kor] *n.* (theat.) bis,
m., repetición, *f.;* inter]. ¡bis!
¡otra vez! ¡que se repita! —, *vt.*
pedir que un actor repita lo
que ha ejecutado.

encounter [in-kaun-tar] *n.*
encuentro, *m.;* duelo, *m.;*
pelea, *f.;* —, *vt.* encontrar; —,
vi. encontrarse.

encourage [in-ka-rich] *vt.* animar, alentar; envalentonar; dar
aliento.

encouragement [in-ka-rich-
ment] *n.* estímulo, aliento, *m.,*
animación, *f.*

encouraging [in-ka-ri-chin] *adj.*
alentador.

encroach [in-krouch] *vt.* usurpar, avanzar gradualmente.

encumber [in-kam-bar] *vt.* embarazar, cargar; estorbar.

encumbrance [in-kam-brans] *n.* impedimento, *m.;* estorbo, *m.,* carga, *f.*

encyclopedia [en-si-klou-pi-dia] *n.* enciclopedia, *f.*

end [end] *n.* fin, *m.;* extremidad, *f.;* cabo, *m.;* término, *m.;* propósito, intento, *m.;* punto, *m.;* **no —,** sinnúmero, *m.;* **to accomplish one's —,** salirse con la suya; **to no —,** en vano; **—,** *vt.* matar, concluir, fenecer; terminar; **—,** *vi.* acabarse, terminarse.

endanger [in-dein-char] *vt.* poner en peligro, arriesgar.

endear [in-diar] *vt.* hacer querer.

endearment [in-dia-ment] *n.* terneza, *f.;* encarecimiento, afecto, *m.*

endeavor [in-de-var] *vi.* esforzarse; intentar; **—,** *n.* esfuerzo, *m.*

ending [en-din] *n.* terminación, conclusión, cesación, *f.;* muerte, *f.*

endless [end-les] *adj.* infinito, perpetuo, sin fin.

endorse [en-dors] *vt.* endosar (una letra de cambio); apoyar, sancionar.

endorsement [en-dors-ment] *n.* endorso.

endorser (of a draft) *n.* cedente (de un giro o letra), *m.*

endow [in-dau] *vt.* dotar.

endowment [in-dou-ment] *n.* dotación, *f.*

endurable [in-diua-ra-bol] *adj.* soportable.

endurance [in-diu-rens] *n.* duración, *f.;* paciencia, *f.;* sufrimiento, *m.*

endure [in-diuar] *vt.* sufrir, soportar; **—,** *vi.* durar; conllevar; sufrir.

enema [e-ni-ma] *n.* lavativa, enema, *f.*

enemy [e-ni-mi] *n.* enemigo, ga; antagonista, *m.* y *f.*

energetic [e-ner-ye-tik] *adj.* enérgico, vigoroso.

energy [e-ner-yi] *n.* energía, fuerza, *f.*

enervate [e-ner-veit] *vt.* enervar, debilitar, quitar las fuerzas.

enfold [in-fould] *vt.* envolver, arrollar; rodear.

enforce [in-fors] *vt.* compeler; hacer cumplir (una ley), poner en vigor.

enforcement [in-fors-ment] *n.* compulsión, coacción, *f.;* fuerza, *f.;* cumplimiento (de una ley), *m.*

engage [in-gueich] *vt.* empeñar, obligar; contratar; **—,** *vi.* comprometerse.

engaged [in-gueichd] *adj.* comprometido, prometido.

engagement [in-gueich-ment] *n.* noviazgo, compromiso, *m.;* cita, *f.;* (theat.) contrato, *m.;* (mil.) combate, *m.*

engaging [in-guei-chin] *adj.* simpático, atractivo.

engender [in-yen-dar] *vt.* y *vi.* engendrar, procrear.

engine [en-yin] *n.* máquina, *f.;* locomotora, *f.;* instrumento, *m.;* — **house,** casa de máquinas; **internal-combustion —,** motor de explosión, motor de combustión interna.

engineer [en-che-niar] *n.* ingeniero, *m.;* maquinista, *m.*

engineering [en-che-nia-rin] *n.* ingeniería, *f.*

England [In-glan] Inglaterra, *f.*

English [in-glish] *n.* y *adj.* inglés, sa; — **language,** inglés, *m.;* — **Channel,** Canal de la Mancha.

Englishman [in-glish-man] *n.* inglés, *m.*

Englishwoman [in-glish-uo-man] *n.* inglesa, *f.*

engrave [in-greiv] *vt.* grabar; esculpir; tallar.

engraver [in-grei-var] *n.* grabador, *m.*

engraving [in-grei-vin] *n.* grabado, *m.;* estampa, *f.*

engrossing [in-grou-sin] *adj.* absorbente.

engulf [in-galf] *vt.* engolfar, tragar, sumir.

enhance [in-jans] *vt.* realzar, elevar, intensificar.

enigma [i-nig-ma] *n.* enigma, *m.*

enigmatic [i-nig-ma-tik] *adj.* enigmático.

enjoy [in-yoi] *vt.* gozar; poseer; saborear; disfrutar de.

enjoyable [in-yoia-bol] *adj.* agradable.

enjoyment [in-yoi-ment] *n.* goce, *m.;* placer, *m.;* fruición, *f.;* usufructo, *m.*

enlarge [in-larch] *vt.* engrandecer, dilatar, extender; ampliar; —, *vi.* extenderse, dilatarse; — **upon,** explayarse.

enlargement [in-larch] *n.* aumento, *m.;* ampliación (de una fotografía, etc.), *f.*

enlighten [in-lai-ten] *vt.* aclarar; iluminar; instruir.

enlightenment [in-lai-ten-ment] *n.* ilustración, *f.;* aclaración, *f.*

enlist [in-list] *vt.* alistar, reclutar; —, *vi.* inscribirse como recluta, engancharse.

enliven [in-lai-ven] *vt.* animar; avivar; alegrar.

enmity [en-mi-ti] *n.* enemistad, *f.;* odio, *m.*

ennoble [i-nou-bel] *vt.* ennoblecer.

enormity [i-nor-mi-ti] *n.* enormidad, *f.;* atrocidad, *f.*

enormous [i-nor-mos] *adj.* enorme.

enough [i-naf] *adj.* bastante, suficiente; —, *adv.* suficientemente; —, *n.* suficiencia, *f.*; — *interj.* ¡basta! ¡suficiente! ¡ya!

enrage [in-reich] *vt.* enfurecer, irritar.

enraged [in-reicht] *adj.* colérico.

enrapture [in-rap-char] *vt.* arrebatar, entusiasmar; encantar.

enrich [in-rich] *vt.* enriquecer; adornar.

enroll [in-roul] *vt.* registrar, inscribir; arrollar.

enrollment [in-roul-ment] *n.* inscripción, *f.*; matriculación, *f.*

ensemble [an-sam-bel] *n.* conjunto, *m.*; traje de mujer compuesto de más de una pieza.

enshrine [en-shrain] *vt.* guardar como reliquia; estimar como cosa sagrada.

ensign [in-sain] *n.* bandera, *f.*; enseña, *f.*; **naval** —, alférez, *m.*; subteniente, *m.*

enslave [in-sleiv] *vt.* esclavizar, cautivar.

ensue [in-siu] *vi.* seguirse; suceder.

ensure [in-suar] *vt.* asegurar.

entail [in-teil] *n.* vínculo, mayorazgo, *m.*; —, *vt.* vincular; ocasionar.

entangle [in-tan-gol] *vt.* enmarañar, embrollar.

enter [en-tar] *vt.* entrar, meter; admitir; registrar; penetrar; —, *vi.* entrar, empeñarse en algo; emprender; aventurar.

enterprise [en-ter-prais] *n.* empresa, *f.*

enterprising [en-ter-prai-sin] *adj.* emprendedor.

entertain [en-ter-tein] *vt.* entretener; obsequiar; divertir.

entertainer [en-ter-tei-nar] *n.* festejador, ra; persona que divierte a otra; cantante, bailarín, etc., que entretiene en una fiesta.

entertaining [en-ter-tei-nin] *adj.* divertido, chistoso.

entertainment [en-ter-tein-ment] *n.* festejo, *m.*; diversión, *f.*, entretenimiento, pasatiempo, *m.*

enthrone [in-zroun] *vt.* entronizar.

enthusiast [in-zu-siast] *n.* entusiasta, *m.* y *f.*

enthusiastic [in-zu-sias-tik] *adj.* entusiasmado, entusiasta.

entice [in-tais] *vt.* halagar; acariciar, excitar, inducir.

enticing [in-tai-sin] *adj.* atractivo, incitante.

entire [in-taiar] *adj.* entero, cumplido, completo, perfecto, todo.

entirety [in-taiar-li] *n.* entereza, integridad, totalidad, *f.*; todo, *m.*

entitle [in-tai-tol] *vt.* intitular; conferir algún derecho; autorizar.

entity [in-ti-ti] *n.* entidad, existencia, *f.*

entrails [en-treils] *n. pl.* entrañas, *f. pl.;* tripa, *f.*

entrance [en-trans] *n.* entrada, *f.;* admisión, *f.;* principio, *m.;* boca, *f.;* ingreso, *m.*

entreat [en-trit] *vt.* rogar, suplicar.

entree o **entrée** [an-trei] *n.* principio (en una comida), *m.,* entrada, *f.,* plato principal.

entrust, intrust [en-trast] *vt.* confiar.

entry [en-tri] *n.* entrada, *f.;* (com.) partida, *f.*

entwine [int-uain] *vt.* entrelazar, enroscar, torcer.

enumerate [e-niu-me-reit] *vt.* enumerar, numerar.

enunciate [i-nan-shieit] *vt.* enunciar, declarar.

envelop [en-va-loup] *vt.* envolver, cubrir.

envelope [en-va-loup] *n.* sobre, *m.,* cubierta, *f.*

enviable [en-via-bol] *adj.* envidiable.

envious [en-vios] *adj.* envidioso.

environment [in-vaia-ron-ment] *n.* medio ambiente, *m.*

environmental [in-vaia-ron-mental] *adj.* ambiental.

environmentalism [in-vaia-ron-men-talism]*n.* ambientalismo, *m.*

environs [in-vaia-ronz] *n. pl.* vecindad, *f.;* alrededores, contornos, *m. pl.*

envoy [en-voi] *n.* enviado, *m.;* mensajero, *m.*

envy [en-vi] *n.* envidia, *f.;* malicia, *f.;* —, *vt.* envidiar.

enzyme [en-saim] *n.* (biol.) enzima, *f.*

epic [e-pik] *adj.* épico; —, *n.* epopeya, *f.*

epicenter [e-pi-sen-tar] *n.* epicentro, *m.*

epidemic [e-pi-der-mik] *adj.* epidémico; —, *n.* epidemia,

epidermis [e-pi-der-mis] *n.* epidermis, *f.*

epigram [e-pi-gram] *n.* epigrama, *m.*

epilepsy [e-pi-lep-si] *n.* epilepsia, *f.*

epileptic [e-pi-lep-tik] *n.* y *adj.* epiléptico, ca.

Episcopalian [i-pis-ko-pa-lian] *n.* episcopal, *m.* y *f.*

episode [e-pi-soud] *n.* episodio, *m.*

epistle [i-pisel] *n.* epístola, *f.*

epitaph [e-pi-taf] *n.* epitafio, *m.*

epithet [e-pi-zet] *n.* epíteto, *m.*

epitome [i-pi-to-mi] *n.* epítome, compendio, *m.;* sinopsis, *f.*

epoch [i-pok] *n.* época, edad,

era, *f.*

equable [e-kua-bol] *adj.* uniforme, parejo, tranquilo.

equal [i-kual] *adj.* igual; justo; semejante; imparcial; —, *n.* par, *m.,* cantidad igual; persona igual; —, *vt.* igualar; compensar.

equality [e-kua-li-ti] *n.* igualdad, uniformidad, *f.*

equalize [i-kua-lais] *vt.* igualar.

equanimity [e-kua-ni-mi-ti] *n.* ecuanimidad, *f.*

equation [i-kuei-shon] *n.* equilibrio, *m.;* (math.) ecuación, *f.*

equator [i-kuei-tar] *n.* ecuador, *m.*

equatorial [e-kua-to-rial] *adj.* ecuatorial.

equestrian [i-kues-trian] *adj.* ecuestre; —, *n.* jinete, *m.*

equidistant [i-kui-dis-tant] *adj.* equidistante.

equilateral [i-kui-la-te-ral] *n.* y *adj.* equilátero, *m.*

equilibrium [i-kui-li-briom] *n.* equilibrio, *m.*

equip [i-kuip] *vt.* equipar, pertrechar; aprestar (un navío).

equipment [i-kuip-ment] *n.* equipo, *m.;* avíos, *m. pl.*

equitable [e-kui-ta-bol] *adj.* equitativo, imparcial.

equity [e-kui-ti] *n.* equidad, justicia, imparcialidad, *f.*

equivalent [i-kui-va-lent] *n.* y *adj.* equivalente, *m.*

equivocal [i-kui-vo-kal] *adj.* equívoco, ambiguo.

equivocate [i-kui-vo-keit] *vt.* equivocar, usar equívocos.

era [ia-ra] *n.* edad, época, era, *f.*

eradicate [i-ra-dieit] *vt.* erradicar, desarraigar, extirpar.

erase [i-reis] *vt.* borrar; cancelar, rayar, tachar.

eraser [i-rei-sar] *n.* goma de borrar, borrador, *m.*

erect [i-rekt] *vt.* erigir; establecer; —, *adj.* derecho, erguido.

erection [i-rek-shon] *n.* erección, *f.;* estructura, construcción, *f.*

erode [i-roud] *vt.* y *vi.* roer, corroer, comer, gastarse.

erosion [i-rou-shon] *n.* erosión, *f.*

err [ar] *vi.* equivocarse, errar; desviarse.

errand [e-rand] *n.* recado, mensaje, *m.;* encargo, *m.;* — **boy,** mensajero, mandadero, *m.*

erratic [i-ra-tik] *adj.* errático, errante; irregular, excéntrico.

error [e-ror] *n.* error, *m.,* equivocación, *f.*

erudite [e-riu-dait] *adj.* erudito.

erudition [e-riu-di-shon] *n.* erudición, *f.*

erupt [i-rapt] *vi.* hacer erupción.

eruption [i-rap-shon] *n.* erupción, *f.;* sarpullido, *m.*

escalator [es-ka-lei-tor] *n.* escalera mecánica; — **clause,** cláusula que permite fluctuaciones en los salarios.

escapade [es-ka-peid] *n.* fuga, escapada, *f.;* travesura, *f.*

escape [is-keip] *vt.* evitar; escapar; —, *vi.* evadirse, salvarse; **to — from danger,** salvarse; —, *n.* escapada, huida, fuga, *f.;* inadvertencia, *f.;* salvamento, *m.;* — **capsule,** cápsula de escape, cápsula de emergencia; **to have a narrow —,** salvarse en una tablita; — **literature,** escapismo, *m.*, literatura huidiza que trata de escapar de la realidad.

escapism [is-kei-pi-sem] *n.* escapismo, *m.*, estilo literario mediante el cual se trata de escapar o huir de la realidad.

escapist [is-kei-pist] *n.* soñador, ra, fantaseador, ra.

escort [es-kort] *n.* escolta; *f.;* acompañante, *m.;* —, *vt.* escoltar, convoyar; acompañar.

Eskimo [es-ki-mou] *n.* y *adj.* esquimal, *m.* y *f.*

esophagus [i-so-fa-gus] *n.* esófago, *m.*

esoteric [e-sou-te-rik] *adj.* esotérico.

especial [is-pe-shal] *adj.* especial, excepcional; **—ly,** *adv.* particularmente; sobre todo.

espionage [es-pio-nash] *n.* espionaje, *m.*

espouse [is-pou-sa] *vt.* desposar.

essay [e-sei] *vt.* ensayar, intentar, probar; —, *n.* ensayo literario; tentativa, *f.*

essence [e-sens] *n.* esencia, *f.;* perfume, *m.;* quid, *m.;* médula, *f.*

essential [i-sen-shal] *adj.* esencial, sustancial, principal; imprescindible; vital; —, *n.* lo esencial.

establish [is-ta-blish] *vt.* establecer, fundar, fijar; confirmar; **to — oneself,** radicarse; establecerse.

establishment [is-ta-blish-ment] *n.* establecimiento, *m.;* fundación, *f ;* institución, *f.*

estate [is-teit] *n.* estado, *m.;* patrimonio, *m.;* hacienda, *f.;* bienes, *m. pl.*

esteem [is-tim] *vt.* estimar, apreciar; —, *n.* estima, *f.;* consideración, *f.*

esteemed [is-timd] *adj.* estimado, considerado.

esthetic [is-zi-tik] *adj.* estético; **—s,** *n. pl.* estética, *f.*

estimate [es-ti-meit] *vt.* estimar, apreciar, tasar; —, *n.* presupuesto, *m.;* cálculo, *m.*

estrange [is-treinch] *vt.* apartar, enajenar, malquistar.

etch [ech] *vt.* grabar al agua fuerte.

etching [e-chin] *n.* aguafuerte, *m.* o *f.;* grabado al agua fuerte.

eternal [i-ter-nal] *adj.* eterno, perpetuo, inmortal.

eternity [i-ter-ni-ti] *n.* eternidad, *f.*

ethereal [i-zia-rial] *adj.* etéreo; vaporoso.

ethical [e-zi-kal] *adj.* ético; —ly, *adv.* moralmente.

ethics [e-ziks] *n. pl.* ética, moralidad, *f.*

Ethiopian [i-ziou-pian] *n.* y *adj.* etiope, *m.* y *f.*

ethnographer [ez-no-gra-far] *n.* etnógrafo, *m.*

ethnologist [ez-no-lo-chist] *n.* etnólogo, *m.*

ethyl [i-zail] *n.* etilo, *m.*

etiquette [e-ti-ket] *n.* etiqueta, *f.*

etymology [e-ti-mo-lo-chi] *n.* etimología, *f.*

eucalyptus [iu-ka-lip-tos] *n.* eucalipto, *m.*

Eucharist [yu-ka-rist] *n.* Eucaristía, *f.*

eucharistic [iu-ka-ris-tik] *adj.* eucarístico.

eulogize [iu-lo-chais] *vt.* elogiar.

eulogy [iu-lo-chi] *n.* elogio, encomio, *m.,* alabanza, *f.*

Europe [iua-rop] Europa, *f.*

European [iua-ro-pian] *n.* y *adj.* europeo, pea.

euthanasia [iu-za-nei-shia] *n.* (med.) eutanasia, *f.*

evacuate [i-va-kueit] *vt.* evacuar.

evacuation [i-va-kuei-shon] *n.* evacuación, *f.*

evacuee [i-va-kui] *n.* evacuado, da, persona desalo-jada de una plaza militar.

evade [i-veid] *vt.* evadir, escapar, evitar.

evaluate [i-va-liueit] *vt.* evaluar.

evaluation [i-va-liuei-shon] *n.* evaluación, *f.*

evanescent [i-va-ne-sent] *adj.* fugitivo; imperceptible.

evangelical [i-van-che-li-kal] *adj.* evangélico.

evangelist [i-van-che-list] *n.* evangelista, *m.* y *f.*

evaporate [i-va-po-reit] *vt.* evaporar, vaporizar; —, *vi.* evaporarse; disiparse; —d milk, leche evaporada, *f.*

evaporation [i-va-po-rei-shon] *n.* evaporación, *f.*

evasion [i-vei-shon] *n.* evasión, *f.;* escape, refugio, *m.;* tergiversación, *f.*

evasive [i-vei-siv] *adj.* evasivo; sofístico.

eve [iv] *n.* tardecita, *f.;* vigilia, víspera, *f.;* Christmas —, Nochebuena, *f.*

even [i-ven] *adj.* llano, igual; par; semejante; —, *adv.* aun, supuesto que; no obstante; — as, como; — now, aun ahora; ahora mismo; —so aun así; —

or odd, pares o nones; — **though,** aun cuando; **not —,** ni siquiera; **—,** *vt.* igualar, allanar.

evening [iv-nin] *adj.* vespertino; **— clothes,** traje de etiqueta; **—,** *n.* tarde, noche, *f.*

evenness [i-ven-nes] *n.* igualdad, uniformidad, *f.*

event [i-vent] *n.* evento, acontecimiento, *m.;* circunstancia, *f.;* caso, *m.;* ocurrencia, *f.,* suceso, *m.;* **in any —,** en todo caso.

eventful [i-vent-ful] *adj.* lleno de acontecimientos; memorable.

eventual [i-ven-chual] *adj.* eventual, fortuito; **—ly,** *adv.* finalmente, con el tiempo.

ever [e-var] *adj.* siempre; **for — and —,** por siempre jamás, eternamente; **— since,** desde que.

evergreen [eva-grin] *adj.* siempre verde; **—,** *n.* (bot.) siempreviva., *f.*

everlasting [eva-las-tin] *adj.* eterno; **—,** *n.* eternidad, *f.*

every [e-vri] *adj.* todo, cada; **— day,** todos los días; **— time,** cada vez.

everybody [e-vri-bo-di] *pron.* cada uno, cada una; todo el mundo.

everyday [e-vri-dei] *adj.* ordinario, rutinario, de todos los días.

everyone [e-vriuan] *pron.* cada cual, cada uno.

everything [e-vri-zin] *n.* todo, *m.*

everywhere [e-vriuear] *adv.* en todas partes, por todas partes, por doquier.

evict [i-vikt] *vt.* despojar jurídicamente; desalojar, expulsar.

eviction [i-vik-shon] *n.* evicción, expulsión, *f.;* despojo jurídico.

evidence [e-vi-dens] *n.* evidencia, *f.;* testimonio, *m.,* prueba, *f.;* **—,** *vt.* evidenciar.

evident [e-vi-dent] *adj.* evidente; patente, manifiesto; indudable.

evil [i-vil] *adj.* malo, depravado, pernicioso; dañoso; **—,** *n.* maldad, *f.;* daño, *m.;* calamidad, *f.;* mal, *m.*

evildoer [i-vil-doar] *n.* malhechor, ra.

evince [i-vins] *vt.* probar, justificar, demostrar.

evoke [i-vouk] *vt.* evocar.

evolution [i-vo-lu-shon] *n.* evolución, *f.;* desarrollo, *m.*

evolve [i-volv] *vt.* y *vi.* desenvolver; desplegarse; emitir.

ewe [iu] *n.* oveja (hembra del carnero), *f.*

exact [ik-sakt] *adj.* exacto, puntual; riguroso; cuidadoso; **—,** *vt.* exigir.

exacting [ik-sak-tin] *adj.* severo, exigente.

exactness, exactitude [ik-saktnes], [ik-sak-ti-tiud] *n.* exactitud, *f.*

exaggeration [ik-sa-che-rei-shon] *n.* exageración, *f.*

exalt [ik-solt] *vt.* exaltar, elevar; alabar; realzar; enaltecer.

exalted [ik-sol-ted] *adj.* sublime.

examination [ik-sa-mi-nei-shon] *n.* examen, *m.;* medical —, reconocimiento médico.

examine [ik-sa-min] *vt.* examinar; escudriñar; ver, revisar.

examiner [ik-sa-mi-nar] *n.* examinador, ra; comprobador, ra.

examining [ik-sa-mi--nin] *adj.* revisor; examinador.

example [ik-sam-pol] *n.* ejemplo, *m.;* **to set an** —, dar el ejemplo.

exasperate [ik-sa-ni-meit] *vt.* exasperar, irritar, enojar, provocar; agravar, amargar.

excavate [eks-ka-veit] *vt.* excavar, cavar, ahondar.

excavation [eks-ka-vei-shon] *n.* excavación, *f.;* cavidad, *f.*

exceed [ik-sid] *vt.* exceder; sobrepujar; rebasar; —, *vi.* excederse.

exceeding [ik-si-din] *adj.* excesivo; —**ly,** *adv.* extremadamente, en sumo grado; sobremanera.

excel [ik-sel] *vt.* sobresalir, exceder; superar.

excellence [ek-se-lens] *n.* excelencia, *f.*

excellent [ek-se-lent] *adj.* excelente; sobresaliente.

except [ik-sept] *vt.* exceptuar, excluir; sacar; —, *vi.* recusar.

excepting [ik-sep-tin] *prep.* menos, salvo, excepto, a excepción de.

exception [ik-sep-shon] *n.* excepción, exclusión, *f.*

exceptional [ik-sep-sho-nal] *adj.* excepcional.

excerpt [ik-serpt] *vt.* extraer; extractar; —, *n.* extracto, *m.*

excess [ik-ses] *n.* exceso, *m.;* intemperancia, *f.;* desmesura, *f.;* sobra, *f.;* — **baggage,** exceso de equipaje.

excessive [ik-se-siv] *adj.* excesivo.

exchange [ik-cheinch] *vt.* cambiar; trocar, permutar; —, *n.* cambio, *m.;* bolsa, lonja, *f.;* — **office,** casa de cambio; **bill of** —, letra de cambio, cédula de cambio; **domestic** —, cambio interior; **foreign** —, cambio exterior o cambio extranjero; **in** — **for,** a cambio de; **rate of** —, tipo de cambio; **stock** —, bolsa, *f.;* **telephone** —, central telefónica.

excite [ik-sait] *vt.* excitar; estimular; agitar.

excitement [ik-sait-mant] *n.* estímulo, *m.;* agitación, *f.;* excitación, conmoción, *f.*

exciting [ik-sai-tin] *adj.* excitante; conmovedor.

exclaim [iks-kleim] *vi.* exclamar; —, *vt.* proferir.

exclamation [eks-kla-mei-shon] *n.* exclamación, *f.;* clamor, *m.;* — **mark,** — **point,** punto de admiración.

exclude [iks-klud] *vt.* excluir; exceptuar.

exclusion [iks-klu-shon] *n.* exclusión, exclusiva, *f.;* excepción *f.*

exclusive [iks-klu-siv] *adj.* exclusivo.

excommunicate [eks-ko-miu-ni-keit] *vt.* excomulgar, descomulgar.

excrement [eks-kri-ment] *n.* excremento, *m.*

excretion [eks-kri-shon] *n.* excremento, *m.;* excreción, *f.*

excruciating [eks-kru-shiei-tin] *adj.* atroz, enorme, grave; muy agudo.

excursion [iks-ker-shon] *n.* excursión, expedición, *f.;* digresión, *f.;* correría, *f.;* jira, *f.*

excusable [iks-kiu-sa-bol] *adj.* excusable, perdonable.

excuse [iks-kius] *vt.* excusar; perdonar; —, *n.* excusa, *f.*

execute [ek-si-kiut] *vt.* ejecutar; llevar a cabo, cumplir.

execution [ek-si-kiu-shon] *n.* ejecución, *f.*

executioner [ek-si-kiu-sho-nar] *n.* ejecutor, *m.;* verdugo, *m.*

executive [ik-se-kiu-tiv] *adj.* y *n.* ejecutivo, *m.*

executor [ik-se-kiu-tar] *n.* testamentario, *m.;* albacea, *m.*

exemplary [ig-sem-pla-ri] *adj.* ejemplar.

exemplify [ig-sem-pli-fai] *vt.* ejemplificar.

exempt [ig-sempt] *adj.* exento, libre por privilegio; —, *vt.* eximir, exentar.

exemption [ig-semp-shon] *n.* exención, franquicia, *f.*

exercise [ek-ser-sais] *n.* ejercicio, *m.;* ensayo, *m.;* tarea, *f.;* práctica, *f.;* —, *vi.* hacer ejercicio; —, *vt.* ejercitar; atarear; practicar; profesar.

exert [ik-sert] *vt.* ejercer; **to — oneself,** esforzarse.

exertion [ik-ser-shon] *n.* esfuerzo, *m.*

exhale [eks-jeil] *vt.* exhalar.

exhaust [ik-sost] *n.* cámara de escape; (auto., avi.) escape, *m.;* — **fan,** expulsor de aire; — **pipe,** tubo de salida de gases; —, *vt.* agotar, consumir.

exhausting [ik-sos-tin] *adj.* enervante, agotador.

exhaustion [ik-sos-shon] *n.* agotamiento, *m.;* extenuación, *f.*

exhaustive [ik-sos-tiv] *adj.* agotador; completo, minucioso.

exhibit [ik-si-bit] *vt.* exhibir; mostrar; —, *n.* memorial, *m.;*

exposición, *f.*

exhibition [ik-si-bi-shon] *n.* exhibición, presentación, exposición, *f.;* espectáculo, *m.*

exhibitionism [ik-si-bi-shonisem] *n.* exhibicionismo, *m.*

exhibitor [ik-si-bi-tar] *n.* expositor, ra.

exhilarate [ik-si-la-reit] *vt.* alegrar, causar alegría.

exhilaration [ik-si-la-rei-shon] *n.* alegría, *f.;* buen humor, regocijo, *in.*

exhort [ik-sort] *vt.* exhortar, excitar.

exhume [ek-siu-meit] *vt.* exhumar, desenterrar.

exile [ek-sail] *n.* destierro, exilio, *m.;* desterrado, da, exiliado, da; —, *vt.* desterrar, exiliar.

exist [ik-sist] *vi.* existir.

existence [ik-sis-tens] *n.* existencia, *f.*

existent [ik-sis-tent] *adj.* existente.

existentialism [ik-sis-ten-shalisem] *n.* existencialismo, *m.*

existing [ik-sis-tin] *adj.* actual, presente; existente. exit, *n.* partida, salida, *f.*

exodus [ek-so-dos] *n.* éxodo, *m.,* salida, *f.*

exonerate [ik-so-ne-reit] *vt.* exonerar, disculpar.

exorbitant [ik-sor-bi-tant] *adj.* exorbitante, excesivo.

exotic [ik-so-tik] *adj.* exótico, extranjero; —, *n.* cosa exótica (como una planta o una palabra).

expand [iks-pand] *vt.* extender, dilatar, expandir.

expansion [iks-pan-shon] *n.* expansión, *f.;* desarrollo, *m.*

expansive [iks-pan-siv] *adj.* expansivo.

expatriation [iks-pei-shi-ei-shon] *n.* expatriación, extrañación.

expect [iks-pekt] *vt.* esperar, aguardar.

expectant [iks-pek-tant] *adj.* expectante, que espera; preñada, encinta, embarazada; — **mother**, mujer embarazada o encinta.

expectation [eks-pek-tei-shon] *n.* expectativa, *f.;* esperanza,

expediency [iks-pi-dien-si] *n.* conveniencia, oportunidad,

expedient [iks-pi-dient] *adj.* oportuno, conveniente; —, *n.* expediente, medio, *m.*

expedition [eks-pi-di-shon] *n.* expedición, excursión, *f.;* cruzada, *f.;* campaña, *f.*

expeditionary [eks-pi-di-shonari]*adj.* expedicionario.

expel [iks-pel] *vt.* expeler, expulsar; desterrar.

expend [iks-pend] *vt.* expender; desembolsar.

expendable [iks-pen-da-bol] *adj.*

(mil.) sacrificable, no indispensable.

expenditure [iks-pen-di-char] *n.*
gasto, *m.*

expense [iks-pens] *n.* gasto, *m.*

expensive [iks-pen-siv] *adj.* caro,
costoso.

experience [iks-pia-riens] *n.*
experiencia, *f.;* práctica, *f.;* —,
vt. experimentar; saber.

experienced [iks-pia-rienst] *adj.*
experimentado; versado, perito.

experiment [iks-pe-ri-ment] *n.*
experimento, *m.;* prueba, *f.* —,
vt. experimentar, hacer la
prueba.

experimental [iks-pe-ri-men-tal]
adj. experimental.

expert [eks-pert] *adj.* experto,
práctico, diestro; perito; —, *n.*
maestro, tra; conocedor,
ra; perito, ta; — **in,** conocedor
de.

expiration [eks-pi-ei-shon] *n.*
expiración, *f.;* muerte, *f.;* vapor,
vaho, *m.;* vencimiento (plazo de
una letra o un pagaré, etc.), *m.*

expire [iks-paiar] *vi.* expirar,
morir; vencerse (una suscripción, etc.).

explanation [eks-pla-nei-shon]
n. explicación, aclaración, *f.*

explicit [iks-pli-sit] *adj.* explícito.

explode [iks-ploud] *vt.* y *vi.* disparar con estallido; volar, estallar; refutar; explotar.

exploit [eks-ploit] *n.* hazaña,
proeza, *f.;* hecho heroico; —, *vt.*
explotar; aprovecharse (de
alguien).

exploitation [eks-ploi-tei-shon]
n. explotación, *f.*

exploration [eks-plo-rei-shon] *n.*
exploración, *f* ; examen, *m.*

explore [iks-plor] *vt.* explorar,
examinar; sondear.

explorer [iks-plo-rar] *n.* explorador, ra.

explosion [iks-plou-shon] *n.*
explosión, *f.*

explosive [iks-plou-siv] *adj.*
explosivo, fulminante; —, *n.*
explosivo, detonante, *m.*

exponent [eks-pou-nent] *n.*
exponente, *m.* y *f.;* (math.)
exponente, *m.*

export [eks-port] *vt.* exportar; —,
n. exportación, *f.;* —**house,**
casa exportadora.

exportation [eks-por-tei-shon] *n.*
exportación, *f.*

exporter [eks-por-tar] *n.* exportador, ra.

expose [iks-pous] *vt.* exponer;
mostrar; descubrir; poner en
peligro.

exposition [iks-pou-si-shon] *n.*
exposición, exhibición, *f.*

exposure [iks-pou-shar] *n.* exposición, *f.*

expound [iks-paund] *vt.* exponer, explicar; interpretar.

express [iks-pres] *vt.* expresar, exteriorizar; representar; —, *adj.* expreso, claro, a propósito; — **car,** furgón, furgón del expreso, vagón expreso; — **company,** compañía de porteo; — **train,** tren rápido o expreso; —, *n.* expreso, correo expreso.

expression [iks-pre-shon] *n.* expresión, *f.;* locución, *f.;* animación del rostro.

expressionless [iks-pre-shon-les] *adj.* sin expresión.

expressive [iks-pre-siv] *adj.* expresivo.

expressly [iks-pres-li] *adv.* expresamente.

expropriate [eks-pro-prieit] *vt.* expropiar, confiscar.

expulsion [iks-pal-shon] *n.* expulsión, *f.*

exquisite [eks-kui-sit] *adj.* exquisito, perfecto, excelente.

extend [iks-tend] *vt.* extender; amplificar; **to — (time),** prorrogar (un plazo); —, *vi.* extenderse; cundir.

extended [iks-ten-did] *adj.* prolongado; extendido.

extension [iks-ten-shon] *n.* extensión, *f.;* prórroga, *f.*

extensive [iks-ten-siv] *adj.* extenso; amplio; general.

extent [iks-tent] *n.* extensión, *f.;* grado, *m.;* **to such an —,** a tal grado.

extenuate [eks-te-nueit] *vt.* extenuar, disminuir, atenuar.

exterior [eks-te-rior] *n.* y *adj.* exterior, *m.*

exterminate [eks-ter-mi-neit] *vt.* exterminar; extirpar.

exterminator [eks-ter-mi-nei-tor] *n.* exterminador, *m.*

external [eks-ter-nal] *adj.* externo, exterior.

extinct [iks-tinkt] *adj.* extinto; abolido.

extinction [iks-tink-shon] *n.* extinción, *f.;* abolición, *f.*

extinguish [iks-tin-güish] *vt.* extinguir; suprimir.

extinguisher [iks-tin-güi-shar] *n.* apagador, extinguidor, *m.;* **fire —,** apagador de incendios.

extol [iks-tol] *vt.* alabar, magnificar, exaltar.

extort [iks-tort] *vt.* sacar por fuerza; adquirir por violencia; arrebatar.

extortion [iks-tor-shon] *n.* extorsión, *f.*

extra [eks-tra] *adj.* extraordinario, adicional; de reserva, de repuesto; —, *n.* suplemento extraordinario de un periódico; algo de calidad extraordinaria; (coll.) actor de cine que desempeña papeles insignificantes; — **mileage,** más millas por unidad de combustible.

extract [eks-trakt] *vt.* extraer; —,

n. extracto, *m.;* compendio, *m.*

extraction [eks-trak-shon] *n.* extracción, *f.;* descendencia, *f.*

extracurricular [eks-tra-ku-rri-cular] *adj.* que no forma parte de un plan de estudios.

extradition [eks-tra-di-shon] *n.* extradición, *f.*

extraordinary [iks-tror-di-na-ri] *adj.* extraordinario.

extravagance [iks-tra-va-gans] *n.* extravagancia, *f.;* derroche, *m.,* profusión de lujo.

extravagant [iks-tra-va-gant] *adj.* extravagante, singular, exorbitante; excesivo; pródigo; gastador, derrochador.

extreme [iks-trim] *adj.* extremo, supremo; último; —, *n.* extremo, *m.;* **to go to —s,** tomar medidas extremas.

extremist [iks-tri-mist] *n.* extremista, radical, *m.*

extremity [iks-tre-mi-ti] *n.* extremidad, *f.*

extricate [eks-tri-keit] *vt.* sacar (de un apuro, etc.); desenredar.

extrovert [eks-trou-vert] *n.* extrovertido, da.

exuberance [iks-tiu-be-rant] *n.* exuberancia, *f.*

exuberant [ik-su-be-rant] *adj.* exuberante, abundantísimo; —ly, *adv.* abundantemente.

exult [ik-salt] *vi.* regocijarse, alegrarse de un triunfo.

exultant [ik-sal-tant] *adj.* regocijado; triunfante, victorioso.

exultation [ek-sal-tei-shon] *n.* exultación, *f.;* regocijo, *m.*

eye [ai] *n.* ojo, *m.;* vista, *f.;* (bot.) yema, *f.,* botón, *m.;* —, *vt.* ojear, contemplar, observar.

eyeball [ai-bol] *n.* niña del ojo.

eyebrow [ai-bro] *n.* ceja, *f.*

eyeful [ai-ful] *n.* completa visión de algo; (coll.) muchacha atractiva.

eyeglasses [ai-glases] *n. pl.* anteojos, lentes, *m. pl.*

eyelash [ai-lash] *n.* pestaña, *f.*

eyelid [ai-lid] *n.* párpado, *m.*

eyesight [ai-sait] *n.* vista, *f.,* potencia visiva.

eye socket [ai-soket] *n.* cuenca del ojo.

eyesore [ai-sor] *n.* adefesio, *m.,* cosa ofensiva a la vista.

eyetooth [ai-tuz] *n.* colmillo, *m.*

eyewitness [ai-uit-nis] *n.* testigo ocular.

F

fable [fei-bol] *n.* fábula, *f.; ficción, f.*

fabric [fa-brik] *n.* tejido, *m.*, tela, *f.*

fabricate [fa-bri-keit] *vt.* fabricar, edificar; inventar (un cuento, una mentira, etc.).

fabulous [fa-biu-los] *adj.* fabuloso.

facade [fa-ad] *n.* fachada, *f.*, frontispicio de un edificio.

face [feis] *n.* cara, faz, *f.;* superficie, *f.;* fachada, *f.;* rostro, *m.;* frente, *f.;* aspecto, *m.;* apariencia, *f.;* atrevimiento, *m.;* esfera (de un reloj), *f.;* **to lose —,** sufrir pérdida de prestigio; **to make —s,** hacer gestos o muecas; **— down,** boca abajo; **— to —,** cara a cara; **— value,** valor nominal o aparente; **—,** *vt.* encararse; hacer frente; **to — about,** dar media vuelta; **to — the street,** dar a la calle.

facet [fa-sit] *n.* faceta, *f.*

facetious [fa-si-shos] *adj.* chistoso, jocoso; gracioso.

facial [fei-shal] *adj.* facial.

facile [fa-sail] *adj.* fácil; afable, complaciente.

facilitate [fa-si-li-teit] *vt.* facilitar.

facility [fa-si-li-ti] *n.* facilidad, ligereza, *f.;* afabilidad, *f.;* destreza, *f.*

facing [fei-sin] *n.* paramento, *m.;* cara, *f.;* guarnición *f.;* forro, m.

facsimile [fak-si-mi-li] *n.* facsímil, *m.*

fact [fakt] *n.* hecho, *m.;* realidad, *f.;* **in —,** en efecto, verdaderamente; **matter of —,** hecho positivo o cierto.

faction [fak-shon] *n.* facción, *f.;* disensión, *f.*

factitious [fak-ti-shos] *adj.* facticio, artificial.

factor [fak-tar] *n.* factor, *m.;* agente, *m.;* (math.) factor, *m.*

factory [fak-to-ri] *n.* fábrica, *f.*, taller, *m.*

factual [fak-chual] *adj.* actual, relacionado a hechos.

faculty [fa-kul-ti] *n.* facultad, *f.;* poder, privilegio, *m.;* profesorado, *m.*

fad [fad] *n.* fruslería, niñería, *f.;* boga, *f.;* novedad, *f.*

fade [feid] *vi.* desteñirse; decaer, marchitarse.

fail [feil] *vt.* abandonar; descuidar; faltar; decepcionar; **—,** *vi.* fallar, fracasar; menguar; debilitarse; perecer; **without —,** sin falta.

failing [fei-lin] *n.* falta, *f.;* defecto, *m.*

failure [fei-liar] *n.* falta, *f.;* culpa, *f.;* quiebra, bancarrota, *f.;* fiasco, *m.;* **to be a —,** quedar o salir deslucido; ser un fracaso.

faint [feint] *vi.* desmayarse; **—,** *adj.* tímido, lánguido; fatigoso,

desfallecido; borroso, sin claridad; —, *n.* desmayo, *m.*

faint-**hearted** [feint-jar-tid] *adj.*
cobarde, medroso, pusi-
lánime; —**ly**, *adv.* medrosamen-
te.

fair [fear] *adj.* hermoso, bello;
blanco; rubio; claro, sereno;
favorable; recto, justo, franco;
— **ball**, (béisbol) pelota que cae
dentro de los límites permitidos
en el juego; — **weather**, (naut.)
bonanza, *f.;* buen tiempo; —, *n.*
feria, exposición, *f.*

fair-**haired** [fear-jeard] *adj.* de
cabellos rubios.

fairly [fea-li] *adv.* positivamente;
favorablemente; justamente,
honradamente; clara-mente;
bastante, tolerablemente; —
well, bastante bien.

fairness [fea-nes] *n.* hermosura,
f.; honradez, *f.;* justicia, *f*

fair-**trade** [fear-treid] *adj.* relativo
al comercio equitativo; — **agre-**
ement, convenio de reciprocidad comercial.

fairy [fea-ri] *n.* hada, *f.;* duende,
m.; —, *adj.* de hadas, relativo a
las hadas; — **tale,** cuento de
hadas.

faith [feiz] *n.* fe, *f.;* fidelidad, sinceridad, *f.;* fervor, *m.*

faithful [feiz-ful] *adj.* fiel, leal; —
ly, *adv.* fielmente.

faithless [feiz-les] *adj.* infiel, pér-

fido, desleal.

fake [feik] *n.* (naut.) aduja, *f.;*
(coll.) imitación fraudulenta; —,
adj. (coll.) falsos fraudulento;
—, *vt.* (coll.) engañar; imitar.

faker [fei-kar] *n.* farsante, *m.* y *f.*

falcon [fol-kon] *n.* halcón, *m.*

fall [fol] *vi.* caer, caerse; perder
el poder; disminuir, decrecer
en precio; **to — asleep**, dormirse; **to — back**, recular; **to —**
back again, recaer; **to — due,**
cumplir, vencer; **to — hea-**
dlong, caer de bruces; **to —**
short, no corresponder a lo
esperado; **to — sick**, enfermar;
to — in love, enamorarse; **to —**
off, menguar, disminuir; caerse; **to — out**, reñir, disputar; **to**
— upon, atacar, asaltar; —, *n.*
caída, *f.;* declive, *m.;* catarata,
f.; otoño, *m.;* — **in prices**, baja,
f.

fallacious [fa-lei-shos] *adj.* falaz,
fraudulento; delusorio.

fallacy [fa-la-si] *n.* falacia, sofis-
tería, *f.,* engaño, *m.*

fallen [fo-len] *adj.* caído; arruinado; — *p.p.* del verbo **fall.**

fallout [fol-aut] *n.* lluvia nuclear,
radiactividad atmosférica.

false [fols] *adj.* falso, pérfido;
postizo; supuesto; — **bottom,**
fondo doble; — **colors**, bandera
falsa; — **teeth**, dientes postizos.

falsehood [fols-jud] *n.* falsedad,

f.; perfidia, *f.;* mentira, *f.*

falsetto [fol-se-tou] *n.* falsete, *m.;* — **voice,** falsete, *m.*

falsification [fol-si-fi-kei-shon] *n.* falsificación, *f.*

falter [fol-tar] *vi.* tartamudear; vacilar, titubear.

faltering [fol-te-rin] *adj.* balbuciente, titubeante.

fame [feim] *n.* fama, *f.;* renombre, *m.*

famed [feimd] *adj.* celebrado, famoso.

familiar [fa-mi-liar] *adj.* familiar, casero; conocido; —**with,** acostumbrado a, versado en, conocedor de.

familiarize [fa-mi-lia-rais] *vt.* familiarizar.

family [fa-mi-li] *n.* familia, *f.;* linaje, *m.;* clase, especie, *f.;* — **name,** apellido, *m.;* — **tree,** árbol genealógico.

famine [fa-min] *n.* hambre, *f.;* carestía, *f.*

famish [fa-mish] *vt.* hambrear.

famous [fei-mos] *adj.* famoso, célebre.

fan [fan] *n.* abanico, *m.;* aventador, ventilador, *m.;* aficionado, da.

fanatic [fa-na-tik] *n. y adj.* fanático, ca; mojigato, ta.

fanciful [fan-si-ful] *adj.* imaginativo, caprichoso; fantástico; — **ly,** *adv.* caprichosamente.

fancy [fan-si] *n.* fantasía, imaginación, imaginativa, *f.;* capricho, *m.;* — **goods,** novedades, modas, *f. pl.;* **foolish —,** quimera, *f.;* —, *vt.* imaginar; gustar de; suponer.

falsification [fal-si-fi-ka-shon] *n.* falsificación, *f.*

fang [fang] *n.* colmillo, *m.;* garra, uña, *f.;* raíz de un diente.

fantastic [fan-tas-tik] *adj.* fantástico; caprichoso.

fantasy [fan-ta-si] *n.* fantasía, *f.*

far [far] *adv.* lejos, a una gran distancia; — **be it from me!** ¡ni lo permita Dios! —, *adj.* lejano, distante, remoto; — **off,** lejano, distante.

faraway [far-a-uei] *adj.* lejano; abstraído.

farce [fars] *n.* farsa, *f.*

fare [fear] *n.* alimento, *m.,* comida, *f.;* viajero, ra; pasaje, *m.;* tarifa, *f.;* —, *vi.* viajar; **to — well (or ill),** irle a uno bien (o mal).

farewell [fear-uel] *n.* despedida, *f* ; —! *interj.* ¡adiós! ¡que le vaya bien!

farfetched [far-fecht] *adj.* forzado, traído de los cabellos.

far-flung [far-flong] *adj.* extendido, de gran alcance.

farm [farm] *n.* tierra arrendada; alquería, *f.;* hacienda, granja, *f.;* —, *vt.* arrendar; tomar en arriendo; cultivar.

farmer [far-mar] *n.* labrador, hacendado; agricultor; **small —** , estanciero, ranchero.

farmhand [farm-jand] *n.* peón de granja.

farming [far-min] *n.* agricultura, *f.*, cultivo, *m.*

far-off [far-of] *adj.* remoto, distante.

far-reaching [far-ri-chin]*adj.* de gran alcance, trascendental.

farsighted [far-sai-tid] *adj.* présbita, présbite; (fig.) precavido; astuto, sagaz, agudo.

farther [far-dar] *adv.* más lejos; más adelante; —, *adj.* más remoto, ulterior.

farthest [far-dest] *adj.* más distante, más remoto; más largo; más extendido; —, *adv.* a la mayor distancia.

fascinate [fa-si-neit] *vt.* fascinar, encantar.

fascination [fa-si-nei-shon] *n.* fascinación, *f.*; encanto, *m.*

fascism [fa-shi-sem] *n.* fascismo, *m.*

fashion [fa-shon] *n.* forma, figura, *f.*; moda, *f.*, estilo, *m.*; uso, *m.*, costumbre, *f.*; condición, *f.*; **latest —**, última moda; —, *vt.* formar, amoldar; confeccionar.

fast [fast] *vi.* ayunar; —, *n.* ayuno, *m.*; —, *adj.* firme, estable, veloz, pronto; disipado,

disoluto; — **clock,** reloj adelantado; — **day,** día de ayuno; —, *adv.* de prisa;— **food,** comida rápida, *f.*

fasten [fasen] *vt.* afirmar, asegurar, atar, fiar; —, *vi.* fijarse.

fastener [fa-se-nar] *n.* asegurador, sujetador, *m.*

fastening [fas-te-nin] *n.* atadura, ligazón, *f.*; nudo, *m.*

fastidious [fas-ti-dios] *adj.* delicado, melindroso; desdeñoso.

fasting [fas-tin] *n.* ayuno, *m.*

fastness [fast-nes] *n.* prontitud, *f.*; ligereza, *f.*; firmeza, *f.*; fortaleza, *f.*

fat [fat] *adj.* gordo, pingüe; **to get —**, echar carnes, engordar; —, *n.* gordo, *m.*, gordura, *f.*; grasa, manteca, *f.*; sebo, *m.*

fatal [fei-tal] *adj.* fatal; funesto.

fatalist [fei-ta-list] *n.* fatalista *m.* y *f.*

fatality [fa-ta-li-ti] *n.* fatalidad, predestinación, *f.*; muerte por accidente.

fate [feit] *n.* destino, *m.*; fatalidad, *f.*, sino, *m.*; suerte, *f.*

fateful [feit-ful] *adj.* fatídico, ominoso, funesto.

father [fa-dar] *n.* padre, *m.*

father-in-law [fa-der-in-lo] *n.* suegro, *m.*

fatherland [fa-der-land] *n.* patria, *f.*

fatherless [fa-der-les] *adj.* huérfano de padre.

fatherly [fa-der-li] *adj.* paternal.

fathom [fa-dom] *n.* braza (medida), *f.;* —, *vt.* sondar; penetrar; **to — a mystery,** desentrañar un misterio.

fathomless [fa-dom-les] *adj.* insondable.

fatigue [fa-tig] *n.* fatiga, *f.,* cansancio, *m.;* —, *vt.* y *vi.* fatigar, cansar, rendirse.

fatness [fat-nes] *n.* gordura, *f.*

fatten [fa-ten] *vt.* cebar, engordar; —, *vi.* engrosarse, engordarse.

fatty [fa-ti] *adj.* grasoso, untoso, craso, pingüe.

faucet [fo-sit] *n.* grifo, *m.;* **water —,** toma, llave, *f.,* caño de agua.

fault [folt] *n.* falta, culpa, *f.;* delito, *m.;* defecto, *m.;* **to find —,** tachar, criticar, poner faltas.

faultfinder [folt-fain-dar] *n.* criticón, ona, censurador, ra.

faultfinding [folt-fain-din] *adj.* caviloso; criticón.

faultless [fol-tles] *adj.* perfecto, cumplido, sin tacha.

faulty [fol-ti] *adj.* culpable, defectuoso.

faun [fon] *n.* fauno, *m.*

fauna [fo-na] *n.* (zool.) fauna, *f.*

faux pas [fou-pa] *n.* paso en falso; (coll.) metida de pata.

favor [fei-var] *n.* favor, beneficio, *m.;* gracia, *f.;* patrocinio, *m.;* **in — of,** a favor de; **in his —,** en su provecho; **your —,** su apreciable, su grata (carta); —, *vt.* favorecer, proteger, apoyar.

favorable [fei-va-ra-bol] *adj.* favorable, provechoso; —**bly,** *adv.* favorablemente.

favorite [fei-vo-rit] *n.* y *adj.* favorito, ta, favorecido, da.

favoritism [fei-vo-ri-tisem] *n.* favoritismo, *m.*

fear [fiar] *vt.* y *vi.* temer, tener miedo; —, *n.* miedo, terror, pavor, *m.*

fearful [fia-ful] *adj.* medroso, temeroso; tímido.

fearless [fia-les] *adj.* intrépido, atrevido; —**ly,** *adv.* sin miedo.

fearsome [fia-som] *adj.* espantoso, horroroso.

feasible [fia-si-bol] *adj.* práctico.

feast [fist] *n.* banquete, *m.;* fiesta, *f.;* —, *vt.* festejar, regalar; —, *vi.* comer opíparamente.

feat [fit] *n.* hecho, *m.;* acción, hazaña, *f.*

feather [fe-dar] *n.* pluma, *f.;* — **bed,** colchón de plumas; —, *vt.* emplumar; enriquecer.

feathered [fe-derd] *adj.* plumado, alado; veloz.

featherweight [fe-da-ueit] *n.* peso pluma, *m.*

feathery [fe-da-ri] *adj.* cubierto de plumas; ligero como una pluma.

feature [fi-char] *n.* facción del rostro; forma, *f.;* rasgo, *m.;* atracción principal; —s, *n. pl.* facciones, *f. pl.,* fisonomía, *f.*

February [fe-brua-ri] febrero, *m.*

federal [fe-de-ral] *adj.* federal.

federate [fe-de-reit] *adj.* confederado; —, *vt.* y *vi.* confederar, confederarse.

federation [fe-de-rei-shon] *n.* confederación, federación, *f.*

fee [fi] *n.* feudo, *m.;* paga, gratificación, *f.;* honorarios, *m. pl.;* derecho, *m.;* cuota, *f.*

feeble-minded [fi-bol-main-ded] *adj.* imbécil, escaso de entendimiento.

feed [fid] *vt.* pacer; nutrir; alimentar, dar de comer; —, *vi.* alimentarse, nutrirse; —, *n.* alimento, *m.;* pasto, *m.*

feeding [fi-din] *n.* nutrición, *f.,* alimento, *m.;* cebadura (para animales), *f.*

feel [fil] *vt.* sentir; palpar; **to —** **like,** tener ganas de; apetecer; —, *vi.* tener sensibilidad; —, *n.* tacto, sentido, *m.*

feeler [fi-lar] *n.* antena, *f.;* (fig.) tentativa, *f.*

feeling [fi-lin] *n.* tacto, *m.;* sensibilidad, *f.;* sentimiento, *m.;* presentimiento *m.*

feet [fit] *n. pl.* de **foot,** pies, *m. pl.*

feign [fein] *vt.* inventar, fingir; simular; —, *vi.* fingirse, disimular.

felicitation [fi-li-si-tei-shon] *n.* felicitación, congratulación, *f.*

felicity [fi-li-si-ti] *n.* felicidad, dicha, *f.*

feline [fi-lain] *adj.* felino, gatuno; —, *n.* gato, animal felino.

fell [fel] *adj.* cruel, bárbaro; —, *n.* cuero, *m.;* piel, *f.;* pellejo, *m.;* —, *vt.* matar las reses; cortar árboles; sobrecargar (en costura); —, *pretérito* del verbo **fall.**

fellow [fe-lou] *n.* compañero, camarada, *m.;* sujeto, *m.;* socio de algún colegio; — **citizen,** conciudadano, na; — **creature,** semejante, *m.;* — **member,** consocio, *m.;* — **student,** condiscípulo, la.

fellowship [fe-lou-ship] *n.* compañía, sociedad, *f.;* beca (en una universidad), *f.;* camaradería, *f.*

felon [fe-lon] *n.* reo de un delito gravísimo.

felony [fe-lo-ni] *n.* delito gravísimo.

felt [felt] *;* —, *pret.* y *p.p.* del verbo **feel.**

female [fi-meil] *n.* hembra, *f.;* —, *adj.* femenino.

feminine [fe-mi-nin] *adj.* femenino; tierno; afeminado, amujerado.

fence [fens] *n.* cerca, palizada, valla, *f.;* perista, *m.;* —, *vt.* cercar; preservar; —, *vi.* esgrimir.

fencer [fen-sar] *n.* esgrimidor, *m.*

fencing [fen-sin] *n.* esgrima, *f.*

fend [fend] *vt.* parar; rechazar, —, *vi.* defenderse.

fender [fen-dar] *n.* guardabarros, guardalodo, guardafango, *m.;* guardafuegos, *m.*

fern [fern] *n.* (bot.) helecho, *m.*

ferocious [fe-ro-shos] *adj.* feroz; fiero.

ferocity [fe-ro-si-ti] *n.* ferocidad, fiereza, *f.*

ferry [fe-ri] *n.* barca de trasporte, barca de trasbordo; —, *vt.* llevar en barca.

ferryboat [fe-ri-bout] *n.* barco para cruzar ríos, etc.

ferryman [fe-ri-man] *n.* barquero, *m.*

fertile [fer-tail] *adj.* fértil, fecundo, productivo.

fertilization [fer-ti-lai-sei-shon] *n.* fertilización, *f.*

fertilize [fer-ti-lais] *vt.* fertilizar.

fertilizer [fer-ti-lai-ser] *n.* abono, fertilizante, *m.*

fervent [fer-vent] *adj.* ferviente; fervoroso; —ly, *adv.* fervientemente, con fervor.

fervid [fer-vid] *adj.* ardiente, vehemente, férvido.

fervor [fer-var] *n.* fervor, ardor, *m.*

fester [fes-tar] *vi.* enconarse, inflamarse.

festival [fes-ti-val] *n.* fiesta, *f.,* festival, *m.*

festive [fes-tiv] *adj.* festivo, alegre.

festivity [fes-ti-vi-ti] *n.* festividad, *f.*

fetch [fech] *vt.* buscar; producir; llevar; arrebatar; —, *n.* estratagema, *f.;* artificio, ardid, *m.*

fetish [fe-tich] *n.* fetiche, *m.,* adoración, ciega de algo.

fetter [fe-tar] *vt.* atar con cadenas.

fetters [fe-ters] *n. pl.* manija, *f.,* grillos, hierros, *m. pl.,* esposas, *f. pl.*

feud [fiud] *n.* riña, contienda, *f.*

feudal [fiu-dal] *adj.* feudal.

feudalism [fiu-da-lisem] *n.* feudalismo, *m.*

fever [fi-var] *n.* fiebre, *f.;* **typhoid** —, tifoidea, fiebre tifoidea.

feverish [fi-ve-rish] *adj.* febril.

few [fiu] *adj.* pocos; **a** —, algunos; — **and far between** poquísimos.

fewer [fiuar] *adj.* menos.

fiancé [fian-sei] *n.* novio, *m.*

fiancée [fian-sei] *n.* novia, *f.*

fib [fib] *n.* mentirilla, *f.*

fiber, fibre [fai-bar] *n.* fibra.

fibroid [fi-broid] *adj.* fibroso

fibrous [fi-bros] *adj.* fibroso.

fickle [fi-kel] *adj.* voluble, inconstante, mudable, frívolo; caprichoso.

fiction [fik-shon] *n.* ficción, *f.;* invención, *f.*

fictitious [fik-ti-shos] *adj.* ficticio; fingido.

fiddle [fi-del] *n.* violín, *m.;* —, *vi.* tocar el violín; jugar nerviosamente con los dedos.

fiddler [fid-lar] *n.* violinista, *m.* y *f.*

fidelity [fi-de-li-ti] *n.* fidelidad, lealtad, *f.*

fidget [fid-yit] *vi.* (coll.) contonearse, moverse inquieta y nerviosamente; —, *n.* agitación nerviosa; persona nerviosa e inquieta.

field [fild] *n.* campo, *m.;* campaña, *f.;* espacio, *m.;* **sown** —, sembrado, *m.;* —, *adj.* campal.

fiend [find] *n.* demonio, *m.;* persona malvada; **dope** —, morfinómano, na.

fiendish [fin-dish] *adj.* diabólico, demoniaco.

fierce [fias] *adj.* fiero, feroz; cruel, furioso.

fiery [fie-ri] *adj.* ardiente, colérico; brioso.

fifteen [fif-tin] *n.* y *adj.* quince, *m.*

fifteenth [fif-tinz] *n.* y *adj.* decimoquinto, *m.*

fifth [fifz] *n.* y *adj.* quinto, *m.;* quinto de galón (medida de vinos y licores); — **column,** quinta columna;— **wheel,** rodete, *m.;* estorbo, *m.,* persona superflua; —**ly,** *adv.* en quinto lugar.

fiftieth [fif-tiez] *n.* y *adj.* quincuagésimo, *m.*

fifty [fif-ti] *n.* y *adj.* cincuenta, *m.*

fig [fig] *n.* higo, *m.;* (coll.) bagatela, *f.;* **I don't care a** —, no me importa un bledo; — **tree,** higuera, *f.*

fight [fait] *vt.* y *vi.* reñir; batallar; combatir; luchar con; —, *vi.* lidiar; —, *n.* batalla, *f.;* combate, *m.,* pelea, *f.;* conflicto, *m.*

fighter [fai-tar] *n.* batallador, ra; peleador, ra; — **plane,** aeroplano de combate.

fighting [fai-tin] *n.* combate, *m.;* riña, *f.;* —, *adj.* pugnante; combatiente.

figment [fig-ment] *n.* invención, *f.,* algo imaginado.

figurative [fi-gu-ra-tiv] *adj.* figurativo, figurado; —**ly,** *adv.* figuradamente.

figure [fi-gar] *n.* figura, forma, hechura, *f.;* imagen, *f.;* cifra, *f.;* **good** —, buen cuerpo; — **of speech,** tropo, *m.,* frase en sentido figurado; —, *vt.* figurar; calcular.

figurehead [fi-ga-jed] *n.* (naut.)

roda, *f.;* figurón de proa; pelele, jefe nominal.

filament [fi-la-ment] *n.* filamento, *m.;* fibra, *f.*

file [fail] *n.* archivo, *m.;* lista, *f.;* (mil.) fila, hilera, *f.;* lima, *f.;* — **case,** fichero, *m.;* — **clerk,** archivero, ra; —, *vt.* archivar; limar; pulir.

filial [fi-lial] *adj.* filial.

filibuster [fi-li-bas-tar] *n.* pirata, filibustero, *m.;* (E.U.A.) prolongadísimo discurso en el congreso para aplazar una ley.

filing [filin] *n.* clasificación, *f.;* archivo, *m.*

fill [fil] *vt.* llenar, henchir; hartar; **to — out,** llenar (un formulario, cuestionario, etc.); **to — up,** colmar; —, *vi.* hartarse; —, *n.* hartura, abundancia, *f.*

filler [fi-lar] *n.* llenador, *m.;* relleno, *m.*

fillet [fi-lit] *n.* faja, tira, banda, *f.;* filete (de pescado), *m.;* (arch.) filete, *m.*

filling [fi-lin] *n.* tapadura, *f.,* relleno, *m.;* orificación (de un diente); tripa, *f.;* — **station,** estación de gasolina.

filly [fi-li] *n.* potranca, *f.*

film [film] *n.* filme, *m.,* película, *f.;* membrana, *f.;* — **festival,** reseña cinematográfica; — **strip,** película auxiliar en clases o conferencias; —, *vt.* fil-

mar.

filter [fil-tar] *n.* filtro, *m.;* —, *vt.* filtrar.

filth, filthiness [filz], [fil-zi-nes] *n.* inmundicia, porquería, *f.;* fango, lodo, *m.*

filthy [fil-zi] *adj.* sucio, puerco.

filtrate [fil-treit] *vt.* filtrar.

fin [fin] *n.* aleta (de un pez), *f.*

final [fai-nal] *adj.* final, último; definitivo; terminal; —**ly,** *adv.* finalmente, por último, al cabo; —**s,** *n. pl.* final, *f.*

finalist [fai-na-list] *n.* finalista, *m. o f.*

finality [fai-na-li-ti] *n.* finalidad, *f.*

finance [fai-nans] *n.* renta, *f.;* economía, *f.;* hacienda pública; finanzas, *f. pl.;* —, *vt.* financiar; costear, sufragar los gastos (de).

financial [fai-nan-shal] *adj.* financiero, pecuniario, económico.

financier [fai-nan-siar] *n.* rentista, hacendista, *m.;* financista, *m.*

financing [fai-nan-sin] *n.* financiamiento, *m.*

find [faind] *vt.* descubrir; proveer; dar con; **to — oneself,** hallarse, estar; verse; **to — out,** descubrir, enterarse (de); —, *n.* hallazgo, descubrimiento, *m.*

finder [fain-dar] *n.* descubridor,

m.; (phot.) visor, *m.*

fine [fain] *adj.* fino; agudo, cortante; claro; trasparente, delicado; elegante; bello; bien criado; bueno; **the — arts,** las bellas artes; —, *n.* multa, *f.;* —, *vt.* multar; —! *interj.* ¡bien! ¡magnífico!

fineness [fain-nes] *n.* fineza, sutileza, perfección, *f.*

finery [fai-ne-ri] *n.* perifollos, *m. pl.;* ropa vistosa.

finger [fin-gar] *n.* dedo, *m.;* — **bowl,** lavadedos, *m.;* —, *vt.* tocar, manosear; manejar.

fingering [fin-gue-rin] *n.* tecleo, *m.;* manoseo, *m.;* (mus.) pulsación, *f.*

fingernail [fin-gar-neil] *n.* uña, *f.;* — **polish,** esmalte para uñas.

fingerprints [fin-gar-prints] *n. pl.* huellas digitales.

finish [fi-nish] *vt.* acabar, terminar, concluir, llevar a cabo; —, *n.* conclusión, *f.,* final, *m.;* pulimento, *m.;* acabado, *m.*

finished [fi-nisht] *adj.* concluido; perfeccionado, refinado; retocado; (coll.) arruinado.

finishing [fi-ni-shin] *n.* última mano; —, *adj.* de retoque; — **school,** colegio de cursos culturales para niñas.

finite [fai-nait] *adj.* limitado, finito.

fire [faiar] *n.* fuego, *m.;* candela, *f.;* incendio, *m.;* quemazón, *f.;* — **alarm,** alarma o llamada de incendios; — **department,** cuerpo de bomberos; — **engine,** bomba de apagar incendios; — **escape,** escalera de salvamento para incendios; **on —,** en llamas; — **extinguisher,** apagador de incendios, matafuegos, *m.;* — **insurance,** seguro contra incendio; — **truck,** autobomba, *f.;* **to catch —,** inflamarse, encenderse; **to open —,** (mil.) hacer una descarga; —, *vt.* quemar, inflamar; —, *vi.* encenderse; (mil.) tirar, hacer fuego.

firearms [faiararm] *n. pl.* armas de fuego.

firebrand [faia-brand] *n.* tizón, *m.;* incendiario, ria; persona sediciosa.

firecracker [faia-kra-kar] *n.* petardo, *m.;* buscapiés, cohete, *m.*

firefly [faia-flai] *n.* luciérnaga, *f*

fireman [faia-man] *n.* bombero, *m.;* (rail.) fogonero, *m.*

fireplace [faia-pleis] *n.* hogar, *m.,* chimenea, *f.*

firepower [faia-pouer] *n.* (mil.) potencia efectiva de disparo.

fireproof [faia-prof] *adj.* a prueba de incendio, incombustible; refractario.

fireside [faia-said] *n.* sitio cerca a la chimenea u hogar; vida de hogar.

firewood [faia-wud] *n.* leña para la lumbre.

fireworks [faia-uorks]*n. pl.* fuegos artificiales.

firing [faia-rin] *n.* encendimiento, *m.;* leña, *f.;* (mil.) descarga, *f.;* — **line,** línea de fuego; — **squad,** pelotón de fusilamiento; piquete de salvas.

firm [ferm] *adj.* firme, estable, constante; seguro; —, *n.* (com.) razón social, casa de comercio; — **name,** razón social.

firmament [fer-ma-ment] *n.* firmamento, *m.*

firmness [ferm-nes] *n.* firmeza, *f.;* constancia, *f.;* fijeza, *f.*

first [ferst] *adj.* primero; primario; delantero; — **aid,** primeros auxilios; — **mate,** piloto, *m.;* —, *adv.* primeramente; — **of all,** ante todo; —**ly,** *adv.* en primer lugar.

first-aid [ferst-eid] *adj.* de primer auxilio; — **kit,** botiquín, *m.*

first-born [ferst-born] *n.* y *adj.* primogénito, ta.

first-class [ferst-clas] *adj.* de primera clase; **private** —, (mil.) soldado de primera.

first cousin [ferst-ka-sin] *n.* primo hermano, prima hermana.

firsthand [ferst-jand] *adj.* directo, de primera mano.

first-rate [ferst-reit] *adj.* primordial; admirable, de primera clase.

fiscal [fis-kal] *adj.* fiscal.

fish [fish] *n.* pez, *m.;* pescado, *m.;* **cured** —, pescado salado; — **globe,** pecera, *f.;* — **market,** pescadería, *f.;* — **pole,** caña de pescar; — **story,** (coll.) cuento increíble, relato fabuloso; —, *vt.* y *vi.* pescar.

fishbone [fish-boun] *n.* espina de pescado.

fisherman [fisher-man] *n.* pescador, *m.*

fishery [fi-she-ri] *n.* pesca, *f.*

fishhook [fish-juk] *n.* anzuelo, *m.*

fishing [fishin] *n.* pesca, *f.;* — **bait,** cebo para pescar; — **line,** sedal, *m.;* — **reel,** carretel, *m.;* — **rod,** caña de pescar; — **tackle,** avíos de pescar.

fission [fi-shon] *n.* desintegración, *f.*

fissure [fi-shar] *n.* grieta, hendedura, *f.;* —, *vt.* y *vi.* agrietar, agrietarse.

fist [fist] *n.* puño, *m.;* —, *vt.* empuñar.

fit [fit] *adj.* apto, idóneo, capaz, cómodo; justo; —, *n.* paroxismo, *m.;* convulsión, *f.;* capricho, *m.;* ataque repentino de

algún mal; —, *vt.* ajustar, acomodar, adaptar; sentar, quedar
bien; **to — out,** proveer; —, *vi.*
convenir, venir; caber.

fitful [fit-ful] *adj.* alternado con
paroxismos; caprichoso;
inquieto.

fitness [fit-nes] *n.* aptitud, conveniencia, *f.;* proporción, *f.;*
oportunidad, *f.*

fitter [fi-tar] *n.* ajustador, *m.;*
arreglador, ra; (naut.) armador,
equipador, *m.;* instalador, *m.;*
costurera, entalladora, *f.*

fitting [fi-tin] *adj.* conveniente,
idóneo, justo; a propósito; adecuado; —, *n.* instalación, *f.;*
ajuste, *m.;* —s, *n. pl.* guarni-
ciones, *f. pl.;* accesorios, avíos,
m. pl.

five [faiv] *n.* y *adj.* cinco, *m.*

fix [fiks] *vt.* fijar, establecer;
componer; **to — up,** concertar;
arreglar, arreglarse; —, *vi.* fijarse, determinarse.

fixation [fik-sei-shon] *n.* fijación,
firmeza, estabilidad, *f.;* (chem.)
fijación, *f.*

fixed [fiks] *adj.* firme, fijo.

fixing [fik-sin] *n.* fijación, *f.;*
ensambladura, *f.*

fixture [fiks-char] *n.* mueble fijo
de una casa; —s, *pl.* instalación, *f.;* enseres, *m. pl.*

fizz [fis] *vi.* sisear; —, *n.* siseo,
m.

fizzle [fi-sel] *n.* fiasco, fracaso,
m.; —, *vi.* sisear; (coll.) fallar.

flabby [fla-bi] *adj.* blando, flojo,
lacio; fofo, débil.

flag [flag] *n.* bandera, *f.;* (naut.)
pabellón, *m.;* — **officer,** (naut.)
jefe de una escuadra; — **of
truce,** bandera de parlamento;
— , *vt.* hacer señales con una
bandera; **to — (a train),** hacer
parar (a un tren) ; — , *vi.* pender; flaquear, debilitarse.

flagging [fla-guin] *adj.* lánguido,
flojo; —, *n.* enlosado, *m.*

flagpole [flag-pol] *n.* asta de bandera.

flagrant [fla-grant] *adj.* flagrante;
notorio.

flagstaff [flag-staf] *n.* asta de
pabellón o de bandera.

flagstone [flag-stoun] *n.* losa, *f.*

flail [fleil] *n.* (agr.) mayal, *m.;* —,
vt. y *vi.* batir, sacudir.

flair [fleir] *n.* afición, inclinación,
f.

flake [fleik] *n.* copo, *m.;* lámina,
f.; **soap** —s, jabón en escamas;
—, *vt.* y *vi.* desmenuzar, des-
menuzarse.

flamboyant [flam-boiant] *adj.* flamante, suntuoso; (arch.) de
líneas ondulantes.

flame [fleim] *n.* llama, *f.;* fuego
(del amor), *m.;* —**thrower,** arro-
jallamas, *m.;* —, *vi.* arder; brillar; flamear, llamear.

flaming [flei-min] *adj.* llameante; flamante, llamativo.

flamingo [fla-min-gou] *n.* (orn.) flamenco, *m.*

flank [flank] *n.* ijada, *f.;* (mil.) flanco, *m.; —, vt.* atacar el flanco; flanquear.

flannel [fla-nel] *n.* franela, *f.;* **thick —,** bayeta, *f.*

flap [flap] *n.* ala (de sombrero), *f.;* bragueta, *f.;* solapa, *f.;* aleta, *f.; —, vt.* y *vi.* aletear; sacudir.

flare [flear] *vi.* lucir, brillar; **—,** *n.* llama, *f.;* (avi.) cohete de señales.

flare-up [flear-ap] *n.* fulguración, *f.;* recrudecimiento (de una enfermedad, etc.), *m.*

flash [flash] *n.* relámpago, *m.;* llamarada, *f.;* borbollón, *m.;* destello, *m.; —* **of lightning,** rayo, relámpago, *m.; —, vt.* enviar (un mensaje) por telégrafo; dar a conocer (noticias) rápidamente; **—,** *vi.* relampaguear, brillar.

flashback [flash-bak] *n.* interrupción de la continuidad de un relato para introducir acontecimientos previos (como en un filme).

flashing [fla-shin] *n.* centelleo, *m.;* tapajuntas (en la construcción de edificios), *m.*

flashlight [flash-lait] *n.* linterna, *f.;* linterna eléctrica de bolsillo; lámpara de intermitencia; **— photography,** fotografía instantánea de relámpago.

flask [flask] *n.* frasco, *m.;* botella, *f.*

flat [flat] *adj.* llano, plano; insípido; **— back,** lomo plano; **— tire,** llanta reventada o desinflada, neumático desinflado; **—,** *n.* llanura, *f.;* piano, *m.;* (naut.) bajío, *m.;* (mus.) bemol, *m.;* apartamiento, departamento, *m.; —***ly,** *adv.* horizontalmente; de plano, francamente.

flat-bottomed [flat-bo-tomd] *adj.* de fondo plano.

flatiron [flat-aion] *n.* plancha (para ropa), *f.*

flatness [flat-nes] *n.* llanura, *f.;* insipidez, *f.*

flatten [fla-ten] *vt.* allanar; abatir; chafar; **—,** *vi.* aplanarse.

flatter [fla-tar] *vt.* adular, lisonjear, echar flores.

flattering [fla-te-rin] *adj.* adulador, lisonjero.

flattery [fla-te-ri] *n.* adulación, lisonja, *f.;* requiebro, *m.;* (coll.) piropo, *m.*

flaunt [flont] *vi.* pavonearse; **—,** *vt.* exhibir con ostentación; **—,** *n.* alarde, *m.*

flavor [flei-var] *n.* sabor, gusto, *m.; —, vt.* sazonar, condimentar.

flavoring [flei-vo-rin] *n.* condimento, *m.;* sabor, *m.*

flaw [flo] *n.* resquebradura, hendidura, *f.;* falta, tacha, *f.;* ráfaga, *f.;* —, *vt.* rajar, hender; —, *vi.* agrietarse, rajarse.

flawless [flo-les] *adj.* sin defecto, sin tacha.

flax [flaks] *n.* lino, *m.;* **to dress** —, rastrillar lino.

flaxen [flak-sen] *adj.* de lino, de hilo; blondo, rubio.

flaxseed [flak-sid] *n.* semilla de lino.

flay [flei] *vt.* desollar, descortezar; censurar severamente.

flea [fli] *n.* pulga, *f.*

fleck [flek] *n.* mancha, raya, *f.;* —, *vt.* manchar, rayar.

flee [fli] *vi.* escapar; huir.

fleece [flis] *n.* vellón, vellocino, *m.,* lana, *f.;* —, *vt.* esquilar; tonsurar; desnudar, despojar.

fleet [flit] *n.* flota, *f.;* —, *adj.* veloz, acelerado, ligero.

fleeting [fli-tin] *adj.* pasajero, fugitivo.

flesh [flesh] *n.* carne, *f.;* — **color,** color de carne; — **wound,** herida superficial o ligera.

flesh-colored [flesh-colord] *adj.* encarnado, de color de carne.

fleshy [flesh-li] *adj.* carnoso, pulposo.

flew [flu] *pretérito* del verbo fly.

flexibility [flek-si-bi-li-ti] *n.* flexibilidad, *f.*

flexible [flek-si-bol] *adj.* flexible, adaptable, movible.

flick [flik] *vt.* dar ligeramente con un látigo; —, *n.* golpe como de un látigo; movimiento rápido.

flicker [fli-kar] *vi.* aletear, fluctuar; —, *n.* aleteo, *m.;* — **of an eyelash,** pestañeo, *m.*

flier [flaiar] *n.* fugitivo, *m.;* volante, *m.;* aviador, ra; tren muy rápido; hoja de anuncios (de una tienda, etc.).

flight [flait] *n.* huida, fuga, *f.;* vuelo, *m.;* bandada (de pájaros); (fig.) elevación, *f.;* — **pattern,** *n.* (avi.) forma de vuelo; — **strip,** (avi.) pita al borde de una carretera para el aterrizaje de emergencia; — **of stairs,** tramo de una escalera.

flimsy [flim-si] *adj.* débil; fútil.

flinch [flinch] *vi.* respingar; desistir, faltar; retirarse; vacilar.

fling [flin] *vt.* lanzar, echar; —, *vi.* lanzarse con violencia; —, *n.* tiro, *m.;* burla, chufleta, *f.;* tentativa, *f.*

flint [flint] *n.* pedernal, *m.;* — **glass,** cristal de piedra.

flip [flip] *vt.* arrojar, lanzar.

flirt [flert] *vt.* arrojar, lanzar; —, *vi.* coquetear; —, *n.* coqueta, *f.,* persona coqueta.

flirtation [fler-tei-shon] *n.* coquetería, *f.,* flirteo, *m.*

flit [flit] *vi.* volar, huir; aletear.

float [flout] *vt.* inundar; —, *vi.* flotar; fluctuar; —, *n.* carro alegórico.

flock [flok] *n.* manada, *f.;* rebaño, *m.;* gentío, *m.;* vedija de lana; —, *vi.* congregarse.

flog [flog] *vt.* azotar.

flogging [flo-guin] *n.* tunda, zurra, *f.*

flood [flad] *n.* diluvio, *m.;* inundación, *f.;* flujo, *m.;* —, *vt.* y *vi.* inundar, inundarse.

floodgate [flad-gueit] *n.* compuerta, *f.*

floodlight [flad-lait] *n.* reflector o lámpara que despide un rayo concentrado de luz.

floor [flar] *n.* pavimento, suelo, piso, *m.;* piso de una casa; — **brush,** escobeta, *f.;* **ground —,** piso bajo; — **show,** espectáculo de variedad en un cabaret; —, *vt.* solar; echar al suelo; (fig.) enmudecer; derrotar.

flooring [flo-rin] *n.* suelo, pavimento, *m.;* ensamblaje de madera para suelos.

flop [flop] *vi.* malograrse, fracasar; caerse; —, *n.* fracaso, *m.,* persona fracasada.

florid [flo-rid] *adj.* florido.

Florida Keys [flo-ri-da-kis] Cayos de la Florida.

flounce [flauns] *n.* volante, adorno plegado (de un vestido);

(Mex.) olán, *m.;* —, *vt.* adornar con volantes u olanes.

flour [flauar] *n.* harina, *f.;* — **mill,** molino de harina.

flourish [fla-rish] *vt.* blandir; agitar; —, *vi.* gozar de prosperidad; crecer lozanamente; jactarse; rasguear; (mus.) preludiar, florear; (mus.) floreo, preludio, *m.;* rasgo (de una pluma), *m.;* lozanía, *f.*

flout [flaut] *vt.* y *vi.* mofar, burlarse; —, *n.* mofa, burla, *f.*

flow [flou] *vi.* fluir, manar; crecer (la marea); ondear, verter; correr; —, *n.* creciente de la marea; abundancia, *f.;* **flujo,** *m.,* corriente, *f.;* caudal, *m.*

flower [flauar] *n.* flor, *f.; (fig.)* lo mejor; — **garden,** jardín de flores, vergel, *m.;* —, *vi.* florear; florecer.

flowerpot [flaua-pot] *n.* tiesto de flores, tiesto, *m.,* maceta, *f.*

flowery [flaua-ri] *adj.* florido.

flown [floun] *p.p.* del verbo fly.

flu [flu] *n.* (coll.) influenza, gripe, *f.,* trancazo, *m.*

fluency [fluen-si] *n.* fluidez, facundia, *f.*

fluent [fluent] *adj.* fluido; fluente, fácil, corriente; **—ly,** *adv.* con fluidez; **to speak (a language) —ly,** hablar (un idioma) a la perfección.

fluff [flaf] *vt.* mullir; —, *n.* pelusa, *f.,* tamo, *m.*

fluffy [fla-fi] *adj.* blando y velloso; fofo.

fluid [fluid] *n.* y *adj.* fluido, *m.*

flunk [flank] *vt.* y *vi.* (coll.)
reprobar; —, *n.* reprobación.

fluorescent [fluo-re-sent] *adj.*
fluorescente.

fluoroscope [fluo-ros-koup] *n.*
fluoroscopio, *m.*

flurry [fla-ri] *n.* ráfaga, *f.;* agitación nerviosa, conmoción, *f.;* —
, *vt.* confundir; alarmar; agitar.

flush [flash] *vt.* sacar agua de
algún lugar; echar agua, limpiar con un chorro de agua
(por ej., un inodoro); animar,
alentar; —, *vi.* sonrojarse,
ruborizarse; fluir repentinamente; —, *n.* rubor, *m.;* conmoción, *f.;* calor intenso (como
de fiebre) ; chorro de agua que
limpia; flor, *f.,* flux, *m.* (de naipes), una mano de naipes
todos del mismo palo; (print.)
composición pareja en el margen izquierdo, composición sin
sangrías; —, *adj.* bien provisto;
vigoroso, lozano; pródigo; parejo.

fluster [flas-tar] *vt.* confundir,
atropellar; —, *vi.* confundirse;
—, *n.* agitación, confusión, *f.*

flute [flut] *n.* flauta, *f.;* (arch.)
estría, *f.;* —, *vt.* estriar.

flutist [flu-tist] *n.* flautista, *m.* y
f.

flutter [fla-tar] *vt.* turbar, desordenar; —, *vi.* revolotear.

fly [flai] *vt.* y *vi.* volar; pasar ligeramente; huir; escapar; **to —
on the beam,** (rad.) volar por la
banda radiofónica; —, *n.*
mosca, *f.;* pliegue, volante, *m.;*
(béisbol) pelota que al ser gol-
peada se eleva.

flying [flai-in] *n.* vuelo, *m.;* aviación, *f.;* —, *adj.* volante, volador; temporal, de pasada;
repentino; — **colors,** bandera
desplegada; **to come off with —
colors,** salir victorioso (en una
prueba, examen, etc.); — **field,**
campo de aviación; — **fish,** pez
volador; **blind —,** vuelo a ciegas, vuelo con instrumentos; —
fortress, (avi.) fortaleza aérea;
— **saucer,** platillo volante o
volador.

fly swatter [flai-suorer]*n.* matamoscas, *m.*

flytrap [flai-trap] *n.* mosquero,
m.

flyweight [flai-ueit] *n.* peso
mosca (boxeador), *m.*

flywheel [flai-uil] *n.* (mech.)
volante, *m.*

foal [foul] *n.* potro, *m.,* potra, *f.;*
—, *vt.* y *vi.* parir una yegua.

foam [foum] *n.* espuma, *f.;* —
rubber, hule espuma, *m.;* —,
vi. hacer espuma.

foamy [fou-mi] *adj.* espumoso.

focal [fou-kal] *adj.* focal.

focus [fou-kos] *n.* foco, *m.*, punto céntrico; enfoque.

fodder [fo-dar] *n.* forraje, *m.*, pastura, *f.*

foe [fou] *n.* adversario, ria, enemigo, ga.

fog [fog] *n.* niebla, neblina, *f.*

foggy [fo-gui] *adj.* nebuloso, brumoso.

foghorn [fog-jorn] *n.* (naut.) sirena, *f.;* pito de los buques.

foible [foi-bol] *n.* debilidad, *f.,* lado flaco.

foil [foil] *vt.* vencer; frustrar; —, *n.* fracaso, *m.;* hoja (de estaño), *f.;* florete, *m.*

foist [foist] *vt.* insertar (subrepticiamente); vender con engaño, colar.

fold [fould] *n.* redil, aprisco, *m.;* plegadura, *f.,* doblez, *m.;* —, *vt.* apriscar el ganado; plegar, doblar.

folder [foul-dar] *n.* plegador, *m.,* plegadera, *f.;* carpeta, *f.*

folding [foul-din] *n.* plegadura, *f.;* — **bed,** catre de tijera o de campaña; cama plegadiza; — **chair,** silla de tijera, silla plegadiza.

foliage [fou-lieich] *n.* follaje, ramaje, *m.*

folk [fouk] *n.* grupo de personas que forman una nación; gente,

f.; **common** —, gente común y corriente; — **music,** música folklórica o tradicional; — **song,** canto folklórico; — **tale,** cuento tradicional o folklórico.

folklore [fou-klar] *n.* folklore, *m.*

follow [fo-lou] *vt.* seguir; acompañar; imitar; —, *vi.* seguirse, resultar, provenir.

follower [fo-louar] *n.* seguidor, ra; imitador, ra; partidario, ria; adherente, *m.* y *f.;* discípulo, la; compañero, ra.

following [fo-louin] *n.* séquito, cortejo, *m.;* profesión, *f.;* —, *adj.* próximo, siguiente.

folly [fo-li] *n.* extravagancia, *f.;* bobería, *f.;* temeridad, *f.;* vicio, *m.*

foment [fou-ment] *vt.* fomentar; proteger.

fond [fond] *adj.* afectuoso; aficionado; demasiado indulgente; **to be — of,** aficionarse, tener simpatía por; —**ly,** *adv.* cariñosamente.

fondle [fon-del] *vt.* mimar, hacer caricias.

fondness [fond-nes] *n.* afecto, *m.;* afición, *f.;* indulgencia, *f.;* bienquerencia, *f.*

font [font] *n.* pila bautismal; fundición, *f.*

food [fud] *n.* alimento, *m.;* comida, *f.;* —**s,** comestibles, *m. pl.,* viandas, *f. pl.*

fool [ful] *n.* loco, ca, tonto, ta, bobo, ba; bufón, ona; —, *vt.* engañar; infatuar; —, *vi.* tontear.

foolhardy [ful-jar-di] *adj.* temerario, atrevido.

foolish [fu-lish] *adj.* bobo, tonto, majadero; —**ly**, *adv.* bobamente, sin juicio.

foolishness [fu-lish-nes] *n.* tontería, *f.*

foolproof [ful-pruf] *adj.* muy evidente, seguro, fácil hasta para un tonto.

foot [fut] *n.* pie, *m.;* pezuña (de vacas, cabras, etc.), *f ;* base, *f.;* extremo, final, *m.;* pie (medida), *m.;* paso, *m.;* — **soldier,** soldado de infantería; **on** —, **by** —, a pie; **square** —, pie cuadrado; —, *vi.* bailar, saltar, brincar; ir a pie; —, *vt.* pasar, caminar por encima; **to** — **the bill,** (coll.) pagar la cuenta.

football [fut-bol] *n.* fútbol, *m.*

foothill [fut-jil] *n.* cerro al pie de una sierra.

foothold [fut-jould] *n.* espacio en que cabe el pie; apoyo, *m.;* afianzamiento, *m.*

footing [fu-tin] *n.* base, *f ;* pisada, *f ;* paso, *m.;* estado, *m.;* condición, *f.;* fundamento, *m.;* afianzamiento *m.*

footnote [fut-nout] *n.* anotación, *f.;* glosa, *f.;* nota, *f.;*

footpath [fut-paz] *n.* senda para peatones.

footprint [fut-print] *n.* huella, pisada, *f.;* vestigio, *m.*

footrest [fut-rest] *n.* apoyo para los pies, escabel, *m.*

footstep [fut-step] *n.* vestigio, *m.;* huella, *f.;* paso, *m.;* pisada, *f.*

footstool [fut-stul] *n.* escabel, *m.,* banquillo para los pies.

footwear [fut-uear] *n.* calzado, *m.*

for [far] *prep.* para; por; —, *conj.* porque, pues; **as** — **me,** en cuanto a mí; **what** —? ¿para qué?

forage [fo-reich] *n.* forraje, *m.;* —, *vt.* forrajear; saquear.

foray [fo-rei] *n.* correría, *f.;* saqueo, *m.;* —, *vt.* saquear.

forbid [fo-bid] *vt.* prohibir, vedar; impedir; **God** —! ¡ni lo quiera Dios!

forbidden [fo-bi-den] *adj.* prohibido.

forbidding [fo-bi-din] *adj.* que prohibe; **repugnante;** formidable, que infunde respeto.

force [fors] *n.* fuerza, *f.;* poder, vigor, *m.;* valor, *m.;* —**s,** tropas, *f. pl.;* **to be in** —, regir; **with full** —, de plano, en pleno vigor; —, *vt.* forzar, violentar; esforzar; obligar; constreñir; **to** — **one's way,** abrirse el paso.

forced [forst] *adj.* forzoso; forzado, estirado; — **landing,** (avi.) aterrizaje forzoso.

forceful [fors-ful] *adj.* fuerte, poderoso; dominante.

forceps [for-seps] *n. pl.* fórceps, *m. pl.*; pinzas, *f. pl.*

forcible [for-si-bol] *adj.* fuerte, eficaz, poderoso, enérgico; — **bly,** *adv.* con energía.

fore [far] *adj.* anterior; (naut.) de proa; —, prefijo que denota anterioridad, por ej., **forerunner,** precursor, *m.*

forearm [for-arm] *n.* antebrazo, *m.*; —, *vt.* armar con anticipación.

forebode [for-boud] *vt.* y *vi.* pronosticar, presagiar.

foreboding [for-bou-din] *n.* corazonada, *f.*; pronóstico, *m.*

forecast [for-kast] *vt.* y *vi.* proyectar, prever; conjeturar de antemano; —, *n.* previsión, *f.*; profecía, *f.*; **weather** —, pronóstico del tiempo.

foreclose [for-klous] *vt.* entablar, decidir un juicio hipotecario.

foreclosure [for-klo-shar] *n.* exclusión, *f.*; juicio hipotecario.

forefather [for-fa-dar] *n.* abuelo, antecesor, antepasado, *m.*

forefinger [for-fin-gar] *n.* dedo índice.

forefront [for-front] *n.* primera fila; parte delantera.

forego [for-gou] *vt.* ceder, abandonar, renunciar a; preceder.

foregoing [for-gouin] *adj.* anterior, precedente.

foregone [for-goun] *adj.* pasado; anticipado, predeterminado; previo.

foreground [for-graund] *n.* delantera, *f.*; primer plano.

forehanded [for-jan-did] *adj.* temprano; oportuno; prudente, frugal.

forehead [for-jed] *n.* frente, *f.*

foreign [fo-ring] *adj.* extranjero; extraño.

foreign-born [fo-ring-born] *adj.* nacido en el extranjero.

foreigner [fo-ri-nar] *n.* extranjero, ra, forastero, ra.

foreleg [for-leg] *n.* pata o pierna delantera.

forelock [for-lok] *n.* mechón de cabello que cae sobre la frente.

foreman [for-man] *n.* presidente del jurado; jefe, capataz, *m.*

foremost [for-moust] *adj.* delantero, primero; —, *adv.* en primer lugar.

forensic [fo-ren-sik] *adj.* forense.

forerunner [for-ra-nar] *n.* precursor, ra; predecesor, ra.

foresee [for-si] *vt.* prever.

foreshadow [for-sha-dou] *vt.* pronosticar, prefigurar.

foreshorten [for-shor-ten] *vt.* escorzar (en dibujo).

foresight [for-sait] *n.* previsión,

f.; presciencia, *f.*

forest [fo-rist] *n.* bosque, *m.;* selva, *f.*

forestation [fors-tei-shon] *n.* silvicultura, forestación, *f.*

forester [fo-res-tar] *n.* guardabosque, *m.*

forestry [fo-ris-tri] *n.* silvicultura, *f.*

foretell [for-tel] *vt.* predecir, profetizar.

forethought [for-zot] *n.* providencia, *f.;* premeditación, *f.*

forever [for-evar] *adv.* por siempre, para siempre.

forevermore [for-evar-mor] *adv.* por siempre jamás.

forewarn [for-uorn] *vt.* prevenir de antemano.

foreword [for-ued] *n.* advertencia, *f.;* prefacio, prólogo, preámbulo, *m.*

forfeit [for-fit] *n.* multa, *f.;* confiscación, *f.;* prenda, *f.;* —, *vt.* confiscar, decomisar; perder; pagar una multa.

forge [forch] *n.* fragua, *f.;* fábrica de metales; —, *vt.* forjar; contrahacer; inventar; falsear; falsificar.

forger [for-yar] *n.* forjador, *m.;* falsario, ria; falsificador, ra.

forgery [for-ye-ri] *n.* falsificación, *f.;* forjadura, *f.*

forget [fo-guet] *vt.* olvidar; descuidar.

forgetful [fo-guet-ful] *adj.* olvidadizo; descuidado.

forgetfulness [fo-guet-ful-nes] *n.* olvido, *m.;* negligencia, *f.*

forgive [fe-guiv] *vt.* perdonar.

forgiveness [fo-gui-ven-nes] *n.* perdón, *m.*

forgiving [fo-gui-vin] *adj.* misericordioso, clemente, que perdona.

forgot [fo-got] *pretérito* del verbo **forget.**

forgotten [fo-go-ten] *p.p.* del verbo **forget.**

fork [fork] *n.* tenedor, *m.;* horca, *f.;* —, *vi.* bifurcarse; **to — out,** (coll.) dar, entregar.

forlorn [for-lorn] *adj.* abandonado, perdido; desdichado, triste.

form [form] *n.* forma, *f.;* esqueleto, modelo, *m.;* modo, *m.;* formalidad, *f.;* método, *m.;* molde, *m.;* patrón, *m.;* — **letter,** carta circular, carta general; **in proper** —, en forma debida; —, *vt.* formar, configurar; idear, concebir; —, *vi.* formarse.

formal [for-mal] *adj.* formal, metódico; ceremonioso; — **dance,** baile de etiqueta.

formality [for-ma-li-ti] *n.* formalidad, *f.;* ceremonia, *f.* format, *n.* formato, *m.*

formation [for-mei-shon] *n.* formación, *f.;* — **flying,** vuelo en formación.

formative [for-ma-tiv] *adj.* formativo.

former [for-mar] *adj.* precedente; anterior, pasado; previo; **the —,** aquél; **—ly,** *adv.* antiguamente, en tiempos pasados, en otro tiempo.

formidable [for-mi-da-bol] *adj.* formidable, temible.

formless [form-les] *adj.* informe, disforme.

formula [for-miu-la] *n.* fórmula, f.

formulate [for-miu-leit] *vt.* formular, articular.

forsake [for-seik] *vt.* dejar, abandonar.

forsaken [for-sei-ken] *adj.* desamparado, abandonado.

fort [fort] *n.* castillo, *m.;* fortaleza, *f.;* fuerte, *m.;* **small —,** fortín, *m.*

forth [forz] *adv.* en adelante; afuera; **and so —,** y así sucesivamente, etcétera.

forthcoming [forz-ka-min] *adj.* próximo, pronto a comparecer.

forthright [forz-rait] *adj.* directo; franco; **—,** *adv.* directamente adelante; con franqueza; inmediatamente.

fortieth [for-tiez] *n.* y *adj.* cuadragésimo, *m.*

fortification [for-ti-fi-kei-shon] *n.* fortificación, *f.*

fortify [for-ti-fai] *vt.* fortificar; corroborar.

fortitude [for-ti-tiud] *n.* fortaleza, *f.;* valor, *m.,* fortitud, *f.*

fortnight [fort-nait] *n.* quincena, *f.,* quince días, dos semanas; **—ly,** *adj.* quincenal; **—ly,** *adv.* cada quince días.

fortress [for-tris] *n.* (mil.) fortaleza, *f.;* castillo, *m.*

fortunate [for-chu-nit] *adj.* afortunado, dichoso; **—ly,** *adv.* felizmente, por fortuna.

fortune [for-chun] *n.* fortuna, *f.;* suerte, *f.;* condición, *f.;* bienes de fortuna.

fortuneteller [for-chun-te-ler] *n.* sortílego, ga, adivino, na.

forty [for-ti] *n.* y *adj.* cuarenta, *m.*

forum [fo-rum] *n.* foro, tribunal, *m.*

forward [for-uard] *adj.* anterior, delantero; precoz; atrevido; pronto, activo, dispuesto; **— pass** (fútbol) lance de la pelota en dirección del equipo contrario; **—,** *n.* delantero (en Rugby, básquetbol); **—,** *adv.* adelante, más allá; hacia adelante; **—,** *vt.* expedir, trasmitir, enviar más adelante.

forwards [for-uards] *adv.* adelante.

fossil [fo-sil] *adj.* y *n.* fósil, *m.*

foster [fos-tar] *vt.* criar, nutrir; alentar; **—,** *adj.* allegado; **—**

brother, hermano de leche; — **child,** hijo de leche, hijo adoptivo; — **father,** padre adoptivo, el que cría y enseña a un hijo ajeno; — **mother,** madre adoptiva.

foul [faul] *adj.* sucio, puerco; impuro, detestable; — **ball,** pelota que cae fuera del primer o tercer ángulo del diamante de béisbol.

found [faund] *vt.* fundar, establecer; edificar; fundir; basar; —, *pretérito* y *p.p.* del verbo **find.**

foundation [faun-dei-shon] *n.* fundación, *f.;* cimiento, fundamento, *m.;* pie, *m.;* fondo, *m.*

founder [faun-dar] *n.* fundador, ra; fundidor, *m.;* —, *vi.* (naut.) irse a pique; caerse; tropezar.

founding [faun-de-rin] *n.* establecimiento, *m.*

fountain [faun-tin] *n.* fuente, *f.;* manantial, *m.;* — **pen,** plumafuente, estilográfica, *f.,* pluma estilográfica.

four [far] *n.* y *adj.* cuatro, *m.;* — **o'clock,** las cuatro; **on all —s,** a gatas.

four-footed [for-fu-tid] *adj.* cuadrúpedo.

fourteen [for-tin] *n.* y *adj.* catorce, *m.*

fourteenth [for-tinz] *n.* y *adj.*

decimocuarto, *m.*

fourth [forz] *n.* y *adj.* cuarto, *m.;* —**ly,** *adv.* en cuarto lugar.

fowl [faul] *n.* ave., *f.*

fox [foks] *n.* zorra, *f.,* zorro, *m.*

foxhound [foks-jaund] *n.* perro zorrero.

fraction [frak-shon] *n.* fracción, *f.*

fractional [frak-sho-nal] *adj.* fraccionario.

fracture [frak-char] *n.* fractura, confracción, rotura, *f.;* —, *vt.* fracturar, romper.

fragile [fra-yail] *adj.* frágil; débil, deleznable.

fragment [frag-ment] *n.* fragmento, trozo, *m.*

fragrance [fra-grans] *n.* fragancia, *f.*

fragrant [fra-grant] *adj.* fragante, oloroso; —**ly,** *adv.* con fragancia.

frail [freil] *adj.* frágil, débil.

frame [freim] *n.* marco, cerco, *m.;* bastidor, *m.;* armazón, *f.;* telar, *m.;* cuadro de vidriera; estructura, *f.;* figura, forma, *f.,* cuerpo, *m.;* forjadura, *f.;* — **of mind,** estado de ánimo; **embroidery —,** bastidor, *m.;* **structural —,** armazón, *f.;* —, *vt.* fabricar, componer; construir, formar; ajustar; idear; poner en bastidor; enmarcar, encuadrar; (coll.) incriminar fraudulentamente; prefijar el resultado (de un concurso, etc.).

France [frans] Francia, f.

franchise [fran-chais] n. franquicia, inmunidad, f.; privilegio, m.

frank [frank] adj. franco, liberal, campechano; —ly, adv. francamente, abiertamente.

frankfurter [frank-fer-tar] n. salchicha, f.

frankness [frank-nes] n. franqueza, ingenuidad, f., candor, m.

frantic [fran-tik] adj. frenético, furioso.

fraternal [fra-ter-nal] adj. fraternal.

fraternity [fra-ter-ni-ti] n. fraternidad, f.

fraternize [fra-ter-nais] vt. y vi. fraternizar, confraternar.

fraud [frod] n. fraude, engaño, m.

fraudulent [fro-diu-lent] adj. fraudulento.

fraught [frot] adj. cargado, lleno.

fray [frei] n. riña, disputa, querella, f.; —, vt. y vi. estregar; romper, romperse; desgastar, desgastarse.

freak [frik] n. fantasía, f.; capricho, m.; monstruosidad, f.

freakish [fri-kish] adj. extravagante, estrambótico.

freckle [fre-kel] n. peca, f.

freckled [fre-kelt] adj. pecoso.

free [fri] adj. libre; liberal; franco, ingenuo; exento, dispensado, privilegiado; gratuito, gratis; — **enterprise,** empresa libre, iniciativa privada; — **lance,** aventurero, ra; persona que escribe para alguna publicación o trabaja para alguna empresa sin contrato u obligación especial; — **on rail,** franco sobre vagón; — **port,** puerto franco o libre; — **thought,** libre pensamiento (esp. en religión); — **trade,** libre cambio; — **trader,** libre cambista; — **verse** verso suelto o libre; — **will,** libre albedrío; voluntariedad, f.; —, vt. libertar; librar; eximir.

freedom [fri-dom] n. libertad, f.; soltura, f.; inmunidad, f.; — **of speech,** libertad de palabra; — **of the press,** libertad de prensa.

free fall [fri-fol] n. caída incontrolada.

freehand [fri-jand] adj. hecho a pulso, sin instrumentos.

free-spoken [fri-spou-ken] adj. dicho sin reserva.

freethinker [fri-zin-kar] n. librepensador, ra.

freeway [fri-uei] n. autopista de acceso limitado.

freewill [fri-uil] adj. espontáneo,

voluntario.

freeze [fris] *vi.* helar, helarse; —, *vt.* helar, congelar.

freezer [fri-sar] *n.* congelador, *m.*, congeladora, *f.*

freight [freit] *n.* carga, *f.;* flete, *m.;* conducción, *f.;* porte, *m.;* — **car,** furgón, *m.*, vagón de mercancías o de carga; — **house,** embarcadero de mercancías; —, *vt.* (naut.) fletar; cargar.

French [french] *adj.* francés, esa; — **doors,** puertas vidrieras dobles; — **language,** francés, *m.;* — **leave,** despedida a la francesa, despedida precipitada o secreta; — **dressing,** salsa francesa (para ensaladas); **the** —, *n. pl.* los franceses, *m. pl.*

Frenchman [french-man] *n.* francés, *m.*

frenzied [fren-sid] *adj.* loco, delirante.

frenzy [fren-si] *n.* frenesí, *m.;* locura, *f.*

frequency [fri-kuen-si] *n.* frecuencia, *f.;* — **modulation,** modulación de frecuencia; **high** —, alta frecuencia.

frequent [fri-kuent] *adj.* frecuente; —**ly,** *adv.* con frecuencia, frecuentemente; —, *vt.* frecuentar.

fresco [fres-kou] *n.* pintura al fresco.

fresh [fresh] *adj.* fresco; nuevo, reciente; — **water,** agua dulce.

freshen [fre-shen] *vt.* refrescar.

freshman [fresh-man] *n.* estudiante de primer año en la escuela superior o universidad; novicio, cia, novato, ta.

freshness [fresh-nes] *n.* frescura, *f.*, frescor, *m.;* (fig.) descaro, *m.*

fresh-water [fresh-uo-tar] *adj.* de agua dulce.

fret [fret] *n.* enojo, *m.;* irritación, *f.;* —, *vt.* frotar; corroer; cincelar; irritar; enojar; —, *vi.* quejarse; enojarse.

fretful [fret-ful] *adj.* enojadizo, colérico; —**ly,** *adv.* de mala gana.

friar [fraiar] *n.* fraile, fray, *m.*

friction [frik-shon] *n.* fricción, rozadura, *f.*

Friday [frai-dei] *n.* viernes, *m.;* **Good F—,** Viernes Santo.

fried [fraid] *adj.* frito; — **potato,** patata o papa frita.

friend [frend] *n.* amigo, ga; **to be close** —**s,** ser uña y carne; **to make** —**s,** trabar amistad, hacerse amigos.

friendless [frend-les] *adj.* sin amigos.

friendliness [frend-li-nes] *n.* amistad, benevolencia, bondad, *f.*

friendly [frend-li] *adj.* amigable, amistoso.

friendship [frend-ship] *n.* amistad, *f.*

frier = **fryer.**

fright [frait] *n.* susto, espanto, pánico, terror, *m.*

frighten [frai-ten] *vt.* espantar; **to — away,** ahuyentar; espantar.

frightful [frait-ful] *adj.* espantoso, horrible.

frigid [fri-chid] *adj.* frío, frígido; **— zone,** zona glacial; **—ly**, *adv.* fríamente.

frill [fril] *n.* faralá, volante, vuelo *m.;* (coll.) adorno excesivo; ostentación en el vestir, en los modales, etc.

frivolity [fri-vo-li-ti] *n.* frivolidad, *f.;* pamplinada, *f.*

frivolous [fri-vo-los] *adj.* frívolo, vano.

frizzle [fri-sel] *vt.* rizar, encrespar.

frock [frok] *n.* toga, túnica, *f.,* sayo, *m.;* vestido, *m.;* **— coat,** casaca, *f.,* levitón, *m.*

frog [frog] *n.* rana, *f.*

frogman [frog-man] *n.* hombre rana, *m.*

from [from] *prep.* de; después; desde; **— now on,** en lo sucesivo, desde ahora en adelante.

front [front] *n.* frente, *f.;* frontispicio, *m.;* portada, *f.;* faz, *f.;* cara, *f.;* **labor —,** frente obrero; **— door,** puerta de entrada; **— seat,** asiento delantero; **in —,** enfrente; **in — of,** delante de; **—,** *vt.* hacer frente; **—,** vi. dar cara.

frontal [fran-tal] *n.* banda en la frente; frontal, *m.;* **—,** *adj.* frontal.

frontier [fron-tiar] *n.* frontera, *f.*

frost [frost] *n.* helada, *f.;* hielo, *m.;* escarcha, *f.;* frialdad de temperamento, austeridad, *f.;* (coll.) indiferencia, *f.;* **—,** *vt.* congelar; cubrir (un pastel o torta) con una capa azucarada.

frostbitten [frost-biten] *adj.* helado, quemado del hielo.

frosted [fros-tid] *adj.* garapiñado.

frosting [frostin] *n.* capa azucarada (para adornar pasteles o tortas), (Mex.) betún, *m.*

frosty [fros-ti] *adj.* helado, frío como el hielo.

froth [froz] *n.* espuma (de algún líquido), *f.;* **—,** *vt.* y *vi.* espumar.

frown [fraun] *vt.* mirar con ceño; **—,** vi. fruncir el entrecejo; **—,** *n.* ceño, *m.;* enojo, *m.;* mala cara.

froze [frous] *pretérito* del verbo **freeze.**

frozen [frou-sen] *adj.* helado; congelado; **— foods,** alimentos congelados; **—,** *p.p.* del verbo **freeze.**

frugal [fru-gal] *adj.* frugal; económico; sobrio.

fruit [frut] *n.* fruto, ta; producto, *m.;* **candied —,** fruta azucarada; **— stand,** puesto de frutas.

fruitful [frut-ful] *adj.* fructífero, fértil; provechoso; útil; **—ly,** *adv.* fructuosamente.

fruitless [frut-les] *adj.* estéril; inútil; infructuoso.

frustrate [fras-treit] *vt.* frustrar; anular.

frustration [fras-trei-shon] *n.* contratiempo, chasco, malogro, *m.*

fry [frai] *vt.* freir.

fryer [frai-er] *n.* pollo para freir.

frying pan [frain-pan] *n.* sartén: *f.*

fuchsia [fak-sha] *n.* (bot.) fucsia, *f.;* color fucsia.

fudge [fadch] *n.* variedad de dulce de chocolate; cuento, embuste, *m.;* **—!** *interj.* ¡que va! (exclamación que indica desdén o menosprecio) .

fuel [fiuel] *n.* combustible, *m.;* **— gauge,** indicador de combustible; **— tank,** depósito de combustible; **— oil,** aceite combustible.

fugitive [fiu-yi-tiv] *n.* y *adj.* fugitivo, va, prófugo, ga.

fulfill [ful-fil] *vt.* colmar; cumplir, realizar.

fulfillment [ful-fil-ment] *n.* cumplimiento, *m.,* realización, *f.*

full [ful] *adj.* lleno, repleto, completo; cumplido; pleno; todo; perfecto; cargado; **— dress,** traje de etiqueta; **— moon,** luna llena, *m.;* **in — swing,** en plena actividad; **— scale,** tamaño natural; **—,** *n.* total, *m.;* **—,** *adv.* entera-mente, del todo.

full-fledged [ful-flecht] *adj.* maduro, con todos los derechos.

full-grown [ful-groun] *adj.* desarrollado, crecido, maduro.

full-length [ful-lengz] *adj.* a todo el largo natural; de cuerpo entero; de largo metraje.

fullness [ful-nes] *n.* plenitud, llenura, abundancia, *f.*

fully [fu-li] *adv.* enteramente; a fondo.

fumble [fam-bel] *vt.* y *vi.* tartamudear; chapucear; andar a tientas.

fume [fium] *n.* humo, vapor, *m.;* cólera, *f* ; **—,** *vt.* ahumar; **—,** *vi.* humear, exhalar; encolerizarse.

fumigate [fiu-mi-gueit] *vt.* fumigar.

fuming [fiu-min] *adj.* humeante.

fun [fan] *n.* chanza, burla, *f.;* chasco *m.;* diversión, *f.;* **to make — of,** burlarse de; **to have —,** divertirse.

function [fank-shon] *n.* función, *f.;* empleo, *m.;* **—.** *vi.* funcionar.

functionary [fank-sho-na-ri] *n.* empleado, *m.;* oficial, funcionario, *m.*

functioning [fank-sho-nin] *n.* funcionamiento, *m.*

fund [fand] *n.* fondo (de dinero), *m.;* —, *vt..* colocar en un fondo.

fundamental [fan-da-men-tal] *adj.* fundamental, básico, cardinal; —**ly**, *adv.* fundamentalmente.

funeral [fiu-ne-ral] *n.* y *adj.* funeral, *m.;* — **car,** carroza, *f ;* — **director,** director de pompas fúnebres.

fungus [fan-gos] *n.* hongo, *m.;* seta, *f.;* fungosidad,

funnel [fa-nel] *n.* embudo, *m.;* cañón (de chimenea), *m.;* (naut.) chimenea, *f.*

funny [fa-ni] *adj.* burlesco, bufón; cómico; — **papers** o **funnies,** historietas cómicas, (Mex.) monitos, *m. pl.;* **to strike as —,** hacer gracia.

fur [far] *n.* piel (para abrigos), *f.;* —, *adj.* hecho de pieles; — **coat,** abrigo de pieles.

furious [fiu-rios] *adj.* furioso, frenético; —**ly**, *adv.* con furia.

furlong [fer-lon] *n.* estadio (octava parte de una milla), *m.*

furlough [fer-lo] *n.* (mil.) licencia, *f.;* permiso, *m.;* —, *vt.* conceder un permiso o licencia (a un soldado, etc.).

furnace [fer-nis] *n.* horno, *m.;* hornaza, *f.*

furnish [fer-nish] *vt.* suplir, proporcionar, surtir, proveer; deparar; equipar; **to — a house,** amueblar una casa.

furnished [fer-nisht] *adj.* amueblado.

furnishings [fer-ni-shins] *n. pl.* mobiliario, *m.;* accesorios, avíos, *m. pl.*

furniture [fer-ni-char] *n.* ajuar, mueblaje, mobiliario, *m.,* muebles *m. pl.;* — **set,** juego de muebles; **piece of —,** mueble, *m.*

furor [fiua-rar] *n.* rabia, *f.;* entusiasmo, *m.*

furrow [fa-rou] *n.* surco, *m.;* —, *vt.* y *vi.* surcar; estriar.

furry [fa-ri] *adj.* parecido a la piel; hecho o guarnecido de pieles.

further [fer-dar] *adj.* ulterior, más distante; —, *adv.* más lejos, más allá; aún; además de eso; —, *vt.* adelantar, promover, ayudar, impulsar, fomentar.

furthermore [fer-der-mar] *adv.* además.

furthest [fer-dest] *adj.* y *adv.* más lejos, más remoto.

furtive [fer-tiv] *adj.* furtivo; secreto; **to look at —ly,** mirar de reojo.

fury [fiu-ri] *n.* furor, *m.;* furia, *f.;* ira, *f.*

fuse [fius] *n.* cohete, *m.;* (elec.) fusible, *m.;* detonador, *m.;* mecha *f.;* espoleta, *f.; —* **box,** caja de fusibles; —, *vt.* y vi. fundir; derretirse.

fuselage [fiu-se-lash] *n.* fuselaje, *m.*

fusion [fiu-shon] *n.* fusión, licuación, *f.*

fuss [fas] *n.* (coll.) alboroto, tumulto, *m.; —* , *vi.* preocuparse por pequeñeces; —, *vt.* (coll.)

molestar con pequeñeces.

fussy [fa-si] *adj.* melindroso; exigente.

futile [fiu-til] *adj.* fútil, vano; frívolo.

future [fiu-char] *adj.* futuro, venidero; —, *n.* lo futuro, el tiempo venidero, porvenir; **in the —,** en adelante, en lo sucesivo.

fuzz [fas] *n.* tamo, *m.,* pelusa, *f.*

G

gab [gab] *n.* (coll.) locuacidad, *f.;* —, *vi.* (coll.) charlar locuazmente.

gabardine [ga-bar-din] *n.* gabardina, *f.; —* **coat,** gabán, *m.,* gabardina, *f.*

gable [ga-bol] *n.* socarrén, alero, *m.*

gadfly [gad-flai] *n.* tábano, *m.*

gadget [gad-chit] *n.* baratija, chuchería, *f.;* utensilio, aparato, *m.;* pieza (de máquina), *f;*

gag [gag] *n.* mordaza, *f.;* (coll.) expresión aguda y jocosa; —, *vt.* tapar la boca con mordaza.

gaily [guei-li] *adv.* alegremente.

gain [guein] *n.* ganancia, *f.;* interés, provecho, beneficio, *m.;* —, *vt.* ganar; conseguir; —, *vi.* enriquecerse; avanzar.

gainful [guein-ful] *adj.* ventajoso, lucrativo.

gait [gueit] *n.* marcha; *f.;* porte, *m.*

gala [ga-la] *adj.* de gala, de fiesta.

galaxy [ga-lak-si] *n.* galaxia, *f.,* vía láctea; — **of** stars, congregación de artistas prominentes.

gale [gueil] *n.* (naut.) ventarrón, *m.;* —**s of laughter,** risotadas, *f. pl.*

gall [gol] *n.* hiel, *f.;* rencor, odio, *m.; —* **bladder,** vesícula biliar; —, *vt.* rozar, ludir; irritar, atosigar.

gallant [ga-lant] *adj.* galante, elegante; gallardo; valeroso; —, *n.* galán, *m.;* cortejo, *m.*

gallantry [ga-lant-li] *n.* galantería, gallardía, *f.;* bravura, *f.*

gallery [ga-le-ri] *n.* galería, *f.;* corredor, *m.*

galley [ga-li] *n.* (naut.) galera, *f.*

gallon [ga-lon] *n.* galón (medida), *m.*

gallop [ga-lop] *n.* galope, *m.;* —, *vi.* galopar.

gallows [ga-lous] *n.* horca, *f.*

galosh [ga-losh] *n.* galocha (generalmente de goma o caucho), *f.,* bota de hule, etc. (para la nieve).

galvanize [gal-va-nais] *vt.* galvanizar.

gamble [gam-bol] vi. jugar por dinero; —, *vt.* aventurar.

gambler [gam-blar] *n.* tahur, ra, jugador, ra.

gambling [gam-blin] *n.* juego por dinero; —, *adj.* de juego; — **house,** casa de juego, casino, *m.*

game [gueim] *n.* juego, *m.;* pasatiempo, *m.;* partida de juego; burla, *f.;* caza, *f.;* — **warden,** guardabosque, *m.;* —, *vi.* jugar.

gamekeeper [gueim-ki-par] *n.* guardabosque, *m.*

gamma [gama] *n.* gama; — **globulin,** globulina gamma; — **rays,** rayos gamma.

gamut [ga-mot] *n.* escala, gama, serie, *f.*

gander [gan-dar] *n.* ánsar, ganso, *m.;* simplón, papanatas, *m.*

gang [gang] *n.* banda, pandilla, patrulla *f.;* — **plow,** arado de reja múltiple.

ganglion [gan-glion] *n.* ganglio *m.*

gangrene [gan-grin] *n.* gangrena, *f.;* —, *vt.* y *vi.* gangrenar, gangrenarse.

gangster [gans-tar] *n.* rufián, *m.*

gap [gap] *n.* boquete, *m.,* brecha, *f.;* laguna, *f.*

gape [gueip] vi. bostezar, boquear; ansiar, hendirse; estar con la boca abierta.

garage [ga-rash] *n.* garaje, garage, *m.,* cochera, *f.*

garb [garb] *n.* atavío, *m.;* vestidura, *f.;* traje, *m.;* apariencia exterior.

garbage [gar-bich] *n.* basura, *f.,* desperdicios, *m. pl.*

garble [gar-bel] *vt.* entresacar, mutilar engañosamente (una cuenta, etc.).

garden [gar-den] *n.* huerto, *m.;* jardín, *m.;* **vegetable** —, huerto de hortalizas; —, vi. cultivar un jardín o un huerto.

gardenia [gar-di-nia] *n.* (bot.) gardenia, *f.*

gardening [gard-nin] *n.* jardinería, *f.*

gargle [gar-guel] *vt.* y *vi.* gargarizar, hacer gárgaras; —, *n.* gárgara, *f.,* gargarismo, *m.*

garish [guea-rish] *adj.* ostentoso y de mal gusto.

garland [gar-land] *n.* guirnalda, f.

garlic [gar-lik] *n.* (bot.) ajo, *m.*

garment [gar-ment] *n.* traje, vestido, *m.; vestidura, f.*

garnish [gar-nish] *vt.* guarnecer, adornar, aderezar; —, *n.* guarnición, *f.; adorno, m.*

garrison [ga-ri-son] *n.* (mil.) guarnición, *f.;* fortaleza, *f.;* —, *vt.* (mil.) guarnecer.

garter [gar-tar] *n.* liga, *f.,* cenojil, *m.;* jarretera, *f.*

gas [gas] *n.* gas, *m.;* **carbonic acid** —, gas carbónico; **chlorine** —, cloro, *m.;* — **burner,** — **jet,** mechero de gas; — **main,** cañería, *f.;* alimentadora de gas; — mask, mascarilla o careta contra gases asfixiantes; — **meter,** medidor de gas; — **pedal,** acelerador (de un auto); —**stove,** estufa o cocina de gas.

gaseous [ga-sios] *adj.* gaseoso.

gash [gash] *n.* cuchillada, *f.;* —, *vt.* dar una cuchillada.

gasket [gas-kit] *n.* relleno, *m.,* empaquetadura, *f.*

gasoline [ga-so-lin] *n.* gasolina, nafta, *f.;* — **tank,** depósito o tanque de gasolina.

gasp [gasp] *vi.* boquear; anhelar; —, *n.* respiración difícil; **last** —, última boqueada.

gaspipe [gas-paip]*n.* tubería de gas.

gastric [gas-trik] *adj.* gástrico.

gate [gueit] *n.* puerta, *f.,* portón, *m.*

gatekeeper [gueit-ki-par] *n.* portero, ra.

gateway [gueit-uei] *n.* entrada, *f.,* paso, *m.;* puerta cochera.

gather [ga-dar] *vt.* recoger, amontonar, **reunir;** fruncir; inferir; arrugar, plegar; —, *vi.* juntarse; supurar.

gathering [ga-ze-rin] *n.* reunión, *f.;* acumulación, *f.;* colecta, *f.*

gaudy [go-di] *adj.* brillante, fastuoso.

gauge, gage [geich], [gouch] *n.* aforo, *m.;* graduador, *m.;* indicador, *m.;* calibrador, *m.;* manómetro, *m.;* calibre, *m.;* **tire** —, medidor de presión de aire de neumático; —, *vt.* aforar; calar; calibrar; graduar, medir.

gaunt [gont] *adj.* flaco, delgado.

gauze [gos] *pretérito* del verbo **give.**

gavel [ga-vel] *n.* mazo, *m.,* gavilla, *f.*

gawk [gok] *n.* majadero, ra; chabacano, na, tonto, ta; —, *vi.* obrar como un majadero; mirar fijamente como un tonto.

gay [guei] *adj.* alegre, festivo; pajarero; **to be** —, estar de buen humor; ser alegre; homo-sexual.

gaze [gueis] *vi.* contemplar, con-siderar; —, *n.* mirada, *f.*

gazelle [ga-sel] *n.* gacela, *f.*

gazette [ga-set] *n.* gaceta, *f.*

gear [guiar] *n.* atavío, *m.;* apara-to, *m.;* engranaje, encaje, *m.,* trasmisión, *f.;* — **case,** caja de engranajes; **changing —s,** cam-bio de velocidad, cambio de marcha; **landing —,** tren de aterrizaje; — **wheel,** rueda den-tada; **in —,** embragado, en juego; **out of —** desembragado, fuera de juego; **to throw out of —,** desencajar, desmontar, des-embragar.

gearshift [guia-shift] *n.* cambio de velocidad, cambio de mar-cha; — **lever,** palanca de cam-bios.

geese [guis] *n. pl.* de **goose,** gan-sos, *m. pl.*

gelatin, gelatine [ye-la-tin] *n.* gelatina, jaletina, *f.*

gelding [guel-din] *n.* caballo capón.

gem [yem] *n.* joya, *f.;* piedra, pie-dra preciosa.

gender [yen-dar] *n.* (gram.) géne-ro, *m.*

gene [yin] *n.* (biol.) gen, *m.*

genealogy [yi-nia-lo-yi] *n.* genea-logía, *f.*

general [ye-ne-ral] *adj.* general, común, usual; — **delivery,** lista de correos; — **partnership,** sociedad colectiva; —, *n.* gene-ral, *m.;* **in —,** por lo común.

generalization [ye-ne-ra-lai-sei-shon] *n.* generalización, *f.*

generalize [ye-ne-ra-lais] *vt.* generalizar.

generate [ye-ne-reit] *vt.* engen-drar; producir; causar.

generation [ye-ne-rei-shon] *n.* generación, *f.*

generator [ye-ne-rei-tor] *n.* engendrador, dinamo o dína-mo, generador, *m.*

generic [ye-ne-rik] *adj.* genérico.

generosity [ye-ne-ro-si-ti] *n.* generosidad, liberalidad, *f.*

generous [ye-ne-ros] *adj.* genero-so.

genesis [ye-ni-sis] *n.* génesis, *f.,* origen, *m.*

genetics [yi-ne-tiks] *n.* genética, *f.*

geniality [ye-ni-a-li-ti] *n.* inge-nuidad, *f.;* alegría, *f.*

genitals [ye-ni-tols] *n. pl.* órga-nos genitales.

genius [yi-nios] *n.* genio, *m.*

genocide [ye-nou-said] *n.* genoci-dio, *m.*

genteel [yen-til] *adj.* gentil, ele-gante.

gentile [yen-tail] *n.* pagano, na, gentil, *m.* y *f.*

Gentile [yen-tail] *n.* persona no

judía.

gentility [yen-ti-li-ti] *n.* gentileza, *f.*; nobleza de sangre.

gentle [yen-tel] *adj.* suave, dócil, manso, moderado; benigno.

gentleman [yen-tel-man] *n.* caballero, gentilhombre, *m.;* — **'s agreement,** obligación moral.

gentleness [yen-tel-nes] *n.* gentileza, *f.;* dulzura, *f.,* suavidad de carácter; nobleza, *f.*

gently [yen-tri] *adv.* suavemente, con dulzura.

genuine [ye-nuin] *adj.* genuino, puro.

genuineness [ye-nuin-nes] *n.* pureza, *f.;* sinceridad, *f.*

genus [ye-nos] *n.* género, *m.,* clase, especie, *f.*

geographer [yio-gra-far] *n.* geógrafo, *m.*

geographic, geographical [yio-gra-fik], [yio-gra-fi-kal] *adj.* geográfico.

geography [yio-gra-fi] *n.* geografía, *f.*

geological [yiou-lo-chi-kal] *adj.* geológico.

geologist [yiou-lo-chist] *n.* geólogo, *m.*

geology [yi-o-lo-chi] *n.* geología, *f.*

geometric, geometrical [yiou-me-trik], [yiou-me-tri-kal] *adj.* geométrico.

geometry [yiou-mi-tri] *n.* geome-tría, *f.;* **solid —,** geometría del espacio; **plane —,** geometría plana.

geriatrics [ye-ria-triks] *n.* geria-tría, *f.*

germ [yerm] *n.* germen, *m.;* microbio, *m.;* — **cell,** célula embrional; — **plasm,** germen plasma.

German [yer-man] *n.* y *adj.* ale-mán, ana; — **measles,** rubéola, *f.,* sarampión benigno.

Germany [yer-ma-ni] Alemania, *f.;* Germania, *f.*

germicide [yer-mi-said] *n.* bacte-ricida, germicida, *m.*

germinate [yer-mi-neit] *vi.* bro-tar, germinar.

gerund [ye-rund] *n.* (gram.) gerundio, *m.*

gestation [yes-tei-shon] *n.* gesta-ción, preñez, *f.*

gesticulate [yes-ti-kiu-leit] *vi.* gesticular; **to — with the hands,** manotear; hacer ade-manes.

gesticulation [yes-ti-kiu-lei-shon] *n.* gesticulación, *f.*

gesture [yes-char] *n.* gesto, movimiento, ademán, *m.*

get [guet] *vt.* obtener, conseguir, alcanzar, coger; agarrar, robar; persuadir; **to go and —,** ir a buscar; —, *vi.* alcanzar; llegar; venir; hacerse, ponerse; preva-lecer; introducirse; **to — along,**

ir pasándola; **to — away,** irse, fugarse, escaparse; **to — together,** reunirse; **to — up,** levantarse.

getaway [guet-auei] *n.* escapada, huida, *f.*

ghastly [gas-tli] *adj.* pálido, cadavérico; espantoso.

ghetto [gue-tou] *n.* ghetto, barrio judío

ghost [goust] *n.* espectro, *m.;* espíritu, *m.;* fantasma, *m.;* — **writer,** escritor o escritora cuyos artículos aparecen bajo el nombre de otra persona.

ghostly [gous-tli] *adj.* espectral, como un espectro.

ghoul [gul] *n.* vampiro, *m.*

giant [yaiant] *n.* gigante, *m.*

giddiness [gui-di-nes] *n.* vértigo, *m.;* inconstancia, *f.*

giddy [gui-di] *adj.* vertiginoso; inconstante.

gift [guift] *n.* don, *m.;* regalo, *m.,* dádiva, *f.;* talento, *m.;* habilidad, *f.;* presente, obsequio, *m.*

gifted [guif-tid] *adj.* hábil, talentoso.

gigantic [yai-gan-tik] *adj.* gigantesco.

giggle [gui-guel] *vi.* reírse disimuladamente; reírse nerviosamente y sin motivo; —, *n.* risilla disimulada o nerviosa.

gigolo [yi-go-lo] *n.* gigoló, *m.*

gild [guild] *vt.* dorar.

gill [yil] *n.* cuarta parte de una pinta; papada, *f.;* —**s,** *pl.* barbas del gallo; agallas de los peces.

gilt [yilt] *n.* y *adj.* dorado, *m.*

gin [yuin] *n.* desmotadora (de algodón), *f.;* ginebra (bebida alcohólica), *f.;* — **rummy,** cierto juego de naipes; —, *vt.* despepitar (algodón, etc.).

ginger [yin-char] *n.* jengibre, *m.;* — **ale,** cerveza de jengibre.

gingerbread [yin-ye-bred] *n.* pan de jengibre.

gingerly [yin-cha-li] *adv.* tímidamente, cautelosamente; —, *adj.* cauteloso, cuidadoso.

gingivitis [yin-yi-vai-tis] *n.* (med.) gingivitis, *f.*

giraffe [yi-raf] *n.* jirafa, *f.*

girder [guer-dar] *n.* viga, *f.*

girdle [guer-del] *n.* faja, *f.;* cinturón, *m.;* —, *vt.* ceñir.

girl [guerl] *n.* muchacha, doncella, niña, *f.;* — **friend,** amiga predilecta, novia potencial; — **guide,** guía, niña guía, *f.;* — **scout,** muchacha exploradora; **young** —, joven, jovencita, *f.*

girlhood [guerl-jud] *n.* niñez, doncellez, *f.,* juventud femenina.

girlish [guer-lish] *adj.* juvenil, propio de una joven o de una niña.

girth [guerz] *n.* cincha, *f.;* circunferencia, f.

gist [yist] n. quid, m.; punto principal de una acusación.

give [guiv] vt. y vi. dar, donar, conceder; abandonar; aplicarse; **to — account**, dar razón; **to — away**, regalar; divulgar; **to — back**, retornar; devolver; **to — birth**, dar a luz; **to — in**, rendirse, ceder; **to — up**, renunciar; rendirse; ceder; transigir; darse por vencido; **to — leave**, permitir; **to — off**, emitir; **to — out**, anunciar públicamente; agotarse, **to — security**, dar fianza.

given [guiven] p.p. del verbo give; **— name**, nombre de pila.

giver [gui-var] n. dador, ra, donador, ra.

gizzard [gi-sard] n. molleja, f., papo (de ave), m.

glacier [gla-siar] n. glaciar, m.

glad [glad] adj. alegre, contento; **I am — to see**, me alegro de ver; **—ly**, adv. con gusto.

gladden [gla-den] vt. alegrar, recrear; regocijar.

gladiator [gla-diei-tar] n. gladiador, m.

gladness [glad-nes] n. alegría, f., regocijo, placer, m.

glamor, glamour [gla-mor] n. encanto, hechizo, m.; elegancia, f.

glamorous [gla-mo-rous] adj.

fascinador, encantador, seductor, tentador.

glance [glans] n. vislumbre, f.; vistazo, m.; ojeada, f.; vista, f.; **at first —**, a primera vista; **—**, vi. lanzar miradas; pasar ligeramente.

gland [gland] n. glándula, f.

glandular [glan-diu-lar] adj. glandular, glanduloso.

glare [glear] n. deslumbramiento, m.; reflejo, m.; mirada feroz y penetrante; **—**, vi. relumbrar, brillar; echar miradas de indignación.

glaring [glea-rin] adj. deslumbrante; manifiesto; penetrante.

glass [glas] n. vidrio, m.; vaso para beber; espejo, m.; **— blower**, soplador de vidrio; **—case**, vidriera, f.; **plate —**, vidrio cilindrado; **water —**, vidrio soluble; **—es**, n. pl. anteojos, m. pl., gafas, f. pl.; **—**, adj. vítreo, de vidrio.

glassware [glas-uear] n. cristalería, f.

glassy [gla-si] adj. vítreo, cristalino, vidrioso.

glaucoma [glo-ko-ma] n. (med.) glaucoma, m.

glazing [glei-sin] n. vidriado, m.

gleam [glim] n. claridad, f.; brillo, destello, centelleo, m.

glee [gli] n. alegría, f.; gozo, m.; jovialidad, f.; canción sin acompañamiento para tres o más voces; — **club,** coro, *m.*

gleeful [gli-ful] *adj.* alegre, gozoso.

glen [glen] *n.* valle, *m.;* llanura, *f.*

glide [glaid] *vi.* resbalar; pasar ligeramente.

glimmer [gli-mar] *n.* vislumbre, *f.;* —, *vi.* vislumbrarse.

glimpse [glimps] *n.* vislumbre, *f.;* ojeada, *f.;* —, *vt.* descubrir, percibir.

glisten [gli-sen] *vi.* relucir, brillar; —, *n.* brillo, *m.*

glitter [gli-tar] *vi.* resplandecer, brillar; —, *n.* brillantez, *f.,* brillo, *m.;* ostentación, *f.*

gloat [glout] *vi.* ojear con admiración; deleitarse.

global [glo-bol] *adj.* global.

globalization [glo-bo-li-cei-shon] *n.* globalización, *f.*

globe [glob] *n.* globo, *m.;* esfera, *f.;* orbe, *m.*

globe-trotter [glob-tro-ter] *n.* trotamundos, *m.* y *f.,* persona que viaja extensamente.

gloom [glum] *n.* oscuridad, *f.;* melancolía, tristeza, *f.*

gloomy [glu-mi] *adj.* sombrío, oscuro; nublado; triste, melancólico; hosco, tenebroso.

glorify [glo-ri-fai] *vt.* glorificar, celebrar.

glorious [glo-rios] *adj.* glorioso, ilustre.

glory [glo-ri] *n.* gloria, fama, celebridad, *f.;* lauro, *m.;* aureola o auréola, *f.*

glossary [glo-sa-ri] *n.* glosario, *m.*

glossy [glo-si] *adj.* lustroso, brillante.

glove [glav] *n.* guante, *m.*

glow [glou] *vi.* arder; inflamarse; relucir; —, *n.* fulgor, *m.;* color vivo; viveza de color; vehemencia de una pasión.

glowworm [glau-uerm] *n.* luciérnaga, *f.*

glucose [glu-kous] *n.* glucosa, *f.*

glue [glu] *n.* cola, *f.,* sustancia glutinosa; —, *vt.* encolar, pegar.

glum [glam] *adj.* tétrico; de mal humor.

glut [glat] *vt.* hartar, saciar; —, *n.* hartura, sobreabundancia, *f.*

glutton [gla-ton] *n.* glotón, ona, tragón, ona.

gluttony [gla-to-ni] *n.* glotonería, *f.*

glycerine [gli-se-rin] *n.* glicerina, *f.*

gnarled [narld] *adj.* nudoso; enredado.

gnash [nash] *vt.* hacer crujir, hacer rechinar.

gnaw [nou] *vt.* roer, mordicar.

go [gou] *vi.* ir, irse, andar, caminar; partir; correr; pasar; **to —**

away, marcharse, salir; **to —
astray,** extraviarse; **to — forward,** ir adelante; **to — back,**
regresar; remontar a; **to —
beyond,** rebasar; trascender, ir
más allá; **to— out,** salir; **to —
without,** pasarse sin; **— to it!** ¡
vamos! ¡a ello! **—,** n. (coll.)
energía, f.; actividad, f.; espíritu, m.; **on the —,** en plena actividad, sin parar, siempre
moviéndose.

goad [goud] n. aguijada, f.; aguijón, m.; garrocha, f.; **—,** vt.
aguijar; estimular, incitar.

goal [goul] n. meta, f ; fin, m.;
tanto, gol, m.; **— line,** raya de
la meta; **— post,** poste de la
meta.

goat [gout] n. cabra, chiva, f.; **he
—,** cabrón, m.

gobbler [go-blar] n. pavo, m.;
glotón, ona.

goblet [go-blit] n. copa, f.; cáliz,
m.

goblin [go-blin] n. duende, m.

God [god] n. Dios, m.; **act of —,**
fuerza mayor; **— willing,** Dios
mediante.

god [god] n. dios, m.

godchild [god-chaild] n. ahijado,
da.

goddaughter [god-dau-tar] n.
ahijada, f.

goddess [go-des] n. diosa, f.

godfather [god-fa-dar] n. padrino, m.

godless [god-les] adj. infiel,
impío, ateo.

godlike [god-laik] adj. divino.

godliness [god-li-nes] n. piedad,
devoción, santidad, f.

godly [god-li] adj. piadoso, devoto, religioso; recto, justificado.

godmother [god-ma-dar] n.
madrina, f.

godsend [god-send] n. bendición,
f., cosa llovida del cielo.

godson [god-san] n. ahijado, m.

goes [gous] 3ª persona del singular del verbo **go.**

goggles [go-guels] n. pl. gafas, f.
pl.

going [gouin] n. paso, m., andadura, f.; partida, f.; progreso,
m.; **—s-on,** (coll.) sucesos,
acontecimientos, m. pl.

gold [gould] n. oro, m.; **— leaf,**
hoja de oro batido; **— mine,**
mina de oro; fuente abundante
de riqueza; **— standard,** patrón
de oro.

golden [goul-den] adj. áureo, de
oro; excelente; **— mean,** moderación, f., justo medio; **— rule,**
regla áurea; **— wedding,** bodas
de oro.

goldfinch [gould-finch] n. (orn.)
cardelina, f., jilguero, m.

goldfish [gould-fish] n. carpa
pequeña dorada.

goldsmith [gould-smiz] n. orífice,

orfebre, *m.*

golf [golf] *n.* golf, *m.;* — **club,** palo o bastón o mazo de golf; — **links,** campo de golf, m.

golfer [golfer] *n.* jugador o jugadora de golf.

gone [gon] *adj.* ido; perdido; pasado; gastado; muerto; —, *p.p.* del verbo **go.**

gong [gong] *n.* campana chinesca.

good [gud] *adj.* bueno, buen, benévolo, bondadoso, cariñoso; conveniente, apto; — **cheer,** jovialidad, *f.,* regocijo, *m.;* — **day,** buenos días; — **evening,** buenas tardes, buenas noches; — **humor,** buen humor; — **luck,** buena suerte; — **morning,** buenos días; — **nature,** temperamento agradable, buen carácter.

good-by, good-bye [gud-bai] *n.* adiós, *m.;* —, *interj.* ¡adiós! ¡hasta luego! ¡hasta después! ¡hasta la vista! ¡vaya con Dios!

goodhearted [gud-jar-tid] *adj.* bondadoso, de buen corazón.

good-looking [gud-lu-kin] *adj.* bien parecido, guapo.

goodly [gud-li] *adj.* considerable, algo numeroso; agradable.

good-natured [gud-nei-chad] *adj.* bondadoso; de buen carácter.

goodness [gud-nes] *n.* bondad, f.

goods [guds] *n. pl.* bienes muebles, *m. pl.;* mercaderías, *f. pl.;* efectos, *m. pl.;* **household** —, enseres, *m. pl.;* **straight of** —, hilo (en costura), *m.*

good-sized [gud-saist] *adj.* de buen tamaño.

goose [gus] *n.* ganso, *m.;* oca, *f.;* tonto, ta; — **flesh,** — **pimples,** (fig.) carne de gallina (producida por el frío o miedo).

gopher [gou-far] *n.* variedad de mamífero roedor.

gore [gor] *n.* sangre cuajada; sesga, *f.;* —, *vt.* acornar, dar cornadas, cornear.

gorgeous [gor-yos] *adj.* primoroso, brillante, vistoso; —**ly,** *adv.* con esplendor y magnificencia.

gorilla [go-ri-la] *n.* (zool.) gorila, f.

gory [go-ri] *adj.* cubierto de sangre grumosa; sangriento.

gospel [gos-pel] *n.* evangelio, *m.*

gossip [go-sip] *n.* charla, *f.;* caramillo, *m.;* chisme, *m.;* murmuración; —, vi. charlar, murmurar, decir chismes.

got [got] *pretérito* y *p.p.* del verbo **get.**

Gothic [go-zik] *adj.* gótico; — **type,** letra gótica.

gouge [gauch] *n.* gubia, gurbia, *f.;* (coll.) ranura o estría hecha con gubia; (coll.) imposición, *f.;* impostor, ra; —, *vt.* escoplear; sacarle (los ojos a alguien);

(coll.) defraudar, engañar.

gourd [guard] *n.* (bot.) calabaza, *f.;* calabacera, *f.*

gout [gaut] *n.* (med.) gota, *f.;* podagra, *f.*

govern [ga-vern] *vt.* y *vi.* gobernar, dirigir, regir; mandar.

government [ga-vern-ment] *n.* gobierno, *m.;* administración pública; — **bonds,** bonos de gobierno; **municipal —,** ayuntamiento, *m.*

governmental [ga-vern-men-tal] *adj.* gubernamental.

governor [ga-ver-nar] *n.* gobernador, *m.;* gobernante, *m.;* (mech.) regulador, *m.;* **—'s office, —'s mansion,** gobernación, *f.*

gown [gaun] *n.* toga, *f.;* vestido de mujer; bata, *f.;* túnica, *f.*

grab [grab] *vt.* agarrar, arrebatar; —, *n.* arrebato, *m.;* cosa arrebatada, gancho para arrancar.

grace [greis] *n.* gracia, *f.;* favor, *m.;* gentileza, *f.;* merced, *f.;* perdón, *m.;* **to say —,** bendecir la mesa; —, *vt.* adornar; agraciar.

graceful [greis-ful] *adj.* que tiene gracia; **—ly,** *adv.* con gracia, elegantemente.

graceless [greis-les]*adj.* sin gracia, desagraciado; réprobo, malvado.

gracious [grei-shos] *adj.* gentil, afable, cortés; —! *interj.* ¡válgame Dios! **—ly,** *adv.* con gentileza.

gradation [gra-dei-shon] *n.* gradación, *f.*

grade [greid] *n.* grado, *m.;* pendiente, *f ;* nivel, *m.;* categoria, *f.;* calidad, *f.;* calificación, *f.;* **— school,** escuela primaria, **passing —,** aprobado, *m.;* —, *vt.* graduar, clasificar.

gradient [grei-dient] *n.* (rail.) pendiente, contrapendiente, *f.;* **falling —,** declive, *m.*

gradual [gra-diual] *adj.* gradual.

graduate [gra-duet] *vt.* graduar; **to be —d,** recibirse; —, *n.* diplomado, da, graduado, da; recibido, da; (chem.) probeta, *f.*

graduation [gra-diu-ei-shon] *n.* graduación, *f.*

graft [graft] *n.* injerto, *m.;* soborno público; —, *vt.* injertar, ingerir.

graham bread [grei-am-bred] *n.* acemita, *f.*

grain [grein] *n.* grano, *m.;* semilla, *f.;* disposición, índole, *f.;* cereal, *m.;* **against the —,** a contrapelo; con repugnancia; **— alcohol,** alcohol de granos.

gram [gram] *n.* gramo (peso), *m.*

grammar [gra-mar] *n.* gramática, *f.;* **— school,** escuela de primera enseñanza, escuela primaria o elemental.

grammatical [gra-ma-ti-kal] *adj.* gramatical.

gramophone [gra-mo-foun] *n.* gramófono, *m.*

grand [grand] *adj.* grande, ilustre; magnífico, espléndido; — **piano,** piano de cola, *m.;* — **slam,** bola, *f.*

grandchild [grand-chaild] *n.* nieto, ta.

granddaughter [gran-do-tar] *n.* nieta, *f.*

grandfather [grand-fa-dar] *n.* abuelo, *m.*

grandiose [gran-di-ous] *adj.* grandioso.

grandmother [gran-ma-dar] *n.* abuela, *f.*

grandparents [gran-pa-rents] *n. pl.* abuelos, *m. pl.*

grandson [gran-san] *n.* nieto, *m.*

grange [greinch] *n.* granja, *f.,* cortijo, *m.,* casa de labranza.

granite [gra-nit] *n.* granito, *m.*

grant [grant] *vt.* conceder; conferir; dar; otorgar; —**ing that,** supuesto que; **to take for** —**ed,** presuponer, dar por sentado; —, *n.* concesión, *f.;* subvención, *f.*

granulate [gra-niu-leit] *vt.* granular.

granulated [gra-niu-lei-ted] *adj.* granulado.

granule [gra-niul] *n.* gránulo, *m.*

grape [greip] *n.* uva, *f.;* **bunch of** —**s,** racimo de uvas.

grapefruit [greip-frut] *n.* toronja, *f.*

grapevine [greip-vain] *n.* parra, vid, viña, *f.;* **through the** —, por vía secreta (aplícase a rumores, etc.).

graph [graf] *n.* diagrama, *m.;* gráfico, *m.*

graphic [gra-fik] *adj.* gráfico; pintoresco; — **arts,** artes gráficas; —**ally,** *adv.* gráficamente.

graphite [gra-fait] *n.* grafito, *m.*

grapple [gra-pel] *vt.* y *vi.* agarrar, agarrarse; luchar.

grasp [grasp] *vt.* empuñar, asir, agarrar; comprender; —, vi. esforzarse a agarrar; —, *n.* puño, puñado, *m.;* poder, *m.*

grasping [gras-pin] *adj.* codicioso.

grass [gras] *n.* hierba, *f.;* herbaje, *m.;* yerba, *f.,* césped, *m.;* — **seed,** semilla de césped; — **widow,** mujer divorciada o separada del marido; mujer cuyo marido está ausente; — **widower,** hombre divorciado o separado de su esposa.

grasshopper [gras-jo-par] *n.* saltamontes, chapulín, *m.*

grassy [gra-si] *adj.* herboso.

grate [greit] *n.* reja, verja, rejilla, *f.;* —, *vt.* rallar; hacer rechinar; enrejar; ofender; irritar.

grateful [greit-ful] *adj.* grato, agradecido.

grater [grei-tar] *n.* rallo, raspador, *m.*

gratification [gra-ti-fi-kei-shon] *n.* gratificación, *f.*

gratify [gra-ti-fai] *vt.* contentar; gratificar; satisfacer.

grating [grei-tin] *n.* rejado, *m.;* reja, *f.;* rejilla, *f.;* —, *adj.* áspero; ofensivo.

gratitude [gra-ti-tiud] *n.* gratitud, *f.,* agradecimiento, *m.*

gratuity [gra-tui-ti] *n.* propina, *f.*

grave [greiv] *n.* sepultura, *f.;* tumba, fosa, *f.;* —, *adj.* grave, serio; —**ly**, *adv.* con gravedad, seriamente.

gravedigger [greiv-di-gar] *n.* sepulturero, *m.*

gravel [gra-vel] *n.* cascajo, *m.;* (med.) piedra, *f.;* mal de piedra; —, *vt.* cubrir con cascajo; (coll.) desconcertar.

gravestone [greiv-stoun] *n.* piedra sepulcral.

graveyard [greiv-yard] *n.* cementerio, panteón, *m.*

gravitate [gra-vi-teit] *vi.* gravitar.

gravitation [gra-vi-tei-shon] *n.* gravitación, *f.*

gravity [gra-vi-ti] *n.* gravedad, *f.;* seriedad, *f*

gravy [gra-vi] *n.* jugo de la carne; salsa, *f.;* — **dish,** salsera, *f.*

gray [grei] *adj.* gris; cano; —, *n.* gris, *m.*

grayish [greish] *adj.* pardusco.

graze [greis] *vt.* pastorear; tocar ligeramente; **to lead (cattle) to** —, pastar (el ganado); —, *vi.* rozar; pacer.

grease [greis] *n.* grasa, *f.;* pringue, *m.;* **to remove** —, desgrasar; —, *vt.* untar, engrasar, lubricar.

greasy [gri-si] *adj.* grasiento, craso, gordo, mantecoso.

great [greit] *adj.* gran, grande; principal; ilustre; noble, magnánimo; colosal; revelante; **G— Bear,** (ast.) Osa Mayor, *f.;* —**ly,** *adv.* muy, mucho; grandemente.

Great Britain [greit-bri-tain] Gran Bretaña, *f.*

great-grandchild [greit-gran-chaild] *n.* bisnieto, ta.

great-grandparent [greit-gran-pa-rent] *n.* bisabuelo, la.

greatness [greit-nes] *n.* grandeza, *f.;* dignidad, *f.;* poder, *m.;* magnanimidad, *f.*

Grecian [gri-shan] *n. y adj.* griego, ga.

Greece [gris] Grecia, *f.*

greed, greediness [grid], [gri-di-nes] *n.* voracidad, *f.;* gula, *f.;* codicia, *f.*

greedy [gri-di] *adj.* voraz, goloso; hambriento; ansioso, deseoso;

insaciable.

Greek [grik] *n.* y *adj.* griego, ga.

green [grin] *adj.* verde, fresco, reciente; no maduro; —, *n.* verde, *m.;* verdor, *m.;* llanura verde; —s, *n. pl.* verduras, *f. pl.*

greenhouse [grin--jaus] *n.* invernáculo, invernadero, *m.*

greenish [gri-nish] *adj.* verdoso.

Greenland [grin-land] Groenlandia, *f.*

Greenlander [grin-lan-dar] *n.* y *adj.* groenlandés, esa.

greens [grins] *n. pl.* verduras, hortalizas, *f. pl.*

greet [grit] *vt.* saludar; —, *vi.* encontrarse y saludarse.

greeting [gri-tin] *n.* salutación, *f.,* saludo, *m.*

gregarious [gri-ga-rios] *adj.* gregario.

grenade [gri-neid] *n.* (mil.) granada, *f.*

grew [gru] *pretérito* del verbo **grow.**

grey [grei] = **gray**

greyhound [grei-jaund] *n.* galgo, lebrel, *m.*

grid [grid] *n.* parrilla, rejilla, *f.;* (elec.) soporte de plomo de las placas de acumuladores.

griddle [gri-del] *n.* plancha, tartera, parrilla, *f.*

grief [grif] *n.* dolor, *m.,* aflicción, pena, *f.;* quebranto, *m.;* congo-

ja, *f.*

grievance [gri-vans] *n.* pesar, *m.;* molestia, *f.;* agravio, *m.;* injusticia, *f ;* perjuicio, *m.*

grieve [griv] *vt.* agraviar, afligir; —, *vi.* afligirse, llorar.

grievous [gri-vos] *adj.* doloroso; enorme; cargoso; —ly, *adv.* penosamente; cruelmente.

grill [gril] *vt.* asar en parrillas; —, *n.* parrilla, *f.*

grille [gril] *n.* enrejado, *m.,* reja, *f.*

grim [grim] *adj.* feo; horrendo; ceñudo; austero.

grimace [gri-meis] *n.* visaje, *m.;* mueca, *f.*

grime [graim] *n.* mugre, *f.;* —, *vt.* ensuciar.

grimness [grim-nes] *n.* austeridad, severidad, *f.*

grimy [grai-mi] *adj.* sucio, manchado.

grin [grin] *n.* sonrisa franca; —, *vi.* sonreir abiertamente, sonreírse francamente.

grind [graind] *vt.* moler; pulverizar; afilar; estregar; mascar.

grinder [grain-dar] *n.* molinero, ra; molinillo, *m.;* amolador, *m.;* muela, *f.;* piedra molar, piedra de afilar.

grip [grip] *vt.* agarrar, empuñar, asir; —, *n.* maleta, *f.*

gripe [graip] *vt.* asir, empuñar; —, *vi.* padecer cólico; (coll.)

lamentarse, quejarse; —**s**, *n.*
pl. cólico, *m.*

gripping [gri-pin] *adj.* emocionante.

grisly [gris-li] *adj.* espantoso,
horroroso.

gristle [gri-sel] *n.* tendón, nervio,
cartílago, *m.*

grit [grit] *n.* moyuelo, *m.*; —**s**, *n.*
pl. maíz, avena o trigo descas-
carado y molido.

gritty [gri-ti] *adj.* arenoso.

grizzled, grizzly [gri-seld], [gris-li]
adj. mezclado con gris, pardus-
co.

groan [graun] *vi.* gemir, suspirar; dar gemidos; —, *n.* gemido,
suspiro, *m.*; quejido, *m.*

grocer [grou-sar] *n.* especiero,
bodeguero, abarrotero, *m.*

grocery [grou-se-ri] *n.* especiería,
abacería, *f.*; bodega, *f.*; —
store, tienda de comestibles,
tienda de abarrotes; —**ries,**
comestibles, *m. pl.*

groggy [gro-gui] *adj.* mareado o
atontado por un golpe (aplícase
generalmente a los pugilistas);
(coll.) medio borracho.

groom [grum] *n.* establero, *m.*;
criado, *m.*; mozo de caballos;
novio, *m.*; —, *vt.* cuidar; aliñar,
asear.

groove [gruv] *n.* muesca, ranura,
f.; rutina, *f.*

grooved [gruvd] *adj.* acanalado,
estriado.

grope [group] *vt.* y *vi.* tentar,
buscar a oscuras; andar a tientas.

gross [grous] *adj.* grueso, corpulento, espeso; grosero; estúpido; — **profits,** beneficio bruto;
— **weight,** peso bruto; —**ly,**
adv. groseramente; en bruto; —
, *n.* gruesa, *f.*; todo, *m.*

grotesque [grou-tesk] *adj.* grotesco.

grouch [grauch] *n.* descontento,
mal humor, *m.*; persona mal-
humorada; —, *vi.* gruñir,
refunfuñar.

grouchy [grau-chi] *adj.* mal
humorado, de mal humor.

ground [graund] *n.* tierra, *f.*;
terreno, suelo, pavimento, *m.*;
fundamento, *m.*; razón fundamental, *f.*; (elec.) tierra, *f.*;
campo (de batalla), *m.*; fondo,
m.; — **control approach,** acceso
de control terrestre; — **floor,**
piso bajo, planta baja; — **hog,**
marmota, *f.*; — **wire,** alambre
de tierra; —**s,** heces, *f pl.*; poso,
sedimento, *m.*; —, *vt.* establecer; traer a tierra; —, *vi.* varar.

groundwork [graund-uek] *n.*
plan, fundamento, *m.*

group [grup] *n.* grupo, *m.*; —, *vt.*
agrupar.

grove [grouv] *n.* arboleda, *f.*;
boscaje, *m.*; **pine** — pinar, *m.*

grovel [gro-vel] *vi.* serpear; arrastrarse; envilecerse.

grow [grou] *vt.* cultivar; —, *vi.* crecer, aumentarse; nacer, brotar; vegetar; adelantar; hacerse, ponerse, volverse; **to — soft, to —tender,** relentecer; enternecerse; **to —up,** crecer; **to — young again,** rejuvenecer.

grower [grouar] *n.* cultivador, *m.*

growing [grouin] *n.* crecimiento, *m.;* cultivo, *m.;* —, *adj.* creciente.

growl [groul] *vi.* regañar, gruñir, rezongar, refunfuñar; —, *n.* gruñido, *m.*

grown [groun] *p.p.* del verbo **grow.**

grown-up [groun-op] *adj.* mayor de edad, maduro; —, *n.* persona mayor de edad, adulto, ta.

growth [grouz] *n.* vegetación, *f.;* crecimiento, *m.;* producto, *m.;* aumento, *m.;* progreso, adelanto, *m.;* nacencia, *f.,* tumor, *m.*

grubby [gru-bi] *adj.* gusarapiento; sucio; desaliñado.

grudge [grach] *n.* rencor, odio, *m.;* envidia, *f.;* **to bear a —,** guardar rencor; —, *vt.* y *vi.* envidiar; repugnar; malquerer.

gruel [gruel] *n.* harina de avena mondada; (Mex.) atole, *m.*

grueling [grue-lin] *adj.* muy severo, agotador.

gruesome [gru-som] *adj.* horrible, espantoso.

grumble [gram-bol] *vi.* gruñir; murmurar.

grumpy [gram-pi] *adj.* regañón, quejoso, ceñudo.

grunt [grant] *vi.* gruñir; gemir.

guarantee [ga-ran-ti] *n.* garante, *m.* y *f.,* fiador, ra; garantía, fianza, *f.;* garantizar.

guarantor [ga-ran-tar] *n.* garante, *m.* y *f.,* fiador, ra; **to be a —,** salir fiador, salir garante.

guaranty [ga-ran-ti] *n.* garante, *m.;* garantía, *f.*

guard [gard] *n.* guarda, *m.* o *f.,* guardia, *f.,* centinela, *m.* y *f.;* rondador, *m.;* vigilante, *m.;* guardafrenos, *m.;* (fútbol) defensa, *m.;* **to be on —,** estar de centinela; estar alerta; —, *vt.* guardar; defender; custodiar; —, *vi.* guardarse; prevenirse; velar; **to — against,** cautelar; precaverse.

guarded [gar-did] *adj.* mesurado, circunspecto.

guardian [gar-dian] *n.* tutor, *m.;* curador, *m.;* guardián (prelado), *m.;* **— saint,** patrón, *m.;* —, *adj.* tutelar; **— angel,** ángel de la guarda.

guardianship [gar-dian-ship] *n.* tutela, *f.*

guerrilla [gue-ri-la] *n.* guerrillero, *m.*

guess [gues] *vt.* y *vi.* conjeturar;

adivinar; —, *n.* conjetura, *f.*

guest [guest]*n.* huésped, da, invitado, da.

guidance [gai-dans] *n.* gobierno, *m.*; dirección, *f.*; — **beam,** (avi.) rayo electrónico orientador.

guide [gaid] *vt.* guiar, dirigir; —, *n.* guía, *m.* y *f.*; conductor, *m.*; **girl** —, guía, niña guía.

guidebook [gaid-buk] *n.* manual (para viajeros), *m.*, guía, *f.*

guidepost [gaid-poust] *n.* poste indicador, hito, *m.*

guild [gild] *n.* gremio, *m.*; comunidad, corporación, *f.*

guile [gail] *n.* engaño, fraude, *m.*

guilt [guilt] *n.* delito, *m.*; culpa, delincuencia, *f.*

guiltless [guil-ti-nes] *adj.* inocente, libre de culpa.

guilty [guil-ti] *adj.* reo, culpable, culpado.

guinea [gui-ni] *n.* guinea (moneda), *f.*; — **pig,** conejillo de Indias, *m.*

guise [gais] *n.* modo, *m.*; manera, *f.*; práctica, *f.*

guitar [gui-tar] *n.* guitarra, *f.*

gulch [galsh] *n.* barranca, quebrada, cañada, *f.*

gulf [galf] *n.* golfo, *m.*; abismo, *m.*, sima, *f.*; torbellino, *m.*

Gulf Stream [galf-strim] *n.* corriente del Golfo (de México).

gull [gal] *n.* (orn.) gaviota, *f.*

gullet [ga-lit] *n.* tragadero, gaz-

nate, *m.*

gullible [ga-li-bol] *adj.* crédulo, fácil de engañar.

gully [ga-li] *n.* barranca, *f.*; —, *vi.* formar canal.

gulp [galp] *n.* trago, *m.*; —, *vt.* engullir, tragar.

gum [gam] *n.* goma, *f.*; encía, *f.*; **chewing** —,   chicle, *m.*, goma de mascar; — **tree,** árbol gomífero.

gun [gan] *n.* arma de fuego; cañón, *m.*; fusil, *m.*; escopeta, *f* pistola, *f* ; revólver, *m.*; — **barrel,** cañón de fusil; — **carriage,** cureña de cañón; — **metal,** bronce de cañones; imitación de cobre.

gunfire [gan-fier] *n.* cañoneo, *m.*

gunner [ga-nar] *n.* artillero, *m.*

gunpowder [gan-pouer] *n.* pólvora, *f.*

gunshot [gan-shot] *n.* tiro de escopeta; herida de arma; alcance de un tiro.

gurgle [guer-guel] *vi.* gorjear; —, *n.* gorjeo, *m.*

gush [gash] *vi.* brotar; chorrear; demostrar afecto exageradamente; —, *n.* chorro, *m.*; efusión, *f.*

gust [gast] *n.* soplo de aire; ráfaga, *f.*

gusto [gas-tou] *n.* gusto, placer, *m.*

gut [gat] *n.* intestino, *m.*, cuerda

de tripa; barriga, *f.;* —*s, n. pl.*
(coll.) valor, *m.,* valentía, fuerza, *f.;* —, *vt.* desventrar, destri-
par.

gutter [ga-tar] *n.* gotera, canal,
f.; zanja, *f.;* caño, *m.;* arroyo de
la calle; —, *vt.* y *vi.* acanalar;
caer en gotas.

guttural [ga-ta-ral] *adj.* gutural.

guy [gai] *n.* (naut.) retenida, *f.;*
tipo, sujeto, *m.*

guzzle [ga-sel] *vt.* y *vi.* beber o

comer con glotonería.

gymnasium [yim-nei-siom] *n.*
gimnasio, *m.*

gymnastic [yim-nas-tik] *adj.*
gimnástico; —*s, n. pl.* gimnástica, gimnasia, *f.*

gynecology [gai-ne-ko-lo-yi] *n.*
(med.) ginecología, *f.*

gypsum [yip-som] *n.* yeso, *m.*

gypsy [yip-si] *n.* y *adj.* gitano,
na; bohemio, mia.

H

habilitate [a-bli-li-teit] *vt.* habilitar.

habit [ja-bit] *n.* hábito, vestido,
m.; uso, *m.; costumbre, f.*

habitable [ja-bi-ta-bol] *adj.* habitable.

habitat [ja-bit] *n.* habitación,
morada, *f.*

habitation [ja-bi-tei-shon] *n.*
habitación, *f.;* domicilio, *m.*

habitual [ja-bi-chual] *adj.* habitual.

had [jad] *pretérito* y *p.p.* del
verbo **have.**

hag [jag] *n.* bruja, hechicera, *f.*

haggard [ja-gard] *adj.* macilento,
ojeroso, trasnochado.

haggle [ja-gal] *vt.* cortar en taja-
das; —, *vi.* regatear.

hail [jeil] *n.* granizo, *m.;* saludo,

m.; —, *vt.* saludar; —, *vi.* granizar; —! *interj.* ¡viva! ¡salve!
¡salud! **Hail Mary,** Ave María.

hailstorm [jeil-storm] *n.* granizada, *f.*

hair [jear] *n.* cabello, pelo, *m.;*
bobbed —, melena, *f.,* pelo
corto; — **ribbon,** cinta para el
cabello; — **trigger,** disparador
muy sensible (con gatillo que
descansa en un pelo); **to comb
one's** —, peinarse; **to cut one's**
-, cortarse el pelo.

hairbrush [jea-brosh] *n.* cepillo
para el cabello.

haircut [jea-kat] *n.* corte de pelo;
to have a —, cortarse el pelo.

hairdo [jea-du] *n.* peinado, *m.*

hairdresser [jea-dre-sar] *n.* pelu-
quero, *m.;* peinador, ra; —'s

shop, peluquería, *f.*; salón de belleza.

hairless [jea-les] *adj.* calvo, sin pelo.

hairpin [jea-pin] *n.* horquilla (para el cabello), *f.*

hair-raising [jea-rei-sin] *adj.* espantoso, aterrador.

hairy [jea-ri] *adj.* peludo, velludo, cabelludo.

half [jaf] *n.* mitad, *f.*; —, *adj.* medio.

half-breed [jaf-brid] *n.* y *adj.* mestizo, za.

halfhearted [jaf-jar-tid] *adj.* indiferente, sin entusiasmo.

half-hour [jaf-auar] *n.* media hora.

half-mast [jaf-mast] *n.* media asta; —, *adj.* a media asta.

half-moon [jaf-mun] *n.* semilunio, *m.*

halfway [jaf-uei] *adv.* a medio camino; —, *adj.* medio; parcial.

halibut [ja-li-bat] *n.* (ichth.) hipogloso, *m.*

halitosis [ja-li-tou-sis] *n.* halitosis, *f.*, mal aliento.

hall [jol] *n.* vestíbulo, *m.*, sala, *f.*; salón, colegio, *m.*; sala, *f.*; cámara, *f.*

hallow [ja-lou] *vt.* consagrar, santificar.

Halloween [ja-louin] *n.* víspera de Todos los Santos.

hallucination [ja-lu-si-nei-shon] *n.* alucinación, *f.*

hallway [jol-uei] *n.* pasillo corredor, *m.*

halo [jei-lou] *n.* halo, *m.*, corona, *f.*

halt [jolt] *vi.* cojear, parar, hacer alto; dudar; —, *n.* cojera, *f.*; parada, *f.*; alto, *m.*; —! *interj.* ¡alto!

halve [jav] *vt.* partir en dos mitades.

halves [javs] *n. pl.* de **half,** mitades, *f. pl.*; **by** —, a medias.

ham [jam] *n.* jamón, *m.*, (anat.) corva, *f.*

hamburger [jam-ber-gar] *n.* hamburguesa, *f.*, carne picada de res.

hamlet [jam-lit] *n.* villorrio, *m.*, aldea, *f.*

hammer [ja-mar] *n.* martillo, *m.*; —, *vt.* martillar; forjar; —, *vi.* trabajar; reiterar esfuerzos.

hammock [ja-mok] *n.* hamaca, *f.*

hamper [jam-par] *n.* cuévano, *m.*, cesto grande (para ropa, etc.); —, *vt.* restringir; estorbar, impedir; entrampar.

hand [jand] *n.* mano, *f.*; palmo (medida), *m.*; carácter de escritura; (coll.) salva de aplausos; poder, *m.*; habilidad, destreza, *f.*; (naut.) marinero, *m.*; obrero, *m.*; mano o manecilla (de un reloj), *f.*; **at** —, a la mano, al lado; — **baggage,** equipaje o bulto de mano; — **grenade,** granada de mano; — **to** —, cuerpo a cuerpo; **in the** —**s of,** en poder de; **on the other** —, en cambio, por otra parte; **with bare** —**s,** a brazo partido; **with one's own** —, de propia mano; **to clap** —**s,** batir palmas, aplaudir; —, *vt.* dar, entregar; alargar; guiar por la mano; **to** — **down,** trasmitir, bajar; pasar más abajo.

handball [jand-bol] *n.* pelota, *f.;* **juego de pelota.**

handbook [jand-buk] *n.* manual, prontuario, *m.*

handcuffs [jand-kaf] *n. pl.* manillas, esposas, *f. pl.*

handful [jand-ful] *n.* manojo, puñado, *m.*

handicap [jan-di-kap] *n.* carrera ciega con caballos de peso igualado; obstáculo, *m.;* ventaja, *f.* (en juegos); lastre (en el golf), *m.*

handicraft [jan-di-kraft] *n.* arte mecánica; destreza manual; mano de obra.

handkerchief [jan-ker-chif] *n.* pañuelo, *m.*

handle [jan-del] *n.* mango, puño, *m.,* asa, manija; palanca, *f.; vt.* manejar; tratar.

handling [jand-lin] *n.* manejo, *m.;* toque, *m.*

handmade [jand-meid] *adj.* hecho a mano.

hand-picked [jand-pikt] *adj.* escogido, selecto, favorecido.

handrail [jand-reil] *n.* barandilla, *f.;* pasamano, *m.*

handset [jand-set] *n.* trasmisor y receptor telefónico.

handshake [jand-sheik] *n.* apretón de manos, *m.*

handsome [jan-som] *adj.* hermoso, bello, gentil, guapo; —**ly,** *adv.* primorosamente; con generosidad.

handwriting [jand-rai-tin] *n.* escritura a mano; caligrafía, *f.;* letra, *f.*

handy [jan-di] *adj.* manual; diestro, mafioso; — **man,** factótum, *m.;* hombre hábil para trabajos de la casa, reparaciones, etc.

hang [jang] *vt.* colgar, suspender; ahorcar; entapizar; —, *vi.* colgar; ser ahorcado; pegarse; quedarse suspenso; depender.

hangar [jan-gar] *n.* (avi.) hangar, *m.;* cobertizo, *m.*

hanger [jan-gar] *n.* alfanje, *m.;* espada ancha; colgador, gancho (para ropa), *m.*

hanging [jan-guin] *adj.* pendiente.

hangings [jan-guins] *n. pl.* tapicería, *f.;* cortinaje, *m.*

hangman [jang-man] *n.* verdugo, *m.*

hangnail [jang-neil] *n.* respigón,

uñero, padrastro, *m.*

hangover [jang-ou-var] *n.* resaca, *f.;* (Mex.) cruda, *f.*

hanker [jan-kar] *vi.* ansiar, apetecer.

hankering [jang-ka-rin] *n.* anhelo, *m.*

haphazard [jap-ja-sard] *n.* accidente, lance, *m.;* —, *adj.* casual, descuidado.

hapless [ja-plis] *adj.* desgraciado, desventurado.

happen [ja-pen] *vi.* acontecer, acaecer, suceder, sobrevenir, caer; **to — to,** acertar, suceder por casualidad.

happening [jap-nin] *n.* suceso, acontecimiento, *m.*

happily [ja-pi-li] *adv.* felizmente.

happiness [ja-pi-nes] *n.* felicidad, dicha, *f.*

happy [ja-pi] *adj.* feliz, bienaventurado; jubiloso.

harangue [ja-rang] *n.* arenga, *f.;* —, *vi.* arengar.

harass [ja-ras] *vt.* cansar, fatigar, sofocar, acosar.

harbinger [jar-bin-char] *n.* precursor, ra.

harbor [jar-bar] *n.* albergue, *m.;* puerto, *m.;* bahía, *f.;* asilo, *m.;* —, *vt.* albergar; hospedar; —, *vi.* tomar albergue.

hard [jard] *adj.* duro, firme; difícil; penoso; cruel, severo, rígido; — **and fast,** rígido; sin excepción; — **cash,** numerario efectivo; — **cider,** sidra fermentada; — **coal,** antracita, *f.;* — **of hearing,** medio sordo, duro de oído; —, *adv.* cerca, a la mano, difícilmente.

hard-boiled [jard-boild] *adj.* cocido hasta endurecerse; — **eggs,** huevos duros.

harden [jar-den] *vt.* y *vi.* endurecer, endurecerse.

hardening [jard-nin] *n.* endurecimiento, *m.*

hardhearted [jard-jar-tid] *adj.* duro de corazón, insensible.

hardly [jard-li] *adv.* apenas; severamente.

hardness [jard-nes] *n.* dureza, *f.;* dificultad, *f.;* inhumanidad, *f.;* severidad, *f.*

hardship [jard-ship] *n.* injuria, opresión, *f.;* injusticia, *f.;* penalidad, *f.;* trabajo, *m.;* molestia, fatiga, *f.*

hardware [jard-uear] *n.* ferretería, *f.;* — **store,** quincallería, ferretería, *f.*

hardwood [jard-wud] *n.* madera dura.

hard-working [jard-workin] *adj.* trabajador.

hardy [jar-di] *adj.* atrevido, bravo, intrépido; fuerte, robusto, vigoroso.

hare [jear] *n.* liebre, *f.*

harem [ja-rim] *n.* harén, *m.*

hark [jark] *vi.* escuchar; —! *interj.* ¡oye! ¡mira!

harlot [jar-lot] *n.* puta, meretriz, prostituta, *f.*

harm [jarm] *n.* mal, daño, *m.;* desgracia, *f.;* perjuicio, *m.;* —, *vt.* dañar, injuriar, ofender.

harmful [jarm-ful] *adj.* dañoso, dañino, perjudicial.

harmless [jarm-les] *adj.* inocente, inofensivo.

harmonic [jar-mo-nik] *adj.* armónico; —s, *n. pl.* armonía, teoría musical.

harmonica [jar-mo-ni-ka] *n.* armónica, *f.*

harmonious [jar-mo-nios] *adj.* armonioso.

harmonize [jar-mo-nais] *vt.* armonizar, concertar, ajustar; concretar; —, *vi.* convenir, corresponder.

harmony [jar-mo-ni] *n.* armonía, *f.*

harp [jarp] *n.* arpa, *f.;* —, *vt.* y *vi.* tocar el arpa; **to — upon**, machacar, porfiar, importunar con insistencia (sobre algo).

harpist [jar-pist] *n.* arpista, *m.* y *f.*

harpoon [jar-pun] *n.* arpón, *m.*

harpy [jar-pi] *n.* arpía, *f.*

harrowing [ja-rouin] *adj.* conmovedor; horripilante.

harsh [jarsh] *adj.* áspero, agrio, rígido, duro, austero.

harshness [jarsh-nes] *n.* aspereza, dureza, rudeza, austeridad, severidad, *f.*

harvest [jar-vist] *n.* cosecha, *f.;* agosto, *m.;* —, *vt.* cosech.

has [jas] *3ra persona* del *singular* del verbo **have.**

haste [jeist] *n.* prisa, *f.;* presteza, *f.;* **to be in** —, estar de prisa.

hasten [jei-sen] *vt.* acelerar, apresurar; —, *vi.* estar de prisa, apresurarse.

hastily [jeis-ti-li] *adv.* pecipitadamente; airadamente.

hasty [jeis-ti] *adj.* pronto, apresurado; colérico.

hat [jat] *n.* sombrero, *m.;* **straw** —, sombrero de paja.

hatchet [ja-chit] *n.* destral, *m.,* hacha pequeña.

hatching [ja-chin] *n.* incubación, cloquera, *f.*

hate [jeit] *n.* odio, aborrecimiento, *m.;* —, *vt.* odiar, detestar.

hateful [jeit-ful] *adj.* odioso, detestable; —ly, *adv.* detestablemente, con tirria.

hatrack [ja-trak] *n.* cuelgasombreros, *m.,* percha para sombreros.

hatred [jei-trid] *n.* odio, aborrecimiento, *m.*

haughty [jo-ti] *adj.* altanero, altivo, orgulloso.

haul [jol] *vt.* tirar, halar o jalar; acarrear; —, *n.* estirón, tirón, *m.;* botín, *m.,* presa, *f.*

haunch [jonch] *n.* anca, *f.*

haunt [jont] *vt.* frecuentar, rondar; —, *n.* guarida, *f.;* lugar frecuentado.

haunted [jon-tid] *adj.* encantado, frecuentado por espantos.

Havana [ja-va-na] Habana, *f.*

have [jav] *vt.* haber, tener; poseer.

haven [jei-ven] *n.* puerto, *m.;* abrigo, asilo, *m.*

havoc [ja-vok] *n.* estrago, *m.;* ruina, *f.*

Hawaiian Islands [ja-uaian] Islas Hawaianas, *f. pl.*

hawk [jok] *n. (orn.)* halcón, gavilán, *m.;* —, *vi.* cazar con halcón; pregonar, llevar y vender mercaderías por las calles.

hawk-eyed [jok-aid] *adj.* lince, agudo; con vista de lince.

hay [jei] *n.* heno, *m.;* — **fever,** romadizo, *m.,* catarro de origen alérgico.

haystack [jei-stak] *n.* almiar, *m.*

hazard [ja-sard] *n.* acaso, accidente, *m.;* riesgo, *m.;* juego de azar a los dados; —, *vt.* arriesgar; aventurar.

hazardous [ja-sar-dos] *adj.* arriesgado, peligroso.

haze [jeis] *n.* niebla, bruma, *f.;* aturdimiento, *m.*

hazel [jei-sel] *n.* avellano, *m.;* —, *adj.* castaño.

hazelnutc[jei-sel-nut] *n.* avellana, *f.*

hazy [jei-si] *adj.* anieblado, oscuro, brumoso; aturdido.

he [ji] *pron.* él.

head [jed] *n.* cabeza, *f.;* jefe, *m.;* juicio, *m.;* talento, *m.;* puño (de bastón), *m.;* fuente, *f.;* nacimiento (de un río), *m.;* **bald** —, calva, *f.;* **from — to foot,** de arriba abajo; — **of hair,** cabellera, *f.;* —**s or tails,** cara o cruz, cara o sello; —, *vt.* gobernar, dirigir; degollar; podar los árboles; encabezar; **to — off,** alcanzar, prevenir.

headache [je-deik] *n.* dolor de cabeza; hemicránea, jaqueca, *f.*

headdress [jed-dres] *n.* cofia, *f.;* tocado, *m.*

heading [je-din] *n.* título, membrete, *m.*

headless [jed-lis] *adj.* descabezado; estúpido.

headlight [jed-lait] *n.* linterna delantera; farol delantero.

headline [jed-lain] *n.* encabezamiento, título (de un periódico, etc.), *m.*

headmaster [jed-mas-tar] *n.* director de una escuela.

headphone [jed-foun] *n.* auricular para la cabeza.

headpiece [jed-pis] *n.* casco, yelmo, *m.;* cabeza, *f.,* intelecto, *m.;* entendimiento, *m.;* (print.)

viñeta, *f.;* auricular telefónico con so-porte para la cabeza.

headquarters [jed-kor-ters] *n.* (mil.) cuartel general; jefatura, administración, *f.;* **police —,** jefatura de policía.

headset [jed-set] *n.* (radio y TV.) casco con auricular.

headstone [jed-stoun] *n.* lápida, *f.*

headstrong [jed-stron] *adj.* testarudo, cabezudo.

headway [jed-uei] *n.* (naut.) salida, marcha, *f.;* avance, progreso, *m.;* intervalo entre dos trenes en una misma ruta.

heal [jil] *vt.* y *vi.* curar, sanar, cicatrizar; **—,** *vi.* recobrar la salud.

health [jelz] *n.* salud, sanidad, salubridad, *f.;* **bill of —,** patente de sanidad; **— officer,** oficial de sanidad o de cuarentena; sanitario, *m.;* **— resort,** centro de salud; **to be in good —,** estar bien de salud; **to be in poor —,** estar mal de salud.

healthful [jelz-ful] *adj.* saludable.

healthy [jel-zi] *adj.* sano; salubre, saludable, lozano.

heap [jip] *n.* montón, *m.;* rima, *f.,* rimero, *m.;* **ash —,** cenicero, *m.;* **—,** *vt.* amontonar, acumular.

hear [jiar] *vt.* oir; entender; acceder; **—,** *vi.* oir; escuchar.

hearing [jia-rin] *n.* oído, *m.,* oreja, *f.;* audiencia, *f.*

hearsay [jia-sei] *n.* rumor, *m.;* fama, *f.;* voz pública; **by —,** de oídas, por oídas.

heart [jart] *n.* corazón, *m.;* alma, *f.;* interior, centro, *m.;* ánimo, valor, *m.;* emoción, *f.;* **by —,** de memoria; **— trouble,** enfermedad del corazón; **to one's —'s content,** a pedir de boca; **with all my —,** con toda mi alma.

heartache [jart-eik] *n.* angustia, congoja, *f.*

heartbeat [jart-bit] *n.* latido del corazón.

heartbreak [jart-breik] *n.* decepción amorosa; pesar, *m.,* aflicción, *f.;* disgusto, *m.*

heartbreaking [jart-brei-kin] *adj.* doloroso, conmovedor.

heartbroken [jart-brou-ken] *adj.* transido de dolor.

heartburn [jart-bern] *n.* acedía, *f.*

heartfelt [jart-felt] *adj.* expresivo, muy sentido, muy sincero.

hearth [jarz] *n.* hogar, *m.,* chimenea, *f.*

heartless [jart-les] *adj.* sin corazón, inhumano. cruel.

heart-rending [jart-rendin] *adj.* agudo, penetrante, desgarrador.

heartsick [jart-sik] *adj.* dolorido, afligido.

heart-to-heart [jart-tu-jart] *adj.* íntimo, sincero, abierto; confidencial.

hearty [jar-ti] *adj.* sincero; sano; vigoroso; campechano; — **meal,** comida sana y abundante.

heat [jit] *n.* calor, *m.;* calefacción, *f.;* ardor, *m.;* vehemencia, *f.;* animosidad, *f.;* (coll.) extremada presión en investigaciones judiciales; carrera, *f.;* — **shield,** cubierta o protector contra el calor; — **wave,** onda cálida; **in** —, en celo (aplícase a los animales) ; **prickly** —, salpullido, *m.;* —, *vt.* calentar; encender.

heater [ji-tar] *n.* escalfador, *m.;* calentador, *m.,* estufa, *f.*

heathen [ji-zen] *n.* gentil, *m.* y *f.,* pagano, na.

heating [ji-tin] *n.* calefacción, *f.;* **central** —, calefacción central.

heave [jiv] *vt.* alzar; elevar; arrojar; (naut.) virar para proa; —, *vi.* palpitar; respirar trabajosamente; —, *n.* esfuerzo para levantarse; suspiro de congoja.

heaven [je-ven] *n.* cielo, *m.;* firmamento, *m.;* —**s!** *interj.* ¡cielos! ¡caramba!

heavenly [je-ven-li] *adj.* celestial, divino.

heaviness [je-vi-nes] *n.*peso, *m.;* (fig.) carga, *f.;* aflicción, *f.;* opresión, *f.*

heavy [je-vi] *adj.* grave, pesado; opresivo, penoso, molesto; triste; tardo, soñoliento; oneroso; **to be** —, pesar.

heavyweight [je-vi-ueit] *adj.* (boxeo) de peso completo; —, *n.* peso completo; (coll.) persona obesa.

hectic [jek-tik] *adj.* inquieto, agitado.

hedge [jedch] *n.* seto, *m.;* barrera, *f.;* —, *vt.* cercar con un seto.

hedgerow [jed-che-rou] *n.* serie de árboles en los cercados.

heed [jid] *vt.* atender, observar; —, *n.* cuidado, *m.;* atención, precaución, *f.;* **to give** —, reparar, atender.

heedless [jid-les] *adj.* descuidado, negligente, imprévido; —**ly,** *adv.* negligentemente.

heel [jil] *n.* talón, carcañal, calcañar, *m.;* (coll.) canalla, bribón, bellaco, *m.,* pérfido villano; **rubber** —, tacón de goma o de caucho; **to take to one's** —**s,** apretar los talones, huir; —, *vt.* poner tacón (a un zapato); (naut.) escorar.

height [jait] *n.* altura, elevación, *f.;* sublimidad, *f.*

heighten [jai-ten] *vt.* realzar; adelantar, mejorar; exaltar.

heinous [jei-nos] *adj.* atroz, odioso.

heir [ear] *n.* heredero, *m.;* — **apparent,** heredero forzoso; — **presumptive,** presunto heredero.

heiress [ea-res] *n.* heredera, *f.*

heirloom [ea-lum] *n.* mueble heredado; reliquia de familia.

helicopter [je-li-kop-tar] *n.* helicóptero, *m.*

helium [je-lium] *n.* (chem.) helio, *m.*

hell [jel] *n.* infierno *m.*

hellish [je-lish] *adj.* infernal, malvado; —**ly,** *adv.* diabólicamente.

hello [ja-lou] *interj.* ¡hola! ¡qué hay! ¡qué hubo! (expresión de saludo).

helmet [jelmit] *n.* yelmo, casco, *m.*

help [jelp] *vt.* y *vi.* ayudar, asistir, socorrer; aliviar, remediar, reparar; evitar; **to — oneself to,** servirse (algún alimento); **I cannot — it,** no puedo remediarlo; —, *n.* ayuda, *f.;* socorro, remedio, *m.*

helper [jel-par] *n.* auxiliador, ra, socorredor, ra. helpful, *adj.* útil, provechoso; saludable.

helpless [jelp-les] *adj.* inútil; imposibilitado.

helpmate [jelp-meit] *n.* compañero, ra; ayudante, *m.* y *f.;* esposa, *f.*

hemisphere [je-mis-fear] *n.* hem-isferio, *m.*

hemlock [jem-lok] *n.* (bot.) abeto, *m.;* (bot.) cicuta, *f.*

hemoglobin [ji-mou-glo-bin] *n.* (med.) hemoglobina, *f.*

hemophilia [ji-mou-fi-lia] *n.* (med.) hemofilia, *f.*

hemorrhage [ji-mou-rach] *n.* hemorragia, *f.*

hemorrhoids [ji-mou-roids] *n. pl.* hemorroides, almorranas, *f. pl.*

hemp [jemp] *n.* cáñamo, *m.*

hen [jen] *n.* gallina, *f.*

hence [jens] *adv.* de aquí; por esto.

henceforth [jens-forz] *adv.* de aquí en adelante; en lo sucesivo.

henchman [jench-man] *n.* secuaz, servil, *m.*

hencoop [jen-kup] *n.* gallinero, *m.*

henna [je-na] *n.* (bot.) alheña, *f.*

hepatitis [je-pa-tai-tis] *n.* (med.) hepatitis, *f.*

her [jar] *pron.* le; la; a ella; —, *adj.* su, de ella.

herald [je-rald] *n.* heraldo, *m.*

herb [jerb] *n.* yerba, hierba, *f.;* — **s,** *pl.* hierbas medicinales.

herbaceous [jer-bei-shos] *adj.* herbáceo.

herbage [jer-beich] *n.* herbaje, *m.,* hierba, *f.*

herbivorous [jer-ba-rios] *adj.* herbívoro.

herculean [jer-kiu-li-nian] *adj.* hercúleo.

herd [jerd] *n.* rebaño, *m.;* manada, *f.;* grey, *f.;* —, *vi.* ir en hatos; asociarse; —, *vt.* guiar (el ganado) en rebaño.

here [jiar] *adv.* aquí, acá.

hereabout, hereabouts [jiar-a-baut], [jiar-a-bauts] *adv.* por aquí, por los alrededores.

hereafter [jia-af-tar] *adv.* en lo futuro; —, *n.* estado venidero, el futuro, *m.*

hereby [jia-bai] *adv.* por esto.

hereditary [je-ri-di-ta-ri] *adj.* hereditario.

heredity [je-ri-di-ty] *n.* derecho de sucesión.

herein [jia-in] *adv.* en esto, aquí dentro.

hereinafter [jia-rin-af-tar] *adv.* después, más adelante.

heresy [je-re-si] *n.* herejía, *f.*

heretic [je-re-tik] *n.* hereje, *m.* y *f.;* —, *adj.* herético.

heretical [ji-re-ti-kal] *adj.* herético.

heretofore [jia-tu-for] *adv.* antes, en tiempos pasa-dos; hasta ahora.

heritage [je-ri-tich] *n.* herencia, *f.*

hermetic [jer-me-tik] *adj.* hermético.

hermit [jer-mit] *n.* ermitaño, eremita, *m.*

hermitage [jer-mi-tich] *n.* ermita, *f.*

hernia [jer-nia] *n.* hernia, rotura, ruptura, *f.*

hero [jia-rou] *n.* héroe, *m.*

heroic [ji-rouik] *adj.* heroico; —s, *n. pl.* expresión o acto extravagantes.

heroine [je-rouin] *n.* heroína, *f.*

heroism [je-roui-sem] *n.* heroísmo, *m.*

heron [je-ron] *n.* garza, *f.*

herring [je-rin] *n.* arenque, *m.*

hers [jers] *pron.* el suyo (de ella).

herself [jer-self] *pron.* sí, ella misma.

hesitant [je-si-teit] *adj.* indeciso, vacilante.

hesitate [je-si-teit] *vi.* vacilar, titubear.

hesitation [je-si-tei-shon] *n.* duda, irresolución, vacilación, *f.,* titubeo, *m.*

hexagon [jek-sa-gon] *n.* hexágono, *m.*

hexameter [jek-sa-mi-tar] *n.* hexámetro, *m.*

hey [jei] *interj.* ¡he! ¡oye!

heyday [jei-dei] *n.* apogeo, auge, *m.,* sumo vigor, suma vitalidad.

hiatus [jai-ei-tos] *n.* abertura, hendidura, *f.;* laguna, *f.;* (gram.) hiato, *m.*

hibernate [jai-ber-neit] *vi.* invernar.

hibernation [jai-ber-nei-shon] *n.*

invernada, f.

hiccough [ji-kap] n. hipo, m.;—, vi. tener hipo.

hickory [jai-ko-ri] n. nogal americano.

hid [jid] *pretérito* del verbo **hide.**

hidden [ji-den] *adj.* escondido; secreto; —, *p.p.* del verbo **hide.**

hide [jaid] *vt.* esconder; apalear; -, *vi.* esconderse; —, *n.* cuero, m.; piel, f.

hide-and-seek [jaid-and-sik] n. juego de escondite, escondite, m.

hideous [jai-dios] *adj.* horrible, macabro.

hierarchy [jaia-rar-ki] n. jerarquía, f.

high [jai] *adj.* alto, elevado; arduo; altivo; noble, ilustre; sublime; caro; — **fidelity,** alta fidelidad; — **frequency,** frecuencia elevada; — **jump,** salto de altura; — **light,** parte subida de una fotografía o pintura; acontecimiento de primordial interés; — **school,** escuela secundaria; —**seas,** alta mar; — **spirits,** alegría, jovialidad, f.; — **tide,** pleamar, f.; — **time,** buena hora; jarana, f.; — **treason,** alta traición; delito de lesa majestad; —**voltage,** alta tensión; — **water,** marea alta, mar llena.

high-grade [jai-greid] *adj.* de alta calidad, excelente.

highlight [jai-lait] *vt.* alumbrar con reflectores eléctricos; destacar, dar realce, dar relieve.

highly [jai-li] *adv.* altamente; en sumo grado; arrogantemente; ambiciosamente; sumamente.

highness [jai-nes] n. altura, f.

high-octane [jai-ok-tein] *adj.* de alto octanaje.

high-pitched [jai-picht] *adj.* agudo; sensitivo.

high-powered [jai-pauerd] *adj.* de alta potencia.

high-pressure [jai-pre-shar] *adj.* de alta presión; intenso, urgente; — **salesman,** vendedor persistente y tenaz.

high-priced [jai-praist] *adj.* caro, de precio elevado.

high school [jai-skul] n. escuela secundaria.

high-speed [jai-spid] *adj.* de gran velocidad.

high-strung [jai-strang] *adj.* nervioso, excitable.

high-water mark [jai-uo-ta-mark] n. colmo, pináculo, m.

highway [jai-uei] n. carretera, f.

hike [jaik] n. caminata, f., paseo a pie (generalmente en el campo).

hilarious [jai-la-rios] *adj.* alegre y bullicioso.

hill [jil] n. collado, cerro, colina, f.

hilly [ji-li] *adj.* montañoso.

him [jim] *pron.* le, lo, a él.

himself [jim-self] *pron.* sí, él mismo.

hind [jind] *adj.* trasero, posterior; —, *n.* cierva (hembra del ciervo), *f.*

hinder [jin-dar] *vt.* impedir, embarazar, estorbar.

hindquarter [jin-kuortar] *n.* cuarto trasero de algunos animales.

hindrance [jin-de-rans] *n.* impedimento, obstáculo, *m.*

hindsight [jin-sait] *n.* mira posterior de una arma de fuego; percepción de la naturaleza y exigencias de un suceso pasado.

hinge [jinch] *n.* charnela, bisagra, *f.*, gozne, *m.*; punto principal, centro, *m.*; —, *vt.* engoznar.

hint [jint] *n.* seña, *f.*; sugestión, insinuación, *f.*; luz, *f.*; aviso, *m.*; buscapié, *m.*; —, *vt.* apuntar, insinuar; sugerir; hacer señas.

hip [jip] *n.* cadera, *f.*

hipbone [jip-boun] *n.* hueso de la cadera.

hippopotamus [ji-po-po-ta-mos] *n.* hipopótamo, *m.*

hire [jaiar] *vt.* alquilar; arrendar; contratar;—, *n.* alquiler, *m.*; salario, *m.*

his [jis] *adj.* su, de él; —, *pron.* el suyo (de él).

hissing [ji-sin] *n.* chifla, *f.*; siseo, *m.*

historian [jis-to-rian] *n.* historiador, *m.*

historic, historical [jis-to-rik], [jis-to-ri-kal] *adj.* histórico.

history [jis-to-ri] *n.* historia, *f.*; narración, *f.*

hit [jit] *vt.* golpear, dar, atinar; —, *vi.* salir bien; encontrar, encontrarse; **to — the target,** dar en el blanco; —, *n.* golpe, *m.*; suerte feliz; alcance, *m.*; (coll.) éxito, *m.*; (béisbol) golpe, *m.*

hitch [jich] *vt.* enganchar, atar, amarrar; —, *n.* impedimento, *m.*; (naut.) nudo o lazo fácil de soltar.

hitchhike [jich-jaik] *vi.* hacer auto-stop, ir por auto-stop.

hither [ji-zar] *adv.* acá; hacia acá; —, *adj.* citerior.

hitherto [ji-zar-tu] *adv.* hasta ahora, hasta aquí.

hive [jaiv] *n.* colmena *f.*; —, *vi.* vivir muchos en un mismo lugar.

hives [jaivs] *n. pl.* (med.) urticaria, *f.*, ronchas, *f. pl.*

hoard [jord] *n.* montón, *m.*; tesoro escondido; —, *vt.* atesorar, acumular.

hoarding [jor-din] *n.* acaparamiento, atesoramiento, *m.*; acumulación de mercancías ante posible escasez.

hoarfrost [jor-frost] *n.* escarcha, *f.*

hoarse [jors] *adj.* ronco; **—ly** *adv.* roncamente.

hoarseness [jors-nes] *n.* ronquera.

hoax [jouks] *n.* burla, *f.*; petardo, *m.*; trufa, *f.*; —, *vt.* engañar, burlar.

hobble [jo-bel] *vi.* cojear; —, *vt.* enredar; —, *n.* dificultad, *f.*; cojera, *f.*; maniota *f.*

hobby [jo-bi] *n.* caballico, *m.*; manía, afición, *f.*

hobnob [job-nob] *vi.* codearse, rozarse.

hobo [jou-bou] *n.* vagabundo, *m.*

hockey [jo-ki] *n.* hockey, *m.*

hocus-pocus [jou-kos-pou-kos] *n.* pasapasa, *m.*; engaño, *m.*, treta, *f.*

hodgepodge [joch-poch] *n.* almodrote, baturrillo, *m.*; morralla, *f.*

hog [jog] *n.* cerdo, puerco, *m.*

hoggish [jo-guish] *adj.* porcuno; egoísta; glotón.

hogshead [jogs-hed] *n.* tonel, *m.*; barrica, *f.*; bocoy, *m.*

hoist [joist] *vt.* alzar; (naut.) izar; —, *n.* monta-cargas, *m.*; cric, *m.*; elevador, *m.*; grúa, *f.*

hold [jould] *vt.* tener, asir; dete-ner; sostener; mantener; juzgar, reputar; poseer; continuar, proseguir; contener; celebrar; sujetar; **to — one's own, mantenerse** firme, no ceder; —, *vi.* valer; mantenerse; durar, abstenerse; adherirse; pos-poner; **to lay —,** echar mano; **— on!,** *interj.* ¡espera! —, *n.* presa, *f.*; mango, *m.*; asa, *f* ; prisión, *f.*; custodia, *f.*; (naut.) bodega, *f.*; apoyo, *m.*; poder, *m.*

holder [joul-dar] *n.* tenedor, posesor; mango, *m.*, asa, *f.*

holding [joul-din] *n.* tenencia, posesión, *f.*; **— company,** compañía tenedora.

holdup [jould-ap] *n.* asalto, salteamiento, *m.*

hole [joul] *n.* agujero, *m.*; cueva, *f.*;

holiday [jou-li-dei] *n.* día de fiesta, día festivo; **—s,** *n. pl.* vacaciones, *f. pl.*; días de fiesta.

holiness [jou-li-nes] *n.* santidad, *f.*

Holland [jo-land] Holanda, *f.*

Hollander [jo-lan-dar] *n.* y *adj.* holandés, esa.

hollow [jo-lou] *adj.* hueco; falso, engañoso, insincero; —, *n.* cavidad, caverna, *f.*; —, *vt.* excavar, ahuecar.

hollow-eyed [jo-lou-aid] *adj.* con los ojos hundidos.

holly [jo-li] *n.* (bot.) acebo, agrifolio, *m.*

hollyhock [jo-li-lok] *n.* (bot.) malva hortense.

holocaust [jo-lo-kost] *n.* holocausto, *m.*

holster [jouls-tar] *n.* funda de pistola.

holy [jou-li] *adj.* santo, pío; consagrado; — **water,** agua bendita; **Holy Week,** Semana Santa; **most —,** santísimo.

homage [jo-mich] *n.* homenaje, culto, *m.*

home [joum] *n.* casa, casa propia, morada, *f.;* patria, *f.;* domicilio, hogar *m.;* **at —,** en casa; **—,** *adj.* doméstico; — **page,** página inicial, *f.*

homeland [joum-land] *n.* patria, *f.,* tierra natal.

homeless [joum-les] *adj.* sin casa, sin hogar.

homemade [joum-meid] *adj.* hecho en casa; casero.

homemaker [joum-mei-kar] *n.* ama de casa.

homeopath [jou-mio-paz] *n.* homeópata, *m.* y *f.*

homerun [joum-ron] *n.* (béisbol) jonrón, cuadrangular, *m.*

homesick [joum-sik] *adj.* nostálgico.

homesickness [joum-sik-nes] *n.* nostalgia por el hogar o el país natal.

homestead [joum-stid] *n.* here-

dad, *f.;* casa solariega; hogar, solar, *m.*

homeward, homewards [joum-uard], [joum-uards] *adv.* hacia casa, hacia su país.

homeward-bound [joum-uard-baund] *adj.* con rumbo al hogar, de regreso.

homework [joum-uek] *n.* tarea, *f.;* trabajo hecho en casa, estudio fuera de la clase.

homicidal [jo-mi-sai-dal] *adj.* homicida.

homicide [jo-mi-said] *n.* homicidio, *m.;* homicida, *m.* y *f.*

homily [jo-mi-li] *n.* homilía, *f.*

homing pigeon [jou-min-pi-chon] *n.* paloma mensajera.

hominy [jo-mi-ni] *n.* maíz de grano, maíz machacado o molido.

homogeneous [jo-mo-yi-nios] *adj.* homogéneo.

homogenize [jo-mo-yi-nais] *vt.* homogenizar.

Honduran [jon-diua-ran] *n.* y *adj.* hondureño, ña.

honest [o-nist] *adj.* honesto, honrado; justo.

honesty [o-nis-ti] *n.* honestidad, justicia, probidad, *f.;* hombría de bien; *f.;* honradez, *f.*

honey [ja-ni] *n.* miel, *f.;* dulzura, *f.;* (coll.) queridito, ta; **like —,** meloso.

honeybee [ja-ni-bi] *n.* abeja

obrera.

honeymoon [ja-ni-mun] *n.* luna de miel.

honeysuckle [ja-ni-sa-kel] *n.* (bot.) madreselva, *f.*

honk [jonk] *n.* graznido de ganso; pitazo de bocina de automóvil.

honor [o-nar] *n.* honra, *f.,* honor, lauro, *m.;* **on my —,** a fe mía; **point of —,** pundonor, *m.;* **—,** *vt.* honrar; **to — (a draft),** (com.) aceptar (un giro o letra de cambio).

honorable [o-no-ra-bol] *adj.* honorable; ilustre; respetable; **— behavior,** caballerosidad, *f.*

honorably [o-no-ra-bli] *adv.* honorablemente.

hood [jud] *n.* caperuza, *f.;* capirote (de graduados), *m.;* capucha (de religioso), *f.;* gorro, *m.;* (auto.) cofre, cubierta del motor; **—,** *vt.* proveer de caperuza; cubrir con caperuza.

hoodwink [jud-uink] *vt.* vendar a uno los ojos; engañar, burlar.

hoof [juf] *n.* pezuña, *f.,* casco de las bestias caballares; **— and mouth disease,** fiebre aftosa.

hook [juk] *n.* gancho, *m.;* anzuelo, *m.;* **by — or crook,** de un modo u otro; **— and eye,** corchete macho y hembra; **—,** *vt.* enganchar.

hooked [jukt] *adj.* enganchado,

encorvado; **— rug,** tapete tejido a mano.

hookup [juk-ap] *n.* empalme, sistema de conexión, *m.;* (rad. y TV.) circuito, *m.,* red de radiodifusoras.

hookworm [juk-uerm] *n.* lombriz intestinal, *f.*

hoop [jup] *n.* cerco, *m.;* cerco de barril; **— skirt,** miriñaque, *m.;* **—,** *vt.* cercar.

hoot [jut] *vi.* gritar; **—,** *n.* grito, *m.*

hop [jop] *n.* salto, *m.;* **—,** *vi.* saltar, brincar.

hope [joup] *n.* esperanza, *f.;* **— chest,** caja en que una mujer guarda trajes, ropa blanca, etc., en anticipación de casamiento; **—,** *vi.* esperar, tener esperanzas.

hopeful [joup-ful] *adj.* lleno de esperanzas, esperanzado; optimista; **—ly,** *adv.* con esperanza; **—,** *n.* joven prometedor por sus buenas cualidades.

hopeless [joup-les] *adj.* desesperado; sin remedio; **—ly,** *adv.* sin esperanza.

horde [jord] *n.* horda, *f.;* enjambre, *m.;* manada, *f.*

horizon [jo-rai-son] *n.* horizonte, *m.*

horizontal [jo-ri-zon-tal] *adj.* horizontal.

hormone [jor-moun] *n.* hormona,

f.

horn [jorn] *n.* cuerno, *m.;* corneta, *f.;* trompeta, *f.;* cacho, *m.;* bocina, *f.;* clarín, *m.*

horned [jornd] *adj.* cornudo.

hornet [jor-nit] *n.* abejón, *m.*

horny [jor-ni] *adj.* hecho de cuerno; calloso.

horoscope [jo-ros-koup] *n.* horóscopo, *m.*

horrible [jo-ri-bol] *adj.* horrible, terrible.

horrid [jo-rid] *adj.* horroroso, horrible.

horrify [jo-ri-fai] *vt.* horrorizar.

horror [jo-rar] *n.* horror, terror, *m.*

horror-stricken [jo-rar-stri-ken] *adj.* horrorizado.

hors d'oeuvre [or-devr] *n. pl.* entremés, *m.;* (Mex.) botana, *f.*

horse [jors] *n.* caballo, *m.;* (mil.) caballería, *f.;* caballete, *m.;* — **race,** carrera de caballos; —, *vi.* cabalgar; —, *vt.* suministrar caballos.

horsefly [jors-flai] *n.* tábano, moscardón, *m.,* moscarda, *f.*

horseplay [jors-plei] *n.* retozo vigoroso; (Sp. Am.) relajo.

horsepower [jors-pauar] *n.* caballo de fuerza.

horseradish [jors-ra-dish] *n.* rábano silvestre, rábano picante.

horseshoe [jors-shu] *n.* herradu-

ra de caballo.

horticulture [jor-ti-kal-char] *n.* horticultura, jardinería, *f.*

hose [jous] *n.* medias, *f.pl.;* manguera, *f.;* tubo flexible.

hosiery [jou-sia-ri] *n.* medias, *f.pl.;* calcetines, *m.pl.*

hospital [jos-pi-tal] *n.* hospital, *m.;* — **ward,** sala **o** crujía de hospital; **maternity —,** casa de maternidad.

hospitality [jos-pi-ta-li-ti] *n.* hospitalidad, *f.*

hospitalization [jos-pi-ta-lai-sei-shon] *n.* hospitalización, *f.*

host [joust] *n.* anfitrión, *m.;* huésped, *m.;* mesonero, *m.;* ejército, *m.;* hostia, *f.*

hostage [jos-tich] *n.* rehén, *m.*

hostel [jos-tel] *n.* posada, hostería, *f.,* hotel, *m.;* **youth —,** posada para jóvenes (movimiento educativo de excursiones de jóvenes).

hostess [jous-tes] *n.* anfitriona, *f.;* posadera, mesonera, patrona, *f.*

hostile [jos-tail] *adj.* hostil; contrario.

hostility [jos-ti-li-ti] *n.* hostilidad, *f.*

hot [jot] *adj.* caliente, cálido; ardiente; picante, picoso, muy condimentado; (coll.) agitado, violento (aplícase a música, bailes, etc.); (coll.) recién robado.

hot-blooded [jot-bla-did] *adj.* excitable, de sangre ardiente.

hot dog [jot-dog] *n.* perro caliente.

hotel [jou-tel] *n.* hotel, *m.*, posada, fonda, *f.*

hotheaded [jot-je-did] *adj.* sañoso, fogoso, exaltado.

hothouse [jot-jaus] *n.* estufa, *f.;* invernadero, *m.*

hot-tempered [jat-tem-perd] *adj.* fogoso, exaltado.

hound [jaund] *n.* sabueso, podenco, *m.;* hombre vil y despreciable.

hour [auar] *n.* hora, *f.;* — **hand,** horario (de un reloj).

hourglass [aua-glas] *n.* reloj de arena; (naut.) ampolleta, *f.*

hourly [aua-li] *adv.* a cada hora; frecuentemente; —, *adj.* que sucede a cada hora, frecuente.

house [jaus] *n.* casa, *f.;* familia, *f.;* linaje, *m.;* cámara (del parlamento), *f.;* **banking** —, casa de banco; **business** —, casa de comercio; **clearing** —, casa de compensación; **commission** —, casa de comisiones; **country** —, casa de campo; **gambling** —, casino, *m.;* — **of correction,** casa de corrección, reformatorio, *m.;* — **party,** fiesta en que los invitados permanecen más de un día, tertulia generalmen-

te en una casa de campo; **H— of Representatives,** Cámara de Representantes; **lodging** —, casa de posada o de huéspedes; **publishing** —, casa editora; **to keep** —, poner casa; ser ama de casa; **whosesale** —, casa mayorista; —, *vt.* y *vi.* albergar; residir.

housefly [jaus-flai] *n.* mosca, *f.*

household [jaus-jould] *n.* familia, *f.;* casa, *f.;* estable-cimiento, *m.;* — **goods,** enseres, *m.pl.;* — **management,** manejo doméstico.

housekeeper [jaus-ki-par] *n.* ama de casa, ama de llaves.

housekeeping [jaus-ki-pin] *n.* gobierno doméstico; manejo casero.

housemaid [jaus-meid] *n.* criada de casa.

housetop [jaus-top] *n.* tejado, *m.*

housewife [jaus-uaif] *n.* ama de casa.

housework [jaus-uek] *n.* quehaceres domésticos, trabajo de casa.

housing [jau-sin] *n.* edificación de casas, alojamiento, *m.;* almacenaje, *m.;* (mech.) cárter, *m.;* cubierta, *f.;* —**s,** gualdrapa, *f.*

hover [jo-var] *vi.* colgar; dudar; rondar.

how [jau] *adv.* cómo, cuán;

cuánto; — **do you do?** ¿cómo le va a usted? — **goes it?** ¿qué tal? — **are you getting along?** ¿qué tal? — **so?** ¿por qué? ¿cómo así?

however [jau-e-var] *conj.* como quiera que; —, *adv.* sin embargo, no obstante.

howl [jaul] *vi.* aullar; reir a carcajadas; —, *n.* aúllo, aullido, *m.*

hub [jab] *n.* cubo, *m.;* centro, *m.;* cubo de una rueda.

hubcap [jab-kap] *n.* tapacubo, *m.*

huckleberry [ja-kel-be-ri] *n.* variedad de gayuba.

huddle [ja-del] *vt.* amontonar en desorden; —, *vi.* amontonarse en confusión; agruparse para recibir señas (en el juego de fútbol); —, *n.* confusión, *f.;* (coll.) conferencia secreta.

hue [jiu] *n.* color, *m.;* tez del rostro; matiz, *m.,* tinta, *f.;* — **and cry,** alarma que se da contra un criminal.

huff [jaf] *n.* arrebato, *m.;* cólera, *f.;* —, *vt.* ofender; tratar con arrogancia; —, *vi.* enojarse, patear de enfado.

hug [jag] *vt.* abrazar, acariciar; —, *n.* abrazo apretado.

huge [jiuch] *adj.* vasto, enorme; gigantesco.

hull [jal] *n.* cáscara, *f.;* (naut.)

casco (de un buque), *m.;* —, *vt.* descortezar.

hum [jam] *vi.* zumbar, susurrar, murmurar; —, *vt.* tararear (una canción, etc.); —, *n.* zumbido, *m.*

human [jiu-man] *n.* y *adj.* humano, na; — **being,** ser humano, *m;* — **resources,** recursos humanos, *m.pl.;* — **rights,** derechos humanos, *m.pl.*

humane [jiu-mein] *adj.* humano, compasivo.

humanist [jiu-ma-nist] *n.* humanista, *m.y f.*

humanitarian [jiu-ma-ni-tearian] *n.* filántropo, pa; —, *adj.* humanitario.

humanity [jiu-ma-ni-ti] *n.* humanidad, *f.*

humanize [jiu-ma-ni-ti] *vt.* hacer humano; civilizar; —, *vi.* humanizarse.

humble [jam-bel] *adj.* humilde, modesto; —, *vt.* humillar; postrar; **to — oneself,** humillarse; doblar o bajar la cerviz.

humbleness [jam-bel-nes] *n.* humildad, *f.*

humbly [jam-bli] *adv.* humildemente.

humid [jiu-mid] *adj.* húmedo.

humidify [jiu-mi-di-fai] *vt.* humedecer.

humidity [jiu-mi-di-ti] *n.* humedad, f.

humiliate [jiu-mi-lieit] *vt.* humillar.

humiliation [jiu-mi-liei-shon] *n.* humillación, mortificación, f., bochorno, *m.*

humility [jiu-mi-li-ti] *n.* humildad, f.

hummingbird [ja-min-berd] *n.* (orn.) colibrí, *m.*

humor [jiu-mar] *n.* humor, *m.;* comicidad, f.; humorada, fantasía, f.; capricho, *m.;* **bad** —, berrinche, *m.*, mal humor; —, *vt.* complacer, dar gusto; matar un antojo.

humorist [jiu-mo-rist] *n.* humorista, *m.y* f.

humorous [jiu-mo-ros] *adj.* humorista, chistoso; —**ly**, *adv.* de buen humor.

hump [jamp] *n.* joroba, f.

humpbacked [jamp-bakt] *adj.* jorobado, giboso.

hunch [janch] *n.* (coll.) idea, corazonada, f., presentimiento, *m.*

hunchback [janch-bak] *n.* joroba, f.; jorobado, da.

hunchbacked = [janch-bakt] **humpbacked.**

hundred [jan-drid] *adj.* cien, ciento; —, *n.* centenar, *m.;* un ciento, *m.*

hundredth [jan-driz] *n.* y *adj.* centésimo, *m.*

hung [jang] *pretérito* y p.p. del verbo **hang.**

Hungary [jan-ga-ri] Hungría, f.

hunger [jan-gar] *n.* hambre, f.; — **strike,** huelga de hambre; —, *vi.* hambrear; anhelar, ansiar.

hungry [jan-gri] *adj.* hambriento; voraz; **to be** —, tener hambre.

hunk [jank] *n.* pedazo grande, trozo, *m.*

hunt [jant] *vt.* cazar; perseguir; buscar; —, *vi.* andar a caza; —, *n.* caza, f.

hunter [jan-tar] *n.* cazador, *m.;* caballo de caza; perro de monte, perro braco.

hunting [jan-tin] *n.* montería, caza, f.; —, *adj.* de caza.

hurdle [jer-del] *n.* zarzo, *m.;* valla, f., obstáculo, *m.;* —**s,** carrera de obstáculos.

hurl [jerl] *vt.* tirar con violencia; arrojar.

hurrah! [ju-ra] *interj.* ¡viva!

hurricane [ja-ri-ken] *n.* huracán, *m.*

hurried [ja-rid] *adj.* apresurado, hecho de prisa.

hurry [ja-ri] *vt.* acelerar, apresurar, precipitar; —, *vi.* atropellarse, apresurarse; —, *n.* precipitación, f.; confusión, f.; urgencia, f.; **in a** —, a prisa; **to be in a** —, tener prisa, estar de prisa, darse prisa.

hurt [jert] *vt.* dañar, hacer daño,

herir; ofender; —, *n*. mal, daño,
perjuicio, *m.;* golpe, *m.;* herida,
f.; —, *adj.* sentido; lastimado;
perjudicado.

husband [jas-band] *n*. marido,
esposo, *m.;* —, *vt.* administrar
con frugalidad.

hush [jash] *n*. silencio, *m.;* —*!*
interj. ¡chitón! ¡silencio! ¡paz!
¡calla! —, *vt.* aquietar; acallar;
—, *vi.* hacer silencio.

husk [jask] *n*. cáscara, *f.;* pellejo, *m.;* —, *vt.* descascarar.

huskiness [jas-ki-nes] *n*. ron-
quedad, ronquera, *f.*

husky [jas-ki] *adj.* cascarudo;
ronco; (coll.) fornido, fuerte; —,
n. persona robusta.

hussy [ja-si] *n*. tunanta, *f.,*
mujer descarada.

hustle [ja-sel] *vt.* y *vi.* bullir;
apurar (un trabajo); apurarse,
andar de prisa.

hut [jat] *n*. cabaña, barraca,
choza, *f.*

hybrid [jai-brid] *n*. y *adj.* híbrido, *m.*

hydraulic [jai-dro-lik] *adj.*
hidráulico; — **engineering,**
hidrotecnia, *f.*

hydrochloric [jai-dro-klo-rik] *adj.*
hidroclórico, clorhídrico.

hydroelectric [jai-dro-i-lek-trik]
adj. hidroeléctrico.

hydrogen [jai-dro-yin] *n*. (chem.)
hidrógeno, *m.;* — **bomb,** bomba

de hidrógeno; **carbureted** —,
hidrocarburo, *m.;* — **peroxide,**
agua oxigenada, peróxido
hidrogenado; — **sulphide,** sul-
fhídrico, *m.*

hyena [jai-ina] *n*. hiena, *f.*

hygiene [jai-yin] *n*. higiene *f.*

hygienic [jai-yi-nIk] *adj.* higiénico.

hymn [jim] *n*. himno, *m.*

hymnal [jim-nal] *n*. himnario, *m.*

hyperbole [jai-per-bo-li] *n*. hipérbole, *f.; exageración, f.*

hypersensitive [jai-per-sen-si-tiv]
adj. excesivamente impresionable.

hypertension [jai-per-ten-shon]
n. hipertensión, *f.*

hyphen [jai-fen] *n*. (gram.) guión,
m.

hyphenate [jai-fe-neit] *vt.* separar con guión.

hypnosis [jip-nou-sis] *n*. hipno-
sis, *f.*

hypnotic [jip-no-tik] *adj.* hipnótico.

hypnotism [jip-no-ti-sem] *n*. hipnotismo, *m.*

hypnotize [jip-no-tais] *vt.* hipnotizar.

hypochondria [jai-pou-kon-dria]
n. hipocondría, *f.*

hypocrisy [ji-po-kri-si] *n*. hipocresía, *f.*

hypocrite [ji-po-krit] *n*. hipócrita,
m. y *f.*

hypocritical [ji-po-kri-tikal] *adj.*
hipócrita.

hypodermic [jai-po-der-mik] *adj.*
hipodérmico; —, *n.* inyección
hipodérmica.

hypothesis [jai-po-zi-sis] *n.* hipótesis, .

hypothetical [jai-pou-ze-tik] *adj.*
hipotético .

hysterectomy [jis-te-rek-to-mi] *n.*
(med.) histerectomía, *f.*

hysteria [jis-tia-ria] *n.* histeria,
f., histerismo, *m.*

hysteric, hysterical [jis-te-rik],
[jis-te-ri-kal] *adj.* histérico.

hysterics [jis-te-riks] *n. pl.* paroxismo histérico.

I

I [ai] *pron.* yo.

iambic [ai-am-bik] *adj.* yámbico.

Iberian [ai-bia-rian] *n.* y *adj.*
ibero, ra.

ice [ais] *n.* hielo, *m.;* granizado,
m.; — **age,** época glacial,*f.;* **dry**
—, hielo seco; — **hockey,** hoc-
key sobre hielo; — **pack,** bolsa
de hielo para aplicaciones frías;
— **pick,** picahielo, *m.;* — **sheet,**
manto de hielo; — **skate,** patín
de hielo; — **water,** agua helada;
—, *vt.* helar; **to** — **a cake,** garapiñar o ponerle betún a un
pastel.

iceberg [ais-berg] *n.* témpano de
hielo.

icebreaker [ais-breiker] *n.* rompehielos, *m.*

ice cream [ais-krim] *n.* helado,
mantecado, *m.,* nieve, *f.*

Iceland [ais-land] Islandia, *f.*

Icelander [ais-lan-dar] *n.* islan-

dés, esa.

Icelandic [ais-lan-dik]*adj.* islán-
dico, islandés.

iceman [ais-men] *n.* repartidor
de hielo.

icing [ai-sin] *n.* capa dulce para
pasteles; (Mex.) betún, *m.*

idea [ai-dia] *n.* idea, *f.;* imagen
mental; concepto, *m.;* **clever** —,
feliz idea.

ideal [ai-dial] *n.* y *adj.* ideal, *m.*

idealism [ai-dia-li-sem] *n.* idealismo, *m.*

idealist [ai-dia-list] *n.* idealista,
m. y *f.*

idealistic [ai-dia-lis-tik] *adj.* idealista.

identical [ai-den-ti-kal] *adj.* idéntico.

identification [ai-den-ti-fi-kei-
shon] *n.* identificación, *f.;* —
card, — **papers,** cédula personal.

identify [ai-den-ti-fai] *vt.* identificar; **to — oneself,** identificarse.

identity [ai-den-ti-ti] *n.* identidad, *f.*

ideology [ai-di-o-lo-yi] *n.* ideología, *f.*, ideario, *m.*

idiocy [i-dio-si] *n.* idiotismo, *m.*

idiom [i-diom] *n.* idioma, *m.;* dialecto, *m.;* modismo, *m.,* frase idiomática.

idiomatic, idiomatical [i-dio-ma-tik], [i-dio-ma-ti-kal] *adj.* idiomático, peculiar a alguna lengua.

idiosyncrasy [i-dio-sin-kra-si] *n.* idiosincrasia, *f.*

idiot [i-diot] *n.* idiota, *m.* y *f.,* necio, cia.

idiotic [i-dio-tik] *adj.* tonto, bobo.

idle [ai-del] *adj.* perezoso, desocupado, holgazán; inútil, vano, frívolo; —, *vi.* holgazanear, estar ocioso.

idleness [ai-del-nes] *n.* ociosidad, pereza, *f.;* negligencia, *f.;* frivolidad, *f.*

idler [aid-lar] *n.* holgazán, ana; (mech.) rueda intermedia.

idol [ai-dol] *n.* ídolo, *m.;* imagen, *f.*

idolatry [ai-do-la-tri] *n.* idolatría, *f.*

idolize [ai-do-lais] *vt.* idolatrar.

idyllic [i-di-lik] *adj.* idílico, como un idilio.

i.e.: that is es decir, esto es.

if [if] *conj.* si; aunque, supuesto que; — **not,** si no.

igloo [i-dlu] *n.* iglú, *m.,* choza esquimal.

ignite [ig-nait] *vt.* y *vi.* encender, abrasar, encenderse.

ignition [ig-ni-shon] *n.* (chem.) ignición, *f.;* (auto.) ignición, *f.;* encendido, *m.;* — **switch,** contacto del magneto.

ignoble [ig-nou-bel] *adj.* innoble; bajo.

ignominy [ig-no-mi-ni] *n.* ignominia, infamia, *f.*

ignorance [ig-no-rans] *n.* ignorancia, *f.*

ignorant [ig-no-rant] *adj.* ignorante, inculto.

ignore [ig-nor] *vt.* pasar por alto, desconocer.

ill [il] *adj.* malo, enfermo, doliente; — **turn,** mala jugada; —, *n.* mal, infortunio; —, *adv.* mal, malamente.

ill-bred [il-bred] *adj.* malcriado, descortés.

ill-disposed [il-dispousd] *adj.* malintencionado, contrario.

illegal [i-li-gal] *adj.* ilegal; —**ly,** *adv.* ilegalmente.

illegible [i-le-ya-bol] *adj.* ilegible; —**bly,** *adv.* de un modo ilegible.

illegitimate [i-li-yi-ti-mit] *adj.* ilegítimo.

ill-fated [il-fei-ded]*adj.* desgraciado, desdichado.

ill-humored [il-jiu-mord] *adj.* malhumorado.

illicit [i-li-sit] *adj.* ilícito; —ly, *adv.* ilícitamente.

illimitable [i-li-mi-ter-bol] *adj.* ilimitado.

illiteracy [i-li-te-ra-si] *n.* analfabetismo, *m.*

illiterate [i-li-te-reit] *adj.* indocto, analfabeto; —, *n.* analfabeto, ta.

ill-mannered [il-ma-nerd] *adj.* malcriado, descortés.

ill-natured [il-nei-chad] *adj.* irascible, de mal carácter.

illness [il-nes] *n.* enfermedad, *f.;* maldad, *f.;* mal, *m.*

illogical [i-lo-yi-kal] *adj.* ilógico.

ill-suited [il-suted] *adj.* inadecuado, inapropiado.

illuminate [i-lu-mi-neit] *vt.* iluminar.

illumination [i-lu-mi-nei-shon] *n.* iluminación, *f.;* alumbra-do, *m.*

illusion [i-lu-shon] *n.* ilusión, *f.;* ensueño, *m.*

illusory [i-lu-so-ri] *adj.* ilusorio.

illustrate [i-lus-treit] *vt.* ilustrar; explicar.

illustration [i-las-trei-shon] *n.* ilustración, *f.;* elucidación, *f.;* ejemplo, *m.;* grabado, *m.*

illustrative [i-las-tra-tiv] *adj.* explicativo.

illustrious [i-las-trios] *adj.* ilustre, insigne, célebre.

ill-will [il-uil] *n.* malevolencia, mala voluntad.

image [i-mich] *n.* imagen, estatua, *f.;* —, *vt.* imaginar.

imagery [i-mi-che-ri] *n.* imagen, pintura, *f.;* vuelos de la fantasía.

imaginable [i-mi-chi-na-bol] *adj.* imaginable, concebible.

imaginary [i-ma-chi-na-ri] *adj.* imaginario.

imagination [i-ma-chi-nei-shon] *n.* imaginación, imaginativa, *f.;* idea fantástica.

imaginative [i-ma-chi-na-tiv] *adj.* imaginativo.

imagine [i-ma-chin] *vt.* imaginar; idear, inventar.

imbecile [im-be-sil] *n.* y *adj.* imbécil, *m.y f.*

imbecility [im-bi-si-li-ti] *n.* imbecilidad, *f.;* idiotismo, *m.*

imbue [im-biu] *vt.* imbuir, infundir.

imitate [i-mi-teit] *vt.* imitar, copiar.

imitation [i-mi-tei-shon] *n.* imitación, copia, *f.*

imitative [i-mi-ter-tiv] *adj.* imitativo, imitado.

imitator [i-mi-tei-tar] *n.* imitador, ra.

immaculate [i-ma-kiu-lit] *adj.*

inmaculado, puro.

immanent [i-ma-nant] *adj.* inmanente.

immaterial [i-ma-tia-rial] *adj.* inmaterial; de poca importancia.

immature [i-ma-chuar] *adj.* inmaduro.

immediate [i-mi-diet] *adj.* inmediato; —**ly**, *adv.* inmediatamente, en seguida, en el acto, acto continuo.

immense [i-mens] *adj.* inmenso; vasto.

immensity [i-men-si-ti] *n.* inmensidad, *f.*

immerse [i-mers] *vt.* sumir, sumergir.

immersion [i-mer-shon] *n.* inmersión, *f.*

immigrant [i-mi-grant] *n.* inmigrante, *m.y f.*

immigrate [i-mi-greit] *vi.* inmigrar.

immigration [i-mi-grei-shon] *n.* inmigración, *f.*

imminent [i-mi-nent] *adj.* inminente.

immobile [i-mou-bail] *adj.* inmóvil.

immoderate [i-mo-de-rit] *adj.* inmoderado, excesivo.

immoral [i-mo-ral] *adj.* inmoral, depravado.

immorality [i-mo-ra-li-ti] *n.* inmoralidad, *f., corrupción de

costumbres.

immortal [i-mor-tal] *adj.* inmortal.

immortality [i-mor-ter-li-ti] *n.* inmortalidad, *f.*

immovable [i-mu-va-bol] *adj.* inmóvil, inmoble; inmovible; —**s**, *n. pl.* bienes raíces.

immune [i-miun] *adj.* inmune, exento.

immunity [i-miu-ni-ti] *n.* inmunidad, franquicia, *f.,* privilegio, *m.*

immunize [i-miu-nais] *vt.* inmunizar.

impact [im-pakt] *n.* impulso, *m.;* choque, *m.*

impair [im-pear] *vt.* empeorar, deteriorar; disminuir.

impale [im-peil] *vt.* empalar (a un reo).

impart [im-part] *vt.* comunicar, dar parte.

impartial [im-par-shal] *adj.* imparcial.

impartiality [im-par-shia-li-ti] *n.* imparcialidad, *f.*

impassable [im-pa-sa-bol] *adj.* intransitable.

impasse [im-pas] *n.* camino intransitable; callejón sin salida; obstáculo insuperable.

impassioned [im-pa-shond] *adj.* apasionado, ardiente.

impassive [im-pa-siv] *adj.* impasible.

impatience [im-pei-shans] *n.* impaciencia, *f.*

impatient [im-pei-shant] *adj.* impaciente.

impeach [im-pich] *vt.* acusar, denunciar, delatar (aplícase especialmente a funcionarios públicos).

impede [im-pid] *vt.* impedir; paralizar.

impediment [im-pe-di-ment] *n.* impedimento, obstáculo, *m.*

impend [im-pend] *vi.* amenazar, aproximar.

impenetrable [im-pe-ni-tra-bol] *adj.* impenetrable.

impenitent [im-pe-ni-tent] *adj.* impenitente; —**ly**, *adv.* sin penitencia.

imperative [im-pe-ra-tiv] *adj.* imperativo, imprescindible; — **mood,** (gram.) modo imperativo.

imperceptible [im-pa-sep-ter-bol] *adj.* imperceptible.

imperfect [im-per-fikt] *adj.* imperfecto, defectuoso; —, *n.* (gram.) pretérito imperfecto.

imperfection [im-pa-fek-shon] *n.* imperfección, *f.*, defecto, *m.*

imperial [im-pi-rial] *adj.* imperial, supremo, soberano.

imperialism [im-pi-ria-li-sem] *n.* imperialismo, *m.*

imperialist [im-pi-ria-list] *n.* y *adj.* imperialista, *m.y f.*

imperil [im-pi-ril] *vt.* arriesgar, poner en peligro.

impersonal [im-per-so-nal] *adj.* impersonal.

impersonate [im-per-so-neit] *vt.* imitar, personificar; re-presentar.

impersonation [im-per-so-nei-shon] *n.* personificación, *f.*; (theat.) imitación, *f.*

impertinence [im-per-ti-nens] *n.* impertinencia, *f.*; descaro, *m.*

impertinent [im-per-ti-nent] *adj.* impertinente; inadecuado, inaplicable; —**ly**, *adv.* impertinentemente; fuera de propósito.

imperturbable [im-per-ter-ba-bol] *adj.* imperturbable; —**bly**, *adv.* sin perturbación.

impervious [im-per-vios] *adj.* impenetrable.

impetuosity [im-pe-tiu-o-si-ti] *n.* impetuosidad, *f.*, ímpetu, *m.*

impetuous [im-pe-tiuos] *adj.* impetuoso; —**ly**, *adv.* a borbotones.

impetus [im-pi-tus] *n.* ímpetu, *m.*

impinge [im-pinch] *vt.* chocar, tropezar; — **upon,** invadir, usurpar, abusar de.

impious [im-pios] *adj.* impío, irreligioso; desapiadado.

implacable [im-pla-ka-bol] *adj.*

implacable, irreconciliable.

implant [im-plant] *vt.* plantar;
injertar; imprimir.

implement [im-pli-ment] *n.*
herramienta, *f.;* utensilio, *m.;*
mueble, *m.;* —**s**, *n. pl.* aperos,
m.pl.; —, *vt.* poner en ejecución, ejecutar, completar, cumplir.

implicate [im-pli-keit] *vt.* implicar, envolver.

implication [im-pli-kei-shon] *n.*
implicación, *f.*

implicit [im-pli-sit] *adj.* implícito.

implied [im-plaid] *adj.* implícito.

implore [im-plor] *vt.* implorar,
suplicar.

impolite [im-po-lait] *adj.* descortés, mal educado.

import [im-port] *vt.* importar; —,
n. importancia, *f.;* artículo
importado; sentido, *m.;* significación, *f.;* — **duties,** derechos
de importación.

importance [im-por-tans] *n.*
importancia, *f.;* trascendencia,
f.

important [im-por-tant] *adj.*
importante.

importation [im-por-tei-shon] *n.*
importación, *f.*

importer [im-por-tar] *n.* importador, ra.

importing [im-por-tin] *adj.*
importador; — **house,** empresa
importadora.

impose [im-pous] *vt.* imponer
(obligaciones, etc.); **to — upon,**
imponerse, abusar de.

imposing [im-pou-sin] *adj.* imponente, que infunde respeto;
tremendo.

imposition [im-po-si-shon] *n.*
imposición, carga, *f.;* impostura, *f.*

impossibility [im-po-si-bi-li-ti] *n.*
imposibilidad; *f.*

impossible [im-po-si-bol] *adj.*
imposible; **to seem —,** parecer
mentira.

impostor [im-pos-tar] *n.* impostor, ra.

impotence [im-po-tans] *n.* impotencia, *f.;* incapacidad, *f.*

impotent [im-po-tent] *adj.* impotente; incapaz; —**ly,** *adv.* sin
poder, impotentemente.

impound [im-paund] *vt.* encerrar, acorralar; depositar o
embargar, poner en custodia
(de algún tribunal).

impoverish [im-po-va-rish] *vt.*
empobrecer.

impractical [im-prak-ti-ksl] *adj.*
impracticable, irrealizable.

impregnable [im-preg-na-bol]
adj. impregnable; inexpugna-
ble.

impregnate [im-preg-neit] *vt.*
impregnar; empreñar.

impresario [im-pre-sa-riou] *n.*
empresario, *m.*

impress [im-pres] *vt.* imprimir, estampar; —, *n.*

impression [im-pre-shon] *n.* impresión, *f.;* edición, *f.*

impressionable [im-pre-sho-na-bol] *adj.* impresionable.

impressive [im-pre-siv] *adj.* penetrante; impresionable; imponente; —**ly,** *adv.* de un modo impresionante.

imprint [im-print] *vt.* imprimir; estampar; —, *n.* florón, *m.,* impresión, *f.;* huella, *f.;* pie de imprenta.

imprison [im-pri-son] *vt.* aprisionar; prender.

imprisonment [im-pri-son-ment] *n.* prisión, *f.,* encierro, *m.*

improbable [im-pro-ba-bol] *adj.* improbable; inverosímil.

impromptu [im-promp-tiu] *adj.* extemporáneo, improvisado.

improper [im-pro-par] *adj.* impropio, indecente.

impropriety [im-pro-prie-ti] *n.* impropiedad, incongruencia, *f.*

improve [im-pruv] *vt.* y *vi.* mejorar, perfeccionar; —, *vi.* progresar.

improved [im-pruvd] *adj.* mejorado, perfeccionado.

improvement [im-pruv-ment] *n.* progreso, mejoramiento, perfeccionamiento, *m.*

improvident [im-pro-vi-dant] *adj.* impróvido.

improvisation [im-pro-vi-sei-shon] *n.* improvisación, *f.*

improvise [im-pro-vais] *vt.* improvisar.

imprudence [im-pru-dans] *n.* imprudencia, *f.*

imprudent [im-pru-dant] *adj.* imprudente.

impulse [im-pals] *n.* impulsión, *f.,* impulso, *m.;* ímpetu, *m.*

impulsive [im-pal-siv] *adj.* impulsivo.

impunity [im-piu-ni-ti] *n.* impunidad, *f.*

impure [im-piuar] *adj.* impuro; impúdico, sucio.

impurity [im-piua-ri-ti] *n.* impureza, *f.*

in [in] *prep.* en; por; a; de; durante; bajo; dentro de; —. *adv.* dentro, adentro.

inability [i-na-bi-li-ti] *n.* inhabilidad, incapacidad, *f.*

inaccessible [in-ak-se-si-bol] *adj.* inaccesible.

inaccuracy [in-a-kiu-ra-si] *n.* inexactitud, incorrección, *f.*

inaccurate [in-a-kiu-reit] *adj.* inexacto.

inactive [in-ak-tiv] *adj.* inactivo; flojo, perezoso, negligente; pasivo.

inactivity [in-ak-ti-vi-ti] *n.* ociosidad, desidia, inactividad, *f.*

inadequacy [in-a-de-kua-si] *n.*

insuficiencia, *f.*

inadequate [in-a-de-kuit] *adj.* inadecuado, defectuoso; imperfecto, insuficiente.

inadvertent [in-ad-ver-tent] *adj.* inadvertido.

inalienable [in-ei-lia-na-bol] *adj.* inajenable, inalienable.

inane [i-nein] *adj.* vacío, sin sentido, tonto.

inanimate [in-a-ni-mit] *adj.* inanimado; exánime.

inarticulate [in-ar-ti-ku-leit] *adj.* inarticulado.

inaudible [in-o-di-bol] *adj.* que no se puede oír; imperceptible.

inaugural [in-o-guiu-ral] *adj.* inaugural.

inaugurate [in-o-guiu-reit] *vt.* inaugurar.

inauguration [in-o-guiu-reishon] *n.* inauguración, *f.*

inborn [in-born] *adj.* innato, ingénito.

in-box [in-boks]*n.* bandeja de entrada, *f.*

inbred [in-bred] *adj.* innato; sin mezcla (de razas, etc.).

incalculable [in-kal-kiu-la-bol] *adj.* incalculable.

incapable [in-kei-pa-bol] *adj.* incapaz, inhábil.

incapacitate [in-ka-pa-si-teit] *vt.* incapacitar; inhabilitar, imposibilitar.

incapacity [in-ka-pa-si-ti] *n.*

incapacidad, insuficiencia, *f.;* estolidez, *f.*

incarcerate [in-kar-se-reit] *vt.* encarcelar, aprisionar.

incarnate [in-kar-neit] *vt.* encarnar.

incarnation [in-kar-nei-shon] *n.* encarnación, encarnadura, *f.*

incense [in-sens] *n.* incienso, *m.;* — **stick,** pebete, *m.;* —, *vt.* exasperar, irritar, provocar; incensar.

incentive [in-sen-siv] *n.* incentivo, estímulo, *m.*

inception [in-sep-shon] *n.* principio, *m.*

incessant [in-se-sant] *adj.* incesante, constante.

incest [in-sest] *n.* incesto, *m.*

inch [inch] *n.* pulgada, *f.;* — **by** —, palmo a palmo; —, *vi.* avanzar o moverse por pulgadas o a pasos muy pequeños.

incidence [in-si-dens] *n.* incidencia, *f.;* — **wires,** (avi.) tirantes o alambres de incidencia.

incident [in-si-dent] *adj.* incidente; dependiente; —, *n.* incidente, *m.;* circunstancia, ocurrencia, *f.*

incidental [in-si-den-tal] *adj.* accidental, casual; contingente; **-ly,** *adv.* incidentalmente.

incinerate [in-si-ne-reit] *vt.* incinerar.

incinerator [in-si-ne-rai-tor] *n.*

incinerador, *m.*

incision [in-si-shon] *n.* incisión, *f.*

incisive [in-sai-siv] *adj.* incisivo, incisorio.

incisor [in-sai-sar] *n.* diente incisivo, *m.*

incite [in-sait] *vt.* incitar, estimular.

incivility [in-si-vi-li-ti] *n.* incivilidad, descortesía, *f.*

inclemency [in-kle-men-si] *n.* inclemencia, severidad, *f.*

inclement [in-kle-ment] *adj.* inclemente.

inclination [in-kli-nei-shon] *n.* inclinación, propensión, *f.;* declive, *m.*

incline [in-klain] *vt.* inclinar; —, *vi.* inclinarse; —, *n.* pendiente, *f.*

inclined [in-klaind] *adj.* inclinado.

inclose [in-klous] *vt.* encerrar, incluir.

inclosure [in-klo-shar] *n.* cercamiento, *m.;* cercado, *m.*

include [in-klaud] *vt.* incluir, comprender.

inclusion [in-klu-shon] *n.* inclusión, *f.*

inclusive [in-klu-siv] *adj.* inclusivo.

incoherence [in-kou-ia-rens] *n.* incoherencia, *f.*

incoherent [in-kou-ia-rent] *adj.* incoherente.

income [in-kam] *n.* renta, *f.,* entradas, *f.pl.;* rendimiento, *m.;* — **tax,** impuesto sobre la renta.

incoming [in-ka-min] *adj.* entrante, que acaba de llegar; — **mail,** correspondencia que acaba de recibirse; — **president,** presidente entrante.

incomparable [in-kom-pa-ra-bol] *adj.* incomparable, excelente; —**bly,** *adv.* incomparablemente.

incompatible [in-kom-pa-ti-bol] *adj.* incompatible; opuesto.

incompetence [in-kom-pe-tens] *n.* incompetencia, *f.*

incomplete [in-kom-plit] *adj.* incompleto, falto, imperfecto.

incomprehensible [in-kom-pri-jen-si-bol] *adj.* incomprensible.

inconceivable [in-ko-si-va-bol] *adj.* incomprensible, inconcebible.

inconclusive [in-kon-klu-siv] *adj.* ineficaz, que no presenta razones concluyentes.

incongruous [in-kon-gruos] *adj.* incongruo.

inconsequential [in-kon-si-kuen-shal] *adj.* inconsecuente.

inconsiderate [in-kon-si-de-reit] *adj.* inconsiderado.

inconsistent [in-kon-sis-tent] *adj.* inconsistente.

inconspicuous [in-kons-pi-kuos]

adj. no conspicuo, que pasa desapercibido.

incontinence [in-kon-ti-nens] *n.* incontinencia, *f.*

inconvenience [in-kon-vi-niens] *n.* inconveniencia, incomodidad, *f.;* —, *vt.* incomodar.

inconvenient [in-kon-vi-nient] *adj.* incómodo, inconveniente.

incorporate [in-kor-po-reit] *vt.* incorporar; —, *vi.* incorporarse; —, *adj.* incorporado.

incorporation [in-kor-po-rei-shon] *n.* incorporación, *f.*

incorrect [in-ko-rekt] *adj.* incorrecto; —ly, *adv.* de un modo incorrecto, incorrectamente.

increase [in-kris] *vt.* acrecentar, aumentar; —, *vi.* crecer, aumentarse; —, *n.* aumento, acrecentamiento, *m.*

increasing [in-kri-sin] *adj.* creciente.

incredible [in-kre-di-bol] *adj.* increíble.

incredulity [in-kre-di-bli] *n.* incredulidad, *f.*

incredulous [in-kre-diu-lis] *adj.* incrédulo.

increment [in-kre-ment] *n.* incremento, *m.*

incriminate [in-kri-mi-neit] *vt.* acriminar, acusar de algún crimen.

incubation [in-kras-tei-shon] *n.* incubación, empolladura, *f.*

incubator [in-kiu-bei-tar] *n.* incubadora, *f.;* empollador, *m.*

inculcate [in-kal-keit] *vt.* inculcar.

incur [in-ker] *vt.* incurrir; ocurrir.

incurable [in-kiua-ra-bol] *adj.* incurable; —bly, *adv.* de un modo incurable.

indebted [in-de-ted] *adj.* endeudado, empeñado, obligado.

indebtedness [in-de-ted-nes] *n.* deuda, obligación, *f.;* pasivo, *m.*

indecency [in-di-sen-si] *n.* indecencia, *f.*

indecent [in-di-sent] *adj.* indecente.

indecision [in-di-si-shon] *n.* irresolución, indecisión, *f.*

indecisive [in-di-sai-siv] *adj.* indeciso.

indeed [in-did] *adv.* verdaderamente, de veras; sí; —no! ¡de ninguna manera!

indefinite [in-de-fi-nit] *adj.* indefinido, indeterminado.

indemnification [in-dem-ni-fi-kei-shon] *n.* indemnización, *f.*

indemnity [in-dem-ni-ti] *n.* indemnidad, *f.;* — bond, contrafianza, *f.*

indent [in-dent] *vt.* mellar; dar mayor margen.

indentation [in-den-tei-shon] *n.* mella, muesca, *f.;* mayor margen.

indenture [in-den-char] *n.* escritura, *f.;* contrato de un aprendiz.

independence [in-di-pen-dens] *n.* independencia, *f.*

independent [in-di-pen-dent] *adj.* independiente.

indescribable [in-dis-krai-ba-bol] *adj.* indescriptible.

indestructible [in-dis-trak-ti-bol] *adj.* indestructible.

index [in-deks] *n.* indicador, *m.;* índice, *m.;* (math.) exponente, *m.;* — **finger,** dedo índice; —, *vt.* arreglar en un índice.

India [in-dia] *n.* India, *f.;* — **rubber,** goma elástica, caucho, *m.*

Indian [in-dian] *n.* y *adj.* indiano, na; indio, dia; — **summer,** veranillo de San Martín, veranillo de San Miguel.

indicate [in-di-keit] *vt.* indicar.

indication [in-di-kei-shon] *n.* indicación, *f.;* indicio, *m.;* señal, *f.*

indicator [in-di-kei-tar] *n.* indicador, apuntador, *m.*

indict [in-dait] *vt.* procesar.

indictment [in-dait-ment] *n.* acusación ante el jurado, denuncia, *f.*

indifference [in-di-fe-rens] *n.* indiferencia, apatía, *f.*

indigenous [in-di-che-nos] *adj.* indígena.

indigestible [in-di-ches-ti-bol] *adj.* indigesto, indigestible.

indigestion [in-di-ches-shon] *n.* indigestión, *f.*

indignant [in-dig-nant] *adj.* airado, indignado.

indignation [in-dig-nei-shon] *n.* indignación, *f.;* despecho, *m.*

indignity [in-dig-ni-ti] *n.* indignidad, *f.*

indigo [in-di-gou] *n.* añil, *m.*

indirect [in-dai-rekt] *adj.* indirecto.

indiscretion [in-dis-kre-shon] *n.* indiscreción, imprudencia, inconsideración, *f.*

indiscriminate [in-dis-kri-mineit] *adj.* indistinto; —**ly,** *adv.* sin distinción, sin discriminación.

indispensable [in-dis-pen-sa-bol] *adj.* indispensable, imprescindible; —**bly,** *adv.* indispensablemente.

indispose [in-dis-pous] *vt.* indisponer.

indisposition [in-dis-pou-si-shon] *n.* indisposición, *f.,* malestar, *m.;* mala gana.

indisputable [in-dis-piu-ta-bol] *adj.* indisputable.

indistinct [in-dis-tinkt] *adj.* indistinto, confuso; borroso.

indistinguishable [in-dis-tin-güi-sha-bol] *adj.* indistinguible.

individual [in-di-vi-diual] *adj.*

individual, —, *n.* individuo, *m.*

individualism [in-di-vi-diua-li-sem] *n.* individualismo, *m.*

individuality [in-di-vi-diua-li-ti] *n.* individualidad, *f.*

indivisible [in-di-vi-si-bol] *adj.* indivisible.

indoctrinate [in-dok-tri-neit] *vt.* doctrinar, adoctrinar; inculcar.

indoor [in-dor] *adj.* interior, de puertas adentro; —s, *adv.* bajo techo, adentro.

indorse [in-dors] *vt.* endosar (una letra, un vale u otro documento).

indorsement [in-dors-ment] *n.* endorso, endoso, *m.*

indorser [in-dor-sar] *n.* (com.) endosante (de un giro), *m.* y *f.*

indubitable [in-diu-bi-ta-bol] *adj.* indubitable, indudable.

induce [in-dius] *vt.* inducir, persuadir; causar.

inducement [in-dius-ment] *n.* motivo, móvil, aliciente, *m.*

induct [in-dakt] *vt.* instalar, iniciar.

induction [in-dak-shon] *n.* iniciación, instalación, *f.;* inducción, deducción, *f.;* ilación, *f.;* — **coil,** carrete de inducción, bobina de inducción.

indulge [in-dalch] *vt.* y *vi.* favorecer; conceder; ser indulgente; **to — in,** entregarse a.

indulgence [in-dal-chens] *n.*

indulgencia, *f.,* mimo, *m.*

indulgent [in-dal-chent] *adj.* indulgente; —**ly,** *adv.* de un modo indulgente.

industrial [in-das-trial] *adj.* industrial.

industrialism [in-das-tria-li-sem] *n.* industrialismo, *m.*

industry [in-das-tri] *n.* industria, *f.*

inebriate [in-i-brieit] *vt.* embriagar.

ineffective [in-i-fek-tiv] *adj.* ineficaz.

inefficiency [in-i-fi-shan-si] *n.* ineficacia, *f.*

inefficient [in-i-fi-shant] *adj.* ineficiente; ineficaz.

ineligibility [in-e-li-chi-bi-li-ti] *n.* ineligibilidad, *f.,* calidad que excluye elección.

ineligible [in-e-li-cha-bol] *adj.* no elegible, que no llena los requisitos para algún puesto.

inept [i-nept] *adj.* inepto.

ineptitude [i-nep-ti-tiud] *n.* ineptitud, *f.*

inequality [i-ni-kuo-li-ti] *n.* desigualdad, disparidad, diferencia, *f.*

inert [i-nert] *adj.* inerte, perezoso; —**ly,** *adv.* indolentemente.

inertia [i-ner-sha] *n.* inercia, *f.*

inescapable [i-nes-kei-padol] *adj.* ineludible.

inevitable [i-ne-vi-tabol] *adj.*

inevitable, fatal, sin remedio; —
bly, *adv.* inevitablemente.

inexcusable [in-iks-kiu-sa-bol]
adj. inexcusable.

inexpensive [in-iks-pen-siv] *adj.*
de poco costo, barato.

inexperience [in-iks-pia-riens] *n.*
inexperiencia, impericia, *f.*

inexperienced [in-iks-pia-rienst]
adj. inexperto, bisoño, sin
experiencia, novel.

inexplicable [in-iks-pli-ka-bol]
adj. inexplicable.

inextricable [in-iks-tri-ka-bol]
adj. intrincado; enmarañado.

infallible [in-fa-li-bol] *adj.* infalible.

infamous [in-fei-mos] *adj.* vil,
infame.

infamy [in-fa-mi] *n.* infamia, *f.*,
oprobio, *m.*

infancy [in-fan-si] *n.* infancia, *f.*

infant [in-fant] *n.* infante, *m.;*
niño, ña.

infanticide [in-fan-ti-said] *n.*
infanticidio, *m.;* infanticida,
m.y f.

infantile [in-fan-tail] *adj.* pueril,
infantil; — **paralysis,** (med.)
parálisis infantil, poliomielitis,
f.

infantry [in-fan-tri] *n.* infantería,
f.

infatuate [in-fa-tiueit] *vt.* infatuar, embobar; fascinar.

infect [in-fekt] *vt.* infectar.

infection [in-fek-shon] *n.* infección, *f.*

infer [in-fer] *vt.* inferir, deducir,
colegir.

inference [in-fe-rens] *n.* inferen-
cia, ilación, *f.;* conclusión lógica, deducción, *f.*

inferior [in-fi-riar] *adj.* inferior;
of — quality, (coll.) de pacotilla,
de calidad inferior; —, *n.* inferior, *m.* o *f.;* oficial subordinado.

inferiority [in-fi-rio-ri-ti] *n.* inferioridad, *f.;* — **complex,** complejo de inferioridad.

infernal [in-fer-nal] *adj.* infernal.

infest [in-fest] *vt.* infestar.

infidel [in-fi-del] *n.* y *adj.* infiel,
pagano, desleal.

infidelity [in-fi-de-li-ti] *n.* infidelidad, *f.;* perfidia, *f.*

infiltrate [in-fil-treit] *vi.* infiltrar-
se, penetrar.

infinite [in-fi-nit] *adj.* infinito,
innumerable; —**ly,** *adv.* infini-
tamente.

infinitesimal [in-fi-ni-te-si-mal]
adj. infinitesimal.

infinitive [in-fi-ni-tiv] *n.* infinitivo, *m.*

infinity [in-fi-ni-ti] *n.* eternidad,
f.; inmensidad, *f.;* infinito, *m.*

infirm [in-ferm] *adj.* enfermo,
débil.

infirmary [in-fer-ma-ri] *n.* enfermería, *f.*

inflame [in-fleim] *vt.* inflamar; —, *vi.* inflamarse.

inflammable [in-fla-ma-bol] *adj.* inflamable.

inflammation [in-fla-mei-shon] *n.* inflamación, *f.,* encendimiento, *m.*

inflammatory [in-fla-ma-to-ri] *adj.* inflamatorio.

inflate [in-fleit] *vt.* inflar, hinchar.

inflation [in-flei-shon] *n.* inflación, *f.;* hinchazón, *f.*

inflexible [in-flek-sa-bol] *adj.* inflexible.

inflict [in-flikt] *vt.* castigar; infligir (penas corporales, etc.).

infliction [in-flik-shon] *n.* imposición, *f.;* castigo, *m.*

inflow [in-flau] *n.* flujo, *m.,* afluencia, *f.;* entrada, *f.*

influence [in-fluens] *n.* influencia, *f.;* —, *vt.* influir; **to — by suggestion,** sugestionar.

influential [in-fluen-shal] *adj.* influyente.

influenza [in-fluen-sa] *n.* (med.) influenza, gripe, *f.,* trancazo, *m.*

influx [in-flaks] *n.* influjo, *m.;* afluencia, *f.;* desembocadura, *f.*

infold [in-fold] *vt.* envolver, abrazar.,

inform [in-form] *vt.* informar, poner en conocimiento; hacer saber, enseñar, poner al corriente, dar razón de; **to — oneself,** enterarse.

informal [in-for-mal] *adj.* íntimo, sin formulismos.

informality [in-for-ma-li-ti] *n.* sencillez, intimidad, *f.,* ausencia de formulismos.

informant [in-for-mant] *n.* denunciador, ra; informante, *m.* y *f.,* informador, ra.

information [in-for-mei-shon] *n.* información, instrucción, *f.;* informe, *m.;* aviso, *m.;* luz, *f.;* — **bureau,** oficina de información.

informed [in-formd] *adj.* sabedor, bien informado.

informer [in-for-mar] *n.* informante, delator, *m.*

infraction [in-frak-shon] *n.* infracción, violación, *f.*

infrared [in-frard] *adj.* infrarrojo.

infrequent [in-fri-kuent] *adj.* raro, insólito.

infuriate [in-fiu-rieit] *vt.* irritar, provocar, enfurecer; sacar de sus casillas.

infusion [in-fiu-shon] *n.* infusión, *f.*

ingenious [in-yi-nios] *adj.* ingenioso; vivo.

ingenuity [in-ye-niu-ti] *n.* ingeniosidad, inventiva, *f.;* ingenuidad *f.;* destreza, *f.*

ingenuous [in-ye-nuos] *adj.* ingenuo, sincero; —**ly,** *adv.*

ingenuamente.

ingrained [in-greind] *adj.* teñido en rama; impregnado.

ingrate [in-greit] *n.* ingrato, ta.

ingratiate [in-grei-shieit] *vt.* hacer aceptar; **to — oneself,** congraciarse.

ingratitude [in-gra-ti-tiud] *n.* ingratitud, *f.*

ingredient [in-gri-dient] *n.* ingrediente, *m.*

inhabit [in-ja-bit] *vt.* habitar, ocupar.

inhabitable [in-ja-bi-ter-bol] *adj.* habitable.

inhabitant [in-ja-bi-tant] *n.* habitante, residente, *m.* y *f.*

inhalation [in-ja-lei-shon] *n.* inhalación, *f.*

inhale [in-jeil] *vt.* aspirar, inhalar.

inhaler [in-jei-lar] *n.* inhalador, *m.*

inherent [in-jia-rant] *adj.* inherente.

inherit [in-je-rit] *vt.* heredar.

inheritance [in-je-ri-tans] *n.* herencia, *f.;* patrimonio, *m.;* — **tax,** impuesto sobre herencia.

inhibit [in-ji-bit] *vt.* inhibir, prohibir.

inhibition [in-ji-bi-shon] *n.* inhibición, prohibición *f.*

inhospitable [in-jos-pi-ter-bol] *adj.* inhospitalario, inhospitable.

inhuman [in-jiu-man] *adj.* inhumano, cruel.

inhumanity [in-jiu-ma-ni-ti] *n.* inhumanidad, crueldad, *f.*

iniquitous [i-ni-kui-tos] *adj.* inicuo, injusto.

iniquity [i-ni-kui-ti] *n.* iniquidad, injusticia, *f.*

initial [i-ni-shal] *adj.* inicial; —, *n.* letra inicial.

initiate [i-ni-shieit] *vt.* principian iniciar.

initiation [i-ni-shi-ei-shon] *n.* principio, *m.;* iniciación, *f.*

initiative [i-ni-sha-tiv] *adj.* iniciativo; —, *n.* iniciativa, *f.*

inject [in-yekt] *vt.* inyectar.

injection [in-yek-shon] *n.* inyección, *f.;* — **pump,** bomba de inyección.

injunction [in-yank-shon] *n.* mandato, entredicho, *m.*

injure [in-yar] *vt.* injuriar, ofender; hacer daño; lastimar.

injured [in-yurd] *adj.* lesionado.

injurious [in-yu-rios] *adj.* injurioso, injusto; perjudicial, nocivo; —**ly,** *adv.* injuriosamente.

injury [in-ya-ri] *n.* injuria, afrenta, sinrazón, ofensa, *f.;* mal, *m.;* perjuicio, *m.;* daño, *m.*

injustice [in-yas-tis] *n.* injusticia, *f.;* agravio, *m.*

ink [ink] *n.* tinta, *f* .; **India —,** tinta china.

inkling [in-klin] *n.* insinuación,

noción vaga.

inland [in-land] *n.* parte interior de un país; —, *adj.* interior; —, *adv.* dentro de un país.

in-law [in-los] *n.* (coll.) pariente politico.

inlet [in-let] *n.* entrada, *f.;* cala, ensenada, *f.*

inmate [in-meit] *n.* inquilino, na; ocupante; preso, sa.

inn [in] *n.* posada, *f.;* mesón, *m.*

innate [i-neit] *adj.* innato, natural, ínsito.

inner [i-nar] *adj.* interior; — **tube,** cámara de aire.

innermost [i-na-moust] *adj.* íntimo, muy interior.

inning [i-nin] *n.* (en juegos) mano, *f.;* (béisbol) entrada, *f.*

innocence [i-no-sens] *n.* inocencia, *f.*

innocent [i-no-sent] *adj.* inocente.

innocuous [i-no-kuos] *adj.* inocuo, inofensivo.

innovation [i-nou-vei-shon] *n.* innovación, *f.*

innumerable [i-niu-me-ra-bol] *adj.* innumerable.

inoculation [i-no-kiu-lei-shon] *n.* inoculación, *f.*

inoffensive [i-no-fen-siv] *adj.* pacífico; inofensivo.

inordinate [i-nor-di-nit] *adj.* desordenado; excesivo.

inorganic [i-nor-ga-nik] *adj.* inorgánico.

inquire [in-kuaiar] *vt.* preguntar (alguna cosa); —, *vi.* inquirir, examinar.

inquirer [in-kuaia-rar] *n.* averiguador, ra, investigador, ra, preguntador, ra.

inquiry [in-kuaia-ri] *n.* interrogación, pregunta, *f.;* investigación, *f.;* pesquisa, *f.*

inquisition [in-kui-si-shon] *n.* inquisición, *f.;* escudriñamiento, *m.*

inquisitive [in-kui-si-tiv] *adj.* curioso, preguntón; —**ly,** *adv.* en forma inquiridora.

inquisitiveness [in-kui-si-tiv-nes] *n.* curiosidad, *f.*

insane [in-sein] *adj.* insano, loco, demente; — **asylum,** casa de locos, manicomio, *m.;* **to go** —, perder la razón.

insanity [in-sa-ni-ti] *n.* insania, locura, *f.*

insatiable [in-sei-sha-bol] *adj.* insaciable.

inscribe [in-skraib] *vt.* inscribir; dedicar; grabar.

inscription [in-skrip-shon] *n.* inscripción, letra, leyenda, *f.;* letrero, *m.;* dedicatoria, *f.*

insect [in-sekt] *n.* insecto, bicho, *m.;* — **killer,** — **poison,** insecticida, *m.*

insecticide [in-sek-ti-said] *n.* insecticida, *m.*

insecure [in-si-kiur] *adj.* inseguro.

insecurity [in-si-kiu-ri-ti] *n.* inseguridad, *f.;* incertidumbre, *f.*

insensible [in-sen-sa-bol] *adj.* insensible; imperceptible.

inseparable [in-se-pa-ra-bol] *adj.* inseparable.

insert [in-sert] *vt.* insertar, ingerir una cosa en otra, meter.

inset [in-set] *vt.* injertar, plantar, fijar; grabar; —, *n.* hoja intercalada en un libro; carta geográfica o lámina dentro de una más grande; intercalación *f.*

inside [in-said] *n.* y *adj.* interior, *m.; f.* (coll.) entrañas, *f. pl.* ; **on the —,** por dentro; **toward the —,** hacia dentro; —, *adv.* adentro, dentro; **— of,** dentro de; **— out,** al revés.

insidious [in-si-dios] *adj.* insidioso.

insight [in-sait] *n.* conocimiento profundo; perspicacia, *f.*

insignia [in-sig-nia] *n. pl.* insignias, *f. pl.* ; estandartes, *m. pl.*

insignificance [in-sig-ni-fi-kans] *n.* insignificancia, *f.;* nulidad, *f.*

insignificant [in-sig-ni-fi-kant] *adj.* insignificante; trivial; **to be —,** ser un cero a la izquierda.

insincere [in-sin-siar] *adj.* poco sincero, hipócrita.

insincerity [in-sin-se-ri-ti] *n.* insinceridad, *f.*

insinuate [in-si-niu-eit] *vt.* insinuar.

insinuation [in-si-niuei-shon] *n.* insinuación, *f.*

insipid [in-si-pid] *adj.* insípido; insulso.

insist [in-sist] *vi.* insistir, persistir, hacer hincapié.

insistent [in-sis-tant] *adj.* insistente, persistente.

insolence [in-so-lens] *n.* insolencia, *f.*

insolent [in-so-lent] *adj.* insolente.

insoluble [in-so-liu-bol] *adj.* insoluble, indisoluble.

insomnia [in-som-nia] *n.* insomnio, *m.*

inspect [ins-pekt] *vt.* reconocer, examinar, inspeccionar.

inspection [ins-pek-shon] *n.* inspección, *f.;* registro, *m.;* **tour of —,** jira de inspección.

inspector [ins-pek-tar] *n.* inspector, superintendente, *m.,* registrador, ra.

inspiration [ins-pa-rei-shon] *n.* inspiración, *f.;* numen, *m.*

instability [ins-ter-bi-li-ti] *n.* instabilidad, inconstancia, *f.*

install [ins-tol] *vt.* instalar.

installation [ins-ter-lei-shon] *n.* instalación, *f.*

installment, instalment [ins-tol-ment] *n.* instalación, *f.;* pago

parcial, plazo, *m.;* entrega, *f ;*
monthly —, mensualidad, *f.;* **on
the — plan,** a crédito, en pagos
parciales, (Mex.) en abonos.

instance [ins-tans] *n.* instancia,
f.; ejemplo, caso, *m.;* instiga-
ción, *f.;* sugestión, *f.;* **for —,**
por ejemplo; **—,** *vt.* citar ejemplos.

instant [ins-tant] *adj.* instante,
urgente; presente; **the 20th —,**
el 20 del presente; **—ly,** *adv.* en
un instante; al punto; **—,** *n.*
instante, momento, *m.*

instantaneous [ins-tan-tei-nios]
adj. instantáneo.

instead of [ins-ted-of] en lugar
de, en vez de.

instigate [ins-ti-gueit] *vt.* instigar, mover.

instigator *[*ins-ti-guei-tar] *n.* ins-
tigador, ra.

instill, instil [ins-til] *vt.* inculcar,
infundir, insinuar.

instinct [ins-tinkt] *n.* instinto,
m.; **—,** *adj.* animado, impulsado; lleno, cargado.

instinctive [ins-tink-tiv] *adj.* instintivo; **—ly,** *adv.* por instinto.

institute [ins-ti-tiut] *vt.* instituir,
establecer; **—,** *n.* instituto, *m.*

institution [ins-ti-tiu-shon] *n.*
institución, *f.*

institutional [ins-ti-tiu-sho-nal]
adj. institucional.

instruct [ins-trakt] *vt.* instruir,

enseñar.

instruction [ins-trak-shon] *n.*
instrucción, enseñanza, *f.*

instructive [ins-trak-tiv] *adj.* instructivo.

instructor [ins-truk-tar] *n.* instructor, *m.*

instrument [ins-tru-ment] *n.*
instrumento, *m.;* contrato, *m.,*
escritura, *f.*

instrumental [ins-tru-men-tal]
adj. instrumental.

insubordinate [in-sa-bor-di-nit]
adj. insubordinado.

insubordination [in-sa-bor-di-
nei-shon] *n.* insubordinación, *f.*

insufferable [in-sa-fe-ra-bol] *adj.*
insufrible, insoportable.

insufficient [in-sa-fi-shant] *adj.*
insuficiente; **—ly,** *adv.* insufi-
cientemente.

insulate [in-siu-leit] *vt.* aislar
(las corrientes eléctricas) .

insulation [in-siu-lei-shon] *n.*
(elec.) aislamiento, *m.*

insulator [in-siu-lei-tar] *n.* (elec.)
aislador, *m.*

insulin [in-siu-lin] *n.* insulina, *f.*

insult [in-salt] *vt.* insultar; **—,** *n.*
insulto, *m.*

insulting [in-sal-tin] *adj.* insul-
tante; **—ly,** *adv.* con insultos,
con insolencia.

insurance [in-shua-rans] *n.*
(com.) seguro, *m.,* seguridad, *f.;*
accident —, seguro contra acci-

dente; **burglary** —, seguro contra robo; **fire** —, seguro contra fuego o incendio; — **agent,** agente de seguros; — **broker,** corredor de seguros; — **policy,** póliza de seguro; — **premium,** prima de seguro; **life** —, seguro de vida.

insure [in-shuar] *vt.* asegurar.

insurgent [in-ser-yent] *n.* y *adj.* insurgente, insurrecto, rebelde, *m.*

insurrection [in-sa-rek-shon] *n.* insurrección, sedición, *f.*

intact [in-takt] *adj.* intacto, entero.

intake [in-teik] *n.* acceso de aire; orificio de entrada o acceso de agua; canal de alimentación; (min.) aereación, *f.;* — **manifold,** válvula múltiple de admisión.

intangible [in-tan-yi-bol] *adj.* intangible.

integral [in-ti-gral] *adj.* íntegro; (chem.) integrante; —**ly,** *adv.* integralmente; —, *n.* todo, *m.*

integrate [in-ti-greit] *vt.* integrar.

integration [in-ti-grei-shon] *n.* integración, *f.*

integrity [in-ti-gri-ti] *n.* integridad, *f.;* pureza, *f.*

intellect [in-ti-lekt] *n.* entendimiento, intelecto, *m.*

intellectual [in-ti-lek-chual] *n.* intelectual, *m.* y *f.;* —, *adj.* intelectual, mental.

intelligence [in-te-li-yens] *n.* inteligencia, *f.;* conocimiento, *m.;* correspondencia, *f.;* — **test,** prueba de inteligencia.

intelligent [in-te-li-yent] *adj.* inteligente.

intemperate [in-tem-pe-reit] *adj.* destemplado; inmoderado.

intend [in-tend] *vt.* intentar; —, *vi.* proponerse; **to** — **(to go, to do, etc.),** pensar (ir, hacer, etc.).

intense [in-tens] *adj.* intenso; vehemente.

intensify [in-ten-si-fai] *vt.* intensificar, hacer más intenso.

intensity [in-ten-si-ti] *n.* intensidad, *f.*

intensive [in-ten-siv] *adj.* completo, concentrado; — **study,** estudio completo.

intent [in-tent] *adj.* atento, cuidadoso; —**ly,** *adv.* con aplicación; —, *n.* intento, designio, *m.*

intention [in-ten-shon] *n.* intención, *f.;* designio, *m.;* (fig.) mira, *f.*

intentional [in-ten-sho-nal] *adj.* intencional; —**ly,** *adv.* de intento, intencionalmente.

intercede [in-ter-sid] *vi.* interceder, mediar.

intercept [in-ter-sept] *vt.* interceptar; impedir.

interchange [in-ter-cheinch] *vt.* alternar, trocar; —, *n.* comercio, *m.*; canje, intercambio, *m.*

intercollegiate [in-ter-co-li-yeit] *adj.* interescolar, interuniversitario.

intercommunicate [in-ter-ko-miu-ni-keit] *vi.* comunicarse mutuamente.

intercourse [in-ter-kors] *n.* comercio, *m.*; comunicación, *f.*; coito, *m.*; contacto carnal.

interdependence [in-ter-di-pendans] *n.* dependencia mutua.

interest [in-te-rest] *vt.* interesar; empeñar; —, *n.* interés, provecho, *m.*; influjo, empeño, *m.*; **compound** —, interés compuesto; **rate of** —, tipo de interés.

interesting [in-te-res-tin] *adj.* interesante, atractivo.

interfere [in-ter-fiar] *vi.* entremeterse, ingerirse, mezclarse, intervenir.

interference [in-ter-fia-rans] *n.* interposición, mediación, ingerencia, *f.*; (rad.) interferencia estática.

interior [in-te-riar] *adj.* interior, interno.

interject [in-ter-yekt] *vt.* interponer.

interjection [in-ter-yek-shon] *n.* (gram.) interjección, *f.*

interlude [in-ter-lud] *n.* interme-

dio, *m.*

intermediate [in-ter-mi-diet] *adj.* intermedio; — **range ballistic missile (IRBM),** proyectil balístico de alcance intermedio; —, *n.* intermediario, ria.

interminable [in-ter-mi-na-bol] *adj.* interminable, ilimitado.

intermingle [in-ter-min-guel] *vt.* y vi. entremezclar; mezclarse.

intermission [in-ter-mi-shon] *n.* intermedio, *m.*

intermittent [in-ter-mi-tent] *adj.* intermitente.

intern [in-tern] *vt.* internar; encerrar; —, *n.* (med.) practicante, *m.*; médico interno (en un hospital).

internal [in-ter-nal] *adj.* interno; — **medicine,** medicina interna.

international [in-ter-nei-sho-nal] *adj.* internacional; — **law,** derecho internacional; — **date line,** línea internacional de cambio de fecha.

internet [in-ter-net] *n.* internet, *m.*

internment [in-tern-ment] *n.* encerramiento, *m.*, concentración, *f.*

intermittent [in-ter-mi-tent] *adj.* intermitente.

internship [in-tern-ship] *n.* práctica que como médicos residentes hacen los posgraduados en un hospital.

interpret [in-ter-prit] *vt.* interpretar.

interpretation [in-ter-pri-tei-shon] *n.* interpretación, *f.;* versión, *f.*

interpreter [in-ter-pri-tar] *n.* intérprete, *m.* y *f.*

interracial [in-ter-rei-shal] *adj.* entre razas.

interrelated [in-ter-ri-lei-tid] *adj.* con relación recíproca.

interrogate [in-te-ro-gueit] *vt.* interrogar, examinar.

interrogation [in-te-ro-guei-shon] *n.* interrogación, pregunta, *f.*

interrogator [in-te-ro-guei-tar] *n.* interrogante, *m.* y *f.*

interrupt [in-te-rapt] *vt.* interrumpir, romper.

interruption [in-te-rap-shon] *n.* interrupción, *f.*

intersect [in-ter-sekt] *vt.* entrecortar; cortar; cruzar.

intersection [in-ter-sek-shon] *n.* intersección, *f.;* bocacalle *f.*

intertwine [in-ter-tuain] *vt.* entretejer.

interval [in-ter-val] *n.* intervalo, *m.;* at —s, a ratos.

intervene [in-ter-vin] *vi.* intervenir; ocurrir.

intervention [in-ter-ven-shon] *n.* intervención, interposición, *f.*

interview [in-ter-viu] *n.* entrevista, *f.*

interwoven [in-ter-uo-ven] *adj.* entretejido, entrelazado.

intestinal [in-tes-tai-nal] *adj.* intestinal.

intestine [in-tes-tain] *adj.* intestino, doméstico; —s, *n. pl.* intestinos, *m. pl.*

intimacy [in-ti-ma-si] *n.* intimidad, confianza, *f.;* familiaridad, *f.*

intimidate [in-ti-mi-deit] *vt.* intimidar.

intimidation [in-ti-mi-dei-shon] *n.* intimidación, *f.*

into [in-tu] *prep.* en, dentro.

intolerable [in-to-le-ra-bol] *adj.* intolerable.

intolerant [in-to-le-rant] *adj.* intolerante.

intonation [in-tou-nei-shon] *n.* entonación, *f.*

intoxicate [in-tok-si-keit] *vt.* embriagar.

intoxicated [in-tok-si-kei-tid] *adj.* bebido, ebrio, borracho.

intoxicating [in-tok-si-kei-tin] *adj.* embriagante; — **liquor,** bebida embriagante.

intoxication [in-tok-si-kei-shon] *n.* embriaguez, *f.;* intoxicación, *f.*

intravenous [in-tra-vi-nos] *adj.* intravenoso; — **shot,** inyección intravenosa.

intrepid [in-tre-pid] *adj.* arrojado, intrépido.

intricacy [in-tri-ka-si] *n.* embrollo, embarazo, *m.;* dificultad, *f.*

intricate [in-tri-ket] *adj.* intrincado, complicado; complejo.

intrinsic [in-trin-sik] *adj.* intrínseco, inherente.

introduce [in-tro-dius] *vt.* introducir, meter; **to — (a person),** presentar (a una persona).

introduction [in-tro-dak-shon] *n.* introducción, *f.;* presentación, *f.;* prólogo, preámbulo, *m.*

introductory [in-tro-dak-ter-ri] *adj.* previo, preliminar, introductorio.

introvert [in-trou-vert] *n.* introvertido, da.

intrude [in-trud] *vi.* entremeterse, introducirse, ingerirse.

intruder [in-tru-dar] *n.* intruso, sa, entremetido, da.

intrusion [in-tru-shon] *n.* intrusión, *f.*

intrust [in-trast] *vt.* confiar.

intuition [in-tui-shon] *n.* intuición, *f.*

inundate [i-nan-deit] *vt.* inundar.

inundation [i-nan-dei-shon] *n.* inundación, *f.*

invade [in-veid] *vt.* invadir, asaltar.

invader [in-vei-dar] *n.* usurpador, ra, invasor, ra.

invalid [in-va-lid] *adj.* inválido; nulo; **— diet,** dieta para inválidos; **—,** *n.* inválido, da.

invalidate [in-va-li-deit] *vt.* invalidar, anular.

invaluable [in-va-liu-a-bol] *adj.* inapreciable.

invasion [in-vei-shion] *n.* invasión, *f.*

invent [in-vent] *vt.* inventar.

invention [in-ven-shon] *n.* invención, *f.;* invento, *m.*

inventive [in-ven-tiv] *adj.* inventivo.

inventor [in-ven-tar] *n.* inventor, *m.;* forjador, *m.*

inventory [in-ven-to-ri] *n.* inventario, *m.*

inverse [in-vers] *adj.* inverso, trastornado.

invert [in-vert] *vt.* invertir, trastrocar.

invertebrate [in-ver-ti-brit] *n.* y *adj.* invertebrado, *m.*

inverted [in-ver-tid] *adj.* invertido, permutado.

invest [in-vest] *vt.* investir; emplear dinero en; (com.) invertir; **to — money,** colocar o invertir dinero.

investigate [in-ves-ti-gueit] *vt.* investigar.

investigation [in-ves-ti-guei-shon] *n.* investigación, pesquisa, *f.*

investigator [in-ves-ti-guei-tar] *n.* pesquisidor, ra, investigador, ra.

investment [in-vest-ment] *n.*

inversión, *f.*

investor [in-ves-tar] *n.* inversionista, *m.* y *f.*

invigorate [in-vi-go-reit] *vt.* vigorizar, dar vigor, fortificar, confortar, robustecer.

invigorating [in-vi-go-rai-tin] *adj.* vigorizante.

invincible [in-vin-si-bol] *adj.* invencible.

invisible [in-vi-si-bol] *adj.* invisible.

invitation [in-vi-tei-shon] *m.*, invitación, *f.*

inviting [in-vai-tin] *adj.* incitante, atractivo, seductor.

invocation [in-vou-kei-shon] *n.* invocación, *f.*

invoice [in-vois] *n.* factura, *f.;* —, *vt.* facturar.

involuntary [in-vo-lun-ta-ri] *adj.* involuntario.

involve [in-volv] *vt.* envolver, implicar.

involved [in-volvd] *adj.* complejo, complexo; implicado, envuelto.

invulnerable [in-val-ne-ra-bol] *adj.* invulnerable.

inward [in-uods] *adj.* interior; interno; —s, *adv.* interiormente; internamente, hacia adentro.

iodine [aia-din] *n.* (chem.) yodo, *m.*

ion [aion] *n.* ion, *m.*

ionization [aiou-nai-sei-shon] *n.*

ionización, *f.*

IQ., IQ: intelligence quotient [ai-kiu], [in-te-li-yens-kuo-shent] cuociente intelectual.

irate [ai-reit] *adj.* iracundo, colérico.

ire [aiar] *n.* ira, iracundia, *f.*

Ireland [aia-land] Irlanda, *f.*

iris [aia-ris] *n.* arco iris; (anat.) iris, *m.;* (bot.) flor de lis.

irish [aia-rish] *n.* y *adj.* irlandés, esa.

irk [erk] *vt.* fastidiar, cansar.

irksome [erk-som] *adj.* tedioso, fastidioso.

iron [aion] *n.* hierro, *m.;* **cast —,** hierro fundido o de fundición; **galvanized —,** hierro galvanizado; **— curtain,** cortina de hierro; **— lung,** pulmón de acero; **— rust,** herrumbre, *f.;* **sheet —,** hierro laminado; **wrought —,** hierro forjado o de fragua; —, *vt.* aplanchar, planchar; poner en grillos.

ironclad [aion-klad] *adj.* blindado, acorazado, o armado de hierro.

ironic [ai-ro-nik] *adj.* irónico.

ironical [ai-ro-ni-kal] *adj.* irónico; —ly, *adv.* con ironía, irónicamente.

irony [ai-ro-ni] *n.* ironía, *f.*

irradiate [i-rei-dieit] *vt.* y *vi.* irradiar, brillar.

irradiated *adj.* irradiado.

irrational [i-ra-sho-nal] *adj.* irracional.

irrefutable [i-ri-fiu-ter-bol] *adj.* irrefutable.

irregular [i-re-guiu-lar] *adj.* irregular.

irregularity [i-re-guiu-la-ri-ti] *n.* irregularidad, *f.*

irrelevance [i-re-le-vans] *n.* calidad de inaplicable.

irrelevant [i-re-le-vant] *adj.* no aplicable; que no prueba nada; no concluyente, desatinado.

irreparable [i-re-pa-ra-bol] *adj.* irreparable.

irrepressible [i-ri-pre-sa-bol] *adj.* irrefrenable.

irreproachable [i-ri-prou-cha-bol] *adj.* irreprochable; intachable.

irresistible [i-ri-sis-ti-bol] *adj.* irresistible.

irrespective [i-ris-pek-tiv] *adj.* independiente; — **of,** sin consideración a, sin tomar en cuenta.

irresponsible [i-ris-pon-si-bol] *adj.* no responsable, irresponsable.

irreverent [i-re-ve-rant] *adj.* irreverente.

irrevocable [i-re-vo-ka-bol] *adj.* irrevocable.

irrigate [i-ri-gueit] *vt.* regar, mojar.

irrigation [i-ri-guei-shon] *n.* riego, *m.;* irrigación, *f.*

irritable [i-ri-ter-bol] *adj.* irritable; colérico.

irritant [i-ri-tant] *n.* (med.) estimulante, *m.*

irritate [i-ri-teit] *vt.* irritar, exasperar, azuzar.

irritation [i-ri-tei-shon] *n.* irritación, *f.*

is [is] 3ra persona del singular del verbo **be.**

island [ai-land] *n.* isla, *f.*

isle [ail] *n.* islote, *m.,* isleta, *f.*

isolate [ai-so-leit] *vt.* aislar, apartar.

isolation [ai-so-lei-shon] *n.* aislamiento, *m.*

isolationist [ai-so-lei-sho-nist] *n.* aislacionista, *m.* y *f.*

isosceles [ai-so-si-lis] *adj.* isósceles.

issue [i-shu] *n.* salida, *f.;* evento, *m.;* fin, término, *m.;* flujo, *m.;* sucesión, *f.;* producto, *m.;* consecuencia, *f.;* punto en debate; (med.) exutorio, *m.;* progenie, *f.;* tirada, edición, *f.;* número (de una publicación); —, *vi.* salir, nacer, prorrumpir, brotar; venir, proceder; provenir; terminarse; —, *vt.* echar; brotar; expedir, despachar; publicar; emitir.

isthmus [isz-mos] *n.* istmo, *m.*

it [it] *pron.* él, ella, ello, lo, la, le.

italic [i-ter-lik] *n.* letra cursiva, bastardilla, *f.*

Italy [i-te-li] Italia, *f.*

itch [ich] *n.* sarna, picazón, *f.;* —, *vi.* picar, tener comezón.

item [ai-tem] *adv.* ítem, otrosí, aun más; —, *n.* artículo, suelto, *m.;* (com.) renglón, *m.*

itemize [ai-te-mais] *vt.* particularizar, detallar, estipular.

itinerant [i-ti-ne-rant] *adj.* ambulante, errante.

itinerary [i-ti-ne-ra-ri] *n.* itinerario, *m.*

its [its] *pron.* el suyo, suyo; —, *adj.* su, de él, de ella.

itself [it-self] *pron.* el mismo, la misma, lo mismo; sí; **by** —, de por sí.

ivory [ai-vo-ri] *n.* marfil, *m.*

ivy [ai-vi] *n.* hiedra, *f.*

J

ab [yab] *n.* pinchazo, *m.;* (boxeo) golpe inverso, *m.;* —, *vt.* pinchar.

jack [yak] *n.* gato, sacabotas, *m.;* martinete, *m.;* cric, *m.,* clavija, *f.;* (coll.) dinero, *m.;* boliche, *m.;* macho, *m.;* burro, *m.;* —**pot,** (póquer) jugada que no puede abrirse mientras un jugador no tenga un par de sotas o algo mejor; **to hit the —pot,** sacarse el premio gordo (en la lotería, etc.).

jackass [ya-kas] *n.* garañón, burro, asno, *m.*

jacket [ya-kit] *n.* chaqueta, *f.,* saco, *m.;* envoltura, *f.;* forro de papel (de un libro).

jackknife [yak-naif] *n.* navaja de bolsillo.

jackrabbit [yak-rabit] *n.* liebre, *f.*

jade [yeid] *n.* jade, *m.;* rocín, *m.;* mujer desacreditada; —, *vt.* cansar.

jag [yag] *n.* diente de sierra; mella, *f.;* diente, *m.;* —, *vt.* dentar.

jagged [ya-guid] *adj.* desigual, dentado.

jaguar [ya-uar] *n.* jaguar, *m.*

jail [yeil] *n.* cárcel, *f.*

jailbird [yeil-berd] *n.* preso, *m.;* criminal, *m.*

jailer [yei-lar] *n.* carcelero, bastonero, *m.*

jalopy [ya-lo-pi] *n.* automóvil destartalado; (Mex.) carcacha, *f.*

jam [yam] *n.* compota, conserva, *f.;* mermelada de frutas; apretadura, *f.;* aprieto, *m.;* **to be in a** —, estar en un aprieto; — **session,** reunión de músicos para improvisar música popular; —, *vt.* apiñar, apretar, estrechar.

jangle [yan-guel] *vi.* reñir, altercar; sonar en discordancia; —, *vt.* hacer sonar; —, *n.* sonido discordante; altercado, *m.*

janitor [ya-ni-tar] *n.* ujier, portero, conserje, *m.*

January [ya-nua-ri] *n.* enero, *m.*

Japan [ya-pan] Japón, *m.*

Japanese [ya-pa-nis] *n.* y *adj.* japonés, esa.

jar [yar] *vi.* chocar; (mus.) discordar; reñir; —, *n.* jarro, *m.;* tinaja, *f.;* riña, *f.;* sonido desapacible; tarro, *m.*

jargon [yar-gon] *n.* jerga, jerigonza, *f.*

jasmine [yas-min] *n.* (bot.) jazmín, *m.*

jasper [yas-par] *n.* (min.) jaspe, *m.*

jaundice [yon-dis] *n.* ictericia, *f.*

jaunt [yont] *n.* excursión, *f.*

javelin [ya-ve-lin] *n.* venablo, *m.,* jabalina, *f.*

jaw [yo] *n.* quijada, *f.;* boca, *f.*

jawbone [yo-boun] *n.* quijada, mandíbula, *f.*

jay [yei] *n.* picaza, urraca, marica, *f.*

jazz [yas] *n.* jazz, *m.*

jealous [ye-los] *adj.* celoso; envidioso; **to be — of,** tener celos de.

jealousy [ye-lo-si] *n.* celos, *m. pl.*

jean [yin] *n.* mezclilla, *f.,* dril, *m.,* tela burda de algodón.

jeans [yins] *n. pl.* pantalones ajustados de dril, generalmente de color azul.

jeep [yip] *n.* (mil.) pequeño automóvil de trasporte.

jelly [ye-li] *n.* jalea, *f.;* gelatina, *f.*

jellyfish [ye-li-fish] *n.* aguamar, *m.;* medusa, *f.*

jeopardize [ye-par-dais] *vt.* arriesgar, poner en riesgo.

jeopardy [ye-par-di] *n.* peligro, riesgo, *m.*

jerk [yerk] *n.* sacudida, sobarbada, *f.,* respingo, *m.;* (coll.) tonto, ta; —, *vt.* y vi. sacudir.

jersey [yer-si] *n.* jersey, *m.,* tejido de punto; ganado vacuno de la isla de Jersey.

jest [yest] *n.* chanza, burla, *f.;* zumba, *f.;* chasco, *m.;* —, *vt.* ridiculizar.

jester [yes-tar] *n.* mofador, ra, bufón, ona.

Jesuit [ye-suit] *n.* jesuita, *m.*

Jesus Christ [yi-sas-kraist] Jesucristo, *m.*

jet [yet] *n.* azabache, *m.;* surtidor, *m.;* — **plane,** avión de retropropulsión; — **propelled,** impulsado por motor de retropropulsión; — **propulsion,** retropropulsión, *f.,* retroimpulso, *m.;* — **stream,** corriente de vientos occidentales veloces

estratosféricos; manga por chorro de aire.

jetty [ye-ti] *n.* muelle, *m.;* rom-
peolas, *m.*

Jew [yu] *n.* judío, día.

jewel [yual] *n.* joya, alhaja, *f.;* —
s, *n. pl.* rubíes (de un reloj),
m. pl.

jeweler [yua-lar] *n.* joyero, *m.*

jewelry [yual-ri] *n.* joyería,
pedrería, *f.;* — **store,** joyería, *f.;*
novelty —, bisutería, joyería de
imitación.

Jewish [yuish] *adj.* judaico, ca,
judío, día.

jiggle [yi-gol] *vt.* mover a tirones;
—, *vi.* moverse a tirones.

jigsaw puzzle [yig-so] *n.* rompecabezas, *m.*

jilt [yilt] *n.* coqueta, *f.;* —, *vt.* dar
calabazas, despedir a un galán;
(coll.) plantar.

jingle [yin-guel] vi. retiñir, resonar; —, *n.* retintín, resonido,
m.; sonaja, *f.*

job [yob] *n.* empleo, *m.;* (Mex.
coll.) chamba, *f.;* destajo, *m.;*
— **lot,** colección, miscelánea de
géneros; *vt.* comprar en calidad
de corredor.

jobber [yo-bar] *n.* agiotista, *m.;*
destajero, *m.*

jobbing [yo-bin] *n.* oficio de comprar y revender.

jobless [yob-les] *adj.* cesante,
sin trabajo.

jockey [yo-ki] *n.* jockey, *m.,* jinete profesional; **disc** o **disk** —,
anunciador de programa
con base en discos; —, *vt.* y *vi.*
engañar, estafar.

jocund [yo-kond] *adj.* jovial; alegre.

jog [yog] *vt.* empujar; dar un
golpe suave; —, *vi.* bambolearse; andar a saltos; —, *n.* empellón, *m.;* traqueo, *m.*

join [yoin] *vt.* juntar, unir; —, *vi.*
unirse, juntarse, asociarse;
confluir.

joint [yoint] *n.* coyuntura, articulación, *f.;* charnela, *f.;* (coll.)
lugar de reunión; (bot.) nudo,
m.; **out of** —, desunido; —, *adj.*
unido; participante; —
account, cuenta en participación; — **heir,** coheredero, ra; —
ly, *adv.* juntamente, conjuntamente, en común; —**ly liable,**
solidario; —, *vt.* juntar, ensamblar; descuartizar.

joke [youk] *n.* chanza, burla,
zumba, *f.;* chasco, *m.;* **to play a**
—, hacer una burla; **to play a**
— **on,** dar broma a; —, vi. bromear.

joker [you-kar] *n.* bromista, *m.* y
f.; comodín (en la baraja), *m.*

jolly [yo-li] *adj.* alegre, jovial.

jolt [yoult] *vt.* y vi. traquear,
sacudir; —, *n.* traqueo, *m.,*
sacudida, *f.*

jostle [yo-sel] *vt.* rempujar, empellar.

jot [yot] *n.* jota, f., cosa mínima; ápice, *m.;* — (**down**), *vt.* apuntar, tomar apuntes, anotar.

journal [yer-nal] *n.* diario, periódico, *m.;* libro diario.

journalism [yer-na-li-sem] *n.* periodismo, *m.*

journalist [yer-na-list] *n.* periodista, *m.* y *f.*

journey [yer-ni] *n.* jornada, *f.;* viaje, *m.;* —, *vi.* viajar.

jovial [you-vial] *adj.* jovial, alegre.

jowl [yaul] *n.* quijada, *f.*

joy [yoi] *n.* alegría, *f.;* júbilo, *m.;* **to give** —, alegrar, causar regocijo; **to wish** —, congratular.

joyful, joyous [yoi-ful], [yoios] *adj.* alegre, gozoso.

Judaism [yu-dei-isem] *n.* judaísmo, *m.*

judge [yadch] *n.* juez, *m.;* —, *vi.* juzgar; inferir.

judgment [yadch-ment] *n.* juicio, *m.;* sentir, *m.;* meollo, concepto, *m.;* opinión, *f.;* decisión, *f.;* **to pass** —, pronunciar la sentencia; juzgar.

judicial [yu-di-shal] *adj.* judicial.

judiciary [yu-di-sha-ri] *n.* magistratura, administración de justicia.

judicious [yu-di-shos] *adj.* juicioso, prudente.

jug [yag] *n.* jarro, *m.*

juggle [ya-guel] *n.* juego de manos; —, *vi.* hacer juegos de manos, escamotear.

juggler [ya-glar] *n.* prestidigitador, *m.;* impostor, estafador, *m.*

jugular [ya-guiu-lar] *adj.* yugular; — **vein,** vena yugular.

juice [yus] *n.* zumo, jugo, *m.*

juicy [yu-si] *adj.* jugoso.

July [yu-lai] *n.* (mes) julio, *m.*

jumble [yam-bel] *vt.* mezclar confusamente; —, *n.* mezcla, confusión, *f.*

jumbo [yam-bou] *n.* persona o cosa excesivamente voluminosa; —, *adj.* colosal, excesivamente voluminoso.

jump [yamp] *vi.* saltar, brincar; convenir, concordar; dar saltos; —, *n.* salto, *m.*

jumping [yam-pin] *n.* salto, brinco, *m.;* —. *adj.* saltante.

junction [yank-shon] *n.* junta, unión, *f.,* empalme, contacto, *m.*

June [yun] *n.* (mes) junio, *m.;* — **bug,** escarabajo americano.

junior [yu-niar] *adj.* más joven; —, *n.* estudiante de tercer año; — **college,** los dos primeros años universitarios; — **high school,** los dos primeros años de escuela secundaria.

juniper [yu-ni-par] *n.* (bot.) junípero, enebro, *m.*, sabina, *f*

junk [yank] *n.* chatarra, *f.,* hierro viejo; cosa despreciable; (naut.) junco, *m.;* — **food,** comida chatarra, *f.*

jurisdiction [yua-ris-dik-shon] *n.* jurisdicción *f.*

jurisprudence [yua-ris-pru-dans] *n.* jurisprudencia, *f.*

jurist [yua-rist] *n.* jurista, *m.* y *f.*, jurisconsulto, *m.* juror, *n.* jurado, *m.*

jury [yua-ri] *n.* junta de jurados; jurado, *m.*

just [yast] *adj.* justo, honrado, virtuoso, derecho; — **as,** como, así como; — **now,** ahora mismo; —**ly,** *adv.* justamente.

justice [yas-tis] *n.* justicia, *f.,* derecho, *m.;* juez, *m.*

justification [yas-ti-fi-kei-shon] *n.* justificación, *f.;* defensa, *f.*

justify [yas-ti-fai] *vt.* justificar.

jut [yat] *vi.* sobresalir.

juvenile [yu-ve-nail] *adj.* juvenil.

juxtapose [yaks-ta-pous] *vt.* yuxtaponer.

K

kangaroo [kan-ga-ru] *n.* canguro, *m.*

katydid [ka-ti-did] *n.* cigarra, *f.*

keen [kin] *adj.* afilado, agudo; penetrante, sutil, vivo; vehemente; satírico, picante; —**ly,** *adv.* con viveza.

keenness [kin-nes] *n.* agudeza, sutileza, perspicacia, *f.;* aspereza, *f.*

keep [kip] *vt.* tener, mantener, retener; preservar, guardar; proteger; detener; conservar; reservar; sostener; observar; solemnizar; **to — accounts,** llevar cuentas; **to — aloof,** apartarse; **to — books,** llevar los libros; **to — house,** poner casa,

ser ama de casa; —, *vi.* perseverar; soler; mantenerse; —, *n.* sustentación, manutención, *f.,* sustento, *m.*

keeper [ki-par] *n.* guardián, tenedor, *m.;* — **of a prison,** carcelero, *m.*

keepsake [kip-seik] *n.* dádiva, *f.,* recuerdo, regalo, *m.*

keg [keg] *n.* barrilito, *m.*

kennel [ke-nel] *n.* perrera, *f.;* jauría, *f.;* zorrera, *f.*

kerchief [ker-chif] *n.* pañuelo, *m.*

kernel [ker-nel] *n.* almendra, pepita, *f.;* meollo, grano, *m.*

kerosene [ke-ro-sin] *n.* querosina, *f.*

ketchup = **catchup.**

kettle [ke-tel] *n.* caldera, marmita, olla, *f.*

key [ki] *n.* llave, *f.;* (mus.) clave, *f.;* clavija, *f.;* chaveta, *f.;* tecla, *f.;* — **ring,** llavero, *m.;* — **word,** palabra clave; **master** —, llave maestra.

keyboard [ki-bord] *n.* teclado de órgano o piano; teclado de máquina de escribir.

keyhole [ki-joul] *n.* agujero de la llave.

keynote [ki-nout] *n.* (mus.) tónica, *f.;* idea básica o fundamental; — **speech,** discurso principal (en una convención, etc.).

Key West [ki-uest] Cayohueso, Cayo Hueso, *m.*

khaki [ka-ki] *n.* y *adj.* kaki, caqui, *m.*

kick [kik] *vt.* acocear; —, vi. patear; (coll.) reclamar, objetar; —, *n.* puntapié, *m.;* patada, *f.;* culatada de armas de fuego; (coll.) efecto estimulador, placer, *m.*

kid [kid] *n.* cabrito *m.;* (coll.) chaval, la; —, *vt.* y *vi.* (coll.) bromear; chancearse.

kidnap [kid-nap] *vt.* secuestrar.

kidnapper [kid-na-par] *n.* secuestrador, ra.

kidnapping [kid-na-pin] *n.* secuestro, *m.*

kidney [kid-ni] *n.* riñón, *m.;* (fig.) clase, índole, especie, *f.;* temperamento, *m.;* — **bean,** judía.

kill [kil] *vt.* matar, asesinar.

killer [ki-lar] *n.* matador, asesino, na, criminal, *m.* y *f.*

killing [ki-lin] *n.* matanza, *f.*

kiln [kiln] *n.* horno, *m.;* **brick** —, horno de ladrillo.

kilogram [ki-lou-gram] *n.* kilogramo, *m.*

kilometer [ki-lou-mi-tar] *n.* kilómetro, *m.*

kilometric [ki-lou-me-trik] *adj.* kilométrico.

kiloton [ki-lou-tan] *n.* kilotonelada, *f.,* kilotón, *m.*

kilowatt [ki-lou-uat] *n.* kilovatio, *m.;* — **hour,** kilovatio-hora, *m.*

kin [kin] *n.* parentesco, *m.;* afinidad, *f.;* **next of** —, pariente más cercano.

kind [kaind] *adj.* benévolo, benigno, bondadoso, afable, cariñoso; —, *n.* género, *m.;* clase, *f.;* especie, naturaleza, *f.;* manera, *f.;* tenor, *m.;* calidad, *f.*

kindergarten [kin-da-gar-ten] *n.* escuela de párvulos; jardín de la infancia.

kindhearted [kaind-jardid] *adj.* bondadoso.

kindle [kin-del] *vt.* y *vi.* encender; arder.

kindliness [kaind-li-nes] *n.* benevolencia, benignidad, *f.*

kindly [kain-dli] *adj.* blando,

suave, tratable; —, *adv.* benig-
namente; bondadosamente.

kindness [kaind-nes] *n.* benevolencia, *f.;* favor, beneficio, *m.;*
have the — to, tenga la bondad
de.

kindred [kain-drid] *n.* parentesco, *m.;* parentela, casta, *f.;* —,
adj. emparentado; parecido.

kinescope [ki-nes-koup] *n.* (TV.)
cinescopio, *m.*

kinetics [ki-ne-tik] *n.* cinética, *f.*

king [king] *n.* rey, *m.;* rey o
doble dama (en el juego de
damas); **—ly,** *adv.* regiamente;
—ly, *adj.* real, suntuoso.

kingdom [king-dom] *n.* reino, *m.*

kingfisher [king-fi-shar] *n.* (orn.)
martín pescador.

king-size [king-sais] *adj.* de
tamaño regio.

kink [kink] *n.* retorcimiento o
ensortijamiento de pelo, alambre, hilo, etc.; peculiaridad, *f.*

kinsfolk [kins-fouk] *n.* parientes,
m. pl.

kinship [kin-ship] *n.* parentela,
f.

kinsman [kins-man] *n.* pariente,
m.

kinswoman [kins-uo-man] *n.*
parienta, *f.*

kiss [kis] *n.* beso, ósculo, *m.;* —,
vt. besar.

kissing [ki-sin] *n.* acción de
besar, besuqueo, *m.*

kit [kit] *n.* estuche, *m.;* **first-aid**
—, botiquín, *m.;* **sewing —,**
costurero, *m.,* estuche de costura.

kitchen [ki-chen] *n.* cocina, *f.;* **—**
police, soldados que asisten en
el trabajo de cocina; trabajo de
cocina en un campamento militar; **— range,** estufa, *f.,* cocina
económica; **— utensils,** trastos,
m. pl. , batería de cocina.

kitchenette [ki-chi-net] *n.* cocina
pequeña.

kite [kait] *n. (orn.)* milano, *m.;*
cometa, birlocha, pandorga, *f.;*
(Mex.) papalote, *m.*

kitten [ki-ten] *n.* gatito, ta; **—,**
vi. parir (la gata).

kitty [ki-ti] *n.* gatito.

knack [nak] *n.* maña, destreza,
f.

knapsack [nap-sak] *n.* mochila,
f.

knead [nid] *vt.* amasar.

knee [ni] *n.* rodilla, *f.;* **— bone,**
rótula, *f.*

kneel [nil] *vi.* arrodillarse, hincar
la rodilla, postrarse.

kneepad [ni-pad] *n.* cojincillo
para las rodillas.

knickerbockers, knickers [ni-ka-
bo-kar], [ni-kars] *n. pl.* calzones cortos, pantalones, *m. pl. ;*
bragas, *f. pl.*

knife [naif] *n.* cuchillo, *m.*

knight [nait] *n.* caballero, paladín, *m.;* — **(in chess),** caballo (en el ajedrez), *m.;* —, *vt.* crear a uno caballero.

knighthood [nait-jud] *n.* caballería, dignidad de caballero.

knit [nit] *vt.* y *vi.* enlazar; atar, unir; trabajar a punto de aguja, tejer.

knitting [ni-tin] *n.* trabajo de punto, tejido con agujas.

knives [naivs] *n. pl.* de **knife,** cuchillos, *m. pl.*

knob [nob] *n.* protuberancia, *f.;* perilla, *f.;* nudo en la madera.

knock [nok] *vt.* y vi. chocar; golpear, tocar; pegar; **to — down,** derribar, tumbar; **to — on the door,** llamar a la puerta; —, *n.* golpe, *m.;* llamada, *f.*

knot [not] *n.* nudo, *m.;* lazo, *m.;* maraña, *f.;* atadura, *f.;* dificultad, *f.;* —, *vt.* enredar, juntar, anudar.

knotted [no-tid] *adj.* nudoso.

know [nou] *vt.* y *vi.* conocer, saber; tener noticia de; **I — positively,** me consta; **to — a thing perfectly,** saber una cosa al dedillo.

know-how [nou-jau] *n.* experiencia y habilidad técnicas.

knowing [nouin] *adj.* instruido, inteligente, entendido, sabedor; **—ly,** *adv.* hábilmente; a sabiendas.

know-it-all [nou-it-ol] *n.* sabelotodo, *m.*

knowledge [no-lich] *n.* conocimiento, saber, *m.;* ciencia, *f.;* inteligencia, habilidad, *f.*

known [naun] *adj.* conocido, sabido.

knuckle [na-kel] *n.* coyuntura, *f.,* nudillo, *m.;* jarrete de ternera.

Korean [ko-ran] *n.* y *adj.* coreano, na.

L

label [lei-bol] *n.* esquela, *f.;* marbete, billete, *m.;* etiqueta, *f.*

labor [lei-bar] *n.* trabajo, *m.;* labor, *f.;* fatiga, *f.;* mano de obra; **hard —,** trabajos forzados; **L— Day,** Día del Trabajo; **— union,** gremio o sindicato obrero; **to be in —,** estar de

parto; —, *vt.* y *vi.* trabajar; afanarse, estar con dolores de parto.

laboratory [la-bo-ra-to-ri] *n.* laboratorio, *m.;* gabinete, *m.*

laborer [lei-ba-rar] *n.* labrador, trabajador, obrero, *m.;* **day —,** jornalero, *m.*

laborious [lei-ba-rios] *adj.* laborioso; difícil.

labyrinth [la-be-rinz] *n.* laberinto, dédalo, *m.*

lace [leis] *n.* lazo, cordón, *m.;* **shoe —,** agujeta, *f.,* cordón de zapato; **— trimming,** adorno de encaje, randa, *f.*

lack [lak] *vt.* y *vi.* carecer, necesitar; faltar algo; **—,** *n.* falta, carencia, *f.;* necesidad, *f.*

lacking [la-kin] *adj.* falto; **to be —,** hacer falta.

lacquer [la-kar] *n.* laca, *f.;* charol, barniz, *m.;* **—,** *vt.* charolar.

lactic [lak-tik] *adj.* lácteo; **— acid,** ácido lácteo.

ladder [la-dar] *n.* escalera portátil.

laden [lei-den] *adj.* cargado; oprimido.

ladle [lei-del] *n.* cucharón, cazo, *m.;* achicador, *m.*

lady [lei-di] *n.* señora, señorita, dama, *f.*

lag [lag] *vi.* moverse lentamente; quedarse atrás, rezagarse.

lagoon [la-gun] *n.* laguna, *f.*

laid [leid] *pretérito* y *p.p.* del verbo **lay.**

lain [lein] *p.p.* del verbo **lie** (yacer, acostarse).

lair [lear] *n.* cubil, *m.*

laity [lei-ti] *n.* estado seglar.

lake [leik] *n.* lago, *m.;* laguna, *f.*

lamb [lam] *n.* cordero, *m.;* carne de cordero.

lame [leim] *adj.* estropeado; cojo; imperfecto; **—,** *vt.* estropear.

lameness [leim-nes] *n.* cojera, *f.;* imperfección, *f.*

lament [la-ment] *vt.* lamentar; **—,** *vi.* lamentarse; **—,** *n.* lamento, *m.*

lamentable [la-men-ta-bol] *adj.* lamentable, deplorable, desconsolador.

lamp [lamp] *n.* lámpara, *f.;* **electric —,** lámpara eléctrica; **— shade,** pantalla, *f.*

lamplight [lamp-lait] *n.* luz de lámpara.

lampoon [lam-pun] *n.* sátira, *f.;* libelo, *m.;* **—,** *vt.* escribir sátiras.

lamppost [lam-poust] *n.* pie de farol, poste de farola.

lance [lans] *n.* lanza, *f.;* lanceta, *f.;* **—,** *vt.* dar un lancetazo; abrir, cortar, perforar; hacer una operación quirúrgica con lanceta.

land [land] *n.* país, *m.;* región, *f.;* territorio, *m.;* tierra, *f.;* **— forces,** tropas de tierra; **— mine,** mina terrestre; **—,** *vt.* y *vi.* desembarcar; saltar en tierra, aterrizar.

landholder [land-joul-dar] *n.* hacendado, *m.*

landing [lan-din] *n.* desembarco,

m.; aterrizaje, *m.;* **emergency — field,** (avi.) campo de emergencia; **— field,** campo de aterrizaje; **— gear,** tren de aterrizaje.

landlady [land-lei-di] *n.* propietaria, arrendadora, *f.;* mesonera, *f.;* posadera, *f.;* casera, *f.*

landlord [land-lord] *n.* propietario, *m.;* posadero, *m.;* casero, *m.*

landowner [land-ou-nar] *n.* hacendado, *m.*

landscape [land-skeip] *n.* paisaje, *m.;* **— gardener,** persona que proyecta y construye jardines o parques; **— gardening,** jardinería, *f.*

landslide [land-slaid] *n.* derrumbe, desprendimiento de tierra; (pol.) mayoría de votos abrumadora.

lane [lein] *n.* callejuela, calle, *f.;* vereda, *f.;* **traffic —,** zona de tránsito.

language [lan-güich] *n.* lengua, *f.;* lenguaje, idioma, *m.*

languid [lan-güid] *adj.* lánguido, débil.

languish [lan-güish] *vi.* entristecerse, afligirse, languidecer.

languishing [lan-güi-shin] *adj.* lánguido.

languor [lan-gor] *n.* languidez, *f.*

lanolin, lanoline [la-nou-lin], [la-nou-lain] *n.* lanolina, *f.*

lantern [lan-tern] *n.* linterna, *f.;* farol, *m.;* **— slide,** diapositiva, *f.;* fotografía positiva.

lap [lap] *n.* falda, *f;* seno, *m.;* regazo, *m.;* (deportes) vuelta, etapa, *f* **—,** *vt.* arrollar, envolver; traslapar, sobreponer; lamer.

lapel [la-pel] *n.* solapa, *f.*

Laplander [lap-lan-dar] *n.* lapón, ona.

lapse [laps] *n.* lapso, *m.;* caída, *f.;* falta ligera; traslación de derecho o dominio; **—,** *vi.* escurrir, manar; deslizarse; caer; caducar; vencerse (un plazo, etc.).

laptop [lap-top] *n.* laptop, *m.*

lard [lard] *n.* manteca, *f.;* lardo, *m.;* gordo, *m.*

larder [lar-dar] *n.* despensa, *f.*

large [larch] *adj.* grande, amplio, vasto; liberal; **at —,** en libertad, suelto; **— type,** tipo de cartel; **—ly,** *adv.* en gran parte.

large-scale [larch-skeil] *adj.* en gran escala.

lark [lark] *n.* (orn.) alondra, *f.*

larkspur [lark-sper] *n.* (bot.) espuela de caballero.

larva [lar-va] *n.* larva, oruga, *f.*

laryngitis [la-rin-yai-tis] *n.* laringitis, *f.*

larynx [la-rinks] *n.* laringe, *f.*

lash [lash] *m.;* sarcasmo, *m.;* **—,** *vt.* azotar; atar; satirizar.

lassitude [la-si-tiud] *n.* lasitud, fatiga, *f.*

lasso [la-su] *n.* lazo, *m.*, reata, *f.*

last [last] *adj.* último, postrero, pasado; — **night,** anoche; — **word,** decisión final; última moda; la última palabra; lo mejor; algo que no se puede mejorar; —**ly,** *adv.* al fin; por último; —, *n.* horma de zapatero; (naut.) carga de un navío; **at** —, al fin, al cabo, por último; —, *vi.* durar, subsistir.

lasting [las-tin] *adj.* duradero, permanente; —**ly,** *adv.* perpetuamente.

latch [lach] *n.* aldaba (de puerta), *f.*; cerrojo, *m.*; —, *vt.* cerrar con aldaba.

late [leit] *adj.* tardío; tardo, lento; difunto; último; — *adv.* tarde; **of** —, de poco tiempo acá; —**ly,** *adv.* poco ha, recientemente.

lateness [leit-nes] *n.* retraso, *m.*, tardanza, *f.*

latent [lei-tant] *adj.* escondido, oculto, latente.

later [lei-tar] *adj.* posterior; —, *adv.* más tarde.

lateral [la-te-ral] *adj.* lateral; —**ly,** *adv.* lateralmente.

latest [lei-tist] *adj.* último; más reciente; — **fashion,** última moda; **at the** —, a más tardar.

latex [lei-teks] *n.* (bot.) látex, *m.*

lather [lei-dar] *n.* espuma de jabón, jabonaduras, *f. pl.* ; —, *vt.* y *vi.* lavar con espuma de jabón; espumar.

Latin [la-tin] *n.* latín (lenguaje), *m.*; —, *n.* y *adj.* latino, na.

Latin-American [la-tin-a-me-ri-kan] *n.* latinoamericano, na.

latitude [la-ti-tiud] *n.* latitud, *f.*

latrine [la-trin] *n.* letrina, *f.*

latter [la-tar] *adj.* posterior, último; **the** —, éste, el último.

lattice [la-tis] *n.* celosía, *f.*; reja, *f.*; enrejado, *m.*; —, *vt.* enrejar.

laudable [lo-da-bol] *adj.* laudable, loable; meritorio.

laudatory [lo-da-to-ri] *adj.* laudatorio.

laugh [laf] *vi.* reir; — **at,** reírse de, burlarse de; —, *n.* risa, risotada, *f.*

laughing [la-fin] *adj.* risueño; — **gas,** óxido nitroso; —, *n.* risa, *f.*; **to burst out** —, soltar una carcajada; —**ly,** *adv.* con risa.

laughter [laf-tar] *n.* risa, risotada; *f.*; **hearty** —, carcajada, *f.*; **outburst of** —, risotada, *f.*

launch [lonch] *vt.* lanzar; —, *vi.* lanzarse; —, *n.* (naut.) lancha, *f.*

launching *n.* (avi.) lanzamiento, *m.*; —, **pad,** plataforma de lanzamiento.

launder [lon-dar] *vt.* lavar (la ropa).

laundromat [lon-dro-mat] *n.* lavandería de auto servicio.

laundry [lon-dri] *n.* lavandería, *f.;* ropa lavada o para lavar.

laurel [lo-rel] *n.* (bot.) lauro, laurel, *m.;* honor, *m.,* fama, *f.*

lava [la-va] *n.* lava, *f.*

lavatory [la-va-to-ri] *n.* lavabo, lavatorio, *m.*

lavender [la-vin-dar] *n.* (bot.) espliego, *m.;* lavándula, *f.;* cantueso, *m.;* —, *adj.* lila.

lavish [la-vish] *adj.* pródigo; gastador; —, *vt.* disipar, prodigar.

law [lo] *n.* ley, *f.;* derecho, *m.;* litigio judicial; jurisprudencia, *f.;* regla, *f.;* **according to —,** procedente, de acuerdo con la ley.

lawbreaker [lo-brei-kar] *n.* delincuente, *m.* y *f.;* trasgresor, ra, persona que infringe la ley.

lawful [lo-ful] *adj.* legal; legítimo.

lawless [lo-les] *adj.* ilegal; anárquico, sin ley.

lawlessness [lo-les-nes] *n.* desobediencia o trasgresión de la ley; ilegalidad, *f.;* desorden, *m.*

lawn [lon] *n.* prado, *m.;* linón, *m.;* césped, *m.;* **— mower,** segadora de césped, corta-césped, *f.*

lawsuit [lo-sut] *n.* proceso, pleito, *m.;* demanda, *f.*

lawyer [lo-yar] *n.* abogado, licenciado, *m.;* jurisconsulto, *m.;* **—**

's office, bufete de abogado.

lax [laks] *adj.* laxo, flojo.

laxative [lak-sa-tiv] *n.* y *adj.* purgante, laxante, *m.*

laxity [lak-si-ti] *n.* laxitud, flojedad, *f.;* relajación, *f.*

lay [lei] *vt.* poner, colocar, extender; calmar, sosegar; imputar; apostar; exhibir; poner (un huevo); **to — claim,** reclamar; pretender; —, *vi.* aovar, poner huevos las aves; —, *pret.* del verbo **lie** (echarse, recostarse).

lay [lei] *adj.* laico, secular, seglar; **— brother,** lego, *m.;* —, *n.* canción, melodía, *f.;* **— of the land,** forma del tendido del terreno o suelo; consideración de la disposición o circunstancia; estado de asuntos.

layer [leiar] *n.* gallina que pone; capa, *f.*

layoff [lei-of] *n.* despedida del trabajo; —, *vt.* despedir del trabajo.

layout [lei-aut] *n.* plan, trazado, esquema, arreglo, *m.;* disposición, distribución, *f.*

laziness [lei-si-nes] *n.* pereza, *f.*

lazy [lei-si] *adj.* perezoso, tardo, pesado.

lead [lid] *vt.* conducir, guiar; gobernar; llevar la batuta; —, *vi.* mandar, tener el mando; ser mano (en el juego de naipes); sobresalir, ser el primero; —, *n.* delantera, *f.;* mano (en los naipes); **to take the —,** tomar la delantera.

lead [lid] *n.* plomo, *m.;* **— pencil,** lápiz, *m.;* **molten —,** plomo derretido.

leaden [le-den] *adj.* hecho de plomo; pesado, estúpido.

leader [li-dar] *n.* líder, guía, conductor, *m.;* jefe general; caudillo, *m.;* **political —,** cacique, *m.*

leadership [li-da-ship] *n.* capacidad dirigente.

leading [li-din] *adj.* principal; capital; **— article,** artículo de fondo de una publicación; **— man, — lady** (theat.) primer actor, primera actriz.

leaf [lif] *n.* folio, *m.;* hoja (de una planta); hoja (de un libro); hoja (de puerta), *f.;* (bot.) fronda, *f.*

leafless *adj.* deshojado, sin hojas.

league [lig] *n.* liga, alianza, *f.;* legua, *f.;* **—,** *vi.* confederarse.

leak [lik] *n.* fuga, *f ;* salida o escape (de gas, líquido, etc.); goteo, *m.;* gotera, *f.;* (naut.) vía de agua; **—,** *vi.* (naut.) hacer agua; gotear, salirse o escaparse (el agua, gas, etc.).

leakage [li-keich] *n.* derrame, escape, goteo, *m.;* merma, *f.;* filtración, *f.;* gotera, fuga, *f.*

leakproof [lik-pruf] *adj.* libre de goteo; a prueba de escape.

leaky [li-ki] *adj.* agujereado, que se gotea.

lean [lin] *vt.* y *vi.* ladear, inclinar, apoyarse; **to — back,** recostarse; **—,** *adj.* magro, seco, chupado.

leaning [li-nin] *n.* ladeo, *m.;* inclinación, tendencia, *f.*

leap [lip] *vi.* saltar, brincar; salir con ímpetu; palpitar; dar brincos; **—,** *n.* salto, *m.;* **— year,** año bisiesto o intercalar.

learn [lern] *vt.* y *vi.* aprender, conocer.

learned [ler-nid] *adj.* docto, instruido.

learning [ler-nin] *n.* literatura, ciencia, erudición, *f.;* saber, *m.;* letras, *f. pl.*

lease [lis] *n.* arriendo, arrendamiento, *m.;* contrato de arrendamiento; **—,** *vt.* arrendar.

leash [lish] *n.* correa, traílla, *f.;* **—,** *vt.* atar con correa.

least [list] *adj.* mínimo; **—,** *adv.* en el grado mínimo; **at —,** a lo menos; **not in the —,** ni en lo más mínimo; **the — posible,** lo menos posible.

leather [le-dar] *n.* cuero, pellejo, *m.*

leave [liv] *n.* licencia, *f.;* permiso, *m.;* des-pedida, *f.;* **— of absence,** licencia, *f.;* permiso para ausentarse; **by your —,** con su permiso; **to give —,** permitir; **to take —,** despedirse; **—,** *vt.* y *vi.* dejar, abandonar; ceder; cesar; salir.

leaves [livs] *n. pl.* de **leaf,** hojas, *f. pl.*

lecture [lek-char] *n.* conferencia, *f.;* corrección, *f.;* reprensión, *f.;* **—,** *vt.* enseñar; censurar, reprender.

ledge [ledch] *n.* capa, tonga, *f.;* borde, *m.;* re-borde, *m.;* anaquel, *m.*

ledger [led-char] *n.* (com.) libro mayor.

leech [lich] *n.* sanguijuela, *f.*

leeway [li-uei] *n.* desviación, *f.;* libertad, *f.;* margen, *m.;* (naut.) deriva, *f.*

left [left] *adj.* siniestro, izquierdo; **— winger,** izquierdista, *m.* y *f.;* **— behind,** rezagado; **—,** *n.* izquierda, *f.;* (pol.) izquierda, *f.;* **on the —,** a la izquierda.

left-handed [left-jandid] *adj.* zurdo; desmañado; insincero, malicioso.

leftist [lef-tist] *n.* y *adj.* (pol.) izquierdista, *m.* y *f.* leftover, *n.* sobrante, *m.;* lo que queda por hacer; sobras, *f. pl.,* restos, *m. pl.*

leg [leg] *n.* pierna, *f.;* pie, *m.;* (math.) cateto, *m.*

legacy [le-ga-si] *n.* legado, *m.,* manda, *f.*

legal [li-gal] *adj.* legal, legítimo; **— tender,** moneda legal; curso legal.

legality [li-ga-li-ti] *n.* legalidad, legitimidad, *f.*

legalize [li-ga-lais] *vt.* legalizar, autorizar.

legend [le-yend] *n.* leyenda, *f.*

legendary [le-yen-da-ri] *adj.* fabuloso, quijotesco, legendario.

legibility [le-yi-bi-li-ti] *n.* legibilidad, *f.*

legible [le-yi-bol] *adj.* legible, que puede leerse.

legion [li-yon] *n.* legión, *f.*

legislate [le-yis-leit] *vt.* legislar.

legislation [le-yis-lei-shon] *n.* legislación, *f.*

legislative [le-yis-la-tiv] *adj.* legislativo.

legislature [le-yis-lei-char] *n.* legislatura, *f.;* cuerpo legislativo.

legitimate [li-yi-ti-meit] *adj.* legítimo; **—,** *vt.* legitimar.

leisure [le-shar] *n.* desocupación, *f.;* ocio, *m.;* comodidad, *f.;* **at —,** cómodamente, con sosiego; **— hours,** horas o ratos libres.

lemon [le-mon] *n.* limón, *m.;* **— drop,** pastilla de limón; **— squeezer,** exprimidor de limones.

lemonade [le-mo-neid] *n.* limonada, *f.*

lend [lend] *vt.* prestar, dar prestado.

lender [len-dar] *n.* prestamista, *m.* y *f.*, prestador, ra.

length [lengz] *n.* longitud, *f.*; largo, *m.*; duración, *f.*; distancia, *f.*; **at —,** finalmente; largamente.

lengthen [len-zen] *vt.* alargar; —, *vi.* alargarse, dilatarse.

lengthwise [lengz-uais] *adv.* longitudinalmente, a lo largo; —, *adj.* colocado a lo largo.

lengthy [leng-zi] *adj.* largo; fastidioso.

leniency [le-nien-si] *n.* benignidad, lenidad, *f.*

lenient [li-niant] *adj.* lenitivo, indulgente.

lens [lens] *n.* lente (vidrio convexo), *m.* y *f.*

lent [lent] *n.* cuaresma, *f.*

lentil [len-til] *n.* (bot.) lenteja, *f.*

leopard [le-pard] *n.* (zool.) leopardo, pardal, *m.* leper, *n.* leproso, sa.

lesion [li-shon] *n.* lesión, *f.*

less [les] *adj.* inferior, menos; —, *adv.* menos.

lessen [le-sen] *vt.* minorar, disminuir; —, *vi.* disminuirse.

lesser [le-sar] *adj.* más pequeño; inferior.

lesson [le-son] *n.* lección, *f.*

let [let] *vt.* dejar, permitir; arren-

dar; **—'s see,** a ver; **—'s go,** vámonos.

letdown [let-daun] *n.* aflojamiento, *m.*; relajación, *f.*; (coll.) decepción, *f.*; desanimación, *f.*

lethal [li-zal] *adj.* letal.

lethargy [le-tar-yi] *n.* letargo, estupor, *m.*

letter [le-tar] *n.* letra, *f.*; carta, *f.*; **air mail —,** carta aérea; **capital —,** mayúscula, *f.*

lettuce [le-tis] *n.* lechuga, *f.*

leucocyte [lu-ko-sait] *n.* (anat.) leucocito, *m.*

level [le-vel] *adj.* llano, igual; nivelado, plano; allanado; —, *n.* llanura, *f.*; plano, *m.*; nivel, *m.*; —, *vt.* allanar; nivelar.

levelheaded [le-vel-je-did] *adj.* discreto, sensato.

leveling [lev-lin] *n.* igualación, nivelación, *f.*; —, *adj.* nivelador.

lever [le-var] *n.* palanca, *f.*; **clutch —,** palanca, *f.*; **firing —,** palanca de desenganche; **operating —, driving —,** palanca de impulsión; **reverse —,** palanca de cambio de marcha.

leverage [le-va-reich] *n.* acción de palanca.

lewd [lud] *adj.* lascivo, disoluto, libidinoso.

lexicon [lek-si-kon] *n.* léxico, diccionario, *m.*

liability [laia-bi-li-ti] *n.* responsabilidad, *f.*; **—les,** (corn.) pasivo, *m.*, créditos pasivos.

liable [laia-bol] *adj.* sujeto, expuesto a; responsable; capaz.

liaison [li-ei-son] *n.* vinculación, coordinación, *f.*

liar [laiar] *n.* embustero, ra, mentiroso, sa.

libel [lai-bol] *n.* libelo, *m.; —, vt.* difamar.

libelous, libellous [lai-be-las] *adj.* difamatorio.

liberal [li-be-ral] *adj.* liberal, generoso; franco; —, *n.* persona de ideas liberales; miembro del Partido Liberal; — **arts,** artes liberales; —**ly,** *adv.* a manos llenas.

liberalism [li-be-ra-li-sem] *n.* liberalismo, *m.*

liberal-minded [li-be-ral-main-did] *adj.* tolerante, de ideas liberales.

liberate [li-be-reit] *vt.* libertar.

liberation [li-be-rei-shon] *n.* liberación, *f.*

liberator [li-be-rei-tar] *n.* libertador, *m.*

liberty [li-ber-ti] *n.* libertad, *f.;* privilegio, *m.;* **to take the — to,** permitirse, tomarse la libertad.

librarian [lai-brea-rian] *n.* bibliotecario, ria.

library [lai-bra-ri] *n.* biblioteca, *f.*

lice [lais] *n. pl.* de louse, piojos.

license, licence [lai-sens] *n.*

licencia, *f.;* permiso, *m.;* **driver's —,** licencia para manejar; — **plate,** placa, *f.*

lick [lik] *vt.* lamer, chupar; (coll.) golpear, tundir; derrotar (en una pelea, etc.).

licking [li-kin] *n.* paliza, *f.*

lid [lid] *n.* tapa, *f.;* tapadera, *f.;* — **(of the eye),** párpado, *m.*

lie [lai] *n.* mentira, *f.;* (coll.) trápala, *f.; —, vi.* mentir; echarse; reposar, acostarse; yacer.

lied [laid] *pret.* del verbo **lie** (mentir).

lieu [lu] *n.* lugar, *m.;* **in — of,** en vez de.

lieutenant [lef-te-nant] *n.* lugarteniente, teniente, *m.;* alférez, *m.;* — **commander,** capitán de corbeta; — **colonel,** teniente coronel; — **general,** teniente general; **second —,** subteniente, *m.*

life [laif] *n.* vida, *f.;* ser, *m.;* vivacidad, *f.;* **for —,** por toda la vida; **from —,** del natural; **high —,** el gran mundo; — **belt,** cinturón salvavidas; — **buoy,** boya, *f.;* — **insurance,** seguro de vida; — **preserver,** salvavidas, *m.;* — **raft,** balsa salvavidas.

lifeboat [laif-bout] *n.* bote salvavidas; lancha salvavidas.

lifeguard [laif-gard] *n.* salvavidas, guardavidas (nadador), *m.*

lifeless [laif-les] *adj.* muerto, inanimado; sin vivacidad.

lifelike [laif-laik] *adj.* natural, que parece vivo.

lifelong [laif-long] *adj.* de toda la vida, que dura toda la vida.

lifesaver [laif-sei-var] *n.* salvavidas, *m.*, miembro del servicio de salvavidas.

life-size [laif-sais] *adj.* de tamaño natural.

lifetime [laif-taim] *n.* duración de la vida; —, *adj.* de por vida, que dura toda la vida.

lift [lift] *vt.* alzar, elevar, levantar; hurtar, robar; —, *n.* acción de levantar, alza, *f.*; ayuda, *f.*; ascensor (hidráulico), *m.*

lifting [lif-tin] *n.* izamiento, *m.*, acción de levantar.

ligament [li-ga-ment] *n.* ligamento, *m.*

light [lait] *n.* luz, *f.*; claridad, *f.*; conocimiento, *m.*; día, *m.*; reflejo, *m.*; candela, *f.*; resplandor, *m.*; — **bulb,** foco, *m.*, bombilla, *f.*; —, *adj.* ligero, leve, fácil; frívolo; superficial; ágil; inconstante; claro; blondo; —, *vt.* encender; alumbrar; —, *vi.* hallar, encontrar; desmontarse; desembarcar.

lighten [lai-ten] *vi.* centellear como relámpago, brillar; aclarar; —, *vt.* iluminar; aligerar; aclarar.

lighter [lai-tar] *n.* encendedor, *m.*; **cigarette** —, encendedor de cigarrillos, mechero, *m.*

lighthearted [lait-jar-tid] *adj.* despreocupado; alegre.

lighthouse [lait-jaus] *n.* (naut.) faro, fanal, *m.*

lighting [lai-tin] *n.* iluminación, *f.*

lightly [lait-li] *adv.* levemente; alegremente; ágilmente.

lightness [lait-nes] *n.* ligereza, *f.*; agilidad, velocidad, *f.*

lightning [lait-nin] *n.* relámpago, *m.*; **heat** —, relámpago sin trueno; — **bug,** luciérnaga, *f.*; — **rod,** pararrayos, *m.*; —, *vi.* relampaguear.

lightweight [lait-ueit] *adj.* de peso ligero.

likable [lai-kabol] *adj.* simpático, agradable.

like [laik] *adj.* semejante; igual; verosímil; —, *n.* semejante, *m.*, parecido, *m.*; **to look** —, parecerse a; —, *prep.* como; —, *vt.* y *vi.* querer, amar; gustar, agradar alguna cosa; **as you** — **it,** como quiera usted; **to be** — **d,** caer en gracia; **to** — **someone,** tener simpatía por.

likelihood [laik-li-jud] *n.* probabilidad, *f.*; indicación, *f.*

likely [lai-ke-li] *adj.* probable, verosímil; —, *adv.* con toda probabilidad.

liken [lai-ken] *vt.* asemejar; comparar.

likeness [laik-nes] *n.* semejanza, *f.;* igualdad, *f.;* retrato fiel.

likewise [laik-uais] *adv.* igualmente, asimismo.

liking [lai-kin] *n.* gusto, agrado, *m.*

lilac [lai-lak] *n.* (bot.) lila, *f.;* —, *adj.* de color lila.

lily [li-li] *n.* lirio, *m.;* — **of the valley,** lirio de los valles, muguete, *m.*

limb [lim] *n.* miembro (del cuerpo), *m.;* pierna, *f.;* rama (de un árbol), *f.*

limber [lim-bar] *adj.* manejable, flexible; —, *vt.* y *vi.* poner manejable, hacer flexible.

lime [laim] *n.* cal, *f.;* variedad de limón; tilo, *m.,* tila, *f.*

limelight [lim-lait] *n.* centro de atención pública. limerick, *n.* verso jocoso.

limestone [lim-stoun] *n.* piedra de cal, caliza, *f.*

limit [li-mit] *n.* límite, término, *m.;* línea, *f.;* **to the** —, hasta no más; —, *vt.* restringir; concretar, confinar.

limitation [li-mi-tei-shon] *n.* limitación, *f.;* restricción, *f.;* coartación, *f.*

limited [li-mi-tid] *adj.* limitado.

limitless [li-mit-les] *adj.* inmenso, ilimitado, sin límite.

limousine [li-mou-sin] *n.* limosina, *f.*

limp [limp] *vi.* cojear; —, *n.* cojera, *f.;* —, *adj.* fláccido, flojo, blando.

limpid [lim-pid] *adj.* limpio, claro, trasparente; límpido.

line [lain] *n.* línea, *f.;* (mil.) línea de batalla; raya, *f.;* contorno, *m.;* cola, *f.;* ferrocarril, *m.;* vía, *f.;* renglón, *m.;* verso, *m.;* linaje, *m.;* cordón (muy delgado), *m.;* **pipe** —, cañería, *f.;* —, *vt.* forrar; revestir; rayar, trazar líneas; —, *vi.* alinearse.

lineage [lai-nich] *n.* linaje, *m.;* descendencia, *f.;* prosapia, *f.;* generación, *f.*

lineal, linear [lai-nial], [lai-niar] *adj.* lineal.

linen [lai-nin] *n.* lienzo, lino, *m.;* tela de hilo; ropa blanca; —, *adj.* de lino, de tela de hilo.

liner [lai-nar] *n.* avión o vapor de travesía.

linger [lin-gar] *vi.* demorarse, tardar, permanecer por un tiempo.

lingerie [lan-che-ri] *n.* ropa interior femenina, ropa íntima, *f.*

lingering [lin-che-rin] *n.* tardanza, dilación, *f.;* —, *adj.* moroso, lento.

linguist [lin-güist] *n.* lingüista, *m.* y *f.*

link [link] *n.* eslabón, *m.;* vínculo, *m.;* anillo de cadena; (mech.) articulación, *f.,* gozne, *m.; —, vt. y vi.* unir, vincular.

linnet [li-nit] *n.* (orn.) pardillo, pardal, *m.*

linoleum [lai-nou-liom] *n.* linóleo, *m.*

linseed [lin-sid] *n.* linaza, *f.; —* **oil,** aceite de linaza.

lint [lint] *n.* hilas, *f. pl.;* hilacha, *f.*

lintel [lin-tel] *n.* lintel o dintel de puerta o ventana.

lion [laion] *n.* león, *m.*

lioness [laio-nes] *n.* leona, *f.*

lip [lip] *n.* labio, *m.;* borde, *m.;* **— reading,** lectura por el movimiento de los labios.

lipstick [lip-stik] *n.* lápiz para los labios, lápiz labial.

liquefy [li-kui-fai] *vt. y vi.* licuar, liquidar; derretir.

liquid [li-kuid] *adj.* liquido; **— air,** aire fluido o líquido; **— fire,** fuego líquido; **— measure,** cántara, *f.,* medida para líquidos; —, *n.* licor, líquido, *m.*

liquidate [li-kui-deit] *vt.* liquidar.

liquidation [li-kui-dei-shon] *n.* (com.) liquidación, *f.*

liquor [li-kuor] *n.* licor, *m.*

Lisbon [lis-bon] Lisboa, *f.*

lisp [lisp] *vi.* balbucear; cecear; —, *n.* ceceo, *m.;* balbuceo, *m.*

list [list] *n.* lista, *f.;* elenco, *m.;* catálogo, *m.;* **— price,** precio de catálogo; —, *vt.* poner en lista; registrar; —, *vi.* (mil.) alistarse.

listen [li-sen] *vi.* escuchar, atender.

listener [lise-nar] *n.* escuchador, ra, oyente, *m. y f.*

listless [list-les] *adj.* indiferente, descuidado.

litany [li-ta-ni] *n.* letanía, *f.*

liter [lis-tar] *n.* litro, *m.*

literacy [li-te-ra-si] *n.* capacidad para leer y escribir.

literal [li-te-ral] *adj.* literal, al pie de la letra, a la letra; **—ly,** *adv.* literalmente.

literary [li-te-ra-ri] *adj.* literario.

literature [li-te-ra-char] *n.* literatura, *f.*

litigation [li-ti-guei-shon] *n.* litigio, pleito, *m.;* litigación, *f.*

litmus [lit-mus] *n.* (chem.) tornasol, *m.*

litter [li-tar] *n.* litéra, cama, *f.;* cama portátil; lechigada, ventregada, *f.; —, vt. y vi.* parir los animales; —, *vt.* desordenar.

little [li-tel] *adj.* pequeño; poco; chico; **a —,** poquito; **— boy,** chico, chiquito, *m.;* **— girl,** chica, chiquita, *f.;* **very —,** muy chico; muy poquito; —, *n.* poco, *m.;* parte pequeña.

liturgy [li-tar-yi] *n.* liturgia, *f.*

live [liv] *vi.* vivir; manifestarse; habitar.

live [laiv] *adj.* vivo; **— wire,** per-

sona lista o muy activa; alambre cargado.

livelihood [laiv-li-jud] *n.* vida, *f.;*
subsistencia, *f.*

liveliness [laiv-li-nes] *n.* vivacidad, *f.*

livelong [liv-long] *adj.* todo; **the
— day,** el día entero.

lively [laiv-li] *adj.* vivo, brioso;
gallardo; anima-do, alegre.

liver [lai-var] *n.* hígado, *m.*

liverwurst [lai-var-rost] *n.* salchicha de hígado.

lives [laivs] *n. pl.* de **life.**

livestock [laiv-stok] *n.* ganadería,
f.; ganado en pie. livid, *adj.* lívido; amoratado.

living [li-vin] *n.* modo de vivir;
subsistencia, *f.;* —, *adj.* vivo;
viviente; — **room,** sala de recibo; salón, *m.;* — **wage,** salario
adecuado para vivir.

lizard [li-zard] *n.* lagarto, *m.;*
lagartija, *f.*

llama [la-ma] *n.* (zool.) llama *f.*

load [loud] *vt.* cargar; llenar;
embarcar; —, *n.* carga, *f.;* cargamento, *m.;* peso, *m.;* — **of a
firearm,** carga (de una arma de
fuego), *f.*

loaf [louf] *n.* pan, bollo de pan,
m.; **meat** —, pan de carne.

loan [loun] *n.* préstamo, —
office, casa de préstamos; —,
vt. prestar.

loathe [loudz] *vt.* aborrecer,

detestar.

loathing [lou-zin] *n.* repugnancia, aversión, *f.*

loathsome [louz-sam] *adj.* detestable, repugnante.

loathly [lou-zi] *adj.* repugnante;
—, *adv.* de mala gana.

loaves [louvs] *n. pl.* de **loaf.**

lobby [lo-bi] *n.* vestíbulo, *m.;* —,
vi. cabildear.

lobe [loub] *n.* lóbulo, *m.*

lobster [lobs-tar] *n.* langosta, *f.*

local [lou-kal] *adj.* local; —, *n.*
(rail.) tren local.

localize [lou-ka-lais] *vt.* localizar.

locally [lou-ka-li] *adv.* localmen-
te.

locate [lou-keit] *vt.* ubicar, colocar, situar; localizar.

located [lou-kei-tid] *adj.* situado,
ubicado.

location [lou-kei-shon] *n.* ubicación, *f.;* localización, colocación, *f.*

lock [lok] *n.* cerradura, cerraja,
f.; llave (de arma de fuego), *f.;*
vedija (de lana), *f.;* mechón (de
cabello), *m.;* compuerta, *f.;*
spring —, cerradura de golpe o
de muelle; —, *vt.* cerrar, cerrar
con llave; **to — out,** cerrar la
puerta a uno para que no
entre; —, *vi.* cerrarse con llave.

locked [lokt] *adj.* cerrado (bajo
llave); encerrado; enganchado;
trabado, entrelazado.

locker [lo-kar] *n.* armario, *m.;* cofre, *m.;* gaveta, *f.* **locket,** *n.* medallón, guardapelo, *m.*

lockjaw [lok-yo] *n.* (med.) tétano, *m.*

locksmith [lok-smiz] *n.* cerrajero, llavero, *m*

locomotion [lou-ko-mou-shon] *n.* locomoción, *f.*

locomotive [lou-ko-mou-tiv] *n.* locomotora, *f.*

locust [lou-kost] *n.* langosta, *f.;* saltamontes, *m.*

lodge [lodch] *n.* casa de guarda en el bosque; casita pequeña; sucursal o casa de una sociedad; —, *vt.* alojar; depositar; presentar; —, *vi.* residir, habitar.

lodger [lod-char] *n.* huésped, *m.* y *f.,* inquilino, na.

lodging [lod-chin] *n.* posada, casa, habitación, *f.;* hospedaje, *m.*

loft [loft] *n.* desván, *m.;* pajar, *m.*

logarithm [lo-ga-ri-zem] *n.* logaritmo, *m.*

logic [lo-yik] *n.* lógica, *f.*

logical [lo-yi-kal] *adj.* lógico, consecuente.

logistics [lo-yis-tiks] *n.* (mil.) logística, *f.*

loin [loin] *n.* ijada, *f.;* ijar, *m.;* — s, *n. pl.* lomos, *m. pl.*

loiter [loi-tar] *vi.* haraganear, holgazanear.

loiterer [loi-ta-rar] *n.* haragán, ana, holgazán, ana.

lollipop [lo-li-pop] *n.* paleta, *f.*

London [lan-don] Londres, *m.*

lone [loun] *adj.* solitario, soltero.

loneliness [loun-li-nes] *n.* soledad, *f.*

lonely = [loun-li] **lonesome.**

lonesome *adj.* solitario, solo; triste, abatido por la soledad.

long [long] *adj.* largo, prolongado; **a — time,** mucho tiempo, un largo rato; —, *adv.* durante mucho tiempo.

long-distance [long-dis-tans] *adj.* de larga distancia; — **call,** llamada de larga distancia.

longer [lon-guer] *adj.* más largo; —, *adv.* más tiempo; **no —,** ya no, no más.

longevity [lon-ye-vi-ti] *n.* longevidad, *f.*

longing [lon-guin] *n.* deseo vehemente, anhelo, *m.*

longitude [lon-gui-tiud] *n.* longitud, *f.*

long-lived [long-livd] *adj.* longevo, muy anciano.

long-range [long-reinch] *adj.* de gran alcance.

long-standing [long-stan-din] *adj.* de larga duración.

look [luk] *vt.* y *vi.* mirar; ver; considerar, pensar, contemplar, esperar; parecer; tener cara de; **as it —s to me,** a mi ver; **— out!** ¡cuidado! **to — after,** echar una vista, cuidar de; **to — bad,** tener mala cara; verse mal; **to — for,** buscar; **to — well,** verse bien; **to — over,** repasar; **—,** n. aspecto, m.; mirada, f.; ojeada, f.

lookout [luk-aut] n. (mil.) centinela, m. y f.; (naut.) vigía, m.

loom [lum] n. telar, m.; **—,** vi. destacarse, descollar; perfilarse; (fig.) amenazar.

loony [lu-ni] adj. (coll.) loco.

loop [lup] n. ojal, m.; aro, anillo, m.; lazo, m.; vuelta, f.

loophole [lup-joul] n. tronera, buhedera, f.; evasiva.

loose [lus] adj. suelto, desatado, holgado, flojo; suelto de vientre; vago, relajado; disoluto; desenredado; **—ly,** adv. sueltamente; **—ly speaking,** en términos generales.

loosen [lu-sen] vt. aflojar, laxar; desliar, desatar.

looseness [lus-nes] n. flojedad, f.; relajación, f.; flujo de vientre.

loot [lut] n. pillaje, botín, m.; **—,** vt. pillar, saquear.

lord [lord] n. señor, m.; amo, dueño, m.; lord (título de nobleza inglés), m.; **—,** vi. señorear, dominar.

lordship [lord-ship] n. excelen-

cia, señoría, f.; dominio, m.; autoridad, f.

lore [lor] n. saber, m.; erudición, f.; conocimiento de hechos y costumbres tradicionales.

lose [lus] vt. perder; disipar, malgastar; **—,** vi. perderse, decaer; **to — face,** perder prestigio; **to — one's senses,** perder la chaveta; **to — one's temper, to — one's composure,** salirse de sus casillas; **to — one's way,** extraviarse, perder el camino; **to — out,** ser derrotado.

loser [lu-sar] n. perdedor, ra; **good —,** buen perdedor, buena perdedora.

loss [los] n. pérdida, f.; daño, m.; **to be at a —,** estar perplejo, estar en duda.

lot [lot] n. suerte, f; lote, m.; cuota, f.; porción, f.; **building —,** solar, m.; **to draw —s,** decidir por suerte, echar a suerte.

lotion [lou-shon] n. loción, f.

lottery [lo-te-ri] n. lotería, rifa, f.

lotus [lo-tus] n. (bot.) loto, m.

loud [laud] adj. ruidoso, alto; clamoroso; (coll.) charro, vulgar; **—ly,** adv. en voz alta.

loudness [laud-nes] n. ruido, m.; (coll.) vulgaridad, f., falta de delicadeza; mal gusto.

loudspeaker [laud-spi-kar] n. altoparlante, m.

lounge [launch] n. sofá, m.; **—**

room, sala de esparcimiento social, *f.;* salón social, *m.;* —, *vi.* holgazanear.

louse [laus] *n. (pl. lice),* piojo, *m.*

lousy [lau-si] *adj.* piojoso; miserable; vil; (coll.) horrible, detestable.

lovable [la-va-bol] *adj.* amable, digno de ser querido.

love [lav] *n.* amor, cariño, *m.;* galanteo, *m.;* —**game,** (tenis) juego a cero; **to fall in** —, enamorarse; **to make** —, cortejar, galantear, enamorar; —, *vt.* amar; gustar de; querer.

lovebird [lav-berd] *n.* (orn.) periquito, *m.*

loveliness [lav-li-nes] *n.* amabilidad, *f.;* agrado, *m.;* belleza, *f.*

lovely [lav-li] *adj.* amable, hermoso, bello.

lover [lo-var] *n.* amante, galán, *m.*

lovesick [lav-sik] *adj.* enamorado; herido de amor.

loving [la-vin] *adj.* amoroso, afectuoso.

low [lau] *adj.* bajo, pequeño; hondo; abatido; vil; —, *vi.* mugir; —, *adv.* a precio bajo; en posición baja.

lower [lauar] *adj.* más bajo; — **berth,** litera o cama baja; — **case,** (print.) caja baja, caja de minúsculas; —, *vt.* bajar, humillar; disminuir; **to** — **(price),**

rebajar (el precio); —, *vi.* disminuirse.

lowermost, lowest [laua-moust], [lau] *adj.* más bajo, ínfimo.

lowland [lau-land] *n.* tierra baja.

lowliness [lau-li-nes] *n.* bajeza, *f.;* humildad, *f.*

lowly [lau-li] *adj.* humilde; —, *adv.* modestamente.

low-pressure [lau-pre-shur] *adj.* de baja presión.

low-priced [lau-praisd] *adj.* barato.

low water [lau-ua-tar] *n.* bajamar, *f.*

loyal [loial] *adj.* leal, fiel; —**ly,** *adv.* lealmente.

loyalist [loia-list] *n.* (pol.) realista, *m.* y *f.*

loyalty [loial-ti] *n.* lealtad, fidelidad, *f.*

lube [liub] *n.* (mech.) aceite lubricante.

lubricant [lu-bri-kant] *n.* y *adj.* lubricante, *m.*

lubricate [lu-bri-keit] *vt.* lubricar, engrasar.

lubrication [lu-bri-kei-shon] *n.* lubricación, *f.*

lucid [lu-sid] *adj.* luciente, luminoso; claro.

luck [lak] *n.* acaso, *m.;* suerte, fortuna, *f.*

luckily [la-ki-li] *adv.* por fortuna, afortunadamente.

luckless [lak-les] *adj.* infeliz,

luxury

desventurado.

lucky [la-ki] *adj.* afortunado, feliz, venturoso, dichoso; **to be —**, tener suerte.

lucrative [lu-kra-tiv] *adj.* lucrativo.

ludicrous [lu-di-kros] *adj.* burlesco; ridículo.

luggage [la-guich] *n.* equipaje, *m.;* **carry-on—**, equipaje de mano, *m.;—* **rack,** porta-equipajes, *m.*

lukewarm [luk-uem] *adj.* tibio; templado.

lull [lal] *vt.* arrullar; adormecer; aquietar; **—**, *n.* pausa, *f.;* momento de calma.

lullaby [la-la-bai] *n.* arrullo, *m.;* canción de cuna.

lumber [lam-bar] *n.* madera de construcción.

lumberjack [lam-ba-yak] *n.* leñador, hachero, *m.*

lumberyard [lam-ba-yard] *n.* depósito de maderas de construcción.

luminous [lu-mi-nos] *adj.* luminoso, resplandeciente.

lump [lamp] *n.* protuberancia, *f.;* chichón, *m.;* **—**, *vt.* amontonar; **—**, *vi.* agrumarse.

lunacy [lu-na-si] *n.* locura, *f.;* frenesí, *m.*

lunatic [lu-na-tik] *adj.* lunático, loco, frenético; fantástico; **—**, *n.* loco, ca.

lunch [lanch] *n.* merienda, colación, *f.;* almuerzo, *m.;* **—**, *vi.* almorzar, merendar.

luncheon [lan-chion] *n.* almuerzo, *m.;* merienda, colación, *f.*

lung [lang] *n.* pulmón, *m.;* **iron —**, pulmón de acero.

lunge [lanch] *n.* embestida, estocada, *f.;* **—**, *vi.* embestir.

lurch [lerch] *n.* abandono, *m.;* vaivén, *m.;* (naut.) bandazo, *m.;* sacudida, *f.;* **—**, *vi.* dar bandazos; caminar con vaivén.

lure [liuar] *n.* señuelo, cebo, *m.;* **—**, *vt.* atraer, inducir.

lurid [liua-rid] *adj.* fantástico, lívido, descolorido.

lurk [lerk] *vi.* espiar, ponerse en acecho.

luscious [la-shos] *adj.* delicioso, sabroso; atractivo, apetitoso.

lush [lash] *adj.* jugoso; suculento.

lust [last] *n.* lujuria, sensualidad, *f.;* libídine, codicia, *f.;* concupiscencia, *f.;* **—**, *vi.* lujuriar.

luster, lustre [las-tar] *n.* lustre, *m.;* brillantez, *f.;* realce, *m.;* viso, *m.*

Lutheran [lu-ze-ran] *n.* y *adj.* luterano, na.

luxurious [lak-su-rios] *adj.* exuberante.

luxury [lak-su-ri] *n.* voluptuosidad, *f.;* exuberancia, *f.;* lujo, *m.*

lyceum [lai-siom] *n.* liceo, *m.*

lying [lai-in] *n.* mentir, *m.*, mentira, *f.;* —, *adj.* mentiroso; tendido, recostado.

lymph [limf] *n.* linfa, *f.*

lymphatic [lim-fa-tik] *adj.* linfático.

lynch [linch] *vt.* linchar.

lynx [links] *n.* lince, *m.*

lyric, lyrical [li-rik], [li-ri-kal] *adj.*

M

macadam [ma-ka-dam] *n.* macádam, *m.*

macaroni [ma-ka-rou-ni] *n.* macarrones, *m. pl.*

macaroon [ma-ka-run] *n.* almendrado, macarrón de almendras.

machination [ma-ki-nei-shon] *n.* maquinación, trama, *f.*

machine [ma-shin] *n.* máquina, *f.;* — gun, ametralladora, *f.;* — tool, herramienta de máquina.

machinery [ma-shi-ne-ri] *n.* maquinaria, mecánica, *f.*

machinist [ma-ki-nist] *n.* maquinista, mecánico, *m.*

mackerel [ma-ke-rel] *n.* (ichth.) escombro, *m.,* caballa, *f.;* (Sp. Am.) macarela, *f.*

mad [mad] *adj.* loco, furioso, rabioso, insensato; stark —, loco rematado; to go —, volverse loco.

madam, madame [ma-dam] *n.* madama, señora, *f.*

madden [ma-den] *vt.* enloquecer, trastornar; enfurecer.

made [meid] *adj.* hecho, fabrica-do, producido; —, *pret.* y *p.p.* del verbo make.

made-up [meid-ap] *adj.* ficticio; artificial; pintado.

madhouse [mad-jaus] *n.* casa de locos, manicomio, *m.*

madman [mad-man] *n.* loco, maniático, *m.*

madness [mad-nes] *n.* locura, manía, *f.;* furor, *m.*

magazine [ma-ga-sin] *n.* revista, *f ;* almacén, depósito, *m.;* (naut.) santabárbara, *f.*

maggot [ma-got] *n.* gusano, *m.;* noción fantástica.

magic [ma-yik] *n.* magia, nigromancia, *f.;* —, *adj.* mágico.

magician [ma-yi-shan] *n.* mago, nigromante, *m.* magistrate, *n.* magistrado, *m.*

magnate [mag-neit] *n.* magnate, *m.*

magnesia [mag-ni-sha] *n.* magnesia, *f.*

magnesium [mag-ni-sham] *n.* magnesio, *m.*

magnet [mag-nit] *n.* imán, *m.,*

piedra imán.

magnetic [mag-ne-ti-kal] *adj.* magnético; — **needle,** calamita, brújula, *f.*

magnetism [mag-ne-ti-sem] *n.* magnetismo, *m.*

magnificence [mag-ni-fi-sens] *n.* magnificencia, *f.*

magnificent [mag-ni-fi-sent] *adj.* magnífico.

magnify [mag-ni-fai] *vt.* amplificar, magnificar; exaltar, exagerar.

magnitude [mag-ni-tiud] *n.* magnitud, grandeza, *f.*

magnolia [mag-nou-lia] *n.* magnolia, *f.*

mahogany [ma-o-ga-ni] *n.* caoba, *f.*

maid [meid] *n.* doncella, joven, *f.;* moza, criada, *f.*

maiden [mei-den] *adj.* virgen, virginal; nuevo; — **name,** nombre de soltera; — **voyage,** primer viaje (de un barco); —, *n.* doncella, joven, *f.*

maidservant [meid-ser-vant] *n.* criada, sirvienta, *f.*

mail [meil] *n.* correo, *m.;* malla, armadura, *f.;* correspondencia, *f.;* cota de malla; **by registered** —, bajo sobre certificado, por correo certificado; **by return** —, a vuelta de correo.

mailbox [meil-boks] *n.* buzón, *m.*

mailman [meil-man] *n.* cartero, *m.*

maim [meim] *vt.* mutilar; estropear; tullir.

main [mein] *adj.* principal; esencial; — **office,** casa matriz; —, *n.* océano, *m.;* alta mar; fuerza, *f.;* **in the** —, en general; —**ly,** *adv.* principalmente, sobre todo.

mainland [mein-land] *n.* continente, *m.*

mainstay [mein-stei] *n.* (naut.) apoyo principal del mastelero; sostén principal; motivo principal.

maintain [mein-tein] *vt.* y *vi.* mantener, sostener; conservar.

maintenance [mein-ti-nans] *n.* mantenimiento, *m.;* protección, *f.;* sustento, *m.;* conservación (de carreteras, caminos, etc.), *f.*

maize [meis] *n.* maíz, *m.*

majestic, majestical [ma-yes-tik], [ma-yes-ti-kal] *adj.* majestuoso; grande; —**ally,** *adv.* majestuosamente.

majesty [ma-yes-ti] *n.* majestad, *f.*

major [mei-yor] *adj.* mayor; —, *n.* (mil.) mayor, *m.*, sargento mayor; (mil.) comandante, *m.;* primera proposición de un silogismo; — **general,** mariscal de campo.

majority [ma-yo-ri-ti] *n.* mayoría, *f.;* pluralidad, *f.;* — (of votes in an election), mayoría absoluta (en una elección).

make [meik] *vt.* hacer, crear, producir, fabricar; ejecutar; obligar; forzar; confeccionar; **to — for,** ir hacia, encaminarse a; **to — believe,** hacer ver, hacer de cuenta; **to — a fool of,** engañar; **to — a point of,** dar importancia a; **to — over,** hacer de nuevo; **to — ready,** preparar; **to — room,** hacer lugar; **to — use of,** servirse de, utilizar; **to — a show of,** ostentar; **to — fun of,** burlarse de; **to — known,** dar a conocer; **to — no difference,** no importar; **to — out,** divisar, columbrar; **to — up,** constituirse, componerse; inventar; contentarse, hacer las paces; maquillar; **—,** *n.* hechura, *f.;* forma, figura, *f.*

make-believe [meik-bi-liv] *n.* disimulo, *m.;* pretexto, *m.*

makeshift [meik-shift] *n.* expediente, medio, *m.;* **—,** *adj.* temporal; mal confeccionado, mal hecho.

makeup [meik-ap] *n.* maquillaje, tocado, *m.*

making [mei-kin] *n.* composición, *f.;* estructura, hechura, *f.*

maladjustment [mal-ad-yas-tid] *n.* mal ajuste; discordancia, *f.;* desequilibrio, *m.*

malady [ma-la-di] *n.* enferme-

dad, *f.*

malaria [ma-la-ria] *n.* malaria, *f.;* paludismo, *m.*

male [meil] *adj.* masculino; **—,** *n.* macho, *m.*

malefactor [ma-li-fak-tor] *n.* malhechor, *m.*

malevolent [ma-le-vo-lent] *adj.* malévolo.

malformed [mal-formd] *adj.* malhecho, contrahecho.

malice [ma-lis] *n.* malicia, *f.*

malicious [ma-li-shos] *adj.* malicioso.

malignant [ma-lig-nant] *adj.* maligno.

malignity [ma-lig-nant-li] *n.* malignidad, *f.*

mall [mol] *n.* plaza comercial, *f.;* centro comercial, *m.*

malnutrition [mal-niu-tri-shon] *n.* desnutrición, *f.*

malt [molt] *n.* malta, *f.,* cebada fermentada.

maltreat [mal-trit] *vt.* maltratar.

mamma, mama [ma-ma] *n.* mamá, *f.*

mammal [ma-mal] *n.* mamífero, *m.*

mammoth [ma-moz] *adj.* enorme, gigantesco; **—,** *n.* mamut, *m.*

man [man] *n.* hombre, *m.;* marido, *m.;* criado, peón, *m.;* **— overboard,** hombre al agua; **mechanical —,** autómata, *m.;*

young —, joven, *m.*; **—,** *vt.* (naut.) tripular, armar.

manage [ma-nich] *vt.* y *vi.* manejar, manipular, gobernar, administrar; dirigir; gestionar.

manageable [ma-ni-ya-bol] *adj.* manejable, dócil, tratable; dirigible.

manager [ma-ni-char] *n.* administrador, director, *m.*; gestor, *m.*; gerente, *m.*; **assistant —,** subgerente, *m.*

managing [ma-na-yin] *adj.* dirigente; gestor.

mandatory [man-da-to-ri] *adj.* obligatorio.

mane [mein] *n.* melena, *f.*; crines del caballo.

maneuver [ma-nu-var] *n.* maniobra, *f.*; **—,** *vt.* y *vi.* maniobrar.

manful [man-ful] *adj.* bravo, valiente.

manganese [man-ga-nis] *n.* manganeso, *m.*

manger [mein-char] *n.* pesebre, *m.*; nacimiento (de Navidad) .

manhandle [man-jan-del] *vt.* maltratar.

manhood [man-jud] *n.* virilidad, *f.*; edad viril; hombría, *f.*; valentía, *f.*; valor, *m.*

mania [mei-nia] *n.* manía, *f.*; tema, *m.*

maniac [mei-niak] *n.* y *adj.* maniático, ca.

manicure [ma-ni-kiuar] *n.* arre-

glo de las uñas; **—,** *vt.* arreglar las uñas.

manicurist [ma-ni-kiuarist] *n.* manicurista, *f.*

manifest [ma-ni-fest] *adj.* manifiesto, patente; **—,** *n.* manifiesto, *m.*; **—,** *vt.* manifestar.

manifestation [ma-ni-fes-teishon] *n.* manifestación, *f.*

manifesto [ma-ni-fes-tou] *n.* manifiesto, *m.*; declaración pública, proclamación, *f.*

manifold [ma-ni-fould] *adj.* muchos, varios, múltiple.

manikin [ma-ni-kin] *n.* maniquí, *m.*

manipulate [ma-ni-piu-leit] *vt.* manejar, manipular.

mankind [man-kaind] *n.* género humano, humanidad, *f.*

manliness [man-li-nes] *n.* valentía, *f.*, valor, *m.*

manly [man-li] *adj.* varonil, valeroso.

man-made [man-meid] *adj.* hecho por el hombre; **— satellite,** satélite artificial.

mannequin [ma-ni-kin] *n.* maniquí, *m.*

manner [ma-nar] *n.* manera, *f.*; modo, *m.*; forma, *f.*; método, *m.*; maña, *f.*; hábito, *m.*; moda, *f.*; especie, *f.*; vía, *f.*; **—s,** *n. pl.* modales, *m. pl.*, urbanidad, crianza, *f.*; **in such a —,** de tal modo; **in the — of,** a fuer de, en son de, a guisa de.

mannerism [ma-ne-ri-sem] *n.* amaneramiento, *m.*

manor [ma-nor] *n.* señorío, *m.;* feudo, *m.*

manpower [man-pauar] *n.* fuerza de trabajo, mano de obra; brazos, *m. pl.;* (mil.) elemento humano.

mansion [man-shon] *n.* casa grande, casa de gran lujo; solar, *m.*

manslaughter [man-slo-tar] *n.* homicidio (sin premeditación), *m.*

mantel, mantelpiece [man-tel], [man-tel-pis] *n.* repisa de chimenea.

mantle [man-tel] *n.* manto, *m.;* capa, *f.*

manual [ma-niual] *n.* manual, *m.;* —, *adj.* manual; — **training,** instrucción en artes y oficios.

manufacture [ma-nu-fak-char] *n.* manufactura, fabricación, *f.;* artefacto, *m.;* —, *vt.* fabricar, manufacturar, hacer.

manufacturer [ma-nu-fak-chu-rar] *n.* fabricante, manufacturero, *m.*

manure [ma-niuar] *n.* abono, estiércol, *m.;* —, *vt.* abonar, estercolar, cultivar.

manuscript [ma-nius-kript] *n.* manuscrito, escrito, *m.;* origi-

nal, *m.*

many [me-ni] *adj.* muchos, muchas; — **a time,** muchas veces; **how** —? ¿cuántos? **as** — **as,** tantos como.

map [map] *n.* mapa, *m.;* carta geográfica; — **maker,** cartógrafo, *m.;* —, *vt.* delinear mapas; trazar, hacer planes.

maple [ma-pel] *n.* arce, *m.;* — **syrup,** jarabe de arce.

mapping [ma-pin] *n.* cartografía, *f.*

mar [mar] *vt.* dañar, corromper; desfigurar.

marble [mar-bel] *n.* mármol, *m.;* canica, bolilla de mármol, bola, *f.;* —, *adj.* marmóreo, de mármol.

March [march] *n.* marzo, *m.*

mare [mear] *n.* yegua, *f.*

margarine [mar-ya-rin] *n.* margarina, *f.*

margin [mar-yin] *n.* margen, *m.* y *f.;* borde, *m.;* orilla, *f.;* —, *vt.* marginar.

marigold [ma-ri-gould] *n.* (bot.) caléndula, *f.*

marijuana, marihuana [ma-ri-jua-na] *n.* marijuana, marihuana, *f.*

marina [ma-ri-na] *n.* dársena para yates.

marine [ma-rin] *n.* marina, *f.;* soldado de marina; —, *adj.* marino.

marionette [ma-rio-net] *n.* (theat.) títere, muñeco, *m.*

marital [ma-ri-tal] *adj.* marital.

maritime [ma-ri-taim] *adj.* marítimo, naval.

mark [mark] *n.* marca, *f.;* señal, nota, *f.;* seña, *f.;* blanco, *m.;* calificación (en escuela o examen), *f.;* — **down,** reducción de precio; **printer's** —, pie de imprenta.

marker [mar-kar] *n.* marca, ficha, *f.;* marcador, *m.*

market [mar-kit] *n.* mercado, *m.;* plaza, *f.;* **meat** —, carnicería, *f.;* — **report,** revista del mercado.

marketable [mar-ki-ta-bol] *adj.* vendible, comercial.

marketing [mar-ki-tin] *n.* mercadotecnia, *f.*

marking [mar-kin] *adj.* marcador.

marksman [marks-man] *n.* tirador, ra.

marksmanship [mars-man-ship] *n.* puntería, *f.*

marmalade [mar-ma-leid] *n.* mermelada, *f.*

marmoset [mar-mo-set] *n.* mono tití.

marmot [mar-mot] *n.* marmota, *f.*

maroon [ma-run] *n.* esclavo fugitivo; negro descendiente de esclavo fugitivo; color rojo oscuro; —, *vt.* abandonar a uno en una costa desierta.

marquis [mar-kuis] *n.* marqués, *m.*

marriage [ma-rich] *n.* matrimonio, casamiento, *m.*

married [ma-rid] *adj.* casado, conyugal; **to get** —, casarse.

marrow [ma-rou] *n.* tuétano, meollo, *m.;* médula, *f.*

marry [ma-ri] *vt.* casar; casarse con; —, *vi.* casarse.

marsh [marsh] *n.* pantano, *m.*

marshal [mar-shal] *n.* mariscal, *m.;* **field** —, capitán general.

marshmallow [marsh-me-lou] *n.* malvavisco, *m.,* altea, *f.*

mart [mart] *n.* emporio, *m.;* comercio, *m.;* feria, *f.*

martial [mar-shal] *adj.* marcial, guerrero; — **law,** ley marcial.

martyr [mar-tar] *n.* mártir, *m.* y *f.*

martyrdom [mar-ta-dom] *n.* martirio, *m.*

marvel [mar-vel] *n.* maravilla, *f.;* prodigio, *m.;* —, *vi.* maravillarse.

marvelous [mar-ve-los] *adj.* maravilloso.

Marxist [mark-sist] *n.* marxista, *m.* y *f.*

mascara [mas-ka-ra] *n.* preparación para teñir las pestañas.

mascot [mas-kot] *n.* mascota, *f.*

masculine [mas-kiu-lin] *adj.* masculino, varonil.

mash [mash] *n.* masa, *f.*; —, *vt.* amasar; mezclar; majar.

mask [mask] *n.* máscara, *f.*; pretexto, *m.*; —, *vt.* enmascarar; disimular, ocultar.

mason [mei-son] *n.* albañil, *m.*; masón, *m.*

masoneria [ma-so-ne-ri-a] *f.*; **stone** —, calicanto, *m.*

masquerade [mas-ke-reid] *n.* mascarada, *f.*; — **ball,** — **dance,** baile de máscaras o de disfraz.

mass [mas] *n.* misa, *f.*; **midnight** —, misa de gallo; **to say** —, cantar o celebrar misa.

mass [mas] *n.* masa, *f.*; montón, *m.*; bulto, *m.*; —**es,** *n. pl.* vulgo, *m.*, las masas, el pueblo en general; — **meeting,** mitin popular, reunión del pueblo en masa; — **production,** fabricación en serie o en gran escala.

massacre [ma-sa-krar] *n.* carnicería, matanza, *f.*; —, *vt.* matar atrozmente, hacer una carnicería.

massage [ma-sach] *n.* masaje, *m.*; soba, *f.*; —, *vt.* sobar, dar masaje.

masseur, masseuse [ma-sar], [ma-sesh] *n.* masajista, *m.* y *f.*

massive [ma-siv] *adj.* macizo, sólido.

mast [mast] *n.* árbol de navío, palo, *m.*; fabuco, *m.*; **topsail** —,

verga de garra; —, *vt.* (naut.) arbolar.

master [mas-tar] *n.* amo, dueño, *m.*; maestro, *m.*; señor, *m.*; señorito, *m.*; (naut.) maestre, *m.*; patrón, *m.*; — **of ceremonies,** maestro de ceremonias; — **hand,** mano maestra, maestría, *f.*; — **stroke,** — **touch,** golpe de maestro o diestro, golpe magistral; —, *vt.* domar, gobernar; dominar; sobreponerse.

masterly [mas-ter-li] *adj.* imperioso, despótico; magistral; —, *adv.* con maestría.

masterpiece [mas-ta-pis] *n.* obra o pieza maestra.

mastery [mas-ta-ri] *n.* superioridad, maestría, *f.*

masticate [mas-ti-keit] *vt.* mascar, masticar.

mat [mat] *n.* estera, esterilla, *f.*; —, *vt.* esterar.

match [mach] *n.* mecha, pajuela, *f.*; fósforo, *m.*; cerilla, *f.*, cerillo, *m.*; torneo, partido, *m.*; contrincante, *m.*; pareja, *f.*; casamiento, *m.*; combate, *m.*; —, *vt.* igualar, aparear; casar; —, *vi.* hermanarse.

matchbox [mach-boks] *n.* cajita de fósforos o cerillos.

matching [ma-chin] *n.* igualación, *f.*; aparejamiento, *m.*

matchless [mach-les] *adj.* incomparable, sin par.

matchmaker [mach-mei-kar] *n.* casamentero, ra; organizador de juegos o certámenes.

mate [meit] *n.* consorte, *m.* o *f.*; compañero, ra; (naut.) piloto, *m.*; **first —,** (naut.) piloto, *m.*; **—,** *vt.* desposar; igualar.

material [ma-te-rial] *adj.* material, físico; **—,** *n.* tela, género, *m.*

materialism [ma-te-ria-li-sem] *n.* materialismo, *m.*

materialize [ma-te-ria-lais] *vt.* consumar, realizar; llevar a efecto.

maternal [ma-ter-nal] *adj.* maternal, materno.

maternity [ma-ter-ni-ti] *n.* maternidad, *f.*

mathematical [ma-ze-ma-ti-kal] *adj.* matemático.

mathematician [ma-ze-ma-ti-shan] *n.* matemático, ca.

mathematics [ma-ze-ma-tiks] *n. pl.* matemáticas, *f. pl.*

matinee [ma-ti-nei] *n.* matiné, *f.*

mating [mei-tin] *n.* apareamiento, *m.;* **— time (of animals),** brama (de los animales), *f.*

matriarch [mei-triark] *n.* matriarca, *f.,* mujer que encabeza una familia, grupo o estado.

matriculation [ma-tri-kiu-lei-shon] *n.* matrícula, matricula-

ción,

matrimonial [ma-tri-mou-nial] *adj.* matrimonial, marital.

matrimony [ma-tri-mou-ni] *n.* matrimonio, casamiento, *m.*

matrix [mei-triks] *n.* matriz, *f.;* molde, *m.*

matron [mei-tron] *n.* matrona, *f.*

matted [ma-tad] *adj.* enredado; desgreñado.

matter [ma-tar] *n.* materia, sustancia, *f.;* asunto, objeto, *m.;* cuestión, importancia, *f* ; **it is no —,** no importa; **what is the —?** ¿de qué se trata? **a — of fact,** hecho positivo o cierto, *m.;* **— of form,** cuestión de fórmula, *f.;* **—,** *vi.* importar.

mattress [ma-tris] *n.* colchón, *m.;* **spring —,** colchón de muelle.

mature [ma-chuar] *adj.* maduro; juicioso; **—,** *vt.* madurar; **—,** *vi.* vencerse (una letra, un documento, etc.).

maturity [ma-chua-ri-ti] *n.* madurez, *f.*

maudlin [mod-lin] *adj.* lloroso, sentimental en extremo.

maul [mol] *vt.* apalear, maltratar a golpes.

mauve [mouv] *adj.* color malva.

maverick [ma-ve-rik] *n.* animal sin marca de hierro.

maxim [mak-sim] *n.* máxima, *f.;* axioma, *m.*

maximum [mak-si-mom] *adj.* máximo.

May [mei] *n.* mayo, *m.*

may [mei] *vi.* poder; ser posible.

maybe [mei-bi] *adv.* quizás, tal vez.

mayonnaise [meiou-neis] *n.* mayonesa, *f.,* salsa mayonesa.

mayor [meiar] *n.* corregidor, alcalde, *m.*

maze [meis] *n.* laberinto, *m.;* perplejidad, *f.*

me [mi] *pron.* mí; me.

meadow [me-dou] *n.* pradera, *f.;* prado, *m.;* vega, *f.*

meager, meagre [mi-gar] *adj.* magro; flaco; momio; seco.

meal [mil] *n.* comida, *f.;* harina, *f.*

mean [min] *adj.* bajo, vil, despreciable; abatido; mediocre; mezquino; de término medio; — **temperature,** promedio de temperatura, *m.;* **in the —time,** — **while,** en el ínterin, mientras tanto; —, *n.* medio, *m.;* —**s,** *pl.* medios, recursos, *m. pl.;* **person of —s,** persona acaudalada; **by all —s,** sin falta; **by no —s,** de ningún modo; —, *vt.* y *vi.* significar; querer decir; intentar; **you don't — it!** ¡calla! ¿de veras?

meander [min-dar] *n.* laberinto, *m.;* camino tortuoso; —, *vt.* y *vi.* serpear, seguir un camino tortuoso; caminar sin rumbo.

meaning [mi-nin] *n.* intención, *f.;* inteligencia, *f.;* sentido, significado, *m.;* significación, *f.*

meanness [min-nes] *n.* bajeza, *f.;* pobreza, *f.;* mezquindad, *f.;* mediocridad, *f.;* pequeñez,

meanwhile [min-uail] *adv.* entretanto, mientras tanto; —, *n.* ínterin, *m.*

measles [mis-lis] *n. pl.* sarampión, *m.;* rubéola, *f.*

measure [me-sar] *n.* medida, *f.;* regla, *f.;* (mus.) compás, *m.;* **in some —,** hasta cierto punto; **liquid —,** medida para líquidos; —, *vt.* medir; ajustar; calibrar; calar.

measurement [me-sa-ment] *n.* medición, *f.;* medida, *f.*

meat [mit] *n.* carne, *f.;* **baked —,** carne asada en horno; **broiled —,** carne asada en parrilla.

meatless [mit-les] *adj.* sin carne; **— day,** día de vigilia.

meaty [mi-ti] *adj.* carnoso, sustancioso.

mechanic [mi-ka-nik] *n.* mecánico, *m.*

mechanical [mi-ka-ni-kal] *adj.* mecánico; rutinario.

mechanics [mi-ka-nisk] *n. pl.* mecánica, *f.*

mechanism [me-ka-ni-sem] *n.* mecanismo, *m.*

mechanize [me-ka-nais] *vt.*

mecanizar.

medal [me-dal] *n.* medalla, *f.*

medallion [mi-da-lion] *n.* medallón, *m.*

meddlesome [me-del-som] *adj.* entremetido, da.

mediate [mi-dieit] *vi.* mediar, promediar.

mediation [mi-diei-shon] *n.* mediación, interposición, *f.*

mediator [mi-diei-tar] *n.* mediador, ra.

medical [me-di-kal] *adj.* médico; — **examination,** reconocimiento o examen médico.

medicinal [me-di-si-nal] *adj.* medicinal.

medicine [me-di-sin] *n.* medicina, *f.;* medicamento, *m.*

medieval [me-dii-val] *adj.* medieval.

mediocre [mi-diou-kar] *adj.* mediocre.

mediocrity [mi-dio-kri-ti] *n.* mediocridad, *f.*

meditate [me-di-teit] *vt.* y *vi.* meditar, idear.

meditation [me-di-tei-shon] *n.* meditación, *f.*

medium [mi-diom] *n.* medio, *m.;* expediente, *m.;* —, *adj.* mediano.

medley [med-li] *n.* mezcla, *f.;* baturrillo, *m.;* (mus.) popurrí, *m.*

meek [mik] *adj.* paciente y tími-

do, corto de ánimo; —**ly,** *adv.* tímida y humildemente.

meet [mit] *vt.* encontrar; convocar; reunir, dar con; —, *vi.* encontrarse, juntarse; **till we — again,** hasta la vista; **to go to** —, ir al encuentro; —, *adj.* idóneo, propio; —, *n.* reunión, *f.*

meeting [mi-tin] *n.* asamblea, *f.;* congreso, *m.;* entrevista, *f.;* sesión, reunión, *f.;* mitin, *m.;* **to call a** —, llamar a junta, convocar a una junta.

megaphone [me-ga-foun] *n.* megáfono, portavoz, *m.*

meld [meald] *n.* mezcla en que se confunden los elementos; —, *vt.* mezclar; acusar (en juegos de naipes).

mellow [me-lou] *adj.* maduro, meloso; tierno, suave, blando; —, *vt.* y *vi.* madurar, madurarse.

melodrama [me-lou-dra-ma] *n.* melodrama, *m.*

melody [me-lo-di] *n.* melodía, *f.*

melon [me-lon] *n.* melón, *m.*

melt [melt] *vt.* derretir, fundir; enternecer; —, *vi.* derretirse, enternecerse.

member [mem-bar] *n.* miembro, *m.;* parte, *f.;* individuo, socio, *m.*

membership [mem-ba-ship] *n.* número de socios, personal de socios.

membrane [mem-brein] *n.* membrana, *f.*

memento [me-men-tou] *n.* memento, *m.*

memo: memorandum [me-mou], [me-mou-ran-dom] memorándum, *m.*

memoir [me-muar] *n.* memoria, relación, narrativa, *f.*

memorable [me-mo-ra-bol] *adj.* memorable.

memorandum [me-mo-ran-dom] *n.* memorándum, *m.;* — **book,**.

memorial [mi-mo-rial] *n.* memoria, *f.;* memorial, *m.;* —, *adj.* conmemorativo.

memorize [mi-mo-rais] *vt.* memorizar; aprender de memoria.

memory [me-mo-ri] *n.* memoria, *f.;* recuerdo, *m.*

men [men] *n. pl.* de **man,** hombres, *m. pl.*

menace [me-nis] *n.* amenaza, *f.;* —, *vt.* amenazar.

menagerie [mi-na-che-ri] *n.* colección de animales; casa de fieras.

mend [mend] *vt.* reparar, remendar, retocar; mejorar, corregir; —, *vi.* enmendarse, corregirse.

menial [mi-nial] *adj.* servil, doméstico.

menstruation [mens-truei-shon] *n.* menstruación, regla, *f.*

mental [men-tal] *adj.* mental, intelectual.

mentality [men-ta-li-ti] *n.* mentalidad, *f.*

mention [men-shon] *n.* mención, *f.;* —, *vt.* mencionar; **don't — it,** no hay de qué.

mentor [men-tar] *n.* mentor, guía, *m.*

menu [me-niu] *n.* menú, *m.,* lista de platos, comida, *f.*

mercantile [mer-kan-tail] *adj.* mercantil.

mercenary [mer-si-na-ri] *adj.* mercenario, venal; —, *n.* mercenario, ria.

merchandise [mer-chan-dais] *n.* mercancía, *f.;* efectos comerciales.

merchant [mer-chant] *n.* comerciante, *m.;* mercader, *m.;* negociante, *m. y f.;* —, *adj.* mercante.

merciful [mer-si-ful] *adj.* misericordioso, compasivo, piadoso; —**ly,** *adv.* misericordiosamente.

merciless [mer-si-les] *adj.* duro de corazón, inhumano; —**ly,** *adv.* cruelmente, sin misericordia.

mercury [mer-kiu-ri] *n.* mercurio, *m.*

mercy [mer-si] *n.* misericordia, piedad, clemencia, *f.;* perdón, *m.;* — **killing,** eutanasia, *f.*

mere [miar] *adj.* mero, puro.

merge [merch] *vt.* unir, juntar,

combinar; —, *vi.* absorberse, fusionarse.

merger [mer-char] *n.* consolidación, combinación, *f.;* fusión, *f.*

meridian [me-ri-dian] *n.* mediodía, *m.;* meridiano, *m.*

merit [me-rit] *n.* mérito, *m.;* merecimiento, *m.;* —, *vt.* merecer.

merited [me-ri-tid] *adj.* meritorio, digno, merecido.

meritorious [me-ri-to-rios] *adj.* meritorio.

mermaid [mer-meid] *n.* sirena, *f.*

merrily [me-ri-li] *adv.* alegremente.

merriment [me-ri-ment] *n.* diversión, *f.;* regocijo, *m.* merry, *adj.* alegre, jovial, festivo.

merry-go-round [me-ri-go-raund] *n.* caballitos, *m. pl.,* tiovivo, carrusel, *m.*

mesa [me-sa] *n.* mesa, meseta, altiplanicie, *f.*

mesh [mesh] *n.* malla, *f.*

mess [mes] *n.* plato de comida; vianda, *f.;* ración o porción (de comida); grupo de personas que comen juntas; comida para un grupo; (coll.) confusión, *f.,* lío, *m.*

message [me-sich] *n.* mensaje, *m.*

messenger [me-sin-yar] *n.* mensajero, ra.

metabolism [me-ta-bo-li-sem] *n.*

metabolismo, *m.*

metal [me-tal] *n.* metal, *m.;* (fig.) coraje, espíritu, *m.*

metallic [mi-ta-lik] *adj.* metálico.

metallurgy [me-ta-ler-yi] *n.* metalurgia, *f.*

metamorphosis [me-ta-mor-fousis] *n.* metamorfosis, *f.*

metaphor [me-ta-for] *n.* metáfora, *f.*

metaphysical [me-ta-fi-si-kal] *adj.* metafísico.

metaphysics [me-ta-fi-siks] *n. pl.* metafísica, *f.*

mete [mit] *vt.* asignar; repartir.

meteor [mi-tiar] *n.* meteoro, *m.*

meteorite [mi-tio-rait] *n.* meteorito, *m.*

meteorology [mi-tio-ro-lo-yi] *n.* meteorología, *f.*

meter [mi-tar] *n.* medidor, *m.;* metro, *m.*

method [me-zod] *n.* método, *m.;* vía, *f.;* medio, *m.*

methodic, methodical [mi-zodik], [mi-zo-di-kal] *adj.* metódico.

Methodist [me-zo-dist] *n.* metodista, *m.* y *f.*

methylene [me-zi-lin] *n.* metileno, *m.*

meticulous [me-zi-ko-los] *adj.* meticuloso.

metric [mi-trik] *adj.* métrico; — **system,** sistema métrico.

metropolis [mi-tro-po-lis] *n.*

metrópoli, capital. *f.*

metropolitan [me-tro-po-li-tan] *n.* (eccl.) metropolitano, *m.*, ciudadano o ciudadana de una metrópoli; —, *adj.* metropolitano.

Mexican [mek-si-kan] *n. y adj.* mexicano, na o mejicano, na.

mica [mai-ka] *n.* (min.) mica, *f.*

mice [mais] *n. pl.* de **mouse,** ratones, *m. pl.*

microbe [mai-kroub] *n.* microbio, bacilo, *m.*

microfilm [mai-krou-film] *n.* microfilme, *m.*

microphone [mai-kro-foun] *n.* micrófono, *m.*

microscope [mai-kros-koup] *n.* microscopio, *m.*

microwave [mai-krou-ueiv] *n.* microonda, *f.*

midday [mid-dei] *n.* mediodía, *m.*

middle [mi-del] *adj.* medio, intermedio; mediocre;—, *n.* medio, centro, *m.;* mitad, *f.;* — **ear,** tímpano del oído.

middle-aged [mi-del-eigd] *adj.* entrado en años, de edad madura.

Middle Ages [mi-del-eiges] *n. pl.* Edad Media.

middle class [mi-del-klas] *n.* clase media.

middleman [mi-del-man] *n.* revendedor, intermediario, *m.*

midget [mid-chit] *n.* enano, na.

midnight [mid-nait] *n.* medianoche, *f.*

midst [midst] *n.* medio, centro, *m.*

midsummer [mid-sa-mar] *n.* solsticio estival; pleno verano.

midway [mid-uei] *n.* avenida central de una exposición en que suelen instalarse diversiones; —, *adj.* medio; —, *adv.* a medio camino.

Midwest, Middle West [mid-uest], [mid-del-uest] *n.* Medio Oeste (de los E.U.A.).

midwife [mid-uaif] *n.* comadre, partera, comadrona, *f.*

midwinter [mid-uin-tar] *n.* pleno invierno, solsticio invernal.

midyear [mid-yiar] *adj.* a mediados de año; — **exam,** examen de medio año.

might [mait] *n.* poder, *m.,* fuerza, *f.;* — **and main,** fuerza máxima; —, *pretérito* del verbo **may.**

mightily [mai-ti-li] *adv.* poderosamente, sumamente.

mighty [mai-ti] *adj.* fuerte, potente.

migraine [mi-grein] *n.* hemicránea, jaqueca, *f.*

migrant [mai-grant] *adj.* migratorio, de paso, nómade, nómada; —, *n.* planta o ave migratoria.

migrate [mai-greit] *vi.* emigrar.

migration [mai-grei-shon] *n.* emigración, *f.*

migratory [mai-grei-to-ri] *adj.* migratorio.

mild [maild] *adj.* indulgente, blando, dulce, apacible, suave, moderado; —**ly,** *adv.* suavemente, moderadamente.

mildew [mil-diu] *n.* moho, tizón, tizoncillo, *m.;* roya, *f.;* —, *vi.* enmohecerse.

mile [mail] *n.* milla, *f.*

mileage [mai-lich] *n.* longitud en millas; kilometraje, *m.*

militant [mi-li-tant] *adj.* militante.

military [mi-li-ta-ri] *adj.* militar; **compulsory — service,** servicio militar obligatorio; — **police,** policía militar.

militia [mi-li-sha] *n.* milicia, *f.*

milk [milk] *n.* leche, *f.;* — **of magnesia,** leche de magnesia; —, *vt.* ordeñar.

milkweed [milk-uid] *n.* titímalo, *m.,* cardo lechero.

Milky Way [mil-ki-uei] *n.* Vía Láctea, Galaxia *f.*

mill [mil] *n.* molino, *m.;* —, *vt.* moler, triturar; batir con el molinillo.

millenium [mi-le-niam] *n.* milenio, *m.*

milligram [mi-li-gram] *n.* miligramo, *m.*

millimeter [mi-li-mi-ter] *n.* milímetro, *m.*

million [mi-lion] *n.* millón, *m.*

millionaire [mi-lio-near] *n.* y *adj.* millonario, ria.

mimeograph [mi-mio-graf] *n.* mimeógrafo, *m.*

mimic [mi-mik] *vt.* imitar, contrahacer; —, *adj.* burlesco, mímico; —, *n.* mimo, *m.*

mimicry [mi-mi-kri] *n.* mímica, *f.;* bufonería, *f.*

mince [mins] *vt.* picar (carne) ; —, *vi.* hablar o pasearse con afectación; andar con pasos muy cortos o muy afectadamente.

mincemeat [mins-mit] *n.* picadillo de carne; picadillo de manzana, pasas, etc. con o sin carne.

mind [maind] *n.* mente, *f.;* entendimiento, *m.;* gusto, afecto, *m.;* voluntad, intención, *f.;* pensamiento, *m.;* opinión, *f.;* ánimo, *m.;* **of sound —,** consciente; —, *vt.* notar, observar, considerar; pensar; obedecer; tener cuidado; importar; **not to —,** no importar; —, *vi.* tener cuidado o cautela; preocuparse; obedecer.

mindful [maind-ful] *adj.* atento, diligente.

mine [main] *pron.* el mío, los míos; —, *n.* mina, *f.;* — **field,**

(mil., naut.) campo de minas; cuenca minera; zona donde se han colocado minas explosivas; **land** —, mina terrestre; —, *vt.* y *vi.* minar, cavar.

miner [mai-nar] *n.* minero, minador, *m.*

mineral [mi-ne-ral] *adj.* mineral; — **oil,** aceite mineral, petróleo, *m.;* — **water,** agua mineral; — **wool,** lana de escoria; —, *n,* mineral, *m.*

mingle [min-guel] *vt.* y *vi.* mezclar, mezclarse.

mingled [min-gueld] *adj.* revuelto, mezclado.

miniature [mi-ni-char] *n.* miniatura, *f.*

minimize [mi-ni-mais] *vt.* reducir a un mínimo, menospreciar.

minimum [mi-ni-mom] *n.* mínimum, mínimo, *m.;* —, *adj.* mínimo; — **wage,** jornal mínimo.

minister [mi-nis-tar] *n.* ministro, pastor, capellán, *m.;* —, *vt.* ministrar; servir; suministrar; proveer; socorrer.

ministry [mi-nis-tri] *n.* ministerio, *m.*

mink [mink] *n.* visón, *m.;* — **coat,** abrigo de visón.

minnow [mi-nou] *n.* (ichth.) gobio pequeño.

minor [mi-nar] *adj.* menor, pequeño; inferior; (mus.)

menor; —, *n.* menor (de edad), *m.* y *f.;* asignatura secundaria en las escuelas.

minority [mai-no-ri-ti] *n.* minoridad, *f.;* minoría, *f.*

mint [mint] *n.* (bot.) menta, *f.;* ceca, *f.,* casa de moneda; —, *vt.* acuñar.

minus [mai-nos] *prep.* menos; **seven** — **four,** siete menos cuatro; —, *adj.* negativo; — **quantity,** cantidad negativa; (coll.) despojado; —, *n.* (math.) el signo menos.

minute [mi-nit] *adj.* menudo, pequeño, nimio; minucioso; — **ly,** *adv.* minuciosamente.

minute [mi-nit] *n.* minuto, *m.;* momento, instante, *m.;* — **book,** libro de minutas.

miracle [mi-ra-kol] *n.* milagro, *m.;* maravilla, *f.*

miraculous [mi-ra-kiu-los] *adj.* milagroso.

mirage [mi-rach] *n.* espejismo, *m.*

mire [maiar] *n.* fango, limo, *m.*

mirror [mi-ror] *n.* espejo, *m.*

mirth [merz] *n.* alegría, *f.;* regocijo, *m.*

mirthful [merz-ful] *adj.* alegre, jovial.

misadventure [mis-ad-ven-char] *n.* desventura, *f.;* infortunio, *m.*

misanthrope [mi-san-zroup] *n.* misántropo, *m.*

misapprehend [mis-a-pri-jend] *vt.* entender mal.

misapprehension [mis-a-pri-jen-shon] *n.* error, yerro, *m.;* interpretación errónea.

misbehave [mis-bi-jeiv] *vi.* portarse mal.

misbehavior [mis-bi-jei-vior] *n.* mal comportamiento.

miscalculate [mis-kal-kiu-leit] *vt.* calcular mal.

miscarriage [mis-ka-rich] *n.* aborto, malparto, *m.;* fracaso, *m.*

miscarry [mis-ka-ri] *vi.* frustrarse, malograrse; abortar, malparir.

miscellaneous [mi-si-lei-nios] *adj.* misceláneo, mezclado.

miscellany [mi-se-la-ni] *n.* miscelánea, *f.*

mischief [mis-chif] *n.* travesura, *f.;* daño, infortunio, *m.*

mischievous [mis-chi-vos] *adj.* travieso, pícaro; dañoso, malicioso, malévolo.

misconception [mis-kon-sep-shon] *n.* equivocación, *f.;* falso concepto.

misconduct [mis-kon-dakt] *n.* mala conducta; —, *vt.* conducir o manejar mal.

misconstrue [mis-kons-tru] *vt.* interpretar mal.

misdeed [mis-did] *n.* delito, *m.*

misdemeanor [mis-di-mi-nor] *n.* mala conducta; culpa, falta, *f.*

misdirect [mis-di-rekt] *vt.* dirigir erradamente.

miser [mi-sar] *n.* avaro, ra.

miserable [mi-sa-ra-bol] *adj.* miserable, infeliz; pobre; mísero; mezquino.

miserly [mi-sar-li] *adj.* mezquino, tacaño.

misery [mi-se-ri] *n.* miseria, *f.;* infortunio, *m.*

misfit [mis-fit] *vt.* y *vi.* quedar mal (un vestido, etc.); —, *n.* mal ajuste; vestimenta que no ajusta o cae bien; desadaptado, da, persona que no se adapta al ambiente.

misfortune [mis-for-chun] *n.* infortunio, revés, *m.;* percance, *m.;* calamidad, *f.;* contratiempo, *m.*

misgiving [mis-gi-vin] *n.* recelo, *m.;* duda, *f.;* presentimiento, *m.;* rescoldo, *m.*

misguide [mis-gaid] *vt.* guiar mal.

mishap [mis-jap] *n.* desventura, *f.;* desastre, contratiempo, *m.*

misinform [mis-in-form] *vt.* informar mal.

misinterpret [mis-in-ter-prit] *vt.* interpretar mal.

misjudge [mis-yach] *vt.* y *vi.* juzgar mal.

mislay [mis-lei] *vt.* colocar mal.

mislead [mis-lid] *vt.* extraviar,

descaminar; engañar.

misleading [mis-li-din] *adj.* engañoso, desorientador.

mismanagement [mis-ma-nich-ment] *n.* mala administración, *f.*; desarreglo, *m.*

misnomer [mis-nou-mar] *n.* nombre o título falso.

misplace [mis-pleis] *vt.* colocar mal, sacar algo de su quicio; extraviar.

mispronounce [mis-pra-nouns] *vt.* pronunciar mal.

misrepresent [mis-re-pri-sent] *vt.* representar mal; tergiversar.

misrepresentation [mis-re-pri-sen-tei-shon] *n.* representación falsa; tergiversación, *f.*

miss [mis] *n.* señorita, *f.*; pérdida, falta, *f.*; —, *vt.* errar, perder; omitir; echar de menos; **to — one's mark,** errar el blanco; **to — (in shooting),** errar el tiro; **—** *vi.* frustrarse, malograrse.

missile [mi-sail] *n.* proyectil, *m.*

missing [mi-sin] *adj.* que falta; perdido; **to be —,** hacer falta, faltar.

mission [mi-shon] *n.* misión, comisión, *f.*; cometido, *m.*

missionary [mi-sho-na-ri] *n.* misionero, *m.*

missive [mi-siv] *n.* carta, misiva, *f.*; —, *adj.* misivo.

misspell [mis-pel] *vt.* deletrear mal, escribir con mala ortogra-

fía.

misstatement [mis-teit-ment] *n.* aserción equivocada o falsa.

misstep [mis-tep] *n.* paso en falso.

mist [mist] *n.* niebla, bruma, *f.*

mistake [mis-teik] *n.* equivocación, *f.*; error, *m.*; —, *vt.* equivocar; —, *vi.* equivocarse, engañarse; **to be —n,** estar equivocado, estar errado.

Mister [mis-tar] *n.* Señor (título), *m.*

mistletoe [mi-sel-tou] *n.* (bot.) muérdago, *m.*, liga, *f.*

mistreat [mis-trit] *vt.* maltratar, injuriar.

mistreatment [mis-trit-ment] *n.* maltrato, maltratamiento, *m.*

mistress [mis-tris] *n.* ama, *f.*; señora, *f.*; concubina, *f.*

mistrial [mis-trial] *n.* anulación de un juicio.

mistrust [mis-trast] *vt.* desconfiar; sospechar; —, *n.* desconfianza, sospecha, *f.*

misty [mis-ti] *adj.* nebuloso, brumoso.

misunderstand [mis-an-der-stand] *vt.* entender mal.

misunderstanding [mis-an-der-standin] *n.* mal entendimiento, *m.*; disensión, *f.*; error, *m.*

misuse [mis-ius] *vt.* maltratar; abusar de algo.

mitt, mitten [mit], [mi-ten] *n.*

mitón, *m.*

mix [miks] *vt.* mezclar.

mixed [mikst] *adj.* mezclado; — **up,** revuelto; confuso, indeciso.

mixer [mik-sar] *n.* mezclador, ra; **concrete —,** mezcladora, hormigonera, mezcladora de hormigón.

mixture [miks-char] *n.* mixtura, mezcla, *f.*

mix-up [miks-ap] *n.* (coll.) confusión, *f.;* conflicto, *m.*

moan [moun] *n.* lamento, gemido, *m.;* —, *vt.* lamentar, gemir; —, *vi.* afligirse, quejarse.

mob [mob] *n.* populacho, *m.,* canalla, *f.;* chusma, gentuza, *f.;* gente baja; —, *vt.* atropellar desordenadamente, formar un tropel.

mobile [mou-bail] *adj.* movedizo, móvil.

mobility [mou-bi-li-ti] *n.* movilidad, *f.*

mobilization [mou-bi-lai-sei-shon] *n.* movilización, *f.*

mobilize [mou-bi-lais] *vt.* (mil.) movilizar.

moccasin [mo-ka-sin] *n.* mocasín, *m.,* abarca, *f.*

mock [mok] *vt.* burlar, chiflar; —, *n.* burla, *f.;* —, *adj.* ficticio, falso.

mockery [mo-ka-ri] *n.* burla, zumba, *f.*

mockingbird [mo-kin-berd] *n.*

(orn.) arrendajo, *m.*

mockingly [mo-kin-li] *adv.* burlonamente, en son de burla.

mock-up [mok-ap] *n.* maqueta, *f.*

mode [moud] *n.* modo, *m.;* forma, *f.;* manera, *f.;* costumbre, *f.;* vía, *f.;* (mus.) modalidad, *f.*

model [mo-del] *n.* modelo, *m.;* pauta, *f.;* muestra, *f.;* patrón, *m.;* tipo, *m.;* —, *vt.* modelar.

modeling [mo-de-lin] *n.* modelado, *m.*

moderate [mo-de-rit] *adj.* moderado; mediocre; —**ly,** *adv.* bastante; moderadamente; —, *vt.* moderar.

moderation [mo-de-rei-shon] *n.* moderación, *f.;* sobriedad, *f.*

moderator [mo-de-rei-tar] *n.* moderador, apaciguador, *m.*

modern [mo-dern] *adj.* moderno, reciente.

modernism [mo-der-ni-sem] *n.* modernismo, *m.*

modernistic [mo-der-nis-tik] *adj.* modernista.

modernize [mo-der-nais] *vt.* modernizar.

modest [mo-dist] *adj.* modesto.

modesty [mo-dis-ti] *n.* modestia, decencia, *f.;* pudor, *m.*

modification [mo-di-fi-kei-shon] *n.* modificación, *f.*

modifier [mo-di-fa-er] *n.* modificador, modificante, *m.*

modify [mo-di-fai] *vt.* modificar.

modulate [mo-diu-leit] *vt.* modular.

modulating [mo-diu-lei-tin] *adj.* modulante.

modulation [mo-diu-lei-shon] *n.* modulación, *f.*

moist [moist] *adj.* húmedo, mojado.

moisten [moi-sen] *vt.* humedecer.

moisture [mois-char] *n.* humedad, *f.; jugosidad, f.*

molar [mou-lar] *adj.* molar; — **tooth,** muela, *f.,* diente molar; — **teeth,** muelas, *f. pl.*

molasses [mo-la-sis] *n.* melaza, *f.*

mold [mould] *n.* moho, *m.;* tierra, *f.;* suelo, *m.;* **molde,** *m.;* matriz, *f.; —, vt.* enmohecer, moldar; formar; —, *vi.* enmohecerse.

molding [moul-din] *n.* molduras, *f. pl.,* cornisamiento, *m.*

moldy [moul-di] *adj.* mohoso, lleno de moho.

mole [moul] *n.* topo, *m.;* lunar, *m.;* muelle, dique, *m.*

molecule [mo-li-kiul] *n.* molécula, *f.*

molest [mou-lest] *vt.* acometer; acosar.

mollify [mo-li-fai] *vt.* ablandar.

mollusk [mo-lusk] *n.* molusco,

m.

molt [moult] *vt.* y *vi.* mudar, estar de muda las aves.

molten [moul-ten] *adj.* derretido.

moment [mou-ment] *n.* momento, rato, *m.;* importancia, *f.*

momentarily [mou-men-ta-ri-li] *adv.* a cada momento, momentáneamente.

momentary [mou-men-ta-ri] *adj.* momentáneo.

momentous [mou-men-tos] *adj.* importante.

momentum [mou-men-tom] *n.* ímpetu, *m.;* fuerza de impulsión de un cuerpo.

monarch [mo-nark] *n.* monarca, *m.*

monarchist [mo-nar-kist] *n.* monarquista, *m.* y *f.*

monarchy [mo-nar-ki] *n.* monarquía, *f.*

monastery [mo-nas-tri] *n.* monasterio, *m.*

Monday [man-dei] *n.* lunes, *m.*

monetary [ma-ni-ta-ri] *adj.* monetario.

money [ma-ni] *n.* moneda, *f.;* dinero, *m.;* plata, *f.;* oro, *m.;* — **chest,** caja, *f.;* — **exchange,** bolsa, *f.;* cambio de moneda; — **order,** libranza o giro postal; **paper** —, papel moneda.

moneyed, monied [ma-nid] *adj.* adinerado, rico.

monitor [mo-ni-tar] *n.* admonitor, *m.;* (naut.) monitor, *m.*

monk [monk] *n.* monje, *m.;* cenobita, *m.* y *f.*

monkey [man-ki] *n.* mono, na; simio, mia; — **wrench,** llave inglesa, llave de tuercas.

monogamy [mo-no-ga-mi] *n.* monogamia, *m.*

monogram [mo-no-gram] *n.* monograma, *m.*

monolith [mo-no-liz] *n.* monolito, *m.*

monologue [mo-no-log] *n.* monólogo, *m.*

monopolist [mo-no-po-list] *n.* monopolista, *m.* y *f.*

monopolize [mo-no-po-lais] *vt.* monopolizar, acaparar.

monopoly [mo-no-po-li] *n.* monopolio, *m.*

monorail [mo-nou-reil] *n.* monorriel, *m.*

monosyllabic [mo-nou-si-la-bik] *adj.* monosilábico; —, *n.* monosílabo, *m.*

monotonous [mo-no-to-nos] *adj.* monótono.

monotony [mo-no-to-ni] *n.* monotonía, *f.*

monoxide [mo-nok-said] *n.* (chem.) monóxido, *m.*

monster [mons-tar] *n.* monstruo, *m.*

monstrosity [mons-tro-si-ti] *n.* monstruosidad, *f.*

monstrous [mons-tros] *adj.* monstruoso.

month [manz] *n.* mes, *m.;* —'s **pay,** —'s **allowance,** mensualidad, *f.;* **next** —, el mes entrante, el mes que viene.

monthly [manz-li] *adj.* mensual; —, *adv.* mensualmente.

monument [mo-niu-ment] *n.* monumento, *m.*

monumental [mo-niu-men-tal] *adj.* monumental.

mood [mud] *n.* (gram.) modo, *m.;* humor, talante, *m.*

moody [mu-di] *adj.* caprichoso; taciturno.

moon [mun] *n.* luna, *f.;* **full** —, plenilunio, *m.,* luna llena.

moonlight [mun-lait] *n.* luz de la luna.

moonshine [mun-shain] *n.* claridad de la luna; (coll.) licor fabricado ilícitamente.

moose [muus] *n.* (zool.) alce, *m.*

mop [mop] *n.* trapeador, *m.;* —, *vt.* trapear, fregar.

mope [moup] *vi.* ir cabizbajo, estar melancólico.

moral [mo-ral] *adj.* moral, ético; — **support,** apoyo moral; —, *n.* moraleja, *f.;* —**s,** *n. pl.* moralidad, conducta, *f.;* conducta moral, costumbres, *f. pl.*

morale [mo-ral] *n.* moralidad, *f.;* animación, *f.;* buen espíritu, entusiasmo entre tropas.

morality [mo-ra-li-ti] *n.* ética,

moralidad, f.

moratorium [mo-ra-to-riom] n. moratoria, f.

morbid [mor-bid] adj. enfermo, morboso, mórbido.

more [mor] adj. más, adicional; —, adv. más, en mayor grado; — **or less,** más o menos; —, n. mayor cantidad; **once** —, una vez más; **there's** — **than enough,** hay de sobra.

moreover [mor-ou-var] adv. además.

morgue [morg] n. depósito de cadáveres.

morning [mor-nin] n. mañana, f.; **good** —, buenos días; —, adj. matutino; — **gown,** bata, f.

morning-glory [mor-nin-glo-ri] n. (bot.) dondiego de día.

morocco, morocco leather [mo-ro-kau], [mo-ro-kau-le-der] n. marroquí, m.

moron [mo-ron] n. idiota, m. y f.; retrasado o retrasada mental.

morose [mo-rous] adj. hosco, sombrío, adusto.

morphine [mor-fin] n. morfina, f.

morsel [mor-sel] n. bocado, m.

mortal [mor-tal] adj. mortal; humano; —**ly,** adv. mortalmente; —, n. mortal, m.

mortality [mor-ta-li-ti] n. mortalidad, f.

mortgage [mor-guich] n. hipoteca, f.; —, vt. hipotecar.

mortician [mor-ti-shan] n. sepulturero, enterrador, m.; agente funerario.

mortification [mor-ti-fai-kei-shon] n. mortificación, f.; (med.) gangrena, f.

mortify [mor-ti-fai] vt. y vi. mortificar, mortificarse.

mortuary [mor-tua-ri] adj. funeral.

mosaic [mou-seik] n. y adj. mosaico, m.

Moscow [mos-kou] Moscú, f.

mosquito [mos-ki-tou] n. mosquito, zancudo, m.

moss [mos] n. (bot.) musgo, m.

mossy [mo-si] adj. musgoso.

most [moust] adj. más; —, adv. sumamente, en sumo grado; —, n. los más; mayor número; mayor valor; **at** —, a lo más, cuando más; —**ly,** adv. por lo común; principalmente.

motel [mou-tel] n. (contracción de motor y hotel) autohotel, hotel para automovilistas.

moth [moz] n. polilla, f.; — **ball,** bola de naftalina para la polilla.

mother [ma-dar] n. madre, f.; — **tongue,** lengua materna.

motherhood [ma-dar-jud] n. maternidad, f.

mother-in-law [ma-dar-in-lo] n. suegra, f.

motherless [ma-da-les] adj. sin

madre, huérfana de madre.

motif [mou-tif] *n.* motivo, tema, *m.*

motion [mou-shon] *n.* movimiento, *m.*, moción, *f.;* vaivén, *m.;* proposición, *f.;* — **picture,** película, *f.,* filme, *m.;* — **pictures,** cinematografía, *f.,* cinematógrafo, *m.;* —, *vt.* hacer señas (para indicar algo).

motionless [mou-shon-les] *adj.* inmoble, inmóvil.

motivate [mou-ti-veit] *vt.* motivar, proveer con un motivo; incitar, inducir, estimular interés activo por medio de intereses relacionados o recursos especiales.

motive [mou-tiv] *adj.* motivo, motor; — **power,** fuerza motriz; —, *n.* motivo, móvil, *m.;* razón, *f.*

motley [mot-li] *adj.* abigarrado, gayado, variado.

motor [mou-tar] *n.* motor, *m.;* — **truck,** autocamión, *m.*

motorboat [mou-to-bout] *n.* lancha de motor.

motorcade [mou-to-keid] *n.* desfile de automóviles.

motorcar [mou-tar-kar] *n.* automóvil, *m.*

motorcycle [mou-to-sai-kel] *n.* motocicleta, *f.*

motorist [mou-to-rist] *n.* automovilista, motorista, *m.* y *f.*

motorize [mou-to-rais] *vt.* motorizar.

motto [mo-tou] *n.* lema, *m.;* mote, *m.;* divisa, *f.*

mount [maunt] *n.* monte, *m.;* montaña, *f.;* montaje, *m.;* —, *vt.* y *vi.* ascender, subir; montar.

mountain [maun-ten] *n.* montaña, sierra, *f.;* monte, *m.;* **range of** —**s,** cadena de montañas.

mountainous [maun-ti-nos] *adj.* montañoso.

mounted [maun-ted] *adj.* montado.

mounting [maun-tin] *n.* montaje, *m.*

mourn [morn] *vt.* deplorar; —, *vi.* lamentar; llevar luto.

mourner [mor-nar] *n.* lamentador, ra; llorón, ona; doliente, *m.* y *f.*

mournful [morn-ful] *adj.* triste; fúnebre.

mourning [mor-nin] *n.* luto, *m.;* **in** —, de luto.

mouse [maus] *n. (pl. mice)* ratón, *m.;* — **trap,** ratonera, *f.*

moustache = **mustache.**

mouth [mauz] *n.* boca, *f.;* entrada, *f.;* embocadura, *f.;* **by word of** —, boca a boca, de palabra; — **organ,** armónica, *f.;* **to make the** — **water,** hacerse agua la boca; —, *vi.* hablar a gritos; —, *vt.* poner en la boca; pronunciar.

mouthful [mauz-ful] *n.* bocado, *m.*

mouthpiece [mauz-pis] *n.* vocero, *m.;* boquilla de un instrumento de música.

movable [mu-va-bol] *adj.* movible, movedizo; —**s**, *n. pl.* bienes muebles, *m. pl.*

move [muv] *vt.* mover; proponer; excitar; persuadir; emocionar; bullir; mover a piedad; —, *vi.* moverse, menearse; andar; marchar un ejército; **to — to and fro,** moverse de un lado para otro; zarandearse; revolverse; —, *n.* movimiento, *m.*

movement [muv-ment] *n.* movimiento, *m.;* moción, *f.* movies, *n. pl.* (coll.) cine, cinematógrafo, *m.*

moving [mu-vin] *n.* movimiento, *m.;* —, *adj.* patético, persuasivo; conmovedor; — **pictures**, cine, cinematógrafo, *m.;* —**ly**, *adv.* patéticamente.

mowing [mouin] *n.* siega, *f.;* — **machine**, guadañadora, *f.*

Mr.: Mister [mister] Sr. Señor.

Mrs.: Mistress [mistres] Sra. Señora.

much [mach] *adj.* mucho; —, *adv.* mucho, con mucho; **so —, as —,** tanto; **too —,** demasiado.

muck [mak] *n.* abono, estiércol, *m.;* basura, *f.*

mucous [ma-kos] *adj.* mocoso, viscoso.

mucus [miu-kos] *n.* moco, *m.,* mucosidad, *f.*

mud [mad] *n.* fango, lodo, *m.*

muddle [ma-del] *vt.* enturbiar; embriagar; enredar; confundir; —, *n.* confusión, *f.;* enredo, *m.*

muddy [ma-di] *adj.* cenagoso; turbio; lodoso.

muffin [ma-fin] *n.* variedad de bizcochuelo o panecillo suave.

muffle [ma-fel] *vt.* embozar; envolver.

muffler [ma-flar] *n.* (auto.) silenciador, *m.;* sordina, *f.;* desconectador, *m.*

mug [mag] *n.* cubilete, *m.;* (coll.) cara, *f.*

muggy [ma-gui] *adj.* húmedo y caluroso.

mulberry [mal-be-ri] *n.* mora, *f.;* — **tree,** morera, *f.*

mule [miul] *n.* mulo, *m.,* mula, *f.*

multimillionaire [mal-ti-mi-lio-near] *n.* multimillonario, ria.

multiple [mal-ti-pel] *adj.* multíplice; múltiple; —, *n.* múltiplo, *m.*

multiplication [mal-ti-pli-kei-shon] *n.* multiplicación, *f.;* — **table,** tabla de multiplicar.

multiplier [mal-ti-plaiar] *n.* multiplicador, *m.*

multiply [mal-ti-plai] *vt.* multiplicar; —, *vi.* propagarse, multiplicarse.

multitude [mal-ti-tiud] *n.* multitud, *f.;* vulgo, *m.*

multitudinous [mal-ti-tiu-di-nos]
adj. numeroso, múltiple.

mumble [mam-bel] *vt.* barbotar,
mascullar; —, *vi.* hablar o decir
entre dientes; gruñir; murmurar.

mummy [ma-mi] *n.* momia, *f*

mumps [mamp] *n. pl.* (med.)
papera, parótida, *f.*

munch [manch] *vt.* masticar a
bocados grandes.

mundane [man-dein] *adj.* mundano.

municipal [miu-ni-si-pal] *adj.*
municipal; — **government,**
ayuntamiento, gobierno municipal.

municipality [miu-ni-si-pal-ti] *n.*
municipalidad, *f.*

mural [miua-ral] *n.* y *adj.* mural,
m.

murder [mer-dar] *n.* asesinato,
homicidio, *m.;* —, *vt.* asesinar,
cometer homicidio.

murderer [mer-da-rar] *n.* asesino, na.

murderous [mer-da-ros] *adj.*
sanguinario, cruel.

murky [mer-ki] *adj.* oscuro,
lóbrego; sombrío; turbio; empañado.

murmur [mar-mar] *n.* murmullo,
m.; cuchicheo, *m.;* —, *vi.* mur-

murar.

muscle [ma-sel] *n.* músculo, *m.*

muscular [mas-kiu-lar] *adj.*
muscular; — **distrophy,** distrofia muscular.

muse [mius] *n.* musa, *f.;* meditación profunda; —, *vi.* meditar,
pensar profundamente.

museum [miu-siom] *n.* museo,
m.

mushroom [mash-rum] *n.* (bot.)
seta, *f.,* hongo, *m.*

music [miu-sik] *n.* música, *f.;* —
hall, sala de concierto; — **staff,**
pentagrama, *m.*

musical [miu-si-kal] *adj.* musical; melodioso; — **comedy,** zar-
zuela, *f.,* comedia musical; —**ly,**
adv. con armonía.

musician [miu-si-shan] *n.* músico, *m.*

musing [miu-sin] *n.* meditación,
f.

musk [mask] *n.* almizcle, *m.*

musket [mas-kit] *n.* mosquete,
fusil, *m.;* (coll.) chopo, *m.*

muskrat [mask-rat] *n.* rata
almizclera.

mussel [ma-sel] *n.* marisco, *m.*

must [mast] *vi.* estar obligado;
ser menester, ser necesario;
convenir.

mustache [mas-tash] *n.* bigote,
mostacho, *m.*

mustard [mas-tard] *n.* mostaza,
f.

muster [mas-tar] *vt.* pasar revista de tropa; agregar; —, *n.* (mil.) revista, *f.;* — **roll,** rol, *m.,* lista de dotación; rol de la tripulación.

musty [mas-ti] *adj.* mohoso, añejo.

mutate [miu-teit] *vt.* trasformar, alterar.

mutation [miu-tei-shon] *n.* mudanza, *f.;* mutación, *f.*

mute [miut] *adj.* mudo, silencioso; —**ly,** *adv.* sin chistar.

mutilate [miu-ti-leit] *vt.* mutilar.

mutinous [miu-ti-nos] *adj.* sedicioso; —**ly,** *adv.* amotinadamente.

mutiny [miu-ti-ni] *n.* motín, tumulto, *m.;* —, *vi.* amotinarse, rebelarse.

mutter [ma-tar] *vt.* y *vi.* murmurar, musitar, hablar entre dientes; —, *n.* murmuración, *f.*

mutton [ma-ton] *n.* carnero, *m.*

mutual [miu-chual] *adj.* mutuo, recíproco; **by — con sent,** de común acuerdo; **— aid association,** asociación de apoyo mutuo, sociedad de beneficencia.

muzzle [ma-sel] *n.* bozal, frenillo, *m.;* hocico, *m.;* —, *vt.* amordazar.

my [mai] *adj.* mi.

myocardium [maio-kar-diom] *n.* miocardio, *m.*

myriad [mi-riad] *n.* miríada, *f.;* gran número.

myrtle [mer-tel] *n.* mirto, arrayán, *m.*

myself [mai-self] *pron.* yo mismo, mí mismo.

mysterious [mis-tia-rios] *adj.* misterioso.

mystery [mis-te-ri] *n.* misterio, *m.*

mystic, mystical [mis-tik], [mis-ti-kal] *adj.* místico.

mysticism [mis-ti-si-zem] *n.* misticismo, *m.*

mystify [mis-ti-fai] *vt.* desconcertar, ofuscar.

myth [miz] *n.* fábula mitológica; mito, *m.*

mythical [mi-zi-kal] *adj.* mítico, fabuloso.

mythology [mi-zo-lo-yi] *n.* mitológía, *f.*

N

nab [nab] *vt.* atrapar, prender.

nag [nag] *n.* rocín, matalón, caballejo, *m.;* —, *vt.* y *vi.* regañar continuamente, molestar, sermonear.

nail [neil] *n.* uña, *f.;* garra, *f.;*

clavo, *m.;* — **file,** lima para las uñas; —, *vt.* clavar.

naive [nai-iv] *adj.* ingenuo.

naked [nei-kid] *adj.* desnudo; evidente; puro, simple; **stark —**, en pelota.

nakedness [nei-kid-nes] *n.* desnudez, *f.*

name [neim] *n.* nombre, *m.;* fama, reputación, *f.*

nameless [neim-les] *adj.* anónimo; sin nombre.

namely [neim-li] *adv.* particularmente; a saber.

nap [nap] *n.* siesta, *f.,* sueño ligero; lanilla, *f.,* flojel, *m.*

nape [neip] *n.* nuca, cerviz, *f.*

napkin [nap-kin] *n.* servilleta, *f.;* **sanitary —,** servilleta higiénica.

Naples [nei-pols] Nápoles, *f.*

narcissus [nar-si-sos] *n.* (bot.) narciso, *m.*

narcosis [nar-kou-sis] *n.* narcosis, *f.*

narcotic [nar-kou-tik] *adj.* narcótico; **—s,** *n. pl.* drogas heroicas, estupefacientes, *m. pl.*

narrate [na-reit] *vt.* narrar, relatar.

narration [na-rei-shon] *n.* narración, *f.;* relación de alguna cosa.

narrative [na-ra-tiv] *n.* cuento, relato, *m.;* —, *adj.* narrativo.

narrator [na-rei-tar] *n.* narrador, ra.

narrow [na-rou] *adj.* angosto, estrecho; avariento; próximo; escrupuloso; **—ly,** *adv.* estrechamente; —, *vt.* estrechar; limitar.

narrowminded [na-rou-mainded] *adj.* mezquino, fanático, intolerante.

narrowness [na-rou-nes] *n.* angostura; pobreza, *f.*

nasal [nei-sal] *adj.* nasal.

nastily [nas-ti-li] *adv.* suciamente; desagradablemente.

nasty [nas-ti] *adj.* sucio, puerco; obsceno; sórdido; desagradable.

nation [nei-shon] *n.* nación, *f.,* país, *m.*

national [na-sho-nal] *adj.* nacional.

nationalism [na-sho-na-li-sem] *n.* nacionalismo, *m.*

nationalist [na-sho-na-li-ti] *n.* nacionalista, *m. y f.*

nationality [na-sho-na-li-ti] *n.* nacionalidad, *f.*

nationalize [na-sho-na-lais] *vt.* nacionalizar.

native [nei-tiv] *adj.* nativo; **— of,** oriundo de; —, *n.* natural, *m. y f.*

native-born [nei-tiv-born] *adj.* natural (de un país o lugar indicado).

nativity [nei-ti-vi-ti] *n.* nacimiento, *m.;* natividad, *f.;* horóscopo,

m.

natural [na-chral] *adj.* natural; sencillo; ilegítimo; ingénito; — **ly,** *adv.* naturalmente; —, *n.* (mus.) becuadro, *m.*

naturalist [na-chra-list] *n.* naturalista, *m.* y *f.*

naturalization [na-chra-lai-sei-shon] *n.* naturalización, *f.;* obtención de la ciudadanía de un país.

naturalize [na-chu-ra-lais] *vt.* y *vi.* naturalizar, naturalizarse.

nature [nei-char] *n.* naturaleza, *f.;* índole, *f.;* modalidad, *f.;* carácter, *m.;* tenor, *m.;* humor, *m.;* genio, *m.;* temperamento, *m.;* **good** —, buen humor.

naught [not] *n.* nada, *f.;* cero, *m.;* —, *adj.* nulo.

naughtiness [no-ti-nes] *n.* picardía, travesura, *f.*

naughty [no-ti] *adj.* travieso, pícaro; desobediente.

nausea [no-sia] *n.* náusea, basca, *f.*

nauseate [no-sieit] *vt.* dar disgusto; nausear.

nautical [no-ti-kal] *adj.* náutico.

naval [nei-val] *adj.* naval.

navel [nei-val] *n.* ombligo, *m.*

navigation [na-vi-guei-shon] *n.* navegación, *f.*

navigator [na-vi-guei-tar] *n.* navegante, *m.*

navy [nei-vi] *n.* marina, *f.;* arma-da, *f.;* — **yard,** arsenal de la marina de guerra.

nay [nei] *adv.* y aun, más aún; —, *n.* no, *m.,* voto negativo; contestación negativa.

Nazi [na-tsi] *n.* y *adj.* nazi, *m.* y *f.*

near [niar] *prep.* cerca de, junto a; —, *adv.* casi; cerca, cerca de; —, *adj.* cercano, próximo, inmediato; allegado.

nearby [nia-li] *adj.* cercano, próximo; —, *adv.* cerca, a la mano.

Near East [nia-ist] Cercano Oriente.

nearly [nia-li] *adv.* casi; por poco.

nearness [nia-nes] *n.* proximidad, *f.;* mezquindad, *f.*

near-sighted [nia-sai-tid] *adj.* miope, corto de vista; — **person,** miope, *m.* y *f.*

neat [nit] *adj.* hermoso, pulido; puro; neto; pulcro; ordenado; —**ly,** *adv.* elegantemente; con nitidez; —, *n.* ganado vacuno.

nebulous [ne-biu-los] *adj.* nebuloso.

necessaries [ne-si-sa-ris] *n. pl.* cosas necesarias; requisitos, *m. pl*

necessarily [ne-si-sa-ri-li] *adv.* necesariamente.

necessary [ne-si-sa-ri] *adj.* necesario; **to be** —, hacer falta, ser preciso, ser menester.

necessity [ni-se-si-ti] *n.* necesidad, *f.*

neck [nek] *n.* cuello, *m.;* **back of the —,** nuca, *f.*

necklace [nek-lis] *n.* collar, *m.*

necktie [nek-tai] *n.* corbata, *f.*

nectar [nek-tar] *n.* néctar, *m.*

need [nid] *n.* necesidad, *f.;* pobreza, *f.; —, vt.* y *vi.* necesitar; requerir.

needle [ni-del] *n.* aguja, *f*

needless [nid-les] *adj.* superfluo, inútil, innecesario.

needlework [ni-del-uek] *n.* costura, *f.;* bordado de aguja.

needy [ni-di] *adj.* indigente, necesitado, pobre.

negation [ni-guei-shon] *n.* negación, *f.*

negative [ne-ga-tiv] *adj.* negativo; —, *n.* negativa, *f.*

neglect [ni-glekt] *vt.* descuidar, desatender; —, *n.* negligencia, *f.*

negligence *n.* negligencia, *f.;* descuido, *m.*

negligent [ne-gli-chent] *adj.* negligente.

negligible [ne-gli-chi-bol] *adj.* insignificante.

negotiable [ni-gou-shia-bol] *adj.* negociable.

negotiate [ni-gou-shieit] *vt.* gestionar; —, *vi.* negociar, comerciar.

negotiation [ni-gou-shiei-shon] *n.* negociación, *f.;* negocio, *m.*

neighbor [nei-bor] *n.* vecino, na; —, *vt.* estar contiguo; colindar con; —, *vi.* tratarse como vecinos.

neighborhood [nei-ba-jud] *n.* vecindad, *f.;* vecindario, *m.;* inmediación, cercanía, *f.*

neighboring [nei-ba-rin] *adj.* cercano, vecino.

neighborly [nei-ba-li] *adj.* sociable, amigable.

neither [nai-dar] *conj.* ni; —, *adj.* ninguno; —, *pron.* ninguno, ni uno ni otro.

nephew [ne-fiu] *n.* sobrino, *m.*

nepotism [ne-po-ti-sem] *n.* nepotismo, *m.*

nerve [nerv] *n.* nervio, *m.;* vigor, *m.;* (coll.) audacia, *f.;* descaro, *m.*

nerve-racking, nerve-wracking [nerv-ra-kin], [nerv-ra-kin] *adj.* exasperante, que pone los nervios de punta.

nervous [ner-vos] *adj.* nervioso; excitable; nervudo.

nervousness [ner-vos-nes] *n.* nerviosidad, *f.*

nest [nest] *n.* nido, *m.;* nidada, *f.; —* **egg,** nidal, *m.;* (fig.) ahorros, *m. pl.*

nestle [ne-sel] *vi.* acurrucarse; —, *vt.* abrigar; acomodar (como en un nido).

net [net] *n.* red, *f.;* malla, *f.; —,*

adj. neto, líquido; — **balance,** saldo líquido; — **cost,** costo neto; — **proceeds,** producto líquido; — **weight,** peso neto.

nether [ne-dar] *adj.* inferior, más bajo.

Netherlands [ne-der-lans] Países Bajos, *m. pl.*

netting [ne-tin] *n.* elaboración de redes; pesca con redes; pedazo de red.

nettle [ne-tel] *n.* ortiga, *f.;* —, *vt.* picar como ortiga; irritar.

network [net-uek] *n.* (rad. y TV.) red radiodifusora, red televisora.

neurosis [niua-rou-sis] *n.* (med.) neurosis, *f.*

neurotic [niua-rou-tik] *adj.* neurótico.

neutral [niu-tral] *adj.* neutral.

neutralize [niu-tra-lais] *vt.* neutralizar.

neutron [niu-tron] *n.* neutrón, *m.;* — **bomb,** bomba de neutrones.

never [ne-var] *adv.* nunca, jamás; — **mind,** no importa; — **a whit,** ni una pizca.

nevermore [ne-va-mor] *adv.* jamás, nunca.

nevertheless [ne-va-de-les] *adv.* a pesar de todo, no obstante, así y todo, con todo, sin embargo.

new [niu] *adj.* nuevo, fresco, reciente, original.

newborn [niu-born] *adj.* recién nacido.

newcomer [niu-ka-mar] *n.* recién llegado, da.

Newfoundland [niu-foun-lan] Terranova, *f.*

newlywed [niu-liuid] *n.* recién casado, da.

newness [niu-nes] *n.* novedad, *f.,* calidad de nuevo.

news [nius] *n. pl.* noticias, nuevas, *f. pl.*

newscast [nius-kast] *n.* radiodifusión de noticias; noticiero, noticiario, *m.*

newspaper [nius-pei-par] *n.* gaceta, *f.;* periódico, *m.;* diario, *m.;* — **clipping,** recorte de periódico.

newsreel [nius-ril] *n.* noticiero, *m.,* película que ilustra las noticias del día.

newsstand [nius-tand] *n.* puesto de periódicos.

new-world [niu-ueld] *adj.* del Nuevo Mundo, relacionado con el Hemisferio Occidental.

New Zealand [niu-si-lan] Nueva Zelanda o Nueva Zelandia, *f.*

next [nekst] *adj.* próximo; entrante, venidero; **the — day,** el día siguiente; —, *adv.* luego, inmediatamente después.

nib [nib] *n.* pico, *m.,* punta, *f.*

nibble [ni-bel] *vt.* y *vi.* mordiscar, picar.

nice [nais] *adj.* delicado, exacto, solícito; circunspecto; tierno; fino; elegante; escrupuloso; — **ly,** *adv.* bastante bien.

niche [nish] *n.* nicho, *m.*

nick [nik] *n.* muesca, *f.;* punto crítico; ocasión oportuna; — **of time,** momento oportuno.

nickel [ni-kel] *n.* níquel, *m.*

nickname [nik-neim] *n.* mote, apodo, *m.;* —, *vt.* poner apodos.

nicotine [ni-ko-tin] *n.* nicotina, *f.*

niece [nis] *n.* sobrina, *f.*

nigh [nai] *adv.* casi.

night [nait] *n.* noche, *f.;* **by** —, de noche; **good** —, buenas noches; — **club,** cabaret, club nocturno; — **letter,** telegrama nocturno; — **owl,** trasnochador, ra; — **school,** escuela de noche o nocturna; — **watch,** sereno, *m.,* vela, *f.*

nightfall [nait-fol] *n.* anochecer, *m.;* caída de la tarde.

nightgown [nait-gaun] *n.* camisón, *m.,* camisa de dormir.

nightingale [nait-tan-gol] *n.* ruiseñor, *m.*

nightly [nait-li] *adv.* por las noches, todas las noches; —, *adj.* nocturno.

nightmare [nait-mear] *n.* pesadilla, *f.*

nimble [nim-bel] *adj.* ligero, activo, listo, ágil.

nine [nain] *n.* y *adj.* nueve, *m.*

nineteen [nain-tin] *n.* y *adj.* diez y nueve, diecinueve, *m.*

nineteenth [nain-tinz] *n.* y *adj.* decimonono, *m.*

ninety [nain-ti] *n.* y *adj.* noventa, *m.*

ninth [nainz] *n.* y *adj.* nono, **noveno,** *m.;* —**ly,** *adv.* en noveno lugar.

nip [nip] *vt.* arañar, rasguñar; morder.

nipping [ni-pin] *adj.* mordaz, picante; sensible (frío).

nipple [ni-pel] *n.* pezón, *m.*

nitrate [ni-treit] *n.* nitrato *m.*

nitrogen [nai-tro-yin] *n.* nitrógeno, *m.;* — **peroxide,** peróxido de nitrógeno.

no [nou] *adv.* no; —, *adj.* ningún, ninguno; **by** —**means, in** — **way,** de ningún modo; — **end,** sinnúmero; — **longer,** no más; **there is** — **such thing,** no hay tal cosa.

nobility [nou-bi-li-ti] *n.* nobleza, *f.*

noble [nou-bel] *adj.* noble; insigne; generoso; solariego; —, *n.* noble, *m.*

nobleman [nou-bel-man] *n.* noble, *m.*

nobleness [nou-bel-nes] *n.* nobleza, caballerosidad, *f.*

nobody [nou-ba-di] *pron.* nadie,

ninguno, na; —, *n.* persona insignificante.

nocturnal [nok-ter-nal] *adj.* nocturno.

nod [nod] *n.* cabeceo, *m.;* señal, *f.;*
—, *vt.* inclinar (la cabeza) en señal de asentimiento; —, *vi.* cabecear.

noise [nois] *n.* ruido, estruendo, *m.;* baraúnda, *f.;* bulla, *f.;* rumor, *m.;* **to make —,** hacer ruido, meter bulla.

noiseless [nois-les] *adj.* silencioso, sin ruido.

noisy [noi-si] *adj.* ruidoso.

nomad [nou-mad] *n.* y *adj.* nómada, *m.* y *f.*

nomadic [nou-ma-dik] *adj.* nómada.

nominal [no-mi-nal] *adj.* nominal.

nominate [no-mi-neit] *vt.* nombrar; proponer (a alguna persona para un puesto, cargo, etc.).

nomination [no-mi-nei-shon] *n.* nominación, *f.;* propuesta, *f.*

nonchalance [non-cha-lans] *n.* indiferencia, *f.*

nonchalant [non-cha-lant] *adj.* indiferente, calmado.

noncombatant [non-kom-ba-tant] *n.* no combatiente, *m.*

noncommissioned [non-ko-mi-shond] *adj.* (mil.) subordinado, sin comisión; — **officer,** sargen-to, cabo, *m.,* oficial nombrado por el jefe de un cuerpo.

noncommittal [non-ko-mi-tal] *adj.* evasivo, esquivo, reservado.

nonconformist [non-kom-for-mist] *n.* y *adj.* disidente, *m.* y *f.*

nondescript [non-dis-kript] *adj.* de difícil descripción o clasificación; —, *n.* persona o cosa que no pertenece a determinada clase o categoría; persona o cosa indescriptible.

none [nan] *pron.* nadie, ninguno.

nonentity [non-en-ti-ti] *n.* nada, nulidad, *f.*

nonintervention [non-in-ta-ven-shon] *n.* no intervención, *f.*

nonpartisan [non-par-ti-san] *adj.* independiente, sin afiliación política; —, *n.* miembro o grupo sin afiliación política.

nonpayment [non-pai-ment] *n.* falta de pago.

nonproductive [non-pro-duk-tiv] *adj.* no productivo.

nonsectarian [non-sek-ta-rian] *adj.* no sectario, que no pertenece a denominación alguna.

nonsense [non-sens] *n.* tontería, *f.;* disparate, absurdo, *m.*

nonsensical [non-sen-si-kal] *adj.* absurdo; tonto.

nonstop [non-stop] *adj.* directo, sin parar o sin etapas; —

flight, vuelo directo.

noodle [nu-del] *n.* tallarín fideo, *m.;* (coll.) cabeza, *f.;* simplón, mentecato, *m.;* — **soup,** sopa de tallarines o de fideos.

nook [nuk] *n.* rincón, ángulo, *m.*

noon [nun] *n.* mediodía, *m.*

noonday [nund-ei] *n.* mediodía, *m.*

noose [nus] *n.* lazo corredizo; —, *vt.* enlazar.

nor [nor] *conj.* ni.

norm [norm] *n.* norma, *f.;* tipo, *m.*

normal [nor-mal] *adj.* normal; — **school,** escuela normal.

north [norz] *n.* norte, *m.*

northeast [norz-ist] *n.* nordeste, *m.*

northeastern [norz-is-tern] *adj.* del nordeste.

northerly, northern [nor-zer-li] [nor-zern] *adj.* septentrional, del norte.

northern lights [nor-zern-laits] *n. pl.* aurora boreal.

North Pole [norz-pol] *n.* Polo Norte, *m.*

northward, northwards [norz-uard], [norz-wards] *adv.* hacia el norte.

northwest [norz-uest] *n.* noroeste, *m.*

northwestern [noz-ues-tern] *adj.* del noroeste.

Norway [nor-uey] Noruega, *f.*

nose [nous] *n.* nariz, *f.;* olfato, *m.;* sagacidad, *f.*

nosebleed [nous-blid] *n.* epistaxis, *f.,* hemorragia nasal.

nose dive [nous-daiv] *n.* clavado de proa; descenso repentino de un aeroplano.

nostalgia [nous-tal-chia] *n.* nostalgia,

nostril [nos-tril] *n.* ventana de la nariz.

not [not] *adv.* no; **if** —, si no; — **any,** ningún; ninguno; — **at all,** de ninguna manera; —**even,** ni siquiera.

notable [nou-ta-bol] *adj.* notable; memorable.

notarize [nou-ta-rais] *vt.* autorizar ante notario.

notary [nou-ta-ri] *n.* notario, *m.*

notation [nou-tei-shon] *n.* notación, *f.*

note [nout] *n.* nota, marca, *f.;* señal, *f.;* aprecio, *m.;* billete, *m.;* consecuencia, *f.;* noticia, *f.;* explicación, *f ;* comentario, *m.;* (mus.) nota, *f.;* **bank** — billete de banco; **counterfeit** —, billete falso; —, *vt.* notar, marcar; observar.

notebook [nout-buk] *n.* cuaderno, librito de apuntes.

noted [nou-tid] *adj.* célebre.

noteworthy [nout-ue-zi] *adj.* notable, digno de encomio, digno de atención.

nothing [na-zin] *n.* nada, *f.*, ninguna cosa; **good for —,** inútil, que no sirve para nada.

notice [nou-tis] *n.* noticia, *f.;* aviso, *m.;* nota, *f.;* **—,** *vt.* observar, reparar, fijarse en.

noticeable [nou-ti-sa-bol] *adj.* notable, reparable.

notification [nou-ti-fi-kei-shon] *n.* notificación, *f.,* aviso, *m.*

notify [nou-ti-fai] *vt.* notificar; requerir.

notion [nou-shon] *n.* noción, *f.;* opinión, *f ;* idea, *f.;* **—s,** *n. pl.* novedades, *f. pl.;* mercería, *f.*

notoriety [no-to-rie-ti] *n.* notoriedad, *f.*

notorious [no-to-rios] *adj.* notorio.

noun [naun] *n.* (gram.) sustantivo, nombre, *m.*

nourish [na-rish] *vt.* nutrir, alimentar.

nourishing [na-ri-shin] *adj.* sustancioso, nutritivo.

novel [no-vel] *n.* novela, *f.;* **—,** *adj.* novedoso, original.

novelist [no-ve-list] *n.* novelista, *m.* y *f.*

novelty [no-vel-ti] *n.* novedad, *f.;* **— jewelry,** bisutería, *f.,* joyas de fantasía; **—ties,** *n. pl.* artículos de fantasía.

November [no-vem-bar] *n.* noviembre, *m.*

novice [no-vis] *n.* novicio, cia;

novato, ta; bisoño, ña.

novocaine [no-vo-kein] *n.* novocaína, *f.*

now [nau] *adv.* ahora, en el tiempo presente; **— and then,** de cuando en cuando; **till —,** hasta ahora, hasta aquí; **—!** *interj.* ¡vaya!

nowadays [naua-deis] *adv.* hoy día, en estos días.

nowhere [nouear] *adv.* en ninguna parte.

nozzle [no-sel] *n.* boquilla (de una manguera, etc.), *f.;* gollete, *m.;* nariz de un animal; (coll.) hocico, *m.*

nuclear [niu-kliar] *adj.* nuclear, nucleario; **— fission,** desintegración nuclearia; **— reactor,** reactor nuclear.

nucleus [niu-klios] *n.* núcleo, *m.*

nude [niud] *adj.* desnudo, en carnes, en cuero, sin vestido; nulo.

nudge [nadch] *vt.* dar a uno un codazo disimuladamente.

nudity [niu-di-ti] *n.* desnudez, *f.*

nugget [na-guit] *n.* pepita, *f.;* **gold —,** pepita de oro.

nuisance [niu-sans] *n.* daño, perjuicio, *m.;* incomodidad, *f.,* estorbo, *m.;* (coll.) lata, *f.,* fastidio, *m.*

null [nal] *adj.* nulo, inválido.

nullify [na-li-fai] *vt.* anular, invalidar.

numb [nam] *adj.* entumecido, entorpecido; —, *vt.* entorpecer, entumecer.

number [nam-bar] *n.* número, *m.;* cantidad, *f.;* cifra, *f.;* **back —**, número atrasado; **round —**, número redondo; —, *vt.* numerar.

numbering [nam-ba-rin] *n.* numeración, *f.*

numberless [nam-ba-les] *adj.* innumerable, sin número.

numeral [niu-me-ral] *adj.* numeral; —, *n.* número, *m.*, cifra,

numerator [niu-me-rei-tar] *n.* (math.) numerador, *m.* numerical, *adj.* numérico.

numerous [niu-me-ros] *adj.* numeroso.

m., estúpido, da.

nun [nan] *n.* monja, religiosa, *f.*

nuptial [nap-shal] *adj.* nupcial; **—s**, *n. pl.* nupcias, *f. pl.*, boda, *f.*

nurse [ners] *n.* ama de cría; enfermera, *f.;* **wet —**, nodriza, nutriz, *f.;* —, *vt.* criar, alimen-

tar, amamantar; cuidar (un enfermo) .

nursery [ner-se-ri] *n.* cuarto dedicado a los niños; guardería infantil; plantel, criadero, *m.;* almáciga, *f.*

nursing [ner-sin] *n.* crianza, *f.;* **— bottle,** mamadera, *f.*, biberón, *m.*

nurture [ner-char] *vt.* criar, educar.

nut [nat] *n.* nuez, *f.;* (mech.) tuerca, *f.;* **lock —**, contratuerca, *f.*

nutcracker [nat-kra-kar] *n.* cascanueces, *m.*

nutmeg [nat-meg] *n.* nuez moscada.

nutriment [niu-tri-ment] *n.* nutrimento, alimento, *m.*

nutrition [niu-tri-shon] *n.* nutrición, *f.*, nutrimento, *m.*

nutritious, nutritive [niu-tri-shos], [niu-tri-tiv] *adj.* nutritivo, alimenticio; sustancioso.

nylon [nai-lon] *n.* nylon, *m.*

nymph [nimf] *n.* ninfa, *f.*

O

oak [ouk] *n.* roble, *m.*, encina, *f.*

oar [or] *n.* remo, *m.*

oarsman [ors-man] *n.* remero, *m.*

oasis [ouei-sis] *n.* oasis, *m.*

oat [out] *n.* avena, *f.*

oath [ouz] *n.* juramento, *m.;* jura, *f.;* blasfemia, *f.;* **to take —**

, prestar juramento.

oatmeal [out-mil] *n.* harina de avena, avena, *f.*

obedience [o-bi-diens] *n.* obediencia, *f.*

obedient [o-bi-dient] *adj.* obediente.

obese [ou-bis] *adj.* obeso, gordo.

obesity [ou-bi-si-ti] *n.* obesidad, gordura, *f.*

obey [o-bei] *vt.* obedecer.

obituary [o-bi-chua-ri] *n.* necrología, *f.;* obituario, *m.*

object [ob-yikt] *n.* objeto, *m.;* punto, *m.;* (gram.) complemento, *m.;* — **lesson,** lección objetiva o práctica, enseñanza objetiva; —, *vt.* objetar, poner reparo; oponer.

objection [ob-yek-shon] *n.* oposición, objeción, réplica, *f.;* **to raise an** —, objetar, poner objeción.

objectionable [ob-yek-sho-na-bol] *adj.* censurable, reprensible.

objective [ob-yek-tiv] *adj.* objetivo; —, *n.* meta, *f.;* fin, objetivo, *m.*

obligate [o-bli-gueit] *vt.* obligar; comprometer.

obligation [o-bli-guei-shon] *n.* obligación, *f.;* compromiso, *m.;* cargo, *m.;* **to be under** —, verse obligado.

oblige [o-blaidch] *vt.* obligar; complacer, favorecer.

obliging [o-blai-yin] *adj.* servicial; condescendiente; —**ly,** *adv.* cortésmente; gustosamente.

oblique [o-blik] *adj.* oblicuo; indirecto.

obliterate [o-bli-te-reit] *vt.* borrar; destruir; (med.) obliterar.

oblivion [o-bli-vion] *n.* olvido, *m.*

oblivious [o-bli-vios] *adj.* abstraído; — **of,** inconsciente de.

obnoxious [ob-nok-sios] *adj.* odioso, aborrecible.

oboe [ou-bou] *n.* (mus.) oboe, obué, *m.*

obscene [ob-sin] *adj.* obsceno, impúdico.

obscenity [ob-si-ni-ti] *n.* obscenidad, *f.*

obscure [obs-kiuar] *adj.* oscuro; —, *vt.* oscurecer.

obscurity [ob-skiua-ri-ti] *n.* oscuridad, *f.*

observance [ob-ser-vans] *n.* observancia, *f.;* costumbre, *f.;* rito, *m.;* ceremonia, *f.*

observant [ob-ser-vant] *adj.* observador, atento.

observation [ob-ser-vei-shon] *n.* observación, *f.*

observatory [ob-ser-va-tri] *n.* observatorio, *m.*

observe [ob-serv] *vt.* observar, mirar; reparar; ver; notar,

guardar (una fiesta, etc.); —,
vi. comentar.

observer [ob-ser-var] *n.* observador, ra.

observing [ob-ser-vin] *adj.* observador.

obsess [ob-ses] *vt.* obsesionar, causar obsesión.

obsession [ob-se-shon] *n.* obsesión, *f.*

obsolete [ob-so-lit] *adj.* anticuado, obsoleto.

obstacle [obs-ta-kol] *n.* obstáculo, *m.;* valla, *f.*

obstetrics [obs-ti-triks] *n.* obstetricia, *f.*

obstinacy [obs-ti-na-si] *n.* obstinación, terquedad, *f.*

obstinate [obs-ti-neit] *adj.* terco.

obstruct [obs-trakt] *vt.* obstruir; impedir; estorbar.

obstruction [obs-trak-shon] *n.* obstrucción, *f.;* impedimento, *m.*

obtain [ob-tein] *vt.* obtener, adquirir, lograr; —, *vi.* estar en uso, prevalecer.

obtainable [ob-tei-na-bol] *adj.* asequible.

obtrusive [ob-tru-siv] *adj.* intruso, importuno.

obtuse [ob-tius] *adj.* obtuso, romo, sin punta; sor-do, apagado.

obvious [ob-vios] *adj.* obvio, evidente, visto.

occasion [o-kei-shon] *n.* ocasión, ocurrencia, *f.;* caso, *m.;* tiempo oportuno; acontecimiento, *m.;* **to give** —, dar pie; —, *vt.* ocasionar, causar.

occasional [o-kei-sho-nal] *adj.* ocasional, casual; —**ly,** *adv.* ocasionalmente, a veces, a ratos.

Occident [ok-si-dent] *n.* occidente, *m.*

Occidental [ok-si-den-tal] *adj.* occidental.

occupancy [o-kiu-pan-si] *n.* toma de posesión.

occupant, occupier [o-kiu-pant], [o-kiu-paiar] *n.* ocupador, ra; poseedor, ra; inquilino, na.

occupation [o-kiu-pei-shon] *n.* ocupación, *f.;* empleo, *m.;* quehacer, *m.*

occupied [o-kiu-paid] *adj.* ocupado.

occupy [o-kiu-pai] *vt.* ocupar, emplear.

occur [o-ker] *vi.* ocurrir; suceder; **to** — **frequently,** acontecer a menudo.

occurrence [o-ka-rans] *n.* ocurrencia, *f.;* incidente, *m.;* caso, *m.*

ocean [ou-shan] *n.* océano, *m.,* alta mar, *m.* o *f.*

oceanic [ou-shia-nik] *adj.* oceánico.

oceanography [ou-sha-no-gra-fi]

n. oceanografía, f.

o'clock [o-klok] del reloj; por el reloj; **two —,** las dos.

octagon [ok-ta-gon] n. octágono, m.

octane [ok-tein] n. (chem.) octano, m.; **— rating,** número empleado para medir las propiedades antidetonantes de combustibles líquidos.

octave [ok-teiv] n. (mus.) octava, f.

October [ok-tou-bar] n. octubre, m.

octopus [ok-to-pos] n. (zool.) pulpo, pólipo, m.

odd [od] adj. impar; raro; particular; extravagante; extraño; **—ly,** adv. raramente.

oddity [o-di-ti] n. rareza, f.

odds [ods] n. pl. diferencia, disparidad f.; ventaja, f.; **— and ends,** trozos o fragmentos sobrantes.

odontologist [o-don-to-lo-chist] n. odontólogo, dentista, m.

odor, odour [ou-dar] n. olor, m.; fragancia, f.

of [of] prep. de; tocante; acerca de.

off [of] adj. y adv. lejos, a distancia; **hands —,** no tocar; **— and on,** de quitaipón; **— flavor,** desabrido; que no tiene el verdadero sabor.

offend [o-fend] vt. ofender, irri-

tar; injuriar; **—,** vi. pecar.

offender [o-fen-dar] n. delincuente, m. y f.; ofensor, ra, trasgresor, ra.

offending [o-fen-din] adj. ofensor.

offense [o-fens] n. ofensa, f.; injuria, f.; delincuencia, f., crimen, delito, m.

offensive [o-fen-siv] adj. ofensivo, injurioso; **—,** n. (mil.) ofensiva, f.

offer [o-far] vt. ofrecer; inmolar; atentar; brindar; **to — one's services,** brindarse; **—,** vi. ofrecerse; **—,** n. oferta, proposición, propuesta, f.

offering [o-fa-rin] n. sacrificio, m.; oferta, f.; propuesta, f.

office [o-fis] n. oficina, f.; oficio, empleo, m.; servicio, m.; cargo, m.; lugar, m.; **doctor's —,** consultorio, m.; **main —,** casa matriz; **— seeker,** pretendiente a un puesto, aspirante; **— supplies,** artículos para escritorio; **secretary's —,** secretaría, f.

officer [o-fi-sar] n. oficial, m.; funcionario, m.; agente de policía.

official [o-fi-shal] adj. oficial; **—,** n. oficial, m.; funcionario, m.; **public —,** funcionario público; **—ly,** adv. oficialmente.

offset [of-set] n. (print.) offset, m.; **—,** vt. balancear, compensar; neutralizar.

offshore [of-shor] *adv.* en la cercanía de la costa.

offspring [of-spring] *n.* linaje, *m.;* descendencia, *f.;* vástago, *m.*

oft, often, oftentimes [of-uord], [o-fen], [o-fen-taims] *adv.* muchas veces, frecuentemente, a menudo.

ogre [ou-gar] *n.* ogro, *m.*

oil [oil] *n.* aceite, *m.;* óleo, *m.;* petróleo, *m.;* **crude —,** aceite crudo; **mineral —,** aceite mineral; **— color,** color preparado con aceite; **— field,** campo de petróleo; cuenca petrolífera; **— painting,** pintura al óleo; **— pipe line,** oleoducto, *m.;* **— silk,** encerado, hule, *m.;* **vegetable —,** aceite vegetal; **—,** *vt.* aceitar, engrasar.

oily [oi-li] *adj.* aceitoso, oleaginoso.

ointment [oint-ment] *n.* ungüento, *m.*

O.K.: all correct [ou-kei] correcto, V.° B.° visto bueno; **approval,** aprobación.

okay [ou-kei] *adj.* y *adv.* bueno, está bien; **—,** *vt.* aprobar; dar el visto bueno; **—,** *n.* aprobación, *f.;* visto bueno, *m.*

old [ould] *adj.* viejo; antiguo; rancio; **— age,** vejez, ancianidad, *f.;* **of —,** antiguamente; **— hand,** experto, ta, persona

experimentada; **— line,** conservador, de ideas antiguas; **— maid,** soltera, solterona, *f.;* persona remilgada; **to become —,** envejecerse, gastarse.

old-fashioned [ould-fa-shond] *adj.* anticuado, fuera de moda.

old-time [ould-taim] *adj.* antiguo, anciano.

old-timer [ould-tai-mer] *n.* antiguo residente, miembro o trabajador; persona anticuada.

olfactory [ol-fak-to-ri] *adj.* olfatorio.

oligarchy [o-li-gar-ki] *n.* oligarquía, *f.*

olive [o-liv] *n.* olivo, *m.;* oliva, aceituna, *f.;* **— branch,** ramo de olivo, emblema de paz;**— oil,** aceite de oliva; **— tree,** olivo, *m.;* **pickled —s,** aceitunas en salmuera.

Olympics [olim-piks] *n. pl.* Olimpiada, *f.,* juegos olímpicos.

omelet, omelette [om-lit] *n.* tortilla de huevos.

omen [ou-men] *n.* agüero, presagio, *m.*

omission [ou-mi-shon] *n.* omisión, *f.;* descuido, *m.;* salto, *m.;* olvido, *m.*

omit [ou-mit] *vt.* omitir.

omnipotent [om-ni-po-tent] *adj.* omnipotente, todopoderoso.

omnivorous [om-ni-vo-ros] *adj.* omnívoro.

on [on] *prep.* sobre, encima, en; de; a; —, *adv.* adelante, sin cesar.

once [uans] *adv.* una vez; — **for all,** una vez por todas; **at —,** en seguida, cuanto antes, a un tiempo; **all at —,** de una vez, de un tirón; — **more,** una vez más; — **upon a time,** érase una vez.

oncoming [on-ka-min] *adj.* próximo, cercano, venidero.

one [uan] *adj.* un, uno; **at — stroke,** de un tirón; — **by —,** uno a uno, uno por uno; — **o'clock,** la una.

oneness [uan-nes] *n.* unidad, *f.*

oneself [uan-self] *pron.* sí mismo; **with —,** consigo.

one-sided [uan-sai-ded] *adj.* unilateral, parcial.

one-way [uan-uei] *adj.* en una sola dirección; — **trip,** viaje sencillo o en un solo sentido; — **ticket,** boleto sencillo.

onion [a-nion] *n.* cebolla, *f.*

onlooker [on-lu-kar] *n.* espectador, ra.

only [oun-li] *adj.* único, solo; mero; —, *adv.* solamente, únicamente.

onto [on-tu] *prep.* encima de, sobre, en.

onward, onwards [on-uard], [on-uards] *adv.* adelante.

onyx [o-niks] *n.* ónice, ónix, *m.*

ooze [us] *n.* fango, *m.*; —, *vi.* escurrir o fluir (algún líquido), manar o correr (algún líquido) suavemente; exudar.

opal [ou-pal] *n.* ópalo, *m.*

opaque [ou-peik] *adj.* opaco.

open [ou-pen] *adj.* abierto; patente, evidente; sincero, franco; cándido; rasgado; — **air,** aire libre; — **house,** fiesta para todos los que quieran concurrir; — **letter,** carta abierta (de protesta o súplica); — **question,** cuestión dudosa o sujeta a duda; — **secret,** secreto que todo el mundo sabe; — **shop,** taller que emplea obreros que pertenezcan o no a un gremio; —**ly,** *adv.* con franqueza, claramente, sin rebozo; —, *vt.* abrir; descubrir; —, *vi.* abrirse, descubrirse.

openhearted [ou-pen-jar-ted] *adj.* franco, sincero, sencillo.

opening [ou-pe-nin] *n.* abertura, grieta, *f*; (com.) salida, *f.*; principio, *m.*; boca *f*; apertura, inauguración, *f.*

open-minded [ou-pen-mauzd] *adj.* liberal; imparcial; receptivo.

opera [o-pe-ra] *n.* ópera, *f.*

opera glasses [o-pe-ra-glases] *n. pl.* gemelos de teatro.

operate [o-pe-reit] *vi.* obrar; operar; —, *vt.* explotar.

operatic [o-pe-ra-tik] *adj.* de ópera, relativo a la ópera.

operation [o-pe-rei-shon] *n.* operación, *f.;* funcionamiento, *m.;* **to have an —,** operarse.

operator [o-pe-rei-tar] *n.* operario, ria; operador, ra.

opiate [o-pieit] *n.* opiato, *m.,* opiata, *f.; —, adj.* opiato.

opinion [o-pi-nion] *n.* opinión, *f.;* juicio, *m.;* parecer, *m.;* sentencia, *f.;* concepto, *m.;* **in my —,** a mi ver; **to give an —,** opinar.

opinionated [o-pi-nio-nei-tid] *adj.* obstinado, pertinaz; doctrinal.

opium [o-piom] *n.* opio, *m.*

opossum [o-po-som] *n.* (zool.) zarigüeya, *f.*

opponent [ou-po-nent] *n.* antagonista, *m.* y *f.;* contrario, ria; contendiente, *m.* y *f.*

opportune [o-por-tiun] *adj.* oportuno, tempestivo, favorable, apropiado.

opportunity [o-por-tiu-ni-ti] *n.* oportunidad, sazón, *f.*

oppose [o-pous] *vi.* oponer, oponerse.

opposite [o-pou-sit] *adj.* fronterizo, opuesto; contrario; frente; de cara; **to take the — side,** llevar la contraria; **—,** *n.* antagonista, *m.* y *f.,* adversario, ria.

opposition [o-po-si-shon] *n.* oposición, *f.;* resistencia, *f.;* impedimento, *m.*

oppress [o-pres] *vt.* oprimir.

oppression [o-pre-shon] *n.* opresión, vejación, *f.*

oppressor [o-pre-sar] *n.* opresor, ra.

optic [op-tik] *adj.* óptico; **—s,** *n. pl.* óptica, *f.*

optical [op-tikal] *adj.* óptico; **— illusion,** ilusión de óptica.

optician [op-ti-shan] *n.* óptico, *m.*

optimism [op-ti-mi-sem] *n.* optimismo, *m.*

optimistic [op-ti-mis-tik] *adj.* optimista.

option [op-shon] *n.* opción, *f.;* deseo, *m.*

optional [op-sho-nal] *adj.* opcional.

optometrist [op-to-me-trist] *n.* optómetra, *m.*

optometry [op-to-me-tri] *n.* optometría, *f.*

opulence [o-piu-lens] *n.* opulencia, riqueza, *f.*

or [or] *conj.* o; ó (entre números); u (antes de o y ho).

oracle [o-ra-kel] *n.* oráculo, *m.*

oral [o-ral] *adj.* oral, vocal; **—ly,** *adv.* de palabra.

orange [o-rindch] *n.* naranja, *f.;* **— juice,** jugo de naranja; **— tree,** naranjo, *m.*

oration [o-rei-shon] *n.* oración,

arenga, *f.*

orator [o-rei-tar] *n.* orador, ra, tribuno, *m.*

oratory [o-ra-to-ri] *n.* oratoria, *f.;* oratorio, *m.;* elocuencia, *f.,* arte oratoria.

orb [orb] *n.* orbe, *m.,* esfera, *f.;* (poet.) ojo, *m.*

orbit [or-bit] *n.* órbita, *f.*

orchard [or-chard] *n.* vergel, huerto, *m.,* huerta, *f.*

orchestra [or-kis-tra] *n.* orquesta, *f.*

orchid [or-kid] *n.* orquídea, *f.*

ordain [or-dein] *vt.* (eccl.) ordenar; establecer.

ordeal [or-dil] *n.* ordalías, *f. pl.;* prueba severa.

order [or-dar] *n.* orden, *m.* y *f.;* regla, *f.;* mandato, *m.;* serie, clase, *f.;* encargo, *m.;* (com.) pedido, *m.;* **in — that,** para que; **out of —,** descompuesto; **rush —,** pedido urgente; **trial —,** pedido de ensayo; **unfilled —,** pedido pendiente; **—,** *vt.* ordenar, arreglar; mandar; pedir, hacer un pedido.

orderly [or-der-li] *adj.* ordenado, regular; **—,** *n.* asistente o criado de hospital.

ordinance [or-di-nans] *n.* ordenanza, *f.*

ordinarily [or-di-nea-ri-li] *adv.* ordinariamente.

ordinary [or-din-ri] *adj.* ordina-

rio; burdo, vulgar; **—,** *n.* ordinario, *m.;* **out of the —,** fuera de lo común.

ordnance [ord-nans] *n.* artillería, *f.;* cañones, *m. pl.,* pertrechos de guerra.

ore [or] *n.* mineral, *m.,* mena, *f.;* **— deposit,** yacimiento, *m.*

organ [or-gan] *n.* órgano, *m.;* **internal —s,** vísceras, *f. pl.;* **— pipe,** cañón de órgano; **— stop,** registro de un órgano.

organic [or-ga-nik] *adj.* orgánico.

organism [or-ga-ni-sem] *n.* organismo, *m.*

organization [or-ga-nai-sei-shon] *n.* organización n, *f.;* organismo, *m.*

organize [or-ga-nais] *vt.* organizar.

orgy [or-yi] *n.* orgía, *f.*

Orient [o-rient] *n.* oriente, *m.*

orient [o-rient] *vt.* orientar.

Oriental [o-rien-tal] *adj.* oriental.

orientation [o-rien-tei-shon] *n.* orientación, posición, *f.*

origin [o-ri-yin] *n.* origen, principio, *m.;* procedencia, *f.;* tronco, *m.*

original [o-ri-yi-nal] *adj.* original, primitivo; ingenioso; **—,** *n.* original, *m.*

originality [o-ri-yi-na-li-ti] *n.* originalidad, *f.*

originate [o-ri-yi-neit] *vt.* originar; **—,** *vi.* originar, provenir, originarse.

oriole [o-rioul] *n. (orn.)* oriol, *m.,* oropéndola, *f.;* (Sp. Am.) turpial, *m.*

ornament [or-na-ment] *n.* ornamento, *m.,* decoración, *f.;* —, *vt.* ornamentar, adornar.

ornamental [or-na-men-tal] *adj.* decorativo.

ornamentation [or-na-men-teishon] *n.* ornamentación, *f.*

ornate [or-neit] *adj.* muy adornado.

orphan [or-fan] *n.* y *adj.* huérfano, na.

orphanage [or-fa-nich] *n.* orfandad, *f.;* orfanato, asilo de huérfanos.

orthodox [or-zo-doks] *adj.* ortodoxo.

orthopedic [or-zoi-pik] *adj.* ortopédico.

oscillate [o-si-leit] *vi.* oscilar, vibrar.

oscillation [o-si-lei-shon] *n.* oscilación, vibración, *f.*

osmosis [os-mou-sis] *n.* osmosis, *f.*

ostentation [os-ten-tei-shon] *n.* ostentación, *f.*

ostentatious [os-ten-tei-shos] *adj.* ostentoso, fastuoso; —**ly,** *adv.* pomposamente, con ostentación.

ostracize [os-tra-sais] *vt.* desterrar, excluir.

ostrich [os-trich] *n.* avestruz, *m.*

other [a-dar] *pron.* y *adj.* otro.

otherwise [a-da-uais] *adv.* de otra manera, por otra parte.

ought [ot] *vi.* deber, ser menester.

ounce [auns] *n.* onza, *f.*

our [auar] *adj.* nuestro.

ours [auar] *pron.* el nuestro.

ourselves [aua-sevs] *pron. pl.* nosotros mismos.

oust [aust] *vt.* quitar; desposeer, desalojar.

out [aut] *adv.* fuera, afuera; —, *adj.* de fuera; —! *interj.* ¡fuera!; —, *n.* acción de sacar o dejar fuera a un jugador (en el juego de béisbol); —, *vt.* expeler, desposeer.

out-box [aut-baks] *n.* bandeja de salida, *f.*

outbreak [aut-breik] *n.* erupción, *f.;* estallido, *m.;* principio, *m.*

outburst [aut-berst] *n.* explosión, *f.*

outcast [aut-kast] *adj.* desechado; desterrado, expulso; —, *n.* desterrado, da.

outcome [aut-kam] *n.* conclusión, *f.;* consecuencia, *f.,* resultado, *m.*

outcry [aut-krai] *n.* clamor, *m.;* gritería, *f.;* venta en subasta pública.

outdated [aut-dei-tid] *adj.* anticuado, atrasado.

outdo [aut-du] *vt.* exceder a otro, sobrepujar.

outdoor [aut-dor] *adj.* al aire libre, fuera de casa, al raso; — **exercise,** ejercicio al aire libre.

outdoors [aut-dors] *adv.* al aire libre, a la intemperie, fuera de la casa; —, *adj.* relativo al aire libre o a la intemperie.

outer [au-tar] *adj.* exterior; — **space,** espacio extraterrestre.

outermost [au-ta-moust] *adj.* extremo; lo más exterior.

outfit [aut-fit] *n.* vestido, *m.,* vestimenta, *f.;* ropa, *f.;* —, *vt.* equipar, ataviar.

outgoing [aut-goin] *n.* salida *f.;* gasto, *m.;* —, *adj.* saliente; — **mail,** correspondencia de salida.

outing [au-tin] *n.* excursión o salida al campo, jira campestre.

outlandish [aut-lan-dish] *adj.* de apariencia exótica; ridículo, grotesco.

outlast [aut-last] *vt.* exceder en duración.

outlaw [aut-lo] *n.* forajido, da; bandido, *m.;* —, *vt.* proscribir.

outlet [aut-let] *n.* salida, *f.;* sangrador, tomadero, *m.*

outline [aut-lain] *n.* contorno, *m.;* bosquejo, *m.;* esbozo, *m.;* silueta, *f.;* —, *vt.* esbozar.

outlined [aut-laind] *adj.* perfilado; delineado.

outlive [aut-liv] *vt.* sobrevivir.

outlook [aut-luk] *n.* perspectiva, *f.*

outlying [aut-lain] *adj.* lejos de la parte central; remoto.

outnumber [aut-nam-bar] *vt.* exceder en número.

out-of-date [aut-of-deit] *adj.* anticuado, pasado o fuera de moda.

out-of-print [aut-ov-print] *adj.* (print.) agotado; — **edition,** edición agotada.

out-of-stock [aut-ov-stok] *adj.* (com.) agotado; sin existencia.

out-of-the-way [aut-ov-de-uei] *adj.* y *adv.* remoto, distante; fuera del camino; poco usual, raro.

outpouring [aut-po-rin] *n.* efusión, *f.*

output [aut-put] *n.* capacidad, *f.,* rendimiento, *m.,* producción total; cantidad producida.

outrage [aut-reich] *n.* ultraje, *m.,* infamia, *f.;* —, *vt.* ultrajar.

outrageous [aut-rei-chos] *adj.* ultrajoso; atroz; —**ly,** *adv.* injuriosamente; enormemente.

outrank [aut-rank] *vt.* sobresalir, exceder en rango, grado o posición.

outright [aut-rait] *adv.* cumplidamente, luego, al momento.

outshine [aut-shain] *vt.* exceder

en brillantez, eclipsar.

outside [aut-said] *n.* superficie, *f.;* exterior, *m.;* apariencia, *f.;* —, *adv.* afuera.

outsider [aut-sai-dar] *n.* foraste-ro, ra, extranjero, ra; persona no perteneciente a determinada institución, partido, etc.

outskirts [aut-skirts] *n. pl.* suburbio, *m.,* parte exterior (de una población, etc.).

outspoken [aut-spo-ken] *adj.* franco; que habla en for-ma atrevida.

outstanding [aut-stan-din] *adj.* sobresaliente, notable, extraor-dinario.

outstretch [aut-strech] *vt.* exten-der, alargar.

outward [aut-uod] *adj.* exterior, externo; —**ly,** *adv.* por fuera, exteriormente.

outweigh [aut-ueit] *vt.* pesar más (que otra cosa); compen-sar.

outworn [aut-uorn] *adj.* usado, gastado, anticuado, ajado.

oval [ou-val] *n.* óvalo, *m.;* —, *adj.* ovalado.

ovary [ou-va-ri] *n.* ovario, *m.*

ovation [ou-vei-shon] *n.* ovación, *f.*

oven [a-ven] *n.* horno, *m.*

over [ou-var] *prep.* sobre, por encima de; **all** —, por todos lados; —, *adv.* demás; — **again,**

otra vez; — **and above,** de sobra; — **and** —, repetidas veces.

overabundance [ou-var-a-ban-dans] *n.* plétora, superabun-dancia, *f.,* exceso, *m.*

overact [ou-ver-akt] *vt.* (theat.) exagerar la actuación.

overbearing [ou-va-bea-rin] *adj.* ultrajoso, despótico.

overboard [ou-va-bord] *adv.* (naut.) al agua, al mar.

overcast [ou-va-kast] *vt.* anu-blar, oscurecer; repulgar; **to be** —, nublarse, estar (el cielo) encapotado.

overcharge [ou-va-charch] *vt.* sobrecargar; poner alguna cosa a precio muy subido.

overcoat [ou-va-kaut] *n.* gabán, abrigo, *m.*

overcome [ou-va-kam] *vt.* vencer; superar; salvar (obstáculos).

overcooked [over-kukd] *adj.* recocido.

overcrowd [ou-va-kraud] *vt.* atestar, llenar demasiado.

overdo [ou-va-du] *vt.* exagerar; cocer demasiado (la carne, etc.) ; —, *vi.* hacer más de lo nece-sario.

overdose [ou-va-dous] *n.* dosis excesiva.

overdue [ou-va-diu] *adj.* (com.) atrasado, vencido; —, **draft,** letra vencida.

overeat [ou-var-it] *vi.* hartarse, comer demasiado.

overestimate [ou-var-es-ti-mit] *vt.* estimar o avaluar en exceso.

overexposure [ou-var-iks-pou-shar] *n.* (phot.) exceso de exposición.

overflow [ou-va-flau] *vt.* inundar; —, *vi.* salir de madre; rebosar desbordar; redundar; —, *n.* inundación, *f.;* superabundancia, *f.*

overflowing [ou-va-flauin] *n.* desbordamiento, *m.*

overgrown *adj.* grandulón, que ha crecido demasiado.

overhang [ou-va-jang] *vt.* estar colgando sobre alguna cosa; salir algo fuera del nivel (de un edificio, etc.).

overhead [ou-va-jed] *adv.* sobre la cabeza, en lo alto; —, *n.* (com.) gastos de administración.

overhear [ou-va-jiar] *vt.* oir algo por casualidad.

overheat [ou-va-jit] *vt.* acalorar, calentar demasiado.

overlapping *n.* acción de traslapar; —, *adj.* traslapado.

overload [ou-va-loud] *vt.* sobrecargar; —, *n.* sobre-carga, *f.,* recargo, *m.*

overlook [ou-va-luk] *vt.* mirar desde lo alto; examinar; repasar; pasar por alto; tolerar; descuidar; desdeñar.

overnight [ou-va-nait] *adv.* de noche, durante o toda la noche; —, *adj.* de una noche.

overpass [ou-va-pas] *vt.* y *vi.* atravesar, cruzar; vencer; trasgredir; exceder, sobrepasar; pasar por alto; —, *n.* puente o camino por encima de un ferrocarril, canal u otra vía.

overpower [ou-va-pauar] *vt.* predominar, oprimir.

overproduction [ou-va-pro-dak-shon] *n.* exceso de producción, sobreproducción, *f.*

overrate [ou-va-reit] *vt.* apreciar o valuar alguna cosa en más de lo que vale.

override [ou-va-raid] *vt.* atropellar; fatigar (un caballo) con exceso; prevalecer; anular, no hacer caso de.

overrule [ou-va-rul] *vt.* predominar, dominar.

overrun [ou-va-ran] *vt.* hacer correrías; cubrir enteramente; inundar; infestar; repasar; —, *vi.* rebosar.

oversee [ou-va-si] *vt.* inspeccionar; examinar.

overseer [ou-va-siar] *n.* superintendente, *m.;* capataz, *m.*

oversight [ou-va-sait] *n.* yerro, *m.;* equivocación, *f.;* olvido, *m.*

oversize [ou-va-sais] *adj.* grande en exceso.

oversleep [ou-va-slip] *vi.* dormir demasiado.

overstatement [ou-va-steit-ment] *n.* declaración exagerada.

overstay [ou-vas-tei] *vt.* permanecer demasiado tiempo.

overstep [ou-va-step] *vt. y vi.* pasar más allá; extralimitarse, excederse.

overstuffed *adj.* relleno o rellenado (aplícase a muebles).

overt [ou-vert] *adj.* abierto, público.

overtake [ou-va-teik] *vt.* alcanzar; coger en el hecho.

overthrow [ou-va-zrou] *vt.* trastornar; demoler; destruir; derribar, derrocar; —, *n.* trastorno, *m.;* ruina, derrota, *f.;* derrocamiento, *m.*

overtime [ou-va-taim] *n.* trabajo en exceso de las horas regulares.

overture [ou-va-tern] *n.* abertura, *f.;* (mus.) obertura, *f.;* proposición formal (de paz, etc.).

overturn [ou-va-tern] *vt.* volcar; subvertir, trastornar.

overweight [ou-va-ueit] *n.* exceso de peso; —, *adj.* demasiado pesado, muy obeso.

overwhelm [ou-va-uelm] *vt.* abrumar; oprimir; sumergir.

overwhelming [ou-va-uel-min] *adj.* abrumador, arrollador, dominante.

overwrought [ou-va-rot] *adj.* sobreexcitado.

ovum [ou-vom] *n.* (biol.) huevo, *m.*

owe [ou] *vt.* deber, tener deudas; estar obligado.

owing [ouin] *adj.* que es debido; — **to,** a causa de.

owl, owlet [oul], [au-lit] *n.* lechuza, *f.,* búho, *m.,* (Mex.) tecolote, *m.*

own [oun] *adj.* propio; **my —,** mío, mía; —, *vt.* reconocer; poseer; **to — up,** confesar.

owner [ou-nar] *n.* dueño, ña, propietario, ria; poseedor, ra.

ownership [ou-na-ship] *n.* dominio, *m.;* propiedad, *f.*

oxen [oksen] *n. pl.* de **ox,** bueyes, *m. pl.*

oxidation [ok-si-dei-shon] *n.* oxidación, *f.*

oxidize [ok-si-dais] *vt.* oxidar.

oxygen [ok-si-yen] *n.* oxígeno, *m.;* — **tent,** tienda de oxígeno.

oxygenize [ok-si-ye-nais] *vt.* oxigenar.

oyster [ois-tar] *n.* ostra, *f.,* ostión, *m.*

ozone [ou-soun] *n.* (chem.) ozona, *f.,* ozono, *m.*

P

pace [peis] *n.* paso, *m.*, marcha, *f.; —, vt.* medir a pasos; —, *vi.* pasear; **to — one's beat,** hacer la ronda.

Pacific [pa-si-fik] *n.* Pacífico, *m.,* Océano Pacífico.

pacific [pa-si-fik] *adj.* pacífico.

pacifist [pa-si-fist] *n.* pacifista, *m.* y *f.*

pacify [pa-si-fai] *vt.* pacificar; asosegar, apaciguar.

pack [pak] *n.* lío, fardo, *m.;* baraja de naipes; muta, perrada, *f.;* cuadrilla, *f.;* carga, *f.;* — **animal,** acémila, *f.,* animal de carga; — **horse,** caballo de carga; — **of cigarettes,** cajetilla de cigarros; — **of wolves,** manada de lobos; —, *vt.* empaquetar; empacar; enfardelar, embalar.

package [pa-kich] *n.* fardo, bulto, *m.;* paquete, *m.*

packer [pa-kar] *n.* empaquetador, embalador, *m.*

packet [pa-kit] *n.* paquete, *m.*

packing [pa-kin] *n.* envase, *m.;* empaque, *m.;* relleno, *m.;* — **house,** empresa empacadora, frigorífico, *m.*

pact [pakt] *n.* pacto, convenio, acuerdo, arreglo, contrato, *m.*

pad [pad] *n.* cojincillo, *m.,* almohadilla, *f.,* relleno, *m.;* — **(of paper),** bloc (de papel), *m.;* —, *vt.* rellenar.

padded [pa-did] *adj.* acojinado, relleno, rellenado (de algodón, paja, papel, etc.).

padding [pa-din] *n.* relleno, *m.*

paddle [pa-del] *vi.* remar; chapotear; — *n.* remo, canalete, *m.;* — **wheel,** rueda de paletas.

padlock [pad-lok] *n.* candado, *m.*

pagan [pei-gan] *n.* y *adj.* pagano, na.

paganism [pei-ga-ni-sem] *n.* paganismo, *m.*

page [peich] *n.* página, *f.;* —, llamar (a alguien en un hotel, etc.).

pageant [pa-chant] *n.* espectáculo público; procesión, *f.*

pageantry [pa-chan-tri] *n.* fausto, *m.,* pompa, *f.*

paid-up [peid-ap] *adj.* pagado, terminado de pagar.

pail [peil] *n.* balde, cubo, *m.,* cubeta, *f.*

pain [pein] *n.* pena, *f ;* castigo, *m.;* dolor, *m.;* —, *vt.* afligir; doler; —, *vi.* causar dolor.

painful [pein-ful] *adj.* dolorido; penoso.

painless [pein-les] *adj.* sin pena; sin dolor.

painstaking [peins-tei-kin] *adj.* laborioso afanoso; es-merado; —**ly**, *adv.* detenidamente.

paint [peint] *vt.* y *vi.* pintar; —, *n.* pintura, *f.*

paintbrush [peint-brush] *n.* brocha, *f.*, pincel, *m.*

painter [pein-tar] *n.* pintor, ra.

painting [pein-tin] *n.* pintura, *f.*

pair [pear] *n.* par, *m.*

pajamas [pa-ya-mas] *n. pl.* pijamas, *m. pl.*

pal [pal] *n.* camarada, compañero, ra, compinche, *m.* y *f.*, amigo, ga; cómplice, confederado, *m.*

palace [pa-lis] *n.* palacio, *m.*

palatable [pa-la-ta-bol] *adj.* sabroso.

palate [pa-lit] *n.* paladar, *m.;* gusto, *m.*

palatial [pa-lei-shal] *adj.* propio de palacios, pala-ciego.

pale [peil] *adj.* pálido; claro; **to turn** —, palidecer; —, *n.* palizada, *f.;* estaca, *f.;* límite, *m.;* —, *vt.* empalizar, cercar, rodear.

paleness [peil-nes] *n.* palidez, *f.*

palette [pa-lit] *n.* paleta (de pintor), *f.*

palisade [pa-li-seid] *n.* palizada, *f.*, palenque, *m.*

pall [pol] *n.* palio de arzobispo; palia, *f.;* —, *vi.* desvanecerse; —, *vt.* y *vi.* saciar.

pallbearer [pol-berer] *n.* el que acompaña a un cadáver.

palliate [pa-lieit] *vt.* paliar.

pallor [pa-lar] *n.* palidez, *f.*

palm [pam] *n.* (bot.) palma, *f.;* victoria, *f.;* palma (de la mano), *f.;* — **oil**, aceite de palma o palmera; —, *vt.* escamotear; tocar con la palma de la mano.

palpable [pal-pa-bol] *adj.* palpable; evidente.

palpitate [pal-pi-teit] *vi.* palpitar.

palpitation [pal-pi-tei-shon] *n.* palpitación, *f.*

palsy [pol-si] *n.* parálisis, perlesía, *f.*

paltry [pol-tri] *adj.* vil; mezquino.

pamper [pam-par] *vt.* mimar.

pamphlet [pam-flit] *n.* folleto, libreto, *m.*

pan [pan] *n.* cazuela, cacerola, sartén, *f.*

panacea [pa-na-shia] *n.* panacea, *f.*

Panamanian [pa-na-mei-nian] *n.* y *adj.* panameño, ña.

pancake [pan-keik] *n.* pancake, hotcake, *m.*

pancreas [pan-krias] *n.* (anat.) páncreas, *m.*

panda [pan-da] *n.* panda, *m.*

pane [pein] *n.* cuadro de vidrio.

pang [pang] *n.* angustia, congoja, *f.*

panhandler [pan-jand-lar] *n.*

pordiosero, ra, mendigo, ga; callejero, ra.

panic [pa-nik] *n.* y *adj.* pánico, *m.*

panicky [pa-ni-ki] *adj.* consternado, aterrorizado.

panic-stricken [pa-niks-tri-ken] *adj.* aterrorizado, pasmado, espantado.

panorama [pa-no-ra-ma] *n.* panorama, *m.*

pansy [pan-si] *n.* (bot.) pensamiento, *m.*, trinitaria, *f.;* (coll.) hombre afeminado.

pant [pant] *vi.* palpitar; jadear; **to — for, to — after,** suspirar por; —, *n.* jadeo, *m.*

panther [pan-zar] *n.* pantera, *f.*

panties [pan-tis] *n. pl.* calzones de mujer.

panting [pan-tin] *adj.* jadeante, anhelante, sin respiración, sin aliento.

pantomime [pan-to-maim] *n.* pantomima, *f.*

pantry [pan-tri] *n.* despensa, *f.*

pants [pants] *n. pl.* pantalones, *m. pl.*

papacy [pa-pa-si] *n.* papado, *m.*

papal [pa-pal] *adj.* papal.

paper [pei-par] *n.* papel, *m.;* periódico, *m.;* **—s,** *n. pl.;* escrituras, *f. pl.;* documento, *m.;* **blotting —,** papel secante; **brown —,** papel de estraza; **carbon —,** papel carbón; **glazed** —, papel satinado; **in a — cover,** a la rústica (encuadernación) ; **litmus —,** (chem.) papel reactivo; **tissue —,** papel de seda; **toilet —** papel de excusado; **vellum —,** papel avitelado; **wrapping —,** papel de envolver; **writing —,** papel de escribir; **— clip,** sujetapapeles, *m.;* **— cutter, — knife,** cortapapel, *m.;* **— money,** papel moneda; —, *adj.* de papel; —, *vt.* entapizar con papel.

paprika [pa-pri-ka] *n.* pimentón, *m.*

par [par] *n.* equivalencia, *f.;* igualdad, *f.;* (golf) número de jugadas para un agujero; **at —,** (com.) a la par; **exchange at —,** cambio a la par; **exchange under —,** cambio con quebrado; **— value,** valor a la par.

parable [pa-ra-bol] *n.* parábola, *f.*

parachute [pa-ra-shut] *n.* paracaídas, *m.;* **— troops,** cuerpo de paracaidistas.

parachutist [pa-ra-shu-tist] *n.* paracaidista, *m.*

parade [pa-reid] *n.* ostentación, pompa, *f.;* desfile, *m.;* (mil.) parada, *f.;* —, *vt.* y *vi.* formar parada; tomar parte en un desfile; pasear; hacer gala.

paradise [pa-ra-dais] *n.* paraíso, *m.*

paradox [pa-ra-doks] *n.* paradoja, *f.*

paraffin [pa-ra-fin] *n.* parafina, *f.*

paragraph [pa-ra-graf] *n.* párrafo, *m.*

parakeet [pa-ra-kit] *n.* periquito,
m.

parallel [pa-ra-lel] *n.* línea para-
lela; —, *adj.* paralelo; —, *vt.*
parangonar.

parallelogram [pa-ra-le-lou-
gram] *n.* paralelogramo, *m.*

paralysis [pa-ra-lai-sis] *n.* parálisis, *f.*

paralytic [pa-ra-li-tik] *adj.* paralítico.

paramount [pa-ra-mount] *adj.*
supremo, superior.

paranoia [pa-ra-noia] *n.* paranoia, *f.*

parapet [pa-ra-pit] *n.* parapeto,
m.; pretil, *m.*

paraphernalia [pa-ra-fe-na-lia]
n. equipo, *m.,* atavíos, adornos,
m. pl.

paraphrase [pa-ra-freis] *n.* pará-
frasis, *f.;* —, *vt.* parafrasear.

paraplegic [pa-ra-ple-yik] *n.* y
adj. parapléjico, ca.

parasite [pa-ra-sait] *n.* parásito,
m.

parcel [par-sel] *n.* paquete, *m.;*
porción, cantidad, *f.;* bulto, *m.;*
lío, *m.;* — **post,** paquete postal;
—, *vt.* partir, dividir.

parchment [parch-ment] *n.* per-

gamino, *m.*

pardon [par-don] *n.* perdón, *m.,*
gracia, *f.;* —, *vt.* perdonar.

pardonable [par-do-na-bol] *adj.*
perdonable.

pare [pear] *vt.* recortar; pelar,
quitar la corteza.

parent [pea-rent] *n.* padre, *m.;*
madre, *f.;* —**s,** *n. pl.* padres, *m.
pl.*

parental [pa-ren-tal] *adj.* paternal; maternal.

parenthesis [pa-ren-zi-sis] *n.*
paréntesis, *m.*

parenthood [pe-rent-jud] *n.*
paternidad o maternidad, *f.*

Paris green [pa-ris-grin] *n.* car-
denillo, *m.,* verde de París.

parish [pa-rish] *n.* parroquia, *f.;*
—, *adj.* parroquial.

park [park] *n.* parque, *m.;* —, *vt.*
estacionar (vehículos).

parking [par-kin] *n.* estacionamiento (de automóviles), *m.;* —
place, lugar de estacionamiento; **no** —, se prohíbe estacio-
narse.

parliament [par-la-ment] *n.* parlamento, *m.;* **member of** —,
parlamentario, *m.*

parliamentary [par-la-men-ta-ri]
adj. parlamentario.

parlor [par-lar] *n.* sala, sala de
recibo, *f.;* **funeral** —, casa mortuoria; **beauty** —, salón de
belleza.

parochial [pa-rou-kial] *adj.* parroquial.

parody [pa-ro-di] *n.* parodia, *f.;* —, *vt.* parodiar.

parole [pa-roul] *n.* libertad que se da a un prisionero; —, *vt.* y *vi.* libertar bajo palabra.

paroxysm [pa-rok-si-sem] *n.* paroxismo, *m.*

parrot [pa-rot] *n.* loro, *m.*

parsimonious [par-si-mou-nios] *adj.* económico, moderado en sus gastos; **—ly,** *adv.* con parsimonia, con economía.

parsley [pars-li] *n.* (bot.) perejil, *m.*

parson [par-son] *n.* párroco, *m.*

part [part] *n.* parte, *f.;* oficio, *m.;* papel, *m.;* raya, *f.,* partido, *m.;* obligación, *f.;* **in—,** parcialmente; **— of speech,** parte de la oración; **— time,** trabajo de unas cuantas horas por día, trabajo temporal por semana; **rear —,** zaga, *f.;* **—s,** *n. pl.* partes, *f. pl.,* paraje, distrito, *m.;* —, *vt.* partir, separar, desunir; —, *vi.* partirse, separarse; **— from,** despedirse; **— with,** deshacerse de.

partake [par-teik] *vt.* y *vi.* participar, tomar parte.

partial [par-shal] *adj.* parcial.

partiality [par-shia-li-ti] *n.* parcialidad, *f.*

participant [par-ti-si-pant] *adj.*

participante; —, *n.* partícipe, participante, *m.* y *f.*

participate [par-ti-si-peit] *vt.* participar.

participation [par-ti-si-pei-shon] *n.* participación, *f.*

participle [par-ti-si-pel] *n.* (gram.) participio, *m.*

particle [par-ti-kel] *n.* partícula, *f.*

particular [par-ti-kiu-lar] *adj.* particular, singular; —, *n.* particular, *m.;* particularidad, *f.*

parting [par-tin] *n.* separación, partida,. *f.*

partisan [par-ti-san] *n.* y *adj.* partidario, ra.

partisanship [par-ti-san-ship] *n.* partidarismo, *m.*

partly [parz-li] *adv.* en parte.

partner [part-nar] *n.* socio, cia, compañero, ra; **active —, managing —,** socio gerente o gestor; **silent —,** socio comanditario.

partnership [part-na-ship] *n.* compañía, sociedad, *f.,* sociedad de comercio, sociedad mercantil, asociación comercial; consorcio, *m.*

partridge [par-trich] *n.* perdiz, *f.*

part-time [par-taim] *adj.* parcial; **— work,** trabajo de medio tiempo.

party [par-ti] *n.* partido, *m.;* parte, *f.;* función, *f.;* tertulia, *f.;*

(mil.) partida, *f.;* — **line,** línea telefónica usada por dos o más abonados.

pass [pas] *vt.* pasar; traspasar; trasferir; —, *vi.* pasar, ocurrir; trascurrir; —, *n.* pasillo, *m.;* paso, camino, *m.;* pase, *m.;* estado, *m.;* condición, *f.;* estocada, *f.;* (fútbol) pase *m.;* **narrow** —, callejón, *m.*

passable [pa-sa-bol] *adj.* pasadero, transitable.

passageway [pa-sich-uei] *n.* pasadizo, pasaje, callejón, *m.;* paso, *m.*

passenger [pa-san-yar] *n.* pasajero, ra.

passer-by [pa-sa-bai] *n.* transeúnte, *m.* y *f.*

passing [pa-sin] *adj.* pasajero, transitorio, momentáneo; casual; que pasa; — **grade,** calificación que permite pasar (el examen, etc.); — **bell,** toque de difuntos; —, *n.* paso, *m.;* **in** —, al paso, al pasar.

passion [pa-shon] *n.* pasión, *f.;* amor, *m.;* celo, ardor, *m.;* **to fly into a** —, montar en cólera.

passionate [pa-sho-nit] *adj.* apasionado; colérico.

passive [pa-siv] *adj.* pasivo.

Passover [pa-sou-var] *n.* Pascua (de los judíos), *f.*

passport [pas-port] *n.* pasaporte, salvoconducto, *m.*

password [pas-ued] *n.* (mil.) seña, contraseña, *f.*

past [past] *adj.* pasado; gastado; — **tense,** (gram.) pretérito, *m.;* — **master,** experto, *m.;* autoridad, *f.;* ex funcionario de una logia o sociedad; — **participle,** participio pasado; — **perfect,** *n.* y *adj.* pretérito perfecto; —, *n.* pasado, *m.;* (gram.) pretérito, *m.;* —, *prep.* más allá de, fuera de.

paste [peist] *n.* pasta, *f.;* engrudo, *m.;* —, *vt.* engrudar, pegar.

pastel [pas-tal] *n.* (arte) pastel, *m.;* pintura al pastel.

pasteurization [pas-ta-rai-seishon] *n.* pasterización, *f.*

pasteurize [pas-ta-rais] *vt.* pasterizar.

pastime [pas-taim] *n.* pasatiempo, *m.;* diversión, *f.;* recreo, *m.;* distracción, *f.*

pastor [pas-tor] *n.* pastor, *m.*

pastoral [pas-to-ral] *adj.* pastoril; pastoral, bucólico; — **poetry,** bucólica, *f.*

pastry [peis-tri] *n.* pastelería, *f.;* — **shop,** repostería, *f.*

pasture [pas-char] *n.* pastura, dehesa, *f.;* —, *vt.* pastar, apacentar; —, *vi.* pastar, pacer.

pasty [peis-ti] *adj.* pastoso.

pat [pat] *adj.* apto, conveniente, propio; (coll.) firme, fijo; imposible de olvidar; **to stand** —, mantenerse firme; —, *n.* golpecillo, *m.;* —, *vt.* dar golpecillos; acariciar con la mano.

patch [pach] *n.* remiendo, *m.;* lunar, *m.;* parche, *m.;* —, *vt.* remendar; **to — up,** remendar; ajustar, solucionar; **to — up a quarrel,** hacer las paces.

patent [pei-tent] *adj.* patente, manifiesto; **— leather,** charol, *m.;* **— medicine,** remedio de patente, medicina patentada; —, *n.* patente, *f.*, privilegio de invención; cédula, *f.;* —, *vt.* patentar.

paternity [pa-ter-ni-ti] *n.* paternidad, *f.*

path [paz] *n.* senda, *f.*, sendero, *m.*

pathetic [pa-ze-tik] *adj.* patético.

pathological [pa-zo-lo-yi-kal] *adj.* patológico.

pathology [pa-zo-lo-yi] *n.* patología, *f.*

pathos [pei-zos] *n.* sentimiento, *m.*

pathway [paz-uei] *n.* vereda, senda, *f.*

patience [pei-shans] *n.* paciencia, *f.*

patient [pei-shant] *adj.* paciente, sufrido; **—ly,** *adv.* con paciencia; —, *n.* enfermo, ma; paciente, doliente, *m.* y *f.*

patio [pa-tiou] *n.* patio, *m.*

patriarch [pei-triak] *n.* patriarca, *m.*

patrician [pa-tri-shan] *n.* y *adj.* patricio, *m.*

patriot [pei-triot] *n.* patriota, *m.*

patriotic [pa-trio-tik] *adj.* patriótico.

patriotism [pa-trio-ti-sem] *n.* patriotismo, *m.*

patrol [pa-troul] *n.* patrulla, *f.;* —, *vi.* y *vt.* patrullar; **— wagon,** camión de policía.

patrolman [pa-troul-man] *n.* rondador, *m.*, guardia municipal, vigilante de policía.

patron [pei-tron] *n.* patrón, protector, *m.;* **— saint,** santo patrón.

patronage [pei-tro-nich] *n.* patrocinio, *m.;* patronato, patronazgo, *m.;* clientela, *f.*

patronize [pa-tro-nais] *vt.* patrocinar, proteger.

patter [pa-tar] *vi.* patalear, patear; charlar; —, *n.* charlatanería, *f.;* serie de golpecitos; pataleo, *m.;* pisadas (de niño), *f. pl.*

pattern [pa-tern] *n.* modelo, *m.;* ejemplar, *m.;* patrón, *m.;* muestra, *f.;* molde, *m.;* tipo, *m.*

paunch [ponch] *n.* panza, *f.;* vientre, *m.*

pauper [po-par] *n.* pobre, *m.* y *f.;* limosnero, ra.

pause [pos] *n.* pausa, *f.;* —, *vi.* pausar; deliberar.

pavement [peiv-ment] *n.* pavi-

mento, piso, empedrado de
calle.

pavilion [pa-vi-lion] *n.* (naut.)
pabellón, *m.;* quiosco, *m.;*
(anat.) pabellón (de la oreja),
m.

paving [pei-vin] *n.* pavimento,
piso, *m.;* pavimentación, *f.*

paw [po] *n.* garra, *f.;* —, manosear alguna cosa con poca
maña.

pawn [pon] *n.* prenda, *f.;* peón
(de ajedrez), *m.;* —, *vt.* empeñar.

pawnbroker [pon-brou-kar] *n.*
prendero, *m.;* prestamista, *m.* y
f.

pawnshop [pon-shop] *n.* casa de
préstamos o empeños.

pay [pei] *vt.* pagar; sufrir (por);
to — back, devolver; pagar
(una deuda); vengarse de; **to —
no attention,** no hacer caso; **to
— off,** despedir; castigar,
recompensar; **to — up,** pagar
por completo; —, *n.* paga, *f.,*
pago, *m.;* sueldo, salario, *m.;*
monthly —, mensualidad,
mesada, *f.;* — **roll,** nómina,
nómina de sueldos.

payable [pei-yabol] *adj.* pagade-
ro.

payday [pei-dei] *n.* día de paga.

payment [pei-ment] *n.* pago, *m.;*
paga, *f.;* recompensa, *f.;* premio, *m.;* pagamento, *m.;* **cash**
—, pago al contado; **down —,**
pago inicial; (Mex.) enganche,
m.; **on — of,** mediante el pago
de; — **in advance,** pago adelantado, anticipo, *m.;* — **in full,**
saldo de cuenta; **terms of —,**
condiciones de pago; **to delay
—, to defer —,** diferir o aplazar
el pago; **to make   —,** efectuar
un pago; **to present for —,** presentar al cobro; **to stop —,** suspender el pago.

pea [pi] chícharo, *m.;* — **green,**
verde claro.

peace [pis] *n.* paz, *f.*

peaceable [pi-sa-bol] *adj.* tranquilo, pacífico.

peaceful [pis-ful] *adj.* pacífico,
apacible, tranquilo; silencioso.

peach [pich] *n.* melocotón,
durazno, *m.;* — **tree,** melocoto-
nero, duraznero, *m.*

peacock [pi-kok] *n.* pavo real,
pavón, *m.*

peak [pik] *n.* cima, *f.;* cúspide, *f.*

peaked [pikt] *adj.* puntiagudo;
endeble.

peal [pil] *n.* campaneo, *m.;*
estruendo, *m.;* re-pique, *m.;* —,
vt. y *vi.* hacer resonar; repicar.

peanut [pi-nat] *n.* cacahuate,
cacahuete, maní, *m.;* — **brittle,**
crocante, *m.,* (Mex.) palanque-
ta, *f.;* — **butter,** mantequilla de
cacahuate o maní.

pear [pear] *n.* pera, *f.;* —

orchard, peral, *m.;* — **tree,** peral, *m.*

pearl [parl] *n.* perla, *f.*

pearly [per-li] *adj.* perlino.

peasant [pe-sant] *n.* labriego, ga, campesino, na.

peat [pit] *n.* turba, *f.*

pebble [pe-bel] *n.* guijarro, *m.,* piedrecilla, *f.*

pecan [pi-kan] *n.* pacana, *f.,* nuez encarcelada.

peck [pek] *n.* picotazo, *m.;* —, *vt.* picotear; picar.

peculiar [pi-kiu-liar] *adj.* peculiar, particular, singular.

peculiarity [pi-kiu-la-li] *n.* particularidad, singularidad, *f.*

pecuniary [pi-kiu-nia-ri] *adj.* pecuniario.

pedagogue [pe-da-gog] *n.* pedagogo, *m.*

pedal [pe-dal] *n.* pedal, *m.;* **gas** —, acelerador (de un auto); —, *adj.* relativo a los pies; —, *vt.* y *vi.* pedalear.

peddle [pe-del] *vt.* y *vi.* vender menudencias de casa en casa.

peddler [ped-lar] *n.* buhonero, vendedor ambulante.

pedestal [pe-dis-tal] *n.* pedestal, *m.,* basa, *f.*

pedestrian [pi-des-trian] *n.* andador, ra, peatón, ona; —, *adj.* pedestre.

pediatrician [pe-dia-tri-shan] *n.* (med.) pediatra, *m.* y *f.*

pediatrics [pe-dia-triks] *n.* (med.) pediatría, *f.*

pedigreed [pe-di-grid] *adj.* de casta escogida; — **dog,** perro de raza fina.

peek [pik] *vi.* atisbar; —, *n.* atisbo, *m.,* atisbadura, *f.*

peel [pil] *vt.* descortezar, pelar; —, corteza, *f.,* pellejo (de frutas), *m.*

peeling [pi-lin] *n.* peladura, mondadura, *f.*

peep [pip] *vi.* asomar; atisbar; clavar la mirada; —, *n.* asomo, *m.;* ojeada, *f.*

peephole [pip-joul] *n.* atisbadero, *m.*

peer [piar] *n.* compañero, *m.;* par (grande de Inglaterra), *m.;* —, *vi.* mirar fijamente; fisgar.

peerless [pia-les] *adj.* incomparable, sin par.

peevish [pi-vish] *adj.* regañón, bronco; enojadizo; —**ly,** *adv.* con impertinencia.

peg [peg] *n.* clavija, espita, estaquilla, *f.,* gancho, *m.;* —, *vt.* clavar.

pelican [pe-li-kan] *n.* pelícano, *m.*

pelt [pelt] *n.* pellejo, cuero, *m.;* —, *vt.* golpear; **to** — **with stones,** apedrear.

pelvic [pel-vik] *adj.* pélvico.

pelvis [pel-vis] *n.* pelvis, *f.*

pen [pen] *n.* pluma, *f.;* corral,

m.; caponera, *f.;* — **name,** seudónimo, *m.;* **ball point —,** pluma atómica, bolígrafo, *m.;* —, *vt.* enjaular, encerrar; escribir.

penal [pi-nal] *adj.* penal.

penalize [pi-na-lais] *vt.* penar, imponer pena a.

penalty [pe-nal-ti] *n.* pena, *f.,* castigo, *m.;* multa, *f.*

penance [pe-nans] *n.* penitencia, *f.;* **to do —,** penar.

penchant [pen-chant] *n.* tendencia, inclinación, *f.*

pencil [pen-sil] *n.* pincel, *m.;* lápiz, *m.;* **mechanical —,** lapicero, *m.;* **— case,** estuche para lápices; **— holder,** lapicero, *m.;* **— sharpener,** sacapuntas, *m.;* —, *vt.* pintar; escribir con lápiz.

pendant [pen-dant] *n.* pendiente, *m.*

pending [pen-din] *adj.* pendiente; indeciso; **— payment,** pendiente de pago; **to be —,** pender.

pendulum [pen-diu-lom] *n.* péndulo, *m.*

penetrate [pe-ni-treit] *vt.* y *vi.* penetrar.

penetration [pe-ni-trei-shon] *n.* penetración, *f.;* sagacidad, *f.*

penguin [pen-güin] *n.* pingüino, pájaro bobo, *m.*

penicillin [pe-ni-si-lin] *n.* (med.) penicilina, *f.*

peninsula [pi-nin-siu-la] *n.* península, *f*

penitence [pe-ni-tans] *n.* penitencia, *f.*

penitentiary [pe-ni-ten-sha-ri] *n.* penitenciaría, *f.;* penitenciario, *m.*

penmanship [pen-man-ship] *n.* caligrafía, *f.*

pennant, pennon [pen-nant], [pe-non] *n.* (naut.) flámula, banderola, *f.;* jirón, gallardete, *m.*

penniless [pe-ni-les] *adj.* falto de dinero, indigente.

penny [pe-ni] *n.* centavo, *m.;* penique, *m.;* dinero, *m.*

pension [pen-shon] *n.* pensión, *f.;* **widow's —,** viudedad, *f.;* —, *vt.* dar alguna pensión.

pensioner [pen-sho-nar] *n.* pensionista, *m.* y *f.,* pensionado, da.

pensive [pen-siv] *adj.* pensativo; reflexivo.

pentagon [pen-ta-gon] *n.* pentágono, *m.*

pentameter [pen-ta-mi-tar] *n.* pentámetro, verso de cinco pies.

penthouse [pent-jaus] *n.* cobertizo, tejadillo, *m.;* habitación construida en un techo.

pent-up [pent-ap] *adj.* acorralado, encerrado, reprimido.

penultimate [pi-nal-ti-mit] *adj.*

penúltimo.

penury [pe-niu-ri] *n.* penuria, carestía, *f.*

people [pi-pol] *n.* gente, *f.;* pueblo, *m.;* nación, *f.;* vulgo, *m.;* —, *vt.* poblar.

pep [pep] [pep] *n.* (coll.) energía, *f.,* vigor, entusiasmo, espíritu, *m.*

pepper [pe-par] *n.* pimienta, *f.;* — **pot,** sopa de carne y legumbres condimentada con pimientos, ají, etc.; **red** —, pimiento, chile, *m.;* —, *vt.* sazonar con pimienta; golpear, azotar.

peppermint [pe-pa-mint] *n.* menta, hierbabuena, *f.;* — **drop,** pastilla de menta.

per [per] *prep,* por; — **annum,** al año; — **capita,** por persona, por cabeza; — **cent,** por ciento (%); — **diem,** por día.

perceive [per-siv] *vt.* percibir, comprender.

percentage [per-sen-tich] *n.* porcentaje, *m.,* tanto por ciento.

perceptible [per-sep-ti-bol] *adj.* perceptible.

perception [per-sep-shon] *n.* percepción, idea, noción, *f.*

perch [perch] *n.* (ichth.) perca, *f.;* (medida) pértica, *f.;* —, *vt.* emperchar; —, *vi.* posarse, encaramarse.

perchance [per-chans] *adv.* (poet.) posiblemente, quizá.

percolator [per-ko-lei-tar] *n.* cafetera filtradora, percolador, colador de café.

percussion [per-ka-shan] *n.* percusión, *f.;* golpe, *m.;* — **cap,** *n.* pistón, *m.;* — **instrument,** instrumento de percusión.

perennial [pe-re-nial] *adj.* perenne, perpetuo.

perfect [per-fekt] *adj.* perfecto, acabado; puro; derecho; —**ly,** *adv.* a fondo; —, *vt.* perfeccionar, acabar.

perfection [per-fek-shon] *n.* perfección, *f.*

perfectionist [per-fek-sho-nist] *n.* persona amante de la perfección.

perforate [per-fo-reit] *vt.* horadar, perforar.

perforation [per-fo-rei-shon] *n.* perforación, *f.*

perform [per-form] *vt.* ejecutar; efectuar; ejercer; hacer; realizar; —, *vi.* representar, hacer papel.

performance [per-for-mans] *n.* ejecución, *f.;* cumplimiento, *m.;* actuación, *f.;* obra, *f.;* representación teatral, función, *f.;* funcionamiento, *m.;* **first** —, estreno, *m.*

performer [per-for-mar] *n.* ejecutor, ra, ejecutante, *m.* y *f.,* actor, *m.,* actriz, *f.*

perfume [per-fium] *n.* perfume,

m.; fragancia, f.; — **bottle,** frasco de perfume; — vt. perfumar.

perfunctory [per-fank-to-ri] adj. descuidado, superficial, negligente.

perhaps [per-japs] adv. quizá, quizás, tal vez.

peril [pe-ril] n. peligro, riesgo, m.

perilous [pe-ri-los] adj. peligroso.

perimeter [pe-ri-mi-tar] n. perímetro, m.

period [pi-riod] n. periodo o período, m.; época, f.; punto, m.; **for a fixed —,** a plazo fijo.

periodic [pia-rio-dik] adj. periódico.

periodical [pia-rio-di-kal] n. y adj. periódico, m.

periodically [pia-rio-di-ka-li] adv. periódicamente.

periphery [pe-ri-fe-ri] n. periferia, f.

perish [pe-rish] vi. perecer; sucumbir.

perishable [pe-ri-sha-bol] adj. perecedero.

periwinkle [pe-ri-uin-kel] n. caracol marino; (bot.) vincapervinca, f.

perjure [per-yar] vt. y vi. perjurar.

perk [perk] vi. levantar la cabeza, pavonearse; **to — up,** reanimarse.

perky [per-ki] adj. garboso, gallardo.

permanent [per-ma-nent] adj. permanente, perenne; — **wave,** permanente, m.

permeate [per-mieit] vt. penetrar, atravesar.

permissible [per-mi-sa-bol] adj. lícito, permitido.

permission [per-mi-shon] n. permiso, m., licencia, f.

permit [per-mit] vt. permitir; —, n. permiso, m., cédula, f.

pernicious [per-ni-shos] adj. pernicioso; perjudicial; — **anemia,** (med.) anemia perniciosa.

peroxide [pe-rok-said] n. peróxido, m.; **hydrogen —,** peróxido hidrogenado; — **blonde,** rubia oxigenada.

perpendicular [per-pen-di-kiu-lar] adj. perpendicular; —, n. línea perpendicular.

perpetrate [per-pi-treit] vt. perpetrar, cometer (algún delito).

perpetual [par-pe-tiual] adj. perpetuo.

perpetuate [par-pe-tiueit] vt. perpetuar, eternizar.

perplex [par-pleks] vt. confundir, embrollar.

persecute [per-si-kiut] vt. perseguir; importunar.

persecution [per-si-kiu-shon] n. persecución, f.

perseverance [per-si-vi-rans] n. perseverancia, f.

persevere [per-si-viar] vi. perseverar; obstinarse.

persimmon [per-si-mon] *n.* variedad de níspero (árbol); níspola (fruto), *f.*

persist [per-sist] *vi.* persistir.

persistency [per-sis-tan-si] *n.* persistencia, *f.*

persistent [per-sis-tant] *adj.* persistente.

person [per-son] *n.* persona, *f.*

personage [per-so-nich] *n.* personaje, *m.*

personal [per-so-nal] *adj.* personal; — **effects,** efectos de uso personal.

personality [per-so-na-li-ti] *n.* personalidad, *f.*

personification [per-so-ni-fi-kei-shon] *n.* personificación, *f.*

personify [per-so-ni-fai] *vt.* personificar.

personnel [per-so-nel] *n.* personal, cuerpo de empleados; tripulación, *f.*

perspective [pers-pek-tiv] *n.* perspectiva, *f.; —, adj.* en perspectiva.

perspiration [pers-pai-rei-shon] *n.* traspiración, *f.,* sudor, *m.*

perspire [pers-paia-rar] *vi.* traspirar, sudar.

persuade [per-sueid] *vt.* persuadir.

persuasion [per-suei-shon] *n.* persuasión, *f.*

persuasive [per-suei-siv] *adj.*

persuasivo; **—ly,** *adv.* de un modo persuasivo.

pertain [per-tein] *vi.* pertenecer; relacionar, tocar.

pertaining [per-tei-nin] *adj.* perteneciente; — **to,** relativo a.

pertinacious [per-ti-nei-shos] *adj.* pertinaz, obstinado.

pertinence [per-ti-nens] *n.* conexión, *f.,* relación de una cosa con otra.

pertinent [per-ti-nant] *adj.* pertinente; perteneciente; **—ly,** *adv.* oportunamente.

perturb [per-terb] *vt.* perturbar.

perusal [pa-ru-shal] *n.* examen, *m.,* ojeada, lectura, *f.*

peruse [pa-rus] *vt.* leer; examinar o estudiar (algo) atentamente.

Peruvian [pa-ru-vian] *n.* y *adj.* peruano, na.

pervade [per-veid] *vt.* penetrar.

pervasive [per-vei-siv] *adj.* penetrante.

perverse [per-vers] *adj.* perverso, depravado.

perversion [per-ver-shon] *n.* perversión, *f.*

pervert [per-vert] *vt.* pervertir, corromper.

pessimism [pe-si-mi-sem] *n.* pesimismo, *m.*

pessimist [pe-si-mist] *n.* pesimista, *m.* y *f.*

pessimistic [pe-si-mis-tik] *adj.*

pesimista.

pest [pest] *n.* peste, pestilencia, *f.;* plaga, *f.,* persona fastidiosa.

pestilence [pes-ti-lens] *n.* pestilencia, *f.*

pestle [pes-tel] *n.* majador, *m.,* mano de almirez;
mortar and —, mortero y majador.

pet [pet] *n.* favorito, ta; animal doméstico, mascota, *f.;* —, *vt.* mimar; acariciar.

petal [pe-tal] *n.* (bot.) pétalo, *m.*

petition [pe-ti-shon] *n.* memorial, *m.;* solicitud, *f.;* petición, súplica, *f.;* **to make a —,** elevar una instancia o solicitud; —, *vt.* suplicar, demandar, pedir; requerir en justicia.

petrify [pe-tri-fai] *vt.* y *vi.* petrificar.

petrol [pe-trol] *n.* gasolina, *f.,* petróleo, *m.*

petroleum [pe-tro-liom] *n.* petróleo, *m.;* **— jelly,** ungüento de petróleo, vaselina, *f.*

pettiness [pe-ti-nes] *n.* pequeñez, *f.;* mezquindad, *f.*

petting [pe-tin] *n.* mimo, *m.;* acción de acariciar.

petty [pe-ti] *adj.* pequeño, corto; mezquino; **— cash,** efectivo para el pago de gastos menores; **— larceny,** hurto, *m.,* ratería, *f.;* **— officer,** oficial de marina entre alférez y teniente.

petulant [pe-tiu-lant] *adj.* petulante; **—ly,** *adv.* con petulancia.

pew [piu] *n.* banco de iglesia.

pewter [piu-tar] *n.* peltre, *m.*

phantasy [fan-ta-si] *n.* fantasía, *f.*

phantom [fan-tom] *n.* espectro, fantasma, *m.;* —, *adj.* espectral.

pharmaceutic, pharmaceutical [far-ma-siu-tik], [far-ma-siu-ti-ka-li] *adj.* farmacéutico.

pharmacist [far-ma-sist] *n.* boticario, farmacéutico, *m.*

pharmacy [far-ma-si] *n.* farmacia, botica, *f.*

pharyngitis [fa-rin-yai-tis] *n.* faringitis, *f.*

pharynx [fa-rinks] *n.* faringe, *f.*

phase [feis] *n.* fase, *f.* aspecto, *m.*

pheasant ['feznt] [fe-sant] *n.* faisán, *m.*

phenomenal [fi-no-mi-nal] *adj.* prominente, fenomenal.

phenomenon [fi-no-mi-nom] *n.* fenómeno, *m.*

philander [fi-lan-dar] *vi.* galantear, coquetear.

philanthropic, philanthropical [fi-lan-zro-pik] *adj.* filantrópico.

philanthropist [fi-lan-zro-pist] *n.* filántropo, pa.

philanthropy [fi-lan-zro-pi] *n.* filantropía, *f.*

philharmonic [fi-lar-mo-nik] *adj.*

filarmónico.

Philippines [fi-li-pins] Filipinas, *f. pl.*

philosopher [fi-lo-so-far] *n.* filósofo, *m.*

philosophize [fi-lo-so-fais] *vi.* filosofar.

philosophy [fi-lo-so-fi] *n.* filosofía, *f.*

phlegm [flem] [flem] *n.* flema, *f.*

phlegmatic, phlegmatical [fleg-ma-tik] *adj.* flemático, lento, apático.

phobia [fou-bia] *n.* fobia, obsesión, *f.*

phone [foun] *n.* teléfono, *m.;* — **call,** telefonema, *m.,* llamada telefónica; —, *vt.* telefonear.

phonetic [fo-ne-tik] *adj.* fonético.

phonetics [fou-ne-tiks] *n. pl.* fonética, *f.*

phonic [fo-nik] *adj.* fónico; —**s,** fonología, *f.*

phosphate [fou-no-graf] *n.* fosfato, *m.*

phosphorescence [fos-fo-re-sens] *n.* fosforescencia, *f.*

phosphorescent [fos-fo-re-sent] *adj.* fosforescente.

phosphoric [fos-fo-rik] *adj.* fosfórico; — **acid,** ácido fosfórico.

phosphorus [fos-fo-ros] *n.* fósforo, *m.*

photo = [fou-tou] **photograph.**

photogenic [fou-tou-ye-nik] *adj.* fotogénico.

photograph [fou-tou-graf] *n.* fotografía, *f.;* retrato, *m.;* —, *vt.* fotografiar, retratar; **to be** —**ed,** retratarse.

photographer [fou-tou-gra-far] *n.* fotógrafo, *m.*

photographic [fou-tou-gra-fik] *adj.* fotográfico.

photography [fo-to-gra-fi] *n.* fotografía, *f.*

phrase [freis] *n.* frase, *f.;* estilo, *m.;* (mus.) frase musical; —, *vt.* expresar; (mus.) dividir en frases musicales.

physic [fi-sik] *n.* medicina, *f.;* medicamento, *m.;* purgante, *m.,* purga, *f.;* —**s,** *n. pl.* física, *f ;* —, *vt.* purgar, dar un purgante; aliviar sanar.

physical [fi-si-kal] *adj.* físico; — **education,** educación física, gimnasia, *f.*

physician [fi-si-shan] *n.* médico, *m.;* **attending** —, médico de cabecera.

physicist [fi-si-sist] *n.* físico, *m.*

physics [fi-siks] *n.* física, *f.*

physiognomy [fi-sio-no-mi] *n.* fisonomía, *f.;* facciones, *f. pl.*

physiological [fi-sio-lo-gikal] *adj.* fisiológico.

physiologist [fi-sio-lo-yist] *n.* fisiólogo, *m.*

physiology [fi-sio-lo-yi] *n.* fisiología, *f.*

physique [fi-sik] *n.* físico, *m.*

pi [pai] *n.* (math.) pi (letra griega).

pi, pie [pai] *n.* (print.) pastel, *m.*,
letras de imprenta en confu-
sión o desorden; —, *vt.* (print.)
empastelar, mezclar desordenadamente las letras de
imprenta.

pianist [pia-nist] *n.* pianista, *m.*
y *f.*

piano [pia-nou] *n.* piano, pianoforte, *m.;* **grand** —, piano , pianola, **player** —, piano mecánico, pianola.

pick [pik] *vt.* escoger, elegir;
recoger, mondar, limpiar; **to** —
a pocket, ratear el bolsillo; —,
vi. picar; **to** — **out,** escoger,
señalar; **to** — **over,** escoger,
examinar; —, *n.* pico (herramienta), *m.;* lo escogido, lo
mejor.

picket [pi-kit] *n.* estaca, *f.;*
piquete, *m.;* (mil.) piquete, *m.;*
guardia de huelguistas; —, *vt.*
cercar con estacas o piquetes;
hacer guardia o colocar guar-
dias de huelguistas; —. *adj.* de
estaca; — **fence,** cerca hecha
de estacas puntiagudas.

pickle [pi-kel] *n.* salmuera, *f.;*
encurtido, *m.;* (coll.) dificultad,
f.; **to be in a** —, (coll.) estar en
un lío; — *vt.* escabechar.

pickpocket [pik-po-kit] *n.* ratero,
ra, ladrón, ona.

pickup [pik-ap] *n.* (auto.) aceleración, *f.*

picnic [pik-nik] *n.* comida,
merienda, *f.;* romería, *f.;* jira o
paseo campestre; día de
campo.

pictorial [pik-to-rial] *adj.* pictóri-
co.

picture [pik-char] *n.* pintura, *f.;*
retrato, *m.;* fotografía, *f.;* cuadro, *m.;* — **frame,** marco, *m.;*
motion —, película, *f.*, filme,
m.; — **gallery,** pinacoteca, *f.*,
salón de pinturas, museo de
cuadros.

picturesque [pik-cha-resk] *adj.*
pintoresco.

pie [pai] *n.* pastel, *m.;* empanada, *f.;* (orn.) urraca, *f.;* — **a la
mode,** pastel servido con helados.

piece [pis] *n.* pedazo, *m.;* pieza,
obra, *f ;* cañón o fusil, *m.;* **to
tear to** —**s,** hacer pedazos; —,
vt. remendar; unir los pedazos.

piecemeal [pis-mil] *adv.* en pedazos; a remiendos.

pier [paiar] *n.* estribo de puente;
muelle, *m.*

pierce [pirs] *vt.* penetrar, agujerear, taladrar; excitar; internar;
traspasar.

piercing [pir-sin] *adj.* penetrante,
conmovedor.

piety [pie-ti] *n.* piedad, devoción,
f.; **affected** —, beatería, *f.*

pig [pig] *n.* cochinillo, lechón, *m.;* cerdo; *m.,* puerco, ca; lingote, *m.;* — **iron,** hierro en lingotes; — **latin,** jerigonza, *f.;* —, *vi.* parir la puerca.

pigeon [pid-chon] *n.* palomo, *m.,* paloma, *f.;* **homing** —, paloma viajera o mensajera.

piggish [pi-guish] *adj.* voraz; puerco; cochino.

piggyback [pi-gui-bak] *adj.* sobre los hombros; —, *n.* trasporte en plataformas de ferrocarril de remolques cargados.

piggy bank [pi-gui-bank] *n.* alcancía (generalmente en forma de cochino), *f.*

pigment [pig-ment] *n.* pigmento, *m.;* solución para pinturas.

pigmy [pig-mi] *n.* y *adj.* pigmeo, mea.

pigsty [pigs-tai] *n.* zahúrda, pocilga, *f.*

pigtail [pig-teil] *n.* cola de cochino, *f.;* trenza de cabello; tabaco torcido.

pile [pail] *n.* estaca *f.;* pila, *f.;* montón, *m.;* pira, *f.;* edificio grande y macizo; pelo, *m.;* pelillo (en las telas de lana), *m.;* rimero, *m.;* —s, *n. pl.* (med.) hemorroides, almorranas, *f. pl.;* —, *vt.* amontonar, apilar.

pilgrim [pil-grim] *n.* peregrino, na.

pilgrimage [pil-gri-mich] *n.* pere-grinación.

pill [pil] *n.* píldora, *f.*

pillage [pi-lich] *n.* pillaje, botín, saqueo, *m.;* —, *vt.* pillar, hurtar.

pillar [pi-lar] *n.* pilar, poste, *m.,* columna, *f.;* fig.) sostén, *m.*

pillow [pi-lou] *n.* almohada, *f.,* cojín, *m.;* cabezal, *m.*

pillowcase, pillowslip [pi-lou-keis], [pi-lous-lip] *n.* funda de almo-hada.

pilot [pai-lot] *n.* piloto, *m.;* —, *vt.* pilotear, pilotar.

pimento, pimiento [pi-men-tou] *n.* pimiento, *m.*

pimple [pim-pel] *n.* barro, grano, *m.*

pin [pin] *n.* alfiler, *m.;* prendedor, *m.;* clavija, *f.;* chaveta, *f.;* — **money,** alfileres, *m. pl.,* dinero para alfileres; **safety** —, imperdible, *m.,* alfiler de gancho; —, *vt.* prender, asegurar con alfileres; fijar con clavija; **to** — **(some one) down,** obligar (a alguien) a resolver.

pince-nez *n.* quevedos, *m. pl.*

pincers, pinchers [pin-sars] *n. pl.* pinzas, tenazuelas, *f. pl.;*

pinch [pinch] *vt.* pellizcar, apretar con pinzas; —, *vi.* ser frugal, escatimar gastos; —, *n.* pellizco, *m.;* pulgarada, *f.;* aprieto, *m.*

pincushion [pin-ku-shon] *n.* alfiletero, *m.*

pine [pain] *n.* (bot.) pino, *m.;* — **needle,** pinocha, *f.;* —, *vi.* languidecer; **to — for,** anhelar, ansiar (alguna cosa).

pineapple [pain-a-pol] *n.* piña, *f.,* ananá, ananás, *m.*

pingpong [ping-pong] *n.* tenis de mesa.

pinhole [pin-joul] *n.* agujero que hace un alfiler; agujero muy pequeño.

pink [pink] *n.* (bot.) clavel, *m.;* —, *adj.* rosa, rosado, sonrosado.

pinnacle [pi-na-kol] *n.* pináculo, chapitel, *m.;* cima, cumbre, *f.*

pint [paint] *n.* pinta (medida de líquidos), *f.*

pioneer [paio-niar] *n.* (mil.) zapador, *m.;* descubridor, explorador, precursor, *m.*

pious [paios] *adj.* pío, devoto, piadoso.

pipe [paip] *n.* tubo, cañón, conducto, caño, *m.;* pipa para fumar; (mus.) churumbela, *f.;* **oil — line,** oleoducto, *m.;* **organ** —, cañón de órgano; — **clay,** arcilla refractaria; — **line,** cañería, tubería, *f.;* — **organ,** órgano de cañones; —, *vt.* y *vi.* tocar (la flauta) ; cantar con voz aguda; —, *vt.* proveer de cañerías; conducir por medio de cañerías; (costura) adornar con vivos.

piper [pai-par] *n.* flautista, *m.* y *f.*

piping [pi-pin] *n.* tubería, *f.;* (costura) vivo, cordoncillo, *m.;* —, *adj.* agudo; — **hot,** hirviente.

piracy [paia-ra-si] *n.* piratería, *f.*

pirate [pai-rit] *n.* pirata, *m.;* —, *vt.* y *vi.* piratear, robar, plagiar.

pirating [pai-ri-tin] *n.* piratería, reproducción ilícita de obras literarias.

pistachio [pis-ta-shiou] *n.* (bot.) alfóncigo, pistacho, *m.*

pistil [pis-til] *n.* (bot.) pistilo, *m.*

pistol [pis-tol] *n.* pistola, *f.,* revólver, *m.;* pistolete, *m.*

piston [pis-ton] *n.* pistón, émbolo, *m.;* — **ring,** anillo de empaquetadura del émbolo o pistón; — **rod,** vástago del émbolo.

pit [pit] *n.* hoyo, *m.;* sepultura, *f.;* patio, *m.;* (min.) pozo, *m.;* **ash** —, cenicero, *m.;* **engine** —, (rail.) cenicero, *m.;* —, *vt.* oponer, poner en juego; marcar, picar.

pitch [pich] *n.* pez, brea, *f.,* alquitrán, *m.;* cima, *f.;* grado de elevación; (mus.) tono, *m.;* (en béisbol) lanzamiento, *m.;* — **pine,** pino de tea, pino rizado; — **pipe,** diapasón vocal; —, *vt.* fijar, plantar; colocar; ordenar; tirar; arrojar; embrear; oscurecer; —, *vi.* caerse alguna cosa hacia abajo; caer de cabeza.

pitcher [pi-char] *n.* cántaro, *m.;* (béisbol) lanzador, *m.*

pitchfork [pich-fork] *n.* horca, horquilla, *f.*

piteous [pi-tios] *adj.* lastimoso; compasivo, tierno.

pitfall [pit-fol] *n.* trampa, *f.,* armadijo, *m.;* peligro insospechado.

pith [piz] *n.* meollo, *m.;* médula, *f.;* energía, *f.*

pithy [pi-zi] *adj.* enérgico; meduloso.

pitiful [pi-ti-ful] *adj.* lastimoso, compasivo.

pitiless [pi-ti-les] *adj.* desapiadado, cruel.

pittance [pi-tans] *n.* pitanza, ración, porcioncilla, *f.*

pitted [pi-tid] *adj.* cavado, picado.

pituitary [pi-tui-ta-ri] *adj.* pituitario; — **gland,** glándula pituitaria.

pity [pi-ti] *n.* piedad, compasión, *f.;* misericordia, *f.;* —, *vt.* compadecer, apiadarse de; —, *vi.* tener piedad.

pivot [pi-vot] *n.* espigón, *m.;* quicio, *m.;* chaveta, *f.;* eje de rotación.

pizza [pi-cha] *n.* torta muy condimentada de la cocina italiana, hecha de harina con salsa de tomate y que generalmente contiene también anchoas, queso, etc.

placard [pla-kard] *n.* cartel, letrero, anuncio, *m.*

place [pleis] *n.* lugar, sitio, *m.;* local, *m.;* colocación, *f.;* posición, *f.;* recinto, *m.;* rango, empleo, *m.;* (mil.) plaza, fortaleza, *f.;* — **kick,** (fútbol) acción de patear la pelota después de colocarla en tierra; **stopping —,** paradero, *m.;* **to take —,** verificarse, tener lugar; —, *vt.* colocar; poner; poner (dinero a ganancias).

placement [pleis-ment] *n.* empleo, *m.;* colocación, *f.*

placid [pla-sid] *adj.* plácido, quieto; —**ly,** *adv.* apaciblemente.

plagiarism [plei-yia-ri-sem] *n.* plagio, *m.*

plagiarize [plei-yia-rais] *vt.* plagiar.

plague [pleig] *n.* peste, plaga, *f.;* —, *vt.* atormentar; infestar, apestar.

plain [plein] *adj.* liso, llano, abierto, sencillo; sincero; puro, simple; común; claro, evidente; — **sailing,** (fig.) camino fácil; — **dealing,** buena fe; llaneza, *f.;* —, *n.* llano, *m.*

plainness [plein-nes] *n.* llaneza, igualdad, *f.;* sinceridad, *f.;* claridad, *f.*

plaintiff [plein-tif] *n.* demandador, ra, demandante, *m.y f.*

plaintive [plein-tiv] *adj.* lamento-
so, lastimoso; **—ly,** *adv.* de
manera lastimosa.

plan [plæn] [plan] *n.* plano, *m.;*
sistema, *m.;* proyecto, plan, *m.;*
planificación, *f.;* delineación (de
un edificio, etc.), *f.;* **—,** *vt.* proyectar, planear; plantear; planificar; **—,** *vi.* proponerse; pensar.

plane [plein] *n.* plano, *m.;* cepillo
de carpintería; aeroplano, *m.;*
— geometry, geometría plana;
reconnaisance —, aeroplano de
reconocimiento; **—,** *vt.* allanar;
acepillar.

planet [pla-nit] *n.* planeta, *m.*

plank [plank] *n.* tablón, *m.;*
(naut.) tablaje, *m.;*
—, *vt.* entablar, asegurar con
tablas.

planned [plænd] [pland] *adj.* pla-
neado.

plant ['plænt] [plant] *n.* mata,
planta, *f.;* planta (del pie), *f.;* **—**
, *vt.* plantar, sembrar.

plantain [plan-tein] *n.* (bot.) llan-
tén, *m.;* plátano, *m.*

plantation [plan-tei-shon] *n.*
plantación, planta, *f.,* plantío,
m.; **coffee —,** cafetal, *m.;* **rub-**
ber —, cauchal, *m.*

planter [plan-tar] *n.* plantador,
m.; colono, *m.;* hacendado, *m.;*

sembrador, ra.

planting [plan-tin] *n.* plantación,
f.

plaque [plæk] [plak] *n.* placa, *f.*

plasma [plas-ma] *n.* (biol.) plasma, *m.;* (min.) plasma, *f.,* pras-
ma, *m.*

plaster [plas-tar] *n.* yeso, *m.;*
emplasto, *m.;* enlucido, estuco,
revoque, *m.;* repello, *m.;* **corn**
—, emplasto para los callos; **—**
cast, vendaje enyesado, yeso,
m.; **— coating,** enlucido, enyesado, *m.;* **— of Paris,** yeso, *m.* ,
yeso mate; **—,** *vt.* enyesar;
emplastar.

plastic [plas-tik] *adj.* plástico,
formativo; **— surgery,** anaplas-
tia, cirugía plástica; **—s,** *n. pl.*
plásticos, *m. pl.*

plate [pleit] *n.* plancha o lámina
de metal; placa, *f.;* clisé, *m.;*
plata labrada; plato, *m.;* **—**
glass, vidrio cilindrado o en
planchas; **—,** *vt.* planchear;
batir hoja.

plateau [pla-tou] *n.* mesa, meseta, *f.*

platform [plat-form] *n.* plataforma, tarima, *f.;* tribunal, *m.;* **—**
scale, báscula, *f.*

platinum [pla-ti-nom] *n.* platino,
m.; **— ore,** platina, *f.*

platonic [pla-to-nik] *adj.* platónico.

platter [pla-tar] *n.* fuente, *f.,*

plato grande.

plausible [plo-si-bol] *adj.* plausible, verosímil; —**bly,** *adv.* plausiblemente.

play [plei] *n.* juego, *m.;* recreo, *m.;* representación dramática, comedia, *f.;* — **on words,** juego de palabras; —, *vt.* y *vi.* jugar; juguetear; burlarse; representar, jugar (un papel); (mus.) tocar, sonar; **to — a joke,** hacer una burla; —**ed out,** exhausto, agotado, postrado; **to — up to,** adular.

player [pleiar] *n.* jugador, ra; comediante, ta, actor, *m.,* actriz, *f.;* (mus.) tocador, ra; ejecutante, *m.* y *f.;* **pelota** —, pelotari, *m.;* **ball** —, jugador o jugadora de pelota; — **piano,** pianola, *f.,* piano mecánico o automático.

playground [plei-graund] *n.* campo de deportes o de juegos.

playhouse [plei-jaus] *n.* teatro, *m.*

playing card [plein-kard] *n.* naipe, *m.,* carta (de baraja), *f.*

playmate [plei-meit] *n.* compañero o compañera de juego.

plaything [plei-zin] *n.* juguete, *m.*

playtime [plei-taim] *n.* hora de recreo.

playwright [plei-zin] *n.* dramaturgo, ga.

plea [pli] *n.* defensa, *f.;* excusa, *f.;* pretexto, efugio, *m.;* ruego, *m.;* argumento, *m.;* súplica, *f.;* petición, *f.*

plead [plid] *vt.* defender en juicio; alegar; suplicar.

pleading [pli-din] *n.* acto de abogar por; alegación, *f.;* —**s,** *n. pl.* debates, litigios, *m. pl.*

pleasant [ple-sant] *adj.* agradable; placentero, alegre; risueño, genial.

please [plis] *vt.* agradar, complacer; placer, gustar; **do as you** —, haga usted lo que guste; **if you** —, con permiso de usted; — **be seated,** favor de tomar asiento.

pleasing [pli-sin] *adj.* agradable, placentero, grato; **to be** —, caer bien.

pleasure [ple-shar] *n.* gusto, placer, *m.;* arbitrio, *m.;* recreo, *m.;* — **trip,** viaje de recreo.

pleat [plit] *vt.* plegar; rizar; —, *n.* pliegue, *m.*

pleating [pli-tin] *n.* plegado, *m.,* plegadura, *f.*

plebeian [pli-bian] *adj.* plebeyo, vulgar, bajo; —, *n.* plebeyo, ya.

pledge [plech] *n.* prenda, *f.;* fianza, *f.;* compromiso, *m.;* garantía, *f.;* empeño, *m.;* —, *vt.* empeñar; dar fianza.

plentiful [plen-ti-ful] *adj.* copioso, abundante; —**ly,** *adv.* con abundancia.

pliers [plaiars] *n. pl.* tenacillas, *f. pl.*

plight [plait] *n.* estado, *m.;* condición, *f.;* apuro, aprieto, *m.;* —, *vt.* empeñar; prometer.

plot [plot] *n.* pedazo pequeño de terreno; plano, *m.;* conspiración, trama, *f.;* complot, *m.;* estratagema, *f.;* —, *vt.* y *vi.* trazar; conspirar, tramar.

plotter [plo-tar] *n.* conspirador, ra.

plough = [plau] **plow.**

plow [plau] *n.* arado, *m.;* —, *vt.* arar, labrar la tierra.

plowboy [plau-boi] *n.* arador, *m.*

plowing [plauin] *n.* rompimiento, *m.;* aradura, *f.*

pluck [plak] *vt.* tirar con fuerza; arrancar; desplumar; —, *n.* asadura, *f.,* hígado y bofes; arranque, tirón, *m.;* valor, *m.,* valentía, *f.*

plucky [pla-ki] *adj.* valiente.

plug [plag] *n.* tapón, tarugo, *m.;* obturador, *m.;* clavija, *f.;* (elec.) tapón, *m.,* clavija eléctrica o de contacto; (radio y TV.) anuncio improvisado; **to — in,** enchufar; **to pull the — of,** desenchufar.

plum [plam] *n.* ciruela, *f.;* — **pudding,** variedad de pudín; — **tree,** ciruelo, *m.*

plumage [pla-mich] *n.* plumaje, *m.*

plumber [plam-bar] *n.* plomero, emplomador, *m.;* fontanero, *m.*

plumbing [pla-min] *n.* plomería, instalación de cañerías.

plume [plum] *n.* pluma, *f.;* plumaje, penacho, *m.;* —, *vt.* desplumar; adornar con plumas.

plunder [plan-dar] *vt.* saquear, pillar, robar; —, *n.* pillaje, botín, *m.,* despojos, *m. pl.*

plunge [planch] *vt.* y *vi.* sumergir, sumergirse, precipitarse.

plunger [plan-yar] *n.* buzo, somorgujador, *m.;* émbolo de bomba.

plural [plua-ral] *adj.* y *n.* plural, *m.*

plurality [plua-ra-li-ti] *n.* pluralidad, *f.;* mayoría relativa.

plus [plas] *prep.* más; —, *adj.* adicional.

plutonium [plu-tou-niom] *n.* plutonio, *m.*

ply [plai] *vt.* trabajar con ahínco; importunar, solicitar; —, *vi.* afanarse; aplicarse; viajar con rutinario fijo.

plywood [plai-wud] *n.* madera enchapada.

pneumatic [niu-ma-tik] *adj.* neumático.

pneumonia [niu-mou-nia] *n.* neumonía, pulmonía, *f.*

poach [pouch] *vt.* medio cocer (huevos); —, *vi.* cazar en vedado.

pocket [po-kit] *n.* bolsillo, *m.;* — **money,** dinero para los gastos menudos; —, *vt.* embolsar.

pocketbook [po-kit-buk] *n.* portamonedas, *m.,* cartera, *f.;* (fig.) dinero, *m.,* recursos económicos.

pocketknife [po-kit-naif] *n.* cortaplumas, *m.*

pod [pod] *n.* vaina, *f.*

podium [po-diom] *n.* (arch.) podio, *m.*

poem [pouem] *n.* poema, *m.*

poet [poet] *n.* poeta, *m.;* bardo, *m.*

poetic, poetical [poe-tik], [poe-ti-kal] *adj.* poético; — **license,** licencia poética.

poetry [poue-tri] *n.* poesía, *f.;* **pastoral** —, bucólica, *f.;* **to write** —, poetizar; trovar.

poignant [poi-ñant] *adj.* picante; punzante; satírico; conmovedor.

poinsettia [poin-se-tia] *n.* (bot.) nochebuena, *f.,* flor de la Pascua.

point [point] *n.* punta, *f.;* punto, *m.;* promontorio, *m.;* puntillo, *m.;* estado, *m.;* pico, *m.;* —**s,** *n. pl.* tantos, *m. pl.;* **main** —, quid, *m.;* **make a** — **of,** tener presente; **stretch a** —, exagerar; — **of honor,** pundonor, *m.;* — **of order,** cuestión de orden o reglamento; — **of view,** punto de vista; **to get to the** —, ir al grano; **to the** —, al grano, en plata; —, *vt.* apuntar; aguzar; **to** — **out,** señalar.

pointed [poin-ted] *adj.* puntiagudo; epigramático; conspicuo; satírico; —**ly,** *adv.* sutilmente, explícitamente.

pointer [poin-tar] *n.* apuntador, *m.*

pointless [point-les] *adj.* obtuso, sin punta; insustancial, insípido, tonto.

poise [pois] *n.* peso, *m.;* equilibrio, *m.;* aplomo, *m.;* reposo, *m.;* —, *vt.* pesar, equilibrar.

poison [poi-son] *n.* veneno, *m.;* — **ivy,** variedad de hiedra venenosa; —, *vt.* envenenar; pervertir.

poisoning [poi-so-nin] *n.* envenenamiento, *m.*

poisonous [pois-nos] *adj.* venenoso.

poke [pouk] *n.* empujón, codazo, *m.;* hurgonazo, *m.;* — **bonnet,** gorra de mujer con ala abovedada al frente; —, *vt.* aguijonear, hurgar; asomar; **to** — **fun at,** burlarse de; —, *vi.* andar asomándose.

poker [pou-kar] *n.* hurgón, *m.;* póquer (juego de naipes), *m.*

Poland [po-lan] Polonia, *f.*

polar [pou-lar] *adj.* polar; — **bear,** oso blanco o polar; —

cap, casquete polar.

Pole [poul] *n.* polaco, ca.

pole [poul] *n.* polo, *m.;* (naut.) palo, *m.;* percha, *f.;* — **vault,** salto de garrocha.

polecat [poul-kat] *n.* gato montés.

polestar [poul-star] *n.* estrella polar.

police [po-lis] *n.* policía, *f.;* — **court,** tribunal de policía; — **dog,** perro de policía; — **headquarters,** jefatura de policía; — **state,** (pol.) estado policía.

policeman [po-lis-man] *n.* policía, *m.,* agente de policía, gendarme, *m.*

policewoman [po-lis-uo-man] *n.* agente femenino de policía.

policy [po-li-si] *n.* política de estado, póliza, *f.;* astucia, *f.;* sistema, *m.;* **insurance** —, póliza de seguro.

policyholder [po-li-si-joul-dar] *n.* asegurado, da, persona que tiene póliza de seguro.

poliomyelitis [pou-liou-maia-laitis] *n.* (med.) poliomielitis, *f.,* parálisis infantil.

polish [po-lish] *vt.* pulir, alisar; limar; charolar; —, *vi.* recibir pulimento; —, *n.* pulimento, *m.;* barniz, lustre, *m.*

Polish [po-lish] *n.* y *adj.* polaco, ca.

polished *adj.* elegante, pulido;

bruñido.

polite [—lait] *adj.* pulido, cortés; —**ly,** *adv.* urbanamente, cortésmente.

politeness [po-lait-nes] *n.* cortesía, *f.*

political [po-li-ti-kal] *adj.* político; — **economy,** economía política; — **group,** bloque, *m.;* — **leader,** cacique, *m.;* — **science,** ciencia política; —**ly,** *adv.* según reglas de política.

politician [po-li-ti-shan] *n.* político, *m.*

politics [po-li-tiks] *n. pl.* política, *f.*

polka [pol-ka] *n.* polca, *f.;* — **dot,** diseño de puntos regularmente distribuidos en una tela; — **dot goods,** tela de bolitas.

poll [poul] *n.* cabeza, *f.;* votación, *f.;* voto, *m.;* —**s,** *n. pl.* comicios, *m. pl.;* —, *vt.* descabezar; desmochar; hacer una encuesta; —, *vi.* dar voto en las elecciones.

pollen [po-len] *n.* (bot.) polen, *m.*

pollination [po-li-nei-shon] *n.* polinización, *f.*

polling [pou-lin] *n.* votación, *f.;* — **booth,** casilla electoral.

pollute [po-lut] *vi.* ensuciar; corromper.

pollution [po-lu-shon] *n.* corrupción, contaminación, *f.*

polo [pou-lou] *n.* juego de polo.

polyester [po-lies-tar] *n.* poliéster, *m.*

polygamist [po-li-ga-mist] *n.* polígamo, ma.

polygamy [po-li-ga-mi] *n.* poligamia, *f.*

pomade [po-meid] *n.* pomada, *f.*

pomegranate [po-ma-gra-nit] *n.* (bot.) granado, *m.*; granada, *f.*

pommel [pa-mel] *n.* perilla de una silla de caballería; pomo de una espada; —, *vt.* golpear.

pomp [pomp] *n.* pompa, *f.*; esplendor, *m.*; solemnidad, *f.*

pompous [pom-pos] *adj.* pomposo.

pond [pond] *n.* charca, *f.*, estanque de agua.

ponder [pon-dar] *vt.* y *vi.* ponderar, considerar, deliberar, meditar.

ponderous [pon-de-ros] *adj.* ponderoso, pesado.

pongee [pon-yii] *n.* variedad de tela de seda.

pontiff [pon-tif] *n.* pontífice, papa, *m.*

pony [po-ni] *n.* haca, *f.*, jaco, *m.*; caballito, *m.*

poodle [pu-del] *n.* perro de lanas.

pool [pul] *n.* charco, *m.*; lago, *m.*; tanque, *m.*; billar, *m.*; vaca, *f.*, dinero o cosas reunidas por varias personas; **swimming** —, alberca, piscina, *f.*; —, *vt.* reunir.

poolroom [pul-rum] *n.* salón de billares.

poor [puar] *adj.* pobre; humilde; de poco valor; deficiente; estéril; mísero; — **farm,** casa de caridad, casa del pobre; **the** —, los pobres, *m. pl.*; **to become** —, venir a menos, empobrecer.

pop [pop] *n.* chasquido, *m.*; bebida gaseosa; —, *vt.* y *vi.* entrar o salir de sopetón; meter alguna cosa repentinamente.

popcorn [pop-korn] *n.* palomitas de maíz, maíz tostado y reventado.

Pope [poup] *n.* papa, *m.*

poplar [pop-lar] *n.* álamo temblón.

poppy [po-pi] *n.* (bot.) adormidera, amapola, *f.*

populace [po-piu-lis] *n.* populacho, *m.*; pueblo, *m.*

popular [po-piu-lar] *adj.* popular.

popularity [po-piu-la-ri-ti] *n.* popularidad, boga, *f.*

popularize [po-piu-la-rais] *vt.* popularizar.

populate [po-piu-leit] *vt.* poblar.

population [po-piu-lei-shon] *n.* población, *f.*, número de habitantes (en una ciudad, país, etc.).

porcelain [pors-lin] *n.* porcelana, china, *f.*, loza fina.

porch [porch] *n.* pórtico, vestíbulo, *m.*

porcupine [por-kiu-pain] *n.* puerco espín.

pore [por] *n.* poro, *m.*

pork [pork] *n.* carne de puerco; **— sausage,** longaniza, *f.,* salchicha de puerco.

porous [po-ros] *adj.* poroso.

porpoise [por-pos] *n.* puerco marino.

port [port] *n.* puerto, *m.*

portable [por-tabol] *adj.* portátil; **— typewriter,** máquina de escribir portátil.

portal [por-tal] *n.* portal, *m.;* portada, *f.;* **— to —,** desde el momento de entrar hasta el de salir (en la fábrica).

portend [por-tend] *vt.* pronosticar, augurar.

portent [por-tent] *n.* portento, prodigio, *m.;* presagio, *m.*

porter [por-tar] *n.* portero, *m.;* mozo, mozo de cuerda.

portfolio [port-fou-liou] *n.* cartera, *f.,* cartera portapapeles; **— (of a minister of state)** cartera (de un ministro de estado).

porthole [port-joul] *n.* claraboya, *f.,* ojo de buey.

portion [por-shon] *n.* porción, parte, *f.;* ración, *f.;* dote, *m.* y *f.;* **—,** *vt.* partir, dividir; dotar.

portly [port-li] *adj.* majestuoso; rollizo, corpulento.

portrait [por-treit] *n.* retrato, *m.;* **to make a — of,** retratar; **to sit for a —,** retratarse.

portray [por-trei] *vt.* retratar.

Portuguese [por-tiu-guis] *n.* y *adj.* portugués, esa; **— language,** portugués, *m.*

pose [pous] *vt.* colocar en determinada posición (para retratar, etc.); proponer; **—,** *vi.* asumir cierta actitud o postura; **—,** *n.* postura, actitud, *f.*

position [po-si-shon] *n.* posición, situación, *f.;* estación, *f ;* orientación, *f.*

positive [po-si-tiv] *adj.* positivo, real, verdadero; definitivo; **—ly,** *adv.* ciertamente.

possess [po-ses] *vt.* poseer.

possession [po-se-shon] *n.* posesión, *f.;* **to take — of,** hacerse dueño de; posesionarse de.

possessive [po-se-siv] *adj.* posesivo.

possessor [po-se-sar] *n.* poseedor, ra.

possibility [po-sa-bi-li-ti] *n.* posibilidad, *f.*

possible [po-si-bol] *adj.* posible; **as soon as —,** cuanto antes; **—bly,** *adv.* quizá, quizás.

post [poust] *n.* correo, *m.;* puesto, *m.;* empleo, *m.;* poste, *m.;* palo, *m.;* **— card,** tarjeta postal; **— office,** oficina de correos, administración de correos;

post-office box apartado de correos, casilla de correos; —, *vt.* fijar; enviar por correo; —**no bills,** se prohibe fijar carteles.

postage [pous-tich] *n.* porte de carta, franqueo, *m.;* — **stamp,** timbre, sello, *m.,* estampilla, *f.,* sello de correo o de franqueo, *m.*

postal [pous-tal] *adj.* postal; — **card,** tarjeta postal.

poster [pous-tar] *n.* cartel, cartelón, letrero, *m.*

posterior [pos-tia-rior] *adj.* posterior, trasero.

postgraduate [poust-gra-dueit] *n.* y *adj.* posgraduado, da.

posthumous [pos-tiu-mos] *adj.* póstumo.

postman [post-man] *n.* cartero, *m.;* correo, *m.*

postmark [post-mark] *n.* sello o marca de la oficina de correos.

post-mortem [poust-mor-tem] *adj.* que sucede después de la muerte; —, *n.* autopsia, *f.*

post office [poust-o-fis] *n.* correo, *m.,* oficina postal, casa de correos.

postpone [poust-poun] *vt.* diferir, suspender; pos-poner; trasladar.

postponement [poust-pounment] *n.* aplazamiento, *m.*

postscript [pous-skript] *n.* posdata, *f.*

postulate [pos-tiu-leit] *n.* postulado, *m.;* —, *vt.* postular.

posture [pos-char] *n.* postura, *f.*

postwar [poust-uor] *adj.* de la posguerra; — **period,** posguerra, *f.*

posy [pou-si] *n.* mote, *m.;* flor, *f.;* ramillete de flores.

pot [pot] *n.* marmita, *f.;* olla, *f.;* tarro, *m.;* — **roast,** carne asada en marmita.

potassium [po-ta-sium] *n.* potasio, *m.*

potato [po-tei-tou] *n.* patata, papa, *f.;* **fried** —**es,** patatas o papas fritas; **mashed** —**es,** puré de patata o de papa; **sweet** —, camote, *m.;* batata, *f* ; boniato, *m.*

potency [pou-tan-si] *n.* potencia, energía, fuerza, *f.;* influjo, *m.*

potent [pou-tant] *adj.* potente, poderoso, eficaz.

potential [po-ten-shal] *adj.* potencial, poderoso.

pothole [pot-jol] *n.* agujero grande.

potion [pou-shon] *n.* poción, bebida medicinal.

potluck [pot-lok] *n.* comida ordinaria; **to take** —, comer varias personas juntas sin formalidad.

potpie [pot-pai] *n.* pastel o fricasé de carne.

potpourri [pou-pu-ri] *n.* popurrí,

m.

potter [po-tar] *n.* alfarero, *m.;* —
's ware, alfarería, *f.*, cacharros,
m. pl.

pottery [po-ta-ri] *n.* alfarería, *f.*

pouch [pauch] *n.* buche, *m.;*
bosillo, *m.*, faltriquera, *f.;*
bolsa, *f.*

poultry [poul-tri] *n.* aves caseras, aves de corral, *f.;* — **yard,**
corral de aves caseras.

pounce [pauns] *n.* garra, *f.;* gra-
silla, *f.;* —, *vt.* apomazar; —, *vi.*
entrar repentinamente; —
upon, precipitarse sobre.

pound [paund] *n.* libra, *f.;* libra
esterlina; corral púbico; —
sterling, libra esterlina; —, *vt.*
machacar; golpear, martillar.

pour [por] *vt.* verter, vaciar; servir (el té); —, *vi.* fluir con rapidez; llover a cántaros.

pout [paut] *vi.* hacer pucheros,
ponerse ceñudo; *n.* puchero,
m., mueca fingida.

poverty [po-ver-ti] *n.* pobreza *f.*

powder [pau-dar] *n.* polvo, *m.;*
pólvora, *f.;* — **case,** polvera.

powdered [pau-dared] *adj.* en
polvo, pulverizado.

power [pauar] *n.* poder, *m.;*
potestad, *f ;* imperio, *m.;*
potencia, *f.;* autoridad, *f.;* valor,
m.; — **dive,** (avi.) picada a todo
motor; **in** —, en el poder; — **of**
attorney, carta poder; — **plant,**

casa de máquinas, de calderas,
de fuerza motriz; motor, *m.;*
the —**s that be,** los superiores,
los que dominan.

powerful [paua-ful] *adj.* poderoso; —**ly,** *adv.* poderosamente,
con mucha fuerza.

powerhouse [poua-jaus] *n.* central, *f.;* casa de máquinas, de
calderas o de fuerza motriz.

powerless [paua-les] *adj.* impotente.

pox [poks] *n.* viruelas, *f. pl.;*
chicken —, viruelas locas; **cow**
—, vacuna, *f.*

past participle p. pdo. participio
pasado.

practicability [prak-ti-ka-bi-li-ti]
n. factibilidad, *f.*

practical [prak-ti-kal] *adj.* práctico; — **joke,** chasco, *m.*, burla,
f., broma pesada; — **nurse,**
enfermera práctica (sin titulo).

practice [prak-tis] *n.* práctica, *f.;*
uso, *m.*, costumbre, *f.;* ejercicio, *m.;* —**s,** *n. pl.* costumbres,
f. pl.; —, *vt.* y *vi.* practicar,
ejercer; ensayar.

practitioner [prak-ti-sho-nar] *n.*
persona que ejerce una profesión; en la Ciencia Cristiana,
persona autorizada para curar.

pragmatic, pragmatical [prag-
ma-tik], [prag-ma-ti-kal] *adj.*
pragmático; entremetido.

prairie [prea-ri] *n.* prado, *m.*,

pampa, *f.*

praise [preis] *n.* fama, *f.;* renombre, *m.;* alabanza, loa, *f.;* —, *vt.* celebrar, alabar, enaltecer, ensalzar, elogiar.

praiseworthy [preis-uez-li] *adj.* digno de alabanza.

praline [pra-lain] *n.* almendra confitada.

prank [prank] *n.* travesura, extravagancia, *f.*

pray [prei] *vt. y vi.* suplicar, rezar, rogar, orar.

prayer [prear] *n.* oración, súplica, *f.;* **the Lord's P—,** el Padre Nuestro, *m.;* — **book,** devocionario, *m.;* capitulario, *m.;* — **meeting,** reunión para orar en común.

preach [prich] *vt. y vi.* predicar.

preacher [pri-char] *n.* predicador, *m.*

preamble [priam-bel] *n.* preámbulo, *m.*

prearrange [pria-reinch] *vt.* preparar de antemano.

precarious [pri-kea-rios] *adj.* precario, incierto.

precaution [pri-ko-shon] *n.* precaución, *f.*

precedence [pre-si-dans] *n.* precedencia, *f.*

precedent [pre-si-dant] *n. y adj.* precedente, *m.*

preceding [pri-si-din] *adj.* precursor.

precinct [pri-sinkt] *n.* lindero, *m.;* barriada, *f.;* distrito electoral.

precious [pre-shos] *adj.* precioso; valioso; — **stone,** piedra preciosa.

precipice [pre-si-pis] *n.* precipicio, *m.*

precipitate [pri-si-pi-tit] *vt.* precipitar; —, *vi.* precipitarse; —, *adj.* precipitado; —, *n.* (chem.) precipitado, *m.*

precipitation [pri-si-pi-tei-shon] *n.* precipitación, impetuosidad, *f.*

precise [pri-sais] *adj.* preciso, exacto.

precision [pri-si-shon] *n.* precisión, *f.*

preclude [pri-klud] *vt.* prevenir, impedir, excluir.

precocious [pri-kou-shos] *adj.* precoz, temprano, prematuro.

predatory [pre-da-to-ri] *adj.* rapaz, voraz.

predecessor [pri-di-se-sar] *n.* predecesor, ra, antecesor, ra.

predestination [pri-des-ti-nei-shon] *n.* predestinación, *f.*

predetermine [pri-di-ter-min] *vt.* predeterminar.

predict [pri-dikt] *vt.* predecir.

prediction [pri-dik-shon] *n.* predicción, *f.*

predilection [pri-di-lek-shon] *n.* predilección, *f.*

predominate [pri-do-mi-neit] *vt.* predominar.

pre-**eminence** [pri-e-mi-nens] *n.* preeminencia, *f.*

pre-**eminent** [pri-e-mi-nent] *adj.* preeminente.

pre-**existence** [pri-ik-sis-tans] *n.* preexistencia, *f.*

prefabricate [pri-fa-bri-keit] *vt.* prefabricar.

preface [pre-fis] *n.* prefacio, preámbulo, prólogo, *m.*; —, *vt.* hacer un prólogo (a un libro, etc.); ser preliminar a.

prefer [pri-fer] *vt.* preferir, proponer, presentar.

preferable [pre-fe-ra-bol] *adj.* preferible, preferente.

preference [pre-fe-rans] *n.* preferencia, *f.*

preferential [pre-fe-ren-shal] *adj.* privilegiado; de preferencia.

preferred *adj.* preferente; predilecto; — stock, acciones preferidas o preferentes.

prefix [pri-fiks] *vt.* prefijar; —, *n.* (gram.) prefijo, *m.*

pregnancy [preg-nan-si] *n.* preñez, gravidez, *f.*

pregnant [preg-nant] *adj.* preñada; fértil.

preheat [pri-jit] *vt.* calentar previamente.

prehistoric [pri-jis-to-rik] *adj.* prehistórico.

prejudice [pre-yu-dis] *n.* prejui-

cio, daño, *m.*; preocupación, *f.*; —, *vt.* perjudicar, hacer daño; preocupar.

preliminary [pri-li-mi-na-ri] *adj.* preliminar.

prelude [pre-liud] *n.* preludio, *m.*; —, *vt.* preludiar.

premature [pre-ma-chuar] *adj.* prematuro.

premeditate [pri-me-di-teit] *vi.* premeditar.

premier [pre-miar] *n.* primer ministro, *m.*

premiere [pre-miar] *n.* estreno, debut, *m.*

premise [pre-mis] *n.* premisa, *f.*; —**s**, *n. pl.* predio, *m.*, propiedad, *f.*

premium [pri-miom] *n.* premio, *m.*; remuneración, *f.*; prima, *f.*; **at a** —, a premio; muy valioso debido a su escasez.

premonition [pri-mo-ni-shon] *n.* presentimiento, *m.*

prenatal [pri-nei-tal] *adj.* antenatal, prenatal.

preoccupation [prio-kiu-pei-shon] *n.* preocupación, *f*

prepaid [pri-peid] *adj.* franco de porte, porte pagado, prepagado.

preparation [pre-pa-rei-shon] *n.* preparación, *f.*; preparativo, *m.*

prepare [pri-pear] *vt.* preparar; —, *vi.* prepararse.

prepay [pri-pei] *vt.* franquear

(una carta); pagar anticipadamente, prepagar.

preponderance [pri-pon-de-rans]
n. preponderancia, *f.*

preposition [pre-po-si-shon] *n.*
preposición, *f.*

preposterous [pri-pos-te-ros] *adj.*
absurdo; —**ly,** *adv.* absurda-
mente; sin razón.

prerequisite [pri-re-kui-sit] *n.*
condición o requisito necesario;
—, *adj.* exigido anticipadamente; necesario para el fin que
uno se propone.

prerogative [pri-ro-ga-tiv] *n.* prerrogativa, *f.*

preschool [pri-skul] *adj.* preesco-
lar.

prescribe [pris-kraib] *vt.* y *vi.*
prescribir, ordenar; (med.)
recetar.

prescription [pris-krip-shon] *n.*
receta medicinal.

presence ['prezns] [pre-sens] *n.*
presencia, *f.*; porte, aspecto,
m.; — **of mind,** serenidad de
ánimo.

present ['preznt] [pre-sent] *n.*
presente, regalo, *m.*; **to make a**
— **of,** regalar; —, *adj.* presente;
at —, en la actualidad; —**ly,**
adv. al presente, luego; —, *vt.*
ofrecer, presentar; regalar; **to**
— **itself,** surgir; **to** — **charges**
against, acusar, denunciar.

presentable [pri-sen-ta-bol] *adj.*
presentable, decente, decoroso.

presentation [pre-san-tei-shon]
n. presentación, *f.*

present-day [pre-sent-dei] *adj.*
corriente, de hoy, del presente.

preserve [pri-serv] *vt.* preservar,
conservar; hacer conservas (de
frutas, etc.); —, *n.* conserva,
confitura, *f.*

preside [pri-said] *vi.* presidir;
dirigir; llevar la batuta.

presidency [pre-si-dan-si] *n.* presidencia, *f.*

president [pre-si-dent] *n.* presidente, *m.;* rector, *m.;* rector de
una escuela.

presidential [pre-si-den-shal]
adj. presidencial.

press [pres] [pres] *vt.* planchar,
aprensar, apretar; oprimir,
angustiar; compeler; importunar; estrechar; —, *vi.* apresurarse; agolparse la gente alrededor de una persona o cosa;
—, *n.* prensa, *f.;* imprenta, *f.;*
Associated P—, Prensa
Asociada; — **agent,** agente de
publicidad.

pressing [pre-sin] *adj.* urgente,
apremiante.

pressure [pre-shar] *n.* presión,
f.; opresión, *f.;* — **cooker,** olla
de cocer a presión, (Mex.) olla
express, *f.*

prestige [pres-tich] *n.* prestigio,
m., reputación, fama, *f.*

presume [pri-sium] *vi.* presumir, suponer.

presumption [pri-samp-shon] *n.* presunción, *f.*

presumptuous [pri-samp-tiuos] *adj.* presuntuoso.

presuppose [pri-su-pous] *vt.* presuponer.

pretend [pri-tend] *vt.* y *vi.* hacer ver, simular; pretender.

pretense, pretence [pri-tens] *n.* pretexto, *m.;* pretensión, *f.*

pretentious [pri-ten-shos] *adj.* pretencioso, presuntuoso, vanidoso.

pretext [pri-tekst] *n.* pretexto, socolor, viso, *m.*

prettily [pri-ti-li] *adv.* bonitamente; agradable-mente.

pretty [pri-ti] *adj.* hermoso, lindo, bien parecido, bonito; —, *adv.* algo, un poco, bastante.

pretzel [pret-zal] *n.* galleta dura y salada general-mente en forma de nudo.

prevail [pri-veil] *vi.* prevalecer, predominar, imperar.

prevailing [pri-vei-lin] *adj.* dominante, prevaleciente (uso, costumbre, etc.).

prevalent [pre-va-lant] *adj.* prevaleciente, que existe extensamente.

prevent [pri-vent] *vt.* prevenir; impedir; remediar.

preventable [pri-ven-tabol]*adj.* prevenible, evitable.

prevention [pri-ven-shon] *n.* prevención, *f.*

preventive [pri-ven-tiv] *adj.* preventivo; —, *n.* preventivo, preservativo, *m.*

preview [pri-viu] *n.* exhibición preliminar.

previous [pri-vios] *adj.* previo; antecedente; —ly, *adv.* de antemano.

prey [prei] *n.* botín, *m.;* rapiña, *f.;* presa, *f.;* —, *vi.* pillar, robar.

price [prais] *n.* precio, premio, valor, *m.;* **best —, lowest —,** último precio; **cost —,** precio de costo; **fixed —,** precio fijo; **high —s,** carestía, *f.;* **— ceiling,** límite máximo de precios; **— fixing,** fijación de precios; **— list,** lista de precios, tarifa, *f.;* **sale —,** precio de venta, precio rebajado; **to set a —,** poner precio; **—,** *vt.* apreciar, valuar.

priceless [prais-les] *adj.* inapreciable.

prick [prik] *vt.* punzar, picar; apuntar; hincar; clavar; —, *n.* puntura, *f.;* picadura, *f.;* punzada, *f.;* púa, *f.;* pinchazo, *m.*

prickly [pri-kli] *adj.* espinoso; **— heat,** salpullido, *m.;* **— pear,** higo chumbo o de pala.

pride [praid] *n.* orgullo, *m.;* vanidad, *f.;* jactancia, *f.;* **to — one-self on,** enorgullecerse de; jactarse de; **to take — in,** preciarse de.

priest [prist] *n.* sacerdote, cura, *m.*

priesthood [prist-jud] *n.* sacerdocio, *m.*

primarily [prai-ma-ri-li] *adv.* primariamente, sobre todo.

primary [prai-ma-ri] *adj.* primario, principal; prime-ro; — **colors,** colores primitivos; — **education,** primera enseñanza; — **election,** elección primaria; — **school,** escuela primaria.

primate [prai-mit] *n.* primado, *m.*

prime [praim] *n.* madrugada, alba, *f.;* (fig.) flor, nata, *f.;* primavera, *f.;* principio, *m.;* —, *adj.* primero; primoroso, excelente; —, *vt.* cebar; preparar, prevenir.

primeval [prai-mi-val] *adj.* primitivo.

priming [prai-min] *n.* cebo, *m.;* preparación, *f.;* cebadura (de una bomba), *f.*

primitive [pri-mi-tiv] *adj.* primitivo.

primrose [prim-rous] *n.* (bot.) primavera, *f.;* color amarillo rojizo; —, *adj.* alegre; — **path,** sendero de placeres.

prince [prins] *n.* príncipe, soberano, *m.*

princess [prin-ses] *n.* princesa, *f.*

principal [prin-si-pal] *adj.* principal; —, *n.* principal, jefe, *m.;* rector, director (de un colegio), *m.;* capital (dinero empleado), *m.*

principally [prin-si-pa-li] *adv.* principalmente, máxime.

principle [prin-si-pol] *n.* principio, *m.;* causa primitiva; fundamento, motivo, *m.*

print [print] *vt.* estampar, imprimir; —, *n.* impresión, estampa, *f.;* copia, *f.;* impreso, *m.;* **out of** —, vendido, agotado (libros, etc.).

printed [prin-tid] *adj.* impreso; — **goods,** estampados, *m. pl.;* — **matter,** impresos, *m. pl.* printer, *n.* impresor, *m.;* —**'s devil,** aprendiz de impresor; —**'s mark,** pie de imprenta.

printing [prin-tin] *n.* tipografía, imprenta, *f.;* impresión, *f.;* — **office,** imprenta, *f.;* — **press,** prensa tipográfica.

printshop *n.* imprenta, *f.*

prior [praiar] *adj.* anterior, precedente; —, *n.* prior (prelado), *m.*

priority [praio-ri-ti] *n.* prioridad, prelación, antelación, *f.*

prism [pri-sem] *n.* prisma, *m.*

prison [pri-son] *n.* prisión, cárcel, *f.;* presidio, *m.*

prisoner [pri-so-nar] *n.* preso, sa, prisionero, ra, cautivo, va.

pristine [pris-tain] *adj.* prístino, primitivo.

privacy [pri-va-si] *n.* retiro, *m.*, posibilidad de aislamiento, independencia, *f.*

private [prai-vit] *adj.* secreto, privado; particular; —, *n.* (mil.) soldado raso; **in** —, secreto; **—ly,** *adv.* en secreto, en particular.

privilege [pri-vi-lich] *n.* privilegio, *m.;* **—d,** *adj.* privilegiado.

prize [prais] *n.* premio, *m.;* precio, *m.;* — **fight,** pugilato, *m.;* — **story,** relato interesante digno de premiarse; —, *vt.* apreciar, valuar.

pro [prou] *prep.* para, pro; —, *adj.* en el lado afirmativo (de un debate, etc.); —, *n.* persona que toma el afirmativo (en algún debate, votación, etc.); **the —s and cons,** el pro y el contra.

probability [pro-ba-bi-li-ti] *n.* probabilidad, *f.*

probable [pro-ba-bol] *adj.* probable, verosímil; **—bly,** *adv.* probablemente.

probation [pro-bei-shon] *n.* prueba, *f.;* examen, *m.;* libertad condicional; noviciado, *m.*

probationer [pro-bei-sho-nar] *n.* novicio, *m.;* delincuente que disfruta de libertad condicional.

problem [pro-blem] *n.* problema, *m.*

problematic, problematical [pro-bli-ma-tik], [pro-bli-ma-tikal] *adj.* problemático.

procedure [pro-si-yar] *n.* procedimiento, *m.;* progreso, proceso, *m.*

proceed [pro-sid] *vi.* proceder; provenir; portarse; originarse; ponerse en marcha; **—s,** *n. pl.* producto, rédito, *m.;* resultado, *m.;* **gross —s,** producto íntegro; **net —s,** producto neto o líquido.

proceeding [pro-si-din] *n.* procedimiento, *m.;* proceso, *m.;* conducta, *f.;* **—s,** *n. pl.* actas, *f. pl.;* expediente, *m.;* memoria, *f.,* o informe, *m.,* (de una conferencia, etc.).

process [prou-ses] *n.* proceso, *m.;* procedimiento, *m.;* progreso, *m.;* —, *vt.* procesar; fabricar, tratar o preparar con un método especial.

procession [pro-se-shon] *n.* procesión, *f.*

proclaim [pro-kleim] *vt.* proclamar; publicar.

proclamation [pro-kla-mei-shon] *n.* proclamación, *f.;* decreto, bando, *m.;* cedulón, *m.*

procrastinate [prou-kras-ti-neit] *vt.* diferir, retardar.

procreation [prou-kriei-shon] *n.*

procreación, producción, *f.*

procurable [pro-kiua-ra-bol] *adj.* asequible.

procure [pro-kiuar] *vt.* adquirir, conseguir.

prod [prod] *n.* pinchazo, aguijón, *m.;* —, *vt.* aguijonear, pinchar; aguzar, instar.

prodigal [pro-di-gal] *adj.* pródigo; —, *n.* disipador, ra; derrochador, ra.

prodigious [pro-di-yos] *adj.* prodigioso.

prodigy [pro-di-yi] *n.* prodigio, *m.;* **infant** —, niño prodigio.

produce [pro-dius] *vt.* producir, criar; rendir; causar; —, *n.* producto, *m.*

producer [pro-diu-sar] *n.* productor, ra.

product [pro-dakt] *n.* producto, *m.;* obra, *f.;* efecto, *m.*

production [pro-dak-shon] *n.* producción, *f.;* producto, *m.;* — **cost,** costo de fabricación o de producción.

productive [pro-dak-tiv] *adj.* productivo.

profane [pro-fein] *adj.* profano; —, *vt.* profanar.

profanity [pro-fa-ni-ti] *n.* blasfemia, impiedad, *f.;* lenguaje profano.

profess [pro-fes] *vt.* profesar; ejercer; declarar.

profession [pro-fe-shon] *n.* profe-

sión, *f.*

professional [pro-fe-sho-nal] *adj.* profesional; —, *n.* profesional, *m.;* actor o actriz profesional.

professor [pro-fe-sar] *n.* profesor, ra, catedrático, *m.*

proficient [pro-fe-shant] *adj.* proficiente, adelantado.

profile [prou-fail] *n.* perfil, *m.;* bosquejo biográfico.

profit [pro-fit] *n.* ganancia, *f.;* provecho, *m.;* ventaja, *f.;* utilidad, *f.;* **net** —, ganancia líquida; — **and loss,** ganancias y pérdidas, *f. pl.;* lucros y daños, *m. pl.;* — **sharing,** distribución de la ganancia entre los empleados; —, *vt. y vi.* aprovechar, servir; ser útil; adelantar; beneficiar; aprovecharse; **to** — **by,** beneficiarse con.

profitable [pro-fi-ta-bol] *adj.* provechoso, ventajoso; productivo; —**bly,** *ad.* provechosamente.

profound [pro-faund] *adj.* profundo.

profuse [pro-fius] *adj.* profuso, pródigo.

profusion [pro-fiu-shon] *n.* prodigalidad, *f.;* abundancia, profusión, *f.*

program, programme [prougram] *n.* programa, *m.*

programming [prou-gra-min] *n.* programación, *f.*

progress [prou-gres] *n.* progreso,

m.; adelanto, *m.*; viaje, curso, *m.*; —, *vi.* progresar.

progressive [pro-gre-siv] *adj.* progresivo.

prohibit [pro-ji-bit] *vt.* prohibir, vedar; impedir.

prohibition [proui-bi-shan] *n.* prohibición, *f.*

project [pro-yekt] *vt.* proyectar, trazar; —, *n.* proyecto, *m.*

projectile [pro-yek-tail] *n.* proyectil, *m.*

projection [pro-yek-shon] *n.* proyección, *f.*; proyectura, *f.*

projector [pro-yek-tar] *n.* proyectista, proyector, *m.*; **movie** —, proyector de cine, cinematógrafo, *m.*

prolific [pro-li-fik] *adj.* prolífico, fecundo.

prologue [prou-log] *n.* prólogo, *m.*

prolong [pro-long] *vt.* prolongar; diferir; prorrogar.

prom *n.* baile de graduación (de un colegio).

promenade [pro-mi-nad] *vi.* pasearse; —, *n.* paseo, *m.*

prominence [pro-mi-nens] *n.* prominencia, eminencia, *f.*

prominent [pro-mi-nent] *adj.* saledizo; conspicuo; **to be** —, sobresalir; ser eminente.

promiscuous [pro-mis-kiuos] *adj.* promiscuo.

promise [pro-mis] *n.* promesa, *f.*;

prometido, *m.*; —, *vt.* prometer.

promising [pro-mi-sin] *adj.* prometedor.

promote [pro-mout] *vt.* promover.

promoter [pro-moutar] *n.* promotor, promovedor, *m.*

promotion [pro-mou-shon] *n.* promoción, *f.*

prompt [prompt] *adj.* pronto, listo, expedito; **—ly,** *adv.* con toda precisión; pronto; —, *vt.* sugerir, insinuar; apuntar (en el teatro).

pronoun [pro-nan] *n.* pronombre, *m.*

pronounce [pro-nauns] *vt.* pronunciar; recitar.

pronouncement [pro-naun-sement] *n.* declaración formal; anuncio oficial.

pronunciation [pro-nan-siei-shon] *n.* pronunciación, *f.*

proof [pruf] *n.* prueba, *f.*; **bomb—,** a prueba de bomba; **water—,** impermeable; **fool—,** fácil (hasta para un tonto).

proofread [pruf-rid] *vt.* corregir pruebas.

proofreader [pruf-ri-der] *n.* corrector o correctora de pruebas.

prop [prop] *vt.* sostener, apuntalar; —, *n.* apoyo; sostén, *m.*

propaganda [pro-pa-gan-da] *n.* propaganda, *f.*; anuncios, *m.*

pl.

propagandist [pro-pa-gan-dist] *n.* y *adj.* propagandista, propagador, ra.

propeller [pro-pe-lar] *n.* propulsor, *m.;* hélice, *f.;* — **blade,** segmento o paleta de hélice.

propensity [pro-pen-si-ti] *n.* propensión, tendencia, *f.*

proper [pro-par] *adj.* propio; conveniente; exacto; decente; debido; **in — form,** en forma debida; **—ly,** *adv.* justamente; adecuadamente.

property [pro-pa-ti] *n.* propiedad, *f.;* bien, *m.;* peculiaridad, cualidad, *f.*

prophecy [pro-fe-si] *n.* profecía, *f.*

prophesy [pro-fi-si] *vt.* profetizar; predicar.

prophet [pro-fit] *n.* profeta, *m.*

prophetic [pro-fe-tik] *adj.* profético.

proponent [pro-pou-nent] *n.* proponente, *m.* y *f.*

proportion [pro-por-shon] *n.* proporción, *f.;* simetría, *f.;* **in —,** a prorrata; **—,** *vt.* proporcionar.

proportional [pro-por-sho-nal] *adj.* proporcional.

proportionate [pro-por-sho-nit] *adj.* proporcionado; en proporciones; **—ly,** *adv.* proporcionalmente.

proportioned *adj.* proporcionado.

proposal [pro-pou-shal] *n.* propuesta, proposición, *f.;* oferta, *f.*

propose [pro-pous] *vt.* proponer.

proposition [pro-po-si-shon] *n.* proposición, propuesta, *f.*

proprietor [pro-praia-tar] *n.* propietario, ria, dueño, ña.

propriety [pro-praia-ti] *n.* propiedad, *f.*

proscription [prous-krip-shon] *n.* proscripción, *f.*

prose [prous] *n.* prosa, *f.*

prosecute [pro-si-kiut] *vt.* proseguir, acusar.

prosecution [pro-si-kiu-shon] *n.* prosecución, *f.*

prosecutor [pro-si-kiu-tar] *n.* acusador, *m.*

prospect [pros-pekt] *n.* perspectiva, *f.;* esperanza, *f.*

prospective [pros-pek-tiv] *adj.* en perspectiva; anticipado.

prosper [pros-par] *vi.* prosperar.

prosperity [pros-pe-ri-ti] *n.* prosperidad, bonanza, *f.*

prosperous [pros-pe-ros] *adj.* próspero, feliz.

prostitution [pros-ti-tiu-shon] *n.* prostitución, *f.*

prostrate [pros-treit] *adj.* postrado, prosternado; **—,** *vt.* postrar; **—,** *vi.* prosternarse, postrarse.

prostrated [pros-trei-ted] *adj.* postrado; decaído.

prostration [pros-trei-shon] *n.*

postración, adinamia, *f.; colap-so, m.*

protect [pro-tekt] *vt.* proteger, amparar.

protection [pro-tek-shon] *n.* protección, *f.*

protective [pro-tek-tiv] *adj.* protector.

protector [pro-tek-tar] *n.* protector, ra; patron, na; defensor, ra.

protein [pro-tein] *n.* proteína, *f.*

protest [prou-test] *vt.* y *vi.* protestar; —, *n.* protesta, *f.; (corn.)* protesto (de una libranza).

Protestant [pro-tes-tant] *n.* y *adj.* protestante, *m.* y *f.*

protocol [prou-to-kol] *n.* protocolo, *m.*

proton [prou-ton] *n.* (elec.) protón, *m.*

protoplasm [prou-to-pla-sem] *n.* protoplasma, *m.*

prototype [prou-tou-taip] *n.* prototipo, *m.*

protract [pro-trakt] *vt.* prolongar, dilatar, diferir.

protrude [pro-trud] *vt.* empujar, impeler; —, *vi.* sobresalir.

protuberance [pro-tiu-be-rans] *n.* protuberancia, *f.*

protuberant [pro-tiu-be-rant] *adj.* prominente, saliente.

proud [praud] *adj.* soberbio, orgulloso.

prove [pruv] *vt.* probar, justifi-car; experimentar; —, *vi.* resultar; salir (bien o mal).

proverb [pro-verb] *n.* proverbio, *m.*

proverbial [pro-ver-bial] *adj.* proverbial.

provide [pro-vaid] *vt.* proveer, surtir; proporcionar; **to — one-self with,** proveerse de.

provided [pro-vai-did] *adj.* provisto; — **that,** con tal que, a condición de que, siempre que, dado que.

providence [pro-vi-dans] *n.* providencia, *f.;* economía, *f.*

provident [pro-vi-dant] *adj.* próvido; providente.

provider [pro-vai-dar] *n.* proveedor, ra.

provincial [pro-vin-shal] *adj.* provincial; —, *n.* provinciano, na.

provision [pro-vi-shon] *n.* provisión, *f.;* precaución, *f.;* —**s,** *n. pl.* comestibles, *m. pl.*

provisional [pro-vi-sho-nal] *adj.* provisional.

provocation [pro-vo-kei-shon] *n.* provocación, *f.*

provocative [pro-vo-ka-tiv] *adj.* provocativo; estimulante; —, *n.* excitante, *m.*

provoke [pro-vouk] *vt.* provocar, incitar.

provoking [pro-vou-kin] *adj.* provocativo; —**ly,** *adv.* de un modo provocativo.

prow [prau] *n.* (naut.) proa, *f.*

prowess [prauis] *n.* proeza, valentía, *f.*

prowl [praul] *vi.* andar en busca de pillaje; ron-dar, vagar; rastrear.

proximity [prok-si-mi-ti] *n.* proximidad, cercanía, *f.*

prudence [pru-dans] *n.* prudencia, *f.; precaución, *f.*

prudent [pru-dant] *adj.* prudente, circunspecto, cauteloso, cauto; —ly, *adv.* con juicio.

prudish [pru-dish] *adj.* mojigato, modesto en extremo.

prune [prun] *vt.* podar; escamondar (los árboles); —, *n.* ciruela seca, ciruela pasa, *f.*

pruning [pru-nin] *n.* poda, *f.*

pry [prai] *vi.* espiar, acechar; curiosear.

psalm [salm] *n.* salmo, *m.*

pseudonym [siu-do-nim] *n.* seudónimo o pseudónimo, *m.*

psychiatrist [sai-kaia-trist] *n.* psiquiatra o siquiatra, *m.y f.*

psychiatry [sai-kaia-tri] *n.* psiquiatría o siquiatría, *f.*

psychic [sai-kik] *adj.* psíquico o síquico.

psychoanalysis [sai-koua-na-li-sis] *n.* psicoanálisis o sicoanálisis, *f.*

psychologic, psychological [sai-ko-lo-yi-kal] *adj.* psicológico o sicológico.

psychologist [sai-ko-lo-yist] *n.* psicólogo, ga o sicólogo, ga.

psychology [sai-ko-lo-yi] *n.* psicología o sicología, *f.*

psychopathic [sai-kou-pa-zik] *adj.* psicopático o sicopático.

puberty [piu-ber-ti] *n.* pubertad, *f.*

public [pa-blik] *adj.* público; común; notorio; — **official,** funcionario público; — **relations,** relaciones con el público; — **spirited,** de espíritu cívico; — **utility,** empresa pública, empresa de servicios públicos; — **works,** obras públicas; —ly, *adv.* públicamente; —, *n.* público, *m.*

publication [pa-bli-kei-shon] *n.* publicación, *f*

publicist [pa-bli-sist] *n.* publicista, *m.* y *f.*

publicity [pa-bli-si-ti] *n.* publicidad, *f.*

publicize [pa-bli-sais] *vt.* publicar.

publish [pa-blish] *vt.* publicar, dar a la prensa.

publisher [pa-bli-shar] *n.* publicador, editor, *m.*

publishing [pa-bli-shin] *n.* publicación, *f.;* —, *adj.* editor, editorial; — **house,** casa editorial; casa editora.

puddle [pa-del] *n.* lodazal, cenagal, *m.; —, vt.* enlodar; enturbiar el agua con lodo.

puff [paf] *n.* bufido, soplo, *m.;* bocanada, *f.;*
powder —, mota para polvos, mota para empolvarse; —, *vt.* hinchar; soplar; ensoberbecer; —, *vi.* inflarse; bufar.

puffy [pa-fi] *adj.* hinchado, entumecido.

pug [pag] *n.* variedad de perro muy pequeño de pelo corto; — **nose,** nariz respingona

pull [pul] *vt.* tirar, jalar; coger; rasgar, desgarrar; **to — off,** arrancar; **to — out,** sacar; —, *n.* tirón, *m.;* sacudida, *f.;* (coll.) influencia, *f.*

pulmonary [pal-ma-na-ri] *adj.* pulmonar.

pulp [palp] *n.* pulpa, *f.;* carne (de fruta), *f.*

pulpit [pal-pit] *n.* púlpito, *m.*

pulsate [pal-seit] *vi.* pulsar, latir.

pulse [pals] *n.* pulso, *m.;* legumbres, *f. pl.*

pulverize [pal-ve-rais] *vt.* pulverizar.

pump [pamp] *n.* bomba, *f.;* zapatilla, *f.;* **air —,** máquina neumática; **feed —,** bomba de alimentación; **tire —,** bomba para neumáticos; **vacuum —,** bomba de vacío; —, *vt.* dar a la bomba; sondear; sonsacar.

pumpkin [pamp-kin] *n.* calabaza, *f.*

pun [pan] *n.* equívoco, chiste, *m.;* juego de palabras; —, *vi.* jugar del vocablo, hacer juego de palabras.

punch [panch] *n.* punzón, *m.;* puñetazo, *m.;* sacabocados, *m.;* ponche, *m.;* —, *vt.* punzar, horadar, taladrar; dar puñetazos.

punctual [pank-tiual] *adj.* puntual, exacto.

punctuality [pank-tiu-a-li-ti] *n.* exactitud, puntualidad, *f.*

punctuate [pank-tiueit] *vi.* puntuar.

punctuation [pank-tu-ei-shon] *n.* puntuación, *f.*

puncture [pank-char] *n.* puntura, *f.;* pinchazo, *m.,* pinchadura, *f.;* perforación, *f.;* —, *vt.* perforar.

punish [pa-nish] *vt.* castigar, penar.

punishable [pa-ni-sha-bol] *adj.* punible, castigable.

punishment [pa-nish-ment] *n.* castigo, *m.;* pena, *f.*

puny [pa-ni] *adj.* insignificante, pequeño; débil.

pup [pap] *n.* cachorrillo, *m.;* —, *vi.* parir la perra.

pupil [piu-pil] *n.* (anat.) pupila, *f.;* pupilo, *m.;* discípulo, la; — **of the eye,** niña del ojo.

puppet [pa-pit] *n.* títere, muñeco, *m.;* — **show,** representación de títeres.

puppy [pa-pi] *n.* perrillo, cachorro, *m.*

purchase [per-chis] *vt.* comprar; mercar.

purchaser [per-chi-sar] *n.* comprador, ra.

purchasing [per-chi-sin] *adj.* comprador; — **power,** poder adquisitivo.

pure [piuar] *adj.* puro; simple, mero; —**ly,** *adv.* puramente.

purée [piua-rei] *n.* puré, *m.*

purgatory [per-ga-to-ri] *n.* purgatorio, *m.*

purge [perch] *vt.* purgar; —, *n.* purga, purgación, *f.;* catártico, purgante, *m.*

purify [piua-ri-fai] *vt.* purificar; —, *vi.* purificarse.

puritan [piu-ri-tan] *n.* puritano, na.

purity [piua-ri-ti] *n.* pureza, *f.*

purple [per-pel] *adj.* purpureo, morado; —, *n.* púrpura, *f.;* —, *vi.* ponerse morado; —, *vt.* teñir de color morado.

purpose [per-pos] *n.* intención, *f.;* designio, proyecto, *m.;* objetivo, *m.;* vista, *f.;* mira, *f.;* efecto, *m.;* **on** —, de propósito, adrede; **to no** —, inútilmente; **to the** —, al propósito, de perilla; —, *vt.* y *vi.* proponerse,

resolver, intentar.

purr [per] *vi.* ronronear (aplicase a los gatos).

purse [pers] *n.* bolsa, *f.;* portamonedas, *m.;* —, *vt.* embolsar.

pursue [per-siu] *vt.* y *vi.* perseguir; seguir; acosar; continuar.

pursuit [per-sut] *n.* perseguimiento, *m.;* ocupación, *f.;* persecución, *f.*

purvey [per-vi] *vt.* y *vi.* proveer, suministrar.

purveyor [per-veiar] *n.* abastecedor, ra, surtidor, ra.

push [pash] *vt.* empujar; apretar; —, *vi.* hacer esfuerzos; **to — ahead, to — through,** pujar, avanzar; —, *n.* impulso, *m.;* — **button,** botón de contacto, botón automático.

pushing [pa-shin] *adj.* emprendedor, agresivo.

puss, pussy [pus], [pu-si] *n.* micho, gato, *m.*

put [put] *vt.* poner, colocar; proponer; imponer, obligar; **to —in order,** poner en orden; **to — in writing,** poner por escrito; **to — on shoes,** calzar; **to — out (a light, etc.),** apagar (una luz, etc.); **to — through,** ejecutar, llevar a cabo; **to — together,** confeccionar, armar.

putty [pa-ti] *n.* almáciga, masilla, *f.;* cemento, *m.;* —, *vt.* enmasillar.

puzzle [pa-sel] *n.* acertijo, enigma, rompecabezas, *m.;* perplejidad, *f.;* **jigsaw —,** rompecabezas, *m.;* **—,** *vt.* embrollar, confundir; **—,** *vi.* confundirse.

puzzling [pa-se-lin] *adj.* enigmá-

tico; engañador.

pygmy [pig-mi] *n.* y *adj.* pigmeo, mea.

pyramid [pi-ra-mid] *n.* pirámide, *f.*

python [pai-zon] *n.* pitón, *m.*

Q

quart [kwart] cuarto de galón.

quack [kwæk] [kuak] *vi.* graznar (como un pato); **—,** *n.* charlatán, curandero, *m.*

quadrangle [kuo-dran-guel] *n.* cuadrángulo, *m.*

quadrant [kuo-drant] *n.* cuadrante, *m.;* (naut.) octante, *m.*

quadrilateral [kuo-dri-la-te-ral] *adj.* cuadrilátero.

quadruple [kuo-dru-pol] *adj.* cuádruplo.

quail [kueil] *n.* codorniz, *f.*

quaint [kueint] *adj.* extraño pero agradable por su sabor de antaño; **—ly,** *adv.* en forma extraña pero agradable.

quake [kueik] *vi.* temblar, tiritar; **—,** *n.* temblor, *m.*

qualify [kuo-li-fai] *vt.* calificar; modificar; templar; **—,** *vi.* habilitarse, llenar los requisitos.

qualitative [kuo-li-ta-tiv] *adj.* cualitativo.

quality [kua-li-ti] *n.* calidad, *f.;*

don, *m.;* condición, *f.;* prenda, *f.;* **average —,** calidad media.

qualm [kualm] *n.* deliquio, desmayo, *m.;* escrúpulo, *m.;* duda, *f.*

quandary [kuon-da-ri] *n.* incertidumbre, duda, *f.;* di-lema, *m.*

quantity [kuon-ti-ti] *n.* cantidad, *f.*

quarantine [kuo-ran-tin] *n.* cuarentena, *f.;* **—,** *vt.* poner en cuarentena; **to — a nation,** declarar cuarentena contra una nación.

quarrel [kuo-rel] *n.* quimera, riña, pelea, contienda, *f.;* **—,** *vi.* reñir, disputar.

quarry [kuo-ri] *n.* cantera, *f.*

quart [kuort] *n.* un cuarto de galón.

quarter [kuor-tar] *n.* cuarto, *m.,* cuarta parte, *f.;* cuartel, *m.;* barriada, *f.;* barrio, *m.;* moneda de E.U.A. que equivale a 25 centavos de dólar; **— of an**

hour, cuarto de hora; —, *vt.* cuartear; acuartelar; dividir en cuatro.

quarterly [kuor-ta-li] *adj.* trimestral.

quartet [kuor-tet] *n.* (mus.) cuarteto, *m.*

quartz [kuorts] *n.* (min.) cuarzo, *m.*

quash [kuosh] *vt.* reprimir, aplastar.

quaver [kuei-var] *n.* estremecimiento, *m.;* (mus.) corchea, *f.;* —, *vi.* gorgoritear, trinar; temblar.

queen [kuin] *n.* reina, *f.;* dama (en el juego de ajedrez), *f.*

queenly [kuin-li] *adj.* majestuoso, como una reina.

queer [kuiar] *adj.* extraño; ridículo; enrevesado; raro; —**ly,** *adv.* en forma rara.

quench [kuench] *vt.* apagar; extinguir, saciar.

query [kue-ri] *n.* pregunta, *f.;* duda, *f.;* —, *vt.* preguntar.

quest [kuest] *n.* pesquisa, inquisición, *f.;* busca, *f.*

question [kues-tion] *n.* cuestión, *f.,* asunto, *m.;* duda, *f.;* pregunta, *f.;* **to ask a —,** hacer una pregunta; **to be a — of,** tratarse de; —, *vi.* preguntar; —, *vt.* dudar, desconfiar, poner en duda.

questionable [kues-tio-na-bol] *adj.* cuestionable, dudoso.

questionnaire [kues-tio-near] *n.* cuestionario, *m.*

quick [kuik] *adj.* listo; rápido; veloz; ligero, pronto; ágil, ardiente, penetrante; —**ly,** *adv.* rápidamente, con presteza; —, *n.* carne viva; parte vital.

quicken [kui-ken] *vt.* vivificar; acelerar; animar.

quicklime [kuik-laim] *n.* cal viva.

quickness [kuik-nes] *n.* ligereza, presteza, *f.;* actividad, *f.;* viveza, penetración.

quicksand [kuik-sand] *n.* arena movediza.

quicksilver [kuik-sil-var] *n.* azogue, mercurio, *m.*

quiet [kuaiat] *adj.* quedo, quieto, tranquilo, llado; —, *n.* calma, serenidad, *f.;* *vt.* tranquilizar.

quietness, quietude [kuaia-tiud] *n.* quietud, tranquilidad, *f.*

quill [kuil] *n.* pluma de ave; cañón, *m.,* pluma, *f.,* (para escribir); púa del puerco espín.

quilt [kuilt] *n.* colcha, *f.;* **crazy —,** centón, *m.*

quince [kuins] *n.* (bot.) membrillo, *m.;* — **jelly,** jalea de membrillo.

quinine [kui-nin] *n.* quinina, *f.*

quintessence [kuin-te-sens] *n.* quintaesencia, *f.*

quintet [kuin-tet] *n.* (mus.) quinteto, *m.*

quintuplets [kuin-tu-plets] *n. pl.* quíntuples, *m.* o *f. pl.*

quirk [kuerk] *n.* desviación, *f.;* pulla, *f.;* sutileza, *f.;* rasgo (como en la escritura).

quit [kuit] *vt.* descargar; desempeñar; absolver; **to — work,** dejar de trabajar; **—,** *vi.* desistir, dejar (de hacer algo).

quite [kuait] *adv.* totalmente, enteramente, absolutamente, bastante.

quiver [kui-var] *n.* temblor, tiritón, *m.;* **—,** *vi.* temblar, retemblar, blandir.

quiz [kuis] *vt.* examinar; **—,** *n.* examen por medio de preguntas.

quota [kuou-ta] *n.* cuota, *f..*

quotable [kuou-ta-bol] *adj.* citable.

quotation [kuo-tei-shon] *n.* citación, cotización, cita, *f.;* **list of —s,** boletín de cotizaciones; **— marks,** comillas, *f. pl.*

quote [kuout] *vt.* citar; **to — (a price),** cotizar (precio).

quotient [kuou-shent] *n.* cociente o cuociente, *m.;* **intelligence —,** cociente intelectual.

R

rabbi [ra-bi] *n.* rabí, rabino, *m.*

rabbit [ra-bit] *n.* conejo, *m.*

rabble [ra-bel] *n.* chusma, gentuza, *f.;* gente baja.

rabid [ra-bid] *adj.* rabioso, furioso.

rabies [rei-bis] *n.* rabia, hidrofobia, *f.*

raccoon [ra-kun] *n.* (zool.) mapache, *m.*

race [reis] *n.* raza, casta, *f.;* carrera, corrida, *f.;* **— track,** corredera, pista, *f.;* **—,** *vi.* competir en un carrera; correr con mucha ligereza; **—,** *vt.* (auto.) acelerar con carga disminuida.

racial [rei-shal] *adj.* racial, de raza.

rack [rak] *n.* tormento, *m.;* rueca, *f.;* cremallera, *f.;* percha, *f.;* destrucción, *f.;* **—,** *vt.* atormentar; trasegar.

racket [ra-kit] *n.* baraúnda, confusión, *f.;* raqueta, *f.;* explotación, *f.;* cualquier ardid fraudulento.

racoon = raccoon.

radar [rei-dar] *n.* radar, *m.*

radiance [rei-dians] *n.* brillo, esplendor, *m.*

radiant [rei-diant] *adj.* radiante, brillante.

radiate [rei-dieit] *vi.* echar rayos, centellear; irradiar.

radiation [rei-diei-shon] *n.* irradiación, *f.;* radiación, *f.*

radiator [rei-diei-tar] *n.* calorífero, calentador, *m.*, estufa, *f.;* (auto.) radiador, *m.;* **steam —,** calorífero de vapor.

radical [ra-di-kal] *adj.* radical; —, *n.* (math.) radical, *m.;* **—ly,** *adv.* radicalmente.

radicalism [ra-di-ka-li-sem] *n.* radicalismo, *m.*

radio [rei-diou] *n.* radio, *m. o f.,* radiocomunicación, *f.;* — **amplifier,** radioamplificador, *m.;* — **announcer,** anunciador de radio; — **beam,** faro radioeléctrico; — **broad-casting station,** estación radiodifusora; — **hookup,** circuito, *m.;* — **listener,** radioescucha, radioyente, *m. y f.;* — **message,** comunicación radioeléctrica; — **receiver,** radiorreceptor, *m.;* — **technician,** radiotécnico, *m.;* — **tube,** válvula de radio.

radioactive [rei-diou-ak-tiv] *adj.* radiactivo.

radioactivity [rei-diou-ak-ti-vi-ti] *n.* radiactividad, *f.*

radiobroadcast [rei-diou-brod-kast] *vt. y vi.* difundir por radiotrasmisión.

radiobroadcasting [rei-diou-brod-kas-tin] *n.* radiodifusión, *f.*

radish [ra-dish] *n.* rábano, *m.*

radium [rei-diom] *n.* (chem.) radio, *m.*

radius [rei-dios] *n.* (math., anat.) radio, *m.*

raffle [ra-fel] *n.* rifa, *f.,* sorteo, *m.;* —, *vt.* rifar, sortear.

raft [raft] *n.* balsa, *f.;* armadía, *f.; (coll.)* gran cantidad; **a — of people,** un gentío, *m.*

rag [rag] *n.* trapo, andrajo, jirón, *m..;* **—s,** *n. pl.* andrajos, *m. pl.*

rage [reich] *n.* rabia, *f.;* furor, *m.;* cólera, *f.;* **to fly into a —,** montar en cólera; —, *vi.* rabiar, encolerizarse.

raging [rei-yin] *n.* furia, rabia, *f.;* **—ly,** *adv.* furiosamente.

ragweed [rag-uid] *n.* (bot.) ambrosía, *f.*

raid [reid] *n.* invasión, *f.;* —, *vt.* invadir, hacer una incursión.

raider [rei-dar] *n.* corsario, *m.*

rail [reil] *n.* baranda, barrera, *f.;* balaustrada, *f.;* (rail.) carril, riel, *m.;* **by —,** por ferrocarril; —, *vt.* cercar con balaustradas; —, *vi.,* injuriar de palabra.

railing [rei-lin] *n.* baranda, *f.,* barandal, pretil, *m.*

railroad [reil-roud] *n.* ferrocarril, *m.;* vía férrea; **electric —** ferrocarril eléctrico; **elevated —,** ferrocarril elevado; — **crossing,** paso a nivel; — **station,** estación de ferrocarril; — **track,** vía férrea.

railway [reil-uei] *n.* ferrocarril, *m.;* **cable —,** funicular —, ferrocarril de cable; — **express,** servicio rápido de carga por ferrocarril; **street —,** ferrocarril urbano.

rain [rein] *n.* lluvia, *f.;* — **water,** agua lluvia, agua llovediza; —, *vi.* llover; **to — heavily,** llover a cántaros; **to stop — ing,** escampar.

rainbow [rein-bou] *n.* arco iris.

raincoat [rein-kout] *n.* impermeable, *m.;* capote, *m.*

raindrop [rein-drop] *n.* gota de lluvia.

rainfall [rein-fol] *n.* aguacero, *m.,* lluvia, *f.;* precipitación pluvial.

rainy [rei-ni] *adj.* lluvioso.

raise [reis] *vt.* levantar, alzar; fabricar, edificar; izar (la bandera); engrandecer, excitar, causar; **to — an objection,** poner objeción, objetar; **to — up,** suspender, alzar.

raisin [rei-san] *n.* pasa (uva seca), *f.*

rake [reik] *n.* rastro, rastrillo, *m.;* tunante, *m.;* —, *vt.* rastrillar; raer; rebuscar.

rally [ra-li] *vt.* (mil.) reunir; ridiculizar; —, *vi.* reunirse; burlarse de alguno.

ram [ram] *n.* ariete, *m.;* **battering —,** brigola, *f.;* —, *vt.* impeler con violencia; pegar contra; atestar, henchir.

ramble [ram-bel] *vi.* vagar; callejear; —, *n.* corre-ría, *f.*

ramification [ra-mi-fi-kei-shon] *n.* ramificación, *f.;* ramal, *m.*

ramp [ramp] *n.* rampa, *f.*

rampage [ram-peich] *n.* conducta violenta o desenfrenada.

rampant [ram-pant] *adj.* desenfrenado; rampante (en heráldica).

rampart [ram-part] *n.* baluarte, *m.;* terraplén, *m.;* (mil.) muralla, *f.*

ramrod [ram-rod] *n.* baqueta, *f.;* atacador, *m.;* (mil.) roquete, *m.*

ran [ran] *pretérito* del verbo **run.**

ranch [ranch] *n.* finca rústica de ganado.

rancher [ran-char] *n.* hacendado, da; ranchero, ra.

rancid [ran-sid] *adj.* rancio.

rancor [ran-kor] *n.* rencor, *m.*

random [ran-dom] *n.* ventura, casualidad, *f.;* **at —,** a trochemoche, al azar.

rang [rang] *pretérito* del verbo **ring.**

range [reindch] *vr.* colocar, ordenar; clasificar; —, *vi.* fluctuar; vagar; —, *n.* clase, *f.;* orden, *m.;* hilera, *f.;* correría, *f.;* alcance, *m.;* línea de un tiro de artillería; cocina económica, estufa, *f.;* — **finder,** telémetro, *m.;*

— **of mountains,** sierra, *f.* cadena de montañas.

ranger [reind-char] *n.* guardabosque, *m.;* (mil.) comando (de E.U.A.), *m.*

rank [rank] *adj.* exuberante; rancio; fétido; vulgar; indecente; —, *n.* fila, hilera, *f.;* clase, *f.;* grado, *m.;* — **and file,** (mil.) individuos de tropa; las masas, *f. pl.*

ransack [ran-sak] *vt.* saquear, pillar.

ransom [ran-som] *vt.* rescatar; —, *n.* rescate, *m.*

rant [rant] *vi.* decir disparates; regañar con vehemencia.

rap [rap] *vt.* y *vi.* dar un golpe vivo y repentino; **to — at the door,** tocar a la puerta; —, *n.* golpe ligero y seco.

rape [reip] *n.* violación, *f.,* estupro, *m.;* —, *vt.* estuprar.

rapid [ra-pid] *adj.* rápido.

rapidity [ra-pi-di-ti] *n.* rapidez, *f.*

rapt [rapt] *adj.* encantado, enajenado.

rapture [rap-char] *n.* rapto, éxtasis, *m.*

rapturous [rap-cha-ros] *adj.* embelesado.

rare [rear] *adj.* raro, extraordinario.

rash [ras-kal] *adj.* precipitado, temerario; —**ly,** *adv.* precipitadamente; —, *n.* brote, *m.;* urti-

caria, *f.;* erupción, *f.;* sarpullido, *m.*

rashness [rash-nes] *n.* temeridad, *f.;* arrojo, *m.*

rasp [rasp] *n.* escofina, *f.;* raspador, *m.;* —, *vt.* raspar; escofinar.

raspberry [ras-be-ri] *n.* frambuesa, *f.*

rat [rat] *n.* rata, *f.*

ratchet [rach] *n.* rueda o diente de engranaje; trinquete, *m.*

rate [reit] *n.* tipo, *m.,* tasa, *f.,* precio, valor, *m.;* grado, *m.;* manera, *f.;* tarifa, *f.;* razón, *f.;* velocidad, *f.;* **at the — of,** a razón de; **at the — of exchange,** al cambio de; **at what — of exchange?** ¿a qué cambio? — **of interest,** tipo de interés; —, *vt.* tasar, apreciar; calcular; calificar; reñir a uno; —, *vi.* ser considerado favorablemente; (coll.) tener influencia.

rather [ra-dar] *adv.* de mejor gana; más bien; antes; antes bien; bastante; mejor dicho.

ratification [ra-ti-fi-kei-shan] *n.* ratificación, *f.*

ratify [ra-ti-fai] *vt.* ratificar.

rating [rei-tin] *n.* valuación, *f.*

ratio [rei-shiou] *n.* proporción, *f.;* razón, *f.;* **direct —** razón directa; **inverse —,** razón inversa.

ration [ra-shon] *n.* (mil.) ración, *f.;* —, *vt.* racionar.

rational [ra-sho-nal] *adj.* racional; razonable.

rationing [ra-sho-nin] *n.* racionamiento, *m.*

rattle [ra-tel] *vt.* y *vi.* hacer ruido; confundir; zumbar; rechinar; **to become —d,** perder la chaveta; confundirse; **—,** *n.* ruido (como el de matracas), *m.*; sonajero, *m.*; matraca, *f.*

rattlesnake [ra-tel-sneik] *n.* culebra de cascabel.

raucous [ro-kos] *adj.* ronco, áspero, bronco; **— voice,** voz ronca y desagradable.

ravage [ra-vich] *vi.* saquear, pillar; asolar; **—,** *n.* saqueo, *m.*

rave [reiv] *vi.* delirar; enfurecerse; echar chispas.

raven [rei-ven] *n.* cuervo, *m.*

ravenous [ra-ve-nos] *adj.* voraz, famélico.

ravine [ra-vin] *n.* barranca, cañada, *f.*

raving [rei-vin] *adj.* furioso, frenético; **—ly,** *adv.* como un loco furioso.

ravish [ra-vish] *vt.* estuprar; arrebatar.

ravishing [ra-vi-shin] *adj.* encantador.

raw [ro] *adj.* crudo; puro; nuevo; **in a — state,** en bruto; **— materials,** primeras materias, materias primas.

ray [rei] *n.* rayo (de luz), *m.*;

(ichth.) raya, *f.*

razor [rei-sar] *n.* navaja de afeitar; **— blade,** hoja de afeitar; **electric —,** afeitadora o rasuradora eléctrica.

reach [riich] *vt.* alcanzar; llegar hasta; **—,** *vi.* extenderse, llegar; alcanzar, penetrar; esforzarse; **—,** *n.* alcance, poder, *m.*; capacidad, *f.*

react [ri-akt] *vi.* reaccionar; resistir; obrar recíprocamente.

reaction [ri-ak-shon] *n.* reacción, *f.*

reactionary [ri-ak-sho-na-ri] *n.* reaccionario, ria; (pol.) derechista, *m.* y *f.*; **—,** *adj.* reaccionario.

reactivate [ri-ak-ti-veit] *vt.* reactivar.

reactor [ri-ak-tar] *n.* reactor, *m.*

read [rid] *vt.* leer; interpretar; adivinar, predecir; **—,** *vi.* leer; estudiar.

read [red] *adj.* leído, erudito; **well — man,** hombre letrado.

readable [ri-da-bol] *adj.* legible.

reader [ri-dar] *n.* lector, ra.

readily [re-di-li] *adv.* prontamente; de buena gana.

readiness [re-di-nes] *n.* facilidad, *f.*; vivacidad del ingenio; voluntad, gana, *f.*; prontitud, *f.*

reading [ri-din] *n.* lectura, *f.*; **— room,** salón de lectura.

readjust [riad-yast] *vt.* recomponer; reajustar.

readjustment [riad-yast-ment] *n.* reajuste, *m.*

ready [re-di] *adj.* listo, pronto; inclinado; fácil; ligero.

real [rial] *adj.* real, verdadero, efectivo; inmueble; — **estate,** bienes raíces o inmuebles.

realism [ria-li-sem] *n.* realismo, *m.*

realist [ria-list] *n.* realista, *m.* y *f.*

realistic [ria-lis-tik] *adj.* realista; natural.

reality [ria-li-ti] *n.* realidad, *f.;* efectividad, *f.*

realization [ria-lai-sei-shon] *n.* comprensión, *f.;* realización, *f.*

realize [ria-lais] *vt.* hacerse cargo de, darse cuenta de; realizar.

really [ria-li] *adv.* realmente, verdaderamente.

realm [relm] *n.* reino, *m.;* dominio, *m.*

reap [rip] *vt.* segar.

reaper [ri-par] *n.* segador, ra.

reappear [ria-piar] *vi.* reaparecer.

reapportion [ria-point] *vt.* asignar o repartir de nuevo.

rear [riar] *n.* retaguardia, *f.;* parte posterior; —, *adj.* posterior.

rearrange [ria-reindch] *vt.* refundir, dar nueva forma (a una comedia, discurso, etc.); volver a arreglar.

rear-view mirror [ria-viu-mi-rar] *n.* (auto.) espejo de retrovisión.

reason [ri-son] *n.* razón, *f.;* causa, *f.;* motivo, *m.;* juicio, *m.;* quid, *m.;* **by — of,** con motivo de, a causa de; **for this —,** por esto; **without —,** sin qué ni para qué, sin razón; —, *vt.* razonar, raciocinar.

reasonable [ri-so-na-bol] *adj.* razonable, lógico.

reasoning [ri-so-nin] *n.* raciocinio, *m.*

reassurance [ria-shua-rans] *n.* confirmación, *f.;* reiteración de confianza; restauración de ánimo.

reassure [ria-shuar] *vt.* tranquilizar, calmar; asegurar de nuevo.

rebate [ri-beit] *n,* rebaja, deducción, *f.,* descuento, *m.;* —, *vt.* descontar, rebajar.

rebel [re-bel] *n.* rebelde, *m.* y *f.,* insurrecto, ta; —, *adj.* insurrecto; —, *vi.* rebelarse; insubordinarse.

rebellion [ri-be-lion] *n.* rebelión, insubordinación, *f.*

rebellious [ri-be-lios] *adj.* rebelde.

rebirth [ri-berz] *n.* renacimiento, *m.*

rebound [ri-baund] *vt.* y *vi.* repercutir; —, *n.* rebote (de una pelota); repercusión, *f.*

rebuild [ri-bild] *vt.* reedificar, reconstruir.

rebuke [ri-biuk] *vt.* reprender, regañar; —, *n.* reprensión, *f.*, regaño, *m.*

recall [ri-kal] *vt.* llamar, hacer volver; revocar; — **to mind,** recapacitar; —, *n.* revocación, *f.*

recant [ri-kant] *vt.* retractarse, desdecirse.

recapitulate [ri-kal-si-treit] *vt.* recapitular.

recapture [ri-kap-char] *n.* represa (de un navío, etc.); —, *vt.* volver a tomar; represar.

recede [ri-sid] *vi.* retroceder; desistir.

receipt [ri-sit] *n.* recibo, *m.;* receta, *f.,* ingreso, *m.;* **to acknowledge** —, acusar recibo.

receivable [ri-si-va-bol] *adj.* admisible; **bills** —, cuentas por cobrar.

receive [ri-siv] *vt.* recibir; aceptar, admitir; cobrar.

receiver [ri-si-var] *n.* receptor, *m.;* recipiente, *m.;* audífono, *m.;* depositario, *m.;* — **in bankruptcy,** síndico, *m.*

recent [ri-sent] *adj.* reciente, nuevo; fresco.

receptacle [ri-sep-ta-kol] *n.* receptáculo, *m.*

reception [ri-sep-shon] *n.* acogi-

da, *f.; recepción, f.*

receptionist [ri-sep-sho-nist] *n.* recepcionista, *f.,* persona encargada de recibir a los visitantes en una oficina.

receptive [ri-sep-tiv] *adj.* receptivo.

recess [ri-ses] *n.* recreo, *m.;* retiro, *m.;* nicho, *m.;* lugar apartado; grieta, *f.;* tregua, *f.;* receso, *m.*

recession [ri-se-shon] *n.* retirada, *f.;* receso, *m.* recipe, *n.* receta de cocina.

recipient [ri-si-piant] *n.* receptor, ra.

reciprocal [ri-si-pro-kal] *adj.* recíproco.

reciprocate [ri-si-pro-keit] *vi.* corresponder; —, *vt.* reciprocar, compensar.

reciprocity [re-si-pro-si-ti] *n.* reciprocidad, *f.*

recital [ri-sai-tal] *n.* recitación, *f.;* concierto musical.

recitation [re-si-tei-shon] *n.* recitación *f.*

recite [ri-sait] *vt.* recitar; referir, relatar; declamar; **to** — **a lesson,** dar una lección.

reckless [re-kles] *adj.* descuidado; audaz; —**ly,** *adv.* audazmente; descuidadamente.

reckon [re-kon] *vt.* contar, numerar; —, *vi.* computar, calcular.

reckoning [rek-nin] *n.* cuenta, *f.;* cálculo, *m.*

reclaim [ri-kleim] *vt.* reformar, corregir; recobrar; hacer utilizable; reclamar.

reclamation [re-kla-mei-shon] *n.* aprovechamiento, *m.,* utilización, *f.;* reclamación, *f.*

recline [ri-klain] *vt. y vi.* reclinar; reposar.

recluse [ri-klus] *adj.* recluso, retirado; —, *n.* recluso, sa.

recognition [re-kog-ni-shon] *n.* reconocimiento, *m.;* agradecimiento, *m.*

recognize [re-kog-nais] *vt.* reconocer.

recoil [ri-koil] *vi.* retirarse; —, *n.* rechazo, *m.*

recollect [re-ko-lekt] *vt. y vi.* recordar; acordarse.

recollect [re-ko-lekt] *vt.* recobrar.

recollection [re-ko-lek-shon] *n.* recuerdo, *m.;* reminiscencia, *f.*

recommend [re-ko-mend] *vt.* recomendar.

recommendation [re-ko-men-dei-shon] *n.* recomendación, *f.*

recompense [re-kom-pens] *n.* recompensa, *f.;* —, *vt.* recompensar.

reconcile [re-kon-sail] *vt.* reconciliar.

reconciliation [re-kon-si-liei-shon] *n.* reconciliación, *f.*

reconsider [ri-kon-si-dar] *vt.* considerar de nuevo.

reconstruct [ri-kon-strakt] *vt.* reedificar, reconstruir.

record [ri-kord] *vt.* registrar; protocolar; grabar.

record [ri-kord] *n.* registro, archivo, *m.;* disco, *m.;* — **player,** tocadiscos, fonógrafo, *m.;* **off the** —, confidencialmente, extraoficialmente (tratándose de una declaración que no debe publicarse) ; —**s,** *n. pl.* anales, *m. pl.;* —, *adj.* sin precedente.

recorder [ri-kor-dar] *n.* registrador, archivero, *m.;* grabadora, *f.*

recount [ri-kaunt] *vt.* referir, contar de nuevo; —, *n.* recuento, *m.*

recourse [ri-kors] *n.* recurso, retorno, *m.*

recover [ri-ka-var] *vt.* recobrar; cobrar; reparar; restablecer; **to — (property),** recobrar (propiedad); **to — one's senses,** volver en si; —, *vi.* convalecer, restablecerse; **to — (health),** sanar, recobrar (la salud), reponerse.

recovery [ri-ka-ve-ri] *n.* convalecencia, *f.;* recobro, *m.;* recuperación, *f.,* restablecimiento, *m.*

recreate [re-krieit] *vt.* recrear, deleitar, divertir.

recreation [re-kriei-shon] *n.* recreación, *f.*

recrimination [ri-kri-mi-nei-shon] *n.* recriminación, *f.*

recruit [ri-krut] *vt.* reclutar; —, *n.* (mil.) recluta, *m.*

recruiting [ri-kru-tin] *n.* recluta, *f.*, reclutamiento, *m.*

rectangle [rek-tan-guel] *n.* rectángulo, *m.*

rectangular [rek-tan-guiu-lar] *adj.* rectangular.

rectify [rek-ti-fai] *vt.* rectificar.

recuperate [ri-ku-pe-reit] *vi.* restablecerse, recuperarse; —, *vt.* recobrar, recuperar.

recur [ri-ker] *vi.* recurrir.

recurrence [ri-ka-rans] *n.* retorno, *m.;* vuelta, *f.;* repetición, *f.*

recurrent [ri-ka-rant] *adj.* periódico, que reaparece de cuando en cuando.

red [red] *adj.* rojo; rubio; colorado; — **herring,** arenque ahumado; acción para distraer la atención del asunto principal; — **lead,** minio, bermellón, *m.;* — **man,** piel roja, *m.,* indio norteamericano; — **pepper,** pimiento, pimentón, *m.;* — **tape,** balduque, *m.;* expedienteo, *m.,* (Mex.) papeleo, *m.;* **R—** **(communist),** *n.* y *adj.* rojo (comunista), *m.*

redbird [red-berd] *n.* (orn.) cardenal, *m.*

red-blooded [red-bla-did] *adj.* valiente, denodado; vigoroso.

redbreast [red-brest] *n.* petirrojo, pechirrojo, *m.*

redden [re-den] *vt.* teñir de color rojo; —, *vi.* ponerse colorado, sonrojarse.

reddish [re-dish] *adj.* rojizo, bermejizo.

redeem [ri-dim] *vt.* redimir, rescatar.

redeemer [ri-di-mar] *n.* redentor, ra, salvador, ra; the **R—,** el Redentor, *m.*

redeeming [ri-di-min] *adj.* redentor.

redemption [ri-dem-shon] *n.* redención, *f.*

red-haired [red-jerd] *adj.* pelirrojo.

redhead [red-jed] *n.* pelirrojo, ja.

red-hot [red-jot] *adj.* candente, ardiente.

redress [ri-dres] *vt.* enderezar; corregir; reformar; rectificar; —, *n.* reforma, corrección, *f.*

reduce [ri-dius] *vt.* reducir; perder peso; disminuir; sujetar; —, *vi.* reducirse.

reduction [ri-dak-shon] *n.* reducción, rebaja, *f.*

redundant [ri-dan-dant] *adj.* redundante, superfluo; **to be —,** redundar.

redwood [red-vud] *n.* (bot.) pino de California.

reed [rid] *n.* caña, *f.;* flecha, *f.*

reef [rif] *vt.* (naut.) tomar rizos a

las velas; —, *n.* arrecife, escollo, *m.*

reek [rik] *n.* humo, vapor, *m.;* —
, *vi.* humear; vahear; oler a.

re-**elect** [rii-lekt] *vt.* reelegir.

re-**election** [rii-lek-shon] *n.* reelección, *f.*

re-**enforce** [riin-fors] *vt.* reforzar.

re-**establish** [riis-ta-blish] *vt.*
restablecer, volver a establecer
una cosa.

refer [ri-fer] *vt.* y *vi.* referir, remitir; dirigir; referirse; — **to,**
véase.

referee [re-fa-rii] *n.* arbitrador,
árbitro, *m.;* —, *vt.* y *vi.* servir
de árbitro o de juez.

reference [re-frans] *n.* referencia,
relación, *f.*

refill [ri-fil] *vt.* rellenar; —, *n.*
relleno, *m.;* repuesto, *m.*

refine [ri-fain] *vt.* y *vi.* refinar,
purificar, purificarse.

refinement [ri-fain-ment] *n.* refinación, *f.;* refinamiento, *m.;*
refinadura, *f.;* elegancia afecta-
da.

refinery [ri-fai-na-ri] *n.* refinería,
f.

reflect [ri-flekt] *vt.* y *vi.* reflejar,
repercutir; reflexionar; recaer;
meditar.

reflection [ri-flek-shon] *n.* reflexión, meditación, *f.;* reflejo, *m.*

reflex [ri-fleks] *n.* y *adj.* reflejo,
m.

reforest [ri-fo-rist] *vt.* repoblar de
árboles.

reform [ri-form] *vt.* reformar; —,
vi. reformarse; —, *n.* reforma, *f.*

reformation [re-for-mei-shon] *n.*
reformación, *f.;* reforma, *f.*

reformatory [ri-for-ma-to-ri] *n.*
reformatorio, *m.*

reformer [ri-for-mar] *n.* reforma-
dor, ra.

refract [ri-frakt] *vt.* refractar,
refringir.

refrain [ri-frein] *vi.* reprimirse,
abstenerse; mesurarse; —, *n.*
estribillo, *m.*

refresh [ri-fresh] *vt.* refrigerar,
refrescar.

refresher [ri-fre-shar] *n.* repaso,
m.; — **course,** curso de repaso.

refreshing [ri-fre-shin] *adj.*
refrescante.

refreshment [ri-fresh-ment] *n.*
refresco, refrigerio, *m.*

refrigerate [ri-fri-ya-reit] *vt.* refrigerar.

refrigeration [ri-fri-ya-reishon] *n.*
refrigeración, *f.*

refrigerator [ri-fri-ya-rei-tar] *n.*
refrigerador, *m.*

refuel [ri-fiual] *vt.* poner nuevo
combustible.

refuge [re-fiuch] *n.* refugio, asilo,
m.; seno, *m.;* recurso, *m.*

refugee [re-fiu-yii] *n.* refugiado,
da.

refund [ri-fand] *vt.* restituir;

devolver, rembolsar.

refurbish [ri-fur-bish] *vt.* renovar, retocar.

refusal [ri-fiu-sal] *n.* repulsa, denegación, *f.;* negativa, *f.*

refuse [ri-fius] *vt.* rehusar, repulsar, negarse a; —, *n.* desecho, *m.,* sobra, *f.;* limpiaduras, *f. pl.;* basura, *f.*

refute [re-fiut] *vt.* refutar; confutar.

regain [ri-guein] *vt.* recobrar, recuperar.

regal [ri-gal] *adj.* real.

regard [ri-gard] *vt.* estimar; considerar; —, *n.* consideración, *f.;* respeto, *m.;* —**s,** *n. pl* recuerdos, *m. pl.,* memorias, *f. pl.;* **in — to,** en cuanto a, respecto a, con respecto a; **in this —,** a este respecto; **to give —s,** dar saludos; **with — to,** a propósito de, relativo a.

regarding [ri-gar-din] *prep.* concerniente a.

regardless [ri-gard-les] *adj.* descuidado, negligente; indiferente; **— of,** a pesar de.

regency [ri-yan-si] *n.* regencia, *f.;* gobierno, *m.*

regeneration [ri-ye-na-rei-shon] *n.* regeneración, *f.;* renacimiento, *m.*

regent [ri-yent] *n.* regente, *m.*

regime [rei-yim] *n.* régimen, *m.;* administración, *f.*

regiment [re-yi-mant] *n.* regimiento, *m.;* —, *vt.* regimentar; asignar a un regimiento o grupo; regimentar (en el sentido del estado totalitario).

region [ri-yon] *n.* región, *f.;* distrito, *m.;* país, *m.*

regional [ri-yo-nal] *adj.* regional.

register [re-yis-tar] *n.* registro, *m.;* **cash —,** caja registradora; —, *vt.* inscribir; registrar; certificar (una carta); —, *vi.* matricularse, registrarse.

registered [re-yis-tad] *adj.* registrado, matriculado; **— letter,** carta certificada.

registration [re-yis-trei-shon] *n.* registro, *m.;* inscripción, *f.;* empadronamiento, *m.*

regress [ri-gres] *n.* retroceso, *m.;* —, *vi.* retrogradar, retroceder.

regret [ri-gret] *n.* arrepentimiento, *m.;* pesar, *m.;* — *vt.* sentir (pena o dolor), lamentar, deplorar.

regretful [ri-gret-ful] *adj.* pesaroso, arrepentido.

regrettable [ri-gre-ta-bol] *adj.* sensible, lamentable, deplorable.

regular [re-guiu-lar] *adj.* regular; ordinario; **— army,** tropas de línea; —, *n.* regular, *m.*

regularity [re-guiu-la-ri-ti] *n.* regularidad, *f.*

regulate [re-guiu-leit] *vt.* regular,

ordenar.

regulation [re-guiu-lei-shon] *n.* reglamentación, *f.,* reglas, *f. pl.;* arreglo, *m.*

rehabilitate [ria-bi-li-teit] *vt.* rehabilitar.

rehabilitation [ria-bi-li-tei-shon] *n.* rehabilitación, *f.*

rehearsal [ri-jer-sal] *n.* repetición, *f.;* (theat.) ensayo, *m.;* **dress —,** último ensayo (con vestuario y demás detalles).

rehearse [ri-jers] *vt.* ensayar.

reign [rein] *n.* reinado, reino, *m.;* **—,** *vi.* reinar, prevalecer, imperar.

reimburse [rim-bers] *vt.* rembolsar.

reimbursement [rim-bers-ment] *n.* rembolso, reintegro, *m.*

rein [rein] *n.* rienda, *f.;* **—,** *vt.* refrenar.

reincarnation [riin-kar-nei-shon] *n.* reencarnación, *f.*

reindeer [rein-diar] *n. sing.* y *pl.* reno (s), rangífero (s), *m.*

reinforced [rein-forsd] *adj.* reforzado, armado; **— concrete,** hormigón armado.

reinforcement [rein-fors] *n.* refuerzo, *m.*

reinstate [riin-steit] *vt.* instalar de nuevo; restablecer.

reissue [ri-ishiu] *n.* reimpresión, *f.;* nueva edición; **—,** *vt.* reimprimir.

reiterate [ri-i-te-reit] *vt.* reiterar.

reject [ri-yekt] *vt.* rechazar, rebatir; despreciar.

rejection [ri-yek-shon] *n.* rechazamiento, rechazo, *m.,* repudiación, *f.*

rejoice [ri-yois] *vt.* y *vi.* regocijar, regocijarse.

rejoicing [ri-yoi-sin] *n.* regocijo, *m.*

rejoin [ri-yoin] *vi.* volver a juntarse; **—,** *vt.* replicar.

rejuvenate [ri-yu-vi-neit] *vt.* y *vi.* rejuvenecer, rejuvenecerse.

relapse [ri-laps] *vi.* recaer; **—,** *n.* reincidencia, recidiva, *f.;* recaída, *f.*

relate [ri-leit] *vt.* y *vi.* relatar, contar; referirse.

related [ri-lei-tid] *adj.* emparentado, relacionado.

relation [ri-lei-shon] *n.* relación, *f.;* parentesco, *m.;* pariente, *m.* y *f.*

relationship [ri-lei-shon] *n.* parentesco, *m.;* relación, *f.*

relative [re-la-tiv] *adj.* relativo; **—ly,** *adv.* relativamente; **—,** *n.* pariente, *m.* y *f.*

relativity [re-la-ti-vi-ti] *n.* relatividad, *f.*

relax [ri-laks] *vt.* relajar, aflojar; **—,** *vi.* descansar, reposar.

relaxation [ri-lak-sei-shon] *n.* reposo, descanso, *m.;* relajación, *f.*

relay [ri-lei] *n.* parada, *f.;* —
race, carrera de relevos; —, *vt.*
trasmitir.

release [ri-lis] *vt.* soltar, libertar;
relevar; dar al público; —, *n.*
soltura, *f.;* descargo, *m.;* permiso para publicar o exhibir (una
noticia, película, etc.).

relent [ri-lent] *vi.* relentecer,
ablandarse.

relentless [ri-lent-les] *adj.* empe-
dernido, inflexible, implacable.

relevant [re-le-vant] *adj.* pertinente; concerniente.

reliability [re-laia-bi-li-ti] *n.* responsabilidad, *f.;* calidad de
digno de confianza.

reliable [ri-laia-bol] *adj.* digno de
confianza, responsable.

reliance [ri-laians] *n.* confianza,
f.

reliant [ri-laiant] *adj.* de confianza; **self—,** responsable, capaz,
con confianza en sí mismo.

relic [re-lik] *n.* reliquia, *f.*

relief [ri-lif] *n.* relieve (escultura),
m.; alivio, consuelo, *m.;* **to be
on —,** recibir ayuda económica
del gobierno; — **map,** mapa de
relieve.

relieve [ri-liv] *vt.* relevar; aliviar,
consolar; socorrer.

religion [ri-li-yon] *n.* religión, *f.;*
culto, *m.*

religious [ri-li-yos] *adj.* religioso;
— **instruction,** catequismo, *m.;*

—ly, *adv.* religiosa-mente.

relinquish [ri-lin-kuish] *vt.*
abandonar, dejar.

relish [re-lish] *n.* sabor, *m.;*
gusto, deleite, *m.;* condimento,
m.; —, *vt.* agradar; saborear; —
, *vi.* saber, tener sabor.

reload [ri-loud] *vt.* volver a cargar.

reluctance [ri-lak-tans] *n.* repugnancia, *f.,* disgusto, *m.*

reluctant [ri-lak-tant] *adj.*
renuente, con disgusto.

rely [ri-lai] *vi.* confiar en; contar
con.

remain [ri-mein] *vi.* quedar, restar, permanecer, durar.

remainder [ri-mein-dar] *n.* resto,
residuo, *m.;* restante, *m.;*
sobra, *f.*

remains [ri-meins] *n. pl.* restos,
residuos, *m. pl.,* sobras, *f. pl.*

remark [ri-mark] *n.* observación,
nota, *f.,* comentario, *m.;* —, *vt.*
notar, observar, comentar.

remarkable [ri-mar-ka-bol] *adj.*
notable, interesante. remedy,
n. remedio, medicamento, *m.;*
cura, *f.;* —, *vt.* remediar.

remember [ri-mem-bar] *vt.*
recordar, tener presente; dar
memorias; —, *vi.* acordarse.

remembrance [ri-mem-brans] *n.*
memoria, *f.;* recuerdo, *m.*

remind [ri-maind] *vt.* acordar,
recordar.

reminder [ri-main-dar] *n.* recuerdo, recordatorio, *m.*

reminisce [re-mi-nis] *vi.* recordar, contar recuerdos.

reminiscence [re-mi-ni-sens] *n.* reminiscencia, *f.*

reminiscent [re-mi-ni-sent] *adj.* recordativo, que recuerda acontecimientos pasados.

remit [ri-mit] *vt.* remitir, enviar; restituir.

remittance [ri-mi-tans] *n.* remesa, *f.;* remisión, *f.*

remnant [rem-nant] *n.* resto, residuo, *m.;* retazo, *m.*

remorse [ri-mors] *n.* remordimiento, *m.;* compunción, *f.;* cargo de conciencia.

remorseless [ri-mors-les] *adj.* insensible a los remordimientos.

remote [ri-mout] *adj.* remoto, lejano; **—ly,** *adv.* remotamente, a lo lejos.

remoteness [ri-mout-nes] *n.* alejamiento, *m.;* distancia, *f.;* lejanía, *f.*

removable [ri-mu-va-bol] *adj.* de quita y pon.

removal [ri-mu-val] *n.* deposición, *f.;* alejamiento, *m.;* acción de quitar.

remove [ri-muv] *vt.* remover, alejar; privar (del empleo); quitar; sacar; **—,** *vi.* mudarse.

rendition [ren-di-shon] *n.* rendición, *f.;* rendimiento, *m.;* ejecución, *f.*

renegade [re-ni-gueid] *n.* renegado da, apóstata, *m.* y *f.*

renew [ri-niu] *vt.* renovar, restablecer, reanudar, instaurar.

renewal [ri-niual] *n.* renovación, *f.;* renuevo, *m.;* prórroga, *f.*

renounce [ri-nauns] *vt.* renunciar.

renovate [re-nou-veit] *vt.* renovar, instaurar.

renown [ri-naun] *n.* renombre, *m.;* celebridad, *f.*

renowned [ri-ound] *adj.* célebre.

rent [rent] *n.* renta, *f.;* arrendamiento, *m.;* rendimiento, *m.;* alquiler, *m.;* rasgón, *m.;* **—,** *vt.* arrendar, alquilar.

rental] [ren-tal] *n.* renta, *f.,* arriendo, alquiler, *m.;* **—,** *adj.* relativo a renta o alquiler.

renter [ren-tar] *n.* inquilino, na, arrendatario, ria.

renunciation [ri-nan-siei-shon] *n.* renuncia, renunciación, *f.*

repair [ri-pear] *vt.* reparar, resarcir, restaurar; **—,** *vi.* ir; regresar; **—,** *n.* reparo, remiendo, *m.,* reparación, compostura, *f.;* **— ship,** buque taller; **— shop,** maestranza, *f.,* taller de reparaciones; **beyond —,** sin posible reparación.

repaired [ri-peard] *adj.* compuesto, remendado.

reparable [ri-pea-ra-bol] *adj.* reparable.

reparation [re-pa-rei-shon] *n.* reparación, *f.,* remedio, *m.*

repatriate [ri-pa-trieit] *vt.* repatriar.

repay [ri-pei] *vt.* volver a pagar, restituir, devolver.

repeal [ri-pil] *vt.* abrogar, revocar; —, *n.* revocación, anulación, cesación, *f.*

repeat [ri-pit] *vt.* repetir.

repeated [ri-pi-tid] *adj.* repetido, reiterado.

repeatedly [ri-pi-tid-li] *adv.* repetidamente, repetidas veces.

repel [ri-pel] *vt.* repeler, rechazar.

repellent [ri-pe-lent] *adj.* repelente, repulsivo.

repent [ri-pent] *vi.* arrepentirse.

repentance [ri-pen-tans] *n.* arrepentimiento, *m.*

repentant [ri-pen-tant] *adj.* arrepentido.

repercussion [ri-per-ka-shon] *n.* repercusión, *f.*

repertoire [re-par-tuar] *n.* repertorio, *m.*

repetition [re-pi-ti-shon] *n.* repetición, reiteración, *f.*

repetitious [re-pi-ti-shous] *adj.* redundante, que contiene repeticiones.

replace [ri-pleis] *vt.* remplazar; reponer; sustituir.

replacement [ri-pleis-ment] *n.* remplazo, *m.,* sustitución, *f.;* pieza de repuesto.

replenish [ri-ple-nish] *vt.* llenar, surtir.

replica [re-pli-ka] *n.* réplica, *f.*

reply [ri-plai] *vt.* contestar, responder; —, *n.* réplica, respuesta, contestación, *f.;* **awaiting your —,** en espera de su respuesta, en espera de sus noticias.

report [ri-port] *vt.* referir, contar; informar; dar cuenta; —, *n.* voz, *f.;* rumor, *m.;* fama, *f.;* relación, *f.;* informe, *m.;* memoria, *f.*

reporter [ri-por-tar] *n.* relator, ra; reportero, *m.;* periodista, *m.* y *f.,* cronista, *m.* y *f.*

represent [re-pri-sent] *vt.* representar.

representation [re-pri-sen-tei-shon] *n.* representación, *f.*

representative [re-pri-sen-ta-tiv] *adj.* representativo; —, *n.* representante, *m.* y *f.;* **House of R—s,** Cámara de Representantes.

repress [ri-pres] *vt.* reprimir, domar.

reprieve [ri-priv] *vt.* suspender una ejecución; demorar un castigo; —, *n.* dilación (de algún castigo), *f.;* suspensión, *f.*

reprimand [re-pri-mand] *vt.* reprender, corregir; regañar; —, *n.* reprensión, *f.;* reprimenda, *f.*

reprint [ri-print] *n.* tirada aparte; reimpresión, *f.;* —, *vt.* reimprimir.

reprisal [ri-prai-sal] *n.* represalia, *f.*

reproach [ri-prouch] *n.* reproche, *m.;* censura, *f.;* —, *vt.* culpar, reprochar; vituperar; improperar.

reproduce [ri-pro-dius] *vt.* reproducir.

reproduction [ri-pro-dak-shon] *n.* reproducción, *f.*

reptile [rep-tail] *n.* reptil, *m.*

republic [ri-pa-blik] *n.* república, *f.*

republican [ri-pa-bli-kan] *n.* y *adj.* republicano, na.

repudiate [ri-piu-dieit] *vt.* repudiar.

repudiation [ri-piu-diei-shon] *n.* repudio, *m.,* repudiación, *f.*

repugnant [ri-pag-nant] *adj.* repugnante; —ly, *adv.* de muy mala gana, con repugnancia.

repulse [ri-pals] *vt.* repulsar, desechar; —, *n.*

repulsion [ri-pal-shon] *n.* repulsión, repulsa, *f.*

repulsive [ri-pal-siv] *adj.* repulsivo.

reputable [ri-piu-ta-bol] *adj.*
honroso, estimable.

reputation [re-piu-tei-shon] *n.* reputación, *f.*

repute [ri-piut] *vt.* reputar.

request [ri-kuest] *n.* solicitud, petición, súplica, *f.;* pedido, *m.;* encargo, *m.;* on —, a solicitud; —, *vt.* rogar, suplicar; pedir, solicitar.

require [ri-kuaiar] *vt.* requerir, demandar.

required [ri-kuaiard] *adj.* obligatorio.

requirement [ri-kuaia-ment] *n.* requisito, *m.;* exigencia, *f.*

requisite [re-kui-sit] *adj.* necesario, indispensable; —, *n.* requisito, *m.*

resale [ri-seil] *n.* reventa, *f.,* venta de segunda mano.

rescue [res-kiu] *n.* rescate, libramiento, recobro, *m.;* —, *vt.* librar, rescatar; socorrer; salvar.

research [ri-serch] *n.* investigación, *f.*

resell [ri-sel] *vt.* revender, volver a vender.

resemblance [ri-sem-blans] *n.* semejanza, *f.*

resemble [ri-sem-bel] *vt.* asemejarse a, parecerse a.

resent [ri-sent] *vt.* resentir.

resentful [ri-sent-ful] *adj.* resentido; vengativo; —ly, *adv.* con resentimiento.

resentment [ri-sent-ment] *n.* resentimiento, *m.;* (fig.) escama, *f.*

reservation [re-sa-vei-shon] *n.* reservación, *f.;* reserva, *f.;* restricción mental.

reserve [ri-serv] *vt.* reservar; —, *n.* reserva, *f.;* sigilo, *m.*

reserved [ri-servd] *adj.* reservado; callado; —**ly,** *adv.* con reserva.

reservoir [ri-ser-vuar] *n.* depósito, *m.;* tanque, *m.*

reset [ri-set] *vt.* reengastar; montar de nuevo; **to — a bone,** reducir un hueso (roto o dislocado); **to — type,** (print.) volver a componer el tipo.

reside [ri-said] *vi.* residir, morar.

residence [re-si-dans] *n.* residencia.

resident [re-si-dent] *n.* y *adj.* residente, *m.* y *f.*

residential [re-si-den-shal] *adj.* residencial.

residual [ri-si-diual] *adj.* residual; —, *n.* residuo, *m.* residue, *n.* residuo, resto, *m.*

resign [ri-sain] *vt.* y *vi.* resignar, renunciar, ceder; resignarse, rendirse, conformarse.

resignation [re-sig-nei-shon] *n.* resignación, *f.;* renuncia, *f.*

resigned [ri-saind] *adj.* resignado.

resilient [ri-si-liant] *adj.* elástico, flexible.

resin [re-sin] *n.* resina, colofonia, *f.,* pez griega.

resist [ri-sist] *vt.* y *vi.* resistir; oponerse.

resistance [ri-sis-tans] *n.* resistencia, *f.;* — **coil,** bobina de resistencia.

resistant [ri-sis-tant] *adj.* resistente.

resolute [re-so-lut] *adj.* resuelto.

resolution [re-so-lu-shon] *n.* resolución, *f.*

resolve [ri-solv] *vt.* resolver; decretar; —, *vi.* resolverse.

resolved [ri-solvd] *adj.* resuelto.

resonance [re-so-nans] *n.* resonancia, *f.*

resonant [re-so-nant] *adj.* resonante.

resort [ri-sort] *vi.* recurrir, frecuentar; —, *n.* centro de recreo; **summer —,** lugar de veraneo; **bathing —,** balneario, *m.*

resound [ri-saund] *vi.* resonar.

resource [ri-sors] *n.* recurso, *m.;* expediente, *m.*

resourceful [ri-sors-ful] *adj.* ingenioso, hábil; fértil en recursos o expedientes; —**ness,** *n.* ingeniosidad, habilidad, expedición, *f.*

respect [ris-pekt] *n.* respecto, *m.;* respeto, *m.;* motivo, *m.;* — **s,** *n. pl.* saludos, *m. pl.,* enhorabuena, *f.;* —, *vt.* apreciar; respetar; venerar.

respectability [ris-pek-ta-bi-li-ti] *n.* respetabilidad, *f.*

respectable [ris-pek-ta-bol] *adj.* respetable; decente; considerable.

respected [ris-pek-tid] *adj.* considerado, apreciado.

respectful [ris-pekt-ful] *adj.* respetuoso; —**ly,** *adv.* respetuosamente.

respecting [ris-pek-tin] *prep.* con respecto a.

respective [ris-pek-tiv] *adj.* respectivo, relativo.

respiration [res-pi-rei-shon] *n.* respiración, *f.*

respirator [res-pi-rei-tar] *n.* respirador, aparato para respiración artificial.

respiratory [ris-pai-ra-to-ri] *adj.* respiratorio; — **ailment,** enfermedad del aparato respiratorio.

respite [ris-pait] *n.* suspensión, *f.;* respiro, *m.;* tregua, *f.;* —, *vt.* suspender, diferir.

resplendent [ris-plen-dent] *adj.* resplandeciente, fulgurante, reluciente.

respond [ris-pond] *vt.* responder; corresponder.

response [ris-pons] *n.* respuesta, réplica, *f.*

responsibility [ris-pon-sa-bi-li-ti] *n.* responsabilidad, *f.;* encargo,

m.; **to assume** —, tomar por su cuenta, asumir responsabilidad.

responsible [ris-pon-si-bol] *adj.* responsable.

responsive [ris-pon-siv] *adj.* sensible, de simpatía.

rest [rest] *n.* reposo, *m.;* sueño, *m.;* quietud, *f.;* (mus.) pausa, *f.;* resto, residuo, restante, *m.,* sobra, *f.;* **the** —, los demás; — **room,** excusado, retrete, *m.;* (Chile) descanso, *m.;* —, *vt.* poner a descansar; apoyar; —, *vi.* dormir, reposar, recostarse; **to** — **upon,** basarse en.

restaurant [res-to-ran] *n.* restaurante, *m.,* fonda, *f.*

restitution [res-ti-tiu-shon] *n.* restitución, *f.*

restless [rest-les] *adj.* inquieto, intranquilo, revuelto.

restoration [res-to-rei-shon] *n.* restauración, *f.*

restore [ris-tor] *vt.* restaurar, restituir, restablecer, devolver, instaurar.

restrain [ris-trein] *vt.* restringir, refrenar; **to** — **oneself,** reprimirse.

restraint [ris-treint] *n.* refrenamiento, *m.,* coerción, *f.;* **without** —, a rienda suelta.

restrict [ris-trikt] *vt.* restringir, limitar.

restriction [ris-trik-shon] *n.* restricción, coartación, f.

result [ri-salt] n. resultado, m.; consecuencia, f.; éxito, m.; —, vi. resultar; redundar en.

resume [ri-sium] vt. resumir, reanudar; empezar de nuevo.

resurrect [re-sa-rekt] vt. resucitar.

resurrection [re-sa-rek-shon] n. resurrección, f.

retail [ri-teil] vt. revender, vender al por menor; —, n. venta al por menor, menudeo, m.; **at** —, al menudeo, al por menor.

retain [ri-tein] vt. retener, guardar.

retaliate [ri-ta-lieit] vi., vengarse, desquitarse.

retaliation [ri-ta-liei-shon] n. venganza, f., desquite, m.

retard [ri-tard] vt. retardar.

retention [ri-ten-shon] n. retención, f.

reticent [re-ti-sant] adj. reticente.

retina [re-ti-na] n. retina (del ojo), f.

retire [ri-taiar] vt. retirar; —, vi. retirarse, sustraerse; jubilarse.

retired [ri-taiad] adj. apartado, retirado.

retirement [ri-taia-ment] n. retiro, retiramiento, m.; jubilación, f.; receso, m.

retrace [ri-treis] vt. volver a trazar; **to — one's steps,** volver

sobre sus huellas.

retract [ri-trakt] vt. retractar, retirar; retraer.

retreat [ri-trit] n. retirada, f.; (eccl.) retiro, m.; —, vi. retirarse.

retribution [re-tri-biu-shon] n. retribución, recompensa, f.; refacción, f.

retrieve [ri-triv] vt. recuperar, recobrar.

retroactive [re-trouak-tiv] adj. retroactivo.

retrospect, retrospection [re-trous-pekt], [re-trous-pek-shon] n. reflexión de las cosas pasadas.

return [ri-tern] vt. retribuir; restituir; volver; devolver; —, vi. regresar; —, n. retorno, regreso, m.; vuelta, f.; recompensa, retribución, f.; recaída, f.

reunion [ri-iu-nion] n. reunión, f.

reunite [ri-iu-nait] vt. reunir, volver a unir; —, vi. reunirse, reconciliarse.

revamp [ri-vamp] vt. meter capellada nueva; remendar, renovar.

reveal [ri-vil] vt. revelar; publicar.

revel [re-vel] vi. andar en borracheras; —, n. borrachera, f.; **drunken** —, orgía, f.

revelation [re-ve-lei-shon] n.

revelación, *f.*

reveler, reveller [rev-lar] *n.* fiestero, ra, parrandero, ra.

revelry [re-val-ri] *n.* borrachera, *f.;* jarana, *f.*

revenge [ri-vench] *vt.* vengar; —, *n.* venganza, *f.*

revengeful [ri-vench-ful] *adj.* vengativo; —**ly**, *adv.* con venganza.

revenue [re-ve-niu] *n.* renta, *f.;* rédito, *m.;* ingreso, *m.;* — **cutter**, guardacostas, *m.;* — **stamp**, sello de impuesto.

reverberate [ri-ver-be-reit] *vt.* y *vi.* reverberar; resonar, retumbar.

revere [ri-vear] *vt.* reverenciar, venerar.

reverence [re-ve-rans] *n.* reverencia, *f.;* —, *vt.* reverenciar.

reverend [re-ve-rend] *adj.* reverendo; venerable; —, *n.* clérigo, abad, *m.;* pastor, *m.*

reverent, reverential [re-ve-rant], [re-ve-ren-shal] *adj.* reverencial, respetuoso.

reversal [ri-ver-shal] *n.* revocación (de una sentencia), *f.;* reversión, *f.*

reverse [ri-vers] *n.* vicisitud, *f.;* contrario, *m.;* reverso (de una moneda), *m.;* revés, *m.;* través, *m.;* contramarcha, *f.;* —, *adj.* inverso; contrario; —, *vt.* invertir, poner al revés; **to — the**

charges (on a phone call), cobrar (una llamada telefónica) al número llamado, pedir (una llamada telefónica) por cobrar; **to put in —,** dar marcha atrás.

reversible [ri-ver-si-bol] *adj.* revocable, reversible.

revert [ri-vert] *vt.* y *vi.* revertir, trastrocar; volverse atrás.

review [ri-viu] *n.* revista, *f.;* reseña, *f.;* repaso, *m.;* **to make a —**, reseñar; —, *vt.* rever; repasar.

revile [ri-vail] *vt.* ultrajar; difamar.

revise [ri-vais] *vt.* revisar, rever; —, *n.* revista, revisión, *f.;* (print.) segunda prueba.

revision [ri-vi-shon] *n.* revisión, *f.*

revival [ri-vai-val] *n.* restauración, *f.;* renacimiento, *m.;* (theat.) nueva representación de una obra antigua.

revive [ri-vaiv] *vt.* avivar; restablecer; (theat.) volver a presentar (una comedia antigua, etc.); —, *vi.* revivir.

revocable [re-vo-kei-bol] *adj.* revocable.

revoke [ri-vouk] *vt.* revocar, anular.

revolt [ri-voult] *vi.* rebelarse; alzarse en armas; —, *n.* rebelión, *f.*

revolting [ri-voul-tin] *adj.* repugnante.

revolution [re-vo-lu-shon] *n.* revolución, *f.*

revolutionary [re-vo-lu-sho-na-ri] *n.* y *adj.* revolucionario, ria.

revolutionize [re-va-lu-sho-nais] *vt.* revolucionar.

revolve [ri-volv] *vt.* revolver; meditar; —, *vi.* girar.

revolver [ri-vol-var] *n.* revólver, *m.*, pistola, *f.*

revulsion [ri-val-shon] *n.* reacción repentina; (med.) revulsión, *f.*

reward [ri-uord] *n.* recompensa, *f.;* fruto, *m.;* pago, *m.;* —, *vt.* recompensar.

rhetoric [re-to-rik] *n.* retórica, *f.*

rhetorical [ri-to-ri-kal] *adj.* retórico.

rheumatic [ru-ma-tik] *adj.* reumático.

rheumatism [ru-ma-ti-sem] *n.* reumatismo, *m.*

rhinoceros [rai-nou-se-ros] *n.* rinoceronte, *m.*

rhyme [raim] *n.* rima, *f.;* poema, *m.;* —, *vi.* rimar.

rhythm [ri-dem] *n.* ritmo, *m.*

rhythmic, rhythmical [riz-mik], [riz-mi-kal] *adj.* rítmico.

rib [rib] *n.* costilla, *f.;* nervio, *m.*, nervadura, (de un puente, barco, etc.), *f.*

ribbon [ri-ban] *n.* listón, *m.*, cinta, *f.;* —s, *n. pl.* perifollos, *m. pl.*

rice [rais] *n.* arroz, *m.;* — **field,** arrozal, *m.;* — **paper,** papel de paja de arroz.

rich [rich] *adj.* rico; opulento; abundante; empalagoso.

riches [ri-chis] *n. pl.* riqueza, *f.;* bienes, *m. pl.*

richness [rich-nes] *n.* riqueza, suntuosidad, *f.* rickets, *n.* raquitismo, *m.*

rid [rid] *vt.* librar, desembarazar.

ridden [ri-den] *p.p.* del verbo **ride.**

riddle [ri-del] *n.* enigma, rompecabezas, acertijo, *m.;* criba, *f.;* (min.) garbillo, *m.;* —, *vt.* acribillar; cribar.

ride [raid] *vi.* cabalgar; andar en coche; **to — a bicycle,** montar en bicicleta; —, *n.* paseo a caballo o en coche.

rider [rai-dar] *n.* cabalgador, *m.;* pasajero (en un auto, autobús, tren, *etc.*), *m.*

ridge [ridch] *n.* espinazo, lomo, *m.;* cordillera, *f.;* arruga, *f.;* —, *vt.* formar lomos o surcos.

ridicule [ri-di-kiul] *n.* ridiculez, *f.;* ridículo, *m.;* —, *vt.* ridiculizar.

ridiculous [ri-di-kiu-los] *adj.* ridículo.

riding [rai-din] *n.* paseo a caballo o en auto; —, *adj.* relativo a la equitación; — **boot,** bota de montar; — **breeches,** pantalo-

nes de equitación o de montar
a caballo; — **habit,** — **outfit,**
traje de montar; — **master,**
profesor de equitación.

rifle [rai-fel] *vt.* robar, pillar;
estriar, rayar; —, *n.* fusil, *m.,*
carabina rayada; — **case,** car-
caj, *m.*; — **corps,** fusilería, *f.*;
— **range,** alcance de proyectil
de rifle; lugar para tirar al
blanco.

rift [rift] *n.* hendidura, *f.;* división, *f.;* disensión, *f.*

rig [rig] *vt.* ataviar; (naut.) aparejar; —, *n.* aparejo, *m.;* traje
ridículo o de mal gusto.

right [rait] *adj.* derecho, recto;
justo; honesto; —! *interj.*
¡bueno! ¡bien! **all** —! ¡bien!
—, *adv.* derechamente, rectamente; ¡justamente; bien; —
away, en seguida, luego; —
now, ahora mismo; **to be** —,
tener razón; **to set** —, poner
en claro; —, *n.* justicia, *f.;*
razón, *f.;* derecho, *m.;* mano
derecha; (pol.) derecha, *f.;* **all**
—**s reserved,** derechos reservados; — **of way,** derecho de vía;
—, *vt.* hacer justicia.

right angle [rait-angol] *n.* ángulo
recto.

righteous [rai-chos] *adj.* justo,
honrado.

right-hand [rait-jand] *adj.* a la
derecha; **to the** — **side,** a la
derecha.

right-wing [rait-uin] *adj.* derechista (en política).

rigid [ri-yid] *adj.* rígido; austero,
severo; —**ly,** *adv.* con rigidez.

rigidity [ri-yi-di-ti] *n.* rigidez,
austeridad, *f.*

rigor [ri-gor] *n.* rigor, *m.;* severidad, *f.*

rigorous [ri-go-ros] *adj.* riguroso.

rim [rim] *n.* margen, *m.* y *f.,* orilla, *f.,* borde, *m.*

rind [raind] *n.* corteza, *f.;* holle-
jo, *m.*

ring [ring] *n.* círculo, cerco, *m.;*
anillo, *m.;* campaneo,
m.;(boxeo) cuadrilátero *m.;*
(mech.) manija, *f.;* — **finger,**
dedo anular; —, *vt.* sonar; **to** —
the bell, tocar la campana,
tocar el timbre; —, *vi.* retiñir,
retumbar; resonar.

ringing [rin-guin] *adj.* sonoro,
resonante; —, *n.* repique, *m.*

ringworm [ring-uerm] *n.* (med.)
empeine, *m.,* tiña, *f.*

rinse [rins] *vt.* lavar, limpiar,
enjuagar.

riot [raiot] *n.* tumulto, bullicio,
m., pelotera, *f.;* orgía, *f.;* borrachera, *f.;* motín, *m.;* —, *vi.*
andar en orgías; causar alboro-
tos; armar motines.

rioter [raio-tar] *n.* amotinador,
ra; revoltoso, sa;(coll.) bullanguero, ra, alborotador, ra.

riotous [raio-tos] *adj.* bullicioso, sedicioso; disoluto; —ly, *adv.* disolutamente.

rip [rip] *vt.* rasgar, lacerar; descoser; —, *n.* rasgadura, *f.;* — cord, (avi.) cuerda que al tirar de ella abre el paracaídas.

ripen [rai-pen] *vt.* y *vi.* madurar.

ripple [ri-pel] *vi.* susurrar; ondular; rizar, ondear; —, *n.* susurro, *m.*

rise [rais] *vi.* levantarse; nacer, salir (los astros); rebelarse; ascender; hincharse; elevarse; resucitar; surgir; to — above, trascender; —, *n.* levantamiento, *m.;* elevación, *f.;* subida, *f.;* salida (del sol), *f.;* causa, *f.*

risen [rai-sen] *p.p.* del verbo rise.

risk [risk] *n.* riesgo, peligro, *m.;* without —, sobre seguro; —, *vt.* arriesgar.

risky [ris-ki] *adj.* peligroso.

rite [rait] *n.* rito, *m.*

ritual [ri-chual] *adj.* y *n.* ritual, *m.*

rival [rai-val] *adj.* competidor; —, *n.* rival, *m.* y *f.;* —, *vt.* competir, emular.

rivalry [rai-val-ri] *n.* rivalidad, *f.*

river [ri-var] *n.* río, *m.;* — basin, cuenca de un río; — bed, cauce, *m.*

riverside [ri-var-said] *n.* ribera, *f.;* —, *adj.* situado a la orilla de un rio.

rivulet [ri-viu-lit] *n.* riachuelo, *m.*

roach [rouch] *n.* (ichth.) escarcho, rubio, *m.;* cucaracha, *f.*

road [roud] *n.* camino, *m.;* camino real; via, *f.;* ruta, *f.;* carretera, *f.;* main —, carretera, *f.;* paved —, carretera pavimentada.

roam [roum] *vt.* y *vi.* corretear; tunar, vagar.

roan [roun] *adj.* roano, ruano.

roar [ror] *vi.* rugir; aullar; bramar; —, *n.* rugido, *m.;* bramido, estruendo, *m.;* mugido, *m.*

roast [roust] *vt.* asar; tostar; — beef, rosbif, *m.*

roaster [rous-tar] *n.* asador, *m.*

rob [rob] *vt.* robar, hurtar.

robber [ro-bar] *n.* ladrón, ona.

robbery [ro-be-ri] *n.* robo, *m.*

robe [roub] *n.* manto, *m.;* toga, *f.;* bata, *f.;* peinador, *m.;* —, *vt.* y *vi.* vestir, vestirse, ataviarse.

robin [ro-bin] *n.* (orn.) petirrojo, pechirrojo, pechicolorado, *m.*

robust [rou-bast] *adj.* robusto.

rock [rok] *n.* roca, *f.;* escollo, *m.;* (naut.) vigía, *m.;* — bottom, el fondo, lo más profundo; — crystal, cuarzo, *m.;* — garden, jardín entre rocas; — salt, sal gema; —, *vt.* mecer; arrullar; conmover; —, *vi.* bambolear, balancearse, oscilar.

rocker [ro-kar] *n.* mecedora, *f.;* cunera, *f.*

rocket [ro-kit] *n.* cohete, volador, *m.;* **space —,** cohete espacial.

rocky [ro-ki] *adj.* peñascoso, pedregoso, rocoso, roqueño; **R— Mountains,** Montañas Rocallosas o Rocosas, *f. pl.*

rod [rod] *n.* varilla, caña, *f.*

rode [roud] *pretérito* del verbo **ride.**

rodent [rou-dent] *n.* roedor, *m.*

role, role [roul] *n.* (theat.) papel, *m.,* parte, *f.;* papel (que desempeña una persona), *m.*

roll [roul] *vt.* rodar; volver; arrollar, enrollar; —, *vi.* rodar; girar; —, *n.* rodadura, *f.;* rollo, *m.;* lista, *f.;* catálogo, *m.;* rasero, *m.;* panecillo, *m.;* **to call the —,** pasar lista.

roller [rou-lar] *n.* rodillo, cilindro, aplanador, *m.;* rodo, *m.;* aplanadora, *f.;* rueda, *f.;* — **bearing,** cojinete de rodillos; — **coaster,** montaña rusa; — **skate,** patín de ruedas, patín, *m.;* — **towel,** toalla sin fin.

rolling [rou-lin] *adj.* rodante; ondulante; — **mill,** taller de laminar; — **pin,** rodillo de pastelero; — **stock,** (rail.) material rodante; —, *n.* rodadura, *f.;* (avi.) balanceo, *m.;* (naut.) balance, *m.*

Roman [rou-man] *adj.* romano; romanesco; —, *n.* romano, na; — **type,** letra redonda.

romance [rou-mans] *n.* romance, *m.;* ficción, *f.;* cuento, *m.;* fábula, *f.;* **R—,** *adj.* romance.

romantic [rou-man-tik] *adj.* romántico; sentimental.

romanticism [rou-man-ti-si-sem] *n.* romanticismo, *m.*

Rome [roum] Roma, *f.*

roof [ruf] *n.* tejado, techo, *m.;* azotea, *f.;* — **of the mouth,** paladar, *m.;* — **garden,** azotea, *f.;* —, *vt.* techar.

roofing [ru-fin] *n.* techado, *m.;* material para techos.

rookie [ru-ki] *n.* bisoño, *m.*

room [rum] *n.* cuarto, *m.* habitación, cámara, *f.;* aposento, *m.;* fugar, espacio, *m.*

roommate [rum-meit] *n.* compañero o compañera de cuarto.

roomy [ru-mi] *adj.* espacioso.

roost [rust] *n.* pértiga del gallinero; —, *vi.* dormir las aves en una pértiga.

rooster [rus-tar] *n.* gallo, *m.*

root [rut] *n.* raíz, *f.;* origen, *m.;* — **beer,** bebida de extractos de varias raíces; **to take —,** echar raíces, prender; radicarse; —, *vt.* y *vi.* arraigar; echar raíces; (coll.) gritar o aplaudir ruidosamente a los jugadores para animarlos; **to — out,** desarraigar.

rope [roup] *n.* cuerda, *f.;* cordel, *m.;* cable, *m.;* soga, *f.,* —, *vt.* atar con un cordel.

rosary [rou-sa-ri] *n.* rosario, *m.*

rose [rous] *n.* (bot.) rosa, *f.;* color de rosa; —, *pretérito* del verbo **rise.**

rosebud [rous-bad] *n.* capullo de rosa.

rosewood [rous-vud] *n.* palo de rosa, palisandro, *m.*

rosin [ro-sin] *n.* resina, *f.,* pez griega.

roster [ros-tar] *n.* lista, *f.;* matrícula, *f.;* registro, *m.*

rosy [rou-si] *adj.* róseo, de color de rosa.

rot [rot] *vi.* pudrirse; —, *n.* morriña, *f.;* putrefacción, *f.*

rotary [rou-ta-ri] *adj.* giratorio; — **press,** máquina rotativa.

rotate [rou-teit] *vt.* y *vi.* girar; alternar; dar vueltas.

rotation [rou-tei-shon] *n.* rotación, *f.*

rotten [ro-ten] *adj.* podrido, corrompido.

rottenness [ro-ten-nes] *n.* podredumbre, putrefacción, *f.*

rotund [rou-tand] *adj.* rotundo, redondo, circular, esférico.

rough [raf] *adj.* áspero; bronco, brusco; bruto, tosco; tempestuoso.

roughness [raf-nes] *n.* aspereza, *f.;* rudeza, tosquedad, *f.;* tem-pestad, *f.*

roulette [ru-let] *n.* ruleta, *f.*

round [raund] *adj.* redondo; circular; cabal; rotundo, franco, sincero; — **number,** número redondo; — **steak,** corte especial de carne de vaca; — **trip,** viaje redondo, viaje de ida y vuelta; **to make** —, redondear; —, *n.* círculo, *m.;* redondez, *f.;* vuelta, *f.*

roundness [raund-nes] *n.* redondez, *f.*

round table [raund-tei-bol] *n.* mesa redonda, reunión de un grupo para discutir problemas de interés mutuo.

route [rut] *n.* ruta, vía, *f.,* camino, *m.;* **en** —, en ruta, en camino.

routine [ru-tin] *n.* rutina, *f.;* hábito, *m.;* —, *adj.* rutinario.

rove [rouv] *vi.* vagar.

row [rau] *n.* riña, camorra, *f.,* zipizape, *m.*

row [rau] *n.* hilera, fila, *f.;* — **of seats,** tendido, *m.;* —, *vt.* y *vi.* (naut.) remar, bogar.

rowdy [rau-di] *n.* alborotador, ra, bullanguero, ra; —, *adj.* alborotoso, bullanguero.

royal [roial] *adj.* real; regio; —**ly,** *adv.* regiamente.

royalty [roial-ti] *n.* realeza, dignidad real; —**ties,** *n. pl.* regalías, *f. pl.,* derechos de autor.

rub [rab] *vt.* estregar, fregar, frotar, raspar, restregar; **to —
against,** rozar; **—,** *n.* frotamiento, *m.;* roce, *m.;* (fig.) tropiezo, obstáculo, *m.;* dificultad, *f.*

rubber [ra-bar] *n.* goma, *f.,*
goma elástica, caucho, hule, *m.;* **hard —,** caucho endurecido; **—band,** liga de caucho; **— cement,** cemento de caucho; **— heel,** tacón de goma o de caucho; **— stamp,** sello de goma; (coll.) persona que obra de una manera rutinaria; **synthetic —,** caucho artificial.

rubbish [ru-bish] *n.* escombro, *m.;* ruinas, *f. pl.;* andrajos, *m. pl.;* cacharro, ripio, *m.*

ruby [ru-bi] *n.* rubí, *m.*

ruddy [ra-di] *adj.* colorado, rubio; lozano.

rude [rud] *adj.* rudo, brutal, rústico, grosero, tosco.

rudeness [rud-nes] *n.* descortesía, *f.;* rudeza, insolencia, *f.;* barbaridad, *f.;* brusquedad, *f.*

rudiment [ru-di-ment] *n.* rudimento, *m.*

ruffle [ra-fel] *vt.* desordenar, desazonar; rizar; fruncir (un volante, una vuelta, etc.); irritar, enojar; **—,** *n.* volante fruncido, vuelta, *f.;* conmoción, *f.;* enojo, enfado, *m.*

rug [rag] *n.* tapete, *m.;* alfombra, *f.;* **steamer —,** manta de viaje.

rugged [ra-guid] *adj.* áspero, tosco; robusto, vigoroso.

ruin [ruin] *n.* ruina, *f.;* perdición, *f.;* escombros, *m. pl.;* **—,**
vt. arruinar; destruir, echar a perder.

ruinous [rui-nos] *adj.* ruinoso.

rule [rul] *n.* mando, *m.;* regla, *f.;* máxima, *f.;* norma, *f.;* férula, *f.;* ordenanza, *f.;* **as a —,** por lo general; **by —,** a regla, por regla; **standard —,** regla fija; **to make it a —,** tener por costumbre; **—,** *vt.* y *vi.* gobernar; reglar; dirigir; imperar, mandar; **—,** *vt.* rayar.

ruler [ru-lar] *n.* gobernador, gobernante, *m.;* mandatario, *m.;* regla, *f.*

ruling [ru-lin] *n.* rayadura, *f.;* (leyes) decisión, *f.;* **—,** *adj.* gobernante, dirigente.

rum [ram] *n.* ron, *m.*

Rumanian [ru-ma-nian] *n.* y *adj.* rumano, na.

rumble [ram-bel] *vi.* crujir, rugir; **— seat,** (auto.) asiento trasero descubierto.

ruminate [ru-mi-neit] *vt.* y *vi.* rumiar.

rumination [ru-mi-nei-shon] *n.* rumiación, *f.*

rummage [ra-midch] *vt.* trastornar, revolver, escudriñar; **—,** *n.* registro, *m.;* **— sale,** venta de artículos usados, venta de remates (con fines caritativos).

rumor [ru-mor] *n.* rumor, *m.;* —, *vt.* divulgar alguna noticia.

rump [ramp] *n.* anca, nalga (de animal), *f.*

rumple [ram-pel] *n.* arruga, *f.;* —, *vt.* arrugar.

run [ran] *vt.* correr; manejar; traspasar; **to — down a pedestrian,** atropellar un peatón, *vi.* correr; fluir, manar; pasar rápidamente; proceder; **to — across,** tropezar con; **to — aground,** encallar; **to — down,** averiguar; alcanzar; pararse (un reloj); descargarse; agotarse; **to — into,** topar, chocar con; **to — off,** escaparse, escurrir; **to — out of,** no tener más (de algo), agotarse (un artículo); **to — the risk of,** arriesgar, aventurar; **to — through,** examinar o ensayar rápidamente; —, *n.* corrida, carrera, *f.;* curso, *m.;* recorrido, *m.;* serie, *f.;* libertad en el uso de cosas; (mus.) escala, *f.;* **in the long —,** a la larga.

runaway [ran-auei] *n.* fugitivo, va, desertor, ra.

rung [rang] *n.* escalón, peldaño (de escalera de mano), *m.;* —, *p.p.* del verbo **ring.**

run-in [ran-in] *n.* riña, *f.*

runner [ra-nar] *n.* corredor, ra; mensajero, ra; alfombra larga y angosta (para una es-calera o pasadizo).

runner-up [ra-nar-ap] *n.* competidor que queda en segundo lugar.

running [ra-nin] *n.* carrera, corrida, *f.;* curso, *m.;* — **board,** estribo, *m.;* — **gear,** juego de ruedas y ejes de un vehículo; — **water,** agua corriente; —, *adj.* corriente, que corre o fluye.

runt [rant] *n.* enano, *m.*

runway [ran-uei] *n.* cauce, *m.;* corredera, *f.;* vía, *f.;* pasadizo para ganado; pasadizo para exhibición de modelos; pista de aviones en un aeropuerto.

rupture [rap-char] *n.* rotura, *f.;* hernia, quebradura, *f.;* —, *vt.* reventar, romper.

rural [ru-ral] *adj.* rural, campestre, rústico.

rush [rash] *n.* (bot.) junco, *m.;* ímpetu, *m.;* prisa, *f.;* — **hour,** hora de tránsito in-tenso; — **order,** pedido urgente, pedido de precisión; —, *vi.* abalanzarse, tirarse; ir de prisa, apresurarse.

russet [ra-sit] *adj.* bermejizo.

Russia [ra-sha] Rusia, *f.*

Russian [ra-shan] *n.* y *adj.* ruso; sa; — **language,** ruso, *m.*

rust [rast] *n.* herrumbre, *f.;* moho, *m.;* (bot.) roya, *f.;* color bermejo; —, *vi.* enmohecerse.

rustic [ras-tik] *adj.* rústico, pardal; —, *n.* patán, rústico, *m.*

rustle [ras-tik] *n.* susurro, *m.;* —, *vi.* crujir, susurrar.

rustproof [rast-pruf] *adj.* a prueba de herrumbre, inoxidable.

rusty [ras-ti] *adj.* mohoso.

rut [rat] *vi.* estar en celo; —, *n.* brama, *f.;* cantinela, rutina, *f.*

rutabaga [ru-ta-bei-ga] *n.* (bot.) naba, *f.*

ruthless [ruz-les] *adj.* cruel, insensible; —**ly,** *adv.* inhumanamente.

rye [rai] *n.* (bot.) centeno, *m.*

S

South America [sauz-ame-ri-ka] S. A. Sud América;

South Africa [sauz-a-fri-ka] Sud Africa.

sabbath [sa-baz] *n.* día de descanso (sábado para los judíos, domingo para los cristianos).

sable [sei-bol] *n.* cebellina, marta, *f.*

sabotage [sa-bo-tash] *n.* sabotaje, *m.*

saccharine [sa-ka-rin] *n.* sacarina, *f.;* —, *adj.* sacarino, azucarado.

sacrament [sa-kra-ment] *n.* sacramento, *m.;* Eucaristía, *f.*

sacred [sei-krid] *adj.* sagrado, sacro; inviolable.

sacrifice [sa-kri-fais] *n.* sacrificio, *m.;* —, *vt.* sacrificar; **to — oneself,** sacrificarse.

sacrilege [sa-kri-lich] *n.* sacrilegio, *m.*

sad [sad] *adj.* triste, melancólico; infausto.

sadden [sa-den] *vt.* entristecer.

saddle [sa-del] *n.* silla, silla de montar; — **horse,** caballo de montar; —, *vt.* ensillar.

saddlebag [sa-del-bag] *n.* alforja, *f.*

sadism [sei-di-sem] *n.* sadismo, *m.*

sadistic [sa-dis-tik] *adj.* sádico.

sadness [sad-nes] *n.* tristeza, *f.;* aspecto tétrico.

safari [sa-fa-ri] *n.* expedición de caza, safari, *m.*

safe [seif] *adj.* seguro; salvo; — **and sound,** sano y salvo; —, *n.* caja fuerte; —**ly,** *adv.* a salvo.

safe-conduct [seif-kon-dakt] *n.* salvoconducto, seguro, *m.,* carta de amparo.

safe-deposit [seif-di-po-sit] *adj.* de seguridad; — **box,** caja de seguridad.

safeguard [seif-gard] *n.* salva-guardia, *f.;* —, *vt.* proteger.

safety [seif-ti] *n.* seguridad, *f.;* salvamento, *m.;* — **belt,** cinto salvavidas; — **island,** platafor-ma de seguridad; refugio, *m.;* — **match,** fósforo de seguridad; — **pin,** alfiler de gancho, imperdible, *m.;* —**razor,** navaja de seguridad.

saffron [sa-fron] *n.* (bot.) aza-frán, *m.*

sag [sag] *n.* desviación, *f.,* pan-deo, seno, *m.;* —, *vi.* empan-darse, combarse; doblegarse.

sage [seich] *n. y adj.* sabio, *m.*

sagebrush [seich-brush] *n.* (bot.) artemisa, *f.*

sail [seil] *n.* vela, *f.;* —, *vi.* nave-gar.

sailboat [seil-bout] *n.* velero, *m.,* buque de vela.

sailing [sei-lin] *n.* navegación, *f.;* partida, salida, *f.;* —, *adj.* de vela.

sailor [sei-lor] *n.* marinero, *m.*

saint [seint] *n.* santo, ta; ángel, *m.;* **patron** —, santo patrón; —, *vt.* canonizar.

saintly [seint-li] *adj.* santo.

sake [seik] *n.* causa, razón, *f.;* amor, *m.,* consideración, *f.;* **for your own** —, por tu propio bien.

salad [sa-lad] *n.* ensalada, *f.;* —

dressing, aderezo, *m.,* salsa para ensalada.

salamander [sa-la-man-dar] *n.* salamandra, *f.*

salary [sa-la-ri] *n.* salario, suel-do, *m.,* paga, *f.*

sale [seil] *n.* venta, *f.;* (com.) rea-lización, *f.;* **auction** —, remate, *m.;* **clearance** —, liquidación, *f.;* — **price,** precio de venta, precio reducido; —**s tax,** impuesto sobre ventas.

salesclerk [seils-klerk] *n.* vende-dor, ra, dependiente, *m. y f.*

salesman [seils-man] *n.* vende-dor, tendero, *m.;* **traveling** —, comisionista, agente viajero.

salicylic [sa-li-si-lik] *adj.* (chem.) salicílico.

salicylate [sa-li-si-lait] *n.* (chem.) salicilato, *m.*

saliva [sa-lai-va] *n.* saliva, *f.*

sallow [sa-lou] *adj.* cetrino, páli-do; — **face,** cara pálida y ama-rillenta.

salmon [sa-mon] *n.* salmón, *m.;* —, *adj.* de color salmón; — **trout,** trucha salmonada.

salon [sa-lon] *n.* salón, *m.,* sala de exhibición; **beauty** —, salón de belleza.

saloon [sa-lun] *n.* cantina, taberna, *f.*

salt [solt] *n.* sal, *f.; (fig.)* sabor, *m.;* gracia, *f.;* agudeza, *f.;* —, *adj.* salado; —, *vt.* salar; salpresar.

saltcellar, saltshaker [solt-se-lar], [solt-shei-ker] *n.* salero, *m.*, receptáculo para sal.

salted [soltid] *adj.* salado; — **fish,** pescado salado; — **meat,** carne salpresa.

salty [sol-ti] *adj.* salado, salobre.

salute [sa-liut] *vt.* saludar; —, *n.* salutación, *f.*, saludo, *m.*

salvage [sal-vich] *n.* salvamento, *m.*; (naut.) derecho de salvamento; —, *vt.* salvar.

salvation [sal-vei-shon] *n.* salvación, *f.*

same [seim] *adj.* mismo; idéntico; propio.

sample [sam-pel] *n.* muestra, *f.*; ejemplo, *m.*

sanatorium [sa-na-to-riom] *n.* sanatorio, *m.*

sanctify [sank-ti-fai] *vt.* santificar.

sanction [sank-shon] *n.* sanción, *f.*; —, *vt.* sancionar.

sanctity [sank-ti-ti] *n.* santidad, santimonia, *f.*

sanctuary [sank-chua-ri] *n.* santuario, *m.*; asilo, *m.*

sand [sand] *n.* arena, *f.*; — **dune,** médano, *m.*, duna, *f.*; — **pit,** arenal, *m.*; —, *vt.* enarenar.

sandal [san-dal] *n.* sandalia, *f.*

sandbag [sand-bag] *n.* saco de arena; —, *vt.* res-guardar con sacos de arena; golpear con sacos de arena.

sandstone [sand-stoun] *n.* piedra arenisca.

sandwich [sand-uich] *n.* sandwich, emparedado, *m.*; —, *vt.* emparedar; intercalar.

sandy [san-di] *adj.* arenoso, arenisco.

sane [sein] *adj.* sano.

sang [sang] *pretérito* del verbo **sing.**

sanitarium [sa-ni-tea-riom] *n.* sanatorio, *m.*

sanitary [sa-ni-ta-ri] *adj.* sanitario; — **napkin,** servilleta higiénica.

sanitation [sa-ni-tei-shon] *n.* saneamiento, *m.*

sanity [sa-ni-ti] *n.* cordura, *f.*; juicio sano, sentido común; **to lose one's** —, volverse loco.

sank [sank] *pretérito* del verbo **sink.**

sapling [sa-plin] *n.* renuevo, vástago, *m.*; mozalbete, *m.*

sapphire [sa-faiar] *n.* zafir, zafiro, *m.*

sarcasm [sar-ka-sem] *n.* sarcasmo, *m.*

sarcastic [sar-kas-tik] *adj.* sarcástico, mordaz, cáustico.

sardine [sar-din] *n.* sardina, *f.*

sash [sash] *n.* faja, *f.*; cinturón, *m.*; cinta, *f.*; bastidor de ventana o de puerta.

sassafras [sa-sa-fras] *n.* sasa-frás, *m.*

sat [sat] *pretérito y p.p.* del verbo **sit.**

Satan [sei-tan] *n.* Satanás, *m.*

satanic [sa-ta-nik] *adj.* diabólico, satánico.

satellite [sa-te-lait] *n.* satélite, *m.*

satiate [sei-shieit] *vt.* saciar, hartar; —, *vi.* saciarse, hartarse.

satin [sa-tin] *n.* raso, *m.*

satire [sa-taiar] *n.* sátira, *f.*

satirical [sa-ti-ri-kal] *adj.* satírico.

satirist [sa-ti-rist] *n.* autor satírico, persona que usa sátira.

satirize [sa-ti-rais] *vt.* satirizar.

satisfaction [sa-tis-fak-shon] *n.* satisfacción, *f.*

satisfactorily [sa-tis-fak-to-ri-li] *adj.* satisfactoriamente.

satisfactory [sa-tis-fak-to-ri] *adj.* satisfactorio; **to be — to you,** ser de su agrado.

satisfy [sa-tis-fai] *vt.* satisfacer.

saturate [sa-cha-reit] *vt.* saturar.

Saturday [sa-te-di] *n.* sábado, *m.*

satyr [sa-tar] *n.* sátiro, *m.*

sauce [sos] *n.* salsa, *f.*

saucepan [sos-pan] *n.* cacerola, *f.*

saucer [so-sar] *n.* plato pequeño.

saucy [so-si] *adj.* atrevido, mal-criado, respondón.

saunter [son-tar] *vi.* callejear, vagar, andar sin rumbo.

sausage [so-sich] *n.* salchicha, *f.;* **pork —,** longaniza, *f.*

savage [sa-vich] *adj.* salvaje, bárbaro; —, *n.* salvaje, *m.*

savagery [sa-vi-geri] *n.* salvajismo, *m.,* salvajez, *f.*

save [seiv] *vt.* salvar; economizar, ahorrar; conservar; —, *prep.* excepto.

saver [sei-var] *n.* libertador, ra; ahorrador, ra.

saving [sei-vin] *adj.* frugal, económico; salvador; —, *prep.* fuera de, excepto; —, *n.* salvamento, *m.;* —**s,** *n. pl.* ahorros, *m. pl.,* economías, *f. pl.;* —**s bank,** caja de ahorros, banco de ahorros.

savior, saviour [sei-viar] *n.* salvador, ra.

Saviour [sei-viar] *n.* Redentor, Salvador, *m.*

savor, savour [sei-var] *n.* olor, *m.;* sabor, *m.;* —, *vt. y vi.* gustar, saborear; **to — of,** oler a, saber a; tener la característica de.

savory [sei-va-ri] *adj.* sabroso.

saw [so] *n.* sierra, *f.;* —, *vt.* serrar; —, *pretérito* del verbo **see.**

sawdust [so-dast] *n.* aserraduras, *f. pl.,* aserrín, *m.*

saxophone [sak-so-foun] *n.* (mus.) saxofón, *m.*

say [sei] *vt.* decir, hablar; proferir; **that is to —,** es decir; **to — mass,** cantar misa; **to — to oneself,** decir para su capote; **—,** *n.* habla, *f.*

saying [seiin] *n.* dicho, proverbio, refrán *m.*

scaffold [ska-fold] *n.* andamio; *m.*

scaffolding [ska-fol-din] *n.* andamiaje, *m.;* construcción de tablados o andamios.

scald [skold] *vt.* escaldar; **—,** *n.* escaldadura, *f.;* quemadura, *f.*

scale [skeil] *n.* balanza, *f.;* escama, *f.;* escala, *f.;* gama, *f.;* lámina delgada; **balance —,** balanza, *f.;* **platform —,** báscula, *f.;* **—,** *vt.* y *vi.* escalar, descostrarse; desconchar (una pared, un techo, etc.) .

scaling [skei-lin] *n.* desconchamiento (de una pared o un techo, etc.); (mil.) escalamiento, *m.;* escamadura, *f.*

scallop [sko-lop] *n.* (ichth.) venera, pechina, *f.;* festón, *m.;* **—,** *vt.* festonear.

scalp [skolp] *n.* cuero cabelludo; **—,** *vt.* escalpar; comprar y revender billetes de teatro, etc., por una ganancia.

scalper [skol-per] *n.* revendedor, *m.,* persona que revende billetes de teatro, etc., por una ganancia; **ticket —,** revendedor, *m.*

scan [skan] *vt.* escudriñar; medir las sílabas de un verso.

scandal [skan-dal] *n.* escándalo, *m.;* infamia, *f.*

scandalize [skan-da-lais] *vt.* escandalizar.

scandalous [skan-da-los] *adj.* escandaloso.

Scandinavia [skan-di-nei-via] Escandinavia, *f.*

scant, scanty [skant], [skan-ti] *adj.* escaso, parco; sórdido.

scapegoat [skeip-gout] *n* víctima inocente; (Mex.) chivo expiatorio.

scar [skar] *n.* cicatriz, *f.;* **—,** *vt.* hacer alguna cicatriz.

scarce [skars] *adj.* raro; **—ly,** *adv.* apenas, escasamente; solamente; pobremente.

scarcity [skar-si-ti] *n.* escasez, *f.*

scare [skear] *n.* susto, *m.;* **to get a —,** llevarse un susto; **—,** *vt.* espantar.

scarecrow [skea-krau] *n.* espantapájaros, mamarracho, *m.*

scarf [skarf] *n.* bufanda, *f.;* chal, *m.,* chalina, *f.*

scatter [ska-tar] *vt.* esparcir, dispersar; disipar; **—,** *vi.* derramarse, disiparse.

scavenger [ska-vin-char] *n.* basurero, *m.,* barrendero, ra;

animal que se alimenta de carroña.

scenario [si-na-riou] *n.* guión, argumento de una película cinematográfica.

scene [sin] *n.* escena, perspectiva, vista, *f.;* paisaje, *m.;* (theat.) escena, *f.;* lugar de un suceso.

scenery [si-na-ri] *n.* vista, *f.;* **paisaje**, *m.;* (theat.) escenografía, decoración, *f.,* bastidores, *m. pl.*

scenic, scenical [si-nik], [si-nikal] *adj.* escénico.

scent [sent] *n.* olfato, *m.;* olor, *m.;* rastro, *m.;* —, *vt.* oler, olfatear; —, *vi.* olfatear.

scepter, sceptre [skep-tar] *n.* cetro, *m.*

sceptic, sceptical = **skeptic, skeptical.**

schedule [she-diul] *n.* plan, programa, *m.;* catálogo, *m.;* horario, itinerario, *m.;* —, *vt.* fijar en un plan o en un programa.

schematic [ski-ma-tik] *adj.* esquemático.

scheme [skim] *n.* proyecto, *m.;* esquema, plan, modelo, *m.;* —, *vt.* proyectar.

schism [ski-sem] *n.* cisma, *m.*

scholar [sko-lar] *n.* estudiante, *m.* y *f.;* literato, ta; erudito, ta.

scholarly [sko-lar-li] *adj.* de estudiante; erudito, muy instruido; —, *adv.* eruditamente.

scholarship [sko-lar-ship] *n.* educación literaria; beca, *f.;* erudición, *f.*

scholastic [sko-las-tik] *adj.* escolástico; estudiantil.

school [skul] *n.* escuela, *f.;* **high** —, escuela secundaria, escuela superior; — *vt.* instruir, enseñar; disciplinar.

schoolhouse [skul-jaus] *n.* escuela (edificio), *f.*

schooling [sku-lin] *n.* instrucción, enseñanza, *f.*

schoolteacher [skul-ti-cher] *n.* maestro o maestra de escuela.

sciatic [skai-atik] *adj.* ciático; — **nerve,** nervio ciático.

science [saians] *n.* ciencia,

scientific [saian-ti-fik] *adj.* científico.

scientist [saian-tist] *n.* hombre de ciencia, científico, ca.

scissors [si-sors] *n. pl.* tijeras, *f. pl.*

scold [skould] *vt.* y *vi.* regañar, reñir, refunfuñar; —, *n.* persona regañona.

scolding [skoul-din] *n.* regaño, *m.;* —, *adj.* regañón.

scoop [skup] *n.* cucharón, *m.;* (naut.) achicador, *m.;* cesta (en el juego de pelota) ; (coll. periodismo) acción de ganar una noticia; —, *vt.* cavar, socavar.

scope [skoup] *n.* alcance, *m.;* rienda suelta; libertad, *f.*

scorch [skorch] *vt.* quemar por encima; tostar; socarrar; calcinar; —, *vi.* quemarse, secarse.

score [skor] *n.* muesca, *f.;* consideración, *f.;* cuenta, *f* ; razón, *f* ; motivo, *m.;* veintena, *f.;* (deportes) tantos, *m. pl.,* puntuación, *f.;* (mus.) partitura, *f.;* —, *vt.* sentar alguna deuda; imputar; señalar con una línea; —, *vi.* hacer tantos (en un juego).

scornful [skorn-ful] *adj.* desdeñoso; —**ly**, *adv.* con desdén.

scorpion [skor-pion] *n.* escorpión, *m.*

Scotch [skoch] *n. y adj.* escocés, esa; —, *n.* whisky escocés.

Scotland [skot-lan] Escocia, *f.*

scoundrel [skaun-drel] *n.* pícaro, ra, bribón, ona, infame, *m. y f.;* canalla, *m.*

scour [skauar] *vt.* fregar, estregar; limpiar; rebuscar, sondear.

scout [skaut] *n.* (mil.) batidor, corredor, *m.,* escucha, *f.;* centinela avanzada; **boy** —, niño explorador, niño de la Asociación de Niños Exploradores; **girl** —, niña exploradora, niña de la Asociación de Niñas Exploradoras; —, *vi.* reconocer secretamente los movimientos del enemigo; (mil.) explorar.

scowl [skaul] *n.* ceño, *m.,* semblante ceñudo; —, *vi.* mirar con ceño.

scramble [skra-bel] *vi.* trepar; arrebatar, disputar; esparcirse en forma irregular; —, *vt.* mezclar confusamente; —**d eggs,** huevos revueltos; —, *n.* disputa, arrebatiña, *f.;* (avi.) despegue rápido de emergencia en operaciones de defensa.

scrap [skrap] *n.* migaja, *f.;* pedacito, *m.;* —**s**, *pl* sobras, *f. pl.,* retazos, *m. pl.;* — **heap,** montón de desechos, pila de desperdicios; — **iron,** — **metal,** chatarra, *f.;* —, *vt.* descartar; —, *vi.* (coll.) disputar, reñir.

scrape [skreip] *vt. y vi.* raer, raspar, arañar; juntar gradualmente (dinero, etc.); —, *n.* dificultad, *f.*

scraper [skrei-par] *n.* raspador, *m.*

scratch [skrach] *vt.* rascar, raspar; borrar; arañar; —, *n.* rasguño, *m.*

scrawl [skrol] *vt. y vi.* garrapatear; —, *n.* garabatos, *m. pl.,* garrapato, *m.*

scream [skrim] *vi.* gritar, chillar, dar alaridos; —, *n.* chillido, grito, alarido, *m.*

screech [skrich] *vi.* chillar, dar alaridos; —, *n.* chillido, grito, alarido, *m.;* — **owl,** lechuza, *f.*

screen [skrin] *n.* pantalla, *f.;*

biombo, *m.;* mampara, *f.;* pantalla de cine; **fire —,** pantalla de chimenea; **—,** *vt.* abrigar, esconder; cribar, cerner, tamizar; seleccionar por eliminación; proyectar en la pantalla.

screw [skru] *n.* tornillo, *m.;* clavo de rosca; rosca, *f.;* **— driver,** destornillador, *m.;* **— propeller,** hélice, *f.;* **to have a — loose,** (coll.) tener un tornillo flojo, ser alocado; **—,** *vt.* atornillar; forzar, apretar.

scribe [skraib] *n.* escritor, *m.;* escriba, *m.;* escribiente, *m.*

script [skript] *n.* (rad. y TV.) guión, argumento, libreto, *m.;* (print.) plumilla inglesa.

scriptural [skrip-cha-ral] *adj.* bíblico.

Scripture [skrip-char] *n.* Escritura Sagrada.

scroll [skroul] *n.* rollo (de papel o pergamino), *m.;* voluta, *f.;* **— saw,** sierra de cinta, sierra de marquetería; **—,** *vt.* decorar con volutas.

scrub [skrab] *vt.* estregar con un estropajo; fregar, restregar; **—,** *n.* estropajo, *m.;* ganapán, *m.;* (Mex.) afanador, *m.*

scruple [skra-pel] *n.* escrúpulo, rescoldo, *m.;* **—,** *vi.* tener escrúpulos de conciencia.

scrutinize [skru-ti-nais] *vt.* escudriñar, examiner; escrutar.

scrutiny [skru-ti-ni] *n.* escrutinio, examen, *m.*

Scuba [sku-ba] *n.* escafandra autónoma.

sculptor [skalp-tar] *n.* escultor, *m.*

sculpture [skalp-char] *n.* escultura, *f.;* **—,** *vt.* esculpir.

scum [skam] *n.* nata, *f.;* espuma, *f.;* escoria, *f.;* **—,** *vt.* espumar.

sea [sii] *n.* mar, *m.* y *f.;* **rough —,** mar alta; **— breeze,** viento de mar; **— food,** marisco o pescado; **— gull,** gaviota, *f.;* **— horse,** hipocampo, *m.;* **— wall,** malecón, *m.;* **—,** *adj.* de mar, marítimo.

seal [sil] *n.* sello, *m.;* (zool.) foca, *f.;* becerro marino; **—,** *vt.* sellar.

sea level [si-level] *n.* nivel del mar.

sealing [si-lin] *n.* caza de focas; selladura, *f.;* **— wax,** lacre, *m.*

seam [sim] *n.* costura, *f.;* cicatriz, *f.;* sutura, *f.;* **—,** *vt.* coser.

seaman [si-man] *n.* marinero, marino, *m.*

seamless [sim-les] *adj.* sin costura; **— hosiery,** medias sin costura.

seamstress [sems-tris] *n.* costurera, *f.*

seaport [si-port] *n.* puerto de mar.

sear [siar] *vt.* cauterizar; quemar; dorar o freír (la superficie de la carne, etc.); secar.

search [serch] *vt.* examinar, registrar; escudriñar, inquirir, tentar, pesquisar; —, *n.* pesquisa, *f.;* busca, *f.;* búsqueda, *f.;* **in — of,** en busca de; — **engine,** motor de búsqueda, *m.*

searchlight [serch-lait] *n.* reflector, *m.*

seashore [si-shor] *n.* ribera, *f.;* litoral, *m.*

seasick [si-sik] *adj.* mareado.

seaside [si-said] *n.* orilla o ribera del mar; —, *adj.* en la costa; del mar; — **resort,** lugar de recreo a la orilla del mar.

season [si-son] *n.* estación, *f.;* tiempo, *m.;* tiempo oportuno; sazón, *f.;* temporada, *f.;* — **ticket,** (theat.) abono para la temporada; (rail.) abono de pasaje; —, *vt.* sazonar; imbuir; curar; condimentar; —, *vi.* sazonarse.

seasonable [si-so-na-bol] *adj.,* oportuno, tempestivo, a propósito.

seasonal [si-so-nal] *adj.* de temporada, estacional.

seasoned [si-sond] *adj.* curado; sazonado; **highly —,** picante, picoso.

seasoning [si-so-nin] *n.* condimento, *m.*

seat [sit] *n.* silla, *f.;* localidad, *f.;* morada, *f.;* domicilio, *m.;* situación, *f.;* **front —,** asiento delantero; **back —,** asiento trasero; — **cover,** cubreasiento, *m.;* —, *vt.* situar; colocar; asentar; sentar.

seating [si-tin] *n.* acción de sentar; material para entapizar sillas; — **capacity,** cabida, *f.;* número de asientos.

seaward [si-uord] *adj.* del litoral; —, —**s,** *adv.* hacia el mar.

seaweed [si-uid] *n.* alga marina.

secede [si-sid] *vi.* apartarse, separarse.

secession [si-se-shon] *n.* separación, *f.;* secesión, *f.*

seclude [si-klud] *vt.* apartar, excluir, recluir.

seclusion [si-klu-shon] *n.* separación, *f.;* reclusión, *f.*

second [se-kond] *adj.* segundo; — **childhood,** segunda infancia, chochera, *f.;* — **hand,** segundero (de un reloj); — **lieutenant,** alférez, subteniente, *m.;* — **nature,** costumbre arraigada; —**ly,** *adv.* en segundo lugar; —, *n.* padrino (en un duelo), *m.;* defensor, *m.;* segundo, *m.;* (mus.) segunda, *f.;* —, *vt.* apoyar, ayudar; **to — the motion,** apoyar la moción.

secondary [se-kon-da-ri] *adj.* secundario; — **school,** escuela secundaria.

second-class [se-kond-klas] *adj.* de segunda clase, mediocre.

secondhand [se-kond-jand] *adj.* de ocasión; usado; de segunda mano; — **dealer,** prendero, ropavejero, *m.;* — **shop,** baratillo, *m.,* tienda de artículos de segunda mano.

secrecy [si-kre-si] *n.* secreto, *m.;* reserva, *f.;* reticencia, *f.*

secret [si-kret] *n.* secreto, *m.;* **in** —, en secreto; —, *adj.* privado; secreto; reservado; — **service,** policía secreta; —**ly,** *adv.* secretamente, a escondidas, de rebozo.

secretariat [se-kre-ta-riat] *n.* secretaría, *f.*

secretary [se-kre-ta-ri] *n.* secretario, ria; **private** —, secretario (o secretaria) particular; —'s **office,** secretaría, *f.*

secrete [si-krit] *vt.* esconder; guardar en secreto; (med.) secretar.

secretion [si-kri-shon] *n.* secreción, *f.*

secretive [si-kra-tiv] *adj.* misterioso; reservado; secretorio.

sect [sekt] [sekt] *n.* secta, *f.*

sectarian, sectary [sek-tea-rian], [sek-ta-ri] *n.* y *adj.* sectario, ria; secuaz, *m.* y *f.*

section [sek-shon] *n.* sección, *f.;* departamento, *m.*

sector [sek-tar] *n.* sector, *m.*

secular [se-kiu-lar] *adj.* secular, seglar.

secure [se-kiuar] *adj.* seguro; salvo; —**ly,** *adv.* en forma segura; —, *vt.* asegurar; conseguir; resguardar.

security [si-kiu-ri-ti] *n.* seguridad, *f.;* defensa, *f.;* confianza, *f.;* fianza, *f.;* **to give** —, dar o prestar fianza; — **risk,** individuo que representa un peligro para la seguridad pública.

sedan [si-dan] *n.* (auto.) sedán, *m.*

sedate [si-deit] *adj.* sosegado, tranquilo.

sedative [se-da-tiv] *n.* y *adj.* sedativo, sedante, calmante, confortante, *m.*

sedentary [se-dan-tri] *adj.* sedentario.

sediment [se-di-ment] *n.* sedimento, *m.;* hez, *f.*

sedimentary [se-di-men-ta-ri] *adj.* sedimentario.

seduce [si-dius] *vt.* seducir; engañar.

seduction [si-dak-shon] *n.* seducción, *f.*

seductive [si-dak-tris] *adj.* seductivo, seductor.

see [sii] *vt.* y *vi.* ver, observar, descubrir; advertir; conocer, juzgar, comprender; presenciar; **let's** —, vamos a ver, a ver; **to** — **to it that,** encargarse

de; —, véase; —! *interj.* ¡mira!
—, silla episcopal; **the Holy S—**
, la Santa Sede.

seed [siid] *n.* semilla, simiente,
f.; origen, *m.;* — **corn,** semilla
para maíz; **to go to —,** (coll.)
degenerar, decaer, echarse a
perder; —, *vi.* granar, sembrar.

seedless [siid-les] *adj.* sin semilla; — **grapes,** uvas sin semilla.

seeing [siin] *n.* vista, *f.;* acto de
ver, ver, *m.;* — **that,** visto que,
en consideración a; — **eye dog,**
perro lazarillo, perro guía (para
los ciegos).

seek [siik] *vt.* y *vi.* buscar; pretender.

seem [siim] *vi.* parecer, semejar-
se; tener cara de.

seeming [sii-min] *n.* apariencia,
f.; —**ly,** *adv.* al parecer.

seen [siin] *p.p.* del verbo **see.**

seep [siip] *vi.* colarse, escurrirse.

seesaw [si-so] *n.* vaivén *m.;*
balancín de sube y baja; —, *vi.*
balancear.

seethe [siiz] *vi.* hervir, bullir.

segment [seg-ment] *n.* segmento,
m.

segregate [se-gri-gueit] *adj.*
segregado, apartado; —, *vt.*
segregar.

segregation [se-gri-guei-shon] *n.*
segregación, separación, *f.*

seismograph [sais-mo-graf] *n.*
sismógrafo, *m.*

seize [siis] *vt.* asir, agarrar,
prender; secuestrar bienes o
efectos; decomisar.

seizure [si-shar] *n.* captura,
toma, *f.;* secuestro, *m.*

seldom [sel-dom] *adv.* raramente, rara vez.

select [si-lekt] *vt.* elegir, escoger;
—, *adj.* selecto, escogido, granado.

selection [si-lek-shon] *n.* selección, *f.;* trozo, *m.*

selective [si-lek-tiv] *adj.* selecti-
vo, relativo a la se-lección; que
escore.

self [self] *adj.* propio, mismo; —,
n. sí mismo.

self-centered [self-sen-terd] *adj.*
egoísta, concentrado en sí
mismo; independiente.

self-confident [self-kon-fident]
adj. que tiene confianza en sí
mismo.

self-conscious [self-kon-shious]
adj. consciente de sí mismo;
tímido, vergonzoso.

self-contained [self-kon-teind]
adj. reservado; independiente;
completo, que contiene todos
sus elementos.

self-controlled [self-kon-troul]
adj. dueño de sí mismo.

self-defense [self-di-fens] *n.*
defensa propia.

self-denial [self-di-naial] *n.*
abnegación, *f.*

self-esteem [self-istim] *n.* amor propio.

self-evident [self-e-vi-dent] *adj.* natural, patente; **to be —,** caerse de suyo.

self-explanatory [self-eks-pla-na-to-ri] *adj.* que se explica por sí mismo.

self-expression [self-iks-pre-shon] *n.* expresión de personalidad; aserción de rasgos individuales.

self-governing [self-go-ver-nin] *adj.* autónomo, que tiene dominio sobre sí mismo.

self-help [self-jelp] *n.* ayuda de sí mismo.

self-improvement [self-im-pruv-ment] *n.* mejoramiento de sí mismo.

self-indulgence [self-in-dal-yans] *n.* intemperancia, *f.;* entrega a la satisfacción de los propios deseos.

selfish [sel-fish] *adj.* interesado; egoísta.

selfishness [sel-fish-nes] *n.* egoísmo, *m.*

self-reliance [self-ri-laians] *n.* confianza en sí mismo.

self-reliant [self-ri-laiant] *adj.* independiente, que confía en sí mismo.

self-respect [self-ris-pekt] *n.* respeto de sí mismo.

self-sacrifice [self-sa-kri-fais] *n.*

abnegación, *f.*

self-satisfied [self-sa-tis-faid] *adj.* satisfecho de sí mismo.

self-starter [self-star-tar] *n.* motor de arranque, arranque automático.

self-sufficient [self-su-fi-shent] *adj.* capaz de mantenerse; independiente; confiado en sí mismo; altanero.

self-taught [self-taut] *adj.* autodidacto.

sell [sel] *vt.* y *vi.* vender; traficar; —, *n.* (coll.) patraña, *f.;* engaño, *m.*

seller [se-lar] *n.* vendedor, ra.

selves [selvs] *n. pl.* de **self.**

semblance [sem-blans] *n.* semejanza, apariencia, *f.*

semester [si-mes-tar] *n.* semestre, *m.*

semiannual [se-mia-nual] *adj.* semianual, semestral.

semicircle [se-mi-ser-kel] *n.* semicírculo, *m.*

semicolon [se-mi-kou-lon] *n.* punto y coma.

semifinal [se-mi-fi-nal] *adj.* semifinal; —s, *n. pl.* semi-finales, *m. pl.*

semimonthly [se-mi-monz-li] *adj.* quincenal; — **pay,** quincena, paga quincenal; —, *adv.* quincenalmente.

seminar [se-mi-nar] *n.* seminario, grupo de estudiantes dirigido por un profesor que hace estudios superiores.

seminary [se-mi-na-ri] *n.* seminario, *m.*

senate [se-neit] *n.* senado, *m.*

senator [se-ni-tar] *n.* senador, *m.*

senatorial [se-ni-to-rial] *adj.* senatorio, senatorial.

send [send] *vt.* enviar, despachar, mandar; producir; trasmitir.

sender [sen-dar] *n.* remitente, *m.* y *f.;* (elec.) trasmisor, *m.*

sending [sen-din] *n.* trasmisión, *f.,* envío, *m.*

senile [si-nail] *adj.* senil.

senior [si-nior] *adj.* mayor; — **high school,** añossuperiores de una escuela secundaria; —, *n.* estudiante de cuarto año.

seniority [si-nio-ri-ti] *n.* antigüedad, ancianidad, *f.*

sensation [sen-sei-shon] *n.* sensación, *f.;* sentimiento, *m.*

sensational [sen-sei-sho-nal] *adj.* sensacional.

sense [sens] *n.* sentido, *m.;* entendimiento, *m.;* razón, *f.;* juicio, *m.;* sentimiento, *m.;* sensatez, *f.;* **common** —, sentido práctico, sentido común; — **of sight,** ver, *m.,* vista, *f.;* — **organ,** órgano sensorio; —, *vt.* percibir; sentir.

senseless [sens-les] *adj.* insensi-

ble.

sensibility [sen-si-bi-li-ti] *n.* sensibilidad, *f.*

sensible [sen-si-bol] *adj.* sensato, juicioso.

sensitive [sen-si-tiv] *adj.* sensible; sensitivo.

sensitize [sen-si-tais] *vt.* sensibilizar.

sensory [sen-so-ri] *adj.* sensorio.

sensual [sen-siual] *adj.* sensual.

sensuality [sen-siua-li-ti] *n.* sensualidad, *f.*

sensuous [sen-siuos] *adj.* sensorio, sensitivo; sensual.

sent ['sent] [sent] *pretérito* y *p.p.* del verbo **send.**

sentence [sen-tens] *n.* sentencia, frase, oración, *f.;* (leyes) sentencia, *f.;* —, *vt.* sentenciar, condenar.

sentiment [sen-ti-mant] *n.* sentimiento, *m.;* opinión, *f.*

sentimental [sen-ti-men-tal] *adj.* sentimental.

sentimentalist [sen-ti-men-ta-list] *n.* sentimentalista, *m.* y *f.*

sentinel [sen-ti-nel] *n.* centinela, *m.* y *f.*

sentry [sen-tri] *n.* centinela, *m.* y *f.*

separable [se-pa-ra-bol] *adj.* separable.

separate [se-pa-reit] *vt.* separar; —, *vi.* separarse; —, *adj.* separado; **under — cover,** por

separado; **—ly,** *adv.* separadamente.

separation [se-pa-rei-shon] *n.*
separación, *f.*

September [sep-tem-bar] *n.* septiembre o setiembre, *m.*

septic [sep-tik] *adj.* séptico; —
tank, foso séptico.

sequel [si-kual] *n.* secuela, consecuencia, *f.;* continuación, *f.*

sequence [si-kuans] *n.* serie,
continuación, *f.*

sequoia [si-kuoia] *n.* secoya, *f.*

serenade [se-re-neid] *n.* serenata, *f.;* (Mex.) gallo, *m.;* —, *vt.*
llevar una serenata o un gallo
(a alguien).

serene [se-rin] *adj.* sereno, tranquilo; **—ly,** *adv.* serenamente.

serenity [se-ri-ni-ti] *n.* serenidad, *f.*

sergeant [sar-yant] *n.* sargento,
m.; alguacil, *m.*

serial [sia-rial] *adj.* que se publica en series; **—,** *n.* publicación
en cuadernos periódicos; película cinematográfica de episo-
dios.

series [sia-ris] *n.* serie, cadena,
f.

sermon [ser-mon] *n.* sermón, *m.*

sermonize [ser-mo-nais] *vt.* y *vi.*
sermonear; regañar; amones-
tar.

serous [se-ros] *adj.* seroso.

serpent [ser-pent] *n.* serpiente,

sierpe, *f.*

serpentine [ser-pen-tain] *adj.*
serpentino; **—,** *n.* (chem.) serpentina, *f.;* **—,** *vi.* serpentear.

serum [si-ram] *n.* suero, *m.*

servant [ser-vant] *n.* criado, da;
servidor, ra; sirviente, ta.

serve [serv] *vt.* y *vi.* servir; asistir o servir (a la mesa); ser a
propósito.

service [ser-vis] *n.* servicio, *m.;*
servidumbre, *f.;* utilidad, *f.;*
culto divino; **at your —,** su servidor, ra, a sus órdenes; **day —**
, servicio diurno; **night —,** servicio nocturno; **— station,** estación de gasolina; estación de
servicios; taller de repuestos y
reparaciones; **to be of —,** ser
útil.

servile [ser-vail] *adj.* servil; **—ly,**
adv. servilmente.

servitude [ser-vi-tiud] *n.* servidumbre, esclavitud, *f.*

sesame [se-sa-mi] *n.* (bot.) sésamo, *m.;* **open —,** sésamo ábrete
(frase mágica de contra-seña).

session [se-shon] *n.* junta, *f.;*
sesión, *f.;* **joint —,** sesión
plena.

set [set] *vt.* poner, colocar, fijar;
establecer, determinar; basar;
—, *vi.* ponerse (el sol o los
astros); tramontar (el sol o los
astros); cuajarse; aplicarse; **to**
— a diamond, montar un dia-

mante; **to — aside,** poner a un lado; **to — back,** hacer retroceder; **to — forward,** hacer adelantar; **to — on fire,** pegar fuego a; **to — the table,** poner la mesa; **to — up,** erigir; sentar; —, *n.* juego, *m.*, con-junto (de cartas), *m.*; servicio (de plata), *m.*; conjunto de varias cosas; colección, *f.*; cuadrilla, bandada, *f.*; **— of dishes,** vajilla, *f.*; —, *adj.* puesto, fijo.

setback [set-bak] *n.* revés, *m.*; (arch.) voladizo, *m.*

setter [se-tar] *n.* perro de ajeo.

setting [se-tin] *n.* establecimiento, *m.*; colocación, *f.*; asentamiento, *m.*; fraguado, *m.*; montadura, *f.*; (theat.) escenario, decorado, *m.*; marco, *m.*; **— of the sun,** puesta del sol.

settle [se-tel] *vt.* colocar, fijar, afirmar; componer; arreglar; calmar; solventar (deudas); —, *vi.* reposarse; establecerse, radicarse; sosegarse.

settlement [se-tel-ment] *n.* establecimiento, *m.*; domicilio, *m.*; contrato, *m.*; arreglo, *m.*; liquidación, *f.*; empleo, *m.*; colonia, *f.*

settler [se-tlar] *n.* colono, *m.*

setup [set-ap] *n.* disposición, *f.*; arreglo, *m.*; organización, *f.*

seven [se-ven] *n.* y *adj.* siete, *m.*

seventeen [se-ven-tin] *n.* y *adj.* diez *y* siete, diecisiete, *m.*

seventeenth [se-ven-tinz] *n.* y *adj.* decimoséptimo, *m.*

seventh [se-venz] *n.* y *adj.* séptimo, *m.*; **— heaven,** séptimo cielo, éxtasis, *m.*

seventy [se-ven-ti] *n.* y *adj.* setenta, *m.*

sever [se-var] *vt.* y *vi.* separar, dividir; cortar; desligar; **to — connections,** romper las relaciones; apartarse.

several [se-ve-ral] *adj.* diversos, varios.

severance [se-ve-rans] *n.* separación, *f.*; **— pay,** compensación de despido (de un empleado, etc.).

severen [si-viar] *adj.* severo, riguroso; serio; áspero; duro, cruel; **—ly,** *adv.* severamente.

severity [si-ve-ri-ti] *n.* severidad, *f.*

sew [sou] *vt.* y *vi.* coser.

sewage [siuich] *n.* inmundicias, *f. pl.*; **— system,** alcantarillado, *m.*

sewer [siuar] *n.* albañal, *m.*; cloaca, *f.*; caño, *m.*

sewing [souin] *n.* costura, *f.*; **— machine,** máquina de coser.

sex [seks] *n.* sexo, *m.*

sexual [sek-siual] *adj.* sexual.

shabby [sha-bi] *adj.* vil, bajo; destartalado; miserable.

shack [shak] *n.* choza, cabaña,

f.; (coll.) casa en mal estado.

shackle [sha-kel] *vt.* encadenar; **—s,** *n. pl.* grillos, *m. pl.*

shade [sheid] *n.* sombra, oscuridad, *f.;* matiz, *m.;* sombrilla, *f.;* umbría, *f.;* —, *vt.* dar sombra; matizar; esconder.

shadow [sha-dou] *n.* sombra, *f.;* protección, *f.;* —, *vt.* sombrear.

shady [shei-di] *adj.* con sombra, sombrío, umbroso; — **character,** individuo sospechoso.

shaft [shaft] *n.* flecha, saeta, *f.*

shake [sheik] *vt.* sacudir; agitar; —, *vi.* temblar; **to — hands,** darse las manos; —, *n.* concusión, sacudida, *f.;* vibración *f.*

shaker [shei-kar] *n.* agitador, *m.;* estremecedor, *m.;* **cocktail** —, coctelera, *f.;* **salt** —, salero, *m.*

shaky [shei-ki] *adj.* titubeante, tembloroso; inestable; (coll.) dudoso, sospechoso.

shall [shal] *vi.* verbo auxiliar para indicar el futuro en la primera persona del singular y del plural, o el imperativo en las demás personas, por ej., **I — eat,** comeré; **we — eat,** comeremos; **he — eat,** comerá de todos modos, tendrá que comer, etc.

shallow [sha-lou] *adj.* somero; poco profundo; —, *n.* bajío (banco de arena), *m.*

shame [sheim] *n.* vergüenza, *f.;* deshonra; **what a —!** ¡qué pena! ¡qué lástima! —, *vt.* avergonzar, deshonrar.

shameful [sheim-ful] *adj.* vergonzoso; deshonroso; **—ly,** *adv.* ignominiosamente.

shameless [sheim-les] *adj.* desvergonzado.

shampoo [sham-pu] *vt.* dar champú, lavar la cabeza; —, *n.* champú, *m.*

shamrock [sham-rok] *n.* trébol, trifolio, *m.*

shank [shank] *n.* pierna, *f.;* asta, *f.;* asta de ancla.

shape [sheip] *vt.* y *vi.* formar; concebir; configurar; dar forma; adaptar; —, *n.* forma, figura, *f.;* modelo, *m.*

shapeless [sheip-les] *adj.* informe, sin forma.

shapely [sheip-li] *adj.* bien hecho, bien formado; — **figure,** buen cuerpo.

share [shear] *n.* parte, porción, cuota, *f.;* (com.) acción, *f.;* reja del arado; participación, *f.;* —, *vt.* y *vi.* repartir, participar; compartir.

shareholder [shea-joul-dar] *n.* (com.) accionista, *m.* y *f.*

shark [shark] *n.* tiburón, *m.;* petardista, *m.*

sharp [sharp] *adj.* agudo, aguzado; astuto; perspicaz, sagaz;

penetrante; picante, acre, mordaz, severo, rígido; vivo, violento; — **bend,** curva cerrada; —, *n.* (mus.) sostenido, *m.;* **two o'clock** —, las dos en punto; — **ly,** *adv.* con filo; ingeniosamente; ásperamente.

sharpen [shar-pen] *vt.* afilar, aguzar.

sharpener [sharp-nar] *n.* aguzador, afilador, amolador, *m.;* máquina de afilar; **pencil** —, tajalápices, sacapuntas, *m.*

sharpness [sharp-nes] *n.* agudeza, *f.;* sutileza, perspicacia, *f.;* acrimonia, *f.*

sharpshooter [sharp-shu-tar] *n.* buen tirador; soldado elegido por su buena puntería.

shatter [sha-tar] *vt.* destrozar, estrellar; —, *vi.* hacerse pedazos; —, *n.* pedazo, fragmento, *m.*

shatterproof [sha-tar-pruf] *adj.* inastillable.

shave [sheiv] *vt.* rasurar, afeitar; raspar; rozar; (fig.) escatimar; —, *n.* afeitada, *f.;* (coll.) escape, *m.*

shaver [shei-var] *n.* barbero, *m.;* usurero, *m.;* (coll.) muchacho, chico, *m.;* **electric** —, rasuradora eléctrica.

shaving [shei-vin] *n.* raedura, acepilladura, *f.;* rasurada, afeitada, *f.;* — **cream,** crema de

afeitar.

shawl [shol] *n.* chal, mantón, *m.*

she [shi] *pron.* ella.

sheath [shiz] *n.* vaina, funda, *f.;* vestido recto y ajustado; —, *vt.* envainar; (naut.) aforrar el fondo de un navío.

sheave [shiv] *n.* rueda de polea, roldana, *f.;* —**s,** *n. pl.* de **sheaf.**

shed [shed] *vt.* verter, derramar; esparcir; —, *n.* sotechado, tejadillo, *m.;* cabaña, barraca, *f.;* cobertizo, *m.;* techo, *m.;* choza, *f.*

sheep [shiip] *n. sing.* y *pl.* oveja(s), *f.,* carnero, *m.;* criatura indefensa y tímida; (coll.) papanatas, *m.*

sheepish [shii-pish] *adj.* vergonzoso; tímido; cortado.

sheepskin [ship-skin] *n.* piel de carnero; (fig.) diploma, *m.*

sheer [shiar] *adj.* puro, claro, sin mezcla; delgado, trasparente; —, *adv.* de un solo golpe; completamente; —, *vi.* desviarse.

sheet [shiit] *n.* pliego de papel; (naut.) escota, *f.;* **bed** —, sábana, *f.;* **blank** —, hoja en blanco; — **anchor,** áncora mayor de un navío; — **glass,** vidrio en lámina; — **iron,** plancha de hierro batido; — **lightning,** relampagueo a manera de fucilazos; — **metal,** hoja metálica; metal en hojas, palastro, *m.,* lámina, *f.;*

— **music,** música publicada en hojas sueltas; — **(of paper), —** **(of metal),** hoja, *f.;* —, *vt.* ensabanar; extender en láminas.

shelf [shelf] *n.* anaquel, estante, *m.;* (naut.) arrecife, *m.;* escollera, *f.;* **corner —,** rinconera, *f.;* **on the —,** (coll.) desechado, archivado.

shell [shel] *n.* cáscara, *f.;* concha, *f.;* corteza, *f.;* bomba, *f.;* cartucho, *m.;* granada, *f.;* **cartridge —,** cápsula, *f.;* — **room,** (naut.) pañol de granadas; **tortoise —,** carey, *m.;* —, *vt.* descascarar, descortezar; bombardear; —, *vi.* descascararse.

shellfish [shel-fish] *n.* marisco, *m.*

shelter [shel-tar] *n.* guarida, *f.;* amparo, abrigo, *m.;* asilo, refugio, *m.;* cubierta, *f.;* —, *vt.* guarecer, abrigar; acoger.

shelve [shelv] *vt.* echar a un lado, arrinconar; desechar.

shelves [shelvs] *n. pl.* de **shelf.**

shelving [shel-vin] *n.* estantería, *f.;* material para anaqueles.

shepherd [she-pard] *n.* pastor, *m.;* —, *vt.* pastorear.

shepherdess [she-par-des] *n.* pastora, ovejera, *f.*

sherbet [sher-bit] *n.* sorbete, *m.*

sheriff [she-rif] *n.* alguacil, *m.,* funcionario administrativo de un condado.

sherry [she-ri] *n.* jerez, vino de Jerez.

shield [shild] *n.* escudo, *m.;* patrocinio, *m.;* —, *vt.* defender; amparar.

shift [shift] *vi.* cambiarse; moverse; trasladarse; ingeniarse; trampear; —, *vt.* mudar; cambiar; trasportar; —, *n.* último recurso; (mech.) cambio de marcha; tanda, *f.;* conmutación, *f.;* artificio, *m.;* astucia, *f.;* efugio, *m.*

shiftless [shift-les] *adj.* perezoso; negligente; des-cuidado.

shimmer [shi-mar] *vi.* brillar tenuemente; —, *n.* luz trémula.

shin [shin] *n.* espinilla, *f.*

shinbone [shin-boun] *n.* tibia, espinilla, *f.*

shine [shain] *vi.* lucir, brillar, resplandecer; —, *vt.* dar lustre (a los zapatos, etc.); —, *n.* brillo, *m.;* resplandor, *m.*

shingle [shin-guel] *n.* ripia, *f.;* tejamaní, tejamanil, *m.;* muestra, *f.,* letrero en un bufete (de un médico, un abogado, etc.); —, *vt.* cubrir (un techo, etc.) con ripias; trasquilar; cinglar.

shingles [shin-guels] *n.* (med.) herpes, *m. o f. pl.*

shining [shai-nin] *adj.* resplandeciente, luciente, reluciente.

shiny [shai-ni] *adj.* brillante, luciente.

ship [ship] *n.* nave, *f.;* bajel, navío, barco, *m.*

shipment [ship-ment] *n.* cargazón, expedición, *f.;* cargamento, *m.;* envio, despacho, embarque, *m.,* remesa, *f.*

shipper [shi-par] *n.* expedidor, remitente, *m.;* (com.) embarcador, *m.*

shipping [shi-pin] *n.* navegación, *f ;* marina, flota, *f.;* expedición, *f.;* embarque, *m.;* — clerk, dependiente encargado de embarques y remisiones; — **company,** compañía naviera; — **expenses,** gastos de expedición; — **room,** departamento de embarques; —, *adj.* naviero.

shipwreck [ship-rek] *n.* naufragio, *m.*

shipwrecked [ship-rekd] *adj.* náufrago; — **person,** náufrago, ga.

shirt [shert] *n.* camisa de hombre; — **store,** camisería, *f ;* **sport** —, camisa sport.

shiver [shi-var] *n.* cacho, pedazo, fragmento, *m.;* estremecimiento, *m.;* —, *vi.* tiritar de miedo o frío; —, *vt.* romper, estrellar.

shivering [shi-ve-rin] *n.* temblor, estremecimiento, *m.*

shoal [shoul] *n.* multitud, *f.;* bajío, *m.;* (naut.) vigía, *f.;* — **of fish,** manada de peces; —, *adj.* bajo, vadoso; —, *vi.*

perder profundidad gradualmente.

shock [shok] *n.* choque, encuentro, *m.;* concusión, *f.;* combate, *m.;* ofensa, *f.;* hacina, *f.;* — **absorber,** amortiguador, *m.;* — **troops,** tropas escogidas, tropas ofensivas o de asalto; — **wave,** onda de choque; —, *vt.* sacudir, ofender.

shocking [sho-kin] *adj.* espantoso, horroroso, horrible, ofensivo, chocante; — **pink,** color rosa subido.

shoe [shu] *n.* zapato, *m.;* herradura de caballo; **old** —, chancla, *f.;* **rubber** —, chanclo, *m.,* zapato de goma; — **polish,** grasa para calzado, betún, *m.;* — **store,** zapatería, *f.;* — **tree,** horma de zapatos; **to put on one's** —**s,** calzarse; —, *vt.* calzar; herrar un caballo.

shoehorn [shu-jorn] *n.* calzador, *m.*

shoelace [shu-leis] *n.* cordón de zapato, agujeta, *f.*

shoemaker [shu-mei-kar] *n.* zapatero, *m.*

shone [shon] *pretérito y p.p.* del verbo **shine.**

shoot [shut] *vt.* tirar, disparar; arrojar, lanzar; fusilar; matar o herir con escopeta; **to** —**at a target,** tirar al blanco; —, *vi.* brotar, germinar; sobresalir;

lanzarse; —, *n.* tiro, *m.;* brote, vástago, tallo, *m.*

shop [shop] *n.* tienda, *f.;* taller, *m.;* **in the** —**s,** en el comercio, en las tiendas; **pastry** —, repostería, *f.;* **confectionery** —, dulcería, *f.;* **beauty** —, salón de belleza; —, *vi.* hacer compras, ir de compras.

shopkeeper [shop-ki-par] *n.* tendero, ra; mercader, *m.*

shoplifter [shop-lif-tar] *n.* ratero, *m.*

shopper [sho-par] *n.* comprador, ra.

shopping [sho-pin] *n.* compras, *f. pl.;* **to go** —, ir de compras.

shopwindow [shop-uin-dou] *n.* vidriera, vitrina, *f.;* aparador, *m.*

shore [shor] *n.* costa, ribera, playa, orilla, *f.;* — **leave,** (naut.) permiso para ir a tierra; —**line,** ribera, costa, *f.*

short [short] *adj.* corto; breve, sucinto, conciso; brusco; **in a** — **while,** dentro de poco, al poco rato; — **circuit,** (elec.) cortocircuito, *m.;* — **cut,** atajo, *m.,* camino corto; medio rápido; **to** —**circuit,** causar un cortocircuito; — **sale,** promesa de venta de valores u otros bienes que no se poseen, pero cuya adquisición se espera pronto; — **wave,** onda corta; **on** — **noti-**

ce, con poco tiempo de aviso; —, *n.* cortocircuito, *m.;* **in** —, en resumen, en concreto, en definitiva; —**ly,** *adv.* brevemente; presto; en pocas palabras; dentro de poco.

shortage [shor-tich] *n.* escasez, falta, *f.;* déficit, *m.*

shorten [shortn] *vt.* acortar; abreviar.

shortening [short-nin] *n.* acortamiento, *m.,* disminución, *f.;* manteca, mantequilla o grasa vegetal usada para pastelería.

shorts [shorts] *n. pl.* calzones cortos; calzoncillos, *m. pl.;* pantalones cortos de mujer.

shortsighted [short-sai-tid] *adj.* corto de vista, miope.

short-term [short-term] *adj.* a corto plazo.

shot [shot] *n.* tiro, *m.;* alcance, *m.;* (coll.) inyección hipodérmica; (coll.) trago de licor; —, *pret. y p.p.* del verbo **shoot.**

shotgun [shot-gan] *n.* escopeta, *f.*

should [shud] *condicional* de **shall** (úsase como auxiliar de otros verbos).

shoulder [shoul-dar] *n.* hombro, *m.;* **round** —**ed,** cargado de espaldas; — **blade,** omóplato, *m.;* —, *vt.* cargar al hombro; soportar.

shout [shaut] *vi.* dar vivas, aclamar; reprobar con gritos; gritar; —, *n.* aclamación, *f.,* grito, *m.*

shove [shav] *vt.* y *vi.* empujar; impeler; —, *n.* empujón, *m.*

shovel [sha-vel] *n.* pala, *f.;* **fire —**, paleta, *f.;* —, *vt.* traspalar.

show [shou] *vt.* mostrar, enseñar, explicar, hacer ver; descubrir, manifestar; probar; —, *vi.* parecer; **to — off,** lucirse; **to — oneself superior to,** sobreponerse a; —, *n.* espectáculo, *m.;* muestra, *f.;* exposición, *f.;* (theat.) función, *f.;* **— bill,** cartelón, cartel, *m.;* **— boat,** buque-teatro, *m.;* **— card,** rótulo, cartel, letrero, *m.*

showcase [shou-keis] *n.* escaparate, mostrador, *m.,* vitrina, *f.*

shower [shauar] *n.* aguacero, chubasco, *m.;* llovizna, *f.;* fiesta de regalos (para una novia, etc.); (fig.) abundancia, *f.;* **— bath,** baño de ducha o de regadera; —, *vi.* llover; —, *vt.* derramar profusamente.

showman [shou-man] *n.* empresario, director de espectáculos públicos; (fig.) buen actor.

showmanship [shou-man-ship] *n.* habilidad para presentar espectáculos.

shown [shoun] *p.p.* del verbo **show.**

showroom [shou-rum] *n.* sala de muestras; sala de exhibición de modelos.

shrank [shrank] *pretérito* del verbo **shrink.**

shrapnel [shrap-nel] *n.* granada de metralla.

shred [shred] *n.* cacho, *m.,* pedazo pequeño; triza, *f.;* jirón, *m.;* —, *vt.* picar, hacer trizas; rallar.

shrew [shru] *n.* mujer de mal genio; (zool.) musgaño, *m.*

shrewd [shrud] *adj.* astuto, sagaz; mordaz.

shrewdness [shrud-nes] *n.* astucia, *f.;* sagacidad, *f.*

shriek [shrik] *vi.* chillar; —, *n.* chillido, *m.*

shrill [shril] *adj.* agudo, penetrante, chillón.

shrimp [shrimp] *n.* camarón, *m.;* hombrecillo, *m.*

shrine [shrain] *n.* relicario, *m.;* tumba de santo; (eccl.) trono, *m.*

shrink [shrink] *vi.* encoger (una tela); encogerse, rehuir; —, *vt.* contraer, encoger.

shrivel [shri-vel] *vt.* y *vi.* arrugar, arrugarse, encogerse.

shrub [shrab] *n.* arbusto, *m.*

shrubbery [shra-be-ri] *n.* arbustos, *m. pl.*

shrug [shrag] *vi.* encogerse de hombros; —, *n.* encogimiento de hombros.

shrunk [shrank] *p.p.* del verbo **shrink.**

shuck [shak] *n.* cáscara, *f.;* descascarar, desgranar.

shudder [sha-dar] *vi.* estremecerse, despeluzarse; —, *n.* despeluzamiento, temblor, estremecimiento, *m.*

shuffle [sha-fel] *vt.* y *vi.* poner en confusión, desordenar; barajar los naipes; trampear; tergiversar; arrastrar (los pies); —, *n.* barajadura, *f.;* treta, *f.*

shuffling [sha-flin] *n.* tramoya, *f.;* acción de arrastrar (los pies).

shun [shan] *vt.* huir, evitar.

shut [shat] *vt.* cerrar, encerrar.

shutdown [shat-daun] *n.* paro, *m.;* cesación de trabajo.

shy [shai] *adj.* tímido; reservado; vergonzoso; contenido; pudoroso.

shyness [shai-nes] *n.* timidez, *f.*

Siamese [saia-mis] *n.* y *adj.* siamés, esa.

sick [sik] *adj.* malo, enfermo; disgustado, aburrido.

sicken [si-ken] *vt.* y *vi.* enfermar, enfermarse.

sickening [sik-nin] *adj.* repugnante, asqueroso, nauseabundo.

sickle [si-kel] *n.* hoz, segadera, *f.*

sickly [si-kli] *adj.* enfermizo, malsano.

sickness [sik-nes] *n.* enfermedad, *f.*

side [said] *n.* lado, *m.;* costado, *m.;* facción, *f.;* partido, *m.;* — **arms,** armas llevadas al cinto; — **dish,** platillo, entremés, *m.;* — **light,** luz lateral; información incidental; — **line,** negocio o actividad accesorios; — **show,** función o diversión secundaria; —, *adj.* lateral, oblicuo; — **by** —, juntos; —, *vi.* apoyar la opinión (de alguien), declararse a favor (de alguien o algún partido).

sideboard [said-bord] *n.* aparador, *m.*

sideburns [said-berns] *n.* patillas, *f. pl.*

sidelong [said-lon] *adj.* lateral; —, *adv.* lateralmente; oblicuamente.

side-step [said-step] *vt.* evitar; —, *vi.* hacerse a un lado.

sidetrack [said-trak] *vt.* (rail.) desviar a un apartadero; arrinconar; apartarse de.

sidewalk [said-uok] *n.* banqueta, acera, vereda, *f.*

sideways [said-ueis] *adv.* de lado, al través.

siding [sai-din] *n.* cobertura exterior de una casa de madera; (rail.) apartadero, desviadero, *m.*

sierra [sie-ra] *n.* sierra, cadena

de montañas.

sigh [sai] *vi.* suspirar, gemir; —, *n.* suspiro, *m.*

sight [sait] *n.* vista, mira, *f.;* perspectiva, *f.;* mamarracho, espantajo, *m.;* **at first** —, a primera vista; **at** —, a presentación; **gun** —, punto (de escopeta), *m.;* **on** —, a la vista; **sense of** —, ver, *m.*, sentido de la vista; — **draft,** letra o giro a la vista.

sightless [sait-les] *adj.* ciego.

sign [sain] *n.* señal, *f.;* indicio, *m.;* tablilla, *f.;*

signal [sig-nal] *n.* señal, seña, *f.;* aviso, *m.;* —, *adj.* insigne, señalado; — **light,** (rail.) farol (de mano o de disco), *m.;* (naut.) fanal, faro, *m.;* — **man,** (rail.) guardavía, *m.;* — **mast,** semáforo, *m.*, mástil de señales.

signature [sig-na-char] *n.* firma, *f.;* seña, *f.;* signatura, *f.*

significance [sig-ni-fi-kans] *n.* importancia, significación, *f.*

significant [sig-ni-fi-kant] *adj.* significativo, importante.

signify [sig-ni-fai] *vt.* significar; —, *vi.* importar.

sign language [sain-lan-ueig] *n.* lenguaje de señales.

signpost [sain-post] *n.* hito, *m.;* pilar de anuncios.

silence [sai-lens] *n.* silencio, *m.;*

—, *vt.* imponer silencio, hacer callar.

silencer [sai-lan-sar] *n.* silenciador, apagador, *m.;* (Mex.) mofle, *m.*

silent [sai-lent] *adj.* silencioso; callado; mudo; — **partner,** socio comanditario.

silhouette [si-luet] *n.* silueta, *f.*

silica [si-li-ka] *n.* (chem.) sílice, *f.*

silk [silk] *n.* seda, *f.*

silkworm [silk-uerm] *n.* gusano de seda.

silky [sil-ki] *adj.* hecho de seda; sedeño, sedoso.

sill [sil] *n.* umbral de puerta; **window** —, repisa de ventana.

silliness [si-li-nes] *n.* simpleza, bobería, tontería, necedad, *f.*

silly [si-li] *adj.* tonto, imbécil, bobo.

silt [silt] *n.* cieno, limo, légamo, *m.*

silver [sil-var] *n.* plata, *f.;* —, *adj.* de plata; — **dollar,** peso fuerte; — **fox,** zorro plateado; piel de zorro plateado; — **nitrate,** nitrato de plata; — **screen,** pantalla cinematográfica; — **wedding,** bodas de plata; **to** — **plate,** platear.

silverware [sil-va-uear] *n.* cuchillería de plata; vajilla de plata.

silvery [sil-va-ri] *adj.* plateado.

similar [si-mi-lar] *adj.* similar;

semejante; —**ly,** *adv.* en forma similar.

similarity [si-mi-la-ri-ti] *n.* semejanza, *f.*

simile [si-mi-li] *n.* semejanza, similitud, *f.;* símil, *m.*

simmer [si-mar] *vi.* hervir a fuego lento.

simple [sim-pel] *adj.* simple, puro, sencillo.

simple-minded [sim-pel-main-ded] *adj.* imbécil, idiota.

simpleton [sim-pel-ton] *n.* simplón, ona, zonzo, za.

simplicity [sim-pli-si-ti] *n.* simplicidad, *f.;* simpleza, llaneza, *f.*

simplify [sim-pli-fai] *vt.* simplificar.

simply [sim-pli] *adv.* simplemente.

simulate [si-miu-leit] *vt.* simular, fingir.

simultaneous [si-mal-tei-nios] *adj.* simultáneo, sincrónico.

sin [sin] *n.* pecado, *m.;* culpa, *f.;* —, *vi.* pecar, faltar.

since [sins] *adv.* desde entonces; —, *conj.* ya que, pues que, pues, puesto que; —, *prep.* desde, después de.

sincere [sin-siar] *adj.* sencillo; sincero, franco; —**ly,** *adv.* sinceramente; —**ly yours,** (despedida de una carta) su seguro servidor, de usted muy sinceramente, etc.

sincerity [sin-se-ri-ti] *n.* sinceridad, *f.;* llaneza, *f.*

sinew [si-niu] *n.* tendón, *m.;* nervio, *m.*

sing [sing] *vt.* y *vi.* cantar; gorjear (los pájaros).

singe [sindch] *vt.* chamuscar, socarrar.

singer [sin-gar] *n.* cantor, *m.;* cantora, *f.;* cantante, *m.* y *f.*

singing [sin-guin] *n.* canto, *m.,* acción de cantar.

single [sin-guel] *adj.* sencillo, simple, solo; soltero, soltera; —**file,** fila india; uno tras otro; —**man,** soltero, *m.;* — **woman,** soltera, *f.;* —, *vt.* singularizar; separar.

single-breasted [sin-guel-brestid] *adj.* de botonadura sencilla (chaqueta u otra prenda similar).

single-handed [sin-guel-jandid] *adj.* sin ayuda.

single-minded [sin-guel-mainded] *adj.* cándido, sencillo; con un solo propósito.

singleness [sin-guel-nes] *n.* sencillez, sinceridad, *f.;* celibato, *m.,* soltería, *f.*

single-track [sin-guel-trak] *adj.* de una sola vía, de un solo carril; — **mind,** mentalidad estrecha.

singsong [sing-song] *n.* sonsonete, *m.;* tonadita, *f.*

singular [sin-guiu-lar] *adj.* singular, peculiar; (gram.) singular.

sinister [si-nis-tar] *adj.* siniestro; hacia la izquierda; viciado; infeliz, funesto.

sink [sink] *vi.* hundirse; sumergirse; bajarse; penetrar; arruinarse, decaer, sucumbir; —, *vt.* hundir, echar a lo hondo; sumergir; deprimir, destruir; —, *n.* fregadero, *m.*

sinner [si-nar] *n.* pecador, ora.

sinus [si-nos] *n.* seno, *m.*, cavidad, *f.*; seno frontal.

sip [sip] *vt.* y *vi.* tomar a sorbos, sorber; —, *n.* sorbo, *m.*

siphon [sai-fon] *n.* sifón, *m.*; — **bottle,** sifón, *m.*, botella de sifón.

sir [ser] *n.* señor, *m.*; **dear** —, muy señor mío, muy señor nuestro.

sire [saiar] *n.* caballero, *m.*; (poet.) padre, *m.*

siren [saia-ran] *n.* sirena, *f.*

sirloin [ser-loin] *n.* lomo de buey o vaca, solomillo, *m.*

sissy [si-si] *n.* marica, *m.*, varón de modales afeminados.

sister [sis-tar] *n.* hermana, *f.*; religiosa, *f.*

sisterhood [sis-ta-jud] *n.* hermandad, *f.*

sister-in-law [sis-ta-in-lo] *n.* cuñada, *f.*

sisterly [sis-ta-li] *adj.* como hermana.

sit [sit] *vi.* sentarse; estar situado.

sit-down strike [sit-daun-straik] *n.* huelga de brazos caídos.

site [sait] *n.* sitio, *m.*; situación, *f.*; emplazamiento, *m.*; localización,

sitting [si-tin] *n.* sesión, junta, *f.*; sentada, *f.*; postura ante un pintor para un retrato; — **room,** sala, *f.*

situate [si-tiu-eit] *vt.* colocar, situar.

situation [si-tiu-ei-shon] *n.* situación, *f.*; ubicación, *f.*

six [siks] *n.* y *adj.* seis, *m.*

sixteen [siks-tiin] *n.* y *adj.* dieciséis, diez y seis, *m.*

sixteenth [siks-tiinz] *n.* y *adj.* decimosexto, *m.*

sixth [siksz] *n.* y *adj.* sexto, *m.*; — **sense,** sexto sentido, sentido intuitivo; —**ly,** *adv.* en sexto lugar.

sixty [siks-ti] *n.* y *adj.* sesenta, *m.*

size [sais] *n.* tamaño, talle, *m.*; calibre, *m.*; dimensión, *f.*; estatura, *f.*; condición, *f.*; variedad de cola o goma; —, *vt.* encolar; ajustar, calibrar.

sized [saist] *adj.* de tamaño especial; preparado con una especie de cola o goma.

sizzle [si-sel] *vi.* chamuscar, sisear; —, *n.* siseo, *m.*

skate [skeit] *n.* patín, *m.; ice* —, patín de hielo; **roller** —, patín de ruedas; —, *vi.* patinar.

skater [skei-tar] *n.* patinador, ra.

skating [skei-tin] *n.* acto de patinar; — **rink,** patinadero, *m.*, pista para patinar.

skeleton [ske-li-ton] *n.* esqueleto, *m.; —* **key,** llave maestra.

skeptical [skep-ti-kal] *adj.* escéptico.

sketch [skech] *n.* esbozo, *m.;* esquicio, *m.;* bosquejo, *m.;* boceto, *m.;* esquema, *m.;* croquis, *m.;* —, *vt.* esbozar.

ski [ski] *n.* esquí, *m.; —* **jump,** salto en esquíes; pista para esquiar; —, *vi.* patinar con esquíes.

skid [skid] *n.* patinaje (de un auto), *m.;* calza o cuña (para detener una rueda), *f.;* —, *vi.* patinar, resbalarse.

skill [skil] *n.* destreza, pericia, *f.*, ingenio, *m.;* maestría, maña, *f.*

skilled [skild] *adj.* práctico, instruido, versado, diestro.

skillet [ski-let] *n.* cazuela, sartén, *f.*

skim [skim] tratar superficialmente; —, *n.* espuma, *f.*

skin [skin] *n.* cutis, *m.;* cuero, *m.;* piel, *f.;* —, *vt.* desollar; (coll.) robarle dinero (a

alguien).

skinned [skind] *adj.* desollado.

skinny [ski-ni] *adj.* flaco, macilento.

skip [skip] *vi.* saltar, brincar; —, *vt.* pasar, omitir; —, *n.* salto, brinco, *m.*

skirmish [sker-mish] *n.* escaramuza, *f.;* tiroteo, *m.;* —, *vi.* escaramuzar.

skirt [skert] *n.* falda, enagua *f.;* —, *vt.* orillar.

skit [skit] *n.* burla, zumba, *f.;* pasquín, *m.;* sainete, *m.*, piececita cómica o dramática.

skittish [ski-tish] *adj.* espantadizo, retozón; caprichoso; frívolo; —**ly,** *adv.* caprichosamente.

skull [skal] *n.* cráneo, *m.;* calavera, *f.*

skullcap [skal-kap] *n.* gorro, *m.;* casquete, *m.*

skunk [skank] *n.* zorrillo, zorrino, *m.;* persona despreciable.

sky [skai] *n.* cielo, firmamento, *m.; —* **blue,** azul celeste.

sky-high [skai-jai] *adj.* muy alto, por las nubes.

skylark [skai-lark] *n.* (zool.) alondra, *f.;* —, *vi.* bromear, retozar.

skyline [skai-lain] *n.* horizonte, *m.;* perspectiva de una ciudad.

skyrocket [skai-ro-kit] *n.* cohete volador; —, *vi.* elevarse súbitamente, por ej., los precios.

skyscraper [skai-skra-par] *n.* rascacielos, *m.*

slab [slab] *n.* losa, *f.;* plancha, *f.*

slack [slak] *adj.* flojo, perezoso, negligente, lento.

slack, slacken [sla-ken] *vt.* y *vi.* aflojar; ablandar; entibiarse; decaer; relajar; aliviar.

slacker [sla-kar] *n.* cobarde, *m.* y *f.;* hombre que elude sus deberes militares en tiempo de guerra.

slam [slam] *n.* capote (en los juegos de naipes), *m.;* portazo, *m.;* —, *vt.* dar capote; empujar con violencia.

slander [slan-dar] *vt.* calumniar, infamar; —, *n.* calumnia, *f.*

slanderer [slan-da-rar] *n.* calumniador, ra, maldiciente, *m.* y *f.*

slang [slang] *n.* vulgarismo, *m.;* jerga, *f.*

slant [slant] *vi.* inclinarse, pender oblicuamente; —, *vt.* sesgar, inclinar.

slap [slap] *n.* manotada, *f.;* — **on the face,** bofetada, *f.;* —, *adv.* de sopetón; —, *vt.* golpear, dar una bofetada.

slash [slash] *vt.* acuchillar; —, *n.* cuchillada, *f.*

slaughter [slo-tar] *n.* carnicería, matanza, *f.;* —, *vt.* matar atrozmente; matar en la carnicería.

slaughterhouse [slo-ta-jaus] *n.* rastro, matadero, degolladero, *m.*

slave [sleiv] *n.* esclavo, va; —, *vi.* trabajar como esclavo.

slavery [slei-va-ri] *n.* esclavitud, *f.*

slaw [slo] *n.* ensalada de col.

slay [slei] *vt.* matar, quitar la vida.

slayer [sleiar] *n.* asesino, na.

sledge [slech] *n.* rastra, *f.;* — **hammer,** macho, acotillo, *m.,* martillo pesado.

sleek [sliik] *adj.* liso, bruñido; —, *vt.* alisar, pulir.

sleep [sliip] *vi.* dormir; **to — soundly,** dormir profundamente, dormir como un bendito; —, *n.* sueño, *m.*

sleeper [slii-par] *n.* persona que duerme, zángano, *m.;* durmiente, *m.;* (rail.) coche dormitorio; éxito inesperado de librería; película insignificante que resulta un éxito pecuniario.

sleepily [slii-pi-li] *adv.* con somnolencia o torpeza, con sueño.

sleepiness [slii-pi-nes] *n.* adormecimiento, *m.;* **to cause —,** adormecer.

sleeping [slii-pin] *n.* sueño, *m.;* — **bag,** talego para dormir a la intemperie; — **car,** coche dormitorio, vagón cama; — **room,** dormitorio, *m.;* — **sickness,** encefalitis letárgica.

sleepless [sliip-les] *adj.* desvela-

do, sin dormir; **to spend a —
night,** pasar la noche en blanco.

sleepwalker [sliip-ua-ker] *n.*
sonámbulo, la.

sleepwalking [sliip-ua-kin] *n.*
sonambulismo, *m.*

sleepy [slii-pi] *adj.* soñoliento; **to
be —,** tener sueño.

sleepyhead [slii-pi-jed] *n.* dormi-
lón, ona.

sleeve [sliiv] *n.* manga, *f.*

sleeveless [sliiv-les] *adj.* sin
mangas.

slender [slen-dar] *adj.* delgado,
sutil, débil, pequeño; escaso; **—
ly,** *adv.* delgadamente.

slice [slais] *n.* rebanada, lonja,
f.; espátula, *f.*

slicing [slai-sin] *adj.* rebanador;
— machine, máquina cortadora
o rebanadora.

slick [slik] *adj.* liso; lustroso; **—,**
vt. hacer liso o lustroso.

slide [slaid] *vi.* resbalar, deslizarse; **—,** *n.* res-balón, *m.;* resba-
ladero, *m.;* corredera, *f.;* **lantern —,** diapositiva, *f.;* **— rule,**
regla de cálculo; **— valve,** válvula corrediza.

sliding [slai-din] *adj.* deslizante,
corredizo, deslizable; **— door,**
puerta corrediza.

slight [slait] *adj.* ligero, leve,
pequeño; **—,** *n.* descuido, *m.;*
—, *vt.* despreciar.

slim [slim] *adj.* delgado, sutil.

slime [slaim] *n.* lodo, *m.;* sustancia viscosa; pecina, *f.*

slimy [slai-mi] *adj.* viscoso,
pegajoso.

slip [slip] *vi.* resbalar; escapar,
huirse; **—,** *vt.* meter; correr; **to
— on,** ponerse; **—,** *n.* resbalón,
m.; tropiezo, *m.;* escapada, *f.;*
patinazo, *m.;* enagua, combinación, *f.;* **— cover,** funda de
mueble.

slipper [sli-par] zapatilla, *f.*

slippery [sli-pe-ri] *adj.* resbaladizo, deleznable, resbaloso.

slit [slit] *vt.* rajar, hender; **—,** *n.*
raja, hendidura, *f.*

sliver [sli-var] *n.* astilla, tira, *f.;*
—, *vt.* rasgar, cortar en tiras.

slobber [slo-bar] *n.* baba, *f.;* **—,**
vt. babosear; **—,** *vi.* babear.

slogan [slou-gan] *n.* lema, mote,
m.; grito de combate; frase
popularizada para anunciar un
producto.

slope [sloup] *n.* sesgo, *m.;* escar-
pa, *f.;* vertiente, *f.;* declive, *m.;*
cuesta, *f.;* **—,** *vt.* sesgar; **—,** *vi.*
inclinarse.

sloping [slou-pin] *adj.* oblicuo;
inclinado.

sloppy [slo-pi] *adj.* lodoso, fangoso; (coll.) desaliñado, descuidado.

slot [slot] *n.* hendidura, *f.;* **—
machine,** máquina automática

con ranura para monedas.

sloth [slouz] *n.* pereza, *f.; (zool.)* perezoso, *m.*

slothful [slouz-ful] *adj.* perezoso.

slouch [slauch] *vt.* y *vi.* estar cabizbajo (como un patán); bambolearse pesadamente; ponerse gacho; —, *n.* persona incompetente y perezosa; joroba, *f.*

slough [slau] *n.* lodazal, cenagal, *m.;* decaimiento espiritual.

slow [slou] *adj.* tardío, lento, torpe, perezoso; — **motion,** velocidad reducida; —, *vt.* y *vi.* retardar, demorar; **to — down,** reducir o acortar la marcha.

slowly [slou-li] *adv.* despacio, despaciosamente, lentamente.

slowness [slou-nes] *n.* lentitud, tardanza, pesadez, *f.*

slug [slag] *n.* holgazán, zángano, *m.; (zool.)* babosa, *f.; (print.)* lingote, *m.;* —, *vt.* aporrear, golpear fuertemente.

slum [slam] *vi.* visitar viviendas o barrios bajos o escuálidos; — s, *n. pl.* barrios bajos; viviendas escuálidas.

slumber [slam-bar] *vi.* dormitar; —, *n.* sueño ligero.

slump [slamp] *n.* hundimiento, *m.;* quiebra, *f.;* baja considerable de precios o actividades en los negocios.

slur [sler] *vt.* ensuciar; pasar ligeramente; —, *n.* (mus.) ligado, *m.;* afrenta, estigma, calumnia, *f.*

slush [slash] *n.* lodo, barro, cieno, *m.*

sly [slai] *adj.* astuto; furtivo.

small [smol] *adj.* pequeño, menudo, chico.

smallpox [smol-poks] *n.* viruelas, *f. pl.*

smart [smart] *n.* escozor, *m.;* —, *adj.* punzante, agudo, agrio; ingenioso; mordaz; doloroso; inteligente; elegante, apuesto; —, *vi.* escocer, arder.

smartness [smart-nes] *n.* agudeza, viveza, sutileza, *f.;* elegancia, *f.*

smash [smash] *vt.* romper, quebrantar; —, *n.* fracaso, *m.;* (tenis) volea alta.

smear [smiar] *vt.* untar; emporcar; manchar; calumniar.

smell [smel] *vt.* y *vi.* oler; percibir; olfatear; —, *n.* olfato, *m.;* olor, *m.;* hediondez, *f.;* **sense of —,** olfato, *m.*

smelt [smelt] *n.* (ichth.) eperlano, *m.;* —, *vt.* fundir (el metal).

smile [smail] *vi.* sonreir, sonreírse; —, *n.* sonrisa, *f.*

smirk [smerk] *vi.* sonreir burlonamente.

smith [smiz] *n.* forjador de metales; **black—,** herrero, *m.*

smog [smog] *n.* combinación de

humo y niebla.

smoke [smouk] *n.* humo, *m.;* vapor, *m.;* — **screen,** cortina de humo; —, *vt.* y *vi.* ahumar; humear; fumar (tabaco).

smoker [smou-kar] *n.* fumador, *m.;* (rail.) coche fumador.

smokestack [smou-kstak] *n.* chimenea, *f.*

smoking [smou-kin] *adj.* fumífero, que despide humo; **no** —, se prohíbe fumar.

smoky [smou-ki] *adj.* humeante; humoso.

smolder [smoul-dar] *vi.* arder sin llama; existir en forma latente; —, *n.* humo, *m.*

smooth [smuch] *adj.* liso, pulido, llano; suave; afable; —, *vt.* allanar; alisar; lisonjear.

smoothly [smuz-li] *adv.* llanamente; con blandura.

smoothness [smuz-nes] *n.* lisura, *f.;* llanura, *f.;* suavidad, *f.*

smother [sma-dar] *vt.* sofocar; apagar; —, *n.* humareda, *f.*

smoulder [smoul-dar] *vi.* arder debajo de la ceniza; existir en forma latente.

smudge [smadch] *vt.* fumigar; ensuciar, tiznar; —, *n.* tiznadura, mugre, *f.*

smuggle [sma-guel] *vt.* contrabandear.

smuggler [sma-glar] *n.* contrabandista, *m.* y *f.*

smuggling [sma-glin] *n.* contrabando, *m.*

snack [snak] *n.* parte, porción, *f.;* tentempié, refrigerio, *m.,* colación, *f.;* merienda, *f.;* —, *vi.* merendar.

snag [snag] *n.* protuberancia, *f.;* raigón de diente; diente que sobresale; rama de un árbol escondida en el fondo de un lago o río; tocón, *m.;* obstáculo inesperado.

snail [sneil] *n.* caracol, *m.*

snake [sneik] *n.* culebra, sierpe, serpiente, *f.;* —, *vi.* culebrear.

snap [snap] *vt.* y *vi.* romper; agarrar; morder; contestar con grosería; chasquear; es-tallar; **to** — **one's fingers,** castañetear los dedos; **to** — **open,** abrirse de golpe; **to** — **a picture,** tomar una instantánea; —, *n.* estallido, *m.;* castañeteo, *m.;* corchete, *m.;* —, *adj.* repentino; — **judgment,** opinión a la ligera.

snapper [sna-par] *n.* (ichth.) pargo, *m.;* corchete.

snapshot [snap-shot] *n.* instantánea, fotografía, *f.*

snare [snear] *n.* lazo, *m.;* trampa, *f.;* garlito, *m.;* trapisonda, *f.;* — **drum,** pequeño tambor militar; **to fall into a** —, caer en la ratonera; —, *vt.* cazar animales con lazos; trapisondear.

snarl [snarl] *vi.* regañar, gruñir;

—, *vt.* enredar; —, *n.* gruñido, *m.;* complicación, *f.*

snatch [snach] *vt.* arrebatar; agarrar; —, arrebatamiento, *m.;* arrebatiña, *f.;* pedazo, *m.;* ratito, *m.*

sneak [snik] *vi.* arrastrar; ratear; **to — out,** salirse a escondidas, tomar las de Villadiego; —, *n.* persona traicionera; **—thief,** ratero, ra.

sneer [sniar] *vi.* hablar con desprecio; fisgarse; —, *n.* fisga, *f.*

sneeze [snis] *vi.* estornudar; —, *n.* estornudo, *m.*

snicker [sni-kar] *vi.* reir a menudo y socarronamente; —, *n.* risita socarrona.

sniff [snif] *vi.* resollar con fuerza.

sniffle [sni-fel] *vi.* aspirar ruidosamente por la nariz; gimotear.

snip [snip] *vt.* tijeretear; —, *n.* tijeretada, *f.;* pedazo pequeño, pedacito, *m.*

sniper [sni-par] *n.* tirador apostado.

snob [snob] *n.* snob, *m.* y *f.,* persona presuntuosa; advenedizo social o intelectual.

snobbish [sno-bish] *adj.* presuntuoso; jactancioso; propio del snob.

snoop [snup] *vi.* (coll.) espiar, fisgar, acechar; escudriñar; —, *n.* (coll.) metiche, fisgón, *m.*

snooze [snus] *n.* sueño ligero; —

, *vi.* dormir ligeramente, dormitar.

snore [snor] *vi.* roncar; —, *n.* ronquido, *m.*

snorkel [snor-kel] *n.* doble tubo de respiración para submarinos; **— pen,** pluma fuente que se llena mediante un tubo aspirante.

snort [snort] *vi.* resoplar, bufar como un caballo fogoso.

snout [snaut] *n.* hocico, *m.;* trompa de elefante; (coll.) nariz, *f.;* boquilla (de manguera, etc.), *f.*

snow [snou] *n.* nieve, *f.;* **— line,** límite de las nieves perpetuas; —, *vi.* nevar.

snowball [snou-bol] *n.* pelota de nieve.

snowbird [snou-berd] *n.* (orn.) variedad de pinzón.

snowfall [snou-fol] *n.* nevada, *f.*

snowflake [snou-fleik] *n.* coro de nieve.

snowplow [snou-plou] *n.* quitanieve, *m.*

snowstorm [snou-storm] *n.* nevada, *f.,* tormenta de nieve.

snow-white [snou-uait] *adj.* níveo, blanco como la nieve.

snowy [snoui] *adj.* nevoso; nevado.

snub [snab] *vt.* desairar, tratar con desprecio; —, *n.* altanería, *f.;* desaire, *m.*

snug [snag] *adj.* abrigado; conveniente, cómodo, agradable, grato.

snuggle [sna-guel] *vi.* acurrucarse; estar como apretado; arrimarse a otro en busca de calor o cariño.

so [sou] *adv.* así; tal; por consiguiente; tanto; **and — forth,** y así sucesivamente; **—, and —,** Fulano de Tal, *m.,* Fulana de Tal, *f.; —* **much,** tanto; **—** **that,** para que, de modo que; **— then,** conque; **that is —,** eso es, así es; **—what?** ¿y qué?

soak [souk] *vt.* y *vi.* remojarse.

soap [soup] *n.* jabón, *m.;* **cake of —,** pastilla de jabón; **—** **bubble,** globo de jabón; **—opera,** (coll.) telenovela, *f.;* radio-novela, *f.;* **—,** *vt.* jabonar, enjabonar.

soapsuds [soup-sods] *n. pl.* jabonaduras, *f. pl.,* espuma de jabón.

soapy [sou-pi] *adj.* jabonoso.

soar [sor] *vi.* remontarse, sublimarse.

soaring [sou-rin] *n.* vuelo muy alto; acción de remontarse.

sob [sob] *n.* sollozo, *m.;* **—,** *vi.* sollozar.

sober [so-bar] *adj.* sobrio; serio; **—ly,** *adv.* sobriamente; juiciosamente.

sobriety [sou-braia-ti] *n.* sobriedad, *f.;* seriedad, gravedad, *f.*

soccer [so-kar] *n.* fútbol inglés, *m.*

sociability [sou-sha-bi-li-ti] *n.* sociabilidad, *f.*

sociable [sou-sha-bol] *adj.* sociable, comunicativo.

social [sou-shal] *adj.* social, sociable; **—** **sciences,** ciencias sociales; **—** **security,** seguro social; **—** **service,** **—** **work,** servicio social, servicio en pro de las clases pobres; **—** **worker,** trabajador social; **—,** *n.* tertulia, *f.*

socialism [sou-sha-li-sem] *n.* socialismo, *m.*

socialist [sou-sha-list] *n.* y *adj.* socialista, *m.* y *f.*

socialistic [sou-sha-lis-tik] *adj.* socialista.

socialize [sou-sha-lais] *vt.* socializar.

society [so-saia-ti] *n.* sociedad, *f.;* compañía, *f.*

sociological [sou-siou-lo-yi-kal] *adj.* sociológico.

sociologist [sou-sio-lo-yist] *n.* sociólogo, ga.

sociology [sou-sio-lo-yi] *n.* sociología, *f.*

sock [sok] *n.* calcetín, *m.;* zueco, *m.;* (coll.) golpe fuerte; **—,** *vt.* golpear con violencia.

socket [so-kit] *n.* cubo, encaje, casquillo, *m.;* alveolo de un diente; encastre, *m.;* **eye —,**

órbita, *f.*, cuenca del ojo; **elec-tric —,** enchufe, *m.*

soda [sou-da] *n.* sosa, soda, *f.;* **baking —,** bicarbonato de sosa o de soda; **— cracker,** galleta de soda; **— fountain,** fuente de sodas; **— water,** gaseosa, *f.*

sodium [sou-diom] *n.* (chem.) sodio, *m.;* **— chloride,** cloruro de sodio, sal de cocina.

sofa [sou-fa] *n.* sofá, *m.*

soft [soft] *adj.* blando, mole, suave; benigno; tierno, compasivo; jugoso; afeminado; **—coal,** hulla grasa, carbón bituminoso; **— drink,** refresco, *m.*, bebida no alcohólica; **— water,** agua dulce, agua no cruda; **—ly,** *adv.* con suavidad, quedamente.

softball [soft-bol] *n.* juego parecido al béisbol que se juega con pelota blanda.

soft-boiled [soft-boild] *adj.* cocido, pasado por agua; **—eggs,** huevos pasados por agua.

soften [so-fen] *vt.* ablandar, mitigar; enternecer; reblandecer, suavizar.

softness [soft-nes] *n.* suavidad, blandura, *f.;* dulzura, *f*

soft-spoken [soft-spoken] *adj.* afable, que habla con dulzura.

soggy [so-gui] *adj.* empapado, mojado.

soil [soil] *vt.* ensuciar, emporcar;

—, *n.* mancha; suelo, *m.*, tierra, *f.*

soiled [soild] *adj.* sucio; **— clothes,** ropa sucia.

sol [sol] *n.* (mus.) sol, *m.;* sol (moneda del Perú), *m.*

solace [so-lis] *vt.* solazar, consolar; **—,** *n.* consuelo, solaz, *m.*

solar [sou-lar] *adj.* solar; **— plexus,** (anat.) plexo solar; **— system,** sistema solar; **— year,** año solar.

sold [sould] *pret.* y *p.p.* del verbo **sell,** vender; **— out,** agotado, vendido.

solder [soul-dar] *vt.* soldar; **—,** *n.* soldadura, *f.*

soldier [soul-diar] *n.* soldado, *m.*

sole [soul] *n.* planta del pie; suela del zapato; **—,** *adj.* único, solo; **—,** *vt.* solar, poner suela al calzado.

sole [soul] *n.* (ichth.) lenguado.

solemn [so-lem] *adj.* solemne.

solemnity [so-lem-ni-ti] *n.* solemnidad, *f.*

solemnize [so-lem-nais] *vt.* solemnizar.

solicit [so-li-sit] *vt.* solicitar; implorar; pedir.

solicitation [so-li-si-tei-shon] *n.* solicitación, *f.*

solicitor [so-li-si-tar] *n.* procurador, solicitador, *m.*

solicitous [so-li-si-tos] *adj.* solícito, diligente.

solicitude [so-li-si-tiud] *n.* solicitud, *f.;* cuidado, *m.*

solid [so-lid] *adj.* sólido, compacto; — **color,** color entero, *m.;* — **geometry,** geometría del espacio; —, *n.* sólido, *m.*

solidarity [so-li-da-ri-ti] *n.* solidaridad, *f.*

solidify [so-li-di-fai] *vt.* congelar; solidar; solidificar.

solidity [so-li-di-ti] *n.* solidez, *f.*

soliloquize [so-li-lo-kuais] *vi.* soliloquiar, hablar a solas.

soliloquy [so-li-lo-kui] *n.* soliloquio, *m.*

solitaire [so-li-tear] *n.* solitario (diamante grueso), *m.;* solitario (juego de una sola persona, generalmente de naipes), *m.*

solitary [so-li-ta-ri] *adj.* solitario, retirado; —, *n.* ermitaño, *m.*

solitude [so-li-tiud] *n.* soledad, *f.;* vida solitaria.

solo [sou-lou] *n.* y *adj.* solo, *m.*

soloist [sou-louist] *n.* solista, *m.* y *f.*

soluble [so-liu-bol] *adj.* soluble.

solution [so-lu-shon] *n.* solución, *f.*

solve [solv] *vt.* solver, disolver; aclarar, resolver.

solvency [sol-ven-si] *n.* solvencia, *f.*

somber [som-bar] *adj.* sombrío, nebuloso, oscuro; lúgubre, triste, tétrico, melancólico.

some [sam] *adj.* algo de, un poco de; algún, alguna; —, *pron.* unos pocos, ciertos, algunos.

somebody [sam-ba-di] *n.* alguien, *m.,* alguno, na.

somehow [sam-jau] *adv.* de algún modo, de alguna manera.

someone [sam-uan] *pron.* alguien, alguna persona.

somersault, somerset [sa-ma-solt], [sa-ma-set] *n.* voltereta, *f* ; salto mortal; —, *vi.* dar un salto mortal.

something [sam-sin] *n.* alguna cosa; algo, *m.;* — **else,** otra cosa, alguna otra cosa.

sometime [sam-taim] *adv.* en algún tiempo.

sometimes [sam-taims] *adv.* algunas veces, a veces.

somewhat [sam-uot] *n.* un poco, algo, algún tanto; —, *adv.* algún tanto. un poco; — **cold,** algo frío, un poco frío.

somewhere [sam-uear] *adv.* en alguna parte.

somnambulism [som-nam-biu-li-sem] *n.* sonambulismo, *m.*

son [son] *n.* hijo, *m.*

sonata [so-na-ta] *n.* (mus.) sonata, *f.*

song [song] *n.* canción, *f.,* canto, *m.;* cántico, *m.;* **Song of Solomon,** Cantar de los Cantares; — **sparrow,** gorrión canoro; — **thrush,** tordo canoro; — **writer,** compositor de canciones.

songbook [song-berd] *n.* cancionero, *m.,* libro de canciones.

sonic [so-nik] *adj.* sónico; — **barrier,** barrera sónica.

son-in-law [san-in-lo] *n.* yerno, *m.*

sonnet [so-nit] *n.* soneto, *m.*

sonorous [so-no-ros] *adj.* sonoro.

soon [sun] *adv.* presto, pronto, prontamente; **as — as,** luego que, en cuanto; **as — as possible,** lo más pronto posible.

sooner [su-ner] *adv.* más pronto, primero; más bien.

soothe [suuz] *vt.* sosegar, calmar, tranquilizar.

sooty [su-ti] *adj.* holliniento, fuliginoso.

sop [sop] *n.* pan mojado, *m.;* soborno, *m.,* adulación, *f.*

sophisticate [so-fis-ti-keit] *n.* persona de mundo.

sophisticated [so-fis-ti-kei-tid] *adj.* artificial, afectado; re-finado y sutil.

sophistication [so-fis-ti-kei-shon] *n.* afectación, *f.;* artificio, *m.* falta de sencillez.

sophomore [so-fo-mor] *n.* estudiante de segundo año de una escuela superior o universidad.

sopping [so-pin] *adj.* ensopado; — **wet,** empapado.

soprano [so-pra-nou] *n.* (mus.) soprano, tiple, *m.;* — **singer,** tiple, soprano, *f.*

sorcerer [sor-se-rer] *n.* hechicero, brujo, *m.*

sorceress [sor-se-res] *n.* hechicera, bruja, *f.*

sorcery [sor-se-ri] *n.* hechizo, encanto, *m.;* hechice-ría, *f.*

sordid [sor-did] *adj.* sórdido, sucio; avariento; —**ly,** *adv.* sórdidamente.

sore [sor] *n.* llaga, úlcera, *f.;* —, *adj.* doloroso, penoso; (coll.) enojado, resentido; — **throat,** carraspera, *f.,* mal de garganta.

sorghum [sor-gom] *n.* (bot.) sorgo, *m.,* zahína, *f.;* melaza de sorgo.

sorority [so-ro-ri-ti] *n.* hermandad de mujeres.

sorrow [so-rou] *n.* pesar, *m.;* tristeza, *f.;* —, *vi.* entristecerse.

sorry [so-ri] *adj.* triste; afligido; miserable; **to be —,** sentir; **to feel — for,** compadecerse (de alguien), tenerle lástima; **I am very —,** lo siento mucho.

sort [sort] *n.* género, *m.,* especie, *f.;* calidad, clase, *f.;* manera, *f.;* —, *vt.* separar, clasificar.

soul [soul] *n.* alma, *f.;* esencia, *f.;* persona, *f.*

sound [saund] *adj.* sano; entero; puro; firme; (com.) solvente; — **barrier,** barrera sónica; —

track, guía sonora (en películas cinematográficas); **— wave,** onda sonora; **—ly,** *adv.* vigorosamente; **—,** *n.* tienta, sonda, *f.;* sonido, ruido, *m.;* son, *m.;* estrecho, *m.;* **at the — of,** al son de; **—,** *vt.* (naut.) sondar; tocar; celebrar; sondar (intenciones) ; **—,** *vi.* sonar, resonar.

sounding [saun-din] *n.* (naut.) sondeo, *m.;* **—,** *adj.* sonante; **— line,** sondaleza, *f.*

soundproof [saund-pruf] *adj.* a prueba de sonido.

soup [sup] *n.* sopa, *f.;* **— plate,** plato sopero; **vegetable —,** sopa de verdura.

sour [sauar] *adj.* agrio, ácido; áspero; **— grapes,** uvas verdes; (fig.) indiferencia hacia algo que no se puede poseer; **—,** *vt.* y *vi.* agriar, acedar; agriarse.

source [sors] *n.* manantial, *m.,* mina, *f.;* principio, origen, *m.*

south [sauz] *n.* sur, sud, mediodía, *m.;* **S—,** la región meridional (en Estados Unidos generalmente la región al sur del Río Ohio); **—,** *adj.* meridional, del sur.

southeast [sauz-ist] *n.* y *adj.* sureste, sudeste, *m.*

southern [sau-zarn] *adj.* meridional.

southerner [sau-zar-nar] *n.* persona de la región meridional (en Estados Unidos generalmente el nacido o que reside al sur del Río Ohio).

southernmost [sauz-moust] *adj.* lo más al sur.

southland [sauz-lan] *n.* región meridional, región del sur.

southward [sauz-uod] *adv.* hacia el sur, con rumbo al sur.

southwest [sauz-uest] *n.* y *adj.* sudoeste, *m.;* **—,** *adv.* del sudoeste; hacia el sudoeste.

souvenir [su-ve-niar] *n.* recuerdo, *m.;* memoria, *f.*

sovereign [so-ve-rein] *n.* y *adj.* soberano, na.

sovereignty [so-ve-rein-ti] *n.* soberanía, *f.*

sow [sou] *vt.* sembrar, sementar; esparcir.

soy [soi] *n.* soja, *f.;* semilla de soja; salsa de soja.

space [speis] *n.* espacio, trecho, *m.;* intersticio, *m.;* lugar, *m.*

spacecraft [speis-kraft] *n.* nave espacial.

space ship [speis-ship] *n.* nave espacial.

spacious [spei-shos] *adj.* espacioso, amplio; **—ly,** *adv.* con bastante espacio.

spade [speid] *n.* laya, azada, *f.;* (en los naipes) espada, *f.;* **—,** *vt.* azadonar.

Spain [spein] España, *f.*

span [span] *n.* palmo, *m.;* espacio, *m.;* — **of a bridge,** tramo, *m.;* —, *vt.* medir a palmos; extenderse sobre; atravesar.

Spaniard [spa-niad] *n.* español, la.

spaniel [spa-niel] *n.* sabueso, *m.*

Spanish [spa-nish] *adj.* español; — **America,** Hispanoamérica, *f.,* América española; — **American,** hispanoamericano, na; — **ballad,** romance, *m.;* — **language,** castellano, *m.*

spank [spank] *n.* palmada, *f.;* —, *vt.* pegar, dar palmadas, dar nalgadas.

spanking [span-kin] *n.* nalgada, *f.*

spar [spar] *n.* espato, *m.;* —, *vi.* boxear.

spare [spear] *vt.* y *vi.* ahorrar, economizar, per-donar; vivir con economía; —, *adj.* es-caso, económico; de reserva; — **time,** tiempo desocupado; — **tire,** neumático o llanta de repuesto o de reserva; — **parts,** piezas de repuesto.

sparerib [spear-rib] *n.* costilla de puerco.

sparing [spea-rin] *adj.* frugal; parco; económico; —**ly,** *adv.* parcamente.

spark [spark] *n.* chispa, *f.;* bujía, *f.;* (poet.) centella, *f.;* (coll.) pisaverde, *m.;* — **plug,** bujía, *f.;* —, *vi.* echar chispas, chispear;

—, *vt.* y *vi.* (coll.) enamorar; cortejar.

sparkle [spar-kel] *n.* centella, chispa, *f.;* —, *vi.* chispear; espumar.

sparkling [spar-klin] *adj.* cente-lleante; efervescente; vivo, ani-mado; — **wine,** vino espumoso; — **personality,** personalidad atrayente.

sparrow [spa-rou] *n.* gorrión, pardal, *m.;* — **hawk,** gavilán, *m.*

sparse [spars] *adj.* escaso; esparcido.

spasm [spa-sem] *n.* espasmo, *m.*

spastic [spas-tik] *adj.* (med.) espástico; espasmódico.

spatula [spa-tiu-la] *n.* espátula, *f.*

speak [spik] *vt.* y *vi.* hablar; decir; conversar; pronunciar; **to** — **plainly,** hablar con claridad; **to** — **in torrents,** hablar a bor-botones; **to** — **to,** dirigirse a.

speaker [spi-kar] *n.* el que habla; orador, ra; **S—of the House,** presidente de la Cámara de Representantes (en E.U.A.).

speaking [spi-kin] *n.* habla, *f.;* oratoria, *f.;* —, *adj.* que habla; — **trumpet,** portavoz, *m.;* — **tube,** tubo acústico.

spear [spiar] *n.* lanza, *f.;* arpón, *m.;* —, *vt.* herir con lanza;

alancear.

spearmint [spia-mint] *n.* hierbabuena, *f.*

special [spe-shal] *adj.* especial,
particular.

special-delivery [spe-shal-de-li-
ve-ri] *adj.* de urgencia; de
entrega inm ediata; — **letter,**
carta urgente, carta de entrega
inmediata; — **stamp,** sello de
entrega inmediata.

specialist [spe-sha-list] *n.* especialista, *m.* y *f.*

specialty [spe-shia-li-ti] *n.* especialidad, *f.,* rasgo característico.

specialize [spe-sha-lais] *vt.* y *vi.*
especializar; especializarse.

specialty [spe-shal-ti] *n.* especialidad, *f.*

species [spi-shis] *n.* especie,
clase, *f.;* género, *m.*

specific [spe-si-fik] *adj.* específico; — **gravity,** densidad específica; peso específico; —, *n.*
específico, *m.;* —**ally,** *adv.*
específicamente.

specification [spe-si-fi-kei-shon]
n. especificación, *f.;* —**s,** *pl.*
pliego de condiciones.

specify [spe-si-fai] *vt.* especificar.

specimen [spe-si-men] *n.* espécimen, *m.,* muestra, *f.;* prueba, *f.*

speck, speckle [spek], [spe-kel]
n. mancha, mácula, tacha, *f.;*
—, *vt.* manchar, abigarrar.

spectacle [spek-ta-kol] *n.* espectáculo, *m.;* exhibición, *f.;* —**s,**
n. pl. anteojos, espejuelos, *m.
pl.,* gafas, *f pl.*

spectacular [spek-ta-kiu-lar] *adj.*
espectacular, aparatoso; grandioso; —, *n.* programa extraordinario (de televisión).

spectator [spek-tei-tar] *n.* espectador, ra.

specter, spectre [spek-tar] *n.*
espectro, *m.*

spectral [spek-tral] *adj.* aduen-
dado; espectrométrico; —
analysis, análisis espectral,
análisis del espectro solar.

spectrum [spek-trom] *n.* espectro, *m.*

speculate [spe-kiu-leit] *vi.* especular; reflexionar.

speculation [spe-kiu-lei-shon] *n.*
especulación, *f.;* especulativa,
f.; meditación, *f.*

speculative [spe-kiu-la-tiv] *adj.*
especulativo; teórico.

speech [spich] *n.* habla, *f.;* discurso, *m.,* oración, arenga, *f.;*
conversación, *f.;* perorata, *f.;*
(theat.) parlamento, *m.;* **to
make a** —, perorar, pronunciar
un discurso.

speechless [spich-les] *adj.* mudo,
sin habla.

speed [spid] *n.* prisa, *f.;* celeri-
dad, rapidez, *f.;* prontitud, *f.;*
velocidad, *f.;* **at full** —, a todo

escape, a toda velocidad, a toda prisa, de corrida; — **limit,** límite de velocidad, velocidad máxima; —, *vt.* apresurar; despachar; ayudar; —, *vi.* darse prisa.

speedboat [spid-bout] *n.* lancha de carrera.

speedily [spi-di-li] *adv.* aceleradamente, de prisa.

speedometer [spi-do-mi-tar] *n.* velocímetro, celerímetro, *m.*

speedway [spid-uei] *n.* autopista, *f.;* autódromo, *m.*

speedy [spi-di] *adj.* veloz, pronto, diligente.

spell [spel] *n.* hechizo, encanto, *m.;* periodo de descanso; periodo corto; —, *vt.* y *vi.* deletrear; hechizar, encantar; (coll.) revezar.

spellbound [spel-baund] *adj.* fascinado, encantado.

spelling [spe-lin] *n.* ortografía, *f.;* deletreo, *m.*

spend [spend] *vt.* gastar; disipar; consumir; **to —(time),** pasar (tiempo); —, *vi.* hacer gastos.

spender [spen-dar] *n.* gastador, ra; derrochador, ra.

spent [spent] *adj.* alcanzado de fuerzas; gastado.

sperm [sperm] *n.* esperma, *f.;* semen, *m.*

spew [spiu] *vt.* y *vi.* vomitar.

sphere [sfiar] *n.* esfera, *f.*

spheric, spherical [sfe-rik], [sfe-ri-kal] *adj.* esférico.

sphinx [sfinks] *n.* esfinge, *f.,* persona de carácter misterioso e indescifrable.

spice [spais] *n.* especia, *f ;* sal, *f.,* picante, *m.;* —**s,** especiería, *f.,* especias, *f. pl.;* —, *vt.* sazonar con especias.

spicy [spai-si] *adj.* especiado; aromático; picante.

spider [spai-dar] *n.* araña, *f.*

spigot [spi-got] *n.* llave, *f.,* grifo, *m.;* espita, *f.*

spike [spaik] *n.* alcayata, escarpia, *f.;* púa metálica de algunos zapatos para deporte; (bot.) variedad de espiga.

spill [spil] *vt.* derramar, verter; —, *n.* clavija, espiga, *f.;* astilla, *f.;* (coll.) vuelco, *m.* spillway, *n.* vertedero lateral; canal de desagüe.

spin [spin] *vt.* hilar; alargar, prolongar; —, *vi.* hilar; girar, dar vueltas; —, *n.* vuelta, *f.;* paseo, *m.;* giro, *m.*

spinach [spi-nich] *n.* espinaca, *f.*

spinal [spai-nal] *adj.* espinal; — **column,** espina dorsal.

spindle [spin-del] *n.* huso, *m.;* quicio, *m.;* carretel, *m.;* — **of a lathe,** (mech.) mandril, *m.*

spine [spain] *n.* espinazo, *m.,* espina, *f.*

spinster [spin-tar] *n.* hilandera,

f.; soltera, *f.;* solterona, *f.*

spiral [spai-ral] *adj.* espiral; —
staircase, escalera de caracol;
—ly, *adv.* en forma espiral.

spire [spaiar] *n.* espira, *f ;* cúspide, cima, *f.;* aguja (de una
torre), *f.*

spirit [spi-rit] *n.* aliento, *m.;*
espíritu, *m.;* ánimo, valor, *m.;*
brío, *m.;* humor, *m.;* fantasma,
m.; **—,** *vt.* incitar, animar; **to —
away,** arrebatar, secuestrar.

spirited [spi-ri-tid] *adj.* vivo,
brioso; **—ly,** *adv.* con espíritu.

spiritual [spi-ri-tiual] *adj.* espiritual.

spiritualism, spiritism [spi-ri-
tiua-li-sem], [spir-ri-tism] *n.*
espiritismo, *m.*

spiritualist [spi-ri-tiua-list] *n.*
espiritualista, *m.* y *f.*

spit [spit] *n.* asador, *m.;* saliva,
f., expectoración, *f.;* **—,** *vt.* y *vi.*
escupir, salivar.

spite [spait] *n.* rencor, *m.,* malevolencia, *f.;* **in — of,** a pesar de,
a despecho de; **—,** *vt.* dar
pesar, mortificar.

spiteful [spait-ful] *adj.* rencoro-
so, malicioso; **—ly,** *adv.* malig-
namente, con tirria.

splash [splash] *vt.* salpicar,
enlodar; **—,** *n.* salpicadura,
rociada, *f.*

splay [splei] *vt.* exponer a la
vista; extender; **—,** *adj.* exten-

dido; desmañado.

spleen [splin] *n.* bazo, *m.;*
esplín, *m.*

splendid [splen-did] *adj.* espléndido, magnífico.

splendor [splen-dor] *m.;* pompa,
f.; brillo, *m.*

splint [splint] *n.* astilla, *f.;*
cabestrillo, *m.*

splinter [splin-tar] *n.* cacho, *m.;*
astilla, *f.;* brizna, *f.;* **—,** *vt.* astillar; **—,** *vi.* astillarse.

split [split] *vt.* hender, rajar; **—,**
vi. henderse; **to — with laughter,** desternillarse de risa; **—,**
n. hendidura, raja, *f.;* **banana
—,** mezcla de helados con jarabe, nueces y plátano.

splotch [sploch] *vt.* manchar,
salpicar; **—,** *n.* mancha, *f.,*
borrón, *m.*

spoil [spoil] *vt.* pillar, robar; despojar; contaminar; arruinar;
dañar; pudrir; mimar demasiado; echar a perder; **—,** *vi.*
corromperse; dañarse, echarse
a perder; **—s,** *n. pl.* despojo,
botín, *m.*

spoke [spouk] *n.* rayo de la
rueda; **—,** *pretérito* del verbo
speak.

spoken [spou-ken] *p.p.* del verbo
speak.

spokesman [spouks-man] *n.*
interlocutor, *m.;* vocero, *m.;*
portavoz, *m.*

sponge [spandch] *n.* esponja, *f.;* —, *vt.* limpiar con esponja.

spongy [spand-chi] *adj.* esponjoso.

sponsor [spon-sar] *n.* fiador, *m.;* padrino, *m.;* madrina, *f;* garante, *m.* y *f.;* persona responsable.

spontaneity [spon-ta-nei-ti] *n.* espontaneidad, voluntariedad, *f.*

spontaneous [spon-tei-nios] *adj.* espontáneo; — **combustion,** combustión espontánea.

spool [spul] *n.* canilla, broca, bobina, *f.,* carrete, carretel, *m.;* — **of thread,** carrete de hilo.

spoon [spun] *n.* cuchara, *f.*

spoonful [spun-ful] *n.* cucharada, *f.*

sporadic [spo-ra-dik] *adj.* esporádico.

sport [sport] *n.* juego, retozo, *m.;* juguete, divertimiento, recreo, pasatiempo, *m.;* deporte, *m.;* —, *adj.* deportivo; — **shirt,** camisa para deportes, camisa sport; —, *vt.* lucir, —, *vi.* chancear, juguetear.

sporting [spor-tin] *adj.* deportivo.

sportive [spor-tiv] *adj.* festivo, juguetón.

sportsman [sports-man] *n.* deportista, *m.;* persona equitativa y generosa en los deportes; buen perdedor.

sportsmanship [sports-man-ship] *n.* espíritu de equidad en los deportes y en los negocios.

spot [spot] *n.* mancha, *f.;* borrón, *m.;* sitio, lugar, *m.;* — **cash,** dinero al contado; — **remover,** quitamanchas, sacámanchas, *m.;* —, *vt.* manchar; (coll.) observar, reconocer.

spotless [spot-les] *adj.* limpio, inmaculado; puro; sin mancha.

spotlight [spot-lait] *n.* luz concentrada; proyector, *m.;* (auto.) faro giratorio; —, *vt.* dar realce.

spotted, spotty [spo-tid], [spo-ti] *adj.* lleno de manchas, sucio; moteado.

spouse [spaus] *n.* esposo, sa.

spout [spaut] *vt.* y *vi.* arrojar agua con mucho ímpetu; borbotar; chorrear; —, *n.* llave de fuente; gárgola, *f.;* bomba marina; chorro de agua; pico (de una cafetera, etc.), *m.*

sprainn [sprein] *vt.* torcer; —, *n.* torcedura, *f.*

sprang [spran] *pretérito* del verbo **spring.**

sprawl [sprol] *vi.* revolcarse; arrastrarse con las piernas extendidas; extenderse irregularmente (como las viñas).

spray [sprei] *n.* rociada, *f.;* ramita, *f;* espuma del mar; rociador; vaporizador, *m.;* — **gun,** pistola pulverizadora; — **net,**

loción para rociar el cabello; —, *vt.* rociar, pulverizar.

spraying [spreiin] *n.* rociada, *f.;* riego, *m.;* pulverización, *f.*

spread [spred] *vt.* extender, desplegar, tender; esparcir, divulgar; regar; untar; propagar; generalizar; —, *vi.* **extenderse, desplegarse;** — **over,** cubrir; —, *n.* extensión, dilatación, *f.;* **sobrecama,** *f.;* —, *adj.* extendido, aumentado.

spreadsheet [spred-shit] *n.* hoja de cálculo, *f.*

spring [sprait-li] *vi.* brotar, arrojar; nacer, provenir; dimanar, originarse; saltar, brincar; —, *vt.* soltar, hacer saltar; revelar (una sorpresa, etc.); **to** — **back,** saltar hacia atrás; **to** — **forward,** arrojarse; **to** — **from,** venir, proceder de; **to** — **a leak,** (naut.) declararse una vía de agua; —, *n.* primavera, *f.;* elasticidad, *f.;* muelle, resorte, *m.;* salto, *m.;* manantial, *m.;* **hot** — **s,** burga, *f.;* — **of water,** fuente *f.*

springboard [sprin-bord] *n.* trampolín, *m.*

springlike [spring-laik] *adj.* primaveral.

springy [sprin-gui] *adj.* elástico.

sprinkle [sprin-kel] *vt.* rociar; salpicar; —, *vi.* lloviznar; —, *n.* rociada, *f.;* lluvia ligera.

sprinkler [sprin-klar] *n.* rociador, *m.;* (Mex.) rehilete (para regar el prado, etc.), *m.*

sprinkling [sprin-klin] *n.* rociada, aspersión, *f.;* —**can,** regadera, *f.*

sprint [sprint] *n.* carrera breve a todo correr; —, *vi.* correr velozmente.

sprout [spraut] *n.* vástago, renuevo, tallo, retoño, *m.;* —**s,** *n. pl.* bretones, *m. pl.;* —, *vi.* brotar, pulular.

sprung [sprang] *p.p.* del verbo **spring.**

spry [sprai] *adj.* activo, listo, vivo, ágil, veloz, ligero.

spur [sper] *n.* espuela, *f.*

spurious [spiua-rios] *adj.* espurio, falso; contrahecho; supuesto; bastardo.

spurn [spern] *vt.* acocear; despreciar, desdeñar.

spurt [spert] *vt.* chorrear, arrojar; —, *vi.* manar a borbotones, borbotar; —, *n.* chorro, *m.;* esfuerzo grande.

spy [spai] *n.* espía, *m.* y *f.;* —, *vt.* y *vi.* espiar; columbrar.

squab [skuob] *adj.* implume; cachigordo, regordete; —, *n.* pichón, *m.,* palomita, *f.;* canapé, sofá, *m.;* cojín, *m.*

squabble [skuob] *vi.* reñir, disputar; —, *n.* riña, disputa, *f.*

squadron [skuo-dron] *n.* (mil.)

escuadrón, *m.*

squalid [skuo-lid] *adj.* sucio, puerco, escuálido.

squall [skuol] *n.* grito desgarrador; chubasco, *m.*; — **of wind**, ráfaga de viento; —, *vi.* chillar.

squalor [skuo-lar] *n.* porquería, suciedad, escualidez, *f.*

squander [skuon-dar] *vt.* malgastar, disipar, derrochar.

square [skuear] *adj.* cuadrado, cuadrángulo; exacto; cabal; equitativo; — **dance**, contradanza, *f.*; baile de figuras; — **root**, raíz cuadrada; — **deal**, trato equitativo; — **foot**, pie cuadrado; —, *n.* cuadro, *m.*; plaza, *f.*

squared [skuead] *adj.* cuadrado.

squash [skuosh] *vt.* aplastar; —, *n.* calabaza, *f.*; calabacera, *f..*

squat [skuot] *vi.* agacharse, sentarse en cuclillas; —, *adj.* agachado; rechoncho.

squawk [skuok] *vi.* graznar; (coll.) quejarse; —, *n.* graznido, *m.*

squeak [skuik] *vi.* chillar; —, *n.* grito, chillido, *m.*

squeal [skuil] *vi.* plañir, gritar; delatar.

squeamish [skui-mish] *adj.* fastidioso; demasiado delicado; remilgado.

squeeze [skuis] *vt.* apretar, comprimir; estrechar; —, *n.* compresión, *f.*, acción de apretar; abrazo, *m.*

squelch [skelch] *vt.* aplastar; hacer callar.

squint [skuint] *adj.* ojizaino; bizco; —, *vi.* mirar de reojo; mirar con los ojos medio cerrados.

squirm [skuerm] *vi.* retorcerse, contorcerse.

squirrel [skui-ral] *n.* ardilla, *f.*

squirt [skuert] *vt.* jeringar; —, *n.* jeringa, *f.*; chorro, *m.*; (coll.) joven grosero; persona insignificante y presuntuosa.

stab [stab] *vt.* dar de puñaladas; —, *n.* puñalada, *f.*

stability [sta-bi-li-ti] *n.* estabilidad, solidez, fijeza, *f.*

stabilize [stei-bi-lais] *vt.* estabilizar, hacer firme.

stable [stei-bol] *n.* establo, *m.*; —, *vt.* poner en el establo; —, *adj.* estable.

stack [stak] *n.* niara, *f.*; (coll.) gran cantidad; montón, *m.*; —, *vt.* hacinar; amontonar.

stadium [stei-diom] *n.* estadio, *m.*

staff [staf] *n.* báculo, palo, *m.*; apoyo, *m.*; cuerpo, *m.*; personal, *m.*; **editorial** —, redacción, *f.*, cuerpo de redacción; **music** —, pentagrama, *m.*; **ruled** —, (mus.) pauta, *f.*; — **officer**, oficial del estado mayor.

stag [stag] *n.* ciervo, *m.;* (coll.) hombre que va a una fiesta sin compañera; — **party,** tertulia para hombres.

stage [steidch] *n.* escenario, *m.*

stagger [sta-gar] *vi.* vacilar, titubear; estar incierto; tambalear; —, *vt.* escalonar, alternar; asustar; hacer vacilar.

stagnant [stag-nant] *adj.* estancado.

stagnate [stag-neit] *vi.* estancarse.

stagnation [stag-nei-shon] *n.* estancamiento, *m.*

stain [stein] *vt.* manchar; empañar la reputación; —, *n.* mancha, tacha, *f.,* borrón, *m.* ; deshonra, *f.*

stainless [stein-les] *adj.* limpio, inmaculado; impecable; inoxidable; — **steel,** acero inoxidable.

stair [stear] *n.* escalón, *m.* ; **—s,** *n. pl.* escalera, *f.;* **back —s,** escalera de servicio, escalera trasera.

staircase [stea-keis] *n.* escalera, *f.*

stairway [stea-uei] *n.* escalera, *f.*

stale [steil] *adj.* añejo, viejo, rancio; —, *vi.* hacerse rancio o viejo; orinar el gana-do; —, *n.* orina de ganado.

stalemate [steil-meit] *n.* tablas (en el juego de ajedrez), *f. pl.* ; empate, *m.* ; —, *vt.* hacer tablas (en el juego de ajedrez); parar, paralizar.

staleness [steil-nes] *n.* vejez, *f.;* rancidez, *f.*

stalk [stok] *vt.* acechar; —, *vi.* ir pavoneándose; —, *n.* paso majestuoso; tallo, pie, tronco, *m.* ; troncho (de ciertas hortalizas).

stall [stol] *n.* pesebre, *m.* ; tienda portátil; tabanco, *m.* ; barraca, *f.;* (avi.) desplome, *m.* ; silla (de coro), *f.;* butaca en el teatro; —, *vt.* meter en el establo; —*vi.* demorarse premeditadamente; (auto.) pararse.

stallion [sta-lion] *n.* caballo padre.

stalwart [stol-uot] *adj.* robusto, vigoroso.

stamen [stei-men] *n.* (bot.) estambre, *m.*

stamina [sta-mi-na] *n.* fuerza vital; vigor, *m.* ; resistencia, *f.*

stammer [sta-mar] *vi.* tartamudear, balbucear.

stamp [stamp] *vt.* patear (los pies); estampar, imprimir, sellar; acuñar; —, *n.* cuño, *m.* ; sello, *m.* ; impresión, *f.;* estampa, *f.;* timbre, *m.* ; **postage —,** sello de correo; **revenue —,** sello de impuesto.

stampede [stam-pid] *n.* huida atropellada, fuga precipitada, estampida, *f.*; —, *vi.* huir en tropel.

stance [stans] *n.* posición, postura, *f.*

stanch [stanch] *vt.* estancar; —, *vi.* estancarse; —, *adj.* sano; leal; firme, seguro; hermético, a prueba de agua.

stand [stand] *vi.* estar de pie o derecho; sostenerse; resistir; permanecer; pararse; hacer alto, estar situado; hallarse; — **by**, estar cerca o listo para ayudar; —, *vt.* sostener; soportar; **to** — **aside,** apartarse; **to** — **in line,** hacer cola; **to** — **out,** resaltar, destacarse; **to** — **still,** estarse parado o quieto; **to** — **up,** ponerse de pie, pararse; —, *n.* puesto, sitio, *m.* ; posición, *f.;* parada, *f.;* tarima, *f.;* estante, *m.*

standard [stan-dard] *n.* estandarte, *m.* ; modelo, *m.* ; norma, *f.;* pauta, *f.;* tipo, *m.* ; regla fija; patrón, *m.* ; **gold** —, patrón de oro; — **equipment,** equipo corriente, equipo regular; — **of living,** nivel de vida; —, *adj.* normal; — **measure,** medida patrón; — **time,** hora normal.

standardization [stan-da-dai-sei-shon] *n.* uniformidad, igualación, *f.*

standardize [stan-da-rais] *vt.* normalizar, regularizar, estan-

dardizar.

stand-by [stand-bai] *n.* cosa o persona con que se puede contar en un momento dado; — **credit,** crédito contingente.

standing [stan-din] *adj.* permanente, fijado, establecido; estancado; — **army,** ejército permanente; — **room,** espacio para estar de pie; —, *n.* duración, *f.;* posición, *f.;* puesto, *m.* ; reputación, *f.*

standpoint [stand-point] *n.* punto de vista.

standstill [stand-stil] *n.* pausa, *f.;* alto, *m.*

stanza [stan-sa] *n.* verso, *m.* , estrofa, *f.*

staple [stei-pel] *n.* materia prima; producto principal; presilla, grapa, *f.;* —**s,** *n. pl.* artículos de primera necesidad; —, *adj.* establecido; principal; —, *vt.* engrapar.

stapler [stei-plar] *n.* engrapador, *m.*

star [star] *n.* estrella, *f.;* asterisco, *m.* ; astro, *m.* ; —, *vt.* decorar con estrellas; marcar con asteriscos; presentar en calidad de estrella; **S— Spangled Banner,** bandera tachonada de estrellas; —, *vi.* (theat.) ser estrella, tomar el papel principal.

starch [starch] *n.* almidón, *m.* ;

—, *vt.* almidonar.

stare [stear] *vt.* clavar la vista; —, *n.* mirada fija.

starfish [star-fish] *n.* estrella de mar.

stark [stark] *adj.* fuerte, áspero; puro; — **mad,** loco rematadamente; —**ly,** *adv.* del todo.

starlet [star-let] *n.* estrella joven de cine.

starlight [star-lait] *n.* luz de las estrellas.

starred, starry [stard], [sta-ri] *adj.* estrellado, como estrellas.

start [start] *vi.* sobrecogerse, sobresaltarse, estremecerse; levantarse de repente; salir los caballos en las carreras; —, *vt.* empezar, comenzar; fomentar; cebar, poner en marcha; **to — off, to — out,** ponerse en marcha; . , *n.* sobresalto, *m.* ; ímpetu, *m.* ; principio, *m.* ; **to get a —,** tomar la delantera.

starter [star-tar] *n.* iniciador, ra; arrancador, ra; principio, *m.* ; (auto.) arranque, *m.* ; **to step on the —,** pisar el arranque.

starting [star-tin] *n.* principio, *m.* ; origen, *m.* ; comienzo, *m.* ; — **point,** punto de partida; poste de salida (en las carreras).

startle [star-tel] *vi.* sobresaltarse, estremecerse de repente; —, *n.* espanto, susto repentino.

startling [star-tlin] *adj.* espantoso, pasmoso, alarmante.

starvation [star-vei-shon] *n.* muerte por hambre, (med.) inanición, *f.*

starve [starv] *vi.* perecer o morirse de hambre.

state [steit] *n.* estado, *m.* ; condición, *f.;* (pol.) Estado, *m.* ; pompa, grandeza, *f.;* situación, *f.;* estación, *f.;* circunstancia, *f.;* —**'s evidence,** (leyes) testimonio en favor del estado en una audiencia; —, *vt.* plantear; fijar; declarar; precisar.

statehouse [steit-jaus] *n.* sede de la legislatura de un estado (en E.U.A.).

statement [steit-ment] *n.* relación, cuenta, *f.;* afirmación, *f.;* (com.) estado de cuenta; relato, *m.* ; manifestación, *f.;* declaración, *f.*

statesmanship [steits-man-ship] *n.* política, *f.;* arte de gobernar.

static [sta-tik] *n.* (rad.) estática, *f.;* —, *adj.* estático.

statics [sta-tiks] *n.* estática, *f.*

station [stei-shon] *n.* estación, *f.;* empleo, puesto, *m.* ; situación, postura, *f.;* grado, *m.* ; condición, *f.;* (rail.) estación, *f.;* paradero, *m.* ; **central —, main —,** central, *f.*

stationary [stei-sho-na-ri] *adj.* estacionario, fijo.

stationery [stei-sho-na-ri] *n.* útiles o efectos de escritorio; papelería, *f.;* — **store,** papelería, *f.*

statistic, statistical [sta-tis-tik], [sta-tis-tikal] *adj.* estadístico.

statistician [sta-tis-ti-shan] *n.* experto en estadística.

statistics [sta-tis-tiks] *n. pl.* estadística, *f.*

statuary [sta-tiua-ri] *n.* estatuario, escultor, *m. ;* escultura de estatuas; grupo de estatuas; —, *adj.* estatuario.

statue [sta-tiu] *n.* estatua, *f.*

stature [sta-char] *n.* estatura, talla, *f.*

status [stei-tos] *n.* posición, condición, *f.;* — **quo,** statu quo.

statute [sta-tiut] *n.* estatuto, *m. ;* reglamento, *m. ;* regla, *f.*

statutory [sta-tiu-to-ri] *adj.* estatuido, establecido por la ley; perteneciente a un estatuto; castigable por el estatuto.

staunch = [stonch] **stanch.**

stay [stei] *n.* estancia, permanencia, *f.;* suspensión (de una sentencia); cesación, *f. ;* apoyo, *m. ;* estribo, *m. ;* — s, corsé, justillo, *m. ;* —, *vi.* quedarse, permanecer, estarse; tardar, detenerse, aguardarse, esperarse; **to — in bed,** guardar cama; —, *vt.* detener, contener; apoyar.

stead [sted] *n.* lugar, sitio, paraje, *m.*

steadfast [sted-fast] *adj.* firme, estable, sólido; —**ly,** *adv.* con constancia.

steadily [ste-di-li] *adv.* firmemente; invariable-mente.

steady [ste-di] *adj.* firme, fijo; —, *vt.* hacer firme.

steak [steik] *n.* bistec, *m.*

steal [stil] *vt.* y *vi.* hurtar, robar; **to — in,** colarse; **to — away,** escabullirse.

stealth [stelz] *n.* hurto, *m. ;* **by —,** a hurtadillas.

stealthily [stel-zi-li] *adv.* a hurtadillas.

stealthy [stel-zi] *adj.* furtivo.

steam [stim] *n.* vapor, *m. ;* —, *adj.* de vapor; — **bath,** baño de vapor; — **boiler,** caldera de una máquina de vapor; — **engine,** bomba de vapor, máquina de vapor; — **fitter,** montador de tubos y calderas de vapor; — **heat,** calefacción por vapor; — **radiator,** calorífero de vapor; — **roller,** aplanadora de vapor; — **shovel,** pala de vapor; — **pressure,** presión del vapor; —, *vi.* vahear; —, *vt.* limpiar con vapor; cocer al vapor.

steamboat [stim-bout] *n.* vapor, *m. ;* buque de vapor.

steamer [sti-mar] *n.* vapor, *m. ;* máquina o carro de vapor; —

rug, manta de viaje.

steamship [stim-ship] *n.* vapor, *m.* ; buque de vapor; — **agency,** agencia de vapores; — **line,** línea de vapores.

steel [stil] *n.* acero.

steep [stip] *adj.* escarpado, pino; (coll.) exorbitante; —, *n.* precipicio, *m.*

steeple [sti-pel] *n.* torre, *f.;* campanario, *m.* ; es-pira,

steer [stiar] *n.* novillo, *m.* ; (coll.) consejo, *m.* ; buey, *m.* ; —, *vt.* gobernar; guiar, dirigir.

steerage [stia-rich] *n.* gobierno, *m.* ; (naut.) antecámara de un navío; proa, *f.*

steering [sti-rin] *n.* dirección, *f.;* —, *adj.* de gobierno (de automóvil, etc.); — **gear,** (naut.) aparato de gobierno; — **wheel,** volante, *m.*

stellar [ste-lar] *adj.* estelar.

stem [stem] *n.* vástago, tallo, *m.* ; estirpe, *f.;* (naut.) branque, *m.* ; —, *vt.* cortar (la corriente) ; estancar.

stencil [sten-sil] *n.* patrón, dechado, *m.* ; patrón estarcidor, estarcidor, *m.* ; estarcido, *m.* ; —, *vt.* estarcir.

step [step] *n.* paso, *m.* ; peldaño, escalón, *m.* ; huella, *f.;* trámite, *m.;* gestión, *f.;* **in** —, de acuerdo; **to be in** —, llevar el paso; *vi.* dar un paso;

andar; —, *vt.* escalonar; **to —in,** entrar; **to — on,** pisar; **to — out,** salir; (coll.) ir de parranda; **to — up,** acelerar, avivar.

stepbrother [step-broder] *n.* medio hermano, hermanastro, *m.*

stepdaughter [step-dau-tar] *n.* hijastra, *f.*

stepfather [step-fadar] *n.* padrastro, *m.*

stepladder [step-la-dar] *n.* escalera de mano; gradilla, *f.*

stepmother [step-madar] *n.* madrastra, *f.*

steppingstone [ste-pin-stoun] *n.* pasadera, *f.;* medio para progresar o adelantar.

stepsister [step-sistar] *n.* media hermana, hermanastra, *f.*

stepson [step-son] *n.* hijastro, *m.*

stereotype [ste-rio-taip] *n.* estereotipia, *f.;* —, *vt.* estereotipar.

sterile [ste-rail] *adj.* estéril.

sterility [ste-ri-li-ti] *n.* esterilidad, *f.*

sterilization [ste-ri-lai-sei-shon] *n.* esterilización, *f.*

sterilize [ste-ri-lais] *vt.* desinfectar, esterilizar.

sterling [ster-lin] *adj.* genuino, verdadero; —, *n.* moneda esterlina; — **silver,** plata esterlina.

stern [stern] *adj.* austero, rígido, severo; ceñudo; —, *n.* (naut.)

popa, *f.*

sternum [stern-nom] (anat.) *n.* esternón, *m.*

steroid [ste-roid] *n.* esteroide, *m.*

stethoscope [ste-zos-koup] *n.* (med.) estetoscopio, *m.*

stew [stiu] *vt.* y *vi.* estofar; guisar; (coll.) mortificarse; —, *n.* guisado, guiso, *m.* ; sancocho, *m.*

stewardess [stiua-des] *n.* camarera; **plane** —, azafata, sobrecargo, aeromoza, *f.*

stick [stik] *n.* palo, bastón, *m.* ; vara, *f.;* **incense** —, pebete, *m.* ; —, *vt.* pegar; picar; punzar; —, *vi.* pegarse; detenerse; perseverar.

sticker [sti-kar] *n.* etiqueta engomada.

sticking [sti-kin] *n.* pegadura, *f.*

sticky [sti-ki] *adj.* viscoso, pegajoso, pegadizo.

stiff [stif] *adj.* tieso; duro, torpe; rígido; obstinado; — **neck,** torticolis o tortícolis, *m.*

stiffen [sti-fen] *vt.* atiesar, endurecer; —, *vi.* endurecerse.

stiffness [stif-nes] *n.* tesura, rigidez, *f.;* obstinación,

stifle [sti-fel] *vt.* sofocar.

stifling [sti-flin] *adj.* sofocante; — **heat,** calor asfixiante.

stigma [stig-ma] *n.* nota de infamia, estigma, *m.* ; borrón, *m.*

still [stil] *vt.* aquietar, aplacar; calmar; —, *adj.* silencioso, tranquilo; —, *n.* silencio, *m.* ; alambique, *m.* ; fotografía para anunciar una película; —, *adv.* todavía; siempre, hasta ahora; no obstante.

stillness [stil-nes] *n.* calma, quietud, *f.*

stilt [stilt] *n.* zanco, *m.*

stimulant [sti-miu-lant] *n.* estimulante, *m.*

stimulate [sti-miu-leit] *vt.* estimular, aguijonear.

stimulation [sti-miu-lei-shon] *n.* estímulo, *m.* ; estimulación, *f.*

stimulus [sti-miu-los] *n.* estímulo, *m.*

sting [sting] *vt.* picar o morder (un insecto); —, *n.* aguijón, *m.;* punzada, remordimiento de conciencia.

stinginess [stin-yi-nes] *n.* tacañería, avaricia, *f.*

stinging [stin-guin] *adj.* picante; mordaz; punzante; —**nettle,** (bot.) ortiga, *f.*

stingy [stin-yi] *adj.* mezquino, tacaño, avaro.

stink [stink] *vi.* heder; —, *n.* hedor, *m.*

stipulation [sti-piu-lei-shon] *n.* estipulación, *f.;* contrato mutuo.

stir [ster] *vt.* mover; agitar; menear; conmover; incitar; —, *vi.* moverse; bullir; —, *n.*

tumulto, *m.* ; turbulencia, *f.;* movimiento, *m.* ; (coll.) cárcel, *f.*

stirring [ste-rin] *adj.* emocionante, animador.

stirrup [sti-rap] *n.* estribo, *m.*

stitch [stich] *vt.* coser, bastear; —, *n.* puntada, *f.;* punto, *m.*

stock [stok] *n.* tronco, *m.* ; injerto, *m.* ; zoquete, *m.* ; mango, *m.* ; corbatín, *m.* ; estirpe, *m.* ; linaje, *m.* ; (com.) capital, principal, *m.* ; fondo, *m.* ; (com.) acción, *f.;* ganado, *m.* ; **in** —, en existencia; **preferred** —**s**, acciones preferentes; — **company,** sociedad anónima; — **exchange,** bolsa, *f.,* bolsa de comercio, bolsa financiera; — **market,** mercado de valores; — **s,** *pl.* acciones en los fondos públicos; **supply** —, provisión, *f.;* **to speculate in** —**s,** jugar a la bolsa; —, *vt.* proveer, abastecer.

stockbroker [stok-brou-kar] *n.* agente de cambio, corredor de bolsa, bolsista, *m.*

stockholder [stok-joul-dar] *n.* accionista, *m.* y *f.*

stocking [sto-kin] *n.* media, *f.*

stockjobbing [stok-yobin] *n.* juego de bolsa, agiotaje, *m.*

stockpile [sok-pail] *n.* acumulación de mercancías de reserva; —, *vt.* acumular mercancías de reserva.

stocky [sto-ki] *adj.* rechoncho.

stockyard [stok-yard] *n.* rastro, *m.* ; corral de gana-do.

stoical [stoi-kal] *adj.* estoico; — **ly,** *adv.* estoicamente.

stoicism [stoui-si-sem] *n.* estoicismo, *m.*

stoke [stouk] *vt.* y *vi.* atizar el fuego.

stole [stoul] *n.* estola, *f.;* —, *pretérito* del verbo **steal.**

stolen [stou-len] *p.p.* del verbo **steal.**

stomach [sto-mak] *n.* estómago, *m.* ; apetito, *m.* ; **on the** —, boca abajo; —, *vt.* aguantar; soportar.

stone [stoun] *n.* piedra, *f.;* canto, *m.* ; (med.) cálculo, *m.* ; pepita, *f.,* hueso de fruta; alhaja, *f.,* piedra preciosa; **hewn** —, cantería, *f.;* **of** —, pétreo; — **fruit,** fruta de hueso; **corner** —, piedra angular; **foundation** —, piedra fundamental; —, *vt.* apedrear; quitar los huesos de las frutas; empedrar; trabajar de albañilería.

stony [stou-ni] *adj.* de piedra, pétreo; duro.

stool [stul] *n.* banquillo.

stoop [stup] *n.* inclinación hacia abajo; abatimiento, *m.* ; escalinata, *f.;* —, *vi.* encorvarse, inclinarse; bajarse; agacharse.

stop [stop] *vt.* detener, parar, diferir; cesar, suspender, paralizar; tapar; —, *vi.* pararse, hacer alto; **to — a clock,** parar un reloj; —, *n.* pausa, *f.;* obstáculo, *m.* ; parada, *f.;* detención, *f.;* — **signal,** señal de alto o de parada; — **light,** luz de parada.

stopover [stop-ou-var] *n.* escala, *f.;* parada en un punto intermediario del camino.

stoppage [sto-pich] *n.* obstrucción, *f.;* impedimento, *m.* ; (rail.) alto, *m.*

stopping [sto-pin] *n.* obstrucción, *f.;* impedimento, *m.* ; (rail.) alto, *m.* ; — **place,** paradero, *m.*

storage [sto-rich] *n.* almacenamiento, *m.* ; almacenaje, *m.* ; **cold —,** cámara frigorífica; — **battery,** batería, *f.,* batería de acumuladores, acumulador, *m.*

store [stor] *n.* abundancia, *f.;* provisión, *f.;* almacén, *m.* ; **department —,** bazar, *m.,* tienda de departamentos; **dry goods —,** mercería, *f.;* —, *vt.* surtir, proveer, abastecer; almacenar.

storehouse [stor-jaus] *n.* almacén, *m.*

storeroom [stor-rum] *n.* almacén, depósito, *m.* ; (naut.) pañol, *m.*

stork [stork] *n.* cigüeña, *f.*

storm [storm] *n.* tormenta, tempestad, borrasca, *f.;* (mil.) asalto, *m.* ; tumulto, *m.* ; — **center,** centro tempestuoso; —, *vi.* haber tormenta.

stormy [stor-mi] *adj.* tempestuoso; violento, turbulento.

story [sto-ri] *n.* cuento, *m.* ; historia, *f.;* crónica, *f.;* fábula, *f.;* (coll.) mentira, *f.;* piso de una casa.

stout [staut] *adj.* robusto, vigoroso; corpulento; fuerte; —**ly,** *adv.* valientemente, obstinadamente; —, *n.* cerveza fuerte; persona corpulenta; vestido propio para personas gruesas.

stoven [stouv] *n.* estufa, *f.;* fogón, *m.* ; hornillo, *m.*

stow [stou] *vt.* meter, colocar; (coll.) dejar; (naut.) estibar.

stowaway [stoua-uei] *n.* polizón, ona.

straddle [stra-del] *vt.* montar a horcajadas; —, *vi.* evitar tomar un partido; —, *n.* el estar a horcajadas.

straggle [stra-guel] *vi.* vagar; extenderse.

straggler [stra-glar] *n.* rezagado, da.

straight [streit] *adj.* derecho, recto; justo; — **line,** línea recta; — **razor,** navaja ordinaria de afeitar; —, *adv.* directamente; en línea recta.

straightaway [streit-a-uei] *n.* curso directo; —, *adj.* derecho, en dirección continua.

straightedge [streit-edch] *n.* regla (para trazar línea recta), f.

straighten [strei-ten] *vt.* enderezar.

straightforward [streit-for-uard] *adj.* derecho; franco; leal.

strain [strein] *vt.* colar, filtrar; cerner, trascolar; apretar (a uno contra sí) ; forzar; violentar; —, *vi.* esforzarse; —, *n.* retorcimiento, *m.* ; raza, *f.*; linaje, *m.* ; estilo, *m.* ; sonido, *m.* ; armonía, *f.*; tensión.

strainer [strei-nar] *n.* colador, *m.* , coladera, *f.*

strait [streit] *adj.* rígido; exacto; escaso; — **jacket**, camisa de fuerza; —, *n.* (geog.) estrecho, *m.* ; aprieto, *m.* , angustia, *f.*; penuria, *f.*

straiten [strei-ten] *vt.* acortar, estrechar, angostar; —**ed cir-cumstances,** circunstancias reducidas, escasos recursos.

strand [strand] *n.* costa, playa, ribera, *f.*; cordón, *m.* ; —, *vi.* encallar; —, *vt.* embarrancar; abandonar; **to be —ed,** perderse, estar uno solo y abandonado.

strange [streinch] *adj.* extraño; curioso; raro; peculiar; —**ly,** *adv.* extraordinariamente.

stranger [strein-char] *n.* extranjero, ra, desconocido, da; forastero, ra.

strangle [stran-guel] *vt.* ahogar, estrangular; — **hold,** (entre luchadores) presa que ahoga al antagonista.

strategic [stra-ti-yik] *adj.* estratégico.

strategy [stra-ti-yi] *n.* estrategia, *f.*

straw [stro] *n.* paja, *f.*; bagatela, *f.*; (Mex.)popote (para tomar líquidos), *m;*—, *adj.* de paja, falso; — **hat,** sombrero de paja; — **vote,** voto no oficial para determinar la opinión pública.

strawberry [stro-be-ri] *n.* fresa, frutilla, *f.*

stray [strei] *vi.* extraviarse; perder el camino; —, *n.* persona descarriada; animal extraviado; —, *adj.* extraviado, perdido, aislado, sin conexión.

streak [strik] *n.* raya, lista, *f.*; —, *vt.* rayar.

stream [strim] *n.* arroyo, río, torrente, raudal, *m.*; corriente, *f.*; a — **of children,** una muchedumbre infantil; **down** —, agua abajo; —, *vt.* y *vi.* correr, fluir; entrar a torrentes.

streamer [stri-mar] *n.* (naut.) flámula, *f.*, gallardete, *m.* ; cinta colgante.

streamlined [strim-laind] *adj.* aerodinámico.

street [strit] *n.* calle, *f.;* — **crossing,** cruce de calle; — **intersection,** bocacalle, *f.*

streetcar [strit-kar] *n.* tranvía, *m.* ; — **conductor,** cobrador, *m.* ; — **line,** línea de tranvía.

strength [strenz] *n.* fuerza, robustez, *f.,* vigor, *m.* ; fortitud, *f.;* potencia, *f.;* fortaleza, resistencia, *f.;* **to gain —,** cobrar fuerzas; **tensile —,** resistencia a la tracción.

strengthen [stren-zen] *vt.* corroborar, consolidar; fortificar; reforzar; —, *vi.* fortalecerse.

strenuous [stre-niuos] *adj.* estrenuo, fuerte; vigoroso; arduo; activo; —**ly,** *adv.* vigorosamente.

streptococcus [strep-to-ko-kos] *n.* estreptococo, *m.*

stress [stres] *n.* fuerza, *f.;* tensión, *f.;* acento, *m.;* —**ed syllable,** sílaba acentuada; —, *vt.* acentuar, dar énfasis, hacer hincapié en.

stretch [strech] *vt.* y *vi.* extender, alargar; estirar; extenderse; esforzarse; —, *n.* extensión, *f.;* esfuerzo, *m.* ; estirón, *m.* ; trecho, *m.*

stretcher [stre-char] *n.* estirador, *m.* ; tendedor, *m.* ; camilla, *f.*

strew [stru] *vt.* esparcir; sembrar.

strict [strikt] *adj.* estricto, estrecho; exacto; riguroso, severo; terminante; — **order,** orden terminante; —**ly,** *adv.* estrictamente, con severidad.

stride [straid] *n.* tranco, *m.* ; adelanto, avance, *m.;* —, *vt.* cruzar, pasar a zancadas; —, *vi.* andar a pasos largos.

strident [strai-dant] *adj.* estridente.

strife [straif] *n.* contienda, disputa, *f.;* rivalidad, *f.*

strike [straik] *vt.* y *vi.* golpear; dar; chocar; declararse en huelga; — **out,** tachar; (béisbol) hacer perder el tanto al bateador que falla en golpear la pelota en tres golpes consecutivos; —, *n.* golpe, *m.;* hallazgo, *m.* ; huelga, *f.*

striking [strai-kin] *adj.* impresionante, sorprendente, llamativo; —**ly,** *adv.* de un modo sorprendente.

string [strin] *n.* cordón, *m.* ; cuerda, *f* ; hilo, *m.* ; hilera, *f.;* fibra, *f.;* — **bean,** habichuela verde, judía, *f.,* (Mex.) ejote, *m.*

stringed [stringd] *adj.* encordado; — **instrument,** instrumento de cuerda.

stringent [strin-yent] *adj.* severo, riguroso, rígido; convincente.

strip [strip] *n.* tira, faja, *f.;* —, *vt.* desnudar, despojar.

stripe [straip] *n.* raya, lista, *f.;* roncha, *f.,* cardenal, *m.* ; azote, *m.* ; —, *vt.* rayar.

striped [straipt] *adj.* rayado.

strive [straiv] *vi.* esforzarse; empeñarse; disputar, contender; oponerse.

stroke [strouk] *n.* golpe, *m.* ; toque (en la pintura), *m.* ; sonido (de reloj), *m.* ; (golf) tirada, *f.;* golpe de émbolo; caricia con la mano; (med.) apoplejía, *f.;* palote, *m.* ; —, *vt.* acariciar.

stroll [stroul] *vi.* tunar, vagar, pasearse; —, *n.* paseo, *m.*

strong [strong] *adj.* fuerte, vigoroso, robusto; concentrado; poderoso; violento; pujante; —ly, *adv.* con fuerza.

struck [strak] *adj.* cerrado o afectado por huelga; golpeado.

structural [strak-cha-ral] *adj.* estructural; construccional; —iron, hierro para construcciones.

structure [strak-char] *n.* estructura, *f.;* edificio, *m.* ; fábrica, *f.*

struggle [strak-guel] *n.* lucha, contienda, *f.,* conflicto, *m.* ; brega, *f.;* —, *vi.* esforzarse; luchar, lidiar; agitarse; contender.

strum [stram] *vt.* (mus.) tocar defectuosamente (un instru-mento de cuerda); rasguear (una guitarra, etc.).

strychnine [strik-nin] *n.* estricnina, *f.*

stub [stab] *n.* tocón, *m.* ; talón, *m.* ; colilla, *f.;* fragmento, *m.* ; —, *vt.* pegar, dar.

stubble [sta-bel] *n.* rastrojo, *m.*

stubborn [sta-bon] *adj.* obstinado, terco, testarudo; enrevesado; cabezón; **to be** —, ser porfiado o terco.

stubby [sta-bi] *adj.* cachigordete; gordo.

stucco [sta-kou] *n.* estuco, *m.*

stuck-up [stuk-up] *adj.* (coll.) arrogante, presumido, presuntuoso.

student [stiu-dent] *n.* estudiante, *m.* y *f.,* alumno, na.

studio [stiu-diou] *n.* estudio de un artista (pintor, escultor, etc.); **moving picture** —, estudio cinematográfico.

study [sta-di] *n.* estudio, *m.* ; aplicación, *f.;* meditación profunda; gabinete, *m.* ; —, *vt.* estudiar, cursar; observar; —, *vi.* estudiar, aplicarse.

stuff [staf] *n.* materia, *f.;* material, *m.* ; efectos. *m. pl.* ; cosas, *f. pl.* ; materia prima; henchir, llenar; cebar; rellenar; —, *vi.* atracarse; tragar; **to — oneself,** hartarse, soplarse.

stuffing [sta-fin] *n.* relleno, *m.*

stuffy [sta-fi] *adj.* mal ventilado; (coll.) enojado y terco; (coll.) estirado, presuntuoso.

stumble [stam-bel] *vi.* tropezar; —, *n.* tropiezo, *m.*

stumbling [stum-blin] *n.* tropezón, *m.* ; — **block,** tropezadero, *m.* ; obstáculo, impedimento, *m.*

stun [stan] *vt.* aturdir; pasmar.

stung [stung] *pretérito,* y *p.p.* del verbo **sting.**

stunning [stu-nin] *adj.* elegante, atractivo; aturdidor.

stunt [stant] *vt.* no dejar crecer; reprimir —, *n.* hazaña, *f.;* — **flying,** acrobacia aérea.

stupefy [stiu-pi-fai] *vt.* atontar, atolondrar.

stupendous [stiu-pen-dos] *adj.* estupendo, maravilloso; —**ly,** *adv.* estupendamente.

stupid [stiu-pid] *adj.* estúpido, tonto, bruto; **to be** —, ser duro de mollera; —, *n.* bobo, ba; tonto, ta; —**ly,** *adv.* estúpidamente.

stupidity [stiu-pi-di-ti] *n.* estupidez, *f.*

sturdily [ster-di-li] *adv.* robustamente, vigorosamente.

sturdy [ster-di] *adj.* fuerte, tieso, robusto, rollizo; determinado, firme.

stutter [sta-tar] *vi.* tartamudear; —, *n.* tartamudeo, *m.*

sty [stai] *n.* zahúrda, pocilga, *f.;* (med.) orzuelo, *m.*

style [stail] *n.* estilo, *m.* ; título, *m.* ; **gnomon,** *m.* ; modo, *m.* ; moda, *f.;* **in** —, a la moda; —, *vt.* intitular, nombrar; confeccionar según la moda.

stylish [stai-lin] *adj.* elegante, a la moda.

stylist [stai-list] *n.* estilista, *m.* y *f.*

stylize [stai-lais] *vt.* estilizar.

suave [suav] *adj.* pulido y cortés; —**ly,** *adv.* pulida cortésmente.

sub [sab] *n.* (coll.) sustituto, ta; submarino, *m.;* subordinado, da.

subconscious [sab-kon-shos] *adj.* subconsciente; —, *n.* subconsciencia, *f.*

subdivide [sab-di-vaid] *vt.* subdividir.

subdivision [sab-di-vi-shon] *n.* subdivisión, *f.*

subdue [sab-diu] *vt.* sojuzgar, rendir, sujetar; conquistar; mortificar.

subhead [sab-jed] *n.* subtítulo, *m.* , título o encabezamiento secundario.

subject [sab-yikt] *n.* sujeto, tema tópico, *m.* ; asignatura, *f.;* materia, *f* ; —, *adj.* sujeto, sometido a; — **matter,** asunto, tema, *m.;* —, *vt.* sujetar, someter; supeditar; rendir, exponer.

subjection [sab-yek-shon] *n.* sujeción, *f.;* supeditación, *f.*

subjective [sab-yek-tiv] *adj.* subjetivo; —, *adv.* subjetivamente.

subjugate [sab-yu-gueit] *vt.* sojuzgar, sujetar.

subjunctive [sab-yank-tiv] *n.* y *adj.* subjuntivo, *m.*

sublease [sab-lis] *vt.* subarrendar; —, *n.* subarriendo, *m.*

sublet [sub-let] *vt.* subarrendar, dar en alquiler.

sublime [sa-blaim] *adj.* sublime, excelso; **—ly,** *adv.* de un modo sublime; —, *n.* sublimidad, *f.;* —, *vt.* hacer sublime, exaltar; purificar; (chem.) sublimar.

submarine [sab-ma-rin] *n.* y *adj.* submarino, sumergible, *m.*

submerge, submerse [sab-merch] *vt.* sumergir.

submission [sab-mi-shon] *n.* sumisión, *f.,* rendimiento, *m.* ; resignación, *f.;* humildad, *f.*

submissive [sab-mi-siv] *adj.* sumiso, obsequioso; **—ly,** *adv.* con sumisión.

submit [sab-mit] *vt.* someter, rendir; —, *vi.* some-terse.

subordinate [sab-or-di-neit] *n.* y *adj.* subordinado, subalterno, inferior, dependiente, *m.* ; —, *vt.* subordinar; someter.

subordination [sab-or-di-nei-shon] *n.* subordinación, *f.*

subpoena, subpena [sab-poi-na] *n.* orden de comparecer, comparendo, *m.* ; —, *vt.* citar para comparecencia, citar con comparendo.

subscribe [sabs-kraib] *vt.* y *vi.* suscribir, certificar con su firma; suscribirse (a una revista, periódico, etc.); consentir; abonarse (a una función de ópera, etc.).

subscriber [sabs-krai-bar] *n.* suscriptor, ra, abonado, da.

subscription [sabs-krip-shon] *n.* suscripción, *f.,* abono, *m.*

subsequent [sab-si-kuent] *adj.* subsiguiente, subsecuente; **—ly,** *adv.* posteriormente.

subservient [sab-ser-viant] *adj.* subordinado; útil.

subside [sab-said] *vi.* apaciguarse; bajar, disminuirse.

subsidiary [sab-si-dia-ri] *adj.* subsidiario, afiliado, auxiliar; —, *n.* auxiliar, *m.*

subsidize [sab-si-dais] *vt.* dar subsidios.

subsidy [sab-si-di] *n.* subsidio, socorro, *m.* , subvención, *f.*

subsist [sab-sist] *vi.* subsistir, existir; —, *vt.* mantener.

subsistence [sab-sis-tans] *n.* existencia, *f.;* subsistencia, *f.*

substance [sabs-tans] *n.* sustancia, *f.;* entidad, *f.;* esencia, *f.*

substantial [sabs-tan-shal] *adj.* sustancial; real, material; sustancioso; fuerte.

substantiate [sabs-tan-shieit] *vt.* corroborar; verificar; comprobar; sustanciar.

substantive [sabs-tan-tiv] *n.* (gram.) sustantivo, *m.*

substitute [sabs-ti-tiut] *vt.* sustituir, remplazar; relevar; —, *n.* sustituto, ta; remplazo, *m.* ; suplente, *m.* ; lugarteniente, *m.* ; sobresaliente, *m.* ; —, *adj.* de sustituto.

substitution [sabs-ti-tiu-shon] *n.* sustitución, *f.*

subterranean, subterraneous [sab-ta-rei-nian], [sab-tar-rei-neous] *adj.* subterráneo; oculto; secreto.

subtitle [sab-tail] *n.* subtítulo, *m.* , título secundario.

subtle [sa-tel] *adj.* sutil, delicado, tenue; agudo, penetrante; astuto.

subtlety [sa-tel-ti] *n.* sutileza, *f.*

subtract [sab-trakt] *vt.* sustraer; (math.) restar.

subtraction [sab-trak-shon] *n.* sustracción, *f.;* (math.) resta, *f.*

suburb [sa-berb] *n.* suburbio, arrabal, *m.;* —s, *pl.* afueras, *f. pl.*

suburban [sa-ber-ban] *adj.* suburbano.

subversive [sab-ver-siv] *adj.* subversivo.

subway [sab-uei] *n.* túnel, *m.* ;

ferrocarril subterráneo; (coll.) metro, *m.*

succeed [sak-sid] *vt.* y *vi.* suceder, seguir; conseguir, lograr, tener éxito.

success [sak-ses] *n.* éxito, *m.* , buen éxito.

successful [sak-ses-ful] *adj.* próspero, dichoso; **to be ,** tener buen éxito; **—ly,** *adv.* con éxito.

succession [sak-se-shon] *n.* sucesión, *f.;* descendencia, *f.;* herencia, *f.*

successive [sak-se-siv] *adj.* sucesivo.

succulent [sa-kiu-lant] *adj.* suculento, jugoso.

succumb [sa-kamb] *vi.* sucumbir.

such [sach] *adj.* y *pron.* tal, semejante; **—** **as,** tal como; **— as (go there, etc.),** los o las que (van allí, etc.); **in — a manner,** de tal modo.

suck [sak] *vt.* y *vi.* chupar, mamar; —, *n. chupada, f.*

sucker [sa-kar] *n.* chupador, ra; persona fácil de engañar; (coll.) caramelo, *m.* , (Mex.) paleta, *f.*

suction [sak-shon] *n.* succión, *f.;* chupada, *f.*

sudden [sa-den] *adj.* repentino, no prevenido; **—ly,** *adv.* de repente, súbitamente, de pronto.

suds [sads] *n. pl.* jabonadura, *f.,*

espuma de jabón.

sue [su] *vt.* y *vi.* poner pleito, demandar.

suede [sueid] *n.* piel de ante.

suffer [sa-far] *vt.* y *vi.* sufrir; tolerar, padecer.

suffering [sa-fe-rin] *n.* sufrimiento, *m.* , pena, *f.;* dolor, *m.* ; —, *adj.* doliente.

suffice [sa-fais] *vt.* y *vi.* bastar, ser suficiente.

sufficient [sa-fi-shent] *adj.* suficiente, bastante.

suffix [sa-fiks] *n.* (gram.) sufijo, *m.* ; —, *vt.* añadir un sufijo.

suffocate [sa-fo-keit] *vt.* sofocar, ahogar; —, *vi.* sofocarse.

suffocation [sa-fo-kei-shon] *n.* sofocación, *f.*

suffrage [sa-frich] *n.* sufragio, voto, *m.*

sugar [shu-gar] *n.* azúcar, *m.* y *f.* (coll.) lisonja, *f.;* **beet** —, azúcar de remolacha; **brown** —, azúcar morena; **cube** —, azúcar cubicado, da; **granulated** —, azúcar granulado, da; **refined** —, azúcar blanco, ca; — **bowl,** azucarero, *m.* , azucarera, *f.;* — **cane,** caña de azúcar;—, *vt.* azucarar; confitar.

sugar-cane [shu-gar-kein] *adj.* de caña de azúcar; — **plantation,** cañaveral, *m.* ; — **juice,** guarapo, *m.*

sugar-coat [shu-gar-kout] *vt.*

azucarar, garapiñar; hermosear lo feo; ocultar la verdad.

sugary [shu-ga-ri] *adj.* azucarado, dulce.

suggest [sa-yest] *vt.* sugerir; proponer.

suggestion [sa-yes-chon] *n.* sugestión, *f.*

suggestive [sa-yes-tiv] *adj.* sugestivo.

suicidal [sui-sai-dal] *adj.* suicida.

suicide [sui-said] *n.* suicidio, *m.* ; suicida, *m.* y *f.;* **to commit —,** suicidarse.

suit [sut] *n.* vestido entero; traje, *m.* ; galanteo, *m.* ; petición, *f.;* pleito, *m.* ; **ready-made —,** traje hecho; — **made to order,** traje a la medida; **to bring —,** formar causa, demandar, entablar un juicio; —, *vt.* y *vi.* adaptar; surtir; ajustarse, acomodarse; convenir; —, *vt.* sentar, caer bien.

suitability [su-ta-bi-li-ti] *n.* conveniencia, *f.;* compatibilidad, *f.*

suitable [su-ta-bol] *adj.* conforme, conveniente, satisfactorio; idóneo; —**bly,** *adv.* apropiadamente, debidamente.

suitcase [sut-keis] *n.* maleta, *f.*

suite [suit] *n.* serie, *f.;* tren, *m.* , comitiva, *f.;* — **of rooms,** habitación de varios cuartos (en un hotel).

suitor [su-tar] *n.* pretendiente, galán, *m.* ; demandante, *m.*

sulk [salk] *n.* mal humor; —, *vi.* ponerse mal-humorado, hacer pucheros.

sulky [sal-ki] *adj.* regañón, mal-humorado, resentido.

sullen [sa-len] *adj.* intratable; hosco; —**ly,** *adv.* de mal humor; tercamente.

sully [sa-li] *vt.* manchar, ensuciar; —, *vi.* empañarse.

sulphate [sal-feit] *n.* sulfato, *m.*

sulphur [sal-far] *n.* azufre, *m.* ; — **dioxide,** gas sulfuroso, bióxido sulfuroso.

sultry [sal-tri] *adj.* caluroso y húmedo; sofocante; (coll.) ardiente, sensual.

sum [sam] *n.* suma, *f.*; monto, *m.* ; (com.) montante, *m.* ; **certain** —, tanto, *m.* ; — **total,** total, *m.* , cifra total; —, *vt.* sumar; recopilar; **to — up,** resumir.

summarize [sa-ma-rais] recopilar.

summary [sa-ma-ri] resumen, *m.*

summation [su-mei-shon] *n.* total, *m.* , suma, *f.*

summer [sa-mar] *n.* verano; —, *adj.* estival, de verano; — **house,** cenadero, quiosco, *m.* ; — **resort,** lugar de veraneo; —, *vi.* veranear.

summersault = [sa-ma-solt] **somersault.**

summit [sa-mit] *n.* ápice, *m.* ; cima, cresta, cumbre, *f.*; — **conference,** conferencia en la cumbre.

summon [sa-mon] *vt.* citar; requerir por auto de juez; convocar, convidar; (mil.) intimar la rendición.

summons [sa-mons] *n. pl.* citación, *f.*; requerimiento, *m.* ; emplazamiento, *m.*

sumptuous [samp-chuos] *adj.* suntuoso.

sun [san] *n.* sol, *m.* ; — **parlor,** — **porch,** solana, *f.*; —, *vt.* asolear; —, *vi.* asolearse; tomar el sol.

sunbeam [san-bim] *n.* rayo de sol.

sunblock [san-blok] *n.* bloqueador solar, *m.*

sunburn [san-burn] *n.* quemadura de sol; —, *vi.* quemarse por el sol.

sunburnt [san-bernt] *adj.* tostado por el sol, asoleado.

sundae [san-dei] *n.* helado cubierto con jarabe y fruta o nueces machacadas.

Sunday [san-di] *n.* domingo, *m.* ; — **School** doctrina dominical, escuela dominical.

sundial [san-dail] *n.* reloj de sol, cuadrante, *m.*

sundown = [san-daun] **sunset.**

sunflower [san-flauar] *n.* girasol, mirasol, tornasol, *m.*

sung [sang] *p.p.* del verbo **sing.**

sunglass [san-gla-ses] *n.* espejo ustorio; —**es,** anteojos contra el sol, gafas para el sol.

sunk [sank] *p.p.* del verbo **sink.**

sunlamp [san-lamp] *n.* lámpara de rayos ultravioletas.

sunless [san-les] *adj.* sin sol, sin luz.

sunlight [san-lait] *n.* luz del sol.

sunny [sa-ni] *adj.* asoleado; brillante; alegre; **it is —,** hace sol.

sunrise [san-rais] *n.* salida del sol.

sunroom [san-rum] *n.* solana, *f.*

sunset [san-set] *n.* puesta del sol, *f.*, ocaso, *m.*

sunshade [san-sheid] *n.* quitasol, *m.* ; pantalla, *f.*; visera contra el sol.

sunshine [san-shain] *n.* luz solar, luz del sol, *f.*

sunshiny [san-shai-ni] *adj.* lleno de sol; resplandeciente como el sol.

sunstroke [san-strouk] *n.* insolación, *f.*

superb [su-perb] *adj.* soberbio, espléndido, excelente.

supercilious [su-per-si-li-oous] *adj.* arrogante, altanero; —**ly,** *adv.* con altivez.

superficial [su-per-fi-shal] *adj.* superficial.

superfluous [su-per-fluos] *adj.* superfluo; prolijo; redundante; —**ly,** *adv.* superfluamente.

superhuman [su-par-jiu-man] *adj.* sobrehumano.

superimpose [su-par-im-pous] *vt.* sobreponer.

superintendent [su-par-in-tendant] *n.* superintendente, mayordomo, *m.*

superior [su-pia-riar] *n.* y *adj.* jefe, superior, *m.*

superiority [su-pe-ri-o-ri-ti] *n.* superioridad, *f.*; arrogancia, *f.*

superlative [su-per-la-tiv] *n.* y *adj.* superlativo, *m.* ; —**ly,** *adv.* en sumo grado.

superman [su-per-man] *n.* superhombre, *m.*

supermarket [su-per-mar-kit] *n.* supermercado, *m.*

supernatural [su-per-na-cha-ral] *adj.* sobrenatural.

supersede [su-per-sid] *vt.* sobreseer; remplazar; invalidar.

supersonic [su-per-so-nik] *adj.* supersónico.

superstition [su-pers-ti-shon] *n.* superstición, *f.*

superstitious [su-pers-ti-shos] *adj.* supersticioso.

supervene [su-per-vin] *vi.* sobrevenir.

supervise [su-per-vais] *vt.* inspeccionar, dirigir, vigilar.

supervision [su-per-vi-shon] *n.* superintendencia, *f.;* dirección, inspección, vigilancia, *f.*

supervisor [su-per-vai-sor] *n.* superintendente, *m. y f.;* inspector, ra.

supper [sa-par] *n.* cena, *f.;* **Last S—,** Ultima Cena; **Lord's S—,** institución de la Eucaristía; **to have —,** cenar.

supple [sa-pel] *adj.* flexible, manejable; blando; **— ,** *vt.* hacer flexible.

supplement [sa-pli-ment] *n.* suplemento, *m. ;* **—,** *vt.* suplir; adicionar.

supplemental, supplementary [sa-pli-men-tal], [sa-pli-men-ta-ri] *adj.* adicional, suplementario.

supplicate [sa-pli-keit] *vt.* suplicar.

supply [sa-plai] *vt.* suplir, completar; surtir; proporcionar; dar, proveer; abastecer; **—,** *n.* surtido, *m. ;* provisión, *f.;* **— and demand,** oferta y demanda.

support [sa-port] *vt.* sostener; soportar, asistir; basar; **—,** *n.* sustento, *m. ;* apoyo, *m.*

supporter [sa-por-tar] *n.* apoyo, *m. ;* protector, ra, defensor, ra.

suppose [sa-pous] *vt.* suponer.

supposed [sa-pousd] *adj.* supuesto.

supposedly [sa-pous-dli] *adv.* según se supone, hipotéticamente.

supposing [sa-po-sin] *conj.* (coll.) en caso de que; **— that,** suponiendo que.

supposition [sa-po-si-shon] *n.* suposición, *f.,* supuesto, *m.*

suppress [sa-pres] *vt.* suprimir; reprimir.

suppression [sa-pre-shon] *n.* supresión, *f.*

supremacy [su-pre-ma-si] *n.* supremacía, *f.*

supreme [su-prim] *adj.* supremo.

surcharge [ser-charch] *vt.* sobrecargar; **—,** *n.* sobre-carga, *f.,* recargo, *m.*

sure [shuar] *adj.* seguro, cierto, certero; firme; estable; **to be —,** sin duda; seguramente; ya se ve; **—ly,** *adv.* sin duda. **sure-footed,** *adj.* seguro, de pie firme.

surf [serf] *n.* (naut.) resaca, *f.;* oleaje, *m.*

surface [ser-fis] *n.* superficie, cara, *f.;* **— tension,** tensión superficial; **—,** *vt.* alisar; **—,** *vi.* emerger, surgir.

surfacing [ser-fi-sin] *n.* recubrimiento (de un camino), *m. ;* revestimiento, *m. ;* alisamiento, *m.*

surge [serch] *n.* ola, onda, *f.;* golpe de mar; **—,** *vi.* embravecerse (el mar); agitarse; surgir.

surgeon [ser-yon] *n.* cirujano, *m.*

surgery [ser-ye-ri] *n.* cirugía, *f.*

surgical [ser-yi-kal] *adj.* quirúr-gico.

surly [ser-yi] *adj.* aspero de genio; insolente.

surmise [ser-mais] *vt.* sospe-char; suponer; —, *n.* sospecha, *f.;* suposición, *f.*

surmount [ser-maunt] *vt.* sobre-pujar; superar.

surname [ser-neim] *n.* apellido*;* —, *vt.* apellidar, dar un apelli-do (a alguien).

surpass [ser-pas] *vt.* sobresalir, sobrepujar, exceder, aventajar, sobrepasar.

surplus [ser-plas] *n.* sobrante, *m.* , sobra, *f.*

surprise [ser-prais] *vt.* sorpren-der; —, *n.* sorpresa.

surprising [ser-prai-sin] *adj.* sor-prendente, inesperado.

surrealism [sa-ria-li-sem] *n.* surrealismo, *m.*

surrender [sa-ren-dar] *vt.* rendir; ceder, renunciar; —, *vi.* rendir-se; —, *n.* rendición, *f.;* sumi-sión, *f.*

surrogate [sa-ro-gueit] *vt.* subro-gar; —, *n.* suplente, sustituto, *m.*

surround [sa-raund] *vt.* circun-dar, cercar, rodear.

surrounding [sa-raun-din] *adj.*

circunstante; que rodea; —, *n.* acción de circundar; —s, *pl.* cercanías, *f. pl.* , alrededores, *m. pl.* ; ambiente, *m.*

surveillance [ser-vei-lans] *n.* vigilancia, *f.*

survey [ser-vei] *vt.* inspeccionar, examinar; apear (tierras); —, *n.* inspección, *f.;* apeo (de tierras), *m.* ; estudio, *m.*

surveying [ser-vein] *n.* agrimen-sura, *f.;* estudio, examen, *m.* ; inspección, *f.*

survival [ser-vai-val] *n.* supervi-vencia, *f.;* — **of the fittest,** supervivencia de los más aptos.

survive [ser-vaiv] *vi.* sobrevivir.

surviving [ser-vai-vin] *adj.* sobre-viviente.

survivor [ser-vai-var] *n.* sobrevi-viente, *m. y f.*

susceptibility [sa-sep-ta-bi-li-ti] *n.* susceptibilidad, *f.*

susceptible [sa-sep-ti-bol] *adj.* susceptible.

suspect [sas-pekt] *vt. y vi.* sos-pechar.

suspend [sas-pend] *vt.* suspen-der, prorrogar, aplazar.

suspenders [sas-pen-dars] *n. pl.* tirantes, *m. pl.*

suspense [sas-pens] *n.* suspen-sión, *f* ; detención, *f.;* incerti-dumbre, duda, *f.;* — **movie,** película de misterio.

suspension [sas-pen-shon] *n.* suspensión, *f.;* — **bridge,** puente colgante; — **of work,** paro, *m.*

suspicion [sas-pi-shon] *n.* sospecha, *f.*

suspicious [sas-pi-shos] *adj.* suspicaz; sospechoso, receloso; **to make** —, dar que pensar.

sustain [sas-tein] *vt.* sostener, sustentar, mantener; apoyar; sufrir.

sustaining [sas-tei-nin] *adj.* que sustenta; — **program,** (rad. y TV.) programa radiofónico que perifonean por su cuenta las radiodifusoras.

sustenance [sas-ti-nans] *n.* sostenimiento, sustento, *m.;* alimentos, *m. pl.*

swab [suob] *n.* (naut.) lampazo, *m.;* (med.) esponja, *f.;* —, *vt.* fregar, limpiar; (naut.) lampacear.

swaddling [sua-dlin] *n.* empañadura, *f.;* — **clothes,** pañales, *m. pl.,* envolturas, *f. pl.*

swallow [suo-lou] *n.* (orn.) golondrina, *f.;* bocado, *m.;* trago, *m.;* —, *vt.* tragar, engullir.

swam [suam] *pretérito* del verbo **swim.**

swamp [suomp] *n.* pantano, fangal, *m.;* —, *vt.* sumergir; abrumar (de trabajo).

swan [suon] *n.* cisne, *m.;* —

song, canto del cisne, *m.;* última obra de un poeta o un músico; — **dive** (natación) salto del ángel.

swank [suank] *adj.* (coll.) elegante; —, *n.* (coll.) moda, *f.;* —, *vi.* (coll.) baladronear.

swanky [suan-ki] *adj.* (coll.) de moda ostentosa; elegante.

swap [suop] *vt.* y *vi.* (coll.) cambalachear, cambiar; (coll.) hacer permutas; —, *n.* (coll.) cambio, trueque, *m.*

swarm [suorm] *n.* enjambre, *m.;* gentío, *m.;* hormiguero, *m.;* —, *vi.* enjambrar; hormiguear de gente; abundar.

sway [suei] *vt.* disuadir; cimbrar; dominar, gobernar; —, *vi.* ladearse, inclinarse; tener influjo; —, *n.* bamboleo, *m.;* poder, imperio, influjo, *m.*

swear [suear] *vt.* y *vi.* jurar; blasfemar.

swearing [suea-rin] *n.* jura, *f.,* juramento, *m.;* blasfemia, *f.*

sweat [suet] *n.* sudor, *m.;* —, *vi.* sudar; trabajar con fatiga.

sweater [sue-tar] *n.* suéter, *m.,* chaqueta de punto de lana.

Swede [suid] *n.* sueco, ca.

Sweden [sui-den] Suecia, *f.*

Swedish [sui-dish] *adj.* sueco; — **language,** sueco, *m.*

sweep [suip] *vt.* y *vi.* barrer; arrebatar, pasar o tocar ligeramente; oscilar; —, *n.* barredura, *f.;* vuelta, *f.;* giro, *m.;* alcance, *m.*

sweeper [sui-par] *n.* barredor, ra; **carpet** —, barredora de alfombra.

sweeping [sui-pin] *adj.* rápido; barredero; vasto; —, *n.* barrido, *m.;* —**s,** *pl.* barreduras, *f. pl.,* desperdicios, *m. pl.*

sweet [suit] *adj.* dulce, grato, meloso, gustoso; suave; oloroso; melodioso; hermoso; amable; — **potato,** batata, *f.,* camote, moniato, buniato, *m.;* — **to have a — tooth,** ser amante del dulce, ser goloso; —, *n.* dulzura, *f.;* querida, *f.;* —**s,** dulces, *m. pl.;* —**ly,** *adv.* dulcemente.

sweeten [sui-ten] *vt.* endulzar; suavizar; aplacar; perfumar.

sweetheart [suit-jart] *n.* querido, da, novio, via; galanteador, *m.*

sweetness [suit-nes] *n.* dulzura, suavidad, *f.*

swell [suel] *vi.* hincharse; ensoberbecerse; embravecerse; —, *vt.* hinchar, inflar, agravar; — **up,** soplar; —, *n.* hinchazón, *f.;* bulto, *m.;* petimetre, *m.;* mar de leva; —, *adj.* (coll.) elegante, a la moda.

swelling [sue-lin] *n.* hinchazón, *f.;* tumor, *m.;* bulto, *m.,* protuberancia, *f.*

swelter [suel-tar] *vi.* sofocarse, ahogarse de calor; sudar.

sweltering [suel-te-rin] *adj.* sofocante.

swept [suept] *adj.* barrido; —, *pretérito* y *p.p.* del verbo **sweep.**

swerve [suerv] *vi.* vagar; desviarse; —, *vt.* desviar, torcer; —, *n.* desviación, *f.*

swift [suift] *adj.* veloz, ligero, rápido; —, *n.* (orn.) vencejo, *m.;* —**ly,** *adv.* velozmente.

swig [suig] *vt.* beber vorazmente; —, *n.* trapo, *m.* swim, *vi.* nadar; abundar en; ser vertiginoso; —, *vt.* pasar a nado.

swimmer [sui-mar] *n.* nadador, ra.

swimming [sui-min] *n.* natación, *f.;* vértigo, *m.;* — pool, piscina o alberca de natación; —**ly,** *adv.* sin dificultad.

swindle [suin-del] *vt.* petardear, estafar; —, *n.* estafa, *f.,* petardo, *m.*

swindler [suin-dlar] *n.* petardista, *m.,* tramposo, sa.

swine [suain] *n. sing.* y *pl.* puerco(s), cochino(s), *m.;* ganado de cerda.

swineherd [suain-jerd] *n.* porquerizo, *m.*

swing [suing] *vi.* balancear, columpiarse, oscilar; mecerse; agitarse; —, *vt.* esgrimir;

mecer; manejar con éxito; **to —
a loan,** lograr obtener un préstamo; **—,** *n.* balanceo, *m.;*
columpio, *m.;* **— bar,** balancín,
m.; **— music,** variedad de jazz.

swinging [suin-guin] *n.* vibración, *f.;* balanceo, *m.;* oscilación, *f.;* **—** *adj.* oscilante.

swipe [suaip] *n.* mango de
bomba; (coll.) golpe fuerte; **—,**
vt. dar golpes fuertes; coil.)
hurtar, robar.

swirl [suerl] *vt.* y *vi.* hacer remo-
linos el agua; arremolinar; **—,**
n. torcimiento, *m.*

switch [suich] *n.* varilla, *f.;* (rail.)
aguja, *f.;* (elec.) interruptor,
conmutador, *m.;* **ignition —,**
contacto de la ignición; **— box,**
caja de interruptores; **—,** *vt.*
varear; desviar; (elec.) cambiar;
to — off, desviar; apagar; **to —
on,** poner, encender.

Switzerland [sui-cha-land]
Suiza, *f.*

Swiss [suis] *n.* y *adj.* suizo, za;
— cheese, queso Gruyère.

swivel [sui-vel] *n.* torniquete, *m.;*
— chair, silla giratoria; **—,** *vt.* y
vi. girar.

swollen [suo-len] *adj.* hinchado,
inflado; **—,** *p.p.* del verbo **swell.**

swoop [suup] *vt.* coger, agarrar;
—, *vi.* precipitarse, caer;**—,** *n.*
acto de echarse un ave de rapi-
ña sobre su presa; **at one —,**

de un golpe.

sword [suord] *n.* espada, *f.*

swordfish [suord-fish] *n.* pez
espada, *m.*

swore [suor] *pretérito* del verbo
swear.

sworn [suorn] p.p. del verbo
swear.

swum [suam] p.p. del verbo
swim.

swung [suang] *pretérito* y *p.p.*
del verbo **swing.**

sycamore [si-ka-mor] *n.* (bot.)
sicómoro, *m.*

syllable [si-la-bol] *n.* sílaba, *f.*

sylph [silf] *n.* silfo, *m.;* sílfide, *f.*

symbol [sim-bol] *n.* símbolo, *m.*

symbolic [sim-bo-lik] *adj.* simbólico.

symbolism [sim-bo-li-sem] *n.*
simbolismo, *m.*

symbolize [sim-bo-lais] *vt.* simbolizar.

symmetrical [si-me-tri-kal] *adj.*
simétrico; **—ly,** *adv.* con simetría.

symmetry [si-mi-tri] *n.* simetría,
f.

sympathetic [sim-pa-ze-tik] *adj.*
que congenia; inclinado a sentir compasión o a condolerse;
—ally, *adv.* con compasión.

sympathize [sim-pa-zais] *vi.*
compadecerse, simpatizar; **—
with,** compadecer.

sympathizer [sim-pa-zai-ser] *n.*

compadecedor, ra, simpatiza-
dor, ra.

sympathy [sim-pa-zi] *n.* compasión, condolencia, *f.;* simpatía,
f.; pésame, *m.*

symphony [sim-fo-ni] *n.* sinfonía, armonía, *f.*

symposium [sim-pou-siom] *n.*
simposia, *f.,* festín o banquete
de los antiguos griegos en
donde se cruzaban ideas; sim-
posio, *m.,* conferencia para discutir un tema; colección de
opinones sobre un mismo
tema.

symptom [simp-tom] *n.* síntoma,
m.

synagogue [si-na-gog] *n.* sinagoga, *f.*

synchronize [sin-kro-nais] *vt.*
sincronizar.

syndicate [sin-di-kit] *n.* sindicato, *m.;* —, *vt.* y *vi.* sindicar.

synonym [si-no-nim] *n.* sinónimo, *m.*

synonymous [si-no-ni-mos] *adj.*

sinónimo; —**ly**, *adv.* en forma
sinónima.

synopsis [si-nop-sis] *n.* sinopsis,
f.; sumario, resumen, *m.*

syntax [sin-taks] *n.* sintaxis, *f.*

synthesis [sin-ze-sis] *n.* síntesis,
f.

synthetic [sin-ze-tik] *adj.* sintético; fabricado; — **rubber,** caucho artificial, caucho sintético.

synthetize [sin-za-sais] *vt.* sinte-
tizar.

syphilis [si-fi-lis] *n.* sífilis, *f.,*
gálico, *m.*

syringe [si-rindch] *n.* jeringa;
hypodermic —, jeringa hipodérmica.

syrup o **sirup** [si-rop] *n.* jarabe,
m.; **cough** —, jarabe para la
tos.

system [sis-tem] *n.* sistema, *m.;*
instalación, *f.*

systematic [sis-te-ma-tik] *adj.*
sistemático, metódico.

systematize [sis-te-ma-tais] *vt.*
sistematizar, sistematar.

T

tab [tab] *n.* pequeña etiqueta o
lengüeta saliente; (coll.) cuenta;
to pick up the —, pagar la
cuenta de varios (en un restaurante, etc.); **to keep — on,**
(coll.) vigilar (a alguien), com-

probar lo que hace.

tabernacle [ta-ba-na-kol] *n.*
tabernáculo, *m.;* templo, *m.*

table [tei-bol] *n.* mesa, *f.;* velador, *m.;* tabla, *f.;* elenco, *m.;* **on
the** —, sobre la mesa; **round** —

, mesa redonda; — **cover,** carpeta, *f.;* — **service,** vajilla, *f.;* **to set the —,** poner la mesa; **—,** *vt.* apuntar en forma sinóptica; poner sobre la mesa.

tablecloth [tei-bol-kloz] *n.* mantel, *m.*

tablespoon [tei-bol-spun] *n.* cuchara, *f.*

tablet [ta-blit] *n.* tableta, *f.;* pastilla, *f.;* plancha, lámina, *f.;* — **of paper,** bloc de papel.

tableware [tei-bol-uear] *n.* servicio de mesa.

tabloid [ta-bloid] *n.* noticiero ilustrado.

taboo, tabu [ta-bu] *n.* tabú, *m.;* **—,** *adj.* prohibido; **—,** *vt.* interdecir, vedar, prohibir.

tabular [ta-biu-lar] *adj.* en forma de tabla, tabular.

tabulate [ta-biu-leit] *vt.* presentar cifras o datos en forma de tabla, tabular.

taciturn [ta-si-tern] *adj.* taciturno, callado.

tack [tak] *n.* tachuela, *f.;* **—,** *vt.* clavar; atar; pegar.

tackle [ta-kel] *n.* todo género de instrumentos o aparejos; **fishing —,** arreos de pescar; (naut.) cordaje, cuadernal, *m.;* jarcia, *f.;* (fútbol norteamericano) atajador, *m.,* jugador en la primera línea de un equipo; **—,** *vt.* asir, forcejear; atajar; aco

meter, emprender, intentar.

tact [takt] *n.* tacto, *m.*

tactful [takt-ful] *adj.* sensato, sigiloso; prudente, con tacto; — **ly,** *adv.* sigilosamente, prudentemente, con tacto.

tactics [tak-tiks] *n. pl.* táctica, *f.*

tactless [takt-les] *adj.* sin tacto, imprudente.

tadpole [tad-poul] *n.* renacuajo, *m.*

taffeta [ta-fi-ta] *n.* tafetán, *m.*

taffy [ta-fi] *n.* melcocha, *f.;* (coll.) zalamería, *f.*

tag [tag] *n.* marbete, *m.,* marca, *f.;* etiqueta, *f.;* juego infantil en que se persigue a un niño hasta tocarlo; (Mex.) juego de la roña; **—,** *vt.* poner marbete.

tail [teil] *n.* cola, *f.,* rabo, *m.;* — **spin,** (avi.) barrena de cola.

taillight [teil-lait] *n.* (auto.) farol de cola, (Mex. coll.) calavera, *f.*

tailor [tei-lar] *n.* sastre, *m.*

tailoring [tei-la-rin] *n.* sastrería, *f.*

tailor-made [tei-la-meid] *adj.* a la medida; como hecho a mano.

taint [teint] *vt.* tinturar, manchar; inficionar; viciar; **—,** *n.* mácula, mancha, *f.*

take [teik] *vt.* tomar, coger, asir; recibir, aceptar; pillar; prender; admitir; aguantar; **—,** *vi.* encaminarse, dirigirse; salir bien; arraigarse; prender (el fuego);

to — **a breath,** resollar; **to —
apart,** desarmar, desmontar; **to
— a walk,** pasear, dar un
paseo; **to — away,** llevar; quitar; **to — charge of,** encargarse
de; **to — for granted,** dar por
sentado; **to — home,** llevar a
casa; **to — off,** (avi.) despegar;
to — out, suprimir; llevar a
pasear; **to — place,** verificarse,
tener lugar; **to —the liberty,**
permitirse; **to — upon oneself,**
encargarse de; **to — it,** (coll.)
sobrellevar, soportar (algo); —,
n. toma, *f.;* presa, *f.;* parte de
una escena filmada o televisada sin interrupción.

taken [tei-ken] *p.p.* del verbo
take.

take-off [teik-of] *n.* caricatura, *f.;*
parodia, *f.;* (avi.) despegue, *m.*

take-out [tei-kaut] *n.* comida
para llevar.

taking [tei-kin] *adj.* agradable,
simpático, cautivador; (coll.)
contagioso; —, *n.* presa, *f.;*
secuestro, *m.;* —**s,** *pl.* colectas,
f. pl., dinero recogido.

talcum [tal-kum] *n.* talco, *m.;* —
powder, polvo de talco.

tale [teil] *n.* cuento, *m.,* fábula,
f.

talent [ta-lent] *n.* talento, *m.;*
ingenio, *m.;* capacidad, habilidad, *f.*

talented [ta-len-tid] *adj.* talento-

so, capaz.

talk [tok] *vi.* hablar, conversar;
charlar; —, *n.* plática, habla, *f.;*
charla, *f.;* fama, *f.;* conferencia,
f., discurso, *m.*

talkative [to-ka-tiv] *adj.* gárrulo,
locuaz, palabrero, hablador,
parlero, charlatán.

talker [to-kar] *n.* charlador, ra.

talking [to-kin] *adj.* hablante; —
machine, fonógrafo, tocadiscos,
m.; — **picture,** película sonora
o hablada.

tall [tol] *adj.* alto, elevado; (coll.)
raro, increíble; — **story,** relato
exagerado e increíble.

tallow [ta-lou] *n.* sebo, *m.;* —, *vt.*
ensebar.

tally [ta-li] *n.* cuenta, *f.;* —
sheet, hoja de apuntes; —, *vt.*
ajustar; tarjar.

talon [ta-lon] *n.* garra del ave de
rapiña.

tame [teim] *adj.* amansado,
domado, domesticado; abatido;
manso; sumiso; —, *vt.* domar,
domesticar.

taming [tei-min] *n.* domadura, *f.*

tamper [tei-mar] *vi.* tramar;
sobornar; entremeterse en lo
que no se debe.

tan [tan] *vt.* curtir, zurrar, tostar, broncear; —, *vi.* broncear-
se, —, *n.* casca, *f.;* color café
claro, color de arena.

tandem [tan-dam] *adv.* uno tras

otro; —, *n.* tándem. *m.*, bicicleta usada por dos ciclistas al mismo tiempo; coche con caballos uno tras otro; —, *adj.* tándem.

tang [tang] *n.* sabor, *m.;* olor fuerte; retintín, *m.;* —, *vi.* retiñir.

tangent [tan-yent] *n.* y *adj.* tangente, *f.*

tangerine [tan-ya-rin] *n.* naranja tangerina o mandarina.

tangible [tan-yi-bol] *adj.* tangible.

tangle [tan-guel] *vt.* enredar, embrollar; —, *vi.* enredarse; —, *n.* enredo, embrollo, *m.;* confusión, *f.;* maraña, *f.*

tango [tan-gou] *n.* tango, *m.*

tank [tank] *n.* (mil.) tanque, *m.,* carro blindado; depósito, tanque, *m.;* cisterna, *f.,* aljibe, *m.;* — car, (rail.) vagón-tanque, *m.;* — **trap,** (mil.) trampa u obstáculo para tanques; —, *vt.* almacenar.

tanned [tand] *adj.* curtido; tostado del sol.

tantalize [tan-ta-lais] *vt.* atormentar a alguno mostrándole placeres que no puede alcanzar.

tantalizing [tan-ta-lai-sin] *adj.* atormentador; tentador.

tantrum [tan-trom] *n.* berrinche, *m.*

tap [tap] *vt.* tocar ligeramente; barrenar; golpear ligeramente; decentar; utilizar, usufructuar; sacar; —, *n.* palmada suave; toque ligero; grifo, *m.;* espita, *f.;* tomadero, *m.;* — **dance,** baile zapateado (común en los E.U.A.).

tape [teip] *n.* cinta, *f.;* cinta de grabar; — **measure,** cinta de medir.

taper [tei-par] *n.* candela, *f.;* cirio, *m.;* taladro de reducción; —, *adj.* cónico; —, *vi.* rematar en punta, ahusar; —, *vt.* dar forma ahusada.

tapestry [ta-pis-tri] *n.* tapiz, *m.;* tapicería, *f.*

tapeworm [teip-uem] *n.* tenia, lombriz solitaria, solitaria, *f.*

tapioca [ta-pio-ka] *n.* tapioca, *f.*

tar [tar] *n.* brea, *f.;* (coll.) marinero, *m.;* alquitrán, *m.,* pez, *f.;* —, *vt.* embrear.

tarantula [ta-ran-tiu-la] *n.* tarántula, *f.*

tardiness [tar-di-nes] *n.* tardanza, *f.*

tardy [tar-di] *adj.* tardo, lento.

target [tar-guit] *n.* rodela, *f.;* blanco (para tirar), *m.;* **to hit the —,** dar en el blanco, acertar.

tariff [ta-rif] *n.* tarifa, *f.,* arancel, *m.*

tarnish [tar-nish] *vt.* deslustrar;

manchar; —, *vi.* deslustrarse; —, *n.* borrón, *m.*, mancha, *f.*

tarpaulin [tar-po-lin] *n.* tela embreada; toldo, *m.*

tarpon [tar-pon] *n.* (ichth.) sábalo, *m.*

tart [tart] *adj.* agrio; acedo, acre; —, *n.* torta, *f.*, pastelillo, *m.*; —**ly,** *adv.* agriamente.

tartar [tar-tar] *n.* tártaro, *m.*; sarro (de los dientes), *m.*

task [task] *n.* tarea, *f.*; quehacer, *m.*; — **force,** tropa o contingente naval a los cuales se asignan tareas de combate.

tassel [ta-sel] *n.* mota, borlita, *f.*; —, *vt.* decorar con borlitas.

taste [teist] *n.* gusto, *m.*; sabor, *m.*; prueba, *f.*; saboreo, *m.*; ensayo, *m.*; —, *vt.* y *vi.* gustar; probar; experimentar; agradar; tener sabor.

tasteful [teist-ful] *adj.* elegante, galano, de buen gusto; —**ly,** *adv.* con buen gusto.

tasteless [teist-les] *adj.* sin sabor; de mal gusto.

tasty [teis-ti] *adj.* sabroso, gustoso.

tatter [ta-tar] *n.* andrajo, *m.*

tattered [ta-tard] *adj.* andrajoso, haraposo.

tattle [ta-tel] *vt.* y *vi.* charlar, parlotear; chismear; —, *n.* charla, *f.*

tattletale [ta-tel-teil]*n.* chismoso,

sa, chismero, ra, soplón, ona, delator, ra.

tattoo [ta-tuu] *n.* tatuaje, *m.*; (mil.) retreta, *f.*; —, *vt.* tatuar.

taunt [tont] *vt.* mofar; ridiculizar; dar chanza; —, *n.* mofa, burla, chanza, *f.*

taut [tot] *adj.* tieso, terco, tirante; nítido, en orden.

tavern [ta-varn] *n.* taberna, *f.*; posada, *f.*

tawny [to-ni] *adj.* moreno; de color tostado.

tax [taks] *n.* impuesto, tributo, gravamen, *m.*, contribución, *f.*; carga, *f.*; **additional** —, recargo, *m.*; **income** —, impuesto sobre la renta; — **rate,** tarifa de impuestos; —, *vt.* imponer tributos o impuestos; agotar (la paciencia); abrumar.

taxable [tak-sa-bol] *adj.* sujeto a impuestos.

taxation [tak-sei-shon] *n.* tributación, *f.*

tax-exempt [taks-ik-sempt] *adj.* exento de impuestos.

taxi [tak-si] *n.* taxímetro, taxi, *m.*, automóvil de plaza o de alquiler; (Mex.) libre, *m.*; —, *vi.* ir en un taxímetro o automóvil de alquiler; (avi.) moverse sobre la superficie.

taxicab [tak-si-kab] *n.* taxímetro, automóvil de alquiler; (Mex.) libre, *m.*

taxpayer [taks-paier] *n.* contri- buyente, *m.* y *f.*, pagador o pagadora de impuestos.

tea [tii] *n.* té, *m.;* — **ball,** bola metálica perforada para el té; — **bag,** bolsita con hojas de té.

teach [tich] *vt.* enseñar, instruir; —, *vi.* ejercer el magisterio.

teacher [ti-char] *n.* maestro, tra, profesor, ra, preceptor, ra, pedagogo, ga.

teaching [ti-chin] *n.* enseñanza, *f.;* —, *adj.* docente; — **staff,** personal docente.

teacup [ti-kap] *n.* taza para té.

teak [tik] *n.* (bot.) teca, *f.*

teakettle [ti-ke-tel] *n.* tetera, *f.*

teal [til] *n.* cerceta, zarceta, *f.*, variedad de ánade silvestre.

team [tim] *n.* tiro de caballos; pareja, *f.;* equipo, *m.*

teamwork [tim-uek] *n.* trabajo de cooperación; auxilio mutuo.

teapot [ti-pot] *n.* tetera, *f.*

tear [tear] *n.* lágrima, *f.;* gota, *f.;* — **bomb,** bomba lacrimógena; — **gas,** gas lacrimógeno.

tear [tear] *vt.* despedazar, lace- rar; rasgar; arrancar; raja, *f.;* jirón, *m.*

teardrop [tia-drop] *n.* lágrima, *f.*

tearful [tia-ful] *adj.* lloroso, lacri- moso; —**ly,** *adv.* con llanto.

tease [tis] *vt.* cardar (lana o lino); molestar, atormentar; dar broma; (coll.) tomar el pelo.

teaspoon [ti-spun] *n.* cucharita, *f.*

teat [tit] *n.* ubre, *f.;* teta, *f.*

technical [tek-ni-kal] *adj.* técni- co; — **staff,** personal técnico.

technicality [tek-ni-ka-li-ti] *n.* asunto técnico; cuestión técni- ca.

technician [tek-ni-shan] *n.* experto, técnico, *m.*

technicolor [tek-ni-ka-lar] *n.* tec- nicolor, *m.*

technique [tek-nik] *n.* técnica, *f.*, método, *m.*

technological [tek-no-lo-yi-kal] *adj.* tecnológico.

technology [tek-no-lo-yi] *n.* tec- nología, *f.*

tedious [ti-dios] *adj.* tedioso, fas- tidioso.

teem [tiim] *vi.* abundar; rebosar.

teenager [tin-ei-char] *n.* joven de 13 a 19 años.

teens [tins] *n. pl.* números y años desde 13 hasta 19; perio- do de 13 a 19 años de edad.

teeter [tin-tar] *vt.* y *vi.* balance- arse; —, *n.* balanceo, *m.;* columpio de sube y baja.

teeth [tiz] *n. pl.* de **tooth,** dien- tes, *m. pl.;* **false** —, dientes postizos; **set of** —, dentadura, *f.*

teethe [tiz] *vi.* endentecer, echar los dientes.

teething [ti-zin] *n.* dentición, *f.;*

— **ring,** chupador, *m.*

telecast [te-li-kast] *vt.* y *vi.* televisar, trasmitir por televisión; —, *n.* teledifusión, *f.*

telegraph [te-li-graf] *n.* telégrafo, *m.;* —, *vi.*

telephone [te-li-foun] *n.* teléfono, *m.;* **dial** —, teléfono automático; — **booth,** cabina telefónica; — **receiver,** receptor, *m.;* — **directory,** directorio de teléfonos, lista de abonados al teléfono; —, *vt.* y *vi.* telefonear.

telescope [te-lis-koup] *n.* telescopio, *m.*

teletype [te-li-taip] *n.* teletipo, *m.;* —, *vt.* enviar un mensaje por teletipo.

televiewer [te-li-viuar] *n.* televidente, *m.* y *f.*

televise [te-li-vais] *vt.* televisar.

television [te-li-vi-shon] *n.* televisión, *f.;* — **set,** telerreceptor, televisor, aparato de televisión.

tell [tel] *vt.* y *vi.* decir; informar, contar; numerar, revelar; mandar; hacer efecto.

teller [te-lar] *n.* relator, ra; computista, *m.* y *f.;* **paying** —, pagador, ra; **receiving** —, recibidor, ra.

telltale [tel-teil] *n.* soplón, ona, delator, ra; —, *adj.* revelador.

temerity [ti-me-ri-ti] *n.* temeridad, *f.*

temper [tem-par] *vt.* templar, moderar; atemperar; —, *n.* temperamento, *m.;* humor, genio, *m.;* **ill** —, mal humor; **to lose one's** —, enojarse; salirse de sus casillas.

temperament [tem-pe-ra-ment] *n.* temperamento, *m.;* carácter, genio, *m.*

temperamental [tem-pe-ra-mental] *adj.* genial; de carácter caprichoso.

temperance [tem-pe-rans] *n.* templanza, moderación, *f.;* sobriedad, *f.*

temperate [tem-pe-rit] *adj.* templado, moderado, sobrio; — **zone,** zona templada.

temperature [tem-pri-char] *n.* temperatura, *f.*

tempered [tem-pard] *adj.* templado, acondicionado; **ill** —, de mal genio; **even** —, parejo, apacible, de buen carácter.

tempest [tem-pist] *n.* tempestad, *f.*

tempestuous [tem-pes-tiuos] *adj.* tempestuoso, proceloso; —**ly,** *adv.* tempestuosamente.

temple [tem-pel] *n.* templo, *m.;* sien, *f.*

temporal [tem-po-ral] *adj.* temporal, provisional; secular, profano; (anat., zool.) temporal.

temporarily [tem-po-ra-li-ti] *adv.* temporalmente, provisionalmente; por lo pronto.

temporary [tem-po-ra-ri] *adj.* provisional, temporario, temporal.

tempt [temptt] *vt.* tentar; provocar.

temptation [temp-tei-shon] *n.* tentación, *f.;* prueba, *f.*

tempting [temp-tin] *adj.* tentador; —**ly,** *adv.* en forma tentadora.

temptress [temp-tres] *n.* tentadora, mujer fascinadora.

ten [ten] *n.* y *adj.* diez, *m.;* (math.) decena, *f.*

tenacious [ti-nei-shos] *adj.* tenaz.

tenacity [ti-na-si-ti] *n.* tenacidad, *f.;* porfía, *f.*

tenant [te-nant] *n.* arrendador, ra, tenedor, ra, inquilino, na; —, *vt.* arrendar.

tend [tend] *vt.* guardar, velar; atender; —, *vi.* tirar, dirigirse; atender.

tendency [ten-den-si] *n.* tendencia, *f.;* inclinación, *f.*

tender [ten-dar] *adj.* tierno, delicado; sensible; —**ly,** *adv.* tiernamente; —, *n.* oferta, propuesta, *f.;* (naut.) patache, *m.;* (rail.) ténder (de una locomotora), *m.;* (com.) lo que se emplea para pagar; —, *vt.* ofrecer, proponer; presentar.

tender-hearted [ten-der-jar-ded] *adj.* compasivo, impresionable.

tenderloin [ten-der-loin] *n.* filete, solomillo, *m.*

tendon [ten-don] *n.* tendón, *m.*

tenement [te-ni-mant] *n.* tenencia, habitación, *f.;* — **house,** casa de vecindad.

tenet [te-nit] *n.* dogma, *m.;* aserción, *f.;* credo, *m.*

tennis [te-nis] *n.* tenis, *m.,* raqueta (juego), *f.;* — **court,** campo de tenis; — **player,** tenista, *m.* y *f.*

tenor [te-nor] *n.* (mus.) tenor, *m.;* tenor, curso, *m.;* contenido, *m.;* sustancia, *f.;* —, *adj.* de tenor.

tense [tens] *adj.* tieso; tenso; —, *n.* (gram.) tiempo, *m.;* **past** —, pasado, *m.;* **present** —, presente, *m.*

tension [ten-shon] *n.* tensión, tirantez, *f.;* (elec.) voltaje, *m.*

tent [tent] *n.* (mil.) tienda de campaña; pabellón, *m.;* (cirugía) tienta, *f.;* **oxygen** —, tienda de oxígeno; —, *vi.* acampar en tienda de campaña.

tentacle [ten-ta-kol] *n.* tentáculo, *m.*

tentative [ten-ta-tiv] *adj.* tentativo; de ensayo; de prueba; —**ly,** *adv.* como prueba.

tenth [tenz] *n.* y *adj.* décimo, ma; —**ly,** *adv.* en décimo lugar.

tenuous [te-niuos] *adj.* tenue, delgado.

tenure [te-niuar] *n.* tenencia, incumbencia, *f.*

tepid [te-pid] *adj.* tibio.

term [term] *n.* término, confín, *m.;* plazo, *m.;* tiempo, periodo, *m.;* estipulación, *f.;* **—s of payment,** condiciones de pago; **to come to —s,** llegar a un acuerdo; **—,** *vt.* nombrar, llamar.

terminal [ter-mi-nal] *adj.* terminal, final; **—,** *n.* terminal, *m.;* (rail.) estación terminal.

terminate [ter-mi-neit] *vt.* y *vi.* terminar, limitar.

terminology [ter-mi-no-lo-yi] *n.* terminología, *f.*

termite [ter-mait] *n.* termita, *f.*

terrace [te-ras] *n.* terraza, *f.,* terrado, *m.;* terraplén, *m.;* **—,** *vt.* terraplenar.

terrestrial [ti-res-trial] *adj.* terrestre, terreno.

terrible [te-ra-bol] *adj.* terrible.

terrier [te-rier] *n.* zorrero, *m.*

terrific [te-ri-fik] *adj.* terrífico, terrible, espantoso; (coll.) tremendo, maravilloso.

terrify [te-ri-fai] *vt.* espantar, llenar de terror.

territory [te-ri-to-ri] *n.* territorio, *m.*

terror [te-ror] *n.* terror, espanto, *m.*

terrorist [te-ro-rist] *n.* terrorista, *m.*

terrorize [te-ro-rais] *vt.* aterrori-zar, aterrar, espantar.

terror-stricken [te-ro-stri-ken] *adj.* aterrorizado, horro-rizado.

terse [ters] *adj.* terso, sucinto.

terseness [ters-nes] *n.* brevedad, concisión, *f.*

test [test] *n.* ensayo, *m.,* prueba, *f.;* examen, *m.;* **— pilot,** piloto de prueba; **— tube,** probeta, *f.;* **—,** *vt.* ensayar, probar; examinar.

Testament [tes-ta-ment] *n.* Testamento, *m.;* **New —,** el Nuevo Testamento; **Old —,** el Viejo Testamento.

testament [tes-ta-ment] *n.* testamento, *m.*

tester [tes-tar] *n.* probador, ra; cielo de cama o de púlpito.

testify [tes-ti-fai] *vt.* testificar, atestiguar; aseverar.

testimonial [tes-ti-mou-nial] *n.* atestación, *f.;* recomendación, *f.,* elogio, *m.;* **—,** *adj.* testimonial.

testimony [tes-ti-mo-ni] *n.* testimonio, *m.*

testing [tes-tin] *n.* ensayo, *m.,* prueba, *f.*

tetanus [te-ta-nos] *n.* tétano, *m.*

tether [te-dar] *n.* correa, maniota, *f.;* traba, *f.;* **—,** *vt.* atar con una correa.

text [tekst] *n.* texto, *m.;* tema, *m.*

textbook [tekst-buk] *n.* texto,

libro de texto.

textile [teks-tail] *adj.* hilable; textil; —, *n.* tejido, *m.*

textual [tekst-chual] *adj.* textual.

texture [tekst-char] *n.* textura, *f.;* tejido, *m.*

thalamus [za-la-mus] *n.* (bot.) tálamo, *m.;* (anat.) tálamo óptico.

thallus [za-lus] *n.* (bot.) talo, *m.*

than [dan] *conj.* que o de (en sentido comparativo).

thank [zank] *vt.* agradecer, dar gracias; — **offering,** ofrecimiento en acción de gracias; —**s,** gracias, *f. pl.;* — **you,** gracias, *f. pl.*

thankful [zank-ful] *adj.* grato, agradecido; —**ly,** *adv.* con gratitud.

thankfulness [zank-ful-nes] *n.* gratitud, *f.*

thankless [zank-les] *adj.* ingrato.

Thanksgiving Day [zanks-gi-bin-dei] *n.* día de dar gracias, día de acción de gracias (en Estados Unidos).

that [dat] *pron.* ése, ésa, eso; aquél, aquélla, aquello; que, quien, el cual, la cual, lo cual; —, *conj.* que, para que; —, *adj.* ese, esa, aquel, aquella; —, *adv.* así de, a tal grado; de este tamaño; **not — large,** no tan grande.

thaw [zo] *n.* deshielo, *m.;* —, *vi.*

derretirse, disolverse; deshelarse; —, *vt.* derretir.

the [da] *art.* el, la, lo; los, las.

theater [zia-tar] *n.* teatro, *m.*

theatrical [zia-tri-kal] *adj.* teatral; fingido para impresionar; —**ly,** *adv.* en forma teatral.

theft [zeft] *n.* robo, *m.*

their [dear] *adj.* su, sus (de ellos o de ellas); —**s,** *pron.* el suyo, los suyos, suyo, suyos (de ellos o ellas).

them [dem] *pron.* (acusativo y dativo de **they**) los, las, les; ellos, ellas.

theme [ziim] *n.* tema, asunto, *m.;* (mus.) motivo, *m.;* — **park,** parque de diversiones, m;— **song,** (rad. y TV.) música que inicia un programa o que sirve de motivo al mismo.

themselves [dem-selvs] *pron. pl.* ellos mismos, ellas mismas; si mismos o mismas.

then [den] *adv.* entonces, después; en tal caso; **now and —,** de cuando en cuando.

theological [zio-lo-yi-kal] *adj.* teológico.

theology [zio-lou-yi] *n.* teología, *f.*

theorem [zio-rem] *n.* teorema, *m.;* **binomial —,** binomio de Newton.

theoretical *adj.* teórico.

theorist [zio-rist] *n.* teórico, *m.*

theorize [zio-rais] *vt.* teorizar.

therapeutic, therapeutical [ze-ra-piu-tik], [ze-ra-piu-ti-kal] *adj.* terapéutico.

therapeutics [ze-ra-piu-tiks] *n.* terapéutica, *f.*

therapy [ze-ra-pi] *n.* terapia, *f.*

there [dear] *adv.* allí, allá; ahí; — **is,** — **are,** hay; —! *interj.* ¡mira! ¡ya lo ves! ¡te lo dije!

thereby [dear-bai] *adv.* por medio de eso; con eso; por lo tanto.

therefrom [dear-from] *adv.* de allí, de allá, de eso.

thermal [zer-mal] *adj.* termal; — **waters,** termas, caldas, *f. pl.*

thermic [zer-mik] *adj.* termal; térmico.

thermometer [zer-mo-mi-tar] *n.* termómetro, *m.*

thermonuclear [zer-mou-niu-kliar] *adj.* termonuclear.

thermos, thermos bottle [zer-mos], [zer-mos-bo-tel] *n.* termos, *m.* thermostat, *n.* termostato, *m.*

thesaurus [zi-so-ros] *n.* tesauro, *m.*

these [dis] *pron. pl.* éstos, éstas; —, *adj.* estos, estas.

thesis [zi-sis] *n.* tesis, *f.*

they [dei] *pron. pl.* ellos, ellas.

thiamine [zia-main] *n.* tiamina, *f.*

thick [zik] *adj.* espeso, denso; grueso; turbio; frecuente; torpe; ronco; **through — and thin,** por toda situación difícil o penosa (expresión que demuestra la lealtad de alguien); —, *n.* la parte más gruesa; —**ly,** *adv.* espesamente; frecuentemente.

thicken [zi-ken] *vi.* y *vt.* espesar, condensar; condensarse, espesarse.

thickening [zi-ke-nin] *n.* sustancia para espesar; acción de espesarse.

thicket [zi-kit] *n.* espesar, matorral, *m.;* maleza, *f.*

thickness [zik-nes] *n.* espesura, densidad, *f.;* grosor, grueso, *m.*

thief [zif] *n.* ladrón, ona.

thieve [ziv] *vt.* y *vi.* hurtar, robar; —**s,** *n. pl.* de **thief.**

thigh [zai] *n.* muslo, *m.*

thighbone [zai-boun] *n.* fémur, *m.*

thimble [zim-bel] *n.* dedal, *m.*

thin [zin] *adj.* delgado, delicado; sutil; flaco; claro; ralo; —, *vt.* enrarecer; atenuar; adelgazar; aclarar.

thine [dain] *pron.* tuyo, tuya, tuyos, tuyas.

thing [zing] *n.* cosa, *f.;* asunto, *m.*

think [zink] *vt.* y *vi.* pensar, imaginar, meditar, considerar; creer, juzgar, opinar.

thinking [zin-kin] *n.* pensamiento, *m.;* juicio, *m.;* opinión, *f.*

thinness [zin-nes] *n.* tenuidad; raleza, *f.;* escasez, *f.*

third [zerd] *n.* y *adj.* tercero, *m.;* — **degree,** (coll.) abuso de autoridad por parte de la policía para obtener información; — **person,** (gram.) tercera persona; tercero, *m.;* —**ly,** *adv.* en tercer lugar.

thirst [zerst] *n.* sed, *f.;* anhelo, *m.;* —, *vi.* tener sed, padecer sed.

thirstiness [zers-ti-nes] *n.* sed, *f.;* anhelo, *m.*

thirsty [zers-ti] *adj.* sediento; **to be** —, tener sed.

thirteen [zer-tiin] *n.* y *adj.* trece, *m.*

thirtieth [zer-tiez] *n.* y *adj.* trigésimo, treintavo, *m.*

thirty [zer-ti] *n.* y *adj.* treinta, *m.*

this [dis] *adj.* este, esta; —, *pron.* éste, ésta; esto.

thorn [zorn] *n.* espino, *m.;* espina, *f.:* — **in the side,** (coll.) molestia, mortificación, *f.;* —, *vt.* pinchar; proveer de espinas.

thorny [zor-ni] *adj.* espinoso; arduo.

thorough [za-ro] *adj.* entero, cabal, perfecto; —**ly,** *adv.* enteramente, cabalmente, detenidamente.

thoroughbred [za-ro-bred] *adj.* de sangre, de casta (de caba-

llos) ; —, *n.* persona bien nacida **o** de buena crianza, persona de sangre **a**zul; caballo u otro animal de casta.

thoroughness [za-ro-nes] *n.* entereza, *f.;* perfección *f.*

those [dous] *adj. pl.* de that, aquellos, aquellas esos, esas; —, *pron.* aquéllos, aquéllas, ésos, ésas.

though [dau] *conj.* aunque, no obstante; **as** —, como que, como si; —, *adv.* sin embargo, no obstante.

thought [zot] *n.* pensamiento, juicio, *m.;* opinión, *f.;* cuidado, *m.;* concepto, *m.;* **to give** — **to,** pensar en; —, *pretérito* y p.p. del verbo **think.**

thoughtful [zot-ful] *adj.* pensativo, meditabundo; pensado; —**ly,** *adv.* de un modo muy pensativo.

thoughtfulness [zot-ful-nes] *n.* meditación profunda; consideración, atención, *f.*

thoughtless [zot-les] *adj.* inconsiderado, descuida-do; insensato; —**ly,** *adv.* sin reflexión.

thousand [zau-sand] *n.* mil, *m.;* millar, *m.;* **per** —, por mil; —, *adj.* mil.

thousandth [zau-sandz] *n.* y *adj.* milésimo, *m.*

thread [zred] *n.* hilo, *m.;* fibra, *f.;* —, *vt.* enhebrar; atravesar.

threat [zret] *n.* amenaza, *f.*

threaten [zre-ten] *vt.* amenazar.

threatening [zret-nin] *n.* amenaza, *f.;* —, *adj.* amenazador; —ly, *adv.* con amenazas.

three [zri] *n.* y *adj.* tres, *m.*

thresh [zresh] *vt.* trillar; desgranar; golpear; batir; sacudir.

thresher [zre-shar] *n.* trillador, *m.*

threshing [zre-shin] *adj.* trillador; — **machine**, trilladora, *f.,* máquina trilladora, trillo, *m.*

threshold [zresh-jould] *n.* umbral, *m.;* entrada, *f.*

threw [zru] *pretérito* del verbo **throw.**

thrift [zrift] *n.* economía, frugalidad, *f.;* —ily, *adv.* económicamente.

thriftiness [zrif-ti-nes] *n.* frugalidad, parsimonia, *f.*

thrifty [zrif-ti] *adj.* frugal, económico; próspero, vigoroso.

thrill [zril] *vt.* emocionar; —, *vi.* estremecerse; —, *n.* estremecimiento, *m.;* emoción, *f.*

thrilling [zri-lin] *adj.* excitante; emocionante; conmovedor.

thrive [zraiv] *vi.* prosperar, adelantar, aprovechar.

thriving [zrai-vin] *adj.* próspero.

throat [zrout] *n.* garganta, *f.;* cuello, *m.;* **sore** —, dolor de garganta.

throb [zrob] *vi.* palpitar; vibrar;

—, *n.* palpitación, *f.;* latido, *m.*

thrombosis [zrom-bou-sis] *n.* (med.) trombosis, *f.*

throne [zroun] *n.* trono, *m.;* —, *vt.* entronizar.

throttle [zro-tel] *n.* gaznate, garguero, *m.;* regulador, *m.;* — **of an engine,** válvula reguladora; —, *vt.* ahogar; estrangular.

through [zru] *prep.* a través, por medio de; por conducto de; —, *adj.* continuo; — **train** tren directo; —, *adv.* del principio al fin, de extremo a extremo; completamente; — **and** —, de un lado a otro, por completo.

throughout [zru-aut] *prep.* por todo, en todo; — **the country,** por todo el país; —, *adv.* en todas partes; en todos sentidos.

throw [zrou] *vt.* echar, arrojar, tirar, lanzar; botar; **to** — **down,** derribar; **to** — **into gear,** engranar; *n.* tiro, *m.,* tirada, *f.;* derribo, *m.*

thrown [zroun] *p.p.* del verbo **throw.**

thrush [zrash] *n.* (orn.) tordo, *m.*

thrust [zrast] *vt.* empujar, impeler; meter; — *vi.* entremeterse, introducirse; **to** — **aside,** rechazar; **to** — **in,** hincar; —, *n.* estocada, *f.;* puñalada, *f.;* lanzada, *f.*

thug [zag] *n.* asesino, *m.;* malhechor, *m.*

thumb [zam] *n.* pulgar, *m.;* — **notches,** muescas para el dedo pulgar (como índice de libros, etc.); —, *vt.* manosear con poca destreza; emporcar con los dedos; to — **a ride,** (coll.) hacer el auto-stop.

thumbtack [zam-tak] *n.* chinche, tachuela, *f.*

thump [zamp] *n.* porrazo, golpe, *m.;* —, *vt.* y *vi.* aporrear, apuñear.

thunder [zan-dar] *n.* trueno, *m.;* estrépito, *m.;* —, *vt.* y *vi.* tronar; atronar; fulminar.

thunderbolt [zan-da-boult] *n.* rayo, *m.*, centella, *f.*

thunderclap [zan-da-klap] *n.* trueno, *m.*

thundercloud [zan-da-klaud] *n.* nube cargada de electricidad.

thundering [zan-da-rin] *adj.* atronador, fulminante.

thundershower [zan-da-sha-uer] *n.* aguacero con truenos, tormenta, *f.*

thunderstorm [zan-das-torm] *n.* temporal, *m.*, tormenta, tronada, tempestad, *f.*

thunderstruck [zan-das-truk] *adj.* atónito, estupefacto.

Thursday [zres-di] *n.* jueves, *m.;* **Holy** —, Jueves Santo.

thus [das] *adv.* así, de este modo.

thwart [duort] *vt.* frustrar, desbaratar; —, *n.* (naut.) banco de remero.

thyroid [zai-roid] *n.* (anat.) tiroides, *m.*, glándula tiroides; —, *adj.* tiroideo.

thyself [daiself] *pron.* ti mismo.

tibia [ti-bia] *n.* (anat.) tibia, *f.*

tick [tik] *n.* garrapata, *f.;* (coll.) tic tac, *m.;* —, *vi.* hacer sonido de tic tac; —, *vt.* marcar en lista.

ticket [ti-ket] *n.* boleto, *m.*, boleta, *f.;* cédula, *f.;* (rail.) billete, *m.*, localidad, *f.;* **round trip** —, boleto de ida y vuelta; **season** —, billete de abono; — **collector,** (rail.) expendedor de billetes; — **office,** (rail.) despacho, *m.*, taquilla, *f.;* — **scalper,** revendedor, *m.;* — **seller,** taquillero, ra; — **window,** taquilla, *f.;* —, *vt.* marcar.

tickle [ti-kel] *vt.* cosquillear, hacer cosquillas; —, *vi.* tener cosquillas; —, *n.* cosquilla, *f.*

tickling [ti-klin] *n.* cosquillas, *f. pl.;* cosquilleo, *m.*

tidal [tai-dal] *adj.* (naut.) de la marea; — **wave,** maremoto, *m.*

tide [taid] *n.* tiempo, *m.;* estación, *f.;* marea, *f.;* **high** —, marea alta, pleamar, *f.;* —, *vt.* llevar; to — **over,** ayudar momentáneamente.

tidings [tai-dins] *n. pl.* noticias,

f. pl.

tidy [tai-di] adj. aseado, pulcro; ordenado; —, vt. arreglar, poner en orden, limpiar; —, vi. asearse.

tie [tai] vt. anudar, atar; enlazar; empatar; amarrar; —, n. nudo, m.; corbata, f.; lazo, m.; (mus.) ligadura, f.; empate, m.

tier [tiar] n. fila, hilera, f.; (theat.) hilera de palcos.

tiger [tai-gar] n. tigre, m.; — **lily,** (bot.) tigridia, f.; — **moth,** variedad grande de polilla.

tight [tait] adj. tirante, tieso, tenso, estrecho; apretado; escaso; (coll.) tacaño; — **squeeze,** apuro, m.

tighten [tai-ten] vt. tirar, estirar; apretar.

tightrope [tait-roup] n. cuerda tiesa; cuerda de volatinero.

tights [taits] n. pl. mallas, calzas, f. pl., trajes ajustados que usan los acróbatas.

tigress [tai-gres] n. hembra del tigre.

tile [tail] n. teja, f.; losa, f., azulejo, m.; —, vt. tejar.

tiling [tai-lin] n. tejado, m.; azulejos, m. pl.

till [til] prep. y conj. hasta que, hasta; — **now,** hasta ahora; —, n. cajón, m.; gaveta para dinero; —, vt. cultivar, labrar, laborar.

tiller [ti-lar] n. agricultor, ra; (naut.) caña del timón; — **rope,** guardín, m.

tilt [tilt] n. declive, m., inclinación, f.; cubierta, f.; justa, f.; —, vt. inclinar, empinar; apuntar la lanza; —, vi. justar.

timber [tim-bar] n. madera, f.; **beam of** —, madero, m.; **building** —, madera de construcciones; — **line,** límite de los bosques; — **wolf,** lobo gris; —, vt. enmaderar.

time [taim] n. tiempo, m.; (mus.) compás, m.; edad, época, f.; hora, f.; vez, f.; **at any** —, cuando quiera; **a long** — **ago,** hace mucho tiempo; **at the proper** —, a su tiempo; **at the same** —, al mismo tiempo, a la vez; **at this** —, al presente; **at** —**s,** a veces; **behind** —, atrasado; **from** — **to** —, de cuando en cuando; **in olden** —**s,** antiguamente; **in** —, a tiempo, de perilla; **on** —, a plazos; **some** — **ago,** tiempo atrás; **spare** —, tiempo desocupado; — **clock,** reloj que indica las horas de entrada y salida de los obreros; — **exposure,** (phot.) exposición de tiempo; **to mark** —, marcar el paso; **to take** —, tomarse tiempo; — **bomb,** bomba de explosión demorada; —, vt. medir el tiempo de; hacer a tiempos regulares; escoger el tiempo.

timeless [taim-les] *adj.* eterno.

timely [taim-li] *adv.* con tiempo; a propósito; —, *adj.* oportuno, tempestivo; a buen tiempo.

timepiece [taim-pis] *n.* reloj, *m.*

timer [tai-mar] *n.* persona o instrumento para registrar el tiempo; regulador o marcador de tiempo.

timesaving [taim-sei-vin] *adj.* que ahorra tiempo; — **device,** dispositivo para ahorrar tiempo.

timetable [taim-tei-bol] *n.* (rail.) horario, itinerario, *m.*

timid [ti-mid] *adj.* tímido, temeroso; —**ly,** *adv.* con timidez.

timidity [ti-mi-di-ti] *n.* timidez, pusilanimidad, *f.*

timing [tai-min] *n.* regulación de tiempo, sincronización, *f.;* coincidencia, *f.*

tin [tin] *n.* estaño, *m.;* hojalata, *f.;* — **can,** lata, *f.;* — **foil,** hoja de estaño; — **plate,** hoja de lata, hojalata, *f.*

tinker [tin-kar] *n.* latonero, *m.;* calderero, remendón, *m.;* —, *vt.* remendar; desabollar; tratar torpemente de componer algo.

tinkle [tin-kel] *vt.* y *vi.* cencerrear; —, *vi.* tintinear; retiñir; —, *n.* retintín, *m.*

tinkling [tin-klin] *n.* retintín, *m.*

tint [tint] *n.* tinta, *f.;* tinte, *m.;* —, *vt.* teñir, colorar.

tiny [tai-ni] *adj.* pequeño, chico.

tip [tip] *n.* punta, extremidad, *f.;* cabo, *m.;* graficación, propina, *f.;* información oportuna; —, *vt.* Golpear ligramente; dar propina; inclinar, ladear; volcar.

tipsy [tip-si] *adj.* algo borracho; inestable.

tiptoe [tip-tou] *n.* punta del pie; **on —,** de puntillas.

tiptop [tip-top] *n.* cumbre, *f.;* —, *adj.* (coll.) excelente, de la más alta calidad.

tire [taiar] *n.* llanta, goma, *f.,* neumático, *m.;* **balloon —,** neumático balón, llanta balón; **change of —,** repuesto, *m.;* **flat —,** pinchazo, *m.,* llanta desinflada; **spare —,** neumático o llanta de repuesto; — **cover,** cubrellanta, *m.;* — **gauge,** medidor de presión en los neumáticos; —, *vt.* cansar, fatigar; proveer con una llanta; —, *vi.* cansarse, fastidiarse; rendirse.

tired [taiad] *adj.* fatigado, cansado; rendido.

tireless [taia-les] *adj.* incansable.

tiresome [taia-som] *adj.* tedioso; molesto.

tissue [ti-shu] *n.* tisú, *m.;* (anat.) tejido, *m.;* — **paper,** papel de seda.

titanic [tai-ta-nik] *adj.* titánico.

tithe [taiz] *n.* diezmo, *m.;* —, *vi.* diezmar.

title [tai-tel] *n.* título, *m.;* — **deed,** derecho de propiedad; — **page,** portada, carátula, *f.,* frontispicio (de un libro), *m.;* — **role,** papel principal; —, *vt.* titular, intitular.

titular [ti-tiu-lar] *n.* y *adj.* titular, *m.*

to [tu] *prep.* a, para; por; de; hasta; en; con; que; —, *adv.* hacia adelante.

toad [toud] *n.* sapo, *m.*

toady [tou-di] *n.* adulador, ra; — **ish,** *adj.* adulador; —, *vi.* y *vt.* adular; ser adulador. **to-and-fro,** *adj.* de acá para allá; de un lado a otro.

toast [toust] *vt.* tostar; brindar; —, *n.* tostada, *f.,* pan tostado; brindis, *m.*

toasted [tous-ted] *adj.* tostado.

toaster [tous-tar] *n.* parrilla, *f.,* tostador, *m.*

tobacco [to-ba-kou] *n.* tabaco, *m.;* **cut** —, picadura, *f.;* — **box,** tabaquera, *f.;* — **pouch,** bolsa para tabaco; — **shop,** tabaquería, *f.*

today, to-day [to-dei] *n.* y *adv.* hoy, *m.;* **a week from** —, dentro de ocho días, de hoy en ocho días.

toddle [to-del] *vi.* andar con pasitos inciertos; tambalearse.

toddler [tod-lar] *n.* el que da pasitos inciertos; niño de uno a tres años de edad.

toe [tou] *n.* dedo del pie; punta del calzado; —, *vt.* tocar con los dedos del pie; **to** — **the line,** comportarse bien, hacer lo que se le manda al pie de la letra.

toenail [tou-neil] *n.* uña del dedo del pie.

together [to-gue-dar] *adv.* juntamente, en compañía de otro; al mismo tiempo; **to get** —, unirse, juntarse.

toil [toil] *vi.* fatigarse, trabajar mucho; afanarse; —, *n.* trabajo, *m.;* fatiga, *f.;* afán, *m.*

toilet [toi-let] *n.* tocado, *m.;* tocador, *m.;* excusado, retrete, *m.;* — **articles,** artículos de tocador; — **paper,** papel de excusado, papel higiénico; — **water,** agua de tocador.

token [tou-ken] *n.* señal, *f.;* memoria, *f.;* recuerdo, *m.;* prueba, *f.;* — **payment,** (com.) pago parcial como reconocimiento de un adeudo; **by the same** —, por lo mismo, por el mismo motivo.

told [tould] *pretérito* y *p.p.* del verbo **tell.**

tolerable [to-le-ra-bol] *adj.* tolerable; mediocre; —**ly,** *adv.* tolerablemente, así así.

tolerance [to-le-rans] *n.* tolerancia, *f.*

tolerate [to-le-reit] *vt.* tolerar.

toleration [to-le-rei-shon] *n.* tolerancia, *f.*

toll [toul] *n.* peaje, *m.;* tañido lento de las campanas; — **bridge**, puente de peaje; — **call**, llamada telefónica de larga distancia; —, *vt.* tocar o doblar una campana; colectar peajes; —, *vi.* sonar las campanas.

tomato [to-mei-tou] *n.* tomate, *m.*, (Mex.) jitomate, *m.;* — **sauce**, salsa de tomate.

tomb [tum] *n.* tumba, *f.;* sepulcro, *m.;* —, *vt.* poner en tumba.

tomboy [tom-boi] *n.* jovencita retozona, marimacho, *m.*

tombstone [tum-stoun] *n.* piedra o lápida sepulcral.

tome [toum] *n.* tomo, *m.*

tomorrow [to-mo-rou] *n.* y *adv.* mañana, *f.;* **day after —,** pasado mañana; — **morning,** mañana por la mañana.

ton [tan] *n.* tonelada, *f.*

tonal [tou-nal] *adj.* tonal.

tone [toun] *n.* tono, *m.;* tono de la voz; acento, *m.;* (mus.) modalidad, *f.;* —, *vt.* cambiar el tono; armonizar el tono; **to —down,** suavizar; **to — up,** animar.

tongs [tongs] *n. pl.* tenazas, *f. pl.*

tongue [tang] *n.* (anat.) lengua, *f.;* lenguaje, *m.;* habla, *f.;* lengua de tierra; **to hold one's —,** callarse; — **twister,** *n.* trabalenguas, *m.*

tonight, to-night [to-nait] *n.* y *adv.* esta noche.

tonnage [ta-nich] *n.* tonelaje, porte de un buque.

tonsil [ton-sil] *n.* tonsila, amígdala, agalla, *f.*

tonsillectomy [ton-si-lek-ta-mi] *n.* amigdalotomía, operación de las amígdalas.

tonsillitis [ton-si-lai-tis] *n.* tonsilitis, amigdalitis, *f.*

too [tu] *adv.* también; — **much,** demasiado; —**many things,** demasiadas cosas.

took [tuk] *pretérito* del verbo **take.**

tool [tul] *n.* herramienta, *f.;* utensilio, *m.;* persona usada como instrumento; — **bag,** talega de herramientas, cartera de herramientas; — **chest,** caja de herramientas; —**s,** pertrechos, *m. pl.;* útiles, bártulos, *m. pl.;* —, *vt.* labrar con herramientas.

tooth [tuz] *n.* diente, *m.;* gusto, *m.;* (mach.) diente de rueda; **molar —,** diente molar; — **powder,** dentífrico, *m.,* polvo dentífrico.

toothache [tuz-eik] *n.* dolor de muelas.

toothbrush [tuz-brash] *n.* cepillo de dientes.

toothless [tuz-les] *adj.* desdentado, sin dientes.

toothpaste [tuz-peist] *n.* dentífrico, *m.*, pasta dentífrica.

toothpick [tuz-pik] palillo de
dientes.

top [top] *n.* cima, cumbre, cresta, *f.;* último grado; cabeza, *f.;*
capota, *f.;* —, *vt.* y *vi.* elevarse
por encima; sobrepujar, exce-
der; descabezar los árboles.

topaz [tou-pas] *n.* topacio, *m.*

topic [to-pik] *n.* tópico, particular, asunto, tema, *m.*

topical [to-pi-kal] *adj.* tópico;
sobre el tema o asunto.

topknot [top-not] *n.* copete, *m.*

topmost [top-moust] *adj.* superior, más alto.

topnotch [top-noch] *adj.* (coll.)
de primera, excelente.

topographer [to-po-gra-far] *n.*
topógrafo, *m.*

topography [to-po-gra-fi] *n.* topografía, *f.*

topple [to-pel] *vi.* volcarse.

top-secret [top-si-krit] *adj.* absolutamente secreto.

torch [torch] *n.* antorcha, hacha,
f.

torchlight [torch-lait] *n.* luz de
antorcha; — **procession,** procesión con antorchas.

tore [tor] *pretérito* del verbo **tear.**

toreador [to-ri-dor] *n.* torero, *m.*

torment [tor-ment] *n.* tormento,

m.; pena, *f.;* —, *vt.* atormentar.

tormentor, tormenter [tor-men-
tar] *n.* atormentador, ra.

torn [torn] *adj.* rasgado, descosido; —, p.p. del verbo **tear.**

tornado [tor-nei-dou] *n.* tornado,
huracán, *m.*

torpedo [tor-pi-dou] *n.* torpedo,
m.; (ichth.) tremielga, *f.;* **to fire
a —,** lanzar un torpedo; **—boat,**
torpedero, *m.;* — **tube,** lanzatorpedos, tubo lanzatorpedos;
— *vt.* torpedear.

torpid [tor-pid] *adj.* entorpecido;
inerte, apático.

torrent [to-rent] *n.* torrente, *m.*

torrential [to-ren-shal] *adj.*
torrencial.

torrid [to-rid] *adj.* tórrido,
ardiente; — **zone,** zona tórrida.

torso [tor-sou] *n.* torso, *m.*

tortoise [tor-tos] *n.* tortuga, *f.;*
carey, *m.;* — **shell,** concha de
tortuga, carey, *m.*

tortuous [tor-tuos] *adj.* tortuoso,
sinuoso.

torture [tor-char] *n.* tortura, *f.;*
suplicio, *m.;* martirio, *m.;* —,
vt. atormentar, torturar, martirizar.

toss [tos] *vt.* tirar, lanzar, arrojar; agitar, sacudir; **to — up,**
lanzar algo al aire; jugar a cara
o cruz; —, *vi.* agitarse; mecerse; —, *n.* sacudida, *f.;* meneo,
m., agitación, *f.*

tot [tot] *n.* niño, ña.

total [tou-tal] *n.* total, *m.;* —, *adj.* entero, completo; — **war,** guerra total; — **loss,** pérdida total; — **weight,** peso total.

totalitarian [tou-ta-li-tea-rian] *n.* y *adj.* totalitario, *m.*

totter [to-tar] *vi.* bambolear; tambalear, vacilar, titubear.

tottering [to-ta-rin] *adj.* vacilante, titubeante; —**ly,** *adv.* en forma tambaleante.

touch [tach] *vt.* tocar, palpar; emocionar, conmover; —, *vi.* aproximarse a; —, *n.* tocamiento, toque, contacto, *m.;* **sense of** —, sentido del tacto; **in** — **with,** en contacto con; **to get in** — **with,** comunicarse con.

touchable [ta-cha-bol] *adj.* tangible.

touching [ta-chin] *adj.* patético, conmovedor.

touchy [ta-chi] *adj.* quisquilloso, melindroso, susceptible.

tough [taf] *adj.* tosco; tieso; vicioso; vigoroso; pendenciero; difícil; — **contest,** concurso reñido; — **battle,** batalla ardua.

toughen [ta-fen] *vi.* hacerse correoso; endurecerse; —, *vt.* hacer tosco; hacer correoso; endurecer.

tour [tuar] *n.* viaje, *m.,* peregrinación, *f.;* vuelta, *f.;* —, *vt.* viajar.

tourist [tu-rist] *n.* turista, *m.* y *f.;* viajero, ra; — **court,** posada para automovilistas.

tournament [tur-na-ment] *n.* torneo, combate, concurso, *m.*

tourniquet [tur-ni-kei] *n.* torniquete, *m.*

tow [tau] *n.* estopa, *f.;* remolque, *m.;* —, *vt.* (naut.) remolcar.

toward, towards [to-uords] *prep.* hacia, con dirección a; cerca de.

towboat [tau-bout] *n.* bote remolcador, *m.*

towel [taual] *n.* toalla, *f.;* **roller** —, toalla sin fin.

tower [tauar] *n.* torre, *f.;* ciudadela, *f.;* **fortified** —, torreón, *m.;* —, *vi.* remontarse; elevarse a una altura; **to** — **above,** sobrepasar mucho en altura.

towline [tau-lain] *n.* cable, *m.,* soga o cadena de remolque.

town [taun] *n.* ciudad, *f.;* pueblo, *m.,* población, *f.;* villa, *f.;* **home** —, ciudad natal; — **council,** ayuntamiento, cabildo, *m.;* — **crier,** pregonero, voceador, *m.;* — **hall,** — **house,** casa de ayuntamiento, casa consistorial, comuna; *f.;* — **planning,** urbanización, *f.*

toxic [tok-sik] *adj.* tóxico.

toxin [tok-sin] *n.* toxina, *f.,* veneno, *m.*

toy [toi] *n.* juguete, *m.;* chuche-

ría, *f.;* miriñaque, *m.;* —, *vi.*
jugar, divertirse.

trace [treis] *n.* huella, pisada, *f.;*
vestigio, *m.,* señal, *f.;* —, *vt.*
delinear, trazar; seguir la pista.

trachea [tra-kia] *n.* (anat.) tráquea, *f.*

tracing [trei-sin] *n.* calco, *m.;*
trazo, *m.*

track [trak] *n.* vestigio, *m.;* huella, pista, *f.;* rodada, *f.;* —
meet, concurso de pista y
campo; **race** —, hipódromo, *m.;*
—, *vt.* rastrear.

tract [trakt] *n.* trecho, *m.;*
región, comarca, *f.;* tratado, *m.;*
(anat.) sistema, *m.*

tractable [trak-ta-bol] *adj.* tratable, manejable.

traction [trak-shon] *n.* acarrea-
miento, *m.,* tracción, *f.;* (med.)
tracción, *f.*

tractor [trak-tar] *n.* tractor, *m.*

trade [treid] *n.* comercio, tráfico,
m.; negocio, trato, *m.,* contratación, *f.;* **board of** —, junta de
comercio; — **name,** nombre de
fábrica; — **price,** precio para el
comerciante; — **school,** escuela
de artes y oficios; — **union,**
gremio, *m.;* — **winds,** vientos
alisios; —, *vi.* comerciar, traficar, negociar, cambiar (una
cosa por otra), (coll.) cambalachear.

trade-mark [treid-mark] *n.*

marca de fábrica.

trader [trei-dar] *n.* comerciante,
traficante, *m.;* navío mercante.

trading [trei-din] *n.* comercio,
m.; —, *adj.* comercial.

tradition [tra-di-shon] *n.* tradición, *f.*

traditional [tra-di-sho-nal] *adj.*
tradicional; —**ly,** *adv.* tradicio-
nalmente.

traffic [tra-fik] *n.* tráfico, *m.,* circulación, *f.;* mercaderías, *f. pl.;*
tránsito, *m.;* trasporte, *m.;*
heavy —, tránsito intenso; **light**
—, tránsito ligero; — **lane,** zona
de tránsito; — **light,** semáforo,
m.; — **sign,** señal de tránsito;
—, *vi.* traficar, comerciar.

tragedian [tra-yi-dian] *n.* actor
trágico; autor de tragedias.

tragedy [tra-yi-di] *n.* tragedia, *f.*

tragic [tra-yik] *adj.* trágico.

tragically [tra-yi-ka-li] *adv.* trági-
camente.

trail [treil] *vt.* y *vi.* rastrear;
arrastrar; —, *n.* rastro, *m.;*
pisada, *f.;* vereda, trocha, *f.;*
sendero, *m.*

trailer [trei-lar] *n.* remolque, acoplado, *m.,* carro de remolque;
persona que sigue una pista o
un rastro.

train [trein] *vt.* arrastrar, amaestrar, enseñar, criar, adiestrar;
disciplinar; entrenar; —, *n.*
(rail.) tren, *m.;* séquito, tren,

m.; serie, f.; cola (de vestido), f.; — **conductor,** *motorista, cobrador, m.; —* **oil,** *aceite de ballena.*

trainer [trei-nar] *n.* enseñador, *m.;* entrenador, *m.*

training [trei-nin] *n.* educación, disciplina, *f.;* entrenamiento, *m.; —, adj.* de instrucción, de entrenamiento.

trait [treit] *n.* rasgo de carácter; toque, *m.*

traitor [trei-tar] *n.* traidor, *m.*

traitorous [trei-to-ros] *adj.* pérfido, traidor, traicionero.

trajectory [tra-yek-to-ri] *n.* trayectoria, *f.*

trammel [tra-mel] *n.* trasmallo, *m.; —s, pl.* obstáculos, impedimentos, *m. pl.; —, vt.* coger, interceptar; impedir.

tramp [tramp] *n.* sonido de pasos pesados; paso fuerte; caminata, *f.;* vagabundo, *m.;* bigardo, *m.; —* **steamer,** vapor que toma carga donde y cuando puede; *—, vi.* vagabundear; *—, vt.* patear.

trance [trans] *n.* rapto, *m.;* éxtasis, *m.;* estado hipnótico.

tranquil [tran-kuil] *adj.* tranquilo.

tranquilizer [tran-kui-lai-sar] *n.* calmante, sedante, *m.*

tranquillity o **tranquility** [tran-kui-li-ti] *n.* tranquilidad, paz,

calma, *f.*

transact [tran-sakt] *vt.* negociar, transigir.

transaction [tran-sak-shon] *n.* transacción, *f.;* negociación, *f.;* tramitación, *f.*

transatlantic [tran-sakt-lan-tik] *adj.* trasatlántico; *—* **airplane,** avión trasatlántico; *—* **liner,** vapor trasatlántico.

transcend [tran-send] *vt.* trascender, pasar; exceder.

transcendent [tran-sen-dant] *adj.* trascendente; sobresaliente.

transcendental [tran-sen-den-tal] *adj.* trascendental; sobresaliente.

transcontinental [trans-kon-ti-nen-tal] *adj.* trascontinental.

transcribe [trans-kraiv] *vt.* trascribir, copiar, trasladar.

transcript [trans-kript] *n.* trasunto, traslado, *m.,* copia (de un documento, etc.), *f.*

transcription [trans-krip-shon] *n.* traslado, *m.;* copia, *f.;* **electrical —,** (rad. y TV.) trascripción eléctrica.

transistor [tran-sis-tor] *n.* transistor, *m.*

transfer [trans-far] *vt.* trasferir, trasportar, trasbordar, trasladar, trasponer; *—, n.* cesión, trasferencia, *f.,* traspaso, *m.;* traslado, *m.*

transferable [trans-fe-ra-bol] *adj.* trasferible.

transfigure [trans-fi-gar] *vt.* trasformar, trasfigurar.

transform [trans-form] *vt.* trasformar; —, *vi.* trasformase.

transformation [trans-for-mei-shon] *n.* trasformación, *f.*

transformer [trans-for-mar] *n.* trasformador, *m.*

transfusion [trans-fiu-shon] *n.* trasfusión, *f.;* **blood** —, trasfusión de sangre.

transgress [trans-gres] *vt.* y *vi.* trasgredir; violar.

transgression [trans-gre-shon] *n.* trasgresión, *f.*

transgressor [trans-gre-sar] *n.* trasgresor, ra.

transient [tran-sient] *adj.* pasajero, transitorio; —, *n.* transeúnte, *m.* y *f.;* —**ly**, *adv.* de un modo transitorio.

transit [tran-sit] *n.* tránsito, *m.;* trámite, *m.;* teodolito, *m.;* — **theodolite,** teodolito, *m.;* —, *vt.* pasar por.

transition [tran-si-shon] *n.* transición, *f.;* tránsito, *m.*

transitive [tran-si-tiv] *adj.* transitivo; —, *n.* verbo transitivo.

transitory [tran-si-to-ri] *adj.* transitorio.

translate [trans-leit] *vt.* trasladar, traducir, verter; interpretar.

translation [trans-lei-shon] *n.* traducción, *f.;* interpretación, *f.*

translator [trans-lei-tar] *n.* traductor, ra.

translucent [trans-lu-sent] *adj.* trasluciente, diáfano.

transmission [trans-mi-shon] *n.* trasmisión, *f.;* — **belt,** correa de trasmisión.

transmit [trans-mit] *vt.* trasmitir.

transmitter [trans-mi-tar] *n.* trasmisor, *m.*

transparency [trans-pa-ren-si] *n.* trasparencia, *f.*

transparent [trans-pa-rent] *adj.* trasparente, diáfano.

transpire [trans-paiar] *vt.* traspirar, exhalar; —, *vi.* (coll.) acontecer.

transplant [trans-plant] *n.* trasplante, *m.;* **corneal** —, trasplante de córnea; —, *vt.* trasplantar.

transport [trans-port] *vt.* trasportar; deportar; llevar; trasponer; —, *n.* trasportación, *f.;* rapto, *m.;* (naut.) trasporte, *m.;* criminal condenado a la deportación; — **company,** empresa porteadora, compañía de trasportes.

transportation [trans-por-tei-shon] *n.* trasportación, *f.,* trasporte, acarreo, *m.*

transpose [trans-pous] *vt.* trasponer; (mus.) trasportar.

transverse [trans-vers] *adj.* tras-verso, travesero; —**ly**, *adv.* trasversalmente.

trap [trap] *n.* trampa, *f.; vt.* hacer caer en la trampa, atrapar.

trapeze [tra-pis] *n.* trapecio, *m.*

trash [trash] *n.* heces, *f. pl.*, des-echo, *m.;* cachivache, cacharro, *m.;* basura, *f.*

trashy [tra-shi] *adj.* vil, despreciable, de ningún valor.

trauma [tro-ma] *n.* (med.) trau-matismo, *m.*, lesión, *f.*

traumatic [tro-ma-tik] *adj.* trau-mático.

travel [tra-vel] *vt.* y *vi.* viajar; **to — over,** recorrer; —, *n.* viaje, *m.*

traveling [tra-ve-lin] *adj.* de viaje; — **companion,** compañe-ro o compañera de viaje; — **salesman,** agente viajero, via-jante, *m.;* — **expenses,** viáticos, *m. pl.*

travesty [tra-vis-ti] *n.* parodia, *f.;* —, *vt.* disfrazar.

trawler [tro-lar] *n.* embarcación para pescar o dragar a la ras-tra; persona que pesca o draga a la rastra.

tray [trei] *n.* bandeja, salvilla, *f.;* batea, *f.;* (Mex.) charola, *f.*

treacherous [tre-cha-ras] *adj.* traidor, pérfido.

treachery [tre-cha-ri] *n.* perfidia, deslealtad, traición, *f.*

tread [tred] *vt.* y *vi.* pisar, apre-tar con el pie; pisotear; patale-ar; caminar con majestad; —, *n.* pisada, *f.*

treason [tri-son] *n.* traición, *f.*

treasure [tre-shar] *n.* tesoro, *m.;* riqueza, *f.;* —, *vt.* atesorar; guardar riquezas.

treasurer [tre-sha-rar] *n.* tesore-ro, ra.

treasury [tre-sha-ri] *n.* tesorería (oficina), *f.*

treat [trit] *vt.* y *vi.* tratar; rega-lar; medicinar; **to — of,** versar sobre, tratar de; —, *n.* trato, *m.;* banquete, festín, *m.*, convi-dada, *f.*

treatise [tria-tris] *n.* tratado, *m.*

treatment [trit-ment] *n.* trato, *m.;* (med.) tratamiento, *m.*

treaty [tri-ti] *n.* tratado, pacto, trato, *m.*

trek [trek] *n.* prolongado viaje; jornada, *f.;* —, *vi.* hacer una jornada ardua.

tremble [trem-bel] *vi.* temblar; estremecerse; —, *n.* temblor, *m.*

trembling [trem-blin] *adj.* tem-bloroso; —, temor, *m.*

tremendous [tre-men-dos] *adj.* tremendo; inmenso; —**ly**, *adv.* de un modo tremendo. tremor, *n.* temblor, estremecimiento,

m.

tremulous [tre-miu-los] *adj.* trémulo, tembloroso; —**ly,** *adv.* temblorosamente.

trench [trench] *n.* foso, *m.;* (mil.) trinchera, *f.;* cauce, *m.;* —, *vt.* cortar; atrincherar; hacer cauces.

trend [trend] *n.* tendencia, *f.,* curso, *m.;* —, *vi.* tender, inclinarse.

trepidation [tre-pi-dei-shon] *n.* trepidación, *f.*

trespass [tres-pas] *vt.* quebrantar, traspasar, violar; —, *n.* trasgresión, violación, *f.*

trespasser [tres-pa-sar] *n.* trasgresor, ra.

triad [traiad] *n.* (mus.) acorde, *m.;* terno, *m.*

trial [traial] *n.* prueba, *f.;* ensayo, *m.;* juicio, *m.;* — **balance,** balance de prueba; — **order,** pedido de ensayo; — **run,** presentación de un espectáculo por algún tiempo como prueba o ensayo; marcha de ensayo.

triangle [traian-guel] *n.* triángulo, *m.;* grupo de tres personas.

triangular [traian-guiu-lar] *adj.* triangular.

tribal [trai-bal] *adj.* tribal, perteneciente a una tribu.

tribe [traib] *n.* tribu, *f.;* raza, casta, *f.*

tribulation [tri-biu-lei-shon] *n.* tribulación, *f.*

tribunal [trai-biu-nal] *n.* tribunal, *m.;* juzgado, *m.*

tribune [tri-biun] *n.* tribuno, *m.;* tribuna, *f.*

tributary [tri-biu-ta-ri] *n.* y *adj.* tributario, *m.*

tribute [tri-biut] *n.* tributo, *m.*

trick [trik] *n.* engaño, fraude, *m.;* superchería, astucia, *f.;* burla, *f.;* maña, *f.;* —, *vt.* engañar; ataviar; hacer juegos de manos; embaucar.

tricky [tri-ki] *adj.* astuto, artificioso; tramposo.

tricycle [trai-si-kol] *n.* triciclo, *m.*

tried [traid] *adj.* ensayado; probado; fiel.

trigger [tri-gar] *n.* gatillo (de una arma de fuego), *m.*

trigonometry [tri-go-no-mi-tri] *n.* trigonometría, *f.*

trilingual [trai-lin-gual] *adj.* trilingüe.

trillion [tri-lion] *n.* trillón, *m.,* la tercera potencia de un millón, o 1,000,000,000,000,000,000 (en la América Ibera, España, Inglaterra, y Alemania); un millón de millones, o 1,000,000,000,000 (en Francia y los Estados Unidos).

trim [trim] *adj.* acicalado, compuesto, bien ataviado; —**ly,** *adv.* lindamente; en buen estado; —, *n.* atavío, adorno, ade-

rezo, *m.*; —, *vt.* preparar; acomodar; adornar, ornar; podar;
recortar, cortar; recortar (el
cabello); (naut.) orientar (las
velas); equilibrar.

trinity [tri-ni-ti] *n.* grupo de tres,
trinidad, *f.*

trinket [trin-kit] *n.* joya, alhaja,
f.; adorno, *m.*; fruslería, chuchería, *f.*; juguete, *m.* trio, *n.*
(mus.) terceto, trío, *m.*

trip [trip] *vt.* echar zancadilla;
hacer tropezar; —, *vi.* tropezar;
dar traspié; —, *n.* zancadilla, *f.*;
traspié, *m.*; resbalón, *m.*; viaje,
m.; **one-way** —, viaje sencillo;
return —, viaje de vuelta;
round —, viaje redondo, viaje
de ida y vuelta.

tripe [traip] *n.* tripas, *f. pl.*,
callos, *m. pl.*; menudo, *m.*

triple [tri-pel] *adj.* tríplice, triple,
triplo; —, *vt.* triplicar.

triplet [tri-plit] *n.* (poet.) terceto,
m.; —**s**, gemelos, trillizos, *m.*
pl.

tripod [trai-pod] *n.* trípode, *m.*

tripping [tri-pin] *adj.* veloz, ágil,
ligero; —, *n.* baile ligero; tropiezo, tropezón, *m.*

trite [trait] *adj.* trivial, usado,
banal.

triumph [traiomf] *n.* triunfo, *m.*;
—, *vi.* triunfar; vencer.

trivial [tri-vial] *adj.* trivial, vulgar.

triviality [tri-via-li-ti] *n.* trivialidad, *f.*

trolley [tro-li] *n.* tranvía, *m.*; —
bus, — **coach,** ómnibus eléctrico.

trombone [trom-boun] *n.* (mus.)
trombón, *m.*

troop [trup] *n.* tropa, *f.*; cuadrilla, turba, *f.*; —, *vi.* atroparse.

trooper [tru-par] *n.* soldado a
caballo, también su caballo;
policía a caballo.

trophy [trou-fi] *n.* trofeo, *m.*

tropic [tro-pik] *n. y adj.* trópico,
m.; **the** —**s,** el trópico.

tropical [tro-pi-kal] *adj.* trópico,
tropical.

trot [trot] *n.* trote, *m.*; —, *vi.* trotar.

trotter [tro-tar] *n.* caballo trotón;
trotador, *m.*

troubadour [tru-ba-dor] *n.*
trovador, *m.*

trouble [tra-bel] *vt.* perturbar;
afligir; incomodar, molestar; —,
vi. incomodarse; —, *n.* turbación, *f.*; disturbio, *m.*; inquietud, *f.*; aflicción, pena, *f.*; congoja, *f.*; trabajo, *m.*; **to be in** —,
verse en apuros.

troubled [tra-beld] *adj.* afligido;
agitado.

troublemaker [tra-bel-mei-kar]
n. perturbador, ra, alborotador,
ra.

troublesome [tra-bel-som] *adj.*

penoso, fatigoso; importuno; fastidioso, molesto, majadero.

troupe [trup] *n.* compañía o tropa, especialmente de actores de teatro.

trousers [trau-sars] *n. pl.* calzones, pantalones, *m. pl.*

trout [traut] *n.* trucha, *f.*

truant [truant] *n.* y *adj.* holgazán, ana, haragán, ana.

truce [trus] *n.* tregua, suspensión de armas.

truck [trak] *vt.* y *vi.* trocar, cambiar; acarrear; trasportar; —, *n.* camión, carretón, *m.;* cambio, trueque, *m.;* **small —,** camioneta, *f.*

trudge [tradch] *vi.* caminar con pesadez y cansancio; —, *n.* paseo fatigoso.

true [tru] *adj.* verdadero, cierto; sincero, exacto; efectivo; — **bill,** acusación de un gran jurado.

truly [tru-li] *adv.* en verdad; sinceramente.

trump [tramp] *n.* triunfo (en el juego de naipes), *m.;* (coll.) excelente persona; —, *vt.* ganar con el triunfo; — **card,** triunfo (en los juegos de naipes), *m.;* **to — up,** forjar, inventar.

trumpet [tram-pit] *n.* trompeta, *f.;* — **creeper,** jazmín trompeta; —, *vt.* trompetear; pregonar con trompeta.

trumpeter [tram-pi-tar] *n.* trom-

petero, *m.*

trunk [trank] *n.* tronco, *m.;* baúl, cofre, *m.;* — **of an elephant,** trompa, *f.;* — **(of trees and plants),** pie, tronco (de los árboles y plantas), *m.;* **auto —,** portaequipajes, maletero, *m.;* —, *adj.* troncal.

trunks [tranks] *n. pl.* calzón corto de hombre; **swimming —,** traje de baño de hombre, taparrabo, *m.*

trust [trast] *n.* confianza, *f.;* cargo, depósito, fideicomiso, *m.;* crédito, *m.;* cometido, *m.;* cuidado, *m.;* asociación comercial para monopolizar la venta de algún género; consorcio, *m.;* **in —,** en administración; **on —,** al fiado; —, *vt.* y *vi.* confiar; encargar y fiar; dar crédito; esperar; —, *vi.* confiarse, fiarse.

trustee [tras-tii] *n.* fideicomisario, depositario, síndico, *m.*

trustful [trast-ful] *adj.* fiel; confiado.

trustiness [tras-ti-nes] *n.* probidad, integridad, *f.*

trusting [tras-tin] *adj.* confiado.

trustworthy [trast-uer-zi] *adj.* digno de confianza.

trusty [tras-ti] *adj.* fiel, leal; seguro.

truth [truz] *n.* verdad, *f.;* fidelidad, *f.;* realidad, *f.;* **in —,** en verdad.

truthful [truz-ful] *adj.* verídico, veraz.

truthfulness [truz-ful-nes] *n.* veracidad, *f.*

try [trai] *vt.* y *vi.* examinar, ensayar, probar; experimentar; tentar; intentar; juzgar; purificar; refinar; —, *vt.* procurar; **to — on clothes,** probarse ropa; —, *n.* prueba, *f.*; ensayo, *m.*

tryout [trai-aut] *n.* prueba, *f.*, ensayo, *m.*

tub [tab] *n.* tina, *f.*; cuba, *f.*; cubo, barreño, *m.*; barreña, *f.*; —, *vt.* y *vi.* (coll.) bañar, bañarse o lavarse en una tina.

tuba [tiu-ba] *n.* (mus.) bombardino, *m.*

tube [tiub] *n.* tubo, cañón, cañuto, caño, *m.*; (rail.) ferrocarril subterráneo, *m.*; **amplifying —,** válvula amplificadora; **electronic —,** tubo electrónico; **inner —,** cámara de aire; **test —,** probeta, *f.*; **vacuum —,** tubo al vacío; —, *vt.* poner en tubo; entubar.

tuber [tiub-er] *n.* tubérculo, *m.*; (anat.) protuberancia, prominencia, *f.*

tubercular [tiu-ber-kiu-lar] *adj.* tísico, tuberculoso.

tuberculosis [tiu-ber-kiu-lou-sis] *n.* (med.) tuberculosis, tisis, *f.*

tuck [tak] *n.* alforza, *f.*; pliegue, *m.*; doblez, *m.*; —, *vt.* arreman-

gar, recoger.

Tuesday [tius-di] *n.* martes, *m.*

tug [tag] *vt.* tirar con fuerza; arrancar; —, *vi.* esforzarse; —, *n.* tirada, *f.*; esfuerzo, *m.*; tirón, *m.*; (naut.) remolcador, *m.*

tugboat [tag-bout] *n.* remolcador, *m.*

tuition [tiui-shon] *n.* instrucción, enseñanza, *f.*; costo de la matrícula y la enseñanza.

tulip [tiu-lip] *n.* tulipán, *m.*

tumble [tam-bel] *vi.* caer, hundirse, voltear; revolcarse; —, *vt.* revolver; rodar; volcar; —, *n.* caída, *f.*; vuelco, *m.*; confusión, *f.*

tumor [tiu-mar] *n.* tumor, *m.*, hinchazón, nacencia, *f.*

tumult [tiu-malt] *n.* tumulto, *m.*; agitación, *f.*; alboroto, *m.*

tumultuous [tiu-mal-tios] *adj.* tumultuoso; alborotado.

tuna [tiu-na] *n.* (bot.) tuna, *f.*; **— fish,** atún, *m.*

tune [tiun] *n.* tono, *m.*; armonía, *f.*; aria, *f.*; **in —,** afinado; —, *vt.* afinar un instrumento musical; armonizar; (rad.) sintonizar.

tungsten [tangs-ten] *n.* tungsteno, volframio, *m.*

tunic [tiu-nik] *n.* túnica, *f.*

tunnel [ta-nel] *n.* túnel, *m.*; galería, *f.*; —, *vi.* construir un túnel.

turbid [ter-bid] *adj.* turbio, cenagoso; turbulento.

turbine [ter-bain] *n.* turbina, *f.;* **blast** —, turbosopladora, *f.*

turbulence [ter-biu-lans] *n.* turbulencia, confusión, *f.*

turbulent [ter-biu-lant] *adj.* turbulento, tumultuoso.

turf [terf] *n.* césped, *m.;* turba, *f.;* hipódromo, *m.;* carreras de caballos; —, *vt.* cubrir con césped.

Turk [terk] *n.* turco, ca.

turkey [ter-ki] *n.* pavo, *m.;* (Mex.) guajolote, *m.;* — **buzzard,** gallinazo, *m.*

Turkey [ter-ki] Turquía, *f.*

Turkish [ter-kish] *adj.* turco; — **bath,** baño turco; — **towel,** toalla rusa.

turmoil [ter-moil] *n.* disturbio, *m.,* baraúnda, confusión, *f.*

turn [tern] *vt.* volver, trocar; verter, traducir; cambiar; tornear; —, *vi.* volver, girar, rodar; voltear; dar vueltas; volverse a, mudarse, trasformarse; dirigirse; **to — back,** regresar, volver atrás; (coll.) virar; **to — down,** poner boca abajo, voltear; rehusar, bajar (la llama de gas, etc.); **to — off,** cerrar; **to — on,** abrir, encender, poner; **to — over,** revolver; **to — pale,** palidecer; **to — the corner,** doblar la esquina; **to — to,** recurrir a; —, *n.* vuelta, *f.;* giro, *m.;* rodeo,

m.; turno, *m.;* vez, *f.;* habilidad, inclinación, *f.;* servicio, *m.;* forma, figura, hechura, *f.;* **a good** —, un favor; **sharp** —, codo, *m.*

turning [tern-nin] *n.* vuelta, *f.;* rodeo, *m.;* recodo, *m.;* —, *adj.* de vuelta; — **point,** punto decisivo.

turnpike [tern-paik] *n.* entrada de camino de portazgo; camino de portazgo.

turntable [tern-tei-bol] *n.* (rail.) plataforma giratoria, tornavía, *f.*

turquoise [ter-kuois] *n.* turquesa, *f.*

turtle [ter-tel] *n.* tortuga, *f.;* galápago, *m.*

turtledove [ter-tel-douv] *n.* tórtola, *f.*

tusk [task] *n.* colmillo, *m.;* diente, *m.*

tussle [ta-sel] *n.* lucha, *f.;* riña, *f.;* agarrada, *f.;* pelea, *f.;* rebatiña, *f.;* —, *vi.* pelear; reñir; agarrarse.

tutor [tiu-tar] *n.* tutor, *m.;* preceptor, *m.;* —, *vt.* enseñar, instruir.

tuxedo [tak-si-dou] *n.* smoking, *m.*

TV., T.V.: television [ti-vi], [te-le-vi-shon] T.V., TV., televisión.

twang [tuang] *vt.* y *vi.* producir un sonido agudo; restallar;

hablar con tono nasal; —, *n.* tañido (de un instrumento), *m.;* tono nasal.

tweak [tuik] *vt.* agarrar y halar con un tirón retorcido; —, *n.* tirón retorcido.

tweed [tuid] *n.* género tejido de lana de superficie áspera y de dos colores; —**s**, *pl.* ropa hecha de paño de lana y de superficie áspera.

twelfth [tuelf] *n.* y *adj.* duodécimo, *m.*

twelve [tuelv] *n.* y *adj.* doce, *m.*

twelvemonth [tuelf-monz] *n.* año, *m.,* doce meses.

twentieth [tuen-tiez] *n.* y *adj.* vigésimo, veintavo, *m.*

twenty [tuen-ti] *n.* y *adj.* veinte, *m.;* — **odd,** veintitantos.

twice [tuais] *adv.* dos veces; al doble.

twig [tuig] *n.* varita, varilla, *f.;* vástago, *m.*

twilight [tuai-lait] *n.* crepúsculo, *m.;* —, *adj.* crepuscular; — **sleep,** narcosis obstétrica parcial.

twin [tuin] *n.* y *adj.* gemelo, la, mellizo, za.

twinkle [tuin-kel] *vi.* centellear; parpadear; —, *n.* centello, *m.;* pestañeo, *m.;* movimiento rápido.

twinkling [tuin-klin] *n.* guiñada, *f.;* pestañeo, *m.;* momento, *m.;*

in the — of an eye, en un abrir y cerrar de ojos.

twirl [tuerl] *vt.* voltear; hacer girar; —, *n.* vuelta, *f.,* giro, *m.*

twist [tuist] *vt.* y *vi.* torcer, retorcer; entretejer; retortijar; **to — one's body,** contorcerse; —, *n.* trenza, *f.;* hilo de algodón; torcedura, *f.;* baile y ritmo popular de los E.U.A.

twisted [tuis-ted] *adj.* torcido; enredado.

twisting [tuis-tin] *adj.* torcedor; —, *n.* torcedura, *f.,* torcimiento, *m.*

twitch [tuich] *vt.* tirar bruscamente, agarrar; arrancar; —, *vi.* crisparse, contorcerse, tener una contracción nerviosa; —, *n.* tirón, *m.,* crispatura, *f.,* contracción nerviosa.

two-faced [tu-feisd] *adj.* falso; de dos caras; disimulado.

twofold [tu-fould] *adj.* doble, duplicado; —, *adv.* al doble.

two-step [tu-step] *n.* paso doble (música y baile).

tycoon [tai-kun] *n.* título dado antiguamente al jefe del ejército japonés; magnate industrial.

type [taip] *n.* tipo, *m.;* letra, *f.;* carácter, *m.;* clase, *f.;* género, *m.;* **bold-faced** —, tipo negro; **canon** —, canon, *m.;* **large** —, tipo de cartel; **light-faced** —, tipo delgado; **lower-case** —, letra minúscula; **Old English —**, letra gótica; **pica —,** tipo cícero; **Roman —,** letra redonda; **upper-case —,** letra mayúscula; **— bar,** línea de tipos; **—,** *vt.* y *vi.* escribir a máquina; **—,** *vt.* clasificar.

typewrite [taip-rait] *vt.* escribir a máquina.

typewriter [taip-rai-ter] *n.* máquina de escribir, *m.* y *f.;* **portable —,** máquina de escribir portátil.

typewritten [taip-ri-ten] *adj.* escrito a máquina.

typhoid [tai-foid] *n.* tifoidea, *f.;* **—,** *adj.* tifoideo; **— fever,** fiebre tifoidea.

typhoon [tai-fun] *n.* tifón, huracán, *m.*

typhus [tai-fus] *n.* (med.) tifus, tifo, *m.*

typical [ti-pi-kal] *adj.* típico; **—ly,** *adv.* en forma típica.

typify [ti-pi-fai] *vt.* simbolizar, representar.

typing [tai-pin] *n.* mecanografía, dactilografía, *f.*

typist [tai-pist] *n.* mecanógrafo, fa.

tyrannic, tyrannical [tai-ra-nik], [tai-ra-nikal] *adj.* tiránico.

tyrannous [tai-ra-nos] *adj.* tiránico, tirano, arbitrario; cruel; injusto.

tyranny [tai-ra-ni] *n.* tiranía, crueldad, opresión, *f.*

tyrant [tai-rant] *n.* tirano, *m.*

U

ubiquitous [iu-bi-kui-tos] *adj.* ubicuo.

udder [a-dar] *n.* ubre, *f.*

ugliness [a-gli-nes] *n.* fealdad, deformidad, *f.;* (coll.) rudeza, *f.*

ugly [a-gli] *adj.* feo, disforme; (coll.) rudo, desagradable.

ulcer [al-sar] *n.* úlcera, *f.*

ulterior [al-tia-riar] *adj.* ulterior; **— motive,** motivo oculto.

ultimate [al-ti-mit] *adj.* último; **—,** *n.* lo último.

ultimatum [al-ti-mei-tom] *n.* ultimatum, *m.;* última condición irrevocable.

ultra [al-tra] *adj.* extremo; excesivo; **—,** *n.* extremista, *m.* y *f.;* persona radical.

ultramodern [al-tra-mo-dern] *adj.* ultramoderno.

ultrasonic [al-tra-so-nik] *adj.* ultrasónico.

ultraviolet [al-tra-vaio-lit] *adj.* ultravioleta, ultraviolado; **— rays,** rayos ultraviolados.

umbilical [am-bi-lai-kal] *adj.*

umbilical; — **cord,** ombligo, *m.*

umbrella [am-bre-la] *n.* para-guas, *m.;* parasol, quitasol, *m.;* — **stand,** portaparaguas, *m.*

umpire [am-paiar] *n.* árbitro, arbitrador, *m.;* —, *vt.* arbitrar.

U.N.: United Nations [iu-en], [iu-nai-tid-nei-shons] ONU, Organización de las Naciones Unidas.

unabashed [a-na-basht] *adj.* desvergonzado, descocado.

unabated [a-na-bei-tid] *adj.* no disminuido, no agotado; cabal.

unable [an-ei-bol] *adj.* incapaz; **to be** —, no poder.

unabridged [a-na-brichd] *adj.* completo, sin abreviar.

unaccompanied [an-a-kam-pa-nid] *adj.* solo, sin acompañan-te.

unaccountable [an-a-kaun-ta-bol] *adj.* inexplicable, extraño.

unacquainted [an-a-kuein-tid] *adj.* desconocido; **I am — with him,** no lo conozco.

unadulterated [an-a-dal-te-rei-tid] *adj.* genuino, puro; sin mezcla.

unaffected [an-a-fek-tid] *adj.* sin afectación, sincero, natural; — **ly,** *adv.* en forma natural, sen-cillamente.

unaided [an-ei-did] *adj.* sin ayuda.

unaltered [an-al-tard] *adj.* inva-riado; sin ningún cambio.

unanimity [iu-na-ni-mi-ti] *n.* unanimidad, *f.*

unanimous [iu-na-ni-mos] *adj.* unánime; —**ly,** *adv.* por acla-mación, por unanimidad.

unapproachable [an-a-prou-cha-bol] *adj.* inaccesible.

unarmed [an-armd] *adj.* inerme, desarmado.

unassisted [an-a-sis-tid] *adj.* sin ayuda, solo; sin auxilio.

unassuming [an-a-siu-min] *adj.* modesto, sencillo, sin preten-siones.

unavoidable [an-a-voi-da-bol] *adj.* inevitable; **to be** —, no tener remedio, no poder evitar-se.

unaware [an-a-uear] *adj.* incau-to; de sorpresa, sin saber.

unawares [an-a-ueas] *adv.* inad-vertidamente; de improviso, inesperadamente.

unbalanced [an-ba-lanst] *adj.* trastornado; no equilibrado.

unbearable [an-bea-ra-bol] *adj.* intolerable.

unbeliever [an-bi-li-var] *n.* incré-dulo, la; infiel, *m.* y *f.*

unbend [an-bend] *vt.* aflojar; —, *vi.* condescender; descansar.

unbending [an-ben-din] *adj.* inflexible.

unbiased [an-baiast] *adj.* impar-cial, exento de prejuicios.

unbind [an-baind] *vt.* desatar; aflojar.

unborn [an-born] *adj.* sin nacer, no nacido todavía.

unbound [an-bound] *adj.* sin encuadernar, a la rústica (aplícase a libros); desatado.

unbounded [an-boun-did] *adj.* infinito; ilimitado.

unbreakable [an-brei-ka-bol] *adj.* irrompible.

unbridle [an-bri-del] *vt.* desenfrenar; —d, *adj.* desenfrenado, licencioso; violento.

unbroken [an-brou-ken] *adj.* indómito; entero; no interrumpido, continuado.

unbuckle [an-ba-kel] *vt.* deshebillar.

unburden [an-ber-den] *vt.* descargar, aliviar.

unbutton [an-ba-ton] *vt.* desabotonar.

uncanny [an-ka-ni] *adj.* extraño, misterioso.

unceasing [an-si-sin] *adj.* sin cesar, continuo; —ly, *adv.* sin tregua.

uncertain [an-ser-ten] *adj.* inseguro; incierto, dudoso; vacilante.

uncertainty [an-ser-tan-ti] *n.* incertidumbre, *f.*

unchecked [an-chekt] *adj.* desenfrenado.

uncivilized [an-si-vi-laist] *adj.* salvaje, incivilizado.

unclaimed [an-kleimd] *adj.* no reclamado, sin reclamar; sin recoger.

uncle [an-kel] *n.* tío, *m.*

unclean [an-klin] *adj.* inmundo, sucio, puerco; obsceno; inmoral.

uncoil [an-koil] *vt.* desarrollar, devanar.

uncomfortable [an-kam-for-ta-bol] *adj.* incómodo; intranquilo; desagradable.

uncommon [an-ko-mon] *adj.* raro, extraordinario, fuera de lo común.

uncompromising [an-kom-pro-mai-sin] *adj.* inflexible; irreconciliable.

unconcern [an-kon-sern] *n.* indiferencia, *f.;* descuido, *m.;* despreocupación, *f.*

unconcerned [an-kon-sernd] *adj.* indiferente.

unconditional [an-kon-di-sho-nal] *adj.* incondicional, absoluto; — **surrender,** rendición absoluta, rendición incondicional.

unconscious [an-kon-shos] *adj.* inconsciente; desmayado.

unconventional [an-kon-ven-sho-nal] *adj.* informal, sin ceremonia, sin formulismos.

uncover [an-ka-var] *vt.* descubrir.

uncultivated [an-kal-ti-vei-tid] *adj.* inculto; sin cultivar.

uncut [an-kat] *adj.* no cortado, entero.

undamaged [an-da-mich] *adj.* ileso, libre de daño.

undaunted [an-don-tid] *adj.* intrépido, atrevido.

undecided [an-di-sai-did] *adj.* indeciso.

undeniable [an-di-naia-bol] *adj.* innegable; indudable; —**bly,** *adv.* innegablemente.

under [an-dar] *prep.* debajo de, bajo; — **penalty of fine,** so pena de multa; — **penalty of death,** so pena de muerte; —, *adv.* debajo, abajo, más abajo.

underage [an-da-rich] *adj.* menor de edad.

undercover [an-da-ka-var] *adv.* bajo cuerda, secretamente.

undercurrent [an-da-ka-rent] *n.* tendencia oculta; corriente submarina.

undercut [an-da-kat] *n.* solomillo, *m.;* puñetazo hacia arriba; —, *vi.* vender a precios más bajos que el competidor; —, *vt.* socavar.

underdeveloped [an-da-di-ve-lopt] *adj.* subdesarrollado; — **countries,** países subdesarrollados.

underdog [an-da-dog] *n.* persona oprimida; el que lleva la peor parte.

underestimate [an-dar-es-ti-mit] *vt.* menospreciar; calcular de menos; subestimar.

underexposure [an-dar-iks-pou-shar] *n.* (phot.) insuficiente exposición.

undergo [an-da-gou] *vt.* sufrir; sostener.

undergraduate [an-da-gra-diueit] *n.* estudiante universitario no graduado.

underground [an-da-graund] *adj.* subterráneo; subrepticio; —, *adv.* debajo de la tierra; en secreto; subrepticiamente; —, *n.* subterráneo, *m.;* ferrocarril subterráneo.

underhand [an-da-jand] *adj.* secreto, clandestino; ejecutado con las manos hacia abajo; fraudulento; injusto; —, *adv.* con las manos hacia abajo; clandestinamente.

underhanded [an-da-jan-did] *adj.* bajo cuerda, por debajo de cuerda, secreto, clandestino; —ly, *adv.* en forma clandestina.

underlie [an-da-lai] *vi.* estar debajo; ser base de.

underline [an-da-lain] *vt.* subrayar.

underling [an-da-lin] *n.* subordinado, *m.;* suboficial, *m.*

underlying [an-da-laiin] *adj.* fundamental, básico; esencial;

yaciente, que yace debajo.

undermine [an-da-main] *vt.*
minar; desprestigiar por debajo
de cuerda.

underneath [an-da-niz] *adv.*
debajo.

undernourished [an-da-na-risht]
adj. malnutrido, desnutrido,
malalimentado.

underpass [an-da-pas] *n.* viaducto, *m.*

underprivileged [an-da-pri-vi-li-
chid] *adj.* desvalido, menestero-
so, necesitado; **the — classes,**
las clases menesterosas.

underrate [an-da-reit] *vt.* menoscabar; deslustrar; menospre-
ciar.

underscore [an-da-skor] *vt.*
subrayar; recalcar.

undersell [an-da-sel] *vt.* vender
por menos (que otro).

undershirt [an-da-shert] *n.*
camiseta, *f.*

underside [an-dar-said] *n.* lado
inferior, fondo de una cosa.

undersigned [an-dar-saind] *n. y
adj.* suscrito, ta.

underskirt [an-da-skert] *n.* enagua, *f.*, refajo, fondo, zagalejo,
m.

understand [an-da-stand] *vt.*
entender, comprender; **do you
—?** ¿entiende Ud.? **we — each
other,** nos comprendemos.

understanding [an-da-stan-din]

n. entendimiento, *m.*, comprensión, *f.*; inteligencia, *f*; conocimiento, *m.*; correspondencia,
f.; meollo, m.; **slow in —,** torpe,
tardo en comprender; **—,** *adj.*
comprensivo; inteligente, perito.

understudy [an-da-sta-di] *n.*
(theat.) sustituto, ta, actor o
actriz que se prepara para remplazar a otro en un momento
dado; **—,** *vt. y vi.* (theat.) prepararse para tomar el papel de
otro en un momento dado.

undertake [an-da-teik] *vt. y vi.*
emprender.

undertaking [an-da-tei-kin] *n.*
empresa, obra, *f.*; empeño, *m.*;
— establishment, funeraria, *f.*

undertone [an-da-toun] *n.* tono
(de voz) bajo; voz baja; color
tenue u opaco.

undertow [an-da-tau] *n.* resaca,
f.

underwater [an-da-ua-ter] *adj.*
subacuático, submarino.

underwear [an-da-uear] *n.* ropa
interior, ropa íntima.

underweight [an-da-ueiz] *adj.* de
bajo peso, que pesa menos del
término medio.

undesirable [an-di-sai-ra-bol]
adj. no deseable, nocivo.

undeveloped [an-da-di-ve-lopt]
adj. no desarrollado; **—
country,** país no explotado; **—**

photograph, fotografía no revelada.

undiluted [an-di-lu-tid] *adj.* puro, sin diluir.

undiminished [an-di-mi-nisht] *adj.* entero, sin disminuir.

undisputed [an-dis-piu-tid] *adj.* incontestable.

undisturbed [an-dis-terbd] *adj.* quieto, tranquilo, sin haber sido estorbado.

undivided [an-di-vai-did] *adj.* indiviso, entero.

undo [an-du] *vt.* deshacer, desatar.

undoing [an-duin] *n.* destrucción, ruina, *f.*

undone [an-dan] *adj.* sin hacer; **to leave nothing —,** no dejar nada por hacer.

undoubted [an-dau-tid] *adj.* evidente; **—ly,** *adv.* sin duda, indudablemente.

undress [an-dres] *vt.* desnudar; **—,** *n.* paños menores.

undulate [an-diu-leit] *vi.* ondear, ondular.

unduly [an-diu-li] *adv.* excesivamente; indebidamente; ilícitamente.

undying [an-daiin] *adj.* inmortal; imperecedero.

unearned [an-ernd] *adj.* inmerecido; que no se ha ganado.

unearth [an-erz] *vt.* desenterrar; revelar; divulgar; descubrir.

uneasiness [an-i-si-nes] *n.* malestar, *m.;* inquietud, intranquilidad, *f.;* desasosiego, *m.*

uneasy [an-i-si] *adj.* inquieto, desasosegado; incómodo; intranquilo.

uneducated [an-e-diu-kei-tid] *adj.* sin educación.

unemployed [an-im-ploid] *adj.* desocupado, sin trabajo; ocioso.

unemployment [an-im-ploi-ment] *n.* desempleo, *m.;* paro, *m.*

unending [an-en-din] *adj.* inacabable, sin fin; eterno, perpetuo.

unequal [an-i-kual] *adj.* desigual.

unequaled [an-i-kuald] *adj.* incomparable.

unerring [an-e-rin] *adj.* infalible.

uneven [an-i-ven] *adj.* desigual; barrancoso; disparejo, impar; **—ly,** *adv.* desigualmente.

unexpected [an-iks-pek-tid] *adj.* inesperado; inopinado; **—ly,** *adv.* de repente.

unexplored [an-iks-plord] *adj.* ignorado, no descubierto, sin explorar.

unfailing [an-fei-lin] *adj.* infalible, seguro.

unfair [an-fear] *adj.* injusto; **—ly,** *adv.* injustamente.

unfaithful [an-feiz-ful] *adj.* infiel, pérfido.

unfamiliar [an-fa-mi-liar] *adj.* desacostumbrado, desconocido.

unfavorable [an-fei-va-ra-bol] *adj.* desfavorable.

unfeeling [an-fi-lin] *adj.* insensible, duro, cruel.

unfit [an-fit] *adj.* inepto, incapaz; inadecuado; indigno; —, *vt.* incapacitar; inhabilitar.

unfold [an-fould] *vt.* desplegar; revelar; desdoblar.

unforeseen [an-for-sin] *adj.* imprevisto.

unforgettable [an-for-ge-ta-bol] *adj.* inolvidable.

unfortunate [an-forch-nit] *adj.* desafortunado, infeliz; malhadado; —ly, *adv.* por desgracia, infelizmente, desgraciadamente.

unfounded [an-faun-did] *adj.* sin fundamento.

unfurl [an-ferl] *vt.* desplegar, extender.

unfurnished [an-fer-nishd] *adj.* sin muebles, no amueblado; — **apartment,** departamento sin amueblar.

ungodly [an-god-li] *adj.* impío.

ungrounded [an-graun-did] *adj.* infundado.

unhappy [an-ja-pi] *adj.* infeliz; descontento, triste.

unharmed [an-jarmd] *adj.* ileso, sano y salvo.

unhealthy [an-jel-zi] *adj.* enfer-mizo; insalubre, malsano.

unheard-of [an-jerd-of] *adj.* inaudito, extraño; no imaginado.

unheeded [an-ji-did] *adj.* despreciado, no atendido.

unhurt [an-jert] *adj.* ileso, sin haber sufrido daño.

unification [iuni-fi-kei-shon] *n.* unificación, *f.*

uniform [iuni-form] *n.* uniforme, *m.;* —, *adj.* uniforme; —ly, *adv.* uniformemente.

uniformity [iuni-for-mi-ti] *n.* uniformidad, *f.*

unilateral [iuni-la-te-ral] *adj.* unilateral.

unify [iuni-fai] *vt.* unificar, unir.

uninjured [an-in-yuad] *adj.* ileso, sin haber sufrido daño.

union [iu-nion] *n.* unión, *f.;* conjunción, *f.;* fusión, *f.*

unionism [iu-nio-ni-sem] *n.* unionismo, *m.,* sindicalismo obrero, agrupación obrera; formación de gremios obreros.

unionize [iu-nio-nais] *vt.* sindicar; unionizar; incorporar en un gremio.

unique [iu-nik] *adj.* único, singular, extraordinario.

unison [iu-ni-son] *n.* unisonancia, *f.;* concordancia, unión, *f.;* **in —,** al unísono.

unit [iu-nit] *n.* unidad, *f.*

unite [iu-nit] *vt.* y *vi.* unir, unirse, juntarse; concretar.

united [iu-nai-tid] *adj.* unido, junto.

United Kingdom [iu-nai-tid-kin-dom] Reino Unido, *m.*

unity [iu-ni-ti] *n.* unidad, concordia, conformidad, *f.*

universal [iu-ni-ver-sal] *adj.* universal; — **joint,** cardán, *m.;* — **ly,** *adv.* universalmente.

universality [iu-ni-ver-sa-li-ti] *n.* universalidad, *f.*

universe [iu-ni-vers] *n.* universo, *m.*

university [iu-ni-ver-si-ti] *n.* universidad, *f.*

unjust [an-yast] *adj.* injusto.

unjustified [an-yas-ti-faid] *adj.* injustificado.

unkempt [an-kempt] *adj.* despeinado; descuidado en el traje; tosco.

unkind [an-kaind] *adj.* poco bondadoso; cruel; —**ly,** *adv.* desfavorablemente; ásperamente.

unknowingly [an-nouin-li] *adv.* sin saberlo; desapercibidamente.

unknown [an-noun] *adj.* desconocido.

unlace [an-leis] *vt.* desenlazar, desamarrar.

unless [an-les] *conj.* a menos que, si no.

unlike [an-laik] *adj.* disímil, des-

emejante; —, *conj.* al contrario de.

unlikely *adj.* improbable; inverosímil.

unlimited [an-li-mi-ted] *adj.* ilimitado.

unload [an-loud] *vt.* descargar.

unlock [an-lok] *vt.* abrir alguna cerradura.

unlucky [an-la-ki] *adj.* desafortunado; siniestro.

unmanageable [an-ma-ne-ya-bol] *adj.* inmanejable, intratable.

unmarried [an-ma-rid] *adj.* soltero; soltera; — **woman,** soltera, *f.;* — **man,** soltero, *m.*

unmask [an-mask] *vt.* desenmascarar, revelar; —, *vi.* desenmascararse, quitarse la máscara.

unmentionable [an-men-sho-na-bol] *adj.* que no se puede mencionar, indigno de mencionarse; —**s,** *n. pl.* cosas que no pueden mencionarse, por ejemplo (en forma jocosa), ropa interior, etc.

unmixed [an-mikst] *adj.* sin mezcla.

unnatural [an-na-chu-ral] *adj.* artificial; contrario a las leyes de la naturaleza.

unnecessary [an-ne-si-sa-ri] *adj.* innecesario, inútil.

unnerve [an-nerv] *vt.* enervar.

unnoticed [an-nou-tist] *adj.* no observado.

unnumbered [an-nam-berd] *adj.* innumerable; sin número.

unobserved [an-ob-servd] *adj.* no observado; inadvertido.

unobtrusive [an-obs-trak-tiv] *adj.* modesto, recatado.

unofficial [an-o-fi-shal] *adj.* extraoficial; particular, privado.

unorthodox [an-or-zo-doks] *adj.* heterodoxo.

unpack [an-pak] *vt.* desempacar; desempaquetar; desenvolver.

unpaid [an-peid] *adj.* pendiente de pago.

unpleasant [an-ple-sant] *adj.* desagradable.

unplug [an-plag] *vt.* desenchufar.

unpopular [an-po-piu-lar] *adj.* impopular.

unprecedented [an-pre-si-dan-tid] *adj.* sin precedente.

unpremeditated [an-pri-me-di-tei-tid] *adj.* sin premeditación.

unproductive [an-pro-dak-tiv] *adj.* estéril, infructuoso.

unprofitable [an-pro-fi-ta-bol] *adj.* inútil, vano, que no rinde utilidad o provecho; —**bly,** *adv.* inútilmente, en forma infructuosa.

unprotected [an-pro-tek-tid] *adj.* sin protección, sin defensa; desvalido.

unpunished [an-pa-nisht] *adj.* impune.

unquenchable [an-kuen-cha-bol] *adj.* inextinguible.

unravel [an-ra-vel] *vt.* desenredar; resolver.

unreal [an-rial] *adj.* fantástico, ilusorio, que no tiene realidad.

unrecognizable [an-re-kog-nai-sa-bol] *adj.* irreconocible.

unreliable [an-ri-laia-bol] *adj.* informal, incumplido.

unrest [an-rest] *n.* inquietud, impaciencia, *f.*; movimiento, *m.*

unrestrained [an-ri-streind] *adj.* desenfrenado; ilimitado.

unripe [an-raip] *adj.* inmaturo; precoz, prematuro; — **fruit,** fruta verde, fruta no madura.

unrivaled [an-rai-vald] *adj.* sin rival, sin igual.

unroll [an-roul] *vt.* desenrollar, desplegar.

unruly [an-ru-li] *adj.* desenfrenado, inmanejable, refractario; desarreglado.

unsavory [an-sei-va-ri] *adj.* desabrido, insípido; ofensivo.

unscathed [an-skaz] *adj.* a salvo; sano y salvo; sin daño o perjuicio.

unscrew [an-skru] *vt.* destornillar, desatornillar, desentornillar.

unscrupulous [an-sku-piu-los] *adj.* sin escrúpulos, inmoral, desalmado.

unseasonable [an-si-so-na-bol] *adj.* fuera de la estación; a destiempo, inoportuno.

unseat [an-sit] *vt.* quitar del asiento; privar del derecho de formar parte de una cámara legislativa.

unseen [an-sin] *adj.* no visto; invisible.

unselfish [an-sel-fish] *adj.* desinteresado, generoso.

unsettled [an-se-teld] *adj.* voluble, inconstante; incierto, indeciso; no establecido; — **accounts,** cuentas por pagar, cuentas no liquidadas.

unshakable [an-shei-ka-bol] *adj.* inmutable, firme, estable, impasible, inconmovible; insacudible.

unsightly [an-sait-li] *adj.* desagradable a la vista, feo.

unskilled [an-skild] *adj.* inexperto, inhábil.

unsound [an-saund] *adj.* falto de salud; falto de sentido; inestable; erróneo, falso.

unsparing [an-spea-rin] *adj.* generoso, liberal; incompasivo, cruel.

unspeakable [an-spi-ka-bol] *adj.* indecible; —**ly,** *adv.* en forma indecible.

unstable [an-stei-bol] *adj.* inestable, inconstante.

unsuitable [an-su-ta-bol] *adj.* inadecuado, impropio.

unsullied [an-sa-lid] *adj.* inmaculado, puro, limpio.

unswerving [an-suer-vin] *adj.* indesviable; leal.

untamed [an-teimd] *adj.* indómito, indomado.

untangle [an-tan-guel] *vt.* desenredar.

unthinking [an-zin-kin] *adj.* desatento, inconsiderado, indiscreto; irreflexivo.

untidy [an-tai-di] *adj.* desaseado, descuidado, desaliñado.

untie [an-tai] *vt.* desatar, deshacer, soltar, desamarrar.

until [an-til] *prep.* hasta; —, *conj.* hasta que.

untimely [an-taim-li] *adj.* intempestivo; prematuro.

untiring [an-tai-rin] *adj.* incansable.

untold [an-tould] *adj.* no relatado, no dicho.

untouched [an-tacht] *adj.* intacto, no tocado.

untried [an-traid] *adj.* no ensayado o probado.

untroubled [an-tra-beld] *adj.* no perturbado, tranquilo, calmado.

untrustworthy [an-trast-uer-zi] *adj.* incumplido, indigno de confianza.

untruth [an-truz] *n.* falsedad,

mentira, f.

unused [an-iusd] *adj.* desacostumbrado.

unusual [an-iu-shual] *adj.* usitado, raro, insólito; poco común; —**ly,** *adv.* excepcionalmente.

unvarying [an-va-rin] *adj.* invariable.

unveil [an-veild] *vt.* y *vi.* descubrir; revelar; quitar el velo (a alguna cosa); estrenar.

unwarranted [an-uo-ran-tid] *adj.* injustificable, inexcusable.

unwelcome [an-uel-kam] *adj.* inoportuno; mal acogido, no recibido con gusto.

unwieldy [an-uil-di] *adj.* pesado, difícil de manejar.

unwilling [an-ui-lin] *adj.* renuente, sin deseos, sin querer; —**ly,** *adv.* de mala gana.

unwind [an-uaind] *vt.* desenredar, desenrollar; desenmarañar; relajar.

unwise [an-uais] *adj.* imprudente; —**ly,** *adv.* sin juicio.

unwittingly [an-ui-tin-li] *adv.* sin saber, sin darse cuenta.

unworthy [an-uer-zi] *adj.* indigno, vil.

unwound [an-uaund] *adj.* sin cuerda; desenrollado.

unwrap [an-rap] *vt.* desenvolver; abrir; revelar.

unwritten [an-ri-ten] *adj.* verbal, no escrito; — **law,** ley de la costumbre, derecho consuetudinario.

unyielding [an-yil-din] *adj.* inflexible.

up [ap] *adv.* arriba, en lo alto; — **to,** hasta; — **to date,** hasta la fecha; hasta ahora, **to make** —, hacer las paces; inventar; compensar; maquillarse; **to bring** —, criar, educar; **to call** —, telefonear; **it is** — **to me,** depende de mí.

upbringing [ap-brin-guin] *n.* educación, crianza, f.

upgrade [ap-greid] *n.* cuesta arriba, pendiente arriba; —, *vt.* ascender en categoría (a un obrero); mejorar un producto para subirle el precio.

upheaval [ap-ji-val] *n.* alzamiento, levantamiento, *m.*; conmoción, f.

uphill [ap-jil] *adj.* difícil, penoso; —, *adv.* en grado ascendente.

uphold [ap-jould] *vt.* levantar en alto; sostener; apoyar, proteger; defender.

upholster [ap-jouls-tar] *vt.* entapizar, tapizar.

upholstery [ap-jouls-te-ri] *n.* tapicería, f., tapizado, *m.*

upkeep [ap-kip] *n.* conservación, f., mantenimiento, *m.*

uplift [ap-lift] *vt.* levantar en alto; mejorar.

upmost [ap-moust] *adj.* lo más

alto; lo más prominente; lo más influyente; —, *adv.* en el lugar más alto; en primer lugar.

upon [a-pon] *prep.* sobre, encima.

upper [a-par] *adj.* superior; más elevado; — **berth,** cama o litera alta (en un tren, un vapor, etc.); — **case,** (print.) caja alta, letras mayúsculas; — **hand,** dominio, *m.*, predominancia, *f.*

upper-case [a-pa-keis] *adj.* (print.) de caja alta, mayúsculo.

upper-class [a-pa-klas] *adj.* aristocrático; relativo a los grados superiores de un colegio.

uppermost [a-pa-moust] *adj.* superior en posición, rango, poder, etc.; **to be** —, predominar.

upright [ap-rait] *adj.* derecho, recto, justo; perpendicular; — **ly,** *adv.* rectamente.

uprising [ap-rai-sin] *n.* subida, *f.;* levantamiento, *m.,* insurrección, *f.*

uproar [ap-ror] *n.* tumulto, alboroto, *m.*

uproot [ap-rut] *vt.* desarraigar, extirpar.

upset [ap-set] *vt.* volcar, trastornar; perturbar; —, *adj.* desordenado; volcano; agitado (de ánimo); —, *n.* trastorno, *m.;*

vuelco, *m.*

upside-down [ap-said-daun] *adj.* de arriba abajo.

upstairs [ap-stears] *adv.* en el piso de arriba, arriba.

upstream [ap-strim] *adv.* aguas arriba, río arriba.

up-to-date [ap-tu-deit] *adj.* moderno, de última moda, reciente.

upturn [ap-tern] *vt.* mejorar; volver hacia arriba; —, *n.* mejoramiento, *m.;* subida, *f.*

upward, upwards [ap-uord], [ap-uords] *adv.* hacia arriba.

uranium [iua-ra-niom] *n.* uranio, *m.*

urban [er-ban] *adj.* urbano.

urbanization [er-ba-ni-sei-shon] *n.* urbanización, *f.*

urchin [er-chin] *n.* pilluelo, *m.;* (coll.) granuja, *m.;* (zool.) erizo, *m.*

urethra [iu-ri-tra] *n.* uretra, *f.*

urge [erch] *vt. y vi.* incitar, hurgar; activar; urgir, instar.

urgency [er-chen-si] *n.* urgencia, *f.;* premura, *f.*

urgent [er-chent] *adj.* urgente; — **ly,** *adv.* urgentemente, con urgencia.

urinal [iu-rai-nal] *n.* orinal, *m.*

urinate [iu-ri-neit] *vi.* orinar, mear.

urn [ern] *n.* urna, *f.*

U.S.A.: United States of America

[iu-es-ei], [iu-nai-tid-steits-of-a-me-ri-ka] E.U.A. Estados Unidos de América.

usable [iu-sa-bol] *adj.* apto, hábil; utilizable.

usage [iu-sich] *n.* uso, *m.;* tratamiento, *m.*

use [ius] *n.* uso, *m.,* utilidad, *f.;* servicio, *m.;* —, *vt.* y *vi.* usar, emplear, servirse de; acostumbrar; soler; **to make — of,** utilizar.

used [iusd] *adj.* usado; de ocasión; **to get — to,** acostumbrarse a.

useful [ius-ful] *adj.* útil; **to make —,** utilizar; —**ly,** *adv.* en forma útil.

usefulness [ius-ful-nes] *n.* utilidad, *f.*

useless [ius-les] *adj.* inútil.

uselessness [ius-les-nes] *n.* inutilidad, *f.*

usual [iu-shual] *adj.* usual, común, usado; general, ordinario; —**ly,** *adv.* de costumbre.

usurp [iu-serp] *vt.* usurpar.

utensil [iu-ten-sil] *n.* utensilio, *m.;* —**s,** *n. pl.* útiles, *m. pl.;* **kitchen —s,** trastos, *m. pl.,* batería de cocina.

uterus [iu-te-rus] *n.* útero, *m.,* matriz, *f.*

utilitarian [iu-ti-li-tea-rian] *adj.* utilitario.

utility [iu-ti-li-ti] *n.* utilidad, *f.;* **public —ies,** servicios públicos.

utilization [iu-ti-li-zei-shon] *n.* utilización, *f.*

utilize [iu-ti-lais] *vt.* utilizar; emplear.

Utopian, utopian [iu-tou-pian] *adj.* utópico; imaginario; —, *n.* utopista, *m.* y *f.*

utter [a-tar] *adj.* acabado; todo; extremo; entero; —, *vt.* proferir; expresar; publicar.

utterance [a-te-rans] *n.* habla, expresión, manifestación, *f.*

utterly [a-ter-li] *adv.* enteramente, del todo.

V

vacancy [va-kan-si] *n.* vacante, *f.;* vacío, *m.*

vacant [va-kant] *adj.* vacío, desocupado, vacante.

vacate [va-keit] *vt.* desocupar; anular, invalidar.

vacation [va-kei-shon] *n.* vacación, *f.,* vacaciones, *f. pl.*

vaccinate [vak-si-neit] *vt.* vacunar.

vaccination [vak-si-nei-shon] *n.* vacuna, *f.;* vacunación, *f.*

vaccine [vak-sin] *n.* vacuna, *f.*

vacillate [vak-si-leit] *vi.* vacilar.

vacuum [va-kium] *n.* vacío, *m.*; — **bottle**, termos, *m.*; — **cleaner**, aspiradora, *f.*; — **pump**, bomba aspirante, bomba de vacío; — **tube**, tubo al vacío.

vagabond [va-ga-bond] *n.* y *adj.* vagabundo, *m.*

vagina [va-yai-na] *n.* (anat.) vagina, *f.*; (bot.) vaina, *f.*

vagrant [vei-grant] *adj.* vagabundo; —, *n.* bribón, *m.*

vague [vei] *adj.* vago; —**ly**, *adv.* vagamente.

vain [vein] *adj.* vano, inútil; vanidoso, presuntuoso; **in** —, en vano.

valence [va-lans] *n.* (chem.) valencia, *f.*

valentine [va-len-tain] *n.* persona a quien se le tributa amor el día de San Valentin (14 de febrero); tarjeta o regalo que se envía el día de San Valentin en señal de amor.

valiant [va-liant] *adj.* valiente, valeroso.

valid [va-lid] *adj.* válido.

validity [va-li-di-ti] *n.* validación, validez, *f.*

valley [va-li] *n.* valle, *m.*, cuenca, *f.*

valor [va-lar] *n.* valor, aliento, brío, *m.*, fortaleza, *f.*

valuable [va-liua-bol] *adj.* precioso, valioso; **to be** —, valer; —**s**, *n. pl.* objetos de valor.

value [va-liu] *n.* valor, precio, importe, *m.*; **real** —, valor efectivo; — **stipulated**, — **agreed on**, valor entendido, *m.*; **face** —, valor nominal o aparente; —, *vt.* valuar, apreciar.

valve [valv] *n.* válvula, *f.*, regulador, *m.*; **safety** —, válvula de seguridad; **slide** —, válvula corrediza; **air** —, válvula de aire.

vampire [vam-paiar] *n.* (zool.) vampiro, *m.*; (fig.) vampiro, *m.*, persona codiciosa; vampiresa, mujer coqueta y aventurera.

van [van] *n.* vagón, *m.*; camión de mudanza.

vandalism [van-da-li-sem] *n.* vandalismo, *m.*

vanguard [van-gard] *n.* vanguardia, *f.*

vanilla [va-ni-la] *n.* vainilla, *f.*

vanish [va-nish] *vi.* desvanecerse, desaparecer.

vanity [va-ni-ti] *n.* vanidad, *f.*; *m.*, polvera, *f.*, estuche o caja de afeites.

vanquish [van-kuish] *vt.* vencer, conquistar.

vantage [van-tich] *n.* ventaja, superioridad, *f.*; — **point**, situación ventajosa.

vapor [vei-par] *n.* vapor, *m.*; exhalación, *f.*

vaporous [vei-pa-ras] *adj.* vaporoso.

variable [vea-ria-bol] *adj.* variable.

variance [va-rians] *n.* discordia, desavenencia, *f.;* diferencia, *f.;* desviación, *f.;* discrepancia, *f.*

variation [va-riei-shon] *n.* variación, mudanza, *f.*

varicose [va-ri-kous] *adj.* varicoso; — **vein,** várice, *f.*

varied [va-rid] *adj.* variado; cambiado, alterado.

variety [va-rai-ti] *n.* variedad, *f.*

various [va-rios] *adj.* varios, diversos, diferentes.

varnish [var-nish] *n.* barniz, *m.;* —, *vt.* barnizar; charolar.

varsity [var-si-ti] *n.* equipo deportivo principal seleccionado para representar a una universidad, etc.

vary [vea-ri] *vt.* y *vi.* variar, diferenciar; cambiar, mudarse, discrepar.

varying [vea-riin] *adj.* variante.

vase [vas] *n.* vaso, jarrón, florero, *m.*

Vaseline [va-si-lin] *n.* Vaselina (marca de fábrica), *f.,* ungüento de petróleo.

vast [vast] *adj.* vasto; inmenso; —**ly,** *adv.* excesivamente; vastamente.

vault [volt] *n.* bóveda, *f.;* cueva, caverna, *f.;* salto, *m.,* voltereta, *f.;* — *vt.* abovedar; —, *vi.* saltar, dar una voltereta.

vaunt [vont] *vi.* jactarse, vanagloriarse.

veal [vil] *n.* ternera, *f.,* ternero, *m.;* — **cutlet,** chuleta de ternera.

vector [vek-tar] *n.* (math., phys.) vector, *m.*

veer [viar] *vi.* (naut.) virar, cambiar (el viento); desviarse.

vegetable [ve-yi-ta-bol] *adj.* vegetal; — **man,** verdulero, *m.;* — **soup,** menestra, *f.,* sopa de verdura; —, *n.* vegetal, *m.;* —**s,** *n. pl.* verduras, hortalizas, *f. pl.*

vegetarian [ve-yi-tea-rian] *n.* y *adj.* vegetariano, na.

vegetation [ve-yi-tei-shon] *n.* vegetación, *f.*

vehemence [vi-mans] *n.* vehemencia, violencia, *f.;* viveza, *f.*

vehement [vi-mant] *adj.* vehemente, violento; —**ly,** *adv.* con vehemencia.

vehicle [vei-kol] *n.* vehículo, *m.*

veil [veil] *n.* velo, *m.;* disfraz, *m.;* —, *vt.* encubrir, ocultar, cubrir con velo.

vein [vein] *n.* vena, *f.;* cavidad, *f.;* inclinación del ingenio; humor, *m.*

veined, veiny [veind], [vei-ni] *adj.* venoso; vetado.

velocity [vi-lo-si-ti] *n* velocidad, *f.*

velvet [vel-vit] *n* terciopelo, *m.;*

—, *adj.* de terciopelo; terciopelado.

velvety [vel-vi-ti] *adj.* terciopelado, aterciopelado.

vendor [ven-dar] *n* vendedor, revendedor, *m.*

venerable [ve-ne-ra-bol] *adj.* venerable.

venerate [ve-na-reit] *vt.* venerar, honrar.

veneration [ve-na-rei-shon] *n.* veneración, *f.;* culto, *m.*

venereal [vi-nia-rial] *adj.* venéreo.

Venetian [vi-ni-shan] *n y adj.* veneciano, na.

Venezuelan [ve-ni-suei-lan] *n y adj.* venezolano, na.

vengeance [ven-yans] *n* venganza, *f.*

vengeful [vench-ful] *adj.* vengativo.

Venice [ve-nis] Venecia, *f.*

venison [ve-ni-son] *n.* carne de venado.

venom [ve-nom] *n.* veneno, *m.*

venomous [ve-no-mos] *adj.* venenoso.

vent [vent] *n.* respiradero, *m.;* salida, *f.;* apertura, *f.;* —, *vt.* dar salida; echar fuera; **to — one's anger,** desahogarse, expresar furia.

ventilate [ven-ti-leit] *vt.* ventilar; discutir, airear.

ventilation [ven-ti-lei-shon] *n.* ventilación, *f.*

ventilator [ven-ti-lei-tar] *n.* ventilador, abanico, *m.*

ventricle [ven-tri-kol] *n.* (anat.) ventrículo, *m.*

ventriloquist [ven-tri-lo-kuist] *n.* ventrílocuo, *m.*

venture [ven-char] *n.* riesgo, *m.;* ventura, *f.;* —, *vi.* osar, aventurarse; —, *vt.* arriesgar.

venturesome, venturous [ven-cha-som], [ven-chu-ras] *adj.* osado, atrevido; **—ly,** *adv.* osadamente.

veranda o verandah [ve-ran-da] *n.* veranda, terraza, galería, *f.,* mirador, *m.*

verb [verb] *n.* (gram.) verbo, *m.*

verbal [ver-bal] *adj.* verbal, literal; **—ly,** *adv.* oralmente de palabra.

verdict [ver-dikt] *n.* veredicto, *m.;* sentencia, *f.;* dictamen, *m.;* fallo (del jurado), *m.*

verdure [ver-diuar] *n.* verdura, *f.,* verdor, *m.*

verge [verdch] *n.* vara, *f.;* fuste, *m.;* borde, *m.;* margen, *m. y f.;* —, *vi.* inclinarse; tirar a, parecerse a (colores etc.).

verify [ve-ri-fai] *vt.* verificar; sustanciar.

veritable [ve-ri-ta-bol] *adj.* verdadero, cierto.

vermilion [ver-mi-lion] *n.* bermellón, *m.;* —, *vt.* teñir de bermellón, teñir de cinabrio.

vermin [ver-min] *n.* bichos, *m. pl.*

vernacular [ver-na-kiu-lar] *adj.* vernáculo, nativo; —, *n.* lengua vernácula; jerga, *f.,* lenguaje propio de un oficio, etc.

versatile [ver-sa-tail] *adj.* polifacético, hábil para muchas cosas; versátil, voluble.

versatility [ver-sa-ti-li-ti] *n.* habilidad para muchas cosas, flexibilidad, *f.*

verse [vers] *n.* verso, *m.;* versículo, *m.;* **blank** —, verso blanco; **free** —, verso suelto o libre.

versed [verst] *adj.* versado.

version [ver-shon] *n.* versión, traducción, *f.*

versus [ver-sos] *prep.* contra.

vertebra [ver-ti-bra] *n.* vértebra, *f.*

vertebral [ver-ti-bral] *adj.* vertebral.

vertebrate [ver-ti-breit] *n. y adj.* vertebrado, *m.*

vertex [ver-teks] *n.* cenit, vértice, *m.*

vertical [ver-ti-kal] *adj.* vertical; **—ly,** *adv.* verticalmente.

vertigo [ver-ti-gou] *n.* vértigo, vahído, *m.*

very [ve-ri] *adj.* idéntico, mismo; verdadero; —, *adv.* muy, mucho, sumamente.

vessel [ve-sel] *n.* vasija, *f.,* vaso, *m.;* buque.

vest [vest] *n.* chaleco, *m.;* —, *vt.* vestir; investir.

veteran [ve-te-ran] *n. y adj.* veterano na.

veterinary [ve-te-ri-na-ri] *n. y adj.* veterinario, *m.*

veto [vi-tou] *n.* veto, *m.*

via [vaia] *prep.* por la via de; por; — **airmail,** por via aérea; — **freight,** por flete o carga.

viaduct [vaia-dakt] *n.* viaducto, *m.*

vial [vaial] *n.* frasco, *m.*

vibrant [vai-brant] *adj.* vibrante.

vibrate [vai-breit] *vt.* vibrar.

vibration [vai-brei-shon] *n.* vibración, *f.*

vibrator [vai-brei-tor] *n.* vibrador, *m.*

vicarious [vi-ka-rios] *adj.* vicario.

vice [vais] *n.* vicio, *m.;* maldad, *f.;* deformidad física; mancha, *f.,* defecto, *m.;* — **versa,** vice-versa, al contrario; —, *prep.* en lugar de.

vice-president [vais-pre-si-dent] *n.* vicepresidente, *m.*

vicinity [vi-si-ni-ti] *n.* vecindad, proximidad, *f.*

vicious [vi-shos] *adj.* vicioso; — **circle,** círculo vicioso; **—ly,** *adj.* de manera viciosa.

vicissitude [vi-si-si-tiud] *n.* vicisitud, *f.*

victim [vik-tim] *n.* víctima, *f.*

victimize [vik-ti-mais] *vt.* sacrificar; engañar.

victor [vik-tar] *n.* vencedor, *m.*

victorious [vik-to-rios] *adj.* victorioso, vencedor.

victory [vik-to-ri] *n.* victoria, *f.*

video [vi-diou] *n.* televisión, *f.*

videotape [vi-diou-teip] *n.* grabación televisada en cinta.

Vienna [vie-na] Viena, *f.*

Viennese [via-nis] *n.* y *adj.* vienés, esa.

view [viu] *n.* vista, *f.;* perspectiva, *f.;* aspecto, *m.;* examen, *m.;* apariencia, *f.;* ver, *m.;* **bird's eye —,** vista a vuelo de pájaro; **in — of,** en vista de; **point of —**, punto de vista; **—**, *vt.* mirar, ver; examinar.

viewpoint [viu-point] *n.* punto de vista.

vigil [vi-yil] *n.* vela, *f.;* vigilia, *f.*

vigilance [vi-yi-lans] *n.* vigilancia, *f.*

vigilant [vi-yi-lant] *adj.* vigilante, atento; **—ly,** *adv.* con vigilancia.

vigor [vi-gar] *n.* vigor, *m.;* robustez, *f.;* energía, *f.*

vigorous [vi-go-ros] *adj.* vigoroso; fuerte.

vile [vail] *adj.* vil, bajo; **—ly,** *adv.* vilmente.

vilify [vi-li-fai] *vt.* envilecer; degradar.

villa [vi-la] *n.* quinta, casa de campo.

village [vi-lech] *n.* aldea, *f.*

villager [vi-li-char] *n.* aldeano, *m.*

villain [vi-lan] *n.* malvado, miserable, *m.*

villainous [vi-la-nos] *adj.* bellaco, vil, ruin; villano; **—ly,** *adv.* vilmente.

vindicate [vin-di-keit] *vt.* vindicar, defender.

vindication [vin-di-kei-shon] *n.* vindicación, *f.;* justificación,

vindictive [vin-dik-tiv] *adj.* vengativo; **—ly,** *adv.* por venganza.

vine [vain] *n.* vid, *f.*

vinegar [vi-ni-gar] *n.* vinagre, *m.*

vineyard [vin-yard] *n.* viña, *f.*, viñedo, *m.*

vinyl [vai-nil] *n.* vinilo, *m.*

viola [vi-ou-la] *n.* (mus.) viola, *f.*

violate [vaio-leit] *vt.* violar.

violation [vaio-lei-shon] *n.* violación, *f.*

violator [vaio-lei-tar] *n.* violador, ra.

violence [vaio-lens] *n.* violencia, *f.*

violent [vaio-lent] *adj.* violento.

violet [vaio-lit] *n.* (bot.) violeta, viola, *f.;* violeta (color), *m.*

violin [vaio-lin] *n.* (mus.) violín, *m.*

violinist [vaio-li-nist] *n.* violinista, *m.* y *f.*

violoncello [vaio-lin] *n.* (mus.)

violoncelo, violonchelo, *m.*

viper [vai-par] *n.* víbora, *f.*

virgin [ver-yin] *n.* virgen, *f.;* —, *adj.* virginal; virgen.

virginal [ver-yi-nal] *adj.* virginal.

virginity [ver-yi-ni-ti] *n.* virginidad, *f.*

virile [vi-rail] *adj.* viril.

virility [vi-ri-li-ti] *n.* virilidad, *f.*

virtual [ver-tiua-li] *adj.* virtual; —ly, *adv.* virtualmente.

virtue [ver-tiu] *n.* virtud, *f.*

virtuous [ver-tiuos] *adj.* virtuoso.

virtuosity [ver-tiuo-si-ti] *n.* virtuosidad, *f.,* disposición extraordinaria para las bellas artes.

virulence [vi-ru-lens] *n.* virulencia, *f.*

virulent [vi-ru-lent] *adj.* virulento.

virus [vaia-ras] *n.* (med.) virus, *m.;* — **pneumonia,** pulmonía a virus.

visa [vi-sa] *n.* visa, *f.,* permiso para entrar en un país; visto bueno.

viscosity [vis-ko-si-ti] *n.* viscosidad, *f.*

vise [vais] *n.* tornillo, torno, *m.*

visibility [vi-si-bi-li-ti] *n.* visibilidad, *f.*

visible [vi-sa-bol] *adj.* visible.

vision [vi-shon] *n.* visión, *f.,* fantasma, *m.;* vista, *f.*

visionary [vi-sho-na-ri] *n.* y *adj.*

visionario, ria.

visit [vi-sit] *vt.* y *vi.* ver; visitar; —, *n.* visita, *f.;* **farewell** —, visita de despedida; **to pay a** —, hacer una visita.

visitation [vi-si-tei-shon] *n.* visitación, *f.;* visita, *f.*

visitor [vi-si-tar] *n.* visitante, *m.* y *f.,* visitador, ra.

vista [vis-ta] *n.* vista, perspectiva, *f.*

visual [vi-shual] *adj.* visual.

visualize [vi-shual] *vt.* vislumbrar, percibir mentalmente percibir con clara visión.

vital [vai-tal] *adj.* vital; — **statistics,** estadística demográfica; —ly, *adv.* vitalmente; —s, *n. pl.* órganos vitales.

vitality [vai-ta-li] *n.* vitalidad, *f.*

vitamin [vi-ta-min] *n.* vitamina, *f.*

vivacious [vi-vei-shos] *adj.* vivaz.

vivacity [vi-va-si-ti] *n.* vivacidad, *f.*

vivid [vi-vid] *adj.* vivo, vivaz; gráfico.

vividness [vi-vid-nes] *n.* vivacidad, intensidad, *f .*

vixen [vik-sen] *n.* zorra, raposa, *f.;* mujer regañona y de mal genio; mujer astuta, arpía, *f.*

vocabulary [vou-ka-biu-la-ri] *n.* vocabulario, *m.*

vocal [vou-kal] *adj.* vocal; — **cords,** cuerdas vocales.

vocalist [vou-ka-list] *n.* cantante, *m.* y *f.*

vocation [vou-kei-shon] *n.* vocación, carrera, profesión, *f.;* oficio, *m.*

vocational [vou-kei-sho-nal] *adj.* práctico, profesional, vocacional; — **school,** escuela de artes y oficios, escuela vocacional; — **training,** instrucción vocacional.

vocative [vo-ka-tiv] *n.* vocativo, *m.*

vogue [voug] *n.* moda, *f.;* boga, *f.*

voice [vois] *n.* voz, *f.;* sufragio, *m.*

voiceless [vois-les] *adj.* sin voz, mudo; que no tiene voz ni voto.

void [void] *adj.* vacío, desocupado; nulo; *n.* vacío, *m.;* —, *vt.* hacer nulo, anular; abandonar, salir; incapacitar; vaciar.

volatile [vo-la-tail] *adj.* volátil; voluble.

volcanic [vol-ka-nik] *adj.* volcánico.

volcano [vol-kei-nou] *n.* volcán, *m.*

volley [vo-li] *n.* descarga de armas de fuego; salva, *f.;* andanada (de insultos, etc.), *f.;* (tenis) voleo, *m.*

volleyball [vo-li-bol] vólibol *m.*

volt [voult] *n.* vuelta (entre jinetes), *f.;* elec.) voltio, *m.*

voltage [voul-tich] *n.* (elec.) vol-

taje, *m.*

volume [vo-lium] *n.* volumen, *m.;* libro, tomo, *m.*

voluminous [vo-liu-mi-nos] *adj.* voluminoso; muy grande.

voluntarily [vo-lon-ta-ri-li] *adv.* voluntariamente.

voluntary [vo-lon-ta-ri] *adj.* voluntario; —, *n.* (mus.) improvisación, *f.;* preludio, *m.*

volunteer [vo-lon-tiar] *n.* (mil.) voluntario, ria; —, *vi.* servir como voluntario; ofrecerse para alguna cosa.

voluptuous [vo-lap-tuos] *adj.* voluptuoso.

vomit [vo-mit] *vt.* y *vi.* vomitar; —, *n.* vómito, *m.;* vomitivo, *m.*

voracious [vo-rei-shos] *adj.* voraz.

vortex [vor-teks] *n.* vórtice, remolino, torbellino, *m.*, vorágine, *f.*

vote [vout] *n.* voto, sufragio, *m.;* —, *vt.* votar.

voter [vou-tar] *n.* votante, *m.* y *f.*

vouch [vauch] *vt.* atestiguar, certificar, afirmar.

voucher [vau-char] *n.* testigo, *m.;* documento justificativo; comprobante, recibo, *m.*

vow [vau] *n.* voto, *m.;* —, *vt.* y *vi.* dedicar, consagrar; hacer votos.

vowel [vauel] *n.* vocal, *f.*

voyage [vo-yich] *n.* viaje por mar;

travesía, f.; —, vi. hacer viaje por mar.

voyager [vo-yi-char] n. navegador, ra, viajero, ra, navegante, m. y f.

vulcanize [val-ka-nais] vt. vulcanizar; **—ed rubber,** caucho vulcanizado.

vulgar [val-gar] adj. vulgar, cursi.

vulgarity [val-ga-ri-ti] n. vulgaridad, f.; bajeza, f.

vulgarize [val-ga-rais] vt. vulgarizar.

vulnerable [val-ne-ra-bol] adj. vulnerable.

vulture [val-char] n. buitre, m.

W

wad [uod] n. atado de paja, heno, etc., m.; borra, f.; taco, m.; (coll.) rollo de papel moneda; riqueza en general; —, vt. acolchar, rellenar; atacar (una arma de fuego).

waddle [uo-del] vi. anadear.

wafer [uei-far] n. hostia, f.; oblea, f.; sello (en farmacias), m.; galletita, f.

waffle [ua-fel] n. barquillo, m.; hojuela, f.

waft [uaft] vt. llevar por el aire o por encima del agua; —, vi. flotar; —, n. banderín, gallardete, m.

wag [uag] vt. mover ligeramente; **to — the tail,** menear la cola; —, n. meneo, m.; bromista, m. y f.

wage [ueich] vt. apostar, emprender; **to — war,** hacer guerra; **—s,** n. pl. sueldo, salario, m., paga, f.; **monthly —s,** mesada, f.; **— earner,** jornalero, m.; asalariado, da.

wager [uei-char] n. apuesta, f.; —, vt. apostar.

waggle [uaguel] vi. anadear, menearse.

wagon [ua-gon] n. carro, m.; carreta, f.

wail [ueil] n. lamento, gemido, m.; —, vi. lamentarse.

waist [ueist] n. cintura, f.; chaqueta, f.

waistcoat [ueist-kout] n. chaleco, m.

waistline [ueist-lain] n. cintura, f.

wait [ueit] vi. esperar, aguardar; quedarse; —, n. acción de esperar; demora, f; **— list,** lista de espera, f.

waiter [uei-tar] n. sirviente, mozo, servidor, mesero, camarero, criado, *m.*

waiting [uei-tin] *n.* espera, *f.;* — **room,** sala de espera.

waitress [uei-tres] *n.* camarera, criada, mesera, *f.*

waive [ueiv] *vt.* abandonar, renunciar (a un derecho, privilegio, etc.); posponer.

waiver [uei-var] *n.* renuncia (a un derecho o privilegio, etc.), *f.*

wake [ueik] *vi.* velar; despertarse; —, *vt.* despertar; —, *n.* vela, *f.;* vigilia, *f.;* velorio, *m.;* (naut.) estela, *f.*

walk [uok] *vt.* y *vi.* pasear, andar, caminar, ir a pie; —, *n.* paseo, *m.,* caminata, *f.;* esfera de acción; **to take a** —, dar un paseo, ir a caminar.

walking [uo-kin] *n.* acción de pasear; paseo, *m.;* **to go** —, dar un paseo, ir de paseo.

wall [uol] *n.* pared, muralla, *f.,* muro, *m.;* —, *vt.* cercar con muros.

wallet [uo-lit] *n.* mochila, *f.;* cartera de bolsillo.

wallow [uo-lou] *vi.* encenagarse.

wallpaper [uol-pei-per] *n.* papel de entapizar.

walnut [uol-nat] *n.* nogal, *m.;* nuez, *f.*

walrus [uol-ras] *n.* (zool.) morsa, *f.*

waltz [uolts] *n.* vals, *m.*

wand [uond] *n.* vara, varita, *f.;* varita mágica; batuta, *f.*

wander [uon-dar] *vi.* vagar, rodar; desviarse, extraviarse.

wanderer [uon-da-rar] *n.* vagamundo, *m.;* peregrino, *m.*

wane [uon] *vi.* disminuir; decaer; menguar; —, *n.* decadencia, *f.;* — **(of the moon)** menguante (de la luna).

want [uont] *vt.* y *vi.* desear, querer, anhelar; faltar; —, *vi.* estar necesitado; sufrir la falta de algo; —, *n.* falta, carencia, *f.;* indifencia, *f.;* deseo, *m.;* necesidad, *f.*

war [uor] *n.* guerra, *f.;* —, *vi.* guerrear; —, *adj.* relativo a la guerra.

ward [uord] *vt.* repeler; **to** — **off,** evitar, desviar; —, *n.* guardia, defensa, *f.;* crujía de hospital; pupilo, *m.*

wardrobe [uor-droub] *n.* guardarropa, *f.,* ropero, *m.;* ropa, *f.,* vestuario, *m.*

ware [uear] *n.* mercadería, *f.;* loza, *f.* ; —**s,** *n. pl.* efectos, *m. pl.,* mercancías, *f. pl.*

warehouse [uea-jaus] *n.* almacén, depósito *m.,* bodega, *f.*

warfare [uea-fear] *n.* guerra, *f.,* conflicto armado.

warily [uea-ri-li] *adv.* prudentemente, con cautela.

warlike [uor-laik] *adj.* guerrero, belicoso, marcial.

Santa Maria Public Library

Customer ID: **********2352

Title: Vela?zquez large print Spanish
and English dictionary Spanish-
English/ingle?s-espan?ol
ID: 32113005891919
Due: 01/02/2016 23:59:59

Title: Ingle | s al minuto : curso
acelerado : manual completo.
ID: 32113008228903
Due: 01/02/2016 23:59:59

Total items: 2
12/12/2015 4:39 PM
Checked out: 3

warm [uorm] *adj.* cálido; caliente; abrigador; cordial, caluroso;
to be —, hacer calor; tener
calor; **—,** *vt.* calentar; **—ly,** *adv.*
calurosamente.

warm-blooded [uorm-bla-ded]
adj. de sangre ardiente; vehemente, entusiasta, fervoroso,
apasionado.

warmhearted [uorm-jar-ted] *adj.*
afectuoso, generoso, benévolo,
de buenos sentimientos.

warmth [uormz] *n.* calor, *m.;*
ardor, fervor, *m.*

warn [uorn] *vt.* avisar; advertir;
prevenir.

warning [uor-nin] *n.* amonestación, *f.;* advertencia, *f.,* aviso,
m.

warrant [uo-rant] *vt.* autorizar;
privilegiar; garantir, garantizar,
asegurar; **—,** *n.* testimonio, *m.;*
justificación, *f.;* decreto de prisión; autorización, *f.*

warranty [uo-ran-ti] *n.* garantía,
seguridad, *f.*

warrior [uo-rior] *n.* guerrero, soldado, batallador, *m.*

wart [uort] *n.* verruga, *f.*

wartime [uor-taim] *n.* época de
guerra.

wary [uea-ri] *adj.* cauto, prudente.

was [uos] 1ª y 3ª persona del
singular del pretérito del verbo
be.

wash [uosh] *vt.* lavar; bañar; **—,**
vi. lavarse; **—,** *n.* lavadura, *f.;*
loción, ablución, *f.;* lavado, *m.;*
variedad de pintura para acuarela; **— bowl, — basin,** lavabo,
m.

washer [uo-shar] *n.* máquina de
lavar ropa; lavadora, *f.;* (mech.)
arandela, *f.*

washerwoman o washwoman
[uo-shar-uo-man], [uo-sha-uo-
man] *n.* lavandera, *f.*

washing [uo-shin] *n.* lavadura,
f.; lavado, *m.;* ropa para lavar;
— machine, máquina de lavar,
lavadora, *f.*

waste [ueist] *vt.* consumir, gastar; malgastar, disipar; destruir, arruinar, asolar; **—,** *vi.*
gastarse; **to — away,** demacrarse; **—,** *n.* desperdicio, *m.;* estopa, *f.;* destrucción, *f.;* despilfarro, *m.;* merma, *f.;* desgaste,
m.; limpiaduras, *f. pl.;* **— pipe,**
tubería de desagüe.

wastebasket [ueist-bas-ket] *n.*
cesto o cesta para papeles.

wasteful [ueist-ful] *adj.* destructivo, pródigo, despilfarrador.

wastefulness [ueist-ful-nes] *n.*
prodigalidad, *f.,* despilfarro, *m.*

wastepaper [ueist-pei-par] *n.*
papel de desecho.

watch [uoch] *n.* desvelo, *m.;* vigilia, vela, *f.;* vigía, *f.;* centinela,
f.; reloj de bolsillo; **wrist —,**

reloj de pulsera; **stop** —, cronógrafo, *m.*; **night** —, vela, *f.*; — **shop**, relojería, *f.*; **to be on the** —, estar alerta; —, *vt.* y *vi.* observar; velar, guardar, custodiar; espiar.

watchdog [uoch-dag] *n.* perro guardián.

watchful [uoch-ful] *adj.* vigilante; cuidadoso; observador.

watchman [uoch-man] *n.* sereno, velador, *m.*

watchtower [uoch-tauer] *n.* atalaya, garita, vigía, *f.*

water [uo-tar] *n.* agua, *f.*; **fresh** —, agua dulce; **hard** —, agua cruda; **mineral** —, agua mineral; **running** —, agua corriente; **salt** —, agua salada; **soda** —, agua de soda; **toilet** —, agua de tocador; — **closet**, común, inodoro, excusado, retrete, *m.*, letrina, *f.*; — **color**, acuarela, *f.*; — **cress**, berro, *m.*; — **faucet**, grifo, grifón, caño de agua, *m.*; — **front**, barrio ribereño; ribera, *f.*; — **heater**, calentador de agua; — **lily**, nenúfar, *m.*, lirio acuático; — **polo**, polo acuático; —, *vt.* regar; abrevar; —, *vi.* llorar; hacer aguada.

water cress [uo-ta-kres] *n.* (bot.) berro, *m.*

waterfall [uo-ta-fol] *n.* cascada, catarata, *f.*, salto de agua; caída de agua.

watering [uo-ta-rin] *n.* riego, *m.*; —, *adj.* que riega; — **pot**, regadera, *f.*

watermelon [uo-ta-me-lon] *n.* sandía, *f.*

waterproof [uo-ta-pruf] *adj.* impermeable, a prueba de agua.

watershed [uo-ta-shed] *n.* vertiente de las aguas; cuenca, *f.*

water ski [uo-ta-ski] *n.* esquí acuático.

waterway [uo-ta-uey] *n.* cañería, *f.*; corriente de agua; vía fluvial.

watt [uot] *n.* vatio, *m.*

wave [ueiv] *n.* ola, onda, *f.*; **short** —, onda corta; **sound** —, onda sonora; — **length**, longitud de onda; —, *vi.* fluctuar; ondear; flamear; **to** — **(to some one)**, saludar (a alguien) agitando la mano.

wavering [uei-ve-rin] *n.* titubeo, *m.*

waving [uei-vin] *n.* ondulación, *f.*

wavy [ueivi] *adj.* ondeado, ondulado.

wax [uaks] *n.* cera, *f.*; — **candle**, vela de cera; — **paper**, —**ed paper**, papel encerado; — **match**, cerilla, *f.*, (Mex.) cerillo, *m.*; fósforo, *m.*; — **taper**, cerilla, *f.*; —, *vt.* encerar; —, *vi.* aumentarse, crecer.

waxen [uak-sen] *adj.* de cera.

waxy [uak-si] *adj.* ceroso.

way [uei] *n.* camino, *m.*, senda, ruta, *f.;* modo, *m.,* forma, *f.;* medio, *m.;* **by the —,** a propósito; **in no —,** de ningún modo, de ninguna manera; **on the —,** al paso, en el camino; **this —,** por aquí; así; **to force one's —,** abrirse el paso; **to give —,** ceder; **right of —,** derecho de vía; **—s and means,** orientación y fines; **— station,** (rail.) estación intermediaria; **to lose one's —,** perderse, extraviarse.

wayside [uei-said] *n.* orilla o borde del camino o sendero; **by the —,** a lo largo del camino o sendero.

wayward [uei-uord] *adj.* caprichoso; desobediente; delincuente.

we [ui] *pron.* nosotros, nosotras.

weak [uik] *adj.* débil, delicado físicamente; flojo; decaído.

weaken [ui-ken] *vt.* debilitar; —, *vi.* aflojarse; ceder; debilitarse.

weakness [uik-nes] *n.* debilidad, *f.*

wealth [uilz] *n.* riqueza, *f.;* bienes, *m. pl.;* bonanza, *f.*

wealthy [uel-zi] *adj.* rico, opulento, adinerado; **— class,** clase acomodada, clase adinerada.

weapon [ue-pon] *n.* arma, *f.;* **—s of war,** pertrechos de guerra.

wear [uear] *vt.* gastar, consumir; usar, llevar, llevar puesto, traer; —, *vi.* consumirse, gastarse; **— and tear,** desgaste producido por el uso; **to — out a person,** fastidiar, aburrir o cansar a una persona; **to — well,** durar (una tela, etc.); —, *n.* uso, *m.*

weariness [uea-ri-nes] *n.* cansancio, rendimiento, *m.*, fatiga, *f.*

wearisome [uea-ri-som] *adj.* cansado, tedioso; laborioso.

weary [uea-ri] *vt.* cansar, fatigar; molestar; —, *adj.* cansado, fatigado, fatigoso.

weasel [ui-sel] *n.* comadreja, *f.*

weather [ue-dar] *n.* tiempo, *m.*, temperatura, *f.;* **bad —,** intemperie, *f.*, mal tiempo; **the — is good,** hace buen tiempo; **— strip,** burlete, *m.;* —, *vt.* sufrir, aguantar (un temporal, adversidad, etc.).

weatherman [ue-dar-men] *n.* meteorologista, *m.*

weave [uiv] *vt.* tejer; trenzar; —, *n.* tejido, *m.*

weaver [ui-var] *n.* tejedor, ra.

web [ueb] *n.* tela, *f.;* tejido, *m.;* red, *f.;* —, *vt.* unir en forma de red; enmarañar, enredar.

web site [ueb-sait] *n.* sitio web, *m.*

wedding [ue-din] *n.* boda, *f.*, casamiento, matrimonio, *m.*, nupcias, *f. pl.;* **silver —,** bodas de plata; **golden —,** bodas de oro; **— cake,** torta o pastel de boda.

wedlock [ued-lok] *n.* matrimonio, *m.*

Wednesday [uens-dei] *n.* miércoles, *m.*

wee [ui] *adj.* pequeñito.

weed [uid] *n.* mala hierba; (coll.) cigarro, tabaco, *m.;* **—s,** *pl.* vestido de luto; **—,** *vt.* escardar.

week [uik] *n.* semana, *f.;* **— end,** fin de semana.

weekday [uik-dei] *n.* día de trabajo; cualquier día de la semana que no sea domingo.

week-end [uik-end] *adj.* de fin de semana.

weekly [ui-kli] *adj.* semanal.

weep [uip] *vi.* llorar, lamentarse.

weeping [ui-pin] *adj.* llorón, plañidero; **— willow,** sauce llorón.

weigh [uei] *vt.* y *vi.* pesar; examinar, considerar.

weight [ueit] *n.* peso, *m.;* pesadez, *f.;* **gross —,** peso bruto; **net —,** peso neto.

weird [uiad] *adj.* extraño, fantástico, sobrenatural, misterioso; que tiene que ver con el destino.

welcome [uel-kom] *adj.* recibido con agrado; **—!** ¡bienvenido! **—,**

n. bienvenida, *f.;* **—,** *vt.* dar la bienvenida.

weld [ueld] *vt.* soldar.

welfare [uel-fear] *n.* prosperidad, *f.;* bienestar, bien, *m.;* **— society,** sociedad benéfica, sociedad de beneficencia; **— state,** estado protector; **— work,** trabajo social, obra de beneficencia.

well [uel] *n.* fuente, *f.;* manantial, *m.;* pozo, *m.,* cisterna, *f.;* cacimba, casimba, *f.;* **—,** *adj.* bueno, sano; **to be —,** estar bien; **—,** *adv.* bien, felizmente; favorablemente; suficientemente; **as — as,** así como, lo mismo que, también como; **— then,** conque; **very —!** ¡está bien! **—!** *interj.* ¡vaya!

well-being [uel-biin] *n.* felicidad, prosperidad, *f.*

well-disposed [uel-dis-pousd] *adj.* favorable, bien dispuesto.

well-done [uel-dan] *adj.* bien cocido.

well-groomed [uel-grumd] *adj.* vestido elegantemente.

well-known [uel-noun] *adj.* notorio, bien conocido.

well-off [uel-of] *adj.* acomodado, rico.

well-timed [uel-taimd] *adj.* oportuno, hecho a propósito.

well-to-do [uel-tu-du] *adj.* acomodado, próspero, rico.

welt [uelt] *n.* ribete, *m.;* roncha, *f.;* —, *vt.* ribetear; (coll.) golpear hasta causar ronchas.

went [uent] *pretérito* del verbo **go.**

were [uer] 2ª persona del singular y todo el plural del *pretérito* del verbo **be.**

west [uest] *n.* poniente, occidente, oeste, *m.;* —, *adj.* occidental.

westerly, western [ues-ter-li], [ues-tern] *adj.* occidental.

West Indies [uest-in-dis] Antillas, *f. pl.*

westward [uest-uod] *adv.* hacia el poniente u occidente.

wet [uet] *adj.* húmedo, mojado; — **blanket,** aguafiestas, *m.* o *f.;* **to get** —, mojarse, empaparse; — **nurse,** nodriza, nutriz, *f.;* —, *n.* humedad, *f.;* —, *vt.* mojar, humedecer.

wet-nurse [uet-ners] *vt.* servir de nodriza, amamantar a un hijo ajeno.

whack [uak] *vt.* aporrear; —, *n.* golpe, *m.;* intento, *m.,* prueba, *f.;* porción, participación, *f.;* **to take a — at it,** intentarlo, hacer la prueba para lograrlo.

whale [ueil] *n.* ballena, *f.*

wharf [uorf] *n.* muelle, *m.*

wharves [uorfs] *n. pl.* de **wharf.**

what [uot] *pron.* qué; cuál; lo que; — **is the matter?** ¿qué pasa?

whatever, whatsoever [uot-e-var], [uot-so-e-var] *pron.* cualquier cosa que, lo que; — *adj.* cualquier.

wheat [uit] *n.* trigo, *m.;* **winter** —, trigo mocho; — **field,** trigal, *m.*

wheel [uil] *n.* rueda, *f.;* — **chair,** silla de ruedas; — **base,** distancia entre ejes; — **and axle,** cabria, *f.;* **driving** —, rueda motriz; **gambling** —, rueda de la fortuna; **gear** —, rueda dentada; **paddle** —, rueda de paletas; **small** —, rodaja, *f.;* **water** —, rodezno, *m.;* — **rope,** (naut.) guardín, *m.;* — **track,** carril, *m.;* **steering** —, volante, *m.;* —, *vt.* rodar, hacer rodar, girar; —, *vi.* girar, dar vueltas.

wheeze [uis] *vi.* resollar con sonido fuerte.

when [uen] *adv.* cuándo; —, *conj.* cuando, mientras que.

whence [uens] *adv.* de donde; de quien.

whenever [uen-e-var] *conj.* cuando quiera que, siempre que; — **you wish,** cuando quiera.

where [uear] *adv.* dónde; en dónde; —, *conj.* donde; en donde.

whereby [uea-bai] *conj.* con lo cual, por donde, por lo cual.

wherever [uear-e-var] *conj.* dondequiera que.

wherewithal [uear-ui-zal] *n.* medios, *m. pl.;* dinero necesario.

whether [ue-dar] *conj.* si; ora.

whey [uei] *n.* suero, *m.*

which [uich] *pron.* que, el cual, la cual, el que, la que; cuál; —, *adj.* cuál de los, qué.

whichever, whichsoever [uich-e-var] [uich-so-e-var] *adj.* cualquier; —, *pron.* cualquiera que.

whiff [uif] *n.* vaharada, *f.;* bocanada de humo, fumada, *f.*

while [uail] *n.* rato, *m.;* vez, *f.;* momento, *m.;* **to be worth —,** valer la pena; —, *conj.* mientras, a la vez que; a medida que; en tanto.

whim [uim] *n.* antojo, capricho, *m.*

whinper [uim-par] *vi.* sollozar, gemir; —, *n.* sollozo, gemido, *m.*

whimsical [uim-si-kal] *adj.* caprichoso, fantástico.

whimsy [uim-si] *n.* fantasía, *f.,* capricho, *m.*

whine [uain] *vi.* lloriquear, lamentarse; —, *n.* quejido, lamento, *m.*

whining [uai-nin] *n.* (coll.) gimoteo, lloriqueo, *m.*

whip [uip] *n.* azote, látigo, *m.;* —, *vi.* andar de prisa.

whipped cream [uipd-krim] *n.* crema batida.

whipping [ui-pin] *n.* flagelación, paliza, *f.*

whirl [uerl] *vt.* y *vi.* girar; hacer girar; moverse rápidamente; —, *n.* giro muy rápido; vuelta, *f.*

whirlpool [uerl-pul] *n.* vórtice, remolino, *m.,* vorágine, olla, *f.*

whirlwind [uerl-uind] *n.* torbellino, remolino, *m.* whisk, *n.* movimiento rápido como de una escobilla; escobilla, *f.,* cepillo, *m.;* —, *vi.* moverse ligera y rápidamente; —, *vt.* batir (huevos, etc.).

whisker [uis-kar] *n.* patilla, *f.,* mostacho, *m.;* —**s,** *pl.* barba, *f.*

whiskey, whisky [uis-ki] *n.* whiskey, *m.,* bebida alcohólica hecha de maíz.

whisper [uis-par] *vi.* susurrar, hablar al oído; —, *n.* cuchicheo, susurro, *m.*

whistle [ui-sel] *vt.* y *vi.* silbar; chiflar; —, *n.* silbido, *m.;* pito, *m.*

white [uait] *adj.* blanco, pálido; cano, canoso; puro; **to become —,** blanquearse; **— clover,** trébol blanco, *m.;* **— feather,** pluma blanca, señal de cobardía; **— gold,** oro blanco, oro aleado con níquel y cinco platino; **— heat,** incandescencia, *f.;* rojo blanco; estado de intensa conmoción física o mental; —

lead, cerusa, *f.,* blanco de plomo; — **lie,** mentirilla, *f.;* — **matter,** (anat.) tejido nervioso blanco (especialmente cerebral y medular); — **oak,** roble blanco; — **pine,** pino blanco; — **poplar,** álamo blanco; — **sauce,** salsa blanca; —, *n.* color blanco; clara de huevo.

white-collar [uait-ko-ler] *adj.* de oficinista; — **worker,** oficinista, *m.* y *f.*

white-haired [uait-jaird] *adj.* canoso, de cabello blanco.

whiten [uai-ten] *vt.* y *vi.* blanquear; blanquearse, emblanquecerse.

whiteness [uait-nes] *n.* blancura, *f.;* palidez, *f.*

whitewash [uait-uosh] *n.* jalbegue, blanquete, enlucimiento, *m.;* —, *vt.* encalar; jalbegar; encubrir.

whitish [uai-tish] *adj.* blanquizco, blanquecino.

whittle [ui-tel] *vt.* cortar con navaja; tallar, tajar, afilar, mondar, sacar punta.

who [ju] *pron.* quien, que; quién.

whoever, whosoever [ju-e-var], [ju-so-e-var] *pron.* quienquiera que, cualquiera que; quien.

whole [joul] *adj.* todo, total; sano, entero; —, *n.* todo, total, *m.;* conjunto, *m.;* — **note** (mus.) redonda, semibreve, *f.;*

— **number,** número entero.

wholehearted [joul-jar-tid] *adj.* sincero, cordial.

wholesale [joul-seil] *n.* venta al por mayor; — **house,** casa al por mayor.

wholesaler [joul-sei-lar] *n.* mayorista, *m.,* comerciante que vende al por mayor.

wholesome [joul-som] *adj.* sano, saludable; —**ly,** *adv.* en forma sana.

whole-wheat [joul-wit] *adj.* de trigo entero.

wholly [jou-li] *adv.* enteramente, totalmente.

whom [jum] *pron.* quien, el que; quién.

whose [jus] *pron.* cuyo, cuya, de quien; de quién.

why [uai] *adv.* ¿por qué? — **not?** ¿pues y qué? ¿por qué no?

wick [uik] *n.* torcida, mecha, *f.,* pabilo, *m.*

wicked [ui-kid] *adj.* malvado, perverso.

wickedness [ui-kid-nes] *n.* perversidad, maldad, *f.*

wicker [ui-kar] *n.* mimbre, *m.;* —, *adj.* de mimbre.

wide [uaid] *adj.* ancho, vasto, extenso; remoto; **far and** —, por todos lados; —**ly,** *adv.* ampliamente.

wide-awake [uaid-a-ueik] *adj.* despierto, alerta, vivo.

wide-eyed [uaid-aid] *adj.* asombrado, con los ojos muy abiertos.

widen [uai-den] *vt.* ensanchar, extender, ampliar.

widespread [uaid-spred] *adj.* extenso, difuso, esparcido, diseminado.

widow [uidou] *n.* viuda, *f.;* —, *vt.* privar a una mujer de su marido.

widower [ui-douar] *n.* viudo, *m.*

widowhood [ui-dou-jud] *n.* viudez, viudedad, *f.*

width [uidz] *n.* anchura, *f.*

wield [uild] *vt.* manejar, empuñar; ejercer.

wife [uaif] *n.* esposa, consorte, mujer, *f.*

wig [uig] *n.* peluca, *f.*

wiggle [ui-guel] *n.* meneo rápido, culebreo, *m.;* —, *vt.* y *vi.* menear, menearse.

wild [uaild] *adj.* silvestre, feroz; desierto; salvaje; —, *n.* desierto, yermo, *m.;* — **boar,** jabalí, *m.;* — **oats,** indiscreciones de la juventud.

wildcat [uaild-kat] *n.* gato montés; (com.) negocio quimérico; (fig.) fiera, *f.;* —, *adj. (com.)* corrompido, quimérico.

wilderness [uail-da-nes] *n.* desierto, *m.,* selva, *f.* wildfire, *n.* fuego griego; conflagración destructiva; **to spread like** —,

esparcirse como relámpago.

wile [uail] *n.* dolo, engaño, *m.;* astucia, *f.*

will [uil] *n.* voluntad, *f.;* albedrío, *m.;* testamento, *m.;* **at** —, a gusto; **against one's** —, contra la voluntad de uno; —, *vt.* legar, dejar en testamento; —, *vi.* verbo auxiliar que indica futuro.

willing [ui-lin] *adj.* deseoso, listo, dispuesto a servir; —**ly,** *adv.* de buen grado, de buena gana.

willingness [ui-lin-nes] *n.* buena voluntad, deseo de servir.

willow [ui-lou] *n.* (bot.) sauce, *m.*

willowy [ui-lou-ui] *adj.* que abunda en sauces; como un sauce; alto y esbelto.

wily [uai-li] *adj.* astuto, insidioso.

win [uin] *vt.* y *vi.* ganar, obtener, conquistar; alcanzar, lograr; **to — the favor (of),** caer en gracia (de).

wince [uins] *vi.* encogerse.

wind [uind] *n.* viento, *m.;* aliento, *m.;* pedo, *m.;* **to break** —, peerse; — **instrument,** instrumento de viento; — **tunnel,** (avi.) túnel aerodinámico.

wind [uind] *vt.* enrollar; dar vuelta, dar cuerda (a un reloj, etc.); torcer; envolver; —, *vi.* caracolear, serpentear; insinuarse; arrollarse; **to — up,**

ultimar (un asunto).

winded [uind-did] *adj.* desalentado, sin fuerzas.

winding [uin-din] *n.* vuelta, revuelta, *f.;* arrollamiento (de un alambre); cuerda (de un reloj, etc.); —, *adj.* tortuoso, sinuoso; —**road,** camino sinuoso; — **sheet,** mortaja, *f.,* sudario, *m.;* — **stair,** escalera de caracol; — **tackle,** (naut.) aparejo de estrelleras.

windmill [uind-mil] *n.* molino de viento.

window [uin-dou] *n.* ventana, *f.;* — **frame,** marco de la ventana; **small** —, ventanilla, *f.;* —**blind,** celosía, *f.,* persiana de ventana; — **shade,** visillo, *m.;* — **shutter,** puertaventana, contraventana, *f.;* —**sill,** repisa de ventana.

windowpane [uin-dou-pein] *n.* vidrio de ventana.

windpipe [uind-paip] *n.* (anat.) tráquea, *f.*

windshield [uind-shild] *n.* guardabrisa, parabrisas, *m.*

windshield wiper [uind-shild-uai-par] *n.* limpiaparabrisas, *m.*

windward [uind-uord] *n.* (naut.) barlovento, *m.;* **to ply to the** —, (naut.) bordear; —, *adv.* (naut.) a barlovento.

windy [uin-di] *adj.* ventoso; **it is** —, hace viento.

wine [uain] *n.* vino, *m.;* **red** —, vino tinto; — **cellar,** bodega, *f.;* — **merchant,** vinatero, *m.*

wing [uing] *n.* ala, *f.;* lado, costado, *m.;* —**s,** *pl.* (theat.) bastidores, *m. pl.;* — **case,** élitro (de un insecto), *m.;* — **chair,** sillón con respaldo en forma de alas; —**spread,** extensión del ala de un aeroplano de un pájaro, etc; —, *vt.* herir superficialmente; —, *vi.* volar.

wink [uink] *vt.* y *vi.* guiñar, pestañear; —, *n.* pestañeo, guiño, *m.*

winner [ui-nar] *n.* ganador, ra, vencedor, ra.

winning [ui-nin] *n.* ganancia, *f.;* lucro, *m.;* —, *adj.* atractivo, encantador; ganador.

winter [uin-tar] *n.* invierno, *m.;* — **wheat,** trigo mocho; —, *adj.* invernal; —, *vi.* invernar, pasar el invierno.

wintry [uin-tri] *adj.* invernal.

wipe [uaip] *vt.* secar, limpiar; borrar; **to — out,** obliterar; arruinar financieramente.

wire [uaiar] *n.* alambre, *m.;* **barbed** —, alambre de púas; **conducting** —, alambre conductor; **live** —, alambre cargado de electricidad; persona muy activa; — **fence,** — **fencing,** alambrado, *m.,* cerca o cercado de alambre; —, *vt.* alambrar; —, *vi.* (coll.) telegrafiar, cablegrafiar.

wireless [uaia-lis] *n.* telegrafía sin hilos, telegrafía inalámbrica, radiotelefonía, *f.;* — **station,** radioemisora, estación radioemisora; — **transmission,** radioemisión.

wiring [uaia-rin] *n.* instalación de alambres eléctricos.

wiry [uaia-ri] *adj.* hecho de alambre; parecido al alambre; flaco pero a la vez fuerte.

wisdom [uis-dom] *n.* sabiduría, prudencia, *f.;* juicio, *m.*

wisdom tooth [uis-dom-tuz] *n.* muela del juicio, muela cordal.

wise [uais] *adj.* sabio, docto, juicioso, prudente, sensato; —, *n.* modo, *m.,* manera, *f.;* —**ly,** *adv.* sabiamente, con prudencia.

wish [uish] *vt.* desear, anhelar, ansiar, querer; **to — a happy Christmas, to — a happy Easter,** desear felices Pascuas; —, *n.* anhelo, deseo, *m.*

wishful [uish-ful] *adj.* deseoso; ávido; — **thinking,** ilusiones, *f. pl.,* buenos deseos.

wisp [uisp] *n.* manojo de paja, de heno, etc.; fragmento, *m.,* pizca, *f.*

wit [uit] *n.* ingenio, *m.,* agudeza, sal, *f.;* **to —,** a saber.

witch [uich] *n.* bruja, hechicera, *f.*

witchcraft [uich-kraft] *n.* brujería, *f.;* sortilegio, *m.* witchery, *n.* hechicería, *f.;* encanto, *m.;* influencia fascinadora.

with [uiz] *prep.* con; por; de; a.

withdraw [uiz-dro] *vt.* quitar; privar; retirar; —, *vi.* retirarse, apartarse, sustraerse.

withdrawal [uiz-droal] *n.* retiro, *m.,* retirada, *f.;* **bank —,** retiro de depósitos del banco.

withhold [uiz-jould] *vt.* detener, impedir, retener.

within [uiz-in] *prep.* dentro de; al alcance de; —**bounds,** a raya; —, *adv.* adentro.

without [uiz-aut] *prep.* sin; fuera de; más allá de; —, *adv.* afuera.

withstand [uid-stand] *vt.* oponer, resistir.

witness [ui-ti-nes] *n.* testimonio, *m.;* testigo, *m.;* **eye —,** testigo ocular; —, *vt.* atestiguar, testificar; presenciar; —, *vi.* servir de testigo.

witty [ui-ti] *adj.* ingenioso, agudo, chistoso.

wives [uaivs] *n. pl.* de **wife.**

wizard [ui-sard] *n.* brujo, hechicero, mago, *m.*

wobble [uo-bal] *vi.* bambolear; —, *n.* bamboleo, *m.*

wobbly [uo-bli] *adj.* instable, que se bambolea.

woe [uou] *n.* dolor, *m.,* aflicción,

f.

woeful [uou-ful] *adj.* triste, funesto; —**ly,** *adv.* dolorosamente.

wolf [vulf] *n.* lobo, *m.;* **she- —,** loba, *f.;* — **pack,** manada de lobos.

wolfram [vul-frum] *n.* wolframio, tungsteno, *m.*

wolves [vulvs] *n. pl.* de **wolf.**

woman [uo-man] *n.* mujer, *f.*

womanhood [uo-man-jud] *n.* la mujer en general.

womankind [uo-man-kaind] *n.* sexo femenino.

womanly [uo-man-li] *adj.* mujeril, femenino.

womb [vum] *n.* útero, *m.,* matriz, *f.*

women [ui-men] *n. pl.* de **woman.**

wonder [uan-dar] *n.* milagro, *m.;* prodigio, *m.;* maravilla, *f.*

wonderful [uan-da-ful] *adj.* maravilloso, prodigioso; —**ly,** *adv.* maravillosamente.

wonderland [uan-da-land] *n.* tierra maravillosa, país de las maravillas o de los prodigios.

won't [uount] contracción de **will not.**

wood [vud] *n.* madera, *f.;* leña, *f.;* — **alcohol,** alcohol metílico; — **louse,** milpiés, *m.,* cochinilla, *f.;* — **pigeon,** paloma zorita; — **pulp,** pulpa de madera; —

thrush, tordo americano; — **turning,** arte de trabajar la madera con el torno para sacar piezas de distintas formas; —**s,** *pl.* bosque, *m.*

woodchuck [wud-chak] *n.* (zool.) marmota, *f.*

woodcut [wud-kat] *n.* grabado en madera; estampa de un grabado en madera.

wooded [wu-ded] *adj.* arbolado.

wooden [wu-den] *adj.* de madera.

woodland [wud-land] *n.* bosque, *m.,* selva, *f.*

woodwork [wud-uek] *n.* obra de madera, obra de carpintería, maderaje, *m.;* molduras, *f. pl.*

wool [wul] *n.* lana, *f.;* — **merchant,** pañero, *m.*

woolen [wu-lan] *adj.* de lana, lanoso.

word [wued] *n.* palabra, voz, *f.;* **by — of mouth,** de palabra; **on my —,** a fe mía, bajo mi palabra; **to leave —,** dejar dicho; —**s (of a song)** letra (de una canción), *f.;* **in other —s,** en otros términos, en otras palabras; —, *vt.* expresar.

wording [uer-din] *n.* dicción, *f.*

wordless [uerd-les] *adj.* sin habla, silencioso.

wordy [uer-di] *adj.* verboso.

wore [uor] *pretérito* del verbo **wear.**

work [uerk] *vi.* trabajar; laborar; funcionar; —, *vt.* trabajar, labrar; laborar; formar; —, *n.* trabajo, *m.*, obra, *f.*; gestión, *f.*; fatiga, *f.*; quehacer, *m.*; **metal** —, metalistería, *f.*; — **of art,** obra de arte.

workable [ue-ka-bol] *adj.* laborable, explotable, factible; que se puede trabajar o hacer funcionar.

workbench [uerk-bench] *n.* banco de taller.

worker [ue-kar] *n.* trabajador, ra, obrero, ra, operario, ria.

working [ue-kin] *n.* funcionamiento, *m.*; trabajo, *m.*; explotación, *f.*; — **day,** día de trabajo.

workman [uek-man] *n.* labrador, *m.*; obrero, *m.*; artífice, *m.*

workmanship [uek-man-ship] *n.* manufactura, *f.*; destreza del artífice; trabajo, *m.*

workout [uek-aut] *n.* ensayo, ejercicio, *m.*

workshop [uek-shop] *n.* taller, *m.*

world [ueld] *n.* mundo, *m.*; universo, *m.*; gente, *f.*; (fig.) mar, *f.*

wordly [ueld-li] *adj.* mundano, profano, terrenal.

world-wide [ueld-uaid] *adj.* mundial, del mundo entero.

worm [uem] *n.* gusano, gorgojo, *m.*; —, *vi.* moverse insidiosa-

mente; —, *vt.* librar de gusanos; efectuar por medios insidiosos.

worm-eaten [uem-i-ten] *adj.* carcomido, apolillado.

wormwood [uem-wud] *n.* (bot.) ajenjo, *m.*

wormy [ue-mi] *adj.* agusanado.

worn [uern] *p.p.* del verbo **wear.**

worn-out [uern-aut] *adj.* raído, gastado; cansado, rendido.

worry [ua-ri] *n.* cuidado, *m.*; preocupación, intranquilidad, *f.*; ansia, *f.*, desasosiego, *m.*; —, *vt.* molestar, atormentar; —, *vi.* preocuparse; **to be worried,** estar con cuidado, estar preocupado.

worse [uers] *adj.* y *adv.* peor; **to get** —, empeorarse; **so much the** —, tanto peor.

worship [uor-ship] *n.* culto, *m.*; adoración, *f.*; **your** —, vuestra merced; —, *vt.* adorar, venerar.

worst [uerst] *adj.* pésimo, malísimo; —, *n.* lo peor, lo más malo; —, *vt.* aventajar; derrotar.

worth [uerz] *n.* valor, precio, *m.*; mérito, *m.*, valía, *f.*; —, *adj.* meritorio, digno; **to be** — **while,** merecer o valer la pena; **to be** — , valer.

worthiness [uer-zi-nes] *n.* dignidad, *f.*; mérito, *m.*

worthless [uerz-les] *adj.* indino, sin valor; — **effort,** esfuerzo inútil; — **person,** persona despreciable.

worth-while [uerz-uail] *adj.* que vale la pena, digno de tenerse en cuenta.

worthy [uer-zi] *adj.* digno, benemérito; merecedor; —, *n.* varón ilustre.

would [wud] *pretérito* de **will,** para expresar deseo, condición, acción.

wound [vaund] *n.* herida, llaga, *f.;* —, *vt.* herir.

wound [vaund] *p.p.* del verbo **wind.**

wove [uouv] *pretérito* del verbo **weave.**

woven [uou-ven] *p.p.* del verbo **weave.**

wrap [rap] *vt.* arrollar; envolver; **to — up,** abrigar, abrigarse; envolver.

wrapper [ra-par] *n.* envolvedor, ra; envoltura, *f.;* bata de casa; forro de un libro.

wrapping [ra-pin] *n.* envoltura, *f.;* cubierta, *f.,* forro exterior.

wrath [raz] *n.* ira, rabia, cólera, *f.*

wreak [rik] *vt.* descargar (la cólera), etc.

wreath [riz] *n.* corona, guirnalda, *f.*

wreck [rek] *n.* naufragio, *m.;* destrucción, *f.;* choque, accidente, *m.;* naufragio, *m.;* —, *vt.*

arruinar; destruir; —, *vi.* arruinarse.

wreckage [re-kidch] *n.* restos, despojos, *m. pl.,* ruinas, *f. pl.*

wren [ren] *n.* (orn.) reyezuelo, *m.*

wrench [rench] *vt.* arrancar; dislocar; torcer; —, *n.* torcedura (del pie, etc.), *f.;* llave, *f.;* **monkey** —, llave inglesa.

wrest [rest] *vt.* arrancar, quitar a fuerza.

wrestle [re-sel] *vi.* luchar; (fig.) pelear; disputar; —, *n.* lucha, *f.*

wrestler [res-lar] *n.* luchador, *m.*

wrestling [res-lin] *n.* lucha, *f.;* **catch-as-catch-can** —, lucha libre; **Greco-Roman** —, lucha grecorromana.

wretch [rech] *n.* pobre infeliz; infame, *m.;* **poor** —! ¡pobre diablo!

wretched [re-chid] *adj.* infeliz, miserable; mezquino; mísero; deplorable, lamentable.

wriggle [ri-guel] *vi.* menearse, agitarse; culebrear.

wring [ring] *vt.* torcer; arrancar; estrujar.

wringer [rin-gar] *n.* exprimidor de ropa.

wrinkle [rin-kel] *n.* arruga, *f.;* —, *vt.* arrugar.

wrist [rist] *n.* muñeca (de la mano), *f.;* — **bandage,** pulsera, venda para la mano; — **watch,** reloj de pulsera.

wristband [rist-band] *n.* puño de camisa.

write [rait] *vt.* escribir; componer; — **off,** cancelar; hacer un descuento por depreciación; — **up,** dar cuenta, completar; alabar en la prensa.

writer [rai-tar] *n.* escritor, ra, autor, ra; novelista, *m.* y *f.*; **prose** —, prosador, ra.

writhe [raidz] *vt.* torcer; —, *vi.* contorcerse.

writing [rai-tin] *n.* escritura, *f.*; escrito, *m.*; manuscrito, *m.*; **in** —, por escrito; **to put in** —, poner por escrito; — **desk,** escritorio, bufete, pupitre, *m.*; — **paper,** papel de escribir.

written [ri-ten] *p.p.* del verbo write.

wrong [rong] *n.* injuria, *f.*; injusticia, *f.*; error, *m.*; —, *adj.* malo, incorrecto, erróneo; injusto; — **side,** revés, *m.*; **to be** —, no tener razón; estar equivocado; —, *vt.* hacer un mal, injuriar; —, —**ly,** *adv.* mal, injustamente; al revés.

wrongdoer [rong-duar] *n.* pecador, ra, malvado, da.

wrongful [rong-ful] *adj.* injusto, inicuo.

wrote [rout] *pretérito* del verbo write.

wrought [rot] *adj.* labrado, hecho; — **iron,** hierro forjado.

wt.: weight P. peso.

X

xerox [se-roks] *vt.* fotocopiar.

Xmas: Christmas [eks-mas] Navidad, Pascua de Navidad.

X ray [eks-rei] *n.* rayo X; radiografía, *f.*

X-ray [eks-rei] *adj.* radiográfico; —**ing,** *n.* radiografía; — **specialist,** radiógrafo; —, *vt.* radiografiar.

xylophone [sai-lo-foun] *n.* (mus.) xilófono, *m.*, variedad de marimba.

Y

yacht [yot] *n.* (naut.) yate, *m.*

yam [yak] *n.* (bot.) batata, *f.*, camote, *m.*

yank [yank] *vt.* (coll.) sacudir, tirar de golpe; **Y—,** *n.* yanqui, *m.* y *f.*

Yankee [yan-ki] *n.* y *adj.* yanqui, *m.* y *f.*

yard [yard] *n.* corral, *m.;* yarda (medida), *f.;* (naut.) verga, *f.;* patio, *m.*

yardstick [yard-stik] *n.* yarda o vara de medir.

yarn [yarn] *n.* estambre, *m.;* (coll.) cuento de aventuras por lo general exageradas o ficticias.

yawn [yon] *vi.* bostezar; —, *n.* bostezo, *m.*

year [yiar] *n.* año, *m.;* **all — round,** todo el año; **many —s ago,** hace muchos años.

yearbook [yia-buk] *n.* libro del año, anuario, *m.*

yearling [yia-lin] *n.* primal, *m.,* animal de un año de edad.

yearly [yia-li] *adj.* anual; —, *adv.* todos los años, anualmente.

yearn [yern] *vi.* anhelar.

yearning [yer-nin] *n.* anhelo, *m.,* deseo ferviente.

yeast [yist] *n.* levadura, *f.;* giste, *m.;* — **cake,** pastilla de levadura.

yell [yel] *vi.* aullar, gritar; —, *n.* grito, aullido, *m.*

yellow [ye-lou] *adj.* amarillo; —, *n.* color amarillo; — **fever,** fiebre amarilla.

yellowish [ye-louish] *adj.* amarillento.

yelp [yelp] *vi.* latir, ladrar; —, *n.*

aullido, latido, *m.*

yen [yen] *n.* yen (unidad monetaria del Japón), *m.;* (coll.) deseo intenso, anhelo, *m.*

yes [yes] *adv.* sí.

yesterday [yes-ta-dei] *adv.* ayer; **day before —,** anteayer.

yet [yet] *adv.* todavía, aún; —, *conj.* sin embargo, con todo.

yield [yild] *vi.* producir, rendir; ceder; sucumbir; darse por vencido; asentir; —, *vt.* producir, rendir; —, *n.* producto, rendimiento, *m.;* (mech.) rendimiento, *m.*

yielding [yil-din] *adj.* condescendiente, que cede.

yodel [you-del] *vt.* cantar con modulación del tono natural al falsete; —, *n.* canto con modulación del tono natural al falsete.

yoke [youk] *n.* yugo, *m.;* yunta, *f.;* férula, *f.;* —, *vt.* uncir; ligar; casar; sojuzgar.

yolk [youk] *n.* yema (de huevo), *f.*

yon, yonder [yon], [yon-dar] *adv.* allí, allá; —, *adj.* de allí, de allá; aquel.

yore [yor] *n.* tiempo antiguo, tiempo atrás; **in days of —,** en tiempo de Maricastaña.

you [yu] *pron.* tú, usted; vosotros, vosotras, ustedes; te, le, lo, la; os, los, las; les; ti.

young [yang] *adj.* joven, mozo; tierno; — **man,** joven, *m.;* — **woman,** joven, señorita, *f.;* — **people,** juventud, *f.*

youngster [yangs-tar] *n.* jovencito, ta, chiquillo, lla, muchacho, cha, jovenzuelo, la.

your [yuar] *adj.* tu, su, vuestro, de usted, de vosotros, de ustedes.

yours [yuas] *pron.* el tuyo, el suyo, el vuestro.

yourself [ya-self] *pron.* tú mismo, usted mismo; vosotros mismos; sí mismo; te, se.

yourselves [ya-selvs] *pron. pl.* de **yourself.**

youth [yuz] *n.* juventud, adolescencia, *f.;* joven, *m.*

youthful [yuz-ful] *adj.* juvenil; — **ly,** *adv.* de un modo juvenil.

yucca [ya-ka] *n.* (bot.) yuca, *f.*

Z

zany [sei-ni] *n. y adj.* tonto, ta, mentecato, ta, bufón, ona.

zeal [sil] *n.* celo, ardor, ahínco, *m.*

zealous [se-los] *adj.* celoso, fervoroso; —**ly,** *adv.* fervorosamente.

zebra [ze-bra] *n.* zebra, cebra, *f.*

zenith [se-niz] *n.* cenit, *m.*

zephyr [se-far] *n.* céfiro, favonio, *m.*

zero [si-rou] *n.* cero, *m.;* — **hour,** (mil.) hora fijada para un ataque, etc.; hora del peligro, hora crítica.

zest [sest] *n.* gusto, *m.,* sabor agudo; gozo, *m.*

zigzag [sig-sag] *n.* zigzag, *m.;* —, *vt. y vi.* hacer un zigzag, ir en forma de zigzag.

zinc [sink] *n.* (chem.) cinc, zinc, *m.;* — **chloride,** cloruro de cinc; — **oxide,** óxido de cinc.

zipper [si-par] *n.* cremallera, *f.;* cierre, *m.;* cierre relámpago.

zodiac [sou-diak] *n.* zodiaco, *m.*

zone [soun] *n.* zona, *f.;* **danger** —, zona del peligro.

zoo [su] *n.* jardín zoológico.

zoological [su-lo-yi-kal] *adj.* zoológico.

zoologist [su-o-lo-yist] *n.* zoólogo, *m.*

zoology [su-o-lo-yi] *n.* zoología, *f.*

zoom [sum] *vi.* (avi.) levantar el vuelo repentinamente; subirse rápidamente o elevarse (como un aeroplano, etc.); zumbir.

zooming [su-min] *n.* subida vertical.